Tax Formula for Individuals

Income (broadly conceived)	$xx,xxx
Less: Exclusions	(x,xxx)
Gross income	$xx,xxx
Less: Deductions *for* adjusted gross income	(x,xxx)
Adjusted gross income	$xx,xxx
Less: The greater of—	
Total itemized deductions	
or standard deduction	(x,xxx)
Personal and dependency exemptions	(x,xxx)
Taxable income	$xx,xxx

Basic Standard Deduction Amounts

	Standard Deduction Amount	
Filing Status	**1996**	**1997**
Single	$4,000	$4,150
Married, filing jointly	6,700	6,900
Surviving spouse	6,700	6,900
Head of household	5,900	6,050
Married, filing separately	3,350	3,450

Amount of Each Additional Standard Deduction

Filing Status	**1996**	**1997**
Single	$1,000	$1,000
Married, filing jointly	800	800
Surviving spouse	800	800
Head of household	1,000	1,000
Married, filing separately	800	800

Personal and Dependency Exemption

1996	**1997**
$2,550	$2,650

1998 ANNUAL EDITION

West's Federal Taxation:

Individual Income Taxes

1998 ANNUAL EDITION

WEST'S FEDERAL TAXATION:
INDIVIDUAL INCOME TAXES

GENERAL EDITORS

William H. Hoffman, Jr., J.D., Ph.D., C.P.A. **James E. Smith,** Ph.D., C.P.A.

Eugene Willis, Ph.D., C.P.A.

CONTRIBUTING AUTHORS

James H. Boyd,
Ph.D., C.P.A.
Arizona State University

D. Larry Crumbley,
Ph.D., C.P.A.
Louisiana State University

Steven C. Dilley,
J.D., Ph.D., C.P.A.
Michigan State University

Mary Sue Gately,
Ph.D., C.P.A.
Texas Tech University

William H. Hoffman, Jr.,
J.D., Ph.D., C.P.A.
University of Houston

David M. Maloney,
Ph.D., C.P.A.
University of Virginia

William A. Raabe,
Ph.D., C.P.A.
Samford University

Boyd C. Randall,
J.D., Ph.D.
Brigham Young University

W. Eugene Seago,
J.D., Ph.D., C.P.A.
Virginia Polytechnic Institute and State University

James E. Smith,
Ph.D., C.P.A.
College of William and Mary

Eugene Willis,
Ph.D., C.P.A.
University of Illinois at Urbana

WEST

SOUTH-WESTERN College Publishing
An International Thomson Publishing Company

Accounting Team Director: Richard Lindgren
Acquisitions Editor: Alex von Rosenberg
Developmental Editor: Esther Craig
Production Editor: Peggy A. Williams
Copyediting: Patricia A. Lewis
Composition: Carlisle Communications, Ltd.
Index: Catalyst Communication Arts
Cover Design: David J. Farr, *ImageSmythe*
Internal Design: LightSource Images
Marketing Manager: Matthew Fillmonov

MacinTax® and *TurboTax*® are registered trademarks of Intuit,® Inc.

Copyright © 1998
by West Educational Publishing Company, an imprint of
South-Western College Publishing
Cincinnati, Ohio

ALL RIGHTS RESERVED

The text of this publication, or any part thereof, may not be reproduced or transmitted in any form or by any means, electronic or mechanical, including photocopying, recording, storage in an information retrieval system, or otherwise, without the prior written permission of the publisher.

ISBN: 0-314-20552-7

1 2 3 4 5 6 7 8 9 WST 5 4 3 2 1 0 9 8 7

Printed in the United States of America

Library of Congress Cataloging-in-Publication Data

Main entry under title:
  West's Federal Taxation.
  Includes index.
  1. Income tax—United States—Law
I. Hoffman, William H.   III.   Willis, Eugene

ISBN 0-314-20552-7, 0-314-20956-5
KF6335.H63   343'.73'04   77-54355

ISSN 0272-0329
1998 ANNUAL EDITION

I(T)P®
International Thomson Publishing
WEST/South-Western College Publishing is an ITP Company.
The ITP trademark is used under license.

PREFACE

The publication of the 1998 Edition marks the twenty-first year of *West's Federal Taxation* (WFT). From a single textbook on Corporations, Partnerships, Estates, and Trusts with an accompanying solutions manual, the WFT series has grown to four major textbooks and a package of more than 50 ancillaries. During this period, WFT has made every effort to improve the quality of the materials and has consistently added attractive innovations. With sales surpassing the one million level, WFT looks forward to continued success in the future in serving you.

This textbook is intended as a basis for a first course in Federal taxation for undergraduate or graduate accounting, business, and law students. With certain modifications in the coverage of the materials, the textbook may be used in a survey course on Federal taxation for undergraduate or graduate students. The materials may also be valuable as a tool for self-study, since they contain numerous clarifying examples adaptable to such an approach.

Tax policy considerations and historical developments are introduced in the textbook only to the extent that they shed light on the reason for a particular rule. The many simple and straightforward examples further clarify the materials by showing how a particular tax rule applies in an actual situation.

Since the original edition was issued in 1978, we have followed a policy of annually revising the text material to reflect statutory, judicial, and administrative changes in the Federal tax law and to correct any errors or other shortcomings. Not only do we encourage user input, we actively seek the advice of users as the basis for improving the textbook.

Tax legislation may be enacted in 1997 or early 1998. If any significant tax legislation is enacted during this period, we will provide you with supplements on a timely basis.

Though the primary emphasis of the textbook is on the income taxation of individuals, Chapter 20 provides an overview of the Federal taxation of other forms of business organization (corporations and partnerships). This chapter could be of particular significance to students who do not plan to take a second course in Federal taxation. For others, Chapter 20 may serve as a lead-in to *West's Federal Taxation: Corporations, Partnerships, Estates, and Trusts.*

ENHANCED PEDAGOGICAL PLAN

In the 1998 edition, we have continued to enhance the pedagogy to assist the student in the learning process and to address the recommendations of the Accounting Education Change Commission (AECC).

- *Learning Objectives.* Each chapter begins with student learning objectives for the chapter. These behavioral objectives provide the students with guidance in learning the key concepts and principles.
- *Chapter Outline.* The learning objectives are followed by a topical outline of the material in the chapter. Page references appear in the outline to provide the student with ready access to each topic.

- *Chapter Introductions.* The introductions link the material in the current chapter to previous chapters and demonstrate its relevance. Frequently, the chapter introduction includes a "real-world" illustration to help convey the relevance of the material.
- *Margin Notes.* Each of the learning objectives appears in the margin where the related material is introduced and helps to guide the student through the chapter.
- *Tax in the News.* Tax in the News items appear in each chapter as a boxed feature to enliven the text discussion. These items are drawn from today's business press and present current issues that are relevant to the chapter material.
- *Ethical Considerations.* Ethical Considerations features appear in each chapter presenting thought-provoking issues related to the chapter topics. In response to the recommendations of the AECC, they also demonstrate that many issues do not have a single correct answer. The questions raised in the Ethical Considerations were selected to provoke discussion and provide opportunities for debate (oral communication) based on the student's value system rather than to provide a defensible answer. To assist the professor in providing guidance for the discussion, the *Instructor's Guide with Lecture Notes* includes material on each Ethical Consideration. This material identifies the issues raised in the Ethical Consideration and, where appropriate, recommends a solution or alternate solutions.
- *Key Terms.* Located before the Problem Materials in each chapter is a list of key terms to assist student learning. When the key term is introduced in the chapter, it appears in bold print. The list of key terms includes page references to the chapter coverage. In addition, each key term is defined in the Glossary (Appendix C).
- *Communication Assignments.* In recognition of the increasing emphasis in accounting and tax education on communication, identified items in the Problem Materials now include a written communication component. Selected Problems, Cumulative Problems, and Research Problems are identified as communication assignments with a "scroll" icon. These problems ask the student to prepare a tax client letter, a memorandum for the tax files, or other written materials. The discussion of the tax research process in Chapter 2 includes an illustration of the client letter and the memo.
- *Decision-Making Problems.* The Problem Materials include decision-making problems that are designed to enhance the student's analytical skills. These problems are identified with a "scales" icon.
- *Issue Recognition Questions.* The Problem Materials include questions that are designed to require the student to identify tax issues. With this issues orientation, such questions can be multifaceted and have no single right answer. These questions are identified with a "lightbulb" icon.
- *Team Projects: Arthur Andersen Tax Challenge Cases.* This feature at the end of the Problem Materials gives students experience working as a team to solve complex real world tax issues. The instructor can choose between two cases that can be ordered from your West representative and provided to students at no cost. Materials for the instructor can be found in the *Instructor's Guide*.
- The Research Problems heading now includes a CD-ROM icon to emphasize that solutions to all the research problems can now be prepared using *West's Federal Taxation on CD-ROM*. *WFT on CD-ROM* includes false leads as well as the necessary cases, Revenue Rulings, and Revenue Procedures as a way of providing a realistic environment for the tax research process.

Preface

- *Internet exercises.* Included as part of the Research Problems for each chapter are questions which require the use of the tax resources of the internet. These exercises are identified with a globe and computer mouse icon.

SPECIAL FEATURES

A variety of other pedagogical devices are used to assist the student in the learning process. We recognize the importance of readability and continue to strive to make our textbook and supplements even more readable and understandable. The following features enhance the readability of the text:

- Including three levels of headings to aid in organization.
- Using bold print in the text to identify key terms the first time each term is used.
- Italicizing other key words to emphasize their importance to the student.
- Avoiding legal terminology except where it is beneficial.
- Using Concept Summaries to synthesize important concepts in chart or tabular form.
- Using Exhibits, Figures, and Tables to enhance presentations.
- Organizing the material in lists with bullets rather than presenting it in lengthy sentences.
- Using examples frequently to help the student understand the tax concept being discussed.
- Using a larger page size to provide a more open, accessible, and student-friendly textbook.

Once knowledge of the tax law has been acquired, it needs to be used. The tax minimization process, however, normally requires careful planning. Because we recognize the importance of planning procedures, most chapters include a separate section (called *Tax Planning Considerations*) illustrating the applications of these procedures to specific areas. While tax planning applications and suggestions appear throughout the chapter, this separate section at the end of the chapter calls the student's attention to the importance of tax planning.

We believe that any basic course in Federal taxation should offer the reader the opportunity to learn and utilize the methodology of tax research. This knowledge is requisite in today's environment with its increased emphasis on the concept of "learning to learn." Chapter 2 and Appendix E are devoted to this methodology. Also, most chapters contain *Research Problems* that require the use of research tools. Solutions to these Research Problems can be found in the *Instructor's Guide*. The effectiveness of the text does not, however, depend on the coverage of tax research procedures. Consequently, the treatment of this subject may be omitted without impairing the continuity of the remaining textual materials.

Although it is not our purpose to approach taxation from the standpoint of preparing tax returns, some familiarity with forms is necessary. Because 1997 forms will not be available until later in the year, most tax return problems in this edition are written for tax year 1996. For the reader's convenience, Appendix B contains a full reproduction of most of the 1996 tax forms frequently encountered in actual practice. The 1996 problems may be solved manually, or many may be solved using the tax return preparation software (*TurboTax* or *MacInTax*) that may be purchased by students who use this textbook.

Appendix F contains two comprehensive tax return problems written for tax year 1996. Each of these problems lends itself for use as a term project because of the sophistication required for satisfactory completion. Solutions to the problems in Appendix F appear in the *Instructor's Guide*.

Most tax textbooks are published in the spring, long before tax forms for the year of publication are available from the government. We believe that students should be exposed to the most current tax forms. As a result, we develop some new problems and provide adopters with reproducible copies of these problems, along with blank tax forms and solutions on the new forms. Shortly after the beginning of 1998, adopters will receive a *Forms Problems Supplement* containing these tax return problems solved on 1997 forms.

WEST'S FEDERAL TAXATION ON CD-ROM

West is continuing to offer this text on CD-ROM. It includes the entire text of the printed version of *West's Federal Taxation: Individual Income Taxes, 1998 Edition* as well as the full text of all referenced cases, code Sections, Regulations, Revenue Procedures, and Revenue Rulings, and all tax forms, tables and schedules from the appendixes. Students can jump directly from the text they're reading to the full text of any of the references included on the disc.

We have expanded the materials on the CD-ROM so that solutions to all of the Research Problems can be prepared using the CD-ROM. In addition to adding the requisite cases, Revenue Rulings, and Revenue Procedures for the solutions, additional cases, Revenue Rulings, and Revenue Procedures are included to serve as "false leads" and provide a realistic environment for the tax research process.

Other features include "notebook" capabilities that allow students to cut and paste from the text, type in their own comments, and convert the text and notes into other word processing packages. Records of all queries are kept which allow viewing and editing of past queries. Each disc has an electronic "book-mark" feature that marks the spot where the student left off and returns to the last page that was viewed when the project is resumed. *WFT on CD-ROM* is fully supported by West's CD-ROM Customer Service Technicians and Research Attorneys. Professors and students can call for any technical or research assistance their projects require.

System requirements include an IBM or compatible PC with a 486 processor or higher; Windows version 3.1 or higher (includes Windows 95); DOS version 3.3 or higher; 4 MB of available RAM, 8 MB recommended (after loading all memory-resident software including device drivers and MSCDEX); minimum of 16 MB of available hard disk space; VGA monitor or better; CD-ROM drive using Microsoft CD-ROM Extensions (MSCDEX) version 2.1 or higher (compatible CD-ROM drives must meet the ISO 9660 standard). To print images off the CD, 1.5 MG RAM on a printer is required.

SUPPLEMENTS

West is continuing to publish the Arthur Andersen Tax Challenge Cases, a set of four capstone cases and their solutions provided to the instructor for classroom use. The cases encompass both tax compliance and tax planning and provide an opportunity for a team approach in solving tax issues and recommending tax strategies. As a technique for further integrating the cases with the textbook coverage of the tax topics in the cases, page references to two of the cases appear at the end of each chapter.

Other products in our 1998 instructional package include the following:

- The *Instructor's Guide with Lecture Notes* contains lecture notes for each chapter, materials on the Ethical Considerations found in the textbook, materials on the two Arthur Andersen Tax Challenge Cases that are page referenced to the textbook, and solutions to Research Problems and Comprehensive Tax Return problems found in the textbook. The lecture notes consist of a lecture outline that the professor can use as the basis for his or her classroom presentation. These lecture notes include not only material covered in the textbook, but also cases and other relevant material and teaching aids. The lecture notes are also available on disc in ASCII files.

- A *Solutions Manual* that has been carefully checked to ensure that it is error-free. The problems are arranged in accordance with the sequence of the material in the chapter. All problems are labeled by topical coverage in a matrix that also indicates which problems are new, modified, or unchanged in the new edition. The matrix also includes the problem number for the unchanged and modified problems in the prior edition. Approximately 20 percent of the problems in the 1998 edition are new or modified. The solutions are referenced to pages in the textbook. The solutions manual is also available on disc in ASCII files.
- A *Test Bank* with questions and solutions referenced to pages in the textbook. The questions are arranged in accordance with the sequence of the material in the chapter. To assist the professor in selecting questions for an examination, all questions are labeled by topical coverage in a matrix that also indicates which questions are new, modified, or unchanged in the new edition. The matrix includes the question number for the unchanged and modified questions in the prior edition. Approximately 20 percent of the questions in the 1998 edition are new or modified.
- *Westest*, a microcomputer test generation program for IBM PCs and compatibles and the Macintosh family of computers.
- *West CD-ROM Federal Tax Library* (Compact Disc with Read-Only Memory) provides a complete tax research library on a desktop. The Federal Tax Library is a set of compact discs with a software package that reads the discs through a PC. Each disc has a remarkable storage capacity-roughly 1,000 times more than a single-sided floppy disc. A brief list of the library contents includes the complete *Internal Revenue Code of 1986*, Regulations, 1986 Tax Reform Act with Amendments and Legislative History, Federal Court Cases on Tax (i.e., District, Circuit, and Supreme), Tax Court Cases, Revenue Rulings, and Revenue Procedures. The library is available to qualified adopters.
- A *Student Study Guide* prepared by Gerald E. Whittenburg, San Diego State University, includes a chapter review of key concepts and self-evaluation tests with solutions that are page referenced to the textbook.
- *Solutions Transparency Masters* for selected complex and cumulative problems, with a larger typeface for greater readability.
- *PowerPoint Presentation Software* allows qualified adopters to create interactive lectures and manipulate graphs, charts, and figures during in-class lectures. The package contains approximately 30 transparency masters per chapter consisting of alternate figures, outlines, and key points.
- *Teaching Transparency Acetates* contain the key charts and tables from the *PowerPoint* package for instructors who wish to use traditional overheads.
- A *Student Note-Taking Guide* includes selected screens from the PowerPoint package consisting of chapter outlines and key points. This unique guide provides students with the core chapter information, so they can concentrate in class on learning key concepts instead of copying basic lecture outlines and transparencies. These have been printed and bound in a manner similar to accounting working papers. The pages include all the information from the PowerPoint screens while still leaving room for student notes.

- *Instructor's Resource Notebook*—this three-ring binder can be used to house all or portions of the supplements and textbook that we will continue to offer in looseleaf form so you can reorganize the book and incorporate your supplemental materials to fit your course lectures.
- *WFT Individual Practice Sets,* 1997–98 edition, prepared by John B. Barrack, University of Georgia, is designed to cover all the common forms that a tax practitioner would use for the average client.
- Limited free use to qualified adopters of WESTLAW, a computer-assisted tax and legal research service that provides access to hundreds of valuable information sources.
- *West's Internal Revenue Code of 1986 and Treasury Regulations: Annotated and Selected 1998 Edition* by James E. Smith, College of William and Mary. This provides the opportunity for the student to be exposed to the Code and the Regulations in a single-volume book, which also contains useful annotations that help the student work with and understand the Code.
- *WFT On-line* puts the most current information in your hands as soon as it is available. Qualified adopters can log onto West Publishing's site on the World Wide Web (http://www.westpub.com/Educate/) and immediately gain access to the most recent taxation information available, including the Code and Regulations, case citations, new court rulings, and other newsworthy items. This information can then be transferred to a word-processing program for editing, printout, and classroom use while the information is still topical.

TAX PREPARATION SOFTWARE

The trend toward using the computer as an essential tool in tax practice has accelerated. To ensure that the *West's Federal Taxation* instructional package continues to set the pace in this important area, the following product is available to be used with the 1998 edition:

- *TurboTax* © for Windows 96.01a by Intuit is a commercial tax preparation package. It teaches students how to prepare over 80 forms, schedules, and worksheets, and automatically performs all mathematical calculations and data transfers. The *TurboTax* package, available for student purchase, includes discs bound with a 200-page workbook containing exercises and problems. The software runs on IBM PCs and compatibles with 512K memory.

This software product is powerful, easy to learn, and easy to use. We believe that tax education can be raised to a higher level through the use of computers and well-designed software. This software package takes the drudgery out of performing the complex computations required to solve difficult tax problems.

To enable students to take advantage of this software product, the 1998 edition contains numerous tax return problems. Problems that lend themselves to computerized solutions are identified by a computer symbol.

ACKNOWLEDGMENTS

We are most appreciative of the many suggestions that we have received for revising the textbook, many of which have been incorporated in past editions and in the 1998 edition. We would also like to thank the people who have painstakingly worked through all the problems and text questions and generally acted as problem checkers to ensure the accuracy of the book and ancillary package. They are Tracey A. Anderson, Indiana University at South Bend; Caroline K. Craig, Illinois State University; Mark B. Persellin, St. Mary's University; Debra L. Sanders, Washington State University; Randall K. Serrett, Fort Lewis College; Thomas Sternburg, University of Illinois at Urbana; and Raymond F. Wacker, Southern Illinois University at Carbondale.

Finally, this 1998 edition would not have been possible without the technical assistance of and manuscript review by Bonnie Hoffman, CPA, Freda Mulhall, CPA, and Nora Smith, M.Ed. We are indebted to them for their efforts.

William H. Hoffman, Jr.
James E. Smith
Eugene Willis

April 1, 1997

About the Editors

William H. Hoffman, Jr., earned B.A. and J.D. degrees from the University of Michigan and M.B.A. and Ph.D. degrees from The University of Texas. He is a licensed CPA and attorney in Texas. His teaching experience includes: The University of Texas (1957–1961), Louisiana State University (1961–1967), and the University of Houston (1967 to present). Professor Hoffman has addressed many tax institutes and conferences and has published extensively in academic and professional journals. His articles appear in *The Journal of Taxation, The Tax Adviser, Taxes—The Tax Magazine, The Journal of Accountancy, The Accounting Review,* and *Taxation for Accountants.*

James E. Smith is the John S. Quinn Professor of Accounting at the College of William and Mary. He has been a member of the Accounting Faculty for twenty-seven years. He received his Ph.D. degree from the University of Arizona.

Jim has served as a discussion leader for Continuing Professional Education programs for the AICPA, Federal Tax Workshops, and various state CPA societies. He has conducted programs in over 40 states for approximately 25,000 CPAs. He has been the recipient of the AICPAs' Outstanding Discussion Leader Award.

Other awards received by Jim include the Virginia Society of CPAs' Outstanding Accounting Educator Award and the James Madison University's Outstanding Accounting Educator Award. He was the President of the Administrators of Accounting Programs Group (AAPG) in 1991–1992. He was the faculty adviser for the William and Mary teams that received first place in the Arthur Andersen Tax Challenge in 1994 and 1995.

Eugene Willis is the Arthur Andersen Alumni Professor of Accountancy at the University of Illinois (Urbana-Champaign). He joined the Illinois faculty in 1975 after receiving his Ph.D. from the University of Cincinnati. He serves as Interim Head of the department. His articles have appeared in leading academic and professional journals, including the *Accounting Review, The Journal of the American Taxation Association, The Journal of Accountancy,* and *The Journal of Taxation.* Professor Willis is co-director of the National Tax Education Program, a continuing education program co-sponsored by the American Institute of CPAs and the University of Illinois.

Contents in Brief

Preface v

PART I INTRODUCTION AND BASIC TAX MODEL

CHAPTER 1 An Introduction to Taxation and Understanding the Federal Tax Law   1–1

CHAPTER 2 Working with the Tax Law   2–1

CHAPTER 3 Tax Determination; Personal and Dependency Exemptions; An Overview of Property Transactions   3–1

PART II GROSS INCOME

CHAPTER 4 Gross Income: Concepts and Inclusions   4–1

CHAPTER 5 Gross Income: Exclusions   5–1

PART III DEDUCTIONS

CHAPTER 6 Deductions and Losses: In General   6–1

CHAPTER 7 Deductions and Losses: Certain Business Expenses and Losses   7–1

CHAPTER 8 Depreciation, Cost Recovery, Amortization, and Depletion   8–1

CHAPTER 9 Deductions: Employee Expenses   9–1

CHAPTER 10 Deductions and Losses: Certain Itemized Deductions   10–1

CHAPTER 11 Passive Activity Losses   11–1

PART IV SPECIAL TAX COMPUTATION METHODS, PAYMENT PROCEDURES, AND TAX CREDITS

CHAPTER 12 Alternative Minimum Tax   12–1

CHAPTER 13 Tax Credits and Payment Procedures   13–1

PART V PROPERTY TRANSACTIONS

CHAPTER 14 Property Transactions: Determination of Gain or Loss and Basis Considerations 14–1

CHAPTER 15 Property Transactions: Nontaxable Exchanges 15–1

CHAPTER 16 Property Transactions: Capital Gains and Losses 16–1

CHAPTER 17 Property Transactions: Section 1231 and Recapture Provisions 17–1

PART VI ACCOUNTING PERIODS, ACCOUNTING METHODS, AND DEFERRED COMPENSATION

CHAPTER 18 Accounting Periods and Methods 18–1

CHAPTER 19 Deferred Compensation 19–1

PART VII CORPORATIONS AND PARTNERSHIPS

CHAPTER 20 Corporations and Partnerships 20–1

Appendixes A–1

Subject Index I–1

Contents

Preface   v

PART I
INTRODUCTION AND BASIC TAX MODEL

CHAPTER 1
An Introduction to Taxation and Understanding the Federal Tax Law 1–1

History of U.S. Taxation	1–2
Early Periods	1–2
Revenue Acts	1–3
Historical Trends	1–3
Criteria Used in the Selection of a Tax Structure	1–4
The Tax Structure	1–5
Tax Base	1–5
Tax Rates	1–5
Incidence of Taxation	1–5
Major Types of Taxes	1–6
Property Taxes	1–6
Ethical Considerations: Tax-Exempt Status Forever?	1–7
Transaction Taxes	1–8
Death Taxes	1–10
Tax in the News: Can a Use Tax Discriminate?	1–10
Gift Taxes	1–12
Ethical Considerations: The Annual Exclusion for Gifts	1–12
Income Taxes	1–13
Employment Taxes	1–15
Tax in the News: Visitors Beware! The City and State You Visit May Not Be All That Friendly	1–15
Other U.S. Taxes	1–16
Proposed U.S. Taxes	1–17
Tax Administration	1–18
Internal Revenue Service	1–18
The Audit Process	1–18
Ethical Considerations: A Nosy (and Unnecessary) Audit	1–20
Statute of Limitations	1–21
Interest and Penalties	1–22
Tax Practice	1–23
Tax in the News: Even the Mighty Can Fall	1–23
Understanding the Federal Tax Law	1–24
Revenue Needs	1–24
Economic Considerations	1–25
Social Considerations	1–26
Equity Considerations	1–27
Political Considerations	1–29
Influence of the Internal Revenue Service	1–31
Influence of the Courts	1–32
Summary	1–33
Problem Materials	1–34

CHAPTER 2
Working with the Tax Law 2–1

Tax Sources	2–2
Statutory Sources of the Tax Law	2–3
Tax in the News: Small Is Beautiful?	2–3
Administrative Sources of the Tax Law	2–7
Tax in the News: Who Are the Bad Guys?	2–9
Ethical Considerations: The Cost of Tax Compliance	2–12
Judicial Sources of the Tax Law	2–13
Ethical Considerations: Choosing Cases for Appeal	2–16

XV

Working with the Tax Law— Tax Research — 2–23
Identifying the Problem — 2–23
Refining the Problem — 2–23
Locating the Appropriate Tax Law Sources — 2–24
Assessing the Validity of the Tax Law Sources — 2–26
Tax in the News: Internal Revenue Code: Interpretation Pitfalls — 2–27
Arriving at the Solution or at Alternative Solutions — 2–30
Communicating Tax Research — 2–31

Working with the Tax Law— Tax Planning — 2–31
Nontax Considerations — 2–33
Tax Avoidance and Tax Evasion — 2–33
Ethical Considerations: Tax Avoidance — 2–34
Follow-Up Procedures — 2–34
Tax Planning—A Practical Application — 2–34
Electronic Tax Research — 2–35
Tax in the News: Tax Research: CD-ROM versus Paper — 2–36

Problem Materials — 2–41

CHAPTER 3
Tax Determination; Personal and Dependency Exemptions; An Overview of Property Transactions — 3–1

Tax Formula — 3–3
Components of the Tax Formula — 3–3
Application of the Tax Formula — 3–8
Individuals Not Eligible for the Standard Deduction — 3–9
Special Limitations for Individuals Who Can Be Claimed as Dependents — 3–9

Personal and Dependency Exemptions — 3–10
Personal Exemptions — 3–10
Dependency Exemptions — 3–10
Ethical Considerations: Claiming a Dependent — 3–12
Tax in the News: The Wrong Way to Claim Dependency Exemptions — 3–13

Tax Determination — 3–16
Tax Table Method — 3–16
Tax Rate Schedule Method — 3–16
Computation of Net Taxes Payable or Refund Due — 3–18
Unearned Income of Children Under Age 14 Taxed at Parent's Rate — 3–19

Filing Considerations — 3–21
Filing Requirements — 3–21
Filing Status — 3–23
Tax in the News: Low-Income Taxpayers Also Suffer from the Marriage Penalty — 3–25

Gains and Losses from Property Transactions—In General — 3–27
Tax in the News: Being Alone Is Not All That Bad! — 3–27

Gains and Losses from Property Transactions—Capital Gains and Losses — 3–28
Definition of a Capital Asset — 3–28
Computation of Net Capital Gains and Losses — 3–29
Capital Loss Limitation — 3–29

Tax Planning Considerations — 3–30
Taking Advantage of Tax Rate Differentials — 3–30
Income of Minor Children — 3–31
Ethical Considerations: A Working Family Is a Happy Family — 3–31
Dependency Exemptions — 3–31
Ethical Considerations: Manipulating Deductions — 3–33

Problem Materials — 3–33

PART II
GROSS INCOME

CHAPTER 4
Gross Income: Concepts and Inclusions — 4–1

Gross Income—What Is It? — 4–3
Definition — 4–3
Economic and Accounting Concepts — 4–3
Comparison of the Accounting and Tax Concepts of Income — 4–4
Tax in the News: Frequent Flyer Miles Frequently Raise Tax Issues — 4–5
Form of Receipt — 4–6
Ethical Considerations: Unreported Income — 4–6
Recovery of Capital Doctrine — 4–6

Year of Inclusion	**4–7**
Taxable Year	4–7
Accounting Methods	4–7
Exceptions Applicable to Cash Basis Taxpayers	4–9
Exceptions Applicable to Accrual Basis Taxpayers	4–12
Income Sources	**4–14**
Personal Services	4–14
Income From Property	4–14
Income Received by an Agent	4–16
Income From Partnerships, S Corporations, Trusts, and Estates	4–16
Ethical Considerations: Whether to Report Income	4–17
Income in Community Property States	4–17
Items Specifically Included in Gross Income	**4–19**
Alimony and Separate Maintenance Payments	4–19
Ethical Considerations: Structuring a Divorce	4–22
Imputed Interest on Below-Market Loans	4–23
Tax in the News: Ex-Spouse and Federal Government Are Big Lottery Winners	4–24
Income From Annuities	4–28
Prizes and Awards	4–32
Group Term Life Insurance	4–33
Unemployment Compensation	4–34
Social Security Benefits	4–34
Tax in the News: A Tax on a Tax	4–35
Tax Planning Considerations	**4–36**
Nontaxable Economic Benefits	4–36
Tax Deferral	4–36
Shifting Income to Relatives	4–38
Accounting for Community Property	4–39
Alimony	4–39
Problem Materials	**4–40**
CHAPTER 5	
Gross Income: Exclusions	**5–1**
Items Specifically Excluded from Gross Income	**5–2**
Statutory Authority	**5–4**
Gifts and Inheritances	**5–4**
General	5–4
Gifts to Employees	5–5
Employee Death Benefits	5–5
Life Insurance Proceeds	**5–6**
General Rule	5–6
Accelerated Death Benefits	5–6
Ethical Considerations: Investing in Death	5–7
Transfer for Valuable Consideration	5–7
Scholarships	**5–8**
General Information	5–8
Timing Issues	5–9
Disguised Compensation	5–9
Qualified Tuition Reduction Plans	5–10
Ethical Considerations: A Caring Dean	5–10
Compensation for Injuries and Sickness	**5–11**
Damages	5–11
Workers' Compensation	5–12
Accident and Health Insurance Benefits	5–13
Employer-Sponsored Accident and Health Plans	**5–13**
Medical Reimbursement Plans	5–14
Long-Term Care Insurance Benefits	5–14
Meals and Lodging	**5–15**
Furnished for the Convenience of the Employer	5–15
Other Housing Exclusions	5–17
Tax in the News: The IRS Finds Compensatory Reason for Providing Employee Meals	5–17
Other Employee Fringe Benefits	**5–18**
Specific Benefits	5–18
Cafeteria Plans	5–18
Flexible Spending Plans	5–19
General Classes of Excluded Benefits	5–19
Tax in the News: Cafeteria Plans and Public Accountants	5–20
Ethical Considerations: Excluding Employee Discounts	5–22
Taxable Fringe Benefits	5–25
Foreign Earned Income	**5–25**
Interest on Certain State and Local Government Obligations	**5–28**
Tax in the News: Foreign Earned Income Exclusion Creates Jobs for U.S. Citizens	5–28
Dividends	**5–29**
General Information	5–29
Stock Dividends	5–30

Educational Savings Bonds	5–30
Qualified State Tuition Programs	5–31
Tax Benefit Rule	5–32
Income from Discharge of Indebtedness	5–32
Tax Planning Considerations	**5–34**
Life Insurance	5–34
Employee Benefits	5–34
Investment Income	5–35
Problem Materials	**5–36**

PART III
DEDUCTIONS

CHAPTER 6
Deductions and Losses: In General — 6–1

Classification of Deductible Expenses	**6–2**
Deductions for Adjusted Gross Income	6–3
Itemized Deductions	6–4
Tax in the News: America's Team	6–4
Trade or Business Expenses and Production of Income Expenses	6–5
Business and Nonbusiness Losses	6–7
Reporting Procedures	6–7
Deductions and Losses—Timing of Expense Recognition	**6–9**
Importance of Taxpayer's Method of Accounting	6–9
Cash Method Requirements	6–9
Accrual Method Requirements	6–10
Disallowance Possibilities	**6–11**
Public Policy Limitation	6–11
Ethical Considerations: To Obey the Law	6–12
Political Contributions and Lobbying Activities	6–14
Excessive Executive Compensation	6–14
Investigation of a Business	6–15
Tax in the News: The Joy of Not Being an Executive of a Publicly Held Corporation	6–15
Hobby Losses	6–16
Rental of Vacation Homes	6–19

Tax in the News: Is a Dream Home in the Mountains or at the Beach for You?	6–19
Ethical Considerations: Renting for One More Day	6–20
Expenditures Incurred for Taxpayer's Benefit or Taxpayer's Obligation	6–23
Ethical Considerations: How the Payment Is Made	6–25
Disallowance of Personal Expenditures	6–25
Disallowance of Deductions for Capital Expenditures	6–26
Transactions Between Related Parties	6–27
Substantiation Requirements	6–28
Expenses and Interest Relating to Tax-Exempt Income	6–29
Tax Planning Considerations	**6–30**
Time Value of Tax Deductions	6–30
Unreasonable Compensation	6–32
Excessive Executive Compensation	6–32
Shifting Deductions	6–32
Hobby Losses	6–32
Capital Expenditures	6–33
Problem Materials	**6–34**

CHAPTER 7
Deductions and Losses: Certain Business Expenses and Losses — 7–1

Bad Debts	**7–3**
Specific Charge-off Method	7–3
Business versus Nonbusiness Bad Debts	7–4
Loans Between Related Parties	7–5
Ethical Considerations: Writing Off a Loan to a Friend	7–6
Loss of Deposits in Insolvent Financial Institutions	7–6
Worthless Securities	**7–7**
Tax in the News: Family Bad Debts Can Be Deducted under the Right Circumstances	7–7
Small Business Stock	7–8
Losses of Individuals	**7–9**
Events That Are Not Casualties	7–10
Theft Losses	7–10
Ethical Considerations: Deducting a Theft Loss	7–11
When to Deduct Casualty Losses	7–11
Measuring the Amount of Loss	7–12

Ethical Considerations: Deducting the Cost of Repairs	7–13
Statutory Framework for Deducting Losses of Individuals	7–15
Personal Casualty Gains and Losses	7–15

Research and Experimental Expenditures 7–17
Expense Method 7–18
Deferral and Amortization Method 7–18

Net Operating Losses 7–19
Tax in the News: Acquiring Racehorses: A Research and Development Expense 7–19
Carryback and Carryover Periods 7–20
Computation of the Net Operating Loss 7–21
Tax in the News: Hobby Loss versus Business NOL 7–21
Ethical Considerations: Net Operating Losses 7–24
Recomputation of Tax Liability for Year to Which Net Operating Loss is Carried 7–24
Calculation of the Remaining Net Operating Loss 7–25

Tax Planning Considerations 7–26
Tax Consequences of the *Groetzinger* Case 7–26
Documentation of Related-Taxpayer Loans, Casualty Losses, and Theft Losses 7–26
Small Business Stock 7–27
Casualty Losses 7–27
Net Operating Losses 7–27

Problem Materials 7–28

CHAPTER 8
Depreciation, Cost Recovery, Amortization, and Depletion 8–1

Overview 8–3

Accelerated Cost Recovery System (ACRS and MACRS) 8–4
General Considerations 8–4
Ethical Considerations: Deducting Depreciation on a Converted Truck 8–5
Eligible Property Under ACRS or MACRS 8–5
Personalty: Recovery Periods and Methods 8–5
Tax in the News: A Seventeenth-Century Ruggeri Bass Violin Is a Tool of Trade Rather Than a Work of Art 8–6
Realty: Recovery Periods and Methods 8–11

Straight-Line Election Under ACRS and MACRS	8–14
Election to Expense Assets	8–15
Business and Personal Use of Automobiles and Other Listed Property	8–17
Tax in the News: A Ferrari as Medical Equipment	8–18
Ethical Considerations: Substantiating Business Mileage	8–22
Alternative Depreciation System (ADS)	8–23

Amortization 8–24
Ethical Considerations: Allocating Intangible Assets When a Business Is Sold 8–25

Depletion 8–25
Intangible Drilling and Development Costs (IDC) 8–26
Depletion Methods 8–26

Reporting Procedures 8–29

Tax Planning Considerations 8–33
Cost Recovery 8–33
Amortization 8–34
Depletion 8–34

Tables 8–35

Problem Materials 8–43

CHAPTER 9
Deductions: Employee Expenses 9–1

Employee versus Self-Employed 9–2
Tax in the News: There Is Safety in Numbers 9–3

Employee Expenses—In General 9–4

Transportation Expenses 9–5
Qualified Expenditures 9–5
Computation of Automobile Expenses 9–6

Travel Expenses 9–7
Definition of Travel Expenses 9–7
Away-From-Home Requirement 9–7
Restrictions on Travel Expenses 9–8
Combined Business and Pleasure Travel 9–10

Moving Expenses 9–11
Distance Test 9–11
Time Test 9–12

Treatment of Moving Expenses	9–12
Ethical Considerations: How Much Is That House Really Worth?	9–13
Education Expenses	**9–13**
General Requirements	9–13
Requirements Imposed by Law or by the Employer for Retention of Employment	9–14
Maintaining or Improving Existing Skills	9–14
Classification of Specific Items	9–15
Other Provisions Dealing With Education	9–15
Entertainment Expenses	**9–15**
Dollar Limitations	9–16
Classification of Expenses	9–16
Restrictions Upon Deductibility	9–17
Ethical Considerations: Reciprocal Entertaining	9–17
Other Employee Expenses	**9–19**
Office in the Home	9–19
Miscellaneous Employee Expenses	9–20
Contributions to Individual Retirement Accounts	9–21
Classification of Employee Expenses	**9–21**
Accountable Plans	9–21
Tax in the News: NBA Referees Enjoy a Nontaxable Pay Raise	9–22
Nonaccountable Plans	9–23
Ethical Considerations: The Frugal Employee	9–23
Reporting Procedures	9–24
Limitations on Itemized Deductions	**9–25**
Miscellaneous Itemized Deductions Subject to the 2 Percent Floor	9–25
Miscellaneous Itemized Deductions Not Subject to the 2 Percent Floor	9–25
Tax Planning Considerations	**9–26**
Self-Employed Individuals	9–26
Shifting Deductions between Employer and Employee	9–26
Transportation and Travel Expenses	9–26
Moving Expenses	9–27
Education Expenses	9–27
Tax in the News: If You Don't Like the Transfer, Be Ready to Pay!	9–27
Entertainment Expenses	9–28
Unreimbursed Employee Business Expenses	9–28
Problem Materials	**9–29**

CHAPTER 10
Deductions and Losses: Certain Itemized Deductions — **10–1**

General Classification of Expenses	**10–2**
Medical Expenses	**10–2**
General Requirements	10–2
Tax in the News: Average Itemized Deductions	10–3
Medical Expenses Defined	10–4
Ethical Considerations: Necessary or Unnecessary Cosmetic Surgery?	10–4
Capital Expenditures for Medical Purposes	10–5
Medical Expenses Incurred for Spouse and Dependents	10–6
Transportation, Meal, and Lodging Expenses for Medical Treatment	10–7
Amounts Paid for Medical Insurance Premiums	10–8
Year of Deduction	10–8
Reimbursements	10–9
Ethical Considerations: Selecting the Reimbursement Year	10–10
Medical Savings Accounts	10–10
Taxes	**10–10**
Deductibility as a Tax	10–11
Property Taxes	10–11
State and Local Income Taxes	10–13
Interest	**10–13**
Allowed and Disallowed Items	10–14
Tax in the News: Deduction for Mortgage Interest Costs Government Billions	10–17
Restrictions on Deductibility and Timing Considerations	10–18
Classification of Interest Expense	10–18
Charitable Contributions	**10–19**
Criteria for a Gift	10–20
Qualified Organizations	10–21
Time of Deduction	10–21
Record-Keeping and Valuation Requirements	10–22
Ethical Considerations: A Second Appraisal	10–23
Limitations on Charitable Contribution Deduction	10–23
Miscellaneous Itemized Deductions	**10–27**
Other Miscellaneous Deductions	**10–28**
Tax in the News: A Ticket to Jail?	10–28

Comprehensive Example of Schedule A	10–29
Overall Limitation on Certain Itemized Deductions	10–29
Tax Planning Considerations	10–32
Effective Utilization of Itemized Deductions	10–32
Utilization of Medical Deductions	10–32
Timing the Payment of Deductible Taxes	10–33
Protecting the Interest Deduction	10–33
Assuring the Charitable Contribution Deduction	10–34
Problem Materials	10–36

CHAPTER 11
Passive Activity Losses — 11–1

The Tax Shelter Problem	11–2
Tax in the News: The Feds May Ask Tax Shelters to Register	11–3
At-Risk Limits	11–4
Ethical Considerations: Manipulating the At-Risk Limits	11–5
Passive Loss Limits	11–6
Classification and Impact of Passive Income and Losses	11–6
Tax in the News: All That Glitters in Tax Reform Is Not Gold	11–7
Taxpayers Subject to the Passive Loss Rules	11–10
Passive Activities Defined	11–11
Ethical Considerations: A Lovers' Triangle and the Passive Loss Rules	11–19
Interaction of the At-Risk and Passive Activity Limits	11–21
Special Passive Activity Rules for Real Estate Activities	11–22
Ethical Considerations: Punching the Time Clock at Year-End	11–23
Dispositions of Passive Interests	11–25
Tax Planning Considerations	11–27
Utilizing Passive Losses	11–27
Problem Materials	11–28

PART IV
SPECIAL TAX COMPUTATION METHODS, PAYMENT PROCEDURES, AND TAX CREDITS

CHAPTER 12
Alternative Minimum Tax — 12–1

Individual Alternative Minimum Tax	12–3
AMT Formula for Alternative Minimum Taxable Income (AMTI)	12–3
AMT Formula: Other Components	12–6
Ethical Considerations: Minimizing the Tax Liability	12–8
AMT Adjustments	12–9
Ethical Considerations: Relationship between the Regular Income Tax Liability and the AMT	12–12
Tax in the News: AMT Turns Winning into Losing	12–16
AMT Preferences	12–20
Ethical Considerations: Taxability of Bond Interest: Regular Income Tax versus AMT	12–21
Tax in the News: Municipal Bonds and the AMT	12–22
Illustration of the AMT Computation	12–23
AMT Credit	12–24
Corporate Alternative Minimum Tax	12–27
AMT Adjustments	12–27
Tax in the News: Who Pays Corporate AMT?	12–29
Tax Preferences	12–30
Exemption	12–31
Other Aspects of the AMT	12–31
Tax Planning Considerations	12–31
Responding to Bob and Carol	12–31
Avoiding Preferences and Adjustments	12–32
Controlling the Timing of Preferences and Adjustments	12–32
Taking Advantage of the AMT/Regular Tax Rate Differential	12–32
Problem Materials	12–33

CHAPTER 13
Tax Credits and Payment Procedures — 13–1

Tax Policy Considerations	13–3
Tax in the News: Incentives Gained through the Reenactment of Tax Credits	13–4
Overview and Priority of Credits	13–5
Refundable versus Nonrefundable Credits	13–5
General Business Credit	13–6
Treatment of Unused General Business Credits	13–7

Specific Business-Related Tax Credit Provisions — 13-7
Tax Credit for Rehabilitation Expenditures — 13-7
Ethical Considerations: Using the Rehabilitation Expenditures Credit — 13-9
Business Energy Credits — 13-9
Work Opportunity Tax Credit — 13-9
Research Activities Credit — 13-10
Low-Income Housing Credit — 13-12
Ethical Considerations: A Win-Win Situation or an Incalculable Loss? — 13-13
Disabled Access Credit — 13-13

Other Tax Credits — 13-14
Earned Income Credit — 13-14
Tax Credit for Elderly or Disabled Taxpayers — 13-16
Tax in the News: "Earned Income Credit" or "Easy Income for Cheats"? — 13-17
Foreign Tax Credit — 13-18
Adoption Expenses Credit — 13-19
Credit for Child and Dependent Care Expenses — 13-20

Payment Procedures — 13-22
Procedures Applicable to Employers — 13-22
Tax in the News: Creativity Gone Awry Leads to Time in Confinement — 13-26
Ethical Considerations: Being Paid Once Every Two Years — 13-28
Procedures Applicable to Self-Employed Persons — 13-33

Tax Planning Considerations — 13-37
Foreign Tax Credit — 13-37
Credit for Child and Dependent Care Expenses — 13-38
Adjustments to Increase Withholding — 13-39
Adjustments to Avoid Overwithholding — 13-39

Problem Materials — 13-40

PART V
PROPERTY TRANSACTIONS

CHAPTER 14
Property Transactions: Determination of Gain or Loss and Basis Considerations — 14-1

Determination of Gain or Loss — 14-3
Realized Gain or Loss — 14-3
Tax in the News: What Is the Amount Realized? — 14-4
Ethical Considerations: Reporting of a Distribution: Dividend versus Return of Capital — 14-6
Recognized Gain or Loss — 14-7
Nonrecognition of Gain or Loss — 14-7
Recovery of Capital Doctrine — 14-8

Basis Considerations — 14-9
Determination of Cost Basis — 14-9
Gift Basis — 14-12
Ethical Considerations: Looking a Gift Horse in the Eye — 14-14
Property Acquired From a Decedent — 14-15
Ethical Considerations: Helping a Friend Increase Basis — 14-16
Disallowed Losses — 14-17
Tax in the News: Reporting of Wash Sales — 14-19
Conversion of Property From Personal Use to Business or Income-Producing Use — 14-20
Additional Complexities in Determining Realized Gain or Loss — 14-21
Summary of Basis Adjustments — 14-23

Tax Planning Considerations — 14-23
Tax Consequences of Alice's Proposed Transaction — 14-23
Cost Identification and Documentation Considerations — 14-25
Selection of Property for Making Gifts — 14-25
Selection of Property for Making Bequests — 14-26
Disallowed Losses — 14-26

Problem Materials — 14-27

CHAPTER 15
Property Transactions: Nontaxable Exchanges — 15-1

General Concept of a Nontaxable Exchange — 15-2

Like-Kind Exchanges—§ 1031 — 15-3
Like-Kind Property — 15-4
Exchange Requirement — 15-5
Boot — 15-5
Tax in the News: Residential or Rental? Depends on Who Wants to Know! — 15-6

Basis and Holding Period of Property Received 15–7

Involuntary Conversions—§ 1033   15–9
Involuntary Conversion Defined   15–10
Tax in the News: A Sound Investment—Not   15–10
Computing the Amount Realized   15–11
Replacement Property   15–11
Time Limitation on Replacement   15–13
Ethical Considerations: Postponing Realized Gain from an Involuntary Conversion   15–13
Nonrecognition of Gain   15–14
Involuntary Conversion of a Personal Residence   15–15
Reporting Considerations   15–15

Sale of a Residence—§ 1034   15–16
Replacement Period   15–16
Tax in the News: IRS Continues to Maintain Strict Interpretation of § 1034   15–17
Principal Residence   15–18
Nonrecognition of Gain Requirements   15–19
Capital Improvements   15–20
Tax in the News: Joint Ownership and a New Spouse: Caution Is Necessary   15–20
Basis and Holding Period of the New Residence   15–21
Reporting Procedures   15–22

Sale of a Residence—§ 121   15–23
Exclusion Requirements   15–23
Ethical Considerations: A Couple's Approach to the § 121 Exclusion   15–24
Relationship to Other Provisions   15–24
Making and Revoking the Election   15–24
Computation Procedure   15–25

Other Nonrecognition Provisions   15–26
Exchange of Stock for Property—§ 1032   15–26
Certain Exchanges of Insurance Policies—§ 1035   15–26
Exchange of Stock for Stock of the Same Corporation—§ 1036   15–26
Certain Reacquisitions of Real Property—§ 1038   15–26
Transfers of Property between Spouses or Incident to Divorce—§ 1041   15–27
Ethical Considerations: Incident to Divorce or Not?   15–27
Rollovers into Specialized Small Business Investment Companies—§ 1044   15–27

Tax Planning Considerations   15–28
Like-Kind Exchanges   15–28
Involuntary Conversions   15–29
Sale of a Personal Residence   15–29

Problem Materials   15–32

CHAPTER 16
Property Transactions: Capital Gains and Losses   16–1

General Considerations   16–2
Rationale for Separate Reporting of Capital Gains and Losses   16–2
General Scheme of Taxation   16–3

Capital Assets   16–3
Definition of a Capital Asset   16–3
Tax in the News: Campaigning on Capital Gains Tax Cuts   16–3
Effect of Judicial Action   16–6
Tax in the News: Is the Art in Corporate Offices Depreciable?   16–6
Statutory Expansions   16–7
Ethical Considerations: Capital Asset Status for Stock Held by Securities Dealers   16–7

Sale or Exchange   16–9
Worthless Securities and § 1244 Stock   16–9
Special Rule—Retirement of Corporate Obligations   16–9
Options   16–10
Patents   16–12
Franchises, Trademarks, and Trade Names   16–13
Lease Cancellation Payments   16–15

Holding Period   16–16
Review of Special Holding Period Rules   16–16
Special Rules for Short Sales   16–17
Tax in the News: A Big Short Sale Against the Box   16–18

Tax Treatment of Capital Gains and Losses of Noncorporate Taxpayers   16–20
Treatment of Capital Gains   16–21
Ethical Considerations: Delaying a Marriage to Get a Tax Advantage   16–22
Ethical Considerations: Indexing Long-Term Capital Gains for Inflation   16–22
Treatment of Capital Losses   16–23

Reporting Procedures	16–24
Tax Treatment of Capital Gains and Losses of Corporate Taxpayers	**16–27**
Tax Planning Considerations	**16–27**
Importance of Capital Asset Status	16–27
Planning for Capital Asset Status	16–27
Effect of Capital Asset Status in Transactions Other Than Sales	16–28
Stock Sales	16–29
Maximizing Benefits	16–29
Year-End Planning	16–30
Problem Materials	**16–30**

CHAPTER 17
Property Transactions: Section 1231 and Recapture Provisions — 17–1

Section 1231 Assets	**17–3**
Relationship to Capital Assets	17–3
Tax in the News: Read the Fine Print to Find the True Tax Treatment	17–3
Justification for Favorable Tax Treatment	17–4
Property Included	17–5
Property Excluded	17–5
Special Rules for Certain § 1231 Assets	17–5
Ethical Considerations: Determining How Long an Asset Has Been Held	17–7
General Procedure for § 1231 Computation	17–8
Tax in the News: Hurricane Blows in a Gain	17–8
Section 1245 Recapture	**17–12**
Ethical Considerations: Does Applying the Recapture Rules Make a Difference?	17–12
Tax in the News: Harried CPA Explains the Unexplainable	17–13
Section 1245 Property	17–14
Observations on § 1245	17–15
Section 1250 Recapture	**17–16**
Computing Recapture on Nonresidential Real Property	17–16
Computing Recapture on Residential Rental Housing	17–18
Section 1250 Recapture Situations	17–19
Considerations Common to §§ 1245 and 1250	**17–20**

Exceptions	17–20
Other Applications	17–21
Ethical Considerations: To Depreciate or Not Depreciate	17–23
Special Recapture Provisions	**17–23**
Special Recapture for Corporations	17–23
Gain From Sale of Depreciable Property between Certain Related Parties	17–23
Intangible Drilling Costs	17–23
Reporting Procedures	**17–24**
Tax Planning Considerations	**17–29**
Timing of § 1231 Gain	17–29
Timing of Recapture	17–29
Postponing and Shifting Recapture	17–29
Avoiding Recapture	17–30
Problem Materials	**17–30**

PART VI
ACCOUNTING PERIODS, ACCOUNTING METHODS, AND DEFERRED COMPENSATION

CHAPTER 18
Accounting Periods and Methods — 18–1

Tax in the News: Acceleration of Income	18–2
Accounting Periods	**18–3**
In General	18–3
Specific Provisions for Partnerships, S Corporations, and Personal Service Corporations	18–4
Ethical Considerations: Required Tax Years	18–6
Making the Election	18–7
Changes in the Accounting Period	18–7
Taxable Periods of Less Than One Year	18–8
Mitigation of the Annual Accounting Period Concept	18–10
Accounting Methods	**18–11**
Permissible Methods	18–11
Cash Receipts and Disbursements Method—Cash Basis	18–11
Accrual Method	18–13

Tax in the News: Tenant Deposits for Retirement Home Were Not Prepaid Income	18–14
Hybrid Method	18–16
Change of Method	18–16
Ethical Considerations: A Change in Accounting Method	18–17
Special Accounting Methods	**18–18**
Installment Method	18–19
Tax in the News: Art Gallery Was Not a Dealer While Its Principal Employee Was in Jail	18–20
Ethical Considerations: A Related-Party Installment Sale Has Unexpected Results	18–25
Disposition of Installment Obligations	18–26
Interest on Deferred Taxes	18–26
Electing Out of the Installment Method	18–26
Long-Term Contracts	18–27
Inventories	**18–31**
Determining Inventory Cost	18–32
The LIFO Election	18–36
Tax Planning Considerations	**18–37**
Taxable Year	18–37
Cash Method of Accounting	18–37
Installment Method	18–37
Completed Contract Method	18–38
Inventories	18–38
Problem Materials	**18–39**

CHAPTER 19
Deferred Compensation — 19–1

Qualified Pension, Profit Sharing, and Stock Bonus Plans	**19–4**
Types of Plans	19–4
Qualification Requirements	19–7
Tax Consequences to the Employee and Employer	19–11
Limitations on Contributions to and Benefits From Qualified Plans	19–15
Ethical Considerations: Personal Benefit versus Employees' Benefit	19–17
Top-Heavy Plans	19–17
Cash or Deferred Arrangement Plans	19–18

Ethical Considerations: Everything Including the Kitchen Sink	19–19
Retirement Plans for Self-Employed Individuals	**19–20**
Coverage Requirements	19–20
Contribution Limitations	19–21
Tax in the News: Selecting Benefit Options	19–21
Individual Retirement Accounts (IRAs)	**19–22**
General Rules	19–22
Tax in the News: The Sooner the Better	19–23
Penalty Taxes for Excess Contributions	19–25
Taxation of Benefits	19–26
Nonqualified Deferred Compensation Plans	**19–27**
Underlying Rationale for Tax Treatment	19–27
Tax Treatment to the Employer and Employee	19–28
Ethical Considerations: Limiting Compensation for Executives But Not for Other Highly Paid Individuals	19–31
Restricted Property Plans	**19–31**
General Provisions	19–31
Substantial Risk of Forfeiture	19–32
Special Election Available	19–32
Employer Deductions	19–33
Stock Options	**19–34**
In General	19–34
Incentive Stock Options	19–34
Tax in the News: Stock Options for Senior Officers	19–35
Nonqualified Stock Options	19–37
Tax Planning Considerations	**19–38**
Deferred Compensation	19–38
Qualified Plans	19–38
Self-Employed Retirement Plans	19–38
Individual Retirement Accounts	19–39
Comparison of § 401(k) Plan With IRA	19–39
Nonqualified Deferred Compensation (NQDC) Plans	19–39
Stock Options	19–41
Flexible Benefit Plans	19–41
Problem Materials	**19–42**

PART VII
CORPORATIONS AND PARTNERSHIPS

CHAPTER 20
Corporations and Partnerships — 20–1

What Is a Corporation? — 20–3
Compliance With State Law — 20–3
The Association Approach — 20–3
Tax in the News: Who Is Taxed on a Basketball Star's Salary? — 20–4
Limited Liability Companies — 20–5
A Simple Way to Select Entity Status — 20–5

Income Tax Considerations — 20–5
General Tax Consequences of Different Forms of Business Entities — 20–5
Individuals and Corporations Compared—An Overview — 20–6
Specific Provisions Compared — 20–7
Deductions Available Only to Corporations — 20–10
Determination of Corporate Tax Liability — 20–12
Ethical Considerations: Where Do Deductions Belong? — 20–13
Corporate Filing Requirements — 20–14
Reconciliation of Corporate Taxable Income and Accounting Income — 20–14

Forming the Corporation — 20–17
Capital Contributions — 20–17
Transfers to Controlled Corporations — 20–18

Operating the Corporation — 20–20
Dividend Distributions — 20–20
Stock Redemptions — 20–22

Liquidating the Corporation — 20–22
General Rule of § 331 — 20–23
Exception to the General Rule — 20–23
Basis Determination—§§ 334 and 338 — 20–23
Effect of the Liquidation on the Corporation — 20–24
Ethical Considerations: Necessity for Filing a Corporate Tax Return — 20–24

The S Election — 20–24
Justification for the Election — 20–24
Operational Rules — 20–26
Tax in the News: One Questionable Use of S Corporation Status — 20–26

Partnerships — 20–29
Nature of Partnership Taxation — 20–29
Partnership Formation — 20–30
Partnership Operation — 20–32

Tax Planning Considerations — 20–34
Corporate versus Noncorporate Forms of Business Organization — 20–34
Regular Corporation versus S Status — 20–35
Use of an Entity to Reduce the Family Income Tax Burden — 20–35
Ethical Considerations: Does a Shifting of Income Occur? — 20–36

Problem Materials — 20–37

APPENDIXES

Tax Rate Schedules and Tables — A–1
Tax Forms — B–1
Glossary of Tax Terms — C–1
Table of Code Sections Cited — D–1
Table of Regulations Cited — D–9
Table of Revenue Procedures and Revenue Rulings Cited — D–13
Citator Example — E–1
Comprehensive Tax Return Problems — F–1
Table of Cases Cited — G–1
Depreciation — H–1
Subject Index — I–1

PART I

Introduction and Basic Tax Model

Part I provides an introduction to taxation in the United States. Although the primary orientation of this text is income taxation, other types of taxes are also discussed briefly. The purposes of the Federal tax law are examined, and the legislative, administrative, and judicial sources of Federal tax law, including their application to the tax research process, are analyzed. Part I concludes with the introduction of the basic tax model for the individual taxpayer.

Chapter 1
An Introduction to Taxation and Understanding the Federal Tax Law

Chapter 2
Working with the Tax Law

Chapter 3
Tax Determination; Personal and Dependency Exemptions; An Overview of Property Transactions

CHAPTER 1

AN INTRODUCTION TO TAXATION AND UNDERSTANDING THE FEDERAL TAX LAW

LEARNING OBJECTIVES

After completing Chapter 1, you should be able to:

1. Understand some of the history, including trends, of the Federal income tax.

2. Know some of the criteria for selecting a tax structure and understand the components of a tax structure.

3. Identify the different taxes imposed in the United States at the Federal, state, and local levels.

4. Understand the administration of the tax law including the audit process utilized by the IRS.

5. Appreciate some of the ethical guidelines involved in tax practice.

6. Recognize the economic, social, equity, and political considerations that justify various aspects of the tax law.

7. Describe the role played by the IRS and the courts in the evolution of the Federal tax system.

OUTLINE

History of U.S. Taxation, 1–2
Early Periods, 1–2
Revenue Acts, 1–3
Historical Trends, 1–3
Criteria Used in the Selection of a Tax Structure, 1–4
The Tax Structure, 1–5
Tax Base, 1–5
Tax Rates, 1–5
Incidence of Taxation, 1–5
Major Types of Taxes, 1–6
Property Taxes, 1–6

Transaction Taxes, 1–8
Death Taxes, 1–10
Gift Taxes, 1–12
Income Taxes, 1–13
Employment Taxes, 1–15
Other U.S. Taxes, 1–16
Proposed U.S. Taxes, 1–17
Tax Administration, 1–18
Internal Revenue Service, 1–18
The Audit Process, 1–18
Statute of Limitations, 1–21
Interest and Penalties, 1–22

Tax Practice, 1–23
Understanding the Federal Tax Law, 1–24
Revenue Needs, 1–24
Economic Considerations, 1–25
Social Considerations, 1–26
Equity Considerations, 1–27
Political Considerations, 1–29
Influence of the Internal Revenue Service, 1–31
Influence of the Courts, 1–32
Summary, 1–33

The primary objective of this chapter is to provide an overview of the Federal tax system. Among the topics discussed are the following:

- A brief history of the Federal income tax.
- The different types of taxes imposed at the Federal, state, and local levels.
- Some highlights of tax law administration.
- Tax concepts that help explain the reasons for various tax provisions.
- The influence that the Internal Revenue Service (IRS) and the courts have had in the evolution of current tax law.

Why does a text devoted primarily to the Federal individual income tax discuss state and local taxes? A simple illustration shows the importance of non-Federal taxes.

EXAMPLE 1

Rick is employed by Flamingo Corporation in San Antonio, Texas, at a salary of $54,000. Rick's employer offers him a chance to transfer to its New York City office at a salary of $60,000. Neither Texas nor San Antonio imposes an income tax, but New York State and New York City do. A quick computation indicates that the additional income taxes (Federal, state, and local) involved approximate $4,000. ▼

Although Rick must consider many nontax factors before he decides on a job change, he should also evaluate the tax climate. How do state and local taxes compare? In this case, what appears to be a $6,000 pay increase is only $2,000 when the additional income taxes of $4,000 are taken into account.

HISTORY OF U.S. TAXATION

EARLY PERIODS

1 LEARNING OBJECTIVE
Understand some of the history, including trends, of the Federal income tax.

The concept of an income tax can hardly be regarded as a newcomer to the Western Hemisphere. An income tax was first enacted in 1634 by the English colonists in the Massachusetts Bay Colony, but the Federal government did not adopt this form of taxation until 1861. In fact, both the Federal Union and the

Confederate States of America used the income tax to raise funds to finance the Civil War. Although modest in its reach and characterized by broad exemptions and low rates, the income tax generated $376 million of revenue for the Federal government during the Civil War.

When the Civil War ended, the need for additional revenue disappeared, and the income tax was repealed. As was true before the war, the Federal government was able to finance its operations almost exclusively from customs duties (tariffs). It is interesting to note that the courts held that the Civil War income tax was not contrary to the Constitution.

When a new Federal income tax on individuals was enacted in 1894, its opponents were prepared to and did again challenge its constitutionality. The U.S. Constitution provided that "... No Capitation, or other direct, Tax shall be laid, unless in Proportion to the Census or Enumeration herein before directed to be taken." In *Pollock v. Farmers' Loan and Trust Co.*,[1] the U.S. Supreme Court found that the income tax was a direct tax that was unconstitutional because it was not apportioned among the states in proportion to their populations.

A Federal corporate income tax, enacted by Congress in 1909, fared better in the judicial system. The U.S. Supreme Court found this tax to be constitutional because it was treated as an excise tax.[2] In essence, it was a tax on the right to do business in the corporate form. As such, it was likened to a form of the franchise tax.[3] The corporate form of doing business had been developed in the late nineteenth century and was an unfamiliar concept to the framers of the U.S. Constitution. Since a corporation is an entity created under law, jurisdictions possess the right to tax its creation and operation. Using this rationale, many states still impose franchise taxes on corporations.

The ratification of the Sixteenth Amendment to the U.S. Constitution in 1913 sanctioned both the Federal individual and corporate income taxes and, as a consequence, neutralized the continuing effect of the *Pollock* decision.

REVENUE ACTS

Following ratification of the Sixteenth Amendment, Congress enacted the Revenue Act of 1913. Under this Act, the first Form 1040 was due on March 1, 1914. The law allowed various deductions and personal exemptions of $3,000 for a single individual and $4,000 for married taxpayers. Rates ranged from a low of 2 percent to a high of 6 percent. The 6 percent rate applied only to taxable income in excess of $500,000![4]

Various revenue acts were passed between 1913 and 1939. In 1939, all of these revenue laws were codified into the Internal Revenue Code of 1939. In 1954, a similar codification of the revenue law took place. The current law is entitled the Internal Revenue Code of 1986, which largely carries over the provisions of the 1954 Code. To date, the Code has been amended several times since 1986. This matter is discussed further in Chapter 2 under Origin of the Internal Revenue Code.

HISTORICAL TRENDS

The income tax has proved to be a major source of revenue for the Federal government. Figure 1–1, which contains a breakdown of the major revenue

---

[1] 3 AFTR 2602, 15 S.Ct. 912 (USSC, 1895). See Chapter 2 for an explanation of the citations of judicial decisions.
[2] *Flint v. Stone Tracy Co.*, 3 AFTR 2834, 31 S.Ct. 342 (USSC, 1911).
[3] See the discussion of state franchise taxes later in the chapter.
[4] This should be contrasted with the highest current tax rate of 39.6%, which applies once taxable income exceeds $271,050.

FIGURE 1-1
Federal Budget Receipts—1997

Individual income taxes	39%
Corporation income taxes	11
Social insurance taxes and contributions	33
Excise taxes	4
Borrowing	9
Other	4
	100%

sources,[5] demonstrates the importance of the income tax. *Estimated* income tax collections from individuals and corporations amount to 50 percent of the total receipts.

The need for revenues to finance the war effort during World War II converted the income tax into a *mass tax*. For example, in 1939, less than 6 percent of the U.S. population was subject to the Federal income tax. In 1945, over 74 percent of the population was subject to the Federal income tax.[6]

Certain changes in the income tax law are of particular significance in understanding the Federal income tax. In 1943, Congress passed the Current Tax Payment Act, which provided for the first pay-as-you-go tax system. A pay-as-you-go income tax system requires employers to withhold for taxes a specified portion of an employee's wages. Persons with income from other than wages must make periodic (e.g., quarterly) payments to the taxing authority (the Internal Revenue Service) for estimated taxes due for the year.

One trend that has caused considerable concern has been the increased complexity of the Federal income tax laws. Often, under the name of tax reform, Congress has added to this complexity by frequently changing the tax laws. Increasingly, this has forced many taxpayers to seek the assistance of tax professionals. At this time, therefore, substantial support exists for tax law simplification.

CRITERIA USED IN THE SELECTION OF A TAX STRUCTURE

2 LEARNING OBJECTIVE
Know some of the criteria for selecting a tax structure and understand the components of a tax structure.

In the eighteenth century, Adam Smith identified the following *canons of taxation,* which are still considered when evaluating a particular tax structure:[7]

- *Equality.* Each taxpayer enjoys fair or equitable treatment by paying taxes in proportion to his or her income level. Ability to pay a tax is the measure of how equitably a tax is distributed among taxpayers.
- *Convenience.* Administrative simplicity has long been valued in formulating tax policy. If a tax is easily assessed and collected and its administrative costs are low, it should be favored. An advantage of the withholding (pay-as-you-go) system is its convenience for taxpayers.

---

[5] Budget of the United States Government for Fiscal Year 1997, Office of Management and Budget (Washington, D.C.: U.S. Government Printing Office, 1996).

[6] Richard Goode, *The Individual Income Tax* (Washington, D.C.: The Brookings Institution, 1964), pp. 2–4.

[7] *The Wealth of Nations,* Book V, Chapter II, Part II (New York: Dutton, 1910).

- *Certainty.* A tax structure is *good* if the taxpayer can readily predict when, where, and how a tax will be levied. Individuals and businesses need to know the likely tax consequences of a particular type of transaction.
- *Economy.* A *good* tax system involves only nominal collection costs by the government and minimal compliance costs on the part of the taxpayer. Although the government's cost of collecting Federal taxes amounts to less than one-half of 1 percent of the revenue collected, the complexity of our current tax structure imposes substantial taxpayer compliance costs.

By these canons, the Federal income tax is a contentious product. *Equality* is present as long as one accepts ability to pay as an ingredient of this component. *Convenience* exists due to a heavy reliance on pay-as-you-go procedures. *Certainty* probably generates the greatest controversy. In one sense, certainty is present since a mass of administrative and judicial guidelines exists to aid in interpreting the tax law. In another sense, however, certainty does not exist since many questions remain unanswered and frequent changes in the tax law by Congress lessen stability. *Economy* is present if only the collection procedure of the IRS is considered. Economy is not present, however, if one focuses instead on taxpayer compliance efforts and costs.

THE TAX STRUCTURE

TAX BASE

A tax base is the amount to which the tax rate is applied. In the case of the Federal income tax, the tax base is *taxable income.* As noted later in the chapter (Figure 1–2), taxable income is gross income reduced by certain deductions (both business and personal).

TAX RATES

Tax rates are applied to the tax base to determine a taxpayer's liability. The tax rates may be proportional or progressive. A tax is *proportional* if the rate of tax remains constant for any given income level.

EXAMPLE 2 Bill has $10,000 of taxable income and pays a tax of $3,000, or 30%. Bob's taxable income is $50,000, and the tax on this amount is $15,000, or 30%. If this constant rate is applied throughout the rate structure, the tax is proportional. ▼

A tax is *progressive* if a higher rate of tax applies as the tax base increases. The Federal income tax, Federal gift and estate taxes, and most state income tax rate structures are progressive.

EXAMPLE 3 If Cora, a married individual filing jointly, has taxable income of $10,000, her tax for 1997 is $1,500 for an average tax rate of 15%. If, however, Cora's taxable income is $50,000, her tax will be $8,644 for an average tax rate of 17.29%. The tax is progressive since higher rates are applied to greater amounts of taxable income. ▼

INCIDENCE OF TAXATION

The degree to which various segments of society share the total tax burden is difficult to assess. Assumptions must be made concerning who absorbs the burden for paying the tax. For example, since dividend payments to shareholders are not deductible by a corporation and are generally taxable to shareholders, the same income is subject to a form of double taxation. Concern over double taxation is valid to the extent that corporations are *not* able to shift the corporate tax to the consumer through higher commodity prices. Many research studies have shown a high degree of shifting of the corporate income tax. When the corporate tax can be shifted, it becomes merely a consumption tax that is borne by the ultimate purchasers of goods.

The progressiveness of the U.S. Federal income tax rate structure for individuals has varied over the years. As late as 1986, for example, there were 15 rates, ranging from 0 to 50 percent. These later were reduced to two rates of 15 and 28 percent. Currently, there are five rates, ranging from 15 to 39.6 percent.

Major Types of Taxes

PROPERTY TAXES

3 Learning Objective
Identify the different taxes imposed in the United States at the Federal, state, and local levels.

Normally referred to as **ad valorem taxes** because they are based on value, property taxes are a tax on wealth, or capital. In this regard, they have much in common with death taxes and gift taxes discussed later in the chapter. Although property taxes do not tax income, the income actually derived (or the potential for any income) may be relevant insofar as it affects the value of the property being taxed.

Property taxes fall into *two* categories: those imposed on realty and those imposed on personalty. Both have added importance since they usually generate a deduction for Federal income tax purposes (see Chapter 10).

Ad Valorem Taxes on Realty. Property taxes on realty are exclusively within the province of the states and their local political subdivisions (e.g., cities, counties, school districts). They represent a major source of revenue for *local* governments, but their importance at the *state* level has waned over the past few years. Some states, for example, have imposed freezes on the upper revaluations of residential housing.

How realty is defined can have an important bearing on which assets are subject to tax. This is especially true in jurisdictions that do not impose ad valorem taxes on personalty. Primarily a question of state property law, **realty** generally includes real estate and any capital improvements that are classified as fixtures. Simply stated, a *fixture* is something so permanently attached to the real estate that its removal will cause irreparable damage. A built-in bookcase might well be a fixture, whereas a movable bookcase would not be a fixture. Certain items such as electrical wiring and plumbing cease to be personalty when installed in a building and become realty.

The following are some of the characteristics of ad valorem taxes on realty:

- Property owned by the Federal government is exempt from tax. Similar immunity usually is extended to property owned by state and local governments and by certain charitable organizations.
- Some states provide for lower valuations on property dedicated to agricultural use or other special uses (e.g., wildlife sanctuaries).
- Some states partially exempt the homestead portion of property from taxation. Modern homestead laws normally protect some or all of a personal residence (including a farm or ranch) from the actions of creditors pursuing claims against the owner.

CHAPTER 1 An Introduction to Taxation and Understanding the Federal Tax Law   1–7

- Lower taxes may apply to a residence owned by an elderly taxpayer (e.g., age 65 and older).
- When non-income-producing property (e.g., a personal residence) is converted to income-producing property (e.g., a rental house), typically the appraised value increases.
- Some jurisdictions extend immunity from tax for a specified period of time (a *tax holiday*) to new or relocated businesses.

ETHICAL CONSIDERATIONS

Tax-Exempt Status Forever?

The Orr family lives in a residence that they have owned for several years. They purchased the residence from St. John's Methodist Church, which had used the house as a parsonage for its minister.

To the Orrs' surprise, since they purchased the residence, they have not received any ad valorem property tax bills from either the city or the county. Is there a plausible reason for this? Explain.

What, if anything, should the Orrs do about the property tax matter?

Unlike the ad valorem tax on personalty (see below), the tax on realty is difficult to avoid. Since real estate is impossible to hide, a high degree of taxpayer compliance is not surprising. The only avoidance possibility that is generally available is associated with the assessed value of the property. For this reason, the assessed value of the property—particularly, a value that is reassessed upward—may be subject to controversy and litigation.

Four methods are currently in use for assessing the value of real estate:

1. Actual purchase or construction price.
2. Contemporaneous sales prices or construction costs of comparable properties.
3. Cost of reproducing a building, less allowance for depreciation and obsolescence from the time of actual construction.
4. Capitalization of income from rental property.

Because all of these methods suffer faults and lead to inequities, a combination of two or more is not uncommon. For example, when real estate values and construction costs are rising, the use of actual purchase or construction price (method 1) places the purchaser of a new home at a definite disadvantage compared with an owner who acquired similar property years before. As another illustration, if the capitalization of income (method 4) deals with property subject to rent controls (e.g., New York City), the property may be undervalued.

The history of the ad valorem tax on realty has been marked by inconsistent application due to a lack of competent tax administration and definitive guidelines for assessment procedures. In recent years, however, some significant improvements have occurred. Some jurisdictions, for example, have computerized their reassessment procedures so they will have an immediate effect on all property located within the jurisdiction. Nevertheless, the property tax area continues to be controversial.

Ad Valorem Taxes on Personalty.
Personalty can be defined as all assets that are not realty. It may be helpful to distinguish between the *classification* of an asset (realty or personalty) and the *use* to which it is put. Both realty and personalty can

be either business use or personal use property. Examples include a residence (realty that is personal use), an office building (realty that is business use), surgical instruments (personalty that is business use), and regular wearing apparel (personalty that is personal use).[8]

Personalty can also be classified as tangible property or intangible property. For ad valorem tax purposes, intangible personalty includes stocks, bonds, and various other securities (e.g., bank shares).

The following generalizations may be made concerning the ad valorem taxes on personalty:

- Particularly with personalty devoted to personal use (e.g., jewelry, household furnishings), taxpayer compliance ranges from poor to zero. Some jurisdictions do not even attempt to enforce the tax on these items. For automobiles devoted to personal use, many jurisdictions have converted from value as the tax base to arbitrary license fees based on the weight of the vehicle. Some jurisdictions also consider the vehicle's age (e.g., automobiles six years or older are not subject to the ad valorem tax because they are presumed to have little, if any, value).
- For personalty devoted to business use (e.g., inventories, trucks, machinery, equipment), taxpayer compliance and enforcement procedures are measurably better.
- Which jurisdiction possesses the authority to tax movable personalty (e.g., railroad rolling stock) always has been and continues to be a troublesome issue.
- A few states levy an ad valorem tax on intangibles such as stocks and bonds. Taxpayer compliance may be negligible if the state lacks means of verifying security transactions and ownership.

TRANSACTION TAXES

Transaction taxes, which characteristically are imposed at the manufacturer's, wholesaler's, or retailer's level, cover a wide range of transfers. Like many other types of taxes (e.g., income taxes, death taxes, and gift taxes), transaction taxes usually are not within the exclusive province of any level of taxing authority (Federal, state, local government). As the description implies, these levies place a tax on transfers of property and normally are determined by multiplying the value involved by a percentage rate.

Federal Excise Taxes.
Long one of the mainstays of the Federal tax system, Federal **excise taxes** had declined in relative importance until recently. In late 1982, 1990, and 1993, Congress substantially increased the Federal excise taxes on such items as tobacco products, fuel and gasoline sales, telephone usage, and air travel passenger tickets. Other Federal excise taxes include the following:

- Manufacturers' excise taxes on trucks, trailers, tires, firearms, sporting equipment, coal, and the gas guzzler tax on automobiles.[9]
- Alcohol taxes.

---

[8] The distinction, important for ad valorem and for Federal income tax purposes, often becomes confused when personalty is referred to as "personal" property to distinguish it from "real" property. This designation does not give a complete picture of what is involved. The description "personal" residence, however, is clearer, since a residence can be identified as being realty. What is meant, in this case, is realty that is personal use property.

[9] The gas guzzler tax is imposed on the manufacturers of automobiles and progresses in amount as the mileage ratings per gallon of gas decrease.

- Luxury tax on automobiles. The tax is 8 percent of the retail price in excess of $36,000 (adjusted each year for inflation). The tax previously was 10 percent and is scheduled to be phased out in yearly increments by year 2003.
- Miscellaneous taxes (e.g., the tax on wagering).

The list of transactions covered, although seemingly impressive, has diminished over the years. At one time, for example, there was a Federal excise tax on admission to amusement facilities (e.g., theaters) and on the sale of such items as leather goods, jewelry, furs, and cosmetics.

When reviewing the list of both Federal and state excise taxes, one should recognize the possibility that the tax laws may be trying to influence social behavior. For example, the gas guzzler tax is intended as an incentive for the automobile companies to build cars that are fuel efficient. Since many consider alcohol and tobacco to be harmful to a person's health, why not increase their cost by imposing excise taxes and thereby discourage their use? Unfortunately, the evidence of the level of correlation between the imposition of an excise tax and consumer behavior is mixed.

State Excise Taxes. Many state and local excise taxes parallel the Federal version. Thus, all states tax the sale of gasoline, liquor, and tobacco products; however, the rates vary significantly. For gasoline products, for example, compare the 39 cents per gallon imposed by the state of Connecticut with the 8 cents per gallon levied by the state of Alaska. For tobacco sales, contrast the 2.5 cents per pack of cigarettes in effect in Virginia with the 82.5 cents per pack applicable in Washington. Given the latter situation, is it surprising that the smuggling of cigarettes for resale elsewhere is so widespread?

Other excise taxes found at some state and local levels include those on admission to amusement facilities; hotel occupancy and the rental of various other facilities; and the sale of playing cards, oleomargarine products, and prepared foods. Most states impose a transaction tax on the transfer of property that requires the recording of documents (e.g., real estate sales).[10] Some extend the tax to the transfer of stocks and other securities.

General Sales Taxes. The distinction between an excise tax and a general **sales tax** is easy to make. One is restricted to a particular transaction (e.g., the 18.4 cents per gallon Federal excise tax on the sale of gasoline), while the other covers a multitude of transactions (e.g., a 5 percent tax on *all* retail sales). In actual practice, however, the distinction is not always that clear. Some state statutes exempt certain transactions from the application of the general sales taxes (e.g., sales of food to be consumed off the premises, sales of certain medicines and drugs). Also, it is not uncommon to find that rates vary depending on the commodity involved. Many states, for example, allow preferential rates for the sale of agricultural equipment or apply different rates (either higher or lower than the general rate) to the sale of automobiles. With many of these special exceptions and classifications of rates, a general sales tax can take on the appearance of a collection of individual excise taxes.

A **use tax** is an ad valorem tax, usually at the same rate as the sales tax, on the use, consumption, or storage of tangible property. The purpose of a use tax is to prevent the avoidance of a sales tax. Every state that imposes a general sales tax

---

[10] This type of tax has much in common with the stamp tax levied by Great Britain on the American colonies during the pre–Revolutionary War period in U.S. history.

> ### TAX IN THE NEWS
>
> #### CAN A USE TAX DISCRIMINATE?
>
> The purpose of the use tax is to keep taxpayers from avoiding state and local sales taxes by purchasing goods out-of-state. Can the rate imposed by a use tax exceed the rate of the sales tax, however? If so, the taxpayer who buys goods out-of-state is worse off than if the purchases are made in-state.
>
> In a recent test of a Missouri use tax, the U.S. Supreme Court found it to be unconstitutional. A use tax cannot be in excess of the sales tax rate because that would discriminate against interstate commerce [*Associated Industries of Missouri v. Lohman*, 93 AFTR2d 94-2061, 114 S.Ct. 1815 (USSC, 1994)].

levied on the consumer also has a use tax. Alaska, Delaware, Montana, New Hampshire, and Oregon have neither tax.

EXAMPLE 4

Susan resides in a jurisdiction that imposes a 5% general sales tax but lives near a state that has no sales or use tax at all. Susan purchases an automobile for $10,000 from a dealer located in the neighboring state. Has she saved $500 in sales taxes? The state use tax is designed to pick up the difference between the tax paid in another jurisdiction and what would have been paid in the state in which Susan resides. ▼

The use tax is difficult to enforce for many purchases and is therefore often avoided. In some cases, for example, it may be worthwhile to make purchases through an out-of-state mail-order business. In spite of shipping costs, the avoidance of the local sales tax that otherwise might be incurred could make the price of such products as computer components cheaper. Some states are taking steps to curtail this loss of revenue. For items such as automobiles (refer to Example 4), the use tax probably will be collected when the purchaser registers the item in his or her home state.

Local general sales taxes, over and above those levied by the state, are common. It is not unusual to find taxpayers living in the same state who pay different general sales taxes due to the location of their residence.

EXAMPLE 5

Pete and Sam both live in a state that has a general sales tax of 3%. Sam, however, resides in a city that imposes an additional general sales tax of 2%. Even though Pete and Sam live in the same state, one is subject to a rate of 3%, while the other pays a tax of 5%. ▼

Severance Taxes. **Severance taxes** are an important source of revenue for many states. These transaction taxes are based on the notion that the state has an interest in its natural resources (e.g., oil, gas, iron ore, coal). Therefore, a tax is imposed when the natural resources are extracted.

DEATH TAXES

A **death tax** is a tax on the right to transfer property or to receive property upon the death of the owner. Consequently, a death tax falls into the category of an excise tax. If the death tax is imposed on the right to pass property at death, it is classified as an **estate tax.** If it taxes the right to receive property from a decedent, it is termed an **inheritance tax.** As is typical of other types of excise taxes, the value of the property transferred provides the base for determining the amount of the death tax.

The Federal government imposes only an estate tax. State governments, however, levy inheritance taxes, estate taxes, or both.

EXAMPLE 6
At the time of her death, Wilma lived in a state that imposes an inheritance tax but not an estate tax. Mary, one of Wilma's heirs, lives in the same state. Wilma's estate is subject to the Federal estate tax, and Mary is subject to the state inheritance tax. ▼

The Federal Estate Tax.
The Revenue Act of 1916 incorporated the estate tax into the tax law. Never designed to generate a large amount of revenue, the tax was originally intended to prevent large concentrations of wealth from being kept within a family for many generations. Whether this objective has been accomplished is debatable. Like the income tax, estate taxes can be reduced through various planning procedures.

The gross estate includes property the decedent owned at the time of death. It also includes life insurance proceeds when paid to the estate or when paid to a beneficiary other than the estate if the deceased-insured had any ownership rights in the policy. Quite simply, the gross estate represents property interests subject to Federal estate taxation.[11] All property included in the gross estate is valued as of the date of death or, if the alternate valuation date is elected, six months later.[12]

Deductions from the gross estate in arriving at the taxable estate include funeral and administration expenses, certain taxes, debts of the decedent, casualty losses[13] incurred during the administration of the estate, transfers to charitable organizations, and, in some cases, the marital deduction. The marital deduction is available for amounts actually passing to a surviving spouse (a widow or widower).

Once the taxable estate has been determined and certain taxable gifts have been added to it, the estate tax can be computed. From the amount derived from the appropriate tax rate schedules, various credits should be subtracted to arrive at the tax, if any, that is due.[14] Although many other credits are also available, probably the most significant is the unified transfer tax credit. The main reason for this credit is to eliminate or reduce the estate tax liability for modest estates. Currently, the amount of the credit is $192,800. Based on the estate tax rates, the credit covers a tax base of $600,000.

EXAMPLE 7
Ned made no taxable gifts before his death in 1997. If Ned's taxable estate amounts to $600,000 or less, no Federal estate tax is due because of the application of the unified transfer tax credit. Under the tax law, the estate tax on a taxable estate of $600,000 is $192,800. ▼

State Death Taxes.
As noted earlier, states usually levy an inheritance tax, an estate tax, or both. The two forms of death taxes differ according to whether the tax is imposed on the heirs or on the estate.

Characteristically, an inheritance tax divides the heirs into classes based on their relationship to the decedent. The more closely related the heir, the lower the

---

[11] For further information on these matters, see *West's Federal Taxation: Corporations, Partnerships, Estates, and Trusts.*
[12] See the discussion of the alternate valuation date in Chapter 14.
[13] For a definition of casualty losses, see the Glossary of Tax Terms in Appendix C.
[14] For tax purposes, it is always crucial to appreciate the difference between a deduction and a credit. A *credit* is a dollar-for-dollar reduction of tax liability. A *deduction*, however, only benefits the taxpayer to the extent of his or her tax bracket. An estate in a 50% tax bracket, for example, would need $2 of deductions to prevent $1 of tax liability from developing. In contrast, $1 of credit neutralizes $1 of tax liability.

rates imposed and the greater the exemption allowed. Some states completely exempt from taxation amounts passing to a surviving spouse.

GIFT TAXES

Like a death tax, a **gift tax** is an excise tax levied on the right to transfer property. In this case, however, the tax is imposed on transfers made during the owner's life and not at death. Also, a gift tax applies only to transfers that are not supported by full and adequate consideration.

EXAMPLE 8 Carl sells property worth $20,000 to his daughter for $1,000. Although property worth $20,000 has been transferred, only $19,000 represents a gift, since this is the portion not supported by full and adequate consideration. ▼

The Federal Gift Tax. First enacted in 1932, the Federal gift tax was intended to complement the estate tax. In the absence of a tax applicable to lifetime transfers by gift, it would be possible to avoid the estate tax and escape taxation entirely.

Only taxable gifts are subject to the gift tax. For this purpose, a taxable gift is measured by the fair market value of the property on the date of transfer less the annual exclusion of $10,000 per donee and, in some cases, less the marital deduction, which allows tax-free transfers between spouses. Each donor is allowed an annual exclusion of $10,000 for each donee.[15]

EXAMPLE 9 On December 31, 1996, Vera (a widow) gives $10,000 to each of her four married children, their spouses, and her eight grandchildren. On January 3, 1997, she repeats the same procedure. Due to the annual exclusion, Vera has not made a taxable gift, although she transferred $160,000 [$10,000 × 16 (number of donees)] in 1996 and $160,000 [$10,000 × 16 (number of donees)] in 1997 for a total of $320,000 ($160,000 + $160,000). ▼

ETHICAL CONSIDERATIONS   The Annual Exclusion for Gifts

Arlene, a wealthy widow, would like to transfer $20,000 of cash to her son, Wilbur, in 1997 without exceeding the $10,000 per donee annual exclusion. To achieve this result, Arlene devises the following scheme: she gives $10,000 to Wilbur and $10,000 to her brother, George, who gives $10,000 to Wilbur.

Will Arlene's scheme succeed? What could go wrong?

A special election applicable to married persons allows one-half of the gift made by the donor-spouse to be treated as being made by the nondonor-spouse. This election to split the gifts of property made to third persons has the effect of increasing the number of annual exclusions available. Also, it allows the use of the nondonor-spouse's unified transfer tax credit and may lower the tax brackets that will apply.

The gift tax rate schedule is the same as that applicable to the estate tax. The schedule is commonly referred to as the *unified transfer tax schedule.*

---

[15] The purpose of the annual exclusion is to avoid the need to report and pay a tax on *modest* gifts. Without the exclusion, the IRS could face a real problem of taxpayer noncompliance.

The Federal gift tax is *cumulative* in effect. What this means is that the tax base for current taxable gifts includes past taxable gifts. Although a credit is allowed for prior gift taxes, the result of adding past taxable gifts to current taxable gifts is to force the donor into a higher tax bracket.[16] Like the Federal estate tax rates, the Federal gift tax rates are progressive (see Example 3 earlier in this chapter).

The unified transfer tax credit is available for all taxable gifts, and as with the Federal estate tax, the amount of this credit is $192,800. There is, however, only one unified transfer tax credit, and it applies both to taxable gifts and to the Federal estate tax. In a manner of speaking, therefore, once the unified transfer tax credit has been exhausted for Federal gift tax purposes, it is no longer available to insulate a decedent from the Federal estate tax.

In summary, transfers by gift and transfers by death are subject to the unified transfer tax. The same rates and credits apply. Further, taxable gifts are added to the taxable estate in arriving at the tax base for applying the unified transfer tax at death.

State Gift Taxes. The states currently imposing a state gift tax are Connecticut, Delaware, Louisiana, New York, North Carolina, and Tennessee. Most of the laws provide for lifetime exemptions and annual exclusions. Like the Federal gift tax, the state taxes are cumulative in effect. But unlike the Federal version, the amount of tax depends on the relationship between the donor and the donee. Like state inheritance taxes, larger exemptions and lower rates apply when the donor and donee are closely related to each other.

INCOME TAXES

Income taxes are levied by the Federal government, most states, and some local governments. The trend in recent years has been to place greater reliance on this method of taxation. This trend is not consistent with what is happening in other countries, and in this sense, our system of taxation is somewhat different.

Income taxes generally are imposed on individuals, corporations, and certain fiduciaries (estates and trusts). Most jurisdictions attempt to assure the collection of income taxes by requiring certain pay-as-you-go procedures (e.g., withholding requirements for employees and estimated tax prepayments for other taxpayers).

On occasion, Congress has seen fit to impose additional taxes on income. Such impositions were justified either by economic considerations or by special circumstances resulting from wartime conditions. During World War II, the Korean conflict, and the Vietnam conflict, excess-profits taxes were imposed in addition to the regular Federal income tax. The taxes were aimed at the profiteering that occurs when the economy is geared to the production of war materials.

Another additional income tax is the surcharge approach. During the period from April 1, 1968, to July 1, 1970, for example, taxpayers were subject to a surcharge of 10 percent of the amount of their regular income tax liability. This led to the strange result that taxpayers had to pay, so to speak, an income tax on their income tax. Justifications for the special tax included the need to restrain what was regarded as an overactive economy, to curtail inflation, and to reduce the Federal deficit.

In light of current budget deficits, the surcharge approach has its advocates in Congress and therefore may be of more than historical interest. The advantage of the surcharge approach is that it represents a temporary solution to the problem.

---

[16] For further information on the Federal gift tax, see *West's Federal Taxation: Corporations, Partnerships, Estates, and Trusts.*

▼ **FIGURE 1–2**
Formula for Federal Income Tax on Individuals

Income (broadly conceived)	$xx,xxx
Less: Exclusions (income that is not subject to tax)	(x,xxx)
Gross income (income that is subject to tax)	$xx,xxx
Less: Certain business deductions (usually referred to as deductions *for* adjusted gross income)	(x,xxx)
Adjusted gross income	$xx,xxx
Less: The greater of certain personal and employee deductions (usually referred to as *itemized deductions*) or The standard deduction (including any additional standard deduction) and	(x,xxx)
Less: Personal and dependency exemptions	(x,xxx)
Taxable income	$xx,xxx
Tax on taxable income (see Tax Rate Schedules in Appendix A)	$ x,xxx
Less: Tax credits (including Federal income tax withheld and other prepayments of Federal income taxes)	(xxx)
Tax due (or refund)	$ xxx

Thus, Congress can impose the tax on a one-shot basis without having to modify the regular income tax rates or base.

Federal Income Taxes. Chapters 3 through 19 deal with the application of the Federal income tax to individuals. The procedure for determining the Federal income tax applicable to individuals is summarized in Figure 1–2.

The application of the Federal corporate income tax does not require the computation of adjusted gross income (AGI) and does not provide for the standard deduction and personal and dependency exemptions. All allowable deductions of a corporation fall into the business-expense category. In effect, therefore, the taxable income of a corporation is the difference between gross income (net of exclusions) and deductions.

Chapter 20 summarizes the rules relating to corporations. For an in-depth treatment of the Federal income tax as it affects corporations, estates, and trusts, see *West's Federal Taxation: Corporations, Partnerships, Estates, and Trusts,* 1998 Edition, Chapters 2 through 9, 12, and 19.

State Income Taxes. All but the following states impose an income tax on individuals: Alaska, Florida, Nevada, South Dakota, Texas, Washington, and Wyoming.

Some of the characteristics of state income taxes are summarized as follows:

- With few exceptions, all states require some form of withholding procedures.
- Most states use as the tax base the income determination made for Federal income tax purposes.
- A minority of states go even further and impose a flat rate upon AGI as computed for Federal income tax purposes. Several apply a rate to the Federal income tax liability. This is often referred to as the piggyback approach to state income taxation. Although the term *piggyback* does not lend itself to precise definition, in this context, it means making use, for state income tax purposes, of what was done for Federal income tax purposes.

CHAPTER 1 An Introduction to Taxation and Understanding the Federal Tax Law   1–15

> ### TAX IN THE NEWS
>
> **VISITORS BEWARE! THE CITY AND STATE YOU VISIT MAY NOT BE ALL THAT FRIENDLY**
>
> Even if you are not a resident, you may be subject to local and state income taxes if you earn money in that jurisdiction. Besides the nonresident who commutes (e.g., a taxpayer who lives in Connecticut but works full-time in New York City), taxpayers who perform services on an itinerant basis may be vulnerable. For example, the Dallas Cowboys are subject to the city of Philadelphia income tax every time they are hosted by the Eagles. This must be particularly distressing to Troy Aikman, who lives in a city (Dallas) and a state (Texas) that do not have an income tax.
>
> Although these situations are commonly referred to as the application of the "jock tax," other persons besides professional athletes get hit. Particularly susceptible are entertainers, doctors, lawyers, lecturers, and anyone who generates large fees and has a high profile. Ordinary professionals are not targeted because the amount of taxes involved would not justify the collection effort.
>
> Is it any wonder that Las Vegas, which has no city or state income tax, is such a popular place to perform highly paid services (e.g., entertainment, prize fighting)?

- Because of the tie-in to the Federal return, the state may be notified of any changes made by the IRS upon audit of a Federal return.
- Most states allow a deduction for personal and dependency exemptions. Some states substitute a tax credit for a deduction.
- A diminishing minority of states allow a deduction for Federal income taxes.
- Most states allow their residents some form of tax credit for income taxes paid to other states.
- The due date for filing generally is the same as for the Federal income tax (the fifteenth day of the fourth month following the close of the tax year).

Nearly all states have an income tax applicable to corporations. It is difficult to determine those that do not because a state franchise tax sometimes is based in part on the income earned by the corporation.[17]

Local Income Taxes. Cities imposing an income tax include, but are not limited to, Baltimore, Cincinnati, Cleveland, Detroit, Kansas City (Mo.), New York, Philadelphia, and St. Louis. The application of a city income tax is not limited to local residents.

EMPLOYMENT TAXES

Classification as an employee usually leads to the imposition of **employment taxes** and to the requirement that the employer withhold specified amounts for income taxes. The rules governing the withholding for income taxes are discussed in Chapter 13. The material that follows concentrates on the two major employment taxes: FICA (Federal Insurance Contributions Act—commonly referred to as the

---
[17] See the discussion of franchise taxes later in the chapter.

Social Security tax) and FUTA (Federal Unemployment Tax Act). Both taxes can be justified by social and public welfare considerations: FICA offers some measure of retirement security, and FUTA provides a modest source of income in the event of loss of employment.

Employment taxes come into play only if two conditions are satisfied. First, is the individual involved an *employee* (as opposed to *self-employed*)? The differences between an employee and a self-employed person are discussed in Chapter 9.[18] Second, if the individual involved is an employee, is he or she covered under FICA or FUTA or both? The coverage of both of these taxes is summarized in Exhibit 13–2 in Chapter 13.[19]

FICA Taxes. The **FICA tax** rates and wage base have steadily increased over the years. It is difficult to imagine that the initial rate in 1937 was only 1 percent of the first $3,000 of covered wages. Thus, the maximum tax due was only $30!

Currently, the FICA tax has two components: Social Security tax (old age, survivors, and disability insurance) *and* Medicare tax (hospital insurance). The Social Security tax rate is 6.2 percent for 1996 and 1997, and the Medicare tax rate is 1.45 percent for these years. The base amount for Social Security is $62,700 for 1996 and $65,400 for 1997. There is no limit on the base amount for the Medicare tax. The employer must match the employee's portion.

A spouse employed by another spouse is subject to FICA. However, children under the age of 18 who are employed in a parent's trade or business are exempted.

FUTA Taxes. The purpose of the **FUTA tax** is to provide funds that the states can use to administer unemployment benefits. This leads to the somewhat unusual situation of one tax being handled by both Federal and state governments. The end result of such joint administration is to compel the employer to observe a double set of rules. Thus, state and Federal returns must be filed and payments made to both governmental units.

In 1997, FUTA applies at a rate of 6.2 percent on the first $7,000 of covered wages paid during the year to each employee. The Federal government allows a credit for FUTA paid (or allowed under a merit rating system) to the state. The credit cannot exceed 5.4 percent of the covered wages. Thus, the amount required to be paid to the IRS could be as low as 0.8 percent (6.2% − 5.4%).

States follow a policy of reducing the unemployment tax on employers who experience stable employment. Thus, an employer with little or no employee turnover might find that the state rate drops to as low as 0.1 percent or, in some states, even to zero. The reason for the merit rating credit is that the state has to pay fewer unemployment benefits when employment is steady.

FUTA differs from FICA in the sense that the incidence of taxation falls entirely upon the employer. A few states, however, levy a special tax on employees to provide either disability benefits or supplemental unemployment compensation, or both.

OTHER U.S. TAXES

To complete the overview of the U.S. tax system, some missing links need to be covered that do not fit into the classifications discussed elsewhere in this chapter.

---

[18] See also Circular E, Employer's Tax Guide, issued by the IRS as Publication 15.

[19] Chapter 13 deals with the self-employment tax (the Social Security and Medicare taxes for self-employed persons).

Federal Customs Duties. One tax that has not yet been mentioned is the tariff on certain imported goods.[20] Generally referred to as customs duties or levies, this tax, together with selective excise taxes, provided most of the revenues needed by the Federal government during the nineteenth century. In view of present times, it is remarkable to note that tariffs and excise taxes alone paid off the national debt in 1835 and enabled the U.S. Treasury to pay a surplus of $28 million to the states.

In recent years, tariffs have served the nation more as an instrument for carrying out protectionist policies than as a means of generating revenue. Thus, a particular U.S. industry might be saved from economic disaster, so the argument goes, by placing customs duties on the importation of foreign goods that can be sold at lower prices. Protectionists contend that the tariff therefore neutralizes the competitive edge held by the producer of the foreign goods.[21]

Protectionist policies seem more appropriate for less-developed countries whose industrial capacity has not yet matured. In a world where a developed country should have everything to gain by encouraging international free trade, such policies may be of dubious value. History shows that tariffs often lead to retaliatory action on the part of the nation or nations affected.

Miscellaneous State and Local Taxes. Most states impose a franchise tax on corporations. Basically, a **franchise tax** is levied on the right to do business in the state. The base used for the determination of the tax varies from state to state. Although corporate income considerations may come into play, this tax most often is based on the capitalization of the corporation (either with or without certain long-term indebtedness).

Closely akin to the franchise tax are **occupational taxes** applicable to various trades or businesses, such as a liquor store license, a taxicab permit, or a fee to practice a profession such as law, medicine, or accounting. Most of these are not significant revenue producers and fall more into the category of licenses than taxes. The revenue derived is used to defray the cost incurred by the jurisdiction in regulating the business or profession in the interest of the public good.

PROPOSED U.S. TAXES

Considerable dissatisfaction with the U.S. Federal income tax has led to several recent proposals that, to say the least, are rather drastic in nature. One proposal would retain the income tax but with substantial change. Two other proposals would replace the Federal income tax with an entirely different system of taxation.

The Flat Tax. Representative Dick Armey (R, Texas) has proposed a **flat tax** that would replace the current graduated income tax with one rate, 17 percent. Large personal exemptions (e.g., approximately $30,000 for a family of four) would allow many low- and middle-income taxpayers to pay no tax. All other deductions would be eliminated, and no tax would be imposed on income from investments.

Various other versions of the flat tax have been suggested that would retain selected deductions (e.g., interest on home mortgages and charitable contributions) and not exclude all investment income from taxation.

---

[20] Less-developed countries that rely principally on one or more major commodities (e.g., oil, coffee) are prone to favor *export* duties as well.

[21] The North American Free Trade Agreement (NAFTA), enacted in 1993, substantially reduced the tariffs on trade between Canada, Mexico, and the United States. The General Agreement on Tariffs and Trade (GATT) legislation enacted in 1994 also reduced tariffs on selected commodities among 124 signatory nations.

The major advantage of the flat tax is its simplicity. Everyone agrees that the current Federal income tax is unbelievably complex. Consequently, compliance costs are disproportionately high.

Value Added Tax. The **value added tax (VAT)** is one of two proposals that would replace the Federal income tax. Under the VAT, a business would pay the tax (approximately 17 percent) on all of the materials and services required to manufacture its product. In effect, the VAT taxes the increment in value as goods move through production and manufacturing stages to the marketplace. Moreover, the VAT paid by the producer will be reflected in the selling price of the goods. Thus, the VAT is a tax on consumption.

Several other countries (e.g., European Union countries) use the VAT either as a supplement to or a replacement for an income tax.

Sales Tax. A **national sales tax** is favored by Representative Bill Archer (R, Texas), who is the current chairman of the House Ways and Means Committee. This tax differs from a VAT in that it would be collected on the final sale of goods and services. Consequently, it is collected from the consumer and not from businesses adding value to the product. Like the VAT, the national sales tax is intended to replace the Federal income tax.

Critics contend that consumption taxes (both a VAT and a national sales tax) impose more of a burden on low-income taxpayers because they must spend larger proportions of their incomes on essential purchases. Representative Archer's proposal would attempt to remedy this inequity by granting some sort of credit or exemption to low-income taxpayers.

TAX ADMINISTRATION

INTERNAL REVENUE SERVICE

4 LEARNING OBJECTIVE
Understand the administration of the tax law including the audit process utilized by the IRS.

The responsibility for administering the Federal tax laws rests with the Treasury Department. Administratively, the IRS is part of the Department of the Treasury and is responsible for enforcing the tax laws. The Commissioner of Internal Revenue is appointed by the President and is responsible for establishing policy and supervising the activities of the entire IRS organization.

The field organization of the IRS includes the following:

- Service Centers (10) that are primarily responsible for processing tax returns, including the selection of returns for audit. The Service Center having proper jurisdiction is where taxpayers must file their Federal tax returns.
- District Directors (33) who are responsible for audits and for the collection of delinquent taxes. Some states have no District Director (e.g., Idaho, Wyoming) while others have more than one (e.g., California, New York).

THE AUDIT PROCESS

Selection of Returns for Audit. Due to budgetary limitations, only a small minority of returns are audited. For the fiscal year ending September 30, 1995, for example, the IRS audited only 0.92 percent of the total returns, down from 1.06 percent in the preceding fiscal year.

The IRS utilizes mathematical formulas and statistical sampling techniques to select tax returns that are most likely to contain errors and to yield substantial amounts of additional tax revenues upon audit.

Though the IRS does not openly disclose all of its audit selection techniques, the following observations may be made concerning the probability of selection for audit:

- Certain groups of taxpayers are subject to audit much more frequently than others. These groups include individuals with gross income in excess of $50,000, self-employed individuals with substantial business income and deductions, and taxpayers with prior tax deficiencies. Also vulnerable are cash businesses (e.g., cafes and small service businesses) where the potential for tax avoidance is high.

EXAMPLE 10 Jack owns and operates a liquor store on a cash-and-carry basis. Since all of Jack's sales are for cash, he might well be a prime candidate for an audit by the IRS. Cash transactions are easier to conceal than those made on credit. ▼

- If information returns (e.g., Form 1099, Form W–2) are not in substantial agreement with reported income, an audit can be anticipated.
- If an individual's itemized deductions are in excess of norms established for various income levels, the probability of an audit is increased.
- Filing of a refund claim by the taxpayer may prompt an audit of the return.
- Certain returns are selected on a random sampling basis under the Taxpayer Compliance Measurement Program (TCMP). The TCMP is used to develop, update, and improve the mathematical formulas and statistical sampling techniques used by the IRS. For the present, the TCMP has been suspended due to a lack of congressional funding.
- Information obtained from other sources (e.g., informants, news items) may lead to an audit. The tax law permits the IRS to pay rewards to persons who provide information that leads to the detection and punishment of those who violate the tax laws. The rewards may not exceed 10 percent of the taxes, fines, and penalties recovered as a result of such information.

EXAMPLE 11 After 15 years of service, Rita is discharged by her employer, Dr. Smith. Shortly thereafter, the IRS receives an anonymous letter informing it that Dr. Smith keeps two separate sets of books, one of which substantially understates his cash receipts. ▼

EXAMPLE 12 During a divorce proceeding, it is revealed that Leo, a public official, kept large amounts of cash in a shoe box at home. This information is widely disseminated by the news media and comes to the attention of the IRS. Needless to say, the IRS would be interested in knowing whether these funds originated from a taxable source and, if so, whether they were reported on Leo's income tax returns. ▼

Types of Audits. Once a return is selected for audit, the taxpayer is notified accordingly. If the issue involved is minor, the matter often can be resolved simply by correspondence (a **correspondence audit**) between the IRS and the taxpayer.

EXAMPLE 13 During 1995, Janet received dividend income from Green Corporation. In early 1996, Green Corporation reported the payment on Form 1099–DIV (an information return for reporting dividend payments), the original being sent to the IRS and a copy to Janet. When preparing her income tax return for 1995, Janet apparently overlooked this particular Form 1099–DIV and failed to include the dividend on Schedule B, Interest and Dividend Income, of Form

1040. In 1997, the IRS sends a notice to Janet calling her attention to the omission and requesting a remittance for additional tax, interest, and penalty. Janet promptly mails a check to the IRS for the requested amount, and the matter is closed. ▼

Other examinations are generally classified as either office audits or field audits. An **office audit** usually is restricted in scope and is conducted in the facilities of the IRS. In contrast, a **field audit** involves an examination of numerous items reported on the return and is conducted on the premises of the taxpayer or the taxpayer's representative.

Upon the conclusion of the audit, the examining agent issues a Revenue Agent's Report (RAR) that summarizes the findings. The RAR will result in a refund (the tax was overpaid), a deficiency (the tax was underpaid), or a *no change* (the tax was correct) finding.

ETHICAL CONSIDERATIONS

A Nosy (and Unnecessary) Audit

In 1998, Thelma, a single professional of moderate means, is notified by the IRS that her 1996 income tax return is to be audited. She is given an appointment and is asked to bring to the local IRS office all substantiation supporting the charitable contributions she claimed as deductions. This is the third year in a row that she has been audited on the charitable contribution issue; each of the prior audits resulted in the issuance of a "no-change" letter by the IRS. Thelma is very devout and gives at least 10 percent of her yearly income to her church.

During the audit, the agent asks Thelma a number of questions that she considers to be inappropriate and even overly personal. Some examples are:

- Bank and savings accounts held, where located, and the average balance of each.
- Type of cars owned and the cost of each.
- Real estate owned and its estimated value.
- Marital history including divorce and property settlements, if any.
- Type and extent of entertainment and other social and recreational activities including vacations taken and their cost.

Flustered and embarrassed, Thelma does her best to cooperate. The audit terminates after the agent makes a cursory examination of the receipts and records that support the charitable contributions she claimed. As in the past, a no-change RAR is issued and the matter is closed.

Comment on the propriety of the conduct of the IRS during the audit. Does a taxpayer have any defense in these types of situations?

Settlement Procedures. If an audit results in an assessment of additional tax and no settlement is reached with the IRS agent, the taxpayer may attempt to negotiate a settlement with the IRS. If an appeal is desired, an appropriate request must be made to the Appeals Division of the IRS. In some cases, a taxpayer may be able to obtain a percentage settlement or a favorable settlement of one or more disputed issues. The Appeals Division is authorized to settle all disputes based on the *hazard of litigation* (the probability of favorable resolution of the disputed issue or issues if litigated).

If a satisfactory settlement is not reached within the administrative appeal process, the taxpayer may wish to litigate the case in the Tax Court, a Federal District Court, or the Court of Federal Claims. However, litigation is recommended only as a last resort because of the legal costs involved and the uncertainty of the final outcome. Tax litigation considerations are discussed more fully in Chapter 2.

STATUTE OF LIMITATIONS

A **statute of limitations** is a provision in the law that offers a party a defense against a suit brought by another party after the expiration of a specified period of time. The purpose of a statute of limitations is to preclude parties from prosecuting stale claims. The passage of time makes the defense of such claims difficult since witnesses may no longer be available or evidence may have been lost or destroyed. Found at the state and Federal levels, such statutes cover a multitude of suits, both civil and criminal.

For our purposes, the relevant statutes deal with the Federal income tax. The two categories involved cover both the period of limitations applicable to the assessment of additional tax deficiencies by the IRS and the period that deals with claims for refunds by taxpayers.

Assessment by the IRS.
Under the general rule, the IRS may assess (impose) an additional tax liability against a taxpayer within *three years* of the filing of the income tax return. If the return is filed early, the three-year period begins to run from the due date of the return (usually April 15 for a calendar year individual taxpayer).

If a taxpayer omits an amount of gross income in excess of 25 percent of the gross income reported on the return, the statute of limitations is increased to six years.

EXAMPLE 14 For 1992, Mark, a calendar year taxpayer, reported gross income of $400,000 on a timely filed income tax return. If Mark omitted more than $100,000 (25% × $400,000), the six-year statute of limitations would apply to the 1992 tax year. ▼

The six-year provision on assessments by the IRS applies only to the omission of income and does not cover other factors that might lead to an understatement of tax liability (e.g., overstatement of deductions and credits).

There is *no* statute of limitations on assessments of tax if *no return* is filed or if a *fraudulent* return is filed.

Limitations on Refunds.
If a taxpayer believes that an overpayment of Federal income tax was made, a claim for refund should be filed with the IRS. A *claim for refund*, therefore, is a request to the IRS that it return to the taxpayer the excessive income taxes paid.[22]

A claim for refund generally must be filed within *three years* from the date the return was filed *or* within *two years* from the date the tax was paid, whichever is later. Income tax returns that are filed early are deemed to have been filed on the date the return was due.

---

[22] The form to use by an individual in filing a claim for refund generally is Form 1040X.

INTEREST AND PENALTIES

Interest rates are determined quarterly by the IRS based on the existing Federal short-term rate. The rates for tax refunds (overpayments) are 1 percent below those applicable to assessments (underpayments). For the first quarter (January 1– March 31) of 1997, the rates were 8 percent for refunds and 9 percent for assessments.[23]

For assessments of additional taxes, the interest begins running on the unextended due date of the return. With refunds, however, no interest is allowed if the overpayment is refunded to the taxpayer within 45 days of the date the return is filed. For this purpose, returns filed early are deemed to have been filed on the due date.

The tax law provides various penalties for lack of compliance by taxpayers. Some of these penalties are summarized as follows:

- For a *failure to file* a tax return by the due date (including extension—see Chapter 3), a penalty of 5 percent per month (up to a maximum of 25 percent) is imposed on the amount of tax shown as due on the return. Any fraction of a month counts as a full month.
- A penalty for a *failure to pay* the tax due (as shown on the return) is imposed in the amount of 0.5 percent per month (up to a maximum of 25 percent). Again, any fraction of a month counts as a full month. During any month in which both the failure to file penalty and the failure to pay penalty apply, the failure to file penalty is reduced by the amount of the failure to pay penalty.

EXAMPLE 15 Adam files his tax return 18 days after the due date of the return. Along with the return, he remits a check for $1,000, which is the balance of the tax he owed. Disregarding the interest element, Adam's total penalties are as follows:

Failure to pay penalty (0.5% × $1,000)		$ 5
Plus:		
Failure to file penalty (5% × $1,000)	$50	
Less failure to pay penalty for the same period	(5)	
Failure to file penalty		45
Total penalties		$50

Note that the penalties for one full month are imposed even though Adam was delinquent by only 18 days. Unlike the method used to compute interest, any part of a month is treated as a whole month. ▼

- A *negligence* penalty of 20 percent is imposed if any of the underpayment was for intentional disregard of rules and regulations without intent to defraud. The penalty applies to just that portion attributable to the negligence.

EXAMPLE 16 Cindy underpaid her taxes for 1996 in the amount of $20,000, of which $15,000 is attributable to negligence. Cindy's negligence penalty is $3,000 (20% × $15,000). ▼

---

[23] The rates applicable after March 31, 1997, were not available when this text went to press.

TAX IN THE NEWS

EVEN THE MIGHTY CAN FALL

Apparently oblivious of the fate that Pete Rose suffered, Darryl Strawberry followed the same road when he failed to report substantial amounts of income from autograph shows and promotional appearances from 1986 to 1992. Charged with tax fraud, Strawberry entered into a plea bargain that resulted in $350,000 in back taxes, interest, and penalties, six months home confinement, and three years probation.

Many criticized the result as being unduly light in that, unlike Pete Rose, Strawberry was not required to serve any time in prison. Conviction on all of the charges against Strawberry could have resulted in a prison sentence as long as 15 years.

- Various fraud penalties may be imposed. *Fraud* is a deliberate action on the part of the taxpayer evidenced by deceit, misrepresentation, concealment, etc. For possible fraud situations, refer to Examples 11 and 12. The burden of proving fraud is on the IRS. This is in contrast to the usual deficiency assessment made by the IRS, where the burden is on the taxpayer to show that he or she does not owe any additional tax.

TAX PRACTICE

The area of tax practice is largely unregulated. Virtually anyone can aid another in complying with the various tax laws. If a practitioner is a member of a profession, such as law or public accounting, he or she must abide by certain ethical standards. Furthermore, the Internal Revenue Code imposes penalties upon the preparers of Federal tax returns who violate proscribed acts and procedures.

5 LEARNING OBJECTIVE
Appreciate some of the ethical guidelines involved in tax practice.

Ethical Guidelines. The American Institute of CPAs has issued numerous guides for CPAs engaged in tax practice. Called "Statements on Responsibilities in Tax Practice," some of these are summarized below.

- Do not take questionable positions on a client's tax return in the hope that the return will not be selected for audit by the IRS. Any positions taken should be supported by a good-faith belief that they have a realistic chance of being sustained if challenged. The client should be fully advised of the risks involved and of the penalties that would result if the position taken is not successful.
- A practitioner can use a client's estimates if they are reasonable under the circumstances. If the tax law requires verification (e.g., receipts), the client should be so advised. In no event should an estimate be given the appearance of greater accuracy than is the case. For example, an estimate of $1,000 should not be deducted on a return as $999.
- Every effort should be made to answer questions appearing on tax returns. A question need not be answered if the information requested is not readily available, the answer is voluminous, or the question's meaning is uncertain. The failure to answer a question on a return cannot be justified on the grounds that the answer could prove disadvantageous to the taxpayer.

- Upon learning of an error on a past tax return, advise the client to correct it. Do not, however, inform the IRS of the error. If the error is material and the client refuses to correct it, consider withdrawing from the engagement. This will be necessary if the error has a carryover effect and prevents the current year's tax liability from being determined correctly.

Statutory Penalties Imposed on Tax Return Preparers. In addition to ethical constraints, a tax return preparer may be subject to certain statutorily sanctioned penalties, including the following:

- Various penalties involving procedural matters. Examples include failing to furnish the taxpayer with a copy of the return; endorsing a taxpayer's refund check; failing to sign the return as a preparer; failing to furnish one's identification number; and failing to keep copies of returns or maintain a client list.
- Understatement of a tax liability based on a position that lacks any realistic possibility of being sustained. If the position is not frivolous, the penalty can be avoided by disclosing it on the return.
- Any willful attempt to understate taxes. This usually results when a preparer disregards or makes no effort to obtain pertinent information from a client.

Understanding the Federal Tax Law

6 LEARNING OBJECTIVE
Recognize the economic, social, equity, and political considerations that justify various aspects of the tax law.

The Federal tax law is a mosaic of statutory provisions, administrative pronouncements, and court decisions. Anyone who has attempted to work with this body of knowledge would have to admit to its complexity. For the person who has to trudge through a mass of rules to find the solution to a tax problem, it may be of some consolation to know that the law's complexity can generally be explained. Whether sound or not, there is a reason for the formulation of every rule. Knowing these reasons, therefore, is a considerable step toward understanding the Federal tax law.

The Federal tax law has as its *major objective* the raising of revenue. But although the fiscal needs of the government are important, other considerations explain certain portions of the law. Economic, social, equity, and political factors also play a significant role. Added to these factors is the marked impact the IRS and the courts have had and will continue to have on the evolution of Federal tax law. These matters are treated in the remainder of the chapter, and, wherever appropriate, the discussion is referenced to subjects covered later in the text.

REVENUE NEEDS

The foundation of any tax system has to be the raising of revenue to cover the cost of government operations. Ideally, annual outlays should not exceed anticipated revenues, thereby leading to a balanced budget with no resulting deficit. Many states have achieved this objective by passing laws or constitutional amendments precluding deficit spending. Unfortunately, the Federal government has no such conclusive prohibition, and mounting annual deficits have become an increasing concern for many.

When enacting most of the recent tax legislation, a deficit-conscious Congress has been guided by the concept of **revenue neutrality**. The concept means that the changes made will neither increase nor decrease the net result reached under the prior rules. Revenue neutrality does not mean that any one taxpayer's tax liability will remain the same. Since the circumstances involved will differ, one taxpayer's increased tax liability could be another's tax savings. Although revenue-neutral tax reform does not reduce deficits, at least it does not aggravate the problem. One can expect budget deficit considerations to play an ever-increasing role in shaping future tax policy.

ECONOMIC CONSIDERATIONS

Using the tax system in an effort to accomplish economic objectives has become increasingly popular in recent years. Generally, proponents of this goal use tax legislation to amend the Internal Revenue Code and promote measures designed to help control the economy or encourage certain activities and businesses.

Control of the Economy.
Congress has used depreciation write-offs as a means of controlling the economy. Theoretically, shorter asset lives and accelerated methods should encourage additional investment in depreciable property acquired for business use. Conversely, longer asset lives and the required use of the straight-line method of depreciation dampen the tax incentive for capital outlays.

A change in the tax rate structure has a more immediate impact on the economy. With lower tax rates, taxpayers are able to retain additional spendable funds. If lower tax rates are accompanied by the elimination of certain deductions, exclusions, and credits, however, the overall result may not be lower tax liabilities.

Encouragement of Certain Activities.
Without passing judgment on the wisdom of any such choices, it is quite clear that the tax law does encourage certain types of economic activity or segments of the economy. For example, the favorable treatment allowed research and development expenditures can be explained by the desire to foster technological progress. Under the tax law, such expenditures can be either deducted in the year incurred or capitalized and amortized over a period of 60 months or more. In terms of the timing of the tax savings, these options usually are preferable to capitalizing the cost with a write-off over the estimated useful life of the asset created. If the asset developed has an indefinite useful life, no write-off would be available without the two options allowed by the tax law.

Is it desirable to encourage the conservation of energy resources? Considering the world energy situation and our own reliance on foreign oil, the answer to this question has to be yes. The concern over energy usage was a prime consideration in the enactment of legislation to make various tax savings for energy conservation expenditures available to taxpayers.

Is preserving the environment a desirable objective? Ecological considerations explain why the tax law permits a 60-month amortization period for costs incurred in the installation of pollution control facilities.

Is it wise to stimulate U.S. exports of goods and services? Considering the pressing and continuing problem of a deficit in the U.S. balance of payments, the answer should be clear. Along this line, Congress has created Foreign Sales Corporations (FSCs), which are designed to encourage domestic exports of goods. The FSC provisions exempt a percentage of profits from export sales from the Federal income tax. Also in an international setting, Congress has deemed it advisable to establish incentives for U.S. citizens who accept employment overseas. Such persons receive generous tax breaks through special treatment of their foreign-source income and certain housing costs.

Is saving desirable for the economy? Saving leads to capital formation and thereby makes funds available to finance home construction and industrial expansion. The tax law encourages saving by according preferential treatment to private retirement plans. Not only are contributions to Keogh (H.R. 10) plans and certain Individual Retirement Accounts (IRAs) deductible, but income from the contributions accumulates free of tax. As noted below, the encouragement of private-sector pension plans can also be justified under social considerations.

Encouragement of Certain Industries. No one can question the proposition that a sound agricultural base is necessary for a well-balanced national economy. Undoubtedly, this can explain why farmers are accorded special treatment under the Federal tax system. Among the benefits are the election to expense rather than capitalize certain soil and water conservation expenditures and fertilizers and the election to defer the recognition of gain on the receipt of crop insurance proceeds.

Encouragement of Small Business. At least in the United States, a consensus exists that what is good for small business is good for the economy as a whole. Whether valid or not, this assumption has led to a definite bias in the tax law favoring small business.

In the corporate tax area, several provisions can be explained by the desire to benefit small business. One provision permits the shareholders of a small business corporation to make a special election that generally will avoid the imposition of the corporate income tax.[24] Furthermore, such an election enables the corporation to pass through its operating losses to its shareholders. The rules governing the election of this special status were liberalized in 1996 by the passage of the Small Business Job Protection Act.

SOCIAL CONSIDERATIONS

Some provisions of the Federal tax law, particularly those dealing with the income tax of individuals, can be explained by social considerations. Some notable examples and their rationales include the following:

- Certain benefits provided to employees through accident and health plans financed by employers are nontaxable to employees. Encouraging such plans is considered socially desirable since they provide medical benefits in the event of an employee's illness or injury.
- Most premiums paid by an employer for group term insurance covering the life of the employee are nontaxable to the employee. These arrangements can be justified on social grounds in that they provide funds for the family unit to help it adjust to the loss of wages caused by the employee's death.
- A contribution made by an employer to a qualified pension or profit sharing plan for an employee receives special treatment. The contribution and any income it generates are not taxed to the employee until the funds are distributed. Such an arrangement also benefits the employer by allowing a tax deduction when the contribution is made to the qualified plan. Private retirement plans are encouraged to supplement the subsistence income level the employee otherwise would have under the Social Security system.[25]

---

[24] Known as the S election, it is discussed in Chapter 20.
[25] The same rationale explains the availability of similar arrangements for self-employed persons (the H.R. 10, or Keogh, plan). See Chapter 19.

- A deduction is allowed for contributions to qualified charitable organizations.[26] The deduction attempts to shift some of the financial and administrative burden of socially desirable programs from the public (the government) to the private (the citizens) sector.
- A tax credit is allowed for amounts spent to furnish care for certain minor or disabled dependents to enable the taxpayer to seek or maintain gainful employment.[27] Who could deny the social desirability of encouraging taxpayers to provide care for their children while they work?
- A tax deduction is not allowed for certain expenditures deemed to be contrary to public policy. This disallowance extends to such items as fines, penalties, illegal kickbacks, bribes to government officials, and gambling losses in excess of gains. Social considerations dictate that the tax law should not encourage these activities by permitting a deduction.

Many other examples could be cited, but the conclusion would be unchanged. Social considerations do explain a significant part of the Federal tax law.

EQUITY CONSIDERATIONS

The concept of equity is relative. Reasonable persons can, and often do, disagree about what is fair or unfair. In the tax area, moreover, equity is most often tied to a particular taxpayer's personal situation. To illustrate, compare the tax positions of those who rent their personal residences with those who own their homes. Renters receive no Federal income tax benefit from the rent they pay. For homeowners, however, a large portion of the house payments they make may qualify for the Federal interest and property tax deductions. Although renters may have difficulty understanding this difference in tax treatment, the encouragement of home ownership can be justified on both economic and social grounds.

In the same vein, compare the tax treatment of a corporation with that of a partnership. Although the two businesses may be of equal size, similarly situated, and competitors in the production of goods or services, they are not treated comparably under the tax law. The corporation is subject to a separate Federal income tax; the partnership is not. Whether the differences in tax treatment can be justified logically in terms of equity is beside the point. The point is that the tax law can and does make a distinction between these business forms.

Equity, then, is not what appears fair or unfair to any one taxpayer or group of taxpayers. It is, instead, what the tax law recognizes. Some recognition of equity does exist, however, and explains part of the law. The concept of equity appears in tax provisions that alleviate the effect of multiple taxation and postpone the recognition of gain when the taxpayer lacks the ability or wherewithal to pay the tax. Provisions that mitigate the effect of the application of the annual accounting period concept and help taxpayers cope with the eroding results of inflation also reflect equity considerations.

Alleviating the Effect of Multiple Taxation.
The income earned by a taxpayer may be subject to taxes imposed by different taxing authorities. If, for example, the taxpayer is a resident of New York City, income might generate Federal, state of New York, and city of New York income taxes. To compensate for this apparent inequity, the Federal tax law allows a taxpayer to claim a deduction for state and local income taxes. The deduction does not, however, neutralize the

---

[26] The charitable contribution deduction is discussed in Chapter 10.   [27] See Chapter 13.

- Listed areas where the IRS will not issue advance letter rulings or determination letters.
- Announced where exempt organizations should send the annual information required to maintain their tax-exempt status.

Letter Rulings. Individual **letter rulings** are issued upon a taxpayer's request for a fee and describe how the IRS will treat a proposed transaction for tax purposes. They apply only to the taxpayer who asks for and obtains the ruling, but post-1984 letter rulings may be substantial authority for purposes of the accuracy-related penalty.[15] Though this procedure may sound like the only real way to carry out effective tax planning, the IRS limits the issuance of individual rulings to restricted, preannounced areas of taxation. The main reason the IRS will not rule in certain areas is that they involve fact-oriented situations. Thus, a ruling may not be obtained on many of the problems that are particularly troublesome for taxpayers.[16]

The law now requires the IRS to make individual rulings available for public inspection after identifying details are deleted.[17] Published digests of private letter rulings can be found in *Private Letter Rulings* (published by RIA), BNA *Daily Tax Reports,* and Tax Analysts & Advocates *Tax Notes. IRS Letter Rulings Reports* (published by Commerce Clearing House) contains both digests and full texts of all letter rulings. *Letter Ruling Review* (published by Tax Analysts) is a monthly publication that selects and discusses the more important of the approximately 300 letter rulings issued each month.

Letter rulings receive multidigit file numbers, which indicate the year and week of issuance as well as the number of the ruling during that week. Consider, for example, Ltr.Rul. 9631025, which deals with the tax on unrelated business income of schools leasing land:

96	**31**	**025**
Year 1996	31st week of issuance	Number of the ruling issued during the 31st week

Other Administrative Pronouncements. *Treasury Decisions* (TDs) are issued by the Treasury Department to promulgate new Regulations, amend or otherwise change existing Regulations, or announce the position of the Government on selected court decisions. Like Revenue Rulings and Revenue Procedures, TDs are published in the *Internal Revenue Bulletin* and subsequently transferred to the *Cumulative Bulletin.*

The IRS publishes other administrative communications in the *Internal Revenue Bulletin* such as Announcements, Notices, LRs (Proposed Regulations), and Prohibited Transaction Exemptions.

Like letter rulings, **determination letters** are issued at the request of taxpayers and provide guidance on the application of the tax law. They differ from letter

---

[15] Notice 90–20, 1990–1 C.B. 328. In this regard, letter rulings differ from Revenue Rulings, which are applicable to *all* taxpayers. Letter rulings may later lead to the issuance of a Revenue Ruling if the holding involved affects many taxpayers. In its Agents' Manual, the IRS indicates that letter rulings may be used as a guide with other research materials in formulating a District Office position on an issue. The IRS is required to charge a taxpayer a fee for letter rulings, determination letters, etc.

[16] Rev.Proc. 97–3, I.R.B. No. 1, 84 contains a list of areas in which the IRS will not issue advance rulings. From time to time, subsequent Revenue Procedures are issued that modify or amplify Rev.Proc. 97–3.

[17] § 6110.

rulings in that the issuing source is the District Director rather than the National Office of the IRS. Also, determination letters usually involve completed (as opposed to proposed) transactions. Determination letters are not published and are made known only to the party making the request.

The following examples illustrate the distinction between letter rulings and determination letters:

EXAMPLE 1

The shareholders of Red Corporation and Green Corporation want assurance that the consolidation of the corporations into Blue Corporation will be a nontaxable reorganization. The proper approach would be to request the National Office of the IRS to issue a letter ruling concerning the income tax effect of the proposed transaction. ▼

EXAMPLE 2

Chris operates a barber shop in which he employs eight barbers. To comply with the rules governing income tax and payroll tax withholdings, Chris wants to know whether the barbers working for him are employees or independent contractors. The proper procedure would be to request a determination letter on their status from the appropriate District Director. ▼

The National Office of the IRS releases **Technical Advice Memoranda (TAMs)** weekly. Although TAMs and letter rulings both give the IRS's determination of an issue, they differ in several respects. Letter rulings deal with proposed transactions and are issued to taxpayers at their request. In contrast, TAMs deal with completed transactions and are often requested in relation to exempt organizations and employee plans. Futhermore, TAMs arise from questions raised by IRS personnel during audits and are issued by the National Office of the IRS to its field personnel rather than to taxpayers. TAMs are not officially published and may not be cited or used as precedent.[18] They are assigned file numbers according to the same procedure used for letter rulings. For example, TAM 9637008 refers to the 8th TAM issued during the 37th week of 1996.

Several internal memoranda that constitute the working law of the IRS now must be released. These General Counsel Memoranda (GCMs) and Technical Advice Memoranda (TAMs) are not officially published, and the IRS indicates that they may not be cited as precedents by taxpayers.[19] However, these working documents do explain the IRS's position on various issues.

ETHICAL CONSIDERATIONS

The Cost of Tax Compliance

Arthur P. Hall of the Tax Foundation points out that since 1954 the income tax code has grown from 103 sections to more than 700 and is now about four inches thick. An additional nine inches of Treasury Regulations explain these four inches of tax law.

Shirley Petersen, former IRS Commissioner, tells of one multinational corporation that had to file a 21,000-page tax return in 30 volumes. "They had to use a truck to deliver it to the IRS," Petersen says.

---

[18] § 6110(j)(3). Post-1984 TAMs may be substantial authority for purposes of avoiding the accuracy-related penalty. Notice 90–20, 1990–1 C.B. 328.

[19] These are unofficially published by the publishers listed in Exhibit 2–1. Such internal memoranda for post-1984 may be substantial authority for purposes of the accuracy-related penalty. Notice 90–20, 1990–1 C.B. 328.

▼ **FIGURE 2–1**
Federal Judicial System

Dr. Hall continues, "Because of complexity and instability, taxpayers cannot be certain about how taxation will affect a business plan or investment. At least 70 percent of the total cost of Federal tax compliance is due to the income tax, indicating that businesses paid an estimated $92.5 billion in 1994 to comply with the Federal tax."

Is it equitable that taxpayers must bear such large compliance costs in order to calculate and pay their income taxes?

JUDICIAL SOURCES OF THE TAX LAW

The Judicial Process in General.
After a taxpayer has exhausted some or all of the remedies available within the IRS (i.e., no satisfactory settlement has been reached at the agent or at the Appeals Division level), the dispute can be taken to the Federal courts. The dispute is first considered by a **court of original jurisdiction** (known as a trial court) with any appeal (either by the taxpayer or the IRS) taken to the appropriate appellate court. In most situations, the taxpayer has a choice of any of *four trial courts:* a **Federal District Court,** the **U.S. Court of Federal Claims,** the **U.S. Tax Court,** or the **Small Cases Division** of the U.S. Tax Court. The trial and appellate court scheme for Federal tax litigation is illustrated in Figure 2–1.

The broken line between the U.S. Tax Court and the Small Cases Division indicates that there is no appeal from the Small Cases Division. The jurisdiction of the Small Cases Division is limited to cases involving amounts of $10,000 or less. The proceedings of the Small Cases Division are informal (e.g., no necessity for the taxpayer to be represented by a lawyer or other tax adviser). Special trial judges rather than Tax Court judges preside over these proceedings. The decisions of the Small Cases Division are not precedents for any other court decision and are not reviewable by any higher court. Proceedings can be more timely and less expensive in the Small Cases Division.

American law, following English law, is frequently *made* by judicial decisions. Under the doctrine of *stare decisis,* each case (except in the Small Cases Division) has precedential value for future cases with the same controlling set of facts. Most Federal and state appellate court decisions and some decisions of trial courts are published. More than 4 million judicial opinions have been published in the United States; over 130,000 cases are published each year.[20] Published court decisions are organized by jurisdiction (Federal or state) and level of court (trial or appellate).

A decision of a particular court is called its holding. Sometimes a decision includes dicta or incidental opinions beyond the current facts. Such passing remarks, illustrations, or analogies are not essential to the current holding. Although the holding has precedential value under *stare decisis,* dicta are not binding on a future court.

Trial Courts. The various trial courts (courts of original jurisdiction) differ in several respects:

- *Number of courts.* There is only one Court of Federal Claims and only one Tax Court, but there are many Federal District Courts. The taxpayer does not select the District Court that will hear the dispute but must sue in the one that has jurisdiction.
- *Number of judges.* Each District Court has only 1 judge, the Court of Federal Claims has 16 judges, and the Tax Court has 19 regular judges. The entire Tax Court, however, will review a case (the case is sent to court conference) only when more important or novel tax issues are involved. Most cases will be heard and decided by one of the 19 judges.
- *Location.* The Court of Federal Claims meets most often in Washington, D.C., whereas a District Court meets at a prescribed seat for the particular district. Each state has at least one District Court, and many of the more populous states have more than one. Therefore, the inconvenience and expense of traveling for the taxpayer and his or her counsel (present with many suits in the Court of Federal Claims) are largely eliminated. Although the Tax Court is officially based in Washington, D.C., the various judges travel to different parts of the country and hear cases at predetermined locations and dates. Although this procedure eases the distance problem for the taxpayer, it may mean a delay before the case comes to trial and is decided.
- *Jurisdiction of the Court of Federal Claims.* The Court of Federal Claims has jurisdiction over any claim against the United States that is based upon the Constitution, any Act of Congress, or any regulation of an executive department. Thus, the Court of Federal Claims hears nontax litigation as well as tax cases. This forum appears to be more favorable for issues having an equitable or pro-business orientation (as opposed to purely technical issues) and for those requiring extensive discovery.[21]
- *Jurisdiction of the Tax Court and District Courts.* The Tax Court hears only tax cases and is the most popular forum. The District Courts hear nontax litigation as well as tax cases. Some Tax Court justices have been appointed from IRS or Treasury Department positions. For these reasons, some people suggest that the Tax Court has more expertise in tax matters.
- *Jury trial.* The only court in which a taxpayer can obtain a jury trial is a District Court. But since juries can only decide questions of fact and not questions of law, even taxpayers who choose the District Court route often

---

[20] Jacobstein, Mersky, and Dunn, *Fundamentals of Legal Research,* 6th ed. (Westbury, N.Y.: The Foundation Press, 1994), p. 11.

[21] T. D. Peyser, "The Case for Selecting the Claims Court to Litigate a Federal Tax Liability," *The Tax Executive* (Winter 1988): 149.

do not request a jury trial. In that event, the judge will decide all issues. Note that a District Court decision is controlling only in the district in which the court has jurisdiction.

- *Payment of deficiency.* For the Court of Federal Claims or a District Court to have jurisdiction, the taxpayer must pay the tax deficiency assessed by the IRS and sue for a refund. A taxpayer who wins (assuming no successful appeal by the Government) recovers the tax paid plus appropriate interest. For the Tax Court, however, jurisdiction is usually obtained without first paying the assessed tax deficiency. In the event the taxpayer loses in the Tax Court (and does not appeal or an appeal is unsuccessful), the deficiency must be paid with appropriate interest. With the elimination of the deduction for personal (consumer) interest, the Tax Court route of delaying payment of the deficiency can become expensive. For example, to earn 11 percent after tax, a taxpayer with a 39.6 percent marginal tax rate would have to earn 18.2 percent. By paying the tax, a taxpayer limits underpayment interest and penalties on the underpayment.
- *Termination of running of interest.* A taxpayer who selects the Tax Court may deposit a cash bond to stop the running of interest. The taxpayer must deposit both the amount of the tax and any accrued interest. If the taxpayer wins and the deposited amount is returned, the Government does not pay interest on the deposit.
- *Appeals.* Appeals from a District Court or a Tax Court decision are to the appropriate U.S. Court of Appeals. Appeals from the Court of Federal Claims go to the Court of Appeals for the Federal Circuit.
- *Bankruptcy.* When a taxpayer files a bankruptcy petition, the IRS, like other creditors, is prevented from taking action against the taxpayer. Sometimes a bankruptcy court may settle a tax claim.

For a summary, see Concept Summary 2–1.

Appellate Courts. The losing party can appeal a trial court decision to a **Circuit Court of Appeals.** The 11 geographical circuits, the circuit for the District of Columbia, and the Federal Circuit[22] appear in Figure 2–2. The appropriate circuit for an appeal depends upon where the litigation originated. For example, an appeal from New York goes to the Second Circuit.

If the Government loses at the trial court level (District Court, Tax Court, or Court of Federal Claims), it need not (frequently does not) appeal. The fact that an appeal is not made, however, does not indicate that the IRS agrees with the result and will not litigate similar issues in the future. The IRS may decide not to appeal for a number of reasons. First, the current litigation load may be heavy, and as a consequence, the IRS may decide that available personnel should be assigned to other, more important cases. Second, the IRS may determine that this is not a good case to appeal. Perhaps the taxpayer is in a sympathetic position or the facts are particularly strong in his or her favor. In that event, the IRS may wait to test the legal issues involved with a taxpayer who has a much weaker case. Third, if the appeal is from a District Court or the Tax Court, the Court of Appeals of jurisdiction could have some bearing on whether the IRS chooses to go forward with an appeal. Based on past experience and precedent, the IRS may conclude that the chance for success on a particular issue might be more promising in another Court of Appeals. If so, the IRS will wait for a similar case to arise in a different jurisdiction.

---

[22] The Court of Appeals for the Federal Circuit was created, effective October 1, 1982, by P.L. 97–164 (4/2/82) to hear decisions appealed from the Claims Court (now the Court of Federal Claims).

Concept Summary 2–1

Federal Judicial System: Trial Courts

Issue	U.S. Tax Court	U.S. District Court	U.S. Court of Federal Claims
Number of judges per court	19*	1	16
Payment of deficiency before trial	No	Yes	Yes
Jury trial available	No	Yes	No
Types of disputes	Tax cases only	Most criminal and civil issues	Claims against the United States
Jurisdiction	Nationwide	Location of taxpayer	Nationwide
IRS acquiescence policy	Yes	Yes	Yes
Appeal route	U.S. Court of Appeals	U.S. Court of Appeals	U.S. Court of Appeals for the Federal Circuit

*There are also 14 special trial judges and 9 senior judges.

ETHICAL CONSIDERATIONS

Choosing Cases for Appeal

The U.S. Government loses a tax case against a prominent citizen in the U.S. District Court of Iowa. The taxpayer, a minister, had set up three separate trusts for each of his three children (i.e., a total of nine trusts). The Government argued that under Reg. § 1.641(a)–0(c) these trusts should be consolidated and treated as three trusts to stop the taxpayer from mitigating the progressive tax structure (e.g., 39.6 percent top tax bracket).

The IRS has decided to appeal a case in this multiple trust area. As one of the attorneys for the Government, you must choose between the Iowa case and a similar multiple trust conflict in the U.S. District Court of Virginia. Here the taxpayer is a CPA who has established four separate trusts for her two children (i.e., a total of eight trusts). See *Estelle Morris Trusts,* 51 T.C. 20 (1968). Factors you are considering are the potential sympathy associated with the minister's profession and a lack thereof associated with the CPA, the facts indicating that the attempt at tax avoidance is more egregious in the Iowa case, and a colleague's opinion that the Virginia case is winnable. Which case will you select? Comment on the fairness of the Government's ability and willingness to select a case to appeal in this fashion.

With the establishment of the Federal Circuit at the appellate level, a taxpayer has an alternative forum to the Court of Appeals of his or her home circuit for the

▼ **FIGURE 2-2**
The Federal Courts of Appeals

appeal. Appeals from both the Tax Court and the District Court go to a taxpayer's home circuit. Now, when a particular circuit has issued an adverse decision, the taxpayer may wish to select the Court of Federal Claims route, since any appeal will be to the Federal Circuit.

District Courts, the Tax Court, and the Court of Federal Claims must abide by the **precedents** set by the Court of Appeals of jurisdiction. A particular Court of Appeals need not follow the decisions of another Court of Appeals. All courts, however, must follow the decisions of the **U.S. Supreme Court.**

Because the Tax Court is a national court (it hears and decides cases from all parts of the country), the observation made in the previous paragraph has caused problems. For many years, the Tax Court followed a policy of deciding cases based on what it thought the result should be, even though its decision might be appealed to a Court of Appeals that had previously decided a similar case differently. A number of years ago this policy was changed in the *Golsen*[23] decision. Now the Tax Court will decide a case as it feels the law should be applied *only* if the Court of Appeals of appropriate jurisdiction has not yet passed on the issue or has previously decided a similar case in accord with the Tax Court's decision. If the Court of Appeals of appropriate jurisdiction has previously held otherwise, the Tax Court will conform under the *Golsen* rule even though it disagrees with the holding.

---

[23] *Jack E. Golsen*, 54 T.C. 742 (1970).

EXAMPLE 3

Emily lives in Texas and sues in the Tax Court on Issue A. The Fifth Court of Appeals is the appellate court of appropriate jurisdiction. The Fifth Court of Appeals has already decided, in a case involving similar facts but a different taxpayer, that Issue A should be resolved against the Government. Although the Tax Court feels that the Fifth Court of Appeals is wrong, under its *Golsen* policy it will render judgment for Emily. Shortly thereafter, Rashad, a resident of New York, in a comparable case, sues in the Tax Court on Issue A. Assume that the Second Court of Appeals, the appellate court of appropriate jurisdiction, has never expressed itself on Issue A. Presuming the Tax Court has not reconsidered its position on Issue A, it will decide against Rashad. Thus, it is entirely possible for two taxpayers suing in the same court to end up with opposite results merely because they live in different parts of the country. ▼

Appeal to the U.S. Supreme Court is by **Writ of Certiorari.** If the Court accepts jurisdiction, it will grant the Writ (*Cert. Granted*). Most often, it will deny jurisdiction (*Cert. Denied*). For whatever reason or reasons, the Supreme Court rarely hears tax cases. The Court usually grants certiorari to resolve a conflict among the Courts of Appeals (e.g., two or more appellate courts have assumed opposing positions on a particular issue) or where the tax issue is extremely important. The granting of a Writ of Certiorari indicates that at least four members of the Supreme Court believe that the issue is of sufficient importance to be heard by the full Court.

The *role* of appellate courts is limited to a review of the record of trial compiled by the trial courts. Thus, the appellate process usually involves a determination of whether the trial court applied the proper law in arriving at its decision. Rarely will an appellate court disturb a lower court's fact-finding determination.

Both the Code and the Supreme Court indicate that Federal appellate courts are bound by findings of facts unless they are clearly erroneous.[24] This aspect of the appellate process is illustrated by a decision of the Court of Appeals for the District of Columbia involving whether a taxpayer was engaged in an activity for profit under § 183.[25] This appeals court specifically held that the "Tax Court's findings of facts are binding on Federal courts of appeals unless clearly erroneous." The Court applauded the Tax Court for the thoroughness of its factual inquiry but could "not place the stamp of approval upon its eventual legal outcome." In reversing and remanding the decision to the Tax Court, the appellate court said that "the language of § 183, its legislative history and the applicable Treasury regulation combine to demonstrate that the court's [Tax Court's] standard is erroneous as a matter of law." The appeals court held that this taxpayer's claims of deductibility were to be evaluated by proper legal standards.

An appeal can have any of a number of possible outcomes. The appellate court could approve (affirm) or disapprove (reverse) the lower court's finding, or it could send the case back for further consideration (remand). When many issues are involved, a mixed result is not unusual. Thus, the lower court could be affirmed (*aff'd*) on Issue A and reversed (*rev'd*) on Issue B, while Issue C is remanded (*rem'd*) for additional fact finding.

When more than one judge is involved in the decision-making process, disagreements are not uncommon. In addition to the majority view, one or more judges may concur (agree with the result reached but not with some or all of the reasoning) or dissent (disagree with the result). In any one case, of course, the

---

[24] §§ 7482(a) and (c). *Comm. v. Duberstein*, 60–2 USTC ¶9515, 5 AFTR2d 1626, 80 S.Ct. 1190 (USSC, 1960). See Rule 52(a) of the Federal Rules of Civil Procedure.

[25] *Dreicer v. Comm.*, 81–2 USTC ¶9683, 48 AFTR2d 5884, 665 F.2d 1292 (CA–DC, 1981).

majority view controls. But concurring and dissenting views can have an influence on other courts or, at some subsequent date when the composition of the court has changed, even on the same court.

Knowledge of several terms is important in understanding court decisions. The term *plaintiff* refers to the party requesting action in a court, and the *defendant* is the party against whom the suit is brought. Sometimes a court uses the terms *petitioner* and *respondent*. In general, "petitioner" is a synonym for "plaintiff," and "respondent" is a synonym for "defendant." At the trial court level, a taxpayer is normally the plaintiff (or petitioner), and the Government is the defendant (or respondent). If the taxpayer wins and the Government appeals as the new petitioner (or appellant), the taxpayer becomes the new respondent.

Judicial Citations—General. Having concluded a brief description of the judicial process, it is appropriate to consider the more practical problem of the relationship of case law to tax research. As previously noted, court decisions are an important source of tax law. The ability to cite and locate a case is, therefore, a must in working with the tax law. Judicial citations usually follow a standard pattern: case name, volume number, reporter series, page or paragraph number, and court (where necessary).

Judicial Citations—The U.S. Tax Court. A good starting point is with the Tax Court. The Tax Court issues two types of decisions: Regular and Memorandum. The Chief Judge decides whether the opinion is issued as a Regular or Memorandum decision. The distinction between the two involves both substance and form. In terms of substance, *Memorandum* decisions deal with situations necessitating only the application of already established principles of law. *Regular* decisions involve novel issues not previously resolved by the Court. In actual practice, however, this distinction is not always preserved. Not infrequently, Memorandum decisions will be encountered that appear to warrant Regular status and vice versa. At any rate, do not conclude that Memorandum decisions possess no value as precedents. Both represent the position of the Tax Court and, as such, can be relied upon.

The Regular and Memorandum decisions issued by the Tax Court also differ in form. Memorandum decisions are officially published in mimeograph form only. Regular decisions are published by the U.S. Government in a series entitled *Tax Court of the United States Reports*. Each volume of these *Reports* covers a six-month period (January 1 through June 30 and July 1 through December 31) and is given a succeeding volume number. But, as was true of the *Cumulative Bulletin*, there is usually a time lag between the date a decision is rendered and the date it appears in bound form. A temporary citation might be necessary to aid the researcher in locating a recent Regular decision. Consider, for example, the temporary and permanent citations for *John D. Beatty*, a decision filed on April 17, 1996:

Temporary Citation { *John D. Beatty*, 106 T.C. ___, No. 14 (1996).
Explanation: Page number left blank because not yet known.

Permanent Citation { *John D. Beatty*, 106 T.C. 268 (1996).
Explanation: Page number now available.

Both citations tell us that the case will ultimately appear in Volume 106 of the *Tax Court of the United States Reports*. But until this volume is bound and made available to the general public, the page number must be left blank. Instead, the temporary citation identifies the case as being the 14th Regular decision issued by the Tax Court since Volume 105 ended. With this information, the decision can easily be located in either of the special Tax Court services published by Commerce Clearing House (recently acquired by the Dutch company Wolter Klower) or Research Institute of America (formerly by Prentice-Hall). Once Volume 106 is released, the permanent citation can be substituted and the number of the case dropped.

Before 1943, the Tax Court was called the Board of Tax Appeals, and its decisions were published as the *United States Board of Tax Appeals Reports* (B.T.A.). These 47 volumes cover the period from 1924 to 1942. For example, the citation *Karl Pauli*, 11 B.T.A. 784 (1928) refers to the 11th volume of the *Board of Tax Appeals Reports*, page 784, issued in 1928.

If the IRS loses in a decision, it may indicate whether it agrees or disagrees with the results reached by the court by publishing an **acquiescence** ("A" or "Acq.") or **nonacquiescence** ("NA" or "Nonacq."), respectively. Until 1991, acquiescences and nonacquiescences were published only for certain Regular decisions of the Tax Court, but the IRS has expanded its acquiescence program to include other civil tax cases where guidance is helpful. The acquiescence or nonacquiescence is published in the *Internal Revenue Bulletin* and the *Cumulative Bulletin* as an *Action on Decision*. The IRS can retroactively revoke an acquiescence.

Most often the IRS issues nonacquiescences to adverse decisions that are not appealed. A nonacquiescence provides a warning to taxpayers that a similar case cannot be settled administratively. A taxpayer will incur fees and expenses appealing within the IRS even though the IRS may be unwilling to litigate a fact pattern similar to a nonacquiesce decision.[26]

Although Memorandum decisions are not published by the U.S. Government, they are published by Commerce Clearing House (CCH) and Research Institute of America (RIA [formerly by Prentice-Hall]). Consider, for example, the three different ways that *Jack D. Carr* can be cited:

Jack D. Carr, T.C.Memo. 1985–19
    The 19th Memorandum decision issued by the Tax Court in 1985.

Jack D. Carr, 49 TCM 507
    Page 507 of Vol. 49 of the CCH *Tax Court Memorandum Decisions.*

Jack D. Carr, RIA T.C.Mem.Dec. ¶85,019
    Paragraph 85,019 of the RIA *T.C. Memorandum Decisions.*

Note that the third citation contains the same information as the first. Thus, ¶85,019 indicates the following information about the case: year 1985, 19th T.C. Memo. decision.[27] Although the RIA citation does not specifically include a volume number, the paragraph citation indicates that the decision can be found in the 1985 volume of the RIA Memorandum decision service.

Judicial Citations—The U.S. District Court, Court of Federal Claims, and Courts of Appeals.

District Court, Court of Federal Claims, Court of Appeals, and Supreme Court decisions dealing with Federal tax matters are reported in both the CCH *U.S. Tax Cases* (USTC), and the RIA *American Federal Tax Reports* (AFTR) series. Federal District Court decisions, dealing with *both* tax and nontax issues, also are published by West Publishing Company in its *Federal Supplement Series*. The following examples illustrate three different ways of citing a District Court case:

---

[26] G. W. Carter, "Nonacquiescence: Winning by Losing," *Tax Notes* (September 19, 1988): 1301–1307.

[27] In this text, the RIA citation for Memorandum decisions of the U.S. Tax Court is omitted. Thus, *Jack D. Carr* would be cited as 49 TCM 507, T.C.Memo. 1985–19.

Simons-Eastern Co. v. U.S., 73–1 USTC ¶9279 (D.Ct.Ga., 1972).

Explanation: Reported in the first volume of the *U.S. Tax Cases* (USTC) published by Commerce Clearing House for calendar year 1973 (73–1) and located at paragraph 9279 (¶9279).

Simons-Eastern Co. v. U.S., 31 AFTR2d 73–640 (D.Ct.Ga., 1972).

Explanation: Reported in the 31st volume of the second series of the *American Federal Tax Reports* (AFTR2d) published by RIA and beginning on page 640. The "73" preceding the page number indicates the year the case was published but is a designation used only in recent decisions.

Simons-Eastern Co. v. U.S., 354 F.Supp. 1003 (D.Ct.Ga., 1972).

Explanation: Reported in the 354th volume of the *Federal Supplement Series* (F.Supp.) published by West Publishing Company and beginning on page 1003.

In all of the preceding citations, note that the name of the case is the same (Simons-Eastern Co. being the taxpayer), as is the reference to the Federal District Court of Georgia (D.Ct.Ga.) and the year the decision was rendered (1972).[28]

Decisions of the Court of Federal Claims[29] and the Courts of Appeals are published in the USTCs, AFTRs, and a West Publishing Company reporter called the *Federal Second Series* (F.2d). Volume 999, published in 1993, is the last volume of the *Federal Second Series*. It is followed by the *Federal Third Series* (F.3d). Beginning with October 1982, the Court of Federal Claims decisions are published in another West Publishing Company reporter entitled the *Claims Court Reporter*. Beginning with Volume 27 on October 30, 1992, the name of the reporter changed to the *Federal Claims Reporter* (abbreviated as Fed.Cl.). The following examples illustrate the different forms:

Finkbohner, Jr. v. U.S., (CA–11, 1986)
86–1 USTC ¶9393 (CCH citation)
57 AFTR2d 86–1400 (RIA citation)
788 F.2d 723 (West citation)

Apollo Computer, Inc. v. U.S., (Fed.Cl., 1994)
95–1 USTC ¶50,015 (CCH citation)
74 AFTR2d 94–7172 (RIA citation)
32 Fed.Cl. 334 (West citation)

Note that *Finkbohner, Jr.* is a decision rendered by the Eleventh Court of Appeals in 1986 (CA–11, 1986), while *Apollo Computer, Inc.* was issued by the Court of Federal Claims in 1994 (Fed.Cl., 1994).

Judicial Citations—The U.S. Supreme Court.

Like all other Federal tax decisions (except those rendered by the Tax Court), Supreme Court decisions are published by Commerce Clearing House in the USTCs and by RIA (formerly by Prentice-Hall) in the AFTRs. The U.S. Government Printing Office also publishes these decisions in the *United States Supreme Court Reports* (U.S.) as does West Publishing Company in its *Supreme Court Reporter* (S.Ct.) and the Lawyer's

---

[28] In this text, the case would be cited in the following form: *Simons-Eastern Co. v. U.S.*, 73–1 USTC ¶9279, 31 AFTR2d 73–640, 354 F.Supp. 1003 (D.Ct.Ga., 1972). Prentice-Hall Information Services is now owned by Research Institute of America. Although recent volumes contain the RIA imprint, many of the older volumes continue to have the P-H imprint.

[29] Before October 29, 1992, the Court of Federal Claims was called the Claims Court. Before October 1, 1982, the Court of Federal Claims was called the Court of Claims.

Co-operative Publishing Company in its *United States Reports, Lawyer's Edition* (L.Ed.). The following illustrates the different ways the same decision can be cited:

U.S. v. The Donruss Co., (USSC, 1969)
69–1 USTC ¶9167 (CCH citation)
23 AFTR2d 69–418 (RIA citation)
89 S.Ct. 501 (West citation)
393 U.S. 297 (U.S. Government Printing Office citation)
21 L.Ed.2d 495 (Lawyer's Co-operative Publishing Co. citation)

The parenthetical reference (USSC, 1969) identifies the decision as having been rendered by the U.S. Supreme Court in 1969. In this text, the citations of Supreme Court decisions will be limited to the CCH (USTC), RIA (AFTR), and West (S.Ct.) versions. For a summary, see Concept Summary 2–2.

Concept Summary 2–2

Judicial Sources

Court	Location	Authority
U.S. Supreme Court	S.Ct. Series (West) U.S. Series (U.S. Gov't.) L.Ed. (Lawyer's Co-op.) AFTR (RIA) USTC (CCH)	Highest authority
U.S. Courts of Appeal	Federal 3d (West) AFTR (RIA) USTC (CCH)	Next highest appellate court
Tax Court (Regular decisions)	U.S. Govt. Printing Office, RIA/CCH separate services	Highest trial court*
Tax Court (Memorandum decisions)	RIA T.C.Memo (RIA) TCM (CCH)	Less authority than regular T.C. decision
U.S. Court of Federal Claims**	Federal Claims Reporter (West) AFTR (RIA) USTC (CCH)	Similar authority as Tax Court
U.S. District Courts	F.Supp. Series (West) AFTR (RIA) USTC (CCH)	Lowest trial court
Small Cases Division of Tax Court	Not published	No precedent value

*Theoretically, the Tax Court, Court of Federal Claims, and District Courts are on the same level of authority. But some people believe that since the Tax Court hears and decides tax cases from all parts of the country (it is a national court), its decisions may be more authoritative than a Court of Federal Claims or District Court decision.
**Before October 29, 1992, the U.S. Claims Court.

WORKING WITH THE TAX LAW—TAX RESEARCH

3 LEARNING OBJECTIVE
Understand the tax research process.

Tax research is the method by which a tax practitioner, student, or professor determines the best available solution to a situation that possesses tax consequences. In other words, it is the process of finding a competent and professional conclusion to a tax problem. The problem may originate from completed or proposed transactions. In the case of a completed transaction, the objective of the research is to determine the tax result of what has already taken place. For example, was the expenditure incurred by the taxpayer deductible or not deductible for tax purposes? When dealing with proposed transactions, the tax research process is directed toward the determination of possible tax consequences. To the extent that tax research leads to a choice of alternatives or otherwise influences the future actions of the taxpayer, it becomes the key to effective tax planning.

Tax research involves the following procedures:

- Identifying and refining the problem.
- Locating the appropriate tax law sources.
- Assessing the validity of the tax law sources.
- Arriving at the solution or at alternative solutions with due consideration given to nontax factors.
- Effectively communicating the solution to the taxpayer or the taxpayer's representative.
- Following up on the solution (where appropriate) in light of new developments.

These procedures are diagrammed in Figure 2–3. The broken lines reflect the steps of particular interest when tax research is directed toward proposed, rather than completed, transactions.

IDENTIFYING THE PROBLEM

Problem identification must start with a compilation of the relevant facts involved.[30] In this regard, *all* of the facts that may have a bearing on the problem must be gathered because any omission could modify the solution to be reached. To illustrate, consider what appears to be a very simple problem.

EXAMPLE 4

Early in December, Fred and Megan review their financial and tax situation with their son, Sam, and daughter-in-law, Dana. Fred and Megan are in the 28% tax bracket. Both Sam and Dana are age 21. Sam, a student at a nearby university, owns some publicly traded stock that he inherited from his grandmother. A current sale would result in approximately $7,000 of gross income. At this point, Fred and Megan provide about 55% of Sam and Dana's support. Although neither is now employed, Sam has earned $960 and Dana has earned $900. The problem: Should the stock be sold, and would the sale prohibit Fred and Megan from claiming Sam and Dana as dependents? ▼

REFINING THE PROBLEM

Initial reaction is that Fred and Megan in Example 4 could *not* claim Sam and Dana as dependents if the stock is sold, since Sam would then have earned more than

---

[30] For an excellent discussion of the critical role of facts in carrying out tax research, see Ray M. Sommerfeld and G. Fred Streuling, *Tax Research Techniques,* Tax Study No. 5 (New York: The American Institute of Certified Public Accountants, 1981), Chapter 2.

FIGURE 2-3
Tax Research Process

the exemption amount under § 151(d).[31] However, Sam is a full-time student, and § 151(c)(1)(B) allows a son or daughter who is a full-time student and is under age 24 to earn more than the exemption amount without penalizing the parents with the loss of the dependency exemption. Thus, Sam could sell the stock without penalizing the parents with respect to the gross income test. However, the $7,000 income from the sale of the stock might lead to the failure of the greater-than-50 percent support test, depending on how much Sam spends for his (or Dana's) support.

Assume, however, that further fact gathering reveals the following additional information:

- Sam does not really need to spend the proceeds from the sale of the stock.
- Sam receives a sizable portion of his own support from a scholarship.

With these new facts, additional research leads to § 152(d) and Reg. § 1.152–1(c), which indicate that a scholarship received by a student is not included for purposes of computing whether the parents furnished more than one-half of the child's support. Further, if Sam does not spend the proceeds from the sale of stock, the unexpended amount is not counted for purposes of the support test. Thus, it appears that the parents would not be denied the dependency exemptions for Sam and Dana.

LOCATING THE APPROPRIATE TAX LAW SOURCES

Once the problem is clearly defined, what is the next step? Although the next step is a matter of individual judgment, most tax research begins with the index

---
[31] See the related discussion in Chapter 3.

volume of the tax service, a keyword search on an on-line tax service, or a CD-ROM search (see the subsequent discussion of Electronic Tax Research). If the problem is not complex, the researcher may bypass the tax service or on-line service and turn directly to the Internal Revenue Code and Treasury Regulations. For the beginner, the latter procedure saves time and will solve many of the more basic problems. If the researcher does not have a personal copy of the Code or Regulations, resorting to the appropriate volume(s) of a tax service will be necessary.[32] The major tax services available are as follows:

Standard Federal Tax Reporter, Commerce Clearing House.

United States Tax Reporter, Research Institute of America (entitled *Federal Taxes* prior to July 1992).

Federal Tax Coordinator 2d, Research Institute of America.

Tax Management Portfolios, Bureau of National Affairs.

Rabkin and Johnson, *Federal Income, Gift and Estate Taxation*, Matthew Bender, Inc.

CCH's Federal Tax Service, Commerce Clearing House.

Mertens Law of Federal Income Taxation, Callaghan and Co.

Working with the Tax Services. In this text, it is not feasible to teach the use of any particular tax service; this ability can be obtained only by practice.[33] However, several important observations about the use of tax services cannot be overemphasized. First, never forget to check for current developments. The main text of any service is not revised frequently enough to permit reliance on that portion as the *latest* word on any subject. Where current developments can be found depends, of course, on which service is being used. Commerce Clearing House's *Standard Federal Tax Reporter* service contains a special volume devoted to current matters. Both RIA's *U.S. Tax Reporter* and *Federal Tax Coordinator 2d* integrate the new developments into the body of the service throughout the year. Second, when dealing with a tax service synopsis of a Treasury Department pronouncement or a judicial decision, remember there is no substitute for the original source.

To illustrate, do not base a conclusion solely on a tax service's commentary on *Simons-Eastern Co. v. U.S.*[34] If the case is vital to the research, look it up. The facts of the case may be distinguishable from those involved in the problem being researched. This is not to say that the case synopsis contained in the tax service is wrong; it might just be misleading or incomplete.

Tax Periodicals. The various tax periodicals are another source of tax information. The best way to locate a journal article pertinent to a tax problem is through Commerce Clearing House's *Federal Tax Articles*. This multivolume service includes a subject index, a Code Section number index, and an author's index. The RIA (formerly P-H) tax service also has a topical "Index to Tax Articles" section

---

[32] Several of the major tax services publish paperback editions of the Code and Treasury Regulations that can be purchased at modest prices. These editions are usually revised twice each year. For an annotated and abridged version of the Code and Regulations that is published annually, see James E. Smith, *West's Internal Revenue Code of 1986 and Treasury Regulations: Annotated and Selected* (St. Paul, Minn.: West Publishing Company, 1997).

[33] The representatives of the various tax services are prepared to provide the users of their services with printed booklets and individual instruction on the use of the materials.

[34] Refer to Footnote 28.

that is organized using the RIA paragraph index system. Also, beginning in 1992, *The Accounting & Tax Index* is available in three quarterly issues plus a cumulative year-end volume covering all four quarters. The original *Accountant's Index* started in 1921 and ended in 1991.

The following are some of the more useful tax periodicals:

The Journal of Taxation
Warren, Gorham and Lamont
31 St. James Avenue
Boston, MA 02116

Tax Law Review
Warren, Gorham and Lamont
31 St. James Avenue
Boston, MA 02116

Trusts and Estates
6151 Powers Ferry Road NW
Atlanta, GA 30339

Oil and Gas Tax Quarterly
Matthew Bender & Co.
2 Park Avenue
New York, NY 10016

The International Tax Journal
Panel Publishers
14 Plaza Road
Greenvale, NY 11548

TAXES—The Tax Magazine
Commerce Clearing House, Inc.
2700 Lake Cook Road
Riverwood, IL 60015

National Tax Journal
5310 East Main Street
Columbus, OH 43213

The Tax Adviser
AICPA
1211 Avenue of the Americas
New York, NY 10036

The Practical Accountant
11 Penn Plaza
New York, NY 10001

Estate Planning
Warren, Gorham and Lamont
31 St. James Avenue
Boston, MA 02116

Taxation for Accountants
Warren, Gorham and Lamont
31 St. James Avenue
Boston, MA 02116

The Tax Executive
1001 Pennsylvania Avenue NW
Suite 320
Washington, D.C. 20004

Journal of Corporate Taxation
Warren, Gorham and Lamont
31 St. James Avenue
Boston, MA 02116

Journal of Taxation for Individuals
Warren, Gorham and Lamont
31 St. James Avenue
Boston, MA 02116

The Tax Lawyer
American Bar Association
750 N. Lake Shore Drive
Chicago, IL 60611

Journal of the American Taxation Association
American Accounting Association
5717 Bessie Drive
Sarasota, FL 34233

Tax Notes
6830 Fairfax Drive
Arlington, VA 22213

ASSESSING THE VALIDITY OF THE TAX LAW SOURCES

Once a source has been located, the next step is to assess it in light of the problem at hand. Proper assessment involves careful interpretation of the tax law with consideration given to its relevance and validity. In connection with validity, an important step is to check for recent changes in the tax law.

Interpreting the Internal Revenue Code. The language of the Code can be extremely difficult to comprehend fully. For example, a subsection [§ 341(e)]

> ## TAX IN THE NEWS
>
> ### INTERNAL REVENUE CODE: INTERPRETATION PITFALLS
>
> One author has noted 10 common pitfalls in interpreting the Code:
> 1. Determine the limitations and exceptions to a provision. Do not permit the language of the Code Section to carry greater or lesser weight than was intended.
> 2. Just because a Section fails to mention an item does not necessarily mean that the item is excluded.
> 3. Read definitional clauses carefully.
> 4. Do not overlook small words such as *and* and *or*. There is a world of difference between these two words.
> 5. Read the Code Section completely; do not jump to conclusions.
> 6. Watch out for cross-referenced and related provisions, since many Sections of the Code are interrelated.
> 7. At times Congress is not careful when reconciling new Code provisions with existing Sections. Conflicts among Sections, therefore, do arise.
> 8. Be alert for hidden definitions; terms in a particular Code Section may be defined in the same Section or in a separate Section.
> 9. Some answers may not be found in the Code; therefore, a researcher may have to consult the Regulations and/or judicial decisions.
> 10. Take careful note of measuring words such as *less than 50 percent*, *more than 50 percent*, and *at least 80 percent*.
>
> SOURCE: Adapted by permission from Henry G. Wong, "Ten Common Pitfalls in Reading the Internal Revenue Code," *Journal of Business Strategy*, July-August 1972, pp. 30–33. Reprinted with permission by Faulkner & Gray, Inc., 11 Penn Plaza, New York, NY 10001.

relating to collapsible corporations contains *one* sentence of more than 450 words (twice as many as in the Gettysburg Address). Within this same subsection is another sentence of 300 words. Research has shown that in one-third of the conflicts reaching the Tax Court, the Court could not discern the intent of Congress by simply reading the statute. Yet the overriding attitude of the Tax Court judges is that the statute comes first. Even when the statute is unworkable, the Court will not rewrite the law.[35]

Assessing the Validity of a Treasury Regulation. It is often stated that Treasury Regulations have the force and effect of law. This statement is certainly true for most Regulations, but some judicial decisions have held a Regulation or a portion thereof invalid. When a court holds a Regulation invalid, it usually does so on the ground that the Regulation is contrary to the intent of Congress when it enacted a particular Code Section. Most often the courts do not question the validity of Regulations because of the belief that "the first administrative interpretation of a provision as it appears in a new act often expresses the general

---

[35] T. L. Kirkpatrick and W. B. Pollard, "Reliance by the Tax Court on the Legislative Intent of Congress," *The Tax Executive* (Summer 1986): 358–359.

understanding of the times or the actual understanding of those who played an important part when the statute was drafted."[36]

Keep the following observations in mind when assessing the validity of a Regulation:

- IRS agents must give the Code and the Regulations issued thereunder equal weight when dealing with taxpayers and their representatives.
- Proposed Regulations provide a preview of future final Regulations, but they are not binding on the IRS or taxpayers.
- In a challenge, the burden of proof is on the taxpayer to show that the Regulation is wrong. However, a court may invalidate a Regulation that varies from the language of the statute and has no support in the Committee Reports.
- If the taxpayer loses the challenge, a 20 percent negligence penalty may be imposed.[37] This accuracy-related penalty applies to any failure to make a reasonable attempt to comply with the tax law and any disregard of rules and regulations.[38]
- Final Regulations tend to be legislative, interpretive, or procedural. **Procedural Regulations** neither establish tax laws nor attempt to explain tax laws. Procedural Regulations are *housekeeping-type instructions* indicating information that taxpayers should provide the IRS as well as information about the internal management and conduct of the IRS itself.
- Some **interpretive Regulations** merely reprint or rephrase what Congress stated in the Committee Reports that were issued when the tax legislation was enacted. Such Regulations are *hard* and *solid* and almost impossible to overturn because they clearly reflect the intent of Congress. An interpretive Regulation is given less deference than a legislative Regulation, however. The Supreme Court has told lower courts to analyze Treasury Regulations carefully before accepting the Treasury's interpretation.[39]
- In some Code Sections, Congress has given the *Secretary or his delegate* the authority to prescribe Regulations to carry out the details of administration or to otherwise complete the operating rules. Under such circumstances, it could almost be said that Congress is delegating its legislative powers to the Treasury Department. Regulations issued pursuant to this type of authority truly possess the force and effect of law and are often called **legislative Regulations** (e.g., consolidated return Regulations).
- Courts tend to apply a legislative reenactment doctrine. A particular Regulation is assumed to have received congressional approval if the Regulation was finalized many years earlier and Congress has not amended the Code Section pertaining to that Regulation.

Assessing the Validity of Other Administrative Sources of the Tax Law.

Revenue Rulings issued by the IRS carry less weight than Treasury Department Regulations. Revenue Rulings are important, however, in that they reflect the position of the IRS on tax matters. In any dispute with the IRS on the interpretation of tax law, therefore, taxpayers should expect agents to follow the results reached in any applicable Revenue Rulings. A 1986 Tax Court decision, however, indicated that Revenue Rulings "typically do not constitute substantive authority

---

[36] *Augustus v. Comm.*, 41–1 USTC ¶9255, 26 AFTR 612, 118 F.2d 38 (CA–6, 1941).
[37] §§ 6662(a) and (b)(1).
[38] § 6662(c).
[39] *U.S. v. Vogel Fertilizer Co.*, 82–1 USTC ¶9134, 49 AFTR2d 82–491, 102 S.Ct. 821 (USSC, 1982); *National Muffler Dealers Assn., Inc.*, 79–1 USTC ¶9264, 43 AFTR2d 79–828, 99 S.Ct. 1304 (USSC, 1979).

for a position."[40] Most Revenue Rulings apply retroactively unless a specific statement indicates the extent to which a ruling is to be applied without retroactive effect.[41]

Actions on Decisions further tell the taxpayer the IRS's reaction to certain court decisions and Revenue Rulings. Recall that the IRS follows a practice of either acquiescing (agreeing) or nonacquiescing (not agreeing) with selected decisions. A nonacquiescence does not mean that a particular court decision is of no value, but it does indicate that the IRS will continue to litigate the issue involved.

Assessing the Validity of Judicial Sources of the Tax Law.
The judicial process as it relates to the formulation of tax law has already been described. How much reliance can be placed on a particular decision depends upon the following variables:

- The level of the court. A decision rendered by a trial court (e.g., a Federal District Court) carries less weight than one issued by an appellate court (e.g., the Fifth Court of Appeals). Unless Congress changes the Code, decisions by the U.S. Supreme Court represent the last word on any tax issue.
- The legal residence of the taxpayer. If, for example, a taxpayer lives in Texas, a decision of the Fifth Court of Appeals means more than one rendered by the Second Court of Appeals. This result occurs because any appeal from a U.S. District Court or the Tax Court would be to the Fifth Court of Appeals and not to the Second Court of Appeals.[42]
- A Tax Court Regular decision carries more weight than a Memorandum decision since the Tax Court does not consider Memorandum decisions to be binding precedents.[43] Furthermore, a Tax Court *reviewed* decision carries even more weight. All of the Tax Court judges participate in a reviewed decision.
- A Circuit Court decision where certiorari has been requested and denied by the U.S. Supreme Court carries more weight than a Circuit Court decision that was not appealed. A Circuit Court decision heard *en banc* (all the judges participate) carries more weight than a normal Circuit Court case.
- Whether the decision represents the weight of authority on the issue. In other words, is it supported by the results reached by other courts?
- The outcome or status of the decision on appeal. For example, was the decision appealed and, if so, with what result?

In connection with the last two variables, the use of a citator is invaluable to tax research.[44] Citators and their use are discussed in Appendix E.

Assessing the Validity of Other Sources.
Primary sources of tax law include the Constitution, legislative history materials, statutes, treaties, Treasury Regulations, IRS pronouncements, and judicial decisions. In general, the IRS considers only primary sources to constitute substantial authority. However, a researcher might wish to refer to *secondary materials* such as legal periodicals, treatises, legal

---

[40] *Nelda C. Stark*, 86 T.C. 243 (1986). See also *Ann R. Neuhoff*, 75 T.C. 36 (1980). For a different opinion, however, see *Industrial Valley Bank & Trust Co.*, 66 T.C. 272 (1976).

[41] Rev.Proc. 87–1, 1987–1 C.B. 503.

[42] Before October 1, 1982, an appeal from the then-named U.S. Court of Claims (the other trial court) was directly to the U.S. Supreme Court.

[43] *Severino R. Nico, Jr.*, 67 T.C. 647 (1977).

[44] The major citators are published by Commerce Clearing House, RIA, and Shepard's Citations, Inc.

opinions, General Counsel Memoranda, and written determinations. In general, secondary sources are not authority.

Until 1990, the IRS considered only primary sources to constitute substantial authority. In Notice 90–20,[45] the IRS expanded the list of substantial authority *for purposes of* the accuracy-related penalty in § 6662 to include a number of secondary materials (e.g., letter rulings, General Counsel Memoranda, the Bluebook). As under former § 6661, "authority" does not include conclusions reached in treatises, legal periodicals, and opinions rendered by tax professionals.

A letter ruling or determination letter is substantial authority only for the taxpayer to whom it is issued, except as noted above with respect to the accuracy-related penalty.

Upon the completion of major tax legislation, the staff of the Joint Committee on Taxation (in consultation with the staffs of the House Ways and Means and Senate Finance Committees) often will prepare a General Explanation of the Act, commonly known as the Bluebook because of the color of its cover. The IRS will not accept this detailed explanation as having legal effect, except as noted above with respect to the accuracy-related penalty. The Bluebook does, however, provide valuable guidance to tax advisers and taxpayers until Regulations are issued, and some letter rulings and General Counsel Memoranda of the IRS cite its explanations.

ARRIVING AT THE SOLUTION OR AT ALTERNATIVE SOLUTIONS

Example 4 raised the question of whether a taxpayer would be denied dependency exemptions for a son and a daughter-in-law if the son sold some stock near the end of the year. A refinement of the problem supplies additional information:

- Sam was a full-time student during four calendar months of the year.
- Sam and Dana anticipate filing a joint return.

Additional research leads to Regulation § 1.151–3(b), which indicates that to qualify as a student, Sam must be a full-time student during each of *five* calendar months of the year at an educational institution. Thus, proceeds from Sam's sale of the stock would cause his parents to lose at least one dependency exemption because Sam's gross income would exceed the exemption amount. The parents still might be able to claim Dana as an exemption if the support test is met.

Section 151(c)(2) indicates that a supporting taxpayer is not permitted a dependency exemption for a married dependent if the married individual files a joint return. Initial reaction is that a joint return by Sam and Dana would be disastrous to the parents. However, more research uncovers two Revenue Rulings that provide an exception if neither the dependent nor the dependent's spouse is required to file a return but does so solely to claim a refund of tax withheld. The IRS asserts that each spouse must have gross income of less than the exemption amount.[46] Therefore, if Sam sells the stock and he and Dana file a joint return, the parents would lose the dependency exemption for both Sam and Dana.

If the stock is not sold until January, both exemptions may still be available to the parents. However, under § 151(d)(2) a personal exemption is not available to a taxpayer who can be claimed as a dependent by another taxpayer (whether actually claimed or not). Thus, if the parents can claim Sam and Dana as dependents, Sam and Dana would lose their personal exemptions on their tax return.

---

[45] 1990–1 C.B. 328; see also Reg. § 1.6661–3(b)(2).

[46] Rev.Rul. 54–567, 1954–2 C.B. 108; Rev.Rul. 65–34, 1965–1 C.B. 86.

CHAPTER 2 Working with the Tax Law   2–31

▼ **FIGURE 2–4**
Tax File Memorandum

> August 16, 1997
>
> **TAX FILE MEMORANDUM**
>
> FROM: John J. Jones
>
> SUBJECT: Fred and Megan Taxpayer
>   Engagement: Issues
>
> Today I talked to Fred Taxpayer with respect to his August 14, 1997 letter requesting tax assistance. He wishes to know if his son, Sam, can sell stock worth $19,000 (basis = $12,000) without the parents losing the dependency exemptions for Sam and Sam's wife, Dana.
>
> Fred Taxpayer is married to Megan, and Sam is a full-time student at a local university. Sam inherited the stock from his grandmother about five years ago. If he sells the stock, he will save the proceeds from the sale. Sam does not need to spend the proceeds if he sells the stock because he receives a $3,000 scholarship that he uses for his own support (i.e., to pay for tuition, books, and fees). Fred and Megan are in the 28% tax bracket and furnish approximately 55% of Sam and Dana's support.
>
> ISSUE: If the stock is sold, would the sale prohibit Fred and Megan from claiming Sam and Dana as dependents? I told Fred that we would have an answer for him within two weeks.

COMMUNICATING TAX RESEARCH

4 LEARNING OBJECTIVE
Communicate the results of the tax research process in a client letter and a tax file memorandum.

Once satisfied that the problem has been researched adequately, the researcher may need to prepare a memo (and/or letter) setting forth the result. The form such a memo takes could depend on a number of considerations. For example, does an employer or professor recommend a particular procedure or format for tax research memos? Is the memo to be given directly to the client or will it first go to the researcher's employer? Whatever form it takes, a good research memo should contain the following elements:

- A clear statement of the issue.
- In more complex situations, a short review of the fact pattern that raises the issue.
- A review of the tax law sources (e.g., Code, Regulations, Revenue Rulings, judicial authority).
- Any assumptions made in arriving at the solution.
- The solution recommended and the logic or reasoning supporting it.
- The references consulted in the research process.

In short, a good tax memo should tell the reader what was researched, the results of that research, and the justification for the recommendation made.[47]

Illustrations of the memos for the tax file and the client letter associated with Example 4 appear in Figures 2–4, 2–5, and 2–6.

WORKING WITH THE TAX LAW—
TAX PLANNING

5 LEARNING OBJECTIVE
Apply tax research techniques and planning procedures.

Tax research and tax planning are inseparable. The *primary* purpose of effective *tax planning* is to reduce the taxpayer's total tax bill. This statement does not mean that the course of action selected must produce the lowest possible tax under the

---
[47] See Chapter 6 of the publication cited in Footnote 30.

▼ **FIGURE 2-5**
Tax File Memorandum

August 26, 1997

TAX FILE MEMORANDUM

FROM: John J. Jones

SUBJECT: Fred and Megan Taxpayer
          Engagement: Conclusions

Section 152(a) provides that in order for a taxpayer to take a dependency exemption, the taxpayer must provide over 50% of the support of the potential dependent. Fred and Megan provide about 55% of the support of their son, Sam, and their daughter-in-law, Dana. If Sam should sell the stock in 1997, he would not need to spend the proceeds for support purposes (i.e., would save the proceeds). Thus, the stock sale would not affect his qualifying for the support test. In calculating the percentage of support provided by Fred and Megan, a $3,000 scholarship received by Sam is not counted in determining the amount of support Sam provides for himself [see Reg. § 1.152–1(c)].

Section 151(c)(1) provides that in order to qualify for a dependency exemption, the potential dependent's gross income must be less than the exemption amount (i.e., $2,650 in 1997). Without the stock sale, the gross income of both Sam ($960) and Dana ($900) will be below the exemption amount in 1997. The $3,000 Sam receives as a scholarship is excluded from his gross income under § 117(a) because he uses the entire amount to pay for his tuition, books, and fees at a local university.

The key issue then is whether the stock, which will generate $7,000 gain for Sam, will cause the gross income test to be violated. The gain will increase Sam's gross income to $7,960 ($7,000 + $960). However, § 151(c)(1)(B) permits a child's gross income to exceed the exemption amount if the child is a student under the age of 24. Under Reg. § 1.151–3(b), to qualify as a student, the person must be a full-time student during each of five calendar months. A telephone call to Megan provided the information that Sam was a student for only four months in 1997. Thus, since Sam is not eligible for the student exception, the sale of the stock by Sam in 1997 would result in Fred and Megan losing the dependency exemption for Sam.

The stock sale would also result in the loss of the dependency exemption for Dana if Sam and Dana file a joint return for 1997 [see § 151(c)(2)].

From a tax planning perspective, Sam should not sell the stock until 1998. This will enable Fred and Megan to claim dependency exemptions on their 1997 return for Sam and Dana. Note, however, that neither Sam nor Dana will be permitted to take a personal exemption deduction on their 1997 tax return since they are claimed as dependents on someone else's return [see § 151(d)(2)]. However, this will not produce any negative tax consequences since their tax liability will be zero if the stock is not sold in 1997.

---

circumstances. The minimization of tax liability must be considered in context with the legitimate business goals of the taxpayer.

A *secondary* objective of effective tax planning is to reduce or defer the tax in the current tax year. Specifically, this objective aims to accomplish one or more of the following: eradicating the tax entirely; eliminating the tax in the current year; deferring the receipt of income; converting ordinary income into capital gains; converting active to passive income; converting passive to active expense; proliferating taxpayers (i.e., forming partnerships and corporations or making lifetime gifts to family members); eluding double taxation; avoiding ordinary income; or creating, increasing, or accelerating deductions. However, this second objective should be approached with considerable reservation and moderation. For example, a tax election in one year may reduce taxes currently, but saddle future years with a disadvantageous tax position.

▼ **FIGURE 2–6**
Client Letter

Hoffman, Smith, and Willis, CPAs
50 Kellogg Boulevard
St. Paul, Minnesota 55164

August 30, 1997

Mr. and Ms. Fred Taxpayer
111 Boulevard
Williamsburg, Virginia 23185

Dear Mr. and Ms. Taxpayer:

This letter is in response to your request for us to review your family's financial and tax situation. Our conclusions are based upon the facts as outlined in your August 14th letter. Any change in the facts may affect our conclusions.

You provide over 50% of the support for your son, Sam, and his wife, Dana. The scholarship Sam receives is not included in determining support. If the stock is not sold, you will qualify for a dependency exemption for both Sam and Dana.

However, if the stock is sold, a gain of approximately $7,000 will result. This amount will result in the gross income requirement being violated (i.e., potential dependent's gross income must not exceed $2,650) for Sam. Therefore, you will not qualify to receive a dependency exemption for Sam. In addition, if Sam sells the stock and he and Dana file a joint return, you also will not qualify for a dependency exemption for Dana.

From a tax planning perspective, Sam should not sell the stock in 1997. Delaying the stock sale will enable you to claim dependency exemptions for both Sam and Dana. If the stock is sold, Sam and Dana should not file a joint return. This will still enable you to qualify for a dependency exemption for Dana.

Should you need more information or need to clarify our conclusions, do not hesitate to contact me.

Sincerely yours,

John J. Jones, CPA
Partner

NONTAX CONSIDERATIONS

There is an honest danger that tax motivations may take on a significance that does not correspond to the true values involved. In other words, tax considerations may impair the exercise of sound business judgment by the taxpayer. Thus, the tax planning process can become a medium through which to accomplish ends that are socially and economically objectionable. All too often, planning seems to lean toward the opposing extremes of placing either too little or too much emphasis on tax considerations. The happy medium—a balance that recognizes the significance of taxes, but not beyond the point where planning detracts from the exercise of good business judgment—turns out to be the promised land that is too infrequently reached.

The remark is often made that a good rule is to refrain from pursuing any course of action that would not be followed were it not for certain tax considerations. This statement is not entirely correct, but it does illustrate the desirability of preventing business logic from being *sacrificed at the altar of tax planning*.

TAX AVOIDANCE AND TAX EVASION

A fine line exists between legal tax planning and illegal tax planning—tax avoidance versus tax evasion. **Tax avoidance** is merely tax minimization through legal techniques. In this sense, tax avoidance is the proper objective of all tax planning. Tax evasion, while also aimed at the elimination or reduction of taxes, connotes the use of subterfuge and fraud as a means to an end. Popular usage—probably because of the common goals involved—has so linked these two concepts that many individuals are no longer aware of the true distinctions between them. Consequently, some taxpayers have been deterred from properly taking advantage of planning possibilities. The now classic words of Judge Learned Hand in *Commissioner v. Newman* reflect the true values the taxpayer should have:

> Over and over again courts have said that there is nothing sinister in so arranging one's affairs as to keep taxes as low as possible. Everybody does so, rich or poor; and all do right, for nobody owes any public duty to pay more than the law demands: taxes are enforced extractions, not voluntary contributions. To demand more in the name of morals is mere cant.[48]

ETHICAL CONSIDERATIONS

Tax Avoidance

In a speech class, a philosophy student argues that tax advisers are immoral because they help people cheat the government. Each time a tax adviser shows a taxpayer a tax planning idea that reduces the client's liability, all other taxpayers have to pay more taxes. Society would be better off if all tax advisers would work at improving our environment or living conditions in the inner cities.

An accounting student argues that the primary purpose of tax planning is to reduce a taxpayer's overall liability. This advisory process can result in avoiding, deferring, or postponing the tax burden until the future. There is nothing illegal or immoral about tax avoidance. Taxpayers have every legal right to be concerned about tax avoidance and to arrange their affairs so as to pay no more taxes than the law demands. There is no difference between reducing a tax expense through the help of a tax adviser and reducing a cost of operating a business with the aid of a cost accountant.

Comment on each student's position.

FOLLOW-UP PROCEDURES

Because tax planning usually involves a proposed (as opposed to a completed) transaction, it is predicated upon the continuing validity of the advice based upon the tax research. A change in the tax law (either legislative, administrative, or judicial) could alter the original conclusion. Additional research may be necessary to test the solution in light of current developments (refer to the broken lines at the right in Figure 2–3).

TAX PLANNING—A PRACTICAL APPLICATION

Returning to the facts of Example 4, what could be done to protect the dependency exemptions for the parents? If Sam and Dana were to refrain from filing a joint return, both could be claimed by the parents. This result assumes that the stock is not sold.

---

[48] *Comm. v. Newman*, 47–1 USTC ¶9175, 35 AFTR 857, 159 F.2d 848 (CA–2, 1947).

An obvious tax planning tool is the installment method. Could the securities be sold using the installment method under § 453 so that most of the gain is deferred into the next year? Under the installment method, certain gains may be postponed and recognized as the cash proceeds are received. The problem is that the installment method is not available for stock traded on an established securities market.[49]

A little more research, however, indicates that Sam can sell the stock and postpone the recognition of gain until the following year by selling short an equal number of substantially identical shares and covering the short sale in the subsequent year with the shares originally held. Selling short means that Sam sells borrowed stock (substantially identical) and repays the lender with the stock held on the date of the short sale. This *short against the box* technique would allow Sam to protect his $7,000 profit and defer the closing of the sale until the following year.[50] Further, if the original shares have been held for the required long-term holding period before the date of the short sale, Sam would be able to obtain long-term capital gain treatment.[51] Thus, some research and planning would reap tax savings for this family. Note the critical role of obtaining the correct facts in attempting to resolve the proper strategy for the taxpayers.

Throughout this text, most chapters include observations on Tax Planning Considerations. Such observations are not all-inclusive but are intended to illustrate some of the ways in which the material covered can be effectively utilized to minimize taxes.

ELECTRONIC TAX RESEARCH

6 LEARNING OBJECTIVE
Have an awareness of electronic tax research.

Computer-based tax research tools now hold a prominent position in tax practice. Electronic tax resources allow the tax library to reflect the tax law itself, including its dynamic and daily changes. Nevertheless, using electronic means to locate tax law sources cannot substitute for developing and maintaining a thorough knowledge of the tax law or for logical and analytical review in addressing open tax research issues.

Accessing tax documents through electronic means offers several important advantages over a strictly paper-based approach:

- Materials generally are available to the practitioner faster through an electronic system, as delays related to typesetting, proofreading, production, and distribution of the new materials are streamlined.
- Some tax documents, such as so-called slip opinions of trial-level court cases and interviews with policymakers, are available only through electronic means.
- Commercial subscriptions to electronic tax services are likely to provide, at little or no cost, additional tax law sources to which the researcher would not have access through stand-alone purchases of traditional material. For example, the full text of private letter rulings are quite costly to acquire in a paper-based format, but electronic publishers may bundle the rulings with other materials for a reasonable cost.

Strict cost comparisons of paper and electronic tax research materials are difficult to construct, especially when the practitioner uses hardware, including work-

---

[49] See Chapter 18 for a discussion of installment sales.
[50] §§ 1233(a) and 1233(b)(2). See Chapter 16 for a discussion of short sales.
[51] Long-term capital gains are eligible for preferential tax treatment. In addition, if Sam had capital losses from other transactions, the capital gains and capital losses could be offset. See the discussion in Chapter 16.

> ### TAX IN THE NEWS
>
> #### TAX RESEARCH: CD-ROM VERSUS PAPER
>
> With the movement toward computer technology, is there any need to conduct tax research using a traditional paper tax service? John Fothergill, a partner in a nine-member accounting firm in Vermont, believes paper tax reporting services still have a place in conducting tax research. In fact, he believes both the traditional and the technology-based approaches are needed. In his opinion, one complements the other.
>
> For the past three years, Fothergill has been using a CD-ROM tax reporting service. His normal research approach is to do a keyword search using the CD-ROM service as the basis for gathering all the pertinent data. If the project is relatively simple, the entire research process is conducted on the CD-ROM service. If the CD-ROM search identifies many keyword "hits," however, he may turn to the paper tax reporting service to narrow the search process after he has used the CD-ROM service. If nothing else, the paper is a lot easier on the eyes.
>
> In addition, if he is introducing himself to a relatively new topic, Fothergill prefers to use paper initially rather than the CD-ROM service. Then, once he is comfortable with the relevant code sections and theory, he may turn to the CD-ROM service for more detailed searching for cases and rulings.
>
> SOURCE: Adapted from "CD-ROM vs. Paper Verdict: They Both Win," *Journal of Accountancy*, August 1996, p. 45.

stations and communications equipment, that is already in place and employed elsewhere in the practice. Over time, though, the convenience, cost, and reliability of electronic research tools clearly will make them the dominant means of finding and analyzing the law in tax practice.

Using Electronic Services. Tax researchers often use electronic means to find sources of the tax law. Usually, the law is found using one of the following strategies:

- *Search* various databases using keywords that are likely to be found in the underlying documents, as written by Congress, the judiciary, or administrative sources.
- *Link* to tax documents for which all or part of the proper citation is known.
- *Browse* the tax databases, examining various tables of contents and indexes in a traditional manner or using cross-references in the documents to jump from one tax law source to another.

Virtually all of the major commercial tax publishers and some of the primary sources of the law itself, such as the Supreme Court and some of the Courts of Appeals, now provide tax materials in electronic formats. Competitive pressures are forcing computer literacy upon tax practitioners, and the user-friendliness of the best of the tax search software is of great benefit to both the daily and the occasional user.

CD-ROM Services. The CD has been a major source of electronic tax data for about a decade. Data compression techniques continue to allow more tax materials to fit on a single disk every year. CCH, RIA, WESTLAW, and others offer vast tax libraries to the practitioner, often in conjunction with a subscription to traditional

▼ EXHIBIT 2–2
CD-ROM Tax Services

Tax CD Service	Description
CCH ACCESS	Includes the CCH tax service, primary sources including treaties, and other subscription materials. Ten to twenty disks.
RIA OnPoint	Includes the RIA topical *Coordinator* and the annotated tax service formerly provided by Prentice-Hall. The Citator has elaborate document-linking features, and major tax treatises also are provided. One to ten disks.
WESTLAW	Code, Regulations, *Cumulative Bulletins*, cases, citator, and editorial material. About a dozen disks.
Kleinrock's	A single disk with all tax statutory, administrative, and judicial law. Another single disk provides tax forms and instructions for Federal and state jurisdictions.

paper-based resources or accompanied by newsletters, training seminars, and ongoing technical support.

At its best, a CD-based tax library provides the archival data that make up a permanent, core library of tax documents. For about $200 a year, the tax CD is updated quarterly, providing more comprehensive tax resources than the researcher is ever likely to need. The CD is comparable in scope to a paper-based library of a decade ago costing perhaps $20,000 to establish and $10,000 per year in perpetuity to maintain. If the library is contained on a small number of disks, it also can offer portability through use on laptop computers. Exhibit 2–2 summarizes the most popular of the CD tax services on the market today.

On-Line Systems. An on-line research system allows a practitioner to obtain virtually instantaneous use of tax law sources by accessing the computer of the service provider. On-line services generally employ price-per-search cost structures, which can average more than $100 per hour, significantly higher than the cost of CD services. Thus, unless a practitioner can pass along related costs to clients or others, on-line searching generally is limited to the most important issues and to the researchers with the most experience and training in search techniques.

Perhaps the best combination of electronic tax resources is to conduct day-to-day work on a CD system, so that the budget for the related work is known in advance, and augment the CD search with on-line access where it is judged to be critical. Exhibit 2–3 lists the most commonly used commercial on-line tax services.

The Internet. The Internet provides a wealth of tax information in several popular forms, sometimes at no direct cost to the researcher. Using so-called browser software that often is distributed with new computer systems and their communication devices, the tax professional can access information provided around the world that can aid the research process.

- *Home pages (sites) on the World Wide Web (WWW)* are provided by accounting and consulting firms, publishers, tax academics and libraries, and governmental bodies as a means of making information widely available or of soliciting subscriptions or consulting engagements. The best pages offer links to other pages and direct contact to the page providers. One of the best pages available to the tax practitioner is the Internal Revenue Service's *Digital Daily*, as illustrated in Exhibit 2–4. This page offers downloadable forms and

▼ **EXHIBIT 2-3**
On-Line Tax Services

On-Line Service	Description
LEXIS/NEXIS	Federal and state statutory, administrative, and judicial material. Extensive libraries of newspapers, magazines, patent records, and medical and economic databases, both U.S. and foreign-based.
WESTLAW	Federal and state statutes, administrative documents, and court opinions. Extensive citator access, editorial material, and gateways to third-party publications. Extensive government document databases.
CCH ACCESS	Includes the CCH tax service, primary sources including treaties, and other subscription materials. Tax and economic news sources, extensive editorial material, and practitioner support tools.

▼ **EXHIBIT 2-4**
The IRS *Digital Daily*

instructions, "plain English" versions of Regulations, and news update items. Exhibit 2–5 lists some of the Web sites that may be most useful to tax researchers and their Internet addresses as of press date.

- *Newsgroups* provide a means by which information related to the tax law can be exchanged among taxpayers, tax professionals, and others who subscribe

CHAPTER 2 Working with the Tax Law

▼ **EXHIBIT 2–5**
Tax-Related Web Sites

Web Site	WWW Address at Press Date (Usually preceded by http://www)	Description
Internal Revenue Service	**irs.ustreas.gov/prod/cover**	News releases, downloadable forms and instructions, tables, and E-mail
Court opinions	The official site of the Fifth Court of Appeals is **tarlton.law.utexas.edu/us5th/us5th**, and the site at **law.emory.edu/fedcts** allows the researcher to link to the site of the jurisdiction that is the subject of the query (see Exhibit 2–6).	
Discussion groups moderated by Tax Analysts	**tax.org/notes**	Policy-oriented discussions of tax laws and proposals to change the law, links to student tax clinics, excerpts from the Tax Notes newsletter, and a tax calendar
Tax Sites Directory	**uni.edu/schmidt/tax.html**	References and links to tax sites on the Internet, including state and Federal tax sites, academic and professional pages, tax forms and software
Tax laws on-line	Regulations are at **http://law.house.gov/cfr.htm**, and the Code is at **fourmilab.ch/ustax/ustax.html**	
Tax World	**omer.actg.uic.edu**	References and links to tax sites on the Internet, including property tax and international tax links
Commercial tax publishers	For instance, **riatax.com** and **cch.com**	Information about products and services available by subscription, newsletter excerpts
Large accounting firms and professional organizations	For instance, the AICPA's page is at **aicpa.org.** and an Ernst and Young Tax Services page is at **ey.com/us/tax/eyustax**	Tax planning newsletters, descriptions of services offered and career opportunities, and exchange of data with clients and subscribers
West Publishing Company	**westpub.com**	Informational updates, newsletters, support materials for subscribers and adopters, and continuing education

to the group's services. Newsgroup members can read the exchanges among other members and offer replies and suggestions to inquiries as desired. Discussions address the interpretation and application of existing law, analysis of proposals and new pronouncements, and reviews of tax software.

- *E-mail capabilities* are available to most tax professionals through an employer's equipment or by a subscription providing Internet access at a low and usually fixed cost for the period. E-mail allows for virtually instantaneous sending and receiving of messages, letters, tax returns and supporting data, spreadsheets, and other documents necessary to solve tax problems.

▼ **EXHIBIT 2-6**
The Emory *Federal Courts Finder*

In many situations, solutions to research problems will benefit from, or require, the use of various electronic tax research tools. A competent tax professional must become familiar and proficient with these tools and be able to use them to meet the expectations of clients and the necessities of work in the modern world.[52]

---

[52] For a more detailed discussion of the use of electronic tax research in the modern tax practice, see W. A. Raabe, G. E. Whittenburg, and J. C. Bost, *West's Federal Tax Research*, 4th ed (St. Paul, Minn.: West Publishing Co., 1997).

CHAPTER 2 Working with the Tax Law

KEY TERMS

Acquiescence, 2–20
Circuit Court of Appeals, 2–15
Court of original jurisdiction, 2–13
Determination letters, 2–11
Federal District Court, 2–13
Finalized Regulations, 2–8
Interpretive Regulations, 2–28
Legislative Regulations 2–28

Letter rulings, 2–11
Nonacquiescence, 2–20
Precedents, 2–17
Procedural Regulations, 2–28
Proposed Regulations, 2–8
Revenue Procedures, 2–10
Revenue Rulings, 2–9
Small Cases Division, 2–13

Tax avoidance, 2–33
Tax research, 2–23
Technical Advice Memoranda (TAMs), 2–12
Temporary Regulations, 2–9
U.S. Court of Federal Claims, 2–13
U.S. Supreme Court, 2–17
U.S. Tax Court, 2–13
Writ of Certiorari, 2–18

PROBLEM MATERIALS

DISCUSSION QUESTIONS

1. Judicial decisions interpreting a provision of the Internal Revenue Code of 1939 or 1954 are no longer of any value in view of the enactment of the Internal Revenue Code of 1986. Assess the validity of this statement.

2. The Small Business Job Protection Act of 1996 became part of the Internal Revenue Code of 1986. Assess the validity of this statement.

3. Why are Committee Reports of Congress important as a source of tax law?

4. Why are certain Code Section numbers missing from the Internal Revenue Code (e.g., §§ 6, 7, 8, 9, 10)?

5. In which Title and Subtitle of the U.S. Code is the income tax portion of the Internal Revenue Code of 1986 found?

6. Paul Jacobs operates a small international firm named Teal, Inc. A new treaty between the United States and Ukraine conflicts with a Section of the Internal Revenue Code. Paul asks you for advice. If he follows the treaty position, does he need to disclose this on his tax return? If he is required to disclose, are there any penalties for failure to disclose? Prepare a letter in which you respond to Paul. Teal's address is 100 International Drive, Tampa, FL 33620.

7. Explain how Regulations are arranged. How would a Proposed Regulation under § 66 be cited?

8. Distinguish between legislative, interpretive, and procedural Regulations.

9. Distinguish between:
   a. Treasury Regulations and Revenue Rulings.
   b. Revenue Rulings and Revenue Procedures.
   c. Revenue Rulings and letter rulings.
   d. Letter rulings and determination letters.

10. Rank the following items from the highest authority to the lowest in the Federal tax law system:
    a. Interpretive Regulation.
    b. Legislative Regulation.

c. Letter ruling.
d. Revenue Procedure.
e. Internal Revenue Code.
f. Proposed Regulation.

11. Interpret each of the following citations:
    a. Rev.Rul. 74–503, 1974–2 C.B. 117.
    b. Rev.Proc. 87–59, 1987–2 C.B. 764.
    c. Ltr.Rul. 8550037.

12. Michelle Zull calls you on the phone. She says that she has found a 1988 letter ruling that agrees with a position she wishes to take on her tax return. She asks you about the precedential value of a letter ruling. Draft a memo for the tax files outlining what you told Michelle.

13. Edith is considering writing the IRS to determine if a proposed divisive reorganization would be tax-free. Outline some relevant tax issues Edith faces in making this decision.

14. a. What are Treasury Decisions (TDs)?
    b. What purpose do they serve?
    c. Where are they published?

15. What are the major differences between letter rulings and determination letters?

16. What is a Technical Advice Memorandum (TAM)?

17. Caleb receives a ninety-day letter after his discussion with an appeals officer. He is not satisfied with the $92,000 settlement offer. Identify the relevant tax research issues facing Caleb.

18. Which of the following would be considered advantages of the Small Cases Division of the Tax Court?
    a. Appeal to the Court of Appeals for the Federal Circuit is possible.
    b. A hearing of a deficiency of $11,200 is considered on a timely basis.
    c. Taxpayer can handle the litigation without using a lawyer or certified public accountant.
    d. Taxpayer can use other Small Cases Division decisions for precedential value.
    e. The actual hearing is conducted informally.
    f. Travel time will probably be reduced.

19. List an advantage and a disadvantage of using the U.S. Tax Court as the trial court for Federal tax litigation.

20. Sam Brown is considering litigating a tax deficiency of approximately $317,000 in the court system. He asks you to provide him with a short description of his alternatives indicating the advantages and disadvantages of each. Prepare your response to Sam in the form of a letter. His address is 200 Mesa Drive, Tuscon, AZ 85714.

21. List an advantage and a disadvantage of using the U.S. Court of Federal Claims as the trial court for Federal tax litigation.

22. A taxpayer lives in Michigan. In a controversy with the IRS, the taxpayer loses at the trial court level. Describe the appeal procedure under the following different assumptions:
    a. The trial court was the Small Cases Division of the U.S. Tax Court.
    b. The trial court was the U.S. Tax Court.
    c. The trial court was a U.S. District Court.
    d. The trial court was the U.S. Court of Federal Claims.

23. Suppose the U.S. Government loses a tax case in the U.S. District Court of South Carolina but does not appeal the result. What does the failure to appeal signify?

24. Because the U.S. Tax Court is a national court, it always decides the same issue in a consistent manner. Assess the validity of this statement.

25. For the U.S. Tax Court, U.S. District Court, and the U.S. Court of Federal Claims, indicate the following:

a. Number of regular judges per court.
b. Availability of a jury trial.
c. Whether the deficiency must be paid before the trial.

26. In which of the following states could a taxpayer appeal the decision of a U.S. District Court to the Second Court of Appeals?
    a. Alaska.
    b. Arkansas.
    c. New York.
    d. South Carolina.
    e. Utah.

27. Explain the fact-finding determination of a Federal Court of Appeals.

28. What is the Supreme Court's policy on hearing tax cases?

29. In assessing the validity of a prior court decision, discuss the significance of the following on the taxpayer's issue:
    a. The decision was rendered by the U.S. District Court of Wyoming. Taxpayer lives in Wyoming.
    b. The decision was rendered by the U.S. Court of Federal Claims. Taxpayer lives in Wyoming.
    c. The decision was rendered by the Second Court of Appeals. Taxpayer lives in California.
    d. The decision was rendered by the U.S. Supreme Court.
    e. The decision was rendered by the U.S. Tax Court. The IRS has acquiesced in the result.
    f. Same as (e) except that the IRS has issued a nonacquiescence as to the result.

30. The IRS may acquiesce or nonacquiesce to what court decisions? Can an acquiescence be withdrawn retroactively?

31. Where can a researcher locate a 1989 U.S. District Court decision?

32. Answer the following questions based upon this citation: *Schuster's Express, Inc.*, 66 T.C. 588 (1976), *aff'd* 562 F.2d 39 (CA–2, 1977), *nonacq.*
    a. In which court did this decision first appear?
    b. Who was the plaintiff?
    c. Who was the respondent?
    d. Did the appellate court agree or disagree with the trial court?
    e. Does the Government agree with the position of the court?

33. Interpret each of the following citations:
    a. 54 T.C. 1514 (1970).
    b. 408 F.2d 1117 (CA–2, 1969).
    c. 69–1 USTC ¶9319 (CA–2, 1969).
    d. 23 AFTR2d 69–1090 (CA–2, 1969).
    e. 293 F.Supp. 1129 (D.Ct. Miss., 1967).
    f. 67–1 USTC ¶9253 (D.Ct. Miss., 1967).
    g. 19 AFTR2d 647 (D.Ct. Miss., 1967).
    h. 56 S.Ct. 289 (USSC, 1935).
    i. 36–1 USTC ¶9020 (USSC, 1935).
    j. 16 AFTR 1274 (USSC, 1935).
    k. 422 F.2d 1336 (Ct.Cls., 1970).

34. Explain the following abbreviations:
    a. CA–2
    b. Fed.Cl.
    c. *aff'd.*
    d. *rev'd.*
    e. *rem'd.*
    f. *Cert. Denied*
    g. *acq.*
    h. B.T.A.
    i. USTC
    j. AFTR
    k. F.3d
    l. F.Supp.
    m. USSC
    n. S.Ct.
    o. D.Ct.

35. Give the Commerce Clearing House citation for the following courts:
    a. Small Cases Division of the Tax Court.
    b. Federal District Court.
    c. U.S. Supreme Court.
    d. U.S. Court of Federal Claims.
    e. Tax Court Memorandum decision.

36. Where can you locate a published decision of the U.S. Court of Federal Claims?

37. Which of the following items can probably be found in the *Cumulative Bulletin*?
    a. Revenue Ruling.
    b. Small Cases Division of the U.S. Tax Court decision.
    c. Letter ruling.
    d. Revenue Procedure.
    e. Proposed Regulation.
    f. District Court decision.
    g. Senate Finance Committee Report.
    h. Acquiescences to Tax Court decisions.
    i. Tax Court Memorandum decision.

38. As part of her course work for a Masters of Tax degree, Ann is required to prepare a 30-page term paper about limited liability partnerships. Identify some relevant research steps Ann may take.

39. Does the U.S. Tax Court or a U.S. District Court have the higher level of authority?

40. Since a Regulation has the force and effect of tax law, can a Regulation be overturned by a court?

41. Determine the level of authority for a Tax Court Memorandum decision, a Tax Court Regular decision, and a Tax Court reviewed decision.

42. When might a researcher need to refer to a citator?

43. Which of the following would be considered differences between the Research Institute of America and Commerce Clearing House citators?
    a. Distinguishes between the various issues in a particular court decision.
    b. Lists all court decisions that cite the court decision being researched.
    c. Allows a researcher to determine the validity of a Revenue Ruling.
    d. Indicates whether a court decision is explained, criticized, followed, or overruled by a subsequent decision.
    e. Pinpoints the exact page on which a decision is cited by another case.

44. List the elements that a good tax research memo should include.

45. Defend the practice by which tax advisers such as CPAs use tax planning techniques to reduce the tax liability of their clients.

46. You inherit a tax problem that was researched five months ago. You believe the answer is correct, but you are unfamiliar with the general area. How would you find some recent articles dealing with the subject area? How do you evaluate the reliability of the authority cited in the research report? How do you determine the latest developments pertaining to the research problem?

47. Constance is developing an outline for younger associates to follow in researching tax issues in her office. Identify the relevant alternatives available to a tax researcher.

PROBLEMS

48. Tom, an individual taxpayer, has just been audited by the IRS and, as a result, has been assessed a substantial deficiency (which has not yet been paid) in additional income taxes. In preparing his defense, Tom advances the following possibilities:
    a. Although a resident of Kentucky, Tom plans to sue in a U.S. District Court in Oregon that appears to be more favorably inclined toward taxpayers.

CHAPTER 2 Working with the Tax Law   2–45

b. If (a) is not possible, Tom plans to take his case to a Kentucky state court where an uncle is the presiding judge.
c. Since Tom has found a B.T.A. decision that seems to help his case, he plans to rely on it under alternative (a) or (b).
d. If he loses at the trial court level, Tom plans to appeal either to the U.S. Court of Federal Claims or to the U.S. Second Court of Appeals because he has relatives in both Washington, D.C., and New York. Staying with these relatives could save Tom lodging expense while his appeal is being heard by the court selected.
e. Whether or not Tom wins at the trial court or appeals court level, he feels certain of success on an appeal to the U.S. Supreme Court.

Evaluate Tom's notions concerning the judicial process as it applies to Federal income tax controversies.

49. Using the legend provided, identify the governmental unit that produces the following tax sources:

Legend

T = U.S. Treasury Department
NO = National Office of the IRS
DD = District Director of the IRS
NA = Not applicable

a. Proposed Regulations.
b. Revenue Procedures.
c. Letter rulings.
d. Determination letters.
e. Technical Advice Memoranda.
f. Treasury Decisions.
g. Revenue Rulings.

50. Using the legend provided, classify each of the following statements (more than one answer per statement may be appropriate):

Legend

D = Applies to the U.S. District Court
T = Applies to the U.S. Tax Court
C = Applies to the U.S. Court of Federal Claims
A = Applies to the U.S. Court of Appeals
U = Applies to the U.S. Supreme Court
N = Applies to none of the above

a. Decides only Federal tax matters.
b. Decisions are reported in the F.3d Series.
c. Decisions are reported in the USTCs.
d. Decisions are reported in the AFTRs.
e. Appeal is by Writ of Certiorari.
f. Court meets most often in Washington, D.C.
g. A jury trial is available.
h. Trial court.
i. Appellate court.
j. Appeal is to the Federal Circuit and bypasses the taxpayer's particular circuit court.
k. Has a Small Cases Division.
l. The only trial court where the taxpayer does not have to pay the tax assessed by the IRS first.

51. Using the legend provided, classify each of the following citations as to the type of court:

Legend

T = Applies to the U.S. Tax Court
D = Applies to the U.S. District Court
C = Applies to the U.S. Court of Federal Claims
A = Applies to the U.S. Court of Appeals
U = Applies to the U.S. Supreme Court
N = Applies to none of the above

a. 241 F.2d 197 (CA–4, 1957).
b. 90 T.C. 1 (1988).
c. 54 S.Ct. 8 (USSC, 1933).
d. 3 B.T.A. 1042 (1926).
e. T.C.Memo. 1954–141.
f. 597 F.2d 760 (Ct.Cl., 1979).
g. Ltr.Rul. 9414051.
h. 354 F.Supp. 1003 (D.Ct. Ga., 1972).
i. Rev.Rul. 74–164.

52. Using the legend provided, classify each of the following tax sources:

Legend

P = Primary tax source
S = Secondary tax source
B = Both
N = Neither

a. Sixteenth Amendment to the Constitution.
b. Tax treaty between the United States and France.
c. Revenue Rulings.
d. General Counsel Memoranda (1988).
e. Tax Court Memorandum decision.
f. *Yale Law Review* article.
g. Temporary Regulations (issued 1994).
h. District Court decision.
i. Small Cases Division of the U.S. Tax Court decision.
j. Senate Finance Committee report.

53. Using the legend provided, classify each of the following citations as to publisher:

Legend

RIA = Research Institute of America
CCH = Commerce Clearing House
W = West Publishing Company
U.S. = U.S. Government
O = Others

CHAPTER 2 Working with the Tax Law

a. 83–2 USTC ¶9600.
b. 52 AFTR2d 83–5954.
c. 67 T.C. 293 (1976).
d. 39 TCM 32 (1979).
e. 416 U.S. 938.
f. RIA T.C.Memo. ¶80,582.
g. 89 S.Ct. 501.
h. 2 Cl.Ct. 600.
i. 415 F.2d 488.
j. 592 F.Supp. 18.
k. Rev.Proc. 77–37, 1977–2 C.B. 568.
l. 21 L.Ed.2d 495.
m. S.Rep. No. 1622, 83rd Cong., 2d Sess. 42 (1954).

RESEARCH PROBLEMS

*Note: **West's Federal Taxation on CD-ROM** can be used in preparing solutions to the Research Problems. Alternatively, tax research materials contained in a standard tax library can be used.*

Research Problem 1. When the same word is used at different places in the Internal Revenue Code, does the word mean the same thing?

Research Problem 2. Determine what is covered in the following subchapters in Chapter 1, Subtitle A of the Internal Revenue Code of 1986:
a. B.
b. D.
c. F.
d. K.
e. P.

Research Problem 3. A particular Code Section, which was passed in 1986, conflicts with a treaty between the United States and France, which was signed in 1991. Which source controls? Where can a researcher find tax treaties?

Research Problem 4. Determine how the term *person* is defined in the Internal Revenue Code of 1986.

Research Problem 5. Go to page 44,274 of the August 25, 1995, issue of the *Federal Register*. What action was taken by the IRS, and what was the subject matter?

Research Problem 6. What do acquiescence, acquiescence in result only, and nonacquiescence mean? What position did the IRS take with respect to *Zabolotny v. Comm.*, 7 F.3d 774 (CA–8, 1993)?

Research Problem 7. Locate the following tax services in your library and indicate the name of the publisher and whether the service is organized by topic or Code Section:
a. *United States Tax Reporter.*
b. *Standard Federal Tax Reporter.*
c. *Federal Tax Coordinator 2d.*
d. *Mertens Law of Federal Income Taxation.*
e. *Tax Management Portfolios.*
f. Rabkin & Johnson, *Federal Income, Gift & Estate Taxation.*
g. *Federal Tax Service.*

Research Problem 8. In the Tax Publications Matrix below, place an X if a court decision can be found in the publication. There may be more than one X in a row for a particular court.

Court	U.S. Govt. Printing Office	West Publishing Company				Research Institute of America			Commerce Clearing House	
		Federal Supp.	Federal 3d	Federal Claims Reporter	S.Ct.	BTA Memo	TC Memo	AFTR	TC Memo	USTC
U.S. Supreme Court										
Court of Appeals										
Court of Federal Claims										
District Court										
Tax Court (Regular decisions)										
Tax Court (Memo decisions)										
Board of Tax Appeal										
BTA Memo										

Research Problem 9. With respect to the changes in the maximum amounts to be expensed under § 179 in 1997 and 1998, what was the House's position, the Senate's position, and the Conference Agreement in the Small Business Job Protection Act of 1996?

Research Problem 10. Locate the following Internal Revenue Code citations and give a brief description of each of them:
 a. § 708(a).
 b. § 1371(a)(1).
 c. § 2503(a).

Research Problem 11. Locate the following Regulation citations and give a brief description of each of them:
 a. Reg. § 1.170–4(A)(b)(2)(ii)(C).
 b. Reg. § 1.672(b)–1.
 c. Reg. § 20.2031–7(F).

Research Problem 12. Find the following item and give a brief description of its contents: Rev.Rul. 78–325, 1978–2 C.B. 124.

Research Problem 13. Did the IRS agree or disagree with the following court decisions?
 a. *Longue Vue Foundation*, 90 T.C. 150 (1988).
 b. *Charles Crowther*, 28 T.C. 1293 (1957).
 c. *Sidney Merians*, 60 T.C. 187 (1973).
 d. *Zabolotny v. Comm.*, 7 F.3d 774 (CA–8, 1993).

Research Problem 14. Determine the reliability of the following decisions:
 a. *Maid of The Mist Corp.*, T.C.Memo. 1977–263, 36 TCM 1068 (1977).
 b. *Albert Lazisky*, 72 T.C. 495 (1979).
 c. *Farm Service Cooperative*, 70 T.C. 145 (1978).
 d. *Tufts v. Comm.*, 81–2 USTC ¶9574 (CA–5, 1981), rev'g 70 T.C. 756 (1978).

Research Problem 15. Find *Francis Levien*, 103 T.C. 120 (1994), and answer these questions.
 a. Who was the petitioner (plaintiff)?
 b. Who was the respondent (defendant)?
 c. What was the court's holding with respect to issue one?
 d. Was this a reviewed decision?
 e. How many judges agreed with the majority opinion?
 f. Who wrote a concurring opinion?
 g. Was this decision entered under Rule 155?

Research Problem 16. During 1997, Frank lived with and supported a 20-year-old woman who was not his wife. He resides in a state that has a statute that makes it a misdemeanor for a man and woman who are not married to each other to live together. May Frank claim his *friend* as a dependent assuming he satisfies the normal tax rules for the deduction? Should Frank consider moving to another state?

Partial list of research aids:
§ 152(b)(5).
John T. Untermann, 38 T.C. 93 (1962).
S.Rept. 1983, 85th Cong., 2d Sess., reprinted in the 1958 Code Cong. & Adm. News 4791, 4804.

Research Problem 17. Using the 1985–1989 volume of CCH's *Federal Tax Articles*, locate Code Section 636, article .012. Who are the authors, in what journal does the article appear, and what principle is discussed in the article?

Use the tax resources of the internet to address the following questions. Do not restrict your search to the World Wide Web, but include a review of newsgroups and general reference materials, practitioner sites and resources, primary sources of the tax law, chat rooms and discussion groups, and other opportunities.

Research Problem 18. Go to each of the following internet locations.
  a. Several primary sources of the tax law, including the U.S. Supreme Court, a circuit Court of Appeal, the Internal Revenue Service, and final Regulations.
  b. Sources of proposed Federal tax legislation.
  c. A collection of tax rules for your state.

Research Problem 19. Go to each of the following internet locations.
  a. Several newspapers and magazines, such as *USA Today*, the *New York Times*, the *Washington Post*, *Newsweek* magazine, your local newspaper, and a local television station.
  b. Other news sources such as *CNN Interactive*, Newspapers OnLine, and a collection of on-line versions of magazines.

Research Problem 20. Go to each of the following internet locations.
  a. The American Institute of CPAs, the American Taxation Association, several tax-related newsgroups, and tax information provided by enrolled agents.
  b. Tax World, the Tax Prophet, Taxing Times, and Dennis Schmidt's internet tax index. Home pages for the professor of your course, Price Waterhouse, Ernst & Young, Deloitte & Touche, a local tax consulting firm, and a local tax law firm.

CHAPTER 3

Tax Determination; Personal and Dependency Exemptions; An Overview of Property Transactions

LEARNING OBJECTIVES

After completing Chapter 3, you should be able to:

1. Understand and apply the components of the Federal income tax formula.

2. Apply the rules for arriving at personal and dependency exemptions.

3. Use the proper method for determining the tax liability.

4. Identify and work with kiddie tax situations.

5. Recognize the filing requirements and the proper filing status.

6. Possess an overview of property transactions.

7. Identify tax planning opportunities associated with the individual tax formula.

OUTLINE

Tax Formula, 3–3

Components of the Tax Formula, 3–3

Application of the Tax Formula, 3–8

Individuals Not Eligible for the Standard Deduction, 3–9

Special Limitations for Individuals Who Can Be Claimed as Dependents, 3–9

Personal and Dependency Exemptions, 3–10

Personal Exemptions, 3–10

Dependency Exemptions, 3–10

Tax Determination, 3–16

Tax Table Method, 3–16

Tax Rate Schedule Method, 3–16

Computation of Net Taxes Payable or Refund Due, 3–18

Unearned Income of Children under Age 14 Taxed at Parents' Rate, 3–19

Filing Considerations, 3–21

Filing Requirements, 3–21

Filing Status, 3–23

Gains and Losses from Property Transactions—In General, 3–27

Gains and Losses from Property Transactions—Capital Gains and Losses, 3–28

Definition of a Capital Asset, 3–28

Computation of Net Capital Gains and Losses, 3–29

Capital Loss Limitation, 3–29

Tax Planning Considerations, 3–30

Taking Advantage of Tax Rate Differentials, 3–30

Income of Minor Children, 3–31

Dependency Exemptions, 3–31

Individuals are subject to Federal income tax based on taxable income. This chapter explains how taxable income and the income tax of an individual taxpayer are determined.

To compute taxable income, it is necessary to understand the tax formula in Figure 3–1. Although the tax formula is rather simple, determining an individual's taxable income can be quite complex. The complexity stems from the numerous provisions that govern the determination of gross income and allowable deductions.

After computing taxable income, the appropriate rates must be applied. This requires a determination of the individual's filing status, since different rates apply for single taxpayers, married taxpayers, and heads of household. The basic tax rate structure is progressive, with rates ranging from 15 percent to 39.6 percent.[1] For

▼ **FIGURE 3–1**
Tax Formula

Income (broadly conceived)	$xx,xxx
Less: Exclusions	(x,xxx)
Gross income	$xx,xxx
Less: Deductions *for* adjusted gross income	(x,xxx)
Adjusted gross income	$xx,xxx
Less: The greater of— Total itemized deductions *or* the standard deduction	(x,xxx)
Personal and dependency exemptions	(x,xxx)
Taxable income	$xx,xxx

---

[1] The 1997 Tax Table was not available from the IRS at the date of publication of this text. The Tax Table for 1996 and the Tax Rate Schedules for 1996 and 1997 are reproduced in Appendix A. For quick reference, the 1996 and 1997 Tax Rate Schedules are also reproduced inside the front cover of this text.

CHAPTER 3 Tax Determination; Personal and Dependency Exemptions   3–3

comparison, the lowest rate structure, which was in effect in 1913–1915, ranged from 1 to 7 percent, and the highest, in effect during 1944–1945, ranged from 23 to 94 percent.

Once the individual's tax has been computed, prepayments and credits are subtracted to determine whether the taxpayer owes additional tax or is entitled to a refund.

When property is sold or otherwise disposed of, a gain or loss may result, which can affect the determination of taxable income. Although property transactions are covered in detail in Chapters 14–17, an understanding of certain basic concepts helps in working with some of the materials to follow. The concluding portion of this chapter furnishes an overview of property transactions, including the distinction between realized and recognized gain or loss, the classification of such gain or loss (ordinary or capital), and treatment for income tax purposes.

TAX FORMULA

1 LEARNING OBJECTIVE
Understand and apply the components of the Federal income tax formula.

Most individuals compute taxable income using the tax formula shown in Figure 3–1. Special provisions govern the computation of taxable income and the tax liability for certain minor children who have unearned income in excess of specified amounts. These provisions are discussed later in the chapter.

Before illustrating the application of the tax formula, a brief discussion of its components is helpful.

COMPONENTS OF THE TAX FORMULA

Income (Broadly Conceived). This includes all the taxpayer's income, both taxable and nontaxable. Although it is essentially equivalent to gross receipts, it does not include a return of capital or receipt of borrowed funds.

EXAMPLE 1   Dave needed money to purchase a house. He sold 5,000 shares of stock for $100,000. He had paid $40,000 for the stock. In addition, he borrowed $75,000 from a bank. Dave has taxable income of $60,000 from the sale of the stock ($100,000 selling price − $40,000 return of capital). He has no income from the $75,000 borrowed from the bank because he has an obligation to repay that amount. ▼

Exclusions. For various reasons, Congress has chosen to exclude certain types of income from the income tax base. The principal income exclusions are discussed in Chapter 5. A partial list of these exclusions is shown in Exhibit 3–1.

Gross Income. The Internal Revenue Code defines gross income broadly as "except as otherwise provided . . ., all income from whatever source derived."[2] The "except as otherwise provided" refers to exclusions. Gross income includes, but is not limited to, the items in the partial list in Exhibit 3–2. It does not include unrealized gains. Gross income is discussed in Chapters 4 and 5.

---
[2] § 61(a).

▼ EXHIBIT 3–1
Partial List of Exclusions from Gross Income

Accident insurance proceeds	Meals and lodging (if furnished for employer's convenience)
Annuities (cost element)	Military allowances
Bequests	Minister's dwelling rental value allowance
Child support payments	
Cost-of-living allowance (for military)	Railroad retirement benefits (to a limited extent)
Damages for personal injury or sickness	Scholarship grants (to a limited extent)
Gifts received	Social Security benefits (to a limited extent)
Group term life insurance, premium paid by employer (for coverage up to $50,000)	Veterans' benefits
Inheritances	Welfare payments
Interest from state and local (i.e., municipal) bonds	Workers' compensation benefits
Life insurance paid on death	

▼ EXHIBIT 3–2
Partial List of Gross Income Items

Alimony	Group term life insurance, premium paid by employer (for coverage over $50,000)
Annuities (income element)	
Awards	Hobby income
Back pay	Interest
Bargain purchase from employer	Jury duty fees
Bonuses	Living quarters, meals (unless furnished for employer's convenience)
Breach of contract damages	
Business income	Mileage allowance
Clergy fees	Military pay (unless combat pay)
Commissions	Notary fees
Compensation for services	Partnership income
Death benefits	Pensions
Debts forgiven	Prizes
Director's fees	Professional fees
Dividends	Punitive damages
Embezzled funds	Rents
Employee awards (in certain cases)	Rewards
Employee benefits (except certain fringe benefits)	Royalties
	Salaries
Estate and trust income	Severance pay
Farm income	Strike and lockout benefits
Fees	Supplemental unemployment benefits
Gains from illegal activities	Tips and gratuities
Gains from sale of property	Travel allowance (in certain cases)
Gambling winnings	Wages

EXAMPLE 2

Beth received the following amounts during the year:

Salary	$30,000
Interest on savings account	900
Gift from her aunt	10,000
Prize won in state lottery	1,000
Alimony from ex-husband	12,000
Child support from ex-husband	6,000
Damages for injury in auto accident	25,000
Increase in the value of stock held for investment	5,000

Review Exhibits 3–1 and 3–2 to determine the amount Beth must include in the computation of taxable income and the amount she may exclude. Then check your answer in footnote 3.[3] ▼

Deductions for Adjusted Gross Income. Individual taxpayers have two categories of deductions: (1) deductions *for* adjusted gross income (deductions to arrive at adjusted gross income) and (2) deductions *from* adjusted gross income.

Deductions *for* adjusted gross income (AGI) include ordinary and necessary expenses incurred in a trade or business, one-half of self-employment tax paid, alimony paid, certain payments to an Individual Retirement Account and Medical Savings Accounts, moving expenses, forfeited interest penalty for premature withdrawal of time deposits, the capital loss deduction, and others.[4] The principal deductions *for* AGI are discussed in Chapters 6, 7, 8, 9, and 11.

Adjusted Gross Income (AGI). AGI is an important subtotal that serves as the basis for computing percentage limitations on certain itemized deductions, such as medical expenses and charitable contributions. For example, medical expenses are deductible only to the extent they exceed 7.5 percent of AGI, and charitable contribution deductions may not exceed 50 percent of AGI. These limitations might be described as a 7.5 percent *floor* under the medical expense deduction and a 50 percent *ceiling* on the charitable contribution deduction.

EXAMPLE 3

Keith earned a salary of $23,000 in the current tax year. He contributed $2,000 to his Individual Retirement Account (IRA) and sustained a $1,000 capital loss on the sale of Wren Corporation stock. His AGI is computed as follows:

Gross income		
Salary		$23,000
Less: Deductions *for* AGI		
IRA contribution	$2,000	
Capital loss	1,000	(3,000)
AGI		$20,000

▼

---

[3] Beth must include $43,900 in computing taxable income ($30,000 salary + $900 interest + $1,000 lottery prize + $12,000 alimony). She can exclude $41,000 ($10,000 gift from aunt + $6,000 child support + $25,000 damages). The unrealized gain on the stock held for investment also is not included in gross income. Such gain will be included in gross income only when it is realized upon disposition of the stock.

[4] § 62.

EXAMPLE 4

Assume the same facts as in Example 3, and that Keith also had medical expenses of $1,800. Medical expenses may be included in itemized deductions to the extent they exceed 7.5% of AGI. In computing his itemized deductions, Keith may include medical expenses of $300 [$1,800 medical expenses − $1,500 (7.5% × $20,000 AGI)]. ▼

Itemized Deductions. As a general rule, personal expenditures are disallowed as deductions in arriving at taxable income. However, Congress has chosen to allow specified personal expenses as **itemized deductions.** Such expenditures include medical expenses, certain taxes and interest, and charitable contributions.

In addition to these personal expenses, taxpayers are allowed itemized deductions for expenses related to (1) the production or collection of income and (2) the management of property held for the production of income.[5] These expenses, sometimes referred to as *nonbusiness expenses,* differ from trade or business expenses (discussed previously). Trade or business expenses, which are deductions *for* AGI, must be incurred in connection with a trade or business. Nonbusiness expenses, on the other hand, are expenses incurred in connection with an income-producing activity that does not qualify as a trade or business. Such expenses are itemized deductions.

EXAMPLE 5

Leo is the owner and operator of a video game arcade. All allowable expenses he incurs in connection with the arcade business are deductions *for* AGI. In addition, Leo has an extensive portfolio of stocks and bonds. Leo's investment activity is not treated as a trade or business. All allowable expenses that Leo incurs in connection with these investments are itemized deductions. ▼

Itemized deductions include, but are not limited to, the expenses listed in Exhibit 3–3. See Chapter 10 for a detailed discussion of itemized deductions.

▼ **EXHIBIT 3–3**
Partial List of Itemized Deductions

Medical expenses in excess of 7.5% of AGI
State and local income taxes
Real estate taxes
Personal property taxes
Interest on home mortgage
Investment interest (to a limited extent)
Charitable contributions (within specified percentage limitations)
Casualty and theft losses in excess of 10% of AGI
Miscellaneous expenses (to the extent such expenses exceed 2% of AGI)
    Union dues
    Professional dues and subscriptions
    Certain educational expenses
    Tax return preparation fee
    Investment counsel fees
    Unreimbursed employee business expenses (after 50% reduction for meals and entertainment)

---

[5] § 212.

Standard Deduction. The **standard deduction,** which is set by Congress, is a specified amount that depends on the filing status of the taxpayer. The effect of the standard deduction is to exempt a taxpayer's income, up to the specified amount, from Federal income tax liability. In the past, Congress has attempted to set the tax-free amount represented by the standard deduction approximately equal to an estimated poverty level,[6] but it has not always been consistent in doing so.

The standard deduction is the sum of two components: the *basic* standard deduction and the *additional* standard deduction.[7] Table 3–1 lists the basic standard deduction allowed for taxpayers in each filing status. All taxpayers allowed a *full* standard deduction are entitled to the applicable amount listed in Table 3–1. The standard deduction amounts are subject to adjustment for inflation each year.

Certain taxpayers are not allowed to claim *any* standard deduction, and the standard deduction is *limited* for others. These provisions are discussed later in the chapter.

A taxpayer who is age 65 or over *or* blind qualifies for an *additional standard deduction* of $800 or $1,000, depending on filing status (see amounts in Table 3–2). Two additional standard deductions are allowed for a taxpayer who is age 65 or over *and* blind. The additional standard deduction provisions also apply for a qualifying spouse who is age 65 or over or blind, but a taxpayer may not claim an additional standard deduction for a dependent.

▼ **TABLE 3–1**
Basic Standard Deduction Amounts

Filing Status	Standard Deduction Amount 1996	1997
Single	$4,000	$4,150
Married, filing jointly	6,700	6,900
Surviving spouse	6,700	6,900
Head of household	5,900	6,050
Married, filing separately	3,350	3,450

▼ **TABLE 3–2**
Amount of Each Additional Standard Deduction

Filing Status	1996	1997
Single	$1,000	$1,000
Married, filing jointly	800	800
Surviving spouse	800	800
Head of household	1,000	1,000
Married, filing separately	800	800

---

[6] S.Rep. No. 92–437, 92nd Cong., 1st Sess., 1971, p. 54. Another purpose of the standard deduction was discussed in Chapter 1 under Influence of the Internal Revenue Service—Administrative Feasibility. The size of the standard deduction has a direct bearing on the number of taxpayers who are in a position to itemize deductions. Reducing the number of taxpayers who itemize also reduces the audit effort required from the IRS. Currently, about 70% of all individual taxpayers choose to use the standard deduction.

[7] § 63(c)(1).

To determine whether to itemize, the taxpayer compares the *total* standard deduction (the sum of the basic standard deduction and any additional standard deductions) to total itemized deductions. Taxpayers are allowed to deduct the *greater* of itemized deductions or the standard deduction. Taxpayers whose itemized deductions are less than the standard deduction compute their taxable income using the standard deduction rather than itemizing.

Example 6

Sara, who is single, is 66 years old. She had total itemized deductions of $4,900 during 1997. Her total standard deduction is $5,150 ($4,150 basic standard deduction plus $1,000 additional standard deduction). Sara should compute her taxable income for 1997 using the standard deduction ($5,150), since it exceeds her itemized deductions ($4,900). ▼

Personal and Dependency Exemptions. Exemptions are allowed for the taxpayer, for the taxpayer's spouse, and for each dependent of the taxpayer. The exemption amount is $2,550 in 1996 and $2,650 in 1997.

APPLICATION OF THE TAX FORMULA

The tax formula shown in Figure 3–1 is illustrated in Example 7.

Example 7

Grace, age 25, is single and has no dependents. She is a high school teacher and earned a $20,000 salary in 1997. Her other income consisted of a $1,000 prize won in a sweepstakes contest and $500 interest on municipal bonds received as a graduation gift in 1992. During 1997, she sustained a deductible capital loss of $1,000. Her itemized deductions are $4,300. Grace's taxable income for the year is computed as follows:

Income (broadly conceived)		
Salary		$20,000
Prize		1,000
Interest on municipal bonds		500
		$21,500
Less: Exclusion—		
Interest on municipal bonds		(500)
Gross income		$21,000
Less: Deduction *for* adjusted gross income—		
Capital loss		(1,000)
Adjusted gross income		$20,000
Less: The greater of—		
Total itemized deductions	$4,300	
or the standard deduction	$4,150	(4,300)
Personal and dependency exemptions		
(1 × $2,650)		(2,650)
Taxable income		$13,050

▼

The structure of the individual income tax return (Form 1040, 1040A, or 1040EZ) differs somewhat from the tax formula in Figure 3–1. On the tax return, gross income generally is the starting point in computing taxable income. With few exceptions, exclusions are not reported on the tax return.

INDIVIDUALS NOT ELIGIBLE FOR THE STANDARD DEDUCTION

The following individual taxpayers are ineligible to use the standard deduction and must therefore itemize:[8]

- A married individual filing a separate return where either spouse itemizes deductions.
- A nonresident alien.
- An individual filing a return for a period of less than 12 months because of a change in annual accounting period.

SPECIAL LIMITATIONS FOR INDIVIDUALS WHO CAN BE CLAIMED AS DEPENDENTS

Special rules apply to the standard deduction and personal exemption of an individual who can be claimed as a dependent on another person's tax return.

When filing his or her own tax return, a *dependent's* basic standard deduction is limited to the greater of $650 or the individual's earned income for the year.[9] However, if the individual's earned income exceeds the normal standard deduction, the standard deduction is limited to the appropriate standard deduction amount shown in Table 3–1. These limitations apply only to the basic standard deduction. A dependent who is 65 or over or blind or both is also allowed the additional standard deduction amount on his or her own return (refer to Table 3–2). These provisions are illustrated in Examples 8 through 11.

EXAMPLE 8 Susan, who is 17 years old and single, is claimed as a dependent on her parents' tax return. During 1997, she received $1,200 interest (unearned income) on a savings account. She also earned $500 from a part-time job. When Susan files her own tax return, her standard deduction is $650 (the greater of $650 or earned income of $500). ▼

EXAMPLE 9 Assume the same facts as in Example 8, except that Susan is 67 years old and is claimed as a dependent on her son's tax return. In this case, when Susan files her own tax return, her standard deduction is $1,650 [$650 (the greater of $650 or earned income of $500) + $1,000 (the additional standard deduction allowed because Susan is 65 or over)]. ▼

EXAMPLE 10 Peggy, who is 16 years old and single, earned $1,000 from a summer job and had no unearned income during 1997. She is claimed as a dependent on her parents' tax return. Her standard deduction is $1,000 (the greater of $650 or earned income). ▼

EXAMPLE 11 Jack, who is a 20-year-old, single, full-time college student, is claimed as a dependent on his parents' tax return. He worked as a musician during the summer of 1997, earning $4,300. Jack's standard deduction is $4,150 (the greater of $650 or $4,300 earned income, but limited to the $4,150 standard deduction for a single taxpayer). ▼

A taxpayer who claims an individual as a dependent is allowed to claim an exemption for the dependent. The dependent cannot claim a personal exemption

---

[8] § 63(c)(6).

[9] § 63(c)(5). The $650 amount is subject to adjustment for inflation each year. The amount was also $650 for 1996.

on his or her own return. Based on the tax formula, Jack in Example 11 would have taxable income of $150, determined as follows:

Gross income	$ 4,300
Less: Standard deduction	(4,150)
Personal exemption	(–0–)
Taxable income	$ 150

PERSONAL AND DEPENDENCY EXEMPTIONS

2 LEARNING OBJECTIVE
Apply the rules for arriving at personal and dependency exemptions.

The use of exemptions in the tax system is based in part on the idea that a taxpayer with a small amount of income should be exempt from income taxation. An exemption frees a specified amount of income from tax ($2,550 in 1996 and $2,650 in 1997). The exemption amount is indexed (adjusted) annually for inflation. An individual who is not claimed as a dependent by another taxpayer is allowed to claim his or her own personal exemption. In addition, a taxpayer may claim an exemption for each dependent.

EXAMPLE 12

Bonnie, who is single, supports her mother and father, who have no income of their own, and claims them as dependents on her tax return. Bonnie may claim a personal exemption for herself plus an exemption for each dependent. On her 1997 tax return, Bonnie may deduct $7,950 for exemptions ($2,650 per exemption × 3 exemptions). ▼

PERSONAL EXEMPTIONS

The Code provides a **personal exemption** for the taxpayer and an exemption for the spouse if a joint return is filed. However, when separate returns are filed, a married taxpayer cannot claim an exemption for his or her spouse *unless* the spouse has no gross income and is not claimed as the dependent of another taxpayer.

The determination of marital status generally is made at the end of the taxable year, except when a spouse dies during the year. Spouses who enter into a legal separation under a decree of divorce or separate maintenance before the end of the year are considered to be unmarried at the end of the taxable year. The following table illustrates the effect of death or divorce upon marital status:

	Marital Status for 1997
• Walt is the widower of Helen who died on January 3, 1997.	Walt and Helen are considered to be married for purposes of filing the 1997 return.
• Bill and Jane entered into a divorce decree that is effective on December 31, 1997.	Bill and Jane are considered to be unmarried for purposes of filing the 1997 return.

DEPENDENCY EXEMPTIONS

As indicated in Example 12, the Code allows a taxpayer to claim a dependency exemption for each eligible individual. A **dependency exemption** may be claimed for each individual for whom the following five tests are met:

- Support.
- Relationship or member of the household.
- Gross income.
- Joint return.
- Citizenship or residency.

A person who dies during the year can still be claimed as a dependent if all of the tests are met. In such a case, no proration is necessary, and the full amount of the exemption is allowed.

Support Test. Over one-half of the support of the individual must be furnished by the taxpayer. Support includes food, shelter, clothing, medical and dental care, education, etc. However, a scholarship received by a student is not included for purposes of computing whether the taxpayer furnished more than half of the child's support.[10]

EXAMPLE 13 Hal contributed $3,400 (consisting of food, clothing, and medical care) toward the support of his son, Sam, who earned $1,500 from a part-time job and received a $2,000 scholarship to attend a local university. Assuming that the other dependency tests are met, Hal can claim Sam as a dependent since he has contributed more than half of Sam's support. The $2,000 scholarship is not included as support for purposes of this test. ▼

If the individual does not spend funds that have been received from any source, the unexpended amounts are not counted for purposes of the support test.

EXAMPLE 14 Emily contributed $3,000 to her father's support during the year. In addition, her father received $2,400 in Social Security benefits, $200 of interest, and wages of $600. Her father deposited the Social Security benefits, interest, and wages in his own savings account and did not use any of the funds for his support. Thus, the Social Security benefits, interest, and wages are not considered as support provided by Emily's father. Emily may claim her father as a dependent if the other tests are met. ▼

Capital expenditures for items such as furniture, appliances, and automobiles are included in total support if the item does, in fact, constitute support.[11]

EXAMPLE 15 Norm purchased a television set costing $150 and gave it to his minor daughter. The television set was placed in the child's bedroom and was used exclusively by her. Norm should include the cost of the television set in determining the support of his daughter. ▼

EXAMPLE 16 Mark paid $6,000 for an automobile that was titled and registered in his name. Mark's minor son is permitted to use the automobile equally with Mark. Since Mark did not give the automobile to his son, the $6,000 cost is not includible as a support item. However, out-of-pocket operating expenses incurred by Mark for the benefit of his son are includible as support. ▼

---

[10] Reg. § 1.152–1(c).
[11] Rev.Rul. 57–344, 1957–2 C.B. 112; Rev.Rul. 58–419, 1958–2 C.B. 57.

ETHICAL CONSIDERATIONS

Claiming a Dependent

Martha is a widow and lives with her only son, Roland, and his family. Martha's only income consists of $70,000 in interest from tax-exempt bonds. She invests all of the income in stocks in her name. The stocks do not pay dividends. Martha's will provides that all of her property is to pass to Roland upon her death. Because of this expectation, Roland provides all of his mother's support. On his return, Roland claims a dependency exemption for his mother.

Is this proper procedure? After all, Martha was in a position to provide all of her support had she chosen to do so.

One exception to the support test involves a **multiple support agreement.** A multiple support agreement permits one of a group of taxpayers who furnish more than half of the support of an individual to claim a dependency exemption for that individual even if no one person provides more than 50 percent of the support.[12] Any person who contributed *more than 10 percent* of the support is entitled to claim the exemption if each person in the group who contributed more than 10 percent files a written consent. This provision frequently enables one of the children of aged dependent parents to claim an exemption when none of the children meets the 50 percent support test. Each person who is a party to the multiple support agreement must meet all other requirements (except the support requirement) for claiming the exemption. A person who does not meet the relationship or member-of-household requirement, for instance, cannot claim the dependency exemption under a multiple support agreement. It does not matter if he or she contributes more than 10 percent of the individual's support.

EXAMPLE 17

Wanda, who resides with her son, Adam, received $6,000 from various sources during 1997. This constituted her entire support for the year. She received support from the following:

	Amount	Percentage of Total
Adam, a son	$2,880	48
Bob, a son	600	10
Carol, a daughter	1,800	30
Diane, a friend	720	12
	$6,000	100

If Adam and Carol file a multiple support agreement, either may claim the dependency exemption for Wanda. Bob may not claim Wanda because he did not contribute more than 10% of her support. Bob's consent is not required in order for Adam and Carol to file a multiple support agreement. Diane does not meet the relationship or member-of-household test and cannot be a party to the agreement. The decision as to who claims Wanda rests with Adam and Carol. It is possible for Carol to claim Wanda, even though Adam furnished more of Wanda's support. ▼

---

[12] § 152(c).

TAX IN THE NEWS

THE WRONG WAY TO CLAIM DEPENDENCY EXEMPTIONS

Bill and Virginia are divorced in 1989, and Virginia is granted custody of their two children. Bill is awarded the dependency exemptions for the children, however, and the court decree instructs Virginia to do whatever is necessary to carry out this result. After the trial is over, Bill has Virginia sign a copy of the divorce decree.

When he files his income tax return, Bill claims the children as his dependents. He attaches a copy of the divorce decree that Virginia signed. When Virginia files her return, she also claims the children as dependents.

Upon audit of Bill's return, the IRS disallows the dependency exemptions for the children on the grounds that Bill failed to provide the key information requested by Form 8332 (Release of Claim to Exemption for Child of Divorced or Separated Parents). Missing information included the children's names and Social Security numbers, the date of the custodial parent's signature, the years for which the exemption claims are released, and an agreement by the custodial parent not to claim the children as exemptions.

Bill challenges the disallowance by the IRS by taking the matter to court. Although sympathetic to Bill's plight, the court holds for the IRS. Bill's remedy is to sue Virginia in the appropriate *state* court to compel her to comply with the original divorce decree. See *William C. White*, 72 TCM 786, T.C.Memo. 1996–438.

Each person who qualifies under the more-than-10 percent rule (except for the person claiming the exemption) must complete Form 2120 (Multiple Support Declaration) waiving the exemption. The person claiming the exemption must attach all Forms 2120 to his or her own return.

A second exception to the 50 percent support requirement can occur for a child of parents who are divorced or separated under a decree of separate maintenance. For decrees executed after 1984, the custodial parent is allowed to claim the exemption unless that parent agrees in writing not to claim a dependency exemption for the child.[13] Thus, claiming the exemption is dependent on whether or not a written agreement exists, *not* on meeting the support test.

EXAMPLE 18 Ira and Rita obtain a divorce decree in 1990. In 1997, their two children are in Rita's custody. Ira contributed over half of the support for each child. In the absence of a written agreement on the dependency exemptions, Rita (the custodial parent) is entitled to the exemptions in 1997. However, Ira may claim the exemptions if Rita agrees in writing. ▼

For the noncustodial parent to claim the exemption, the custodial parent must complete Form 8332 (Release of Claim to Exemption for Child of Divorced or Separated Parents). The release can apply to a single year, a number of specified years, or all future years. The noncustodial parent must attach a copy of Form 8332 to his or her return.

---

[13] § 152(e).

Relationship or Member-of-the-Household Test. To be claimed as a dependent, an individual must be either a relative of the taxpayer or a member of the taxpayer's household. The Code contains a detailed listing of the various blood and marriage relationships that qualify. Note, however, that the relationship test is met if the individual is a relative of either spouse. Once established by marriage, a relationship continues regardless of subsequent changes in marital status.

The following individuals may be claimed as dependents of the taxpayer if the other tests for dependency are met:[14]

- A son or daughter of the taxpayer or a descendant of either, such as a grandchild.
- A stepson or stepdaughter of the taxpayer.
- A brother, sister, stepbrother, or stepsister of the taxpayer.
- The father or mother of the taxpayer or an ancestor of either, such as a grandparent.
- A stepfather or stepmother of the taxpayer.
- A nephew or niece of the taxpayer.
- An uncle or aunt of the taxpayer.
- A son-in-law, daughter-in-law, father-in-law, mother-in-law, brother-in-law, or sister-in-law of the taxpayer.
- An individual who, for the entire taxable year of the taxpayer, has as his or her principal place of abode the home of the taxpayer and is a member of the taxpayer's household. This does not include an individual who, at any time during the taxable year, was the spouse of the taxpayer.

The following rules are also prescribed in the Code:[15]

- A legally adopted child is treated as a natural child.
- A foster child qualifies if the child's principal place of abode is the taxpayer's household.

Gross Income Test. The dependent's gross income must be less than the exemption amount ($2,650 in 1997).[16] The gross income test is measured by income that is taxable. In the case of scholarships, for example, it excludes the nontaxable portion (e.g., amounts received for books and tuition) but includes the taxable portion (e.g., amounts received for room and board).

A parent may claim a dependency exemption for his or her child, even when the child's gross income exceeds $2,650, if the parent provided over half of the child's support and the child, at year-end, is under age 19 or is a full-time student under age 24. If the parent claims a dependency exemption, the dependent child may not claim a personal exemption on his or her own income tax return.

A child is defined as a son, stepson, daughter, stepdaughter, adopted son, or adopted daughter and may include a foster child.[17] For the child to qualify as a student for purposes of the dependency exemption, he or she must be a full-time student at an educational institution during some part of five calendar months of the year.[18] This exception to the gross income test for dependent children who are under age 19 or full-time students under age 24 permits a child or college student

---

[14] § 152(a). However, under § 152(b)(5), a taxpayer may not claim someone who is a member of his or her household as a dependent if their relationship is in violation of local law. For example, the dependency exemption was denied because the taxpayer's relationship to the person claimed as a dependent constituted *cohabitation*, a crime under applicable state law. *Cassius L. Peacock, III*, 37 TCM 177, T.C.Memo. 1978–30.

[15] § 152(b)(2).
[16] § 151(c)(1).
[17] Reg. § 1.151–3(a).
[18] Reg. §§ 1.151–3(b) and (c).

to earn money from part-time or summer jobs without penalizing the parent with the loss of the dependency exemption.

Joint Return Test. If a dependent is married, the supporting taxpayer (e.g., the parent of a married child) generally is not permitted a dependency exemption if the married individual files a joint return with his or her spouse.[19] The joint return rule does not apply, however, if the following conditions are met:

- The reason for filing is to claim a refund for tax withheld.
- No tax liability would exist for either spouse on separate returns.
- Neither spouse is required to file a return.

See Table 3–4 later in the chapter and the related discussion concerning income level requirements for filing a return.

EXAMPLE 19

Paul provides over half of the support of his son Quinn. He also provides over half of the support of Vera, who is Quinn's wife. During the year, both Quinn and Vera had part-time jobs. In order to recover the taxes withheld, they file a joint return. If Quinn and Vera are not required to file a return, Paul is allowed to claim both as dependents. ▼

Citizenship or Residency Test. To be a dependent, the individual must be either a U.S. citizen, a U.S. resident, or a resident of Canada or Mexico for some part of the calendar year in which the taxpayer's tax year begins.

Phase-out of Exemptions. Several provisions of the tax law are intended to increase the tax liability of more affluent taxpayers who might otherwise enjoy some benefit from having some of their taxable income subject to the lower income tax brackets (e.g., 15 percent, 28 percent). One such provision phases out personal and dependency exemptions as AGI exceeds specified threshold amounts. For 1996 and 1997, the phase-out *begins* at the following threshold amounts:

	1996	1997
Joint returns/Surviving spouse	$176,950	$181,800
Head of household	147,450	151,500
Single	117,950	121,200
Married, filing separately	88,475	90,900

These threshold amounts are indexed for inflation each year.

Exemptions are phased out by 2 percent for each $2,500 (or fraction thereof) by which the taxpayer's AGI exceeds the threshold amounts. For a married taxpayer filing separately, the phase-out is 2 percent for each $1,250 or fraction thereof.

The allowable exemption amount can be determined with the following steps:

1. AGI − threshold amount = excess amount
2. Excess amount ÷ $2,500 = reduction factor [rounded up to the next whole increment (e.g., 18.1 = 19)] × 2 = phase-out percentage
3. Phase-out percentage (from step 2) × exemption amount = amount of exemptions phased out
4. Exemption amounts − phase-out amount = allowable exemption deduction

---

[19] § 151(c)(2).

EXAMPLE 20

Frederico is married but files a separate return. His AGI is $110,900. He is entitled to one personal exemption.

1. $110,900 − $90,900 = $20,000 excess amount
2. [($20,000 ÷ $1,250) × 2] = 32% (phase-out percentage)
3. 32% × $2,650 = $848 amount of exemption phased out
4. $2,650 − $848 = $1,802 allowable exemption deduction ▼

Note that the exemption amount is completely phased out when the taxpayer's AGI exceeds the threshold amount by more than $122,500 ($61,250 for a married taxpayer filing a separate return), calculated as follows:

$122,501 ÷ $2,500 = 49.0004, rounded to 50 and multiplied by 2 = 100%
(phase-out percentage)

EXAMPLE 21

Bill and Isabella file a joint return claiming two personal exemptions and one dependency exemption for their child. Their AGI equals $305,800.

$305,800 − $181,800 = $124,000 excess amount

Since the excess amount exceeds $122,500, the exemptions are completely phased out. ▼

TAX DETERMINATION

TAX TABLE METHOD

3 LEARNING OBJECTIVE
Use the proper method for determining the tax liability.

Most taxpayers compute their tax using the **Tax Table.** Eligible taxpayers compute taxable income (as shown in Figure 3–1) and *must* determine their tax by reference to the Tax Table. The following taxpayers, however, may not use the Tax Table method:

- An individual who files a short period return (see Chapter 18).
- Individuals whose taxable income exceeds the maximum (ceiling) amount in the Tax Table. The 1996 Tax Table applies to taxable income below $100,000 for Form 1040.
- An estate or trust.

The 1997 Tax Table was not available at the date of publication of this text. Therefore, the 1996 Tax Table will be used to illustrate the tax computation using the Tax Table method.

EXAMPLE 22

Pedro, a single taxpayer, is eligible to use the Tax Table. For 1996, he had taxable income of $25,025. To determine Pedro's tax using the Tax Table (see Appendix A), find the $25,000 to $25,050 income line. The first column to the right of the taxable income column is for single taxpayers. Pedro's tax for 1996 is $3,887. ▼

TAX RATE SCHEDULE METHOD

The **Tax Rate Schedules** contain rates of 15, 28, 31, 36, and 39.6 percent. Separate schedules are provided for the following filing statuses: single, married filing jointly, married filing separately, and head of household. The rate schedules for 1996 and 1997 are reproduced inside the front cover of this text and also in Appendix A.

The rate schedules are adjusted for inflation each year. Comparison of the 1996 and 1997 schedules for single taxpayers shows that the top amount to which the 15 percent bracket applies rose from $24,000 in 1996 to $24,650 in 1997. Thus,

▼ **TABLE 3-3**
1997 Tax Rate Schedule for Single Taxpayers

If Taxable Income Is		The Tax Is:	Of the Amount Over
Over	But Not Over		
$ –0–	$ 24,650	15%	$ –0–
24,650	59,750	$ 3,697.50 + 28%	24,650
59,750	124,650	13,525.50 + 31%	59,750
124,650	271,050	33,644.50 + 36%	124,650
271,050		86,348.50 + 39.6%	271,050

inflation allowed $650 ($24,650 − $24,000) more taxable income to be subject to the lowest 15 percent rate.

The 1997 rate schedule for single taxpayers is reproduced in Table 3–3. This schedule is used to illustrate the tax computations in Examples 23, 24, and 25.

▼ **EXAMPLE 23**

Pat is single and had $18,000 of taxable income in 1997. His tax is $2,700 ($18,000 × 15%). ▼

Several terms are used to describe tax rates. The rates in the Tax Rate Schedules are often referred to as *statutory* (or nominal) rates. The *marginal* rate is the highest rate that is applied in the tax computation for a particular taxpayer. In Example 23, the statutory rate and the marginal rate are both 15 percent.

▼ **EXAMPLE 24**

Chris is single and had taxable income of $41,450 in 1997. Her tax is $8,401.50 [$3,697.50 + 28%($41,450 − $24,650)]. ▼

The *average* rate is equal to the tax liability divided by taxable income. In Example 24, Chris had statutory rates of 15 percent and 28 percent, and a marginal rate of 28 percent. Chris's average rate was 20.3 percent ($8,401.50 tax liability ÷ $41,450 taxable income).

Note that $3,697.50, which is the starting point in the tax computation in Example 24, is 15 percent of the $24,650 taxable income in the first bracket. Income in excess of $24,650 is taxed at a 28 percent rate. This reflects the *progressive* (or graduated) rate structure on which the U.S. income tax system is based. A tax is progressive if a higher rate of tax applies as the tax base increases.

▼ **EXAMPLE 25**

Carl is single and had taxable income of $81,900 in 1997. His tax is $20,392 [$13,525.50 + 31%($81,900 − $59,750)]. Note that the effect of this computation is to tax part of Carl's income at 15%, part at 28%, and part at 31%. An alternative computational method provides a clearer illustration of the progressive rate structure:

Tax on $24,650 at 15%	$ 3,697.50
Tax on $59,750 − $24,650 at 28%	9,828.00
Tax on $81,900 − $59,750 at 31%	6,866.50
Total	$20,392.00

▼

A special computation limits the effective tax rate on long-term capital gain. The beneficial tax treatment of long-term capital gain is discussed in detail in Chapter 16.

COMPUTATION OF NET TAXES PAYABLE OR REFUND DUE

The pay-as-you-go feature of the Federal income tax system requires payment of all or part of the taxpayer's income tax liability during the year. These payments take the form of Federal income tax withheld by employers or estimated tax paid by the taxpayer or both.[20] The payments are applied against the tax from the Tax Table or Tax Rate Schedules to determine whether the taxpayer will get a refund or pay additional tax.

Employers are required to withhold income tax on compensation paid to their employees and to pay this tax over to the government. The employer notifies the employee of the amount of income tax withheld on Form W–2 (Wage and Tax Statement). The employee should receive this form by January 31 after the year in which the income tax is withheld.

If taxpayers receive income that is not subject to withholding or income from which not enough tax is withheld, they must pay estimated tax. These individuals must file Form 1040–ES (Estimated Tax for Individuals) and pay in quarterly installments the income tax and self-employment tax estimated to be due (see Chapter 13 for a thorough discussion).

The income tax from the Tax Table or the Tax Rate Schedules is reduced first by the individual's tax credits. There is an important distinction between tax credits and tax deductions. Tax credits reduce the tax liability dollar-for-dollar. Tax deductions reduce taxable income on which the tax liability is based.

EXAMPLE 26

Gail is a taxpayer in the 28% tax bracket. As a result of incurring $1,000 in child care expenses (see Chapter 13 for details), she is entitled to a $200 child care credit ($1,000 child care expenses × 20% credit rate). She also contributed $1,000 to the American Cancer Society and included this amount in her itemized deductions. The child care credit results in a $200 reduction of Gail's tax liability for the year. The contribution to the American Cancer Society reduces taxable income by $1,000 and results in a $280 reduction in Gail's tax liability ($1,000 reduction in taxable income × 28% tax rate). ▼

Tax credits are discussed in Chapter 13. The following are several of the more common credits:

- Earned income credit.
- Credit for child and dependent care expenses.
- Credit for the elderly.
- Foreign tax credit.

EXAMPLE 27

Kelly, age 30, is a head of household with two dependents. During 1997, Kelly had the following: taxable income, $30,000; income tax withheld, $3,950; estimated tax payments, $600; and credit for child care expenses, $200. Kelly's net tax payable is computed as follows:

Income tax (from 1997 Tax Rate Schedule, Appendix A)		$ 4,500
Less: Tax credits and prepayments—		
Credit for child care expenses	$ 200	
Income tax withheld	3,950	
Estimated tax payments	600	(4,750)
Net taxes payable or (refund due if negative)		$ (250)

▼

---

[20] § 3402 for withholding; § 6654 for estimated payments.

UNEARNED INCOME OF CHILDREN UNDER AGE 14 TAXED AT PARENTS' RATE

4 LEARNING OBJECTIVE
Identify and work with kiddie tax situations.

Before the Tax Reform Act (TRA) of 1986, a dependent child could claim an exemption on his or her own return even if claimed as a dependent by the parents. This enabled a parent to shift investment income (such as interest and dividends) to a child by transferring ownership of the assets producing the income. The child would pay no tax on the income to the extent that it was sheltered by the child's exemption.

For pre-1987 years, an additional tax motivation existed for shifting income from parents to children. Although a child's unearned income in excess of the exemption amount was subject to tax, it was taxed at the child's rate, rather than the parents' rate.

To reduce the tax savings that result from shifting income from parents to children, the net **unearned income** (commonly called investment income) of certain minor children is taxed as if it were the parents' income.[21] Unearned income includes such income as taxable interest, dividends, capital gains, rents, royalties, pension and annuity income, and income (other than earned income) received as the beneficiary of a trust. This provision, commonly referred to as the **kiddie tax,** applies to any child for any taxable year if the child has not reached age 14 by the close of the taxable year, has at least one living parent, and has unearned income of more than $1,300. The *kiddie tax* provision does not apply to a child age 14 or older. However, the limitation on the use of the standard deduction and the unavailability of the personal exemption do apply to such a child as long as he or she is eligible to be claimed as a dependent by a parent.

The term *parent* is defined in the Senate Finance Committee Report as a parent or stepparent of the child. No statutory definition exists for the term.

Net Unearned Income.
Net unearned income of a dependent child is computed as follows:

Unearned income
Less: $650
Less: The greater of
- $650 of the standard deduction *or*
- The amount of allowable itemized deductions directly connected with the production of the unearned income

Equals: Net unearned income

If net unearned income is zero (or negative), the child's tax is computed without using the parent's rate. If the amount of net unearned income (regardless of source) is positive, the net unearned income will be taxed at the parent's rate. The $650 amounts in the preceding formula are subject to adjustment for inflation each year (refer to footnote 9).

Tax Determination.
If a child under age 14 has net unearned income, there are two options for computing the tax on the income. A separate return may be filed for the child, or the parents may elect to report the child's income on their own return. If a separate return is filed for the child, the tax on net unearned income (referred to as the *allocable parental tax*) is computed as though the income had

[21] § 1(g).

been included on the parents' return. Form 8615 (reproduced in Appendix B) is used to compute the tax. The steps required in this computation are illustrated below.

EXAMPLE 28

Olaf and Olga have a child, Hans (age 10). In 1997, Hans received $2,800 of interest and dividend income and paid investment-related fees of $200. Olaf and Olga had $69,450 of taxable income, not including their child's investment income. Olaf and Olga do not make the parental election.

1. **Determine Hans's net unearned income**

Gross income (unearned)	$ 2,800
Less: $650	(650)
Less: The greater of	
• $650 or	
• Investment expense	(650)
Equals: Net unearned income	$ 1,500

2. **Determine allocable parental tax**

Parents' taxable income	$ 69,450
Plus: Hans's net unearned income	1,500
Equals: Revised taxable income	$ 70,950
Tax on revised taxable income	$ 14,510
Less: Tax on parents' taxable income	(14,090)
Allocable parental tax	$ 420

3. **Determine Hans's nonparental source tax**

Hans's AGI	$ 2,800
Less: Standard deduction	(650)
Less: Personal exemption	(–0–)
Equals: Taxable income	$ 2,150
Less: Net unearned income	(1,500)
Nonparental source taxable income	$ 650
Equals: Tax ($650 × 15% rate)	$ 98

4. **Determine Hans's total tax liability**

Nonparental source tax (step 3)	$ 98
Allocable parental tax (step 2)	420
Total tax	$ 518

Election to Claim Certain Unearned Income on Parent's Return. If a child under age 14 is required to file a tax return and meets all of the following requirements, the parent may elect to report the child's unearned income that exceeds $1,300 on the parent's own tax return:

- Gross income is from interest and dividends only.
- Gross income is more than $650 but less than $6,500.
- No estimated tax has been paid in the name and Social Security number of the child, and the child is not subject to backup withholding (see Chapter 13).

If the parental election is made, the child is treated as having no gross income and then is not required to file a tax return.

The parent(s) must also pay an additional tax equal to the smaller of $97.50 or 15 percent of the child's gross income over $650. Parents who have substantial itemized deductions based on AGI (see Chapter 10) may find that making the parental election increases total taxes for the family unit. Taxes should be calculated both with the parental election and without it to determine the appropriate choice.

Other Provisions. If parents have more than one child subject to the tax on net unearned income, the tax for the children is computed as shown in Example 28 and then allocated to the children based on their relative amounts of income. For children of divorced parents, the taxable income of the custodial parent is used to determine the allocable parental tax. This parent is the one who may elect to report the child's unearned income. For married individuals filing separate returns, the individual with the greater taxable income is the applicable parent.

FILING CONSIDERATIONS

5 LEARNING OBJECTIVE
Recognize the filing requirements and the proper filing status.

Under the category of filing considerations, the following questions need to be resolved:

- Is the taxpayer required to file an income tax return?
- If so, which form should be used?
- When and how should the return be filed?
- In computing the tax liability, which column of the Tax Table or which Tax Rate Schedule should be used?

The first three questions are discussed under Filing Requirements, and the last is treated under Filing Status.

FILING REQUIREMENTS

General Rules. An individual must file a tax return if certain minimum amounts of gross income have been received. The general rule is that a tax return is required for every individual who has gross income that equals or exceeds the sum of the exemption amount plus the applicable standard deduction.[22] For example, a single taxpayer under age 65 must file a tax return in 1997 if gross income equals or exceeds $6,800 ($2,650 exemption plus $4,150 standard deduction). Table 3–4 lists the income levels[23] that require tax returns under the general rule and under certain special rules.

The additional standard deduction for being age 65 or older is considered in determining the gross income filing requirements. For example, note in Table 3–4 that the 1997 filing requirement for a single taxpayer age 65 or older is $7,800 ($4,150 basic standard deduction + $1,000 additional standard deduction + $2,650 exemption). However, the additional standard deduction for blindness is not taken into account. The 1997 filing requirement for a single taxpayer under age 65 and blind is $6,800 ($4,150 basic standard deduction + $2,650 exemption).

A self-employed individual with net earnings of $400 or more from a business or profession must file a tax return regardless of the amount of gross income.

---

[22] The gross income amounts for determining whether a tax return must be filed are adjusted for inflation each year.

[23] § 6012(a)(1).

TABLE 3–4
Filing Levels

Filing Status	1996 Gross Income	1997 Gross Income
Single		
Under 65 and not blind	$ 6,550	$ 6,800
Under 65 and blind	6,550	6,800
65 or older	7,550	7,800
Married, filing joint return		
Both spouses under 65 and neither blind	$11,800	$12,200
Both spouses under 65 and one or both spouses blind	11,800	12,200
One spouse 65 or older	12,600	13,000
Both spouses 65 or older	13,400	13,800
Married, filing separate return		
All—whether 65 or older or blind	$ 2,550	$ 2,650
Head of household		
Under 65 and not blind	$ 8,450	$ 8,700
Under 65 and blind	8,450	8,700
65 or older	9,450	9,700
Qualifying widow(er)		
Under 65 and not blind	$ 9,250	$ 9,550
Under 65 and blind	9,250	9,550
65 or older	10,050	10,350

Even though an individual has gross income below the filing level amounts and therefore does not owe any tax, he or she must file a return to obtain a tax refund of amounts withheld. A return is also necessary to obtain the benefits of the earned income credit allowed to taxpayers with little or no tax liability. Chapter 13 discusses the earned income credit.

Filing Requirements for Dependents. Computation of the gross income filing requirement for an individual who can be claimed as a dependent on another person's tax return is subject to more complex rules. Such an individual must file a return if he or she has *either* of the following:

- Earned income only and gross income that is more than the total standard deduction (including any additional standard deduction) that the individual is allowed for the year.
- Unearned income only and gross income of more than $650 plus any additional standard deduction that the individual is allowed for the year.
- Both earned and unearned income and gross income of more than the larger of earned income (but limited to the applicable basic standard deduction) or $650, plus any additional standard deduction that the individual is allowed for the year.

Thus, the filing requirement for a dependent who has no unearned income is the total of the *basic* standard deduction plus any *additional* standard deduction, which includes both the additional deduction for blindness and the deduction for being age 65 or older. For example, the 1997 filing requirement for a single dependent who is under 65 and not blind is $4,150, the amount of the basic standard deduction for 1997. The filing requirement for a single dependent under 65 and blind is $5,150 ($4,150 basic standard deduction + $1,000 additional standard deduction).

Selecting the Proper Form.
The 1997 tax forms had not been released at the date of publication of this text. The following comments apply to 1996 forms. It is possible that some provisions will change for the 1997 forms.

Individual taxpayers file a return on either Form 1040 (the long form), Form 1040A (the short form), or Form 1040EZ. Taxpayers who cannot use either Form 1040EZ or Form 1040A must use Form 1040. These forms are reproduced in Appendix B. Examine the forms to determine which form is appropriate for a particular taxpayer.

When and Where to File.
Tax returns of individuals are due on or before the fifteenth day of the fourth month following the close of the tax year. For the calendar year taxpayer, the usual filing date is on or before April 15 of the following year.[24] When the due date falls on a Saturday, Sunday, or legal holiday, the last day for filing falls on the next business day. If the return is mailed to the proper address with sufficient postage and is postmarked on or before the due date, it is deemed timely filed. Congress has directed the IRS to prescribe rules governing the filing of returns using the various private parcel delivery services (e.g., DHL, UPS).

If a taxpayer is unable to file the return by the specified due date, a four-month extension of time can be obtained by filing Form 4868 (Application for Automatic Extension of Time to File U.S. Individual Income Tax Return).[25] Further extensions may be granted by the IRS upon a showing of good cause by the taxpayer. For this purpose, Form 2688 (Application for Extension of Time to File U.S. Individual Income Tax Return) should be used. An extension of more than six months will not be granted if the taxpayer is in the United States.

Although obtaining an extension excuses a taxpayer from a penalty for failure to file, it does not insulate against the penalty for failure to pay.[26] If more tax is owed, the filing of Form 4868 should be accompanied by an additional remittance to cover the balance due.

The return should be sent or delivered to the Regional Service Center of the IRS for the area where the taxpayer lives.[27]

If an individual taxpayer needs to file an amended return (e.g., because of a failure to report income or to claim a deduction or tax credit), Form 1040X is filed. The form generally must be filed within three years of the filing date of the original return or within two years from the time the tax was paid, whichever is later.

FILING STATUS

The amount of tax will vary considerably depending on which Tax Rate Schedule is used. This is illustrated in the following example.

---

[24] § 6072(a).
[25] Reg. § 1.6081–4.
[26] For an explanation of these penalties, refer to Chapter 1.
[27] The Regional Service Centers and the geographical area each covers can be found in *Your Federal Income Tax*, IRS Publication 17 for 1996 or at http://www.irs.ustreas.gov.

Example 29

The following amounts of tax are computed using the 1997 Tax Rate Schedules for a taxpayer (or taxpayers in the case of a joint return) with $40,000 of taxable income (see Appendix A).

Filing Status	Amount of Tax
Single	$7,995.50
Married, filing joint return	6,000
Married, filing separate return	8,522
Head of household	6,903.50

Rates for Single Taxpayers. A taxpayer who is unmarried or separated from his or her spouse by a decree of divorce or separate maintenance and does not qualify for another filing status must use the rates for single taxpayers. Marital status is determined as of the last day of the tax year, except when a spouse dies during the year. In that case, marital status is determined as of the date of death. State law governs whether a taxpayer is considered married, divorced, or legally separated.

Under a special relief provision, however, married persons who live apart may be able to qualify as single. Married taxpayers who are considered single under the *abandoned spouse rules* are allowed to use the head of household rates. See the discussion of this filing status under Abandoned Spouse Rules later in the chapter.

Rates for Married Individuals. The joint return (Tax Rate Schedule Y, Code § 1(a)) was originally enacted in 1948 to establish equity between married taxpayers in common law states and those in community property states. Before the joint return rates were enacted, taxpayers in community property states were in an advantageous position relative to taxpayers in common law states because they could split their income. For instance, if one spouse earned $100,000 and the other spouse was not employed, each spouse could report $50,000 of income. Splitting the income in this manner caused the total income to be subject to lower marginal tax rates. Each spouse would start at the bottom of the rate structure.

Taxpayers in common law states did not have this income-splitting option, so their taxable income was subject to higher marginal rates. This inconsistency in treatment was remedied by the joint return provisions. The progressive rates in the joint return Tax Rate Schedule are constructed based on the assumption that income is earned equally by the two spouses.

If married individuals elect to file separate returns, each reports only his or her own income, exemptions, deductions, and credits, and each must use the Tax Rate Schedule applicable to married taxpayers filing separately. It is generally advantageous for married individuals to file a joint return, since the combined amount of tax is lower. However, special circumstances (e.g., significant medical expenses incurred by one spouse subject to the 7.5 percent limitation) may warrant the election to file separate returns. It may be necessary to compute the tax under both assumptions to determine the most advantageous filing status.

When Congress enacted the rate structure available to those filing joint returns, it intended to favor married taxpayers. In certain situations, however, the parties would incur less tax if they were not married and filed separate returns. The additional tax that a joint return can cause, commonly called the **marriage penalty,** can develop when *both* spouses have larger taxable incomes.

TAX IN THE NEWS

LOW-INCOME TAXPAYERS ALSO SUFFER FROM THE MARRIAGE PENALTY

The inequity of the marriage penalty is not limited to taxpayers with high incomes (see Example 30).

Consider, for example, Albert and June, each of whom has one dependent child. During 1997, Albert and June both earn wages of $10,000. Neither has any deductions *for* AGI.

Situation A shows the income tax result if Albert and June are married and file a joint return. Situation B assumes Albert and June are not married, qualify for head-of-household status, and file accordingly, with each claiming one child as a dependent. Because the Tax Tables for 1997 were not yet available, the Tax Rate Schedules were used to compute the tax.

The harsh effect of the marriage penalty is apparent. Albert and June are $2,839 better off (refunds totaling $4,420 versus $1,581) by not being married. This result is remarkable when one considers that AGI of only $20,000 is involved!

	Situation A	Situation B		
	If They Are Married	If They Are Not Married		
Their Taxes:		Albert	June	Total
Adjusted gross income	$20,000	$10,000 +	$10,000 =	$20,000
Personal and dependency exemptions	10,600	5,300 +	5,300 =	10,600
Standard deduction	6,900	6,050 +	6,050 =	12,100
Taxable income	2,500	–0– +	–0– =	–0–
Taxes owed	375	–0– +	–0– =	–0–
Earned income tax credit*	1,956	2,210 +	2,210 =	4,420
Refund	$ 1,581	$2,210 +	$2,210 =	$4,420

*See Chapter 13 for a discussion of the earned income tax credit. The credits above were calculated following the procedure utilized in Example 19 of Chapter 13.

EXAMPLE 30

John and Betty are employed, and each earns taxable income of $55,000. If they *are not married* and file separate returns, each has a tax liability of $12,196, or a total of $24,392 ($12,196 × 2). If they are married to each other, the filing of a joint return produces a tax of $25,756 on taxable income of $110,000 ($55,000 + $55,000). Thus, being married results in $1,364 ($25,756 − $24,392) more tax! ▼

Although some have suggested changes to lessen the impact of the marriage penalty, any remedy is apt to make the tax law more complex.

The Code places some limitations on deductions, credits, etc., when married individuals file separately. If either spouse itemizes deductions, the other spouse must also itemize. Married taxpayers who file separately cannot take either of the following:

- The credit for child and dependent care expenses (in most instances).
- The earned income credit.

The joint return rates also apply for two years following the death of one spouse, if the surviving spouse maintains a household for a dependent child.[28] This is referred to as **surviving spouse** status.

EXAMPLE 31

Fred dies in 1996 leaving Ethel with a dependent child. For the year of Fred's death (1996), Ethel files a joint return with Fred (presuming the consent of Fred's executor is obtained). For the next two years (1997 and 1998), Ethel, as a surviving spouse, may use the joint return rates. In subsequent years, Ethel may use the head-of-household rates if she continues to maintain a household as her home that is the domicile of the child. ▼

Rates for Heads of Household. Unmarried individuals who maintain a household for a dependent (or dependents) are entitled to use the **head-of-household** rates.[29] The tax liability using the head-of-household rates falls between the liability using the joint return Tax Rate Schedule and the liability using the Tax Rate Schedule for single taxpayers.

To qualify for head-of-household rates, a taxpayer must pay more than half the cost of maintaining a household as his or her home. The household must also be the principal home of a dependent relative.[30] As a general rule, the dependent must live in the taxpayer's household for over half the year.

There are two exceptions to these requirements. One exception is that an *unmarried child* (child also means grandchild, stepchild, or adopted child) need not be a dependent in order for the taxpayer to qualify as a head of household.

EXAMPLE 32

Nancy maintains a household where she and Dan, her nondependent unmarried son, reside. Since Dan is not married, Nancy qualifies for the head-of-household rates. ▼

Another exception to the general rule is that head-of-household status may be claimed if the taxpayer maintains a *separate home* for his or her *parent or parents* if at least one parent qualifies as a dependent of the taxpayer.[31]

EXAMPLE 33

Rick, an unmarried individual, lives in New York City and maintains a household in Detroit for his dependent parents. Rick may use the head-of-household rates even though his parents do not reside in his New York home. ▼

Head-of-household status is not changed during the year by death of the dependent. As long as the taxpayer provided more than half of the cost of maintaining the household prior to the dependent's death, head-of-household status is preserved.

Abandoned Spouse Rules. When married persons file separate returns, several unfavorable tax consequences result. For example, the taxpayer must use the Tax Rate Schedule for married taxpayers filing separately. To mitigate such harsh treatment, Congress enacted provisions commonly referred to as the

---

[28] § 2(a).
[29] § 2(b).
[30] As defined in § 152(a). See § 2(b)(1)(A).
[31] § 2(b)(1)(B).

TAX IN THE NEWS

BEING ALONE IS NOT ALL THAT BAD!

Alice York's marriage to Scott was anything but blissful. In fact, after the birth of their first (and only) child, Mark, the animosity became so intense that Scott moved out. That was two years ago, and Alice has not seen or heard from him since.

Alice has a good job that keeps her quite busy. As a consequence, she has not bothered to take the time to obtain a divorce. She files her income tax return using "single" status and claims a dependency exemption for Mark. She also claims a child care credit for the day care expenses she incurs on account of Mark.

The IRS challenges the filing status Alice uses and also contends that a child care credit can only be taken by a married person if a joint return is filed. Alice goes to court and is victorious. The court finds that Alice is an "abandoned spouse." As such, she is to be considered a "single" person for both filing status and child care credit purposes. See *Mary Lee Sharer*, 68 TCM 686, T.C.Memo. 1994–453.

---

abandoned spouse rules. These rules allow a married taxpayer to file as a head of household if all of the following conditions are satisfied:

- The taxpayer does not file a joint return.
- The taxpayer paid more than one-half the cost of maintaining his or her home for the tax year.
- The taxpayer's spouse did not live in the home during the last six months of the tax year.
- The home was the principal residence of the taxpayer's child, stepchild, or adopted child for more than half the year.
- The taxpayer could claim the child, stepchild, or adopted child as a dependent.[32]

GAINS AND LOSSES FROM PROPERTY TRANSACTIONS—IN GENERAL

6 LEARNING OBJECTIVE
Possess an overview of property transactions.

Gains and losses from property transactions are discussed in detail in Chapters 14 through 17. Because of their importance in the tax system, however, they are introduced briefly at this point.

When property is sold or otherwise disposed of, gain or loss may result. Such gain or loss has an effect on the income tax position of the party making the sale or other disposition when the *realized* gain or loss is *recognized* for tax purposes.

---

[32] The dependency requirement does not apply, however, if the taxpayer could have claimed a dependency exemption except for the fact that the exemption was claimed by the noncustodial parent under a written agreement. Refer to Example 18 and the related discussion.

Without realized gain or loss, generally, there can be no recognized gain or loss. The concept of realized gain or loss is expressed as follows:

$$\text{Amount realized from the sale} - \text{Adjusted basis of the property} = \text{Realized gain (or loss)}$$

The amount realized is the selling price of the property less any costs of disposition (e.g., brokerage commissions) incurred by the seller. Simply stated, adjusted basis of the property is determined as follows:

	Cost (or other original basis) at date of acquisition[33]
Add:	Capital additions
Subtract:	Depreciation (if appropriate) and other capital recoveries (see Chapter 8)
Equals:	Adjusted basis at date of sale or other disposition

All realized gains are recognized (taxable) unless some specific part of the tax law provides otherwise (see Chapter 15 dealing with certain nontaxable exchanges). Realized losses may or may not be recognized (deductible) for tax purposes, depending on the circumstances involved. Generally, losses realized from the disposition of personal use property (property neither held for investment nor used in a trade or business) are not recognized.

EXAMPLE 34

During the current year, Ted sells his sailboat (adjusted basis of $4,000) for $5,500. Ted also sells one of his personal automobiles (adjusted basis of $8,000) for $5,000. Ted's realized gain of $1,500 from the sale of the sailboat is recognized. On the other hand, the $3,000 realized loss on the sale of the automobile is not recognized and will not provide Ted with any deductible tax benefit. ▼

Once it has been determined that the disposition of property results in a recognized gain or loss, the next step is to classify the gain or loss as capital or ordinary. Although ordinary gain is fully taxable and ordinary loss is fully deductible, the same may not hold true for capital gains and capital losses.

GAINS AND LOSSES FROM PROPERTY TRANSACTIONS—CAPITAL GAINS AND LOSSES

For tax years beginning after 1992, preferential tax treatment may apply to gains on capital assets that have been held for more than a year. The maximum rate on *net capital gain* (see Chapter 16 for details) is 28 percent. This provision could save 11.6 percent for taxpayers in the 39.6 percent bracket.

DEFINITION OF A CAPITAL ASSET

Capital assets are defined in the Code as any property held by the taxpayer *other than* property listed in § 1221. The list in § 1221 includes inventory, accounts receivable, and depreciable property or real estate used in a business. Thus, the sale or exchange of assets in these categories usually results in ordinary income or loss treatment (see Chapter 17).

---

[33] Cost usually means purchase price plus expenses related to the acquisition of the property and incurred by the purchaser (e.g., brokerage commissions). For the basis of property acquired by gift or inheritance and other basis rules, see Chapter 14.

EXAMPLE 35

Kelly owns a pizza parlor. During the current year, he sells two automobiles. The first automobile, which had been used as a pizza delivery car for three years, was sold at a loss of $1,000. Because this automobile is an asset used in his business, Kelly has an ordinary loss deduction of $1,000, rather than a capital loss deduction. The second automobile, which Kelly had owned for two years, was his personal car. It was sold for a gain of $800. The personal car is a capital asset. Therefore, Kelly has a capital gain of $800. ▼

The principal capital assets held by an individual taxpayer include assets held for personal (rather than business) use, such as a personal residence or an automobile, and assets held for investment purposes (e.g., corporate securities and land).

COMPUTATION OF NET CAPITAL GAINS AND LOSSES

Capital gains and losses must be classified as short term (those on assets held for one year or less) and long term (those on assets held for more than one year). Short-term capital losses (STCL) are offset against short-term capital gains (STCG). The result is either net short-term capital gain (NSTCG) or net short-term capital loss (NSTCL).

Long-term capital losses (LTCL) are offset against long-term capital gains (LTCG), and the result is either net long-term capital gain (NLTCG) or net long-term capital loss (NLTCL).

Several combinations are possible after this first round of offsetting. For example, if the taxpayer has NSTCL and NLTCG, these amounts are offset. Likewise, if the taxpayer has NLTCL and NSTCG, a similar offsetting is required. In general, the offsetting continues as long as there is gain in any category and loss in any other category.

EXAMPLE 36

In the current year, Polly has the following capital gains and losses: STCL of $4,000, STCG of $3,000, LTCG of $6,000, and LTCL of $2,000. This results in NSTCL of $1,000 ($4,000 STCL − $3,000 STCG) and NLTCG of $4,000 ($6,000 LTCG − $2,000 LTCL). The $1,000 NSTCL is used to offset the $4,000 NLTCG, resulting in an excess of NLTCG over NSTCL of $3,000. ▼

CAPITAL LOSS LIMITATION

Noncorporate Capital Losses. Capital losses are first offset against capital gains (as illustrated in Example 36). If, after this offsetting, an individual taxpayer has net capital losses, such losses are deductible as a deduction *for* AGI to a maximum of $3,000 per year. Any unused amounts are carried over for an indefinite period.

EXAMPLE 37

During the year, Tina has $1,000 of NLTCL and $2,000 of NSTCL. Tina's other income is $100,000. Her capital loss deduction for the year is $3,000, consisting of the $2,000 NSTCL and $1,000 NLTCL. ▼

When a taxpayer has both short-term and long-term capital losses, and the losses together exceed $3,000, the short-term losses must be used first in applying the $3,000 limitation.

EXAMPLE 38

Matt has NSTCL of $2,500 and NLTCL of $5,000 for the year. His other income is $50,000. Matt uses the losses as follows:

NSTCL	$2,500
NLTCL	500
Maximum capital loss deduction	$3,000

The remaining NLTCL of $4,500 ($5,000 NLTCL − $500 used) may be carried forward for an indefinite period until used. See Chapter 16 for a detailed discussion of capital loss carryovers. ▼

Corporate Capital Losses. Corporate taxpayers may offset capital losses only against capital gains. Capital losses in excess of capital gains may not be used to reduce ordinary income of a corporation. A corporation's unused capital losses are subject to a carryback and carryover. Capital losses are initially carried back three years and then carried forward five years to offset capital gains that arise in those years. See Chapters 16 and 20 for a discussion of capital losses of corporate taxpayers.

TAX PLANNING CONSIDERATIONS

TAKING ADVANTAGE OF TAX RATE DIFFERENTIALS

It is natural for taxpayers to be concerned about the tax rates they are paying. How does a tax practitioner communicate information about rates to clients? There are several possibilities.

The marginal rate (refer to Examples 23 through 25) provides information that can help a taxpayer evaluate a particular course of action or structure a transaction in the most advantageous manner.

7 LEARNING OBJECTIVE
Identify tax planning opportunities associated with the individual tax formula.

EXAMPLE 39
Due to his salary, Ron is in the 28% marginal tax bracket for 1996. He is considering selling corporate stock he has held as an investment for four years for a $10,000 gain in December. If he sells the stock, his income tax increases by $2,800 ($10,000 gain × 28% marginal rate), and he has $7,200 of after-tax income ($10,000 − $2,800 tax). ▼

EXAMPLE 40
Assume the same facts as in Example 39 and that Ron plans to retire early in 1997. Upon retirement, Ron's only source of income will be nontaxable Social Security benefits and municipal bond interest. If Ron waits until 1997 to sell the stock, his tax on the gain is $1,500 ($10,000 gain × 15% marginal rate), and his after-tax income is $8,500 ($10,000 gain − $1,500 tax). By being aware of the effect of marginal tax rates, Ron can save $1,300 in tax. ▼

The marginal rate analysis illustrated in Examples 39 and 40 for an income item can also help a taxpayer obtain the greatest tax benefit from a deductible expense. For example, a taxpayer who is in the 15 percent bracket this year and expects to be in the 31 percent bracket next year should, if possible, defer payment of deductible expenses until next year to maximize the tax benefit of the deduction.

A note of caution is in order with respect to shifting income and expenses between years. Congress has recognized the tax planning possibilities of such shifting and has enacted many provisions to limit a taxpayer's ability to do so. Some of these limitations on the shifting of income are discussed in Chapters 4, 5, and 18. Limitations that affect a taxpayer's ability to shift deductions are discussed in Chapters 6 through 11 and in Chapter 18.

A taxpayer's *effective rate* can be an informative measure of the effectiveness of tax planning. The effective rate is computed by dividing the taxpayer's tax liability by the total amount of income. A low effective rate can be considered an indication of effective tax planning.

One way of lowering the effective rate is to exclude income from the tax base. For example, a taxpayer might consider investing in tax-free municipal bonds rather than taxable corporate bonds. Although pre-tax income from corporate bonds is usually higher, after-tax income may be higher if the taxpayer invests in tax-free municipals.

Another way of lowering the effective rate is to make sure that the taxpayer's expenses and losses are deductible. For example, losses on investments in passive activities may not be deductible (see Chapter 11). Therefore, a taxpayer who plans to invest in an activity that will produce a loss in the early years should take steps to ensure that the business is treated as active rather than passive. Active losses are deductible while passive losses are not.

INCOME OF MINOR CHILDREN

Taxpayers can use several strategies to avoid or minimize the effect of the rules that tax the unearned income of certain minor children at the parents' rate. The kiddie tax rules do not apply once a child reaches age 14. Parents should consider giving a younger child assets that defer taxable income until the child reaches age 14. For example, U.S. government Series EE savings bonds can be used to defer income until the bonds are cashed in (see Chapter 4).

Growth stocks typically pay little in the way of dividends. However, the profit on an astute investment may more than offset the lack of dividends. The child can hold the stock until he or she reaches age 14. If the stock is sold then at a profit, the profit is taxed at the child's low rates.

Taxpayers in a position to do so can employ their children in their business and pay them a reasonable wage for the work they actually perform (e.g., light office help, such as filing). The child's earned income is sheltered by the standard deduction, and the parents' business is allowed a deduction for the wages. The kiddie tax rules have no effect on earned income, even if it is earned from the parents' business.

ETHICAL CONSIDERATIONS

A Working Family Is a Happy Family

Leo and Cora own and operate an automobile dealership in a small community. Because the business is very competitive and many potential customers are attracted to big city discounters, Leo finds it necessary to advertise a lot.

The advertising for the dealership occasionally stresses a "family theme." In these commercials, Leo and Cora appear together with their three children to convey to the viewer the family orientation of the business. The dealership pays the children for their performances. Each child receives a salary that approximates the amount of the standard deduction available to a single person. The salaries are deposited in the children's respective savings accounts. All of the children are under the age of 19, and one is under age 14.

What are Leo and Cora trying to accomplish? Will it work? Should it work?

DEPENDENCY EXEMPTIONS

The Joint Return Test. A married person can be claimed as a dependent only if that individual does not file a joint return with his or her spouse. If a joint return has been filed, the damage may be undone if separate returns are substituted on a timely basis (on or before the due date of the return).

EXAMPLE 41 While preparing a client's 1996 income tax return on April 8, 1997, the tax practitioner discovered that the client's daughter filed a joint return with her husband in late January of 1997. Presuming the daughter otherwise qualifies as the client's dependent, the exemption is not lost if she and her husband file separate returns on or before April 15, 1997. ▼

An initial election to file a joint return must be considered carefully in any situation in which the taxpayers might later decide to amend their return and file separately. As indicated above, separate returns may be substituted for a joint return only if the amended returns are filed on or before the normal due date of the return. If the taxpayers in Example 41 attempt to file separate returns after April 15, 1997, the returns will not be accepted, and the joint return election is binding.[34]

Keep in mind that the filing of a joint return will not be fatal to the dependency exemption if the parties are filing solely to recover all income tax withholdings, are not required to file a return, and no tax liability would exist on separate returns.

The Gross Income Test. The exception to the gross income test for a person under the age of 19 or a full-time student under the age of 24 applies only to a child of the taxpayer. The term *child* is limited to a son, stepson, daughter, stepdaughter, adopted son, or adopted daughter and may include a foster child.

EXAMPLE 42 Austin provides more than 50% of the support of his son, Irvin, and his daughter-in-law, Donna, who live with him. Donna, age 22, is a full-time student and earns $3,000 from a part-time job. Irvin and Donna do not file a joint return. Austin may claim Irvin as a dependent but not Donna. Although students under the age of 24 are excepted from the gross income test, this applies only to a "child" of the taxpayer. Donna does not come within the exception because she is not Austin's child. ▼

Can the fact that the parties live in a community property state make a difference?

EXAMPLE 43 Assume the same facts as in Example 42 except that all parties live in Nevada, a community property jurisdiction. Now Austin can claim both Irvin and Donna as his dependents. Since Donna's income is only $1,500 (her half of the community), she now satisfies the gross income test (less than $2,650 for 1997). ▼

The Support Test. Adequate records of expenditures for support should be maintained in the event a dependency exemption is questioned on audit by the IRS. The maintenance of adequate records is particularly important for exemptions arising from multiple support agreements.

Relationship to the Deduction for Medical Expenses. Generally, medical expenses are deductible only if they are paid on behalf of the taxpayer, his or her spouse, and their dependents. Since deductibility may rest on dependency status, planning is important in arranging multiple support agreements.

EXAMPLE 44 During the year, Zelda will be supported by her two sons (Vern and Vito) and her daughter (Maria). Each will furnish approximately one-third of the required support. If the parties decide that the dependency exemption should be claimed by the daughter under a multiple support agreement, any medical expenses incurred by Zelda should be paid by Maria. ▼

---

[34] Reg. § 1.6013–1(a)(1).

In planning a multiple support agreement, take into account which of the parties is most likely to exceed the 7.5 percent limitation (see Chapter 10). In Example 44, for instance, Maria might be a poor choice if she and her family do not expect to incur many medical and drug expenses of their own.

ETHICAL CONSIDERATIONS

Manipulating Deductions

Jason and his two sisters furnish more than 50 percent of the support of their widowed mother. Their mother lives with Jason, and his sisters sign Form 2120 enabling him to claim her as a dependent. During the year, the mother incurred medical expenses that were paid by one of Jason's sisters.

In completing his income tax return for the tax year, Jason claims his mother's medical expenses along with his own. Although he did not pay the expenses, Jason reasons that he could have done so from the funds he furnished for his mother's support.

Comment on the propriety of what Jason has done.

One exception permits the deduction of medical expenses paid on behalf of someone who is not a spouse or a dependent. If the person could be claimed as a dependent *except* for the gross income or joint return test, the medical expenses are, nevertheless, deductible. For additional discussion, see Chapter 10.

KEY TERMS

Abandoned spouse, 3–27

Dependency exemption, 3–10

Head of household, 3–26

Itemized deductions, 3–6

Kiddie tax, 3–19

Marriage penalty, 3–24

Multiple support agreement, 3–12

Personal exemption, 3–10

Standard deduction, 3–7

Surviving spouse, 3–26

Tax Rate Schedules, 3–16

Tax Table, 3–16

Unearned income, 3–19

PROBLEM MATERIALS

DISCUSSION QUESTIONS

1. A friend of yours remarks that the current top rate of 39.6% is the highest the Federal income tax has ever been. Please comment.
2. Rearrange the following components to show the formula for arriving at the amount of Federal taxable income:
    a. Deductions *for* AGI.
    b. The greater of the standard deduction or itemized deductions.
    c. Income (broadly conceived).
    d. Adjusted gross income.
    e. Exclusions.
    f. Personal and dependency exemptions.
    g. Gross income.

3. During the year, Ned inherits $5,000 from a great uncle. To help Ned come up with a $15,000 down payment on a condominium, Ned's mother lends him an additional $10,000. How do these transactions affect Ned's gross income for the year?

4. During the year, Mildred's stock investment increased in value by $13,000. She also sold some stock for $4,500; the stock had cost $4,000. How do these facts affect Mildred's gross income?

5. Jason and Kara (both age 64) will itemize their deductions on a joint return for 1997. Since they will not have certain itemized deductions next year, they expect their income tax liability to increase. Comment on their expectation.

6. Al and Melissa are husband and wife, and both are employed. They do not live in a community property state. Since Melissa incurred most of their itemized deductions (e.g., medical, charitable), Al feels that they would save taxes if they filed separate returns. On such returns, Al would claim the standard deduction, and Melissa would itemize her deductions *from* AGI. Comment on this proposed course of action.

7. Discuss the marital status of the parties under the following circumstances:
   a. One spouse dies during the year.
   b. The spouses are divorced during the year.

8. If an individual who may qualify as a dependent does not spend funds that he or she has received (e.g., wages or Social Security benefits), are these unexpended amounts considered in applying the support test? Are they included in applying the gross income test?

9. Freda purchased a stereo system for her son Wes, age 16. The stereo was placed in Wes's room and used exclusively by him. Freda also purchased a new sports car, titled and registered in her own name, that was used 90% of the time by Wes. Should the cost of these items be considered as support in determining whether Freda may claim Wes as a dependent?

10. Carol provided 75% of the support of Debra, her niece. Debra was a full-time student during the year and earned $3,800 from a part-time job. Can Carol claim Debra as a dependent?

11. Besides what he furnishes on his own, Walter receives support from his daughter (20%) and his son (25%). Can either the daughter or the son claim Walter as a dependent under a multiple support agreement? Why or why not?

12. After Hugh and Ashley were divorced, Ashley disappeared with their two children. Under the divorce decree (issued in 1996), Hugh is awarded the dependency exemptions for the two children. Does Hugh have a problem? Explain.

13. A taxpayer who is divorced continues to support his former mother-in-law. May he claim her as a dependent? Suppose she does not live with him. Does this make any difference?

14. Roberto, who is single, is a U.S. citizen and resident. He provides almost all of the support of his parents and two aunts, who are citizens and residents of Guatemala. Roberto's parents and aunts are seriously considering moving to and becoming residents of Mexico. Would such a move have any impact on Roberto? Why or why not?

15. What perceived abuse is the kiddie tax designed to correct?

16. A single individual age 65 or over and blind is required to file a Federal income tax return in 1997 if he or she has gross income of $7,800 or more (refer to Table 3–4).
    a. Explain how the $7,800 filing requirement was computed.
    b. In general, explain the effect of the additional standard deduction on the determination of gross income requirements for filing.

17. Comment on the so-called marriage penalty in connection with the following:
    a. What it is.
    b. When it is likely to occur.
    c. What income level (i.e., low, modest, high) could be vulnerable.

18. Baron and Cheryl are both professionals who have held jobs since they graduated from college five years ago. For several years, they have been engaged to be married. Both would like to tie the knot, but Cheryl is hesitant because of a "marriage penalty" she has heard about. Baron feels Cheryl's fears are unfounded and says they should be able to avoid any such penalty by filing separate returns as married persons. Comment on Baron and Cheryl's situation.

19. In 1997, Ginger's husband dies. Ginger plans to file as a surviving spouse for tax years 1997 through 1999. Ginger's only dependent is her mother, who lives with her. Comment on any misconceptions Ginger may have regarding the tax law.

20. Jacob is single and lives alone in an apartment. He maintains the home where his parents live, but only his mother qualifies as Jacob's dependent. When Jacob files his own return, he chooses single status since *both* of his parents do not qualify as dependents. Comment on Jacob's filing status.

21. Several years ago, after a particularly fierce argument, Fran's husband moved out and has not been heard from or seen since. Because Fran cannot locate her husband, she has been using "married, filing separate" status when filing her income tax return. Comment on Fran's status.

22. During the current year, Andre had a $7,000 long-term capital loss on the sale of common stock he had held as an investment. In addition, he had a $3,000 loss on the sale of his personal automobile, which he had owned for a year. How do these transactions affect Andre's taxable income?

23. Ten years ago, Ann purchased a personal residence for $140,000. In the current year, she sells the residence for $105,000. Ann's friend tells her she has a recognizable loss of $35,000 from the sale. Do you agree with the friend's comment? Elaborate.

24. List some assets that are not capital assets and some that are capital assets. Why is it important to determine whether an asset is an ordinary asset or a capital asset?

25. During the current year, Kate earned a salary of $40,000. She sold 20 shares of Robin Corporation common stock that she had purchased two years ago at a loss of $2,500 and sold her personal automobile at a gain of $1,500. Compute Kate's AGI.

26. If Cole has a salary of $41,000, net short-term capital gain of $1,000, and net long-term capital losses of $8,500, what is his AGI?

27. Lloyd and Nell would like to start building a college fund for their three grandchildren by making gifts to them. Since the grandchildren are all under the age of 14, they are concerned about the implications of the kiddie tax. What do you suggest?

28. Perry is divorced and has living with him his married daughter, Celia, and her husband, Clark. During the year, Celia earned $3,100 from a part-time job and filed a separate return to recover her withholdings. Clark has no income. Perry can prove that he provided more than 50% of Celia and Clark's support. Perry did not claim Celia as his dependent because he believed she failed the gross income test. Perry filed his return using single taxpayer status. All parties reside in California. Comment on Perry's tax position.

29. Erica and her two brothers equally furnish all of the support of their mother. Erica is married and has four children. Her brothers are single and claim the standard deduction. Erica's mother is not in good health. What suggestions can you make regarding the tax position of the parties?

PROBLEMS

30. Compute the taxpayer's taxable income for 1997 in each of the following cases:
    a. Jack is married and files a joint return with his wife Alice. Jack and Alice have two dependent children. They have AGI of $50,000 and $8,300 of itemized deductions.
    b. Pete is an unmarried head of household with two dependents. He has AGI of $45,000 and itemized deductions of $5,200.

c. Iris, age 22, is a full-time college student who is claimed as a dependent by her parents. She earns $4,200 from a part-time job and has interest income of $1,500.

d. Matt, age 20, is a full-time college student who is claimed as a dependent by his parents. He earns $2,500 from a part-time job and has interest income of $4,100. His itemized deductions related to the investment income are $700.

Note: Problems 31 and 32 can be solved by referring to Figure 3–1, Exhibits 3–1 through 3–3, Tables 3–1 and 3–2, and the discussion under Deductions for Adjusted Gross Income in this chapter.

31. Compute taxable income for 1997 for Baron on the basis of the following information. His filing status is head of household.

Salary	$62,000
Alimony paid	2,400
Casualty loss (deductible portion)	9,500
Interest on home mortgage	5,200
Property taxes on home	2,400
State and local income taxes	1,600
Number of dependents	3
Age	46

32. Compute taxable income for 1997 for Renee on the basis of the following information. Her filing status is single.

Inheritance received from mother	$20,000
Gift received from aunt	15,000
Cash dividends from stock investments	18,000
Interest income from savings accounts and money market deposits	16,000
Interest on state and local bonds	9,000
Lottery winnings	3,000
Charitable contributions	4,300
Number of dependents	1
Age	66

33. Determine the amount of the standard deduction allowed for 1997 in each of the following independent situations. In each case, assume the taxpayer is claimed as another person's dependent.

   a. Mona, age 16, has income as follows: $710 interest from a savings account and $800 from a part-time job.

   b. Aaron, age 18, earns $4,300 from a part-time job.

   c. Irving, age 71 and single, has income as follows: $3,100 nontaxable Social Security benefits and $1,050 from a part-time job.

   d. Maureen, age 67, is single and blind and has cash dividends of $1,300 from a stock investment.

34. Determine the number of personal and dependency exemptions in each of the following independent situations:

   a. Wesley, age 45, provides all of the support of Doreen (age 70) who does not live with him. Doreen was Wesley's mother-in-law before his divorce.

   b. Carol, age 50, provides all of the support of two cousins, Rick and Jane. Jane lives with Carol but Rick does not.

   c. Ron, age 66, provides all of the support of Cynthia and Leona who live with him. Cynthia is Ron's wife, and Leona is unrelated but is a close friend of the family and a member of their church. Ron files a separate return. Neither Cynthia nor Leona has any income, and neither files a return.

d. Nicole, age 60, provides all of the support of Alan, age 66 and blind, and Grace, age 89. Alan, Nicole's husband, died in February of the current year. Grace is Alan's mother and lives in a nursing home. Nicole files a separate return.

35. Compute the number of personal and dependency exemptions in each of the following independent situations:
    a. Roberto, a U.S. citizen and resident, contributes 100% of the support of his parents who are citizens of Mexico and live there.
    b. Pablo, a U.S. citizen and resident, contributes 100% of the support of his parents who are citizens of Guatemala. Pablo's father is a resident of Guatemala, and his mother is a legal resident of the United States.
    c. Marlena, a U.S. citizen and resident, contributes 100% of the support of her parents who are also U.S. citizens but are residents of Germany.

36. Determine the number of personal and dependency exemptions in each of the following independent situations:
    a. Warren and Terri provide more than half of the support of their children, Demi and Paul. Demi, age 19, earns $3,200 from a part-time job. Paul, age 21, earns $2,700 from a part-time job.
    b. Hortense, age 64 and widowed, furnishes more than half of the support of her father, age 88 and blind. The father receives Social Security benefits of $4,300, interest on a savings account of $2,300, and interest on tax-exempt bonds of $9,000.
    c. Dennis and Ava provide more than half of the support of their son, Henry. Henry, age 25, is a full-time student in medical school. During the year, Henry receives $2,500 in dividends from stock investments.
    d. Earl provides more than half of the support of his nephew, Brad, who lives with him. Brad, age 17 and a full-time student, earns $2,500 from a part-time job.

37. Doug and Mae are married and file a joint return. They have three children and Mae's parents who qualify as their dependents. If Doug and Mae's AGI is $200,000, what is their allowable exemption deduction for 1997?

38. Melvin and Sarah Turner are married and file a joint return. Transactions for 1997 are as follows:

Salaries ($42,000 for Melvin and $39,000 for Sarah)	$81,000
Lottery winnings	1,200
Inheritance from Melvin's father	30,000
Gift from Sarah's mother	10,000
Short-term capital loss from sale of stock held as an investment	3,000

    The Turners provided all of the support of their 20-year-old married daughter, Maryanne, and her husband, Boyd. Maryanne and Boyd live with the Turners, and neither has any gross income. The Turners also furnish over half of the support of Sarah's aunt who lives in a nursing home. The aunt, age 76, has interest of $2,700 from State of Alabama bonds. Melvin is age 65, while Sarah is 45. If the Turners have itemized deductions of $7,000, what is their taxable income for 1997?

39. Bob, age 13, is a full-time student supported by his parents who claim him on their tax return for 1997. Bob's parents present you with the following information and ask that you prepare Bob's 1997 Federal income tax return:

Wages from summer job	$2,100
Interest on savings account at First National Bank	950
Interest on City of Chicago bonds Bob received as a gift from his grandfather two years ago	750
Dividend from Owl Corporation	200

a. What is Bob's taxable income for 1997?
b. Bob's parents file a joint return for 1997 on which they report taxable income of $66,000. Compute Bob's 1997 tax liability.

40. Walter and Nancy provide 70% of the support of their daughter (age 21) and son-in-law (age 22). The son-in-law (John) is a full-time student at a local university, while the daughter (Irene) holds various part-time jobs from which she earns $3,000. Walter and Nancy engage you to prepare their tax return for 1997. During a meeting with them in late March of 1998, you learn that John and Irene do not file a joint return. What tax advice would you give based on the following assumptions:
a. All parties live in Louisiana (a community property state).
b. All parties live in New Jersey (a common law state).

41. Don is a wealthy executive who had taxable income of $200,000 in 1997. He is considering transferring title in a duplex he owns to his son Sam, age 16. Sam has no other income and is claimed as a dependent by Don. Net rent income from the duplex is $10,000 a year, which Sam will be encouraged to place in a savings account. Will the family save income taxes in 1997 if Don transfers title in the duplex to Sam? Explain.

42. Compute the 1997 tax liability for each of the following taxpayers:
a. Norm and Nancy, both age 46, are married, have two dependent children, and file a joint return. Their combined salaries totaled $66,000. They had deductions *for* AGI of $7,000 and total itemized deductions of $7,100.
b. Clark, age 45, is single and has no dependents. He had a salary of $52,000, deductions *for* AGI of $3,000, and total itemized deductions of $4,100.
c. David and Susan, both age 65, are married, have no dependents, and file a joint return. Their combined salaries were $92,000. They had deductions *for* AGI of $2,000 and itemized deductions of $8,500.

43. Dustin and Vicki are married and file a joint return. Dustin is age 70, and Vicki is age 65. Their income is as follows: $32,000 (cash dividends from stock investments); $12,000 (interest income on certificates of deposits); and $18,000 (interest income on City of Detroit bonds). In addition, they incur a long-term capital loss of $2,500 on the sale of stock held as an investment. They furnish more than half of the support of Vicki's cousin who does not live with them. If they have itemized deductions of $8,000, determine their taxable income for 1997.

44. Peter, age 12, is claimed as a dependent on his parents' 1997 Federal income tax return, on which they reported taxable income of $95,000. During the summer, Peter earned $2,500 from a job as a model. His only other income consisted of $1,700 in interest on a savings account. Compute Peter's taxable income and tax liability.

45. Carmen, who is 12 years old, is claimed as a dependent on her parents' tax return. During 1997, she received $12,200 in dividends and interest and had no investment expenses related to this income. She also earned $2,000 wages from a part-time job. Compute the amount of income that is taxed at Carmen's parents' rate.

46. Tyler became 14 years of age on December 20, 1997. During 1997, he had income as follows: $4,300 from a part-time job as a model for teen clothing and $4,000 interest on a certificate of deposit. Since Tyler banks his income, his parents furnish all of his support. Tyler's parents claim him as a dependent and are in the 28% tax bracket. If Tyler files his own return, how much tax does he owe?

47. Bruce Smith and Wanda Brown are young professionals who are employed in well-paying jobs. They have been dating each other for several years and are considering getting married in December 1997 or January 1998. For 1997, their respective AGIs are $65,000 and $68,000. They anticipate earning the same income in 1998. In both years, they will claim the standard deduction.
    Bruce and Wanda solicit your tax advice. Specifically, they wish to know what Federal income tax results from their getting married in 1997 or in 1998. Prepare a letter to

Wanda (4339 Elm St., Apt. 39A, Cincinnati, OH 45221) setting forth the tax determination under each choice.

48. Which of the following individuals are required to file a tax return for 1997? Should any of these individuals file a return even if filing is not required? Why?
    a. Sam is married and files a joint return with his spouse, Lana. Both Sam and Lana are 67 years old. Their combined gross income was $14,000.
    b. Bobby is a dependent child under age 19 who received $4,000 in wages from a part-time job.
    c. Mike is single and is 67 years old. His gross income from wages was $6,700.
    d. Marge is a self-employed single individual with gross income of $4,500 from an unincorporated business. Business expenses amounted to $4,000.

49. Which of the following taxpayers must file a Federal income tax return for 1997?
    a. Bob, age 19, is a full-time college student. He is claimed as a dependent by his parents. He earned $4,100 wages during the year.
    b. Anita, age 12, is claimed as a dependent by her parents. She earned interest of $1,200 during the year.
    c. Earl, age 16, is claimed as a dependent by his parents. He earned wages of $2,700 and interest of $1,100 during the year.
    d. Karen, age 16 and blind, is claimed as a dependent by her parents. She earned wages of $2,600 and interest of $1,200 during the year.
    e. Pat, age 17, is claimed as a dependent by her parents. She earned interest of $300 during the year. In addition, she earned $550 during the summer operating her own business at the beach, where she painted caricatures of her customers.

50. In each of the following situations, classify Darlene's filing status for tax year 1997:
    a. Darlene is a widow and maintains a household in which her two dependent children live. Darlene's husband died in 1995.
    b. Same as (a) except that Darlene's husband died in 1993 (not 1995).
    c. Darlene is single and lives alone. She maintains the household of her parents, only one of whom qualifies as her dependent.
    d. Darlene is married, but her husband disappeared for parts unknown in 1996. Darlene maintains the household in which she and her dependent children live.

51. In each of the following situations, classify Isaac's filing status for tax year 1997:
    a. Isaac lives alone. He has not seen or heard from his wife since 1996.
    b. Isaac's wife died in January 1997. He maintains the home in which he and his dependent child live.
    c. Isaac's wife died in 1993. He maintains the home in which he and his unmarried child live. The child does not qualify as Isaac's dependent.
    d. Isaac is divorced and lives alone. He also maintains a home in which his dependent child lives.

52. Henry died on January 1, 1995. He was survived by his wife, Sue, and their 19-year-old son, Mike, who was a college sophomore. Mike was a full-time student in 1996 and earned $3,000 for the year. In 1997, Mike reduced his school load and became a part-time student. He earned $5,200 in 1997. Mike continues to live with his mother, who provides over half of his support. What is Sue's filing status in 1995, 1996, and 1997?

53. Tracy, age 66, is a widow. Her husband died in 1995. Tracy maintains a home in which she and her 28-year-old son reside. Her son Gary is a piano player at a local nightclub, where he earned $12,000 during 1997. Gary contributed $3,000 of his income toward household expenses and put the remainder in a savings account that he used to return to college full-time to pursue a master's degree in music starting in August 1997. Tracy contributed $12,000 toward household expenses. What is the most favorable filing status available to Tracy for 1997, and how many exemptions may she claim?

54. Hazel, age 39, is single. She maintains a household that is the residence of her two children, Fran, age 8, and Sam, age 11. The children are claimed as dependents by their father, who provides $2,000 child support for each of them. During 1997, Hazel earned a salary of $95,000. Other items that affected her taxable income are as follows:

Total itemized deductions	$ 6,700
Capital gains	
Short-term	1,300
Long-term	3,100
Capital losses	
Short-term	(4,800)
Long-term	(4,000)
Interest income	3,100

Hazel provides all the support for her mother, Mabel, who lives in a nursing home. Mabel qualifies as Hazel's dependent.
a. Compute Hazel's AGI and taxable income for 1997.
b. What is Hazel's filing status for 1997?

55. Tina, age 61, earned a salary of $63,000 in 1997. She sold common stock that she had owned for 10 months at a loss of $1,500 and sold a pleasure boat that she had bought in 1988 at a loss of $4,000. Tina also sold an antique desk for a gain of $10,000. She acquired the desk in 1953. Compute Tina's AGI for 1997.

56. Lee is a single, cash basis calendar year taxpayer. For the years 1996 and 1997, he expects AGI of $20,000 and the following itemized deductions:

Church pledge	$2,300
Interest on home mortgage	1,200
Property taxes	500

Discuss the tax consequences of the alternatives below. Assume for purposes of this problem that the interest and taxes are deductible in the year of payment.
a. In 1996, Lee pays his church pledge for 1996 and 1997 ($2,300 for each year).
b. Lee does nothing different.

57. Gina, a cash basis taxpayer, is single and has no dependents. She provides you with the following estimates for 1996 and 1997:

	1996	1997
Adjusted gross income	$56,000	$60,000
Charitable contributions	2,200	2,400
Interest on home mortgage	1,000	850
Property taxes	700	700

Can Gina decrease taxable income over the two-year period by prepaying her 1997 charitable contributions in 1996?

CUMULATIVE PROBLEMS

58. Leroy and Marcia Roper, 4030 Beachside Drive, Longboat Key, FL 33548, file a joint return for 1997. Leroy, age 64, is the manager for a Motel 10. His Social Security number is 344-99-7642. Marcia, who is age 66, is the manager of Marie's Beauty Salon. Her Social Security number is 354-55-7890. Transactions for 1997 are as follows:

Leroy's salary	$ 50,000
Marcia's salary	44,000
Interest on City of Sarasota bonds	1,100
Life insurance proceeds received on the death of Marcia's mother	100,000
Inheritance from Marcia's mother	140,000
Collection of a loan (Leroy had made an interest-free loan to his brother several years ago)	5,000

The Ropers sold some stock investments during 1997. The results are summarized below.

Name of Corporation	Date Purchased	Date Sold	Cost	Selling Price
Green Co.	7/1/96	2/1/97	$ 5,000	$7,000
Blue Co.	9/1/95	5/1/97	8,000	9,000
Amber Co.	12/1/96	6/1/97	10,000	6,000

The Ropers' itemized deductions for 1997 are as follows:

Charitable contributions (cash)	$1,200
Interest on home mortgage	4,800
Property taxes on home	3,000
Casualty loss (deductible portion)	3,100

The Ropers' son, Steven (Social Security number 371–85–0033), lived with them during 1997 except for the nine months he was away at college. Steven, age 23, is a law student and received a $12,000 scholarship to cover books and tuition. The rest of his support was furnished by the Ropers, who estimate that they spent about $10,000 on it.

Compute the Ropers' taxable income for 1997. Suggested software (if available): *TurboTax* or *MacInTax*.

59. Horace Fern, age 43, lives at 321 Grant Avenue, Cheyenne, WY 82002. Horace's mother Kate (age 65) lived with him until her death in August 1996. Up to the time of her death, Kate qualified as Horace's dependent. Horace maintained the household where he and his mother lived.

Horace is a manager for Bison Lumber Company at a yearly salary of $62,000. Because his job duties will be expanded, Bison plans to increase Horace's salary by 10% starting in 1997.

During 1996, Horace paid $3,300 ($300 each month) in alimony to Janet, his ex-wife. As Janet was remarried in late November, Horace's alimony obligation has terminated.

Besides his salary, Horace received interest income of $5,700 from Western Bank and $6,300 from First Savings Bank on $200,000 in certificates of deposit (CDs) he owns. Horace received the CDs as a gift from his mother several years ago.

Except as otherwise noted, Horace's expenditures for 1996 are summarized below:

Interest on home mortgage	$3,300
Property taxes on home	1,300
Charitable contributions	1,800

Relevant Social Security numbers are as follows:

Horace Fern	520–31–4596
Kate Fern	520–32–3214
Janet Fern	520–33–4432

Federal income taxes withheld from Horace's salary amounted to $10,900. He also paid estimated tax of $300 each quarter.

Part 1—Tax Computation

Compute Horace's net tax payable or refund due for 1996. Horace does not wish to contribute to the Presidential Election Campaign Fund. If he has overpaid, he wants the amount refunded. If you use tax forms for your computations, you will need Form 1040 and Schedules A and B. Suggested software (if available): *TurboTax* or *MacInTax*.

Part 2—Tax Planning

In addition to preparing the return for 1996, Horace has asked you to advise him regarding his tax situation for 1997. He is particularly concerned about the tax effects of the following:

- The death of Kate.
- The cessation of alimony payments due to Janet's remarriage.
- The salary increase.
- Interest income on the CDs.

Write a letter to Horace in which you summarize (in approximate amounts) how much more (or less) he will owe in income taxes for 1997. Also include recommendations on what can be done to mitigate the tax consequences resulting from the investment in CDs. Assume that Horace's itemized deductions will remain constant in 1997.

RESEARCH PROBLEMS

Note: ***West's Federal Taxation on CD-ROM*** *can be used in preparing solutions to the Research Problems. Alternatively, tax research materials contained in a standard tax library can be used.*

Research Problem 1. In the state of Texas, a lawsuit was instituted charging that the state schools for the mentally retarded furnished inadequate, unsafe, and improper care, treatment, and education. As part of the settlement of this suit, the Texas Department of Mental Health offered to pay a fixed daily amount to third-party providers of these services. Under this arrangement, the taxpayers received $16,425 during the year for the care of their mentally retarded daughter. This amount covered a daily per diem for food and board, medical expenses, cost of special food, clothing, transportation, special laundry, home repairs, and other living expenses. The daughter lived with the taxpayers and during the year attended classes at a special school operated by the local school district.

Although the taxpayers did not pay for more than 50% of their daughter's support, they claimed her as a dependent for the year. The taxpayers contend that the amount they received from the state is a scholarship and, therefore, should not be taken into account in applying the support test. The IRS disagrees. What is the appropriate result?

Partial list of research aids:
§ 152(d).
Rev.Rul. 61–186, 1961–2 C.B. 30.
Rev.Rul. 64–221, 1964–2 C.B. 46.

Research Problem 2. Lori and Mike Wise were husband and wife until they were divorced in 1991. As part of the divorce settlement, Mike agreed to be liable for any income taxes that might be assessed against them by the IRS for joint returns filed in the past.

Lori and Mike filed joint returns every year they were married. For tax year 1990, however, each initially filed as "married persons filing separate." Upon further reflection, they replaced the separate returns with a joint return.

In January 1997, the IRS audits the joint return the Wises filed for tax year 1990. As a result of the audit, a deficiency of $480,000 is assessed against the taxpayers. Since Mike is not available, the full amount of the deficiency is assessed against Lori.

Lori objects to the assessment against her on three grounds. First, she maintains that she neither signed the return nor authorized the use of her signature. Second, Lori feels that the assessment should be made against Mike. After all, under the divorce decree Mike has assumed any liability for additional taxes imposed. Third, the assessment is precluded by the three-year statute of limitations.

Regarding Lori's first contention, she offers no proof other than her own statement. Also, no evidence exists that she filed a separate return for 1990.
   a. Discuss the validity of each of Lori's three defenses in a letter to her. As much as possible, express your advice in nonlegal terms. Lori Wise lives at 3126 Kingsride Rd., Funston, UT 84602.
   b. Prepare a memo containing legal substantiation for your position. The memo is for inclusion in your firm's client files.

Research Problem 3. Judy and Greg married in 1986 and have since resided in California. In October 1992, Judy filed in state court to have her marriage to Greg annulled. The annulment was granted in May 1993. Under California law, an annulment voids the marriage and, in effect, treats it as if it never occurred.

Judy files her Federal income tax return for calendar year 1992 using "single" status. Upon audit of the return, the IRS contends that Judy's correct filing status is "married filing separate." Who is correct and why?

Partial list of research aids:
Code § 7703(a)(1).
Reg. § 1.6013–4(a)(1).
Harold K. Lee, 64 T.C. 552 (1975).
Betty J. Shackelford, 70 TCM 945, T.C.Memo. 1995–484.

Use the tax resources of the internet to address the following questions. Do not restrict your search to the World Wide Web, but include a review of newsgroups and general reference materials, practitioner sites and resources, primary sources of the tax law, chat rooms and discussion groups, and other opportunities.

Research Problem 4. Many tax advisors with materials on the internet propose tax planning techniques by which to minimize liabilities under the kiddie tax. Summarize the most effective of these proposals, and cite the providers of such information.

Research Problem 5. Find an internet site that receives and answers technical tax questions from the public. Pose a question of the site with respect to whether a dependency exemption is available in a described situation, or whether head-of-household status can be used. How quickly did the site provider respond? Did they apply the law correctly to your query?

Research Problem 6. Find an internet site that computes an individual's Federal income taxes at no charge. Submit a set of facts to the site using data from one of your assignment problems. Did the internet tax calculator match the answer you had derived previously?

TEAM PROJECT: ARTHUR ANDERSEN TAX CHALLENGE CASES

For more information on the Arthur Andersen Tax Challenge Cases, refer to Chapter 1, page 1–38.

Information related to tax issues and problems that are discussed in this chapter may be found in the

Day and Ball case on pages 2, 3, 4, and 7
Miller case on pages 1, 3, 4, and 16

Read and analyze the case you have been assigned and *identify* any issues and problems that are related to material covered in this chapter. If the information provided in the case is complete, prepare answers for this part of the case at this time. If you need information that is contained in the later parts of the case, write a memo summarizing the questions or problems so you can prepare a complete answer at a later date.

PART II
GROSS INCOME

Part II presents the income component of the basic tax model. Included in this presentation are the determination of what is income and the statutory exclusions that are permitted in calculating gross income. Because the taxpayer's accounting method and accounting period affect when income is reported, an introductory discussion of these topics is also included.

Chapter 4
Gross Income: Concepts and Inclusions

Chapter 5
Gross Income: Exclusions

CHAPTER 4

GROSS INCOME: CONCEPTS AND INCLUSIONS

LEARNING OBJECTIVES

After completing Chapter 4, you should be able to:

1. Explain the concepts of gross income and realization and distinguish between the economic, accounting, and tax concepts of gross income.

2. Describe the cash and accrual methods of accounting and the related effects of the choice of taxable year.

3. Identify who should pay the tax on a particular item of income in various situations.

4. Apply the Internal Revenue Code provisions on alimony, loans made at below-market interest rates, annuities, prizes and awards, group term life insurance, unemployment compensation, and Social Security benefits.

5. Identify tax planning strategies for minimizing gross income.

OUTLINE

Gross Income—What Is It?, 4-3
Definition, 4-3
Economic and Accounting Concepts, 4-3
Comparison of the Accounting and Tax Concepts of Income, 4-4
Form of Receipt, 4-6
Recovery of Capital Doctrine, 4-6

Year of Inclusion, 4-7
Taxable Year, 4-7
Accounting Methods, 4-7
Exceptions Applicable to Cash Basis Taxpayers, 4-9
Exceptions Applicable to Accrual Basis Taxpayers, 4-12

Income Sources, 4-14
Personal Services, 4-14
Income from Property, 4-14
Income Received by an Agent, 4-16
Income from Partnerships, S Corporations, Trusts, and Estates, 4-16
Income in Community Property States, 4-17

Items Specifically Included in Gross Income, 4-19
Alimony and Separate Maintenance Payments, 4-19
Imputed Interest on Below-Market Loans, 4-23

Income from Annuities, 4-28
Prizes and Awards, 4-32
Group Term Life Insurance, 4-33
Unemployment Compensation, 4-34
Social Security Benefits, 4-34

Tax Planning Considerations, 4-36
Nontaxable Economic Benefits, 4-36
Tax Deferral, 4-36
Shifting Income to Relatives, 4-38
Accounting for Community Property, 4-39
Alimony, 4-39

Mr. Zarin lost over $2,500,000 of his own money gambling. The casino then allowed him to gamble on credit. After several months, his liability to the casino totaled more than $3,400,000. Following protracted negotiations, the casino agreed to settle its claim against Mr. Zarin for a mere $500,000. Although Mr. Zarin had paid for gambling losses of $3,000,000, the IRS had the audacity to ask him to pay tax on $2,900,000; that is, the amount the casino marked down his account.[1] Mr. Zarin undoubtedly had difficulty understanding how he could be deemed to have income in this situation.

Given an understanding of the income tax formula, though, one can see how the "free" gambling Mr. Zarin enjoyed could constitute income. The starting point in the formula is the determination of gross income rather than "net income." Once gross income is determined, the next step is to determine the allowable deductions. In Mr. Zarin's way of thinking, these steps were collapsed.

This chapter is concerned with the first step in the computation of taxable income—the determination of gross income. Questions that are addressed include the following:

- What: What is income?
- When: In which tax period is the income recognized?
- Who: Who must include the item of income in gross income?

The Code provides an all-inclusive definition of gross income in § 61. Chapter 5 presents items of income that are specifically excluded from gross income (exclusions).

---

[1] *Zarin v. Comm.*, 90-2 USTC ¶50,530, 66 AFTR2d 90-5679, 916 F.2d 110 (CA-3, 1990).

GROSS INCOME—WHAT IS IT?

DEFINITION

1 **LEARNING OBJECTIVE**
Explain the concepts of gross income and realization and distinguish between the economic, accounting, and tax concepts of gross income.

Section 61(a) of the Internal Revenue Code defines the term **gross income** as follows:

> Except as otherwise provided in this subtitle, gross income means all income from whatever source derived.

This definition is derived from the language of the Sixteenth Amendment to the Constitution.

Supreme Court decisions have made it clear that all sources of income are subject to tax unless Congress specifically excludes the type of income received:

> The starting point in all cases dealing with the question of the scope of what is included in "gross income" begins with the basic premise that the purpose of Congress was to use the full measure of its taxing power.[2]

Although at this point we know that *income* is to be broadly construed, we still do not have a satisfactory definition of the term *income*. Congress left it to the judicial and administrative branches to thrash out the meaning of income. Early in the development of the income tax law, a choice was made between two competing models: economic income and accounting income.

ECONOMIC AND ACCOUNTING CONCEPTS

The term **income** is used in the Code but is not separately defined. Thus, early in the history of our tax laws, the courts were required to interpret "the commonly understood meaning of the term which must have been in the minds of the people when they adopted the Sixteenth Amendment to the Constitution."[3] In determining the definition of income, the Supreme Court rejected the economic concept of income.

Economists measure income (**economic income**) by first determining the fair market value of the individual's net assets at the beginning and end of the year (change in net worth). Then, to arrive at economic income, this change in net worth is added to the goods and services that person actually consumed during the period. Economic income also includes imputed values for such items as the rental value of an owner-occupied home and the value of food a taxpayer might grow for personal consumption.[4]

EXAMPLE 1

Helen's economic income is calculated as follows:

Fair market value of Helen's assets on December 31, 1997	$220,000	
Less liabilities on December 31, 1997	(40,000)	
Net worth on December 31, 1997		$180,000
Fair market value of Helen's assets on January 1, 1997	$200,000	
Less liabilities on January 1, 1997	(80,000)	
Net worth on January 1, 1997		(120,000)

---

[2] *James v. U.S.*, 61–1 USTC ¶9449, 7 AFTR2d 1361, 81 S.Ct. 1052 (USSC, 1961).

[3] *Merchants Loan and Trust Co. v. Smietanka*, 1 USTC ¶42, 3 AFTR 3102, 41 S.Ct. 386 (USSC, 1921).

[4] See Henry C. Simons, *Personal Income Taxation* (Chicago: University of Chicago Press, 1933), Ch. 2–3.

Increase in net worth	$60,000
Consumption	
Food, clothing, and other personal expenditures	25,000
Imputed rental value of Helen's home she owns and occupies	12,000
Economic income	$97,000

The need to value assets annually would make compliance with the tax law burdensome and would cause numerous controversies between the taxpayer and the IRS over valuation. In addition, using market values to determine income for tax purposes could result in liquidity problems. That is, the taxpayer's assets may increase in value even though they are not readily convertible into the cash needed to pay the tax (e.g., commercial real estate). Thus, the IRS, Congress, and the courts have rejected the economic concept of income as impractical.

In contrast, the accounting concept of income is founded on the realization principle.[5] According to this principle, income (**accounting income**) is not recognized until it is realized. For realization to occur, (1) an exchange of goods or services must take place between the accounting entity and some independent, external group, and (2) in the exchange the accounting entity must receive assets that are capable of being objectively valued. Thus, the mere appreciation in the market value of assets before a sale or other disposition is not sufficient to warrant income recognition. In addition, the imputed savings that arise when an individual creates assets for his or her own use (e.g., feed grown for a farmer's own livestock) are not income because no exchange has occurred. The courts and the IRS have ruled, however, that embezzlement proceeds and buried treasures found satisfy the realization requirement and, therefore, must be recognized as income.[6]

The Supreme Court expressed an inclination toward the accounting concept of income when it adopted the realization requirement in *Eisner v. Macomber*:

> Income may be defined as the gain derived from capital, from labor, or from both combined, provided it is understood to include profit gained through a sale or conversion of capital assets.... Here we have the essential matter: not a gain accruing to capital; not a *growth* or *increment* of value *in* investment; but a gain, a profit, something of exchangeable value, *proceeding from* the property, *severed from* the capital however invested or employed, and *coming in,* being *"derived"*—that is, *received* or *drawn by* the recipient for his separate use, benefit and disposal—*that is,* income derived from the property.[7]

In summary, *income* represents an increase in wealth recognized for tax purposes only upon realization.

COMPARISON OF THE ACCOUNTING AND TAX CONCEPTS OF INCOME

Although income tax rules frequently parallel financial accounting measurement concepts, differences do exist. Of major significance, for example, is the fact that unearned (prepaid) income received by an accrual basis taxpayer often is taxed in the year of receipt. For financial accounting purposes, such prepayments are not treated as income until earned.[8] Because of this and other differences, many

---

[5] See the American Accounting Association Committee Report on the "Realization Concept," *The Accounting Review* (April 1965): 312–322.

[6] *Rutkin v. U.S.*, 52–1 USTC ¶9260, 41 AFTR2d 596, 72 S.Ct. 571 (USSC, 1952); Rev.Rul. 61, 1953–1 C.B. 17.

[7] 1 USTC ¶32, 3 AFTR 3020, 40 S.Ct. 189 (USSC, 1920).

[8] Similar differences exist in the deduction area.

TAX IN THE NEWS

FREQUENT FLYER MILES FREQUENTLY RAISE TAX ISSUES

Frequent flyer miles are awarded in many different situations. An individual may accumulate miles based on trips taken for nonbusiness travel and use the miles to purchase a ticket for other personal travel. An employee may accumulate miles while traveling for the employer and be allowed to use the miles for personal travel. This can become a substantial fringe benefit, estimated to be worth about $.02 per mile traveled, or over $6 per hour for jet travel. The taxpayer may even accumulate frequent flyer miles for using a particular credit card to pay for other goods and services.

Charley v. Comm. is the only source of authority dealing directly with the tax consequences of receiving frequent flyer points. In *Charley* the taxpayer and his wife were controlling shareholders in a corporation. Mr. Charley was also an employee of the corporation and was required to make numerous business trips. He was allowed to convert the business miles to his personal use in the following manner: The employer would purchase a coach ticket, which Mr. Charley would upgrade to first class using frequent flyer miles he had accumulated from other business travel. The company would bill the client Mr. Charley was serving for the price of a first class ticket. The excess of the price of first class over coach fare was credited to Mr. Charley's personal account at the travel agency, which he could use to purchase other tickets or receive as a cash refund.

The Tax Court and the appellate court reasoned that the transactions can reasonably be viewed from at least two different perspectives: (1) Mr. Charley received additional compensation that was credited to his account at the travel agency; (2) Mr. Charley received property (frequent flyer miles) that he sold to the travel agent for the right to draw upon his account. Under either view, Mr. Charley experienced an increase in wealth, which was realized when his account at the travel agency was credited.

The courts refused to decide whether as a general proposition the receipt of frequent flyer credits always generates income. It seems clear, however, that when the employer deducts the cost of the airline tickets and the employee receives the benefit of the frequent flyer miles, the employee has realized income. Whether the IRS will seek to tax that income is a different matter. Not only might the cost of enforcing the law exceed the additional revenue, but collecting the tax could also create much ill will toward the IRS.

SOURCE: *Charley v. Comm.*, 96–2 USTC ¶50,399, 78 AFTR2d. 96–5694, 91 F.3d 72 (CA–9, 1996) aff'g 66 TCM 1429, T.C.Memo. 1993–558.

---

corporations report financial accounting income that is substantially different from the amounts reported for tax purposes (see Chapter 20, Reconciliation of Taxable Income and Accounting Income).

The Supreme Court provided an explanation for some of the variations between accounting and taxable income in a decision involving inventory and bad debt adjustments:

> The primary goal of financial accounting is to provide useful information to management, shareholders, creditors, and others properly interested; the major responsibility of the accountant is to protect these parties from being misled. The primary goal of the income tax system, in contrast, is the equitable collection of revenue.... Consistently

with its goals and responsibilities, financial accounting has as its foundation the principle of conservatism, with its corollary that 'possible errors in measurement [should] be in the direction of understatement rather than overstatement of net income and net assets'. In view of the Treasury's markedly different goals and responsibilities, understatement of income is not destined to be its guiding light.

... Financial accounting, in short, is hospitable to estimates, probabilities, and reasonable certainties; the tax law, with its mandate to preserve the revenue, can give no quarter to uncertainty.[9]

FORM OF RECEIPT

Gross income is not limited to cash received. "It includes income realized in any form, whether in money, property, or services. Income may be realized [and recognized], therefore, in the form of services, meals, accommodations, stock or other property, as well as in cash."[10]

EXAMPLE 2 Ostrich Corporation allowed Bill, an employee, to use a company car for his vacation. Bill realized income equal to the rental value of the car for the time and mileage. ▼

EXAMPLE 3 Terry owed $10,000 on a mortgage. The creditor accepted $8,000 in full satisfaction of the debt. Terry realized income of $2,000 from retiring the debt.[11] ▼

ETHICAL CONSIDERATIONS

Unreported Income

The roof of your office building recently experienced some damage as the result of a storm. You are negotiating with a carpenter who has quoted two prices for the repair work: $600 if you pay in cash ("folding money") and $700 if you pay by check. The carpenter observes that the IRS can more readily discover his receipt of a check. Thus, he hints that he will report the receipt of the check (but not the cash). The carpenter has a full-time job and will do the work after hours and on the weekend. He comments that he should be allowed to keep all he earns after regular working hours. Evaluate what you should do including whether you have an ethical obligation to pay the higher price.

RECOVERY OF CAPITAL DOCTRINE

The Constitution grants Congress the power to tax income but does not define the term. Because the Constitution does not define income, it would seem that Congress could simply tax gross receipts. Although Congress does allow certain deductions, none are constitutionally required. However, the Supreme Court has held that there is no income subject to tax until the taxpayer has recovered the capital invested.[12] This concept is known as the **recovery of capital doctrine.**

In its simplest application, this doctrine means that sellers can reduce their gross receipts (selling price) by the adjusted basis of the property sold.[13] This net amount, in the language of the Code, is gross income.

---

[9] *Thor Power Tool Co. v. Comm.*, 79–1 USTC ¶9139, 43 AFTR2d 79–362, 99 S.Ct. 773 (USSC, 1979).

[10] Reg. § 1.61–1(a).

[11] Reg. § 1.61–12. See *U.S. v. Kirby Lumber Co.*, 2 USTC ¶814, 10 AFTR 458, 52 S.Ct. 4 (USSC, 1931). Exceptions to this general rule are discussed in Chapter 5.

[12] *Doyle v. Mitchell Bros. Co.*, 1 USTC ¶17, 3 AFTR 2979, 38 S.Ct. 467 (USSC, 1916).

[13] For a definition of adjusted basis, see the Glossary of Tax Terms in Appendix C.

CHAPTER 4 Gross Income: Concepts and Inclusions   4–7

EXAMPLE 4

Dave sold common stock for $15,000. He had purchased the stock for $12,000. Dave's gross receipts are $15,000. This amount consists of a $12,000 recovery of capital and $3,000 of gross income. ▼

Collections on annuity contracts and installment payments received from sales of property must be allocated between recovery of capital and income. Annuities are discussed in this chapter, and installment sales are discussed in Chapter 18.

YEAR OF INCLUSION

TAXABLE YEAR

2 LEARNING OBJECTIVE
Describe the cash and accrual methods of accounting and the related effects of the choice of taxable year.

The annual accounting period or **taxable year** is a basic component of our tax system.[14] Generally, an entity must use the *calendar year* to report its income. However, a *fiscal year* (a period of 12 months ending on the last day of any month other than December) can be elected if the taxpayer maintains adequate books and records. This fiscal year option generally is not available to partnerships, S corporations, and personal service corporations, as discussed in Chapter 18.[15]

Determining the particular year in which the income will be taxed is important for determining when the tax must be paid. But the year each item of income is subject to tax can also affect the total tax liability over the entity's lifetime. This is true for the following reasons:

- With a progressive rate system, a taxpayer's marginal tax rate can change from year to year.
- Congress may change the tax rates.
- The relevant rates may change because of a change in the entity's status (e.g., a person may marry or a business may be incorporated).
- Several provisions in the Code are dependent on the taxpayer's gross income for the year (e.g., whether the person can be claimed as a dependent, as discussed in Chapter 3).

ACCOUNTING METHODS

The year an item of income is subject to tax often depends upon which acceptable **accounting method** the taxpayer regularly employs.[16] The three primary methods of accounting are (1) the cash receipts and disbursements method, (2) the accrual method, and (3) the hybrid method. Most individuals use the cash receipts and disbursements method of accounting, whereas most corporations use the accrual method. The Regulations require the accrual method for determining purchases and sales when inventory is an income-producing factor.[17] Some businesses employ a hybrid method that is a combination of the cash and accrual methods of accounting.

In addition to these overall accounting methods, a taxpayer may choose to spread the gain from the sale of property over the collection periods by using the installment method of income recognition. Contractors may either spread profits from contracts over the periods in which the work is done (the percentage of completion method) or defer all profit until the year in which the project is

---

[14] See Accounting Periods in Chapter 18.
[15] §§ 441(a) and (d).
[16] See Accounting Methods in Chapter 18.

[17] Reg. § 1.446–1(c)(2)(i). Other circumstances in which the accrual method must be used are presented in Chapter 18.

completed (the completed contract method, which can be used only in limited circumstances).[18]

The IRS has the power to prescribe the accounting method to be used by the taxpayer. Section 446(b) grants the IRS broad powers to determine if the accounting method used *clearly reflects income*:

> Exceptions—If no method of accounting has been regularly used by the taxpayer, or *if the method used does not clearly reflect income, the computation of taxable income shall be made under such method as, in the opinion of the Secretary . . . does clearly reflect income.*

A change in the method of accounting requires the consent of the IRS.[19]

Cash Receipts Method.
Under the **cash receipts method,** property or services received are included in the taxpayer's gross income in the year of actual or constructive receipt by the taxpayer or agent, regardless of whether the income was earned in that year.[20] The income received need not be reduced to cash in the same year. All that is necessary for income recognition is that property or services received have a fair market value—a cash equivalent.[21] Thus, if a cash basis taxpayer receives a note in payment for services, he or she has income in the year of receipt equal to the fair market value of the note. However, a creditor's mere promise to pay (e.g., an account receivable), with no supporting note, is not usually considered to have a fair market value.[22] Thus, the cash basis taxpayer defers income recognition until the account receivable is collected.

EXAMPLE 5

Dana, an accountant, reports her income by the cash method. In 1997, she performed an audit for Orange Corporation and billed the client for $5,000, which was collected in 1998. In 1997, Dana also performed an audit for Blue Corporation. Because of Blue's precarious financial position, Dana required Blue to issue an $8,000 secured negotiable note in payment of the fee. The note had a fair market value of $6,000. Dana collected $8,000 on the note in 1998. Dana's gross income for the two years is as follows:

	1997	1998
Fair market value of note received from Blue	$6,000	
Cash received		
From Orange on account receivable		$ 5,000
From Blue on note receivable		8,000
Less: Recovery of capital		(6,000)
Total gross income	$6,000	$ 7,000

Generally, a check received is considered a cash equivalent. Thus, a cash basis taxpayer must recognize the income when the check is received. This is true even though the taxpayer receives the check after banking hours.[23]

Accrual Method.
Under the **accrual method,** an item is generally included in the gross income for the year in which it is earned, regardless of when the income

---

[18] §§ 453(a) and (b), § 453A, and Reg. § 1.451–3. See Chapter 18 for limitations on the use of the installment method and the completed contract method.
[19] § 446(e). See Chapter 18.
[20] *Julia A. Strauss,* 2 B.T.A. 598 (1925). See the Glossary of Tax Terms in Appendix C for a discussion of the terms "cash equivalent doctrine" and "constructive receipt."
[21] Reg. §§ 1.446–1(a)(3) and (c)(1)(:).
[22] *Bedell v. Comm.,* 1 USTC ¶359, 7 AFTR 8469, 30 F.2d 622 (CA–2, 1929).
[23] *Charles F. Kahler,* 18 T.C. 31 (1952).

is collected. The income is earned when (1) all the events have occurred that fix the right to receive such income and (2) the amount to be received can be determined with reasonable accuracy.[24]

Generally, the taxpayer's rights to the income accrue when title to property passes to the buyer or the services are performed for the customer or client.[25] If the rights to the income have accrued but are subject to a potential refund claim (e.g., under a product warranty), the income is reported in the year of sale, and a deduction is allowed in subsequent years when actual claims accrue.[26]

Where the taxpayer's rights to the income are being contested (e.g., when a contractor fails to meet specifications), the year in which the income is subject to tax depends upon whether payment has been received. If payment has not been received, no income is recognized until the claim is settled. Only then is the right to the income established.[27] However, if the payment is received before the dispute is settled, the court-made **claim of right doctrine** requires the taxpayer to recognize the income in the year of receipt.[28]

Example 6

A contractor completed a building in 1997 and presented a bill to the customer. The customer refused to pay the bill and claimed that the contractor had not met specifications. A settlement with the customer was not reached until 1998. No income would accrue to the contractor until 1998. If the customer paid for the work and then filed suit for damages, the contractor could not defer the income (the income would be taxable in 1997). ▼

The measure of accrual basis income is generally the amount the taxpayer has a right to receive. Unlike the cash basis, the fair market value of the customer's obligation is irrelevant in measuring accrual basis income.

Example 7

Assume the same facts as in Example 5, except Dana is an accrual basis taxpayer. Dana must recognize $13,000 ($8,000 + $5,000) income in 1997, the year her rights to the income accrued. ▼

Hybrid Method. The **hybrid method** is a combination of the accrual method and the cash method. Generally, when the hybrid method is used, inventory is an income-producing factor. Therefore, the Regulations require that the accrual method be used for determining sales and cost of goods sold. In this circumstance, to simplify record keeping, the taxpayer accounts for inventory using the accrual method and uses the cash method for all other income and expense items (e.g., dividend and interest income). The hybrid method is primarily used by small businesses.

EXCEPTIONS APPLICABLE TO CASH BASIS TAXPAYERS

Constructive Receipt. Income that has not actually been received by the taxpayer is taxed as though it had been received—the income is constructively received—under the following conditions:

- The amount is made readily available to the taxpayer.
- The taxpayer's actual receipt is not subject to substantial limitations or restrictions.[29]

---

[24] Reg. § 1.451–1(a).
[25] *Lucas v. North Texas Lumber Co.*, 2 USTC ¶484, 8 AFTR 10276, 50 S.Ct. 184 (USSC, 1930).
[26] *Brown v. Helvering*, 4 USTC ¶1222, 13 AFTR 851, 54 S.Ct. 356 (USSC, 1933).
[27] *Burnet v. Sanford and Brooks*, 2 USTC ¶636, 9 AFTR 603, 51 S.Ct. 150 (USSC, 1931).
[28] *North American Oil Consolidated Co. v. Burnet*, 3 USTC ¶943, 11 AFTR 16, 52 S.Ct. 613 (USSC, 1932).
[29] Reg. § 1.451–2(a).

The rationale for the **constructive receipt** doctrine is that if the income is available, the taxpayer should not be allowed to postpone the income recognition. For instance, a taxpayer is not permitted to defer income for December services by refusing to accept payment until January. However, determining whether the income is *readily available* and whether *substantial limitations or restrictions exist* necessitates a factual inquiry that leads to a judgment call.[30] The following are some examples of the application of the constructive receipt doctrine.

EXAMPLE 8 Ted is a member of a barter club. In 1997, Ted performed services for other club members and earned 1,000 points. Each point entitles him to $1 in goods and services sold by other members of the club; the points can be used at any time. In 1998, Ted exchanged his points for a new color TV. Ted must recognize $1,000 income in 1997 when the 1,000 points were credited to his account.[31] ▼

EXAMPLE 9 On December 31, an employer issued a bonus check to an employee but asked her to hold it for a few days until the company could make deposits to cover the check. The income was not constructively received on December 31 since the issuer did not have sufficient funds in its account to pay the debt.[32] ▼

EXAMPLE 10 Rick owned interest coupons that matured on December 31. The coupons could be converted to cash at any bank at maturity. Thus, the income is constructively received on December 31.[33] ▼

EXAMPLE 11 Dove Company mails dividend checks on December 31, 1997. The checks will not be received by shareholders until January. The shareholders do not realize income until 1998.[34] ▼

The constructive receipt doctrine does not reach income that the taxpayer is not yet entitled to receive even though he or she could have contracted to receive the income at an earlier date.

EXAMPLE 12 Sara offered to pay Ivan $100,000 for land in December 1997. Ivan refused but offered to sell the land to Sara on January 1, 1998, when he would be in a lower tax bracket. If Sara accepts Ivan's offer, the gain is taxed to Ivan in 1998 when the sale is completed.[35] ▼

Income set apart or made available is not constructively received if its actual receipt is subject to *substantial restrictions*. The life insurance industry has used substantial restrictions as a cornerstone for designing life insurance contracts with favorable tax features. Ordinary life insurance policies provide (1) current protection—an amount payable in the event of death—and (2) a savings feature—a cash surrender value payable to the policyholder if the policy is terminated during his or her life. The annual increase in cash surrender value is not taxable because the policyholder must cancel the policy to actually receive the increase in value. Because the cancellation requirement is a substantial restriction, the policyholder does not constructively receive the annual increase in cash surrender value.[36] Employees often receive from their employers property subject to substantial restrictions. Generally, no income is recognized until the restrictions lapse.[37]

---

[30] *Baxter v. Comm.*, 87–1 USTC ¶9315, 59 AFTR2d 87–1068, 816 F.2d 493 (CA–9, 1987).
[31] Rev.Rul. 80–52, 1980–1 C.B. 100.
[32] *L. M. Fischer*, 14 T.C. 792 (1950).
[33] Reg. § 1.451–2(b).
[34] Reg. § 1.451–2(b).
[35] *Cowden v. Comm.*, 61–1 USTC ¶9382, 7 AFTR2d 1160, 289 F.2d 20 (CA–5, 1961).
[36] *Theodore H. Cohen*, 39 T.C. 1055 (1963).
[37] § 83(a). See also the discussion of Restricted Property Plans in Chapter 19.

EXAMPLE 13 Carlos is a key employee of Red, Inc. The corporation gave stock with a value of $10,000 to Carlos. The stock could not be sold, however, for five years. Carlos will not be required to recognize income until the restrictions lapse at the end of five years. ▼

Original Issue Discount. Lenders frequently make loans that require a payment at maturity of more than the amount of the original loan. The difference between the amount due at maturity and the amount of the original loan is actually interest but is referred to as **original issue discount.** Under the general rules of tax accounting, the cash basis lender would not report the original issue discount as interest income until the year the amount is collected, although an accrual basis borrower would deduct the interest as it is earned. However, the Code puts the lender and borrower on parity by requiring that the original issue discount be reported when it is earned, regardless of the taxpayer's accounting method.[38] The interest "earned" is calculated by the effective interest rate method.

EXAMPLE 14 On January 1, 1997, Mark, a cash basis taxpayer, paid $82,645 for a 24-month certificate. The certificate was priced to yield 10% (the effective interest rate) with interest compounded annually. No interest was paid until maturity, when Mark received $100,000. Thus, Mark's gross income from the certificate is $17,355 ($100,000 − $82,645). Mark's income earned each year is calculated as follows:

1997 (.10 × $82,645) =	$ 8,264
1998 [.10 × ($82,645 + $8,264)] =	9,091
	$17,355

▼

The original issue discount rules do not apply to U.S. savings bonds (discussed in the following paragraphs) or to obligations with a maturity date of one year or less from the date of issue.[39] See Chapter 16 for additional discussion of the tax treatment of original issue discount.

Series E and Series EE Bonds. Certain U.S. government savings bonds (Series E before 1980 and Series EE after 1979) are issued at a discount and are redeemable for fixed amounts that increase at stated intervals. No interest payments are actually made. The difference between the purchase price and the amount received on redemption is the bondholder's interest income from the investment.

The income from these savings bonds is generally deferred until the bonds are redeemed or mature. Furthermore, Series E bonds can be exchanged within one year of their maturity date for Series HH bonds, and the interest on the Series E bonds can be further deferred until maturity of the Series HH bonds.[40] Thus, U.S. savings bonds have attractive income deferral features not available with corporate bonds and certificates of deposit issued by financial institutions.

Of course, the deferral feature of government bonds issued at a discount is not an advantage if the investor has insufficient income to be subject to tax as the income accrues. In fact, the deferral may work to the investor's disadvantage if he or she has other income in the year the bonds mature or the bunching of the bond interest into one tax year creates a tax liability. Fortunately, U.S. government bonds

---

[38] §§ 1272(a)(3) and 1273(a).
[39] § 1272(a)(2).
[40] Treas. Dept. Circulars No. 1–80 and No. 2–80, 1980–1 C.B. 714, 715. Note that interest is paid at semiannual intervals on the Series HH bonds and must be included in income as received. Refer to Chapter 5 for a discussion of the savings bond interest exclusion.

have a provision for these investors. A cash basis taxpayer can elect to include in gross income the annual increment in redemption value.[41]

EXAMPLE 15

Kate purchases Series EE U.S. savings bonds for $500 (face value of $1,000) on January 2 of the current year. If the bonds are redeemed during the first six months, no interest is paid. At December 31, the redemption value is $519.60.

If Kate elects to report the interest income annually, she must report interest income of $19.60 for the current year. If she does not make the election, she will report no interest income for the current year. ▼

When a taxpayer elects to report the income from the bonds on an annual basis, the election applies to all such bonds the taxpayer owns at the time of the election and to all such securities acquired subsequent to the election. A change in the method of reporting the income from the bonds requires permission from the IRS.

Amounts Received under an Obligation to Repay. The receipt of funds with an obligation to repay that amount in the future is the essence of borrowing. Because the taxpayer's assets and liabilities increase by the same amount, no income is realized when the borrowed funds are received. Because amounts paid to the taxpayer by mistake and customer deposits are often classified as borrowed funds, receipt of the funds is not a taxable event.

EXAMPLE 16

A landlord receives a damage deposit from a tenant. The landlord does not recognize income until the deposit is forfeited because the landlord has an obligation to repay the deposit if no damage occurs.[42] However, if the deposit is in fact a prepayment of rent, it is taxed in the year of receipt. ▼

EXCEPTIONS APPLICABLE TO ACCRUAL BASIS TAXPAYERS

Prepaid Income. For financial reporting purposes, advance payments received from customers are reflected as prepaid income and as a liability of the seller. However, for tax purposes, the prepaid income often is taxed in the year of receipt.

EXAMPLE 17

In December 1997, a tenant paid his January 1998 rent of $1,000. The accrual basis landlord must include the $1,000 in his 1997 income for tax purposes, although the unearned rent income is reported as a liability on the landlord's December 31, 1997, balance sheet. ▼

Taxpayers have repeatedly argued that deferral of income until it is actually earned properly matches revenues and expenses. Moreover, a proper matching of income with the expenses of earning the income is necessary to clearly reflect income, as required by the Code. The IRS responds that § 446(b) grants it broad powers to determine whether an accounting method clearly reflects income. The IRS further argues that generally accepted financial accounting principles should not dictate tax accounting for prepaid income because of the practical problems of collecting Federal revenues. Collection of the tax is simplest in the year the taxpayer receives the cash from the customer or client.

Over 40 years of litigation, the IRS has been only partially successful in the courts. In cases involving prepaid income from services to be performed at the demand of customers (e.g., dance lessons to be taken at any time in a 24-month

---

[41] § 454(a).
[42] *John Mantell*, 17 T.C. 1143 (1952).

period), the IRS's position has been upheld.[43] In such cases, the taxpayer's argument that deferral of the income was necessary to match the income with expenses was not persuasive because the taxpayer did not know precisely when each customer would demand services and, thus, when the expenses would be incurred. However, taxpayers have had some success in the courts when the services were performed on a fixed schedule (e.g., a baseball team's season-ticket sales).[44] In some cases involving the sale of goods, taxpayers have successfully argued that the prepayments were mere deposits[45] or in the nature of loans.[46]

Against this background of mixed results in the courts, congressional intervention, and taxpayers' strong resentment of the IRS's position, in 1971 the IRS modified its prepaid income rules, as explained in the following paragraphs.

Deferral of Advance Payments for Goods.
Generally, a taxpayer can elect to defer recognition of income from *advance payments for goods* if the method of accounting for the sale is the same for tax and financial reporting purposes.[47]

EXAMPLE 18
Brown Company will ship goods only after payment for the goods has been received. In December 1997, Brown received $10,000 for goods that were not shipped until January 1998. Brown can elect to report the income for tax purposes in 1998, assuming the company reports the income in 1998 for financial reporting purposes. ▼

Deferral of Advance Payments for Services.
Revenue Procedure 71–21[48] permits an accrual basis taxpayer to defer recognition of income for *advance payments for services* to be performed by the end of the tax year following the year of receipt. No deferral is allowed if the taxpayer might be required to perform any services, under the agreement, after the tax year following the year of receipt of the advance payment. In addition, prepaid rent and prepaid interest cannot be deferred under this revenue procedure.

EXAMPLE 19
Yellow Corporation, an accrual basis taxpayer, sells its services under 12-month, 18-month, and 24-month contracts. The corporation provides services to each customer every month. In April of 1997, Yellow Corporation sold the following customer contracts:

Length of Contract	Total Proceeds
12 months	$6,000
18 months	3,600
24 months	2,400

Fifteen hundred dollars of the $6,000 may be deferred ($3/12 \times \$6,000$), and $1,800 of the $3,600 may be deferred ($9/18 \times \$3,600$) because those amounts will not be earned until 1998. However, the entire $2,400 received on the 24-month contracts is taxable in the year of

---

[43] *American Automobile Association v. U.S.*, 61–2 USTC ¶9517, 7 AFTR2d 1618, 81 S.Ct. 1727 (USSC, 1961); *Schlude v. Comm.*, 63–1 USTC ¶9284, 11 AFTR2d 751, 83 S.Ct. 601 (USSC, 1963).

[44] *Artnell Company v. Comm.*, 68–2 USTC ¶9593, 22 AFTR2d 5590, 400 F.2d 981 (CA–7, 1968). See also *Boise Cascade Corp. v. U.S.*, 76–1 USTC ¶9203, 37 AFTR2d 76–696, 530 F.2d 1367 (Ct. Cls., 1976).

[45] *Veenstra & DeHavaan Coal Co.*, 11 T.C. 964 (1948).

[46] *Consolidated-Hammer Dry Plate & Film Co. v. Comm.*, 63–1 USTC ¶9494, 11 AFTR2d 1518, 317 F.2d 829 (CA–7, 1963); *Comm. v. Indianapolis Power & Light Co.*, 90–1 USTC ¶50,007, 65 AFTR2d 90–394, 110 S.Ct. 589 (USSC, 1990).

[47] Reg. § 1.451–5(b). See Reg. § 1.451–5(c) for exceptions to this deferral opportunity. The financial accounting conformity requirement is not applicable to contractors who use the completed contract method.

[48] 1971–2 C.B. 549.

receipt (1997), since a part of the income will still be unearned by the end of the tax year following the year of receipt (part will be earned in 1999). ▼

In summary, Revenue Procedure 71–21 will result in conformity of tax and financial accounting in a very limited number of prepaid income cases. It is not apparent why prepaid rents and interest may not be deferred, why revenues under some service contracts may be spread over two years, and why revenues under longer service contracts must be reported in one year. Although Revenue Procedure 71–21 has reduced the number of controversies involving prepaid income, a consistent policy has not yet evolved.

INCOME SOURCES

PERSONAL SERVICES

3 LEARNING OBJECTIVE
Identify who should pay the tax on a particular item of income in various situations.

It is a well-established principle of taxation that income from personal services must be included in the gross income of the person who performs the services. This principle was first established in a Supreme Court decision, *Lucas v. Earl*.[49] Mr. Earl entered into a binding agreement with his wife under which Mrs. Earl was to receive one-half of Mr. Earl's salary. Justice Holmes used the celebrated **fruit and tree metaphor** to explain that the fruit (income) must be attributed to the tree from which it came (Mr. Earl's services). A mere **assignment of income** does not shift the liability for the tax.

Services of an Employee. Services performed by an employee for the employer's customers are considered performed by the employer. Thus, the employer is taxed on the income from the services provided to the customer, and the employee is taxed on any compensation received from the employer.[50]

EXAMPLE 20

Dr. Shontelle incorporated her medical practice and entered into a contract to work for the corporation for a salary. All patients contracted to receive their services from the corporation, and those services were provided through the corporation's employee, Dr. Shontelle. The corporation must include the patients' fees in its gross income. Dr. Shontelle must include her salary in her gross income. The corporation will be allowed a deduction for the reasonable salary paid to Dr. Shontelle (see the discussion of unreasonable compensation in Chapter 6). ▼

Services of a Child. In the case of a child, the Code specifically provides that amounts earned from personal services must be included in the child's gross income. This result applies even though the income is paid to other persons (e.g., the parents).[51]

INCOME FROM PROPERTY

Income from property (interest, dividends, rent) must be included in the gross income of the *owner* of the property. If a father clips interest coupons from bonds shortly before the interest payment date and gives the coupons to his son, the

---

[49] 2 USTC ¶496, 8 AFTR 10287, 50 S.Ct. 241 (USSC, 1930).
[50] *Sargent v. Comm.*, 91–1 USTC ¶50,168, 67 AFTR2d 91–718, 929 F.2d 1252 (CA–8, 1991).
[51] § 73. For circumstances in which the child's unearned income is taxed at the parents' rate, see Unearned Income of Certain Minor Children Taxed at Parents' Rate in Chapter 3.

interest will still be taxed to the father. A father who assigns rents from rental property to his daughter will be taxed on the rent since he retains ownership of the property.[52]

Often income-producing property is transferred after income from the property has accrued but before the income is recognized under the transferor's method of accounting. The IRS and the courts have developed rules to allocate the income between the transferor and the transferee.

Interest. According to the IRS, interest accrues daily. Therefore, the interest for the period that includes the date of the transfer is allocated between the transferor and transferee based on the number of days during the period that each owned the property.

EXAMPLE 21

Floyd, a cash basis taxpayer, gave his son, Seth, bonds with a face amount of $10,000 and an 8% stated annual interest rate. The gift was made on January 31, 1997, and the interest was paid on December 31, 1997. Floyd must recognize $68 in interest income (8% × $10,000 × $31/366$). Seth will recognize $732 in interest income ($800 − $68). ▼

When the transferor must recognize the income from the property depends upon the method of accounting and the manner in which the property was transferred. In the case of a gift of income-producing property, the donor must recognize his or her share of the accrued income at the time it would have been recognized had the donor continued to own the property.[53] However, if the transfer is a sale, the transferor must recognize the accrued income at the time of the sale. This results because the accrued interest will be included in the sales proceeds.

EXAMPLE 22

Assume the same facts as in Example 21, except the interest that was payable as of December 31 was not actually or constructively received by the bondholders until January 3, 1998. As a cash basis taxpayer, Floyd generally does not recognize interest income until it is received. If Floyd had continued to own the bonds, the interest would have been included in his 1998 gross income, the year it would have been received. Therefore, Floyd must include the $68 accrued income in his gross income as of January 3, 1998.

Further assume that Floyd sold identical bonds on the date of the gift. The bonds sold for $9,900, including accrued interest. On January 31, 1997, Floyd must recognize the accrued interest of $68 on the bonds sold. Thus, the selling price of the bonds is $9,832 ($9,900 − $68). ▼

Dividends. A corporation is taxed on its earnings, and the shareholders are taxed on the dividends paid to them from the corporation's after-tax earnings. The dividend can take the form of an actual dividend or a constructive dividend (e.g., shareholder use of corporate assets).

Unlike interest, dividends do not accrue on a daily basis because the declaration of a dividend is at the discretion of the corporation's board of directors. Generally, dividends are taxed to the person who is entitled to receive them—the shareholder of record as of the corporation's record date.[54] Thus, if a taxpayer sells stock after a dividend has been declared but before the record date, the dividend generally will be taxed to the purchaser.

---

[52] *Galt v. Comm.*, 54–2 USTC ¶9457, 46 AFTR 633, 216 F.2d 41 (CA–7, 1954); *Helvering v. Horst*, 40–2 USTC ¶9787, 24 AFTR 1058, 61 S.Ct. 144 (USSC, 1940).

[53] Rev.Rul. 72–312, 1972–1 C.B. 22.

[54] Reg. § 1.61–9(c). The record date is the cutoff for determining the shareholders who are entitled to receive the dividend.

a. What effect does the settlement have on Liz's gross income?
b. Assume Liz also collected $30,000 of damages for slander to her personal reputation caused by the bill collector misrepresenting the facts to Liz's employer and other creditors. Is this $30,000 included in Liz's gross income?

41. Determine the taxpayer's taxable damages in each of the following cases:
    a. Orange Corporation collected $500,000 for damages to its business reputation.
    b. Don collected $100,000 in lost wages caused by age discrimination by his employer. Under the relevant law, a successful plaintiff can recover only lost wages.
    c. Kirby was injured in an automobile accident and collected $10,000 for loss of the use of his left arm, $15,000 for pain and suffering, $9,000 in lost wages, $5,000 for medical expenses, and $10,000 of punitive damages. Kirby had deducted none of the medical expenses.
    d. Nell received $10,000 of damages for invasion of her privacy by a photographer and $5,000 of punitive damages.
    e. Joanne received compensatory damages of $50,000 and punitive damages of $200,000 from a cosmetic surgeon who botched her nose job.

42. Rex, age 45, is an officer of Blue Company, which provided him with the following nondiscriminatory fringe benefits in 1997:
    a. Hospitalization insurance for Rex and his dependents. The cost of coverage for Rex was $450, and the additional cost for Rex's dependents was $400.
    b. Reimbursement of $700 from an uninsured medical reimbursement plan available to all employees.
    c. Group term life insurance protection of $120,000. (Each employee received coverage equal to twice his or her annual salary.)
    d. Salary continuation payments of $2,600 while Rex was hospitalized for an illness.

    While Rex was ill, he collected $1,600 on a salary continuation insurance policy he had purchased. Determine the amounts Rex must include in gross income.

43. The UVW Union and HON Corporation are negotiating contract terms. Assume the union members are in the 28% marginal tax bracket and all benefits are provided on a nondiscriminatory basis. Write a letter to the UVW Union members explaining the tax consequences of the options discussed below. The union's address is 905 Spruce Street, Washington, D.C. 20227.
    a. The company would impose a $100 deductible on medical insurance benefits. Most employees incur more than $100 each year in medical expenses.
    b. Employees would get an additional paid holiday with the same annual income (the same pay but less work).
    c. An employee who did not need health insurance (because the employee's spouse works and receives family coverage) would be allowed to receive the cash value of the coverage.

44. Sally and Bill are married and file joint returns. In 1997, Bill, an accountant, has a salary of $75,000, and Sally receives a salary of $25,000 as an apartment manager. What are the tax consequences of the following benefits that Bill and Sally's employers provide?
    a. Bill receives a reimbursement of $5,000 for child care expenses. Sally and Bill have three children who are not yet school age.
    b. Bill and Sally are provided a free membership at a local fitness and exercise club that allows them to attend three aerobic exercise sessions per week. The value of this type of membership is $450.
    c. Bill is provided free parking at work. The value of the parking is $1,500 per year.
    d. Sally is provided with a free apartment. Living in this apartment is a condition of her employment. Similar apartments rent for $1,000 per month.

45. Determine the taxpayer's gross income for each of the following:
    a. Alice is the manager of a plant. The company owns a house one mile from the plant (rental value of $6,000) that Alice is allowed to occupy.

b. Pam works for an insurance company that allows employees to eat in the cafeteria for $.50 a meal. Generally, the cost to the insurance company of producing a meal is $5.00, and a comparable meal could be purchased for $4.00. Pam ate 150 meals in the cafeteria during the year.

c. Wade is a Methodist minister and receives a housing allowance of $600 per month from his church. Wade is buying his home and uses the $600 to make house payments ($450) and to pay utilities ($150).

d. Floyd is a college professor and lives in campus housing. He is not charged rent. The fair market value of the house is $100,000, and the annual rental value is $7,200.

46. Does the taxpayer recognize gross income in the following situations?
    a. Ann is a registered nurse working in a community hospital. She is not required to take her lunch on the hospital premises, but she can eat in the cafeteria at no charge. The hospital adopted this policy to encourage employees to stay on the premises and be available in case of emergencies. During the year, Ann ate most of her meals on the premises. The total value of those meals was $750.
    b. Ira is the manager of a hotel. His employer will allow him to live in one of the rooms rent-free or to receive a $600 per month cash allowance for rent. Ira elected to live in the hotel.
    c. Seth is a forest ranger and lives in his employer's cabin in the forest. He is required to live there, and because there are no restaurants nearby, the employer supplies Seth with groceries that he cooks and eats on the premises.
    d. Rocky is a partner in the BAR Ranch (a partnership). He is the full-time manager of the ranch. BAR has a business purpose for Rocky's living on the ranch.

47. Betty is considering taking an early retirement offered by her employer. She would receive $1,500 per month, indexed for inflation. However, she would no longer be able to use the company's health facilities, and she would be required to pay her hospitalization insurance of $6,000 each year. Betty and her husband will file a joint return and take the standard deduction. She currently receives a salary of $37,500 a year, and her employer pays for all of her hospitalization insurance. If she retires, Betty would not be able to use her former employer's exercise facilities because of the commuting distance. She would like to continue to exercise, however, and will therefore join a health club at a cost of $50 per month. Betty and her husband have other sources of income and are in and will remain in the 28% marginal tax bracket. She currently pays Social Security taxes of 7.65% on her salary, but her retirement pay would not be subject to this tax. She will earn about $9,000 a year from a part-time job. Betty would like to know whether she should accept the early retirement offer.

48. Sparrow, Inc., has a wide variety of fringe benefits available to its employees. However, not all of the employees actually need the benefits. For example, some employees have working spouses whose employers provide health insurance benefits for the employee's families. In addition, Sparrow reimburses up to $5,000 for child care costs, but not all of the employees have children. Some employees have expressed a strong interest in long-term care insurance. Sparrow's management has asked you to write a memo explaining how the company can accommodate the varying needs of its employees at the lowest after-tax cost to the employee. Sparrow's address is 300 Harbor Drive, Vermillion, SD 57069.

49. Ed is employed by FUN Bowling Lanes, Inc. Determine Ed's gross income in each of the following situations:
    a. Ed's children are allowed to use the lanes without charge. Each child can also bring a friend without charge. This benefit is available to all employees. During the year, the children bowled 100 games, and the usual charge was $1.50 per game. Friends of Ed's children bowled 90 games.
    b. The company has a lunch counter. Ed is allowed to take home the leftover donuts each night. The company's cost was $450, and the value of the donuts Ed took home was $100.
    c. The company pays Ed's subscription to *Bowling Lanes Management*, a monthly journal.

CHAPTER 5 Gross Income: Exclusions

50. Thrush Corporation has 10 employees and is considering offering group hospitalization benefits. The average cost is $3,000 per employee per year. Three of the employees are shareholders and are in the 40% (combined Federal and state) income tax bracket; they currently pay for their own health insurance. The corporation is in the 34% marginal tax bracket. The remaining 7 employees who are not shareholders are considering taking a $1,500 per year pay cut in exchange for the hospitalization benefits. These employees are in the 30% (combined Federal and state) income tax bracket.
    a. Evaluate this proposal for the 7 employees.
    b. Write a memo explaining the after-tax effects on the employees and the corporation of providing health insurance to all employees. Thrush's address is 500 Fern Avenue, Scranton, PA 18509.

51. Tara's employer provides a flexible benefits plan. Under the plan, medical and dental expenses incurred during the year that are not covered by the company's group health insurance plan will be paid by the flexible benefits plan. At the first of each year, the employee must set the amount to be covered by the plan. The employee's monthly salary is reduced by one-twelfth of the identified flexible benefit amount for the year. Tara thinks it is highly unlikely that she can accurately estimate her medical and dental expenses not covered by the company's group health insurance plan, but she feels these costs will probably be in the range of $1,500 to $2,500. She expects to be in the 28% marginal tax bracket. Tara would like your advice regarding how much she should reduce her salary in exchange for the expanded dental and medical benefits.

52. Snowbird Corporation would like you to review its employee fringe benefits program with regard to the effects of the plan on the company's president (Polly), who is also the majority shareholder:
    a. All employees receive free tickets to State University football games. Polly is seldom able to attend the games and usually gives her tickets to her nephew. The cost of Polly's tickets for the year was $75.
    b. The company pays all parking fees for its officers but not for other employees. The company paid $1,200 for Polly's parking for the year.
    c. Employees are allowed to use the copy machine for personal purposes as long as the privilege is not abused. Polly is president of a trade association and made extensive use of the copy machine to prepare mailings to members of the association. The cost of the copies was $900.
    d. The company is in the household moving business. Employees are allowed to ship goods without charge whenever there is excess space on a truck. Polly purchased a dining room suite for her daughter. Company trucks delivered the furniture to the daughter. Normal freight charges would have been $600.
    e. The company has a storage facility for household goods. Officers are allowed a 20% discount on charges for storing their goods. All other employees are allowed a 10% discount. Polly's discounts for the year totaled $400.

53. Eli works for a company that operates a cruise ship. All employees are allowed to take a one-week cruise each year at no cost to the employee. The employee is provided with a room, meals, and general recreation on the ship. Determine the tax consequences of Eli accepting a trip under the following assumptions:
    a. Eli must travel on a standby basis; that is, Eli can travel only if the ship is not completely booked. The room Eli occupies has maid service, and the sheets and towels are changed each day.
    b. Eli takes his meals with the other customers who pay a fixed amount for the cruise that includes meals and lodging.
    c. The recreation consists of the use of the pool, dancing, and bingo games.
    d. All guests must pay for their drinks and snacks between meals, but Eli and the other employees are given a 20% discount.
    e. Employees at Eli's level and above are provided with free parking at the pier. Parking for the week would cost $70. This group comprises about 25% of all employees of the company.

54. George, a U.S. citizen, is employed by Pelican, Inc., a global company. His salary for 1997 is $60,000 and his 1998 salary is $80,000. George's first foreign assignment is to St. Petersburg, Russia, and began on July 1, 1997. He works in St. Petersburg until December 31, 1998. Being a workaholic, George did not take any vacation during this period.
    a. Compute George's 1997 salary that is includible in his gross income.
    b. Compute George's 1998 salary that is includible in his gross income.

55. Determine Hazel's gross income from the following receipts for the year:

Gain on sale of Augusta County bonds	$ 600
Interest on U.S. government savings bonds	900
Interest on state income tax refund	150
Interest on Augusta County bonds	900
Patronage dividend from Potato Growers Cooperative	1,700

    The patronage dividend was received in March of the current year for amounts paid and deducted in the previous year as expenses of Hazel's profitable cash basis farming business.

56. Determine Jack's gross income from the following items:
    a. Jack owns 100 shares of Roadrunner Company common stock. The company has a dividend reinvestment plan. Under the plan, Jack can receive an $18 cash dividend or an additional share of stock with a fair market of $18. Jack elected to take the stock.
    b. Jack owns 100 shares of Bat Corporation. The company declared a dividend, and Jack was to receive an additional share of the company's common stock with a fair market value of $18. Jack did not have the option to receive cash. However, a management group announced a plan to repurchase all available shares for $18 each. The offer was part of a takeover defense.
    c. Jack also collected $125 on a corporate debenture. The corporation had been in bankruptcy for several years. Jack had correctly deducted the cost of the bond in a prior year because the bankruptcy judge had informed the bondholders they would not receive anything in the final liquidation. Later the company collected on an unanticipated claim and had the funds to make partial payment on the bonds.

57. Lynn Schwartz recently inherited $25,000. She is considering using the money to finance a college education for her 5-year-old child. Lynn does not expect her gross income to ever exceed $40,000 a year. She is very concerned with the safety of the principal and has decided to invest the $25,000 in Series EE U.S. government savings bonds. The bonds earn 5% interest each year. At the end of 13 years, when Lynn's child is 18 and ready to go to college, the bonds will be worth $44,375. This would pay a substantial portion of the cost of a 4-year college education at that time. Write a letter to Lynn advising her as to whether the Series EE bonds will be an appropriate investment for financing her child's college education, including whether the bonds should be purchased in Lynn's name or in the child's name (with Lynn as custodian). Lynn's address is 100 Myrtle Cove, Fairfield, CT 06432.

58. Starting in 1990, Chuck and Luane have been purchasing Series EE bonds in their name to use for the higher education of their daughter (Susie who currently is age 18). During the year, they cash in $12,000 of the bonds to use for freshman year tuition, fees, and room and board. Of this amount, $5,000 represents interest. Of the $12,000, $8,000 is used for tuition and fees, and $4,000 is used for room and board. Their AGI, before the educational savings bond exclusion, is $80,000.
    a. Determine the tax consequences for Chuck and Luane, who will file a joint return, and for Susie.
    b. Assume that Chuck and Luane purchased the bonds in Susie's name. Determine the tax consequences for Chuck and Luane and for Susie.
    c. How would your answer for (a) change if Chuck and Luane file separate returns?

59. Carlos made payments to the Qualified State Tuition Program for the benefit of his son, Ramon. Carlos contributed $4,000 each year for a four-year period. This will satisfy Ramon's tuition and fees for four years of college. At the time of Ramon's freshman year, the tuition and fees have increased to $6,000 per year. Determine the effect on Carlos and Ramon's gross income for Ramon's freshman year.

60. How does the tax benefit rule apply in the following cases?
    a. In 1997, Wilma paid Vera $5,000 for locating a potential client. The deal fell through, and in 1998, Vera refunded the $5,000 to Wilma.
    b. In 1997, Wilma paid an attorney $300 for services in connection with a title search. Because the attorney was negligent, Wilma incurred some additional costs in acquiring the land. In 1998, the attorney refunded his $300 fee to Wilma.
    c. In 1997, Wilma received a $90 dividend with respect to 1997 premiums on her life insurance policy.
    d. In 1998, a cash basis farmer received a $400 patronage dividend with respect to 1997 purchases of cattle feed.

61. Mary and her two sisters, Cary and Gladys, were injured in a car accident in 1997, and each sustained injuries requiring $1,200 in medical expenses. Because the claim was not settled until 1998, each sister had completed her 1997 income tax return before the settlement. Mary does not itemize deductions. Cary does itemize deductions, but the $1,200 medical expense did not exceed the 7.5%-of-AGI threshold; consequently, the deduction did not result in a reduction of her tax liability. Gladys also itemizes deductions. Because of other medical expenses, the $1,200 expense pushed her $800 over the 7.5%-of-AGI threshold. Therefore, Gladys benefited from the deduction by having her taxes reduced. In 1998, each sister received a $1,200 insurance settlement for her injuries. How much of the $1,200 settlement received does each sister need to include in gross income?

62. Fran, who is in the 36% tax bracket, recently collected $100,000 on a life insurance policy she carried on her father. She currently owes $120,000 on her personal residence and $120,000 on business property. National Bank holds the mortgage on both pieces of property and has agreed to accept $100,000 in complete satisfaction of either mortgage. The interest rate on the mortgages is 8%, and both mortgages are payable over 10 years. What would be the tax consequences of each of the following alternatives, assuming Fran currently deducts the mortgage interest on her tax return?
    a. Retire the mortgage on the residence.
    b. Retire the mortgage on the business property.

    Which alternative should Fran select?

63. Robin Company is experiencing financial troubles and is considering negotiating the following with its creditors. Determine the tax consequences to Robin of the following plan:
    a. The Motor Finance Company will cancel $1,500 in accrued interest. Robin had deducted the interest in the prior year. Motor Finance Company will also reduce the principal on the note by $1,000. The note financed the purchase of equipment from a local dealer.
    b. The Trust Land Company, which sold Robin land and buildings, will reduce the mortgage on the building by $15,000.
    c. Ridge, the sole shareholder in the corporation, will cancel a $50,000 receivable from the corporation in exchange for additional stock.

CUMULATIVE PROBLEMS

64. Oliver W. Hand was divorced from Sandra D. Hand on May 12, 1996. On September 6, 1997, Oliver married Beulah Crane. Oliver and Beulah will file a joint return for 1997. Oliver's Social Security number is 262-60-3814. Beulah's number is 259-68-4184, and she will adopt "Hand" as her married name. The Hands live at 210 Mason Drive, Atlanta, GA 30304. Sandra's Social Security number is 219-74-1361.

Oliver is 50 and is employed by Atom, Inc., as an electrical engineer. His salary for 1997 was $60,000. Beulah is 35 and earned $37,000 as a marriage counselor in 1997. She was employed by Family Counselors, Inc.

The divorce agreement required Oliver to make 132 monthly payments to Sandra. The payments are $1,200 per month for 84 months, at which time the payments decrease to $1,000 per month. Oliver and Sandra have a 14-year-old daughter, Daisy Hand. If Daisy should die before she attains age 21, Oliver's remaining payments to Sandra would be reduced to $1,000 per month. Sandra was granted custody of Daisy and can document that she provided $2,000 of support for Daisy. Oliver made 12 payments in 1997.

Oliver's employer provided him with group term life insurance coverage in the amount of $100,000 in 1997.

Beulah's employer provided Beulah with free parking in a parking garage adjacent to the office building where Beulah works. The monthly charge to the general public is $65.

Oliver received dividends of $40 on Red Corporation stock he owned before marriage, and Beulah received dividends of $50 on her separately owned White Corporation stock. They received dividends of $600 on jointly owned Blue Corporation stock, which they acquired after marriage. Oliver and Beulah live in a common law state.

Combined itemized deductions for Oliver and Beulah in 1997 were as follows:

State income taxes withheld		
Oliver	$3,200	
Beulah	1,200	$4,400
Real estate taxes on residence		1,500
Home mortgage interest (paid to Atlanta Federal Savings and Loan)		4,020
Cash contributions to church		900

In 1997, Beulah received a refund of 1996 state income taxes of $700. She had deducted state income taxes withheld as an itemized deduction on her 1996 return. Oliver received a $500 refund on his 1996 state income taxes. He had used the standard deduction in 1996.

Additional information:

- Oliver's employer withheld Federal income tax of $10,650 and $4,590 of FICA (Social Security) tax. Beulah's employer withheld $4,580 of Federal income tax and $2,831 of FICA tax.

Part 1—Tax Computation
Compute the Hands' net tax payable (or refund due) for 1997. Suggested software (if available): *TurboTax* or *MacInTax*.

Part 2—Tax Planning
Assume the Hands came to you in early December of 1997 seeking tax planning advice for 1997 and 1998. They provide you with the following information:

a. All the facts previously presented will be essentially the same in 1998 except for the items described in (b), (c), (d), and (e).
b. Oliver inherited $100,000 from his mother on December 1. He will use part of his inheritance to pay off the mortgage on the Hands' residence on January 3, 1998. Consequently, there will be no mortgage interest expense in 1998.
c. Oliver expects a 4% salary increase in 1998, and Beulah expects a 10% increase.
d. The Hands have pledged to contribute $2,400 to their church in 1998 (as opposed to $900 contributed in 1997). However, they could use Oliver's inherited funds to pay the pledge before the end of 1997 if you advise them to do so to achieve an overall tax savings.

e. The Hands acquired 100 shares of ABC Corporation stock on July 5, 1997, at a total cost of $2,000. The value of the stock has increased rapidly, and it is now worth $5,000. The Hands plan to sell the stock and ask whether they should sell it in 1997 or wait until 1998.

Advise the Hands as to the appropriate tax planning strategy for 1997 and 1998. Support your recommendations by computing their tax liabilities for 1997 and 1998 considering the various available alternatives. Suggested software (if available): *TurboTax* or *MacInTax*.

65. Albert S. Moore (Social Security number 363–22–1141) is 35 years old and is married to Bonnie B. Moore (Social Security number 259–50–4284). The Moores live at 215 Harper's Road, Newport News, VA 23100. They file a joint return and have two dependent children (Bobby and Cindy). In 1997, Albert and Bonnie had the following transactions:
   a. Albert received $90,000 in salary from Plum Steel Company. He worked on a construction project in Mexico from July 1, 1996 through December 31, 1997. Withholding for Federal income tax was $11,000. The proper amount of FICA taxes was withheld.
   b. Albert and Bonnie received $1,200 of interest on U.S. government bonds and $600 of interest on Montgomery County School bonds.
   c. Bonnie was involved in an automobile accident in 1996 and incurred $12,000 of medical expenses. Insurance paid $8,000 of the expenses, and Albert and Bonnie deducted the remaining $4,000 on their 1996 return. During 1997, Bonnie received a settlement from the other driver's insurance company. She received $12,000 for her medical expenses, $65,000 as compensatory damages for the physical injury, and $35,000 of punitive damages.
   d. Bonnie received 10 shares of Cherry, Inc., as a stock dividend. The shares received had a fair market value of $360. Bonnie had the option of receiving cash equal to the value of the shares, but chose not to do so.
   e. Albert paid $9,000 of alimony to his first wife, Rosa T. Monroe (Social Security number 800–60–2580).
   f. Albert and Bonnie's itemized deductions were as follows:

   - State income taxes paid and withheld totaled $2,400. In addition, a $600 overpayment for their 1996 state taxes (deducted on the 1996 Federal return) was applied to their 1997 liability.

   - Real estate taxes on their principal residence were $1,500.

   - Interest on their principal residence was $3,600.

   - Cash contributions to the church were $2,200.

   Part 1—Tax Computation

   Compute the Moores' net tax payable (or refund due) for 1997. Suggested software (if available): *TurboTax* or *MacInTax*.

   Part 2—Tax Planning
   Assume the Moores provided you with the above information late in 1997. They are considering selling Orange, Inc., stock purchased in November 1997 for $6,000. The stock has a present and projected fair market value of $4,000. The sale could occur in late 1997 or early 1998. They do not expect any major changes in their income situation, except Albert's salary will increase to $125,000 and he will be working in the United States for the entire year. Write a letter to the Moores that contains your advice and prepare a memo for the tax files.

RESEARCH PROBLEMS

*Note: **West's Federal Taxation on CD-ROM** can be used in preparing solutions to the Research Problems. Alternatively, tax research materials contained in a standard tax library can be used.*

Research Problem 1. David Hobson is the minister at the First Baptist Church. As part of his compensation, David receives an $800 per month housing allowance. David is purchasing his residence, and he uses the $800 each month to make mortgage and property tax payments. The mortgage interest and property taxes are deducted (as itemized deductions) on David's tax return. The examining IRS agent thinks David would be enjoying a double benefit if the housing allowance is excluded and the itemized deductions are allowed. In addition, the agent contends that the housing allowance exclusion should apply only where the church provides the residence or the minister uses the funds to pay rent. Therefore, the agent maintains that David should include in gross income the $800 received each month. David has asked your assistance in this matter. Write a letter to David that contains your advice and prepare a memo for the tax files. David's address is 982 Richmond Drive, Hollis, OK 73550.

Research Problem 2. The Beige Real Estate Company borrowed $1,400,000 from the First National Bank to purchase a building. The loan was without recourse; that is, if Beige did not pay the mortgage, the bank could repossess the property. But if the fair market value of the property repossessed was less than the amount of the debt, Beige would not be responsible for the difference. When the fair market value of the property was $800,000 and the balance on the mortgage was $1,000,000, Beige was unable to make its monthly loan payment. After much negotiation, the bank reduced the principal to $800,000, which enabled Beige to make its payment in a timely manner. The IRS added $200,000 of income from discharge of indebtedness to Beige's taxable income for the year. Beige contends it has no gross income because the fair market value of the building is not more than the reduced principal of the debt. Advise Beige on who is correct.

Partial list of research aids:
Rev.Rul. 91–31, 1991–1 C.B. 19.

Research Problem 3. Cardinal City was experiencing cash-flow problems. Therefore, the city offered property owners a 3% discount if they would pay their property taxes six months before the due date. Electric Utilities, Inc., took advantage of the offer and received a $65,000 discount. The company deducted the undiscounted amount of the taxes and excluded the discount from gross income. The company reasons that the discount represents interest on local government obligations and thus is nontaxable under § 103. Evaluate the company's position.

Research Problem 4. Snipe Company is closing one of its plants. The company's management is very concerned about employee morale at other plants. To minimize the damage to employee relations, the company has decided to pay the costs of "outplacement services" for the employees of the plant to be closed. The services include the use of a consultant in writing resumés, identifying potential employers, and writing to those employers. The company has asked your advice as to whether the employees would be required to include the costs of the services in their gross incomes.

Use the tax resources of the internet to address the following questions. Do not restrict your search to the World Wide Web, but include a review of newsgroups and general reference materials, practitioner sites and resources, primary sources of the tax law, chat rooms and discussion groups, and other opportunities.

Research Problem 5. Go to the IRS site on the internet and download instructions and regulations relative to educational savings bonds and qualified state tuition programs. Summarize one of the key provisions in these materials in outline format.

Research Problem 6. Employers often use the internet as a means of attracting applications from potential employees. Locate an internet site offering employment opportunities, ideally one provided by a well-known corporation. How does the employer promote its fringe benefit and cafeteria plan packages? Contrast several such sites.

TEAM PROJECT: ARTHUR ANDERSEN TAX CHALLENGE CASES

For more information on the Arthur Andersen Tax Challenge Cases, refer to Chapter 1, page 1–38.

Information related to tax issues and problems that are discussed in this chapter may be found in the

Day and Ball case on pages 3, 5, 17, and 30
Miller case on pages 2, 3, 11, 13, 14, 15, 22, and 29

Read and analyze the case you have been assigned and *identify* any issues and problems that are related to material covered in this chapter. If the information provided in the case is complete, prepare answers for this part of the case at this time. If you need information that is contained in the later parts of the case, write a memo summarizing the questions or problems so you can prepare a complete answer at a later date.

PART III
DEDUCTIONS

Part III presents the deduction component of the basic tax model. Deductions are classified as business versus nonbusiness, "for" versus "from," employee versus employer, active versus passive, and reimbursed versus unreimbursed. The effect of each of these classifications is analyzed. The presentation includes not only the deductions that are permitted, but also limitations and disallowances associated with deductions. Because deductions can exceed gross income, the treatment of losses is also included.

Chapter 6
Deductions and Losses: In General

Chapter 7
Deductions and Losses: Certain Business Expenses and Losses

Chapter 8
Depreciation, Cost Recovery, Amortization, and Depletion

Chapter 9
Deductions: Employee Expenses

Chapter 10
Deductions and Losses: Certain Itemized Deductions

Chapter 11
Passive Activity Losses

CHAPTER 6

DEDUCTIONS AND LOSSES: IN GENERAL

LEARNING OBJECTIVES

After completing Chapter 6, you should be able to:

1. Differentiate between deductions *for* and *from* adjusted gross income and understand the relevance of the differentiation.

2. Describe the cash and accrual methods of accounting.

3. Apply the Internal Revenue Code deduction disallowance provisions associated with the following: public policy limitations, political activities, excessive executive compensation, investigation of business opportunities, hobby losses, vacation home rentals, payment of others' expenses, personal expenditures, capital expenditures, related-party transactions, and expenses related to tax-exempt income.

4. Identify tax planning opportunities for maximizing deductions and minimizing the disallowance of deductions.

OUTLINE

Classification of Deductible Expenses, 6-2
Deductions for Adjusted Gross Income, 6-3
Itemized Deductions, 6-4
Trade or Business Expenses and Production of Income Expenses, 6-5
Business and Nonbusiness Losses, 6-7
Reporting Procedures, 6-7
Deductions and Losses—Timing of Expense Recognition, 6-9
Importance of Taxpayer's Method of Accounting, 6-9
Cash Method Requirements, 6-9

Accrual Method Requirements, 6-10
Disallowance Possibilities, 6-11
Public Policy Limitation, 6-11
Political Contributions and Lobbying Activities, 6-14
Excessive Executive Compensation, 6-14
Investigation of a Business, 6-15
Hobby Losses, 6-16
Rental of Vacation Homes, 6-19
Expenditures Incurred for Taxpayer's Benefit or Taxpayer's Obligation, 6-23
Disallowance of Personal Expenditures, 6-25

Disallowance of Deductions for Capital Expenditures, 6-26
Transactions between Related Parties, 6-27
Substantiation Requirements, 6-28
Expenses and Interest Relating to Tax-Exempt Income, 6-29
Tax Planning Considerations, 6-30
Time Value of Tax Deductions, 6-30
Unreasonable Compensation, 6-32
Excessive Executive Compensation, 6-32
Shifting Deductions, 6-32
Hobby Losses, 6-32
Capital Expenditures, 6-33

CLASSIFICATION OF DEDUCTIBLE EXPENSES

1 LEARNING OBJECTIVE
Differentiate between deductions *for* and *from* adjusted gross income and understand the relevance of the differentiation.

The tax law has an all-inclusive definition of income; that is, income from whatever source derived is includible in gross income. Income cannot be excluded unless there is a specific statement to that effect in the Internal Revenue Code.

Similarly, deductions are disallowed unless a specific provision in the tax law permits them. The inclusive definition of income and the exclusive definition of deductions may not seem fair to taxpayers, but it is the structure of the tax law.

The courts have held that whether and to what extent deductions are allowed depends on legislative grace.[1] In other words, any exclusions from income and all deductions are gifts from Congress!

It is important to classify deductible expenses as **deductions for adjusted gross income** (AGI) or **deductions from adjusted gross income.** Deductions *for* AGI can be claimed whether or not the taxpayer itemizes. Deductions *from* AGI result in a tax benefit only if they exceed the taxpayer's standard deduction. If itemized deductions (*from* AGI) are less than the standard deduction, they provide no tax benefit.

EXAMPLE 1
Steve is a self-employed CPA. Ralph is one of Steve's employees. During the year, Steve and Ralph incur the following expenses:

	Steve	Ralph
Dues to American Institute of CPAs and State Society of CPAs	$ 400	$ 300
Subscriptions to professional journals	500	200
Registration fees for tax conferences	800	800
	$1,700	$1,300

---

[1] *New Colonial Ice Co. v. Helvering,* 4 USTC ¶1292, 13 AFTR 1180, 54 S.Ct. 788 (USSC, 1934).

Steve does not reimburse any of his employees for dues, subscriptions, or educational programs.

Steve's expenses are classified as a deduction *for* AGI. Therefore, he can deduct the $1,700 on his Federal income tax return. Ralph's expenses are classified as deductions *from* AGI. Ralph will be able to benefit from the $1,300 of expenses on his Federal income tax return only if he itemizes deductions. If he takes the standard deduction instead, the $1,300 of expenses will have no effect on the calculation of his taxable income. Even if Ralph does itemize deductions, he must reduce the $1,300 of expenses, which are classified as miscellaneous itemized deductions, by 2% of his AGI. As this example illustrates, whether a deduction is classified as *for* AGI or *from* AGI can affect the benefit the taxpayer receives from the deduction. ▼

Deductions *for* AGI are also important in determining the *amount* of itemized deductions because many itemized deductions are limited to amounts in excess of specified percentages of AGI. Examples of itemized deductions that are limited by AGI are medical expenses and personal casualty losses. Itemized deductions that are deductible only to the extent that they exceed a specified percentage of AGI are increased when AGI is decreased. Likewise, when AGI is increased, these itemized deductions are decreased.

EXAMPLE 2

Tina earns a salary of $20,000 and has no other income. She itemizes deductions during the current year. Medical expenses for the year are $1,800. Since medical expenses are deductible only to the extent they exceed 7.5% of AGI, Tina's medical expense deduction is $300 [$1,800 − (7.5% × $20,000)]. If Tina had a $2,000 deduction *for* AGI, her medical expense deduction would be $450 [$1,800 − (7.5% × $18,000)], or $150 more. If the $2,000 deduction was *from* AGI, her medical expense deduction would remain $300 since AGI is unchanged. ▼

DEDUCTIONS FOR ADJUSTED GROSS INCOME

To understand how deductions of individual taxpayers are classified, it is necessary to examine the role of § 62. The purpose of § 62 is to classify various deductions as deductions *for* AGI. It does not provide the statutory authority for taking the deduction. For example, § 212 allows individuals to deduct expenses attributable to income-producing property. Section 212 expenses that are attributable to rents or royalties are classified as deductions *for* AGI. Likewise, a deduction for trade or business expenses is allowed by § 162. These expenses are classified as deductions *for* AGI.

If a deduction is not listed in § 62, it is an itemized deduction, *not* a deduction *for* AGI. Following is a *partial* list of the items classified as deductions *for* AGI by § 62:

- Expenses attributable to a trade or business carried on by the taxpayer. A trade or business does not include the performance of services by the taxpayer as an employee.
- Expenses incurred by a taxpayer in connection with the performance of services as an employee if the expenses are reimbursed and other conditions are satisfied.
- Deductions that result from losses on the sale or exchange of property by the taxpayer.
- Deductions attributable to property held for the production of rents and royalties.
- The deduction for payment of alimony.
- Certain contributions to pension, profit sharing, and annuity plans of self-employed individuals.
- The deduction for certain retirement savings allowed by § 219 (e.g., IRAs).

> ## TAX IN THE NEWS
>
> ### AMERICA'S TEAM
>
> A political football is in the air with respect to tax reform, and it appears almost everybody wants to play. The "football" is the Federal income tax system.
>
> Numerous players, both Democrats and Republicans, are trying out for the team. The prospects include Rep. Bill Archer (chairman of the House Ways and Means Committee), Sen. Pete Domenici, Rep. Dick Armey (House Majority Leader), and Rep. Dick Gephardt (House Minority Leader). Even Newt Gingrich (Speaker of the House) is weighing what position he would like to play. Other members of Congress are expected to jockey for positions on the team. On the sidelines now but hoping to participate are Jack Kemp and Bill Bradley.
>
> A debate is raging over the rules of the game. Should the current income tax system be reformed or should it be replaced? Should the replacement be a flat tax, a consumption tax, or a value added tax? It is almost impossible to read a newspaper or turn on the TV without encountering a discussion of someone's tax proposal. Archer has stated, "I want to tear the income tax out by its roots," and Armey has said, "America needs nothing less than a completely new tax system." Not only are the players willing to take on the reform of the Federal income tax system, but some would like to go even further and repeal the Sixteenth Amendment to the U.S. Constitution.
>
> A key element in all of the proposals is simplicity. One method advocated for advancing simplicity is the elimination of deductions (a foundation of the flat tax proposals). As the legislative process goes forward, it will be interesting to observe the lobbying and debate over deductions and other components of the current Federal income tax system and to see what results finally emerge from the process.

- The penalty imposed on premature withdrawal of funds from time savings accounts or deposits.
- The deduction for moving expenses.

These items are covered in detail in various chapters in the text.

ITEMIZED DEDUCTIONS

The Code defines itemized deductions as the deductions allowed other than "the deductions allowable in arriving at adjusted gross income."[2] Thus, if a deduction is not properly classified as a deduction *for* AGI, then it is classified as an itemized deduction.

Section 212 Expenses.
Section 212 allows deductions for ordinary and necessary expenses paid or incurred for the following:

- The production or collection of income.
- The management, conservation, or maintenance of property held for the production of income.
- Expenses paid in connection with the determination, collection, or refund of any tax.

---
[2] § 63(d).

Section 212 expenses related to rent and royalty income are deductions *for* AGI.[3] Expenses paid in connection with the determination, collection, or refund of taxes related to the income of sole proprietorships, rents and royalties, or farming operations are deductions *for* AGI. All other § 212 expenses are itemized deductions (deductions *from* AGI). For example, investment-related expenses (e.g., safe deposit box rentals) are deductible as itemized deductions attributable to the production of investment income.[4]

Deductible Personal Expenses. Taxpayers are allowed to deduct certain expenses that are primarily personal in nature. These expenses, which generally are not related to the production of income, are deductions *from* AGI (itemized deductions). Some of the more frequently encountered deductions in this category include the following:

- Contributions to qualified charitable organizations (not to exceed a specified percentage of AGI).
- Medical expenses (in excess of 7.5 percent of AGI).
- Certain state and local taxes (e.g., real estate taxes and state and local income taxes).
- Personal casualty losses (in excess of an aggregate floor of 10 percent of AGI and a $100 floor per casualty).
- Certain personal interest (e.g., mortgage interest on a personal residence).

Itemized deductions are discussed in detail in Chapter 10.

TRADE OR BUSINESS EXPENSES AND PRODUCTION OF INCOME EXPENSES

Section 162(a) permits a deduction for all ordinary and necessary expenses paid or incurred in carrying on a trade or business. These include reasonable salaries paid for services, expenses for the use of business property, and one-half of self-employment taxes paid (see Chapter 13). Such expenses are deducted *for* AGI.

It is sometimes difficult to determine whether an expenditure is deductible as a trade or business expense. The term "trade or business" is not defined in the Code or Regulations, and the courts have not provided a satisfactory definition. It is usually necessary to ask one or more of the following questions to determine whether an item qualifies as a trade or business expense:

- Was the use of the particular item related to a business activity? For example, if funds are borrowed for use in a business, the interest is deductible as a business expense.
- Was the expenditure incurred with the intent to realize a profit or to produce income? For example, expenses in excess of the income from raising horses are not deductible if the activity is classified as a personal hobby rather than a trade or business.
- Were the taxpayer's operation and management activities extensive enough to indicate the carrying on of a trade or business?

Section 162 *excludes* the following items from classification as trade or business expenses:

- Charitable contributions or gifts.
- Illegal bribes and kickbacks and certain treble damage payments.
- Fines and penalties.

---

[3] § 62(a)(4).   [4] Reg. § 1.212–1(g).

A bribe paid to a domestic official is not deductible if it is illegal under the laws of the United States. Foreign bribes are deductible unless they are unlawful under the Foreign Corrupt Practices Act of 1977.[5]

Ordinary and Necessary Requirement. The terms **ordinary and necessary** are found in both §§ 162 and 212. To be deductible, any trade or business expense must be "ordinary and necessary." In addition, compensation for services must be "reasonable" in amount.

Many expenses that are necessary are *not* ordinary. Neither "ordinary" nor "necessary" is defined in the Code or Regulations. The courts have held that an expense is *necessary* if a prudent businessperson would incur the same expense and the expense is expected to be appropriate and helpful in the taxpayer's business.[6]

EXAMPLE 3

Pat purchased a manufacturing concern that had just been adjudged bankrupt. Because the business had a poor financial rating, Pat satisfied some of the obligations to employees and outside salespeople incurred by the former owners. Pat had no legal obligation to pay these debts, but felt this was the only way to keep salespeople and employees. The Second Court of Appeals found that the payments were necessary in that they were both appropriate and helpful.[7] However, the Court held that the payments were *not* ordinary but were in the nature of capital expenditures to build a reputation. Therefore, no deduction was allowed. ▼

An expense is *ordinary* if it is normal, usual, or customary in the type of business conducted by the taxpayer and is not capital in nature.[8] However, an expense need not be recurring to be deductible as ordinary.

EXAMPLE 4

Albert engaged in a mail-order business. The post office judged that his advertisements were false and misleading. Under a fraud order, the post office stamped "fraudulent" on all letters addressed to Albert's business and returned them to the senders. Albert spent $30,000 on legal fees in an unsuccessful attempt to force the post office to stop. The legal fees (though not recurring) were ordinary business expenses because they were normal, usual, or customary in the circumstances.[9] ▼

For § 212 deductions, the law requires that expenses bear a reasonable and proximate relationship to (1) the production or collection of income or to (2) the management, conservation, or maintenance of property held for the production of income.[10]

EXAMPLE 5

Wendy owns a small portfolio of investments, including 10 shares of Hawk, Inc., common stock worth $1,000. She incurred $350 in travel expenses to attend the annual shareholders' meeting at which she voted her 10 shares against the current management group. No deduction is permitted because a 10-share investment is insignificant in value in relation to the travel expenses incurred.[11] ▼

---

[5] § 162(c)(1).
[6] *Welch v. Helvering,* 3 USTC ¶1164, 12 AFTR 1456, 54 S.Ct. 8 (USSC, 1933).
[7] *Dunn and McCarthy, Inc. v. Comm.,* 43–2 USTC ¶9688, 31 AFTR 1043, 139 F.2d 242 (CA–2, 1943).
[8] *Deputy v. DuPont,* 40–1 USTC ¶9161, 23 AFTR 808, 60 S.Ct. 363 (USSC, 1940).
[9] *Comm. v. Heininger,* 44–1 USTC ¶9109, 31 AFTR 783, 64 S.Ct. 249 (USSC, 1943).
[10] Reg. § 1.212–1(d).
[11] *J. Raymond Dyer,* 36 T.C. 456 (1961).

Reasonableness Requirement. The Code refers to **reasonableness** solely with respect to salaries and other compensation for services.[12] But the courts have held that for any business expense to be ordinary and necessary, it must also be reasonable in amount.[13]

What constitutes reasonableness is a question of fact. If an expense is unreasonable, the excess amount is not allowed as a deduction. The question of reasonableness generally arises with respect to closely held corporations where there is no separation of ownership and management.

Transactions between the shareholders and the closely held company may result in the disallowance of deductions for excessive salaries and rent expense paid by the corporation to the shareholders. The courts will view an unusually large salary in light of all relevant circumstances and may find that the salary is reasonable despite its size.[14] If excessive payments for salaries and rents are closely related to the percentage of stock owned by the recipients, the payments are generally treated as dividends.[15] Since dividends are not deductible by the corporation, the disallowance results in an increase in the corporate taxable income. Deductions for reasonable salaries will not be disallowed *solely* because the corporation has paid insubstantial portions of its earnings as dividends to its shareholders.

EXAMPLE 6

Sparrow Corporation, a closely held corporation, is owned equally by Lupe, Carlos, and Ramon. The company has been highly profitable for several years and has not paid dividends. Lupe, Carlos, and Ramon are key officers of the company, and each receives a salary of $200,000. Salaries for similar positions in comparable companies average only $100,000. Amounts paid the owners in excess of $100,000 may be deemed unreasonable, and, if so, a total of $300,000 in salary deductions by Sparrow is disallowed. The disallowed amounts are treated as dividends rather than salary income to Lupe, Carlos, and Ramon because the payments are proportional to stock ownership. Salaries are deductible by the corporation, but dividends are not. ▼

BUSINESS AND NONBUSINESS LOSSES

Section 165 provides for a deduction for losses not compensated for by insurance. As a general rule, deductible losses of individual taxpayers are limited to those incurred in a trade or business or in a transaction entered into for profit. Individuals are also allowed to deduct losses that are the result of a casualty. Casualty losses include, but are not limited to, fire, storm, shipwreck, and theft. See Chapter 7 for a further discussion of this topic. Deductible personal casualty losses are reduced by $100 per casualty, and the aggregate of all personal casualty losses is reduced by 10 percent of AGI. A personal casualty loss is an itemized deduction. See Concept Summary 6–2 near the end of the chapter for the classification of expenses.

REPORTING PROCEDURES

All deductions *for* and *from* AGI wind up on pages 1 and 2 of Form 1040. All deductions *for* AGI are reported on page 1. The last line on page 1 is adjusted gross income.

---

[12] § 162(a)(1).
[13] *Comm. v. Lincoln Electric Co.*, 49–2 USTC ¶9388, 38 AFTR 411, 176 F.2d 815 (CA–6, 1949).
[14] *Kennedy, Jr. v. Comm.*, 82–1 USTC ¶9186, 49 AFTR2d 82–628, 671 F.2d 167 (CA–6, 1982), *rev'g* 72 T.C. 793 (1979).
[15] Reg. § 1.162–8.

The first item on page 2 is also adjusted gross income. Itemized deductions are entered next, followed by the deduction for personal and dependency exemptions. The result is taxable income.

Most of the deductions *for* AGI on page 1 originate on supporting schedules. Examples include business expenses (Schedule C) and rent, royalty, partnership, and fiduciary deductions (Schedule E). Other deductions *for* AGI, such as IRAs, Keogh retirement plans, and alimony, are entered directly on page 1 of Form 1040.

All itemized deductions on page 2 are carried over from Schedule A. Some Schedule A deductions originate on other forms. Examples include home mortgage interest, investment interest, noncash charitable contributions in excess of $500, casualty losses, and unreimbursed employee expenses.

Form 1040 becomes a summary of the detailed information entered on the other schedules and forms. See Figure 6–1.

▼ **FIGURE 6–1**
Format of Form 1040

Form 1040, Page 1
- Income from All Sources
- Less: Deductions for AGI (partial list):
  - IRAs
  - Keogh Retirement Plans
  - Alimony
  - Moving Expenses
  - Penalty on Early Withdrawal of Savings
- Equals: Adjusted Gross Income

Form 1040, Page 2
- Adjusted Gross Income
- Less: Standard Deduction or Itemized Deductions
- Exemptions
- Equals: Taxable Income

Schedule B — Interest and Dividends
Schedule C — Business Income
Schedule D — Capital Gains and Losses
Schedule E — Rents, Royalties, etc.
Schedule F — Farm Income

Schedule A
- Medical Expenses
- Taxes
- Interest → Home Mortgage Interest
- Form 4952 — Investment Interest
- Charitable Contributions
- Form 8283 — Noncash Charitable Contributions
- Casualty Losses
- Form 4684 — Casualties and Thefts
- Miscellaneous Itemized Deductions
- Form 2106 or Form 2106–EZ — Employee Business Expenses
- Equals: Total Itemized Deductions

DEDUCTIONS AND LOSSES—TIMING OF EXPENSE RECOGNITION

IMPORTANCE OF TAXPAYER'S METHOD OF ACCOUNTING

LEARNING OBJECTIVE 2
Describe the cash and accrual methods of accounting.

A taxpayer's **accounting method** is a major factor in determining taxable income. The method used determines when an item is includible in income and when an item is deductible on the tax return. Usually, the taxpayer's regular method of record keeping is used for income tax purposes.[16] The taxing authorities do not require uniformity among all taxpayers. They do require that the method used clearly reflect income and that items be handled consistently.[17] The most common methods of accounting are the cash method and the accrual method.

Throughout the portions of the Code dealing with deductions, the phrase "paid or incurred" is used. *Paid* refers to the cash basis taxpayer who gets a deduction only in the year of payment. *Incurred* concerns the accrual basis taxpayer who obtains the deduction in the year in which the liability for the expense becomes certain (refer to Chapter 4).

CASH METHOD REQUIREMENTS

The expenses of cash basis taxpayers are deductible only when they are actually paid with cash or other property. Promising to pay or issuing a note does not satisfy the actually paid requirement.[18] However, the payment can be made with borrowed funds. At the time taxpayers charge expenses on their credit cards, they are allowed to claim the deduction. They are deemed to have simultaneously borrowed money from the credit card issuer and constructively paid the expenses.[19]

Although the cash basis taxpayer must have actually or constructively paid the expense, payment does not assure a current deduction. Cash basis and accrual basis taxpayers cannot take a current deduction for capital expenditures except through amortization, depletion, or depreciation over the life (actual or statutory) of the asset. The Regulations set forth the general rule that an expenditure that creates an asset having a useful life that extends substantially beyond the end of the tax year must be capitalized.[20]

EXAMPLE 7
John, a cash basis taxpayer, rents property from Carl. On July 1, 1997, John paid $2,400 rent for the 24 months ending June 30, 1999. The prepaid rent extends 18 months after the close of the tax year—substantially beyond the year of payment. Therefore, John must capitalize the prepaid rent and amortize the expense on a monthly basis. His deduction for 1997 is $600. ▼

The Tax Court and the IRS took the position that an asset that will expire or be consumed by the end of the tax year following the year of payment must be prorated. The Ninth Court of Appeals held that such expenditures are currently deductible, however, and the Supreme Court apparently concurs (the one-year rule for prepaid expenses).[21]

---

[16] § 446(a).
[17] §§ 446(b) and (e); Reg. § 1.446–1(a)(2).
[18] *Page v. Rhode Island Trust Co., Exr.*, 37–1 USTC ¶9138, 19 AFTR 105, 88 F.2d 192 (CA–1, 1937).
[19] Rev.Rul. 78–39, 1978–1 C.B. 73. See also Rev.Rul. 80–335, 1980–2 C.B. 170, which applies to pay-by-phone arrangements.
[20] Reg. § 1.461–1(a).
[21] *Zaninovich v. Comm.*, 80–1 USTC ¶9342, 45 AFTR2d 80–1442, 616 F.2d 429 (CA–9, 1980), rev'g 69 T.C. 605 (1978). Cited by the Supreme Court in *Hillsboro National Bank v. Comm.*, 83–1 USTC ¶9229, 51 AFTR2d 83–874, 103 S.Ct. 1134 (USSC, 1983).

EXAMPLE 8

Assume the same facts as in Example 7 except that John was required to pay only 12 months rent in 1997. He paid $1,200 on July 1, 1997. The entire $1,200 would be deductible in 1997. ▼

The payment must be required, not a voluntary prepayment, to obtain the current deduction under the one-year rule.[22] The taxpayer must also demonstrate that allowing the current deduction will not result in a material distortion of income. Generally, the deduction will be allowed if the item is recurring or was made for a business purpose rather than to manipulate income.[23]

As Chapter 18 explains, not all taxpayers are allowed to use the cash method.[24]

ACCRUAL METHOD REQUIREMENTS

The period in which an accrual basis taxpayer can deduct an expense is determined by applying the *all events test* and the *economic performance test*. A deduction cannot be claimed until (1) all the events have occurred to create the taxpayer's liability and (2) the amount of the liability can be determined with reasonable accuracy. Once these requirements are satisfied, the deduction is permitted only if economic performance has occurred. The economic performance test is met only when the service, property, or use of property giving rise to the liability is actually performed for, provided to, or used by the taxpayer.[25]

EXAMPLE 9

On December 22, 1997, Chris's entertainment business sponsored a jazz festival in a rented auditorium at a local college. His business is responsible for cleaning up the auditorium after the festival and for reinstalling seats that were removed so more people could attend the festival. Since the college is closed over the Christmas holidays, the company hired by Chris to perform the work did not begin these activities until January 2, 1998. The cost to Chris is $1,200. Chris cannot deduct the $1,200 until 1998, when the services are performed. ▼

An exception to the economic performance requirements allows certain *recurring items* to be deducted if the following conditions are met:

- The item is recurring in nature and is treated consistently by the taxpayer.
- Either the accrued item is not material, or accruing it results in better matching of income and expenses.
- All the events have occurred that determine the fact of the liability and the amount of the liability can be determined with reasonable accuracy.
- Economic performance occurs within a reasonable period (but not later than 8½ months after the close of the taxable year).[26]

EXAMPLE 10

Rick, an accrual basis, calendar year taxpayer, entered into a monthly maintenance contract during the year. He makes a monthly accrual at the end of every month for this service and pays the fee sometime between the first and fifteenth of the following month when services are performed. The amount involved is immaterial, and all the other tests are met. The December 1997 accrual is deductible even though the service is performed on January 12, 1998. ▼

---

[22] *Bonaire Development Co. v. Comm.*, 82–2 USTC ¶9428, 50 AFTR2d 82–5167, 679 F.2d 159 (CA–9, 1982).
[23] *Keller v. Comm.*, 84–1 USTC ¶9194, 53 AFTR2d 84–663, 725 F.2d 1173 (CA–8, 1984), *aff'g* 79 T.C. 7 (1982).
[24] § 448.
[25] § 461(h).
[26] § 461(h)(3)(A)

CHAPTER 6 Deductions and Losses: In General

EXAMPLE 11

Rita, an accrual basis, calendar year taxpayer, shipped merchandise sold on December 30, 1997, via Greyhound Van Lines on January 2, 1998, and paid the freight charges at that time. Since Rita reported the sale of the merchandise in 1997, the shipping charge should also be deductible in 1997. This procedure results in a better matching of income and expenses. ▼

Reserves for estimated expenses (frequently employed for financial accounting purposes) generally are not allowed for tax purposes because the economic performance test cannot be satisfied.

EXAMPLE 12

Blackbird Airlines is required by Federal law to test its engines after 3,000 flying hours. Aircraft cannot return to flight until the tests have been conducted. An unrelated aircraft maintenance company does all of the company's tests for $1,500 per engine. For financial reporting purposes, the company accrues an expense based upon $.50 per hour of flight and credits an allowance account. The actual amounts paid for maintenance are offset against the allowance account. For tax purposes, the economic performance test is not satisfied until the work has been done. Therefore, the reserve method cannot be used for tax purposes. ▼

DISALLOWANCE POSSIBILITIES

3 LEARNING OBJECTIVE
Apply the Internal Revenue Code deduction disallowance provisions associated with the following: public policy limitations, political activities, excessive executive compensation, investigation of business opportunities, hobby losses, vacation home rentals, payment of others' expenses, personal expenditures, capital expenditures, related-party transactions, and expenses related to tax-exempt income.

The tax law provides for the disallowance of certain types of expenses. Without specific restrictions in the tax law, taxpayers might attempt to deduct certain items that in reality are personal expenditures. For example, specific tax rules are provided to determine whether an expenditure is for trade or business purposes or related to a personal hobby.

Certain disallowance provisions are a codification or extension of prior court decisions. After the courts denied deductions for payments considered to be in violation of public policy, the tax law was changed to provide specific authority for the disallowance of these deductions. Discussions of specific disallowance provisions in the tax law follow.

PUBLIC POLICY LIMITATION

Justification for Denying Deductions.
The courts developed the principle that a payment that is in violation of public policy is not a necessary expense and is not deductible.[27] Although a bribe or fine, may be appropriate, helpful, and even contribute to the profitability of an activity, the courts held that to allow such expenses would frustrate clearly defined public policy. A deduction would dilute the effect of the penalty since the government would be indirectly subsidizing a taxpayer's wrongdoing.

Accordingly, the IRS was free to restrict deductions if, in its view, the expenses were contrary to public policy. But since the law did not explain which actions violated public policy, taxpayers often had to go to court to determine whether or not their expense fell into this category.

Furthermore, the public policy doctrine could be arbitrarily applied in cases where no clear definition had emerged. To solve these problems, Congress enacted legislation that attempts to limit the use of the doctrine. Under the legislation,

---

[27] *Tank Truck Rentals, Inc. v. Comm.*, 58–1 USTC ¶9366, 1 AFTR2d 1154, 78 S.Ct. 507 (USSC, 1958).

deductions are disallowed for certain specific types of expenditures that are considered contrary to public policy:

- Bribes and kickbacks including those associated with Medicare or Medicaid (in the case of foreign bribes and kickbacks, only if the payments violate the U.S. Foreign Corrupt Practices Act of 1977).
- Fines and penalties paid to a government for violation of law.

EXAMPLE 13

Brown Corporation, a moving company, consistently loads its trucks with weights in excess of the limits allowed by state law. The additional revenue more than offsets the fines levied. The fines are for a violation of public policy and are not deductible. ▼

- Two-thirds of the treble damage payments made to claimants resulting from violation of the antitrust law.[28]

To be disallowed, the bribe or kickback must be illegal under either Federal or state law and must also subject the payer to a criminal penalty or the loss of license or privilege to engage in a trade or business. For a bribe or kickback that is illegal under state law, a deduction is denied only if the state law is generally enforced.

EXAMPLE 14

During the year, Keith, an insurance salesman, paid $5,000 to Karen, a real estate broker. The payment represented 20% of the commissions Keith earned from customers referred by Karen. Under state law, the splitting of commissions by an insurance salesperson is an act of misconduct that could warrant a revocation of the salesperson's license. Keith's $5,000 payments to Karen are not deductible provided the state law is generally enforced. ▼

ETHICAL CONSIDERATIONS

To Obey the Law

Clyde owns a trucking firm that operates in the Mid-Atlantic states. One of his major customers frequently ships goods between Charlotte and Baltimore. Occasionally, the customer sends last-minute shipments that are outbound for Europe on a freighter sailing from Baltimore. To satisfy the delivery schedule in these cases, Clyde's drivers must substantially exceed the speed limit. Clyde's business pays for any related speeding tickets. Twice within the past year, drivers have had their license suspended for 30 days for driving at such excessive speeds. Clyde's firm continues to pay the driver's salary during such suspension periods.

Clyde believes that it is necessary to conduct his business in this manner if it is to be profitable, maintain the support of his drivers, and maintain the goodwill of his customers. Evaluate Clyde's business practices.

Legal Expenses Incurred in Defense of Civil or Criminal Penalties. To deduct legal expenses, the taxpayer must be able to show that the origin and character of the claim are directly related to a trade or business, an income-producing activity, or the determination, collection, or refund of a tax. Personal legal expenses are not deductible. Thus, legal fees incurred in connection with a

---

[28] §§ 162(c), (f), and (g).

criminal defense are deductible only if the crime is associated with the taxpayer's trade or business or income-producing activity.[29]

EXAMPLE 15

Debra, a financial officer of Blue Corporation, incurred legal expenses in connection with her defense in a criminal indictment for evasion of Blue's income taxes. Debra may deduct her legal expenses because she is deemed to be in the trade or business of being an executive. The legal action impairs her ability to conduct this business activity.[30] ▼

Deductible legal expenses associated with the following are deductible *for* AGI:

- Ordinary and necessary expenses incurred in connection with a trade or business.
- Ordinary and necessary expenses incurred in conjunction with rental or royalty property held for the production of income.

All other deductible legal expenses are deductible *from* AGI. For example, legal expenses generally are deductible *from* AGI if they are for fees for tax advice relative to the preparation of an individual's income tax return. Contrast this with the deduction *for* classification of legal fees for tax advice relative to the preparation of the portion of the tax return for a sole proprietor's trade or business (Schedule C) or an individual's rental or royalty income (Schedule E).

Expenses Relating to an Illegal Business.

The usual expenses of operating an illegal business (e.g., a numbers racket) are deductible.[31] However, § 162 disallows a deduction for fines, bribes to public officials, illegal kickbacks, and other illegal payments.

EXAMPLE 16

Sam owns and operates an illegal gambling establishment. In connection with this activity, he had the following expenses during the year:

Rent	$ 60,000
Payoffs to the police	40,000
Depreciation on equipment	100,000
Wages	140,000
Interest	30,000
Criminal fines	50,000
Illegal kickbacks	10,000
Total	$430,000

All of the usual expenses (rent, depreciation, wages, and interest) are deductible; payoffs, fines, and kickbacks are not deductible. Of the $430,000 spent, $330,000 is deductible and $100,000 is not. ▼

An exception applies to expenses incurred in illegal trafficking in drugs.[32] *Drug dealers* are not allowed a deduction for ordinary and necessary business expenses incurred in their business. In arriving at gross income from the business,

---

[29] *Comm. v. Tellier*, 66–1 USTC ¶9319, 17 AFTR2d 633, 86 S.Ct. 1118 (USSC, 1966).
[30] Rev.Rul. 68–662, 1968–2 C.B. 69.
[31] *Comm. v. Sullivan*, 58–1 USTC ¶9368, 1 AFTR2d 1158, 78 S.Ct. 512 (USSC, 1958).
[32] § 280E.

however, dealers may reduce total sales by the cost of goods sold.[33] In this regard, no distinction is made between legal and illegal businesses in calculating gross income. Treating cost of goods sold as a negative income item rather than as a deduction item produces the unseemly result that a drug dealer's taxable income is reduced by cost of goods sold.

POLITICAL CONTRIBUTIONS AND LOBBYING ACTIVITIES

Political Contributions. Generally, no business deduction is permitted for direct or indirect payments for political purposes.[34] Historically, the government has been reluctant to accord favorable tax treatment to business expenditures for political purposes. Allowing deductions might encourage abuses and enable businesses to have undue influence upon the political process.

Lobbying Expenditures. The Revenue Reconciliation Act of 1993 (RRA of 1993) generally repealed the lobbying deduction (certain expenses incurred to influence legislation).[35] Any lobbying expenses incurred in attempting to influence state or Federal legislation or the actions of certain high-ranking public officials (e.g., the President, Vice-President, cabinet-level officials, and the two most senior officials in each agency of the executive branch) are no longer deductible. The disallowance also applies to a pro rata portion of the membership dues of trade associations and other groups that are used for lobbying activities.

EXAMPLE 17

Egret Company pays a $10,000 annual membership fee to the Free Trade Group, a trade association for plumbing wholesalers. The trade association estimates that 70% of its dues are allocated to lobbying activities. Thus, Egret Company's deduction is limited to $3,000 ($10,000 × 30%). ▼

There are three exceptions to this repeal of the lobbying expenses deduction. An exception is provided for influencing local legislation (e.g., city and county governments). Second, the disallowance provision does not apply to activities devoted solely to monitoring legislation. Third, a *de minimis* exception is provided for annual in-house expenditures (lobbying expenses other than those paid to professional lobbyists or any portion of dues used by associations for lobbying) if such expenditures do not exceed $2,000. If the in-house expenditures exceed $2,000, none of the in-house expenditures can be deducted.

EXCESSIVE EXECUTIVE COMPENSATION

The deduction of executive compensation is subject to two limitations. As discussed earlier in this chapter, the compensation of shareholder-employees of closely held corporations is subject to the reasonableness requirement. The second limitation, the so-called millionaires provision, applies to publicly held corporations (a corporation that has at least one class of stock registered under the Securities Act of 1934).[36]

The millionaires provision does not limit the amount of compensation that can be paid to an employee. Instead, it limits the amount the employer can deduct for

---

[33] Reg. § 1.61–3(a). Gross income is defined as sales minus cost of goods sold. Thus, while § 280E prohibits any deductions for drug dealers, it does not modify the normal definition of gross income.

[34] § 276.

[35] § 162(e).

[36] § 162(m). This millionaires provision was added by the Revenue Reconciliation Act of 1993 (RRA of 1993).

TAX IN THE NEWS

THE JOY OF NOT BEING AN EXECUTIVE OF A PUBLICLY HELD CORPORATION

Being rich without being a top executive of a publicly held corporation has its advantages. Wealthy nonexecutives need not worry about loss of position, prestige, and income as a result of mergers and acquisitions. Nor do they have to be concerned that an employer will limit their compensation because it is excessive and therefore not deductible.

Wealthy nonexecutives, with their estimated gross income for 1995 and 1996, include the following individuals and groups, who appear on *Forbes* magazine's list of best paid entertainers and authors:

Oprah Winfrey	$171 million
Steven Spielberg	150 million
Beatles	130 million
Michael Jackson	90 million
Rolling Stones	77 million
Eagles	75 million
Arnold Schwarzenegger	74 million
David Copperfield	74 million
Jim Carrey	63 million
Michael Crichton	59 million

SOURCE: Adapted from "Oprah's Paycheck Tops Salary List," *Newport News Daily Press*, September 9, 1996, p. A2.

---

the compensation of a covered executive to $1 million annually. Covered employees include the chief executive officer and the four other most highly compensated officers.

Employee compensation *excludes* the following:

- Commissions based on individual performance.
- Certain performance-based compensation based on company performance according to a formula approved by a board of directors compensation committee (comprised solely of two or more outside directors) and by shareholder vote. The performance attainment must be certified by this compensation committee.
- Payments to tax-qualified retirement plans.
- Payments that are excludible from the employees' gross income (e.g., certain fringe benefits).

INVESTIGATION OF A BUSINESS

Investigation expenses are expenses paid or incurred to determine the feasibility of entering a new business or expanding an existing business. They include such costs as travel, engineering and architectural surveys, marketing reports, and various legal and accounting services. How such expenses are treated for tax purposes depends on a number of variables, including the following:

- The current business, if any, of the taxpayer.
- The nature of the business being investigated.
- The extent to which the investigation has proceeded.
- Whether or not the acquisition actually takes place.

If the taxpayer is in a business the *same as or similar to* that being investigated, all investigation expenses are deductible in the year paid or incurred. The tax result is the same whether or not the taxpayer acquires the business being investigated.[37]

EXAMPLE 18　Terry, an accrual basis sole proprietor, owns and operates three motels in Georgia. In the current year, Terry incurs expenses of $8,500 in investigating the possibility of acquiring several additional motels located in South Carolina. The $8,500 is deductible in the current year whether or not Terry acquires the motels in South Carolina. ▼

When the taxpayer is *not* in a business that is the same as or similar to the one being investigated, the tax result depends on whether the new business is acquired. If the business is not acquired, all investigation expenses generally are nondeductible.[38]

EXAMPLE 19　Lynn, a retired merchant, incurs expenses in traveling from Rochester, New York, to California to investigate the feasibility of acquiring several auto care centers. If no acquisition takes place, none of the expenses are deductible. ▼

If the taxpayer is *not* in a business that is the same as or similar to the one being investigated and actually acquires the new business, the expenses must be capitalized. At the election of the taxpayer, the expenses may be amortized over a period of 60 months or more, beginning with the month in which the business is started.[39]

EXAMPLE 20　Tina owns and operates 10 restaurants located in various cities throughout the Southeast. She travels to Atlanta to discuss the acquisition of an auto dealership. In addition, she incurs legal and accounting costs associated with the potential acquisition. After incurring total investigation costs of $12,000, she acquires the auto dealership on October 1, 1997.

Tina must capitalize the $12,000 of investigation expenses for the auto dealership. If she elects to amortize the expenses over 60 months, she can deduct $600 ($12,000 × 3/60) in 1997. ▼

HOBBY LOSSES

Business or investment expenses are deductible only if the taxpayer can show that the activity was entered into for the purpose of making a profit. Certain activities may have either profit-seeking or personal attributes, depending upon individual circumstances. Examples include raising horses and operating a farm used as a weekend residence. While personal losses are not deductible, losses attributable to profit-seeking activities may be deducted and used to offset a taxpayer's other income. For this reason, the tax law limits the deductibility of **hobby losses.**

---

[37] § 195. *York v. Comm.*, 58–2 USTC ¶9952, 2 AFTR2d 6178, 261 F.2d 421 (CA–4, 1958).

[38] Rev.Rul. 57–418, 1957–2 C.B. 143; *Morton Frank*, 20 T.C. 511 (1953); and *Dwight A. Ward*, 20 T.C. 332 (1953).

[39] § 195.

General Rules. If an individual can show that an activity has been conducted with the intent to earn a profit, losses from the activity are fully deductible. The hobby loss rules apply only if the activity is not engaged in for profit. Hobby expenses are deductible only to the extent of hobby income.[40]

The Regulations stipulate that the following nine factors should be considered in determining whether an activity is profit-seeking or a hobby:[41]

- Whether the activity is conducted in a businesslike manner.
- The expertise of the taxpayers or their advisers.
- The time and effort expended.
- The expectation that the assets of the activity will appreciate in value.
- The taxpayer's previous success in conducting similar activities.
- The history of income or losses from the activity.
- The relationship of profits earned to losses incurred.
- The financial status of the taxpayer (e.g., if the taxpayer does not have substantial amounts of other income, this may indicate that the activity is engaged in for profit).
- Elements of personal pleasure or recreation in the activity.

The presence or absence of a factor is not by itself determinative of whether the activity is profit-seeking or a hobby. Rather, the decision is a subjective one that is based on an analysis of the facts and circumstances.

Presumptive Rule of § 183. The Code provides a rebuttable presumption that an activity is profit-seeking if the activity shows a profit in at least three of any five prior consecutive years.[42] If the activity involves horses, a profit in at least two of seven consecutive years meets the presumptive rule. If these profitability tests are met, the activity is presumed to be a trade or business rather than a personal hobby. In this situation, the IRS bears the burden of proving that the activity is personal rather than trade or business related.

EXAMPLE 21

Camille, an executive for a large corporation, is paid a salary of $200,000. Her husband is a collector of antiques. Several years ago, he opened an antique shop in a local shopping center and spends most of his time buying and selling antiques. He occasionally earns a small profit from this activity but more frequently incurs substantial losses. If the losses are business related, they are fully deductible against Camille's salary income on a joint return. In resolving this issue, consider the following:

- Initially determine whether the antique activity has met the three-out-of-five years profit test.
- If the presumption is not met, the activity may nevertheless qualify as a business if the taxpayer can show that the intent is to engage in a profit-seeking activity. It is not necessary to show actual profits.
- Attempt to fit the operation within the nine criteria prescribed in the Regulations and listed above. These criteria are the factors considered in trying to rebut the § 183 presumption. ▼

Determining the Amount of the Deduction. If an activity is deemed to be a hobby, the expenses are deductible only to the extent of the gross income from the hobby. These expenses must be deducted in the following order:

---

[40] § 183(b)(2).
[41] Reg. §§ 1.183–2(b)(1) through (9).
[42] § 183(d).

- Amounts deductible under other Code sections without regard to the nature of the activity, such as property taxes and home mortgage interest.
- Amounts deductible under other Code sections if the activity had been engaged in for profit, but only if those amounts do not affect adjusted basis. Examples include maintenance, utilities, and supplies.
- Amounts that affect adjusted basis and would be deductible under other Code sections if the activity had been engaged in for profit.[43] Examples include depreciation, amortization, and depletion.

These deductions are deductible *from* AGI as itemized deductions to the extent they exceed 2 percent of AGI.[44] If the taxpayer uses the standard deduction rather than itemizing, all hobby loss deductions are wasted.

EXAMPLE 22

Jim, the vice president of an oil company, has AGI of $80,000. He decides to pursue painting in his spare time. He uses a home studio, comprising 10% of the home's square footage. During the current year, Jim incurs the following expenses:

Frames	$ 350
Art supplies	300
Fees paid to models	1,000
Home studio expenses:	
Total property taxes	900
Total home mortgage interest	10,000
Depreciation on 10% of home	500
Total home maintenance and utilities	3,600

During the year, Jim sold paintings for a total of $3,200. If the activity is held to be a hobby, Jim is allowed deductions as follows:

Gross income		$ 3,200
Deduct: Taxes and interest (10% of $10,900)		(1,090)
Remainder		$ 2,110
Deduct: Frames	$ 350	
Art supplies	300	
Models' fees	1,000	
Maintenance and utilities (10%)	360	(2,010)
Remainder		$ 100
Depreciation ($500, but limited to $100)		(100)
Net income		$ -0-

Jim includes the $3,200 of income in AGI, making his AGI $83,200. The taxes and interest are itemized deductions, deductible in full. The remaining $2,110 of expenses are reduced by 2% of his AGI ($1,664); so the net deduction is $446. Since the property taxes and home mortgage interest are deductible anyway, the net effect is a $2,754 ($3,200 less $446) increase in taxable income. ▼

EXAMPLE 23

Assume that Jim's activity in Example 22 is held to be a business. The business is located in a small office building he owns. Expenses are property taxes of $90, mortgage interest of $1,000, frames of $350, art supplies of $300, models' fees of $1,000, maintenance and utilities

---

[43] Reg. § 1.183–1(b)(1).

[44] Reg. § 1.67–1T(a)(1)(iv) and Rev.Rul. 75–14, 1975–1 C.B. 90.

TAX IN THE NEWS

IS A DREAM HOME IN THE MOUNTAINS OR AT THE BEACH FOR YOU?

Most of us have dreamed of having a second home in the mountains or at the beach. The general attitude is that we deserve a second home and that it would be a healthy environment for the kids. Then we encounter the reality of paying for it.

One frequently prescribed technique is to rent a vacation home to others when you are not using it. Supposedly, the second home will generate rent income to use for the mortgage payments and deductions (e.g., mortgage interest and property taxes) on your income tax return, while providing a vacation getaway.

Unfortunately, the dream can become a nightmare. More than likely, the vacation home will be subject to both the § 280A limitation on deducting expenses in excess of rental income and the § 469 passive activity loss provision (see Chapter 11). To make matters worse, the vacation home is unlikely to be self-sustaining (i.e., cash inflows including tax benefits do not at least equal cash outflows). Therefore, those who view the vacation home as a cool investment are likely to be disappointed.

Thomas Ochsenschlanger, a partner in the Washington office of Grant Thornton, recommends discussing the financial aspects of a vacation home with your accountant *before* buying the property.

SOURCE: Adapted from Scott R. Schmedel, "Dream Second Home Can Be a Tax-Return Nightmare," *Wall Street Journal*, March 8, 1996, pp. C1 and C15.

---

of $360, and depreciation of $500. Under these circumstances, Jim could deduct expenses totaling $3,600. All these expenses would be trade or business expenses deductible *for* AGI. His reduction in AGI would be as follows:

Gross income		$ 3,200
Less: Taxes and interest	$1,090	
Other business expenses	2,010	
Depreciation	500	(3,600)
Reduction in AGI		($ 400)

RENTAL OF VACATION HOMES

Restrictions on the deductions allowed for part-year rentals of personal **vacation homes** were written into the law to prevent taxpayers from deducting essentially personal expenses as rental losses. Many taxpayers who owned vacation homes had formerly treated the homes as rental property and generated rental losses as deductions *for* AGI. For example, a summer cabin would be rented for 2 months per year, used for vacationing for 1 month, and left vacant the rest of the year. The taxpayer would then deduct 11 months' depreciation, utilities, maintenance, etc., as rental expenses, resulting in a rental loss. Section 280A eliminates this treatment by allowing deductions on residences used primarily for personal purposes only to the extent of the income generated. Only a break-even situation is allowed; no losses can be deducted.

There are three possible tax treatments for residences used for both personal and rental purposes. The treatment depends upon the *relative time* the residence is used for personal purposes versus rental use.

Primarily Personal Use. If the residence is *rented* for *less than 15 days* in a year, it is treated as a personal residence. The rent income is excluded from gross income, and mortgage interest and real estate taxes are allowed as itemized deductions, as with any personal residence.[45] No other expenses (e.g., depreciation, utilities, maintenance) are deductible. Although this provision exists primarily for administrative convenience, several bills have been introduced in Congress since 1993 that would have repealed this exclusion from gross income.

EXAMPLE 24

Dixie owns a vacation cottage on the lake. During the current year, she rented it for $1,600 for two weeks, lived in it two months, and left it vacant the remainder of the year. The year's expenses amounted to $6,000 mortgage interest expense, $500 property taxes, $1,500 utilities and maintenance, and $2,400 depreciation. Since the property was not rented for at least 15 days, the income is excluded, the mortgage interest and property tax expenses are itemized deductions, and the remaining expenses are nondeductible personal expenses. ▼

ETHICAL CONSIDERATIONS

Renting for One More Day

June is a widow who lives in Williamsburg, Virginia. For the past five years (since the death of her husband), she has rented her home for one week to a professional golfer who is participating in the A–B Golf Classic. The rent income is $1,500. During this week, June visits her sister in Charlotte. A neighbor who is a CPA advises June that she does not need to report the $1,500 on her Federal income tax return because she did not rent her house for more than two weeks during the year.

In 1997, June has the opportunity to rent the house for $2,800 for an additional week in December to the golfer and his family who would like to spend Christmas in Williamsburg. She checks with her CPA neighbor to verify she will not have to include the rent income in her gross income. June agrees to rent her house and to visit her sister through New Year's Day.

The golfer and his family arrived on December 20 and were scheduled to depart on December 27. On December 26, the golfer's wife calls June at her sister's, explains that their two-year-old child is ill, and asks if they can rent for an additional day until the child feels better. June says yes, of course, but indicates she will not accept any rent for the additional day.

When June returns home on January 2, 1998, she finds the check on her kitchen counter is for $3,200 rather than for $2,800. The check is enclosed in a Christmas card from the golfer and his family.

On her 1997 Federal income tax return, June does not report any rent income or deduct any rental expenses. According to her records, she rented her house for exactly two weeks.

Can you justify June's treatment of the rent income and expenses?

Primarily Rental Use. If the residence is *rented* for 15 days or more in a year and is *not used* for personal purposes for more than the greater of (1) 14 days or (2) 10 percent of the total days rented, the residence is treated as rental property.[46]

---

[45] § 280A(g).

[46] § 280A(d) and Prop.Reg. § 1.280A–3(c).

CHAPTER 6 Deductions and Losses: In General

The expenses must be allocated between personal and rental days if there are any personal use days during the year. The deduction of the expenses allocated to rental days can exceed rent income and result in a rental loss. The loss may be deductible under the passive activity loss rules (discussed in Chapter 11).

EXAMPLE 25

Assume instead that Dixie in Example 24 rented the cottage for 120 days and lived in it for 13 days. The cottage is primarily rental use since she rented it for 15 days or more and did not use it for personal purposes for more than 14 days. ▼

EXAMPLE 26

Assume instead that Dixie in Example 24 rented the cottage for 200 days and lived in it for 19 days. The cottage is primarily rental use since she rented it for 15 days or more and did not use it for personal purposes for more than 20 days (10% of the rental days). ▼

EXAMPLE 27

Assume instead that Dixie in Example 24 used the cottage for 12 days and rented it for 48 days for $4,800. Since she rented the cottage for 15 days or more but did not use it for more than 14 days, the cottage is treated as rental property. The expenses must be allocated between personal and rental days.

	Percentage of Use	
	Rental 80%	Personal 20%
Income	$4,800	$–0–
Expenses		
Mortgage interest ($6,000)	($4,800)	($1,200)
Property taxes ($500)	(400)	(100)
Utilities and maintenance ($1,500)	(1,200)	(300)
Depreciation ($2,400)	(1,920)	(480)
Total expenses	($8,320)	($2,080)
Rental loss	($3,520)	$–0–

Dixie deducts the $3,520 rental loss *for* AGI (assuming she meets the passive activity loss rules, discussed in Chapter 11). She also has an itemized deduction for property taxes of $100 associated with the personal use. The mortgage interest of $1,200 associated with the personal use is not deductible as an itemized deduction because the cottage is not a qualified residence (qualified residence interest) for this purpose (see Chapter 10). The portion of utilities and maintenance and depreciation attributable to personal use is not deductible. ▼

Personal/Rental Use. If the residence is rented for 15 days or more in a year *and* is used for personal purposes for more than the greater of (1) 14 days or (2) 10 percent of the total days rented, it is treated as a personal/rental use residence. The expenses must be allocated between personal days and rental days. Expenses are allowed only to the extent of rent income.

EXAMPLE 28

Assume instead that Dixie in Example 24 rented the property for 30 days and lived in it for 30 days. The residence is classified as personal/rental use property since she used it more than 14 days and rented it for 15 days or more. The expenses must be allocated between rental use and personal use, and the rental expenses are allowed only to the extent of rent income. ▼

If a residence is classified as personal/rental use property, the expenses that are deductible anyway (e.g., real estate taxes and mortgage interest) must be deducted first. If a positive net income results, otherwise nondeductible expenses that do not affect adjusted basis (e.g., maintenance, utilities, insurance) are allowed next. Finally, if any positive balance remains, depreciation is allowed.

Expenses must be allocated between personal and rental days before the limits are applied. The courts have held that real estate taxes and mortgage interest, which accrue ratably over the year, are allocated on the basis of 365 days.[47] The IRS, however, disagrees and allocates real estate taxes and mortgage interest on the basis of total days of use.[48] Other expenses (utilities, maintenance, depreciation, etc.) are allocated on the basis of total days used.

Example 29

Jason rents his vacation home for 60 days and lives in the home for 30 days. The limitations on personal/rental use residences apply. Jason's gross rent income is $10,000. For the entire year (not a leap year), the real estate taxes are $2,190; his mortgage interest expense is $10,220; utilities and maintenance expense equals $2,400; and depreciation is $9,000. Using the IRS approach, these amounts are deductible in this specific order:

Gross income	$10,000
Deduct: Taxes and interest (60/90 × $12,410)	(8,273)
Remainder to apply to rental operating expenses and depreciation	$ 1,727
Deduct: Utilities and maintenance (60/90 × $2,400)	(1,600)
Balance	$ 127
Deduct: Depreciation (60/90 × $9,000 = $6,000 but limited to above balance)	(127)
Net rent income	$ -0-

The nonrental use portion of real estate taxes and mortgage interest ($4,137 in this case) is deductible if the taxpayer elects to itemize (see Chapter 10). The personal use portion of utilities, maintenance, and depreciation is not deductible in any case. Also note that the basis of the property is not reduced by the $5,873 depreciation not allowed ($6,000 − $127) because of the above limitation. (See Chapter 14 for a discussion of the reduction in basis for depreciation allowed or allowable.) ▼

Example 30

Using the court's approach in allocating real estate taxes and mortgage interest, Jason, in Example 29, would have this result:

Gross income	$10,000
Deduct: Taxes and interest (60/365 × $12,410)	(2,040)
Remainder to apply to rental operating expenses and depreciation	$ 7,960
Deduct: Utilities and maintenance (60/90 × $2,400)	(1,600)
Balance	$ 6,360
Deduct: Depreciation (60/90 × $9,000, but limited to $6,360)	(6,000)
Net rent income	$ 360

Jason can deduct $10,370 ($12,410 paid − $2,040 deducted as expense in computing net rent income) of personal use mortgage interest and real estate taxes as itemized deductions. ▼

Note the contrasting results in Examples 29 and 30. The IRS's approach (Example 29) results in no rental gain or loss and an itemized deduction for real

---

[47] Bolton v. Comm., 82−2 USTC ¶9699, 51 AFTR2d 83−305, 694 F.2d 556 (CA−9, 1982).

[48] Prop.Reg. § 1.280A−3(d)(4).

estate taxes and mortgage interest of $4,137. In Example 30, Jason has net rent income of $360 and $10,370 of itemized deductions. The court's approach decreases his taxable income by $10,010 ($10,370 itemized deductions less $360 net rent income). The IRS's approach reduces his taxable income by only $4,137.

EXAMPLE 31

Assume instead that Jason in Example 29 had not lived in the home at all during the year. The house is rental property. The rental loss is calculated as follows:

Gross income	$10,000
Expenses	
Taxes and interest	($12,410)
Utilities and maintenance	(2,400)
Depreciation	(9,000)
Total expenses	($23,810)
Rental loss	($13,810)

Whether any of the rental loss would be deductible depends upon whether Jason actively participated in the rental activity and met the other requirements for passive activity losses (discussed in Chapter 11). ▼

Conversion to Rental Property. A related issue is whether or not a taxpayer's *primary residence* is subject to the preceding rules if it is converted to rental property. If the vacation home rules apply, a taxpayer who converts his or her personal residence to rental property during the tax year, without any tax avoidance motive, could have the allowable deductions limited to the rent income. This would occur if the personal use exceeded the greater of 14 days or 10 percent of rental days test (a likely situation). The Code, however, provides that during a *qualified rental period*, any personal use days are not counted as personal use days in terms of classifying the use of the residence as *personal/rental use* rather than as *primarily rental use*.[49] In effect, the deduction for expenses of the property incurred during a qualified rental period is not subject to the personal use test of the vacation home rules. A qualified rental period is a consecutive period of 12 or more months. The period begins or ends in the taxable year in which the residence is rented or held for rental at a fair price. The residence must not be rented to a related party. If the property is sold before the 12-month period expires, the qualified rental period is the actual time rented.

EXAMPLE 32

Rhonda converts her residence to rental property on May 1 and rents it for the remainder of 1997 for $5,600 and for all of 1998 for $8,400. The house would be classified as personal/rental use property (personal use days during 1997 are greater than both 14 days and 10% of rental days) except that this is a qualified rental period. Therefore, Rhonda's deduction for rental expenses is not limited to the gross income of $5,600 in 1997. ▼

See Concept Summary 6–1 for a summary of the vacation home rules.

EXPENDITURES INCURRED FOR TAXPAYER'S BENEFIT OR TAXPAYER'S OBLIGATION

An expense must be incurred for the taxpayer's benefit or arise from the taxpayer's obligation. An individual cannot claim a tax deduction for the payment of the expenses of another individual.

---

[49] § 280A(d).

Concept Summary 6-1

Vacation/Rental Home

- **Was the residence rented for 15 or more days during the year?**
  - **No** → Treat as a second home. Income is excludible. Itemize taxes and interest.
  - **Yes** → **Were personal use days more than the greater of 14 days or 10% of the total rental days?**
    - **No** → Property is a rental activity. → Allocate expenses to personal use. Taxes are itemized deductions. → Remaining expenses and income are from rental activity subject to at-risk and passive activity loss rules. → Report on Schedule E.
    - **Yes** → **Does rental portion of taxes and interest expenses* exceed rent income?**
      - **Yes** → Deduct interest and taxes only to extent of income. Other expenses are nondeductible. Remainder of taxes and interest are itemized deductions.
      - **No** → **Does rental portion of all other expenses** except depreciation exceed remaining net income?**
        - **Yes** → Deduct only to extent of remaining net income. Itemize personal part of interest and taxes. Remainder is nondeductible.
        - **No** → **Does rental portion of depreciation** exceed remaining net income?**
          - **Yes** → Deduct only to extent of remaining net income. Itemize personal part of interest and taxes. Remainder is nondeductible.
          - **No** → Remaining net income is passive rental activity subject to at-risk and passive activity loss rules. → Report on Schedule E.

*Allocated on the basis of 365 (366 in a leap year) days (court) or total days of use (IRS).
**Allocated on the basis of total days of use.

EXAMPLE 33

During the current year, Fred pays the interest on his son, Vern's, home mortgage. Neither Fred nor Vern can take a deduction for the interest paid. Fred is not entitled to a deduction because the mortgage is not his obligation. Vern cannot claim a deduction because he did not pay the interest. The tax result would have been more favorable had Fred made a cash gift to Vern and let him pay the interest. Then Vern could have deducted the interest, and Fred might not have been liable for any gift taxes depending upon the amount involved. A deduction would have been created with no cash difference to the family. ▼

One exception to this disallowance rule is the payment of medical expenses for a dependent. Such expenses are deductible by the payer subject to the normal rules that limit the deductibility of medical expenses (see Chapter 10).[50]

ETHICAL CONSIDERATIONS

How the Payment Is Made

Dan and Jeff both have sons who graduated from college recently and are employed by the same company in a rural community where rental housing is not readily available. Each father loans his son $10,000; the sons combine their resources and use the $20,000 as a down payment on a house that they buy together.

During 1997, the sons make all the mortgage payments on their house until December when they are furloughed from their jobs. Dan gives his son $900 to use to pay his share of the mortgage payment, and Jeff pays $900 directly to the mortgage company for his son. In each of these $900 amounts, $800 represents interest on the mortgage.

Over lunch recently, Dan and Jeff were discussing their sons' real estate investment and the $900 mortgage payment each father had funded. Jeff indicated that since he had paid the mortgage payment directly, he was going to deduct the $800 of interest on his Form 1040. After this conversation, Dan concludes that, in substance, he and Jeff have done the same thing. Accordingly, Dan calls his son and tells him that he wants to deduct the $800 on his tax return. Though Dan's son is not pleased, he agrees to permit his father to take the deduction and says he will not deduct the mortgage interest on his own return.

Evaluate the propriety of the position taken by Dan.

DISALLOWANCE OF PERSONAL EXPENDITURES

Section 262 states that "except as otherwise expressly provided in this chapter, no deduction shall be allowed for personal, living, or family expenses." To justify a deduction, an individual must be able to identify a particular section of the Code that sanctions the deduction (e.g., charitable contributions, medical expenses). Sometimes the character of a particular expenditure is not easily determined.

EXAMPLE 34

During the current year, Howard pays $1,500 in legal fees and court costs to obtain a divorce from his wife, Vera. Involved in the divorce action is a property settlement that concerns the disposition of income-producing property owned by Howard. In a similar situation, the Tax Court held that the taxpayer could not deduct any such costs.[51] "Although fees primarily related to property division concerning his income-producing property, they weren't ordinary and necessary expenses paid for conservation or maintenance of property held for production of income. Legal fees incurred in defending against claims that arise from a taxpayer's marital relationship aren't deductible expenses regardless of possible consequences on taxpayer's income-producing property." ▼

The IRS has clarified the issue of the deduction of legal fees incurred in connection with a divorce.[52] To be deductible, an expense must relate solely to tax advice in a divorce proceeding. For example, legal fees attributable to the determination of dependency exemptions of children are deductible if the fees are distinguishable from the general legal fees incurred in obtaining a divorce. Other

---

[50] § 213(a).
[51] *Harry H. Goldberg*, 29 TCM 74, T.C.Memo. 1970–27.
[52] Rev.Rul. 72–545, 1972–2 C.B. 179.

examples are the costs of creating a trust to make periodic alimony payments and the determination of the tax consequences of a property settlement. Therefore, it is advisable to request an itemization of attorney's fees to substantiate a deduction for the tax-related amounts.

DISALLOWANCE OF DEDUCTIONS FOR CAPITAL EXPENDITURES

The Code specifically disallows a deduction for "any amount paid out for new buildings or for permanent improvements or betterments made to increase the value of any property or estate."[53] The Regulations further define capital expenditures to include those expenditures that add to the value or prolong the life of property or adapt the property to a new or different use.[54] Incidental repairs and maintenance of the property are not capital expenditures and can be deducted as ordinary and necessary business expenses. Repairing a roof is a deductible expense, but replacing a roof is a capital expenditure subject to depreciation deductions over its useful life. The tune-up of a delivery truck is an expense; a complete overhaul probably is a capital expenditure.

Capitalization versus Expense. When an expenditure is capitalized rather than expensed, the deduction is at best deferred and at worst lost forever. Although an immediate tax benefit for a large cash expenditure is lost, the cost may be deductible in increments over a longer period of time.

If the expenditure is for a tangible asset that has an ascertainable life, it is capitalized and may be deducted as depreciation (or cost recovery) over the life of the asset (for depreciation) or over a statutory period (for cost recovery under either ACRS or MACRS).[55] Land is not subject to depreciation (or cost recovery) since it does not have an ascertainable life.

EXAMPLE 35 Stan purchased a prime piece of land located in an apartment-zoned area. Stan paid $500,000 for the property, which had an old but usable apartment building on it. He immediately had the building demolished at a cost of $100,000. The $500,000 purchase price and the $100,000 demolition costs must be capitalized, and the basis of the land is $600,000. Since land is a nondepreciable asset, no deduction is allowed. More favorable tax treatment might result if Stan rented the apartments in the old building for a period of time to attempt to establish that there was no intent to demolish the building. If Stan's attempt is successful, it might be possible to allocate a substantial portion of the original purchase price of the property to the building (a depreciable asset). When the building is later demolished, any remaining adjusted basis can be deducted as an ordinary (§ 1231) loss. (See Chapter 17 for a discussion of the treatment of § 1231 assets.) ▼

If the expenditure is for an intangible asset (e.g., copyright, patent, covenant not to compete, goodwill), the capitalized expenditure can be amortized, regardless of whether or not the intangible asset has an ascertainable life. Prior to the effect of RRA of 1993, intangible assets with indeterminate lives (e.g., goodwill) could not be amortized.

Intangible assets, referred to as § 197 intangibles, are amortized over a 15-year statutory period using the straight-line method.[56] This statutory change has

---

[53] § 263(a)(1).
[54] Reg. § 1.263(a)–1(b).
[55] See Chapter 8 for the discussion of depreciation and cost recovery.
[56] § 197.

produced both positive and negative results. On the positive side, goodwill is now subject to amortization. On the negative side, intangibles with an actual life shorter than 15 years must be amortized over the longer 15-year statutory period (e.g., a covenant not to compete with a 5-year life).

TRANSACTIONS BETWEEN RELATED PARTIES

The Code places restrictions on the recognition of gains and losses from **related-party transactions.** Without these restrictions, relationships created by birth, marriage, and business would provide endless possibilities for engaging in financial transactions that produce tax savings with no real economic substance or change. For example, to create an artificial loss, a wife could sell investment property to her husband at a loss and deduct the loss on their joint return. Her husband could then hold the asset indefinitely, and the family would sustain no real economic loss. A complex set of laws has been designed to eliminate such possibilities.

Losses. The Code provides for the disallowance of any "losses from sales or exchanges of property . . . directly or indirectly" between related parties.[57] When the property is subsequently sold to a nonrelated party, any gain recognized is reduced by the loss previously disallowed. Any disallowed loss not used by the related-party buyer to offset his or her recognized gain on a subsequent sale or exchange to an unrelated party is permanently lost.

EXAMPLE 36 Freida sells common stock with a basis of $1,000 to her son, Bill, for $800. Bill sells the stock several years later for $1,100. Freida's $200 loss is disallowed upon the sale to Bill, and only $100 of gain ($1,100 selling price − $800 basis − $200 disallowed loss) is taxable to him upon the subsequent sale. ▼

EXAMPLE 37 George sells common stock with a basis of $1,050 to his son, Ray, for $800. Ray sells the stock eight months later to an unrelated party for $900. Ray's gain of $100 ($900 selling price − $800 basis) is not recognized because of George's previously disallowed loss of $250. Note that the offset may result in only partial tax benefit upon the subsequent sale (as in this case). If the property had not been transferred to Ray, George could have recognized a $150 loss upon the subsequent sale to the unrelated party ($1,050 basis − $900 selling price). ▼

EXAMPLE 38 Pete sells common stock with a basis of $1,000 to an unrelated third party for $800. Pete's son repurchased the same stock in the market on the same day for $800. The $200 loss is not allowed because the transaction is an indirect sale between related parties.[58] ▼

Unpaid Expenses and Interest. The law prevents related taxpayers from engaging in tax avoidance schemes where one related taxpayer uses the accrual method of accounting and the other uses the cash basis. An accrual basis, closely held corporation, for example, could borrow funds from a cash basis individual shareholder. At the end of the year, the corporation would accrue and deduct the interest, but the cash basis lender would not recognize interest income since no interest had been paid. Section 267 specifically defers the deduction of the

---

[57] § 267(a)(1).
[58] *McWilliams v. Comm.*, 47–1 USTC ¶9289, 35 AFTR 1184, 67 S.Ct. 1477 (USSC, 1947).

accruing taxpayer until the recipient taxpayer must include it in income; that is, when it is actually paid to the cash basis taxpayer. This *matching* provision applies to interest as well as other expenses, such as salaries and bonuses.

This deduction deferral provision does not apply if both of the related taxpayers use the accrual method or both use the cash method. Likewise, it does not apply if the related party reporting income uses the accrual method and the related party taking the deduction uses the cash method.

Relationships and Constructive Ownership.
Section 267 operates to disallow losses and defer deductions only between related parties. Losses or deductions generated by similar transactions with an unrelated party are allowed. *Related parties* include the following:

- Brothers and sisters (whether whole, half, or adopted), spouse, ancestors (parents, grandparents), and lineal descendants (children, grandchildren) of the taxpayer.
- A corporation owned more than 50 percent (directly or indirectly) by the taxpayer.
- Two corporations that are members of a controlled group.
- A series of other complex relationships between trusts, corporations, and individual taxpayers.

Constructive ownership provisions are applied to determine whether the taxpayers are related. Under these provisions, stock owned by certain relatives or related entities is *deemed* to be owned by the taxpayer for purposes of applying the loss and expense deduction disallowance provisions. A taxpayer is deemed to own not only his or her stock but the stock owned by his or her lineal descendants, ancestors, brothers and sisters or half-brothers and half-sisters, and spouse. The taxpayer is also deemed to own his or her proportionate share of stock owned by any partnership, corporation, estate, or trust of which he or she is a member. An individual is deemed to own any stock owned, directly or indirectly, by his or her partner. However, constructive ownership by an individual of the partnership's and the other partner's shares does not extend to the individual's spouse or other relatives (no double attribution).

EXAMPLE 39
The stock of Sparrow Corporation is owned 20% by Ted, 30% by Ted's father, 30% by Ted's mother, and 20% by Ted's sister. On July 1 of the current year, Ted loaned $10,000 to Sparrow Corporation at 8% annual interest, principal and interest payable on demand. For tax purposes, Sparrow uses the accrual basis, and Ted uses the cash basis. Both are on a calendar year. Since Ted is deemed to own the 80% owned by his parents and sister, he constructively owns 100% of Sparrow Corporation. If the corporation accrues the interest within the taxable year, no deduction can be taken until payment is made to Ted. ▼

SUBSTANTIATION REQUIREMENTS

The tax law is built on a voluntary system. Taxpayers file their tax returns, report income and take deductions to which they are entitled, and pay their taxes through withholding or estimated tax payments during the year. The taxpayer has the burden of proof for substantiating expenses deducted on the returns and must retain adequate records. Upon audit, the IRS will disallow any undocumented or unsubstantiated deductions. These requirements have resulted in numerous conflicts between taxpayers and the IRS.

Some events throughout the year should be documented as they occur. For example, it is generally advisable to receive a pledge payment statement from one's church, in addition to a canceled check (if available) for proper documentation of a charitable contribution.[59] In addition, for charitable contributions, a donor must obtain a receipt from the donee for contributions of $250 or more. Other types of deductible expenditures may require receipts or some other type of support.

Specific and *more stringent* rules for deducting travel, entertainment, and gift expenses are discussed in Chapter 9. Certain mixed-use (both personal and business use) and listed property are also subject to the adequate records requirement (discussed in Chapter 8).

EXPENSES AND INTEREST RELATING TO TAX-EXEMPT INCOME

Certain income, such as interest on municipal bonds, is tax-exempt.[60] The law also allows the taxpayer to deduct expenses incurred for the production of income.[61] Deduction disallowance provisions, however, make it impossible to make money at the expense of the government by excluding interest income and deducting interest expense.[62]

EXAMPLE 40

Sandy, a taxpayer in the 36% bracket, purchased $100,000 of 6% municipal bonds. At the same time, she used the bonds as collateral on a bank loan of $100,000 at 8% interest. A positive cash flow would result from the tax benefit as follows:

Cash paid out on loan	($8,000)
Cash received from bonds	6,000
Tax savings from deducting interest expense (36% of $8,000 interest expense)	2,880
Net positive cash flow	$ 880

To eliminate the possibility illustrated in Example 40, the Code specifically disallows as a deduction the expenses of producing tax-exempt income. Interest on any indebtedness incurred or continued to purchase or carry tax-exempt obligations also is disallowed.

Judicial Interpretations. It is often difficult to show a direct relationship between borrowings and investment in tax-exempt securities. Suppose, for example, that a taxpayer borrows money, adds it to existing funds, buys inventory and stocks, then later sells the inventory and buys municipal bonds. A series of transactions such as these can completely obscure any connection between the loan and the tax-exempt investment. One solution would be to disallow interest on any debt to the extent that the taxpayer holds any tax-exempt securities. This approach would preclude individuals from deducting part of their home mortgage interest if they owned any municipal bonds. The law was not intended to go to such extremes. As a result, judicial interpretations have tried to be reasonable in disallowing interest deductions.

In one case, a company used municipal bonds as collateral on short-term loans to meet seasonal liquidity needs.[63] The Court disallowed the interest deduction on the grounds that the company could predict its seasonal liquidity needs. The

---

[59] Rev.Proc. 92–71, 1992–2 C.B. 437, addresses circumstances where checks are not returned by a financial institution or where electronic transfers are made.
[60] § 103.
[61] § 212.
[62] § 265.
[63] *The Wisconsin Cheeseman, Inc. v. U.S.*, 68–1 USTC ¶9145, 21 AFTR2d 383, 388 F.2d 420 (CA–7, 1968).

company could anticipate the need to borrow the money to continue to carry the tax-exempt securities. The same company *was* allowed an interest deduction on a building mortgage, even though tax-exempt securities it owned could have been sold to pay off the mortgage. The Court reasoned that short-term liquidity needs would have been impaired if the tax-exempt securities were sold. Furthermore, the Court ruled that carrying the tax-exempt securities bore no relationship to the long-term financing of a construction project.

EXAMPLE 41

In January of the current year, Alan borrowed $100,000 at 8% interest. He used the loan proceeds to purchase 5,000 shares of stock in White Corporation. In July, he sold the stock for $120,000 and reinvested the proceeds in City of Denver bonds, the income from which is tax-exempt. Assuming the $100,000 loan remained outstanding throughout the entire year, Alan cannot deduct the interest attributable to the period in which he held the bonds. ▼

TIME VALUE OF TAX DEDUCTIONS

TAX PLANNING CONSIDERATIONS

4 LEARNING OBJECTIVE
Identify tax planning opportunities for maximizing deductions and minimizing the disallowance of deductions.

Cash basis taxpayers often have the ability to make early payments for their expenses at the end of the tax year. This permits the payments to be deducted currently instead of in the following tax year. In view of the time value of money, a tax deduction this year may be worth more than the same deduction next year. Before employing this strategy, the taxpayer must consider next year's expected income and tax rates and whether a cash-flow problem may develop from early payments. Thus, the time value of money as well as tax rate changes must be considered when an expense can be paid and deducted in either of two years.

EXAMPLE 42

Jena pledged $5,000 to her church's special building fund. She can make the contribution in December 1997 or January 1998. Jena is in the 36% tax bracket in 1997, and in the 31% bracket in 1998. She itemizes in both years. Assume Jena's discount rate is 8%. If she takes the deduction in 1997, she saves $365 ($1,800 − $1,435), due to the decrease in the tax rates and the time value of money.

	1997	1998
Contribution	$5,000	$5,000
Tax bracket	.36	.31
Tax savings	$1,800	$1,550
Discounted @ 8%	1.0	.926
Savings in present value	$1,800	$1,435

▼

EXAMPLE 43

Assume the same facts as in Example 42, except that Jena is in the 31% bracket in both 1997 and 1998. By taking the deduction in 1997, Jena saves $115 ($1,550 − $1,435), due to the time value of money.

	1997	1998
Contribution	$5,000	$5,000
Tax bracket	.31	.31
Tax savings	$1,550	$1,550
Discounted @ 8%	1.0	.926
Savings in present value	$1,550	$1,435

▼

Concept Summary 6–2

Classification of Expenses

Expense Item	Deductible For AGI	Deductible From AGI	Not Deductible	Applicable Code §
Investment expenses				
Rent and royalty	X			§ 62(a)(4)
All other investments		X[4]		§ 212
Employee expenses				
Commuting expenses			X	§ 262
Travel and transportation[1]		X[4,5]		§ 162(a)(2)
Reimbursed expenses[1]	X			§ 62(a)(2)(A)
Moving expenses	X			§ 62(a)(15)
Entertainment[1]		X[4,5]		§ 162(a)
All other employee expenses[1]		X[4,5]		§ 162(a)
Certain expenses of performing artists	X			§ 62(a)(2)(B)
Trade or business expenses	X			§§ 162 and 62(a)(1)
Casualty losses				
Business	X			§ 165(c)(1)
Personal		X[6]		§ 165(c)(3)
Tax determination				
Collection or refund expenses	X[8]	X[4]		§§ 212 and 62(a)(1) or (4)
Bad debts	X			§§ 166 and 62(a)(1) or (3)
Medical expenses		X[7]		§ 213
Charitable contributions		X		§ 170
Taxes				
Trade or business	X			§§ 162 and 62(a)(1)
Personal taxes				
Real property		X		§ 164(a)(1)
Personal property		X		§ 164(a)(2)
State and local income		X		§ 164(a)(3)
Investigation of a business[2]	X			§§ 162 and 62(a)(1)
Interest				
Business	X			§§ 162 and 62(a)(1)
Personal		X[3]	X[9]	§ 163(a), (d), and (h)
All other personal expenses			X	§ 262

1. Deduction *for* AGI if reimbursed, an adequate accounting is made, and employee is required to repay excess reimbursements.
2. Provided certain criteria are met.
3. Subject to the excess investment interest and the qualified residence interest provisions.
4. Subject (in the aggregate) to a 2%-of-AGI floor imposed by § 67.
5. Only 50% of meals and entertainment are deductible.
6. Subject to a 10%-of-AGI floor and a $100 floor.
7. Subject to a 7.5%-of-AGI floor.
8. Only the portion relating to business, rental, or royalty income or losses.
9. Other personal interest is disallowed.

UNREASONABLE COMPENSATION

In substantiating the reasonableness of a shareholder-employee's compensation, an internal comparison test is sometimes useful. If it can be shown that nonshareholder-employees and shareholder-employees in comparable positions receive comparable compensation, it is indicative that compensation is not unreasonable.

Another possibility is to demonstrate that the shareholder-employee has been underpaid in prior years. For example, the shareholder-employee may have agreed to take a less-than-adequate salary during the unprofitable formative years of the business. He or she would expect the "postponed" compensation to be paid in later, more profitable years. The agreement should be documented, if possible, in the corporate minutes.

Keep in mind that in testing for reasonableness, the *total* pay package must be considered. Look at all fringe benefits or perquisites, such as contributions by the corporation to a qualified pension plan. Even though those amounts are not immediately available to the covered shareholder-employee, they must be taken into account.

EXCESSIVE EXECUTIVE COMPENSATION

With the $1 million limit on the deduction of compensation of covered employees, many corporations and their executives must engage in additional tax planning. Previously, concerns over the deductibility of compensation related primarily to closely held corporations. The $1 million limit applies specifically to publicly held corporations. In many instances, it is now necessary for these corporations to restructure the compensation packages of their top executives in order to deduct payments in excess of $1 million. Opportunities include compensation payable on a commission basis, certain other performance-based compensation, payments to qualified retirement plans, and payments that are excludible fringe benefits.

SHIFTING DEDUCTIONS

Taxpayers should manage their obligations to avoid the loss of a deduction. Deductions can be shifted among family members, depending upon which member makes the payment. For example, a father buys a condo for his daughter and puts the title in both names. The taxpayer who makes the payment gets the deduction for the property taxes. If the condo is owned by the daughter only and her father makes the payment, neither is entitled to a deduction. In this case, the father should make a cash gift to the daughter who then makes the payment to the taxing authority.

HOBBY LOSSES

To demonstrate that an activity has been entered into for the purpose of making a profit, a taxpayer should treat the activity as a business. The business should engage in advertising, use business letterhead stationery, and maintain a business phone.

If a taxpayer's activity earns a profit in three out of five consecutive years, the presumption is that the activity is engaged in for profit. It may be possible for a cash basis taxpayer to meet these requirements by timing the payment of expenses or the receipt of revenues. The payment of certain expenses incurred before the end of the year might be made in the following year. The billing of year-end sales might be delayed so that collections are received in the following year.

Keep in mind that the three-out-of-five-years rule under § 183 is not absolute. All it does is shift the presumption. If a profit is not made in three out of five years, the losses may still be allowed if the taxpayer can show that they are due to the nature of the business. For example, success in artistic or literary endeavors can take a long time. Also, due to the present state of the economy, even full-time farmers and ranchers are often unable to show a profit. How can one expect a part-time farmer or rancher to do so?

Merely satisfying the three-out-of-five-years rule does not guarantee that a taxpayer is automatically home free. If the three years of profits are insignificant relative to the losses of other years, or if the profits are not from the ordinary operation of the business, the taxpayer is vulnerable. The IRS may still be able to establish that the taxpayer is not engaged in an activity for profit.

EXAMPLE 44

Ashley had the following gains and losses in an artistic endeavor:

1993	($ 50,000)
1994	(65,000)
1995	400
1996	200
1997	125

Under these circumstances, the IRS might try to overcome the presumption. ▼

If Ashley in Example 44 could show conformity with the factors enumerated in the Regulations or could show evidence of business hardships (e.g., injury, death, or illness), the government cannot override the presumption.[64]

CAPITAL EXPENDITURES

On the sale of a sole proprietorship where the sales price exceeds the fair market value of the tangible assets and stated intangible assets, a planning opportunity may exist for both the seller and the buyer. The seller's preference is for the excess amount to be allocated to goodwill. Goodwill is a capital asset whereas a covenant not to compete produces ordinary income treatment (see Chapter 16).

Because both a covenant and goodwill are amortized over a statutory 15-year period, the tax results of a covenant and goodwill are the same for the buyer. However, the buyer should recognize that an allocation to goodwill rather than a covenant may provide a tax benefit to the seller. Therefore, the seller and buyer, in negotiating the sales price, should factor in the tax benefit to the seller of having the excess amount labeled goodwill rather than a covenant not to compete. Of course, if the noncompetition aspects of a covenant are important to the buyer, part of the excess amount can be assigned to a covenant.

---

[64] *Faulconer, Sr. v. Comm.*, 84–2 USTC ¶9955, 55 AFTR2d 85–302, 748 F.2d 890 (CA–4, 1984), *rev'g* 45 TCM 1084, T.C.Memo. 1983–165.

KEY TERMS

Accounting method, 6–9

Deductions *for* adjusted gross income, 6–2

Deductions *from* adjusted gross

income, 6–2

Hobby losses, 6–16

Ordinary and necessary, 6–6

Reasonableness, 6–7

Related-party transactions, 6–27

Vacation home, 6–19

PROBLEM MATERIALS

DISCUSSION QUESTIONS

1. "All income must be reported and all deductions are allowed unless specifically disallowed in the Code." Discuss.

2. Discuss the difference in the tax treatment of deductions *for* and deductions *from* AGI.

3. Does an expenditure that is classified as a deduction *from* AGI produce the same tax benefit as an expenditure that is classified as a deduction *for* AGI?

4. Classify each of the following expenditures as a deduction *for* AGI, a deduction *from* AGI, or not deductible:
    a. Allison pays qualified moving expenses of $3,000.
    b. Emalie gives $1,000 to the Girl Scouts.
    c. Amos pays alimony of $2,500 per month to his former spouse.
    d. Arnold pays $600 for real estate taxes levied by the county on his personal residence.
    e. April gives $1,000 to a family whose house was destroyed by a fire.

5. Classify each of the following expenditures as a deduction *for* AGI, a deduction *from* AGI, or not deductible:
    a. Amos contributes $500 to his H.R. 10 plan (i.e., a retirement plan for a self-employed individual).
    b. Keith pays $500 of child support to his former wife, Renee, for the support of their son, Chris.
    c. Judy pays $500 for professional dues that are reimbursed by her employer.
    d. Ted pays $500 as the monthly mortgage payment on his personal residence. Of this amount, $100 represents a payment on principal, and $400 represents an interest payment.
    e. Lynn pays $500 to a moving company for moving her household goods to Detroit where she is starting a new job.

6. Larry and Susan each invest $10,000 in separate investment activities. They each incur deductible expenses of $800 associated with their respective investments. Explain why Larry's expenses are properly classified as deductions *from* AGI (itemized deductions) and Susan's expenses are appropriately classified as deductions *for* AGI.

7. List the three items that § 162 specifically excludes from classification as a trade or business expense.

8. Raven, Inc., an aircraft manufacturer, retains Major General Ryan and Lieutenant General Morales as consultants. Each is paid $200,000 during the year. General Ryan is on active duty with the U.S. Air Force, while General Morales is retired from the Bolivian Air Force. Each is on the procurement committee for his country's air force. Raven has submitted bids for the sale of its fighter aircraft to the United States and Bolivia.
    a. Under what circumstances can Raven deduct the payments?
    b. If deductible, are the payments deductible *for* AGI or *from* AGI?

CHAPTER 6 Deductions and Losses: In General   6–35

9. Wendy, a machinist employed by Silver Airlines, owns 25 shares of Silver Airlines stock. Silver has 900,000 shares of stock outstanding. Wendy spends $800 to travel to Chicago for Silver's annual meeting. Her expenses would have been $500 more, but she was permitted to fly free on Silver. She attended both days of the shareholders' meeting and actively participated. What are the tax consequences of the trip for Wendy?

10. Sam and Vera are the owners of a corporation. To reduce the corporation's taxable income, they pay a $1,000 salary each month to their 7-year-old daughter, Peg. Why is this salary disallowed as a deduction?

11. Which of the following losses are deductible?
    a. Loss on the sale of a factory building used in a trade or business.
    b. Loss on the sale of a truck held for personal use.
    c. Loss from the destruction by a tornado of a warehouse used in a trade or business.
    d. Loss on the destruction by fire of the taxpayer's residence.
    e. Loss on the sale of Lavender Corporation stock held as an investment.

12. Mary Kate owns a building that she leases to an individual who operates a grocery store. Rent income is $10,000 and rental expenses are $6,000. On what Form 1040 schedule or schedules are the income and expenses reported?

13. Distinguish between the timing for the recording of a deduction under the cash method versus the accrual method.

14. Landry, a cash basis taxpayer, decides to reduce his taxable income for 1997 by buying $10,000 worth of supplies on December 28, 1997. The supplies will be used up in 1998.
    a. Can Landry deduct this expenditure in 1997?
    b. Would your answer differ if Landry bought the supplies because a supplier was going out of business and had given him a significant discount on the supplies?

15. What is the significance of the all events and economic performance tests?

16. James provides a one-year warranty on the vacuum cleaners manufactured by his company. Claims under the warranty typically amount to 2% of sales. Can James use the reserve method to account for the warranty expense?

17. Lemon, Inc., is a soft-drink distributor. Lemon's delivery trucks frequently are required to park in "No Parking" zones in order to make their deliveries. Occasionally, the trucks are ticketed and Lemon pays the parking fine. Can Lemon deduct these fines?

18. Ted is an agent for an airline manufacturer and is negotiating a sale with a representative of the U.S. government and with a representative of a developing country. Ted's company has sufficient capacity to handle only one of the orders. Both orders will have the same contract price. Ted believes that if his employer will authorize a $500,000 payment to the representative of the foreign country, he can guarantee the sale. He is not sure that he can obtain the same result with the U.S. government. Identify the relevant tax issues for Ted.

19. Edna obtains a divorce from Ralph for which she incurs legal fees of $10,000. Distinguish between the types of expenses associated with the divorce that are deductible by Edna and those that are not deductible.

20. Stuart, an insurance salesman, is arrested for allegedly robbing a convenience store. He hires an attorney who is successful in getting the charges dropped. Is the attorney's fee deductible?

21. Linda operates a drug-running operation. Which of the following expenses she incurs can reduce taxable income?
    a. Bribes paid to border guards.
    b. Salaries to employees.
    c. Price paid for drugs purchased for resale.
    d. Kickbacks to police.
    e. Rent on an office.

22. Gordon anticipates that being positively perceived by the individual who is elected mayor will be beneficial for his business. Therefore, he contributes to the campaigns of

both the Democratic and the Republican candidates. The Republican candidate is elected mayor. Can Gordon deduct any of the political contributions he made?

23. Melissa, the owner of a sole proprietorship that has 20 employees, does not provide health insurance for her employees. She is going to spend $1,500 lobbying in opposition to health care legislation that would require her to provide employee health insurance. Discuss the tax advantages and disadvantages of her paying the $1,500 to a professional lobbyist rather than spending the $1,500 on in-house lobbying expenditures.

24. What limits exist on the deductibility of executive compensation? Do the limits apply to all types of business entities? Are there any exceptions to the limitations?

25. What is the significance of one's present occupation in the deductibility of expenses incurred in investigating another business?

26. Amanda had been raising quarter horses for three years. Each year, her losses were about $15,000. She projects that her losses for the current year will be about $10,000. However, if she sells a promising mare before the end of the year, the $10,000 projected loss can be converted into a $4,000 projected profit. Without the perceived need to produce a current-year profit, Amanda would prefer to keep the mare for breeding purposes. Identify the relevant tax issues for Amanda.

27. Discuss the tax treatment of the rental of a vacation home if it is:
    a. Rented 10 days during the year.
    b. Rented 130 days during the year; used personally for 12 days.
    c. Rented for 250 days; used personally for 40 days.

28. Karen and Andy own a beach house. They have an agreement with a rental agent to rent it up to 200 days per year. For the past three years, the agent has been successful in renting it for 200 days. Karen and Andy use the beach house for one week during the summer and one week during Thanksgiving. Their daughter, Sarah, a college student, has asked if she and some friends can use the beach house for the week of spring break. Advise Karen and Andy how they should respond and identify any relevant tax issues.

29. Contrast the differing results obtained in a personal/rental situation by allocating property taxes and mortgage interest on the IRS's basis and the court's basis. Which method would the taxpayer prefer?

30. Hank was transferred from Phoenix to North Dakota on March 1 of the current year. He immediately put his home in Phoenix up for rent. The home was rented May 1 to November 30 and was vacant during the month of December. It was rented again on January 1 for six months. What expenses, if any, can Hank deduct on his return? Which deductions are *for* AGI and which ones are *from* AGI?

31. Erika would like to help her daughter Hillary and son-in-law James with what she hopes are short-term financial problems. This assistance will be in the form of paying their monthly mortgage payments for the past six months. If the payments are not made, the mortgage company will foreclose on their residence. Erika's preference is to make the payments directly to the mortgage company. However, she is willing to give the money to Hillary and James who then would pay the arrearages. Advise Erika on which option, if any, offers preferential tax treatment to her.

32. Explain which, if any, legal fees incurred obtaining a divorce are deductible. Are they deductible *for* or *from* AGI?

33. Igor repaired the roof on his factory at a cost of $1,500 in the current year. During the same year, Raisa replaced the roof on her small rental house for $1,500. Both taxpayers are on the cash basis. Are their expenditures treated the same on their tax returns? Why or why not?

34. Ella owns 60% of the stock of Peach. The stock has declined in value since Ella purchased it five years ago. She is going to sell 5% of her stock to a relative to pay her 12-year-old daughter's private school tuition. Ella is also going to make a gift of 10% of her stock to another relative. Identify the relevant tax issues for Ella.

35. Tara sold 100 shares of Eagle Company stock to Frank, her brother, for $20,000. She had originally paid $16,000 for the stock. Frank later sold the stock for $15,000 on the open market. What are the tax consequences to Tara and Frank? Would your answer differ if Tara had sold the stock to Frank for its fair market value of $12,000?

36. Helen owns 20% of Black Corporation; 20% of Black's stock is owned by Sara, Helen's mother; 15% is owned by Richard, Helen's brother; the remaining 45% is owned by unrelated parties. Helen is on the cash basis, and Black Corporation is on the accrual basis. On December 31, 1997, Black accrued Helen's salary of $5,000 and paid it on April 4, 1998. Both are on a calendar year. What is the tax effect to Helen and Black?

PROBLEMS

37. Sandra is an attorney. She incurs the following expenses when she and her employee, Fred, attend the American Bar Association convention in San Francisco:

    Conference registration:
        Sandra $200
        Fred   200
    Airline tickets from Pittsburgh to San Francisco:
        Sandra   700
        Fred   400
    Lodging in San Francisco:
        Sandra   450
        Fred   250

    Calculate the effect of these expenses on Sandra's AGI.

38. Calvin received the following income and incurred and paid the following expenses during the current tax year:

Salary income	$60,000
Dividend income	4,000
Interest income	3,000
Contributions to First Church	2,500
Real estate taxes on personal residence	1,800
Alimony paid to former spouse	12,000
Retirement plan contribution	2,000
Mortgage interest on personal residence	6,000
State income taxes	3,500
Loss on the sale of stock	900

    Calculate Calvin's AGI.

39. Sam and his wife Vera own all of the stock of Thrush. Vera is the president and Sam is the vice-president. Vera and Sam are paid salaries of $400,000 and $300,000, respectively, each year. They consider the salaries to be reasonable based on a comparison with salaries paid for comparable positions in comparable companies. They project Thrush's taxable income for next year, before their salaries, to be $800,000. They decide to place their four teenage children on the payroll and to pay them total salaries of $100,000. The children will each work about five hours per week for Thrush.
    a. What are Sam and Vera trying to achieve by hiring the children?
    b. Calculate the tax consequences of hiring the children on Thrush, and on Sam and Vera's family.

40. Amber incurs the following losses during the current tax year:

Loss on the sale of Brown stock	$ 500
Theft loss of uninsured car used in Amber's business	1,200
Loss on the sale of Amber's personal use car	2,000
Loss on the sale of Amber's personal residence	10,000

Calculate Amber's deductible losses.

41. The income statement for Karl's business reported the following revenues and expenses for 1997, the initial year of operations:

Sales revenue (including $8,000 credit sales uncollected at year-end)	$60,000
Wage expenses ($1,000 unpaid at year-end)	22,000
Office expenses (supplies, copying, etc.)	2,000
Bad debt expense (consists of reserve established for $3,000 with write-offs of $500)	3,000
Utilities and telephone expense*	6,000
Insurance expense*	4,000
Rent expense (January 1, 1997–January 31, 1998)	9,750

*Amount incurred = amount paid.

a. Calculate Karl's AGI using the accrual method.
b. Calculate Karl's AGI using the cash method.

42. Doris is the owner of a sole proprietorship that uses the cash method. She leases an office building for $24,000 for an 18-month period on October 1, 1997. In order to obtain this favorable lease rate, she pays the $24,000 at the inception of the lease. How much rent expense may Doris deduct on her 1997 tax return?

43. Duck, an accrual basis corporation, sponsored a rock concert on December 29, 1997. Gross receipts were $300,000. The following expenses were incurred and paid as indicated:

Expense		Payment Date
Rental of coliseum	$ 25,000	December 21, 1997
Cost of goods sold:		
Food	30,000	December 30, 1997
Souvenirs	60,000	December 30, 1997
Performers	100,000	January 5, 1998
Cleaning of coliseum	10,000	February 1, 1998

Since the coliseum was not scheduled to be used again until January 15, the company with which Duck had contracted did not actually perform the cleanup until January 8–10, 1998.

Calculate Duck's net income from the concert for tax purposes for 1997.

44. Doug incurred and paid the following expenses during the year:

- $50 for a ticket for running a red light while he was commuting to work.
- $100 for a ticket for parking in a handicapped parking space.
- $200 to an attorney to represent him for the two aforesaid tickets.
- $500 to an attorney to draft a lease agreement with a tenant for a one-year lease on an apartment that Doug owns.

Determine the amount that Doug can deduct for each of these payments.

45. Marcia, an attorney with a leading New York law firm, is convicted of failing to file Federal income tax returns for 1994–1996. Her justification for failing to do so was the pressures of her profession (80–90 hour workweeks). She is assessed taxes, interest, and penalties of $90,000 by the IRS. In addition, she incurs related legal fees of $60,000. Determine the amount that Marcia can deduct, and classify it as a deduction *for* or a deduction *from* AGI.

46. David runs an illegal numbers racket. His gross revenues were $500,000. He incurred the following expenses:

Illegal kickbacks	$20,000
Salaries	80,000
Rent	24,000
Utilities and telephone	9,000
Bribes to police	25,000
Interest	6,000
Depreciation on equipment	12,000

    a. What is his net income from this business that is includible in taxable income?
    b. If the business was an illegal drug operation and cost of goods sold was $100,000, how would your answer differ?

47. Polly made the following political contributions:

To national Republican Party	$1,000
To national Democratic Party	1,000
To local candidate for mayor	500
To candidate for state senate	200
To candidate for school board	100

    How much can Polly deduct?

48. Edward, an attorney, is hired by a major accounting firm to represent it and its clients in dealing with members of the U.S. Congress. The accounting firm is supporting liability reform that would limit the "joint and several" liability of professionals such as attorneys and CPAs. During the year, Edward is paid $10,000 for this representation. The firm also reimburses Edward $2,500 for meal and entertainment expenses incurred in meeting with members of Congress and their staffs. In addition, the firm pays Edward $5,000 for his work in opposing legislation that would adversely affect several of its major clients. What is the amount of these payments that the firm may deduct?

49. Amber, a publicly held corporation, currently pays its president an annual salary of $900,000. In addition, it contributes $20,000 annually to a defined contribution pension plan for him. As a means of increasing company profitability, the board of directors decides to increase the president's compensation. Two proposals are being considered. Under the first proposal, the salary and pension contribution for the president would be increased by 30%. Under the second proposal, Amber would implement a performance-based compensation program that is projected to provide about the same amount of additional compensation and pension contribution for the president.
    a. Evaluate the alternatives from the perspective of Amber, Inc.
    b. Prepare a letter to Amber's board of directors that contains your recommendations. Address the letter to the board chairperson, Agnes Riddle, whose address is 100 James Tower, Cleveland, OH 44106.

50. Jenny, the owner of a very successful restaurant chain, is exploring the possibility of expanding the chain into a city in the neighboring state. She incurs $20,000 of expenses associated with this investigation. Based on the regulatory environment for restaurants in the city, she decides not to do so. During the year, she also investigates opening a hotel that will be part of a national hotel chain. Her expenses for this are $15,000. The hotel begins operations on December 1. Determine the amount that Jenny can deduct in the current year for investigating these two businesses.

51. Tim traveled to a neighboring state to investigate the purchase of two restaurants. His expenses included travel, legal, accounting, and miscellaneous expenses. The total was $12,000. He incurred the expenses in March and April 1997.
    a. What can Tim deduct in 1997 if he was in the restaurant business and did not acquire the two restaurants?
    b. What can Tim deduct in 1997 if he was in the restaurant business and acquired the two restaurants and began operating them on July 1, 1997?
    c. What can Tim deduct in 1997 if he did not acquire the two restaurants and was not in the restaurant business?
    d. What can he deduct in 1997 if he acquired the two restaurants, but was not in the restaurant business when he acquired them? Operations began on July 1, 1997.

52. Alfred, who is single, conducts an activity that is appropriately classified as a hobby. The activity produces the following revenues and expenses:

Revenue	$10,000
Property taxes	3,000
Materials and supplies	2,000
Utilities	1,000
Advertising	2,500
Insurance	500
Depreciation	4,000

    Without regard to this activity, Alfred's AGI is $40,000. Determine how much income Alfred must report, the amount of the expenses he is permitted to deduct, and his taxable income.

53. Samantha is an executive with an AGI of $100,000 before consideration of income or loss from her miniature horse business. Her income comes from winning horse shows, stud fees, and sales of yearlings. Her home is on 20 acres, 18 of which she uses to pasture the horses and upon which she has erected stables, paddocks, fences, tack houses, and so forth.

    Samantha uses an office in her home that is 10% of the square footage of the house. She uses the office exclusively for keeping records of breeding lines, histories, and show and veterinary records. Her records show the following income and expenses for the current year:

Income from fees, prizes, and sales	$22,000
Expenses	
Entry fees	1,000
Feed and veterinary bills	4,000
Supplies	900
Publications and dues	500
Travel to horse shows (no meals)	2,300
Salaries and wages of employees	8,000
Depreciation on horse equipment	3,000
Depreciation on horse farm improvements	7,000
Depreciation on 10% of home	1,000
Total home mortgage interest	24,000
Total property taxes on home	2,200
Total property taxes on horse farm improvements	800

    The mortgage interest is only on her home. The horse farm improvements are not mortgaged.
    a. How must Samantha treat the income and expenses of the operation if the miniature horse activity is held to be a hobby?
    b. How would your answer in (a) differ if the horse operation was held to be a business?

CHAPTER 6 Deductions and Losses: In General

54. Ashley, who lives in a summer resort area, **rented her personal residence for two weeks** while she was visiting Paris. Rent income was $2,000. Related expenses for the year were as follows:

Real property taxes	$ 3,000
Mortgage interest	6,000
Utilities	2,400
Insurance	1,200
Repairs	600
Depreciation	12,000

    Determine the effect on Ashley's AGI.

55. In 1997, Anna rented her vacation home for 60 days, used it personally for 20 days, and left it vacant for 285 days. She had the following income and expenses:

Rent income	$ 6,000
Expenses	
Real estate taxes	2,000
Interest on mortgage	9,000
Utilities	600
Repairs	1,000
Roof replacement	12,000
Depreciation	8,000

    a. Compute Anna's net rent income or loss and the amounts she can itemize on her tax return, using the court's approach in allocating property taxes and interest.
    b. How would your answer in (a) differ using the IRS's method of allocating property taxes and interest?

56. How would your answer in Problem 55 differ if Anna had rented the house for 90 days and had used it personally for 12 days?

57. Chee, single, age 40, had the following income and expenses in 1997:

Income	
Salary	$ 43,000
Rental of vacation home (rented 60 days, used personally 60 days, vacant 245 days)	4,000
Municipal bond interest	2,000
Dividend from General Motors	400
Expenses	
Interest	
On home mortgage	8,400
On vacation home	4,758
On loan used to buy municipal bonds	3,100
Taxes	
Property tax on home	2,200
Property tax on vacation home	1,098
State income tax	3,300
Charitable contributions	1,100
Tax return preparation fee	300
Utilities and maintenance on vacation home	2,600
Depreciation on rental 50% of vacation home	3,500

    Calculate Chee's taxable income for 1997 before personal exemptions.

58. During the current year, Robert pays the following amounts associated with his own residence and that of his daughter, Anne:

- Property taxes:
  On home owned by Robert — $3,000
  On home owned by Anne — 1,500

- Mortgage interest:
  Associated with Robert's home — 8,000
  Associated with Anne's home — 4,500

- Repairs to:
  Robert's home — 1,200
  Anne's home — 700

- Utilities:
  Robert's home — 2,700
  Anne's home — 1,600

- Replacement of roof:
  Robert's home — 4,000

a. Which of these expenses can Robert deduct?
b. Which of these expenses can Anne deduct?
c. Are the deductions *for* AGI or *from* AGI (itemized)?
d. How could the tax consequences be improved?

59. Lee incurred the following expenses in the current tax year. Indicate, in the spaces provided, whether each expenditure is deductible *for* AGI, *from* AGI, or not deductible.

	Expense Item	Deductible For AGI	Deductible From AGI	Not Deductible
a.	Lee's personal medical expenses			
b.	Lee's dependent daughter's medical expenses			
c.	Real estate taxes on rental property			
d.	Real estate taxes on Lee's personal residence			
e.	Real estate taxes on daughter's personal residence			
f.	Lee's state income taxes			
g.	Interest on rental property mortgage			
h.	Interest on Lee's personal residence mortgage			
i.	Interest on daughter's personal residence mortgage			
j.	Interest on business loans			
k.	Charitable contributions			
l.	Depreciation on rental property			
m.	Utilities & maintenance on:			
	(1) Rental property			
	(2) Lee's home			
	(3) Daughter's home			
n.	Depreciation on auto used in Lee's business			
o.	Depreciation on Lee's personal auto			
p.	Depreciation on daughter's personal auto			

60. Janet Saxon sold stock (basis of $40,000) to her brother, Fred, for $32,000.
    a. What are the tax consequences to Janet?
    b. What are the tax consequences to Fred if he later sells the stock for $42,000? For $28,000? For $36,000?
    c. Write a letter to Janet in which you inform her of the tax consequences if she sells the stock to Fred for $32,000 and explain how a sales transaction could be structured that would produce better tax consequences for her. Janet's address is 32 Country Lane, Lawrence, KS 66045.

61. The Robin Corporation is owned as follows:

Irene	20%
Paul, Irene's husband	20%
Sylvia, Irene's mother	15%
Ron, Irene's father	25%
Quinn, an unrelated party	20%

    Robin is on the accrual basis, and Irene and Paul are on the cash basis. Irene and Paul each loaned the Robin Corporation $10,000 out of their separate funds. On December 31, 1997, Robin accrued interest at 7% on both loans. The interest was paid on February 4, 1998. What is the tax treatment of this interest expense/income to Irene, Paul, and Robin?

62. What is Kim's constructive ownership of Wren Corporation, given the following information?

Shares owned by Kim	900
Shares owned by Sam, Kim's uncle	600
Shares owned by Barbara, Kim's partner	30
Shares owned by Vera, Kim's granddaughter	670
Shares owned by unrelated parties	800

63. Chris has a brokerage account and buys on the margin, which resulted in an interest expense of $9,000 during the year. Income generated through the brokerage account was as follows:

Municipal interest	$35,000
Taxable dividends and interest	65,000

    How much investment interest can Chris deduct?

64. Jay's sole proprietorship has the following assets

	Basis	Fair Market Value
Cash	$ 10,000	$ 10,000
Accounts receivable	18,000	18,000
Inventory	25,000	30,000
Patent	22,000	40,000
Land	50,000	75,000
	$125,000	$173,000

    The building in which Jay's business is located is leased. The lease expires at the end of the year.
    Jay is age 70 and would like to retire. He expects to be in the 36% tax bracket. Jay is negotiating the sale of the business with Lois, a key employee. They have agreed on the fair market value of the assets, as indicated above, and agree the total purchase price should be about $200,000.

a. Advise Jay regarding how the sale should be structured.
b. Advise Lois regarding how the purchase should be structured.
c. What might they do to achieve an acceptable compromise?

CUMULATIVE PROBLEMS

65. John and Mary Jane Sanders are married, filing jointly. Their address is 204 Shoe Lane, Blacksburg, VA 24061. They are expecting their first two children (twins) in early 1998. John's salary in 1997 was $85,000, from which $11,000 of Federal income tax and $3,600 of state income tax were withheld. Mary Jane made $40,000 and had $4,000 of Federal income tax and $2,000 of state income tax withheld. The appropriate amount of FICA tax was withheld for John and for Mary Jane.

John and Mary Jane are both covered by their employer's medical insurance policies with all of the premiums being paid by the employers. The premiums were $3,600 for John and $3,200 for Mary Jane. Mary Jane received medical benefits of $2,400 under the plan. John was not ill during 1997.

John makes alimony payments of $30,000 per year to June, his former wife. He also makes child support payments of $12,000 for his son, Rod, who lives with June except for two months in the summer when he visits John and Mary Jane.

Mary Jane's father lived with them until his death in October. His only sources of income were salary of $1,600, $500 of unemployment compensation benefits, and Social Security benefits of $3,200. Of this amount, he deposited $3,000 in a savings account. The remainder of his support, including funeral expenses of $5,000, was provided by John and Mary Jane.

Other income received by the Sanders was as follows:

• Interest on certificates of deposit	$ 900
• Dividend income	600
• Share of partnership taxable income (distributions from the partnership to Mary Jane were $200)	300
• Award received by Mary Jane from employer for outstanding suggestion for cutting costs	1,000

They made charitable contributions of $3,500 during the year and paid an additional $700 in state income taxes in 1997 upon filing their 1996 state income tax return. Their deductible home mortgage interest was $9,000, and their property taxes came to $2,400. They had no other deductible expenses.

Part 1—Tax Computation
Calculate their tax (or refund) due for 1997. Suggested software (if available): *TurboTax* or *MacInTax*.

Part 2—Tax Planning
Assume that they come to you for advice in December 1997. John has learned that he will receive a $15,000 bonus. He wants to know if he should take it in December 1997 or in January 1998. Mary Jane will quit work on December 31 to stay home with the twins. Their itemized deductions will decrease by $2,000 because Mary Jane will not have state income taxes withheld. Mary Jane does not expect to receive the employee award in 1998. She expects the medical benefits received to be $4,500. The Sanders expect all of their other income items to remain the same in 1998. Write a letter to John and Mary Jane that contains your advice and prepare a memo for the tax files. Suggested software (if available): *TurboTax* or *MacInTax*.

66. Helen Archer, age 30, is single and lives at 120 Sanborne Avenue, Springfield, IL 60740. Her Social Security number is 648–11–9981. Helen has been divorced from her former husband, Albert, for three years. She has a son, Jason, who is age 8. His Social Security number is 648–98–3471. Helen does not wish to contribute $3 to the Presidential Election Campaign Fund.

Helen, an advertising executive, earned a salary of $75,000 in 1996. Her employer withheld $9,900 in Federal income tax, $3,200 in state income tax, and the appropriate amount of FICA tax.

Helen has legal custody of Jason. Jason lives with his father during summer vacation. Albert indicates that his expenses for Jason are $10,000. Helen can document that she spent $4,500 for Jason's support during 1996.

Helen's mother died on January 7, 1996. Helen inherited assets worth $200,000 from her mother. As the sole beneficiary of her mother's life insurance policy, Helen received insurance proceeds of $100,000. Her mother's cost basis for the life insurance policy was $40,000. Helen's favorite aunt gave her $10,000 for her thirtieth birthday in October.

On November 8, 1996, Helen sells for $19,000 Amber stock that she had purchased for $20,000 from her first cousin, Walt, on December 5, 1991. His cost basis for the stock was $12,000, and the stock was worth $20,000 on December 5, 1991. On December 1, 1996, Helen sold Falcon stock for $15,000. She had acquired the stock on July 2, 1996, for $9,000.

An examination of Helen's records reveals the following information:

- Received interest income of $3,500 from First Savings Bank.
- Received dividend income of $1,200 from Amber.
- Received $1,700 of interest income on City of Springfield school bonds.
- Received alimony of $20,000 from Albert.

From her checkbook records, she determines that she made the following payments during 1996.

- Charitable contributions of $1,500 to First Presbyterian Church and $800 to the American Red Cross.
- Mortgage interest on her residence of $6,500.
- Property taxes of $1,900 on her residence and $800 on her car.
- Sales taxes of $1,700.
- Estimated Federal income taxes of $10,000 and estimated state income taxes of $1,000.
- Medical expenses of $4,000 for her and $500 for Jason. Eight hundred dollars of her medical expenses were reimbursed by her medical insurance policy in December.

Calculate Helen's net tax payable or refund due for 1996. If you use tax forms, you will need Form 1040 and Schedules A, B, and D. Suggested software (if available): *TurboTax* or *MacInTax*.

RESEARCH PROBLEMS

Note: **West's Federal Taxation on CD-ROM** *can be used in preparing solutions to the Research Problems. Alternatively, tax research materials contained in a standard tax library can be used.*

Research Problem 1. Noel is an employee of the U.S. Immigration Service and is stationed at Dorval International Airport in Montreal. Noel received a Living Quarters Allowance (LQA) of $10,000. An LQA is a stipend provided to qualifying Federal employees stationed abroad who are not otherwise provided with housing and is excludible from gross income under § 912(1)(C).

Noel and Janet, his spouse, purchased a house in Montreal and lived in it during the tax year. They deducted mortgage interest of $9,000 and property taxes of $2,000. A Revenue Agent disallowed a portion of these deductions under § 265 (Expenses and Interest Relating to Tax-Exempt Income). The disallowed amount was the portion that was allocable to the tax-exempt LQA. Advise Noel on the appropriate treatment of the disallowed property taxes and mortgage interest.

Research Problem 2. Gray Chemical Company manufactured pesticides that were toxic. Over the course of several years, the toxic waste contaminated the air and water around the company's plant. Several employees suffered toxic poisoning, and the Environmental Protection Agency cited the company for violations. In court, the judge found Gray guilty and imposed fines of $15 million. The company voluntarily set up a charitable fund for the purpose of bettering the environment and funded it with $8 million. The company incurred legal expenses in setting up the foundation and defending itself in court. The court reduced the fine from $15 million to $7 million.

Gray Chemical Company deducted the $8 million paid to the foundation and the legal expenses incurred. The IRS disallowed both deductions on the grounds that the payment was, in fact, a fine and in violation of public policy.

Gray's president, Ted Jones, has contacted you regarding the deductibility of the $7 million fine, the $8 million payment to the foundation, and the legal fees. Write a letter to Mr. Jones that contains your advice and prepare a memo for the tax files. Gray's address is 200 Lincoln Center, Omaha, NE 68182.

Partial list of research aids:
§§ 162(a) and (f).
Reg. § 1.162–21(b).

Research Problem 3. Rex and Agnes Harrell purchased a beach house at Duck, North Carolina, in early 1996. Although they intended to use the beach house occasionally for recreational purposes, they also planned to rent it through the realty agency that had handled the purchase in order to help pay the mortgage payments, property taxes, and maintenance costs. Rex is a surgeon, and Agnes is a counselor.

The beach house was in need of substantial repairs. Rather than hiring a contractor, Rex and Agnes decided they would make the repairs themselves. During both high school and college, Rex had worked summers in construction. In addition, he had taken an advanced course in woodworking and related subjects from a local community college several years ago.

During 1996, according to a log maintained by the Harrells, they occupied the beach house on 38 days and rented it on 49 days. The log also indicated that on 24 of the 38 days that they occupied the beach house, one or both of them were engaged in work on the beach house. Their two teenage children were with them on all of these days, but did not help with the work being done. On their 1996 income tax return, Rex and Agnes, who filed a joint return, treated the beach house as a rental property and deducted a pro rata share of the property taxes, mortgage interest, utilities, maintenance and repairs, and depreciation in determining their net loss from the beach home. A Revenue Agent has limited the deductions to the rent income. He contends that the 14-day personal use provision was exceeded and that many of the alleged repairs were capital expenditures. Advise the Harrells on how they should respond to the IRS.

Research Problem 4. Sam and Vera were engaged to be married. While Vera was on a four-day business trip to Madison County, she met Tex. They fell in love and were married the following week in Las Vegas. Vera returned the engagement ring to Sam who was devastated. He sued Vera for breach of promise to marry. Can Sam deduct the attorney's fees associated with the lawsuit?

Research Problem 5. Tom and Jane owned a second home in a resort area in Florida. During the year, they vacationed there for 27 days. Their vacation home was leased to the resort rental company under a 30-month lease. The rental agreement provided that the resort was to pay Tom and Jane a fixed annual rent of $21,000 plus 40% of rent income in excess of $52,500. For any day that Tom and Jane used the vacation home, they were required to pay the resort $10 (limited to four weeks). For any personal use in excess of four weeks, they were required to pay the resort 80% of the regular rental amount. The resort rental agent rented their vacation home to tourists for 200 days during the year.

Based on the rental agreement, Tom and Jane's accountant concluded that the vacation home should be classified as primarily rental use property rather than personal/rental use property. The accountant concluded that for § 280A purposes the vacation home was rented for 338 days (i.e., 365 days – 27 days) rather than for only 200 days. Therefore, Tom and Jane were able to take deductions on the vacation home in excess of the rent income. On audit, the IRS treated the property as personal/rental use property and disallowed the excess deductions.

Advise Tom and Jane on how they should respond to the IRS.

Use the tax resources of the internet to address the following questions. Do not restrict your search to the World Wide Web, but include a review of newsgroups and general reference materials, practitioner sites and resources, primary sources of the tax law, chat rooms and discussion groups, and other opportunities.

Research Problem 6. Locate and read a recent judicial or administrative ruling regarding the deductibility of hobby losses. Look for rulings that deal with horse breeding, professional sports teams, or art collecting activities. Which criteria did the ruling emphasize in upholding or reversing the taxpayers deduction for such losses?

Research Problem 7. The $1 million maximum compensation deduction does not seem to have deterred large corporations from remunerating their executives at very high levels of pay. What techniques are being used to work around the millionaires provision? Are executives taking pay cuts, or are their salaries being deferred or changed in nature due to § 162(m)?

TEAM PROJECT: ARTHUR ANDERSEN TAX CHALLENGE CASES

For more information on the Arthur Andersen Tax Challenge Cases, refer to Chapter 1, page 1–38.

Information related to tax issues and problems that are discussed in this chapter may be found in the

Day and Ball case on pages 2, 3, 5, and 20–24
Miller case on pages 1, 11–12 and 31

Read and analyze the case you have been assigned and *identify* any issues and problems that are related to material covered in this chapter. If the information provided in the case is complete, prepare answers for this part of the case at this time. If you need information that is contained in the later parts of the case, write a memo summarizing the questions or problems so you can prepare a complete answer at a later date.

CHAPTER 7

DEDUCTIONS AND LOSSES: CERTAIN BUSINESS EXPENSES AND LOSSES

LEARNING OBJECTIVES

After completing Chapter 7, you should be able to:

1. Determine the amount, classification, and timing of the bad debt deduction.

2. Understand the tax treatment of worthless securities including § 1244 stock.

3. Distinguish between deductible and nondeductible losses of individuals.

4. Identify a casualty and determine the amount, classification, and timing of casualty and theft losses.

5. Recognize and apply the alternative tax treatments for research and experimental expenditures.

6. Determine the amount of the net operating loss and recognize the impact of the carryback and carryover provisions.

7. Identify tax planning opportunities in deducting certain business expenses, business losses, and personal losses.

OUTLINE

Bad Debts, 7-3

Specific Charge-Off Method, 7-3

Business versus Nonbusiness Bad Debts, 7-4

Loans between Related Parties, 7-5

Loss of Deposits in Insolvent Financial Institutions, 7-6

Worthless Securities, 7-7

Small Business Stock, 7-8

Losses of Individuals, 7-9

Events That Are Not Casualties, 7-10

Theft Losses, 7-10

When to Deduct Casualty Losses, 7-11

Measuring the Amount of Loss, 7-12

Statutory Framework for Deducting Losses of Individuals, 7-15

Personal Casualty Gains and Losses, 7-15

Research and Experimental Expenditures, 7-17

Expense Method, 7-18

Deferral and Amortization Method, 7-18

Net Operating Losses, 7-19

Carryback and Carryover Periods, 7-20

Computation of the Net Operating Loss, 7-21

Recomputation of Tax Liability for Year to Which Net Operating Loss Is Carried, 7-24

Calculation of the Remaining Net Operating Loss, 7-25

Tax Planning Considerations, 7-26

Tax Consequences of the *Groetzinger* Case 7-26

Documentation of Related-Taxpayer Loans, Casualty Losses, and Theft Losses, 7-26

Small Business Stock, 7-27

Casualty Losses, 7-27

Net Operating Losses, 7-27

Working with the tax formula for individuals requires the proper classification of items that are deductible *for* adjusted gross income (AGI) and items that are deductions *from* AGI (itemized deductions). Business expenses and losses, discussed in this chapter, are reductions of gross income to arrive at the taxpayer's AGI. Expenses and losses incurred in connection with a transaction entered into for profit and attributable to rents and royalties are deducted *for* AGI. All other expenses and losses incurred in connection with a transaction entered into for profit are deducted *from* AGI.

The situation of Robert P. Groetzinger provides an interesting insight into the importance of the proper classification for the individual taxpayer. In January 1978, Groetzinger terminated his employment with a private company and devoted virtually all of his working time to pari-mutuel wagering on dog races. He had no other profession or employment, and his only sources of income, apart from his gambling winnings, were interest, dividends, and sales from investments. During the tax year in question, he went to the track six days a week and devoted 60 to 80 hours per week to preparing and making wagers on his own account.

The tax question that this case presents is whether Groetzinger's gambling activities constitute a trade or business. If the gambling is a trade or business, his gambling losses are deductions *for* AGI. If the gambling activity is not a trade or business, the losses are itemized deductions, and Groetzinger's taxes increase by $2,142.[1]

Deductible losses on personal use property are deducted as an itemized deduction. Itemized deductions are deductions *from* AGI. While the general coverage of itemized deductions is in Chapter 10, casualty and theft losses on personal use property are discussed in this chapter.

In determining the amount and timing of the deduction for bad debts, proper classification is again important. A business bad debt is classified as a deduction *for* AGI, and a nonbusiness bad debt is classified as a short-term capital loss.

---

[1] *Groetzinger v. Comm.*, 85-2 USTC ¶9622, 56 AFTR2d 85-5683, 771 F.2d 269 (CA-7, 1985).

BAD DEBTS

1 LEARNING OBJECTIVE
Determine the amount, classification, and timing of the bad debt deduction.

If a taxpayer sells goods or provides services on credit and the account receivable subsequently becomes worthless, a **bad debt** deduction is permitted only if income arising from the creation of the account receivable was previously included in income.[2] No deduction is allowed, for example, for a bad debt arising from the sale of a product or service when the taxpayer is on the cash basis because no income is reported until the cash has been collected. Permitting a bad debt deduction for a cash basis taxpayer would amount to a double deduction because the expenses of the product or service rendered are deducted when payments are made to suppliers and to employees, or at the time of the sale.

EXAMPLE 1

Tracy, an individual engaged in the practice of accounting, performed accounting services for Pat for which she charged $8,000. Pat never paid the bill, and his whereabouts are unknown.

If Tracy is an accrual basis taxpayer, the $8,000 is included in income when the services are performed. When it is determined that Pat's account will not be collected, the $8,000 is expensed as a bad debt.

If Tracy is a cash basis taxpayer, the $8,000 is not included in income until payment is received. When it is determined that Pat's account will not be collected, the $8,000 is not deducted as a bad debt expense since it was never recognized as income. ▼

A bad debt can also result from the nonrepayment of a loan made by the taxpayer or from purchased debt instruments.

SPECIFIC CHARGE-OFF METHOD

Taxpayers (other than certain financial institutions) may use only the **specific charge-off method** in accounting for bad debts. Certain financial institutions are allowed to use the **reserve method** for computing deductions for bad debts.

A taxpayer using the specific charge-off method may claim a deduction when a specific business debt becomes either partially or wholly worthless or when a specific nonbusiness debt becomes wholly worthless.[3] For the business debt, the taxpayer must satisfy the IRS that the debt is partially worthless and must demonstrate the amount of worthlessness.

If a business debt previously deducted as partially worthless becomes totally worthless in a future year, only the remainder not previously deducted can be deducted in the future year.

In the case of total worthlessness, a deduction is allowed for the entire amount in the year the debt becomes worthless. The amount of the deduction depends on the taxpayer's basis in the bad debt. If the debt arose from the sale of services or products and the face amount was previously included in income, that amount is deductible. If the taxpayer purchased the debt, the deduction is equal to the amount the taxpayer paid for the debt instrument.

One of the more difficult tasks is determining if and when a bad debt is worthless. The loss is deductible only in the year of partial or total worthlessness

---

[2] Reg. § 1.166–1(e).

[3] § 166(a) and Reg. § 1.166.

> **CONCEPT SUMMARY 7–1**
>
> **Specific Charge-Off Method**
>
> | | |
> |---|---|
> | Expense deduction and account write-off | The expense arises and the write-off takes place when a specific business account becomes either partially or wholly worthless or when a specific nonbusiness account becomes wholly worthless. |
> | Recovery of accounts previously written off | If the account recovered was written off during the current taxable year, the write-off entry is reversed. If the account recovered was written off during a previous taxable year, income is created subject to the tax benefit rule. |

for business debts and only in the year of total worthlessness for nonbusiness debts. Legal proceedings need not be initiated against the debtor when the surrounding facts indicate that such action will not result in collection.

EXAMPLE 2   In 1995, Ross loaned $1,000 to Kay, who agreed to repay the loan in two years. In 1997, Kay disappeared after the note became delinquent. If a reasonable investigation by Ross indicates that he cannot find Kay or that a suit against Kay would not result in collection, Ross can deduct the $1,000 in 1997. ▼

Bankruptcy is generally an indication of at least partial worthlessness of a debt. Bankruptcy may create worthlessness before the settlement date. If this is the case, the deduction may be taken in the year of worthlessness.

EXAMPLE 3   In Example 2, assume Kay filed for personal bankruptcy in 1996 and that the debt is a business debt. At that time, Ross learned that unsecured creditors (including Ross) were ultimately expected to receive 20¢ on the dollar. In 1997, settlement is made and Ross receives only $150. He should deduct $800 ($1,000 loan – $200 expected settlement) in 1996 and $50 in 1997 ($200 balance – $150 proceeds). ▼

If a receivable has been written off as uncollectible during the current tax year and is subsequently collected during the current tax year, the write-off entry is reversed. If a receivable has been written off as uncollectible, the collection of the receivable in a later tax year may result in income being recognized. Income will result if the deduction yielded a tax benefit in the year it was taken. See Examples 38 and 39 in Chapter 5.

BUSINESS VERSUS NONBUSINESS BAD DEBTS

A **nonbusiness bad debt** is a debt unrelated to the taxpayer's trade or business either when it was created or when it became worthless. The nature of a debt depends on whether the lender was engaged in the business of lending money or whether there is a proximate relationship between the creation of the debt and the lender's trade or business. The use to which the borrowed funds are put by the debtor is of no consequence. Loans to relatives or friends are the most common type of nonbusiness bad debt.

EXAMPLE 4 José loaned his friend, Esther, $1,500. Esther used the money to start a business, which subsequently failed. Even though proceeds of the loan were used in a business, the loan is a nonbusiness bad debt because the business was Esther's, not José's. ▼

The distinction between a business bad debt and a nonbusiness bad debt is important. A **business bad debt** is deductible as an ordinary loss in the year incurred, whereas a nonbusiness bad debt is always treated as a short-term capital loss. Thus, regardless of the age of a nonbusiness bad debt, the deduction may be of limited benefit due to the capital loss limitations on deductibility in any one year. The maximum amount of a net short-term capital loss that an individual can deduct against ordinary income in any one year is $3,000 (see Chapter 16 for a detailed discussion). Although no deduction is allowed when a nonbusiness bad debt is partially worthless, the taxpayer is entitled to deduct the net amount of the loss upon final settlement.

The following example is an illustration of business bad debts adapted from the Regulations.[4]

EXAMPLE 5 In 1996, Leif sold his business but retained a claim (note or account receivable) against Bob. The claim became worthless in 1997. Leif's loss is treated as a business bad debt because the debt was created in the conduct of his former trade or business. Leif is accorded business bad debt treatment even though he was holding the note as an investor and was no longer in a trade or business when the claim became worthless. ▼

The nonbusiness bad debt provisions are *not* applicable to corporations. It is assumed that any loans made by a corporation are related to its trade or business. Therefore, any bad debts of a corporation are business bad debts.

LOANS BETWEEN RELATED PARTIES

Loans between related parties (especially family members) raise the issue of whether the transaction was a *bona fide* loan or a gift. The Regulations state that a bona fide debt arises from a debtor-creditor relationship based on a valid and enforceable obligation to pay a fixed or determinable sum of money. Thus, individual circumstances must be examined to determine whether advances between related parties are gifts or loans. Some considerations are these:

- Was a note properly executed?
- Was there a reasonable rate of interest?
- Was collateral provided?
- What collection efforts were made?
- What was the intent of the parties?

EXAMPLE 6 Lana loans $2,000 to her widowed mother for an operation. Lana's mother owns no property and is not employed, and her only income consists of Social Security benefits. No note is issued for the loan, no provision for interest is made, and no repayment date is mentioned. In the current year, Lana's mother dies leaving no estate. Assuming the loan is not repaid, Lana cannot take a deduction for a nonbusiness bad debt because the facts indicate that no debtor-creditor relationship existed. ▼

---

[4] Reg. § 1.166–5(d).

ETHICAL CONSIDERATIONS

Writing Off a Loan to a Friend

Loans to family members and friends raise concerns with respect to whether a deductible bad debt exists. The fact that the debtor is a family member or friend does not preclude a deduction for a bad debt. However, evidence must show that the debt is bona fide and that it is in fact worthless.

Frank, an engineer, loans $8,000 to Chris, a friend from high school who is a musician. Chris uses the money to cut a record. The loan, which is evidenced by a formal written instrument, has a maturity date of three years and an 8 percent interest rate.

The record is unsuccessful, and at the maturity date, Chris does not repay the loan. Frank writes Chris twice requesting repayment. Frank hears from another friend that Chris is now divorced and has a drinking problem.

Frank decides to give up trying to collect the loan. Since Frank's combined Federal and state tax rate is 44 percent, he decides he can live without $4,480 ($8,000 × 56%). He deducts the $8,000 as a nonbusiness bad debt on his Federal and state tax returns.

Evaluate the financial and ethical aspects of what Frank has done.

LOSS OF DEPOSITS IN INSOLVENT FINANCIAL INSTITUTIONS

Qualified individuals can *elect* to deduct losses on deposits in qualified financial institutions as personal casualty losses in the year in which the amount of the loss can be reasonably estimated. If the election is made to treat a loss on a deposit as a personal casualty loss, no bad debt deduction for the loss is allowed.[5] As a personal casualty loss, the loss is subject to the $100 per event floor and the 10 percent-of-AGI aggregate floor. Both floors limiting casualty losses are explained later in the chapter. The amount of loss to be recognized under the election is the difference between (1) the taxpayer's basis in the deposit and (2) a reasonable estimate of the amount to be received.

A *qualified individual* is any individual other than:

- An owner of 1 percent or more of the value of the stock of the institution in which the loss was sustained.
- An officer of the institution.
- Certain relatives and other persons who are tax-related to such owners and officers.

A *qualified financial institution* is a commercial bank, thrift institution, insured credit union, or any similar institution chartered and supervised under Federal or state law. A *deposit*, for purposes of this provision, is any deposit, withdrawal certificate, or withdrawable or repurchasable share of or in a qualified financial institution. The term *insolvent* generally denotes a situation where the liabilities exceed the fair market value of the assets.

If the individual does not elect to deduct the loss as a casualty loss, it is treated as a nonbusiness bad debt and, hence, as a short-term capital loss. As a short-term capital loss, it is subject to the capital loss limitation rules (see the discussion in Chapter 16).

---

[5] § 165(l).

TAX IN THE NEWS

FAMILY BAD DEBTS CAN BE DEDUCTED UNDER THE RIGHT CIRCUMSTANCES

A father who lived in Tennessee loaned his daughter $37,500 for a skating rink business. Although the loan was not evidenced by a note with a market rate of interest and a specified repayment schedule, the father had a long history of making such loans to his relatives and of being repaid (e.g., 8 other loans between 1985 and 1988). The daughter was a skater and thought she would be qualified to run this type of business. The daughter repaid $2,000, but the business failed two years later. No subsequent payments were made, and the daughter declared bankruptcy under Chapter 7 the following year.

The father deducted the $35,500 on his income tax return as a nonbusiness bad debt. According to the IRS, the father made no attempt to collect the debt. Therefore, since this was a family situation, the IRS disallowed the deduction.

The Tax Court sided with the father. Since the daughter declared bankruptcy, attempts by the father to collect would have been futile. Buttressing the father's position even prior to the bankruptcy was his familiarity with the daughter's business affairs (i.e., the amount of her outstanding debts, her frequent requests to borrow additional funds, and her landlord's seizure of her business assets). He knew that even if he tried to collect, he would be unsuccessful. In addition, the fact that he had made loans to other family members that had been repaid supported his position that he expected to be repaid.

SOURCE: *Loy E. Bowman*, T.C. Memo. 1995–259, 69 TCM 2886.

WORTHLESS SECURITIES

2 LEARNING OBJECTIVE
Understand the tax treatment of worthless securities including § 1244 stock.

A loss is allowed for securities that become *completely* worthless during the year (**worthless securities**).[6] Such securities are shares of stock, bonds, notes, or other evidence of indebtedness issued by a corporation or government. The losses generated are treated as capital losses deemed to have occurred on the *last day* of the taxable year. By treating the loss as having occurred on the last day of the taxable year, a loss that would otherwise have been classified as short term (if the date of worthlessness was used) may be classified as a long-term capital loss. Capital losses may be of limited benefit due to the $3,000 capital loss limitation.

EXAMPLE 7

Ali, a calendar year taxpayer, owns stock in Owl Corporation (a publicly held company). The stock was acquired as an investment on November 30, 1996, at a cost of $5,000. On April 1, 1997, the stock became worthless. Since the stock is deemed to have become worthless as of December 31 of 1997, Ali has a capital loss from an asset held for 13 months (a long-term capital loss). ▼

---
[6] § 165(g).

Concept Summary 7–2

Bad Debt Deductions

```
Does a valid debt exist (a debtor-creditor relationship)? --No--> A
        |
       Yes
        v
Is the debt really worthless? --No--> A
        |
       Yes
        v
Is the debt evidenced by a security? --Yes--> See § 165(g) dealing with worthless securities (discussed on page 7–7)
        |
        No
        v
Is the creditor a corporation? --Yes--> C
        |
        No
        v
Is the debt a deposit of a qualified individual in a qualified financial institution? --Yes--> Is an election made to treat the loss as a personal casualty? --Yes--> D
        |                                                                                             |
        No                                                                                           No
        v                                                                                             v
Is the debt created or incurred in connection with the creditor's trade or business? --No--> B
        |
       Yes
        v
        C
```

Legend to Tax Treatment

- **A**: No deduction allowed
- **B**: Nonbusiness bad debt (treated as a short-term capital loss)
- **C**: Business bad debt (treated as an ordinary deduction)
- **D**: Personal casualty loss

SMALL BUSINESS STOCK

The general rule is that shareholders receive capital gain or loss treatment upon the sale or exchange of stock. However, it is possible to receive an ordinary loss deduction if the loss is sustained on **small business stock (§ 1244 stock)**. This loss could arise from a sale of the stock or from the stock becoming worthless. Only *individuals*[7] who acquired the stock *from* the corporation are eligible to receive

---

[7] The term "individuals" for this purpose includes a partnership but not a trust or an estate.

ordinary loss treatment under § 1244. The ordinary loss treatment is limited to $50,000 ($100,000 for married individuals filing jointly) per year. Losses on § 1244 stock in excess of the statutory limits receive capital loss treatment.

The corporation must meet certain requirements for the loss on § 1244 stock to be treated as an *ordinary*—rather than a capital—loss. The major requirement is that the total amount of money and other property received by the corporation for stock as a contribution to capital (or paid-in surplus) does not exceed $1 million. The $1 million test is made at the time the stock is issued. Section 1244 stock can be common or preferred stock. Section 1244 applies only to losses. If § 1244 stock is sold at a gain, the Section has no application, and the gain is capital gain.

EXAMPLE 8

On July 1, 1995, Iris, a single individual, purchased 100 shares of Eagle Corporation common stock for $100,000. The Eagle stock qualified as § 1244 stock. On June 20, 1997, Iris sold all of the Eagle stock for $20,000. Because the Eagle stock is § 1244 stock, Iris would have $50,000 of ordinary loss and $30,000 of long-term capital loss. ▼

LOSSES OF INDIVIDUALS

3   LEARNING OBJECTIVE
Distinguish between deductible and nondeductible losses of individuals.

An individual may deduct the following losses under § 165(c):

- Losses incurred in a trade or business.
- Losses incurred in a transaction entered into for profit.
- Losses caused by fire, storm, shipwreck, or other casualty or by theft.

An individual taxpayer may deduct losses to property used in the taxpayer's trade or business or losses to property used in a transaction entered into for profit. Examples include a loss on property used in a proprietorship, a loss on property held for rent, or a loss on stolen bearer bonds. Note that an individual's losses on property used in a trade or business or on transactions entered into for profit are not limited to losses caused by fire, storm, shipwreck, or other casualty or by theft.

An individual taxpayer suffering losses from damage to nonbusiness property can deduct only those losses attributable to fire, storm, shipwreck, or other casualty or theft. Although the meaning of the terms *fire, storm, shipwreck,* and *theft* is relatively free from dispute, the term *other casualty* needs further clarification. It means casualties analogous to fire, storm, or shipwreck. The term also includes accidental loss of property provided the loss qualifies under the same rules as any other casualty. These rules are that the loss must result from an event that is (1) identifiable; (2) damaging to property; and (3) sudden, unexpected, and unusual in nature.

A *sudden event* is one that is swift and precipitous and not gradual or progressive. An *unexpected event* is an event that is ordinarily unanticipated and occurs without the intent of the individual who suffers the loss. An *unusual event* is one that is extraordinary and nonrecurring and does not commonly occur during the activity in which the taxpayer was engaged when the destruction occurred.[8] Examples include hurricanes, tornadoes, floods, storms, shipwrecks, fires, auto accidents, mine cave-ins, sonic booms, and vandalism. Weather that causes damages (drought, for example) must be unusual and severe for the particular region. Damage must be to the taxpayer's property to qualify as a **casualty loss.**

---

[8] Rev.Rul. 72–592, 1972–2 C.B. 101.

A taxpayer can take a deduction for a casualty loss from an automobile accident only if the damage was not caused by the taxpayer's willful act or willful negligence.

EXAMPLE 9

Ted parks his car on a hill and fails to set the brake properly and to curb the wheels. As a result of Ted's negligence, the car rolls down the hill and is damaged. The repairs to Ted's car should qualify for casualty loss treatment since Ted's act of negligence appears to be simple rather than willful. ▼

EVENTS THAT ARE NOT CASUALTIES

4 LEARNING OBJECTIVE
Identify a casualty and determine the amount, classification, and timing of casualty and theft losses.

Not all acts of God are treated as casualty losses for income tax purposes. Because a casualty must be sudden, unexpected, and unusual, progressive deterioration (such as erosion due to wind or rain) is not a casualty because it does not meet the suddenness test.

Examples of nonsudden events that generally do not qualify as casualties include disease and insect damages. When the damage was caused by termites over a period of several years, some courts have disallowed a casualty loss deduction.[9] On the other hand, some courts have held that termite damage over periods of up to 15 months after infestation constituted a sudden event and was, therefore, deductible as a casualty loss.[10] Despite the existence of some judicial support for the deductibility of termite damage as a casualty loss, the current position of the IRS is that termite damage is not deductible.[11]

Other examples of events that are not casualties are losses resulting from a decline in value rather than an actual loss of the property. No loss was allowed where the taxpayer's home declined in value as a result of a landslide that destroyed neighboring homes but did no actual damage to the taxpayer's home.[12] Similarly, a taxpayer was allowed a loss for the actual flood damage to his property but not for the decline in market value due to the property's being flood-prone.[13]

THEFT LOSSES

Theft includes, but is not necessarily limited to, larceny, embezzlement, and robbery.[14] Theft does not include misplaced items.[15]

Theft losses are computed like other casualty losses (discussed in the following section), but the *timing* for recognition of the loss differs. A theft loss is deducted in the year of discovery, not the year of the theft (unless, of course, the discovery occurs in the same year as the theft). If, in the year of the discovery, a claim exists (e.g., against an insurance company) and there is a reasonable expectation of recovering the adjusted basis of the asset from the insurance company, no deduction is permitted.[16] If, in the year of settlement, the recovery is less than the asset's adjusted basis, a partial deduction may be available. If the recovery is greater than the asset's adjusted basis, gain may be recognized.

---

[9] *Fay v. Helvering,* 41–2 USTC ¶9494, 27 AFTR 432, 120 F.2d 253 (CA–2, 1941); *U.S. v. Rogers,* 41–1 USTC ¶9442, 27 AFTR 423, 120 F.2d 244 (CA–9, 1941).

[10] *Rosenberg v. Comm.,* 52–2 USTC ¶9377, 42 AFTR 303, 198 F.2d 46 (CA–8, 1952); *Shopmaker v. U.S.,* 54–1 USTC ¶9195, 45 AFTR 758, 119 F. Supp. 705 (D.Ct.Mo., 1953).

[11] Rev.Rul. 63–232, 1963–2 C.B. 97.

[12] *H. Pulvers v. Comm.,* 69–1 USTC ¶9222, 23 AFTR2d 69–678, 407 F.2d 838 (CA–9, 1969).

[13] *S. L. Solomon,* 39 TCM 1282, T.C.Memo. 1980–87.

[14] Reg. § 1.165–8(d).

[15] *Mary Francis Allen,* 16 T.C. 163 (1951).

[16] Reg. §§ 1.165–1(d)(2) and 1.165–8(a)(2).

EXAMPLE 10   Keith's new sailboat, which he uses for personal purposes, was stolen from the storage marina in December 1995. He discovered the loss on June 3, 1996, and filed a claim with his insurance company that was settled on January 30, 1997. Assuming there is a reasonable expectation of full recovery, no deduction is allowed in 1996. A partial deduction may be available in 1997 if the actual insurance proceeds are less than the lower of the fair market value or the adjusted basis of the asset. (Loss measurement rules are discussed later in this chapter.) ▼

ETHICAL CONSIDERATIONS

Deducting a Theft Loss

Theft losses of personal use assets are itemized deductions in the year of discovery. The taxpayer must show that the property was actually stolen. Losses due to mislaying or losing property cannot be deducted. If there is no positive proof that a theft occurred, all of the details and evidence should be presented. If the reasonable inferences point to a theft, the Tax Court has allowed a deduction. If the inferences point to a mysterious (unexplained) disappearance, however, the deduction will be disallowed.

A taxpayer went shopping in a major city, riding the subway to and from the city. During the day, he purchased items using money from his wallet. When he arrived home, his wallet was missing. He is considering claiming a theft loss deduction for the wallet and the money it contained.

WHEN TO DEDUCT CASUALTY LOSSES

General Rule. Generally, a casualty loss is deducted in the year the loss occurs. However, no casualty loss is permitted if a reimbursement claim with a *reasonable prospect of full recovery* exists.[17] If the taxpayer has a partial claim, only part of the loss can be claimed in the year of the casualty, and the remainder is deducted in the year the claim is settled.

EXAMPLE 11   Brian's new sailboat was completely destroyed by fire in 1997. Its cost and fair market value were $10,000. Brian's only claim against the insurance company was on a $7,000 policy that was not settled by year-end. The following year, 1998, Brian settled with the insurance company for $6,000. He is entitled to a $3,000 deduction in 1997 and a $1,000 deduction in 1998. If Brian held the sailboat for personal use, the $3,000 deduction in 1997 would be reduced first by $100 and then by 10% of his 1997 AGI. The $1,000 deduction in 1998 would be reduced by 10% of his 1998 AGI (see the following discussion on the $100 and 10% floors). ▼

If a taxpayer receives reimbursement for a casualty loss sustained and deducted in a previous year, an amended return is not filed for that year. Instead, the taxpayer must include the reimbursement in gross income on the return for the year in which it is received to the extent that the previous deduction resulted in a tax benefit.

EXAMPLE 12   Fran had a deductible casualty loss of $5,000 on her 1996 tax return. Fran's taxable income for 1996 was $60,000. In June 1997, Fran was reimbursed $3,000 for the prior year's casualty loss. Fran would include the entire $3,000 in gross income for 1997 because the deduction in 1996 produced a tax benefit. ▼

---

[17] Reg. § 1.165–1(d)(2)(i).

Disaster Area Losses. An exception to the general rule for the time of deduction is allowed for **disaster area losses,** which are casualties sustained in an area designated as a disaster area by the President of the United States.[18] In such cases, the taxpayer may *elect* to treat the loss as having occurred in the taxable year immediately *preceding* the taxable year in which the disaster actually occurred. The rationale for this exception is to provide immediate relief to disaster victims in the form of accelerated tax benefits.

If the due date, plus extensions, for the prior year's return has not passed, a taxpayer makes the election to claim the disaster area loss on the prior year's tax return. If the disaster occurs after the prior year's return has been filed, it is necessary to file either an amended return or a refund claim. In any case, the taxpayer must show clearly that such an election is being made.

Disaster loss treatment also applies in the case of a personal residence that has been rendered unsafe for use as a residence because of a disaster. This provision applies when, within 120 days after the President designates the area as a disaster area, the state or local government where the residence is located orders the taxpayer to demolish or relocate the residence.[19]

MEASURING THE AMOUNT OF LOSS

Amount of Loss. The rules for determining the amount of a loss depend in part on whether business use, income-producing use, or personal use property was involved. Another factor that must be considered is whether the property was partially or completely destroyed.

If business property or property held for the production of income (e.g., rental property) is *completely destroyed*, the loss is equal to the adjusted basis of the property at the time of destruction.

EXAMPLE 13

Vicki's automobile, which was used only for business purposes, was destroyed by fire. Vicki had unintentionally allowed her insurance coverage to expire. The fair market value of the automobile was $9,000 at the time of the fire, and its adjusted basis was $10,000. Vicki is allowed a loss deduction of $10,000 (the basis of the automobile). The $10,000 loss is a deduction *for* AGI. ▼

A different measurement rule applies for *partial destruction* of business property and income-producing property and for *partial* or *complete destruction* of personal use property. In these situations, the loss is the *lesser* of the following:

- The adjusted basis of the property.
- The difference between the fair market value of the property before the event and the fair market value immediately after the event.

EXAMPLE 14

Kelly's uninsured automobile, which was used only for business purposes, was damaged in a wreck. At the date of the wreck, the fair market value of the automobile was $12,000, and its adjusted basis was $9,000. After the wreck, the automobile was appraised at $4,000. Kelly's loss deduction is $8,000 (the lesser of the adjusted basis or the decrease in fair market value). The $8,000 loss is a deduction *for* AGI. ▼

The deduction for the loss of property that is part business and part personal must be computed separately for the business portion and the personal portion.

---

[18] § 165(h).   [19] § 165(k).

Any insurance recovery reduces the loss for business, production of income, and personal use losses. In fact, a taxpayer may realize a gain if the insurance proceeds exceed the amount of the loss. Chapter 17 discusses the treatment of net gains and losses on business property and income-producing property.

A taxpayer is not permitted to deduct a casualty loss for damage to insured personal use property unless he or she files a *timely insurance claim* with respect to the damage to the property. This rule applies to the extent that any insurance policy provides for full or partial reimbursement for the loss.[20]

Generally, an appraisal before and after the casualty is needed to measure the amount of the loss. However, the *cost of repairs* to the damaged property is acceptable as a method of establishing the loss in value provided the following criteria are met:

- The repairs are necessary to restore the property to its condition immediately before the casualty.
- The amount spent for such repairs is not excessive.
- The repairs do not extend beyond the damage suffered.
- The value of the property after the repairs does not, as a result of the repairs, exceed the value of the property immediately before the casualty.[21]

ETHICAL CONSIDERATIONS

Deducting the Cost of Repairs

Twenty years ago, Mary purchased a home for $140,000. The house was fairly new and fully landscaped. On July 15, of the current year, a severe storm blew down several large pine trees in front of the home. Mary paid a local nursery $4,000 to replace the trees with comparable trees. Because Mary's homeowners insurance excludes damage to trees, Mary intends to deduct $4,000 as a casualty loss on her Federal income tax return.

Reduction for $100 and 10 Percent-of-AGI Floors. The amount of the loss for personal use property must be further reduced by a $100 *per event* floor and a 10 percent-of-AGI *aggregate* floor.[22] The $100 floor applies separately to each casualty and applies to the entire loss from each casualty (e.g., if a storm damages both a taxpayer's residence and automobile, only $100 is subtracted from the total amount of the loss). The losses are then added together, and the total is reduced by 10 percent of the taxpayer's AGI. The resulting loss is the taxpayer's itemized deduction for casualty and theft losses.

EXAMPLE 15

Rocky, who had AGI of $30,000, was involved in a motorcycle accident. His motorcycle, which was used only for personal use and had a fair market value of $12,000 and an adjusted basis of $9,000, was completely destroyed. He received $5,000 from his insurance company. Rocky's casualty loss deduction is $900 [$9,000 basis − $5,000 insurance − $100 floor − $3,000 (.10 × $30,000 AGI)]. The $900 casualty loss is an itemized deduction (*from* AGI). ▼

When a nonbusiness casualty loss is spread between two taxable years because of the *reasonable prospect of recovery* doctrine, the loss in the second year is

---

[20] § 165(h)(4)(E).
[21] Reg. § 1.165−7(a)(2)(ii).
[22] § 165(c)(3).

not reduced by the $100 floor. This result occurs because this floor is imposed per event and has already reduced the amount of the loss in the first year. However, the loss in the second year is still subject to the 10 percent floor based on the taxpayer's second-year AGI (refer to Example 11).

Taxpayers who suffer qualified disaster area losses can elect to deduct the losses in the year preceding the year of occurrence. The disaster loss is treated as having occurred in the preceding taxable year. Hence, the 10 percent of AGI floor is determined by using the AGI of the year for which the deduction is claimed.[23]

Multiple Losses. The rules for computing loss deductions where multiple losses have occurred are explained in Examples 16 and 17.

EXAMPLE 16

During the year, Tim had the following casualty losses:

Asset	Adjusted Basis	Fair Market Value of Asset Before the Casualty	Fair Market Value of Asset After the Casualty	Insurance Recovery
A	$900	$600	$-0-	$400
B	300	800	250	100

Assets A and B were used in Tim's business at the time of the casualty. The following losses are allowed:

Asset A: $500. The complete destruction of a business asset results in a deduction of the adjusted basis of the property (reduced by any insurance recovery) regardless of the asset's fair market value.

Asset B: $200. The partial destruction of a business (or personal use) asset results in a deduction equal to the lesser of the adjusted basis ($300) or the decline in value ($550), reduced by any insurance recovery ($100).

Both Asset A and Asset B losses are deductions *for* AGI. The $100 floor and the 10%-of-AGI floor do not apply because the assets are business assets. ▼

EXAMPLE 17

During the year, Emily had AGI of $20,000 and the following casualty losses:

Asset	Adjusted Basis	Fair Market Value of Asset Before the Casualty	Fair Market Value of Asset After the Casualty	Insurance Recovery
A	$ 900	$ 600	$ -0-	$ 200
B	2,500	4,000	1,000	-0-
C	800	400	100	250

Assets A, B, and C were held for personal use, and the losses to these three assets are from three different casualties. The loss for each asset is computed as follows:

Asset A: $300. The lesser of the adjusted basis of $900 or the $600 decline in value, reduced by the insurance recovery of $200, minus the $100 floor.

---

[23] § 165(i).

Asset B: $2,400. The lesser of the adjusted basis of $2,500 or the $3,000 decline in value, minus the $100 floor.

Asset C: $0. The lesser of the adjusted basis of $800 or the $300 decline in value, reduced by the insurance recovery of $250, minus the $100 floor.

Emily's itemized casualty loss deduction for the year is $700:

Asset A loss	$ 300
Asset B loss	2,400
Asset C loss	–0–
Total loss	$ 2,700
Less: 10% of AGI (10% × $20,000)	(2,000)
Itemized casualty loss deduction	$ 700

STATUTORY FRAMEWORK FOR DEDUCTING LOSSES OF INDIVIDUALS

Casualty and theft losses incurred by an individual in connection with a trade or business are deductible *for* AGI.[24] These losses are not subject to the $100 per event and the 10 percent-of-AGI limitations.

Casualty and theft losses incurred by an individual in a transaction entered into for profit are not subject to the $100 per event and the 10 percent-of-AGI limitations. If these losses are attributable to rents or royalties, the deduction is *for* AGI.[25] However, if these losses are not connected with property held for the production of rents and royalties, they are deductions *from* AGI. More specifically, these losses are classified as other miscellaneous itemized deductions. An example of this type of loss would be the theft of a security. The aggregate of certain miscellaneous itemized deductions is subject to a 2 percent-of-AGI floor (explained in Chapter 9).

Casualty and theft losses attributable to personal use property are subject to the $100 per event and the 10 percent-of-AGI limitations. These losses are itemized deductions, but they are not subject to the 2 percent-of-AGI floor.[26]

PERSONAL CASUALTY GAINS AND LOSSES

If a taxpayer has personal casualty and theft gains as well as losses, a special set of rules applies for determining the tax consequences. A **personal casualty gain** is the recognized gain from a casualty or theft of personal use property. A **personal casualty loss** for this purpose is a casualty or theft loss of personal use property after the application of the $100 floor. A taxpayer who has both gains and losses for the taxable year must first net (offset) the personal casualty gains and personal casualty losses. If the gains exceed the losses, the gains and losses are treated as gains and losses from the sale of capital assets. The capital gains and losses are short term or long term, depending on the period the taxpayer held each of the assets. In the netting process, personal casualty and theft gains and losses are not netted with the gains and losses on business and income-producing property.

---

[24] § 62(a)(1).
[25] § 62(a)(4).
[26] § 67(b)(3).

EXAMPLE 18

During the year, Cliff had the following personal casualty gains and losses (after deducting the $100 floor):

Asset	Holding Period	Gain or (Loss)
A	Three months	($ 300)
B	Three years	(2,400)
C	Two years	3,200

Cliff would compute the tax consequences as follows:

Personal casualty gain	$ 3,200
Personal casualty loss ($300 + $2,400)	(2,700)
Net personal casualty gain	$ 500

Cliff would treat all of the gains and losses as capital gains and losses and would have the following:

Short-term capital loss (Asset A)	$ 300
Long-term capital loss (Asset B)	2,400
Long-term capital gain (Asset C)	3,200

If personal casualty losses exceed personal casualty gains, all gains and losses are treated as ordinary items. The gains—and the losses to the extent of gains—are treated as ordinary income and ordinary loss in computing AGI. Losses in excess of gains are deducted as itemized deductions to the extent the losses exceed 10 percent of AGI.[27]

EXAMPLE 19

During the year, Hazel had AGI of $20,000 and the following personal casualty gain and loss (after deducting the $100 floor):

Asset	Holding Period	Gain or (Loss)
A	Three years	($2,700)
B	Four months	200

Hazel would compute the tax consequences as follows:

Personal casualty loss	($2,700)
Personal casualty gain	200
Net personal casualty loss	($2,500)

Hazel would treat the gain and the loss as ordinary items. The $200 gain and $200 of the loss would be included in computing AGI. Hazel's itemized deduction for casualty losses would be computed as follows:

Casualty loss in excess of gain ($2,700 − $200)	$ 2,500
Less: 10% of AGI (10% × $20,000)	(2,000)
Itemized deduction	$ 500

---

[27] § 165(h).

Concept Summary 7–3

Casualty Gains and Losses

	Business Use or Income-Producing Property	**Personal Use Property**
Event creating the loss	Any event.	Casualty or theft.
Amount	The lesser of the decline in fair market value or the adjusted basis, but always the adjusted basis if the property is totally destroyed.	The lesser of the decline in fair market value or the adjusted basis.
Insurance	Insurance proceeds received reduce the amount of the loss.	Insurance proceeds received (or for which there is an unfiled claim) reduce the amount of the loss.
$100 floor	Not applicable.	Applicable per event.
Gains and losses	Gains and losses are netted (see detailed discussion in Chapter 17).	Personal casualty and theft gains and losses are netted.
Gains exceeding losses		The gains and losses are treated as gains and losses from the sale of capital assets.
Losses exceeding gains		The gains—and the losses to the extent of gains—are treated as ordinary items in computing AGI. The losses in excess of gains, to the extent they exceed 10% of AGI, are itemized deductions.

RESEARCH AND EXPERIMENTAL EXPENDITURES

5 LEARNING OBJECTIVE
Recognize and apply the alternative tax treatments for research and experimental expenditures.

Section 174 covers the treatment of research and experimental expenditures. The Regulations define **research and experimental expenditures** as follows:

> . . . all such costs incident to the development of an experimental or pilot model, a plant process, a product, a formula, an invention, or similar property, and the improvement of already existing property of the type mentioned. The term does not include expenditures such as those for the ordinary testing or inspection of materials or products for quality control or those for efficiency surveys, management studies, consumer surveys, advertising, or promotions.[28]

Expenses in connection with the acquisition or improvement of land or depreciable property are not research and experimental expenditures. Rather, they increase the basis of the land or depreciable property. However, depreciation on a building used for research may be a research and experimental expense. Only the depreciation that is a research and experimental expense (not the cost of the asset) is subject to the three alternatives discussed on the following page.

---
[28] Reg. § 1.174–2(a)(1).

The law permits the following *three alternatives* for the handling of research and experimental expenditures:

- Expensed in the year paid or incurred.
- Deferred and amortized.
- Capitalized.

If the costs are capitalized, a deduction is not available until the research project is abandoned or is deemed worthless. Since many products resulting from research projects do not have a definite and limited useful life, a taxpayer should ordinarily elect to write off the expenditures immediately or to defer and amortize them. It is generally preferable to elect an immediate write-off of the research expenditures because of the time value of the tax deduction.

The law also provides for a research activities credit. The credit amounts to 20 percent of certain research and experimental expenditures.[29] (The credit is discussed more fully in Chapter 13.)

EXPENSE METHOD

A taxpayer can elect to expense all of the research and experimental expenditures incurred in the current year and all subsequent years. The consent of the IRS is not required if the method is adopted for the first taxable year in which such expenditures were paid or incurred. Once the election is made, the taxpayer must continue to expense all qualifying expenditures unless a request for a change is made to, and approved by, the IRS. In certain instances, a taxpayer may incur research and experimental expenditures before actually engaging in any trade or business activity. In such instances, the Supreme Court has applied a liberal standard of deductibility and permitted a deduction in the year of incurrence.[30]

DEFERRAL AND AMORTIZATION METHOD

Alternatively, research and experimental expenditures may be deferred and amortized if the taxpayer makes an election.[31] Under the election, research and experimental expenditures are amortized ratably over a period of not less than 60 months. A deduction is allowed beginning with the month in which the taxpayer first realizes benefits from the experimental expenditure. The election is binding, and a change requires permission from the IRS.

EXAMPLE 20

Gold Corporation decided to develop a new line of adhesives. The project was begun in 1997. Gold incurred the following expenses in 1997 in connection with the project:

Salaries	$25,000
Materials	8,000
Depreciation on machinery	6,500

Gold incurred the following expenses in 1998 in connection with the project:

Salaries	$18,000
Materials	2,000
Depreciation on machinery	5,700

---

[29] § 41. See the information in Chapter 13 on the termination date for the research activities credit.

[30] *Snow v. Comm.*, 74–1 USTC ¶9432, 33 AFTR2d 74–1251, 94 S.Ct. 1876 (USSC, 1974).

[31] § 174(b)(2).

TAX IN THE NEWS

ACQUIRING RACEHORSES: A RESEARCH AND DEVELOPMENT EXPENSE

A medical doctor who specialized in oncology and hematology purchased interests in thoroughbred racehorses. He acquired the interests believing that the horses could become champions based on their bloodlines. On his Schedule C, he deducted $165,000 as research and development expenses.

In a notice of deficiency, the IRS disallowed the $165,000 deduction based on the determination that expenses for purchasing racehorses are not research and development expenses.

The Tax Court sided with the IRS, finding that none of the $165,000 was expended on research costs and, therefore, no portion of the expenditure was deductible.

SOURCE: *Patrick F. and Arlene Gwon Sheehy*, 72 TCM 178, T.C.Memo. 1996–334.

The benefits from the project will be realized starting in March 1999. If Gold Corporation elects a 60-month deferral and amortization period, there will be no deduction prior to March 1999, the month benefits from the project begin to be realized. The deduction for 1999 would be $10,867, computed as follows:

Salaries ($25,000 + $18,000)	$43,000
Materials ($8,000 + $2,000)	10,000
Depreciation ($6,500 + $5,700)	12,200
Total	$65,200
$65,200 × (10 months/60 months) =	$10,867

The option to treat research and experimental expenditures as deferred expense is usually employed when a company does not have sufficient income to offset the research and experimental expenses. Rather than create net operating loss carryovers that might not be utilized because of the 15-year limitation on such carryovers, the deferral and amortization method may be used. The deferral of research and experimental expenditures should also be considered if the taxpayer expects higher tax rates in the future.

NET OPERATING LOSSES

6 LEARNING OBJECTIVE
Determine the amount of the net operating loss and recognize the impact of the carryback and carryover provisions.

The requirement that every taxpayer file an annual income tax return (whether on a calendar year or a fiscal year) may result in certain inequities for taxpayers who experience cyclical patterns of income or expense. Inequities result from the application of a progressive rate structure to taxable income determined on an annual basis. A **net operating loss (NOL)** in a particular tax year would produce no tax benefit if the Code did not provide for the carryback and carryforward of such losses to profitable years.

EXAMPLE 21

Juanita has a business and realizes the following taxable income or loss over a five-year period: Year 1, $50,000; Year 2, ($30,000); Year 3, $100,000; Year 4, ($200,000); and Year 5, $380,000. She is married and files a joint return. Hubert also has a business and has a taxable income pattern of $60,000 every year. He, too, is married and files a joint return. Note that both Juanita and Hubert have total taxable income of $300,000 over the five-year period. Assume there is no provision for carryback or carryover of NOLs. Juanita and Hubert would have the following five-year tax bills:

Year	Juanita's Tax	Hubert's Tax
1	$ 8,644	$11,444
2	–0–	11,444
3	22,656	11,444
4	–0–	11,444
5	124,791	11,444
	$156,091	$57,220

The computation of tax is made without regard to any NOL benefit. Rates applicable to 1997 are used to compute the tax.

Even though Juanita and Hubert realized the same total taxable income ($300,000) over the five-year period, Juanita had to pay taxes of $156,091, while Hubert paid taxes of only $57,220. ▼

To provide partial relief from this inequitable tax treatment, a deduction is allowed for NOLs.[32] This provision permits NOLs for any one year to be offset against taxable income of other years. The NOL provision is intended as a form of relief for business income and losses. Thus, only losses from the operation of a trade or business (or profession), casualty and theft losses, or losses from the confiscation of a business by a foreign government can create an NOL. In other words, a salaried individual with itemized deductions and personal exemptions in excess of gross income is not permitted to deduct the excess amounts as an NOL. On the other hand, a personal casualty loss is treated as a business loss and can therefore create (or increase) an NOL for an individual.

CARRYBACK AND CARRYOVER PERIODS

General Rules. An NOL must be applied initially to the three taxable years preceding the year of the loss (unless an election is made not to carry the loss back at all). It is carried first to the third prior year, then to the second prior year, then to the immediately preceding tax year (or until used up). If the loss is not fully used in the carryback period, it must be carried forward to the first year after the loss year, and then forward to the second, third, etc., year after the loss year. The carryover period is 15 years. A loss sustained in 1997 is used in this order: 1994, 1995, 1996, 1998 through 2012.

If the loss is being carried to a preceding year, an amended return is filed on Form 1040X, or a quick refund claim is filed on Form 1045. In any case, a refund of taxes previously paid is requested. When the loss is carried forward, the current return shows an NOL deduction for the prior year's loss.

---

[32] § 172.

TAX IN THE NEWS

HOBBY LOSS VERSUS BUSINESS NOL

The income and deductions of a sole proprietor's trade or business are reported on Schedule C of Form 1040. Schedule C is a red flag for IRS auditors, who believe sole proprietors have many temptations and opportunities to hide cash income and exaggerate expense deductions. An IRS study found that sole proprietors filed 5.5 percent of Form 1040s in 1988, but accounted for 31 percent of unreported personal tax liabilities. For 1995, the audit rate for all Form 1040s was 1.67 percent. But if a Schedule C was included, the rate increased to 4.13 percent.

The distinction between NOLs and hobby losses is another problem area on Schedule C. About 25 percent of Schedule Cs show losses. If these losses are trade or business losses, they qualify for NOL treatment if the Form 1040 taxable income is negative.

Not all of these losses should be reported on Schedule C, however. Some of them are hobby losses. If the IRS decides your business is really a hobby, your expense deductions may not exceed your hobby income. The deductions that are allowed (other than property taxes and mortgage interest) are classified as miscellaneous itemized deductions, which are subject to the 2 percent floor.

SOURCE: Adapted from Scott Schmedel, "Schedule C Can Be Taxing, But There's Hope—Really," *Wall Street Journal,* April 5, 1996, p. C1.

Sequence of Use of NOLs. Where there are NOLs in two or more years, the rule is always to use the earliest year's loss first until it is completely absorbed. The later years' losses can then be used until they also are absorbed or lost. Thus, one year's return could show NOL carryovers from two or more years. Each loss is computed and applied separately.

Election to Forgo Carryback. A taxpayer can *irrevocably elect* not to carry back an NOL to any of the three prior years. In that case, the loss is available as a carryover for 15 years. A taxpayer would make the election if it is to his or her tax advantage. For example, a taxpayer might be in a low marginal tax bracket in the carryback years but expect to be in a high marginal tax bracket in future years. Therefore, it would be to the taxpayer's advantage to use the NOL to offset income in years when the tax rate is high rather than use it when the tax rate is relatively low.

COMPUTATION OF THE NET OPERATING LOSS

Since the NOL provisions apply solely to business-related losses, certain adjustments must be made so that the loss more closely resembles the taxpayer's *economic* loss. The required adjustments for corporate taxpayers are usually insignificant because a corporation's tax loss is generally similar to its economic loss. However, in computing taxable income, individual taxpayers are allowed deductions for such items as personal and dependency exemptions and itemized deductions that do not reflect actual business-related economic losses.

To arrive at the NOL for an individual, taxable income must be adjusted by adding back the following items:[33]

1. No deduction is allowed for personal and dependency exemptions. These amounts do not reflect economic, or business, outlays and hence must be added back.
2. The NOL carryover or carryback from another year is not allowed in the computation of the current year's NOL.
3. Capital losses and nonbusiness deductions are limited in determining the current year's NOL. These limits are as follows:
    a. The excess of nonbusiness capital losses over nonbusiness capital gains must be added back.
    b. The excess of nonbusiness deductions over the sum of nonbusiness income and *net* nonbusiness capital gains must be added back. *Net nonbusiness capital gains* are the excess of nonbusiness capital gains over nonbusiness capital losses. *Nonbusiness income* includes such passive items as dividends and interest. It does not include such items as salaries, rents, and gains and losses on the sale or exchange of business assets. *Nonbusiness deductions* are total itemized deductions less personal casualty and theft losses.

    A taxpayer who does not itemize deductions computes the excess of nonbusiness deductions over nonbusiness income by substituting his or her standard deduction for total itemized deductions.
    c. The excess of business capital losses over the sum of business capital gains and the excess of nonbusiness income and net nonbusiness capital gains over nonbusiness deductions must be added back.
    d. The add-back for net nonbusiness capital losses and excess business capital losses does not include net capital losses not included in the current year computation of taxable income because of the capital loss limitation provisions (discussed in Chapter 16).

The capital loss and nonbusiness deduction limits are illustrated in Examples 22 through 25.

EXAMPLE 22 For 1997, taxpayer and spouse have $6,000 of nonbusiness capital losses and $4,000 of nonbusiness capital gains. They must add back $2,000 ($6,000 − $4,000) in determining the excess of nonbusiness capital losses over nonbusiness capital gains. ▼

EXAMPLE 23 For 1997, taxpayer and spouse have $2,000 of nonbusiness capital gains, $1,000 of nonbusiness capital losses, $2,000 of interest income, and no itemized deductions. They must add back $3,900 {$6,900 standard deduction − [$2,000 interest income + $1,000 ($2,000 − $1,000) net nonbusiness capital gains]}. Note that, in this example, there is no excess of nonbusiness capital losses over nonbusiness capital gains. ▼

EXAMPLE 24 For 1997, taxpayer and spouse have $2,000 of nonbusiness capital gains, $1,000 of nonbusiness capital losses, $9,000 of interest income, $9,500 of itemized deductions (none of which are personal casualty and theft losses), $4,000 of business capital losses, and $1,000 of business capital gains. They must add back $2,500 {$4,000 business capital losses − [$1,000 business capital gains + ($9,000 nonbusiness income + $1,000 net nonbusiness capital gains − $9,500 nonbusiness deductions)]}. Note that, in this example, there is no excess of nonbusiness capital losses over nonbusiness capital gains, nor is there an excess of nonbusiness deductions over the sum of nonbusiness income and net nonbusiness capital gains. ▼

---

[33] § 172(d); Reg. § 1.172–3(a).

EXAMPLE 25

For 1997, taxpayer and spouse have $2,000 of nonbusiness capital gains, $3,000 of nonbusiness capital losses, $8,000 of interest income, $9,000 of itemized deductions (none of which are personal casualty and theft losses), $8,000 of business capital losses, and $4,000 of business capital gains. They must add back $1,000 ($9,000 − $8,000), the excess of nonbusiness deductions over nonbusiness income, and $3,000, the excess of combined capital losses. Because of the capital loss limitations, only $3,000 of the loss would have been used in computing taxable income for the year. ▼

Example 26 illustrates the computation of an NOL.

EXAMPLE 26

James opened a retail store in 1996 and experienced an NOL of $185 for that year. James had no taxable income for 1993, 1994, or 1995. James is married, has no dependents, and files a joint return. For 1997, James and his wife had the following taxable income:

Gross income from the business	$ 67,000	
Less: Business expenses	(71,000)	($ 4,000)
Salary from a part-time job		875
Interest on savings account		525
Nonbusiness long-term capital gain		1,000
NOL carryover from 1996		(185)
Net loss on rental property		(100)
Adjusted gross income		($ 1,885)
Less: Itemized deductions		
Interest expense	$ 3,000	
Taxes	4,300	
Casualty loss	2,000	
Total itemized deductions		(9,300)
Exemptions (2 × $2,650)		(5,300)
Taxable income		($16,485)

James's NOL is computed as follows:

Taxable income				($16,485)
Add:				
Net operating loss from 1996			$ 185	
Personal exemptions (2)			5,300	
Excess of nonbusiness deductions over nonbusiness income				
Total itemized deductions		$ 9,300		
Less: Casualty loss		(2,000)		
		$ 7,300		
Less: Interest	$ 525			
Less: Long-term capital gain	1,000	(1,525)	5,775	11,260
Net operating loss				($ 5,225)

The NOL can be thought of as follows:

Business loss	($ 4,000)
Rental loss	(100)
Casualty loss	(2,000)
Salary income	875
Net operating loss	($ 5,225)

▼

ETHICAL CONSIDERATIONS

Net Operating Losses

Adam is aware that the net operating loss carryback and carryover provisions enable him to carry back current period losses for 3 years and to carry the losses forward for 15 years. He also is aware of the time value of money concept. In addition, he recognizes that certain adjustments must be made in converting negative taxable income into an NOL.

Adam discusses with you, his accountant, the projections for his new business for the next five years, which show losses in the first two years, profits in the subsequent three years, and a cumulative profit of $90,000 for the five-year period. Adam indicates that if he delays certain transactions (by modifying the contract dates) from Years 1 and 2 into Years 3 and 4, he can convert the losses for the first two years into small profits with the cumulative projected profits for the five years remaining at $90,000. He raises the issues with you of the benefit and appropriateness of doing so.

RECOMPUTATION OF TAX LIABILITY FOR YEAR TO WHICH NET OPERATING LOSS IS CARRIED

When an NOL is carried back to a nonloss year, the taxable income and income tax for the carryback year must be recomputed by including the NOL as a deduction *for* AGI. Several deductions (such as medical expenses and charitable contributions) are based on the amount of AGI. When an NOL is carried back, all such deductions *except* the charitable contributions deduction must be recomputed on the basis of the new AGI after the NOL has been applied. The deduction for charitable contributions is determined without regard to any NOL carryback but with regard to any other modification affecting AGI. Furthermore, any tax credits limited by or based upon the tax must be recomputed, based on the recomputed tax.

EXAMPLE 27

Peggy sustained an NOL of $11,000 in 1998. Because Peggy had no taxable income in 1995 or 1996, the loss is carried back to 1997. For 1997, the joint income tax return of Peggy and her husband was as follows:

Salary income		$10,000
Dividends		4,000
Net long-term capital gain		1,400
Adjusted gross income		$15,400
Itemized deductions		
Charitable contributions	$2,700	
Interest	4,800	
Taxes	1,420	(8,920)
Exemptions (2 × $2,650)		(5,300)
Taxable income		$ 1,180
Tax (married filing jointly)		$ 177

Peggy's new tax liability for the carryback year is computed as follows:

Adjusted gross income		$ 15,400
Less: Net operating loss		(11,000)
Recomputed adjusted gross income		$ 4,400
Itemized deductions		
Charitable contributions	$2,700	
Interest	4,800	
Taxes	1,420	(8,920)
Exemptions (2 × $2,650)		(5,300)
Recomputed taxable income		$ (9,820)
Tax		$ -0-
Tax originally paid and refund claim		$ 177

CALCULATION OF THE REMAINING NET OPERATING LOSS

After computing the amount of the refund claim for the initial carryback year, it is then necessary to determine the extent to which any NOL remains to carry over to future years. The amount of this carryover loss is the excess of the NOL over the taxable income of the year to which the loss is being applied. However, the taxable income of the year to which the loss is being applied must be determined with the following *modifications*:

- No deduction is allowed for excess capital losses over capital gains.
- No deduction is allowed for the NOL that is being carried back. However, deductions are allowed for NOLs occurring before the loss year.
- Any deductions claimed that are based on or limited by AGI must be determined after making the preceding adjustments. However, charitable contributions do not take into account any NOL carryback.
- No deduction is allowed for personal and dependency exemptions.

EXAMPLE 28

Referring to the facts in Example 27, the NOL carryover from 1997 available for future years would be ($4,520), computed as follows:

Salary income		$10,000
Dividends		4,000
Net long-term capital gain		1,400
Adjusted gross income		$15,400
Itemized deductions		
Charitable contributions	$2,700	
Interest	4,800	
Taxes	1,420	(8,920)
Exemptions (not allowed)		-0-
Modified taxable income		$ 6,480
Net operating loss		($11,000)
Modified taxable income		6,480
Net operating loss to carry forward		($ 4,520)

Since the ending figure is negative, it represents the NOL remaining to carry over to 1999 or later years.

Concept Summary 7–4

Computation of Net Operating Loss

Taxable income shown on the return
Add back:

1. Personal and dependency exemptions.
2. Net operating loss carryover or carryback from another year.
3. The excess of nonbusiness capital losses over nonbusiness capital gains.
4. The excess of nonbusiness deductions over the sum of nonbusiness income plus *net* nonbusiness capital gains.
5. The excess of business capital losses over the sum of business capital gains plus the excess of nonbusiness income and *net* nonbusiness capital gains over nonbusiness deductions. The add-back from the total of items 3 and 5 will not exceed $3,000 because of the capital loss limitation rules.

Equals the net operating loss

Tax Planning Considerations

Learning Objective 7
Identify tax planning opportunities in deducting certain business expenses, business losses, and personal losses.

TAX CONSEQUENCES OF THE *GROETZINGER* CASE

In the *Groetzinger* case discussed earlier in the chapter, the court established that the appropriate tests for determining if gambling is a trade or business are whether an individual engages in gambling full-time in good faith, with regularity, and for the production of income as a livelihood, and not as a mere hobby. The court held that Robert Groetzinger satisfied the tests because of his constant and large-scale effort. Skill was required and was applied. He did what he did for a livelihood, though with less than successful results. His gambling was not a hobby, a passing fancy, or an occasional bet for amusement. Therefore, his gambling was a trade or business, and hence, he was able to deduct his gambling losses *for* AGI. If the court had ruled that Groetzinger's gambling was not a trade or business, his gambling losses would have been limited to his gambling winnings and would have been classified as itemized deductions.

DOCUMENTATION OF RELATED-TAXPAYER LOANS, CASUALTY LOSSES, AND THEFT LOSSES

Since non-bona fide loans between related taxpayers may be treated as gifts, adequate documentation is needed to substantiate a bad debt deduction if the loan subsequently becomes worthless. Documentation should include proper execution of the note (legal form) and the establishment of a bona fide purpose for the loan. In addition, it is desirable to stipulate a reasonable rate of interest and a fixed maturity date.

Since a theft loss is not permitted for misplaced items, a loss should be documented by a police report and evidence of the value of the property (e.g., appraisals, pictures of the property, newspaper clippings). Similar documentation of the value of property should be provided to support a casualty loss deduction because the amount of loss is measured, in part, by the decline in fair market value of the property.

Casualty loss deductions must be reported on Form 4684 (see Appendix B).

SMALL BUSINESS STOCK

Because § 1244 limits the amount of loss classified as ordinary loss on a yearly basis, a taxpayer might maximize the benefits of § 1244 by selling the stock in more than one taxable year. The result could be that the losses in any one taxable year would not exceed the § 1244 limits on ordinary loss.

EXAMPLE 29

Mitch, a single individual, purchased small business stock in 1995 for $150,000 (150 shares at $1,000 per share). On December 20, 1997, the stock is worth $60,000 (150 shares at $400 per share). Mitch wants to sell the stock at this time. Mitch earns a salary of $80,000 a year, has no other capital transactions, and does not expect any in the future. If Mitch sells all of the small business stock in 1997, his recognized loss will be $90,000 ($60,000 − $150,000). The loss will be characterized as a $50,000 ordinary loss and a $40,000 long-term capital loss. In computing taxable income for 1997, Mitch could deduct the $50,000 ordinary loss but could deduct only $3,000 of the capital loss. The remainder of the capital loss could be carried over and used in future years subject to the $3,000 limitation if Mitch has no capital gains. If Mitch sells 82 shares in 1997, he will recognize an ordinary loss of $49,200 [82 × ($1,000 − $400)]. If Mitch then sells the remainder of the shares in 1998, he will recognize an ordinary loss of $40,800 [68 × ($1,000 − $400)]. Mitch could deduct the $49,200 ordinary loss in computing 1997 taxable income and the $40,800 ordinary loss in computing 1998 taxable income. ▼

CASUALTY LOSSES

A special election is available for taxpayers who sustain casualty losses in an area designated by the President as a disaster area. This election affects only the timing, not the calculation, of the deduction. The deduction can be taken in the year before the year in which the loss occurred. Thus, an individual can take the deduction on the 1996 return for a loss occurring between January 1 and December 31, 1997. The benefit, of course, is a faster refund (or reduction in tax). It will also be advantageous to carry the loss back if the taxpayer's tax rate in the carryback year is higher than the tax rate in the year of the loss.

To find out if an event qualifies as a disaster area loss, one can look in any of the major tax services, the Weekly Compilation of Presidential Documents, or the *Internal Revenue Bulletin.*

NET OPERATING LOSSES

In certain instances, it may be advisable for a taxpayer to elect not to carry back an NOL. For an individual, the benefits from the loss carryback could be scaled down or lost due to the economic adjustments that must be made to taxable income for the year to which the loss is carried. For example, a taxpayer should attempt to minimize the number of taxable years to which an NOL is carried. The more years to which the NOL is applied, the more benefits are lost from adjustments for items such as personal and dependency exemptions.

The election not to carry back the loss might also be advantageous if there is a disparity in marginal tax rates applicable to different tax years.

EXAMPLE 30

Abby sustained an NOL of $10,000 in Year 4. Her marginal tax bracket in Year 1 was 15%. In Year 5, however, she expects her bracket to be 39.6% due to a large profit she will make on a business deal. If Abby carries her loss back, her refund will be $1,500 (15% × $10,000). If she elects not to carry it back to Year 1 but chooses, instead, to carry it forward, her savings will be $3,960 (39.6% × $10,000). Even considering the time value of an immediate tax refund, Abby appears to be better off using the carryover approach. ▼

KEY TERMS

Bad debt, 7-3
Business bad debt, 7-5
Casualty loss, 7-9
Disaster area losses, 7-12
Net operating loss (NOL), 7-19
Nonbusiness bad debt, 7-4
Personal casualty gain, 7-15
Personal casualty loss, 7-15
Research and experimental expenditures, 7-17
Reserve method, 7-3
Section 1244 stock, 7-8
Small business stock, 7-8
Specific charge-off method, 7-3
Theft loss, 7-10
Worthless securities, 7-7

PROBLEM MATERIALS

DISCUSSION QUESTIONS

1. Explain whether a bad debt deduction is allowed for a debt arising from the sale of inventory by an accrual basis taxpayer.

2. Discuss when a deduction may be taken for a business debt.

3. Discuss the tax treatment for the recovery of an account receivable previously written off as uncollectible.

4. Discuss the difference between business and nonbusiness bad debts. How is the distinction determined? How is each treated on the return?

5. What factors are to be considered in determining whether a bad debt arising from a loan between related parties is, in fact, a bad debt?

6. Sam used the cash method of accounting for Federal income tax purposes and filed a joint Federal income tax return for the current year. On February 27 of the current year, Sam instituted a civil lawsuit against Dave, alleging fraud in the handling of a real estate project in which Sam had invested. On June 19 of the current year, a default judgment was entered against Dave and in favor of Sam. Under its terms, Sam was to recover from Dave general damages of $20,000 and punitive damages of $50,000. During the current year, Sam did not recover from Dave any of either the general or the punitive damages. Identify the relevant tax issues for Sam.

7. Discuss a taxpayer's options for the tax treatment of a loss incurred on a deposit in a qualified financial institution. Also note the consequences of each option.

8. Macy owns § 1244 stock in a corporation. The stock becomes completely worthless during the current year. Discuss the tax consequences of Macy's worthless § 1244 stock.

9. Discuss the ordinary loss limitations on the sale of § 1244 stock and the advantages of such a characterization.

10. Discuss whether a taxpayer can take a deduction for a casualty loss from an accident caused by the taxpayer's negligence.

11. Jim discovers that his sea wall, which protects his personal residence from the ocean, has been extensively damaged by the ocean. Discuss whether he may take a deduction for the damage to the wall.

12. Discuss the provision for determining the year in which a theft loss is deductible.

13. Discuss the tax treatment when a casualty loss is deducted in a prior year and a reimbursement is received in the current year.

14. Discuss the tax consequences of property being partially destroyed in determining the amount of a casualty loss assuming no insurance proceeds are received.

15. How is a personal casualty loss computed? A business casualty loss? What effect do insurance proceeds have on both types of losses?

16. Discuss the tax consequences of not making an insurance claim when insured business property is subject to a loss.

17. Discuss the circumstances under which the cost of repairs to the damaged property can be used to measure the amount of a casualty loss.

18. During May of the current year, personal use property was stolen from Jim's home. Later in the year, Jim's home and two personal use cars were damaged by a severe storm. Discuss how the $100 floor applies to these casualties.

19. If a taxpayer is required to spread a personal casualty loss between two years under the reasonable prospect of recovery doctrine, how will the $100 per event floor and the 10%-of-AGI limitation be treated?

20. Bonnie sustained a loss on a duplex damaged by fire. She owns the duplex and lives in one unit. She rents out the other unit to a tenant. Discuss the tax treatment of the loss on Bonnie's individual tax return.

21. Discuss the tax treatment of a loss resulting from the theft of a security from an individual.

22. When casualty losses exceed casualty gains, only the amount of the casualty loss in excess of casualty gains is subject to the 10%-of-AGI floor. Discuss the significance of netting losses against gains in this manner rather than having the entire casualty loss subject to the 10%-of-AGI floor.

23. Monte opened a personal savings account at First National Bank many years ago. Last year, First National's banking license was revoked. In January of this year, Monte was informed that First National had been put into compulsory liquidation. The liquidation was precipitated by the embezzlement of funds by First National's former president. In February Monte submitted a claim for $12,459 to the liquidators of First National. In May of the current year, the liquidators advised Monte that they would keep him informed as to the progress of the liquidation and his prospects of recovery. The letter also stated that claimants would be notified if the liquidators were unable to agree to their claims. In November of the current year, Monte was notified that at the present time the liquidators could not predict with any degree of certainty how much of their funds depositors might eventually recover. Identify the relevant tax issues for Monte.

24. Fred and Diane purchased their home many years ago. The property included a large black oak tree approximately 80 feet in height and about 100 years old. The tree was the dominant feature of the front yard, where it stood alone next to the street. Because of the age and stature of the tree, Fred and Diane had it inspected regularly by a tree expert. In August of the current year, Fred noticed that the entire top or crown of the tree had turned brown. Because none of the leaves on other trees in the area had turned brown, Fred called the tree expert to inspect the tree. The inspection showed that the tree had been attacked by woodborers and was beyond saving and effectively dead. Identify the relevant tax issues for Fred and Diane.

25. Why do most taxpayers elect to write off research and experimental expenditures rather than capitalize and amortize such amounts? Are there some situations in which the capitalization and amortization approach would be preferable?

26. If a business does not elect to expense or amortize research expenditures, what is the possibility of writing off such expenditures?

27. Power and Light, a public utility company, planned a research and development project. To obtain a construction permit to expand its facilities, the company filed an application with state regulatory agencies and conducted various studies to support its application as required by the agencies. Because the taxpayer's expansion involved

both the construction of a nuclear power plant and the installation of an ultrahigh voltage electric transmission line, the agencies required that the company conduct several types of environmental impact studies for site selection. The studies measured specific site conditions and the resulting environmental impact of the construction and operation of the project. The company conducted part of the studies directly and used a research organization to conduct the remainder of the studies on its behalf. Identify the relevant tax issues for Power and Light.

28. Discuss the types of losses that can create an NOL.

29. Discuss the periods to which NOLs may be carried. Can the taxpayer elect not to carry an NOL back to any one year? What possible benefit might result from not carrying a loss back to a particular year?

30. Why are such items as nonbusiness deductions and personal and dependency exemptions not allowed in computing the NOL?

31. If an individual has no nonbusiness capital transactions for the year, discuss the treatment of the excess of nonbusiness income over nonbusiness deductions with respect to the NOL.

32. Discuss the recomputation of the tax liability for the year to which an NOL is carried.

33. Discuss the calculation of the NOL remaining after a carryback to a particular tax year.

PROBLEMS

34. Several years ago John Johnson loaned his friend Sara $20,000 to help her make a business investment. In May of the current year, Sara filed for bankruptcy, and John was notified that he could expect to receive no more than 60 cents on the dollar. As of the end of the current year, John has not received any payments. John has contacted you about the possibility of taking a bad debt deduction of $8,000 for the current year.

    Write a letter to John that contains your advice as to whether he can claim a bad debt deduction of $8,000 for the current year. Also, prepare a memo for the tax files. John's address is 100 Tyler Lane, Erie, PA 16563.

35. In 1995, Morgan loaned the Peach Company $50,000. In 1996, Morgan was told that he would probably receive $5,000 of the loan. In 1997, Morgan received $3,000 in final settlement on the loan. Determine Morgan's possible deductions with respect to the loan for 1995, 1996, and 1997.

36. In 1996, Wilma deposited $117,500 with a commercial bank. On July 1, 1997, Wilma was notified that the bank was insolvent, and subsequently she received only $100,000 of the deposit. Wilma also has a salary of $5,000, long-term capital gain of $12,000, and itemized deductions (other than casualty and theft) of $7,000. Determine whether Wilma should elect to treat the loss on the deposit as a personal casualty loss or as a bad debt.

37. Zenith, a single taxpayer, had the following items for 1997:

    - Salary of $75,000.
    - Gain of $15,000 on the sale of § 1244 stock acquired three years ago.
    - Loss of $70,000 on the sale of § 1244 stock acquired two years ago.
    - Stock acquired on December 20, 1996, for $2,500 became worthless on April 3, 1997.

    Determine Zenith's AGI for 1997.

38. Mary, a single taxpayer, purchased 10,000 shares of § 1244 stock several years ago at a cost of $20 per share. In November of the current year, Mary received an offer to sell the stock for $12 per share. She has the option of either selling all of the stock now or selling half of the stock now and half of the stock in January of next year. Mary will receive a salary of $80,000 for the current year and $90,000 next year. Mary will have long-term capital gains of $8,000 for the current year and $10,000 next year. If Mary's goal is to

minimize her AGI for the two years, determine whether Mary should sell all of her stock this year or half of her stock this year and half next year.

39. When Helen returned from a vacation in Hawaii on November 8, 1997, she discovered that a burglar had stolen her silver, stereo, and color television. In the process of removing these items, the burglar damaged some furniture that originally cost $1,400. Helen's silver cost $12,000 and was valued at $16,500; the stereo system cost $8,400 and was valued at $6,200; the television cost $840 and was worth $560. Helen filed a claim with her insurance company and was reimbursed in the following amounts on December 20, 1997.

Silver	$2,800
Stereo	5,600
Television	490

The insurance company disputed the reimbursement claimed by Helen for the damaged furniture, but she protested and was finally paid $280 on January 30, 1998. The repairs to the furniture totaled $1,550. Helen's AGI for 1997 was $20,000, and it was $500 for 1998. How much can Helen claim as a casualty and theft loss? In which year?

40. Olaf owns a 500-acre farm in Minnesota. A tornado hit the area and destroyed a farm building and some farm equipment and damaged a barn. Fortunately for Olaf, the tornado occurred after he had harvested his corn crop. Applicable information is as follows:

Item	Adjusted Basis	FMV Before	FMV After	Insurance Proceeds
Building	$80,000	$100,000	$ -0-	$60,000
Equipment	60,000	50,000	-0-	25,000
Barn	90,000	120,000	90,000	25,000

Because of the extensive damage caused by the tornado, the President designated the area as a disaster area.

Olaf, who files a joint return with his wife Anna, had $90,000 of taxable income last year. Their taxable income for the current year, excluding the loss from the tornado, is $220,000.

Determine the amount of Olaf and Anna's loss and the year in which they should take the loss.

41. On January 7 of the current year, Wade dropped off to sleep while driving home from a business trip. Luckily, he was only slightly injured in the resulting accident, but his car was completely destroyed.

Wade had purchased the car new two years ago and had driven it 64,000 miles at the time of the accident. Of these miles, 28,000 were business miles; the remaining miles were personal miles. The car cost $7,200 new. Wade has taken $1,985 of depreciation for the business use of the car. The fair market value at the time of the accident was $4,000. Wade carried zero deductible collision insurance on the car. He made no claim on his insurance policy because he was afraid that his insurance premiums would increase if he did.

After Wade's release from the hospital the day after the accident, he could not find his wallet (cost $65, fair replacement value $30) or its contents, which included $350 in cash and $500 in traveler's checks. The traveler's checks were replaced by the issuing company. He also was unable to locate the stone from his diamond ring. The stone cost his wife $2,500 when purchased nine years ago and was worth $6,400 at the time of the loss.

a. Determine the amount of Wade's deductible loss *for* AGI.
b. Determine the amount of the loss deductible *from* AGI, assuming AGI for the year is $25,000.

42. On November 1 of the current year, Sam Smith was involved in an accident with his personal use automobile. Sam had purchased the car for $25,000. The automobile had a fair market value of $19,000 before the accident and $12,000 after the accident. The car was covered by an insurance policy that had a $1,000 deductible clause. Sam is afraid that the policy will be canceled if he makes a claim for the damages. Therefore, he is considering not filing a claim. Sam believes that the casualty loss deduction will help mitigate the loss of the insurance reimbursement. Sam's AGI for the current year is $25,000.

Write a letter to Sam that contains your advice with respect to the tax consequences of filing versus not filing a claim for the insurance reimbursement for the damages to his car. Also, prepare a memo for the tax files. Sam's address is 450 Colonel's Way, Warrensburg, MO 64093.

43. Green Corporation, a manufacturing company, decided to develop a new line of fireworks. Because of the danger involved, Green purchased an isolated parcel of land for $300,000 and constructed a building for $1,220,000. The building was to be used for research and experimentation in creating the new fireworks. The project was begun in 1997. Green had the following expenses in 1997 in connection with the project:

Salaries	$160,000
Utilities	20,000
Materials	40,000
Insurance	50,000
Cost of market survey to determine profit potential for new fireworks line	20,000
Depreciation on the building	30,000

Green had the following expenses in 1998 in connection with the project:

Salaries	$200,000
Utilities	30,000
Materials	40,000
Insurance	30,000
Depreciation on the building	31,000

The benefits from the project will be realized starting in June 1999.
  a. If Green Corporation elects to expense research and experimental expenditures, determine the amount of the deduction for 1997, 1998, and 1999.
  b. If Green Corporation elects a 60-month deferral and amortization period, determine the amount of the deduction for 1997, 1998, and 1999.

44. Juan and Rosa, who file a joint return, had the following items for 1997:

Juan's salary	$40,000
Rosa's salary	50,000
Interest income from State of Ohio bonds	5,000

During the year, a fire damaged Juan and Rosa's personal residence. The amount of their itemized deduction associated with the casualty was $125,000. They had no other itemized deductions.
  a. Determine Juan and Rosa's taxable income for 1997.
  b. Determine Juan and Rosa's NOL for 1997.

45. Bill, a single taxpayer, had the following items of income and expense during 1997:

Gross receipts from business	$170,000
Business expenses	200,000
Bill's salary	20,000
Itemized deductions (no casualty or theft)	10,000

a. Determine Bill's taxable income for 1997.
b. Determine Bill's NOL for 1997.

46. Gus, who is married and files a joint return, owns a grocery store. In 1997, his gross sales were $286,000 and operating expenses were $310,000. Other items on his 1997 return were as follows:

Nonbusiness capital gains (short-term)	$10,000
Nonbusiness capital losses (long-term)	9,000
Itemized deductions	10,000
Ordinary nonbusiness income	4,000
Salary from part-time job	10,000

During the years 1994 and 1995, Gus had no taxable income. In 1996, Gus had taxable income of $24,000 computed as follows:

Net business income		$ 60,000
Interest income		2,000
Adjusted gross income		$ 62,000
Less: Itemized deductions		
Charitable contributions of $40,000, limited to 50% of AGI	$31,000	
Medical expenses of $6,550, limited to the amount in excess of 7.5% of AGI ($6,550 − $4,650)	1,900	
Total itemized deductions		(32,900)
Exemptions (2 × 2,550)		(5,100)
Taxable income		$ 24,000

a. What is Gus's 1997 NOL?
b. Determine Gus's recomputed taxable income for 1996.

47. During 1997, Rick and his wife Sara had the following items of income and expense to report:

• Gross receipts from business	$400,000
• Business expenses	525,000
• Interest income from bank savings accounts	8,000
• Sara's salary	50,000
• Long-term capital gain on stock held as an investment	4,000
• Itemized deductions	15,000

a. Assuming Rick and Sara file a joint return, what is their taxable income for 1997?
b. What is the amount of Rick and Sara's NOL for 1997?

48. Assume that in addition to the information in Problem 47, Rick had no taxable income for the years 1994 and 1995 and $6,600 of taxable income for 1996 computed as follows:

Salary		$ 25,000
Capital loss		(1,000)
Adjusted gross income		$ 24,000
Less: Itemized deductions		
Charitable contributions of $20,000, limited to 50% of AGI	$12,000	
Medical expenses of $2,100, limited to the amount in excess of 7.5% of AGI ($2,100 − $1,800)	300	
Total itemized deductions		(12,300)
Exemptions (2 × $2,550)		(5,100)
Taxable income		$ 6,600

Determine the amount of Rick and Sara's 1997 NOL to be carried forward to 1998.

49. Robert and Susan Reid had an NOL of $20,000 in 1997. They had no taxable income for the years 1994 and 1995 and $18,300 of taxable income for 1996 computed as follows:

Salary		$ 50,000
Capital loss		(2,000)
Adjusted gross income		$ 48,000
Less: Itemized deductions		
Charitable contributions of $40,000, limited to 50% of AGI	$24,000	
Medical expenses of $4,200, limited to the amount in excess of 7.5% of AGI ($4,200 − $3,600)	600	
Total itemized deductions		(24,600)
Exemptions (2 × $2,550)		(5,100)
Taxable income		$ 18,300

Write a letter to Robert and Susan informing them of the amount of the remaining NOL to be carried forward if the loss is applied against the 1996 taxable income. Also, prepare a memo for the tax files. Their address is 201 Jerdone Avenue, Conway, SC 29526.

50. Fran is single and had the following income and deductions for 1997:

Business receipts	$ 90,000
Business expenses	130,000
Dividends from domestic corporations	20,000
Interest received from bank savings account	6,000
Itemized deductions	30,000
1996 NOL carried to 1997	20,000

  a. What is Fran's taxable income for 1997?
  b. What is Fran's NOL for 1997?

51. Soong, single and age 32, had the following items for the tax year 1997:

- Salary of $40,000.

- Interest income from U.S. government bonds of $2,000.

- Dividends from a foreign corporation of $500.

- Sale of small business § 1244 stock on October 20, 1997, for $10,000. The stock had been acquired two years earlier for $65,000.

- Business bad debt of $3,000.
- Nonbusiness bad debt of $5,000.
- Sale of small business § 1244 stock on November 12, 1997, for $4,000. The stock had been acquired on June 5, 1997, for $800.
- Sale of common stock on December 4, 1997, for $40,000. The stock was acquired four years ago for $18,000.
- Total itemized deductions of $8,000.

Determine Soong's NOL for 1997.

52. Nell, single and age 38, had the following income and expense items in 1997:

Nonbusiness bad debt	$ 6,000
Business bad debt	2,000
Nonbusiness long-term capital gain	4,000
Nonbusiness short-term capital loss	3,000
Salary	40,000
Interest income	1,000

Determine Nell's AGI for 1997.

53. Assume that in addition to the information in Problem 52, Nell had the following items in 1997:

Personal casualty gain on an asset held for four months	$10,000
Personal casualty loss on an asset held for two years	1,000

Determine Nell's AGI for 1997.

54. Assume that in addition to the information in Problems 52 and 53, Nell had the following items in 1997:

Personal casualty loss on an asset held for five years	$50,000
Interest expense on home mortgage	3,000

Determine Nell's taxable income and NOL for 1997.

55. Jed, age 55, is married with no children. During 1997, Jed had the following income and expense items:
   a. Three years ago, Jed loaned a friend $10,000 to help him purchase a new car. In June of the current year, Jed learned that his friend had been declared bankrupt and had left the country. There is no possibility that Jed will ever collect any of the $10,000.
   b. In December of last year, Jed purchased some stock for $5,000. In March of the current year, the company was declared bankrupt, and Jed was notified that his shares of stock were worthless.
   c. Several years ago, Jed purchased some § 1244 stock for $120,000. This year, he sold the stock for $30,000.
   d. In July of this year, Jed sold some land that he had held for two years for $60,000. He had originally paid $42,000 for the land.
   e. Jed received $40,000 of interest income from State of Minnesota bonds.
   f. In September, Jed's home was damaged by an earthquake. Jed's basis in his home was $430,000. The value of the home immediately before the quake was $610,000. After the quake, the home was worth $540,000. Because earthquake damage was an exclusion on Jed's homeowners insurance policy, he received no insurance recovery.
   g. Jed received a salary of $80,000.
   h. Jed made a charitable contribution of $4,000.

If Jed files a joint return for 1997, determine his NOL for the year.

CUMULATIVE PROBLEMS

56. Alan Rice, age 45 and single, lives at 230 Wood Lane, Salt Lake City, UT 84201. His Social Security number is 885–33–3774. Alan had the following items for the year 1997:

    - Salary of $100,000.
    - Business bad debt of $8,000.
    - Nonbusiness bad debt of $5,000.
    - Sale of § 1244 stock resulting in a loss of $70,000. The stock was acquired two years earlier.
    - Dividends of $10,000 from domestic corporations.
    - Interest income of $3,000 from First Interstate Bank.
    - Long-term capital gain of $21,000.
    - NOL carryover from 1996 of $12,000.
    - On January 1, 1997, a fire severely damaged a two-story building owned by Alan, who occupied the second story of the building as a residence. He had recently opened a flower shop on the ground level. The following information is available with respect to the incident:

Asset	Adjusted Basis	Fair Market Value Before	Fair Market Value After
Building	$70,000	$130,000	$50,000
Inventory	35,000	55,000	None
Store equipment	3,000	2,500	None
Home furnishings	12,600	7,000	800
Personal auto	8,900	7,800	7,600

    - Alan's fire insurance policy paid the following amounts for damages covered by the policy:

Building	$50,000	(policy maximum)
Inventory	30,000	(policy maximum)
Store equipment	None	
Home furnishings	1,000	(policy maximum)
Personal auto	None	

    - Other itemized deductions of $3,000.
    - Alan's employer withheld $10,000 of Federal income tax.

    Compute Alan's 1997 Federal income tax payable (or refund due). Suggested software (if available): *TurboTax* or *MacInTax*.

57. Jane Smith, age 40, is single and has no dependents. She is employed as a legal secretary by Legal Services, Inc. She owns and operates Typing Services located near the campus of San Jose State University at 1986 Campus Drive. She is a cash basis taxpayer. Jane lives at 2020 Oakcrest Road, San Jose, CA 95134. Jane's Social Security number is 123–89–6666. Jane indicates that she wishes to designate $3 to the Presidential Election Campaign Fund. During 1996, Jane had the following income and expense items:
    a. $50,000 salary from Legal Services, Inc.
    b. $20,000 gross receipts from her typing services business.
    c. $700 cash dividend from Buffalo Mining Company, a Canadian corporation.
    d. $1,000 Christmas bonus from Legal Services, Inc.

e. $60,000 life insurance proceeds on the death of her sister.
f. $5,000 check given to her by her wealthy aunt.
g. $100 won in a bingo game.
h. Expenses connected with the typing service:

Office rent	$7,000
Supplies	4,400
Utilities and telephone	4,680
Wages to part-time typists	5,000
Payroll taxes	500
Equipment rentals	3,000

i. $9,000 interest expense on a home mortgage (paid to San Jose Savings and Loan).
j. $5,000 fair market value of silverware stolen from her home by a burglar on October 12, 1996. Jane had paid $4,000 for the silverware on July 1, 1987. She was reimbursed $1,500 by her insurance company.
k. Jane had loaned $2,100 to a friend, Joan Jensen, on June 3, 1993. Joan declared bankruptcy on August 14, 1996, and was unable to repay the loan.
l. Legal Services, Inc., withheld Federal income tax of $8,500 and the required amount of FICA tax.
m. Alimony of $10,000 received from her former husband, Ted Smith.
n. Interest income of $800 on City of San Jose bonds.
o. Jane made estimated tax payments of $1,000.

Part 1—Tax Computation
Compute Jane Smith's 1996 Federal income tax payable (or refund due). If you use tax forms for your computations, you will need Forms 1040 and 4684 and Schedules A, C, and D. Suggested software (if available): *TurboTax* or *MacInTax*.

Part 2—Tax Planning
In 1997, Jane plans to continue her job with Legal Services, Inc. Therefore, items a, d, and l will recur in 1997. Jane plans to continue her typing services business (refer to item b) and expects gross receipts of $26,000. She projects that all business expenses (refer to item h) will increase by 10%, except for office rent, which, under the terms of her lease, will remain the same as in 1996. Items e, f, g, j, and k will not recur in 1997. Items c, i, m, and n will be approximately the same as in 1996.

Jane would like you to compute the minimum amount of estimated tax she will have to pay for 1997 so that she will not have to pay any additional tax upon filing her 1997 Federal income tax return. Write a letter to Jane that contains your advice and prepare a memo for the tax files. Suggested software (if available): *TurboTax* or *MacInTax*.

RESEARCH PROBLEMS

*Note: **West's Federal Taxation on CD-ROM** can be used in preparing solutions to the Research Problems. Alternatively, tax research materials contained in a standard tax library can be used.*

Research Problem 1. While Ralph was in the process of obtaining a divorce, his wife, without Ralph's knowledge, had the furniture removed from his apartment. Discuss whether Ralph would be entitled to a tax deduction for the loss of the furniture.

Partial list of research aids:
Landis G. Brown, 30 TCM 257, T.C.Memo. 1971–60.
Jerry L. Goode, 42 TCM 1209, T.C.Memo. 1981–548.

Research Problem 2. Janice Jones is single and a very successful executive. For the past five years, her taxable income has exceeded $160,000. Lately, Janice has been seeing a lot of Jim Johnson. Jim suffered a financial setback a few years ago, and as a result, he has $500,000 of NOL carryforwards. Janice wants to know if she marries Jim and they file a joint return, will she be able to use Jim's NOL carryforwards to offset her income? Discuss the potential tax consequences.

Research Problem 3. George Johnson, a Minnesota resident, parked his car on a lake while he was watching an iceboat race. During the race, the ice beneath his car unexpectedly gave way, and the car sank to the bottom of the lake. Write a letter to George advising him as to whether he can claim a casualty loss for the damage to the car. Also, prepare a memo for the tax files. George's address is 100 Apple Lane, St. Paul, MN 55123.

Research Problem 4. John Smith was engaged to be married to Nancy Brown. In contemplation of marriage, Nancy deposited $20,000 in a bank account for John, to be used after their marriage. Sometime thereafter, the engagement was broken off, and John used the $20,000 for himself. Nancy has attempted to collect the $20,000 from John without success, and now John has filed for bankruptcy. Discuss the possibility of Nancy's claiming the $20,000 as a nonbusiness bad debt on her income tax return.

Research Problem 5. John had $175,000 of personal savings on deposit in Swan Savings and Loan Association. During the current year, an employee embezzled large sums of money from Swan. As a result, Swan was declared insolvent. At the present, it appears that John will recover only $100,000 of his deposit. John was an officer of Swan for most of the current year. Just after Swan was declared insolvent and placed in conservatorship, John resigned his position as an officer. Evaluate the possibility of John taking the $75,000 loss as a theft or casualty loss on his tax return.

Use the tax resources of the internet to address the following questions. Do not restrict your search to the World Wide Web, but include a review of newsgroups and general reference materials, practitioner sites and resources, primary sources of the tax law, chat rooms and discussion groups, and other opportunities.

Research Problem 6. Find a newspaper article that discusses tax planning for casualty losses when a disaster area designation is made. Does the article convey the pertinent tax rules correctly? Then list all of the locations identified in the last two years by the President as Federal disaster areas.

Research Problem 7. Scan several publications that are read by owners of small businesses. Some of the articles in these publications address tax-related issues such as how to structure a new business. Do these articles do an adequate job of conveying the benefits of issuing § 1244 small business stock? Prepare a short memo explaining the use of § 1244 stock and post it to a newsgroup that is frequented by inventors, engineers, and others involved in start-up corporations.

TEAM PROJECT: ARTHUR ANDERSEN TAX CHALLENGE CASES

For more information on the Arthur Andersen Tax Challenge Cases, refer to Chapter 1, page 1–38.

Information related to tax issues and problems that are discussed in this chapter may be found in the

Day and Ball case on pages: none
Miller case on pages: none

Read and analyze the case you have been assigned and *identify* any issues and problems that are related to material covered in this chapter. If the information provided in the case is complete, prepare answers for this part of the case at this time. If you need information that is contained in the later parts of the case, write a memo summarizing the questions or problems so you can prepare a complete answer at a later date.

CHAPTER 8

Depreciation, Cost Recovery, Amortization, and Depletion

LEARNING OBJECTIVES

After completing Chapter 8, you should be able to:

1. Understand the rationale for the cost consumption concept and identify the relevant time periods for depreciation, ACRS, and MACRS.

2. Determine the amount of cost recovery under ACRS and MACRS.

3. Recognize when and how to make the § 179 expensing election, calculate the amount of the deduction, and apply the effect of the election in making the MACRS calculation.

4. Identify listed property and apply the deduction limitations on listed property and on luxury automobiles.

5. Determine when and how to use the alternative depreciation system (ADS).

6. Identify intangible assets that are eligible for amortization and calculate the amount of the deduction.

7. Determine the amount of depletion expense including being able to apply the alternative tax treatments for intangible drilling and development costs.

8. Perform the reporting procedures for cost recovery.

9. Identify tax planning opportunities for cost recovery, amortization, and depletion.

OUTLINE

Overview, 8-3

Accelerated Cost Recovery System (ACRS and MACRS), 8-4

General Considerations, 8-4

Eligible Property under ACRS or MACRS, 8-5

Personalty: Recovery Periods and Methods, 8-5

Realty: Recovery Periods and Methods, 8-11

Straight-Line Election under ACRS and MACRS, 8-14

Election to Expense Assets, 8-15

Business and Personal Use of Automobiles and Other Listed Property, 8-17

Alternative Depreciation System (ADS), 8-23

Amortization, 8-24

Depletion, 8-25

Intangible Drilling and Development Costs (IDC), 8-26

Depletion Methods, 8-26

Reporting Procedures, 8-29

Tax Planning Considerations, 8-33

Cost Recovery, 8-33

Amortization, 8-34

Depletion, 8-34

Tables, 8-35

---

1 LEARNING OBJECTIVE
Understand the rationale for the cost consumption concept and identify the relevant time periods for depreciation, ACRS, and MACRS.

The Internal Revenue Code provides for a deduction for the consumption of the cost of an asset through depreciation, cost recovery, amortization, or depletion. These deductions are applications of the recovery of capital doctrine (discussed in Chapter 4).

A distinction is made between tangible and intangible property. Tangible property is any property with physical substance (e.g., equipment, buildings), while intangible property lacks such substance (e.g., goodwill, patents).

The **depreciation** rules were completely overhauled by the Economic Recovery Tax Act of 1981 (ERTA). Hence, *most* property placed in service after December 31, 1980, is subject to the accelerated **cost recovery** system (ACRS). However, property placed in service before January 1, 1981, that is still in use, as well as *certain* property placed in service after December 31, 1980, is subject to the pre-ERTA depreciation rules. The Tax Reform Act (TRA) of 1986 completely revised the ACRS rules for property placed in service after December 31, 1986 (MACRS). Therefore, a knowledge of all of the depreciation and cost recovery rules may be needed as Example 1 illustrates.

EXAMPLE 1

The Brown Company owns machinery purchased in 1980. The machinery has a 20-year useful life. The business also owns equipment purchased in 1986 that has a 15-year cost recovery life. In 1990, the business purchased a computer. To compute the depreciation and cost recovery for 1997, Brown will use the pre-ERTA depreciation rules for the machinery, the pre-TRA of 1986 cost recovery rules (ACRS) for the equipment, and the post-TRA of 1986 cost recovery rules (MACRS) for the computer. ▼

This chapter initially focuses on the ACRS and MACRS rules.[1] The chapter then concludes with a discussion of the amortization of intangible property and the depletion of natural resources.

ACRS was one of many provisions in ERTA that were intended to stimulate the economy. The following features of ACRS result in accelerated write-offs:

- Cost recovery periods are shorter than the estimated useful lives required under the pre-1981 depreciation system.

---

[1] § 168. Pre-ERTA depreciation rules under § 167 are covered in Appendix H.

Concept Summary 8–1

Depreciation and Cost Recovery: Relevant Time Periods

System	Date Property Is Placed in Service
§ 167 depreciation	Before January 1, 1981, and *certain* property placed in service after December 31, 1980.
Original accelerated cost recovery system (ACRS)	After December 31, 1980, and before January 1, 1987.
Modified accelerated cost recovery system (MACRS)	After December 31, 1986.

- The use of salvage value, required under the pre-1981 depreciation system, is eliminated under ACRS.
- For many assets, the methods for computing ACRS deductions are more generous than the allowable methods for computing depreciation.

For assets placed in service after 1986, ACRS is replaced with MACRS. The basic effect of MACRS is to somewhat dampen the economic stimulus effect of ACRS. MACRS cost recovery periods are generally longer than ACRS cost recovery periods. In addition, the cost recovery methods available under MACRS are, in most cases, not as generous as the methods available under ACRS.

Overview

Taxpayers may write off the cost of certain assets that are used in a trade or business or held for the production of income. A write-off may take the form of depreciation (or cost recovery), depletion, or amortization. Tangible assets, other than natural resources, are *depreciated*. Natural resources, such as oil, gas, coal, and timber, are *depleted*. Intangible assets, such as copyrights and patents, are *amortized*. Generally, no write-off is allowed for an asset that does not have a determinable useful life.

ACRS and MACRS provide separate cost recovery tables for realty (real property) and personalty (personal property). Realty generally includes land and buildings permanently affixed to the land. Write-offs are not available for land because it does not have a determinable useful life. Cost recovery allowances for real property, other than land, are based on recovery lives specified in the law. The IRS provides tables that specify cost recovery allowances for most types of realty.

Personalty is defined as any asset that is not realty.[2] Personalty includes furniture, machinery, equipment, and many other types of assets. Do not confuse personalty (or personal property) with *personal use* property. Personal use property is any property (realty or personalty) that is held for personal use rather than for use in a trade or business or an income-producing activity. Write-offs are not allowed for personal use assets.

---
[2] Refer to Chapter 1 for a further discussion.

In summary, both realty and personalty can be either business use/income-producing property or personal use property. Examples include a residence (realty that is personal use), an office building (realty that is business use), a dump truck (personalty that is business use), and regular wearing apparel (personalty that is personal use). It is imperative that this distinction between the *classification* of an asset (realty or personalty) and the *use* to which the asset is put (business or personal) be understood.

ACCELERATED COST RECOVERY SYSTEM (ACRS AND MACRS)

GENERAL CONSIDERATIONS

2 LEARNING OBJECTIVE
Determine the amount of cost recovery under ACRS and MACRS.

Under the **accelerated cost recovery system (ACRS)**, the cost of an asset is recovered over a predetermined period that is generally shorter than the useful life of the asset or the period the asset is used to produce income. The ACRS system was designed to encourage investment, improve productivity, and simplify the law and its administration. However, the pre-ACRS depreciation rules will continue to apply in the following situations:

- Property placed in service after 1980 whose life is not based on years (e.g., units-of-production method).
- The remaining depreciation on property placed in service by the taxpayer before 1981.
- Personal property acquired after 1980 if the property was owned or used during 1980 by the taxpayer or a related person (antichurning rule).[3]
- Property that is amortized (e.g., leasehold improvements).

The basis for cost recovery generally is the adjusted cost basis used to determine gain if property is sold or otherwise disposed of. The basis is reduced by the amount of the cost recovery deducted.

Cost Recovery Allowed or Allowable. The basis of cost recovery property must be reduced by the cost recovery allowed and by not less than the allowable amount. The *allowed* cost recovery is the cost recovery actually taken, whereas the *allowable* cost recovery is the amount that could have been taken under the applicable cost recovery method. If the taxpayer does not claim any cost recovery on property during a particular year, the basis of the property must still be reduced by the amount of cost recovery that should have been deducted (the allowable cost recovery).

EXAMPLE 2

On March 15, Jack paid $10,000 for a copier to be used in his business. The copier is five-year property. Jack elected to use the straight-line method of cost recovery, but did not take cost recovery in years three or four. Therefore, the allowed cost recovery (cost recovery actually deducted) and the allowable cost recovery are as follows:

---

[3] § 168(f). The antichurning rules may also require the use of pre-TRA of 1986 ACRS rules on property placed in service after December 31, 1986 (property that otherwise would be subject to MACRS).

	Cost Recovery Allowed	Cost Recovery Allowable
Year 1	$1,000	$1,000
Year 2	2,000	2,000
Year 3	–0–	2,000
Year 4	–0–	2,000
Year 5	2,000	2,000
Year 6	1,000	1,000

If Jack sold the copier for $800 in year seven, he would recognize an $800 gain ($800 amount realized – $0 adjusted basis) because the adjusted basis of the copier is zero. ▼

Cost Recovery Basis for Personal Use Assets Converted to Business or Income-Producing Use. If personal use assets are converted to business or income-producing use, the basis for cost recovery and for loss is the *lower* of the adjusted basis or the fair market value at the time the property was converted. As a result of this lower-of-basis rule, losses that occurred while the property was personal use property will not be recognized for tax purposes through the cost recovery of the property.

EXAMPLE 3

Hans acquires a personal residence for $120,000. Four years later, when the fair market value is only $100,000, he converts the property to rental use. The basis for cost recovery is $100,000, since the fair market value is less than the adjusted basis. The $20,000 decline in value is deemed to be personal (since it occurred while the property was held for personal use) and therefore nondeductible. ▼

ETHICAL CONSIDERATIONS

Deducting Depreciation on a Converted Truck

Bill purchased a new truck several years ago and has always used the truck for personal use. This year Bill started a business and used the truck almost exclusively for business. Because he has not taken any depreciation on his truck and because the cost of a new truck is significantly more than he paid for his truck, Bill wants to use the original cost of the truck for purposes of determining depreciation on his tax return. Evaluate the equity and the appropriateness of Bill's perspective.

ELIGIBLE PROPERTY UNDER ACRS OR MACRS

Assets used in a trade or business or for the production of income are eligible for cost recovery if they are subject to wear and tear, decay or decline from natural causes, or obsolescence. Assets that do not decline in value on a predictable basis or that do not have a determinable useful life (e.g., land, stock, antiques) are not eligible for cost recovery.

PERSONALTY: RECOVERY PERIODS AND METHODS

Classification of Property: ACRS. ACRS provides that the cost of eligible personalty (and certain realty) is recovered over 3, 5, 10, or 15 years. Property is classified by recovery period as follows:

TAX IN THE NEWS

A Seventeenth-Century Ruggeri Bass Violin Is a Tool of Trade Rather Than a Work of Art

In September 1995, the U.S. Third Circuit Court of Appeals affirmed a Tax Court decision, holding that a valuable bass violin could be depreciated when it is used as a tool of trade by a professional musician. The depreciation was allowed even though the instrument actually increased in value while the musician owned it. The key factor appears to be that the taxpayer viewed the instrument as a tool of his trade that was subject to normal wear and tear and not as a work of art.

The petitioner, Brian P. Liddle, who was a professional musician with the Philadelphia Orchestra, purchased the violin for $28,000 in 1984. The violin was built in the seventeenth century by Franceso Ruggeri. Ruggeri studied stringed instrument construction under Nicolo Amati of Cremona, who also instructed Antonio Stradivari.

In early 1996, physicists at the School of Engineering and Design at Southbank University in London reported what musicians have long known—the sound of wooden instruments improves with use. The vibrations cause physical changes to wood that lower its damping coefficient. Lower damping sustains notes: each note can be heard for a longer interval of time. Vibrations redistribute moisture in the wood. When the wood is left alone, it eventually returns to its original state. The researchers concluded that the instrument must be played continuously for the enhanced resonance to be maintained.

The IRS also announced in 1996 that it will continue to challenge depreciation deductions claimed by professional musicians for antique instruments that have no determinable useful lives. The Service believes that the *Liddle* case (and the *Simon* case) was wrongly decided, claiming that "although ACRS statutorily eliminated the concept of salvage value by permitting the entire cost of an asset to be recovered, . . . it did not diverge from the concept that to be entitled to depreciation, property had to have a determinable useful life."

---

3 years	Autos, light-duty trucks, R & D equipment, racehorses over 2 years old and other horses over 12 years old, and personalty with an ADR* midpoint life of 4 years or less.[4]
5 years	Most other equipment except long-lived public utility property. Also includes single-purpose agricultural structures and petroleum storage facilities, which are designated as § 1245 property under the law.
10 years	Public utility property with an ADR midpoint life greater than 18 but not greater than 25 years, burners and boilers using coal as a primary fuel if used in a public utility power plant and if replacing or converting oil- or gas-fired burners or boilers, railroad tank cars, mobile homes, and realty with an ADR midpoint life of 12.5 years or less (e.g., theme park structures).
15 years	Public utility property with an ADR midpoint life exceeding 25 years (except certain burners and boilers using coal as a primary fuel).

*ADR refers to the Asset Depreciation Range system.

---

[4] Rev.Proc. 83-35, 1983-1 C.B. 745 is the source for the ADR midpoint lives.

Taxpayers who own 10-year or 15-year ACRS property continue to compute cost recovery allowances under the ACRS rules. However, all cost has already been recovered on any 3-year or 5-year ACRS property.

Taxpayers had the choice of using (1) the straight-line method over the regular or optional (see below) recovery period or (2) a prescribed accelerated method over the regular recovery period. These two methods are both part of the ACRS system, but a convenient name is not provided for either method. Hereafter, the straight-line method will be referred to as the *optional* (or *elective*) *straight-line method*. The method using percentages prescribed in the Code will be referred to as the *statutory percentage method*.

The rates to be used in computing the deduction under the statutory percentage method are shown in Table 8–1 (all tables are located at the end of the chapter prior to the Problem Materials) and are based on the 150 percent declining-balance method, using the **half-year convention**[5] and an assumption of zero salvage value. The rates in the cost recovery tables at the end of the chapter reflect the relevant methods, conventions, and assumptions.

EXAMPLE 4

Green Utilities acquired 15-year public utility property in 1985 at a cost of $100,000. The property was placed in service on September 1, 1985. Green's cost recovery allowance for 1997 is determined from Table 8–1. The cost recovery percentage for 1997 (recovery year 13) is 6%, and the cost recovery allowance is $6,000 ($100,000 cost × 6%). ▼

Note that in 1985, Green got a half-year's cost recovery deduction (since the half-year convention is reflected in the percentages in Table 8–1) although it held the property only four months.

In the year that personal property is disposed of, no cost recovery is allowed.

EXAMPLE 5

Assume the same facts as in the previous example and that the property is sold in May 1998. Green is not allowed a cost recovery deduction for the property in 1998. ▼

Reduction of Basis for Investment Tax Credit. For personalty placed in service after 1982 and before January 1, 1986, taxpayers were required to reduce the basis of the property for the ACRS write-off by one-half the amount of the investment tax credit taken on the property.[6] The investment tax credit was not allowed on realty.

EXAMPLE 6

Beige Electric Company acquired property on September 4, 1985, for $100,000. The property was 15-year ACRS property, and Beige claimed a $10,000 investment tax credit ($100,000 × 10% investment tax credit rate). The basis of the property was reduced by $5,000 (one-half of the $10,000 investment tax credit). Therefore, the basis for cost recovery was $95,000. The cost recovery for 1997 is $5,700 [$95,000 × 6% (Table 8–1)]. ▼

As an alternative to reducing the basis of the property, a taxpayer could elect to take a *reduced* investment tax credit. Under this election, the investment tax credit was 8 percent (rather than 10 percent) for recovery property other than three-year property and 4 percent (instead of 6 percent) for three-year property. In Example 6, if the reduced investment tax credit election were made, Beige's cost recovery basis would be $100,000 rather than $95,000.

---

[5] The half-year convention assumes all property is placed in service at mid-year and thus provides for a half-year's cost recovery.

[6] § 48(q).

TRA of 1986 generally repealed the investment tax credit for property placed in service after December 31, 1985. Therefore, the reduction of basis for the investment tax credit does not apply to such property.

Classification of Property: MACRS. The general effect of TRA of 1986 was to lengthen asset lives. The **modified accelerated cost recovery system (MACRS)** provides that the cost recovery basis of eligible personalty (and certain realty) is recovered over 3, 5, 7, 10, 15, or 20 years. Property is classified by recovery period under MACRS as follows (see Exhibit 8–1 for examples):[7]

3-year 200% class	ADR midpoints of 4 years and less.[8] Excludes automobiles and light trucks. Includes racehorses more than 2 years old and other horses more than 12 years old.
5-year 200% class	ADR midpoints of more than 4 years and less than 10 years, adding automobiles, light trucks, qualified technological equipment, renewable energy and biomass properties that are small power production facilities, research and experimentation property, semiconductor manufacturing equipment, and computer-based central office switching equipment.
7-year 200% class	ADR midpoints of 10 years and more and less than 16 years, adding single-purpose agricultural or horticultural structures and property with no ADR midpoint not classified elsewhere. Includes railroad track and office furniture, fixtures, and equipment.
10-year 200% class	ADR midpoints of 16 years and more and less than 20 years.
15-year 150% class	ADR midpoints of 20 years and more and less than 25 years, including sewage treatment plants, and telephone distribution plants and comparable equipment used for the two-way exchange of voice and data communications.
20-year 150% class	ADR midpoints of 25 years and more, other than real property with an ADR midpoint of 27.5 years and more, and including sewer pipes.

Accelerated depreciation is allowed for these six MACRS classes of property. Two hundred percent declining-balance is used for the 3-, 5-, 7-, and 10-year classes, with a switchover to straight-line depreciation when it yields a larger amount. One hundred and fifty percent declining-balance is allowed for the 15- and 20-year classes, with an appropriate straight-line switchover.[9]

Taxpayers may *elect* the straight-line method to compute cost recovery allowances for each of these classes of property. Certain property is not eligible for accelerated cost recovery and must be depreciated under an alternative depreciation system (ADS). Both the straight-line election and ADS are discussed later in the chapter.

The original ACRS system gave the taxpayer a half-year of cost recovery for the tax year an asset was placed in service but allowed the taxpayer to recover the balance of the cost recovery basis over the years remaining in the property's recovery period. No cost recovery deduction was permitted for the year of disposition or retirement of the property. Thus, conceptually, the taxpayer was considered to have placed property in service at the beginning of the recovery

---

[7] § 168(e).
[8] Rev.Proc. 87–56, 1987–2 C.B. 674 is the source for the ADR midpoint lives.
[9] § 168(b).

▼ **EXHIBIT 8–1**
Cost Recovery Periods: MACRS

Class of Property	Examples
3-year	Tractor units for use over-the-road.
	Any horse that is not a racehorse and is more than 12 years old at the time it is placed in service.
	Any racehorse that is more than 2 years old at the time it is placed in service.
	Breeding hogs.
	Special tools used in the manufacturing of motor vehicles such as dies, fixtures, molds, and patterns.
5-year	Automobiles and taxis.
	Light and heavy general-purpose trucks.
	Buses.
	Trailers and trailer-mounted containers.
	Typewriters, calculators, and copiers.
	Computers and peripheral equipment.
	Breeding and dairy cattle.
7-year	Office furniture, fixtures, and equipment.
	Breeding and work horses.
	Agricultural machinery and equipment.
	Single-purpose agricultural or horticultural structures.
	Railroad track.
10-year	Vessels, barges, tugs, and similar water transportation equipment.
	Assets used for petroleum refining or for the manufacture of grain and grain mill products, sugar and sugar products, or vegetable oils and vegetable oil products.
15-year	Land improvements.
	Assets used for industrial steam and electric generation and/or distribution systems.
	Assets used in the manufacture of cement.
	Assets used in pipeline transportation.
	Electric utility nuclear production plant.
	Municipal wastewater treatment plant.
20-year	Farm buildings except single-purpose agricultural and horticultural structures.
	Gas utility distribution facilities.
	Water utilities.
	Municipal sewer.

period but was allowed only a half-year's worth of cost recovery for the year it was placed in service.

By contrast, MACRS views property as placed in service in the middle of the first year.[10] Thus, for example, the statutory recovery period for three-year property begins in the middle of the year an asset is placed in service and ends three years later. In practical terms, this means that taxpayers must wait an extra year to recover the cost of depreciable assets. That is, the actual write-off periods are 4, 6, 8, 11, 16, and 21 years. MACRS also allows for a half-year of cost recovery in the year of disposition or retirement.

The procedure for computing the cost recovery allowance under MACRS is the same as under the original ACRS method. The cost recovery basis is multiplied by the percentages that reflect the applicable cost recovery method and the applicable convention. The percentages are shown in Table 8–2.

---
[10] § 168(d)(4)(A).

EXAMPLE 7 Kareem acquires a five-year class asset on April 10, 1997, for $30,000. Kareem's cost recovery deduction for 1997 is $6,000 [$30,000 × .20 (Table 8–2)]. ▼

EXAMPLE 8 Assume the same facts as in Example 7, and that Kareem disposes of the asset on March 5, 1999. Kareem's cost recovery deduction for 1999 is $2,880 [$30,000 × ½ × .192 (Table 8–2)]. ▼

Mid-Quarter Convention. Under the original ACRS rules for personal property, the half-year convention was used no matter when property was acquired during the year. Thus, if a substantial dollar amount of assets was acquired late in the tax year, the half-year convention still applied. The law now contains a provision to curtail the benefits of such a tax strategy. If more than 40 percent of the value of property other than eligible real estate (see Realty: Recovery Periods and Methods: MACRS for a discussion of eligible real estate) is placed in service during the last quarter of the year, a **mid-quarter convention** applies.[11] Property acquisitions are then grouped by the quarter they were acquired for cost recovery purposes. Acquisitions during the first quarter are allowed 10.5 months of cost recovery; the second quarter, 7.5 months; the third quarter, 4.5 months; and the fourth quarter, 1.5 months. The percentages are shown in Table 8–3.

EXAMPLE 9 Silver Corporation acquires the following five-year class property in 1997:

Property Acquisition Dates	Cost
February 15	$ 200,000
July 10	400,000
December 5	600,000
Total	$1,200,000

If Silver Corporation uses the statutory percentage method, the cost recovery allowances for the first two years are computed as indicated below. Since more than 40% ($600,000/ $1,200,000 = 50%) of the acquisitions are in the last quarter, the mid-quarter convention applies.

1997

February 15	[$200,000 × .35 (Table 8–3)]	$ 70,000
July 10	($400,000 × .15)	60,000
December 5	($600,000 × .05)	30,000
Total		$160,000

1998

February 15	[$200,000 × .26 (Table 8–3)]	$ 52,000
July 10	($400,000 × .34)	136,000
December 5	($600,000 × .38)	228,000
Total		$416,000

▼

---

[11] § 168(d)(3).

When property to which the mid-quarter convention applies is disposed of, the property is treated as though it were disposed of at the midpoint of the quarter. Hence, in the quarter of disposition, cost recovery is allowed for one-half of the quarter.

EXAMPLE 10

Assume the same facts as in Example 9, except that Silver Corporation sells the $400,000 asset on November 30 of 1998. The cost recovery allowance for 1998 is computed as follows:

February 15	[$200,000 × .26 (Table 8–3)]	$ 52,000
July 10	[$400,000 × .34 × (3.5/4)]	119,000
December 5	($600,000 × .38)	228,000
Total		$399,000

REALTY: RECOVERY PERIODS AND METHODS

ACRS. Under the original ACRS rules, realty was assigned a 15-year recovery period. Real property other than low-income housing is depreciated using the 175 percent declining-balance method, with a switchover to straight-line depreciation when it yields a larger amount. Low-income housing is depreciated using the 200 percent declining-balance method, with an appropriate straight-line switchover. In either case, zero salvage value is assumed. Statutory percentages for real property are shown in Table 8–4, which contains rates for low-income housing as well as for other 15-year real estate. As explained later in the chapter, taxpayers were allowed to elect the straight-line method for real property.

The half-year convention does not apply to 15-year real property. As a result, Table 8–4 is structured differently from Tables 8–1 and 8–2. The cost recovery deduction for 15-year real property is based on the month the asset is placed in service rather than on the half-year convention. No cost recovery is allowed for the month in which an asset is disposed of if the asset is disposed of before the end of the recovery period.

EXAMPLE 11

Alicia purchased a warehouse for $100,000 on January 1, 1984. The cost recovery allowance for the years 1984 through 1997, using the statutory percentage method, is as follows (see Table 8–4 for percentages).

1984—$12,000 (12% × $100,000)
1985—$10,000 (10% × $100,000)
1986—$9,000 (9% × $100,000)
1987—$8,000 (8% × $100,000)
1988—$7,000 (7% × $100,000)
1989—$6,000 (6% × $100,000)
1990—$6,000 (6% × $100,000)
1991—$6,000 (6% × $100,000)
1992—$6,000 (6% × $100,000)
1993—$5,000 (5% × $100,000)
1994—$5,000 (5% × $100,000)
1995—$5,000 (5% × $100,000)
1996—$5,000 (5% × $100,000)
1997—$5,000 (5% × $100,000)

EXAMPLE 12 Assume the same facts as in Example 11, except the property is low-income housing. Cost recovery deductions using the statutory percentage method for 1984 through 1997 are as follows (see Table 8–4 for percentages):

1984—$13,000 (13% × $100,000)
1985—$12,000 (12% × $100,000)
1986—$10,000 (10% × $100,000)
1987—$9,000 (9% × $100,000)
1988—$8,000 (8% × $100,000)
1989—$7,000 (7% × $100,000)
1990—$6,000 (6% × $100,000)
1991—$5,000 (5% × $100,000)
1992—$5,000 (5% × $100,000)
1993—$5,000 (5% × $100,000)
1994—$4,000 (4% × $100,000)
1995—$4,000 (4% × $100,000)
1996—$4,000 (4% × $100,000)
1997—$4,000 (4% × $100,000)

The Deficit Reduction Act of 1984 changed the recovery period for real property to 18 years. This applies generally to property placed in service after March 15, 1984. However, the 15-year recovery period was retained for low-income housing as well as for other real property placed in service before March 16, 1984.

Eighteen-year real property placed in service after June 22, 1984, is subject to a **mid-month convention**.[12] This means that real property placed in service at any time during a particular month is treated as if it were placed in service in the middle of the month. This allows for one-half month's cost recovery for the month the property is placed in service. If the property is disposed of before the end of the recovery period, one-half month's cost recovery is permitted for the month of disposition regardless of the specific date of disposition. Statutory percentages for 18-year real property with a mid-month convention are shown in Table 8–5.

EXAMPLE 13 Rex purchased a building for $300,000 and placed it in service on August 21, 1984. The first year's cost recovery using the statutory percentage method is $12,000 [$300,000 × 4% (Table 8–5)]. ▼

EXAMPLE 14 Assume the same facts as in Example 13 and that Rex disposes of the building on May 3, 1997. The cost recovery in the year of disposition is $4,500 ($300,000 × 4% × 4.5/12). ▼

Public Law 99–121 extended the minimum recovery period for real property (except low-income housing) from 18 years to 19 years. This applies to property placed in service after May 8, 1985, and before January 1, 1987. Statutory percentages for 19-year real property are shown in Table 8–6. Because the percentages are determined using a mid-month convention, the computation of cost recovery is mechanically the same as for 18-year property with the mid-month convention.

---

[12] A transitional rule, which provides for a full-month convention, is effective for property placed in service after March 15, 1984, and before June 23, 1984. The cost recovery tables for property placed in service during this period are not included in this chapter.

Concept Summary 8-2

Statutory Percentage Method under ACRS and MACRS

ACRS

	Personal Property	Real Property 15-Year	Real Property 18-Year	Real Property 19-Year
Convention	Half-year	Full-month	Mid-month	Mid-month
Cost recovery deduction in the year of disposition	None	Full-month up to month of disposition	Half-month for month of disposition	Half-month for month of disposition

MACRS

	Personal Property	Real Property*
Convention	Half-year or mid-quarter	Mid-month
Cost recovery deduction in the year of disposition	Half-year for year of disposition or half-quarter for quarter of disposition	Half-month for month of disposition

*Straight-line method must be used.

MACRS. Under MACRS, the cost recovery period for residential rental real estate is 27.5 years, and the straight-line method is used for computing the cost recovery allowance. **Residential rental real estate** includes property where 80 percent or more of the gross rental revenues are from nontransient dwelling units (e.g., an apartment building). Hotels, motels, and similar establishments are not residential rental property. Low-income housing is classified as residential rental real estate. Nonresidential real estate has a recovery period of 31.5 years (39 years for such property placed in service after May 12, 1993) and is also depreciated using the straight-line method.[13]

Some items of real property are not treated as real estate for purposes of MACRS. For example, single-purpose agricultural structures are in the 7-year MACRS class. Land improvements are in the 15-year MACRS class.

All eligible real estate is depreciated using the mid-month convention. Regardless of when during the month the property is placed in service, it is deemed to have been placed in service at the middle of the month. In the year of disposition, a mid-month convention is also used.

Cost recovery is computed by multiplying the applicable rate (Table 8–7) by the cost recovery basis.

Example 15

Alec acquired a building on April 1, 1993, for $800,000. If the building is classified as residential rental real estate, the cost recovery allowance for 1997 is $29,088 (.03636 × $800,000). If the building is classified as nonresidential real estate, the 1997 cost recovery allowance is $25,400 (.03175 × $800,000). (See Table 8–7 for percentages.) ▼

---

[13] §§ 168(b), (c), and (e).

As part of the deficit reduction legislation of the Clinton administration (Revenue Reconciliation Act of 1993), nonresidential real estate placed in service after May 12, 1993, is subject to a 39-year recovery period. Property placed in service before 1994 that was subject to a binding contract to construct or purchase, as of May 12, 1993, may still be treated as 31.5-year property under the prior rules.

EXAMPLE 16

Assume the same facts as in Example 15, except Alec acquired the nonresidential building on November 19, 1997. The 1997 cost recovery allowance is $2,568 [$800,000 × .00321 (Table 8–7)]. ▼

STRAIGHT-LINE ELECTION UNDER ACRS AND MACRS

ACRS. Under ACRS, taxpayers could *elect* to write off an asset using the straight-line method rather than the statutory percentage method. The straight-line recovery period could be the same as the prescribed recovery period under the statutory percentage method, or a longer period. The allowable straight-line recovery periods for each class of property are summarized as follows:

3-year property	3, 5, or 12 years
5-year property	5, 12, or 25 years
10-year property	10, 25, or 35 years
15-year property	15, 35, or 45 years
18-year real property and low-income housing (placed in service after March 15, 1984)	18, 35, or 45 years
19-year real property and low-income housing (placed in service after May 8, 1985)	19, 35, or 45 years

If the straight-line option was elected for personal property, the half-year convention applies in computing the cost recovery deduction. The effect of electing the straight-line method for personal property is to extend the statutory recovery period by one year (e.g., three to four and five to six years). There is no cost recovery deduction in the year of the disposition of the property.

EXAMPLE 17

On May 6, 1986, Owl Utilities paid $20,000 for coal-fired boilers to replace gas-fired boilers (10-year property). Owl elected to compute the cost recovery allowance using the optional straight-line method and the regular cost recovery period. Owl's cost recovery allowance for 1986 was $1,000 ($20,000 basis × 10% straight-line rate × ½ year). The cost recovery allowance for 1997 is $1,000 ($20,000 basis × 10% straight-line rate × ½ year). These cost recovery allowances reflect the half-year convention for the first and last years of the cost recovery period. ▼

For each class of personal property, the straight-line election applied to *all* assets in a *particular class* that were placed in service during the year for which the election was made. The election applies for the entire recovery period of these assets. The election is not binding for personal property of the same class placed in service in another tax year.

Under the straight-line option for 15-year *real* property, the first year's cost recovery deduction and the cost recovery deduction for the year of disposition are computed on the basis of the number of months the property was in service during the year.

EXAMPLE 18

Kate acquired a store building on October 1, 1983, at a cost of $150,000. She elected the straight-line method using a recovery period of 15 years. Kate's cost recovery deduction for 1983 was $2,500 [($150,000 ÷ 15) × 3/12]. ▼

EXAMPLE 19 Assume the same facts as in Example 18 and that Kate disposes of the asset on September 30, 1997. Kate's cost recovery deduction for 1997 is $7,500 [($150,000 ÷ 15) × 9/12]. ▼

Under the straight-line option for 18-year or 19-year real property, the cost recovery allowances in the year the property is placed in service and in the year of disposition are computed in the same manner (except for the use of different rates) as under the statutory percentage method. Note that 18-year and 19-year real property use a mid-month convention, whereas 15-year real property uses a full-month convention. Table 8–8 contains the applicable percentages to be used under the straight-line option for 19-year real property. (The tables that contain the percentages for 18-year real property using the straight-line method over 18, 35, and 45 years and 19-year real property using the straight-line method over 35 and 45 years are not reproduced in this text.)

EXAMPLE 20 Ned acquired 19-year real property on October 1, 1986, at a cost of $150,000. He elected the straight-line method of cost recovery. Ned's cost recovery deduction for 1986 was $1,650 [$150,000 × 1.1% (Table 8–8)]. ▼

EXAMPLE 21 Assume the same facts as in Example 20 and that Ned disposes of the asset on September 20, 1997. Ned's cost recovery deduction for 1997 is $5,631 {[$150,000 × 5.3% × (8.5/12)] (Table 8–8)}. ▼

The straight-line election for 15-year, 18-year, or 19-year real property may be made on a *property-by-property* basis within the same year.

MACRS. Although MACRS requires straight-line depreciation for all eligible real estate as previously discussed, the taxpayer may *elect* to use the straight-line method for personal property.[14] The property is depreciated using the class life (recovery period) of the asset with a half-year convention or a mid-quarter convention, whichever is applicable. The election is available on a class-by-class and year-by-year basis. The percentages for the straight-line election with a half-year convention appear in Table 8–9.

EXAMPLE 22 Terry acquires a 10-year class asset on August 4, 1997, for $100,000. He elects the straight-line method of cost recovery. Terry's cost recovery deduction for 1997 is $5,000 ($100,000 × .050). His cost recovery deduction for 1998 is $10,000 ($100,000 × .100). (See Table 8–9 for percentages.) ▼

ELECTION TO EXPENSE ASSETS

3 LEARNING OBJECTIVE
Recognize when and how to make the § 179 expensing election, calculate the amount of the deduction, and apply the effect of the election in making the MACRS calculation.

Section 179 (Election to Expense Certain Depreciable Business Assets) permits the taxpayer to elect to write off up to $18,000 in 1997[15] of the acquisition cost of *tangible personal property* used in a trade or business. Amounts that are expensed under § 179 may not be capitalized and depreciated. The **§ 179 expensing** election is an annual election and applies to the acquisition cost of property placed in service that year. The immediate expense election is not available for real property or for property used for the production of income.[16]

---

[14] § 168(b)(5).

[15] This amount was $10,000 for property placed in service in tax years beginning before January 1, 1993, and was $17,500 for property placed in service in tax years beginning after December 31, 1992, and before January 1, 1997.

[16] §§ 179(b) and (d). The amount shown is per taxpayer, per year. On a joint return, the statutory amounts apply to the couple. If the taxpayers are married and file separate returns, each spouse is eligible for 50% of the statutory amount.

Concept Summary 8–3

Straight-Line Election under ACRS and MACRS

ACRS

	Personal Property	Real Property 15-Year	Real Property 18-Year	Real Property 19-Year
Convention	Half-year	Full-month	Mid-month	Mid-month
Cost recovery deduction in the year of disposition	None	Full-month up to month of disposition	Half-month for month of disposition	Half-month for month of disposition
Elective or mandatory	Elective	Elective	Elective	Elective
Breadth of election	Class by class	Property by property	Property by property	Property by property

MACRS

	Personal Property	Real Property
Convention	Half-year or mid-quarter	Mid-month
Cost recovery deduction in the year of disposition	Half-year for year of dispositon or half-quarter for quarter of disposition	Half-month for month of disposition
Elective or mandatory	Elective	Mandatory
Breadth of election	Class by class	

EXAMPLE 23

Kelly acquires machinery (five-year class) on February 1, 1997, at a cost of $40,000 and elects to expense $18,000 under § 179. Kelly's statutory percentage cost recovery deduction for 1997 is $4,400 [($40,000 cost − $18,000 expensed) × .200]. (See Table 8–2 for percentage.) Kelly's total deduction for 1997 is $22,400 ($18,000 + $4,400). ▼

For tax years beginning in 1997, an increase in the maximum § 179 amount is being phased in as follows:

Tax Year Beginning in	Maximum Expense Deduction
1997	$18,000
1998	$18,500
1999	19,000
2000	20,000
2001 or 2002	24,000
2003 and thereafter	25,000

Annual Limitations. Two additional limitations apply to the amount deductible under § 179. First, the ceiling amount on the deduction is reduced dollar-for-dollar when property (other than eligible real estate) placed in service during the taxable year exceeds $200,000. Second, the amount expensed under § 179 cannot exceed the aggregate amount of taxable income derived from the conduct of any trade or business by the taxpayer. Taxable income of a trade or business is computed without regard to the amount expensed under § 179. Any § 179 expensed amount in excess of taxable income is carried forward to future taxable years and added to other amounts eligible for expensing (and is subject to the ceiling rules for the carryforward years).

EXAMPLE 24

Jill owns a computer service and operates it as a sole proprietorship. In 1997, she will net $11,000 before considering any § 179 deduction. If Jill spends $204,000 on new equipment, her § 179 expense deduction is computed as follows:

§ 179 deduction before adjustment	$18,000
Less: Dollar limitation reduction ($204,000 − $200,000)	(4,000)
Remaining § 179 deduction	$14,000
Business income limitation	$11,000
§ 179 deduction allowed	$11,000
§ 179 deduction carryforward ($14,000 − $11,000)	$ 3,000

Effect on Basis. The basis of the property for cost recovery purposes is reduced by the § 179 amount after it is adjusted for property placed in service in excess of $200,000. This adjusted amount does not reflect any business income limitation.

EXAMPLE 25

Assume the same facts as in Example 24 and that the new equipment is five-year class property. Jill's statutory percentage cost recovery deduction for 1997 is $38,000 [($204,000 − $14,000) × .200]. (See Table 8–2 for percentage.) ▼

Conversion to Personal Use. Conversion of the expensed property to personal use at any time results in recapture income (see Chapter 17). A property is converted to personal use if it is not used predominantly in a trade or business. Regulations provide for the mechanics of the recapture.[17]

BUSINESS AND PERSONAL USE OF AUTOMOBILES AND OTHER LISTED PROPERTY

4 LEARNING OBJECTIVE
Identify listed property and apply the deduction limitations on listed property and on luxury automobiles.

Limits exist on ACRS and MACRS deductions for automobiles and other listed property that are used for both personal and business purposes.[18] If the listed property is *predominantly used* for business, the taxpayer is allowed to use the statutory percentage method to recover the cost. In cases where the property is *not predominantly used* for business, the cost is recovered using a straight-line recovery.

Listed property includes the following:

- Any passenger automobile.
- Any other property used as a means of transportation.
- Any property of a type generally used for purposes of entertainment, recreation, or amusement.
- Any computer or peripheral equipment, with the exception of equipment used exclusively at a regular business establishment, including a qualifying home office.

---

[17] Reg. § 1.179–1(e). [18] § 280F.

TAX IN THE NEWS

A FERRARI AS MEDICAL EQUIPMENT

Babies do not always arrive during office hours. Obstetricians frequently need to get to the delivery room quickly. The question is whether "quickly" requires a red Ferrari sports car.

On August 26, 1995, the *Newport News Daily Press* reported that a Chesapeake obstetrician purchased a red Ferrari and then wrote off the cost on his corporate tax return. On the return, the doctor claimed the purchase price was for an ultrasound machine and treated the amount as a business expense. From the *Daily Press* and other local media reports, it is unclear whether the $85,000 amount was expensed or whether it was capitalized and deducted as cost recovery.

- Any cellular telephone or other similar telecommunications equipment.
- Any other property specified in the Regulations.[19]

Automobiles and Other Listed Property Used Predominantly in Business. For listed property to be considered as predominantly used in business, its business usage must exceed 50 percent.[20] The use of listed property for production of income does not qualify as business use for purposes of the more-than-50 percent test. However, if the more-than-50 percent test is met, both production of income and business use percentages are used to compute the cost recovery deduction.

EXAMPLE 26

On September 1, 1997, Emma places in service listed five-year recovery property. The property cost $10,000. If Emma uses the property 40% for business and 25% for the production of income, the property is not considered as predominantly used for business. The cost is recovered using straight-line cost recovery. If, however, Emma uses the property 60% for business and 25% for the production of income, the property is considered as used predominantly for business. Therefore, she may use the statutory percentage method. Emma's cost recovery allowance for the year is $1,700 ($10,000 × .200 × 85%). ▼

The method for determining the percentage of business usage for listed property is specified in the Regulations. The Regulations provide that for automobiles a mileage-based percentage is to be used. Other listed property is to use the most appropriate unit of time (e.g., hours) the property is actually used (rather than available for use).[21]

The law places special limitations on the cost recovery deduction for passenger automobiles. These statutory dollar limits were imposed on passenger automobiles because of the belief that the tax system was being used to underwrite automobiles whose cost and luxury far exceeded what was needed for their business use.

A *passenger automobile* is any four-wheeled vehicle manufactured for use on public streets, roads, and highways with an unloaded gross vehicle weight rating of 6,000 pounds or less.[22] This definition specifically excludes vehicles used

---

[19] § 280F(d)(4).
[20] § 280F(b)(4).
[21] Reg. § 1.280F–6T(e).
[22] § 280F(d)(5).

directly in the business of transporting people or property for compensation such as taxicabs, ambulances, hearses, and trucks and vans as prescribed by the Regulations.

The following limits apply to the cost recovery deductions for passenger automobiles for 1997:[23]

Year	Recovery Limitation
1	$3,160
2	5,000
3	3,050
Succeeding years until the cost is recovered	1,775

These limits are imposed before any percentage reduction for personal use. In addition, the limitation in the first year includes any amount the taxpayer elects to expense under § 179.[24] If the passenger automobile is used partly for personal use, the personal use percentage is ignored for the purpose of determining the unrecovered cost available for deduction in later years.

EXAMPLE 27

On July 1, 1997, Dan places in service an automobile that cost $20,000. The car is always used 80% for business and 20% for personal use. The cost recovery for the automobile would be as follows:

1997—$2,528 [$20,000 × 20% (limited to $3,160) × 80%]
1998—$4,000 [$20,000 × 32% (limited to $5,000) × 80%]
1999—$2,440 [$20,000 × 19.2% (limited to $3,050) × 80%]
2000—$1,420 [$20,000 × 11.52% (limited to $1,775) × 80%]
2001—$1,420 [$20,000 × 11.52% (limited to $1,775) × 80%]
2002—$1,420 [$5,240 unrecovered cost ($20,000 − $14,760*) (limited to $1,775) × 80%]

*($3,160 + $5,000 + $3,050 + $1,775 + $1,775). Although the statutory percentage method appears to restrict the deduction to $922 [$20,000 × 5.76% (limited to $1,775) × 80%], the unrecovered cost of $5,240 (limited to $1,775) multiplied by the business usage percentage is deductible. At the start of 2000 (year 4), there is an automatic switch to the straight-line cost recovery method. Under this method, the unrecovered cost up to the maximum allowable limit ($1,775) is deductible in the last year of the recovery period (2002 or year 6). Because the limit may restrict the deduction, any remaining unrecovered cost is deductible in the next or succeeding year(s), subject to the maximum allowable yearly limit ($1,775), multiplied by the business usage percentage.

The total cost recovery for the years 1997–2002 is $13,228. ▼

The cost recovery limitations are maximum amounts. If the regular calculation produces a lesser amount of cost recovery, the lesser amount is used.

EXAMPLE 28

On April 2, 1997, Gail places in service an automobile that cost $10,000. The car is always used 70% for business and 30% for personal use. The cost recovery allowance for 1997 is $1,400 ($10,000 × 20% × 70%), which is less than $2,212 ($3,160 × 70%). ▼

Note that the cost recovery limitations apply *only* to passenger automobiles and not to other listed property.

---

[23] § 280F(a)(2). The 1996 indexed amounts are $3,060, $4,900, $2,950, and $1,775.

[24] § 280F(d)(1).

Automobiles and Other Listed Property Not Used Predominantly in Business. The cost of listed property that does not pass the more-than-50 percent business usage test in the year the property is placed in service must be recovered using the straight-line method.[25] The straight-line method to be used is that required under the alternative depreciation system (explained later in the chapter). This system requires a straight-line recovery period of five years for automobiles. However, even though the straight-line method is used, the cost recovery allowance for passenger automobiles cannot exceed the dollar limitations.

EXAMPLE 29

On July 27, 1997, Fred places in service an automobile that cost $20,000. The auto is used 40% for business and 60% for personal use. The cost recovery allowance for 1997 is $800 [$20,000 × 10% (Table 8–11) × 40%]. ▼

EXAMPLE 30

Assume the same facts as in Example 29, except that the auto cost $50,000. The cost recovery allowance for 1997 is $1,264 [$50,000 × 10% (Table 8–11) = $5,000 (limited to $3,160) × 40%]. ▼

If the listed property fails the more-than-50 percent business usage test, the straight-line method must be used for the remainder of the property's life. This applies even if at some later date the business usage of the property increases to more than 50 percent. Even though the straight-line method must continue to be used, however, the amount of cost recovery will reflect the increase in business usage.

EXAMPLE 31

Assume the same facts as in Example 29, except that in 1998, Fred uses the auto 70% for business and 30% for personal use. Fred's cost recovery allowance for 1998 is $2,800 [$20,000 × 20% (Table 8–11) × 70%]. ▼

Change from Predominantly Business Use. If the business use percentage of listed property falls to 50 percent or lower after the year the property is placed in service, the property is subject to *cost recovery recapture*. The amount required to be recaptured and included in the taxpayer's return as ordinary income is the excess cost recovery.

Excess cost recovery is the excess of the cost recovery deduction taken in prior years using the statutory percentage method over the amount that would have been allowed if the straight-line method had been used since the property was placed in service.[26]

EXAMPLE 32

Seth purchased a car on January 22, 1997, at a cost of $20,000. Business usage was 80% in 1997, 70% in 1998, 40% in 1999, and 60% in 2000. Statutory percentage cost recovery deductions in 1997 and 1998 are $2,528 (80% × $3,160) and $3,500 (70% × $5,000), respectively. Seth's excess cost recovery to be recaptured as ordinary income in 1999 is $1,628, calculated as follows:

1997	
Statutory percentage allowance	$ 2,528
Straight-line ($20,000 × 10% × 80%)	(1,600)
Excess	$ 928

---

[25] § 280F(b)(2).

[26] § 280F(b)(3).

1998

Statutory percentage allowance	$ 3,500
Straight-line ($20,000 × 20% × 70%)	(2,800)
1998 excess	$ 700
1997 excess	928
Total excess	$ 1,628

After the business usage of the listed property drops below the more-than-50 percent level, the straight-line method must be used for the remaining life of the property.

EXAMPLE 33

Assume the same facts as in Example 32. Seth's cost recovery allowance for the years 1999 and 2000 would be $1,220 and $1,065, computed as follows:

1999—$1,220   [($20,000 × 20%) limited to $3,050 × 40%]
2000—$1,065   [($20,000 × 20%) limited to $1,775 × 60%]

Leased Automobiles. A taxpayer who leases a passenger automobile must report an *inclusion amount* in gross income. The inclusion amount is computed from an IRS table for each taxable year for which the taxpayer leases the automobile. The purpose of this provision is to prevent taxpayers from circumventing the cost recovery dollar limitations by leasing, instead of purchasing, an automobile.

The dollar amount of the inclusion is based on the fair market value of the automobile and is prorated for the number of days the auto is used during the taxable year. The prorated dollar amount is then multiplied by the business and income-producing usage percentage to determine the amount to be included in gross income.[27] The taxpayer deducts the lease payments, multiplied by the business and income-producing usage percentage. The net effect is that the annual deduction for the lease payment is reduced by the inclusion amount.

EXAMPLE 34

On April 1, 1997, Jim leases and places in service a passenger automobile worth $40,000. The lease is to be for a period of five years. During the taxable years 1997 and 1998, Jim uses the automobile 70% for business and 30% for personal use. Assuming the dollar amounts from the IRS table for 1997 and 1998 are $188 and $412, Jim must include $99 in gross income for 1997 and $288 for 1998, computed as follows:

1997 $188 × (275/365) × 70% = $99
1998 $412 × (365/365) × 70% = $288

In addition, Jim can deduct 70% of the lease payments each year because this is the business use percentage. ▼

Substantiation Requirements. Listed property is now subject to the substantiation requirements of § 274. This means that the taxpayer must prove the business usage as to the amount of expense or use, the time and place of use, the business purpose for the use, and the business relationship to the taxpayer of persons using the property. Substantiation requires adequate records or sufficient evidence corroborating the taxpayer's statement. However, these substantiation requirements do not apply to vehicles that, by reason of their nature, are not likely to be used more than a *de minimis* amount for personal purposes.[28]

---

[27] Reg. § 1.280F–7T(a).

[28] §§ 274(d) and (i).

Concept Summary 8-4

Listed Property Cost Recovery

```
                    Listed
                   Property
                      |
                      v
             Is the Property
           Used Predominantly
              for Business?
           /                   \
         No                    Yes
         /                       \
  Is the Property          Is the Property
   a Passenger              a Passenger
   Automobile?              Automobile?
    /      \                 /         \
   No      Yes              No         Yes
   A        B               C           D
```

Legend to Tax Treatment

A Straight-line cost recovery reduced by the personal use percentage.

B Straight-line cost recovery subject to the recovery limitations ($3,160, $5,000, $3,050, $1,775) and reduced by the personal use percentage.

C Statutory percentage cost recovery reduced by the personal use percentage.

D Statutory percentage cost recovery subject to the recovery limitations ($3,160, $5,000, $3,050, $1,775) and reduced by the personal use percentage.

ETHICAL CONSIDERATIONS

Substantiating Business Mileage

John, a physician, uses his car to go from his office to the hospital to see patients. He makes this trip at least once and quite often two or three times a day. In addition, he uses the car for commuting to his office from home and for other personal use.

Last year, as instructed by his CPA, John maintained a mileage log that he kept in the glove compartment of his car. He recorded his business mileage at the end of each day.

This year John maintained the mileage log for the month of January and compared it with his log for last year. This year's mileage was within 10 miles of last year's. Concluding that maintaining the log was a waste of time, John recorded no entries for the rest of 1997.

At his annual meeting with his CPA to discuss his 1997 tax return, John said that his business mileage and personal use mileage were "the same as last year." Evaluate what John has done.

ALTERNATIVE DEPRECIATION SYSTEM (ADS)

5 LEARNING OBJECTIVE
Determine when and how to use the alternative depreciation system (ADS).

The **alternative depreciation system (ADS)** must be used for the following:[29]

- To calculate the portion of depreciation treated as an alternative minimum tax (AMT) adjustment for purposes of the corporate and individual AMT (see Chapters 12 and 20).
- To compute depreciation allowances for property for which any of the following is true:
  - Used predominantly outside the United States.
  - Leased or otherwise used by a tax-exempt entity.
  - Financed with the proceeds of tax-exempt bonds.
  - Imported from foreign countries that maintain discriminatory trade practices or otherwise engage in discriminatory acts.
- To compute depreciation allowances for earnings and profits purposes (see Chapter 20).

In general, ADS depreciation is computed using straight-line recovery without regard to salvage value. However, for purposes of the AMT, depreciation of personal property is computed using the 150 percent declining-balance method with an appropriate switch to the straight-line method.

The taxpayer must use the half-year or the mid-quarter convention, whichever is applicable, for all property other than eligible real estate. The mid-month convention is used for eligible real estate. The applicable ADS rates are found in Tables 8–10, 8–11, and 8–12.

The recovery periods under ADS are as follows:[30]

- The ADR midpoint life for property that does not fall into any of the following listed categories.
- Five years for qualified technological equipment, automobiles, and light-duty trucks.
- Twelve years for personal property with no class life.
- Forty years for all residential rental property and all nonresidential real property.

Taxpayers may *elect* to use the 150 percent declining-balance method to compute the regular income tax rather than the 200 percent declining-balance method that is available for personal property. Hence, if the election is made, there will be no difference between the cost recovery for computing the regular income tax and the AMT. However, taxpayers who make this election must use the ADS recovery periods in computing the cost recovery for the regular income tax, and the ADS recovery periods generally are longer than the regular recovery periods under MACRS.

The following are examples of the classification of property by class life for the ADS recovery periods:[31]

3-year	Special tools used in the manufacture of motor vehicles, breeding hogs.
5-year	Automobiles, light general-purpose trucks.
7-year	Breeding and dairy cattle.
9.5-year	Computer-based telephone central office switching equipment.
10-year	Office furniture, fixtures, and equipment, railroad track.
12-year	Racehorses more than 2 years old at the time they are placed in service.

---

[29] § 168(g).
[30] The class life for certain properties described in § 168(e)(3) is specially determined under § 168(g)(3)(B).
[31] Rev.Proc. 87–56, 1987–2 C.B. 674 is the source for the recovery periods.

EXAMPLE 35

On March 1, 1997, Abby purchases computer-based telephone central office switching equipment for $80,000. If Abby uses statutory percentage cost recovery (assuming no § 179 election), the cost recovery allowance for 1997 is $16,000 [$80,000 × 20% (Table 8–2, 5-year class property)]. If Abby elects to use ADS 150% declining-balance cost recovery (assuming no § 179 election), the cost recovery allowance for 1997 is $6,312 [$80,000 × 7.89% (Table 8–10, 9.5-year class property)]. ▼

In lieu of depreciation under the regular MACRS method, taxpayers may *elect* straight-line under ADS for property that qualifies for the regular MACRS method. The election is available on a class-by-class and year-by-year basis for property other than eligible real estate. The election for eligible real estate is on a property-by-property basis. One reason for making this election is to avoid a difference between deductible depreciation and earnings and profits depreciation.

EXAMPLE 36

Polly acquires an apartment building on March 17, 1997, for $700,000. She takes the maximum cost recovery allowance for determining taxable income. Polly's cost recovery allowance for computing 1997 taxable income is $20,153 [$700,000 × .02879 (Table 8–7)]. However, Polly's cost recovery for computing her earnings and profits is only $13,853 [$700,000 × .01979 (Table 8–12)]. ▼

AMORTIZATION

6 LEARNING OBJECTIVE
Identify intangible assets that are eligible for amortization and calculate the amount of the deduction.

Prior to the Revenue Reconciliation Act of 1993 (RRA of 1993), the tax treatment of intangible assets had become a source of much controversy between taxpayers and the IRS. Disputes arose as to whether a covenant not to compete (an amortizable asset) was separate and distinct from goodwill and going-concern value (a nonamortizable asset) or merely a transfer of goodwill.

Under RRA of 1993, taxpayers can claim an **amortization** deduction on intangible assets called "amortizable § 197 intangibles." The amount of the deduction is determined by amortizing the adjusted basis of such intangibles ratably over a 15-year period beginning in the month in which the intangible is acquired.[32]

An *amortizable § 197 intangible* is any § 197 intangible acquired after August 10, 1993, and held in connection with the conduct of a trade or business or for the production of income. Section 197 intangibles include goodwill and going-concern value, franchises (except sports franchises), trademarks, and trade names. Covenants not to compete, copyrights, and patents are also included if they are acquired in connection with the acquisition of a business. Generally, self-created intangibles are not § 197 intangibles. The 15-year amortization period applies regardless of the actual useful life of an amortizable § 197 intangible. No other depreciation or amortization deduction is permitted with respect to any amortizable § 197 intangible except those permitted under the 15-year amortization rules.

EXAMPLE 37

On June 1, 1997, Neil purchased and began operating the Falcon Cafe. Of the purchase price, $90,000 is correctly allocated to goodwill. The deduction for amortization for 1997 is $3,500 [($90,000/15) × (7/12)]. ▼

---

[32] § 197(a).

ETHICAL CONSIDERATIONS

Allocating Intangible Assets When a Business Is Sold

Marge and Stan are negotiating Stan's purchase of Marge's business. Both are in the 36 percent tax bracket. They have agreed that the tangible assets of the business are worth $100,000. Marge's adjusted basis for these assets is $70,000. The only other asset of the business is the going-concern value. Marge believes that this asset is worth about $50,000. Stan believes that it is worth somewhat less, probably about $40,000.

Marge and Stan are handling their own negotiations since they do not believe in wasting money on attorneys or CPAs when such professional services are not required. Stan knows from an MBA class he took five years ago that goodwill is not deductible, but that a covenant not to compete can be deducted over the covenant period. Stan believes that Marge, who is age 67 and in poor health, is going to retire. In order to maximize the tax benefits to himself, Stan increases his offer from $140,000 to $145,000 (i.e., "we'll split the difference") if Marge will agree to sign a five-year covenant with $45,000 of the $145,000 purchase price allocated to the covenant. Marge, who believes that the tax consequences of the sale ($145,000 amount realized − $70,000 adjusted basis = $75,000 recognized gain) will be the same regardless of whether the $45,000 is for goodwill or for a covenant, accepts the offer. Evaluate the decisions made by Marge and Stan.

DEPLETION

7 LEARNING OBJECTIVE
Determine the amount of depletion expense including being able to apply the alternative tax treatments for intangible drilling and development costs.

Natural resources (e.g., oil, gas, coal, gravel, timber) are subject to **depletion**, which is simply a form of depreciation applicable to natural resources. Land generally cannot be depleted.

The owner of an interest in the natural resource is entitled to deduct depletion. An owner is one who has an economic interest in the property.[33] An economic interest requires the acquisition of an interest in the resource in place and the receipt of income from the extraction or severance of that resource. Like depreciation, depletion is a deduction *for* adjusted gross income.

Although all natural resources are subject to depletion, oil and gas wells are used as an example in the following paragraphs to illustrate the related costs and issues.

In developing an oil or gas well, the producer must make four types of expenditures.

- Natural resource costs.
- Intangible drilling and development costs.
- Tangible asset costs.
- Operating costs.

Natural resources are physically limited, and the costs to acquire them (e.g., oil under the ground) are, therefore, recovered through depletion. Costs incurred in making the property ready for drilling such as the cost of labor in clearing the property, erecting derricks, and drilling the hole are **intangible drilling and development costs (IDC)**. These costs generally have no salvage value and are a

---
[33] Reg. § 1.611–1(b).

lost cost if the well is dry. Costs for tangible assets such as tools, pipes, and engines are capital in nature. These costs must be capitalized and recovered through depreciation (cost recovery). Costs incurred after the well is producing are operating costs. These costs would include expenditures for such items as labor, fuel, and supplies. Operating costs are deductible when incurred (on the accrual basis) or when paid (on the cash basis).

The expenditures for depreciable assets and operating costs pose no unusual problems for producers of natural resources. The tax treatment of depletable costs and intangible drilling and development costs is quite a different matter.

INTANGIBLE DRILLING AND DEVELOPMENT COSTS (IDC)

Intangible drilling and development costs (IDC) can be handled in one of two ways at the option of the taxpayer. They can be *either* charged off as an expense in the year in which they are incurred *or* capitalized and written off through depletion. The taxpayer makes the election in the first year such expenditures are incurred either by taking a deduction on the return or by adding them to the depletable basis. No formal statement of intent is required. Once made, the election is binding on both the taxpayer and the IRS for all such expenditures in the future. If the taxpayer fails to make the election to expense IDC on the original timely filed return the first year such expenditures are incurred, an automatic election to capitalize them has been made and is irrevocable.

As a general rule, it is more advantageous to expense IDC. The obvious benefit of an immediate write-off (as opposed to a deferred write-off through depletion) is not the only advantage. Since a taxpayer can use percentage depletion, which is calculated without reference to basis (see Example 41), the IDC may be completely lost as a deduction if they are capitalized.

DEPLETION METHODS

There are two methods of calculating depletion: cost and percentage. Cost depletion can be used on any wasting asset (and is the only method allowed for timber). Percentage depletion is subject to a number of limitations, particularly for oil and gas deposits. Depletion should be calculated both ways, and generally the method that results in the *larger* deduction is used. The choice between cost and percentage depletion is an annual election.

Cost Depletion. **Cost depletion** is determined by using the adjusted basis of the asset.[34] The basis is divided by the estimated recoverable units of the asset (e.g., barrels, tons) to arrive at the depletion per unit. The depletion per unit then is multiplied by the number of units sold (*not* the units produced) during the year to arrive at the cost depletion allowed. Cost depletion, therefore, resembles the units-of-production method of calculating depreciation.

EXAMPLE 38

On January 1, 1997, Pablo purchased the rights to a mineral interest for $1,000,000. At that time, the remaining recoverable units in the mineral interest were estimated to be 200,000. The depletion per unit is $5 [$1,000,000 (adjusted basis) ÷ 200,000 (estimated recoverable units)]. If during the year 60,000 units were mined and 25,000 were sold, the cost depletion would be $125,000 [$5 (depletion per unit) × 25,000 (units sold)]. ▼

---

[34] § 612.

▼ **EXHIBIT 8–2**
Sample of Percentage Depletion Rates

22% Depletion	
Cobalt	Sulfur
Lead	Tin
Nickel	Uranium
Platinum	Zinc
15% Depletion	
Copper	Oil and gas
Gold	Oil shale
Iron	Silver
14% Depletion	
Borax	Magnesium carbonates
Calcium carbonates	Marble
Granite	Potash
Limestone	Slate
10% Depletion	
Coal	Perlite
Lignite	Sodium chloride
5% Depletion	
Gravel	Pumice
Peat	Sand

If the taxpayer later discovers that the original estimate was incorrect, the depletion per unit for future calculations must be redetermined based on the revised estimate.[35]

EXAMPLE 39

Assume the same facts as in Example 38. In 1998, Pablo realizes that an incorrect estimate was made. The remaining recoverable units now are determined to be 400,000. Based on this new information, the revised depletion per unit is $2.1875 [$875,000 (adjusted basis) ÷ 400,000 (estimated recoverable units)]. Note that the adjusted basis is the original cost ($1,000,000) reduced by the depletion claimed in 1997 ($125,000). If 30,000 units are sold in 1998, the depletion for the year would be $65,625 [$2.1875 (depletion per unit) × 30,000 (units sold)]. ▼

Percentage Depletion. Percentage depletion (also referred to as statutory depletion) is a specified percentage provided for in the Code. The percentage varies according to the type of mineral interest involved. A sample of these percentages is shown in Exhibit 8–2. The rate is applied to the gross income from the property, but in no event may percentage depletion exceed 50 percent of the taxable income from the property before the allowance for depletion.[36]

---

[35] § 611(a).
[36] § 613(a). Special rules apply for certain oil and gas wells under § 613A (e.g., the 50% ceiling is replaced with a 100% ceiling, and the percentage depletion may not exceed 65% of the taxpayer's taxable income from all sources before the allowance for depletion).

EXAMPLE 40

Assuming gross income of $100,000, a depletion rate of 22%, and other expenses relating to the property of $60,000, the depletion allowance is determined as follows:

Gross income	$100,000
Less: Other expenses	(60,000)
Taxable income before depletion	$ 40,000
Depletion allowance [the lesser of $22,000 (22% × $100,000) or $20,000 (50% × $40,000)]	(20,000)
Taxable income after depletion	$ 20,000

The adjusted basis of the property is reduced by $20,000, the depletion allowed. If the other expenses had been only $55,000, the full $22,000 could have been deducted, and the adjusted basis would have been reduced by $22,000. ▼

Note that percentage depletion is based on a percentage of the gross income from the property and makes no reference to cost. Thus, when percentage depletion is used, it is possible to deduct more than the original cost of the property. If percentage depletion is used, however, the adjusted basis of the property (for computing cost depletion) must be reduced by the amount of percentage depletion taken until the adjusted basis reaches zero.

Effect of Intangible Drilling Costs on Depletion.
The treatment of IDC has an effect on the depletion deduction in two ways. If the costs are capitalized, the basis for cost depletion is increased. As a consequence, the cost depletion is increased. If IDC are expensed, they reduce the taxable income from the property. This reduction may result in application of the provision that limits depletion to 50 percent (100 percent for certain oil and gas wells) of taxable income before deducting depletion.

EXAMPLE 41

Iris purchased the rights to an oil interest for $1,000,000. The recoverable barrels were estimated to be 200,000. During the year, 50,000 barrels were sold for $2,000,000. Regular expenses amounted to $800,000, and IDC were $650,000. If the IDC are capitalized, the depletion per unit is $8.25 ($1,000,000 + $650,000 ÷ 200,000 barrels), and the following taxable income results:

Gross income	$2,000,000
Less: Expenses	(800,000)
Taxable income before depletion	$1,200,000
Cost depletion ($8.25 × 50,000) = $412,500	
Percentage depletion (15% × $2,000,000) = $300,000	
Greater of cost or percentage depletion	(412,500)
Taxable income	$ 787,500

If the IDC are expensed, the taxable income is $250,000, calculated as follows:

Gross income	$ 2,000,000
Less: Expenses, including IDC	(1,450,000)
Taxable income before depletion	$ 550,000
Cost depletion [($1,000,000 ÷ 200,000 barrels) × 50,000 barrels] = $250,000	

CHAPTER 8 Depreciation, Cost Recovery, Amortization, and Depletion

Percentage depletion (15% of $2,000,000 = $300,000, limited to 100% of $550,000 taxable income before depletion) = $300,000

Greater of cost or percentage depletion	(300,000)
Taxable income	$ 250,000

For further restrictions on the use or availability of the percentage depletion method, see § 613.

REPORTING PROCEDURES

8 LEARNING OBJECTIVE
Perform the reporting procedures for cost recovery.

Sole proprietors engaged in a business should file a Schedule C, Profit or Loss from Business, to accompany Form 1040. Schedule C for 1996 is presented because the 1997 form was not yet available.

The top part of page 1 requests certain key information about the taxpayer (e.g., name, address, Social Security number) and the business methods involved (e.g., accounting method and inventory method used). Part I provides for the reporting of items of income. If the business requires the use of inventories and the computation of cost of goods sold (see Chapter 18 for when this is necessary), Part III must be completed and the cost of goods sold amount transferred to line 4 of Part I.

Part II allows for the reporting of deductions. Some of the deductions discussed in Chapters 7 and 8 and their location on the form are bad debts (line 9), depletion (line 12), and depreciation (line 13). Other expenses (line 27) include those items not already covered (see lines 8–26). An example would be research and experimental expenditures.

If depreciation is claimed, it should be supported by completing Form 4562. Form 4562 for 1996 is presented because the 1997 form was not yet available. The amount listed on line 21 of Form 4562 is then transferred to line 13 of Part II of Schedule C.

EXAMPLE 42

Thomas Andrews, Social Security number 123–45–6789, was employed as an accountant until July 1995, when he opened his own practice. His address is 279 Mountain View, Ogden, UT 84201. Andrews keeps his books on the accrual basis and had the following revenue and business expenses in 1996:

a. Revenue from accounting practice, $80,000.
b. Bad debts, $2,000.
c. Automobile expenses, $3,000.
d. Insurance, $800.
e. Office supplies, $4,000.
f. Rent, $12,000.
g. Furniture and fixtures acquired on July 15, 1995, for $8,000. Andrews used the statutory percentage cost recovery method.
h. Business automobile acquired on May 20, 1995, for $10,000. Andrews used the statutory percentage cost recovery method. The automobile, which was driven 12,000 miles during 1996, was used only for business purposes.
i. Microcomputer acquired on May 7, 1996, for $21,500. Andrews elects § 179 and uses the statutory percentage cost recovery method.

(Remember that the statutory ceiling amount for § 179 expensing for 1996 is $17,500.)

Andrews would report the above information on Schedule C and Form 4562 as illustrated on the following pages. ▼

Form 4562 — Depreciation and Amortization (Including Information on Listed Property)

OMB No. 1545-0172
1996
Attachment Sequence No. 67

Department of the Treasury
Internal Revenue Service (99)

▶ See separate instructions. ▶ Attach this form to your return.

Name(s) shown on return: Thomas Andrews
Business or activity to which this form relates: Accounting Services
Identifying number: 123-45-6789

Part I — Election To Expense Certain Tangible Property (Section 179)
(Note: If you have any "listed property," complete Part V before you complete Part I.)

1	Maximum dollar limitation. If an enterprise zone business, see page 2 of the instructions	$17,500
2	Total cost of section 179 property placed in service. See page 2 of the instructions	$21,500
3	Threshold cost of section 179 property before reduction in limitation	$200,000
4	Reduction in limitation. Subtract line 3 from line 2. If zero or less, enter -0-	–0–
5	Dollar limitation for tax year. Subtract line 4 from line 1. If zero or less, enter -0-. If married filing separately, see page 2 of the instructions	$17,500

(a) Description of property	(b) Cost (business use only)	(c) Elected cost
6 5-Year Class Prop.-Microcomputer	$21,500	$17,500

7	Listed property. Enter amount from line 27	
8	Total elected cost of section 179 property. Add amounts in column (c), lines 6 and 7	$17,500
9	Tentative deduction. Enter the smaller of line 5 or line 8	$17,500
10	Carryover of disallowed deduction from 1995. See page 2 of the instructions	
11	Business income limitation. Enter the smaller of business income (not less than zero) or line 5 (see instructions)	$17,500
12	Section 179 expense deduction. Add lines 9 and 10, but do not enter more than line 11	$17,500
13	Carryover of disallowed deduction to 1997. Add lines 9 and 10, less line 12 ▶	

Note: Do not use Part II or Part III below for listed property (automobiles, certain other vehicles, cellular telephones, certain computers, or property used for entertainment, recreation, or amusement). Instead, use Part V for listed property.

Part II — MACRS Depreciation For Assets Placed in Service ONLY During Your 1996 Tax Year (Do Not Include Listed Property.)

Section A—General Asset Account Election

14 If you are making the election under section 168(i)(4) to group any assets placed in service during the tax year into one or more general asset accounts, check this box. See page 2 of the instructions ▶ ☐

Section B—General Depreciation System (GDS) (See page 3 of the instructions.)

(a) Classification of property	(b) Month and year placed in service	(c) Basis for depreciation (business/investment use only—see instructions)	(d) Recovery period	(e) Convention	(f) Method	(g) Depreciation deduction
15a 3-year property						
b 5-year property		4,000	5-Year	HY	200DB	800
c 7-year property						
d 10-year property						
e 15-year property						
f 20-year property						
g 25-year property			25 yrs.		S/L	
h Residential rental property			27.5 yrs.	MM	S/L	
			27.5 yrs.	MM	S/L	
i Nonresidential real property			39 yrs.	MM	S/L	
				MM	S/L	

Section C—Alternative Depreciation System (ADS) (See page 4 of the instructions.)

16a Class life					S/L	
b 12-year			12 yrs.		S/L	
c 40-year			40 yrs.	MM	S/L	

Part III — Other Depreciation (Do Not Include Listed Property.) (See page 4 of the instructions.)

17	GDS and ADS deductions for assets placed in service in tax years beginning before 1996	1,959
18	Property subject to section 168(f)(1) election	
19	ACRS and other depreciation	

Part IV — Summary (See page 4 of the instructions.)

20	Listed property. Enter amount from line 26	3,200
21	Total. Add deductions on line 12, lines 15 and 16 in column (g), and lines 17 through 20. Enter here and on the appropriate lines of your return. Partnerships and S corporations—see instructions	23,459
22	For assets shown above and placed in service during the current year, enter the portion of the basis attributable to section 263A costs	

For Paperwork Reduction Act Notice, see page 1 of the separate instructions.   Cat. No. 12906N   Form **4562** (1996)

Form 4562 (1996) Page **2**

Part V — Listed Property—Automobiles, Certain Other Vehicles, Cellular Telephones, Certain Computers, and Property Used for Entertainment, Recreation, or Amusement

*Note: For any vehicle for which you are using the standard mileage rate or deducting lease expense, complete **only** 23a, 23b, columns (a) through (c) of Section A, all of Section B, and Section C if applicable.*

Section A—Depreciation and Other Information (Caution: *See page 5 of the instructions for limitations for automobiles.*)

23a Do you have evidence to support the business/investment use claimed? ☒ Yes ☐ No **23b** If "Yes," is the evidence written? ☒ Yes ☐ No

(a) Type of property (list vehicles first)	(b) Date placed in service	(c) Business/investment use percentage	(d) Cost or other basis	(e) Basis for depreciation (business/investment use only)	(f) Recovery period	(g) Method/ Convention	(h) Depreciation deduction	(i) Elected section 179 cost
24 Property used more than 50% in a qualified business use (See page 5 of the instructions.):									
Automobile	5/20/95	100 %	10,000	10,000	5-YR	200DB-HY	3,200	
		%						
		%						
25 Property used 50% or less in a qualified business use (See page 5 of the instructions.):									
		%				S/L –		
		%				S/L –		
		%				S/L –		

26 Add amounts in column (h). Enter the total here and on line 20, page 1 . . . . . . **26** 3,200

27 Add amounts in column (i). Enter the total here and on line 7, page 1 . . . . **27**

Section B—Information on Use of Vehicles

Complete this section for vehicles used by a sole proprietor, partner, or other "more than 5% owner," or related person.
If you provided vehicles to your employees, first answer the questions in Section C to see if you meet an exception to completing this section for those vehicles.

		(a) Vehicle 1	(b) Vehicle 2	(c) Vehicle 3	(d) Vehicle 4	(e) Vehicle 5	(f) Vehicle 6
28	Total business/investment miles driven during the year (DO NOT include commuting miles)	12,000					
29	Total commuting miles driven during the year	–0–					
30	Total other personal (noncommuting) miles driven	–0–					
31	Total miles driven during the year. Add lines 28 through 30.	12,000					
		Yes No	Yes No	Yes No	Yes No	Yes No	Yes No
32	Was the vehicle available for personal use during off-duty hours?	X					
33	Was the vehicle used primarily by a more than 5% owner or related person?	X					
34	Is another vehicle available for personal use?	X					

Section C—Questions for Employers Who Provide Vehicles for Use by Their Employees

*Answer these questions to determine if you meet an exception to completing Section B for vehicles used by employees who are **not** more than 5% owners or related persons.*

		Yes	No
35	Do you maintain a written policy statement that prohibits all personal use of vehicles, including commuting, by your employees?		
36	Do you maintain a written policy statement that prohibits personal use of vehicles, except commuting, by your employees? See page 6 of the instructions for vehicles used by corporate officers, directors, or 1% or more owners		
37	Do you treat all use of vehicles by employees as personal use?		
38	Do you provide more than five vehicles to your employees, obtain information from your employees about the use of the vehicles, and retain the information received?		
39	Do you meet the requirements concerning qualified automobile demonstration use? See page 6 of the instructions . .		

Note: If your answer to 35, 36, 37, 38, or 39 is "Yes," you need not complete Section B for the covered vehicles.

Part VI — Amortization

(a) Description of costs	(b) Date amortization begins	(c) Amortizable amount	(d) Code section	(e) Amortization period or percentage	(f) Amortization for this year
40 Amortization of costs that begins during your 1996 tax year:						

41 Amortization of costs that began before 1996 . . . . **41**

42 Total. Enter here and on "Other Deductions" or "Other Expenses" line of your return . . . **42**

8–32 PART III Deductions

SCHEDULE C (Form 1040)
Department of the Treasury
Internal Revenue Service (99)

Profit or Loss From Business
(Sole Proprietorship)

▶ Partnerships, joint ventures, etc., must file Form 1065.
▶ Attach to Form 1040 or Form 1041. ▶ See Instructions for Schedule C (Form 1040).

OMB No. 1545-0074
1996
Attachment Sequence No. 09

Name of proprietor: *Thomas Andrews*
Social security number (SSN): 123 : 45 : 6789

A Principal business or profession, including product or service (see page C-1)
Accounting Services

B Enter principal business code (see page C-6) ▶

C Business name. If no separate business name, leave blank.
Andrews Accounting Services

D Employer ID number (EIN), if any

E Business address (including suite no. or room no.) ▶ *270 Mountain View*
City, town or post office, state, and ZIP code *Ogden, UT 84201*

F Accounting method: (1) ☐ Cash (2) ☒ Accrual (3) ☐ Other (specify) ▶

G Did you "materially participate" in the operation of this business during 1996? If "No," see page C-2 for limit on losses. ☒ Yes ☐ No

H If you started or acquired this business during 1996, check here ▶ ☐

Part I Income

1	Gross receipts or sales. Caution: If this income was reported to you on Form W-2 and the "Statutory employee" box on that form was checked, see page C-2 and check here ▶ ☐	1	80,000
2	Returns and allowances	2	
3	Subtract line 2 from line 1	3	80,000
4	Cost of goods sold (from line 42 on page 2)	4	
5	Gross profit. Subtract line 4 from line 3	5	80,000
6	Other income, including Federal and state gasoline or fuel tax credit or refund (see page C-2)	6	
7	Gross income. Add lines 5 and 6 ▶	7	80,000

Part II Expenses. Enter expenses for business use of your home **only** on line 30.

8	Advertising	8		19	Pension and profit-sharing plans	19	
9	Bad debts from sales or services (see page C-3)	9	2,000	20	Rent or lease (see page C-4):		
				a	Vehicles, machinery, and equipment	20a	
10	Car and truck expenses (see page C-3)	10	3,000	b	Other business property	20b	12,000
11	Commissions and fees	11		21	Repairs and maintenance	21	
12	Depletion	12		22	Supplies (not included in Part III)	22	
13	Depreciation and section 179 expense deduction (not included in Part III) (see page C-3)	13	23,459	23	Taxes and licenses	23	
				24	Travel, meals, and entertainment:		
				a	Travel	24a	
14	Employee benefit programs (other than on line 19)	14		b	Meals and entertainment		
15	Insurance (other than health)	15	800	c	Enter 50% of line 24b subject to limitations (see page C-4)		
16	Interest:						
a	Mortgage (paid to banks, etc.)	16a		d	Subtract line 24c from line 24b	24d	
b	Other	16b		25	Utilities	25	
17	Legal and professional services	17		26	Wages (less employment credits)	26	
18	Office expense	18	4,000	27	Other expenses (from line 48 on page 2)	27	
28	Total expenses before expenses for business use of home. Add lines 8 through 27 in columns ▶					28	45,259
29	Tentative profit (loss). Subtract line 28 from line 7					29	34,741
30	Expenses for business use of your home. Attach **Form 8829**					30	
31	Net profit or (loss). Subtract line 30 from line 29.					31	34,741
	• If a profit, enter on **Form 1040, line 12**, and ALSO on **Schedule SE, line 2** (statutory employees, see page C-5). Estates and trusts, enter on **Form 1041, line 3**.						
	• If a loss, you MUST go on to line 32.						
32	If you have a loss, check the box that describes your investment in this activity (see page C-5).						
	• If you checked 32a, enter the loss on **Form 1040, line 12**, and ALSO on **Schedule SE, line 2** (statutory employees, see page C-5). Estates and trusts, enter on **Form 1041, line 3**.		32a ☐ All investment is at risk.				
	• If you checked 32b, you MUST attach **Form 6198**.		32b ☐ Some investment is not at risk.				

For Paperwork Reduction Act Notice, see Form 1040 instructions.   Cat. No. 11334P   Schedule C (Form 1040) 1996

TAX PLANNING CONSIDERATIONS

COST RECOVERY

Cost recovery schedules should be reviewed annually for possible retirements, abandonments, and obsolescence.

EXAMPLE 43

An examination of the cost recovery schedule of Eagle Company reveals the following:

- Asset A was abandoned when it was discovered that the cost of repairs would be in excess of the cost of replacement. Asset A had an adjusted basis of $3,000.
- Asset J became obsolete this year, at which point, its adjusted basis was $8,000.

Assets A and J should be written off for an additional expense of $11,000 ($3,000 + $8,000). ▼

LEARNING OBJECTIVE 9
Identify tax planning opportunities for cost recovery, amortization, and depletion.

Because of the deductions for cost recovery, interest, and ad valorem property taxes, investments in real estate can be highly attractive. In figuring the economics of such investments, one should be sure to take into account any tax savings that result.

EXAMPLE 44

In early January 1996, Vern purchased residential rental property for $170,000 (of which $20,000 was allocated to the land and $150,000 to the building). Vern made a down payment of $25,000 and assumed the seller's mortgage for the balance. Under the mortgage agreement, monthly payments of $1,000 are required and are applied toward interest, taxes, insurance, and principal. Since the property was already occupied, Vern continued to receive rent of $1,200 per month from the tenant. Vern actively participates in this activity and hence comes under the special rule for a rental real estate activity with respect to the limitation on passive activity losses (refer to Chapter 11). Vern is in the 31% tax bracket.

During 1997, Vern's expenses were as follows:

Interest	$10,000
Taxes	800
Insurance	1,000
Repairs and maintenance	2,200
Depreciation ($150,000 × .03636)	5,454
Total	$19,454

The deductible loss from the rental property is computed as follows:

Rent income ($1,200 × 12 months)	$ 14,400
Less expenses (see above)	(19,454)
Net loss	($ 5,054)

But what is Vern's overall position for the year when the tax benefit of the loss is taken into account? Considering just the cash intake and outlay, it is summarized as follows:

Intake—		
Rent income		$14,400
Tax savings [31% (income tax bracket) × $5,054 (loss from the property)]		1,567 $ 15,967
Outlay—		
Mortgage payments ($1,000 × 12 months)	$12,000	
Repairs and maintenance	2,200	(14,200)
Net cash benefit		$ 1,767 ▼

It should be noted, however, that should Vern cease being an active participant in the rental activity, the passive activity loss rules would apply, and Vern could lose the current period benefit of the loss.

AMORTIZATION

When a business is purchased, goodwill and covenants not to compete are both subject to a statutory amortization period of 15 years. Therefore, the purchaser does not derive any tax benefits when part of the purchase price is assigned to a covenant rather than to goodwill.

Thus, from the purchaser's perspective, bargaining for a covenant should be based on legal rather than tax reasons. Note, however, that from the seller's perspective, goodwill is a capital asset and the covenant is an ordinary income asset.

Since the amortization period for both goodwill and a covenant is 15 years, the purchaser may want to attempt to minimize these amounts if the purchase price can be assigned to assets with shorter lives (e.g., inventory, receivables, and personalty). Conversely, the purchaser may want to attempt to maximize these amounts if part of the purchase price will otherwise be assigned to assets with longer recovery periods (e.g., realty) or to assets not eligible for cost recovery (e.g., land).

DEPLETION

Since the election to use the cost or percentage depletion method is an annual election, a taxpayer can use cost depletion (if higher) until the basis is exhausted and then switch to percentage depletion in the following years.

EXAMPLE 45

Assume the following facts for Melissa:

Remaining depletable basis	$ 11,000
Gross income (10,000 units)	100,000
Expenses (other than depletion)	30,000

Since cost depletion is limited to the basis of $11,000 and if the percentage depletion is $22,000 (assume a 22% rate), Melissa would choose the latter. Her basis is then reduced to zero. In future years, however, she can continue to take percentage depletion since percentage depletion is taken without reference to the remaining basis. ▼

The election to expense intangible drilling and development costs is a one-time election. Once the election is made to either expense or capitalize the intangible drilling and development costs, it is binding on all future expenditures. The permanent nature of the election makes it extremely important for the taxpayer to determine which treatment will provide the greatest tax advantage. (Refer to Example 41 for an illustration of the effect of using the two different alternatives for a given set of facts.)

CHAPTER 8 Depreciation, Cost Recovery, Amortization, and Depletion

TABLES

Summary of Tables

Table 8–1	Original ACRS statutory percentage table for personalty. Applicable depreciation method: 150 percent declining-balance switching to straight-line. Applicable recovery periods: 3, 5, 10, 15 years. Applicable convention: half-year.
Table 8–2	Modified ACRS statutory percentage table for personalty. Applicable depreciation methods: 200 or 150 percent declining-balance switching to straight-line. Applicable recovery periods: 3, 5, 7, 10, 15, 20 years. Applicable convention: half-year.
Table 8–3	Modified ACRS statutory percentage table for personalty. Applicable depreciation method: 200 percent declining-balance switching to straight-line. Applicable recovery periods: 3, 5, 7 years. Applicable convention: mid-quarter.
Table 8–4	Original ACRS statutory percentage table for realty. Applicable depreciation methods: 200 or 175 percent declining-balance switching to straight-line. Applicable recovery period: 15 years. Applicable convention: full-month.
Table 8–5	Original ACRS statutory percentage table for realty. Applicable depreciation method: 175 percent declining-balance switching to straight-line. Applicable recovery period: 18 years. Applicable convention: mid-month.
Table 8–6	Original ACRS statutory percentage table for realty. Applicable depreciation method: 175 percent declining-balance switching to straight-line. Applicable recovery period: 19 years. Applicable convention: mid-month.
Table 8–7	Modified ACRS straight-line table for realty. Applicable depreciation method: straight-line. Applicable recovery periods: 27.5, 31.5, 39 years. Applicable convention: mid-month.
Table 8–8	Original ACRS optional straight-line table for realty. Applicable depreciation method: straight-line. Applicable recovery period: 19 years. Applicable convention: mid-month.
Table 8–9	Modified ACRS optional straight-line table for personalty. Applicable depreciation method: straight-line. Applicable recovery periods: 3, 5, 7, 10, 15, 20 years. Applicable convention: half-year.
Table 8–10	Alternative minimum tax declining-balance table for personalty. Applicable depreciation method: 150 percent declining-balance switching to straight-line. Applicable recovery periods: 3, 5, 9.5, 10 years. Applicable convention: half-year.
Table 8–11	Alternative depreciation system straight-line table for personalty. Applicable depreciation method: straight-line. Applicable recovery periods: 5, 9.5, 12 years. Applicable convention: half-year.
Table 8–12	Alternative depreciation system straight-line table for realty. Applicable depreciation method: straight-line. Applicable recovery period: 40 years. Applicable convention: mid-month.

▼ TABLE 8–1
ACRS Statutory Percentages for Property Other Than 15-Year Real Property, 18-Year Real Property, or 19-Year Real Property Assuming Half-Year Convention

For Property Placed in Service after December 31, 1980, and before January 1, 1987

The Applicable Percentage for the Class of Property Is:

Recovery Year	3-Year	5-Year	10-Year	15-Year Public Utility
1	25	15	8	5
2	38	22	14	10
3	37	21	12	9
4		21	10	8
5		21	10	7
6			10	6
7			9	6
8			9	6
9			9	6
10			9	6
11				6
12				6
13				6
14				6
15				6

▼ TABLE 8–2
MACRS Accelerated Depreciation for Personal Property Assuming Half-Year Convention

For Property Placed in Service after December 31, 1986

Recovery Year	3-Year (200% DB)	5-Year (200% DB)	7-Year (200% DB)	10-Year (200% DB)	15-Year (150% DB)	20-Year (150% DB)
1	33.33	20.00	14.29	10.00	5.00	3.750
2	44.45	32.00	24.49	18.00	9.50	7.219
3	14.81*	19.20	17.49	14.40	8.55	6.677
4	7.41	11.52*	12.49	11.52	7.70	6.177
5		11.52	8.93*	9.22	6.93	5.713
6		5.76	8.92	7.37	6.23	5.285
7			8.93	6.55*	5.90*	4.888
8			4.46	6.55	5.90	4.522
9				6.56	5.91	4.462*
10				6.55	5.90	4.461
11				3.28	5.91	4.462
12					5.90	4.461
13					5.91	4.462
14					5.90	4.461
15					5.91	4.462
16					2.95	4.461
17						4.462
18						4.461
19						4.462
20						4.461
21						2.231

*Switchover to straight-line depreciation.

▼ TABLE 8-3
MACRS Accelerated Depreciation for Personal Property Assuming Mid-Quarter Convention

For Property Placed in Service after December 31, 1986 (Partial Table*)

3-Year

Recovery Year	First Quarter	Second Quarter	Third Quarter	Fourth Quarter
1	58.33	41.67	25.00	8.33
2	27.78	38.89	50.00	61.11

5-Year

Recovery Year	First Quarter	Second Quarter	Third Quarter	Fourth Quarter
1	35.00	25.00	15.00	5.00
2	26.00	30.00	34.00	38.00

7-Year

Recovery Year	First Quarter	Second Quarter	Third Quarter	Fourth Quarter
1	25.00	17.85	10.71	3.57
2	21.43	23.47	25.51	27.55

*The figures in this table are taken from the official tables that appear in Rev.Proc.87-57, 1987-2 C.B. 687. Because of their length, the complete tables are not presented.

▼ TABLE 8-4
ACRS Statutory Percentages for 15-Year Real Property

For Property Placed in Service after December 31, 1980, and before January 1, 1987: 15-Year Real Property—Low Income Housing

And the Month in the First Recovery Year the Property Is Placed in Service Is:

If the Recovery Year Is:	1	2	3	4	5	6	7	8	9	10	11	12
1	13	12	11	10	9	8	7	6	4	3	2	1
2	12	12	12	12	12	12	12	13	13	13	13	13
3	10	10	10	10	11	11	11	11	11	11	11	11
4	9	9	9	9	9	9	9	9	10	10	10	10
5	8	8	8	8	8	8	8	8	8	8	8	9
6	7	7	7	7	7	7	7	7	7	7	7	7
7	6	6	6	6	6	6	6	6	6	6	6	6
8	5	5	5	5	5	5	5	5	5	5	6	6
9	5	5	5	5	5	5	5	5	5	5	5	5
10	5	5	5	5	5	5	5	5	5	5	5	5
11	4	5	5	5	5	5	5	5	5	5	5	5
12	4	4	4	5	4	5	5	5	5	5	5	5
13	4	4	4	4	4	4	5	4	5	5	5	5
14	4	4	4	4	4	4	4	4	4	5	4	4
15	4	4	4	4	4	4	4	4	4	4	4	4
16	—	—	1	1	2	2	2	3	3	3	4	4

▼ TABLE 8-4 (Continued)

For Property Placed in Service after December 31, 1980, and before March 16, 1984: 15-Year Real Property—Other Than Low-Income Housing

	1	2	3	4	5	6	7	8	9	10	11	12
1	12	11	10	9	8	7	6	5	4	3	2	1
2	10	10	11	11	11	11	11	11	11	11	11	12
3	9	9	9	9	10	10	10	10	10	10	10	10
4	8	8	8	8	8	8	9	9	9	9	9	9
5	7	7	7	7	7	7	8	8	8	8	8	8
6	6	6	6	6	7	7	7	7	7	7	7	7
7	6	6	6	6	6	6	6	6	6	6	6	6
8	6	6	6	6	6	6	5	6	6	6	6	6
9	6	6	6	6	5	6	5	5	5	6	6	6
10	5	6	5	6	5	5	5	5	5	5	6	5
11	5	5	5	5	5	5	5	5	5	5	5	5
12	5	5	5	5	5	5	5	5	5	5	5	5
13	5	5	5	5	5	5	5	5	5	5	5	5
14	5	5	5	5	5	5	5	5	5	5	5	5
15	5	5	5	5	5	5	5	5	5	5	5	5
16	—	—	1	1	2	2	3	3	4	4	4	5

▼ TABLE 8-5
ACRS Cost Recovery Table for 18-Year Real Property

For Property Placed in Service after June 22, 1984, and before May 9, 1985: 18-Year Real Property (18-Year 175% Declining Balance) (Assuming Mid-Month Convention)

And the Month in the First Recovery Year the Property Is Placed in Service is:

If the Recovery Year Is:	1	2	3	4	5	6	7	8	9	10	11	12
The Applicable Percentage Is (Use the Column for the Month in the First Year the Property Is Placed in Service):

Year	1	2	3	4	5	6	7	8	9	10	11	12
1	9	9	8	7	6	5	4	4	3	2	1	0.4
2	9	9	9	9	9	9	9	9	9	10	10	10.0
3	8	8	8	8	8	8	8	8	9	9	9	9.0
4	7	7	7	7	7	8	8	8	8	8	8	8.0
5	7	7	7	7	7	7	7	7	7	7	7	7.0
6	6	6	6	6	6	6	6	6	6	6	6	6.0
7	5	5	5	5	6	6	6	6	6	6	6	6.0
8	5	5	5	5	5	5	5	5	5	5	5	5.0
9	5	5	5	5	5	5	5	5	5	5	5	5.0
10	5	5	5	5	5	5	5	5	5	5	5	5.0
11	5	5	5	5	5	5	5	5	5	5	5	5.0
12	5	5	5	5	5	5	5	5	5	5	5	5.0
13	4	4	4	5	4	4	5	4	4	4	5	5.0
14	4	4	4	4	4	4	4	4	4	4	4	4.0
15	4	4	4	4	4	4	4	4	4	4	4	4.0
16	4	4	4	4	4	4	4	4	4	4	4	4.0
17	4	4	4	4	4	4	4	4	4	4	4	4.0
18	4	3	4	4	4	4	4	4	4	4	4	4.0
19		1	1	1	2	2	2	3	3	3	3	3.6

TABLE 8-6
ACRS Cost Recovery Table for 19-Year Real Property

For Property Placed in Service after May 8, 1985, and before January 1, 1987
19-Year Real Property (19-Year 175% Declining Balance)
(Assuming Mid-Month Convention)

If the Recovery Year Is:	1	2	3	4	5	6	7	8	9	10	11	12
	\multicolumn{12}{l}{The Applicable Percentage Is (Use the Column for the Month in the First Year the Property Is Placed in Service):}
1	8.8	8.1	7.3	6.5	5.8	5.0	4.2	3.5	2.7	1.9	1.1	0.4
2	8.4	8.5	8.5	8.6	8.7	8.8	8.8	8.9	9.0	9.0	9.1	9.2
3	7.6	7.7	7.7	7.8	7.9	7.9	8.0	8.1	8.1	8.2	8.3	8.3
4	6.9	7.0	7.0	7.1	7.1	7.2	7.3	7.3	7.4	7.4	7.5	7.6
5	6.3	6.3	6.4	6.4	6.5	6.5	6.6	6.6	6.7	6.8	6.8	6.9
6	5.7	5.7	5.8	5.9	5.9	5.9	6.0	6.0	6.1	6.1	6.2	6.2
7	5.2	5.2	5.3	5.3	5.3	5.4	5.4	5.5	5.5	5.6	5.6	5.6
8	4.7	4.7	4.8	4.8	4.8	4.9	4.9	5.0	5.0	5.1	5.1	5.1
9	4.2	4.3	4.3	4.4	4.4	4.5	4.5	4.5	4.5	4.6	4.6	4.7
10	4.2	4.2	4.2	4.2	4.2	4.2	4.2	4.2	4.2	4.2	4.2	4.2
11	4.2	4.2	4.2	4.2	4.2	4.2	4.2	4.2	4.2	4.2	4.2	4.2
12	4.2	4.2	4.2	4.2	4.2	4.2	4.2	4.2	4.2	4.2	4.2	4.2
13	4.2	4.2	4.2	4.2	4.2	4.2	4.2	4.2	4.2	4.2	4.2	4.2
14	4.2	4.2	4.2	4.2	4.2	4.2	4.2	4.2	4.2	4.2	4.2	4.2
15	4.2	4.2	4.2	4.2	4.2	4.2	4.2	4.2	4.2	4.2	4.2	4.2
16	4.2	4.2	4.2	4.2	4.2	4.2	4.2	4.2	4.2	4.2	4.2	4.2
17	4.2	4.2	4.2	4.2	4.2	4.2	4.2	4.2	4.2	4.2	4.2	4.2
18	4.2	4.2	4.2	4.2	4.2	4.2	4.2	4.2	4.2	4.2	4.2	4.2
19	4.2	4.2	4.2	4.2	4.2	4.2	4.2	4.2	4.2	4.2	4.2	4.2
20	0.2	0.5	0.9	1.2	1.6	1.9	2.3	2.6	3.0	3.3	3.7	4.0

▼ TABLE 8–7
MACRS Straight-Line Depreciation for Real Property Assuming Mid-Month Convention*

For Property Placed in Service after December 31, 1986: 27.5-Year Residential Real Property

The Applicable Percentage Is (Use the Column for the Month in the First Year the Property Is Placed in Service):

Recovery Year(s)	1	2	3	4	5	6	7	8	9	10	11	12
1	3.485	3.182	2.879	2.576	2.273	1.970	1.667	1.364	1.061	0.758	0.455	0.152
2–18	3.636	3.636	3.636	3.636	3.636	3.636	3.636	3.636	3.636	3.636	3.636	3.636
19–27	3.637	3.637	3.637	3.637	3.637	3.637	3.637	3.637	3.637	3.637	3.637	3.637
28	1.970	2.273	2.576	2.879	3.182	3.485	3.636	3.636	3.636	3.636	3.636	3.636
29	0.000	0.000	0.000	0.000	0.000	0.000	0.152	0.455	0.758	1.061	1.364	1.667

For Property Placed in Service after December 31, 1986, and before May 13, 1993: 31.5-Year Nonresidential Real Property

The Applicable Percentage Is (Use the Column for the Month in the First Year the Property Is Placed in Service):

Recovery Year(s)	1	2	3	4	5	6	7	8	9	10	11	12
1	3.042	2.778	2.513	2.249	1.984	1.720	1.455	1.190	0.926	0.661	0.397	0.132
2–19	3.175	3.175	3.175	3.175	3.175	3.175	3.175	3.175	3.175	3.175	3.175	3.175
20–31	3.174	3.174	3.174	3.174	3.174	3.174	3.174	3.174	3.174	3.174	3.174	3.174
32	1.720	1.984	2.249	2.513	2.778	3.042	3.175	3.175	3.175	3.175	3.175	3.175
33	0.000	0.000	0.000	0.000	0.000	0.000	0.132	0.397	0.661	0.926	1.190	1.455

For Property Placed in Service after May 12, 1993: 39-Year Nonresidential Real Property

The Applicable Percentage Is (Use the Column for the Month in the First Year the Property Is Placed in Service):

Recovery Year(s)	1	2	3	4	5	6	7	8	9	10	11	12
1	2.461	2.247	2.033	1.819	1.605	1.391	1.177	0.963	0.749	0.535	0.321	0.107
2–39	2.564	2.564	2.564	2.564	2.564	2.564	2.564	2.564	2.564	2.564	2.564	2.564
40	0.107	0.321	0.535	0.749	0.963	1.177	1.391	1.605	1.819	2.033	2.247	2.461

*The official tables contain a separate row for each year. For ease of presentation, certain years are grouped in these tables. In some instances, this will produce a difference of .001 for the last digit when compared with the official tables.

TABLE 8-8
ACRS Cost Recovery Table for 19-Year Real Property: Optional Straight-Line

For Property Placed in Service after May 8, 1985, and before January 1, 1987: 19-Year Real Property for Which an Optional 19-Year Straight-Line Method Is Elected (Assuming Mid-Month Convention)

If the Recovery Year Is:	\multicolumn{12}{c}{And the Month in the First Recovery Year the Property Is Placed in Service Is:}
	1	2	3	4	5	6	7	8	9	10	11	12
	\multicolumn{12}{l}{The Applicable Percentage Is (Use the Column for the Month in the First Year the Property Is Placed in Service):}
1	5.0	4.6	4.2	3.7	3.3	2.9	2.4	2.0	1.5	1.1	.7	.2
2	5.3	5.3	5.3	5.3	5.3	5.3	5.3	5.3	5.3	5.3	5.3	5.3
3	5.3	5.3	5.3	5.3	5.3	5.3	5.3	5.3	5.3	5.3	5.3	5.3
4	5.3	5.3	5.3	5.3	5.3	5.3	5.3	5.3	5.3	5.3	5.3	5.3
5	5.3	5.3	5.3	5.3	5.3	5.3	5.3	5.3	5.3	5.3	5.3	5.3
6	5.3	5.3	5.3	5.3	5.3	5.3	5.3	5.3	5.3	5.3	5.3	5.3
7	5.3	5.3	5.3	5.3	5.3	5.3	5.3	5.3	5.3	5.3	5.3	5.3
8	5.3	5.3	5.3	5.3	5.3	5.3	5.3	5.3	5.3	5.3	5.3	5.3
9	5.3	5.3	5.3	5.3	5.3	5.3	5.3	5.3	5.3	5.3	5.3	5.3
10	5.3	5.3	5.3	5.3	5.3	5.3	5.3	5.3	5.3	5.3	5.3	5.3
11	5.3	5.3	5.3	5.3	5.3	5.3	5.3	5.3	5.3	5.3	5.3	5.3
12	5.3	5.3	5.3	5.3	5.3	5.3	5.3	5.3	5.3	5.3	5.3	5.3
13	5.3	5.3	5.3	5.3	5.3	5.3	5.3	5.3	5.3	5.3	5.3	5.3
14	5.2	5.2	5.2	5.2	5.2	5.2	5.2	5.2	5.2	5.2	5.2	5.2
15	5.2	5.2	5.2	5.2	5.2	5.2	5.2	5.2	5.2	5.2	5.2	5.2
16	5.2	5.2	5.2	5.2	5.2	5.2	5.2	5.2	5.2	5.2	5.2	5.2
17	5.2	5.2	5.2	5.2	5.2	5.2	5.2	5.2	5.2	5.2	5.2	5.2
18	5.2	5.2	5.2	5.2	5.2	5.2	5.2	5.2	5.2	5.2	5.2	5.2
19	5.2	5.2	5.2	5.2	5.2	5.2	5.2	5.2	5.2	5.2	5.2	5.2
20	.2	.6	1.0	1.5	1.9	2.3	2.8	3.2	3.7	4.1	4.5	5.0

TABLE 8-9
MACRS Straight-Line Depreciation for Personal Property Assuming Half-Year Convention*

For Property Placed in Service after December 31, 1986

MACRS Class	% First Recovery Year	Other Recovery Years — Years	Other Recovery Years — %	Last Recovery Year — Year	Last Recovery Year — %
3-year	16.67	2–3	33.33	4	16.67
5-year	10.00	2–5	20.00	6	10.00
7-year	7.14	2–7	14.29	8	7.14
10-year	5.00	2–10	10.00	11	5.00
15-year	3.33	2–15	6.67	16	3.33
20-year	2.50	2–20	5.00	21	2.50

*The official table contains a separate row for each year. For ease of presentation, certain years are grouped in this table. In some instances, this will produce a difference of .01 for the last digit when compared with the official table.

TABLE 8-10
Alternative Minimum Tax: 150% Declining-Balance Assuming Half-Year Convention

For Property Placed in Service after December 31, 1986 (Partial Table*)

Recovery Year	3-Year 150%	5-Year 150%	9.5-Year 150%	10-Year 150%
1	25.00	15.00	7.89	7.50
2	37.50	25.50	14.54	13.88
3	25.00*	17.85	12.25	11.79
4	12.50	16.66*	10.31	10.02
5		16.66	9.17*	8.74*
6		8.33	9.17	8.74
7			9.17	8.74
8			9.17	8.74
9			9.17	8.74
10			9.16	8.74
11				4.37

*The figures in this table are taken from the official table that appears in Rev.Proc. 87–57, 1987–2 C.B. 687. Because of its length, the complete table is not presented.
*Switchover to straight-line depreciation.

TABLE 8-11
ADS Straight-Line for Personal Property Assuming Half-Year Convention

For Property Placed in Service after December 31, 1986 (Partial Table*)

Recovery Year	5-Year Class	9.5-Year Class	12-Year Class
1	10.00	5.26	4.17
2	20.00	10.53	8.33
3	20.00	10.53	8.33
4	20.00	10.53	8.33
5	20.00	10.52	8.33
6	10.00	10.53	8.33
7		10.52	8.34
8		10.53	8.33
9		10.52	8.34
10		10.53	8.33
11			8.34
12			8.33
13			4.17

*The figures in this table are taken from the official table that appears in Rev.Proc. 87–57, 1987–2 C.B. 687. Because of its length, the complete table is not presented. The tables for the mid-quarter convention also appear in Rev.Proc. 87–57.

TABLE 8-12
ADS Straight-Line for Real Property Assuming Mid-Month Convention

For Property Placed in Service after December 31, 1986

Recovery Year	Month Placed in Service											
	1	2	3	4	5	6	7	8	9	10	11	12
1	2.396	2.188	1.979	1.771	1.563	1.354	1.146	0.938	0.729	0.521	0.313	0.104
2-40	2.500	2.500	2.500	2.500	2.500	2.500	2.500	2.500	2.500	2.500	2.500	2.500
41	0.104	0.312	0.521	0.729	0.937	1.146	1.354	1.562	1.771	1.979	2.187	2.396

KEY TERMS

Accelerated cost recovery system (ACRS), 8-4

Alternative depreciation system (ADS), 8-23

Amortization, 8-24

Cost depletion, 8-26

Cost recovery, 8-2

Depletion, 8-25

Depreciation, 8-2

Half-year convention, 8-7

Intangible drilling and development costs (IDC), 8-25

Listed property, 8-17

Mid-month convention, 8-12

Mid-quarter convention, 8-10

Modified accelerated cost recovery system (MACRS), 8-8

Percentage depletion, 8-27

Residential rental real estate, 8-13

Section 179 expensing, 8-15

PROBLEM MATERIALS

DISCUSSION QUESTIONS

1. Distinguish between cost recovery, amortization, and depletion.

2. Discuss whether personal use property is subject to cost recovery.

3. Henry purchased a rental home for $67,000 from Amy. He made a down payment of $17,000 and borrowed $50,000 from James with a mortgage on the home as collateral. The note secured by the mortgage contained an acceleration clause, which provided that the loan would become due if Henry were to sell or convey the property. Several years later, Henry sold the house to John. To avoid triggering the acceleration clause, Henry and John wove a complicated web to deceive James. As part of this plan, the sales agreement provided that Henry would continue to claim the depreciation on his tax return. Henry also owned property where he maintained his office. Last year, because the property generated a loss, Henry did not deduct the depreciation on the property. During the current year, Henry sold this property at a gain. Identify the relevant tax issues for Henry.

4. If a personal use asset is converted to business use, why is it necessary to compute cost recovery on the lower of fair market value or adjusted basis at the date of conversion?

5. Discuss whether an antique is eligible for cost recovery.

6. Discuss the half-year convention as it is used in the ACRS rules.

7. On January 1, 1987, Aaron, a calendar year taxpayer, purchased a machine (15-year property). In June 1997, Aaron traded the old machine for a new machine (15-year property). Aaron paid $500,000 cash in addition to the first machine as a trade-in for the second machine. Identify the relevant tax issues for Aaron.

8. Discuss why the cost of three-year class property is recovered over four years under MACRS.

9. Discuss when the mid-quarter convention must be used.

10. Discuss the computation of cost recovery in the year of sale of an asset when the mid-quarter convention is being used.

11. Discuss the test for determining whether real property is residential rental real estate or nonresidential real estate.

12. Discuss the mid-month convention as it is used in the MACRS rules.

13. Alan is engaged in the sale of rental warehouse space and related services. When he sought a bank loan to expand one of his warehouses, the lender required Alan to abate the problem of exposed and damaged asbestos-containing pipe insulation in the warehouse. Accordingly, Alan incurred costs of $200,000 to employ an asbestos contractor to remedy the problem. The contractor rewrapped and encapsulated the damaged or punctured areas of asbestos-containing pipe insulation and removed insulation that was too damaged to be rewrapped. The pipes requiring encapsulation amounted to less than 25% of the total pipes in the warehouse. Identify the relevant tax issues for Alan.

14. Discuss the applicable conventions if a taxpayer elects to use straight-line cost recovery for property placed in service after December 31, 1986.

15. If a taxpayer makes a straight-line election under MACRS, discuss the possibility of taking a cost recovery deduction, for personal and real property, in the year of disposition.

16. Discuss whether an election made one year to use straight-line cost recovery under ACRS for personal property of a particular class is binding for property of the same class placed in service in another tax year.

17. Discuss whether an election to use straight-line cost recovery under MACRS can be applied on an asset-by-asset basis.

18. Discuss the maximum § 179 expensing amount.

19. Discuss the limitation on the § 179 amount that can be expensed and its impact on the basis of the property.

20. John was employed as a financial officer for an investment bank. By the middle of the year, John realized that he was going to be terminated by the bank. Therefore, he began preparing for a career in financial consulting as a sole practitioner. John became interested in consulting for a marina, but believing that boat owners formed a close fraternity, he decided that he could obtain such work only by acquiring a boat himself. Accordingly, he purchased a 23-foot Sea Ray Boat for $25,000. During the year, John used the boat only once to visit marinas on the lake to discuss potential employment as a consultant. A few days after this one excursion, John injured his back and was unable to use the boat for the remainder of the year. John was unsuccessful in his attempts to obtain a consulting position with any of the marinas.

    At the beginning of the year, John also purchased a new car to be used for personal purposes. After John was terminated from the bank in September, he began using the car for business purposes.

    Identify the relevant tax issues for John.

21. What are the tax consequences of listed property failing to meet the predominantly business use test?

22. Discuss what factors are used in determining whether the more-than-50% business use test has been satisfied.

23. If a taxpayer does not pass the more-than-50% business use test on an automobile, discuss whether the statutory dollar limitations on cost recovery are applicable.

24. Discuss the tax consequences that result when a passenger automobile, which failed the more-than-50% business usage test during the first two years, satisfies the test for the third year.

25. With the increase in the maximum § 179 expensing amount, discuss whether § 179 should be elected for a passenger automobile.

26. Explain the reason for the inclusion amount with respect to leased passenger automobiles.

27. Explain how an inclusion amount is determined with respect to leased passenger automobiles.

28. Discuss the substantiation requirements for listed property.

29. Explain the amortization period of a § 197 intangible if the actual useful life is less than 15 years.

30. What is the amortization period for self-created goodwill?

31. Discuss the options for handling intangible drilling and development costs.

32. Briefly discuss the differences between cost depletion and percentage depletion.

PROBLEMS

33. On January 1, 1993, Black Company acquired an asset (three-year property) for $10,000 for use in its business. In the years 1993 and 1994, Black took $3,333 and $4,445 of cost recovery. The allowable cost recovery for the years 1995 and 1996 was $1,481 and $741, but Black did not take the deductions. In those years, Black had net operating losses, and the company wanted to "save" the deductions for later years. On January 1, 1997, the asset was sold for $2,000. Calculate the gain or loss on the sale of the asset in 1997.

34. Eve acquired a personal residence in 1991 for $180,000. In January 1997, when the fair market value was $160,000, she converted the residence to rental property.
    a. Calculate the amount of cost recovery that can be taken in 1997.
    b. What would your answer be if the property were worth $200,000 in 1997?

35. Jim acquired a 15-year class asset on March 1, 1986, for $40,000. He did not elect immediate expensing under § 179. On November 10, 1997, Jim sells the asset.
    a. Determine Jim's cost recovery for 1986.
    b. Determine Jim's cost recovery for 1997.

36. Walt purchased a tugboat for use in his business on March 15, 1997, for $500,000. He does not elect immediate expensing under § 179. On February 16, 2003, Walt sells the tug.
    a. Determine Walt's cost recovery for 1997.
    b. Determine Walt's cost recovery for 2003.

37. Juan acquires a five-year class asset on December 2, 1997, for $150,000. This is the only asset acquired by Juan during the year. He does not elect immediate expensing under § 179. On July 15, 1998, Juan sells the asset.
    a. Determine Juan's cost recovery for 1997.
    b. Determine Juan's cost recovery for 1998.

38. Debra acquired a building for $300,000 (exclusive of land) on January 1, 1984. Calculate the cost recovery using the statutory percentage method for 1984 and 1997 if:
    a. The real property is low-income housing.
    b. The real property is a factory building.

39. On December 2, 1984, Wade purchased and placed in service a warehouse. The warehouse cost $850,000. Wade used the statutory percentage cost recovery method. On July 7, 1997, Wade sold the warehouse.
    a. Determine Wade's cost recovery for 1984.
    b. Determine Wade's cost recovery for 1997.

40. On November 1, 1997, Sam purchases and places in service a building that is used as a warehouse. The cost of the building is $2.5 million. Determine Sam's cost recovery for 1997.

41. Pat acquires a warehouse on November 1, 1997, at a cost of $4.5 million. On January 30, 2008, Pat sells the warehouse. Calculate Pat's cost recovery for 1997. For 2008.

42. James acquired an apartment building on March 10, 1997, for $1.3 million. Calculate James's cost recovery for 1997.

43. Lori, who is single, is thinking of acquiring a new copier (five-year class property) for $30,000 in either December of 1997 or January of 1998. Lori expects the taxable income derived from her business (without regard to the amount expensed under § 179) to always be about $100,000. Lori will elect immediate expensing under § 179. Lori acquired seven-year property for $130,000 in March 1997.
    a. Determine Lori's total deduction with respect to the copier if she acquires the copier in 1997.
    b. Determine her total deduction with respect to the copier if she acquires the copier in 1998.
    c. What is your advice to Lori?

44. Jack owns a small business that he operates as a sole proprietor. In 1997, Jack will net $10,000 of business income before consideration of any § 179 deduction. Jack spends $207,000 on new equipment in 1997. If Jack also has $3,000 of § 179 deduction carryforwards from 1996, determine his § 179 expense deduction for 1997 and the amount of any carryforward.

45. Olga is the proprietor of a small business. In 1997, her business income, before consideration of any § 179 deduction, is $6,000. Olga spends $202,000 on new equipment and furniture for 1997. If Olga elects to take the § 179 deduction on a desk that cost $20,000 (included in the $202,000), determine her total cost recovery for 1997 with respect to the desk.

46. On March 10, 1997, Yoon purchased three-year class property for $20,000. On December 15, 1997, Yoon purchased five-year class property for $50,000. He has net business income of $19,000 before consideration of any § 179 deduction.
    a. Calculate Yoon's cost recovery for 1997, assuming he does not make the § 179 election or use straight-line cost recovery.
    b. Calculate Yoon's cost recovery for 1997, assuming he does elect to use § 179 and does not elect to use straight-line cost recovery.
    c. Assuming Yoon's marginal tax rate is 36%, determine his tax benefit from electing § 179.

47. On July 1, 1997, Wilma places in service a computer (five-year class property). The computer cost $20,000. Wilma used the computer 65% for business. The remainder of the time, she used the computer for personal purposes. If Wilma does not elect § 179, determine her cost recovery deduction for the computer for 1997.

48. John Johnson is considering acquiring an automobile at the beginning of 1997 that he will use 100% of the time as a taxi. The purchase price of the automobile is $25,000. John has heard of cost recovery limits on automobiles and wants to know how much of the $25,000 he can deduct in the first year. Write a letter to John in which you present your calculations. Also, prepare a memo for the tax files. John's address is 100 Morningside, Clinton, MS 39058.

49. On February 16, 1997, Ron purchased and placed into service a new car. The purchase price was $18,000. Ron drove the car 12,000 miles during the remainder of the year, 9,000 miles for business and 3,000 miles for personal use. Ron used the statutory percentage method of cost recovery. Calculate the total deduction Ron may take for 1997 with respect to the car.

50. On June 5, 1997, Leo purchased and placed in service a $19,000 car. The business use percentage for the car is always 100%. Compute Leo's cost recovery deduction in 2003.

51. On June 14, 1997, Helen purchased and placed in service a new car. The purchase price was $16,000. The car was used 75% for business and 25% for personal use in both 1997 and 1998. In 1999, the car was used 40% for business and 60% for personal use. Compute the cost recovery deduction for the car in 1999 and the cost recovery recapture.

52. In 1997, Paul purchased a computer (five-year property) for $120,000. The computer was used 60% for business, 20% for income production, and 20% for personal use. In 1998, the usage changed to 40% for business, 30% for income production, and 30% for personal use. Compute the cost recovery deduction for 1998 and any cost recovery recapture. Assume Paul did not make a § 179 election on the computer in 1997.

53. Sally purchased a computer (five-year property) for $3,000. Sally could use the computer 100% of the time in her business, or she could allow her family to also use the computer. Sally estimates that if her family uses the computer, the business use will be 40% and the personal use will be 60%. Determine the tax cost to Sally, in the year of acquisition, of allowing her family to use the computer. Assume that Sally would not elect § 179 limited expensing and that her marginal tax rate is 31%.

54. Midway through 1997, Abdel leases and places in service a passenger automobile. The lease will run for five years, and the payments are $430 per month. During 1997, Abdel uses the car 70% for business use and 30% for personal use. Assuming the inclusion dollar amount from the IRS table is $76, determine the tax consequences to Abdel from the lease for the year 1997.

55. Use the information given in Problem 54, but assume the inclusion dollar amount is $167. Abdel uses the car 60% for business use and 40% for personal use in 1998. Determine Abdel's tax consequences from the lease in 1998.

56. Dennis Harding is considering acquiring an automobile that he will use 100% for business. The purchase price of the automobile would be $30,500. If Dennis leased the car for five years, the lease payments would be $350 per month. Dennis will acquire the car on January 1, 1997. The inclusion dollar amounts from the IRS table for the next five years are $111, $244, $363, $435, and $503. Dennis desires to know the effect on his adjusted gross income of purchasing versus leasing the car for the next five years. Write a letter to Dennis and present your calculations. Also, prepare a memo for the tax files. His address is 150 Avenue I, Memphis, TN 38112.

57. On March 5, 1997, Nell purchased equipment for $60,000. The equipment is 7-year class property and has an ADS midpoint of 9.5 years. Determine Nell's cost recovery deduction for computing 1997 taxable income using the straight-line method under the alternative depreciation system and assuming she does not make a § 179 election.

58. In 1997, Muhammad purchased a light-duty truck for $12,000. The truck is used 100% for business. Muhammad did not make a § 179 election with respect to the truck. If Muhammad uses the statutory percentage method, determine his cost recovery deduction for 1997 for computing taxable income and for computing his alternative minimum tax.

59. In June 1997, Cardinal, Inc., purchased and placed in service railroad track costing $600,000.
    a. Calculate Cardinal's cost recovery deduction for 1997 for computing taxable income, assuming Cardinal does not make the § 179 election or use straight-line cost recovery.
    b. Calculate Cardinal's cost recovery deduction for 1997 for computing taxable income, assuming Cardinal does not make the § 179 election but does elect to use ADS 150% declining-balance cost recovery.

60. Jamie purchased $60,000 of office furniture for her business in June of the current year. Jamie understands that if she elects to use the alternative depreciation system to compute her regular income tax, there will be no difference between the cost recovery for computing the regular income tax and the AMT. Jamie wants to know the *regular*

income tax cost, after three years, of using ADS rather than MACRS. Assume that Jamie does not elect § 179 limited expensing and that her marginal tax rate is 31%.

61. On August 1, 1997, Jake acquired a dental practice from Bob for $250,000. The purchase price was allocated $200,000 to the tangible assets of the practice and $50,000 to the goodwill. Determine Jake's deduction for the amortization of the goodwill for 1997.

62. Mike Saxon is negotiating the purchase of a business. The final purchase price has been agreed upon, but the allocation of the purchase price to the assets is still being discussed. Appraisals on a warehouse range from $1.2 to $1.5 million. If a value of $1.2 million is used for the warehouse, the remainder of the purchase price, $800,000, will be allocated to goodwill. If $1.5 million is allocated to the warehouse, goodwill will be $500,000. Mike wants to know what effect each alternative will have on cost recovery and amortization during the first year. Under the agreement, Mike will take over the business on January 1 of next year. Write a letter to Mike in which you present your calculations and recommendation. Also, prepare a memo for the tax files. Mike's address is 200 Rolling Hills Drive, Shavertown, PA 18708.

63. Wes acquired a mineral interest during the year for $5 million. A geological survey estimated that 250,000 tons of the mineral remained in the deposit. During the year, 80,000 tons were mined, and 45,000 tons were sold for $6 million. Other expenses amounted to $4 million. Assuming the mineral depletion rate is 22%, calculate Wes's lowest taxable income.

64. Chris purchased an oil interest for $2,000,000. Recoverable barrels were estimated to be 500,000. During the year, 120,000 barrels were sold for $3,840,000, regular expenses (including cost recovery) were $1,240,000, and IDC were $1,000,000. Calculate Chris's taxable income under the expensing and capitalization methods of handling IDC.

CUMULATIVE PROBLEMS

65. John Smith, age 31, is single and has no dependents. At the beginning of 1997, John started his own excavation business and named it Earth Movers. John lives at 1045 Center Street, Lindon, UT, and his business is located at 381 State Street, Lindon, UT. The zip code for both addresses is 84059. John's Social Security number is 321–09–6456, and the business identification number is 98–1234567. John is a cash basis taxpayer. During 1997, John had the following items in connection with his business:

Fees for services	$290,000
Building rental expense	36,000
Office furniture and equipment rental expense	6,000
Office supplies	2,500
Utilities	3,000
Salary for secretary	35,000
Salary for equipment operators	78,000
Payroll taxes	9,000
Fuel and oil for the equipment	20,000
Purchase of three front-end loaders on January 15, 1997, for $175,000. John made the election under § 179.	175,000
Purchase of a new dump truck on January 18, 1997	30,000

During 1997, John had the following additional items:

Interest income from First National Bank	$8,000
Dividends from Exxon	2,500
Quarterly estimated tax payments	11,500

On October 8, 1997, John inherited IBM stock from his Aunt Mildred. John had been her favorite nephew. According to the data provided by the executor of Aunt Mildred's estate, the stock had been valued for estate tax purposes at $90,000. John is considering selling the IBM stock for $95,000 on December 29, 1997, and using $60,000 of the proceeds to purchase an Acura NSX. He would use the car 100% for business. John wants to know what effect these transactions would have on his 1997 adjusted gross income.

Write a letter to John in which you present your calculations. Also, prepare a memo for the tax files. Suggested software (if available): *TurboTax* or *MacInTax*.

66. Bob Brown, age 30, is single and has no dependents. He was employed as a barber until May 1996 by Hair Cuts, Inc. In June 1996, Bob opened his own styling salon, the Style Shop, located at 465 Willow Drive, St. Paul, MN 55455. Bob is a cash basis taxpayer. He lives at 1021 Snelling Avenue, St. Paul, MN 55455. His Social Security number is 321–56–7102. Bob does not wish to designate $3 to the Presidential Election Campaign Fund. During 1996, Bob had the following income and expense items:
   a. $25,000 salary from Hair Cuts, Inc.
   b. $3,000 Federal income tax withheld by Hair Cuts, Inc.
   c. $50,000 gross receipts from his own hair styling business.
   d. Expenses connected with Bob's hair styling business:

   - $900 laundry and cleaning
   - $7,000 rent
   - $2,000 supplies
   - $800 utilities and telephone

   e. Bob purchased and installed a fancy barber chair (five-year class property) on June 3, 1996. The chair cost $8,000. Bob did not make the § 179 election.
   f. Bob purchased and installed furniture and fixtures (seven-year class property) on June 5, 1996. These items cost $20,000. Bob did make the § 179 election.
   g. Bob's itemized deductions are as follows:

Property taxes on his residence	$2,000
Mortgage interest on his residence	4,000
State income taxes	2,500
Charitable contributions	1,500

   h. Bob made estimated tax payments of $5,500.

   Compute Bob Brown's 1996 Federal income tax payable (or refund due). If you use tax forms for your computations, you will need Forms 1040 and 4562 and Schedules A, C, and SE. Suggested software (if available): *TurboTax* or *MacInTax*..

RESEARCH PROBLEMS

Note: **West's Federal Taxation on CD-ROM** *can be used in preparing solutions to the Research Problems. Alternatively, tax research materials contained in a standard tax library can be used.*

Research Problem 1. Harry Pickart, who is one of your clients, is considering building a golf course in the resort area of Sun River, Oregon. Because the land is unimproved, all of the sand traps, greens, fairways, and tees will need to be constructed. Write a letter to Harry that contains your advice on whether any deductions can be taken for the landscaping improvements. Also, prepare a memo for the tax files. His mailing address is P.O. Box 100, Sun River, OR 97600.

Research Problem 2. Doug operates a restaurant in a small town. In May of the current year, Doug had a new septic tank installed for the restaurant. The town plans to construct a sewage system in five years. At that time, Doug will be required to be connected to the town system, and his septic tank will be obsolete. Doug believes that depreciation should represent wear, tear, and obsolescence, and, hence, he believes he should use a five-year life for the depreciation of the septic tank. Discuss the proper period and method for depreciating the septic tank.

Partial list of research aids:
J. O. Miller, 56 TCM 1242, T.C.Memo. 1989–66.
Rev.Proc. 87–56, 1987–2 C.B. 674.

Research Problem 3.   Sandra purchased the following personal property during 1997:

Date	Asset	Cost
June 1	Machine A	$20,000
July 10	Machine B	10,000
November 15	Machine C	25,000

Sandra elects to take the § 179 expense on Machine C. Discuss what convention Sandra must use to determine her cost recovery deduction for 1997.

Research Problem 4.   Ella owns a business that rents televisions and appliances to the general public. A person who rents from Ella's business enters into a rent-to-own contract. Under the contract, renters pay a monthly rent as long as they want to use the television or appliance. After a specified number of payments, the renter will own the television or appliance. Ella would like to know whether she can compute depreciation on the televisions and appliances using the income forecast method.

Research Problem 5.   Alfred acquires $50,000 of machinery and equipment for his sole proprietorship. In addition, the Golden Partnership, in which Alfred is a 20% partner, acquires $100,000 of machinery and equipment during the year. Both Alfred's sole proprietorship and Golden Partnership would like to elect the maximum § 179 limited expensing for the tax year. The net income of the partnership is $300,000, and the sole proprietorship has net income of $150,000. Advise Alfred of the amount of § 179 deductions he can take on his income tax return and the source (i.e., sole proprietorship, partnership, or both).

Use the tax resources of the internet to address the following questions. Do not restrict your search to the World Wide Web, but include a review of newsgroups and general reference materials, practitioner sites and resources, primary sources of the tax law, chat rooms and discussion groups, and other opportunities.

Research Problem 6.   Locate a financial calculator program that assesses the wisdom of buying versus leasing a new car. Install the program on your computer and become familiar with it. Use the program to work through Problem 56 in this chapter.

Research Problem 7.   Changes to depreciation systems often are discussed by policy makers and observers of the tax system. Outline the terms and policy objectives of one of the changes currently proposed by the Treasury, a member of Congress, or a tax policy think tank.

TEAM PROJECT: ARTHUR ANDERSEN TAX CHALLENGE CASES

For more information on the Arthur Andersen Tax Challenge Cases, refer to Chapter 1, page 1–38.

Information related to tax issues and problems that are discussed in this chapter may be found in the

Day and Ball case on pages 7 and 20

Read and analyze the case you have been assigned and *identify* any issues and problems that are related to material covered in this chapter. If the information provided in the case is complete, prepare answers for this part of the case at this time. If you need information that is contained in the later parts of the case, write a memo summarizing the questions or problems so you can prepare a complete answer at a later date.

CHAPTER 9

Deductions: Employee Expenses

LEARNING OBJECTIVES

After completing Chapter 9, you should be able to:

1. Distinguish between employee and self-employed status.
2. Recognize deductible transportation expenses.
3. Know how travel expenses are treated.
4. Determine the moving expense deduction.
5. Differentiate between deductible and nondeductible education expenses.
6. Understand how entertainment expenses are treated.
7. Identify other employee expenses.
8. Appreciate the difference between accountable and nonaccountable employee plans.
9. Work with the limitations on miscellaneous itemized deductions.
10. Develop tax planning ideas related to employee business expenses.

OUTLINE

Employee versus Self-Employed, 9-2

Employee Expenses—In General, 9-4

Transportation Expenses, 9-5

Qualified Expenditures, 9-5

Computation of Automobile Expenses, 9-6

Travel Expenses, 9-7

Definition of Travel Expenses, 9-7

Away-from-Home Requirement, 9-7

Restrictions on Travel Expenses, 9-8

Combined Business and Pleasure Travel, 9-10

Moving Expenses, 9-11

Distance Test, 9-11

Time Test, 9-12

Treatment of Moving Expenses, 9-12

Education Expenses, 9-13

General Requirements, 9-13

Requirements Imposed by Law or by the Employer for Retention of Employment, 9-14

Maintaining or Improving Existing Skills, 9-14

Classification of Specific Items, 9-15

Other Provisions Dealing with Education, 9-15

Entertainment Expenses, 9-15

Dollar Limitations, 9-16

Classification of Expenses, 9-16

Restrictions upon Deductibility, 9-17

Other Employee Expenses, 9-19

Office in the Home, 9-19

Miscellaneous Employee Expenses, 9-20

Contributions to Individual Retirement Accounts, 9-21

Classification of Employee Expenses, 9-21

Accountable Plans, 9-21

Nonaccountable Plans, 9-23

Reporting Procedures, 9-24

Limitations on Itemized Deductions, 9-25

Miscellaneous Itemized Deductions Subject to the 2 Percent Floor, 9-25

Miscellaneous Itemized Deductions Not Subject to the 2 Percent Floor, 9-25

Tax Planning Considerations, 9-26

Self-Employed Individuals, 9-26

Shifting Deductions between Employer and Employee, 9-26

Transportation and Travel Expenses, 9-26

Moving Expenses, 9-27

Education Expenses, 9-27

Entertainment Expenses, 9-28

Unreimbursed Employee Business Expenses, 9-28

Considering the large number of taxpayers affected, the tax treatment of job-related expenses is unusually complex. To resolve this matter in a systematic fashion, a number of key questions must be asked:

- Is the taxpayer an *employee* or *self-employed*?
- If an employee, what expenses *qualify* as deductions?
- How are the expenses that qualify *classified* for tax purposes?
- To the extent the expenses are classified as deductions *from* AGI, are they subject to any *limitation*?

Once these questions have been posed and answered, the chapter considers various planning procedures available to maximize the deductibility of employee expenses.

EMPLOYEE VERSUS SELF-EMPLOYED

1 LEARNING OBJECTIVE
Distinguish between employee and self-employed status.

When one person performs services for another, the person performing the service is either an employee or self-employed (i.e., an **independent contractor**). Failure to recognize employee status can have serious consequences. Not only can interest and penalties result, but a government career can be abruptly squelched. Such was the case with several persons that President Clinton nominated to his cabinet during his first term. Zoe Baird (Attorney General), Kimba Wood (Attorney

TAX IN THE NEWS

THERE IS SAFETY IN NUMBERS

Concerned that having workers reclassified from independent contractor to employee status could have ruinous economic effects on small businesses, Congress enacted § 530 of the Revenue Act of 1978. This provision imposes a moratorium on IRS examinations of an individual's employment classification under certain circumstances.

In time, however, Congress came to believe that the IRS had unduly narrowed the protection provided by the § 530 moratorium. Accordingly, in the Small Business Job Protection Act of 1996, some of the previously established safe harbors are reiterated and amplified.

One such safe harbor justifies not treating a worker as an employee if that is the recognized practice in a significant segment of the taxpayer's industry. Although the IRS had interpreted "significant" to mean at least 50 percent, the 1996 Act substitutes a 25 percent yardstick.

Not only is there safety in numbers, but the numbers are also less than the IRS thought suitable.

General), and Retired Admiral Bobby Inman (Secretary of Defense) all had to withdraw from consideration when it was revealed that they had failed to report and pay payroll taxes on their household employees.

The problem is likely to intensify since businesses are increasingly relying on the services of self-employed persons for numerous reasons. Unlike employees, self-employed persons do not have to be included in various fringe benefit programs (e.g., group term life insurance) and retirement plans. Since they are not covered by FICA and FUTA (see Chapter 1), these payroll costs are avoided.

The IRS is very much aware of the tendency of businesses to wrongly classify workers as self-employed rather than as employees. In terms of tax consequences, employment status also makes a great deal of difference to the persons who perform the services. Expenses of self-employed taxpayers, to the extent allowable, are classified as deductions *for* AGI and are reported on Schedule C (Profit or Loss From Business) of Form 1040.[1] With the exception of reimbursement under an accountable plan (see later in the chapter), expenses of employees are deductions *from* AGI. They are reported on Form 2106 (Employee Business Expenses) and Schedule A (Itemized Deductions) of Form 1040.[2]

But when does an employer-employee relationship exist? Such a relationship exists when the employer has the right to specify the end result and the ways and means by which that result is to be attained.[3] An employee is subject to the will and control of the employer with respect not only to what shall be done but also to how it shall be done. If the individual is subject to the direction or control of another only to the extent of the end result but not as to the means of accomplishment, an employer-employee relationship does not exist. An example is the preparation of a taxpayer's return by an independent CPA.

---

[1] §§ 62(a)(1) and 162(a). See Appendix B for a reproduction of Schedule C.

[2] See Appendix B for a reproduction of Form 2106 and Schedule A.
[3] Reg. § 31.3401(c)–(1)(b).

Certain factors indicate an employer-employee relationship. They include (1) the right to discharge without legal liability the person performing the service, (2) the furnishing of tools or a place to work, and (3) payment based on time spent rather than the task performed. Each case is tested on its own merits, and the right to control the means and methods of accomplishment is the definitive test. Generally, physicians, lawyers, dentists, contractors, subcontractors, and others who offer services to the public are not classified as employees.

EXAMPLE 1 Arnold is a lawyer whose major client accounts for 60% of his billings. He does the routine legal work and income tax returns at the client's request. He is paid a monthly retainer in addition to amounts charged for extra work. Arnold is a self-employed individual. Even though most of his income comes from one client, he still has the right to determine how the end result of his work is attained. ▼

EXAMPLE 2 Ellen is a lawyer hired by Arnold to assist him in the performance of services for the client mentioned in Example 1. Ellen is under Arnold's supervision; he reviews her work and pays her an hourly fee. Ellen is an employee of Arnold. ▼

EXAMPLE 3 Frank is a licensed practical nurse who works as a private-duty nurse. He is under the supervision of the patient's doctor and is paid by the patient. Frank is not an employee of either the patient (who pays him) or the doctor (who supervises him). The ways and means of attaining the end result (care of the patient) are under his control. ▼

Employees in a special category are also allowed to file Schedule C to report income and deduct expenses *for* AGI. These employees are called **statutory employees** because they are not common law employees under the rules explained above. The wages or commissions paid to statutory employees are not subject to Federal income tax withholding but are subject to Social Security tax.[4]

EMPLOYEE EXPENSES—IN GENERAL

Once the employment relationship is established, employee expenses fall into one of the following categories:

- Transportation.
- Travel.
- Moving.
- Education.
- Entertainment.
- Other.

These expenses are discussed below in the order presented.

Keep in mind, however, that these expenses are not necessarily limited to employees. A deduction for business transportation, for example, is equally available to taxpayers who are self-employed.

---

[4] See Circular E, *Employer's Tax Guide* (IRS Publication 15), for further discussion of statutory employees.

TRANSPORTATION EXPENSES

QUALIFIED EXPENDITURES

2 LEARNING OBJECTIVE
Recognize deductible transportation expenses.

An employee may deduct unreimbursed employment-related transportation expenses as an itemized deduction *from* AGI. **Transportation expenses** include only the cost of transporting the employee from one place to another when the employee is *not* away from home *in travel status*. Such costs include taxi fares, automobile expenses, tolls, and parking.

Commuting Expenses. Commuting between home and one's place of employment is a personal, nondeductible expense. The fact that one employee drives 30 miles to work and another employee walks six blocks is of no significance.[5]

EXAMPLE 4 Geraldo is employed by Sparrow Corporation. He drives 22 miles each way to work. The 44 miles he drives each workday are nondeductible commuting expenses. ▼

The rule that disallows a deduction for commuting expenses has several exceptions. An employee who uses an automobile to transport heavy tools to work and who otherwise would not drive to work is allowed a deduction, but only for the additional costs incurred to transport the work implements. Additional costs are those exceeding the cost of commuting by the same mode of transportation without the tools. For example, the rental of a trailer for transporting tools is deductible, but the expenses of operating the automobile generally are not deductible.[6] The Supreme Court has held that a deduction is permitted only when the taxpayer can show that the automobile would not have been used without the necessity to transport tools or equipment.[7]

Another exception is provided for an employee who has a second job. The expenses of getting from one job to another are deductible. If the employee goes home between jobs, the deduction is based on the distance between jobs.

EXAMPLE 5 In the current year, Cynthia holds two jobs, a full-time job with Blue Corporation and a part-time job with Wren Corporation. During the 250 days that she works (adjusted for weekends, vacation, and holidays), Cynthia customarily leaves home at 7:30 A.M. and drives 30 miles to the Blue Corporation plant, where she works until 5:00 P.M. After dinner at a nearby cafe, Cynthia drives 20 miles to Wren Corporation and works from 7:00 to 11:00 P.M. The distance from the second job to Cynthia's home is 40 miles. Her deduction is based on 20 miles (the distance between jobs). ▼

If the taxpayer is required to incur a transportation expense to travel between work stations, that expense is deductible.

EXAMPLE 6 Thomas, a general contractor, drives from his home to his office, then drives to three building sites to perform his required inspections, and finally drives home. The costs of driving to his office and driving home from the last inspection site are nondeductible commuting expenses. The other transportation costs are deductible. ▼

---

[5] *Tauferner v. U.S.*, 69–1 USTC ¶9241, 23 AFTR2d 69–1025, 407 F.2d 243 (CA–10, 1969).
[6] Rev.Rul. 75–380, 1975–2 C.B. 59.
[7] *Fausner v. Comm.*, 73–2 USTC ¶9515, 32 AFTR2d 73–5202, 93 S.Ct. 2820 (USSC, 1973).

Likewise, the commuting costs from home to a temporary work station and from the temporary work station to home are deductible.[8]

EXAMPLE 7

Vivian works for a firm in downtown Denver and commutes to work. She occasionally works in a customer's office. On one such occasion, Vivian drove directly to the customer's office, a round-trip distance from her home of 40 miles. She did not go into her office, which is a 52-mile round-trip. Her mileage for going to and from the temporary work station is deductible. ▼

Also deductible is the reasonable travel cost between the general working area and a temporary work station outside that area.[9] What constitutes the general working area depends on the facts and circumstances of each situation. Furthermore, if an employee customarily works on several temporary assignments in a localized area, that localized area becomes the regular place of employment. Transportation from home to these locations becomes a personal, nondeductible commuting expense.

EXAMPLE 8

Sam, a building inspector in Minneapolis, regularly inspects buildings for building code violations for his employer, a general contractor. During one busy season, the St. Paul inspector became ill, and Sam was required to inspect several buildings in St. Paul. The expenses for transportation for the trips to St. Paul are deductible. ▼

COMPUTATION OF AUTOMOBILE EXPENSES

A taxpayer has two choices in computing automobile expenses. The actual operating cost, which includes depreciation (cost recovery), gas, oil, repairs, licenses, and insurance, may be used. Records must be kept that detail the automobile's personal and business use. Only the percentage allocable to business transportation and travel is allowed as a deduction. Complex rules for the computation of depreciation (discussed in Chapter 8) apply if the actual expense method is used.

Use of the **automatic mileage method** is the second alternative. For 1997 the deduction is based on 31.5 cents per mile for all business miles.[10] Parking fees and tolls are allowed in addition to expenses computed using the automatic mileage method.

Generally, a taxpayer may elect either method for any particular year. However, the following restrictions apply:

- The vehicle must be owned by the taxpayer.
- If two or more vehicles are in use (for business purposes) at the *same* time (not alternately), a taxpayer may not use the automatic mileage method.
- A basis adjustment is required if the taxpayer changes from the automatic mileage method to the actual operating cost method. Depreciation is considered allowed for the business miles in accordance with the following schedule for the most recent five years:

---

[8] Rev.Rul. 90-23, 1990-1 C.B. 28 as amplified by Rev.Rul. 94-47, 1994-2 C.B. 18.

[9] Rev.Rul. 190, 1953-2 C.B. 303 as amplified by Rev.Rul. 94-47, 1994-2 C.B. 18.

[10] Rev.Proc. 96-63, I.R.B. No. 53, 46. The rate was 31 cents a mile for 1996.

Year	Rate per Mile
1997	12 cents
1996	12 cents
1995	12 cents
1994	12 cents
1993	11.5 cents

EXAMPLE 9

Tim purchased his automobile in 1994 for $15,000. It is used 90% for business purposes. Tim drove the automobile for 10,000 business miles in 1996; 8,500 miles in 1995; and 6,000 miles in 1994. At the beginning of 1997, the basis of the business portion is $10,560.

Cost ($15,000 × 90%)	$13,500
Less depreciation:	
1996 (10,000 miles × 12 cents)	(1,200)
1995 (8,500 miles × 12 cents)	(1,020)
1994 (6,000 × 12 cents)	(720)
Adjusted business basis 1/1/97	$10,560

- Use of the automatic mileage method in the first year the auto is placed in service is considered an election to exclude the auto from the MACRS method of depreciation (discussed in Chapter 8).
- A taxpayer may not switch to the automatic mileage method if the MACRS statutory percentage method or the election to expense under § 179 has been used.

TRAVEL EXPENSES

DEFINITION OF TRAVEL EXPENSES

3 LEARNING OBJECTIVE
Know how travel expenses are treated.

An itemized deduction is allowed for unreimbursed travel expenses related to a taxpayer's employment. **Travel expenses** are more broadly defined in the Code than are transportation expenses. Travel expenses include transportation expenses and meals and lodging while away from home in the pursuit of a trade or business. Meals cannot be lavish or extravagant under the circumstances. Transportation expenses (as previously discussed) are deductible even though the taxpayer is not away from home. A deduction for travel expenses is available only if the taxpayer is away from his or her tax home. Travel expenses also include reasonable laundry and incidental expenses.

AWAY-FROM-HOME REQUIREMENT

The crucial test for the deductibility of travel expenses is whether or not the employee is away from home overnight. "Overnight" need not be a 24-hour period, but it must be a period substantially longer than an ordinary day's work and must require rest, sleep, or a relief-from-work period.[11] A one-day business trip is not travel status, and meals and lodging for such a trip are not deductible.

---

[11] *U.S. v. Correll*, 68–1 USTC ¶9101, 20 AFTR2d 5845, 88 S.Ct. 445 (USSC, 1967); Rev.Rul. 75–168, 1975–1 C.B. 58.

Temporary Assignments. The employee must be away from home for a temporary period. If the taxpayer-employee is reassigned to a new post for an indefinite period of time, that new post becomes his or her tax home. *Temporary* indicates that the assignment's termination is expected within a reasonably short period of time. The position of the IRS is that the tax home is the business location, post, or station of the taxpayer. Thus, travel expenses are not deductible if a taxpayer is reassigned for an indefinite period and does not move his or her place of residence to the new location.

EXAMPLE 10
Malcolm's employer opened a branch office in San Diego. Malcolm was assigned to the new office for three months to train a new manager and to assist in setting up the new office. He tried commuting from his home in Los Angeles for a week and decided that he could not continue driving several hours a day. He rented an apartment in San Diego, where he lived during the week. He spent weekends with his wife and children at their home in Los Angeles. Malcolm's rent, meals, laundry, incidentals, and automobile expenses in San Diego are deductible. To the extent that Malcolm's transportation expense related to his weekend trips home exceeds what his cost of meals and lodging would have been, the excess is personal and nondeductible. ▼

EXAMPLE 11
Assume that Malcolm in Example 10 was transferred to the new location to become the new manager permanently. His wife and children continued to live in Los Angeles until the end of the school year. Malcolm is no longer "away from home" because the assignment is not temporary. His travel expenses are not deductible. ▼

To curtail controversy in this area, the Code specifies that a taxpayer "*shall not* be treated as *temporarily* away from home during any period of employment if such period exceeds 1 year."[12]

Determining the Tax Home. Under ordinary circumstances, determining the location of a taxpayer's tax home does not present a problem. The tax home is the area in which the taxpayer derives his or her principal source of income. When the taxpayer has more than one place of employment, the tax home is based on the amount of time spent in each area.

It is possible for a taxpayer never to be away from his or her tax home. In other words, the tax home follows the taxpayer.[13] Thus, all meals and lodging remain personal and are not deductible.

EXAMPLE 12
Bill is employed as a long-haul truck driver. He is single, stores his clothes and other belongings at his parents' home, and stops there for periodic visits. Most of the time, Bill is on the road, sleeping in his truck and in motels. It is likely that Bill is never in travel status, as he is not away from home. Consequently, none of his meals and lodging are deductible. ▼

RESTRICTIONS ON TRAVEL EXPENSES

The possibility always exists that taxpayers will attempt to treat vacation or pleasure travel as deductible business travel. To prevent such practices, the law contains restrictions on certain travel expenses.

---

[12] § 162(a). Added by the Comprehensive National Energy Policy Act of 1992.

[13] *Moses Mitnick*, 13 T.C. 1 (1949).

Conventions. For travel expenses to be deductible, a convention must be directly related to the taxpayer's trade or business.[14]

EXAMPLE 13
Dr. Hill, a pathologist who works for a hospital in Ohio, travels to Las Vegas to attend a two-day session on recent developments in estate planning. No deduction is allowed for Dr. Hill's travel expenses. ▼

EXAMPLE 14
Assume the same facts as in Example 13 except that the convention deals entirely with recent developments in forensic medicine. Under these circumstances, a travel deduction is allowed. ▼

If the proceedings of the convention are videotaped, the taxpayer must attend convention sessions to view the videotaped materials along with other participants. This requirement does not disallow deductions for costs (other than travel, meals, and entertainment) of renting or using videotaped materials related to business.

EXAMPLE 15
A CPA is unable to attend a convention at which current developments in taxation are discussed. She pays $200 for videotapes of the lectures and views them at home later. The $200 is an itemized deduction if the CPA is an employee. If she is self-employed, the $200 is a deduction *for* AGI. ▼

The Code places stringent restrictions on the deductibility of travel expenses of the taxpayer's spouse or dependent.[15] Generally, the accompaniment by the spouse or dependent must serve a bona fide business purpose, and the expenses must be otherwise deductible.

EXAMPLE 16
Assume the same facts as in Example 14 with the additional fact that Dr. Hill is accompanied by Mrs. Hill. Mrs. Hill is not employed, but possesses secretarial skills and takes notes during the proceedings. No deduction is allowed for Mrs. Hill's travel expenses. ▼

EXAMPLE 17
Modify the facts in Example 16 to make Mrs. Hill a nurse trained in pathology, who is employed by Dr. Hill as his assistant. Now, Mrs. Hill's travel expenses qualify as deductions. ▼

Education. Travel as a form of education is not deductible.[16] If, however, the education qualifies as a deduction, the travel involved is allowed.

EXAMPLE 18
Greta, a German teacher, travels to Germany to maintain general familiarity with the language and culture. No travel expense deduction is allowed. ▼

EXAMPLE 19
Jean-Claude, a scholar of French literature, travels to Paris to do specific library research that cannot be done elsewhere and to take courses that are offered only at the Sorbonne. The travel costs are deductible, assuming that the other requirements for deducting education expenses (discussed later in the chapter) are met. ▼

---

[14] § 274(h)(1).
[15] § 274(m)(3).
[16] § 274(m)(2).

COMBINED BUSINESS AND PLEASURE TRAVEL

To be deductible, travel expenses need not be incurred in the performance of specific job functions. Travel expenses incurred in attending a professional convention are deductible by an employee if attendance is connected with services as an employee. For example, an employee of a law firm can deduct travel expenses incurred in attending a meeting of the American Bar Association.

Domestic Travel. Travel deductions have been used in the past by persons who claimed a tax deduction for what was essentially a personal vacation. As a result, several provisions have been enacted to govern deductions associated with combined business and pleasure trips. If the business/pleasure trip is from one point in the United States to another point in the United States, the transportation expenses are deductible only if the trip is *primarily for business*.[17] If the trip is primarily for pleasure, no transportation expenses qualify as a deduction. Meals, lodging, and other expenses are allocated between business and personal days.

EXAMPLE 20 In the current year, Hana travels from Seattle to New York primarily for business. She spends five days conducting business and three days sightseeing and attending shows. Her plane and taxi fare amounts to $560. Her meals amount to $100 per day, and lodging and incidental expenses are $150 per day. She can deduct the transportation charges of $560, since the trip is primarily for business (five days of business versus three days of sightseeing). Meals are limited to five days and are subject to the 50% cutback (discussed later in the chapter) for a total of $250 [5 days × ($100 × 50%)], and other expenses are limited to $750 (5 days × $150). If Hana is an employee, the unreimbursed travel expenses are miscellaneous itemized deductions. ▼

EXAMPLE 21 Assume Hana goes to New York for a two-week vacation. While there, she spends several hours renewing acquaintances with people in her company's New York office. Her transportation expenses are not deductible. ▼

Foreign Travel. When the trip is *outside the United States*, special rules apply.[18] Transportation expenses must be allocated between business and personal unless (1) the taxpayer is away from home for seven days or less *or* (2) less than 25 percent of the time was for personal purposes. No allocation is required if the taxpayer has no substantial control over arrangements for the trip or the desire for a vacation is not a major factor in taking the trip. If the trip is primarily for pleasure, no transportation charges are deductible. Days devoted to travel are considered business days. Weekends, legal holidays, and intervening days are considered business days, provided that both the preceding and succeeding days were business days.

EXAMPLE 22 In the current year, Robert takes a trip from New York to Japan primarily for business purposes. He is away from home from June 10 through June 19. He spends three days vacationing and seven days conducting business (including two travel days). His airfare is $2,500, his meals amount to $100 per day, and lodging and incidental expenses are $160 per day. Since Robert is away from home for more than seven days and more than 25% of his time is devoted to personal purposes, only 70% (7 days business/10 days total) of the transportation is deductible. His deductions are as follows:

---

[17] Reg. § 1.162–2(b)(1). [18] § 274(c) and Reg. § 1.274–4.

Transportation (70% × $2,500)		$1,750
Lodging ($160 × 7)		1,120
Meals ($100 × 7)	$ 700	
Less: 50% cutback (discussed later)	(350)	350
Total		$3,220

If Robert is gone the same period of time but spends only two days (rather than three) vacationing, no allocation of transportation is required. Since the pleasure portion of the trip is less than 25% of the total, all of the airfare qualifies for the travel deduction. ▼

Certain restrictions are imposed on the deductibility of expenses paid or incurred to attend conventions located outside the North American area. The expenses are disallowed unless it is established that the meeting is directly related to a trade or business of the taxpayer. Disallowance also occurs unless the taxpayer shows that it is as reasonable for the meeting to be held in a foreign location as within the North American area.

The foreign convention rules do not operate to bar a deduction to an employer if the expense is compensatory in nature. For example, a trip to Rome won by a top salesperson is included in the gross income of the employee and is fully deductible by the employer.

MOVING EXPENSES

4 LEARNING OBJECTIVE
Determine the moving expense deduction.

Moving expenses are deductible for moves in connection with the commencement of work at a new principal place of work.[19] Both employees and self-employed individuals can deduct these expenses. To be eligible for a moving expense deduction, a taxpayer must meet two basic tests: distance and time.

DISTANCE TEST

To meet the distance test, the taxpayer's new job location must be at least 50 miles farther from the taxpayer's old residence than the old residence was from the former place of employment. In this regard, the location of the new residence is not relevant. This eliminates a moving deduction for taxpayers who purchase a new home in the same general area without changing their place of employment. Those who accept a new job in the same general area as the old job location are also eliminated.

EXAMPLE 23

Harry is permanently transferred to a new job location. The distance from Harry's former home to his new job (80 miles) exceeds the distance from his former home to his old job (30 miles) by at least 50 miles. Harry has met the distance test for a moving expense deduction. (See the following diagram.)

[19] § 217(a).

If Harry is not employed before the move, his new job must be at least 50 miles from his former residence. In this instance, Harry has met the distance test if he was not previously employed. ▼

TIME TEST

To meet the time test, an employee must be employed on a full-time basis at the new location for 39 weeks in the 12-month period following the move. If the taxpayer is a self-employed individual, he or she must work in the new location for 78 weeks during the next two years. The first 39 weeks must be in the first 12 months. The time test is suspended if the taxpayer dies, becomes disabled, or is discharged or transferred by the new employer through no fault of the employee.

A taxpayer might not be able to meet the 39-week test by the due date of the tax return for the year of the move. For this reason, two alternatives are allowed. The taxpayer can take the deduction in the year the expenses are incurred, even though the 39-week test has not been met. If the taxpayer later fails to meet the test, either (1) the income of the following year is increased by an amount equal to the deduction previously claimed for moving expenses, or (2) an amended return is filed for the year of the move. The second alternative is to wait until the test is met and then file an amended tax return for the year of the move.

TREATMENT OF MOVING EXPENSES

What Is Included. "Qualified" moving expenses include *reasonable* expenses of:

- Moving household goods and personal effects.
- Traveling from the former residence to the new place of residence.

For this purpose, *traveling* includes lodging, but not meals, for the taxpayer and members of the household.[20] It does not include the cost of moving servants or others who are not members of the household. The taxpayer can elect to use actual auto expenses (no depreciation is allowed) or the automatic mileage method. In this case, moving expense mileage is limited in 1997 to 10 cents per mile (ten cents in 1996) for each car. These expenses are also limited by the reasonableness standard. For example, if one moves from Texas to Florida via Maine and takes six weeks to do so, the transportation and lodging must be allocated between personal and moving expenses.

EXAMPLE 24

Jill is transferred by her employer from the Atlanta office to the San Francisco office. In this connection, she spends the following amounts:

Cost of moving furniture	$2,800
Transportation	700
Meals	200
Lodging	300

Jill's total qualified moving expense is $3,800 ($2,800 + $700 + $300). ▼

---

[20] § 217(b).

CHAPTER 9 Deductions: Employee Expenses 9–13

The moving expense deduction is allowed regardless of whether the employee is transferred by the existing employer or is employed by a new employer. It is allowed if the employee moves to a new area and obtains employment or switches from self-employed status to employee status (and vice versa). The moving expense deduction is also allowed if an individual is unemployed before obtaining employment in a new area.

ETHICAL CONSIDERATIONS

How Much Is That House Really Worth?

Justin is a key management-level employee of Condor Corporation, a national retailer of jewelry. Condor is encountering a great deal of difficulty with its West Coast operations and would like to transfer Justin from its Chicago office to its Los Angeles office. Justin is hesitant to relocate because he anticipates a loss from the sale of his Chicago residence. When Condor offers to purchase the residence for its cost of $350,000, Justin accepts the transfer. Condor also pays all of his other moving expenses. The Form W–2 issued by Condor to Justin contains no information regarding the transfer from Chicago to Los Angeles. One year after purchasing the residence, Condor sells it for $310,000.

What are the parties probably trying to accomplish? Should it work? Will it work?

How Treated. Qualified moving expenses that are paid (or reimbursed) by the employer are not reported as part of the gross income of the employee.[21] Moving expenses that are paid (or reimbursed) by the employer and are not qualified moving expenses are included in the employee's gross income and are not deductible. The employer is responsible for allocating the reimbursement between the qualified and nonqualified moving expenses. Reimbursed qualified moving expenses are separately stated on the Form W–2 given to the employee for the year involved. Qualified moving expenses that are not reimbursed and those of self-employed taxpayers are deductions *for* AGI.[22]

Form 3903 is used to report the details of the moving expense deduction if the employee is not reimbursed or a self-employed person is involved.

EDUCATION EXPENSES

GENERAL REQUIREMENTS

5 LEARNING OBJECTIVE
Differentiate between deductible and nondeductible education expenses.

An employee can deduct expenses incurred for education (**education expenses**) as ordinary and necessary business expenses provided the expenses are incurred for either of two reasons:

1. To maintain or improve existing skills required in the present job.
2. To meet the express requirements of the employer or the requirements imposed by law to retain his or her employment status.

---

[21] §§ 132(a)(6) and (g).   [22] § 62(a)(15).

Education expenses are *not* deductible if the education is for either of the following purposes:

1. To meet the minimum educational standards for qualification in the taxpayer's existing job.
2. To qualify the taxpayer for a new trade or business.[23]

Fees incurred for professional qualification exams (the bar exam, for example) and fees for review courses (such as a CPA review course) are not deductible.[24] If the education incidentally results in a promotion or raise, the deduction still can be taken as long as the education maintained and improved existing skills and did not qualify a person for a new trade or business. A change in duties is not always fatal to the deduction if the new duties involve the same general work. For example, the IRS has ruled that a practicing dentist's education expenses incurred to become an orthodontist are deductible.[25]

REQUIREMENTS IMPOSED BY LAW OR BY THE EMPLOYER FOR RETENTION OF EMPLOYMENT

Teachers are permitted to deduct education expenses if additional courses are required by the employer or are imposed by law. Many states require a minimum of a bachelor's degree and a specified number of additional courses to retain a teaching job. In addition, some public school systems have imposed a master's degree requirement and require teachers to make satisfactory progress toward a master's degree in order to keep their positions. If the required education is the minimum degree required for the job, no deduction is allowed.

A taxpayer classified as an Accountant I who went back to school to obtain a bachelor's degree was not allowed to deduct the expenses. Although some courses tended to maintain and improve his existing skills in his entry-level position, the degree was the minimum requirement for his job.[26]

Expenses incurred for education required by law for various professions will also qualify for deduction.

EXAMPLE 25 In order to satisfy the State Board of Public Accountancy rules for maintaining her CPA license, Nancy takes an auditing course sponsored by a local college. The cost of the education is deductible. ▼

MAINTAINING OR IMPROVING EXISTING SKILLS

The "maintaining or improving existing skills" requirement in the Code has been difficult for both taxpayers and the courts to interpret. For example, a business executive is permitted to deduct the costs of obtaining an M.B.A. on the grounds that the advanced management education is undertaken to maintain and improve existing management skills. The executive is eligible to deduct the costs of specialized, nondegree management courses that are taken for continuing education or to maintain or improve existing skills. Expenses incurred by the executive to obtain a law degree are not deductible, however, because the education constitutes training for a new trade or business. The Regulations deny a self-employed accountant a deduction for expenses relating to law school.[27]

---

[23] Reg. §§ 1.162–5(b)(2) and (3).
[24] Reg. § 1.212–1(f) and Rev.Rul. 69–292, 1969–1 C.B. 84.
[25] Rev.Rul. 74–78, 1974–1 C.B. 44.
[26] Reg. § 1.162–5(b)(2)(iii) Example (2); *Collin J. Davidson*, 43 TCM 743, T.C.Memo. 1982–119.
[27] Reg. § 1.162–5(b)(3)(ii) Example (1).

2. The amount of miscellaneous expenses deductible after the 2%-of-AGI rule is applied.

The amount under item 1 is $1,320 [$120 (safe deposit box rental) + $1,200 (investment counsel fee)]. The item 2 amount is $1,170 [$2,770 (total of miscellaneous expenses) − $1,600 (2% of $80,000 AGI)].

Then, Gina's investment expenses are calculated as follows:

Deductible miscellaneous deductions investment expense (the lesser of item 1 or item 2)	$1,170
Plus: Ad valorem tax on investment property	3,000
Total investment expenses	$4,170

Gina's net investment income is $13,830 ($18,000 investment income − $4,170 investment expenses). ▼

After net investment income is determined, deductible investment interest expense can be calculated.

EXAMPLE 20

Adam is a single person employed by a law firm. His investment activities for the year are as follows:

Net investment income	$30,000
Investment interest expense	44,000

Adam's investment interest deduction is $30,000. ▼

The amount of investment interest disallowed is carried over to future years. In Example 20, therefore, the amount that is carried over to the following year is $14,000 ($44,000 investment interest expense − $30,000 allowed). No limit is placed on the length of the carryover period. The investment interest expense deduction is determined by completing Form 4952 (see Appendix B).

Qualified Residence Interest. *Qualified residence interest* is interest paid or accrued during the taxable year on indebtedness (subject to limitations) *secured* by any property that is a qualified residence of the taxpayer. Qualified residence interest falls into two categories: (1) interest on acquisition indebtedness and (2) interest on home equity loans. Before discussing each of these categories, however, the term qualified residence must be defined.

A *qualified residence* includes the taxpayer's principal residence and one other residence of the taxpayer or spouse. The *principal residence* is one that meets the requirement for nonrecognition of gain upon sale under § 1034 (see Chapter 15). The *one other residence,* or second residence, refers to one that is used as a residence if not rented or, if rented, meets the requirements for a personal residence under the rental of vacation home rules (refer to Chapter 6). A taxpayer who has more than one second residence can make the selection each year of which one is the qualified second residence. A residence includes, in addition to a house in the ordinary sense, cooperative apartments, condominiums, and mobile homes and boats that have living quarters (sleeping accommodations and toilet and cooking facilities).

Although in most cases interest paid on a home mortgage would be fully deductible, there are limitations.[23] Interest paid or accrued during the tax year on

---

[23] § 163(h)(3).

aggregate **acquisition indebtedness** of $1 million or less ($500,000 for married persons filing separate returns) is deductible as qualified residence interest. Acquisition indebtedness refers to amounts incurred in acquiring, constructing, or substantially improving a qualified residence of the taxpayer.

Qualified residence interest also includes interest on **home equity loans.** These loans utilize the personal residence of the taxpayer as security. Because the funds from home equity loans can be used for personal purposes (e.g., auto purchases, medical expenses), what would otherwise have been nondeductible consumer interest becomes deductible qualified residence interest.

However, interest is deductible only on the portion of a home equity loan that does not exceed the *lesser of*:

- The fair market value of the residence, reduced by the acquisition indebtedness, *or*
- $100,000 ($50,000 for married persons filing separate returns).

EXAMPLE 21

Larry owns a personal residence with a fair market value of $150,000 and an outstanding first mortgage of $120,000. Therefore, his equity in his home is $30,000 ($150,000 − $120,000). Larry issues a lien on the residence and in return borrows $15,000 to purchase a new family automobile. All interest on the $135,000 of debt is treated as qualified residence interest. ▼

EXAMPLE 22

Leon and Pearl, married taxpayers, took out a mortgage on their home for $200,000 in 1983. In March of the current year, when the home had a fair market value of $400,000 and they owed $195,000 on the mortgage, Leon and Pearl took out a home equity loan for $120,000. They used the funds to purchase a boat to be used for recreational purposes. The boat, which does not have living quarters, does not qualify as a personal residence. On a joint return, Leon and Pearl can deduct all of the interest on the first mortgage since it is acquisition indebtedness. Of the $120,000 home equity loan, only the interest on the first $100,000 is deductible. The interest on the remaining $20,000 is not deductible because it exceeds the statutory ceiling of $100,000. ▼

Interest Paid for Services. Mortgage loan companies commonly charge a fee for finding, placing, or processing a mortgage loan. Such fees are often called **points** and are expressed as a percentage of the loan amount. Borrowers often have to pay points to obtain the necessary financing. To qualify as deductible interest, the points must be considered compensation to a lender solely for the use or forbearance of money. The points cannot be a form of service charge or payment for specific services if they are to qualify as deductible interest.[24]

Points must be capitalized and are amortized and deductible ratably over the life of the loan. A special exception permits the purchaser of a personal residence to deduct qualifying points in the year of payment.[25] The exception also covers points paid to obtain funds for home improvements.

EXAMPLE 23

During 1997, Thelma purchased a new residence for $130,000 and paid points of $2,600 to obtain mortgage financing. At Thelma's election, the $2,600 can be claimed as an interest deduction for tax year 1997. ▼

---

[24] Rev.Rul. 67–297, 1967–2 C.B. 87.   [25] § 461(g)(2).

> ### TAX IN THE NEWS
>
> #### DEDUCTION FOR MORTGAGE INTEREST COSTS GOVERNMENT BILLIONS
>
> Homeowners are allowed to deduct mortgage interest and real property taxes on their homes. On the other hand, tenants are not allowed to deduct the interest and taxes passed through to them by their landlords in the form of rent. These deductions are leading targets of many proponents of tax reform, who argue that it is not equitable to allow mortgage interest and property tax deductions to homeowners while denying comparable deductions to renters. Another issue, frequently debated in Congress, is the cost of the mortgage interest deduction. The Joint Committee on Taxation (refer to Chapter 2) estimates that the home mortgage interest deduction will cost the government $333.1 billion in lost revenue over the five years from 1996 through 2000.
>
> SOURCE: The staff of the Joint Committee on Taxation.

Points paid to *refinance* an existing home mortgage cannot be immediately expensed, but must be capitalized and amortized as interest expense over the life of the new loan.[26]

EXAMPLE 24 Sandra purchased her residence four years ago, obtaining a 30-year mortgage at an annual interest rate of 12%. In the current year, Sandra refinances the mortgage in order to reduce the interest rate to 9%. To obtain the refinancing, she had to pay points of $2,600. The $2,600 paid comes under the usual rule applicable to points. The $2,600 must be capitalized and amortized over the life of the mortgage. ▼

The rules governing the deductibility of points *paid by a seller* to help a buyer finance the purchase of the residence were changed in 1994.[27] Under prior rules, such points were not deductible by the buyer, but were treated by the seller as a reduction of the selling price of the property.

The IRS changed its position on this issue, retroactive to tax years beginning after December 31, 1990. In effect, points paid by the seller are treated as an adjustment to the price of the residence, and the buyer is treated as having used cash to pay the points that were paid by the seller. A buyer may deduct seller-paid points in the tax year in which they are paid if several conditions are met. Refer to Revenue Procedure 94–27 for a complete list of these conditions (see footnote 27 for citation).

Prepayment Penalty. When a mortgage or loan is paid off in full in a lump sum before its term (early), the lending institution may require an additional payment of a certain percentage applied to the unpaid amount at the time of prepayment. This is known as a prepayment penalty and is considered to be interest (e.g., personal, qualified residence, investment) in the year paid. The general rules for deductibility of interest also apply to prepayment penalties.

---

[26] Rev.Rul. 87–22, 1987–1 C.B. 146.

[27] Rev.Proc. 94–27, 1994–1 C.B. 613.

Interest Paid to Related Parties.
Nothing prevents the deduction of interest paid to a related party as long as the payment actually took place and the interest meets the requirements for deductibility. Recall from Chapter 6 that a special rule for related taxpayers applies when the debtor uses the accrual basis and the related creditor is on the cash basis. If this rule is applicable, interest that has been accrued but not paid at the end of the debtor's tax year is not deductible until payment is made and the income is reportable by the cash basis recipient.

Tax-Exempt Securities.
The tax law provides that no deduction is allowed for interest on debt incurred to purchase or carry tax-exempt securities.[28] A major problem for the courts has been to determine what is meant by the words *to purchase or carry*. Refer to Chapter 6 for a detailed discussion of these issues.

RESTRICTIONS ON DEDUCTIBILITY AND TIMING CONSIDERATIONS

Taxpayer's Obligation.
Allowed interest is deductible if the related debt represents a bona fide obligation for which the taxpayer is liable.[29] Thus, a taxpayer may not deduct interest paid on behalf of another individual. For interest to be deductible, both the debtor and creditor must intend for the loan to be repaid. Intent of the parties can be especially crucial between related parties such as a shareholder and a closely held corporation. A shareholder may not deduct interest paid by the corporation on his or her behalf.[30] Likewise, a husband may not deduct interest paid on his wife's property if he files a separate return, except in the case of qualified residence interest. If both husband and wife consent in writing, either the husband or the wife may deduct the allowed interest on the principal residence and one other residence.

Time of Deduction.
Generally, interest must be paid to secure a deduction unless the taxpayer uses the accrual method of accounting. Under the accrual method, interest is deductible ratably over the life of the loan.

EXAMPLE 25

On November 1, 1997, Ramon borrows $1,000 to purchase appliances for a rental house. The loan is payable in 90 days at 12% interest. On the due date in January 1998, Ramon pays the $1,000 note and interest amounting to $30. Ramon can deduct the accrued portion ($2/3 \times \$30 = \$20$) of the interest in 1997 only if he is an accrual basis taxpayer. Otherwise, the entire amount of interest ($30) is deductible in 1998. ▼

Prepaid Interest.
Accrual method reporting is imposed on cash basis taxpayers for interest prepayments that extend beyond the end of the taxable year.[31] Such payments must be allocated to the tax years to which the interest payments relate. These provisions are intended to prevent cash basis taxpayers from *manufacturing* tax deductions before the end of the year by prepaying interest.

CLASSIFICATION OF INTEREST EXPENSE

Whether interest is deductible *for* AGI or as an itemized deduction *(from)* depends on whether the indebtedness has a business, investment, or personal purpose. If the indebtedness is incurred in relation to a business (other than performing services as an employee) or for the production of rent or royalty income, the

---

[28] § 265(a)(2).
[29] *Arcade Realty Co.*, 35 T.C. 256 (1960).
[30] *Continental Trust Co.*, 7 B.T.A. 539 (1927).
[31] § 461(g)(1).

Concept Summary 10-1

Deductibility of Personal, Investment, and Mortgage Interest

Type	Deductible	Comments
Personal (consumer) interest	No	Includes any interest that is not home mortgage interest, investment interest, or business interest. Examples include car loans, credit cards, etc.
Investment interest (*not* related to rental or royalty property)	Yes	Itemized deduction; limited to net investment income for the year; disallowed interest can be carried over to future years.
Investment interest (related to rental or royalty property)	Yes	Deduction *for* AGI; limited to net investment income for the year; disallowed interest can be carried over to future years.
Qualified residence interest on acquisition indebtedness	Yes	Deductible as an itemized deduction; limited to indebtedness of $1 million.
Qualified residence interest on home equity indebtedness	Yes	Deductible as an itemized deduction; limited to indebtedness equal to lesser of $100,000 or FMV of residence minus acquisition indebtedness.

interest is deductible *for* AGI. If the indebtedness is incurred for personal use, such as qualified residence interest, any deduction allowed is reported on Schedule A of Form 1040 if the taxpayer elects to itemize. If the taxpayer is an employee who incurs debt in relation to his or her employment, the interest is considered to be personal, or consumer, interest. Business expenses appear on Schedule C of Form 1040, and expenses related to rents or royalties are reported on Schedule E.

If a taxpayer deposits money in a certificate of deposit (CD) that has a term of one year or less and the interest cannot be withdrawn without penalty, the full amount of the interest must still be included in income, even though part of the interest is forfeited due to an early withdrawal. However, the taxpayer will be allowed a deduction *for* AGI as to the forfeited amount.

CHARITABLE CONTRIBUTIONS

6 Learning Objective
Understand charitable contributions and their related measurement problems and percentage limitations.

Individuals and corporations are allowed to deduct contributions made to qualified *domestic* organizations.[32] Contributions to qualified charitable organizations serve certain social welfare needs and thus relieve the government of the cost of providing these needed services to the community.

The **charitable contribution** provisions are among the most complex in the tax law. To determine the amount deductible as a charitable contribution, several important questions must be answered:

- What constitutes a charitable contribution?
- Was the contribution made to a qualified organization?
- When is the contribution deductible?
- What record-keeping and reporting requirements apply to charitable contributions?

---
[32] § 170.

- How is the value of donated property determined?
- What special rules apply to contributions of property that has increased in value?
- What percentage limitations apply to the charitable contribution deduction?

These questions are addressed in the sections that follow.

CRITERIA FOR A GIFT

A *charitable contribution* is defined as a gift made to a qualified organization.[33] The major elements needed to qualify a contribution as a gift are a donative intent, the absence of consideration, and acceptance by the donee. Consequently, the taxpayer has the burden of establishing that the transfer was made from motives of *disinterested generosity* as established by the courts.[34] This test is quite subjective and has led to problems of interpretation (refer to the discussion of gifts in Chapter 5).

Benefit Received Rule. When a donor derives a tangible benefit from a contribution, he or she cannot deduct the value of the benefit.

EXAMPLE 26 Ralph purchases a ticket at $100 for a special performance of the local symphony (a qualified charity). If the price of a ticket to a symphony concert is normally $35, Ralph is allowed only $65 as a charitable contribution. ▼

An exception to this benefit rule provides for the deduction of an automatic percentage of the amount paid for the right to purchase athletic tickets from colleges and universities.[35] Under this exception, 80 percent of the amount paid to or for the benefit of the institution qualifies as a charitable contribution deduction.

EXAMPLE 27 Janet donates $500 to State University's athletic department. The payment guarantees that she will have preferred seating on the 50-yard line. Subsequently, Janet buys four $35 game tickets. Under the exception to the benefit rule, she is allowed a $400 (80% of $500) charitable contribution deduction for the taxable year.

If, however, Janet's $500 donation includes four $35 tickets, that portion [$140 ($35 × 4)] and the remaining portion of $360 ($500 − $140) are treated as separate amounts. Thus, Janet is allowed a charitable contribution deduction of $288 (80% of $360). ▼

Contribution of Services. No deduction is allowed for a contribution of one's services to a qualified charitable organization. However, unreimbursed expenses related to the services rendered may be deductible. For example, the cost of a uniform (without general utility) that is required to be worn while performing services may be deductible, as are certain out-of-pocket transportation costs incurred for the benefit of the charity. In lieu of these out-of-pocket costs for an automobile, a standard mileage rate of 12 cents per mile is allowed.[36] Deductions are permitted for transportation, reasonable expenses for lodging, and the cost of meals while away from home incurred in performing the donated services. The travel may not involve a significant element of personal pleasure, recreation, or vacation.[37]

---

[33] § 170(c).
[34] *Comm. v. Duberstein*, 60–2 USTC ¶9515, 5 AFTR2d 1626, 80 S.Ct. 1190 (USSC, 1960).
[35] § 170(l).
[36] § 170(i).
[37] § 170(j).

EXAMPLE 28

Grace, a delegate representing her church in Miami, Florida, travels to a two-day national meeting in Denver, Colorado, in February. After the meeting, Grace spends two weeks at a nearby ski resort. Under these circumstances, none of the transportation, meals, or lodging is deductible since the travel involved a significant element of personal pleasure, recreation, or vacation. ▼

Nondeductible Items. In addition to the benefit received rule and the restrictions placed on contribution of services, the following items may *not* be deducted as charitable contributions:

- Dues, fees, or bills paid to country clubs, lodges, fraternal orders, or similar groups.
- Cost of raffle, bingo, or lottery tickets.
- Cost of tuition.
- Value of blood given to a blood bank.
- Donations to homeowners associations.
- Gifts to individuals.
- Rental value of property used by a qualified charity.

QUALIFIED ORGANIZATIONS

To be deductible, a contribution must be made to one of the following organizations:[38]

- A state or possession of the United States or any subdivisions thereof.
- A corporation, trust, or community chest, fund, or foundation that is situated in the United States and is organized and operated exclusively for religious, charitable, scientific, literary, or educational purposes or for the prevention of cruelty to children or animals.
- A veterans' organization.
- A fraternal organization operating under the lodge system.
- A cemetery company.

The IRS publishes a list of organizations that have applied for and received tax-exempt status under § 501 of the Code.[39] This publication is updated frequently and may be helpful in determining if a gift has been made to a qualifying charitable organization.

Because gifts made to needy individuals are not deductible, a deduction will not be permitted if a gift is received by a donee in an individual capacity rather than as a representative of a qualifying organization.

TIME OF DEDUCTION

A charitable contribution generally is deducted in the year the payment is made. This rule applies to both cash and accrual basis individuals. A contribution is ordinarily deemed to have been made on the delivery of the property to the donee. For example, if a gift of securities (properly endorsed) is made to a qualified charitable organization, the gift is considered complete on the day of

---

[38] § 170(c).
[39] Although this *Cumulative List of Organizations*, IRS Publication 78 (available by purchase from the Superintendent of Documents, U.S. Government Printing Office, Washington, DC 20402), may be helpful, qualified organizations are not required to be listed. Not all organizations that qualify are listed in this publication.

delivery or mailing. However, if the donor delivers the certificate to his or her bank or broker or to the issuing corporation, the gift is considered complete on the date the stock is transferred on the books of the corporation.

A contribution made by check is considered delivered on the date of mailing. Thus, a check mailed on December 31, 1997, is deductible on the taxpayer's 1997 tax return. If the contribution is charged on a bank credit card, the date the charge is made determines the year of deduction.

RECORD-KEEPING AND VALUATION REQUIREMENTS

Record-Keeping Requirements. No deduction is allowed for contributions of $250 or more unless the taxpayer obtains *written substantiation* of the contribution from the charitable organization. The substantiation must specify the amount of cash and a description (but not value) of any property other than cash contributed. The substantiation must be obtained before the earlier of (1) the due date (including extensions) of the return for the year the contribution is claimed or (2) the date such return is filed.[40]

Additional information is required if the value of the donated property is over $500 but not over $5,000. Also, the taxpayer must file Section A of Form 8283 (Noncash Charitable Contributions) for such contributions.

For noncash contributions with a claimed value in excess of $5,000 ($10,000 in the case of nonpublicly traded stock), the taxpayer must obtain a qualified appraisal and must file Section B of Form 8283. This schedule must show a summary of the appraisal and must be attached to the taxpayer's return. Failure to comply with these reporting rules may result in disallowance of the charitable contribution deduction. Additionally, significant overvaluation exposes the taxpayer to rather stringent penalties.

Valuation Requirements. Property donated to a charity is generally valued at fair market value at the time the gift is made. The Code and Regulations give very little guidance on the measurement of the fair market value except to say, "The fair market value is the price at which the property would change hands between a willing buyer and a willing seller, neither being under any compulsion to buy or sell and both having reasonable knowledge of relevant facts."

Generally, charitable organizations do not attest to the fair market value of the donated property. Nevertheless, the taxpayer must maintain reliable written evidence of the following information concerning the donation:

- The fair market value of the property and how that value was determined.
- The amount of the reduction in the value of the property (if required) for certain appreciated property and how that reduction was determined.
- Terms of any agreement with the charitable organization dealing with the use of the property and potential sale or other disposition of the property by the organization.
- A signed copy of the appraisal if the value of the property was determined by appraisal. Only for a contribution of art with an aggregate value of $20,000 or more must the appraisal be attached to the taxpayer's return.

---

[40] § 170(f)(8).

ETHICAL CONSIDERATIONS

A Second Appraisal

Ken donated a painting to the Hamilton City Art Museum. He acquired the painting 20 years ago at a cost of $10,000. Ken had the painting appraised by the owner of a Hamilton art store, a qualified art appraiser, who estimated its value at $50,000. Ken believed the painting was worth more than $50,000, so he had it appraised by an art dealer from Chicago. The Chicago art dealer, also a qualified art appraiser, appraised the painting at a value of $120,000. Ken itemized deductions and took a charitable contribution deduction of $120,000. Was Ken justified in taking a deduction based on the higher appraisal?

LIMITATIONS ON CHARITABLE CONTRIBUTION DEDUCTION

In General. The potential charitable contribution deduction is the total of all donations, both money and property, that qualify for the deduction. After this determination is made, the actual amount of the charitable contribution deduction that is allowed for individuals for the tax year is limited as follows:

- If the qualifying contributions for the year total 20 percent or less of AGI, they are fully deductible.
- If the qualifying contributions are more than 20 percent of AGI, the deductible amount may be limited to either 20 percent, 30 percent, or 50 percent of AGI, depending on the type of property given and the type of organization to which the donation is made.
- In any case, the maximum charitable contribution deduction may not exceed 50 percent of AGI for the tax year.

To understand the complex rules for computing the amount of a charitable contribution, it is necessary to understand the distinction between capital gain property and ordinary income property. In addition, it is necessary to understand when the 50 percent, 30 percent, and 20 percent limitations apply. If a taxpayer's contributions for the year exceed the applicable percentage limitations, the excess contributions may be carried forward and deducted during a five-year carryover period. These topics are discussed in the sections that follow.

Ordinary Income Property. *Ordinary income property* is any property that, if sold, will result in the recognition of ordinary income. The term includes inventory for sale in the taxpayer's trade or business, a work of art created by the donor, and a manuscript prepared by the donor. It also includes, *for purposes of the charitable contribution calculation,* a capital asset held by the donor for less than the required holding period for long-term capital gain treatment. To the extent that disposition of property results in the recognition of ordinary income due to the recapture of depreciation, it is ordinary income property.[41]

If ordinary income property is contributed, the deduction is equal to the fair market value of the property less the amount of ordinary income that would have been reported if the property were sold. In most instances, the deduction is limited to the adjusted basis of the property to the donor.

---

[41] For a more complete discussion of the difference between ordinary income and capital gain property, see Chapter 16.

EXAMPLE 29 Tim owned stock in White Corporation that he donated to a university on May 1, 1997. Tim had purchased the stock for $2,500 on March 3, 1997, and the stock had a value of $3,600 when he made the donation. Since he had not held the property long enough to meet the long-term capital gain requirement, Tim would have recognized a short-term capital gain of $1,100 if he had sold the property. Since short-term capital gain property is treated as ordinary income property for charitable contribution purposes, Tim's charitable contribution deduction is limited to the property's adjusted basis of $2,500 ($3,600 − $1,100 = $2,500). ▼

In Example 29, suppose the stock had a fair market value of $2,300 (rather than $3,600) when it was donated to charity. Because the fair market value now is less than the adjusted basis, the charitable contribution deduction is $2,300.

Capital Gain Property.   **Capital gain property** is any property that would have resulted in the recognition of long-term capital gain or § 1231 gain if the property had been sold by the donor. As a general rule, the deduction for a contribution of capital gain property is equal to the fair market value of the property.

Two major exceptions disallow the deductibility of the appreciation on long-term capital gain property. One exception concerns certain private foundations. Private foundations are organizations that traditionally do not receive their funding from the general public (e.g., the Ford Foundation). Generally, foundations fall into two categories: operating and nonoperating. A private *operating* foundation is one that spends substantially all of its income in the active conduct of the charitable undertaking for which it was established. Other private foundations are *nonoperating* foundations. However, if a private nonoperating foundation distributes the contributions it receives according to special rules within two and one-half months following the year of the contribution, the organization is treated the same as public charities and private operating foundations. Often, only the private foundation knows its status (operating or nonoperating) for sure, and the status can change from year to year.

If capital gain property is contributed to a private nonoperating foundation, the taxpayer must reduce the contribution by the long-term capital gain that would have been recognized if the property had been sold at its fair market value. The effect of this provision is to limit the deduction to the property's adjusted basis.[42]

EXAMPLE 30 Walter purchases stock for $800 on January 1, 1975, and donates it to a private nonoperating foundation on June 21, 1997, when it is worth $2,000. Walter's charitable contribution is $800 ($2,000 − $1,200), the stock's basis. ▼

If, in Example 30, Walter had donated the stock to either a public charity or a private operating foundation, his charitable contribution would be $2,000, the fair market value of the stock.

A second exception applying to capital gain property relates to *tangible personalty*. Tangible personalty is all property that is not realty (land and buildings) and does not include intangible property such as stock or securities. If tangible personalty is contributed to a public charity such as a museum, church, or university, the charitable deduction may have to be reduced. The amount of the reduction is the long-term capital gain that would have been recognized if the property had been sold for its fair market value. The reduction is required *if* the

---

[42] For a limited period, taxpayers who donate *qualified appreciated stock* to private nonoperating foundations may deduct the fair market value of the stock. Qualified appreciated stock is stock for which market quotations are readily available on an established securities market. This provision applies to stock contributed from July 1, 1996, through May 31, 1997.

property is put to an unrelated use. The term *unrelated use* means a use that is unrelated to the exempt purpose or function of the charitable organization.

A taxpayer in this instance must establish that the property is not in fact being put to an unrelated use by the donee. The taxpayer must also establish that at the time of the contribution it was reasonable to anticipate that the property would not be put to an unrelated use. For a contribution of personalty to a museum, if the work of art is the kind of art normally retained by the museum, it is reasonable for a donor to anticipate that the work of art will not be put to an unrelated use. This is the case even if the object is later sold or exchanged by the museum.[43]

EXAMPLE 31

Myrtle contributes a Picasso painting, for which she paid $20,000, to a local museum. She had owned the painting for four years. It had a value of $30,000 at the time of the donation. The museum displayed the painting for two years and subsequently sold it for $50,000. The charitable contribution is $30,000. It is not reduced by the unrealized appreciation since the painting was put to a related use even though it was later sold by the museum. ▼

Fifty Percent Ceiling. Contributions made to public charities may not exceed 50 percent of an individual's AGI for the year. Excess contributions may be carried over to the next five years. The 50 percent ceiling on contributions applies to the following types of public charities:

- A church or a convention or association of churches.
- An educational organization that maintains a regular faculty and curriculum.
- A hospital or medical school.
- An organization supported by the government that holds property or investments for the benefit of a college or university.
- A Federal, state, or local governmental unit.
- An organization normally receiving a substantial part of its support from the public or a governmental unit.

In the remaining discussion of charitable contributions, public charities and private foundations (both operating and nonoperating) that qualify for the 50 percent ceiling will be referred to as *50 percent organizations*.

The 50 percent ceiling also applies to contributions to the following organizations:

- All private operating foundations.
- Certain private nonoperating foundations that distribute the contributions they receive to public charities and private operating foundations within two and one-half months following the year they receive the contribution.
- Certain private nonoperating foundations in which the contributions are pooled in a common fund and the income and principal sum are paid to public charities.

Thirty Percent Ceiling. A 30 percent ceiling applies to contributions of cash and ordinary income property to private nonoperating foundations that are not 50 percent organizations. The 30 percent ceiling also applies to contributions of appreciated capital gain property to 50 percent organizations unless the taxpayer makes a special election (see below).

---

[43] Reg. § 1.170A–4(b)(3)(ii)(b).

In the event the contributions for any one tax year involve both 50 percent and 30 percent property, the allowable deduction comes first from the 50 percent property.

EXAMPLE 32

During the year, Lisa made the following donations to her church: cash of $2,000 and unimproved land worth $30,000. Lisa had purchased the land four years ago for $22,000 and held it as an investment. Therefore, it is long-term capital gain property. Lisa's AGI for the year is $50,000. Disregarding percentage limitations, Lisa's potential deduction is $32,000 [$2,000 (cash) + $30,000 (fair market value of land)].

In applying the percentage limitations, however, the *current* deduction for the land is limited to $15,000 [30% (limitation applicable to long-term capital gain property) × $50,000 (AGI)]. Thus, the total deduction is $17,000 ($2,000 cash + $15,000 land). Note that the total deduction does not exceed $25,000, which is 50% of Lisa's AGI. ▼

Under a special election, a taxpayer may choose to forgo a deduction of the appreciation on capital gain property. Referred to as the *reduced deduction election*, this enables the taxpayer to move from the 30 percent limitation to the 50 percent limitation.

EXAMPLE 33

Assume the same facts as in Example 32, except that Lisa makes the reduced deduction election. Now the deduction becomes $24,000 [$2,000 (cash) + $22,000 (basis in land)] because both donations fall under the 50% limitation. Thus, by making the election, Lisa has increased her charitable contribution deduction by $7,000 [$24,000 − $17,000 (Example 32)]. ▼

Although the reduced deduction election appears attractive, it should be considered carefully. The election sacrifices a deduction for the appreciation on long-term capital gain property that might eventually be allowed. Note that in Example 32, the potential deduction was $32,000, yet in Example 33 only $24,000 is allowed. The reason the potential deduction is decreased by $8,000 ($32,000 − $24,000) is that no carryover is allowed for the amount sacrificed by the election.

Twenty Percent Ceiling. A 20 percent ceiling applies to contributions of appreciated long-term capital gain property to private nonoperating foundations that are not 50 percent organizations.

Contribution Carryovers. Contributions that exceed the percentage limitations for the current year can be carried over for five years. In the carryover process, such contributions do not lose their identity for limitation purposes. Thus, if the contribution originally involved 30 percent property, the carryover will continue to be classified as 30 percent property in the carryover year.

EXAMPLE 34

Assume the same facts as in Example 32. Because only $15,000 of the $30,000 value of the land was deducted in the current year, the balance of $15,000 may be carried over to the following year. But the carryover will still be treated as long-term capital gain property and is subject to the 30%-of-AGI limitation. ▼

In applying the percentage limitations, current charitable contributions must be claimed first before any carryovers can be considered. If carryovers involve more than one year, they are utilized in a first-in, first-out order.

Concept Summary 10-2

Determining the Deduction for Contributions of Appreciated Property by Individuals

If the Type of Property Contributed Is:	And the Property Is Contributed to:	The Contribution Is Measured by:	But the Deduction Is Limited to:
1. Capital gain property	A 50% organization	Fair market value of the property	30% of AGI
2. Ordinary income property	A 50% organization	The basis of the property*	50% of AGI
3. Capital gain property (and the property is tangible personal property put to an unrelated use by the donee)	A 50% organization	The basis of the property*	50% of AGI
4. Capital gain property (and the reduced deduction is elected)	A 50% organization	The basis of the property	50% of AGI
5. Capital gain property	A private nonoperating foundation that is not a 50% organization	The basis of the property*	The lesser of: 1. 20% of AGI 2. 50% of AGI minus other contributions to 50% organizations

*If the fair market value of the property is less than the adjusted basis (i.e., the property has declined in value instead of appreciating), the fair market value is used.

MISCELLANEOUS ITEMIZED DEDUCTIONS

7 LEARNING OBJECTIVE
List the business and personal expenditures that are deductible either as miscellaneous itemized deductions or as other itemized deductions.

No deduction is allowed for personal, living, or family expenses.[44] However, a taxpayer may incur a number of expenditures related to employment. If an employee or outside salesperson incurs unreimbursed business expenses or expenses that are reimbursed under a nonaccountable plan, including travel and transportation, the expenses are deductible as **miscellaneous itemized deductions**.[45] Certain other expenses also fall into the special category of miscellaneous itemized deductions. Some are deductible only if, in total, they exceed 2 percent of the taxpayer's AGI. These miscellaneous itemized deductions include (but are not limited to) the following:

- Professional dues to membership organizations.
- Uniforms or other clothing that cannot be used for normal wear.

---
[44] § 262.
[45] Actors and performing artists who meet certain requirements are not subject to this rule.

TAX IN THE NEWS

A TICKET TO JAIL?

If you won the lottery, would you be willing to pay the income tax due on your winnings? Apparently, a Massachusetts lottery winner was not. In 1985, Phillip won $2.7 million, payable over 20 years. He reported a $135,000 annual payment on his 1989 Federal income tax return and deducted gambling losses of $200,000. As a result of the alleged $65,000 gambling loss, Phillip filed for a $26,000 tax refund. This is a violation of the tax law, which limits the deduction of gambling losses to the amount of gambling winnings. However, there was a more serious problem with his tax-saving strategy. Upon audit, Phillip presented the IRS with $200,000 in losing lottery tickets to substantiate his loss. The IRS alleges that he paid $500 to rent the tickets from a Massachusetts man who collected losing lottery tickets. His accountant wrote a note to the owner indicating that Phillip was borrowing the tickets and would return them in good condition. Now Phillip faces up to five years in prison and a $250,000 fine. His accountant, a former IRS agent, faces up to eight years in prison and a $500,000 fine.

SOURCE: Ross Kerber, "Lottery Winner's Alleged Scheme May Be Just the Ticket . . . to Jail," *Wall Street Journal,* March 14, 1996, p. B1.

- Fees incurred for the preparation of one's tax return or fees incurred for tax litigation before the IRS or the courts.
- Job-hunting costs.
- Fee paid for a safe deposit box used to store papers and documents relating to taxable income-producing investments.
- Investment expenses that are deductible under § 212 as discussed in Chapter 6.
- Appraisal fees to determine the amount of a casualty loss or the fair market value of donated property.
- Hobby losses up to the amount of hobby income (see Chapter 6).
- Unreimbursed employee expenses (see Chapter 9).

Certain employee business expenses that are reimbursed are not itemized deductions, but are deducted *for* AGI. Employee business expenses are discussed in depth in Chapter 9.

OTHER MISCELLANEOUS DEDUCTIONS

Certain expenses and losses do not fall into any category of itemized deductions already discussed but are nonetheless deductible. The following expenses and losses are deductible on line 27 of Schedule A as Other Miscellaneous Deductions.

- Gambling losses up to the amount of gambling winnings.
- Impairment-related work expenses of a handicapped person.
- Federal estate tax on income in respect of a decedent.
- Deduction for repayment of amounts under a claim of right if more than $3,000 (discussed in Chapter 18).
- The unrecovered investment in an annuity contract when the annuity ceases by reason of death, discussed in Chapter 4.

Unlike the expenses and losses discussed previously under Miscellaneous Itemized Deductions, the above expenses and losses are not subject to the 2 percent-of-AGI floor.

COMPREHENSIVE EXAMPLE OF SCHEDULE A

Harry and Jean Brown, married filing jointly, had the following transactions for the current year:

• Medicines that required a prescription	$ 430
• Doctor and dentist bills paid and not reimbursed	2,120
• Medical insurance premium payments	1,200
• Contact lenses	175
• Transportation for medical purposes (380 miles × 10 cents/mile + $5.00 parking)	43
• State income tax withheld	620
• Real estate taxes	1,580
• Interest paid on qualified residence mortgage	2,840
• Charitable contributions in cash	860
• Transportation in performing charitable services (860 miles × 12 cents/mile + $15.80 parking and tolls)	119
• Unreimbursed employee expenses (from a Form 2106)	870
• Tax return preparation	150
• Safe deposit box (used for keeping investment documents and tax records)	170

The Browns' AGI is $40,000. Their completed 1996 Schedule A on the following page reports itemized deductions totaling $7,377.

OVERALL LIMITATION ON CERTAIN ITEMIZED DEDUCTIONS

8 LEARNING OBJECTIVE
Recognize the limitation on certain itemized deductions applicable to high-income taxpayers.

Congress has enacted several provisions limiting tax benefits for high-income taxpayers. These limitations include the exemption phase-out (refer to Chapter 3) and a phase-out of itemized deductions. The phase-out of itemized deductions (also referred to as a cutback adjustment) applies to taxpayers whose AGI exceeds $121,200 ($60,600 for married taxpayers filing separately).[46] The limitation applies to the following frequently encountered itemized deductions:[47]

- Taxes.
- Home mortgage interest, including points.
- Charitable contributions.
- Unreimbursed employee expenses subject to the 2 percent-of-AGI floor.
- All other expenses subject to the 2 percent-of-AGI floor.

---

[46] For 1996, the limitation applied if AGI exceeded $117,950 ($58,975 for married taxpayers filing separately).

[47] Other deductions subject to the limitation include Federal estate tax on income in respect of a decedent, certain amortizable bond premiums, the deduction for repayment of certain amounts, certain unrecovered investments in an annuity, and impairment-related work expenses.

Schedule A—Itemized Deductions

SCHEDULES A&B (Form 1040)
Department of the Treasury
Internal Revenue Service (99)

(Schedule B is on back)
▶ Attach to Form 1040. ▶ See Instructions for Schedules A and B (Form 1040).

OMB No. 1545-0074
1996
Attachment Sequence No. 07

Name(s) shown on Form 1040: *Harry and Jean Brown*
Your social security number: 371 : 30 : 3987

Medical and Dental Expenses

Caution: Do not include expenses reimbursed or paid by others.

Line	Description	Amount	Total
1	Medical and dental expenses (see page A-1)	3,968	
2	Enter amount from Form 1040, line 32	40,000	
3	Multiply line 2 above by 7.5% (.075)	3,000	
4	Subtract line 3 from line 1. If line 3 is more than line 1, enter -0-		968

Taxes You Paid
(See page A-1.)

Line	Description	Amount	Total
5	State and local income taxes	620	
6	Real estate taxes (see page A-2)	1,580	
7	Personal property taxes		
8	Other taxes. List type and amount ▶		
9	Add lines 5 through 8		2,200

Interest You Paid
(See page A-2.)

Note: Personal interest is not deductible.

Line	Description	Amount	Total
10	Home mortgage interest and points reported to you on Form 1098	2,840	
11	Home mortgage interest not reported to you on Form 1098. If paid to the person from whom you bought the home, see page A-2 and show that person's name, identifying no., and address ▶		
12	Points not reported to you on Form 1098. See page A-3 for special rules		
13	Investment interest. If required, attach Form 4952. (See page A-3.)		
14	Add lines 10 through 13		2,840

Gifts to Charity

If you made a gift and got a benefit for it, see page A-3.

Line	Description	Amount	Total
15	Gifts by cash or check. If you made any gift of $250 or more, see page A-3	860	
16	Other than by cash or check. If any gift of $250 or more, see page A-3. If over $500, you **MUST** attach Form 8283	119	
17	Carryover from prior year		
18	Add lines 15 through 17		979

Casualty and Theft Losses

19	Casualty or theft loss(es). Attach Form 4684. (See page A-4.)	

Job Expenses and Most Other Miscellaneous Deductions
(See page A-4 for expenses to deduct here.)

Line	Description	Amount	Total
20	Unreimbursed employee expenses—job travel, union dues, job education, etc. If required, you **MUST** attach Form 2106 or 2106-EZ. (See page A-4.) ▶ *Form 2106 $870*	870	
21	Tax preparation fees	150	
22	Other expenses—investment, safe deposit box, etc. List type and amount ▶ *Safe deposit box, $170*	170	
23	Add lines 20 through 22	1,190	
24	Enter amount from Form 1040, line 32	40,000	
25	Multiply line 24 above by 2% (.02)	800	
26	Subtract line 25 from line 23. If line 25 is more than line 23, enter -0-		390

Other Miscellaneous Deductions

Line	Description
27	Other—from list on page A-4. List type and amount ▶

Total Itemized Deductions

28 Is Form 1040, line 32, over $117,950 (over $58,975 if married filing separately)?
 NO. Your deduction is not limited. Add the amounts in the far right column for lines 4 through 27. Also, enter on Form 1040, line 34, the **larger** of this amount or your standard deduction.
 YES. Your deduction may be limited. See page A-5 for the amount to enter.

▶ 28 **7,377**

For Paperwork Reduction Act Notice, see Form 1040 instructions.   Cat. No. 11330X   Schedule A (Form 1040) 1996

The following deductions are *not* subject to the limitation on itemized deductions:

- Medical and dental expenses.
- Investment interest expense.
- Nonbusiness casualty and theft losses.
- Gambling losses.

Taxpayers subject to the limitation must reduce itemized deductions by the lesser of:

- 3 percent of the amount by which AGI exceeds $121,200 ($60,600 if married filing separately).
- 80 percent of itemized deductions that are affected by the limit.

The overall limitation is applied after applying all other limitations to itemized deductions that are affected by the overall limitation. Other limitations apply to charitable contributions, certain meals and entertainment expenses, and certain miscellaneous itemized deductions.

EXAMPLE 35

Herman, who is single, had AGI of $200,000 for 1997. He incurred the following expenses and losses during the year:

Medical expenses before 7.5%-of-AGI limitation	$16,000
State and local income taxes	3,200
Real estate taxes	2,800
Home mortgage interest	7,200
Charitable contributions	2,000
Casualty loss before 10% limitation (after $100 floor)	21,500
Unreimbursed employee expenses subject to 2%-of-AGI limitation	4,300
Gambling losses (Herman had $3,000 gambling income)	7,000

Herman's itemized deductions *before* the overall limitation are computed as follows:

Medical expenses [$16,000 − (7.5% × $200,000)]	$ 1,000
State and local income taxes	3,200
Real estate taxes	2,800
Home mortgage interest	7,200
Charitable contributions	2,000
Casualty loss [$21,500 − (10% × $200,000)]	1,500
Unreimbursed employee expenses ($4,300 − (2% × $200,000)]	300
Gambling losses ($7,000 loss limited to $3,000 of gambling income)	3,000
Total itemized deductions before overall limitation	$21,000

Herman's itemized deductions subject to the overall limitation are as follows:

State and local income taxes	$ 3,200
Real estate taxes	2,800
Home mortgage interest	7,200
Charitable contributions	2,000
Unreimbursed employee expenses	300
Total	$15,500

Herman must reduce this amount by the smaller of the following:

• 3% ($200,000 AGI − $121,200)	$2,364
• 80% of itemized deductions subject to limitation ($15,500 × .80)	12,400

Therefore, the amount of the reduction is $2,364, and Herman has $18,636 of deductible itemized deductions, computed as follows:

Deductible itemized deductions subject to overall limitation ($15,500 − $2,364)	$13,136
Itemized deductions not subject to overall limitation:	
Medical expenses	1,000
Casualty loss	1,500
Gambling losses	3,000
Deductible itemized deductions	$18,636

TAX PLANNING CONSIDERATIONS

9 LEARNING OBJECTIVE
Identify tax planning procedures that can maximize the benefit of itemized deductions.

EFFECTIVE UTILIZATION OF ITEMIZED DEDUCTIONS

Since an individual may use the standard deduction in one year and itemize deductions in another year, it is frequently possible to obtain maximum benefit by shifting itemized deductions from one year to another. For example, if a taxpayer's itemized deductions and the standard deduction are approximately the same for each year of a two-year period, the taxpayer should use the standard deduction in one year and shift itemized deductions (to the extent permitted by law) to the other year. The individual could, for example, prepay a church pledge for a particular year to shift the deduction to the current year or avoid paying end-of-the-year medical expenses to shift the deduction to the following year.

UTILIZATION OF MEDICAL DEDUCTIONS

When a taxpayer anticipates that medical expenses will approximate the percentage floor, much might be done to generate a deductible excess. Any of the following procedures can help build a deduction by the end of the year:

- Incur the obligation for needed dental work or have needed work carried out.[48] Orthodontic treatment, for example, may have been recommended for a member of the taxpayer's family.
- Have elective remedial surgery that may have been postponed from prior years (e.g., tonsillectomies, vasectomies, correction of hernias, hysterectomies).
- Incur the obligation for capital improvements to the taxpayer's personal residence recommended by a physician (e.g., an air filtration system to alleviate a respiratory disorder).

As an aid to taxpayers who may experience temporary cash-flow problems at the end of the year, the use of bank credit cards is deemed to be payment for purposes of timing the deductibility of charitable and medical expenses.

---

[48] Prepayment of medical expenses does not generate a current deduction unless the taxpayer is under an obligation to make the payment.

EXAMPLE 36

On December 13, 1997, Marge (a calendar year taxpayer) purchases two pairs of prescription contact lenses and one pair of prescribed orthopedic shoes for a total of $305. These purchases are separately charged to Marge's credit card. On January 6, 1998, Marge receives her statement containing these charges and makes payment shortly thereafter. The purchases are deductible as medical expenses in the year charged (1997) and not in the year the account is settled (1998). ▼

Recognizing which expenditures qualify for the medical deduction also may be crucial to exceeding the percentage limitations.

EXAMPLE 37

Mortimer employs Lana (an unrelated party) to care for his incapacitated and dependent mother. Lana is not a trained nurse but spends approximately one-half of the time performing nursing duties (e.g., administering injections and providing physical therapy) and the rest of the time doing household chores. An allocable portion of Lana's wages that Mortimer pays (including the employer's portion of FICA taxes) qualifies as a medical expense. ▼

To assure a deduction for the entire cost of nursing home care for an aged dependent, it is helpful if the transfer of the individual to the home is for medical reasons and is recommended by a doctor. In addition, the nursing home facilities should be adequate to provide the necessary medical and nursing care. To assure a deduction for all of the nursing home expenses, it is necessary to show that the individual was placed in the home for required medical care rather than for personal or family considerations.

Proper documentation is required to substantiate medical expenses. The taxpayer should keep all receipts for credit card or other charge purchases of medical services and deductible drugs as well as all cash register receipts. In addition, medical transportation mileage should be recorded.

If a taxpayer or a dependent of the taxpayer must be institutionalized in order to receive adequate medical care, it may be good tax planning to make a lump-sum payment that will cover medical treatment for future periods. It is advisable to negotiate a contract with the institution so that the expense is fixed and the payment is not a mere deposit.

TIMING THE PAYMENT OF DEDUCTIBLE TAXES

It is sometimes possible to defer or accelerate the payment of certain deductible taxes, such as state income tax, real property tax, and personal property tax. For instance, the final installment of estimated state income tax is generally due after the end of a given tax year. Accelerating the payment of the final installment could result in larger itemized deductions for the current year.

EXAMPLE 38

Jenny, who is single, expects to have itemized deductions of $3,900 in 1997 and $2,500 in 1998. She plans to pay $900 as the final installment on her 1997 estimated state income tax, which is due on January 15, 1998. If Jenny does not pay the final installment until 1998, she will not itemize in either 1997 or 1998. However, if she pays the final installment in December 1997, her itemized deductions will be $4,800 ($3,900 + $900) in 1997, and she will benefit from itemizing. ▼

PROTECTING THE INTEREST DEDUCTION

Although the deductibility of prepaid interest by a cash basis taxpayer has been severely restricted, a notable exception allows a deduction for points paid by the buyer to obtain financing for the purchase or improvement of a principal residence in the year of payment. However, such points must actually be paid by the taxpayer obtaining the loan and must represent a charge for the use of money. It has been held that points paid from the mortgage proceeds do not satisfy the payment requirement.[49] Also, the portion of the points attributable to service charges does not represent deductible interest.[50] Taxpayers financing home purchases or improvements usually should direct their planning toward avoiding these two hurdles to immediate deductibility.

In rare instances, a taxpayer may find it desirable to forgo the immediate expensing of points in the year paid. Instead, it could prove beneficial to capitalize the points and write them off as interest expense over the life of the mortgage.

EXAMPLE 39

Gerald purchases a home on December 15, 1997, for $95,000 with $30,000 cash and a 15-year mortgage of $65,000 financed by the Greater Metropolis National Bank. Gerald pays two points in addition to interest allocated to the period from December 15 until December 31, 1997, at an annual rate of 10%. Since Gerald does not have enough itemized deductions to exceed the standard deduction for 1997, he should elect to capitalize the interest expense by amortizing the points over 15 years. In this instance, Gerald would deduct $86.67 for 1998, as part of his qualified residence interest expense [$1,300 (two points) divided by 15 years], if he elects to itemize that year. ▼

Because personal (consumer) interest is not deductible, taxpayers should consider making use of home equity loans. Recall that these loans utilize the personal residence of the taxpayer as security. Since the tracing rules do not apply to home equity loans, the funds from these loans can be used for personal purposes (e.g., auto loans, education). By making use of home equity loans, therefore, what would have been nondeductible consumer interest becomes deductible qualified residence interest.

ASSURING THE CHARITABLE CONTRIBUTION DEDUCTION

For a charitable contribution deduction to be available, the recipient must be a qualified charitable organization. Sometimes the mechanics of how the contribution is carried out can determine whether or not a deduction results.

EXAMPLE 40

Fumiko wants to donate $5,000 to her church's mission in Kobe, Japan. In this regard, she considers three alternatives:

1. Send the money directly to the mission.
2. Give the money to her church with the understanding that it is to be passed on to the mission.
3. Give the money directly to the missionary in charge of the mission who is currently in the United States on a fund-raising trip.

If Fumiko wants to obtain a deduction for the contribution, she should choose alternative 2. A direct donation to the mission (alternative 1) is not deductible because the mission is a foreign charity. A direct gift to the missionary (alternative 3) does not comply since an individual cannot be a qualified charity for income tax purposes.[51] ▼

When making noncash donations, the type of property chosen can have decided implications in determining the amount, if any, of the deduction.

---

[49] *Alan A. Rubnitz,* 67 T.C. 621 (1977). Seller-paid points may also be deductible by the buyer under the provisions of Rev.Proc. 94–27, cited in footnote 27.

[50] *Donald L. Wilkerson,* 70 T.C. 240 (1978).
[51] *Thomas E. Lesslie,* 36 TCM 495, T.C.Memo. 1977–111.

EXAMPLE 41

Sam wants to give $60,000 in value to his church in some form other than cash. In this connection, he considers four alternatives:

1. Stock held for two years as an investment with a basis of $100,000 and a fair market value of $60,000.
2. Stock held for five years as an investment with a basis of $10,000 and a fair market value of $60,000.
3. The rent-free use for a year of a building that normally leases for $5,000 a month.
4. A valuable stamp collection held as an investment and owned for 10 years with a basis of $10,000 and a fair market value of $60,000. The church plans to sell the collection if and when it is donated.

Alternative 1 is ill-advised as the subject of the gift. Even though Sam would obtain a deduction of $60,000, he would forgo the potential loss of $40,000 that would be recognized if the property were sold.[52] Alternative 2 makes good sense since the deduction still is $60,000 and none of the $50,000 of appreciation that has occurred must be recognized as income. Alternative 3 yields no deduction at all and is not a wise choice. Alternative 4 involves tangible personalty that the recipient does not plan to use. As a result, the amount of the deduction is limited to $10,000, the stamp collection's basis.[53] ▼

For property transfers (particularly real estate), the ceiling limitations on the amount of the deduction allowed in any one year (50 percent, 30 percent, or 20 percent of AGI, as the case may be) could be a factor to take into account. With proper planning, donations can be controlled to stay within the limitations and therefore avoid the need for a carryover of unused charitable contributions.

EXAMPLE 42

Andrew wants to donate a tract of unimproved land held as an investment to the University of Maryland (a qualified charitable organization). The land has been held for six years and has a current fair market value of $300,000 and a basis to Andrew of $50,000. Andrew's AGI for the current year is estimated to be $200,000, and he expects much the same for the next few years. In the current year, he deeds (transfers) an undivided one-fifth interest in the real estate to the university. ▼

What has Andrew in Example 42 accomplished for income tax purposes? In the current year, he will be allowed a charitable contribution deduction of $60,000 (⅕ × $300,000), which will be within the applicable limitation of AGI (30% × $200,000). Presuming no other charitable contributions for the year, Andrew has avoided the possibility of a carryover. In future years, Andrew can arrange donations of undivided interests in the real estate to stay within the bounds of the percentage limitations. The only difficulty with this approach is the need to revalue the real estate each year before the donation, since the amount of the deduction is based on the fair market value of the interest contributed at the time of the contribution.

It may be wise to avoid a carryover of unused charitable contributions, if possible, because that approach may be dangerous in several respects. First, the carryover period is limited to five years. Depending on the taxpayer's projected AGI rather than actual AGI, some of the amount carried over may expire without tax benefit after the five-year period has ended. Second, unused charitable contribution carryovers do not survive the death of the party making the donation and as a consequence are lost.

---

[52] *LaVar M. Withers*, 69 T.C. 900 (1978).
[53] No reduction of appreciation is necessary in alternative 2 since stock is intangible property and not tangible personalty.

EXAMPLE 43

Tiffany dies in October 1997. In completing her final income tax return for 1997, Tiffany's executor determines the following information: AGI of $104,000 and a donation by Tiffany to her church of stock worth $60,000. Tiffany had purchased the stock two years ago for $50,000 and held it as an investment. Tiffany's executor makes the reduced deduction election and, as a consequence, claims a charitable contribution deduction of $50,000. With the election, the potential charitable contribution deduction of $50,000 ($60,000 − $10,000) is less than the 50% ceiling of $52,000 ($104,000 × 50%). If the executor had not made the election, the potential charitable contribution deduction of $60,000 would have been reduced by the 30% ceiling to $31,200 ($104,000 × 30%). No carryover of the $28,800 ($60,000 − $31,200) would have been available. ▼

KEY TERMS

Acquisition indebtedness, 10–16

Capital gain property, 10–24

Charitable contribution, 10–19

Home equity loans, 10–16

Investment income, 10–14

Investment interest, 10–13

Medical expense, 10–2

Miscellaneous itemized deductions, 10–27

Net investment income, 10–14

Ordinary income property, 10–23

Points, 10–16

Qualified residence interest, 10–13

PROBLEM MATERIALS

DISCUSSION QUESTIONS

1. Dan, a self-employed individual taxpayer, prepared his own income tax return for the past year and asked you to check it over for accuracy. Your review indicates that Dan failed to claim certain business entertainment expenses.
   a. Will the correction of this omission affect the amount of medical expenses Dan can deduct? Explain.
   b. Would it matter if Dan were employed rather than self-employed?

2. Pat incurred the following expenses during the year: $450 for an annual physical exam, $80 for a dental checkup, $600 for a weight reduction program, $1,800 for alcohol rehabilitation, and $200 for a stop-smoking clinic. Which of these expenses qualify for the medical deduction? Explain.

3. Nathan sustained serious facial damage in a skiing accident. To restore his physical appearance, he had cosmetic surgery. At the same time, he also had surgery to remove wrinkles from under his eyes caused by age. Can Nathan claim the cost of these procedures as a medical expense?

4. Sam, age 83, was placed in a nursing home by his children. What factors should be considered in determining whether any of the nursing home expenses are deductible?

5. Andres was injured in an automobile accident and is confined to a wheelchair. Because he lives alone, he must have extensive modifications made to various rooms in his home, including the kitchen, bathrooms, and hallways. Do the capital expenditures incurred to modify his home constitute a valid medical expense? If so, how much of the expense is deductible?

6. Susan, a sole proprietor of an antique shop, has two dependent children. During the year, she paid health insurance premiums of $1,400 for her own coverage and $2,000 for

coverage of her children. How will these premium payments affect Susan's taxable income computation?

7. Rebecca took her daughter, Susan, from Chicago to Rochester, Minnesota, for surgery at the Mayo Clinic. She incurred expenses for gasoline, highway tolls, and meals while traveling. Rebecca stayed in a motel near the clinic for six days while Susan was hospitalized. Discuss the extent to which transportation, meals, and lodging costs incurred by Susan and Rebecca are deductible as medical expenses (ignore the 7.5% floor).

8. Erin incurred medical expenses in 1997 and received a reimbursement from her insurance company in 1998. Under what circumstances must Erin report all or part of the reimbursement in gross income for 1998? Under what circumstances may she exclude the reimbursement from gross income for 1998?

9. By December 1, Anna had medical expenses of $5,000, of which $1,000 was reimbursed by her insurance company. She expects her AGI for the year to be $60,000 and her other itemized deductions to be $5,300. Can you suggest any tax planning ideas that will enable Anna to increase her medical expense deduction for the year?

10. A local opthalmologist's advertising campaign included a certificate for a free radial keratotomy for the lucky winner of a drawing. Ahmad held the winning ticket, which was drawn in December 1996. Ahmad had no vision problems and was uncertain what he should do with the prize. In February 1997, Ahmad's daughter, who lives with his former wife, was diagnosed with a vision problem that could be treated either with prescription glasses or a radial keratotomy. The divorce decree requires that Ahmad pay for all medical expenses incurred for his daughter. Identify the relevant tax issues for Ahmad.

11. The city required Heather to pay $3,000 for the cost of a new sidewalk in front of her personal residence. What effect will this $3,000 have on Heather from a tax perspective?

12. Donald owns a principal residence in Chicago, a vacation lodge in New Mexico, and a yacht (with living quarters) on Lake Michigan. All three properties have mortgages on which Donald pays interest. Discuss any limitations that apply to Donald's mortgage interest deduction, and suggest any strategy Donald should consider to maximize his deduction.

13. Ed borrows $20,000 and purchases an automobile. Jack borrows $20,000 to purchase a diamond engagement ring for his fiancée. Ed qualifies for an interest deduction on the amount he borrowed, but Jack does not. Can you offer any explanation for the difference?

14. Jerry purchased a personal residence from Kim. In order to sell the residence, Kim agreed to pay $3,000 in points related to Jerry's mortgage. Discuss the deductibility of the points.

15. Ellen borrows $50,000 from her parents for a down payment on a condominium. She paid interest of $4,200 in 1995, $0 in 1996, and $11,000 in 1997. The IRS disallows the deduction. Can you offer any explanation for the disallowance?

16. The city of Ogden was devastated by a tornado in April 1996, leaving many families in need of food, clothing, shelter, and other necessities. Betty contributed $500 to a family whose home was completely destroyed by the tornado. Jack contributed $700 to the family's church, which gave the money to the family. Discuss the deductibility of these contributions.

17. Lola purchased a ticket to a fund-raising banquet and dance for the Pittsburgh Symphony, a public charity. The ticket cost $250, and the normal cost of such an event is $50. How much can Lola deduct as a charitable contribution?

18. Bill pays tuition to a parochial school run by his church so that his children can attend the school. The church is a qualified charity. Can Bill deduct any portion of the tuition payments as a charitable contribution?

19. Zina decided to have a garage sale to get rid of a number of items that she no longer needed, including books, old stereo equipment, clothing, bicycles, and furniture. She scheduled the sale for Friday and Saturday, but was forced to close at noon Friday because of a torrential downpour. She had collected $500 for the items she sold before closing. The heavy rains continued through the weekend, and Zina was unable to continue the sale. She had not enjoyed dealing with the people who came to the sale on Friday morning, so she donated the remaining items to several local organizations. Zina has asked your advice on how she should treat these events on her tax return. List some of the tax issues you would discuss with her.

20. Paula contributed Orange Corporation common stock to the United Way. In addition, she contributed tables and chairs from her proprietorship's inventory to the high school in her city. Should Paula's charitable contribution deduction for these contributions be determined by the basis or fair market value of the contributed items?

21. During the year, Shirley donated five dresses to the Salvation Army. She had purchased the dresses three years ago at a cost of $1,200 and worn them as personal attire. Because the dresses are long-term capital assets, Shirley plans to deduct $1,200 on her income tax return. Comment on Shirley's understanding of the tax law governing charitable contributions.

22. The Skins Game, which involves four of the top golfers on the PGA Tour, is held each year on the weekend after Thanksgiving. Total prize money amounts to $510,000, and the leading money winner also receives an automobile as a prize. The announcers point out that 10% of the money won by each player goes to charity. In addition, on some holes, the winner of the hole receives the keys to an automobile, which goes to the player's favorite charity. Identify the relevant tax issues for the players. Consider the following possibilities with respect to the car won by the leading money winner: (1) he might keep the car for his own use and sell his present car; (2) he might sell the new car; (3) he might give the car to a friend or relative; (4) he might donate the car to charity; or (5) he might give the car to his caddy.

23. Henry is a television evangelist. In August 1996, the IRS ruled that his organization was no longer a qualified charitable organization because of violations of the tax law. Miguel donated $10,000 to Henry's organization in September 1996. At the time, he did not know that Henry's organization had been disqualified as a charitable organization. In 1997, Henry was jailed for mail fraud. Miguel has filed a civil suit demanding return of the $10,000 plus $100,000 in damages. Identify the relevant tax issues for Miguel.

PROBLEMS

24. Antonio and Carmen are married and together have AGI of $80,000 in 1997. They have no dependents and file a joint return. During the year, they paid $1,200 for medical insurance, $7,000 in doctor bills and hospital expenses, and $1,200 for prescribed medicine and drugs.
    a. In December 1997, Antonio and Carmen received an insurance reimbursement of $1,500 for hospitalization expenses. Determine the deduction allowable for medical expenses paid during the year.
    b. Assume instead that Antonio and Carmen received the $1,500 insurance reimbursement in February 1998. Determine the deduction allowable for medical expenses incurred in 1997.
    c. Assume again that Antonio and Carmen received the $1,500 insurance reimbursement in February 1998. Discuss whether the reimbursement will be included in their gross income for 1998.

25. Frank, a widower, had a serious stroke and is no longer capable of caring for himself. He has three sons, all of whom live in different states. Because they are unable to care for Frank in their homes, his sons have placed him in a nursing home equipped to provide medical and nursing care facilities. Total nursing home expenses amount to $45,000 per year. Of this amount, $18,000 is directly attributable to medical and nursing

care. Frank's Social Security benefits are used to pay for $12,000 of the nursing home charges. He has no other income. His sons plan to split the remaining medical expenses equally.
  a. What portion of the nursing home charges is potentially deductible as a medical expense?
  b. Can you provide Frank's sons with a tax planning idea for maximizing the deduction for his medical expenses?

26. Ken developed a severe asthmatic condition, and his physician advised him to install a special air conditioning, heating, and filtration system in his home. The cost of installing the system was $6,000, and the increase in the value of the residence was determined to be $2,000. Ken's AGI for the year was $30,000.
  a. How much of the expenditure can Ken deduct as a medical expense?
  b. Assume the same facts as in (a), except that Ken was paralyzed in an automobile accident and the expenditures were incurred to build entrance and exit ramps and widen the hallways in his home to accommodate his wheelchair. How much of the expenditure can Ken deduct as a medical expense?

27. For calendar year 1997, Ruth was a self-employed real estate broker with no employees. She had $70,000 net profit from real estate transactions and paid $4,000 in medical insurance premiums on a policy covering 1997. How much of these premiums may Ruth deduct as a deduction *for* AGI and how much may she deduct as an itemized deduction?

28. During the current year, Sara incurred and paid the following expenses for Seth (her son), Emma (her mother), and herself:

Surgery for Seth	$3,200
Trout Valley Academy charges for Seth:	
Tuition	9,000
Room, board, and other expenses	6,600
Psychiatric treatment	7,200
Doctor bills for Emma	2,700
Prescription drugs for Sara, Seth, and Emma	1,300
Insulin for Emma	950
Nonprescription drugs for Sara, Seth, and Emma	800
Charges at Riverview Nursing Home for Emma:	
Medical care	6,500
Lodging	8,200
Meals	3,300

Seth qualifies as Sara's dependent, and Emma would also qualify except that she receives $6,100 of taxable retirement benefits from her former employer. Seth's psychiatrist recommended Trout Valley Academy because of its small class sizes and specialized psychiatric treatment program that is needed to treat Seth's illness. Emma is a paraplegic and diabetic, and Riverview offers the type of care that she requires.

Upon the recommendation of a physician, Sara has an air filtration system installed in her personal residence. She suffers from severe allergies. In connection with this equipment, Sara incurs and pays the following amounts during the year:

Filtration system and cost of installation	$6,800
Increase in utility bills due to the system	550
Cost of certified appraisal	370

The system has an estimated useful life of 10 years. The appraisal was to determine the value of Sara's residence with and without the system. The appraisal states that the system increased the value of Sara's residence by $1,000. Ignoring the 7.5% floor, what is the total of Sara's expenses that qualifies for the medical expense deduction?

29. In May, Rebecca's daughter, Susan, sustained a serious injury that made it impossible for her to continue living alone. Susan, who is a novelist, moved back into Rebecca's home after the accident. Susan has begun writing a new novel based on her recent experiences. To accommodate Susan, Rebecca incurred significant remodeling expenses (widening hallways, building a separate bedroom and bathroom, making kitchen appliances accessible to Susan). In addition, Rebecca had an indoor swimming pool constructed so Susan could do rehabilitation exercises prescribed by her physician.

In September, Susan underwent major reconstructive surgery in Denver. The surgery was performed by Dr. Rama Patel, who specializes in treating injuries of the type sustained by Susan. Rebecca drove Susan from Champaign, Illinois, to Denver, a total of 1,100 miles, in Susan's specially equipped van. They left Champaign on Tuesday morning and arrived in Denver on Thursday afternoon. Rebecca incurred expenses for gasoline, highway tolls, meals, and lodging while traveling to Denver. Rebecca stayed in a motel near the clinic for eight days while Susan was hospitalized. Identify the relevant tax issues based on this information and prepare a list of questions that you would need to ask Rebecca and Susan in order to advise them as to the resolution of any issues you have identified.

30. In Lawrence County, the real property tax year is the calendar year. The real property tax becomes a personal liability of the owner of real property on January 1 in the current real property tax year, 1997. The tax is payable on July 1, 1997. On June 30, 1997, Jason sells his house to Carolyn for $250,000. On July 1, 1997, Carolyn pays the entire real estate tax of $9,125 for the year ending December 31, 1997.
    a. How much of the property taxes may Jason deduct?
    b. How much of the property taxes may Carolyn deduct?

31. Assume the same facts as in Problem 30.
    a. What is Carolyn's basis for the residence?
    b. How much did Jason realize from the sale of the residence?

32. Andrea, who uses the cash method of accounting, lives in a state that imposes an income tax. In April 1997, she files her state income tax return for 1996 and pays an additional $1,000 in state income taxes. During 1997, her withholdings for state income tax purposes amount to $7,400, and she pays estimated state income tax of $700. In April 1998, she files her state return for 1997 claiming a refund of $1,800. Andrea receives the refund in August 1998.
    a. Assuming Andrea itemizes deductions in 1997, how much may she claim as a deduction for state income taxes on her Federal return for calendar year 1997 (filed in April 1998)?
    b. Assuming Andrea itemized deductions in 1997, how will the refund of $1,800 that she received in 1998 be treated for Federal income tax purposes?
    c. Assume Andrea itemizes deductions in 1997 and elects to have the $1,800 refund applied toward her 1998 state income tax liability. How will the $1,800 be treated for Federal income tax purposes?
    d. Assuming Andrea did not itemize deductions in 1997, how will the refund of $1,800 received in 1998 be treated for Federal income tax purposes?

33. Sandra incurred $19,500 of interest expense related to her investments in 1997. Her investment income included $5,000 of interest, $3,000 of dividends, and a $7,500 net capital gain on the sale of securities.
    a. What is the maximum amount that Sandra can treat as investment income for the year?
    b. What other tax factors should Sandra consider in deciding whether to elect to include net capital gain in her investment income?

34. Maria has AGI of $72,000, which includes dividends and interest income of $16,200. In addition to investment interest expense of $14,000, she paid $2,700 of city ad valorem property tax on stocks and bonds and had the following miscellaneous itemized expenses:

Safe deposit box rental (to hold investment securities)	$ 75
Investment counsel fee	1,000
Professional dues and subscriptions	765
Tax return preparation fees	600

Determine Maria's investment expense deduction and discuss the treatment of any portion of the investment interest expense that is disallowed due to the investment interest limitation.

35. Sid and Sara, married taxpayers, took out a mortgage on their home for $100,000 in 1988. In March of the current year, when the home had a fair market value of $200,000 and they owed $85,000 on the mortgage, Sid and Sara took out a home equity loan for $110,000. They used the funds to purchase a motor home to be used for recreational purposes. What is the maximum amount on which they can deduct home equity interest?

36. Ella purchased her residence five years ago, obtaining a 20-year mortgage at an annual interest rate of 10%. On January 2, 1997, Ella refinanced with a 15-year mortgage in order to reduce the interest rate to 8.25%. To obtain the refinancing, she was required to pay points of $2,500. How much, if any, of the $2,500 points can Ella deduct in 1997?

37. Erin donates $1,000 to State University's athletic department. The payment guarantees that Erin will have preferred seating on the 50-yard line.
    a. Assume Erin subsequently buys four $50 game tickets. How much can she deduct as a charitable contribution to the university's athletic department?
    b. Assume that Erin's $1,000 donation includes four $50 tickets. How much can she deduct as a charitable contribution to the university's athletic department?

38. Sara owned stock in Rhino Corporation with a basis of $3,750. She donated the stock to a qualified charitable organization on August 1, 1997.
    a. What is the amount of Sara's deduction, assuming that she had purchased the stock on June 3, 1997, and the stock had a fair market value of $4,800 when she made the donation.
    b. Assume the same facts as in (a), except that Sara had purchased the stock on June 3, 1996.
    c. Assume the same facts as in (a), except that the stock had a fair market value of $3,450 (rather than $4,800) when Sara donated it to the charity.

39. Darby contributed a painting to an art museum in 1997. She had owned the painting for 20 years, and it had a value of $120,000 at the time of the donation. The museum displayed the painting in its impressionist gallery.
    a. Assume that Darby's AGI is $230,000 and her basis for the painting is $80,000. Would you recommend that she make the reduced deduction election?
    b. Assume that Darby's AGI is $230,000 and her basis for the painting is $115,000. Would you recommend that she make the reduced deduction election?

40. During the year, Al made the following contributions to his church:

Cash	$20,000
Stock in Thrush Corporation (a publicly traded corporation)	30,000

    The stock in Thrush Corporation was acquired as an investment three years ago at a cost of $10,000. Al's AGI is $70,000.
    a. What is Al's charitable contribution deduction?
    b. How are excess amounts, if any, treated?

41. Steven, who had AGI of $180,000 in 1997, contributed stock in Azure Corporation (a publicly traded corporation) to State University, a qualified charitable organization. The stock was worth $105,000, and Steven had acquired it as an investment two years ago at a cost of $84,000.
    a. What is the total amount that Steven can deduct as a charitable contribution, assuming he carries over any disallowed contribution from 1997 to future years?

b. What is the maximum amount that Steven can deduct as a charitable contribution in 1997?
c. What factors should Steven consider in deciding how to treat the contribution for Federal income tax purposes?
d. Assume Steven dies in December 1997. What advice would you give the executor of his estate with regard to possible elections that can be made relative to the contribution?

42. On December 30, 1997, Roberta purchased four tickets to a charity ball sponsored by the city of San Diego for the benefit of underprivileged children. Each ticket cost $200 and had a fair market value of $35. On the same day as the purchase, Roberta gave the tickets to the minister of her church for personal use by his family. At the time of the gift of the tickets, Roberta pledged $4,000 to the building fund of her church. The pledge was satisfied by check dated December 31, 1997, but not mailed until January 3, 1998.
a. Presuming Roberta is a cash basis and calendar year taxpayer, how much can she deduct as a charitable contribution for 1997?
b. Would the amount of the deduction be any different if Roberta is an accrual basis taxpayer? Explain.

43. In December each year, Sandy Wren contributes 10% of her gross income to her church. Sandy, who is in the 36% marginal tax bracket, is considering the following alternatives as charitable contributions in December 1997:

	Fair Market Value
1. Cash donation	$12,000
2. Unimproved land held for six years ($2,000 basis)	12,000
3. Purple Corporation stock held for eight months ($2,000 basis)	12,000
4. Silver Corporation stock held for two years ($17,000 basis)	12,000

Sandy has asked you to help her decide which of these potential contributions will be most advantageous taxwise. Rank the four alternatives, and write a letter to Sandy communicating your advice to her. Her address is 1201 Baywatch Drive, Chicago, IL 60606.

44. Manuel and Rosa Garcia, both age 45, are married and have no dependents. They have asked you to advise them whether they should file jointly or separately in 1997. They present you with the following information:

	Manuel	Rosa	Joint
Salary	$40,000		
Business net income		$100,000	
Interest income	400	1,200	$2,200
Deductions *for* AGI	2,000	13,000	
Medical expenses	9,500	600	
State income tax	800	2,000	
Real estate tax			3,400
Mortgage interest			5,200
Unreimbursed employee expenses	1,100		

If they file separately, Manuel and Rosa will split the real estate tax and mortgage interest deductions equally. Write Manuel and Rosa a letter in which you make and explain a recommendation on filing status for 1997. Manuel and Rosa reside at 5904 Stevens Avenue, Durham, NC 27707.

45. For calendar year 1997, Clyde and Trisha file a joint return reflecting AGI of $160,000. Their itemized deductions are as follows:

Medical expenses	$14,000
Casualty loss (not covered by insurance)	17,000
Interest on home mortgage	10,000
Property taxes on home	10,000
Charitable contributions	12,000
State income tax	15,000

    After all necessary adjustments are made, what is the amount of itemized deductions Clyde and Trisha may claim?

46. Kareem and Veneia are married and file a joint return. For 1997, they have AGI of $305,520. Their itemized deductions for the year total $39,000 and consist of the following:

Medical expenses	$32,000
Interest on home mortgage	3,000
State income tax	4,000

    After all necessary adjustments are made, what is the amount of itemized deductions Kareem and Veneia may claim?

47. Ben and Laura are married and file a joint return. For 1997, they have AGI of $358,450, which included net investment income of $41,000 before deducting investment interest. Compute Ben and Laura's allowable itemized deductions for 1997 based on the following information:

Investment interest	$11,000
Casualty loss (after applicable limitations)	8,000
Qualified residence interest	5,400
Property taxes	4,700
Charitable contributions	2,900
State income taxes	5,300

48. Andy, who is single, had AGI of $180,000 for 1997. He incurred the following expenses and losses during the year:

Medical expenses before 7.5%-of-AGI limitation	$15,000
State and local income taxes	2,600
Real estate taxes	3,400
Home mortgage interest	6,600
Charitable contribution	3,500
Casualty loss before 10% limitation (after $100 floor)	20,600
Unreimbursed employee expenses subject to 2%-of-AGI limitation	4,100
Gambling losses (Andy had $3,500 gambling income)	7,000

    Calculate Andy's allowable itemized deductions for the year.

CUMULATIVE PROBLEMS

49. Alice and Bruce Byrd are married taxpayers, ages 47 and 45, who file a joint return. Their Social Security numbers are 034–48–4382 and 016–50–9556, respectively. They live at 473 Revere Avenue, Ames, MA 01850. Alice is the office manager for a dental clinic and earns an annual salary of $45,000. Bruce is the manager of a fast-food outlet owned and operated by Plymouth Corporation. His annual salary is $36,000.

The Byrds have two children, Cynthia (age 23 and S.S. no. 017–44–9126) and John (age 22 and S.S. no. 017–27–4148), who live with them. Both children are full-time students at a nearby college. Alice's mother, Myrtle Jones (age 74 and S.S. no. 016–15–8266), also lives with them. Her sole source of income is from Social Security benefits, which she deposits in a savings account.

During 1996, a particularly harsh storm struck the Ames area. As a result, the Byrds suffered severe flood damage to the basement and foundation of their personal residence, which was purchased in 1987 at a cost of $80,000. Based on an appraisal, the fair market value of the house was $115,000 before the storm and $90,000 after. The Byrds' homeowner's insurance policy does not cover damage due to flooding. The cost of the appraisal was $300.

During 1996, the Byrds furnished one-third of the total support of Bruce's widower father, Sam Byrd (age 70 and S.S. no. 034–82–8583). Sam lives alone and receives the rest of his support from Bruce's sister and brother (one-third each). They have signed a multiple support agreement allowing Bruce to claim Sam as a dependent for 1996. Sam died in November, and Bruce received life insurance proceeds of $270,000 on December 28.

The Byrds had the following expenses relating to their personal residence during 1996:

Property taxes	$2,800
Interest on home mortgage	6,500
Repairs to roof	1,000
Utilities	3,800
Fire and theft insurance	1,100

Medical expenses for 1996 include:

Medical insurance premiums	$4,100
Doctor bill for Sam incurred in 1995 and not paid until 1996	1,600
Operation for Sam	5,900

The operation for Sam represents the one-third Bruce contributed toward his father's support.

Other relevant information follows:

- On December 1, 1996, Myrtle gave Alice and Bruce a tract of undeveloped land (basis of $30,000 and fair market value of $90,000).

- Alice and Bruce had $2,600 ($1,400 for Alice and $1,200 for Bruce) withheld from their salaries for state income taxes. When they filed their 1995 state return in 1996, they paid additional tax of $280.

- During 1996, Alice and Bruce attended a dinner dance sponsored by the Ames Police Disability Association (a qualified charitable organization). The Byrds paid $100 for the tickets. Cost of comparable entertainment would normally be $40. The Byrds contributed $1,700 to their church and gave used clothing (cost of $800 and fair market value of $200) to the Salvation Army. All donations are supported by receipts.

- In 1996, the Byrds received interest income of $1,450 from a savings account they maintained.

- Alice's employer requires that all employees wear uniforms to work. During 1996, Alice spent $340 on new uniforms and $102 on laundry charges. Bruce paid $120 for an annual subscription to the *Journal of Franchise Management*. Neither Alice's nor Bruce's employers reimburse for employee expenses.

- Alice and Bruce had $6,500 ($3,500 for Alice and $3,000 for Bruce) of Federal income tax withheld in 1996 and paid no estimated Federal income tax. Neither Alice nor Bruce wishes to designate $3 to the Presidential Election Campaign Fund.

CHAPTER 10 Deductions and Losses: Certain Itemized Deductions

Part 1—Tax Computation
Compute net tax payable or refund due for Alice and Bruce Byrd for 1996. If they have overpaid, the amount is to be refunded. If you use tax forms for your computations, you will need Form 1040, Schedules A and B, and Form 4684. Suggested software (if available): *TurboTax* or *MacInTax*.

Part 2—Tax Planning
Alice and Bruce are planning some significant changes for 1997. They have provided you with the following information and asked you to project their taxable income and tax liabiliy for 1997.

Myrtle became seriously ill in December 1996 and is no longer able to care for herself. As a result, Alice plans to take a one-year leave of absence from work during 1997 to care for her. The Byrds will use $70,000 of the life insurance proceeds they received as a result of Sam's death and pay off their mortgage in early January 1997. They will invest the remaining $200,000 in short-term certificates of deposit (CDs) and use the interest for living expenses during 1997. They expect to earn total interest of $13,500 on the CDs. Bruce has been awarded a 5% raise for 1997, and withholdings on his salary will increase accordingly.

The Byrds will not incur any additional costs related to the flood damage or Sam's medical problem. Alice will not work at all during 1997, so none of her job-related expenses or withholdings will continue. The Byrds do not expect to owe additional state income tax when they file their 1996 return, but they do expect their charitable contributions and medical insurance premiums to continue at the 1996 level. Assume all other income and deduction items will continue at the same level in 1997 unless you have information that indicates otherwise.

50. Paul and Donna Decker are married taxpayers, ages 44 and 42, who file a joint return for 1997. The Deckers live at 1121 College Avenue, Carmel, IN 46032. Paul is an assistant manager at Carmel Motor Inn, and Donna is a teacher at Carmel Elementary School. They present you with W-2 Forms that reflect the following information:

	Paul	**Donna**
Salary	$35,000	$38,000
Federal tax withheld	6,092	5,400
State income tax withheld	700	760
FICA (Social Security) withheld	2,678	2,907
Social Security numbers	222-11-4567	333-11-9872

Donna is the custodial parent of two children from a previous marriage who reside with the Deckers through the school year. The children, Larry and Jane Parker, reside with their father, Bob, during the summer. Relevant information for the children follows:

	Larry	**Jane**
Age	11	9
Social Security numbers	305-11-4567	303-11-9872
Months spent with Deckers	9	9

Under the divorce decree, Bob pays child support of $150 per month per child during the nine months the children live with the Deckers. Bob says he spends $200 per month per child during the three summer months they reside with him. Donna and Paul can document that they provide $1,800 support per child per year. The divorce decree is silent as to which parent can claim the exemption for the children.

In August, Paul and Donna added a suite to their home to provide more comfortable accommodations for Hannah Snyder (263–33–4738), Donna's mother, who had moved in with them in February 1996 after the death of Donna's father. Not wanting to borrow money for this addition, Paul sold 300 shares of Acme Corporation stock for $50 per share on May 3, 1997, and used the proceeds of $15,000 to cover construction costs. The Deckers had purchased the stock on April 27, 1996, for $22 per share. They received dividends of $550 on the jointly owned stock a month before the sale.

Hannah, who is 66 years old, received $7,200 in Social Security benefits during the year, of which she gave the Deckers $1,700 to use toward household expenses and deposited the remainder in her personal savings account. The Deckers determine that they have spent $1,500 of their own money for food, clothing, medical expenses, and other items for Hannah. They do not know what the rental value of Hannah's suite would be, but they estimate it would be at least $300 per month.

The Deckers received $2,100 interest on City of Indianapolis bonds they had bought in 1995. Paul had heard from a friend that municipal bonds were paying good rates and that municipal bond interest was not taxable. To finance the purchase of the bonds, he borrowed $20,000 from the bank and paid $1,760 interest during 1997. Other interest paid during the year included the following:

Home mortgage interest (paid to Carmel Federal Savings & Loan)	$4,890
Interest on an automobile loan (paid to Carmel National Bank)	920
Interest on Citibank Visa card	855

Donna's uncle died on November 11, 1997, and left her 50 shares of Thrush Corporation stock worth $70 per share. Her uncle's basis in the stock was $34 per share. Donna received $530 in dividends on the stock in December 1997.

In July, Paul hit a submerged rock while boating. Fortunately, he was thrown from the boat, landed in deep water, and was uninjured. However, the boat, which was uninsured, was destroyed. Paul had paid $18,000 for the boat in June 1996, and its value was appraised at $14,500 on the date of the accident.

The Deckers paid doctor and hospital bills of $4,100 and were reimbursed $1,600 by their insurance company. They spent $780 for prescription drugs and medicines and $1,440 for premiums on their health insurance policy. They have filed additional claims of $700 with their insurance company and have been told they will receive payment for that amount in January 1998. Included in the amounts paid for doctor and hospital bills were payments of $360 for Hannah and $750 for the children.

Additional information of potential tax consequence follows:

Real estate taxes paid	$1,900
Cash contributions to church	800
Appraised value of books donated to public library	450
Paul's unreimbursed employee expenses to attend hotel management convention:	
Airfare	340
Hotel	130
Meals	95
Registration fee	100
Refund of state income tax for 1996 (the Deckers itemized on their 1996 return)	910

Compute net tax payable or refund due for the Deckers for 1997. If they have overpaid, the amount is to be credited toward their taxes for 1998. Suggested software (if available): *TurboTax* or *MacInTax*.

RESEARCH PROBLEMS

Note: ***West's Federal Taxation on CD-ROM*** *can be used in preparing solutions to the Research Problems. Alternatively, tax research materials contained in a standard tax library can be used.*

Research Problem 1. Jane suffers from a degenerative spinal disorder. Her physician recommended the installation of a swimming pool at her residence for her use to prevent the onset of permanent paralysis. Jane's residence had a market value of approximately $500,000 before the swimming pool was installed. The swimming pool was built, and an appraiser estimated that the value of Jane's home increased by $98,000 because of the addition.

The pool cost $194,000, and Jane claimed a medical deduction of $96,000 on her tax return. Upon audit of the return, the IRS determined that an adequate pool should have cost $70,000 and would increase the property value by only $31,000. Thus, the IRS claims that Jane should be entitled to a deduction of only $39,000.
   a. Is there any ceiling limitation on the amount deductible as a medical expense?
   b. Can capital expenditures be deducted as medical expenses?
   c. What is the significance of a "minimum adequate facility"? Should aesthetic or architectural qualities be considered in this determination?

Research Problem 2. Tom and Mary Smith, whose son was found murdered in a parking lot, offered a $100,000 reward for the city police to use to obtain for information leading to the arrest and conviction of the murderer. As a result of the reward, a person who had overheard the murderer telling a friend about the crime reported the conversation to the police. The murderer was arrested and convicted, and the Smiths contributed the money to the police department. Can the Smiths treat this payment as a charitable contribution?

Research Problem 3. In January, Ron, a fireman, was injured in the line of duty as a result of interference by a homeowner. He incurred medical expenses of $6,500 related to his injuries. Ron sued the homeowner and was awarded damages of $26,500 in December. The court indicated that $6,500 of the award was for payment of Ron's medical expenses and $20,000 was for punitive damages. Ron has prepared his return for the year and has asked you to review it. You notice that Ron has not reported any part of the award as income and has included the medical expense in computing his itemized deductions. Write a brief summary of the advice you should give Ron.

Research Problem 4. Falcon Corporation is the owner and operator of a large daily metropolitan newspaper. For at least 80 years, Falcon has collected and maintained a "clippings library." The library is a collection of past news items from Falcon's and other newspapers. The 7,800,000 items are well-preserved, cataloged, and cross-listed under various categories. Falcon estimates that it has spent in excess of $10 million compiling and organizing the library. However, since this amount was deducted as incurred, the income tax basis of the library is zero. The fair market value of the library is $3 million.

Falcon Corporation contributes the clippings library to the state historical society (a qualified organization) and claims a charitable contribution deduction of $3 million. Upon audit, the IRS disallows the entire amount of the deduction because the basis of the property is zero. Who is correct?

Partial list of research aids:
§§ 170(e)(1)(A) and 1221(3).

Research Problem 5. The city of Cincinnati wished to establish a scenic corridor along portions of Interstate 75, but did not have the funds to purchase all of the land involved and to make the necessary improvements (e.g., terracing and other landscaping). Likewise, the city was fearful of any personal liability that might result from the operation of the scenic corridor. If, however, state funding could be obtained to cover the improvements and liability costs, the project would be carried out. State funding was possible but not probable.

In 1995, all but one of the property owners affected by the project donated the necessary land to the city. The city purchased the land of the one owner who refused to make a donation. The city agreed to return the land to the donors in the event the project was not carried out. By 1997, it became certain that state funding would not be forthcoming. Therefore, the city returned the land to the donors, except for the parcel it had purchased.

William Baird, one of the donors, claimed a charitable deduction for the fair market value of the land transferred in 1995. Upon audit of William's 1995 income tax return, the IRS disallowed the deduction and assessed the penalty for overvaluation. Is the IRS correct?

a. Write a letter to William that contains your tax advice. His address is 405 Westwood, Cincinnati, OH 45999.
b. Prepare a memo for your firm's tax files.

Partial list of research aids:
§ 6659 [now § 6662(b)(3)].
Reg. § 1.170A–1(e).
Ronald W. McCrary, 92 T.C. 827 (1989).

Use the tax resources of the internet to address the following questions. Do not restrict your search to the World Wide Web, but include a review of newsgroups and general reference materials, practitioner sites and resources, primary sources of the tax law, chat rooms and discussion groups, and other opportunities.

Research Problem 6. Homeowners believe that their deductions for property taxes and mortgage interest related to their residence increase property values. Advocates of a flat tax system, though, maintain that a repeal of such deductions actually would benefit homeowners. On what basis is this argument made? Outline the strongest points on both sides of this debate.

Research Problem 7. Look over the web pages of several large charities. Print some of the most effective materials by which such organizations solicit charitable contributions over the internet. Concentrate especially on the solicitation of gifts of appreciated securities and on the use of private foundations as the recipients of large charitable gifts.

TEAM PROJECT: ARTHUR ANDERSEN TAX CHALLENGE CASES

For more information on the Arthur Andersen Tax Challenge Cases, refer to Chapter 1, page 1-38.

Information related to tax issues and problems that are discussed in this chapter may be found in the

Day and Ball case on pages 2, 3, 4, 7, 11, 12, 25–28, and 33
Miller case on pages 2, 3, 11–15, 24–27, 29–30, 34, and 38

Read and analyze the case you have been assigned and *identify* any issues and problems that are related to material covered in this chapter. If the information provided in the case is complete, prepare answers for this part of the case at this time. If you need information that is contained in the later parts of the case, write a memo summarizing the questions or problems so you can prepare a complete answer at a later date.

CHAPTER 11

PASSIVE ACTIVITY LOSSES

LEARNING OBJECTIVES

After completing Chapter 11, you should be able to:

1. Discuss tax shelters and the reasons for at-risk and passive loss limitations.
2. Explain the at-risk limitation.
3. Describe how the passive loss rules limit deductions for losses, and identify the taxpayers subject to these restrictions.
4. Discuss the definition of passive activities and the rules for identifying an activity.
5. Analyze and apply the tests for material participation.
6. Understand the nature of rental activities under the passive loss rules.
7. Recognize the relationship between the at-risk and passive activity limitations.
8. Discuss the special treatment available to real estate activities.
9. Determine the proper tax treatment upon the disposition of a passive activity.
10. Suggest tax planning strategies to minimize the effect of the passive loss limitations.

OUTLINE

The Tax Shelter Problem, 11–2
At-Risk Limits, 11–4
Passive Loss Limits, 11–6
Classification and Impact of Passive Income and Losses, 11–6
Taxpayers Subject to the Passive Loss Rules, 11–10

Passive Activities Defined, 11–11
Interaction of the At-Risk and Passive Activity Limits, 11–21
Special Passive Activity Rules for Real Estate Activities, 11–22

Dispositions of Passive Interests, 11–25
Tax Planning Considerations, 11–27
Utilizing Passive Losses, 11–27

THE TAX SHELTER PROBLEM

1 LEARNING OBJECTIVE
Discuss tax shelters and the reasons for at-risk and passive loss limitations.

Before Congress enacted legislation to reduce or eliminate their effectiveness, **tax shelters** were popular investments for tax avoidance purposes because they could generate deductions and other benefits that could be used to offset income from other sources. Because of the tax avoidance potential of many tax shelters, they were attractive to wealthy taxpayers in high income tax brackets. Many tax shelters merely provided an opportunity for "investors" to buy deductions and credits in ventures that were not expected to generate a profit, even in the long run.

Although it may seem odd that a taxpayer would intentionally invest in an activity that was designed to produce losses, there is a logical explanation. The typical tax shelter operated as a partnership and relied heavily on nonrecourse financing.[1] Accelerated depreciation and interest expense deductions generated large losses in the early years of the activity. At the very least, the tax shelter deductions deferred the recognition of any net income from the venture until the activity was sold. In the best of situations, the investor could realize additional tax savings by offsetting other income (e.g., salary, interest, and dividends) with deductions flowing from the tax shelter. Ultimately, the sale of the investment would result in capital gain. The following examples illustrate what was possible *before* Congress enacted legislation to curb tax shelter abuses.

EXAMPLE 1

Bob, who earned a salary of $100,000 as a business executive and dividend income of $15,000, invested $20,000 for a 10% interest in a cattle-breeding tax shelter. Through the use of $800,000 of nonrecourse financing and available cash of $200,000, the partnership acquired a herd of an exotic breed of cattle costing $1 million. Depreciation, interest, and other deductions related to the activity resulted in a loss of $400,000, of which Bob's share was $40,000. Bob was allowed to deduct the $40,000 loss, even though he had invested and stood to lose only $20,000 if the investment turned sour. The net effect of the $40,000 deduction from the partnership was that a portion of Bob's salary and dividend income was "sheltered," and as a result, he was required to calculate his tax liability on only $75,000 of income [$115,000 (salary and dividends) − $40,000 (deduction)] rather than $115,000. If this deduction were available under current law and if Bob was in the 39.6% income tax bracket, this deduction would generate a tax savings of $15,840 ($40,000 × 39.6%) in the first year alone! ▼

---

[1] Nonrecourse debt is an obligation for which the borrower is not personally liable. An example of nonrecourse debt is a liability on real estate acquired by a partnership without the partnership or any of the partners assuming any liability for the mortgage. The acquired property generally is pledged as collateral for the loan.

TAX IN THE NEWS

THE FEDS MAY ASK TAX SHELTERS TO REGISTER

Investment bankers and other tax advisers who devise intricate tax-saving deals for clients often require them to sign confidentiality agreements. Representative Bill Archer, the Texas Republican who heads the House Ways and Means Committee, supports requiring advisers to register such deals confidentially with the IRS as "tax shelters." Tax advisers say such pacts are meant to keep competitors from learning of complex tax strategies, but the House budget committee suggests that many also conceal various "inappropriate corporate tax benefits" that cost the government billions.

This requirement would be in addition to the current law that requires investment promoters to register as tax shelters deals that yield inordinate tax benefits relative to the amount invested. Many corporate tax advisers say the idea is too intrusive and would be too time-consuming. Penalty rules already require taxpayers to alert the IRS on their returns if they take overly aggressive positions.

SOURCE: Information from *Wall Street Journal*, May 24, 1995, p. A1.

A review of Example 1 shows that the taxpayer took a *two-for-one* write-off ($40,000 deduction, $20,000 investment). In the heyday of tax shelters, promoters often promised *multiple* write-offs for the investor.

The first major provision aimed at tax shelters was the **at-risk limitation.** Its objective is to limit a taxpayer's deductions to the amount at risk, that is, the amount the taxpayer stands to lose if the investment turns out to be a financial disaster.

EXAMPLE 2

Returning to the facts of Example 1, under the current at-risk rules Bob would be allowed to deduct $20,000 (i.e., the amount that he could lose if the business failed). This deduction would reduce his other income and as a result, Bob would have to report only $95,000 of income ($115,000 − $20,000). The remaining nondeductible $20,000 loss and any future losses flowing from the partnership would be suspended under the at-risk rules and would be deductible in the future only as his at-risk amount increased. ▼

The second major attack on tax shelters came with the passage of the passive activity loss rules. These rules were intended to halt an investor's ability to benefit from the mismatching of an entity's expenses and income that often occurs in the early years of the business. Congress observed that despite the at-risk limitations, investors could still deduct losses flowing from an entity and thereby defer their tax liability on other income. In effect, passive activity rules have essentially made the term *tax shelter* obsolete. Now such ventures where investors are not involved in the day-to-day operations of the business are generally referred to as passive investments, or *passive activities*, rather than tax shelters.

The **passive loss** rules require the taxpayer to segregate all income and losses into three categories: active, passive, and portfolio. In general, the passive loss limits disallow the deduction of passive losses against active or portfolio income, even when the taxpayer is at risk to the extent of the loss. Normally, passive losses can only offset passive income.

EXAMPLE 3

Returning to the facts of Example 1, the passive activity loss rules further restrict Bob's ability to claim the $20,000 tax deduction shown in Example 2. Because Bob is a passive investor and does not materially participate in any meaningful way in the activities of the cattle-breeding operation, the $20,000 loss allowed under the at-risk rules is disallowed under the passive loss rules. The passive loss is disallowed because Bob does not generate any passive income that could absorb his passive loss. Further, his salary (active income) and dividends (portfolio income) cannot be used to absorb any of the passive loss. Consequently, Bob's current year taxable income must reflect his nonpassive income of $115,000, and he receives no current benefit from his share of the partnership loss. However, all is not lost because Bob's share of the entity's loss is *suspended*; it is carried forward and can be deducted in the future when he has passive income or sells his interest in the activity. ▼

This chapter explores the nature of the at-risk limits and passive activity loss rules and their impact on investors. An interesting consequence of these rules is that now investors evaluating potential investments must consider mainly the economics of the venture instead of the tax benefits or tax avoidance possibilities that an investment may generate.

AT-RISK LIMITS

LEARNING OBJECTIVE 2
Explain the at-risk limitation.

The at-risk provisions limit the deductibility of losses from business and income-producing activities. These provisions, which apply to individuals and closely held corporations, are designed to prevent taxpayers from deducting losses in excess of their actual economic investment in an activity. In the case of an S corporation or a partnership, the at-risk limits apply at the owner level. Under the at-risk rules, a taxpayer's deductible loss from an activity for any taxable year is limited to the amount the taxpayer has at risk at the end of the taxable year (the amount the taxpayer could actually lose in the activity).

While the amount at risk generally vacillates over time, the initial amount considered at risk consists of the following:[2]

- The amount of cash and the adjusted basis of property contributed to the activity by the taxpayer.
- Amounts borrowed for use in the activity for which the taxpayer is personally liable or has pledged as security property not used in the activity.

This amount generally is increased each year by the taxpayer's share of income and is decreased by the taxpayer's share of losses and withdrawals from the activity. In addition, because general partners are jointly and severally liable for recourse debts of the partnership, their at-risk amounts are increased when the partnership increases its debt and are decreased when the partnership reduces its debt. However, a taxpayer generally is not considered at risk with respect to borrowed amounts if either of the following is true:

- The taxpayer is not personally liable for repayment of the debt (e.g., nonrecourse debt).
- The lender has an interest (other than as a creditor) in the activity.

---
[2] § 465(b)(1).

An important exception provides that in the case of an activity involving the holding of real property, a taxpayer is considered at risk for his or her share of any *qualified nonrecourse financing* that is secured by real property used in the activity.[3]

Subject to the passive activity rules discussed later in the chapter, a taxpayer may deduct a loss as long as the at-risk amount is positive. However, once the at-risk amount is exhausted, any remaining loss cannot be deducted until a later year. Any losses disallowed for any given taxable year by the at-risk rules may be deducted in the first succeeding year in which the rules do not prevent the deduction—that is, when and to the extent of a positive at-risk amount.

EXAMPLE 4

In 1997, Sue invests $40,000 in an oil partnership that, by the use of nonrecourse loans, spends $60,000 on deductible intangible drilling costs applicable to her interest. Assume Sue's interest in the partnership is subject to the at-risk limits but is not subject to the passive loss limits. Since Sue has only $40,000 of capital at risk, she cannot deduct more than $40,000 against her other income and must reduce her at-risk amount to zero ($40,000 at-risk amount − $40,000 loss deducted). The nondeductible loss of $20,000 ($60,000 loss generated − $40,000 loss allowed) can be carried over to 1998. ▼

EXAMPLE 5

In 1998, Sue has taxable income of $15,000 from the oil partnership and invests an additional $10,000 in the venture. Her at-risk amount is now $25,000 ($0 beginning balance + $15,000 taxable income + $10,000 additional investment). This enables Sue to deduct the carryover loss and requires her to reduce her at-risk amount to $5,000 ($25,000 at-risk amount − $20,000 carryover loss allowed). ▼

An additional complicating factor is that previously allowed losses must be recaptured to the extent the at-risk amount is reduced below zero.[4] That is, previous losses that were allowed must be offset by the recognition of enough income to bring the at-risk amount up to zero. This rule applies in such situations as when the amount at risk is reduced below zero by distributions to the taxpayer or when the status of indebtedness changes from recourse to nonrecourse.

ETHICAL CONSIDERATIONS

Manipulating the At-Risk Limits

At a social function, you encounter your friend Juan. You have known for some time that Juan has an investment in a venture that could make him subject to the at-risk rules. Not wanting to appear "nosy," you make an oblique reference to his investment. He laughs and says, "That hasn't been a problem. At the end of every year, I make a contribution to the partnership to raise my at-risk basis, and then on January 2 of the following year, I get that money back. This approach has worked well for me every year, and the IRS has never caught on. As I've always said, 'there's more than one way to skin a cat.' " As a respected tax accountant in the community, you frown on such techniques with your clients and will not sign tax returns that involve such manipulation. However, Juan is not one of your clients. How do you respond to Juan's confession?

---

[3] § 465(b)(6).   [4] § 465(e).

Concept Summary 11–1

Calculation of At-Risk Amount

Increases to a taxpayer's at-risk amount:

- Cash and the adjusted basis of property contributed to the activity.
- Amounts borrowed for use in the activity for which the taxpayer is personally liable or has pledged as security property not used in the activity.
- Taxpayer's share of amounts borrowed for use in the activity that is qualified nonrecourse financing.
- Taxpayer's share of the activity's income.

Decreases to a taxpayer's at-risk amount:

- Withdrawals from the activity.
- Taxpayer's share of the activity's loss.
- Taxpayer's share of any reductions of debt for which recourse against the taxpayer exists or reductions of qualified nonrecourse debt.

Passive Loss Limits

Learning Objective 3
Describe how the passive loss rules limit deductions for losses, and identify the taxpayers subject to these restrictions.

CLASSIFICATION AND IMPACT OF PASSIVE INCOME AND LOSSES

Classification. The passive loss rules require income and losses to be classified into three categories: active, passive, and portfolio. **Active income** includes, but is not limited to, the following:

- Wages, salary, commissions, bonuses, and other payments for services rendered by the taxpayer.
- Profit from a trade or business in which the taxpayer is a material participant.
- Gain on the sale or other disposition of assets used in an active trade or business.
- Income from intangible property if the taxpayer's personal efforts significantly contributed to the creation of the property.

Portfolio income includes, but is not limited to, the following:

- Interest, dividends, annuities, and royalties not derived in the ordinary course of a trade or business.
- Gain or loss from the disposition of property that produces portfolio income or is held for investment purposes.

Section 469 provides that income or loss from the following activities is treated as *passive*:

- Any trade or business or income-producing activity in which the taxpayer does not materially participate.
- Subject to certain exceptions, all rental activities, whether the taxpayer materially participates or not.

Although the Code defines rental activities as passive activities, several exceptions allow losses from certain real estate rental activities to be offset against nonpassive

TAX IN THE NEWS

ALL THAT GLITTERS IN TAX REFORM IS NOT GOLD

Tax reform, a topic often on the lips of politicians, has been of particular interest recently as various versions of the "flat tax" have been proposed. Theoretical, practical, and political arguments have been presented by both supporters and opponents of the flat tax, but often the implications of any particular plan are difficult to understand. For example, investors in financial instruments producing interest, dividend, and capital gain income could benefit under some flat tax proposals because they exclude such income from taxation. Individuals who invest in real estate may not be as fortunate, however.

Under certain proposals, the taxpayer could claim a deduction for the full cost of the building and land in the year of purchase, rather than having to capitalize these assets and depreciating only the building over a prolonged period of time. If the entity holding the property is a partnership or S corporation, the deduction would flow through to the entity's owners. The result would be a huge loss at the owner level. For real estate investors, however, the losses may not be deductible in the current year due to the passive activity loss rules. The losses would generate no current benefit unless the investor had a like amount of passive income. Under a flat tax regime, the appeal of real estate investments relative to financial investments could decline.

(active or portfolio) income. The exceptions are discussed under Special Passive Activity Rules for Real Estate Activities later in the chapter.

General Impact. Deductions or expenses generated by passive activities can be deducted only to the extent of income from all of the taxpayer's passive activities. Any excess may not be used to offset income from active sources or portfolio income. Instead, any unused passive losses are suspended and carried forward to future years to offset passive income generated in those years. Otherwise, suspended losses may be used only when a taxpayer disposes of his or her entire interest in an activity. In that event, all current and suspended losses related to the activity may offset active and portfolio income.

EXAMPLE 6 Kim, a physician, earned $150,000 from her full-time practice. She also received $10,000 in dividends and interest from various portfolio investments, and her share of a passive loss from a tax shelter not limited by the at-risk rules was $60,000. Because the loss is a passive loss, it is not deductible against her other income. The loss is suspended and is carried over to the future. If Kim has passive income from this investment or from other passive investments in the future, she can offset the suspended loss against that passive income. If she does not have passive income to offset this suspended loss in the future, she will be allowed to offset the loss against other types of income when she eventually disposes of the passive activity. ▼

Impact of Suspended Losses. When a taxpayer disposes of his or her entire interest in a passive activity, the actual economic gain or loss from the investment, including any suspended losses, can finally be determined. As a result, under the passive loss rules, upon a fully taxable disposition, any overall loss realized from the activity by the taxpayer is recognized and can be offset against any income.

A fully taxable disposition generally involves a sale of the property to a third party at arm's length and thus, presumably, for a price equal to the property's fair market value. Gain recognized upon a transfer of an interest in a passive activity generally is treated as passive and is first offset by the suspended losses from that activity.

EXAMPLE 7

Rex sells an apartment building with an adjusted basis of $100,000 for $180,000. In addition, he has suspended losses of $60,000 associated with that building. His total gain, $80,000, and his taxable gain, $20,000, are calculated as follows:

Net sales price	$ 180,000
Less: Adjusted basis	(100,000)
Total gain	$ 80,000
Less: Suspended losses	(60,000)
Taxable gain (passive)	$ 20,000

If current and suspended losses of the passive activity exceed the gain realized or if the sale results in a realized loss, the amount of

- any loss from the activity for the tax year (including losses suspended in the activity disposed of)

in excess of

- net income or gain for the tax year from all passive activities (without regard to the activity disposed of)

is treated as a loss that is not from a passive activity. In computing the loss from the activity for the year of disposition, any gain or loss recognized is included.

EXAMPLE 8

Dean sells an apartment building with an adjusted basis of $100,000 for $150,000. In addition, he has current and suspended losses of $60,000 associated with that building and has no other passive activities. His total gain, $50,000, and his deductible loss, $10,000, are calculated as follows:

Net sales price	$ 150,000
Less: Adjusted basis	(100,000)
Total gain	$ 50,000
Less: Suspended losses	(60,000)
Deductible loss	($ 10,000)

The $10,000 deductible loss is offset against Dean's active income and portfolio income. ▼

Carryovers of Suspended Losses. In the above examples, it was assumed that the taxpayer had an interest in only one passive activity, and as a result, the suspended loss was related exclusively to the activity that was disposed of. Taxpayers often own interests in more than one activity, however, and in that case, any suspended losses must be allocated among the activities in which the taxpayer has an interest. The allocation to an activity is made by multiplying the disallowed passive activity loss from all activities by the following fraction:

$$\frac{\text{Loss from activity}}{\text{Sum of losses for taxable year from all activities having losses}}$$

EXAMPLE 9 Diego has investments in three passive activities with the following income and losses for 1996:

Activity A	($30,000)
Activity B	(20,000)
Activity C	25,000
Net passive loss	($25,000)
Allocated to:	
Activity A ($25,000 × $30,000/$50,000)	$15,000
Activity B ($25,000 × $20,000/$50,000)	10,000
Total suspended losses	($25,000)

Suspended losses are carried over indefinitely and are offset in the future against any passive income from the activities to which they relate.[5]

EXAMPLE 10 Assume the same facts as in Example 9 and that Activity A produces $10,000 of income in 1997. Of the suspended loss of $15,000 from 1996 for Activity A, $10,000 is offset against the income from this activity. If Diego sells Activity A in early 1998, then the remaining $5,000 suspended loss is used in determining his taxable gain or loss. ▼

Passive Credits. Credits arising from passive activities are limited in much the same way as passive losses. Passive credits can be utilized only against regular tax attributable to passive income,[6] which is calculated by comparing the tax on all income (including passive income) with the tax on income excluding passive income.

EXAMPLE 11 Sam owes $50,000 of tax, disregarding net passive income, and $80,000 of tax, considering both net passive and other taxable income (disregarding the credits in both cases). The amount of tax attributable to the passive income is $30,000.

Tax due (before credits) including net passive income	$ 80,000
Less: Tax due (before credits) without including net passive income	(50,000)
Tax attributable to passive income	$ 30,000

Sam in the preceding example can claim a maximum of $30,000 of passive activity credits; the excess credits are carried over. These passive activity credits (such as the low-income housing credit and rehabilitation credit) can only be used against the *regular* tax attributable to passive income. If a taxpayer has a net loss from passive activities during a given year, no credits can be used. Likewise, if a taxpayer has net passive income but the alternative minimum tax applies to that year, no passive activity credits can be used. (The alternative minimum tax is discussed in Chapter 12.)

Carryovers of Passive Credits. Tax credits attributable to passive activities can be carried forward indefinitely much like suspended passive losses. Unlike passive losses, however, passive credits are lost forever when the activity is disposed of in a taxable transaction where loss is recognized. Credits are allowed on dispositions only when there is sufficient tax on passive income to absorb them.

---

[5] § 469(b).   [6] § 469(d)(2).

EXAMPLE 12 Alicia sells a passive activity for a gain of $10,000. The activity had suspended losses of $40,000 and suspended credits of $15,000. The $10,000 gain is offset by $10,000 of the suspended losses, and the remaining $30,000 of suspended losses is deductible against Alicia's active and portfolio income. The suspended credits are lost forever because the sale of the activity did not generate any tax. This is true even if Alicia has positive taxable income or is subject to the alternative minimum tax. ▼

EXAMPLE 13 If Alicia in Example 12 had realized a $100,000 gain on the sale of the passive activity, the suspended credits could have been used to the extent of regular tax attributable to the net passive income.

Gain on sale	$100,000
Less: Suspended losses	(40,000)
Taxable gain	$ 60,000

If the tax attributable to the taxable gain of $60,000 is $15,000 or more, the entire $15,000 of suspended credits can be used. If the tax attributable to the gain is less than $15,000, the excess of the suspended credit over the tax attributable to the gain is lost forever. ▼

When a taxpayer has adequate regular tax liability from passive activities to trigger the use of suspended credits, the credits lose their character as passive credits. They are reclassified as regular tax credits and made subject to the same limits as other credits (discussed in Chapter 13).

TAXPAYERS SUBJECT TO THE PASSIVE LOSS RULES

The passive loss rules apply to individuals, estates, trusts, personal service corporations, and closely held C corporations.[7] Passive income or loss from investments in S corporations or partnerships (see Chapter 20) flows through to the owners, and the passive loss rules are applied at the owner level.

Personal Service Corporations. Application of the passive loss limitations to **personal service corporations** is intended to prevent taxpayers from sheltering personal service income by creating personal service corporations and acquiring passive activities at the corporate level.

EXAMPLE 14 Five tax accountants, who earn a total of $1 million a year in their individual practices, form a personal service corporation. Shortly after its formation, the corporation invests in a passive activity that produces a $200,000 loss during the year. Because the passive loss rules apply to personal service corporations, the corporation may not deduct the $200,000 loss against the $1 million of active income. ▼

Determination of whether a corporation is a *personal service corporation* is based on rather broad definitions. A personal service corporation is a corporation that meets *both* of the following conditions:

- The principal activity is the performance of personal services.
- Such services are substantially performed by employee-owners.

Generally, personal service corporations include those in the fields of health, law, engineering, architecture, accounting, actuarial science, performing arts, and

---
[7] § 469(a).

consulting.[8] A corporation is treated as a personal service corporation if more than 10 percent of the stock (by value) is held by employee-owners.[9] A shareholder is treated as an employee-owner if he or she is an employee or shareholder on *any day* during the testing period.[10] For these purposes, shareholder status and employee status do not even have to occur on the same day.

Closely Held C Corporations.
Application of the passive loss rules to closely held (non-personal service) corporations is also intended to prevent individuals from incorporating to avoid the passive loss limitations. A corporation is classified as a **closely held corporation** if at any time during the taxable year, more than 50 percent of the value of its outstanding stock is owned, directly or indirectly, by or for not more than five individuals. Closely held C corporations (other than personal service corporations) may offset passive losses against *active* income, but not against portfolio income.

EXAMPLE 15

Silver Corporation, a closely held (non-personal service) C corporation, has $500,000 of passive losses from a rental activity, $400,000 of active income, and $100,000 of portfolio income. The corporation may offset $400,000 of the $500,000 passive loss against the $400,000 of active business income, but may not offset the remainder against the $100,000 of portfolio income. Thus, $100,000 of the passive loss is suspended ($500,000 passive loss − $400,000 offset against active income). ▼

Application of the passive loss limitations to closely held corporations prevents taxpayers from transferring their portfolio investments to such corporations in order to offset passive losses against portfolio income.

PASSIVE ACTIVITIES DEFINED

4 LEARNING OBJECTIVE
Discuss the definition of passive activities and the rules for identifying an activity.

Section 469 specifies that the following types of activities are to be treated as passive:

- Any trade or business or income-producing activity in which the taxpayer does not materially participate.
- Subject to certain exceptions, all rental activities.

To understand the meaning of the term *passive activity* and the impact of the rules, one must address the following issues, each of which is the subject of statutory or administrative guidance:

- What constitutes an activity?
- What is meant by material participation?
- When is an activity a rental activity?

Even though guidance is available to help the taxpayer deal with these issues, their resolution is anything but simple.

Identification of an Activity.
Identifying what constitutes an activity is a necessary first step in applying the passive loss limitations. Taxpayers who are involved in complex business operations need to be able to determine whether a given segment of their overall business operations constitutes a separate activity or is to be treated as part of a single activity. Proper treatment is necessary in order to determine whether income or loss from an activity is active or passive.

---

[8] § 448(d)(2).
[9] § 469(j)(2).
[10] § 269A(b)(2).

EXAMPLE 16 Ben owns a business with two separate departments. Department A generates net income of $120,000, and Department B generates a net loss of $95,000. Ben participates for 700 hours in the operations of Department A and for 100 hours in Department B. If Ben is allowed to treat the departments as components of a single activity, he can offset the $95,000 loss from Department B against the $120,000 income from Department A. ▼

EXAMPLE 17 Assume the same facts as in the previous example. If Ben is required to treat each department as a separate activity, because he is a material participant in Department A (having devoted 700 hours to it) the $120,000 profit is active income. However, he is not considered a material participant in Department B (100 hours), and the $95,000 loss is a passive loss. Ben cannot offset the $95,000 passive loss from Department B against the $120,000 of active income from Department A. (A complete discussion of the material participation rules follows.) ▼

Recall that on the disposition of a passive activity, a taxpayer is allowed to offset suspended losses from the activity against other types of income. Therefore, identifying what constitutes an activity is of crucial importance for this purpose too.

EXAMPLE 18 Linda owns a business with two departments. Department A has a net loss of $125,000 in the current year, and Department B has a $70,000 net loss. She disposes of Department B at the end of the year. Assuming Linda is allowed to treat the two departments as separate passive activities, she can offset the passive loss from Department B against other types of income in the following order: gain from disposition of the passive activity, other passive income, and nonpassive income. This treatment leaves her with a suspended loss of $125,000 from Department A. If Departments A and B are treated as components of the same activity, however, on the disposal of Department B, its $70,000 net loss would be suspended along with the other $125,000 of suspended loss of the activity. ▼

The current rules used to delineate what constitutes an activity for purposes of the passive loss limitations are provided in Regulations.[11] These guidelines state that, in general, a taxpayer can treat one or more trade or business activities or rental activities as a single activity if those activities form an *appropriate economic unit* for measuring gain or loss. To determine what ventures form an appropriate economic unit, all of the relevant facts and circumstances must be considered. Taxpayers may use any reasonable method in applying the facts and circumstances. However, the following five factors are given the greatest weight in determining whether activities constitute an appropriate economic unit. It is not necessary to meet all of these conditions in order to treat multiple activities as a single activity.

- Similarities and differences in types of business conducted in the various trade or business or rental activities.
- The extent of common control over the various activities.
- The extent of common ownership of the activities.
- The geographical location of the different units.
- Interdependencies among the activities.

The following examples, adapted from the Regulations, illustrate the application of the general rules for grouping activities.[12]

---

[11] Reg. § 1.469–4.

[12] Reg. § 1.469–4(c)(3).

EXAMPLE 19 George owns a men's clothing store and a video game parlor in Chicago. He also owns a men's clothing store and a video game parlor in Milwaukee. Reasonable methods of applying the facts and circumstances test may result in any of the following groupings:

- All four activities may be grouped into a single activity.
- The clothing stores may be grouped into an activity, and the video parlors may be grouped into a separate activity.
- The Chicago activities may be grouped into an activity, and the Milwaukee activities may be grouped into a separate activity.
- Each of the four activities may be treated as a separate activity. ▼

EXAMPLE 20 Sharon is a partner in a business that sells snack items to drugstores. She also is a partner in a partnership that owns and operates a warehouse. Both partnerships, which are under common control, are located in the same industrial park. The predominant part of the warehouse business is warehousing items for the snack business, and it is the only warehousing business in which Sharon is involved. Sharon should treat the snack business and the warehousing business as a single activity. ▼

Regrouping of Activities. Taxpayers should carefully consider all tax factors in deciding how to group their activities. Once activities have been grouped, they cannot be regrouped unless the original grouping was clearly inappropriate or there has been a material change in the facts and circumstances. If a regrouping is necessary for either of these reasons, the taxpayer is required to disclose to the IRS all information relevant to the regrouping.

The Regulations also grant the IRS the right to regroup activities when both of the following conditions exist.[13]

- The taxpayer's grouping fails to reflect one or more appropriate economic units.
- One of the primary purposes of the taxpayer's grouping is to avoid the passive loss limitations.

The following example, adapted from the Regulations, illustrates a situation where the IRS would exercise its prerogative to regroup a taxpayer's activities.

EXAMPLE 21 Baker, Edwards, Andrews, Clark, and Henson are physicians who operate their own separate practices. Each of the physicians owns interests in activities that generate passive losses, so they devise a plan to set up an entity that will generate passive income. They form the BEACH Partnership to acquire and operate X-ray equipment, and each receives a limited partnership interest. They select an unrelated person to operate the X-ray business as a general partner, and none of the limited partners participates in the activity. Substantially all of the services provided by BEACH are provided to the physicians who own limited partnership interests, and fees are set at a level that assures a profit for BEACH. Each physician treats his medical practice and his interest in the partnership as separate activities and offsets losses from passive investments against the passive income from the partnership. The IRS would interpret the physicians' separate groupings as attempts to avoid the passive loss limitations and would regroup each medical practice and the services performed by the partnership as an appropriate economic unit. ▼

Special Grouping Rules for Rental Activities. Two rules deal specifically with the grouping of rental activities. These provisions are designed to prevent

---
[13] Reg. § 1.469–4(f).

taxpayers from grouping rental activities, which are generally passive, with other businesses in a way that would result in a tax advantage.

First, a rental activity may be grouped with a trade or business activity only if one activity is insubstantial in relation to the other. That is, the rental activity must be insubstantial in relation to the trade or business activity, or the trade or business activity must be insubstantial in relation to the rental activity. The Regulations provide no clear guidelines as to the meaning of insubstantial.[14]

EXAMPLE 22

Schemers, a firm of CPAs, owns a building in downtown Washington, D.C., in which they conduct their practice of public accounting. The firm also rents space on the street level of the building to several retail establishments. Of the total revenue generated by the firm, 95% is associated with the practice of public accounting, and 5% is related to the rental operation. It is likely that the rental activity would be considered insubstantial relative to the accounting practice and the two ventures could be grouped as one nonrental activity. This grouping could be advantageous to the firm, particularly if the rental operation generated a loss! ▼

Second, taxpayers generally may not treat an activity involving the rental of real property and an activity involving the rental of personal property as a single activity.

5 LEARNING OBJECTIVE
Analyze and apply the tests for material participation.

Material Participation. If an individual taxpayer materially participates in a nonrental trade or business activity, any loss from that activity is treated as an active loss that can be offset against active or portfolio income. If a taxpayer does not materially participate, however, the loss is treated as a passive loss, which can only be offset against passive income. Therefore, controlling whether a particular activity is treated as active or passive is an important part of the tax strategy of a taxpayer who owns an interest in one or more businesses. Consider the following examples.

EXAMPLE 23

Dewayne, a corporate executive, earns a salary of $200,000 per year. In addition, he owns a separate business in which he participates. The business produces a loss of $100,000 during the year. If Dewayne materially participates in the business, the $100,000 loss is an active loss that may be offset against his active income from his corporate employer. If he does not materially participate, the loss is passive and is suspended. Dewayne may use the suspended loss in the future only when he has passive income or disposes of the activity. ▼

EXAMPLE 24

Kay, an attorney, earns $250,000 a year in her law practice. She owns interests in two activities, A and B, in which she participates. Activity A, in which she does *not* materially participate, produces a loss of $50,000. Kay has not yet met the material participation standard for Activity B, which produces income of $80,000. However, she can meet the material participation standard if she spends an additional 50 hours in Activity B during the year. Should Kay attempt to meet the material participation standard for Activity B? If she continues working in Activity B and becomes a material participant, the $80,000 income from the activity is *active*, and the $50,000 passive loss from Activity A must be suspended. A more favorable tax strategy is for Kay to *not meet* the material participation standard for Activity B, thus making the income from that activity passive. This enables her to offset the $50,000 passive loss from Activity A against the passive income from Activity B. ▼

---
[14] Reg. § 1.469–4(d).

It is possible to devise numerous scenarios in which the taxpayer could control the tax outcome by increasing or decreasing his or her participation in different activities. Examples 23 and 24 demonstrate some of the possibilities. The conclusion reached in most analyses of this type is that taxpayers will benefit by having profitable activities classified as passive, so that any passive losses can be used to offset passive income. If the activity produces a loss, however, the taxpayer will benefit if it is classified as active so the loss is not subject to the passive loss limitations.

As discussed above, a nonrental trade or business in which a taxpayer owns an interest must be treated as a passive activity unless the taxpayer materially participates. As the Staff of the Joint Committee on Taxation explained, a material participant is one who has "a significant nontax economic profit motive" for taking on activities and selects them for their economic value. In contrast, a passive investor mainly seeks a return from a capital investment (including a possible reduction in taxes) as a supplement to an ongoing source of livelihood.[15] Even if the concept or the implication of being a material participant is clear, the precise meaning of the term **material participation** can be vague. As enacted, § 469 requires a taxpayer to participate on a *regular, continuous, and substantial* basis in order to be a material participant. In many situations, however, it is difficult or impossible to gain any assurance that this nebulous standard is met.

In response to this dilemma, Temporary Regulations[16] provide seven tests which are intended to help taxpayers cope with these issues. Material participation is achieved by meeting any one of the tests. These tests can be divided into three categories:

- Tests based on current participation.
- Tests based on prior participation.
- Test based on facts and circumstances.

Tests Based on Current Participation. The first four tests are quantitative tests that require measurement, in hours, of the taxpayer's participation in the activity during the year.

1. *Does the individual participate in the activity for more than 500 hours during the year?*

The purpose of the 500-hour requirement is to restrict deductions from the types of trade or business activities Congress intended to treat as passive activities. The 500-hour standard for material participation was adopted for the following reasons:[17]

- Few investors in traditional tax shelters devote more than 500 hours a year to such an investment.
- The IRS believes that income from an activity in which the taxpayer participates for more than 500 hours a year should not be treated as passive.

2. *Does the individual's participation in the activity for the taxable year constitute substantially all of the participation in the activity of all individuals (including nonowner employees) for the year?*

---

[15] *General Explanation of the Tax Reform Act of 1986 ("Blue Book")*, prepared by The Staff of the Joint Committee on Taxation, May 4, 1987, H.R. 3838, 99th Cong., p. 212.

[16] Temp. and Prop.Reg § 1.469–5T(a). The Temporary Regulations are also Proposed Regulations. Temporary Regulations have the same effect as final Regulations. Refer to Chapter 2 for a discussion of the different categories of Regulations.

[17] T.D. 8175, 1988–1 C.B. 191.

EXAMPLE 25 Ned, a physician, operates a separate business in which he participates for 80 hours during the year. He is the only participant and has no employees in the separate business. Ned meets the material participation standard of Test 2. If he had employees, it would be difficult to apply Test 2, because the Temporary Regulations do not define the term *substantially all.* ▼

3. *Does the individual participate in the activity for more than 100 hours during the year, and is the individual's participation in the activity for the year not less than the participation of any other individual (including nonowner employees) for the year?*

EXAMPLE 26 Adam, a college professor, owns a separate business in which he participates 110 hours during the year. He has an employee who works 90 hours during the year. Adam meets the material participation standard under Test 3, but probably does not meet it under Test 2 because his participation is only 55% of the total participation. It is unlikely that 55% would meet the *substantially all* requirement of Test 2. ▼

Tests 2 and 3 are included because the IRS recognizes that the operation of some activities does not require more than 500 hours of participation during the year.

4. *Is the activity a significant participation activity for the taxable year, and does the individual's aggregate participation in all significant participation activities during the year exceed 500 hours?*

A **significant participation activity** is a trade or business in which the individual's participation exceeds 100 hours during the year. This test treats taxpayers whose aggregate participation in several significant participation activities exceeds 500 hours as material participants. Test 4 thus accords the same treatment to an individual who devotes an aggregate of more than 500 hours to several significant participation activities as to an individual who devotes more than 500 hours to a single activity.

EXAMPLE 27 Mike owns five different businesses. He participated in each activity during the year as follows:

Activity	Hours of Participation
A	110
B	140
C	120
D	150
E	100

Activities A, B, C, and D are significant participation activities, and Mike's aggregate participation in those activities is 520 hours. Therefore, Activities A, B, C, and D are not treated as passive activities. Activity E is not a significant participation activity (not more than 100 hours), so it is not included in applying the 500-hour test. Activity E is treated as a passive activity, unless Mike meets one of the other material participation tests for that activity. ▼

EXAMPLE 28 Assume the same facts as in the previous example, except that Activity A does not exist. All of the activities are now treated as passive. Activity E is not counted in applying the more-than-500-hour test, so Mike's aggregate participation in significant participation activities is 410 hours (140 in Activity B + 120 in Activity C + 150 in Activity D). He could meet the significant participation test for Activity E by participating for one more hour in the activity. This would cause Activities B, C, D, and E to be treated as nonpassive activities. However, before deciding whether to participate for at least one more hour in Activity E, Mike should assess how the participation would affect his overall tax liability. ▼

Tests Based on Prior Participation. Tests 5 and 6 are based on material participation in prior years. Under these tests, a taxpayer who is no longer a participant in an activity can continue to be *classified* as a material participant. The IRS takes the position that material participation in a trade or business for a long period of time is likely to indicate that the activity represents the individual's principal livelihood, rather than a passive investment. Consequently, withdrawal from the activity, or reduction of participation to the point where it is not material, does not change the classification of the activity from active to passive.

5. *Did the individual materially participate in the activity for any 5 taxable years (whether consecutive or not) during the 10 taxable years that immediately precede the taxable year?*

EXAMPLE 29 Dawn, who owns a 50% interest in a restaurant, was a material participant in the operations of the restaurant from 1991 through 1995. She retired at the end of 1995 and is no longer involved in the restaurant except as an investor. Dawn will be treated as a material participant in the restaurant in 1996. Even if she does not become involved in the restaurant as a material participant again, she will continue to be treated as a material participant in 1997, 1998, 1999, and 2000. In 2001 and later years, Dawn's share of income or loss from the restaurant will be classified as passive unless she materially participates in those years. ▼

6. *Is the activity a personal service activity, and did the individual materially participate in the activity for any three preceding taxable years (whether consecutive or not)?*

As indicated above, the material participation standards differ for personal service activities and other businesses. An individual who was a material participant in a personal service activity for *any three years* prior to the taxable year continues to be treated as a material participant after withdrawal from the activity.

EXAMPLE 30 Evan, a CPA, retires from the EFG Partnership after working full-time in the partnership for 30 years. As a retired partner, he will continue to receive a share of the profits of the firm for the next 10 years, even though he will not participate in the firm's operations. Evan also owns an interest in a passive activity that produces a loss for the year. He continues to be treated as a material participant in the EFG Partnership, and his income from the partnership is active income. Therefore, he is not allowed to offset the loss from his passive investment against the income from the EFG Partnership. ▼

Facts and Circumstances Test. Test 7 is a facts and circumstances test to determine whether the taxpayer has materially participated.

7. *Based on all the facts and circumstances, did the individual participate in the activity on a regular, continuous, and substantial basis during the year?*

The Temporary Regulations do not define what constitutes regular, continuous, and substantial participation except to say that the taxpayer's activities will *not* be considered material participation under Test 7 in the following three circumstances:[18]

- The taxpayer satisfies the participation standards (whether or not a *material participant*) of any Code section other than § 469.
- The taxpayer manages the activity, unless
    - no other person receives compensation for management services, and
    - no individual spends more hours during the tax year managing the activity than does the taxpayer.
- The taxpayer participates in the activity for 100 hours or less during the tax year.

A part of the Temporary Regulations has been reserved for further development of this test. Presumably, additional guidelines will be issued in the future. For the time being, taxpayers should rely on Tests 1 through 6 in determining whether the material participation standards have been met.

Participation Defined. Participation generally includes any work done by an individual in an activity that he or she owns. Participation does not include work if it is of a type not customarily done by owners *and* if one of its principal purposes is to avoid the disallowance of passive losses or credits. Also, work done in an individual's capacity as an investor (e.g., reviewing financial reports in a nonmanagerial capacity) is not counted in applying the material participation tests. However, participation by an owner's spouse counts as participation by the owner.[19]

EXAMPLE 31

Tom, who is a partner in a CPA firm, owns a computer store that has operated at a loss during the year. In order to offset this loss against the income from his CPA practice, Tom would like to avoid having the computer business classified as a passive activity. Through December 15, he has worked 400 hours in the business in management and selling activities. During the last two weeks of December, he works 80 hours in management and selling activities and 30 hours doing janitorial chores. Also during the last two weeks in December, Tom's wife participates 40 hours as a salesperson. She has worked as a salesperson in the computer store in prior years, but has not done so during the current year. If any of Tom's work is of a type not customarily done by owners *and* if one of its principal purposes is to avoid the disallowance of passive losses or credits, it is not counted in applying the material participation tests. It is likely that Tom's 480 hours of participation in management and selling activities will count as participation, but the 30 hours spent doing janitorial chores will not. However, the 40 hours of participation by his wife will count, and Tom will qualify as a material participant under the more-than-500-hour rule (480 + 40 = 520). ▼

Limited Partners. A *limited* partner is one whose liability to third-party creditors of the partnership is limited to the amount the partner has invested in the partnership. Such a partnership must have at least one *general* partner, who is fully liable in an individual capacity for the debts of the partnership to third parties. Generally, a *limited partner* is not considered a material participant unless he or she qualifies under Test 1, 5, or 6 in the above list. However, a *general partner* may qualify as a material participant by meeting any of the seven tests. If an unlimited,

---

[18] Temp. and Prop.Reg. § 1.469–5T(b)(2).

[19] Temp. and Prop.Reg. § 1.469–5T(f)(3).

or general, partner also owns a limited interest in the same limited partnership, all interests are treated as a general interest.[20]

ETHICAL CONSIDERATIONS

A Lovers' Triangle and the Passive Loss Rules

The troubled marriage of John and Eleanor finally reached an impasse, and they mutually agreed to divorce. Shortly after the divorce was finalized, John married Kristen. The three have known each other for years from working together to harvest the grapes of a vineyard owned by John. Prior to the divorce, each had worked 200 hours in the vineyard in the current year. Because the investment generates a loss for the current year, John wants to classify it as an active rather than a passive loss. In order for the loss to be classified as active, the participation of John and Eleanor together must exceed 500 hours. John claims that meeting that threshold is no problem. He worked 200 hours and Eleanor, who was his wife when the work was done, worked 200 hours. Kristen, who files a joint return with John, worked 200 hours. "Besides," says John, "there is nothing in the law that says I can't do this." John feels it is proper to aggregate Eleanor's and Kristen's participation with his own. This makes the loss deductible in full. As John's tax return preparer, how do you react?

6 LEARNING OBJECTIVE
Understand the nature of rental activities under the passive loss rules.

Rental Activities Defined. As discussed previously, § 469 specifies that, subject to certain exceptions, all rental activities are to be treated as passive activities.[21] A **rental activity** is defined as any activity where payments are received principally for the use of tangible (real or personal) property.[22] Importantly, an activity that is classified as a rental activity is subject to the passive activity loss rules, even if the taxpayer involved is a material participant.

EXAMPLE 32
Sarah owns an apartment building and spends an average of 60 hours a week in its operation. Assuming that the apartment building operation is classified as a rental activity, it is automatically subject to the passive activity rules, even though Sarah spends more than 500 hours a year in its operation. ▼

As suggested, Temporary Regulations provide that in certain circumstances activities involving rentals of real and personal property are *not* to be *treated* as rental activities.[23]

EXAMPLE 33
Dan owns a videotape business. Because the average period of customer use is seven days or less, Dan's videotape business is not treated as a rental activity. ▼

The fact that Dan's videotape business in the previous example is not treated as a rental activity does not necessarily mean that it is classified as a nonpassive activity. Instead, the videotape business is treated as a trade or business activity subject to the material participation standards. If Dan is a material participant, the business is treated as active. If he is not a material participant, it is treated as a passive activity.

---

[20] Temp. and Prop.Reg. § 1.469–5T(e)(3)(ii).
[21] § 469(c)(2).
[22] § 469(j)(8).
[23] Temp. and Prop.Reg. § 1.469–1T(e)(3)(ii).

Therefore, activities covered by any of the following six exceptions provided by the Temporary Regulations are not *automatically* treated as passive activities because they would not be classified as rental activities. Instead, the activities are subject to the material participation tests.

1. *The average period of customer use for the property is seven days or less.*

   Under this exception, activities involving the short-term use of tangible property such as automobiles, videocassettes, tuxedos, tools, and other such property are not treated as rental activities. The provision also applies to short-term rentals of hotel or motel rooms.

   This exception is based on the presumption that a person who rents property for seven days or less is generally required to provide *significant services* to the customer. Providing such services supports a conclusion that the person is engaged in a service business rather than a rental business.

2. *The average period of customer use for the property is 30 days or less, and the owner of the property provides significant personal services.*

   For longer-term rentals, the presumption that significant services are provided is not automatic, as it is in the case of the seven-day exception. Instead, the taxpayer must be able to *prove* that significant personal services are rendered in connection with the activity. Relevant facts and circumstances include the frequency with which such services are provided, the type and amount of labor required to perform the services, and the value of the services relative to the amount charged for the use of the property. Significant personal services include only services provided by *individuals*.[24]

3. *The owner of the property provides extraordinary personal services. The average period of customer use is of no consequence in applying this test.*

   Extraordinary personal services are services provided by individuals where the customers' use of the property is incidental to their receipt of the services. For example, a patient's use of a hospital bed is incidental to his or her receipt of medical services. Another example is the use of a boarding school's dormitory, which is incidental to the scholastic services received.

4. *The rental of the property is treated as incidental to a nonrental activity of the taxpayer.*

   Rentals of real property incidental to a nonrental activity are not considered a passive activity. The Temporary Regulations provide that the following rentals are not passive activities.[25]

   - *Property held primarily for investment.* This occurs where the principal purpose for holding the property is the expectation of gain from the appreciation of the property and the gross rent income is less than 2 percent of the lesser of (1) the unadjusted basis or (2) the fair market value of the property.

EXAMPLE 34

Ramon invests in vacant land for the purpose of realizing a profit on its appreciation. He leases the land during the period it is held. The land's unadjusted basis is $250,000, and the fair market value is $350,000. The lease payments are $4,000 per year. Because gross rent income is less than 2% of $250,000, the activity is not a rental activity. ▼

---

[24] Temp. and Prop.Reg. § 1.469–1T(e)(3)(iv).

[25] Temp. and Prop.Regs. §§ 1.469–1T(e)(3)(vi)(B) through (E).

- *Property used in a trade or business.* This occurs where the property is owned by a taxpayer who is an owner of the trade or business using the rental property. The property must also have been used in the trade or business during the year or during at least two of the five preceding taxable years. The 2 percent test above also applies in this situation.

EXAMPLE 35 A farmer owns land with an unadjusted basis of $250,000 and a fair market value of $350,000. He used it for farming purposes in 1995 and 1996. In 1997, he leased the land to another farmer for $4,000. The activity is not a rental activity. ▼

- *Property held for sale to customers.* If property is held for sale to customers and rented during the year, the rental of the property is not a rental activity. If, for instance, an automobile dealer rents automobiles held for sale to customers to persons who are having their own cars repaired, the activity is not a rental activity.

- *Lodging rented for the convenience of an employer.* If an employer provides lodging for an employee incidental to the employee's performance of services in the employer's trade or business, no rental activity exists.

- A partner who rents property to a partnership that is used in the partnership's trade or business does not have a rental activity.

These rules were written to prevent taxpayers from converting active or portfolio income into a passive activity for the purpose of offsetting other passive losses.

5. *The taxpayer customarily makes the property available during defined business hours for nonexclusive use by various customers.*

EXAMPLE 36 Pat is the owner-operator of a public golf course. Some customers pay daily greens fees each time they use the course, while others purchase weekly, monthly, or annual passes. The golf course is open every day from sunrise to sunset, except on certain holidays and on days when the course is closed due to inclement weather conditions. Pat is not engaged in a rental activity, regardless of the average period customers use the course. ▼

6. *The property is provided for use in an activity conducted by a partnership, S corporation, or joint venture in which the taxpayer owns an interest.*

EXAMPLE 37 Joe, a partner in the Skyview Partnership, contributes the use of a building to the partnership. The partnership has net income of $30,000 during the year, of which Joe's share is $10,000. Unless the partnership is engaged in a rental activity, none of Joe's income from the partnership is income from a rental activity. ▼

INTERACTION OF THE AT-RISK AND PASSIVE ACTIVITY LIMITS

7 LEARNING OBJECTIVE
Recognize the relationship between the at-risk and passive activity limitations.

The determination of whether a loss is suspended under the passive loss rules is made after application of the at-risk rules, as well as other provisions relating to the measurement of taxable income. A loss that is not allowed for the year because the taxpayer is not at risk with respect to it is suspended under the at-risk provision and not under the passive loss rules. Further, a taxpayer's basis is reduced by deductions (e.g., depreciation) even if the deductions are not currently usable because of the passive loss rules.

EXAMPLE 38

Jack's adjusted basis in a passive activity is $10,000 at the beginning of 1996. His loss from the activity in 1996 is $4,000. Since Jack had no passive activity income, the $4,000 cannot be deducted. At year-end, Jack has an adjusted basis and an at-risk amount of $6,000 in the activity and a suspended passive loss of $4,000. ▼

EXAMPLE 39

Jack in Example 38 had a loss of $9,000 in the activity in 1997. Since the $9,000 exceeds his at-risk amount ($6,000) by $3,000, that $3,000 loss is disallowed by the at-risk rules. If Jack has no passive activity income, the remaining $6,000 is suspended under the passive activity rules. At year-end, he has a $3,000 loss suspended under the at-risk rules, $10,000 of suspended passive losses, and an adjusted basis and an at-risk amount in the activity of zero. ▼

EXAMPLE 40

Jack in Example 39 realized $1,000 of passive income in 1998. Because the $1,000 increases his at-risk amount, $1,000 of the $3,000 unused loss can be reclassified as a passive loss. If he has no other passive income, the $1,000 income is offset by $1,000 of suspended passive losses. At the end of 1998, Jack has no taxable passive income, $2,000 ($3,000 − $1,000) of unused losses under the at-risk rules, $10,000 of (reclassified) suspended passive losses ($10,000 + $1,000 of reclassified unused at-risk losses − $1,000 of passive losses offset against passive income), and an adjusted basis and an at-risk amount in the activity of zero. ▼

EXAMPLE 41

In 1999, Jack had no gain or loss from the activity in Example 40. He contributed $5,000 more to the passive activity. Because the $5,000 increases his at-risk amount, the $2,000 of losses suspended under the at-risk rules is reclassified as passive. Jack gets no passive loss deduction in 1999. At year-end, he has no suspended losses under the at-risk rules, $12,000 of suspended passive losses ($10,000 + $2,000 of reclassified suspended at-risk losses), and an adjusted basis and an at-risk amount of $3,000 ($5,000 additional investment − $2,000 of reclassified losses). ▼

SPECIAL PASSIVE ACTIVITY RULES FOR REAL ESTATE ACTIVITIES

8 LEARNING OBJECTIVE
Discuss the special treatment available to real estate activities.

The passive loss limits contain two exceptions related to real estate activities. These exceptions allow all or part of real estate rental losses to be offset against active or portfolio income, even though the activity is a passive activity.

Material Participation in a Real Property Trade or Business.
Losses from real estate rental activities are *not* treated as passive losses for certain real estate professionals.[26] To qualify for nonpassive treatment, a taxpayer must satisfy both of the following requirements:

- More than half of the personal services that the taxpayer performs in trades or businesses are performed in real property trades or businesses in which the taxpayer materially participates.
- The taxpayer performs more than 750 hours of services in these real property trades or businesses as a material participant.

Taxpayers who do not satisfy the above requirements must continue to treat losses from real estate rental activities as passive losses.

---
[26] § 469(c)(7).

EXAMPLE 42

During the current year, Della performed personal service activities as follows: 900 hours as a personal financial planner, 550 hours in a real estate development and leasing business, and 600 hours in real estate rental activities. Any loss Della incurred in either real estate activity will *not* be subject to the passive loss rules, since more than 50% of her personal services were devoted to real property trades or businesses, and her material participation in those real estate activities exceeded 750 hours. Thus, any loss from the real estate rental activity could offset active and portfolio sources of income. ▼

As discussed earlier, a spouse's work is taken into consideration in satisfying the material participation requirement. However, the hours worked by a spouse are *not* taken into account when ascertaining whether a taxpayer has worked for more than 750 hours in real property trades or businesses during a year.[27] Services performed by an employee are not treated as being related to a real estate trade or business unless the employee performing the services owns more than a 5 percent interest in the employer. Additionally, a closely held C corporation may also qualify for the passive loss relief if more than 50 percent of its gross receipts for the year are derived from real property trades or businesses in which it materially participates.

ETHICAL CONSIDERATIONS

Punching the Time Clock at Year-End

As the end of the tax year approaches, Ralph, a successful full-time real estate developer and investor, recognizes that his and his wife's income tax situation could be bleak for the year. Unless they are able to generate more hours of participation in one of his rental activities, they will not reach the material participation threshold for the apartment rentals. Consequently, the tax losses from the venture will not be deductible. To accomplish this goal, he suggests the following plan to his wife, Jane:

- He will document the hours throughout the year during which he was merely thinking about the rentals.
- During the week, Jane will visit the apartment rentals to oversee the operations of the buildings (i.e., in a management role).
- On weekends, Ralph *and* Jane will visit the same units to assess the operations. For the weekend duties, Ralph plans to count both his and Jane's hours toward his tally of participation hours.
- Also on the weekends, they will drive around the community looking for other potential apartment rental properties to buy. Again, both his and Jane's hours will be counted.

Ralph contends that the law clearly allows the efforts of one's spouse to count as that of the taxpayer for purposes of the material participation tests. There is nothing in the law that requires a taxpayer to be efficient in his participation hours. How do you react?

Rental Real Estate Activities. The second exception is more significant in that it is not restricted to real estate professionals. This exception allows individuals to deduct up to $25,000 of losses on real estate rental activities against active and

---

[27] § 469(c)(7)(B) and Reg. § 1.469–9.

portfolio income.[28] The potential annual $25,000 deduction is reduced by 50 percent of the taxpayer's AGI in excess of $100,000. Thus, the entire deduction is phased out at $150,000 of AGI. If married individuals file separately, the $25,000 deduction is reduced to zero unless they lived apart for the entire year. If they lived apart for the entire year, the loss amount is $12,500 each, and the phase-out begins at $50,000. AGI for purposes of the phase-out is calculated without regard to IRA deductions, Social Security benefits, and net losses from passive activities.

To qualify for the $25,000 exception, a taxpayer must meet the following requirements.[29]

- Actively participate in the real estate rental activity.
- Own 10 percent or more (in value) of all interests in the activity during the entire taxable year (or shorter period during which the taxpayer held an interest in the activity).

The difference between *active participation* and *material participation* is that the former can be satisfied without regular, continuous, and substantial involvement in operations as long as the taxpayer participates in making management decisions in a significant and bona fide sense. In this context, relevant management decisions include such decisions as approving new tenants, deciding on rental terms, and approving capital or repair expenditures.

The $25,000 allowance is available after all active participation rental losses and gains are netted and applied to other passive income. If a taxpayer has a real estate rental loss in excess of the amount that can be deducted under the real estate rental exception, that excess is treated as a passive loss.

EXAMPLE 43

Brad, who has $90,000 of AGI before considering rental activities, has $85,000 of losses from a real estate rental activity in which he actively participates. He also actively participates in another real estate rental activity from which he has $25,000 of income. He has other passive income of $36,000. The net rental loss of $60,000 is offset by the $36,000 of passive income, leaving $24,000 that can be deducted against other income. ▼

The $25,000 offset allowance is an aggregate of both deductions and credits in deduction equivalents. The deduction equivalent of a passive activity credit is the amount of deductions that reduces the tax liability for the taxable year by an amount equal to the credit.[30] A taxpayer with $5,000 of credits and a tax bracket of 28 percent would have a deduction equivalent of $17,857 ($5,000 ÷ 28%).

If the total deduction and deduction equivalent exceed $25,000, the taxpayer must allocate on a pro rata basis, first among the losses (including real estate rental activity losses suspended in prior years) and then to credits in the following order: (1) credits other than rehabilitation and low-income housing credits, (2) rehabilitation credits, and (3) low-income housing credits.

EXAMPLE 44

Kevin is an active participant in a real estate rental activity that produces $8,000 of income, $26,000 of deductions, and $1,500 of credits. Kevin, who is in the 28% tax bracket, may deduct the net passive loss of $18,000 ($8,000 − $26,000). After deducting the loss, he has an available deduction equivalent of $7,000 ($25,000 − $18,000 passive loss). Therefore, the maximum amount of credits that he may claim is $1,960 ($7,000 × 28%). Since the actual credits are less than this amount, Kevin may claim the entire $1,500 credit. ▼

---

[28] § 469(i).
[29] § 469(i)(6).
[30] § 469(j)(5).

EXAMPLE 45

Kelly, who is in the 28% tax bracket, is an active participant in three separate real estate rental activities. The relevant tax results for each activity are as follows:

- Activity A: $20,000 of losses.
- Activity B: $10,000 of losses.
- Activity C: $4,200 of credits.

Kelly's deduction equivalent from the credits is $15,000 ($4,200 ÷ 28%). Therefore, the total passive deductions and deduction equivalents are $45,000 ($20,000 + $10,000 + $15,000), which exceeds the maximum allowable amount of $25,000. Consequently, Kelly must allocate pro rata first from among losses and then from among credits. Deductions from losses are limited as follows:

- Activity A {$25,000 × [$20,000 ÷ ($20,000 + $10,000)]} = $16,667.
- Activity B {$25,000 × [$10,000 ÷ ($20,000 + $10,000)]} = $8,333.

Since the amount of passive deductions exceeds the $25,000 maximum, the deduction balance of $5,000 and passive credit of $4,200 must be carried forward. Kelly's suspended losses and credits by activity are as follows:

	Total	A	B	C
Allocated losses	$30,000	$20,000	$10,000	$ -0-
Allocated credits	4,200	-0-	-0-	4,200
Utilized losses	(25,000)	(16,667)	(8,333)	-0-
Suspended losses	5,000	3,333	1,667	-0-
Suspended credits	4,200	-0-	-0-	4,200

DISPOSITIONS OF PASSIVE INTERESTS

9 LEARNING OBJECTIVE
Determine the proper tax treatment upon the disposition of a passive activity.

Recall from an earlier discussion that if a taxpayer disposes of an entire interest in a passive activity, any suspended losses (and in certain cases, suspended credits) may be utilized when calculating the final economic gain or loss on the investment. In addition, if a loss ultimately results, that loss can be offset against other types of income. However, the consequences may differ if the activity is disposed of in a transaction that is other than a fully taxable transaction. The following discusses the treatment of suspended passive losses in other types of dispositions.

Disposition of a Passive Activity at Death. A transfer of a taxpayer's interest in an activity by reason of the taxpayer's death results in suspended losses being allowed (to the decedent) to the extent they exceed the amount, if any, of the step-up in basis allowed.[31] Suspended losses are lost to the extent of the amount of the basis increase. The losses allowed generally are reported on the final return of the deceased taxpayer.

EXAMPLE 46

A taxpayer dies with passive activity property having an adjusted basis of $40,000, suspended losses of $10,000, and a fair market value at the date of the decedent's death of $75,000. The increase (i.e., step-up) in basis (see Chapter 14) is $35,000 (fair market value at date of death in excess of adjusted basis). None of the $10,000 suspended loss is deductible by either the decedent or the beneficiary. The suspended losses ($10,000) are lost because they do not exceed the step-up in basis ($35,000). ▼

---

[31] § 469(g)(2).

EXAMPLE 47 A taxpayer dies with passive activity property having an adjusted basis of $40,000, suspended losses of $10,000, and a fair market value at the date of the decedent's death of $47,000. Since the step-up in basis is only $7,000 ($47,000 − $40,000), the suspended losses allowed are limited to $3,000 ($10,000 suspended loss at time of death − $7,000 increase in basis). The $3,000 loss available to the decedent is reported on the decedent's final income tax return. ▼

Disposition of a Passive Activity by Gift. In a disposition of a taxpayer's interest in a passive activity by gift, the suspended losses are added to the basis of the property.[32]

EXAMPLE 48 A taxpayer makes a gift of passive activity property having an adjusted basis of $40,000, suspended losses of $10,000, and a fair market value at the date of the gift of $100,000. The taxpayer cannot deduct the suspended losses in the year of the disposition. However, the suspended losses transfer with the property and are added to the adjusted basis of the property. ▼

Installment Sale of a Passive Activity. An installment sale of a taxpayer's entire interest in a passive activity triggers the recognition of the suspended losses.[33] The losses are allowed in each year of the installment obligation in the ratio that the gain recognized in each year bears to the total gain on the sale.

EXAMPLE 49 Stan sold his entire interest in a passive activity for $100,000. His adjusted basis in the property was $60,000. If he uses the installment method, his gross profit ratio is 40% ($40,000/$100,000). If Stan received a $20,000 down payment, he would recognize a gain of $8,000 (40% of $20,000). If the activity had a suspended loss of $25,000, Stan would deduct $5,000 [($8,000 ÷ $40,000) × $25,000] of the suspended loss in the first year. ▼

Passive Activity Changes to Active. If a formerly passive activity becomes an active one, suspended losses are allowed to the extent of income from the now active business.[34] If any of the suspended loss remains, it continues to be treated as a loss from a passive activity. The excess suspended loss can be deducted from passive income or carried over to the next tax year and deducted to the extent of income from the now active business in the succeeding year(s). The activity must continue to be the same activity.

Nontaxable Exchange of a Passive Activity. In a nontaxable exchange of a passive investment, the taxpayer keeps the suspended losses, which generally become deductible when the acquired property is sold. If the activity of the old and new property are the same, suspended losses can be used.

EXAMPLE 50 A taxpayer exchanged a duplex for a limited partnership interest in a § 721 nonrecognition transaction (see Chapter 20 for details). The suspended losses from the duplex are not deductible until the limited partnership interest is sold. Two separate activities exist: a real estate rental activity and a limited partnership activity. If the taxpayer had continued to own the duplex and the duplex had future taxable income, the suspended losses would have become deductible before the time of disposition. ▼

EXAMPLE 51 In a § 1031 nontaxable exchange (see Chapter 15 for details), a taxpayer exchanged a duplex for an apartment building. The suspended losses from the duplex are deductible against future taxable income of the apartment building. The same activity exists. ▼

---

[32] § 469(j)(6).
[33] § 469(g)(3).
[34] § 469(f).

Concept Summary 11-2

Passive Activity Loss Rules: General Concepts

What is the fundamental passive activity rule?	Passive activity losses may be deducted only against passive activity gains. Losses not allowed are suspended and used in future years.
Who is subject to the passive activity rules?	Individuals. Estates. Trusts. Personal service corporations. Closely held C corporations.
What is a passive activity?	Trade or business or income-producing activity in which the taxpayer does not materially participate during the year, or rental activities, subject to certain exceptions, regardless of the taxpayer's level of participation.
What is an activity?	One or more trade or business or rental activities that comprises an appropriate economic unit.
How is an appropriate economic unit determined?	Based on a reasonable application of the relevant facts and circumstances.
What is material participation?	In general, the taxpayer participates in a regular, continuous, and substantial basis. More specifically, when the taxpayer meets the conditions of one of the seven tests provided in the Regulations.
What is a rental activity?	In general, an activity where payments are received for the use of tangible property. More specifically, a rental activity that does *not* meet one of the six exceptions provided in the Regulations. Special rules apply to rental real estate.

Tax Planning Considerations

10 Learning Objective
Suggest tax planning strategies to minimize the effect of the passive loss limitations.

UTILIZING PASSIVE LOSSES

Taxpayers who have passive activity losses (PALs) should adopt a strategy of generating passive activity income that can be sheltered by existing passive losses. One approach is to buy an interest in a passive activity that is generating income (referred to as passive income generators, or PIGs). Then the PAL can be offset against income from the PIG. From a tax perspective, it would be foolish to buy a loss-generating passive activity (PAL) unless one has other passive income (PIG) to shelter or the activity is rental real estate that can qualify for the $25,000 exception or the exception available to real estate professionals.

A taxpayer with existing passive losses might consider buying rental property. If a large down payment is made and the straight-line method of MACRS (discussed in Chapter 8) is elected, a positive net income could be realized. The income would be sheltered by other passive losses, depreciation expense would be spread out evenly and preserved for future years, and depreciation recapture (discussed in Chapter 17) would be avoided upon the sale of the property. Future gain realized upon the sale of the rental property could be sheltered by existing suspended passive losses.

Taxpayers with passive losses should consider all other trades or businesses in which they have an interest. If they show that they do not materially participate in the activity, the activity becomes a passive activity. Any income generated could be sheltered by existing passive losses and suspended losses. Family partnerships in which certain members do not materially participate would qualify. The silent partner in any general partnership engaged in a trade or business would also qualify.

As the chapter has shown, the passive loss rules can have a dramatic effect on a taxpayer's ability to claim passive losses currently. However, several steps can be taken to mitigate their impact:

- Replace passive activity debt with home equity indebtedness.
- Carefully select the year in which a passive activity is to be disposed of at a gain, as it can be to the taxpayer's advantage to wait until sufficient passive losses have been generated to completely offset the gain recognized on the asset's disposition.
- Keep accurate records of all sources of income and losses, particularly any suspended passive losses and credits and the activities to which they relate, so that their potential tax benefit will not be lost.

Finally, because of the restrictive nature of the passive activity loss rules, it may be advantageous for a taxpayer to use a vacation home enough to convert it to a second residence. This would enable all of the qualified interest and real estate taxes to be deducted without limitation. However, this strategy would lead to the loss of other deductions, such as repairs, maintenance, and insurance.

KEY TERMS

Active income, 11–6
At-risk limitation, 11–3
Closely held corporation, 11–11
Extraordinary personal services, 11–20

Material participation, 11–15
Passive loss, 11–3
Personal service corporation, 11–10
Portfolio income, 11–6

Rental activity, 11–19
Significant participation activity, 11–16
Tax shelters, 11–2

PROBLEM MATERIALS

DISCUSSION QUESTIONS

1. Congress has passed two major provisions to inhibit taxpayers' ability to use tax shelters to reduce or defer Federal income tax. Explain.

2. Alice invested $50,000 for a 25% interest in a partnership in which she is not a material participant. The partnership borrowed $100,000 from a bank and used the proceeds to acquire a building. What is Alice's at-risk amount if the $100,000 was borrowed on a recourse loan?

3. What constitutes a taxpayer's initial at-risk amount, and what causes increases and decreases in the amount at risk?

4. Roy invested $15,000 in a cattle-feeding operation that used nonrecourse notes to purchase $150,000 in feed, which was fed to the cattle and expensed. His share of the expense was $27,000. How much can Roy deduct?

5. Explain the meaning of the terms *active income, portfolio income,* and *passive income.*

6. Manuel owns an interest in an activity that produces a $100,000 loss during the year. Would he generally prefer to have the activity classified as active or passive? Discuss.

7. Felicia owns a passive activity that she acquired several years ago. She has incurred losses on the activity since its acquisition. This is the only passive activity she has ever owned. How will these passive losses affect Felicia's taxable income when she disposes of the activity?

8. What is a suspended loss? Why is it important to allocate suspended losses in cases where a taxpayer has interests in more than one passive activity?

9. On the taxable disposition of a passive activity, what happens to the suspended losses? The suspended credits?

10. Discuss whether the passive loss rules apply to the following: individuals, closely held C corporations, S corporations, partnerships, and personal service corporations.

11. Gray Corporation has $100,000 of active income and a $55,000 passive loss for the year. Under what circumstances is the corporation prohibited from deducting the loss? Under what circumstances is the corporation allowed to deduct the loss?

12. The Regulations set forth a *facts and circumstances test* for determining what constitutes an activity. Describe this test and comment on the significance of the term *appropriate economic unit*.

13. Discuss what constitutes a passive activity.

14. Under what circumstances may the IRS regroup activities in a different way than the taxpayer has grouped them? Give an example of a situation to which the regrouping rule would be applied.

15. What is the significance of the term *material participation*? Why is the extent of a taxpayer's participation in an activity important in determining whether a loss from the activity is deductible or nondeductible?

16. Why did the IRS adopt the more-than-500-hour standard for material participation?

17. Jan, an attorney, operates a separate business that she acquired nine years ago. She has one part-time employee in the business. Jan participated for 130 hours in the business during the current year, and the business incurred a loss of $20,000. Under what circumstances will the loss be deductible as an active loss?

18. Rene retired from public accounting after a long and successful career of 45 years. As part of her retirement package, she continues to share in the profits and losses of the firm, albeit at a lower rate than when she was working full-time. Because Rene wants to stay busy during her retirement years, she has invested and works in a local hardware business, operated as a partnership. Unfortunately, the business has recently gone through a slump and has not been generating profits. Identify relevant tax issues for Rene.

19. Some types of work are counted in applying the material participation standards, and some types are not counted. Discuss and give examples of each type.

20. During the current year, Alan is determined to make better use of the tax losses that tend to flow from the various businesses that he owns. He is particularly sensitive to the limitations that the passive loss rules place on the deductibility of losses because of the disaster that occurred last year: his accountant informed him that he would not be able to claim any of the losses on his income tax return because of his lack of material participation. He has even suggested to his wife that she may have to put in some time at the businesses if his goals are to be accomplished. Identify the tax issues that Alan faces.

21. What are *significant personal services*, and what role do they play in determining whether a rental activity is treated as a passive activity?

22. What are *extraordinary personal services*, and what is their importance in determining whether a rental activity is treated as a passive activity?

23. How is passive activity defined in the Code, and what aspects of the definition have been clarified by final or Temporary Regulations?

24. Laura owns an apartment building and a videotape rental business. She participates for more than 500 hours in the operations of each activity. Are the businesses active or passive?

25. Hilda incurred a loss of $60,000 on a real estate rental activity during the current year. Under what circumstances can Hilda treat the entire loss as nonpassive?

26. In the current year, George and Susie White, both successful CPAs, made a cash investment for a limited partnership interest in a California avocado grove. In addition to the cash generated from the investors, the grove's management borrowed a substantial sum to purchase assets necessary for its operation. The Whites' investment adviser told them that their share of the tax loss in the first year alone would be in excess of their initial cash investment, followed by several more years of losses. They feel confident that their interest in the avocado grove is a sound investment. Identify the tax issues facing the Whites.

27. Rick, a full-time real estate professional, earns $5,000 for development services rendered to an S corporation that owns and manages apartment units. He also owns an interest in the entity. His share of the S corporation's losses for the year totals $5,000. Identify the issues that are relevant in determining how the items of income and loss are treated for tax purposes.

28. Can an employer treat services performed by an employee as being related to a real estate trade or business?

29. Matt owns a small apartment building that generated a loss during the year. Under what circumstances can Matt deduct a loss from the rental activity, and what limitations apply?

30. What are the differences between material participation and active participation under the passive loss rules?

31. Betty and Steve received a substantial windfall due to a recent inheritance. Because they have always loved spending time at the beach, they plan to devote some of the newly available cash to a beach-related investment. Their analysis identifies two possibilities that seem to be logical given their particular situation. They could purchase a beach cottage and use it for both personal and rental purposes; or they could pool their money with Steve's brother and purchase several cottages, one of which would be held strictly for personal use, while the others would be held solely for rental use. Identify the tax issues facing Betty and Steve.

PROBLEMS

32. Last year Kelly earned a salary of $200,000 and invested $40,000 for a 20% interest in a partnership that is not a passive activity. Through the use of $800,000 of nonrecourse financing, the partnership acquired assets worth $1 million. Depreciation, interest, and other deductions related to the activity resulted in a loss of $150,000, of which Kelly's share was $30,000. In the current year, Kelly's share of the partnership's loss was $15,000. How much of the loss from the partnership can Kelly deduct?

33. In the current year, Bill Parker (54 Oak Drive, St. Paul, MN 55162) is considering making an investment of $60,000 in Best Choice Partnership. The prospectus provided by Bill's broker indicates that the partnership investment is not a passive activity and that Bill's share of the entity's loss in the current year will likely be $40,000, while his share of the partnership loss next year will probably be $25,000. Write a letter to Bill in which you indicate how the losses would be treated for tax purposes in the current and next years.

34. Carmen wishes to invest $25,000 in a relatively safe venture and has discovered two alternatives that would produce the following reportable income and loss over the next three years:

Year	Alternative 1 Income (Loss)	Alternative 2 Income (Loss)
1	($15,000)	($45,000)
2	(15,000)	20,000
3	45,000	40,000

She is interested in the after-tax effects of these alternatives over a three-year horizon. Assume that Carmen's investment portfolio produces sufficient passive income to offset any potential passive loss that may arise from these alternatives, that her cost of capital is 8% (the present value factors are 0.92593, 0.85734, and 0.79383), that she is in the 28% tax bracket, that each investment alternative possesses equal growth potential, and that each alternative exposes her to comparable financial risk. In addition, assume that in the loss years for each alternative, there is no cash flow from or to the investment (i.e., the loss is due to depreciation), while in those years when the income is positive, cash flows to Carmen equal the amount of the income. Based on these facts, compute the present value of these two investment alternatives and determine which option Carmen should choose.

35. Tina acquired passive Activity A in January 1992 and Activity B in September 1993. Until 1996, Activity A was profitable. Activity A produced a loss of $200,000 in 1996 and a loss of $100,000 in 1997. Tina has passive income from Activity B of $20,000 in 1996 and $40,000 in 1997. After offsetting passive income, how much of the net losses may she deduct?

36. In 1992, Kay acquired an interest in a partnership in which she is not a material participant. The partnership was profitable until 1996. Kay's basis in her partnership interest at the beginning of 1996 was $40,000. In 1996, Kay's share of the partnership loss was $35,000. In 1997, her share of the partnership income was $15,000. How much can Kay deduct in 1996 and 1997?

37. Bob, an attorney, earned $200,000 from his law practice in the current year. He received $45,000 in dividends and interest during the year. In addition, he incurred a loss of $50,000 from an investment in a passive activity acquired three years ago. What is Bob's net income for the current year after considering the passive investment?

38. Sarah has $100,000 that she wishes to invest, and she is considering the following two options:

    - Option A—Investment in Bluebird Equity Mutual fund, which would be expected to produce dividends of $8,000 per year.

    - Option B—Investment in Redbird Limited Partnership (buys, sells, and operates avocado groves). Sarah's share of the partnership's income and loss over the next three years is expected to be:

Year	Income (Loss)
1	($ 8,000)
2	(2,000)
3	34,000

Sarah is interested in the after-tax effects of these alternatives over a three-year horizon. Assume that Sarah's investment portfolio produces no passive income, that her cost of capital is 8% (the present value factors are 0.92593, 0.85734, and 0.79383), that she is in the 31% tax bracket, that each investment alternative possesses equal growth potential, and that each alternative exposes her to comparable financial risk. Based on these facts, compute the present value of these two investment alternatives and determine which option Sarah should choose.

39. Hazel has two investments in nonrental passive activities. Activity A, which was acquired seven years ago, was profitable until the current year. Activity B was acquired this year. Currently, Hazel's share of the loss from Activity A is $10,000, and her share of the loss from Activity B is $6,000. What is the total of Hazel's suspended losses from these activities as of the end of the current year?

40. Leanne has investments in four passive activity partnerships purchased several years ago. Last year, the income and losses were as follows:

Activity	Income (Loss)
A	$30,000
B	(30,000)
C	(15,000)
D	(5,000)

In the current year, she sold her interest in Activity D for a $10,000 gain. Activity D, which had been profitable until last year, had a current loss of $1,500. How will the sale of Activity D affect Leanne's taxable income in the current year?

41. Leon sells his interest in a passive activity for $100,000 during the year. Determine the tax effect based on each of the following sets of independent facts:
    a. His adjusted basis in this investment is $35,000. Losses from prior years that were not deductible due to the passive loss restrictions total $40,000.
    b. His adjusted basis in this investment is $75,000. Losses from prior years that were not deductible due to the passive loss restrictions total $40,000.
    c. His adjusted basis in this investment is $75,000. Losses from prior years that were not deductible due to the passive loss restrictions total $40,000. In addition, suspended credits total $10,000.

42. Brown Corporation, a personal service corporation, earned active income of $500,000 in the current year. The corporation received $60,000 in dividends during the year. In addition, Brown incurred a loss of $80,000 from an investment in a passive activity acquired three years ago. What is Brown's income for the current year after considering the passive investment?

43. White, Inc., earned $400,000 from operations in the current year. White also received $36,000 in dividends and interest on various portfolio investments. During the year, White paid $150,000 to acquire a 20% interest in a passive activity that produced a $200,000 loss.
    a. How will this affect White's taxable income, assuming the corporation is a personal service corporation?
    b. How will this affect White's taxable income, assuming the corporation is a closely held, non-personal service corporation?

44. Green Corporation, a closely held, non-personal service corporation, earned active income of $50,000 in the current year. Green received $60,000 in dividends during the year. In addition, Green incurred a loss of $80,000 from an investment in a passive activity acquired last year. What is Green's net income for the current year after considering the passive investment?

45. Greg Reynolds (66 Hanover Street, Cincinnati, OH 45230), a syndicated radio talk show host, earns a $400,000 salary in the current year. He works approximately 30 hours per week in this job, which leaves him time to participate in several businesses he acquired in the current year. He owns a movie theater and a drugstore in Cincinnati. He also owns a movie theater and a drugstore in Indianapolis and a drugstore in Louisville. A preliminary analysis on December 1 of the current year shows projected income and losses for the various businesses as follows:

	Income (Loss)
Cincinnati movie theater (95 hours participation)	$56,000
Cincinnati drugstore (140 hours participation)	(89,000)
Indianapolis movie theater (90 hours participation)	34,000
Indianapolis drugstore (170 hours participation)	(41,000)
Louisville drugstore (180 hours participation)	(15,000)

Greg has full-time employees at each of the five businesses listed above. Consider all possible groupings for Greg's activities. Write a letter to him suggesting the grouping method and other strategies that will provide the greatest tax advantage. Greg does not know much about the tax law, so you should provide a concise, nontechnical explanation.

46. Ann acquired an activity four years ago. The loss from the activity was $50,000 in the current year. She had AGI of $140,000 before considering the loss from the activity. The activity is a service station, and Ann is a material participant. What is her AGI after considering this activity?

47. Lee acquired a 20% interest in the ABC Partnership for $60,000 in 1992. The partnership was profitable until 1997, and Lee's amount at risk in the partnership interest was $120,000 at the end of 1996. ABC incurred a loss of $400,000 in 1997 and reported income of $200,000 in 1998. Assuming Lee is not a material participant in ABC, how much of his loss from ABC Partnership is deductible in 1997 and 1998, respectively?

48. Ken has a $40,000 loss from an investment in a partnership in which he does not participate. He paid $30,000 for his interest in the partnership. How much of the loss is disallowed by the at-risk rules? How much is disallowed by the passive loss rules?

49. Last year, Fran invested $40,000 for an interest in a partnership in which she is a material participant. Her share of the partnership's loss for the year was $50,000. In the current year, Fran's share of the partnership's income is $30,000. What is the effect on her taxable income for the current year?

50. Soong, a physician, earned $200,000 from his practice. He also received $18,000 in dividends and interest on various portfolio investments. During the year, he paid $45,000 to acquire a 20% interest in a partnership that produced a $300,000 loss.
    a. Compute Soong's AGI assuming he does not participate in the operations of the partnership.
    b. Compute Soong's AGI assuming he is a material participant in the operations of the partnership.

51. Sam invested $150,000 in a passive activity five years ago. On January 1, 1996, his amount at risk in the activity was $30,000. His shares of the income and losses in the activity were as follows:

Year	Income (Loss)
1996	($40,000)
1997	(30,000)
1998	50,000

How much can Sam deduct in 1996 and 1997? What is his taxable income from the activity in 1998? Keep in mind the at-risk rules as well as the passive loss rules.

52. Joe Cook (125 Hill Street, Charleston, WV 25311) acquired an activity four years ago. The loss from the activity was $50,000 in the current year. He had AGI of $140,000 before considering the loss from the activity. The activity is an apartment building in an

exclusive part of the city, and Joe is an active participant. Write a letter to Joe in which you explain what his AGI is after the loss is considered.

53. Beth acquired an activity four years ago. The loss from the activity was $50,000 in the current year. She had AGI of $140,000 before considering the loss from the activity. The activity is an apartment building, and Beth is not an active participant. What is her AGI after considering the activity?

54. During the current year, Donald worked 1,200 hours as a computer consultant, 600 hours in a real estate development business, and 500 hours in real estate rental activities. He earned $60,000 as a computer consultant, but lost $18,000 in the development business and $26,000 in the real estate rental business. How should Donald treat the losses on his current Federal income tax return?

55. During the current year, Maria Castro worked 1,200 hours as a computer consultant, 320 hours in a real estate development business, and 400 hours in real estate rental activities. Jorge, her husband, worked 250 hours in the real estate development business and 180 hours in the real estate rental business. Maria earned $60,000 as a computer consultant, but the Castros lost $18,000 in the development business and $26,000 in the real estate rental business. How should they treat the losses on their current joint Federal income tax return?

56. Hal and Wanda are married with no dependents and live together in Ohio, which is not a community property state. Since Wanda has large medical expenses, they seek your advice about filing separately to save taxes. Their income and expenses for 1997 are as follows:

Hal's salary	$ 30,000
Wanda's salary	50,000
Dividends and interest (joint)	1,800
Rental loss from actively managed apartments (joint)	(20,000)
Wanda's unreimbursed medical expenses	6,500
All other itemized deductions:*	
Hal	8,000
Wanda	2,000

*None subject to limitations.

Determine whether Hal and Wanda should file jointly or separately for 1997.

57. Lucy and Leon have owned a beach cottage on the New Jersey shore for several years and have always used it as a family retreat. When they acquired the property, they had no intentions of renting it, but because their family circumstances have changed, they are considering using the cottage for only two weeks a year and renting it for the remainder of the year. Their AGI is currently approximately $80,000 per year, and they are in the 36% tax bracket (combined Federal and state). Their financial records indicate that interest and real estate taxes have totaled $8,000 per year, and Lucy and Leon expect these expenditures to continue at this level into the foreseeable future. In addition, if they rent the property, their *incremental* revenue and expenses are projected to be:

Rent income	$ 20,000
Rental commissions	(3,000)
Maintenance expenses	(12,000)
Depreciation expense	(10,000)
	($ 5,000)

If they do convert the cottage to rental property, they insist that they will be actively involved in key rental and maintenance decisions. Given the tax effects of converting the property to rental use, would the cash flow resulting from renting the property be enough to meet the $12,000 annual mortgage payment? This is an important factor in Lucy and Leon's decision.

58. Ida, who has AGI of $80,000 before considering rental activities, is active in three separate real estate rental activities and is in the 28% tax bracket. She had $12,000 of losses from Activity A, $18,000 of losses from Activity B, and income of $10,000 from Activity C. She also had $2,100 of tax credits from Activity A. Calculate her deductions and credits allowed and the suspended losses and credits.

59. Ella has $105,000 of losses from a real estate rental activity in which she actively participates. She has other rental income of $25,000 and other passive income of $32,000. How much rental loss can Ella deduct against active and portfolio income (ignoring the at-risk rules)? Does she have any suspended losses to carry over?

60. Faye died owning an interest in a passive activity property with an adjusted basis of $160,000, suspended losses of $16,000, and a fair market value of $170,000. What can be deducted on her final income tax return?

61. Last year, Nina gave her son a passive activity with an adjusted basis of $100,000. Fair market value of the activity was $180,000, and the activity had suspended losses of $25,000. In the current year, her son realized income of $12,000 from the passive activity. What is the effect on Nina and her son last year and in the current year?

62. Tonya sold a passive activity in the current year for $150,000. Her adjusted basis was $50,000. She used the installment method of reporting the gain. The activity had suspended losses of $12,000. Tonya received $60,000 in the year of sale. What is her gain? How much of the suspended losses can she deduct?

RESEARCH PROBLEMS

Note: *West's Federal Taxation on CD-ROM* can be used in preparing solutions to the Research Problems. Alternatively, tax research materials contained in a standard tax library can be used.

Research Problem 1. Leon Lane (77 Lakeview Drive, Salt Lake City, UT 84109) is a married individual who files a separate return for the taxable year. He is employed full-time as an attorney. Leon, who also owns an interest in a minor league baseball team, does no work in connection with the activity during the year. He anticipates that the activity will result in a loss for the taxable year. Leon pays his wife to work as an office receptionist in connection with the activity for an average of 20 hours a week during the year. Write a letter to Leon and explain whether he will be allowed to deduct his share of the loss from the activity.

Research Problem 2. Bill owns an interest in a small engine repair shop in which he works 425 hours during the year. He has four full-time employees at the repair shop. Bill also owns an apartment building to which he devotes 1,300 hours during the year. He has no employees for the apartment activity. Are these activities active or passive? In your response, consider the impact of the significant participation activity rules.

Research Problem 3. Over the years, Bill Johnson (30 Brookfield Drive, Hampton, VA 23666) has taken great pride in his ability to spot exceptional rental real estate investments, particularly in terms of their appreciation potential. As a result, he has accumulated several properties. In the early years of his investment activities, he was able to devote only a limited amount of time to these ventures. In the current year, he retires from his full-time job and is able to devote most of his time to the management and operation of the rental activities. Bill summarizes the relevant tax attributes of each of the properties as follows:

Property	Suspended Passive Losses	Expected Current Year's Income (Loss)
A	None	$25,000
B	($20,000)	15,000
C	(40,000)	(15,000)

Bill is astute enough to know that he is a qualifying real estate professional for the current year and materially participates in all three properties within the meaning of § 469(c)(7)(A). However, he is uncertain whether he should treat the properties as three separate activities or aggregate them and treat them as one activity.

Write a letter to Bill to assist him in making the decision. Because of Bill's expertise in the tax law, feel free to use technical language in your letter.

Partial list of research aids:
 Reg. § 1.469–9(e).

Use the tax resources of the internet to address the following questions. Do not restrict your search to the World Wide Web, but include a review of newsgroups and general reference materials, practitioner sites and resources, primary sources of the tax law, chat rooms and discussion groups, and other opportunities.

Research Problem 4. Scan the materials offered in several newsgroups frequented by tax consultants. In what context are "tax shelters" still discussed by these professionals? Do these advisors adequately take into account the rules of §§ 465 and 469? Post a message to one of these newsgroups explaining the interaction of these two sections in a paragraph or two.

Research Problem 5. Download and print a copy of Form 8582 and its instructions. Use these materials to complete the requirements of Problem 58.

TEAM PROJECT: ARTHUR ANDERSEN TAX CHALLENGE CASES

For more information on the Arthur Andersen Tax Challenge Cases, refer to Chapter 1, page 1–38.

Information related to tax issues and problems that are discussed in this chapter may be found in the

Day and Ball case on pages: none
Miller case on pages: none

Read and analyze the case you have been assigned and *identify* any issues and problems that are related to material covered in this chapter. If the information provided in the case is complete, prepare answers for this part of the case at this time. If you need information that is contained in the later parts of the case, write a memo summarizing the questions or problems so you can prepare a complete answer at a later date.

PART IV

SPECIAL TAX COMPUTATION METHODS, PAYMENT PROCEDURES, AND TAX CREDITS

Part IV presents several topics that relate to the theme of tax liability determination. The taxpayer must calculate the tax liability in accordance with the basic tax formula and also in accordance with the tax formula for the alternative minimum tax (AMT). The basic tax formula was presented in Part I, and the AMT formula is covered in Part IV. Tax credits reduce the amount of the calculated tax liability. The specific procedures for the timing of the payment of the tax liability are also discussed.

Chapter 12
Alternative Minimum Tax

Chapter 13
Tax Credits and Payment Procedures

CHAPTER 12

ALTERNATIVE MINIMUM TAX

LEARNING OBJECTIVES

After completing Chapter 12, you should be able to:

1. Explain the rationale for the alternative minimum tax (AMT).
2. Understand the formula for computing the AMT for individuals.
3. Identify the adjustments made in calculating the AMT.
4. Identify the tax preferences that are included in calculating the AMT.
5. Apply the formula for computing the AMT and illustrate Form 6251.
6. Describe the role of the AMT credit in the alternative minimum tax structure.
7. Understand the basic features of the corporate AMT.
8. Identify tax planning opportunities to minimize the AMT.

OUTLINE

Individual Alternative Minimum Tax, 12-3

AMT Formula for Alternative Minimum Taxable Income (AMTI), 12-3

AMT Formula: Other Components, 12-6

AMT Adjustments, 12-9

AMT Preferences, 12-20

Illustration of the AMT Computation, 12-23

AMT Credit, 12-24

Corporate Alternative Minimum Tax, 12-27

AMT Adjustments, 12-27

Tax Preferences, 12-30

Exemption, 12-31

Other Aspects of the AMT, 12-31

Tax Planning Considerations, 12-31

Responding to Bob and Carol, 12-31

Avoiding Preferences and Adjustments, 12-32

Controlling the Timing of Preferences and Adjustments, 12-32

Taking Advantage of the AMT/Regular Tax Rate Differential, 12-32

1 LEARNING OBJECTIVE
Explain the rationale for the alternative minimum tax (AMT).

Bob and Carol are unmarried individuals who work for the same employer and have the same amount of gross income and the same amount of deductions. Bob's tax return is prepared by Adam, and Carol's tax return is prepared by Eve. While discussing their tax liability one day at lunch, Carol is dismayed to learn that she paid $15,000 more in Federal income taxes than Bob did for the tax year. Carol meets with Eve that evening. Eve reviews Carol's tax return and assures her that her tax liability was properly calculated.

The above events raise a number of interesting questions for Bob and Carol that can be answered after completing this chapter. Why didn't Bob and Carol have the same tax liability? Were both tax returns properly prepared? Should Carol consider replacing her tax return preparer Eve with Adam? Is it possible and/or desirable for Carol to file an amended return? Should Bob do anything?

The tax law contains many incentives that are intended to influence the economic and social behavior of taxpayers (refer to Chapter 1). Some taxpayers have been able to take advantage of enough of these incentives to avoid or minimize any liability for Federal income tax. Although these taxpayers were reducing taxes legally, Congress became concerned about the inequity that results when taxpayers with substantial economic incomes can avoid paying any income tax. The **alternative minimum tax (AMT)** was enacted as a backup to the regular income tax. The rationale for the AMT was expressed as follows:

> [T]he minimum tax should serve one overriding objective: to ensure that no taxpayer with substantial economic income can avoid significant tax liability by using exclusions, deductions, and credits. Although these provisions may provide incentives for worthy goals, they become counterproductive when taxpayers are allowed to use them to avoid virtually all tax liability. The ability of high-income taxpayers to pay little or no tax undermines respect for the entire tax system and, thus, for the incentive provisions themselves. In addition, even aside from public perceptions... it is inherently unfair for high-income taxpayers to pay little or no tax due to their ability to utilize tax preferences.[1]

The individual AMT is discussed in the first part of this chapter. The corporate AMT is similar to the individual AMT, but differs in several important ways. Details of the corporate AMT are presented in the last part of the chapter.

---

[1] *General Explanation of the Tax Reform Act of 1986 ("Blue Book")*, prepared by The Staff of the Joint Committee on Taxation, May 4, 1987, H.R. 3838, 99th Cong., pp. 432-433.

Individual Alternative Minimum Tax

AMT FORMULA FOR ALTERNATIVE MINIMUM TAXABLE INCOME (AMTI)

2 LEARNING OBJECTIVE
Understand the formula for computing the AMT for individuals.

The AMT is separate from, but parallel to, the regular income tax system.[2] Most income and expense items are treated the same way for both regular income tax and AMT purposes. For example, a taxpayer's salary is included in computing taxable income and is also included in alternative minimum taxable income (AMTI). Alimony paid is allowed as a deduction *for* AGI for both regular income tax and AMT purposes. Certain itemized deductions, such as gambling losses, are allowed for both regular income tax and AMT purposes.

On the other hand, some income and expense items are treated differently for regular income tax and AMT purposes. For example, interest income on bonds issued by state, county, or local governments is *excluded* in computing taxable income. However, interest on such bonds is *included* in computing AMTI if the bonds are private activity bonds issued after August 7, 1986. The deduction for personal and dependency exemptions is *allowed* for regular income tax purposes, but is *disallowed* for AMT purposes.

In other cases, certain items are considered in both the regular income tax and AMT computations, but the amounts are different. For example, the completed contract method can be used to report income from some long-term contracts for regular income tax purposes, but the percentage of completion method is required for AMT purposes. Thus, the amount of income included in taxable income will differ from the amount included in AMTI. Depreciation is allowed as a deduction for both regular income tax and AMT purposes, but the *amount* of the regular income tax deduction will be different from the amount of the AMT deduction. Medical expenses are deductible in calculating both taxable income and AMTI, but the floor on the deduction is different.

The parallel but separate nature of the AMT means that AMTI will differ from taxable income. It is possible to compute AMTI by direct application of the AMT provisions, using the following formula:

Gross income computed by applying the AMT rules

Minus: Deductions computed by applying the AMT rules

Equals: AMTI before tax preferences

Plus: Tax preferences

Equals: Alternative minimum taxable income

While the direct approach for computing AMTI appears quite logical, both the tax law and the tax forms provide a very different approach. Both of these use taxable income as the starting point for computing AMTI, as shown in Figure 12–1. This indirect approach for computing AMTI is analogous to the indirect approach used in calculating a net operating loss.

The purpose of the AMT formula is to *reconcile* taxable income to AMTI. This reconciliation is similar to a bank reconciliation, which reconciles a checkbook balance to a bank balance by considering differences between the depositor's records and the bank's records. The reconciliation of taxable income to AMTI is accomplished by entering reconciling items to account for differences between regular income tax provisions and AMT provisions. These reconciling items are

[2] § 55.

▼ FIGURE 12-1
Alternative Minimum Taxable Income (AMTI) Formula

> Taxable income
> **Plus:** Positive AMT adjustments
> **Minus:** Negative AMT adjustments
> **Equals:** Taxable income after AMT adjustments
> **Plus:** Tax preferences
> **Equals:** Alternative minimum taxable income

referred to as **AMT adjustments** or **tax preferences**. *Adjustments* can be either positive or negative, as shown in the formula in Figure 12–1. Tax preferences are always positive.

Adjustments. The concept of AMT adjustments was introduced in the Tax Reform Act of 1986. Most adjustments relate to *timing differences* that arise because of *separate* regular income tax and AMT treatments. Adjustments that are caused by timing differences will eventually *reverse*; that is, positive adjustments will be offset by negative adjustments in the future, and vice versa.[3]

For example, **circulation expenditures** can give rise to a timing difference that requires an AMT adjustment. For regular income tax purposes, circulation expenditures can be deducted in the year incurred. For AMT purposes, however, circulation expenditures must be deducted over a three-year period. This difference in treatment will be used to illustrate the role of adjustments in the formula for computing AMTI.

EXAMPLE 1 Bob had taxable income of $100,000 in 1996. In computing taxable income, he deducted $30,000 of circulation expenditures incurred in 1996. Bob's allowable deduction for AMT purposes was only $10,000. Therefore, an AMT adjustment was required in 1996 as follows:

Taxable income		$100,000
+AMT adjustment:		
Circulation expenditures deducted for regular income tax purposes	$ 30,000	
−Circulation expenditures allowed for AMT purposes	(10,000)	
Positive adjustment		20,000
=AMTI before tax preferences		$120,000
+Tax preferences		−0−
AMTI		$120,000

Analysis of this computation shows that the allowable AMT deduction is $20,000 less than the allowable regular income tax deduction. Therefore, AMTI will be $20,000 greater than taxable income. This is accomplished by entering a positive AMT adjustment of $20,000. ▼

EXAMPLE 2 Assume that Bob from Example 1 has taxable income of $95,000 in 1997. He is allowed to deduct $10,000 of circulation expenditures for AMT purposes, but is not allowed a deduction for regular income tax purposes because all $30,000 was deducted in 1996. Therefore, a *negative* AMT adjustment is required.

---
[3] § 56.

Taxable income			$ 95,000
−AMT adjustment:			
Circulation expenditures allowed for regular income tax purposes		$ −0−	
Circulation expenditures deducted for AMT purposes		(10,000)	
Negative adjustment			(10,000)
=AMTI before tax preferences			$ 85,000
+Tax preferences			−0−
AMTI			$ 85,000

Analysis of this computation shows that the allowable AMT deduction is $10,000 more than the allowable regular income tax deduction. Therefore, AMTI will be $10,000 less than taxable income. This is accomplished by entering a negative AMT adjustment of $10,000. ▼

As noted previously, timing differences eventually reverse. Therefore, total positive adjustments will be offset by total negative adjustments with respect to a particular item.

EXAMPLE 3 Refer to Examples 1 and 2. The difference in regular income tax and AMT treatments of circulation expenditures will result in AMT adjustments over a three-year period.

Year	Income Tax Deduction	AMT Deduction	AMT Adjustment
1996	$30,000	$10,000	+$20,000
1997	−0−	10,000	−10,000
1998	−0−	10,000	−10,000
Total	$30,000	$30,000	$ −0−

As the last column illustrates, if positive and negative AMT adjustments with respect to a particular item are caused by a timing difference, they will eventually net to zero. ▼

The adjustments for circulation expenditures and other items are discussed in detail under AMT Adjustments.

Although most adjustments relate to timing differences, there are exceptions. See the subsequent discussion of such items under Itemized Deductions. Adjustments that do not relate to timing differences result in a permanent difference between taxable income and AMTI.

Tax Preferences. Some deductions and exclusions allowed to taxpayers for regular income tax purposes provide extraordinary tax savings. Congress has chosen to single out these items, which are referred to as tax preferences.[4] The AMT is designed to take back all or part of the tax benefits derived through the use of preferences in the computation of taxable income for regular income tax purposes. This is why taxable income, which is the starting point in computing AMTI, is increased by tax preference items. The effect of adding these preference items is to disallow for *AMT purposes* those preferences that were allowed in the

[4] § 57.

▼ **FIGURE 12-2**
Alternative Minimum Tax Formula

> Regular taxable income
> **Plus or minus:** Adjustments
> **Equals:** Taxable income after AMT adjustments
> **Plus:** Tax preferences
> **Equals:** Alternative minimum taxable income
> **Minus:** Exemption
> **Equals:** Alternative minimum tax base
> **Times:** 26% or 28% rate
> **Equals:** Tentative minimum tax before foreign tax credit
> **Minus:** Alternative minimum tax foreign tax credit
> **Equals:** Tentative minimum tax
> **Minus:** Regular tax liability*
> **Equals:** Alternative minimum tax (if amount is positive)

*This is the regular tax liability for the year reduced by any allowable foreign tax credit.

regular income tax computation. Tax preferences include the following items, which are discussed in detail under AMT Preferences:

- Percentage depletion in excess of the property's adjusted basis.
- Excess intangible drilling costs reduced by 65 percent of the net income from oil, gas, and geothermal properties.
- Interest on certain private activity bonds.
- Excess of accelerated over straight-line depreciation on real property placed in service before 1987.
- Excess of accelerated over straight-line depreciation on *leased* personal property placed in service before 1987.
- Excess of amortization allowance over depreciation on pre-1987 certified pollution control facilities.
- Fifty percent exclusion from gross income associated with gains on the sale of certain small business stock.

AMT FORMULA: OTHER COMPONENTS

To convert AMTI to AMT, other formula components including the exemption, rates, credit, and regular tax liability must be considered. The impact of each of these components is depicted in the AMT formula in Figure 12-2.

The relationship between the regular tax liability and the tentative AMT is key to the AMT formula. If the regular tax liability exceeds tentative AMT, then the AMT is zero. If the tentative AMT exceeds the regular tax liability, the amount of the excess is the AMT. In essence, the taxpayer will pay whichever tax liability is greater—that calculated using the regular income tax rules or that calculated using the AMT rules. However, both the tax law and Form 6251 adopt this excess approach with the taxpayer paying the regular tax liability plus any AMT.

▼ EXAMPLE 4

Anna, an unmarried individual, has regular taxable income of $100,000. She has positive adjustments of $40,000 and tax preferences of $25,000. Calculate her AMT for 1997.

Anna's regular tax liability is $26,003. Her AMT is calculated as follows:

Taxable income (TI)	$100,000
Plus: Adjustments	40,000
Equals: TI after AMT adjustments	$140,000
Plus: Tax preferences	25,000
Equals: AMTI	$165,000
Minus: AMT exemption ($33,750 − $13,125)	(20,625)*
Equals: AMT base	$144,375
Times: AMT rate	× 26%
Equals: Tentative AMT	$ 37,538
Minus: Regular tax liability	(26,003)
Equals: AMT	$ 11,535

*Discussed below under Exemption Amount.

Anna will pay the IRS a total of $37,538, consisting of her regular tax liability of $26,003 plus her AMT of $11,535. ▼

Exemption Amount. The exemption amount can be thought of as a materiality provision. As such, it enables a taxpayer with a small amount of positive adjustments and tax preferences to avoid being subject to the burden of the AMT.

The *initial* exemption amount is $45,000 for married taxpayers filing joint returns, $33,750 for single taxpayers, and $22,500 for married taxpayers filing separate returns.[5] However, the exemption is *phased out* at a rate of 25 cents on the dollar when AMTI exceeds these levels:

- $112,500 for single taxpayers.
- $150,000 for married taxpayers filing jointly.
- $75,000 for married taxpayers filing separately.

The phase-out of the exemption amount is an application of the wherewithal to pay concept. As a taxpayer's income level increases, so does his or her ability to pay income taxes.

The following example explains the calculation of the phase-out of the AMT exemption.

EXAMPLE 5

Hugh, who is single, has AMTI of $192,500 for the year. His $33,750 initial exemption amount is reduced by $20,000 [($192,500 − $112,500) × 25% phase-out rate]. Hugh's AMT exemption is $13,750 ($33,750 exemption − $20,000 reduction). ▼

The following table shows the beginning and end of the AMT exemption phase-out range for each filing status.

		Phase-out	
Status	**Exemption**	**Begins at**	**Ends at**
Married, joint	$45,000	$150,000	$330,000
Single or head of household	33,750	112,500	247,500
Married, separate	22,500	75,000	165,000

---

[5] § 55(d).

AMT Rate Schedule. A graduated, two-tier AMT rate schedule applies to noncorporate taxpayers. A 26 percent rate applies to the first $175,000 of the AMT base ($87,500 for married, filing separately), and a 28 percent rate applies to the AMT base in excess of $175,000 ($87,500 for married, filing separately).[6]

Regular Tax Liability. The AMT is equal to the tentative minimum tax minus the *regular tax liability*. In most cases, the regular tax liability is equal to the amount of tax from the Tax Table or Tax Rate Schedules decreased by any foreign tax credit allowable for regular income tax purposes. Only the foreign tax credit is allowed as a reduction of the tentative minimum tax. Therefore, taxpayers who pay AMT lose the benefit of all other nonrefundable credits. Furthermore, the foreign tax credit cannot offset more than 90 percent of the tentative minimum tax.

In an AMT year, the taxpayer's total tax liability is equal to the tentative minimum tax (refer to Figure 12–2). The tentative minimum tax consists of two potential components: the regular tax liability and the AMT. The disallowance of credits does not affect a taxpayer's total liability in an AMT year. However, it does decrease the amount of the AMT and, as a consequence, reduces the minimum tax credit (discussed subsequently) available to be carried forward. Thus, for AMT purposes, the government denies all the credits (except the foreign tax credit) that apply in computing the regular income tax liability.

It is also possible that taxpayers who have adjustments and preferences but *do not pay* AMT will lose the benefit of some or all of their nonrefundable credits. This result occurs because a taxpayer may claim nonrefundable credits only to the extent that his or her regular tax liability exceeds the tentative minimum tax.[7]

EXAMPLE 6 Vern has total nonrefundable credits of $10,000, regular tax liability of $33,000, and tentative minimum tax of $25,000. He can claim only $8,000 of the nonrefundable credits in the current year. The disallowed $2,000 credit is lost unless a carryover provision applies. ▼

ETHICAL CONSIDERATIONS

Minimizing the Tax Liability

Billy, a single individual, projects his taxable income for 1997 to be approximately $300,000. He also has positive adjustments and tax preferences of $200,000. Billy anticipates taxable income for 1998 to be about the same with no adjustments or tax preferences for AMT purposes. He is evaluating several proposed transactions that would have the effect of reducing his 1997 tax liability.

One such transaction involves an office building for which he is currently negotiating a lease. The starting date for the lease will be July 1, 1997. The annual rent is going to be around $20,000 with an 18-month prepayment clause. Though Billy favors a five-year lease, a real estate agent has suggested that he lease the office building for an 18-month period with a 42-month renewal option. The real estate agent indicates that there are tax advantages (i.e., Billy can deduct the $30,000 of rent paid at the inception of the lease) as well as business reasons for structuring the transaction this way.

Billy takes the agent's advice and calculates his projected tax liability for 1997 with the 18-month lease with the renewal option and with the five-year lease. Based on his calculations, his regular income tax liability and AMT under each option would be as follows:

---

[6] § 55(b)(1). [7] § 26(a).

CHAPTER 12 Alternative Minimum Tax

	18-Month Lease	5-Year Lease
Regular income tax liability	$ 85,971	$ 93,853
AMT	42,129	39,847
Total	$128,100	$133,700

Is it appropriate for Billy to avoid taxes in this manner? Is is wise? Would you be willing to prepare and sign Billy's tax return showing the lease transaction as proposed by the real estate agent?

AMT ADJUSTMENTS

3 LEARNING OBJECTIVE
Identify the adjustments made in calculating the AMT.

Direction of Adjustments. It is necessary to determine not only the amount of an adjustment, but also whether the adjustment is positive or negative. Careful study of Example 3 reveals the following pattern with regard to *deductions:*

- If the deduction allowed for regular income tax purposes exceeds the deduction allowed for AMT purposes, the difference is a positive adjustment.
- If the deduction allowed for AMT purposes exceeds the deduction allowed for regular income tax purposes, the difference is a negative adjustment.

Conversely, the direction of an adjustment attributable to an *income* item can be determined as follows:

- If the income reported for regular income tax purposes exceeds the income reported for AMT purposes, the difference is a negative adjustment.
- If the income reported for AMT purposes exceeds the income reported for regular income tax purposes, the difference is a positive adjustment.

Circulation Expenditures. For regular income tax purposes, circulation expenditures, other than those the taxpayer elects to charge to a capital account, may be expensed in the year incurred.[8] These expenditures include expenses incurred to establish, maintain, or increase the circulation of a newspaper, magazine, or other periodical.

Circulation expenditures are not deductible in the year incurred for AMT purposes. In computing AMTI, these expenditures must be capitalized and amortized ratably over the three-year period beginning with the year in which the expenditures were made.[9]

The AMT adjustment for circulation expenditures is the amount expensed for regular income tax purposes minus the amount that can be amortized for AMT purposes. The adjustment can be either positive or negative (refer to Examples 1, 2, and 3). A taxpayer can avoid the AMT adjustments for circulation expenditures by electing to write off the expenditures over a three-year period for regular income tax purposes.[10]

Depreciation of Post-1986 Real Property. For real property placed in service after 1986 (MACRS property), AMT depreciation is computed under the

---

[8] § 173(a).
[9] § 56(b)(2)(A)(i).
[10] § 59(e)(2)(A).

alternative depreciation system (ADS), which uses the straight-line method over a 40-year life. The depreciation lives for regular tax purposes are 27.5 years for residential rental property and 39 years for all other real property.[11] The difference between AMT depreciation and regular income tax depreciation is treated as an adjustment in computing the AMT. The differences will be positive during the regular income tax life of the asset because the cost is written off over a shorter period for regular income tax purposes. For example, during the 27.5-year income tax life of residential real property, the regular income tax depreciation will exceed the AMT depreciation because AMT depreciation is computed over a 40-year period.

Table 8–7 is used to compute regular income tax depreciation on real property placed in service after 1986. For AMT purposes, depreciation on real property placed in service after 1986 is computed under the ADS (refer to Table 8–12).

EXAMPLE 7

In January 1997, Sara placed in service a residential building that cost $100,000. Depreciation for 1997 for regular income tax purposes is $3,485 ($100,000 cost × 3.485% from Table 8–7). For AMT purposes, depreciation is $2,396 ($100,000 cost × 2.396% from Table 8–12). In computing AMTI for 1997, Sara has a positive adjustment of $1,089 ($3,485 regular income tax depreciation − $2,396 AMT depreciation). ▼

After real property has been held for the entire depreciation period for regular income tax purposes, the asset will be fully depreciated. However, the depreciation period under the ADS is 41 years due to application of the half-year convention, so depreciation will continue for AMT purposes. This causes negative adjustments after the property has been fully depreciated for regular income tax purposes.

EXAMPLE 8

Assume the same facts as in the previous example, and compute the AMT adjustment for 2025 (the twenty-ninth year of the asset's life). Regular income tax depreciation is zero (refer to Table 8–7). AMT depreciation is $2,500 ($100,000 cost × 2.500% from Table 8–12). Therefore, Sara has a negative AMT adjustment of $2,500 ($0 regular income tax depreciation − $2,500 AMT depreciation). ▼

After real property is fully depreciated for both regular income tax and AMT purposes, the positive and negative adjustments that have been made for AMT purposes will net to zero.

Depreciation of Post-1986 Personal Property. For most personal property placed in service after 1986 (MACRS property), the modified ACRS (MACRS) deduction for regular income tax purposes is based on the 200 percent declining-balance method with a switch to straight-line when that method produces a larger depreciation deduction for the asset. Refer to Table 8–2 for computing regular income tax depreciation.

For AMT purposes, the taxpayer must use the ADS. This method is based on the 150 percent declining-balance method with a similar switch to straight-line for all personal property.[12] Refer to Table 8–10 for percentages to be used in computing AMT depreciation.

All personal property placed in service after 1986 may be taken into consideration in computing one net adjustment. Using this netting process, the AMT adjustment for a tax year is the difference between the total MACRS depreciation

---

[11] The 39-year life generally applies to nonresidential real property placed in service on or after May 13, 1993.

[12] § 56(a)(1).

for all personal property computed for regular income tax purposes and the total ADS depreciation computed for AMT purposes. When the total of MACRS deductions exceeds the total of ADS deductions, the amount of the adjustment is positive. When the total of ADS deductions exceeds the total of MACRS deductions, the adjustment for AMTI is negative.

The MACRS deduction for personal property is larger than the ADS deduction in the early years of an asset's life. However, the ADS deduction is larger in the later years. This is so because ADS lives (based on class life) are longer than MACRS lives (based on recovery period).[13] Over the ADS life of the asset, the same amount of depreciation is deducted for both regular income tax and AMT purposes. In the same manner as other timing adjustments, the AMT adjustments for depreciation will net to zero over the ADS life of the asset.

The taxpayer may elect to use the ADS for regular income tax purposes. If this election is made, no AMT adjustment is required because the depreciation deduction is the same for regular income tax and for the AMT. The election eliminates the burden of maintaining two sets of tax depreciation records.

Pollution Control Facilities. For regular income tax purposes, the cost of certified pollution control facilities may be amortized over a period of 60 months. For AMT purposes, the cost of these facilities placed in service after 1986 must be depreciated under the ADS over the appropriate class life, determined as explained above for depreciation of post-1986 property.[14] The required adjustment for AMTI is equal to the difference between the amortization deduction allowed for regular income tax purposes and the depreciation deduction computed under the ADS. The adjustment may be positive or negative.

Expenditures Requiring 10-Year Write-off for AMT Purposes. Certain expenditures that may be deducted in the year incurred for regular income tax purposes must be written off over a 10-year period for AMT purposes. These rules apply to (1) mining exploration and development costs and (2) research and experimental expenditures.

In computing taxable income, taxpayers are allowed to deduct certain mining exploration and development expenditures. The deduction is allowed for expenditures paid or incurred during the taxable year for exploration (ascertaining the existence, location, extent, or quality of a deposit or mineral) and for development of a mine or other natural deposit, other than an oil or gas well.[15] Mining development expenditures are expenses paid or incurred after the existence of ores and minerals in commercially marketable quantities has been disclosed.

For AMT purposes, however, mining exploration and development costs must be capitalized and amortized ratably over a 10-year period.[16] The AMT adjustment for mining exploration and development costs that are expensed is equal to the amount expensed minus the allowable expense if the costs had been capitalized and amortized ratably over a 10-year period. This provision does not apply to costs relating to an oil or gas well.

EXAMPLE 9

In 1997, Eve incurs $150,000 of mining exploration expenditures and deducts this amount for regular income tax purposes. For AMT purposes, these mining exploration expenditures must be amortized over a 10-year period. Eve must make a positive adjustment for AMTI of $135,000 ($150,000 allowed for regular income tax − $15,000 for AMT) for 1997, the first

---

[13] Class lives and recovery periods are established for all assets in Rev.Proc. 87–56, 1987–2 C.B. 674.
[14] § 56(a)(5).
[15] §§ 617(a) and 616(a).
[16] § 56(a)(2).

year. In each of the next nine years for AMT purposes, Eve is required to make a negative adjustment of $15,000 ($0 allowed for regular income tax − $15,000 for AMT). ▼

To avoid the AMT adjustments for mining exploration and development costs, a taxpayer may elect to write off the expenditures over a 10-year period for regular income tax purposes.[17]

Similar rules apply to computation of the adjustment for research and experimental expenditures.

Use of Completed Contract Method of Accounting.
For a long-term contract, taxpayers are required to use the percentage of completion method for AMT purposes.[18] However, in limited circumstances, taxpayers can use the completed contract method for regular income tax purposes.[19] Thus, a taxpayer recognizes a different amount of income for regular income tax purposes than for AMT purposes. The resulting AMT adjustment is equal to the difference between income reported under the percentage of completion method and the amount reported using the completed contract method. The adjustment can be either positive or negative, depending on the amount of income recognized under the different methods.

A taxpayer can avoid an AMT adjustment on long-term contracts by using the percentage of completion method for regular income tax purposes rather than the completed contract method.

ETHICAL CONSIDERATIONS

Relationship between the Regular Income Tax Liability and the AMT

Allie, who was an accounting major in college, is the controller of a medium-size construction corporation. She prepares the corporate tax return each year. Due to reporting a home construction contract using the completed contract method, the corporation is subject to the AMT in 1997. Allie files the 1997 corporate return in early February 1998. The total tax liability is $58,000 ($53,000 regular income tax liability + $5,000 AMT).

In early March, Allie reads an article on minimizing income taxes. Based on this article, she decides that it would be beneficial for the corporation to report the home construction contract using the percentage of completion method on its 1997 return. Although this will increase the corporation's 1997 income tax liability, it will minimize the total income tax liability over the two-year construction period. Therefore, Allie files an amended return on March 14, 1998. Evaluate Allie's actions from both a tax avoidance and an ethical perspective.

Incentive Stock Options.
Incentive stock options (ISOs) are granted by employers to help attract new personnel and retain those already employed. At the time an ISO is granted, the employer corporation sets an option price for the corporate stock. If the value of the stock increases during the option period, the employee can obtain stock at a favorable price by exercising the option. Employees

---

[17] §§ 59(e)(2)(D) and (E).
[18] § 56(a)(3).

[19] See Chapter 18 for a detailed discussion of the completed contract and percentage of completion methods of accounting.

are generally restricted as to when they can dispose of stock acquired under an ISO (e.g., a certain length of employment may be required). Therefore, the stock may not be freely transferable until some specified period has passed. See Chapter 19 for details regarding ISOs.

The exercise of an ISO does not increase regular taxable income.[20] However, for AMT purposes, the excess of the fair market value of the stock over the exercise price is treated as an adjustment in the first taxable year in which the rights in the stock are freely transferable or are not subject to a substantial risk of forfeiture.[21]

EXAMPLE 10

In 1995, Manuel exercised an ISO that had been granted by his employer, Gold Corporation. Manuel acquired 1,000 shares of Gold stock for the option price of $20 per share. The stock became freely transferable in 1997. The fair market value of the stock at the date of exercise was $50 per share. For AMT purposes, Manuel has a positive gain adjustment of $30,000 ($50,000 fair market value − $20,000 option price) for 1997. The transaction does not affect regular taxable income in 1995 or 1997. ▼

No adjustment is required if the taxpayer exercises the option and disposes of the stock in the same tax year because the bargain element gain is reported for both regular income tax and AMT purposes in that tax year.

The regular income tax basis of stock acquired through exercise of ISOs is different from the AMT basis. The regular income tax basis of the stock is equal to its cost, whereas the AMT basis is equal to the fair market value on the date the options are exercised. Consequently, the gain or loss upon disposition of the stock is different for regular income tax purposes and AMT purposes.

EXAMPLE 11

Assume the same facts as in the previous example and that Manuel sells the stock for $60,000 in 1999. His gain for regular income tax purposes is $40,000 ($60,000 amount realized − $20,000 regular income tax basis). For AMT purposes, the gain is $10,000 ($60,000 amount realized − $50,000 AMT basis). Therefore, Manuel has a $30,000 negative adjustment in computing AMT in 1999 ($40,000 regular income tax gain − $10,000 AMT gain). Note that the $30,000 negative adjustment upon disposition in 1999 offsets the $30,000 positive adjustment upon exercise of the ISO in 1997. ▼

Adjusted Gain or Loss. When property is sold during the year or a casualty occurs to business or income-producing property, gain or loss reported for regular income tax may be different than gain or loss determined for the AMT. This difference occurs because the adjusted basis of the property for AMT purposes must reflect any current and prior AMT adjustments for the following:[22]

- Depreciation.
- Circulation expenditures.
- Research and experimental expenditures.
- Mining exploration and development costs.
- Amortization of certified pollution control facilities.

A negative gain or loss adjustment is required if:

- the gain for AMT purposes is less than the gain for regular income tax purposes;

---

[20] § 421(a).
[21] § 56(b)(3).
[22] § 56(a)(7).

- the loss for AMT purposes is more than the loss for regular income tax purposes; or
- a loss is computed for AMT purposes and a gain is computed for regular income tax purposes.

Otherwise, the AMT gain or loss adjustment is positive.

EXAMPLE 12 In January 1997, Kate paid $100,000 for a duplex acquired for rental purposes. Regular income tax depreciation in 1997 was $3,485 ($100,000 cost × 3.485% from Table 8–7). AMT depreciation was $2,396 ($100,000 cost × 2.396% from Table 8–12). For AMT purposes, Kate made a positive adjustment of $1,089 ($3,485 regular income tax depreciation − $2,396 AMT depreciation). ▼

EXAMPLE 13 Kate sold the duplex on December 20, 1998, for $105,000. Regular income tax depreciation for 1998 is $3,485 [($100,000 cost × 3.636% from Table 8–7) × (11.5/12)]. AMT depreciation for 1998 is $2,396 [($100,000 cost × 2.500% from Table 8–12) × (11.5/12)]. Kate's positive AMT adjustment for 1998 is $1,089 ($3,485 regular income tax depreciation − $2,396 AMT depreciation). ▼

Because depreciation on the duplex differs for regular income tax and AMT purposes, the adjusted basis is different for regular income tax and AMT purposes. Consequently, the gain or loss on disposition of the duplex is different for regular income tax and AMT purposes.

EXAMPLE 14 The adjusted basis of Kate's duplex for regular income tax purposes is $93,030 ($100,000 cost − $3,485 depreciation for 1997 − $3,485 depreciation for 1998). For AMT purposes, the adjusted basis is $95,208 ($100,000 cost − $2,396 depreciation for 1997 − $2,396 depreciation for 1998). The regular income tax gain is $11,970 ($105,000 amount realized − $93,030 regular income tax basis). The AMT gain is $9,792 ($105,000 amount realized − $95,208 AMT basis). Because the regular income tax and AMT gain on the sale of the duplex differ, Kate must make a negative AMT adjustment of $2,178 ($11,970 regular income tax gain − $9,792 AMT gain). Note that this negative adjustment offsets the $2,178 total of the two positive adjustments for depreciation ($1,089 in 1997 + $1,089 in 1998). ▼

Passive Activity Losses. Losses on passive activities are not deductible in computing either the regular income tax or the AMT. This does not, however, eliminate the possibility of adjustments attributable to passive activities.

The rules for computing taxable income differ from the rules for computing AMTI. It follows, then, that the rules for computing a loss for regular income tax purposes differ from the AMT rules for computing a loss. Therefore, any *passive loss* computed for regular income tax purposes may differ from the passive loss computed for AMT purposes.[23]

EXAMPLE 15 Soong acquired two passive activities in 1997. He received net passive income of $10,000 from Activity A and had no AMT adjustments or preferences in connection with the activity. Activity B had gross income of $27,000 and operating expenses (not affected by AMT adjustments or preferences) of $19,000. Soong claimed MACRS depreciation of $20,000 for Activity B; depreciation under the ADS would have been $15,000. In addition, Soong deducted $10,000 of percentage depletion in excess of basis. The following comparison illustrates the differences in the computation of the passive loss for regular income tax and AMT purposes for Activity B.

---
[23] See Chapter 11.

CHAPTER 12 Alternative Minimum Tax

	Regular Income Tax	AMT
Gross income	$ 27,000	$ 27,000
Deductions:		
Operating expenses	($ 19,000)	($ 19,000)
Depreciation	(20,000)	(15,000)
Depletion	(10,000)	–0–
Total deductions	($ 49,000)	($ 34,000)
Passive loss	($ 22,000)	($ 7,000)

Because the adjustment for depreciation ($5,000) applies and the preference for depletion ($10,000) is not taken into account in computing AMTI, the regular income tax passive activity loss of $22,000 for Activity B is reduced by these amounts, resulting in a passive activity loss of $7,000 for AMT purposes. ▼

For regular income tax purposes, Soong would offset the $10,000 of net passive income from Activity A with $10,000 of the passive loss from Activity B. For AMT purposes, he would offset the $10,000 of net passive income from Activity A with the $7,000 passive activity loss allowed from Activity B, resulting in passive activity income of $3,000. Thus, in computing AMTI, Soong makes a positive passive loss adjustment of $3,000 [$10,000 (passive activity loss allowed for regular income tax) – $7,000 (passive activity loss allowed for the AMT)]. To avoid duplication, the AMT adjustment for depreciation and the preference for depletion are *not* reported separately. They are accounted for in determining the AMT passive loss adjustment.

EXAMPLE 16

Assume the same facts as in the previous example. For regular income tax purposes, Soong has a suspended passive loss of $12,000 [$22,000 (amount of loss) – $10,000 (used in 1997)]. This suspended passive loss can offset passive income in the future or can offset active or portfolio income when Soong disposes of the loss activity (refer to Chapter 11). For AMT purposes, Soong's suspended passive loss is $0 [$7,000 (amount of loss) – $7,000 (amount used in 1997)]. ▼

Alternative Tax Net Operating Loss Deduction. In computing taxable income, taxpayers are allowed to deduct net operating loss (NOL) carryovers and carrybacks (refer to Chapter 7). The regular income tax NOL must be modified, however, in computing AMTI. The starting point in computing the **alternative tax NOL deduction (ATNOLD)** is the NOL computed for regular income tax purposes. The regular income tax NOL is then modified for AMT adjustments and tax preferences with the result being the ATNOLD. Thus, preferences and adjustment items that have benefited the taxpayer in computing the regular income tax NOL are added back, thereby reducing or eliminating the ATNOLD.[24]

EXAMPLE 17

In 1997, Adam incurred an NOL of $100,000. Adam had no AMT adjustments, but his deductions included tax preferences of $18,000. His ATNOLD carryback to 1994 is $82,000 ($100,000 regular income tax NOL – $18,000 tax preferences deducted in computing the NOL). ▼

In Example 17, if the adjustment was not made to the regular income tax NOL, the $18,000 in tax preference items deducted in 1997 would have the effect of

---
[24] § 56(a)(4).

TAX IN THE NEWS

AMT Turns Winning into Losing

A taxpayer who was discharged (i.e., fired) by his employer filed a wrongful discharge suit against the employer. The taxpayer was successful and was awarded taxable back pay and benefits of $250,000. In winning the taxable part of the judgment, he incurred attorney's fees of $245,100.

In filing his Form 1040, the taxpayer included the $250,000 in gross income net of the $245,100 (i.e., included a net $4,900 in gross income). Thus, although he was required to pay $245,100 in attorney's fees, he did receive a tax benefit by reducing his gross income.

Unfortunately, the Tax Court agreed with the IRS that the attorney's fees are appropriately classified as miscellaneous itemized deductions (*Kenneth J. Alexander*, 69 TCM 1792, T.C.Memo. 1995–51). Classifying the attorney's fees in this manner resulted in an AMT of $57,441.

---

reducing AMTI in the year (or years) the 1997 NOL is utilized. This would weaken the entire concept of the AMT.

A ceiling exists on the amount of the ATNOLD that can be deducted in the carryback or carryforward year. The deduction is limited to 90 percent of AMTI (before the ATNOLD) for the carryback or carryforward year.

EXAMPLE 18 Assume the same facts as in the previous example. Adam's AMTI (before the ATNOLD) in 1994 is $90,000. Therefore, of the $82,000 ATNOLD carried back to 1994 from 1997, only $81,000 ($90,000 × 90%) can be used in recalculating the 1994 AMT. The unused $1,000 of 1997 ATNOLD is now carried to 1995 for use in recalculating the 1995 AMT. ▼

A taxpayer who has an ATNOLD that is carried back or over to another year must use the ATNOLD against AMTI in the carryback or carryforward year even if the regular income tax, rather than the AMT, applies.

EXAMPLE 19 Matt's ATNOLD for 1998 (carried over from 1997) is $10,000. AMTI before considering the ATNOLD is $25,000. If Matt's regular income tax exceeds the AMT, the AMT does not apply. Nevertheless, Matt's ATNOLD of $10,000 is "used up" in 1998 and is not available for carryover to a later year. ▼

For regular income tax purposes, the NOL can be carried back 3 years and forward 15 years. However, the taxpayer may elect to forgo the 3-year carryback. These rules generally apply to the ATNOLD as well, except that the election to forgo the 3-year carryback is available for the ATNOLD only if the taxpayer elected it for the regular income tax NOL.

Itemized Deductions. Most of the itemized deductions that are allowed for regular income tax purposes are allowed for AMT purposes. Itemized deductions that are allowed for AMT purposes include the following:

- Casualty losses.
- Gambling losses.
- Charitable contributions.

CHAPTER 12 Alternative Minimum Tax

- Medical expenses in excess of 10 percent of AGI.
- Estate tax on income in respect of a decedent.
- Qualified interest.

Taxes (state, local, foreign income, and property taxes) and miscellaneous itemized deductions that are subject to the 2 percent-of-AGI floor are not allowed in computing AMT.[25] A positive AMT adjustment in the total amount of the regular income tax deduction for each is required.

If the taxpayer's gross income includes the recovery of any tax deducted as an itemized deduction for regular income tax purposes, a negative AMT adjustment in the amount of the recovery is allowed for AMTI purposes.[26] For example, state, local, and foreign income taxes can be deducted for regular income tax purposes, but cannot be deducted in computing AMTI. Because of this, any refund of such taxes from a prior year is not included in AMTI. Therefore, in calculating AMTI, the taxpayer must make a negative adjustment for an income tax refund that has been included in computing regular taxable income. Under the tax benefit rule, a tax refund is included in taxable income to the extent that the taxpayer obtained a tax benefit by deducting the tax in a prior year.

Cutback Adjustment. The 3 percent cutback adjustment that applies to regular income tax itemized deductions of certain high-income taxpayers (refer to Chapter 10) does not apply in computing AMT.[27] The effect of the 3 percent cutback adjustment is to disallow a portion of the taxpayer's itemized deductions for regular income tax purposes. Because this cutback adjustment does not apply for AMT purposes, taxable income, which is the starting point for computing AMTI, must be reduced by the amount of the disallowed deductions. Although this reduction has the same effect on AMTI as a negative adjustment, it is not shown on Form 6251 as such. Instead, it is shown on a separate line (line 18) as a subtraction from taxable income.

Medical Expenses. The rules for determining the AMT deductions for medical expenses are sufficiently complex to require further explanation. For regular income tax purposes, medical expenses are deductible to the extent they exceed 7.5 percent of AGI. However, for AMT purposes, medical expenses are deductible only to the extent they exceed 10 percent of AGI.[28]

EXAMPLE 20

Joann incurred medical expenses of $16,000 in 1997. She had AGI of $100,000 for the year. Her AMT adjustment for medical expenses is computed as follows:

	Regular Income Tax	**AMT**
Medical expenses incurred	$16,000	$ 16,000
Less reduction:		
$100,000 AGI × 7.5%	(7,500)	
$100,000 AGI × 10%		(10,000)
Medical expense deduction	$ 8,500	$ 6,000

Joann's AMT adjustment for medical expenses is $2,500 ($8,500 regular income tax deduction − $6,000 AMT deduction). ▼

---

[25] § 56(b)(1)(A).
[26] § 56(b)(1)(D).
[27] § 56(b)(1)(F).
[28] § 56(b)(1)(B).

Interest in General. The AMT itemized deduction allowed for interest expense includes only qualified housing interest and investment interest to the extent of net investment income that is included in the determination of AMTI.[29] Any interest that is deducted in calculating the regular income tax that is not permitted in calculating the AMT is treated as a positive adjustment.

In computing regular taxable income, taxpayers who itemize can deduct the following types of interest (refer to Chapter 10):

- Qualified residence interest.
- Investment interest, subject to the investment interest limitations (discussed under Investment Interest below).

Housing Interest. Under current regular income tax rules, taxpayers who itemize can deduct *qualified residence interest* on up to two residences. The deduction is limited to interest on acquisition indebtedness up to $1 million and home equity indebtedness up to $100,000. Acquisition indebtedness is debt that is incurred in acquiring, constructing, or substantially improving a qualified residence of the taxpayer and is secured by the residence. Home equity indebtedness is indebtedness secured by a qualified residence of the taxpayer, but does not include acquisition indebtedness.

EXAMPLE 21

Gail, who used the proceeds of a mortgage to acquire a personal residence, paid mortgage interest of $112,000 in 1997. Of this amount, $14,000 is attributable to acquisition indebtedness in excess of $1 million. For regular income tax purposes, Gail may deduct mortgage interest of $98,000 ($112,000 total − $14,000 disallowed). ▼

The mortgage interest deduction for AMT purposes is limited to *qualified housing interest*, rather than *qualified residence interest*. Qualified housing interest includes only interest incurred to acquire, construct, or substantially improve the taxpayer's principal residence and such interest on one other qualified dwelling used for personal purposes. A home equity loan qualifies only if it meets the definition of qualified housing interest, which frequently is not the case. When additional mortgage interest is incurred (e.g., a mortgage refinancing), interest paid is deductible as qualified housing interest for AMT purposes only if:

- The proceeds are used to acquire or substantially improve a qualified residence.
- Interest on the prior loan was qualified housing interest.
- The amount of the loan was not increased.

A positive AMT adjustment is required in the amount of the difference between qualified *residence* interest allowed as an itemized deduction for regular income tax purposes and qualified *housing* interest allowed in the determination of AMTI.

Investment Interest. Investment interest is deductible for regular income tax purposes and for AMT purposes to the extent of qualified net investment income.

EXAMPLE 22

For the year, Dan had net investment income of $16,000 before deducting investment interest. He incurred investment interest expense of $30,000 during the year. His investment interest deduction is $16,000. ▼

---

[29] § 56(b)(1)(C).

Even though investment interest is deductible for both regular income tax and AMT purposes, an adjustment is required if the amount of investment interest deductible for regular income tax purposes differs from the amount deductible for AMT purposes. For example, an adjustment will arise if proceeds from a home equity loan are used to purchase investments. Interest on a home equity loan is deductible as qualified residence interest for regular income tax purposes, but is not deductible for AMT purposes unless the proceeds are used to acquire or substantially improve a qualified residence. For AMT purposes, however, interest on a home equity loan is deductible as investment interest expense if proceeds from the loan are used for investment purposes.

To determine the AMT adjustment for investment interest expense, it is necessary to compute the investment interest deduction for both regular income tax and AMT purposes. This computation is illustrated in the following example.

EXAMPLE 23

Tom had $20,000 interest income from corporate bonds and $5,000 dividends from preferred stock. He reported the following amounts of investment income for regular income tax and AMT purposes:

	Regular Income Tax	AMT
Corporate bond interest	$20,000	$20,000
Preferred stock dividends	5,000	5,000
Net investment income	$25,000	$25,000

Tom incurred investment interest expense of $10,000 related to the corporate bonds. He also incurred $4,000 interest on a home equity loan and used the proceeds of the loan to purchase preferred stock. For regular income tax purposes, this $4,000 is deductible as qualified residence interest. His *investment* interest expense for regular income tax and AMT purposes is computed below:

	Regular Income Tax	AMT
To carry corporate bonds	$10,000	$10,000
On home equity loan to carry preferred stock	–0–	4,000
Total investment interest expense	$10,000	$14,000

Investment interest expense is deductible to the extent of net investment income. Because the amount deductible for regular income tax purposes ($10,000) differs from the amount deductible for AMT purposes ($14,000), an AMT adjustment is required. The adjustment is computed as follows:

AMT deduction for investment interest expense	$14,000
Regular income tax deduction for investment interest expense	(10,000)
Negative AMT adjustment	$ 4,000

As discussed subsequently under AMT Preferences, the interest on private activity bonds is a tax preference for AMT purposes. Such interest can also affect the calculation of the AMT investment interest deduction in that it is included in the calculation of net investment income.

Other Adjustments. The standard deduction is not allowed as a deduction in computing AMTI.[30] Although a person who does not itemize is rarely subject to the AMT, it is possible. In such a case, the taxpayer is required to enter a positive adjustment for the standard deduction in computing the AMT.

The personal and dependency exemption amount deducted for regular income tax purposes is not allowed in computing AMT.[31] Therefore, taxpayers must enter a positive AMT adjustment for the personal and dependency exemption amount claimed in computing the regular income tax. A separate exemption (see Exemption Amount) is allowed for AMT purposes. To allow both the regular income tax exemption amount and the AMT exemption amount would result in extra benefits for taxpayers.

EXAMPLE 24 Eli, who is single, has no dependents and does not itemize deductions. He earned a salary of $106,800 in 1997. Based on this information, Eli's taxable income for 1997 is $100,000 ($106,800 − $4,150 standard deduction − $2,650 exemption). ▼

EXAMPLE 25 Assume the same facts as in Example 24. In addition, assume Eli's tax preferences for the year totaled $150,000. Eli's AMTI is $256,800 ($100,000 taxable income + $4,150 adjustment for standard deduction + $2,650 adjustment for exemption + $150,000 tax preferences). ▼

AMT PREFERENCES

4 LEARNING OBJECTIVE
Identify the tax preferences that are included in calculating the AMT.

Percentage Depletion. Congress originally enacted the percentage depletion rules to provide taxpayers with incentives to invest in the development of specified natural resources. Percentage depletion is computed by multiplying a rate specified in the Code times the gross income from the property (refer to Chapter 8). The percentage rate is based on the type of mineral involved. The basis of the property is reduced by the amount of depletion taken until the basis reaches zero. However, once the basis of the property reaches zero, taxpayers are allowed to continue taking percentage depletion deductions. Thus, over the life of the property, depletion deductions may greatly exceed the cost of the property.

The percentage depletion preference is equal to the excess of the regular income tax deduction for percentage depletion over the adjusted basis of the property at the end of the taxable year.[32] Basis is determined without regard to the depletion deduction for the taxable year. This preference item is figured separately for each piece of property for which the taxpayer is claiming depletion.

EXAMPLE 26 Kim owns a mineral property that qualifies for a 22% depletion rate. The basis of the property at the beginning of the year is $10,000. Gross income from the property for the year is $100,000. For regular income tax purposes, Kim's percentage depletion deduction (assume it is not limited by taxable income from the property) is $22,000. For AMT purposes, Kim has a tax preference of $12,000 ($22,000 − $10,000). ▼

Intangible Drilling Costs. In computing the regular income tax, taxpayers are allowed to deduct certain intangible drilling and development costs in the year incurred, although such costs are normally capital in nature (refer to Chapter 8).

---

[30] § 56(b)(1)(E).
[31] § 56(b)(1)(E).
[32] § 57(a)(1). Note the preference label does not apply to percentage depletion on oil and gas wells for independent producers and royalty owners as defined in § 613A(c).

The deduction is allowed for costs incurred in connection with oil and gas wells and geothermal wells.

For AMT purposes, excess intangible drilling costs (IDC) for the year are treated as a preference.[33] The preference for excess IDC is computed as follows:

IDC expensed in the year incurred

Minus: Deduction if IDC were capitalized and amortized over 10 years

Equals: Excess of IDC expense over amortization

Minus: 65% of net oil and gas and geothermal income

Equals: Tax preference item

EXAMPLE 27 Ben, who incurred IDC of $50,000 during the year, elected to expense that amount. His net oil and gas income for the year was $60,000. Ben's tax preference for IDC is $6,000 [($50,000 IDC − $5,000 amortization) − (65% × $60,000 income)]. ▼

A taxpayer can avoid the preference for IDC by electing to write off the expenditures over a 10-year period for regular income tax purposes.

Interest on Private Activity Bonds.
Income from private activity bonds is not included in taxable income, and expenses related to carrying such bonds are not deductible for regular income tax purposes. However, interest on private activity bonds is included as a preference in computing AMTI. Therefore, expenses incurred in carrying the bonds are offset against the interest income in computing the tax preference.[34]

The Code contains a lengthy, complex definition of private activity bonds.[35] In general, **private activity bonds** are bonds issued by states or municipalities with more than 10 percent of the proceeds being used for private business use. For example, a bond issued by a city whose proceeds are used to construct a factory that is leased to a private business at a favorable rate is a private activity bond.

ETHICAL CONSIDERATIONS

Taxability of Bond Interest: Regular Income Tax versus AMT

Jason, who is single and in the 31 percent tax bracket, recently inherited $1 million of bonds from his mother. Rather than changing investments, Jason decides to retain the investment in municipal bonds for the time being.

The Form 1099 he received from the municipality has confused Jason about the tax treatment of the bond interest. He thought that all municipal bonds were tax-exempt, but from an article that he read recently, he is now aware that certain such bonds are not tax-exempt for Federal income tax purposes. Rereading the article, Jason notes that bonds classified as private activity bonds are excludible from gross income for regular income tax purposes but are a tax preference for AMT purposes. Jason has asked the issuer for clarification on the status of the bonds, but has received no answer. He checks his mother's tax return for the past three years and finds that none of her returns included a Form 6251.

---

[33] § 57(a)(2).
[34] § 57(a)(5).
[35] § 141.

Since he wants to file his return this week, Jason has to decide how to report the bond interest. He knows that he is going to be subject to the AMT with some of his income being taxed at the 28 percent rate. He is considering resolving his dilemma by not treating the bonds as private activity bonds. His justification for his position is that his mother was an astute businesswoman and she did not report the bond interest on her tax returns as private activity bond interest. If Jason does not treat the bonds as private activity bonds, the bond interest will not be subject to either the regular income tax or the AMT. Evaluate Jason's proposal.

Depreciation. For real property and leased personal property placed in service before 1987, there is an AMT preference for the excess of accelerated depreciation over straight-line depreciation.[36] However, examination of the cost recovery tables for pre-1987 real property (refer to Chapter 8) reveals that from the eighth year on, accelerated depreciation will not exceed straight-line depreciation. Consequently, taxpayers no longer have preferences attributable to pre-1987 real property.

Accelerated depreciation on pre-1987 leased personal property was computed using specified ACRS percentages (refer to Table 8-1, Chapter 8). AMT depreciation was based on the straight-line method, which was computed using the half-year convention, no salvage value, and a longer recovery period.[37] As a result, in the early years of the life of the asset, the cost recovery allowance used in computing the regular income tax was greater than the straight-line depreciation deduction allowed in computing AMT. The excess depreciation was treated as a tax preference item. For all leased personal property placed in service before 1987 (3-year, 5-year, and 10-year), except for 15-year public utility property, the cost

---

TAX IN THE NEWS

MUNICIPAL BONDS AND THE AMT

A number of investment and tax advisers are warning investors who have municipal bonds in their portfolios (either directly or through mutual funds) that the bonds may not be as tax-exempt as they think.

According to current predictions, more and more taxpayers are likely to become subject to the AMT in the future with municipal bond investors being among the hardest hit. Private activity bond interest that is tax-exempt for regular income tax purposes is subject to taxation under the AMT. A prime reason investors are attracted to private activity bonds is that they offer a higher yield than other municipal bonds. But if the interest results in the taxpayer paying the AMT, this seemingly higher yield might actually be lower.

Congress's Joint Committee on Taxation estimates that the number of taxpayers subject to the AMT will increase from about 600,000 currently to 6.2 million in 2006. The two factors expected to cause this surge are inflation (the AMT exemption is not indexed for inflation) and President Clinton's 1993 tax increase, which included an increase in the AMT rates.

SOURCE: Adapted from Charles Gasparino, "Tax-Free Status of Some Munis May Be Fleeting," *Wall Street Journal*, November 11, 1996, p. C1.

---

[36] § 57(a)(6).
[37] The specified lives for AMT purposes are 5 years for 3-year property, 8 years for 5-year property, 15 years for 10-year property, and 22 years for 15-year property.

recovery period has expired. Since there is no excess depreciation, there is no tax preference for AMT purposes.

EXAMPLE 28

Paul acquired personal property on January 1, 1986, at a cost of $30,000. The property, which was placed in service as leased personal property on January 1, was 10-year ACRS property. Paul's 1986 depreciation deduction for regular income tax purposes was $2,400 ($30,000 cost × 8% rate from Table 8–1). For AMT purposes, the asset was depreciated over the AMT life of 15 years using the straight-line method with the half-year convention. Thus, AMT depreciation for 1986 was $1,000 [($30,000 ÷ 15) × ½ year convention]. Paul's tax preference for 1986 was $1,400 ($2,400 − $1,000). ACRS depreciation for 1997 is $0 ($30,000 × 0% ACRS rate), and straight-line depreciation is $2,000 ($30,000 ÷ 15). Thus, Paul's tax preference for 1997 is $0 since there is no excess depreciation. ▼

The preference item for excess depreciation on leased personal property is figured separately for each piece of property. No preference is reported in the year the taxpayer disposes of the property.

Fifty Percent Exclusion for Certain Small Business Stock. Fifty percent of the gain on the sale of certain small business stock is excludible from gross income for regular income tax purposes. The excluded amount is a tax preference for AMT purposes.[38]

ILLUSTRATION OF THE AMT COMPUTATION

5 LEARNING OBJECTIVE
Apply the formula for computing the AMT and illustrate Form 6251.

The computation of the AMT is illustrated in the following example.

EXAMPLE 29

Hans Sims, who is single, had taxable income for 1997 as follows:

Salary		$ 92,000
Interest		8,000
Adjusted gross income		$100,000
Less itemized deductions:		
Medical expenses ($17,500 − 7.5% of $100,000 AGI)[a]	$10,000	
State income taxes	4,000	
Interest[b]		
Home mortgage (for qualified housing)	20,000*	
Investment interest	3,300*	
Contributions (cash)	5,000*	
Casualty losses ($14,000 − 10% of $100,000 AGI)	4,000*	(46,300)
		$ 53,700
Less exemption		(2,650)
Taxable income		$ 51,050

[a]Total medical expenses were $17,500, reduced by 7.5% of AGI, resulting in an itemized deduction of $10,000. However, for AMT purposes, the reduction is 10%, which leaves an AMT itemized deduction of $7,500 ($17,500 − 10% of $100,000 AGI). Therefore, an adjustment of $2,500 ($10,000 − $7,500) is required for medical expenses disallowed for AMT purposes.

[b]In this illustration, all interest is deductible in computing AMTI. Qualified housing interest is deductible. Investment interest ($3,300) is deductible to the extent of net investment income included in the minimum tax base. For this purpose, the $8,000 of interest income is treated as net investment income.

---

[38]§ 57(a)(7).

Deductions marked by an asterisk are allowed as *alternative minimum tax itemized deductions,* and AMT adjustments are required for the other itemized deductions. Thus, adjustments are required for state income taxes and for medical expenses to the extent the medical expenses deductible for regular income tax purposes are not deductible in computing AMT (see note a above). In addition to the items that affected taxable income, Hans had $35,000 interest on private activity bonds (an exclusion tax preference). AMTI is computed as follows:

Taxable income		$ 51,050
Plus: Adjustments		
	State income taxes	4,000
	Medical expenses (see note a above)	2,500
	Personal exemption	2,650
Plus: Tax preference (interest on private activity bonds)		35,000
Equals: AMTI		$ 95,200
Minus: AMT exemption		(33,750)
Equals: Minimum tax base		$ 61,450
Times: AMT rate		× 26%
Equals: Tentative AMT		$ 15,977
Minus: Regular income tax on taxable income		(11,090)
Equals: AMT		$ 4,887

The solution to Example 29 is also presented on Form 6251. Though this example is for 1997, 1996 tax forms are used because the 1997 tax forms were not available at the time of this writing.

Note that the $2,650 personal exemption amount is a positive adjustment in the Example 29 solution, but does not appear as an adjustment in Form 6251. This difference occurs because line 16 of Form 6251 includes the amount from line 35 of Form 1040. Line 35 of Form 1040 is taxable income before the deduction for personal and dependency exemptions.

AMT CREDIT

6 LEARNING OBJECTIVE
Describe the role of the AMT credit in the alternative minimum tax structure.

As discussed previously, timing differences give rise to adjustments to the minimum tax base. In later years, the timing differences reverse, as was illustrated in several of the preceding examples. To provide equity for the taxpayer when timing differences reverse, the regular income tax liability may be reduced by a tax credit for prior years' minimum tax liability attributable to timing differences. The **alternative minimum tax credit** may be carried over indefinitely. Therefore, there is no need to keep track of when the minimum tax credit arose.[39]

EXAMPLE 30

Assume the same facts as in Example 3. Also assume that in 1996, Bob paid AMT as a result of the $20,000 positive adjustment arising from the circulation expenditures. In 1997, $10,000 of the timing difference reverses, resulting in regular taxable income that is $10,000 greater than AMTI. Because Bob has already paid AMT as a result of the write-off of circulation expenditures, he is allowed an AMT credit in 1997. The AMT credit can offset Bob's regular income tax liability in 1997 to the extent that his regular income tax liability exceeds his tentative AMT. ▼

---

[39] § 53.

Concept Summary 12-1

AMT Adjustments and Preferences for Individuals

Adjustments	Positive	Negative	Both*
Circulation expenditures			X
Depreciation of post-1986 real property			X
Depreciation of post-1986 personal property			X
Pollution control facilities			X
Mining exploration and development costs			X
Research and experimental expenditures			X
Completed contract method			X
Incentive stock options	X**		
Adjusted gain or loss			X
Passive activity losses			X
Alternative tax NOLD			X
Itemized deductions:			
Medical expenses	X		
State income tax	X		
Property tax on realty	X		
Property tax on personalty	X		
Miscellaneous itemized deductions	X		
Tax benefit rule for state income tax refund		X	
Cutback adjustment		X	
Qualified residence interest that is not qualified housing interest	X		
Qualified residence interest that is AMT investment interest	X	X	
Private activity bond interest that is AMT investment interest		X	
Standard deduction	X		
Personal exemptions and dependency deductions	X		
Preferences			
Percentage depletion in excess of adjusted basis	X		
Intangible drilling costs	X		
Private activity bond interest income	X		
Depreciation on pre-1987 leased personal property	X		
§ 1202 exclusion for certain small business stock	X		

*Timing differences.
**While the adjustment is a positive adjustment, the AMT basis for the stock is increased by the amount of the positive adjustment.

Form 6251 — Alternative Minimum Tax—Individuals
Department of the Treasury
Internal Revenue Service

▶ See separate instructions.
▶ Attach to Form 1040 or Form 1040NR.

OMB No. 1545-0227
1996
Attachment Sequence No. **32**

Name(s) shown on Form 1040: *Hans Sims*

Your social security number:

Part I — Adjustments and Preferences

1	If you itemized deductions on Schedule A (Form 1040), go to line 2. Otherwise, enter your standard deduction from Form 1040, line 34, here and go to line 6	
2	Medical and dental. Enter the smaller of Schedule A (Form 1040), line 4 **or** 2½% of Form 1040, line 32	2,500
3	Taxes. Enter the amount from Schedule A (Form 1040), line 9	4,000
4	Certain interest on a home mortgage not used to buy, build, or improve your home	
5	Miscellaneous itemized deductions. Enter the amount from Schedule A (Form 1040), line 26	
6	Refund of taxes. Enter any tax refund from Form 1040, line 10 or line 21	( )
7	Investment interest. Enter difference between regular tax and AMT deduction	
8	Post-1986 depreciation. Enter difference between regular tax and AMT depreciation	
9	Adjusted gain or loss. Enter difference between AMT and regular tax gain or loss	
10	Incentive stock options. Enter excess of AMT income over regular tax income	
11	Passive activities. Enter difference between AMT and regular tax income or loss	
12	Beneficiaries of estates and trusts. Enter the amount from Schedule K-1 (Form 1041), line 8	
13	Tax-exempt interest from private activity bonds issued after 8/7/86	35,000
14	Other. Enter the amount, if any, for each item below and enter the total on line 14. **a** Charitable contributions **b** Circulation expenditures **c** Depletion **d** Depreciation (pre-1987) **e** Installment sales **f** Intangible drilling costs **g** Long-term contracts **h** Loss limitations **i** Mining costs **j** Patron's adjustment **k** Pollution control facilities **l** Research and experimental **m** Tax shelter farm activities **n** Related adjustments	
15	**Total Adjustments and Preferences.** Combine lines 1 through 14 ▶	41,500

Part II — Alternative Minimum Taxable Income

16	Enter the amount from **Form 1040, line 35.** If less than zero, enter as a (loss) ▶	53,700
17	Net operating loss deduction, if any, from Form 1040, line 21. Enter as a positive amount	
18	If Form 1040, line 32, is over $117,950 (over $58,975 if married filing separately), and you itemized deductions, enter the amount, if any, from line 9 of the worksheet for Schedule A (Form 1040), line 28	( )
19	Combine lines 15 through 18 ▶	95,200
20	Alternative tax net operating loss deduction. See page 5 of the instructions	
21	**Alternative Minimum Taxable Income.** Subtract line 20 from line 19. (If married filing separately and line 21 is more than $165,000, see page 5 of the instructions.) ▶	95,200

Part III — Exemption Amount and Alternative Minimum Tax

22	**Exemption Amount.** (If this form is for a child under age 14, see page 6 of the instructions.) If your filing status is: And line 21 is not over: Enter on line 22: Single or head of household $112,500 $33,750 Married filing jointly or qualifying widow(er) 150,000 45,000 Married filing separately 75,000 22,500 If line 21 is **over** the amount shown above for your filing status, see page 6 of the instructions.	33,750
23	Subtract line 22 from line 21. If zero or less, enter -0- here and on lines 26 and 28 ▶	61,450
24	If line 23 is $175,000 or less ($87,500 or less if married filing separately), multiply line 23 by 26% (.26). Otherwise, multiply line 23 by 28% (.28) and subtract $3,500 ($1,750 if married filing separately) from the result	15,977
25	Alternative minimum tax foreign tax credit. See page 6 of the instructions	
26	Tentative minimum tax. Subtract line 25 from line 24 ▶	15,977
27	Enter your tax from Form 1040, line 38 (excluding any amount from Form 4972), minus any foreign tax credit from Form 1040, line 41	11,090
28	**Alternative Minimum Tax.** (If this form is for a child under age 14, see page 7 of the instructions.) Subtract line 27 from line 26. If zero or less, enter -0-. Enter here and on Form 1040, line 46 ▶	4,887

For Paperwork Reduction Act Notice, see separate instructions.   Cat. No. 13600G   Form **6251** (1996)

The AMT credit is applicable only for the AMT that results from timing differences. It is not available in connection with **AMT exclusions,** which represent permanent differences rather than timing differences between the regular income tax liability and the AMT. These AMT exclusions include the following:

- The standard deduction.
- Personal exemptions.
- Medical expenses, to the extent deductible for regular income tax purposes but not deductible in computing AMT.
- Other itemized deductions not allowable for AMT purposes, including miscellaneous itemized deductions, taxes, and interest expense.
- Excess percentage depletion.
- Tax-exempt interest on specified private activity bonds.

EXAMPLE 31 Don, who is single, has zero taxable income for 1997. He also has positive timing adjustments of $300,000 and AMT exclusions of $100,000. His AMT base is $400,000 because his AMT exemption is phased out completely due to the level of AMTI. Don's tentative AMT is $108,500 [($175,000 × 26% AMT rate) + ($225,000 × 28% AMT rate)]. ▼

To determine the amount of AMT credit to carry over, the AMT must be recomputed reflecting only the AMT exclusions and the AMT exemption amount.

EXAMPLE 32 Assume the same facts as in the previous example. If there had been no positive timing adjustments for the year, Don's tentative AMT would have been $17,225 [($100,000 AMT exclusions − $33,750 exemption) × 26% AMT rate]. Don may carry over an AMT credit of $91,275 ($108,500 AMT − $17,225 related to AMT exclusions) to 1998 and subsequent years. ▼

CORPORATE ALTERNATIVE MINIMUM TAX

7 LEARNING OBJECTIVE
Understand the basic features of the corporate AMT.

The AMT applicable to corporations is similar to that applicable to noncorporate taxpayers. However, there are several important differences:

- The corporate AMT rate is 20 percent versus a top rate of 28 percent for noncorporate taxpayers.[40]
- The AMT exemption for corporations is $40,000 reduced by 25 percent of the amount by which AMTI exceeds $150,000.[41]
- Tax preferences applicable to noncorporate taxpayers are also applicable to corporate taxpayers, but some adjustments differ (see below).

Although there are computational differences, the corporate AMT and the noncorporate AMT have the identical objective: to force taxpayers who are more profitable than their taxable income reflects to pay additional tax. The formula for determining the corporate AMT appears in Figure 12–3.

AMT ADJUSTMENTS

Adjustments Applicable to Individuals and Corporations.
The following adjustments that were discussed in connection with the individual AMT also apply to the corporate AMT:

---
[40] § 55(b)(1)(B). [41] §§ 55(d)(2) and (3).

FIGURE 12-3
AMT Formula for Corporations

Taxable income
Plus: Income tax NOL deduction
Plus or minus: AMT adjustments
Plus: Tax preferences
Equals: AMTI before ATNOLD
Minus: ATNOLD (limited to 90% of AMTI before ATNOLD)
Equals: AMTI
Minus: Exemption
Equals: AMT base
Times: 20% rate
Equals: Tentative minimum tax before AMT foreign tax credit
Minus: AMT foreign tax credit (limited to 90% of AMT before AMT foreign tax credit)
Equals: Tentative minimum tax
Minus: Regular tax liability before credits minus regular foreign tax credit
Equals: AMT if positive

- Excess of MACRS over ADS depreciation on real and personal property placed in service after 1986.
- Pollution control facilities placed in service after 1986 (AMT requires ADS depreciation over the asset's ADR life; 60-month amortization is allowed for regular income tax purposes).
- Mining and exploration expenditures (AMT requires amortization over 10 years versus immediate expensing allowed for regular income tax purposes).
- Income on long-term contracts (AMT requires percentage of completion method; completed contract method is allowed in limited circumstances for regular income tax purposes).
- Dispositions of assets (if gain or loss for AMT purposes differs from gain or loss for regular income tax purposes).
- Allowable ATNOLD (which cannot exceed 90 percent of AMTI before deduction for ATNOLD).

Adjustments Applicable Only to Corporations. Three AMT adjustments are applicable only to corporations:[42]

- The adjusted current earnings (ACE) adjustment.
- The Merchant Marine capital construction fund adjustment.
- The adjustment for special deductions allowed to Blue Cross/Blue Shield organizations.

The latter two adjustments apply to specific types of corporations and are not discussed in the chapter. On the other hand, the **ACE adjustment** generally applies to all corporations[43] and is expected to have a significant impact on both tax and financial accounting.

Corporations are subject to an AMT adjustment equal to 75 percent of the excess of ACE over AMTI before the ACE adjustment.[44] Historically, the govern-

---
[42] § 56(c).
[43] The ACE adjustment does not apply to S corporations. § 56(g)(6).
[44] § 56(g).

TAX IN THE NEWS

WHO PAYS CORPORATE AMT?

During 1995, the question of whether the corporate AMT should be repealed was the subject of much debate. Among the issues discussed were the amount of revenue generated, the related compliance costs, and the number of corporations subject to the AMT.

According to a Government Accounting Office report, only about 30,000 of the 2.1 million corporations potentially subject to the AMT (i.e., less than 1.5 percent) paid any AMT for the period 1987–1992. Approximately 2,000 corporations paid 85 percent of the corporate AMT during that period.

Proponents of the corporate AMT claimed these statistics showed that the corporations that should be paying the AMT (i.e., large corporations) are doing so. Opponents claimed the same statistics supported their position that the compliance costs borne by the mass of corporations do not justify the continuation of this tax system. Truly, "beauty is in the eye of the beholder."

---

ment has not required conformity between tax accounting and financial accounting. For many years, the only *direct* conformity requirement was that a corporation that used the LIFO method for tax accounting also had to use LIFO for financial accounting.[45] Through the ACE adjustment, Congress is *indirectly* imposing a conformity requirement on corporations. While a corporation may still choose to use different methods for tax and financial accounting purposes, it may no longer be able to do so without incurring AMT as a result of the ACE adjustment. Thus, a corporation may incur AMT not only because of specifically targeted adjustments and preferences, but also as a result of any methods that cause ACE to exceed AMTI before the ACE adjustment.

The ACE adjustment can be either a positive or a negative amount. AMTI is increased by 75 percent of the excess of ACE over unadjusted AMTI. Or AMTI is reduced by 75 percent of the excess of unadjusted AMTI over ACE. The negative adjustment is limited to the aggregate of the positive adjustments under ACE for prior years, reduced by the previously claimed negative adjustments. See Concept Summary 12–2. Thus, the ordering of the timing differences is crucial because any lost negative adjustment is permanent. Unadjusted AMTI is AMTI without the ACE adjustment or the ATNOLD.[46]

EXAMPLE 33

A calendar year corporation has the following data:

	1996	1997	1998
Pre-adjusted AMTI	$3,000	$3,000	$3,100
Adjusted current earnings	4,000	3,000	2,000

In 1996, because ACE exceeds unadjusted AMTI by $1,000, $750 (75% × $1,000) is included as a positive adjustment to AMTI. No adjustment is necessary for 1997. As unadjusted AMTI exceeds ACE by $1,100 in 1998, there is a potential negative adjustment to AMTI of

---

[45] § 472(c).

[46] §§ 56(g)(1) and (2).

Concept Summary 12-2

Determining the ACE Adjustment*

```
Calculate Taxable Income
          ↓
Calculate AMTI by adjusting Taxable
Income as required by § 56 and § 58
and increasing Taxable Income by § 57
tax preference items
          ↓
Calculate Adjusted Current Earnings
by adjusting AMTI as required (many
of the adjustments based on earnings
and profits adjustments)
          ↓
Is Adjusted Current Earnings AMTI
greater than pre-adjustment AMTI?
    Yes ↙         ↘ No
Increase AMTI by 75% of the excess of    Decrease AMTI by 75% of the excess of
Adjusted Current Earnings over AMTI      AMTI (pre-adjustment) over Adjusted
(pre-adjustment)                         Current Earnings to extent of net
                                         previous increases
```

*Adapted from "Corporate Alternative Minimum Tax: The Impact of Current Earnings Adjustment on Oil and Gas Companies" by Gallun and Zachry, which appeared in the September 1989 issue of the *Oil and Gas Tax Quarterly*, published and copyrighted 1989 by Matthew Bender & Co,. and appears here with their permission.

$825 ($1,100 × 75%). Since the total increases to AMTI for prior years equal $750 and there are no previously claimed negative adjustments, only $750 of the potential negative adjustment reduces AMTI for 1998. Further, $75 of the negative amount is lost forever. ▼

ACE should not be confused with current earnings and profits. Although many items are treated in the same manner, certain variations exist. For example, Federal income taxes, deductible in computing earnings and profits, are not deductible in determining ACE.

The starting point for computing ACE is AMTI, which is defined as regular taxable income after AMT adjustments (other than the ATNOLD and ACE adjustments) and tax preferences. The resulting figure is adjusted for several items in order to arrive at ACE.

TAX PREFERENCES

AMTI includes designated tax preference items. In some cases, this has the effect of subjecting nontaxable income to the AMT. Tax preference items that apply to individuals also apply to corporations.

EXAMPLE 34

The following information applies to Brown Corporation (a calendar year taxpayer) for 1997:

Taxable income	$200,000
Mining exploration costs	50,000
Percentage depletion claimed (the property has a zero adjusted basis)	70,000
Interest on City of Elmira (Michigan) private activity bonds	30,000

Brown Corporation's AMTI for 1997 is determined as follows:

Taxable income		$200,000
Adjustments:		
Excess mining exploration costs [$50,000 (amount expensed) − $5,000 (amount allowed over a 10-year amortization period)]		45,000
Tax preferences:		
Excess depletion	$70,000	
Interest on private activity bonds	30,000	100,000
AMTI		$345,000

EXEMPTION

The tentative AMT is 20 percent of AMTI that exceeds the corporation's exemption amount. The exemption amount for a corporation is $40,000 reduced by 25 percent of the amount by which AMTI exceeds $150,000.

EXAMPLE 35

Blue Corporation has AMTI of $180,000. The exemption amount is reduced by $7,500 [25% × ($180,000 − $150,000)], and the amount remaining is $32,500 ($40,000 − $7,500). Thus, Blue Corporation's AMT base (refer to Figure 12–3) is $147,500 ($180,000 − $32,500). ▼

Note that the exemption phases out entirely when AMTI reaches $310,000.

OTHER ASPECTS OF THE AMT

Foreign tax credits can be applied against only 90 percent of tentative AMT liability. The 90 percent limit does not apply to certain corporations meeting specified requirements for tax years beginning after March 31, 1990.

All of a corporation's AMT is available for carryover as a minimum tax credit. This is so regardless of whether the adjustments and preferences originate from timing differences or AMT exclusions.

EXAMPLE 36

In Example 34, the AMTI exceeds $310,000, so no exemption is allowed. The tentative minimum tax is $69,000 (20% of $345,000). The regular income tax liability is $61,250, and the AMT liability is $7,750 ($69,000 − $61,250). The amount of the minimum tax credit carryover is $7,750, which is all of the current year's AMT. ▼

TAX PLANNING CONSIDERATIONS

RESPONDING TO BOB AND CAROL

The chapter began with a set of circumstances involving Bob and Carol that raised a number of interesting questions. By now, the student should have arrived at a logical reason for the difference in Bob and Carol's tax liabilities and expect the following to happen to Bob.

8 **LEARNING OBJECTIVE**
Identify tax planning opportunities to minimize the AMT.

Bob contacts Adam, his tax return preparer, and explains in an excited voice that he has received a bill from the IRS for $15,000 plus interest associated with the underpayment of his tax liability. Adam has Bob fax him a copy of the IRS deficiency notice. He checks Bob's tax file and then calls Bob to explain that Bob does owe the IRS the $15,000 plus interest. Somehow Bob's tax return was prepared without including a Form 6251 (the alternative minimum tax). Adam suggests that Bob stop by his office later that afternoon to discuss the disposition of the matter further.

AVOIDING PREFERENCES AND ADJUSTMENTS

Several strategies and elections are available to help taxpayers avoid having preferences and adjustments.

- A taxpayer who is in danger of incurring AMT liability should not invest in tax-exempt private activity bonds unless doing so makes good investment sense. Any AMT triggered by interest on private activity bonds reduces the yield on an investment in the bonds. Other tax-exempt bonds or taxable corporate bonds might yield a better after-tax return.
- A taxpayer may elect to expense certain costs in the year incurred or to capitalize and amortize the costs over some specified period. The decision should be based on the present discounted value of after-tax cash flows under the available alternatives. Costs subject to elective treatment include circulation expenditures, mining exploration and development costs, and research and experimental expenditures.

CONTROLLING THE TIMING OF PREFERENCES AND ADJUSTMENTS

The AMT exemption often keeps items of tax preference from being subject to the AMT. To use the AMT exemption effectively, taxpayers should avoid bunching preferences and positive adjustments in any one year. To avoid this bunching, taxpayers should attempt to control the timing of such items when possible.

TAKING ADVANTAGE OF THE AMT/REGULAR TAX RATE DIFFERENTIAL

A taxpayer who cannot avoid triggering the AMT in a given year can usually save taxes by taking advantage of the rate differential between the AMT and the regular income tax.

EXAMPLE 37
Peter, a real estate dealer who expects to be in the 31% tax bracket in 1998, is subject to the AMT in 1997. He is considering the sale of a parcel of land (inventory) at a gain of $100,000. If he sells the land in 1998, he will have to pay tax of $31,000 ($100,000 gain × regular income tax rate). However, if he sells the land in 1997, he will pay tax of $26,000 ($100,000 gain × 26% AMT rate). Thus, accelerating the sale into 1997 will save Peter $5,000 in tax. ▼

EXAMPLE 38
Cora, who expects to be in the 39.6% tax bracket in 1998, is subject to the AMT in 1997. She is going to contribute $10,000 in cash to her alma mater, State University. If Cora makes the contribution in 1998, she will save tax of $3,960 ($10,000 contribution × 39.6% regular income tax rate). However, if she makes the contribution in 1997, she will save tax of $2,600 ($10,000 contribution × 26% AMT rate). Thus, deferring the contribution until 1998 will save Cora $1,360 in tax. ▼

CHAPTER 12 Alternative Minimum Tax

This deferral/acceleration strategy should be considered for any income or expenses where the taxpayer can control the timing. This strategy applies to corporations as well as to individuals.

KEY TERMS

ACE adjustment, 12-28

Alternative minimum tax (AMT), 12-2

Alternative minimum tax credit, 12-24

Alternative tax NOL deduction (ATNOLD), 12-15

AMT adjustments, 12-4

AMT exclusions, 12-27

Circulation expenditures, 12-4

Incentive stock options (ISOs), 12-12

Private activity bonds, 12-21

Tax preferences, 12-4

PROBLEM MATERIALS

DISCUSSION QUESTIONS

1. Since there is a regular income tax, why is there a need for an AMT?
2. Distinguish between the direct method of calculating the AMT and the indirect method.
3. What is the difference between AMT adjustments and tax preferences?
4. Identify which of the following are tax preferences:
   a. Fifty percent exclusion associated with gains on the sale of certain small business stock.
   b. Exclusion on the receipt of property by gift.
   c. Exclusion associated with payment of premiums by the employer on group term life insurance for coverage not in excess of $50,000.
   d. Percentage depletion in excess of the property's adjusted basis.
   e. Tax-exempt interest on certain private activity bonds.
5. Identify which of the following are tax preferences:
   a. Exclusion on the receipt of property by inheritance.
   b. Exclusion to employee on the employer's contribution to the employee's pension plan.
   c. Excess of deduction for circulation expenditures for regular income tax purposes over the deduction for AMT purposes.
   d. Excess of amortization allowance over depreciation on pre-1987 certified pollution control facilities.
   e. Excess of accelerated over straight-line depreciation on real property placed in service before 1987.
6. Describe the tax formula for the AMT.
7. If the regular income tax liability exceeds the tentative AMT, there is no AMT liability, and the total income tax liability is equal to the regular income tax liability. Evaluate the correctness of this statement.
8. For the exemption amount, indicate the following:
   a. Purpose for the exemption.
   b. Amount of the exemption.
   c. Reason for the phase-out of the exemption.

9. What are the AMT rates for an individual taxpayer? To what levels of income do the rates apply?

10. How do nonrefundable tax credits affect the calculation of the AMT?

11. How can an individual taxpayer avoid having an AMT adjustment for circulation expenditures?

12. Tom, who owns and operates a sole proprietorship, acquired machinery and placed it in service in February 1997. If Tom has to pay AMT in 1997, will he be required to make an AMT adjustment for depreciation on the machinery? Explain.

13. Rick, who is single, incurs mining exploration and development costs associated with his energy company. He would expense the costs in the current year in order to reduce his regular income tax, but is aware that this would create a positive adjustment for AMT purposes. His AGI is large enough to reduce the AMT exemption amount to zero. Therefore, he is considering electing to amortize the mining exploration and development costs over 10 years to avoid having to pay any AMT. Advise Rick.

14. Certain taxpayers have the option of using either the percentage of completion method or the completed contract method for reporting profit on long-term contracts. What impact could the AMT have on this decision?

15. Megan, a corporate executive, plans to exercise an incentive stock option granted by her employer to purchase 100 shares of the corporation's stock for an option price of $20 per share. The stock is currently selling for $65 per share.
    a. Explain the possible consequences of this action on Megan's regular income tax and AMT.
    b. Would your response differ if Megan exercises the option and disposes of the stock in the same tax year?

16. Lucy acquired a machine for $30,000 for use in her business two years ago and depreciated it using an accelerated method under MACRS. When she sold the machine at a gain this year, should her recognized gain for regular income tax purposes be the same as her recognized gain for AMT purposes?

17. Carol is going to be subject to the AMT in 1997. She owns an investment building and is considering disposing of it and investing in other realty. Based on an appraisal of the building's value, the realized gain would be $20,000. Ed has offered to purchase the building from Carol with the closing date being December 29, 1997. Ed wants to close the transaction in 1997 because certain beneficial tax consequences will result only if the transaction is closed prior to the beginning of 1998. Abby has offered to purchase the building with the closing date being January 2, 1998. The building has a $25,000 greater AMT adjusted basis. For regular income tax purposes, Carol expects to be in the 28% tax bracket. What are the relevant tax issues that Carol faces in making her decision?

18. Passive activity losses are not deductible in computing either taxable income or AMTI. Explain why an adjustment for passive activity losses may be required for AMT purposes.

19. What effect do adjustments and preferences have on the calculation of the ATNOLD?

20. The following itemized deductions are allowed for regular income tax purposes: medical expenses, state and local income taxes, real estate taxes, personal property taxes, home mortgage interest, investment interest, charitable contributions of cash, charitable contributions of long-term capital gain property, casualty losses, unreimbursed employee business expenses, and gambling losses. Which of these itemized deductions can result in an AMT adjustment?

21. Matt, who is single, has always elected to itemize deductions rather than take the standard deduction. In prior years, his itemized deductions always exceeded the standard deduction by a substantial amount. As a result of paying off the mortgage on his residence, he projects that his itemized deductions for 1997 will exceed the standard deduction by only $500. Matt anticipates that the amount of his itemized deductions

will remain about the same in the foreseeable future. Matt's AGI is $150,000. He is investing the amount of his former mortgage payment each month in tax-exempt bonds. A friend recommends that Matt buy a beach house in order to increase his itemized deductions. What are the relevant tax issues for Matt?

22. In computing the alternative tax itemized deduction for interest, it is possible that some interest allowed as an itemized deduction for regular income tax purposes will not be allowed. Explain.

23. Could computation of the AMT ever require an adjustment for the standard deduction or personal and dependency exemptions? Explain.

24. Alvin owns a mineral deposit that qualifies for the 15% percentage depletion rate. Under what circumstances will the depletion deduction for regular income tax purposes and AMT purposes not be the same?

25. Ira received a gift of $100,000 from his Aunt Lillian. He is going to invest the proceeds in either taxable bonds earning interest at an 8% rate or tax-exempt bonds earning interest at a 6% rate. What are the relevant tax issues for Ira?

26. What is the purpose of the AMT credit? Briefly describe how the credit is computed.

27. Discuss the similarities and differences between the individual AMT and the corporate AMT.

28. Some observers believe the ACE adjustment will cause corporations to change some of the methods they use for financial accounting and tax accounting purposes. Comment.

29. What is the ACE adjustment, and does it apply to both the individual taxpayer and the corporate taxpayer?

30. Is it ever advisable for a taxpayer to defer deductions from an AMT year into a non-AMT year where the regular income tax applies? Explain and give an example of how such a deferral might be accomplished.

PROBLEMS

31. Use the following data to calculate Rachel's AMT base:

Taxable income	$130,000
Positive AMT adjustments	50,000
Negative AMT adjustments	20,000
AMT preferences	25,000

    Rachel is not married.

32. Arthur East, an unmarried individual who is age 66, has taxable income of $100,000. He has AMT positive adjustments of $60,000 and tax preferences of $40,000.
    a. What is Arthur's AMT?
    b. What is the total amount of Arthur's tax liability?
    c. Draft a letter to Arthur explaining why he must pay more than the regular income tax liability. Arthur's address is 100 Colonel's Way, Conway, SC 29526.

33. Calculate the AMT for the following cases. The taxpayer has regular taxable income of $500,000 and does not have any credits.

Filing Status	Tentative AMT	
	Case 1	Case 2
Single	$190,000	$175,000
Married, filing jointly	190,000	175,000

34. Calculate the exemption amount for the following cases for a single taxpayer, a married taxpayer filing jointly, and a married taxpayer filing separately.

Case	AMTI
1	$100,000
2	200,000
3	400,000

35. Leona has nonrefundable credits of $30,000 for 1997. Her regular income tax liability before credits is $35,000, and her tentative AMT is $26,000.
    a. What is the amount of Leona's AMT?
    b. What is the amount of Leona's regular income tax liability after credits?

36. Angela, who is single, incurs circulation expenditures of $123,000 during 1997. She is in the process of deciding whether to expense the $123,000 or to capitalize it and elect to deduct it over a three-year period. Angela already knows that she will be subject to the AMT for 1997 at the 28% rate. Angela is in the 31% bracket for regular income tax purposes this year and expects to remain in that bracket in the future. Advise Angela on whether she should elect the three-year write-off rather than expensing the $123,000 in 1997.

37. Vito owns and operates a news agency (as a sole proprietorship). During 1997, he incurred expenses of $60,000 to increase circulation of newspapers and magazines that his agency distributes. For regular income tax purposes, he elected to expense the $60,000 in 1997. In addition, he incurred $30,000 in circulation expenditures in 1998 and again elected expense treatment. What AMT adjustments will be required in 1997 and 1998 as a result of the circulation expenditures?

38. Lance is a landlord who owns two apartment buildings. He acquired Longwood Acres on February 21, 1986, for $300,000, with $60,000 of the cost allocated to the land. He acquired Colony Square on April 5, 1993, for $800,000, and $200,000 of the cost was allocated to land. Neither apartment complex is low-income housing. Lance elected to write off the cost of each building as fast as possible. What is the effect of depreciation (cost recovery) on Lance's AMTI for 1997?

39. In March 1997, Helen Carlon acquired equipment for her business at a cost of $250,000. The equipment is 5-year class property for regular income tax purposes and 9.5-year class property for AMT purposes.
    a. If Helen depreciates the equipment using the method that will produce the greatest deduction for 1997, what is the amount of the AMT adjustment?
    b. How can Helen reduce the AMT adjustment to $0? What circumstances would motivate her to do so?
    c. Draft a letter to Helen regarding the choice of depreciation methods. Helen's address is 500 Monticello Avenue, Glendale, AZ 85306.

40. In 1997, Gary incurred $180,000 of mining and exploration expenditures. He elects to deduct the expenditures as quickly as the tax law allows for regular income tax purposes.
    a. How will Gary's treatment of mining and exploration expenditures affect his regular income tax and AMT computations for 1997?
    b. How can Gary avoid having AMT adjustments related to the mining and exploration expenditures?
    c. What factors should Gary consider in deciding whether to deduct the expenditures in the year incurred?

41. Rust Company is a real estate construction company with average annual gross receipts of $3 million. Rust uses the completed contract method on a contract that requires 18 months to complete. The contract is for $500,000 with estimated costs of $300,000. At the end of 1997, $180,000 of costs have been incurred. The contract is completed in 1998 with the total costs being $295,000. Determine the amount of adjustments for AMT purposes for 1997 and 1998.

CHAPTER 12 Alternative Minimum Tax

42. In 1995, Diego exercised an incentive stock option, acquiring 1,000 shares of stock at an option price of $65 per share. The fair market value of the stock at the date of exercise was $92 per share. In 1997, the rights in the stock become freely transferable and are not subject to a substantial risk of forfeiture. Diego sells the 1,000 shares of stock in 1998 for $100 per share. How do these transactions affect Diego's AMTI in 1995, 1997 and 1998?

43. In 1997, Lori exercised an incentive stock option that had been granted by her employer, Black Corporation. Lori acquired 100 shares of Black stock for the option price of $175 per share. The rights in the stock become freely transferable and not subject to a substantial risk of forfeiture in 1997. The fair market value of the stock at the date of exercise was $210 per share. Lori sells the stock for $320 per share in 1997. What is the amount of her AMT adjustment in 1997, and what is her recognized gain on the sale for regular income tax purposes and AMT purposes?

44. Bobby sells an apartment building for $500,000. His adjusted basis is $300,000 for regular income tax purposes and $330,000 for AMT purposes.
    a. Calculate Bobby's gain for regular income tax purposes.
    b. Calculate Bobby's gain for AMT purposes.
    c. Calculate Bobby's AMT adjustment, if any.

45. Freda acquired a passive activity in 1997. Gross income from operations of the activity was $150,000. Operating expenses, not including depreciation, were $135,000. Regular income tax depreciation of $37,500 was computed under MACRS. AMT depreciation, computed under ADS, was $24,000. Compute Freda's passive loss deduction and passive loss suspended for regular income tax purposes and for AMT purposes.

46. Wally and Gloria incur and pay medical expenses in excess of insurance reimbursements during the year as follows:

    | For Wally | $8,000 |
    | For Gloria (spouse) | 3,000 |
    | For Chuck (son) | 1,000 |
    | For Carter (Gloria's father) | 9,000 |

    Wally and Gloria's AGI is $200,000. They file a joint return. Chuck and Carter are Wally and Gloria's dependents.
    a. What is Wally and Gloria's medical expense deduction for regular income tax purposes?
    b. What is Wally and Gloria's medical expense deduction for AMT purposes?
    c. What is the amount of the AMT adjustment for medical expenses?

47. Wolfgang had the following itemized deductions for 1997:

    | Medical expenses [$5,000 − (7.5% × $50,000)] | $ 1,250 |
    | State income taxes | 3,000 |
    | Charitable contributions | 5,000 |
    | Home mortgage interest on his personal residence | 6,000 |
    | Casualty loss | 1,500 |
    | Miscellaneous itemized deductions [$3,500 − 2%($50,000)] | 2,500 |
    | | $19,250 |

    a. Calculate Wolfgang's itemized deductions for AMT purposes.
    b. What is the amount of the AMT adjustment?

48. Tom, who is single, owns a personal residence in the city. He also owns a cabin near a ski resort in the mountains. He uses the cabin as a vacation home. In February 1997, he borrowed $60,000 on a home equity loan and used the proceeds to pay off credit card obligations and other debt. During 1997, he paid the following amounts of interest:

On his personal residence	$12,000
On the cabin	4,800
On the home equity loan	5,000
On credit card obligations	1,200

What amount, if any, must Tom recognize as an AMT adjustment in 1997?

49. Walter and Edith, who are married with two dependents, had AGI of $110,000 in 1997. Their AGI included net investment income of $10,000 and gambling income of $2,500. They incurred the following expenses during the year, all of which resulted in itemized deductions for income tax purposes:

Medical expenses (before 7.5%-of-AGI floor)	$9,500
State income taxes	2,800
Personal property tax	900
Real estate tax	9,100
Interest on personal residence	8,600
Interest on home equity loan (proceeds were used to buy a new fishing boat)	1,800
Investment interest expense	2,600
Charitable contribution (cash)	4,200
Unreimbursed employee expenses (before 2%-of-AGI floor)	3,800

a. What is the amount of Walter and Edith's AMT adjustment for itemized deductions in 1997, and is it positive or negative?
b. Assume the same facts as in (a) and that Walter and Edith also earned interest of $5,000 on private activity bonds. They borrowed the money to buy these bonds and paid interest of $3,900 on the loan. Determine the effect on AMTI.

50. Gail pays investment interest of $45,000. She has interest income of $12,000 on taxable bonds, $6,000 on tax-exempt bonds that are private activity bonds, and $5,000 on tax-exempt bonds that are not private activity bonds. Her other investment expenses are $3,000, none of which relates to the tax-exempt bonds.
a. What is Gail's deduction for investment interest for regular income tax purposes?
b. What is the amount of her investment interest carryover for regular income tax purposes?
c. What is the amount of the adjustment for AMT purposes?

51. Bill, who is single with no dependents, had AGI of $100,000 in 1997. His AGI included net investment income of $15,000 and gambling income of $1,100. Bill incurred the following expenses during the year, all of which resulted in itemized deductions for income tax purposes:

Medical expenses (before 7.5%-of-AGI floor)	$11,000
State income taxes	3,200
Personal property tax	2,000
Real estate tax	8,400
Interest on personal residence	12,200
Interest on vacation home (never rented to others)	3,800
Interest on home equity loan (proceeds were used to buy a new automobile)	2,700
Investment interest expense	3,300
Charitable contribution	5,000
Casualty loss (after $100 floor, before 10%-of-AGI floor)	13,000
Unreimbursed employee expenses (before 2%-of-AGI floor)	2,400
Gambling losses	900

CHAPTER 12 Alternative Minimum Tax   **12–39**

What is the amount of Bill's AMT adjustment for itemized deductions in 1997, and is it positive or negative?

52. Peggy, who is single and has no dependents, had taxable income of $102,000 and tax preferences of $72,500 in 1997. She did not itemize deductions for regular income tax purposes. Compute Peggy's AMT exemption and AMTI for 1997.

53. Carl, who is single, has no dependents and does not itemize deductions. He had a personal exemption of $2,650 and taxable income of $82,000 in 1997. His tax preferences totaled $118,000. What is Carl's AMTI for 1997?

54. Emily owns a coal mine that had a basis of $12,000 at the beginning of the year. The property qualifies for a 15% depletion rate. Gross income from the property was $140,000, and net income before the percentage depletion deduction was $60,000. What is Emily's tax preference for excess depletion?

55. Amos incurred and expensed intangible drilling costs (IDC) of $70,000. His net oil and gas income was $60,000. What is the amount of Amos's tax preference item for IDC?

56. Pat, who is single and has no dependents, had a salary of $90,000 in 1997. She had interest and dividend income of $6,000, gambling income of $4,000, and $40,000 interest income from private activity bonds. Pat presents the following additional information:

Medical expenses (before 7.5%-of-AGI floor)	$12,000
State income taxes	4,100
Real estate taxes	2,800
Mortgage interest on residence	3,100
Investment interest expense	1,800
Gambling losses	5,100

Compute Pat's tentative minimum tax for 1997 (rounded to the nearest dollar).

57. Jack, who is single with no dependents and does not itemize, provides you with the following information for 1997:

Short-term capital loss	$ 5,000
Long-term capital gain	25,000
Municipal bond interest received on private activity bonds acquired in 1990	9,000
Dividends from General Motors	1,500
Excess of FMV over cost of incentive stock options (the rights became freely transferable and not subject to a substantial risk of forfeiture in 1997)	35,000

What is the total amount of Jack's tax preference items and AMT adjustments for 1997?

58. Rosa and Steve, who are married, had taxable income of $150,000 for 1997. They had positive AMT adjustments of $40,000, negative AMT adjustments of $10,000, and tax preference items of $67,500.
   a. Compute their AMTI.
   b. Compute their tentative minimum tax.

59. Tara, who is single, has no dependents and does not itemize. She has the following items relative to her tax return for 1997:

Bargain element from the exercise of an incentive stock option (no restrictions apply to the stock)	$ 45,000
Accelerated depreciation on leased equipment acquired before 1987 (straight-line depreciation would have yielded $26,000)	41,000
Percentage depletion in excess of property's adjusted basis	50,000
Taxable income for regular income tax purposes	121,000

a. Determine Tara's AMT adjustments and preferences for 1997.
b. Calculate the AMT (if any) for 1997.

60. Larry, who is single, has the following items for 1997:

   Income
Salary	$105,000
Interest from bank	12,000
Interest on corporate bonds	7,000
Dividends	6,000
Short-term capital gain	8,000

   Expenses
Unreimbursed employee business expenses (no meals or entertainment)	4,000
Total medical expenses	24,000
State income taxes	6,500
Real property taxes	6,800
Home mortgage (qualified housing) interest	7,200

   Casualty loss on vacation home
Decline in value	20,000
Adjusted basis	70,000
Insurance proceeds	12,000
Tax preferences	116,000

   Compute Larry's tax liability for 1997 before credits or prepayments.

61. Lynn is single and has no dependents. Based on the financial information presented below, compute Lynn's AMT for 1997.

   Income:
Salary	$33,000
Taxable interest on corporate bonds	1,800
Dividend income	1,900
Business income	64,000

   Expenditures:
Medical expenses	12,000
State income taxes	6,000
Real estate taxes	8,500
Mortgage (qualified housing) interest	9,200
Investment interest	5,500
Cash contributions to various charities	2,900

   Additional information:
   a. The $64,000 business income is from Acme Office Supplies Company, a sole proprietorship Lynn owns and operates. Acme claimed MACRS depreciation of $3,175 on real property used in the business. ADS depreciation on the property would have been $2,500.
   b. Lynn received interest of $30,000 on City of Columbus private activity bonds.

62. Bonnie, who is single, had taxable income of $0 in 1997. She has positive timing adjustments of $200,000 and AMT exclusion items of $100,000 for the year. What is the amount of Bonnie's AMT credit for carryover to 1998?

63. Browne Corporation, a calendar year taxpayer, has AMTI (before the ACE adjustment) of $600,000 for 1997. Browne's ACE is $1,500,000. What is Browne's tentative minimum tax for 1997?

64. Gray Corporation (a calendar year corporation) reports the following information for the years listed below:

	1996	1997	1998
Unadjusted AMTI	$3,000	$2,000	$5,000
Adjusted current earnings	4,000	3,000	2,000

Compute the ACE adjustment for each year.

65. In each of the following independent situations, determine the tentative AMT:

	AMTI (Before the Exemption Amount)
Quincy Corporation	$150,000
Redland Corporation	160,000
Tanzen Corporation	320,000

66. Amber, Inc., has taxable income of $200,000. During the year, Amber paid dividends of $30,000. The corporation had $20,000 of positive AMT adjustments and $25,000 of tax preferences.
    a. Calculate Amber's regular income tax liability.
    b. Calculate Amber's AMTI and AMT.

CUMULATIVE PROBLEMS

67. Ron T. Freeman, age 38, is divorced and has no dependents. He pays alimony of $24,000 per year to his former wife, Kate. Kate's husband was killed in a hunting accident in 1997. At the time of the accident, their baby was only six weeks old. Ron decided to invest $5,000 each year in a mutual fund in Kate's baby's name to be used as a college fund. He made the initial $5,000 investment in 1997. Ron's Social Security number is 444–11–2222, and Kate's is 555–67–2222. Ron's address is 201 Front Street, Missoula, MT 59812. He is independently wealthy as a result of having inherited sizable holdings in real estate and corporate stocks and bonds. Ron is a minister at First Methodist Church, but he accepts no salary from the church. However, he does reside in the church's parsonage free of charge. The rental value of the parsonage is $600 a month. The church also provides him a cash grocery allowance of $150 a week. Examination of Ron's financial records provides the following information for 1997:
    a. On January 16, 1997, Ron sold 2,000 shares of stock for a gain of $30,000. The stock was acquired four years ago.
    b. He received $40,000 of interest on private activity bonds.
    c. He received gross rent income of $145,000 from an apartment complex he owns and manages.
    d. Expenses related to the apartment complex, which he acquired in 1983, were $190,000.
    e. Ron's dividend and interest income (on a savings account) totaled $26,000.
    f. On October 9, 1995, Ron exercised his rights under Egret Corporation's incentive stock option plan. For an option price of $20,000, he acquired stock worth $55,000. The stock became freely transferable in 1997.
    g. Ron had the following potential itemized deductions *from* AGI:

        • $3,000 fair market value of stock contributed to Methodist church (basis of stock was $2,000). He owned the stock for five years.

        • $2,000 interest on consumer purchases.

- $2,900 state and local taxes.
- $7,000 medical expenses (before 7.5% floor) for himself and $4,000 of hospital expenses associated with Kate's deceased husband.
- $100 for a safe deposit box that is used to store investments and related legal documents.
- $10,000 of losses associated with playing the state lottery. Ron had no winnings during 1997. Any net winning would be contributed to the church.

Compute Ron's tax liability, including AMT if applicable, before prepayments or credits, for 1997.

68. Robert M. and Jane R. Armstrong live at 1802 College Avenue, Carmel, IN 46302. They are married and file a joint return for 1996. The Armstrongs have two dependent children, Ellen J. and Sean M., who are 10-year-old twins. Ellen's Social Security number is 333-42-3368, and Sean's is 333-42-3369.

Robert (224-36-9987) is a factory foreman, and Jane (443-56-3421) is a computer systems analyst. The Armstrongs' W-2 forms for 1996 reflect the following information:

	Robert	Jane
Salary (Indiana Foundry, Inc.)	$55,000	
Salary (Carmel Computer Associates)		$74,000
Federal income tax withheld	6,600	13,600
Social Security wages	55,000	62,700
Social Security withheld	3,410	3,888
Medicare wages	55,000	74,000
Medicare tax withheld	798	1,073
State wages	55,000	74,000
State income tax withheld	1,650	2,220

In addition to their salaries, the Armstrongs had the following income items in 1996:

Interest income (Carmel Sanitation District Bonds)	$14,500
Interest income (Carmel National Bank)	1,000
Dividend income (Able Computer Corporation)	2,500
Gambling income	2,000

Jane inherited $200,000 from her grandfather in January and invested the money in the Carmel Sanitation District Bonds, which are private activity bonds.

The Armstrongs incurred the following expenses during 1996:

Medical expenses (doctor and hospital bills)	$17,000
Real property tax on personal residence	4,500
Mortgage interest on personal residence (reported on Form 1098)	4,000
Investment interest expense	1,900
Contributions to Salvation Army	20,000
Gambling losses	1,750

On March 1, Robert and Jane contributed Ace stock to the Carmel Salvation Army, a public charity. They had acquired the stock on February 9, 1979, for $1,500. The stock was listed on the New York Stock Exchange at a value of $20,000 on the date of the contribution.

Robert received a gift of 25 acres of land from his Uncle Sam on May 15. The appraised value of the land at the date of the gift was $63,000, and Uncle Sam's adjusted basis was $10,000. Uncle Sam was not required to pay any gift tax.

Use Forms 1040, 4952, 6251, and 8283 and Schedules A and B to compute the tax liability (including AMT) for Robert and Jane Armstrong for 1996. Suggested software (if available): *TurboTax* or *MacInTax*. Write a letter to the Armstrongs indicating whether they have a refund or balance due for 1996, and suggest possible tax planning strategies for 1997.

RESEARCH PROBLEMS

Note: **West's Federal Taxation on CD-ROM** *can be used in preparing solutions to the Research Problems. Alternatively, tax research materials contained in a standard tax library can be used.*

Research Problem 1. Tony is a full-time gambler whose only source of income is money that he wins from his gambling activities. The IRS contends that Tony's gambling losses should be treated as itemized deductions for purposes of computing the AMT. Tony argues that the gambling losses should be treated as trade or business expenses. Write a letter to Tony that contains your advice on the classification of the gambling losses. Also prepare a memo for the tax files. Tony's address is 200 Cole Lane, Wichita Falls, TX 76308.

Research Problem 2. Carol owns two warehouses that were placed in service before 1987. Accelerated depreciation for 1997 on Warehouse A was $12,000, and straight-line depreciation would have been $8,000. On Warehouse B, accelerated depreciation was $6,000, and straight-line depreciation would have been $7,500. What was the amount of Carol's tax preference for excess depreciation in 1997?

Research Problem 3. Stuart is a journalist for a metropolitan newspaper. He has a degree in journalism from a major midwestern university.

For the past 10 years, Stuart has prepared his own income tax return. He finds doing so to be challenging and stimulating and believes that he pays lower taxes than he would if he hired a tax return preparer.

His 1996 return is audited. Although it included an AMT form (Form 6251), Stuart had not prepared it properly. Data from his Form 1040 were transferred to the wrong line in several places. In other cases, positive adjustments were not included because Stuart had failed to calculate them (e.g., did not recalculate itemized deductions for AMT purposes and did not have a positive adjustment for the personal exemption). Based on the IRS's calculation, a deficiency of $3,000 was assessed. Stuart's response to the IRS is that Form 6251 is ambiguous and misleading and, therefore, he should not be liable for the AMT. Evaluate Stuart's argument.

Partial list of research aids:
William M. Christine, 66 TCM 1025, T.C.Memo. 1993–473.

Research Problem 4. On his 1996 Federal income tax return, Walter deducted state income taxes of $8,000 for amounts withheld and estimated tax payments made in 1996. When he filed his 1996 state income tax return in April 1997, he discovered that he had overpaid his state income taxes by $1,500. Rather than having the $1,500 refunded to him, he treated it as a 1997 estimated tax payment. The year 1996 was not an AMT year for Walter.

In preparing his 1997 Federal income tax return, Walter is confused about how he should treat the $1,500 in calculating his Federal income tax liability. He knows that under the § 111 tax benefit rule, he should include the $1,500 in gross income in calculating his taxable income. However, since he is going to be subject to the AMT, he is uncertain as to how he should treat the $1,500 in calculating AMT. He thinks that the amount could be treated as a negative adjustment in converting taxable income to AMTI if 1996 had been an AMT year. Since it was not, Walter is unsure of the treatment.

Advise Walter on the appropriate treatment of the $1,500 in calculating his 1997 Federal income tax liability.

Use the tax resources of the internet to address the following questions. Do not restrict your search to the World Wide Web, but include a review of newsgroups and general reference materials, practitioner sites and resources, primary sources of the tax law, chat rooms and discussion groups, and other opportunities.

Research Problem 5. Locate an outstanding proposal to modify the structure or scope of the AMT on individuals. Describe the proposal, the entity making the proposal, and potential motivations for submitting the modification to Congress.

Research Problem 6. Go to one of the tax newsgroups and post a short note on one of the following items, relative to individuals who are subject to the AMT.
  a. Interest deductions on vacation homes.
  b. Charitable contributions of appreciated securities.
  c. Tax preparation fees.

TEAM PROJECT: ARTHUR ANDERSEN TAX CHALLENGE CASES

For more information on the Arthur Andersen Tax Challenge Cases, refer to Chapter 1, page 1–38.

Information related to tax issues and problems that are discussed in this chapter may be found in the

Miller case on pages 3, 19, 21, 39 and 41

Read and analyze the case you have been assigned and *identify* any issues and problems that are related to material covered in this chapter. If the information provided in the case is complete, prepare answers for this part of the case at this time. If you need information that is contained in the later parts of the case, write a memo summarizing the questions or problems so you can prepare a complete answer at a later date.

CHAPTER 13

TAX CREDITS AND PAYMENT PROCEDURES

LEARNING OBJECTIVES

After completing Chapter 13, you should be able to:

1. Explain how tax credits are used as a tool of Federal tax policy.

2. Distinguish between refundable and nonrefundable credits and understand the order in which they can be used by taxpayers.

3. Describe various business-related tax credits.

4. Describe several other tax credits that are available primarily to individual taxpayers.

5. Understand the tax withholding and payment procedures applicable to employers.

6. Understand the payment procedures applicable to self-employed persons.

7. Identify tax planning opportunities related to tax credits and payment procedures.

OUTLINE

Tax Policy Considerations, 13-3

Overview and Priority of Credits, 13-5

Refundable versus Nonrefundable Credits, 13-5

General Business Credit, 13-6

Treatment of Unused General Business Credits, 13-7

Specific Business-Related Tax Credit Provisions, 13-7

Tax Credit for Rehabilitation Expenditures, 13-7

Business Energy Credits, 13-9

Work Opportunity Tax Credit, 13-9

Research Activities Credit, 13-10

Low-Income Housing Credit, 13-12

Disabled Access Credit, 13-13

Other Tax Credits, 13-14

Earned Income Credit, 13-14

Tax Credit for Elderly or Disabled Taxpayers, 13-16

Foreign Tax Credit, 13-18

Adoption Expenses Credit, 13-19

Credit for Child and Dependent Care Expenses, 13-20

Payment Procedures, 13-22

Procedures Applicable to Employers, 13-22

Procedures Applicable to Self-Employed Persons, 13-33

Tax Planning Considerations, 13-37

Foreign Tax Credit, 13-37

Credit for Child and Dependent Care Expenses, 13-38

Adjustments to Increase Withholding, 13-39

Adjustments to Avoid Overwithholding, 13-39

As explained in Chapter 1, Federal tax law often serves other purposes besides merely raising revenue for the government. Evidence of equity, social, and economic considerations, among others, is found throughout the tax law. These considerations also bear heavily in the area of **tax credits.** Consider the following examples:

EXAMPLE 1

Paul and Peggy, husband and wife, are both employed outside the home. Their combined salaries are $50,000. However, after paying for child care expenses of $2,000 on behalf of their daughter, Polly, the net economic benefit from both spouses working is $48,000. The child care expenses are, in a sense, business related in that they would not have been incurred if both spouses did not work outside the home. If no tax benefits are associated with the child care expenditures, $50,000 is subject to tax.

Another couple, Alicia and Diego, also have a child, John. Diego stays at home to care for John (the value of those services is $2,000) while Alicia earns a $48,000 salary. Because the value of Diego's services rendered is not subject to tax, only Alicia's earnings of $48,000 are subject to tax. ▼

The credit for child and dependent care expenses is allowed to mitigate the inequity felt by working taxpayers who must pay for child care services in order to work outside the home.

EXAMPLE 2

Olaf is a retired taxpayer who received $10,000 of Social Security benefits as his only source of income in 1997. His Social Security benefits are excluded from gross income. Therefore, Olaf's income tax is $0. In 1997, Olga, a single taxpayer 66 years of age, has, as her sole source of income, $10,000 from a pension plan funded by her former employer. Assuming Olga has no itemized deductions or deductions *for* AGI, her income tax for 1997 (before credits) is $330, based on the following computation:

Pension plan benefits	$10,000
Less: Basic standard deduction	(4,150)
Additional standard deduction	(1,000)
Personal exemption	(2,650)
Taxable income	$ 2,200
Income tax (at 15%)	$ 330

The tax credit for elderly or disabled taxpayers was enacted to mitigate this inequity.

EXAMPLE 3

Jane is a single parent who depends on the government's "safety net" for survival—she receives Aid for Dependent Children in the amount of $10,000 per year. However, she very much wishes to work. Jane has located a job that will pay $10,500 per year and has found an individual to care for her child at no cost. But, with the $803.25 ($10,500 × 7.65%) payroll deduction for Social Security and Medicare taxes, the economic benefit from working is less than remaining reliant on the government ($9,696.75 as compared to $10,000). ▼

To help offset the effect of Social Security and Medicare taxes on wages of the working poor and to provide an incentive to work, the earned income credit is used to increase the after-tax earnings of qualified individuals. In addition, the earned income credit helps offset the regressive nature of certain taxes, such as the Social Security and Medicare taxes, which impose a relatively larger burden on low-income taxpayers than on more affluent taxpayers.

These three tax credits and many of the other important tax credits available to individuals and other types of taxpayers are a major focus of this chapter. The chapter begins by discussing important tax policy considerations relevant to tax credits. Tax credits are categorized as being either refundable or nonrefundable. The distinction between refundable and nonrefundable credits is important because it may affect the taxpayer's ability to enjoy a tax benefit from a particular credit.

Next an overview of the priority of tax credits is presented. The credit portion of the chapter continues with a discussion of the credits available to businesses and to individual taxpayers and the ways in which credits enter into the calculation of the tax liability.

The Federal tax system has long been based on the pay-as-you-go concept. That is, taxpayers or their employers are required to make regular deposits with the Federal government during the year as payment toward the tax liability that will be determined at the end of the tax year. These deposits are in effect refundable credits. In addition to presenting the procedures used in calculating these payments and the special problems self-employed persons encounter in estimating their payments, the penalties on underpayment are discussed.

TAX POLICY CONSIDERATIONS

1 LEARNING OBJECTIVE
Explain how tax credits are used as a tool of Federal tax policy.

Congress has generally used tax credits to achieve social or economic objectives or to provide equity for different types of taxpayers. For example, the disabled access credit was enacted to accomplish a social objective: to encourage taxpayers to renovate older buildings so they would be in compliance with the Americans with Disabilities Act. This Act requires businesses and institutions to make their facilities more accessible to persons with various types of disabilities. In another example, the foreign tax credit, which has been a part of the law for decades, has as its purpose the economic and equity objectives of mitigating the burden of multiple taxation of a single flow of income.

A tax credit should not be confused with an income tax deduction. Certain expenditures of individuals (e.g., business expenses) are permitted as deductions from gross income in arriving at adjusted gross income (AGI). Additionally, individuals are allowed to deduct certain nonbusiness and investment-related expenses *from* AGI. While the tax benefit received from a tax deduction depends on the tax rate, a tax credit is not affected by the tax rate of the taxpayer.

> ### TAX IN THE NEWS
>
> **INCENTIVES GAINED THROUGH THE REENACTMENT OF TAX CREDITS**
>
> Over the years, Congress has enacted tax credits with the intention of providing incentives for taxpayers to pursue certain types of behaviors considered beneficial to society. Some of these credits, such as the foreign tax credit and the credit for child and dependent care expenses, have had long, uninterrupted histories.
>
> Other tax credits have had a checkered history of being enacted on a temporary basis, then expiring, and later being reenacted when a continuing need is shown. For example, the research activities credit expired for qualifying expenditures incurred after June 30, 1995, only to be reenacted again for the period July 1, 1996 through May 31, 1997. This credit's proponents claim that it is needed to encourage companies to pursue cutting-edge research that could lead to technological advances beneficial to the overall economic security of the nation.
>
> Other lesser-known credits, having expired, were also reenacted by recent legislation. An example is the orphan drug tax credit, which is touted as being just as important as the research activities credit, but at a personal level. Supporters of this credit claim it encourages companies to develop special drugs to fight rare diseases such as Huntington's and Lou Gehrig's disease. Without the credit, the supporters say, companies would be unable to recoup their investment because the drugs created would benefit so few people.

EXAMPLE 4

Assume Congress wishes to encourage a certain type of expenditure. One way to accomplish this objective is to allow a tax credit of 25% for such expenditures. Another way is to allow an itemized deduction for the expenditures. Assume Abby's tax rate is 15%, while Bill's tax rate is 39.6%. In addition, assume that Carmen does not incur enough qualifying expenditures to itemize deductions. The following tax benefits are available to each taxpayer for a $1,000 expenditure:

	Abby	Bill	Carmen
Tax benefit if a 25% credit is allowed	$250	$250	$250
Tax benefit if an itemized deduction is allowed	150	396	–0–

As these results indicate, tax credits provide benefits on a more equitable basis than do tax deductions. Equally apparent is that the deduction approach in this case benefits only taxpayers who itemize deductions, while the credit approach benefits all taxpayers who make the specified expenditure. ▼

For many years, Congress has used the tax credit provisions of the Code liberally in implementing tax policy. Although budget constraints and economic considerations often have dictated the repeal of some credits, other credits, such as those applicable to expenses incurred for child and dependent care, have been kept to respond to important social policy considerations. Other credits, such as the one available to low-income workers, have been retained based on economic and equity considerations. Finally, as the myriad of tax proposals that are always before Congress make clear, the use of tax credits as a tax policy tool continues to evolve as economic and political circumstances change.

OVERVIEW AND PRIORITY OF CREDITS

REFUNDABLE VERSUS NONREFUNDABLE CREDITS

2 LEARNING OBJECTIVE
Distinguish between refundable and nonrefundable credits and understand the order in which they can be used by taxpayers.

As illustrated in Exhibit 13–1, certain credits are refundable while others are nonrefundable. **Refundable credits** are paid to the taxpayer even if the amount of the credit (or credits) exceeds the taxpayer's tax liability.

EXAMPLE 5
Ted, who is single, had taxable income of $21,000 in 1997. His income tax from the 1997 Tax Rate Schedule is $3,150. During 1997, Ted's employer withheld income tax of $3,500. Ted is entitled to a refund of $350 because the credit for tax withheld on wages is a refundable credit. ▼

Nonrefundable credits are not paid if they exceed the taxpayer's tax liability.

EXAMPLE 6
Tina is single, age 67, and retired. Her taxable income for 1997 is $1,320, and the tax on this amount is $198. Tina's tax credit for the elderly is $225. This credit can be used to reduce her net tax liability to zero, but it will not result in a refund, even though the credit ($225) exceeds Tina's tax liability ($198). This result occurs because the tax credit for the elderly is a nonrefundable credit. ▼

Some nonrefundable credits, such as the foreign tax credit, are subject to carryover provisions if they exceed the amount allowable as a credit in a given year. Other nonrefundable credits, such as the tax credit for the elderly (refer to Example 6), are not subject to carryover provisions and are lost if they exceed the

▼ **EXHIBIT 13–1**
Partial Listing of Refundable and Nonrefundable Credits

Refundable Credits

Taxes withheld on wages
Earned income credit

Nonrefundable Credits

Credit for child and dependent care expenses
Credit for the elderly or disabled
Adoption expenses credit
Foreign tax credit
General business credit, which is the sum of the following:
- Tax credit for rehabilitation expenditures
- Business energy credits
- Work opportunity tax credit*
- Research activities credit**
- Low-income housing credit
- Disabled access credit

*Not available under current law for employees hired after September 30, 1997.
**Scheduled to expire after May 31, 1997.

limitations. Because some credits are subject to carryover provisions while others are not, the order in which credits are offset against the tax liability is important. The Code provides that nonrefundable credits are to be offset against a taxpayer's income tax liability in the order shown in Exhibit 13–1.

GENERAL BUSINESS CREDIT

As shown in Exhibit 13–1, the **general business credit** is comprised of a number of other credits, each of which is computed separately under its own set of rules. The general business credit combines these credits into one amount to limit the amount of business credits that can be used to offset a taxpayer's income tax liability. The idea behind combining the credits is to prevent a taxpayer from completely avoiding an income tax liability in any one year by offsetting it with business credits that would otherwise be available.

Two special rules apply to the general business credit. First, any unused credit must be carried back 3 years, then forward 15 years. Second, for any tax year, the general business credit is limited to the taxpayer's *net income tax* reduced by the greater of:[1]

- The *tentative minimum tax*.
- 25 percent of *net regular tax liability* that exceeds $25,000.[2]

In order to understand the general business credit limitation, several terms need defining:

- *Net income tax* is the sum of the regular tax liability and the alternative minimum tax reduced by certain nonrefundable tax credits.
- *Tentative minimum tax* for this purpose is reduced by the foreign tax credit allowed.
- *Regular tax liability* is determined from the appropriate tax table or tax rate schedule, based on taxable income. However, the regular tax liability does not include certain taxes (e.g., alternative minimum tax).
- *Net regular tax liability* is the regular tax liability reduced by certain nonrefundable credits (e.g., credit for child and dependent care expenses, foreign tax credit).

EXAMPLE 7

Floyd's general business credit for the current year is $70,000. His net income tax is $150,000, tentative minimum tax is $130,000, and net regular tax liability is $150,000. He has no other tax credits. Floyd's general business credit allowed for the tax year is computed as follows:

Net income tax	$ 150,000
Less: The greater of	
• $130,000 (tentative minimum tax)	
• $31,250 [25% × ($150,000 − $25,000)]	(130,000)
Amount of general business credit allowed for tax year	$ 20,000

Floyd then has $50,000 ($70,000 − $20,000) of unused general business credits that may be carried back or forward as discussed below. ▼

---

[1] § 38(c).
[2] This amount is $12,500 for married taxpayers filing separately unless one of the spouses is not entitled to the general business credit.

TREATMENT OF UNUSED GENERAL BUSINESS CREDITS

Unused general business credits are initially carried back three years (to the earliest year in the sequence first) and are applied to reduce the tax liability during these years. Thus, the taxpayer may receive a tax refund as a result of the carryback. Any remaining unused credits are then carried forward 15 years.[3]

A FIFO method is applied to the carryovers, carrybacks, and utilization of credits earned during a particular year. The oldest credits are used first in determining the amount of the general business credit. The FIFO method minimizes the potential for loss of a general business credit benefit due to the expiration of credit carryovers, since the earliest years are used before the current credit for the taxable year.

EXAMPLE 8

This example illustrates the use of general business credit carryovers.

General business credit carryovers		
1994	$ 4,000	
1995	6,000	
1996	2,000	
Total carryovers	$12,000	
1997 general business credit		$40,000
Total credit allowed in 1997 (based on tax liability)	$50,000	
Less: Utilization of carryovers		
1994	(4,000)	
1995	(6,000)	
1996	(2,000)	
Remaining credit allowed	$38,000	
Applied against		
1997 general business credit		(38,000)
1997 unused amount carried forward to 1998		$ 2,000

SPECIFIC BUSINESS-RELATED TAX CREDIT PROVISIONS

3 LEARNING OBJECTIVE
Describe various business-related tax credits.

Each component of the general business credit is determined separately under its own set of rules. The components are explained here in the order listed in Exhibit 13–1.

TAX CREDIT FOR REHABILITATION EXPENDITURES

Taxpayers are allowed a tax credit for expenditures incurred to rehabilitate industrial and commercial buildings and certified historic structures. The **rehabilitation expenditures credit** is intended to discourage businesses from moving from older, economically distressed areas (e.g., inner city) to newer locations and to encourage the preservation of historic structures. The current operating features of this credit follow:[4]

---

[3] § 39(a)(1).   [4] § 47.

Rate of the Credit for Rehabilitation Expenses	Nature of the Property
10%	Nonresidential buildings and residential rental property, other than certified historic structures, originally placed in service before 1936
20%	Nonresidential and residential certified historic structures

When taking the credit, the basis of a rehabilitated building must be reduced by the full rehabilitation credit allowed.[5]

EXAMPLE 9

Juan spent $60,000 to rehabilitate a building (adjusted basis of $40,000) that had originally been placed in service in 1932. He is allowed a credit of $6,000 (10% × $60,000) for rehabilitation expenditures. Juan then increases the basis of the building by $54,000 [$60,000 (rehabilitation expenditures) − $6,000 (credit allowed)]. If the building were a historic structure, the credit allowed would be $12,000 (20% × $60,000), and the building's depreciable basis would increase by $48,000 [$60,000 (rehabilitation expenditures) − $12,000 (credit allowed)]. ▼

To qualify for the credit, buildings must be substantially rehabilitated. A building has been *substantially rehabilitated* if qualified rehabilitation expenditures exceed the greater of:

- The adjusted basis of the property before the rehabilitation expenditures, or
- $5,000.

Qualified rehabilitation expenditures do not include the cost of acquiring a building, the cost of facilities related to a building (such as a parking lot), and the cost of enlarging an existing building. Stringent rules apply concerning the retention of internal and external walls.

Recapture of Tax Credit for Rehabilitation Expenditures.

The rehabilitation credit taken must be recaptured if the rehabilitated property is disposed of prematurely or if it ceases to be qualifying property. The **rehabilitation expenditures credit recapture** is based on a holding period requirement of five years and is added to the taxpayer's regular tax liability in the recapture year. In addition, the recapture amount is *added* to the adjusted basis of the rehabilitation expenditures for purposes of determining the amount of gain or loss realized on the property's disposition.

The portion of the credit recaptured is a specified percentage of the credit that was taken by the taxpayer. This percentage is based on the period the property was held by the taxpayer, as shown in Table 13–1.

EXAMPLE 10

On March 15, 1994, Rashad placed in service $30,000 of rehabilitation expenditures on a building qualifying for the 10% credit. A credit of $3,000 ($30,000 × 10%) was allowed, and the basis of the building was increased by $27,000 ($30,000 − $3,000). The building was sold on December 15, 1997. Rashad must recapture a portion of the rehabilitation credit based on the schedule in Table 13–1. Because he held the rehabilitated property for more than three years but less than four, 40% of the credit, or $1,200, must be added to his 1997 tax liability. Also, the adjusted basis of the rehabilitation expenditures is increased by the $1,200 recapture amount. ▼

---

[5] § 50(c).

▼ **TABLE 13–1**
Recapture Calculation for Rehabilitation Expenditures Credit

If the Property Is Held for	The Recapture Percentage Is
Less than 1 year	100
One year or more but less than 2 years	80
Two years or more but less than 3 years	60
Three years or more but less than 4 years	40
Four years or more but less than 5 years	20
Five years or more	0

ETHICAL CONSIDERATIONS

Using the Rehabilitation Expenditures Credit

The tax credit for rehabilitation expenditures is available to help offset the costs related to substantially rehabilitating certain buildings. The credit is calculated on the rehabilitation expenditures incurred and not on the acquisition cost of the building itself.

You are a developer who buys, sells, and does construction work on real estate in the inner city of your metropolitan area. A potential customer approaches you about acquiring one of your buildings that easily could qualify for the 20 percent rehabilitation credit on historic structures. The stated sales price of the structure is $100,000 (based on appraisals ranging from $80,000 to $120,000), and the rehabilitation expenditures, if the job is done correctly, would be about $150,000.

Your business has been slow recently due to the sluggish real estate market in your area, and the potential customer makes the following proposal: if you reduce the sales price of the building to $75,000, he will pay you $175,000 to perform the rehabilitation work. Although the buyer's total expenditures would be the same, he would benefit from this approach by obtaining a larger tax credit ($25,000 increased rehabilitation costs × 20% = $5,000).

It has been a long time since you have sold any of your real estate. How will you respond?

BUSINESS ENERGY CREDITS

For many years, **business energy credits** have been allowed to encourage the conservation of natural resources and the development of alternative energy sources (to oil and natural gas). Over the years, some of these credits have expired while new ones have been added. The most important business energy credits that remain are the 10 percent credits for solar energy property and geothermal property.

WORK OPPORTUNITY TAX CREDIT

The **work opportunity tax credit** was enacted to encourage employers to hire individuals from one or more of a number of targeted and economically disadvantaged groups who start work after September 30, 1996 and before October 1, 1997. Examples of such targeted persons include qualified ex-felons, high-risk youths, food stamp recipients, veterans, summer youth employees, and persons receiving certain welfare benefits.[6]

Computation of the Work Opportunity Tax Credit: General.
The credit generally is equal to 35 percent of the first $6,000 of wages (per eligible employee) for the first 12 months of employment. Thus, the credit is not available for any wages paid to an employee after the first year of employment. If the employee's first year overlaps two of the employer's tax years, however, the employer may take the credit over two tax years. If the credit is elected, the employer's tax deduction for wages is reduced by the amount of the credit. For an employer to qualify for the credit, the employees must be certified by a designated local agency as being members of one of the targeted groups.

EXAMPLE 11
In January 1997, Green Company hires four individuals who are certified to be members of a qualifying targeted group. Each employee is paid wages of $8,000 during the year. Green Company's work opportunity credit is $8,400 [($6,000 × 35%) × 4 employees]. If the tax credit is taken, Green must reduce its deduction for wages paid by $8,400. No credit is available for wages paid to these employees after their first year of employment. ▼

EXAMPLE 12
On June 1, 1997, Maria, a calendar year taxpayer, hired Joe, a member of a targeted group, and obtained the required certification. During the last seven months of 1997, Joe is paid $3,500. Maria is allowed a credit of $1,225 ($3,500 × 35%). Joe continues to work for Maria in 1998 and is paid $7,000 through May 31. Because up to $6,000 of first-year wages are eligible for the credit, Maria is also allowed a 35% credit on $2,500 [$6,000 − $3,500 (wages paid in 1997)] of wages paid in 1998, or $875 ($2,500 × 35%). None of Joe's wages paid after May 31, the end of the first year of employment, is eligible for the credit. Likewise, under current law, no credit is allowed for wages paid to persons newly hired after September 30, 1997. ▼

Computation of the Work Opportunity Tax Credit: Qualified Summer Youth Employees.
The credit for qualified summer youth employees is allowed on wages for services during any 90-day period between May 1 and September 15. The maximum wages eligible for the credit are $3,000 per summer youth employee. The credit rate is 35 percent. If the employee continues employment after the 90-day period as a member of another targeted group, the amount of the wages eligible for the general work opportunity tax credit as a member of the new target group is reduced by the wages paid to the employee as a qualified summer youth employee.

A *qualified summer youth employee* must be age 16 or 17 on the hiring date. An additional requirement for qualifying is that the individual's principal place of abode must be within an empowerment zone or an enterprise community.

RESEARCH ACTIVITIES CREDIT

To encourage research and experimentation, usually described as research and development (R & D), a credit is allowed for certain qualifying expenditures paid or incurred from July 1, 1996 through May 31, 1997. The **research activities credit** is the *sum* of two components: an incremental research activities credit and a basic research credit.[7]

---

[6]§ 51.

[7]§ 41.

Incremental Research Activities Credit. The incremental research activities credit applies at a 20 percent rate to the *excess* of qualified research expenses for the taxable year (the credit year) over the base amount.

In general, *research expenditures* qualify if the research relates to discovering technological information that is intended for use in the development of a new or improved business component of the taxpayer. Such expenses qualify fully if the research is performed in-house (by the taxpayer or employees). If the research is conducted by persons outside the taxpayer's business (under contract), only 65 percent of the amount paid qualifies for the credit.[8]

EXAMPLE 13

George incurs the following research expenditures for the tax year.

In-house wages, supplies, computer time	$50,000
Paid to Cutting Edge Scientific Foundation for research	30,000

George's qualified research expenditures are $69,500 [$50,000 + ($30,000 × 65%)]. ▼

Beyond the general guidelines described above, the Code does not give specific examples of qualifying research. However, the credit is *not* allowed for research that falls into certain categories, including the following:[9]

- Research conducted after the beginning of commercial production of the business component.
- Surveys and studies such as market research, testing, and routine data collection.
- Research conducted *outside* the United States.
- Research in the social sciences, arts, or humanities.

Determining the *base amount* involves a relatively complex series of computations. In addition, when the research credit is available for less than a full tax year, as is the case under current law, the base amount is adjusted further. A discussion of these computations is beyond the scope of this presentation.

EXAMPLE 14

Jack, a calendar year taxpayer, incurs qualifying research expenditures of $200,000 during 1997. Assuming the base amount is $100,000, the incremental research activities credit is $20,000 [($200,000 − $100,000) × 20%]. ▼

Qualified research and experimentation expenditures are not only eligible for the 20 percent credit, but can also be *expensed* in the year incurred.[10] In this regard, a taxpayer has two choices:[11]

- Use the full credit and reduce the expense deduction for research expenses by 100 percent of the credit.
- Retain the full expense deduction and reduce the credit by the product of 50 percent of the credit times the maximum corporate tax rate.

As an alternative to the expense deduction, the taxpayer may *capitalize* the research expenses and *amortize* them over 60 months or more. In this case, the amount capitalized and subject to amortization is reduced by the full amount of the credit *only* if the credit exceeds the amount allowable as a deduction.

---

[8] § 41(b)(3)(A). In the case of payments to a qualified research consortium, 75% of the amount paid qualifies for the credit.
[9] § 41(d).
[10] § 174. Also refer to the discussion of rules for deducting research and experimental expenditures in Chapter 7.
[11] § 280C(c).

EXAMPLE 15

Assume the same facts as in Example 14, which shows that the potential incremental research activities credit is $20,000. The expense that the taxpayer can deduct and the credit amount are as follows:

	Credit Amount	Deduction Amount
• Full credit and reduced deduction $20,000 − $0 $200,000 − $20,000	$20,000	$180,000
• Reduced credit and full deduction $20,000 − [(.50 × $20,000) × .35] $200,000 − $0	16,500	200,000
• Full credit and capitalize and elect to amortize costs over 60 months $20,000 − $0 ($200,000/60) × 12	20,000	40,000

Basic Research Credit. Corporations (other than S corporations or personal service corporations) are allowed an additional 20 percent credit for basic research payments from July 1, 1996 through May 31, 1997, in *excess* of a base amount. This credit is not available to individual taxpayers. *Basic research payments* are defined as amounts paid in cash to a qualified basic research organization, such as a college or university or a tax-exempt organization operated primarily to conduct scientific research.

Basic research is defined generally as any original investigation for the advancement of scientific knowledge not having a specific commercial objective. The definition excludes basic research conducted outside the United States and basic research in the social sciences, arts, or humanities. This reflects the intent of Congress to encourage high-tech research in the United States.

The calculation of this additional credit for basic research expenditures is complex and is based on expenditures in excess of a specially defined base amount.[12] The portion of the basic research expenditures not in excess of the base amount is treated as a part of the qualifying expenditures for purposes of the regular credit for incremental research activities.

EXAMPLE 16

Orange Corporation, a qualifying corporation, pays $75,000 to a university for basic research. Assume that Orange's base amount for the basic research credit is $50,000. The basic research activities credit allowed is $5,000 [($75,000 − $50,000) × 20%]. The $50,000 of basic research expenditures that equals the base amount are treated as research expenses for purposes of the regular incremental research activities credit. ▼

LOW-INCOME HOUSING CREDIT

To encourage building owners to make affordable housing available for low-income individuals, Congress has made a credit available to owners of qualified low-income housing projects.[13]

More than any other, the **low-income housing credit** is influenced by nontax factors. For example, certification of the property by the appropriate state or local

---

[12] § 41(e).   [13] § 42.

agency authorized to provide low-income housing credits is required. These credits are issued based on a nationwide allocation.

The amount of the credit is based on the qualified basis of the property. The qualified basis depends on the number of units rented to low-income tenants. Tenants are low-income tenants if their income does not exceed a specified percentage of the area median gross income. The amount of the credit is determined by multiplying the qualified basis by the applicable percentage; the credit is allowed over a 10-year period if the property continues to meet the required conditions.

EXAMPLE 17

Sarah spends $100,000 to build a qualified low-income housing project completed January 1, 1997. The entire project is rented to low-income families. The credit rate for property placed in service during January 1997 is 8.48%.[14] Sarah may claim a credit of $8,480 ($100,000 × 8.48%) in 1997 and in each of the following nine years. Generally, first-year credits are prorated based on the date the project is placed in service. A full year's credit is taken in each of the next nine years, and any remaining first-year credit is claimed in the eleventh year. ▼

Recapture of a portion of the credit may be required if the number of units set aside for low-income tenants falls below a minimum threshold, if the taxpayer disposes of the property or the interest in it, or if the taxpayer's amount at risk decreases.

ETHICAL CONSIDERATIONS

A Win-Win Situation or an Incalculable Loss?

John and Susie rent a unit at an apartment complex owned by Mitch Brown, who has been Susie's friend since they attended business school together. One day Mitch told John and Susie about the thousands of tax dollars that he has saved by claiming the low-income housing credit for his investment in the apartment complex. Susie was pleased that Mitch had reduced his tax burden because she believes that the government rarely uses its resources wisely. Inadvertently, though, Mitch let slip that the complex "qualified" for the credit only because he overstated the percentage of low-income tenants living in the facility. Mitch admitted that by claiming that John and Susie were low-income tenants (even though they weren't), the percentage of low-income tenants was just enough for Mitch to "qualify" for the credit. Mitch said that because John and Susie were his friends, he was passing along some of his tax savings to them in the form of lower rent.

John and Susie know that if they report Mitch, he will not only lose the economic benefit of the credit, but he will also have legal troubles. Further, if Mitch were to be sentenced to prison for the tax fraud, his children would necessarily become guardians of the state. In addition, John and Susie would have to pay higher rent. Evaluate the courses of action available to John and Susie.

DISABLED ACCESS CREDIT

The **disabled access credit** is designed to encourage small businesses to make their businesses more accessible to disabled individuals. The credit is available for

---

[14] Rev.Rul. 97–1, I.R.B. No. 2, 1. The rate is subject to adjustment every month by the IRS.

any eligible access expenditures paid or incurred by an eligible small business. The credit is calculated at the rate of 50 percent of the eligible expenditures that exceed $250 but do not exceed $10,250. Thus, the maximum amount for the credit is $5,000 ($10,000 × 50%).[15]

An *eligible small business* is one that during the previous year either had gross receipts of $1 million or less or had no more than 30 full-time employees. An eligible business can include a sole proprietorship, partnership, regular corporation, or S corporation.

Eligible access expenditures are generally any reasonable and necessary amounts that are paid or incurred to make certain changes to facilities. These changes must involve the removal of architectural, communication, physical, or transportation barriers that would otherwise make a business inaccessible to disabled and handicapped individuals. Examples of qualifying projects include installing ramps, widening doorways, and adding raised markings on elevator control buttons. However, eligible expenditures do *not* include amounts that are paid or incurred in connection with any facility that has been placed into service after the enactment (November 5, 1990) of the provision.

To the extent a disabled access credit is available, no deduction or credit is allowed under any other provision of the tax law. The adjusted basis for depreciation is reduced by the amount of the credit.

EXAMPLE 18

This year Red, Inc., an eligible business, made $11,000 of capital improvements to business realty that had been placed in service in June 1990. The expenditures were intended to make Red's business more accessible to the disabled and were considered eligible expenditures for purposes of the disabled access credit. The amount of the credit is $5,000 [($10,250 − $250) × 50%]. Although $11,000 of eligible expenditures were incurred, only the excess of $10,250 over $250 qualifies for the credit. Further, the depreciable basis of the capital improvement is $6,000 because the basis must be reduced by the amount of the credit [$11,000 (cost) − $5,000 (amount of the credit)]. ▼

OTHER TAX CREDITS

EARNED INCOME CREDIT

4 LEARNING OBJECTIVE
Describe several other tax credits that are available primarily to individual taxpayers.

The **earned income credit,** which has been a part of the law for many years, consistently has been justified as a means of providing tax equity to the working poor. More recently, the credit has also been designed to help offset regressive taxes that are a part of our tax system, such as the gasoline and Social Security taxes. In addition, the credit has been intended to encourage economically disadvantaged individuals to become contributing members of the workforce.[16] Not only is the current earned income credit more generous than previous versions, it is also touted as being easier to compute.

In 1997, the earned income credit is determined by multiplying a maximum amount of earned income by the appropriate credit percentage (see Table 13–2). Generally, earned income includes employee compensation and net earnings from self-employment but excludes items such as interest, dividends, pension benefits, and alimony. If a taxpayer has children, the credit percentage used in the calculation depends on the number of qualifying children. Thus, in 1997, the

---

[15] § 44.   [16] § 32.

TABLE 13–2
Earned Income Credit and Phase-out Percentages

Tax Year	Number of Qualifying Children	Maximum Earned Income	Credit Percentage	Phase-out Begins	Phase-out Percentage	Phase-out Ends
1997	One child	$6,500	34.00	$11,930	15.98	$25,760
	Two or more children	9,140	40.00	11,930	21.06	29,290
	No qualifying children	4,340	7.65	5,430	7.65	9,770
1996	One child	6,330	34.00	11,610	15.98	25,078
	Two or more children	8,890	40.00	11,610	21.06	28,495
	No qualifying children	4,220	7.65	5,280	7.65	9,500

maximum earned income credit for a taxpayer with one qualifying child is $2,210 ($6,500 × 34%) and $3,656 ($9,140 × 40%) for a taxpayer with two or more qualifying children. However, the maximum earned income credit is phased out completely if the taxpayer's earned income or AGI exceeds certain thresholds as shown in Table 13–2.[17] To the extent that the greater of earned income or AGI exceeds $11,930 in 1997, the difference, multiplied by the appropriate phase-out percentage, is subtracted from the maximum earned income credit.

EXAMPLE 19

In 1997, Grace, who otherwise qualifies for the earned income credit, receives wages of $14,000 and has no other income. She has one qualifying child. Grace's earned income credit is $2,210 ($6,500 × 34%) reduced by $331 [($14,000 − $11,930) × 15.98%]. Thus, Grace's earned income credit is $1,879. If Grace has two or more qualifying children, the calculation would produce a credit of $3,656 ($9,140 × 40%) reduced by $436 [($14,000 − $11,930) × 21.06%]. Thus, Grace's earned income credit would be $3,220. ▼

Earned Income Credit Table. It is not necessary to compute the credit as was done in Example 19. As part of the tax simplification process, the IRS issues an Earned Income Credit Table for the determination of the appropriate amount of the earned income credit. This table and a worksheet are included in the instructions to both Form 1040 and Form 1040A.

Eligibility Requirements. *Eligibility* for the credit may depend not only on the taxpayer meeting the earned income and AGI thresholds, but on whether he or she has a qualifying child. A *qualifying child* must meet the following tests:

- *Relationship test.* The individual must be a son, daughter, descendant of the taxpayer's son or daughter, stepson, stepdaughter, or an eligible foster child of the taxpayer. A legally adopted child of the taxpayer is considered the same as a child by blood.
- *Residency test.* The qualifying child must share the taxpayer's principal place of abode, which must be located within the United States, for more than one-half of the tax year of the taxpayer. Temporary absences (e.g., due to illness or

---

[17] § 32(a)(2)(B). AGI is modified for the purpose of this calculation. See § 32(c)(5).

education) are disregarded for purposes of this test. For foster children, however, the child must share the taxpayer's home for the entire year.
- *Age test.* The child must not have reached the age of 19 (24 in the case of a full-time student) as of the end of the tax year. In addition, a child who is permanently and totally disabled at any time during the year is considered to meet the age test.

In addition to being available for taxpayers with qualifying children, the earned income credit is also available to certain *workers without children*. However, this provision is available only to taxpayers aged 25 through 64 who cannot be claimed as a dependent on another taxpayer's return. As shown in Table 13–2, the credit for 1997 is calculated on a maximum earned income of $4,340 times 7.65 percent and reduced by 7.65 percent of earned income over $5,430. This credit is phased out completely at $9,770.

EXAMPLE 20

Walt, who is single, 28 years of age, and is not claimed as a dependent on anyone else's return, earns $6,500 during 1997. Even though he does not have any qualifying children, he qualifies for the earned income credit. His credit is $332 ($4,340 × 7.65%) reduced by $82 [($6,500 − $5,430) × 7.65%]. Thus, Walt's earned income credit is $250. If, instead, Walt's earned income is $4,900, his earned income credit is $332. In this situation, there is no phase-out of the maximum credit because his earned income is not in excess of $5,430. ▼

Advance Payment. The earned income credit is a form of negative income tax (a refundable credit for taxpayers who do not have a tax liability). An eligible individual may elect to receive advance payments of the earned income credit from his or her employer (rather than receiving the credit from the IRS upon filing the tax return). The amount that can be received in advance is limited to 60 percent of the credit that is available to a taxpayer with only one qualifying child. If this election is made, the taxpayer must file a certificate of eligibility (Form W–5) with his or her employer and *must* file a tax return for the year the income is earned.

TAX CREDIT FOR ELDERLY OR DISABLED TAXPAYERS

The credit for the elderly was originally enacted in 1954 as the retirement income credit to provide tax relief on retirement income for individuals who were not receiving substantial benefits from tax-free Social Security payments.[18]

Currently, the **tax credit for the elderly or disabled** applies to the following:

- Taxpayers age 65 or older.
- Taxpayers under age 65 who are retired with a permanent and total disability and who have disability income from a public or private employer on account of the disability.

The *maximum* allowable credit is $1,125 (15% × $7,500 of qualifying income), but the credit will be less for a taxpayer who receives Social Security benefits or has AGI exceeding specified amounts. Under these circumstances, the base used in the credit computation is reduced. Many taxpayers receive Social Security benefits or have AGI high enough to reduce the base for the credit to zero.

The eligibility requirements and the tax computation are somewhat complicated. Consequently, an individual may elect to have the IRS compute his or her tax and the amount of the tax credit.

---

[18] § 22. This credit is not subject to indexation.

TAX IN THE NEWS

"EARNED INCOME CREDIT" OR "EASY INCOME FOR CHEATS"?

The earned income credit was designed to mitigate the effects of the regressive tax system on low-income taxpayers and to encourage individuals to seek work rather than welfare. Currently, however, the benefits the credit provides are being underused and abused.

To be considered a success, the earned income credit would have to be used by those persons it is intended to help. For example, workers who have a qualifying child and income below a certain amount are allowed to receive advance payment of the credit. However, less than 1 percent of qualifying Americans take advantage of this advance payment opportunity. Some commentators contend that the provisions, which have been changed 10 times since 1976, have become overly complex, difficult to comply with, and almost unusable by the low-income workers the credit is intended to aid. Estimates show that 14 percent of persons qualifying for the credit fail to claim it.

On the other hand, others who don't qualify have found the lure of the credit too good to pass up. In a recent IRS study, one-half of the electronically filed returns that claimed the earned income credit contained errors suspected to be intentional. In fact, some of the tax fraud schemes involving the credit have been initiated by persons in prison. One IRS investigation uncovered a scam operating out of the Maine Correctional Center. A dozen current and former inmates were indicted for improperly seeking refunds for earned income credit claims. Another taxpayer convicted of cheating the government by improperly using the credit testified before Congress that the earned income tax credit could stand for "easy income for cheats!"

▼ **TABLE 13–3**
Base Amounts for Tax Credit for Elderly or Disabled Taxpayers

Status	Base Amount
Single, head of household, or surviving spouse	$5,000
Married, joint return, only one spouse qualified	5,000
Married, joint return, both spouses qualified	7,500
Married, separate returns, spouses live apart the entire year	3,750 each

The credit generally is based on an initial amount (referred to as the *base amount*) and the filing status of the taxpayer in accordance with Table 13–3. To qualify for the credit, married taxpayers who live together must file a joint return. For taxpayers under age 65 who are retired on permanent and total disability, the base amounts could be less than those shown in Table 13–3 because these amounts are limited to taxable disability income.

This initial base amount is *reduced* by (1) Social Security, Railroad Retirement, and certain excluded pension benefits and (2) one-half of the taxpayer's AGI in excess of a threshold amount, which is a function of the taxpayer's filing status. The credit may be calculated using the procedure presented in the following template:

Base amount ($3,750, $5,000, or $7,500—see Table 13-3)	_____
Less: Qualifying nontaxable benefits	_____
One-half of excess of AGI over: $7,500 for single, head of household, or surviving spouse taxpayers $10,000 for married taxpayers $5,000 for married taxpayers filing separately	_____
Total reductions	_____
Balance subject to credit	_____
Multiply balance subject to credit by 15%—this is the tax credit allowed	_____

EXAMPLE 21

Paul and Peggy, husband and wife, are both over age 65 and received Social Security benefits of $2,400 in the current year. On a joint return, they reported AGI of $14,000.

Base amount ($3,750, $5,000, or $7,500—see Table 13-3)		$ 7,500
Less: Qualifying nontaxable benefits	$2,400	
One-half of excess of AGI over: $7,500 for single, head of household, or surviving spouse taxpayers $10,000 for married taxpayers $5,000 for married taxpayers filing separately	2,000	
Total reductions		(4,400)
Balance subject to credit		$ 3,100
Multiply balance subject to credit by 15%—this is the tax credit allowed		$ 465

Schedule R of Form 1040 (see Appendix B) is used to calculate and report the credit.

FOREIGN TAX CREDIT

Both individual taxpayers and corporations may claim a tax credit for foreign income tax paid on income earned and subject to tax in another country or a U.S. possession.[19] As an alternative, a taxpayer may claim a deduction instead of a credit.[20] In most instances, the **foreign tax credit (FTC)** is advantageous since it provides a direct offset against the tax liability.

The purpose of the FTC is to mitigate double taxation since income earned in a foreign country is subject to both U.S. and foreign taxes. However, the ceiling limitation formula may result in some form of double taxation or taxation at rates in excess of U.S. rates when the foreign tax rates are higher than the U.S. rates. This is a distinct possibility because U.S. tax rates are lower than those of many foreign countries.

Other special tax treatments applicable to taxpayers working outside the United States include the foreign earned income exclusion (refer to Chapter 5) and

---

[19] Section 27 provides for the credit, but the qualifications and calculation procedure for the credit are contained in §§ 901–908.

[20] § 164.

limitations on deducting expenses of employees working outside the United States (refer to Chapter 9). Recall from the earlier discussion that a taxpayer may not take advantage of *both* the FTC and the foreign earned income exclusion.

Computation. Taxpayers are required to compute the FTC based upon an overall limitation.[21] The FTC allowed is the *lesser* of the foreign taxes imposed or the *overall limitation* determined according to the following formula:

$$\frac{\text{Foreign-source taxable income}}{\text{Worldwide taxable income}} \times \text{U.S. tax before FTC}$$

For individual taxpayers, worldwide taxable income in the overall limitation formula is determined *before* personal and dependency exemptions are deducted.

EXAMPLE 22

In 1997, Carlos, a calendar year taxpayer, has $10,000 of income from Country Y, which imposes a 15% tax, and $20,000 from Country Z, which imposes a 50% tax. He has taxable income of $59,400 from within the United States, is married filing a joint return, and claims two dependency exemptions. Thus, although Carlos's taxable income for purposes of determining U.S. tax is $89,400, taxable income amounts used in the limitation formula are not reduced by personal and dependency exemptions. Thus, for this purpose, taxable income is $100,000 [$89,400 + (4 × $2,650)]. Assume that Carlos's U.S. tax before the credit is $19,676. Overall limitation:

$$\frac{\text{Foreign-source taxable income}}{\text{Worldwide taxable income}} = \frac{\$30,000}{\$100,000} \times \$19,676 = \$5,903$$

In this case, $5,903 is allowed as the FTC because this amount is less than the $11,500 of foreign taxes imposed [$1,500 (Country Y) + $10,000 (Country Z)]. ▼

Thus, the overall limitation may result in some of the foreign income being subjected to double taxation. Unused FTCs [e.g., the $5,597 ($11,500 − $5,903) from Example 22] can be carried back two years and forward five years.[22]

Only foreign income taxes, war profits taxes, and excess profits taxes (or taxes paid in lieu of such taxes) qualify for the credit. In determining whether or not a tax is an income tax, U.S. criteria are applied. Thus, value added taxes (VAT), severance taxes, property taxes, and sales taxes do not qualify because they are not regarded as taxes on income. Such taxes may be deductible, however.

ADOPTION EXPENSES CREDIT

Beginning in 1997, qualifying adoption expenses paid or incurred by a taxpayer may give rise to the **adoption expenses credit**.[23] The provision is intended to assist taxpayers who incur nonrecurring costs directly associated with the adoption process, such as adoption fees, attorney fees, court costs, social service review costs, and transportation costs.

Up to $5,000 of costs incurred to adopt an eligible child qualify for the credit.[24] An eligible child is one who is:

- under 18 years of age at the time of the adoption or
- physically or mentally incapable of taking care of himself or herself.

---

[21] § 904.
[22] § 904(c) and Reg. § 1.904–2(g), Example 1.
[23] § 23.
[24] § 23(b)(1). The maximum amount of qualifying expenses increases to $6,000 for a "child with special needs." See § 23(d)(3).

A taxpayer can claim the credit in the year following the year in which expenses are paid or incurred. The credit can also be claimed in the year in which the adoption becomes final for expenses paid or incurred in that year. A married couple must file a joint return.

EXAMPLE 23 In late 1997, Sam and Martha pay $2,500 in legal fees, adoption fees, and other expenses directly related to the adoption of an infant daughter, Susan. In 1998, they pay an additional $1,000, and in 1999, the year in which the adoption becomes final, they pay $3,000. Sam and Martha are eligible for a $2,500 credit in 1998 and a $2,500 credit in 1999. ▼

The amount of the credit that is otherwise available is phased out for taxpayers whose AGI (modified for this purpose) exceeds $75,000, and the credit is completely eliminated when the AGI reaches $115,000. The resulting credit is calculated by reducing the allowable credit (determined without this reduction) by the allowable credit multiplied by the ratio of the excess of the taxpayer's AGI over $75,000 to $40,000.

EXAMPLE 24 Assume the same facts as in the previous example, except that Sam and Martha's AGI is $100,000 in each of the relevant years. As a result, their available credits in 1998 and 1999 are reduced from $2,500 to $938 {$2,500 − [$2,500($25,000/$40,000)]}. Therefore, over the two-year period, the adoption expenses credit totals $1,876 ($938 × 2). ▼

The credit is nonrefundable and is available to taxpayers only in a year in which this credit and the other nonrefundable credits do not exceed the taxpayer's tax liability. However, any unused adoption expenses credit may be carried over for up to five years, being utilized on a first-in, first-out basis.

CREDIT FOR CHILD AND DEPENDENT CARE EXPENSES

A credit is allowed to taxpayers who incur employment-related expenses for child or dependent care.[25] The **credit for child and dependent care expenses** is a specified percentage of expenses incurred to enable the taxpayer to work or to seek employment. Expenses on which the credit for child and dependent care expenses is based are subject to limitations.

Eligibility. To be eligible for the credit, an individual must maintain a household for either of the following:

- A dependent under age 13.
- A dependent or spouse who is physically or mentally incapacitated.

Generally, married taxpayers must file a joint return to obtain the credit. The credit may also be claimed by the custodial parent for a nondependent child under age 13 if the noncustodial parent is allowed to claim the child as a dependent under a pre-1985 divorce agreement or under a waiver in the case of a post-1984 agreement.

Eligible Employment-Related Expenses. Eligible expenses include amounts paid for household services and care of a qualifying individual that are incurred to enable the taxpayer to be employed. Child and dependent care expenses include expenses incurred in the home, such as payments for a housekeeper. Out-of-the-home expenses incurred for the care of a dependent under the age of 13 also

---

[25] § 21.

qualify for the credit. In addition, out-of-the-home expenses incurred for an older dependent or spouse who is physically or mentally incapacitated qualify for the credit if that person regularly spends at least eight hours each day in the taxpayer's household. This makes the credit available to taxpayers who keep handicapped older children and elderly relatives in the home instead of institutionalizing them. Out-of-the-home expenses incurred for services provided by a dependent care center will qualify only if the center complies with all applicable laws and regulations of a state or unit of local government.

Child care payments to a relative are eligible for the credit unless the relative is a dependent of the taxpayer or the taxpayer's spouse or is a child (under age 19) of the taxpayer.

EXAMPLE 25 Wilma is an employed mother of an eight-year-old child. She pays her mother, Rita, $1,500 per year to care for the child after school. Wilma does not claim Rita as a dependent. Wilma pays her daughter Eleanor, age 17, $900 for the child's care during the summer. Of these amounts, only the $1,500 paid to Rita qualifies as employment-related child care expenses. ▼

Earned Income Ceiling. The total for qualifying employment-related expenses is limited to an individual's earned income. For married taxpayers, this limitation applies to the spouse with the *lesser* amount of earned income. Special rules are provided for taxpayers with nonworking spouses who are disabled or are full-time students. If a nonworking spouse is physically or mentally disabled or is a full-time student, he or she is *deemed* to have earned income for purposes of this limitation. The deemed amount is $200 per month if there is one qualifying individual in the household or $400 per month if there are two or more qualifying individuals in the household. In the case of a student-spouse, the student's income is *deemed* to be earned only for the months that the student is enrolled on a full-time basis at an educational institution.

Calculation of the Credit. In general, the credit is equal to a percentage of *unreimbursed* employment-related expenses up to $2,400 for one qualifying individual and $4,800 for two or more individuals. The credit rate varies between 20 percent and 30 percent, depending on the taxpayer's AGI. The following chart shows the applicable percentage for taxpayers as AGI increases:

Adjusted Gross Income		
Over	But Not Over	Applicable Rate of Credit
$ 0	$10,000	30%
10,000	12,000	29%
12,000	14,000	28%
14,000	16,000	27%
16,000	18,000	26%
18,000	20,000	25%
20,000	22,000	24%
22,000	24,000	23%
24,000	26,000	22%
26,000	28,000	21%
28,000	No limit	20%

EXAMPLE 26

Nancy, who has two children under age 13, worked full-time while her spouse, Ron, was attending college for 10 months during the year. Nancy earned $21,000 and incurred $5,000 of child care expenses. Ron is *deemed* to be fully employed and to have earned $400 for each of the 10 months (or a total of $4,000). Since Nancy and Ron have AGI of $21,000, they are allowed a credit rate of 24%. Nancy and Ron are limited to $4,000 in qualified child care expenses (the lesser of $4,800 or $4,000). Therefore, they are entitled to a tax credit of $960 (24% × $4,000) for the year. ▼

Dependent Care Assistance Program. Recall from Chapter 5 that a taxpayer is allowed an exclusion from gross income for a limited amount reimbursed for child or dependent care expenses. However, the taxpayer is not allowed both an exclusion from income and a child and dependent care credit on the same amount. The $2,400 and $4,800 ceilings for allowable child and dependent care expenses are reduced dollar for dollar by the amount of reimbursement.[26]

EXAMPLE 27

Assume the same facts as in Example 26, except that of the $5,000 paid for child care, Nancy was reimbursed $2,500 by her employer under a qualified dependent care assistance program. Under the employer's plan, the reimbursement reduces Nancy's taxable wages. Thus, Nancy and Ron have AGI of $18,500 ($21,000 − $2,500). The maximum amount of child care expenses for two or more dependents of $4,800 is reduced by the $2,500 reimbursement, resulting in a tax credit of $575 [25% × ($4,800 − $2,500)]. ▼

Reporting Requirements. The credit is claimed by completing and filing Form 2441, Credit for Child and Dependent Care Expenses (see Appendix B).

PAYMENT PROCEDURES

5 LEARNING OBJECTIVE
Understand the tax withholding and payment procedures applicable to employers.

The tax law contains elaborate rules that require the prepayment of various Federal taxes. Consistent with the pay-as-you-go approach to the collection of taxes, these rules carry penalties for lack of compliance.[27] Prepayment procedures fall into two major categories: those applicable to employers and those applicable to self-employed persons. For employers, both payroll taxes (FICA and FUTA) and income taxes may be involved. With self-employed taxpayers, the focus is on the income tax and the self-employment tax.

PROCEDURES APPLICABLE TO EMPLOYERS

Employment taxes include FICA (Federal Insurance Contributions Act) and FUTA (Federal Unemployment Tax Act). The employer usually is responsible for withholding the employee's share of FICA (commonly referred to as Social Security tax) and appropriate amounts for income taxes. In addition, the employer must match the FICA portion withheld and fully absorb the cost of FUTA. The sum of the employment taxes and the income tax withholdings must be paid to the IRS at specified intervals.

The key to employer compliance in this area involves the resolution of the following points:

---

[26] § 21(c).
[27] See, for example, § 3403 (employer liable for any taxes withheld and not paid over to the IRS), § 6656 (up to 15% penalty on amounts withheld and not paid over), and § 6654 (penalty for failure by an individual to pay estimated income taxes).

Concept Summary 13-1

Tax Credits

Credit	Computation	Comments
Tax withheld on wages (§ 31)	Amount is reported to employee on W-2 form.	Refundable credit.
Earned income (§ 32)	Amount is determined by reference to Earned Income Credit Table published by IRS. Computations of underlying amounts in Earned Income Credit Table are illustrated in Example 19.	Refundable credit. A form of negative income tax to assist low-income taxpayers. Earned income and AGI must be less than certain threshold amounts. Generally, one or more qualifying children must reside with the taxpayer.
Child and dependent care (§ 21)	Rate ranges from 20% to 30% depending on AGI. Maximum base for credit is $2,400 for one qualifying individual, $4,800 for two or more.	Nonrefundable personal credit. No carryback or carryforward. Benefits taxpayers who incur employment-related child or dependent care expenses in order to work or seek employment. Eligible dependents include children under age 13 or dependent (any age) or spouse who is physically or mentally incapacitated.
Elderly or disabled (§ 22)	15% of sum of base amount minus reductions for (a) Social Security and other nontaxable benefits and (b) excess AGI. Base amount is fixed by law (e.g., $5,000 for a single taxpayer).	Nonrefundable personal credit. No carryback or carryforward. Provides relief for taxpayers not receiving substantial tax-free retirement benefits.
Adoption expenses (§ 23)	Up to $5,000 of costs incurred to adopt an eligible child qualify for the credit. Taxpayer claims the credit in the year following the year in which expenditures are paid or incurred, and in the year in which the adoption becomes final for expenses paid or incurred in that year.	Nonrefundable credit. Purpose is to assist taxpayers who incur nonrecurring costs associated with the adoption process.
Foreign tax (§ 27)	Foreign income/total worldwide taxable income × U.S. tax = overall limitation. Lesser of foreign taxes imposed or overall limitation.	Nonrefundable credit. Unused credits may be carried back two years and forward five years. Purpose is to prevent double taxation of foreign income.
General business (§ 38)	May not exceed net income tax minus the greater of tentative minimum tax or 25% of net regular tax liability that exceeds $25,000.	Nonrefundable credit. Components include tax credit for rehabilitation expenditures, business energy credits, work opportunity tax credit, research activities credit, low-income housing credit, and disabled access credit. Unused credit may be carried back 3 years and forward 15 years. FIFO method applies to carryovers, carrybacks, and credits earned during current year.

Concept Summary 13-1

Tax Credits—Continued

Credit	Computation	Comments
Investment (§ 46)	Qualifying investment times energy percentage or rehabilitation percentage, depending on type of property. Part of general business credit and subject to its limitations.	Nonrefundable credit. Part of general business credit and therefore subject to same carryback, carryover, and FIFO rules. Energy percentage is 10%. Regular rehabilitation rate is 10%; rate for certified historic structures is 20%.
Research activities (§ 41)	Incremental credit is 20% of excess of computation year expenditures minus the base amount. Basic research credit is allowed to certain corporations for 20% of cash payments to qualified organizations that exceed a specially calculated base amount. To qualify for the credit, research expenditures must be made from July 1, 1996 through May 31, 1997.	Nonrefundable credit. Part of general business credit and therefore subject to same carryback, carryover, and FIFO rules. Purpose is to encourage high-tech research in the United States.
Low-income housing (§ 42)	Appropriate rate times eligible basis (portion of project attributable to low-income units).	Nonrefundable credit. Part of general business credit and therefore subject to same carryback, carryover, and FIFO rules. Credit is available each year for 10 years. Recapture may apply. Purpose is to encourage construction of housing for low-income individuals.
Disabled access (§ 44)	Credit is 50% of eligible access expenditures that exceed $250, but do not exceed $10,250. Maximum credit is $5,000.	Nonrefundable credit. Part of general business credit and therefore subject to same carryback, carryover, and FIFO rules. Available only to eligible small businesses. Purpose is to encourage small businesses to become more accessible to disabled individuals.
Work opportunity (§ 51)	Credit is limited to 35% of the first $6,000 of wages paid to each eligible employee. Under current law, the employee must begin work after September 30, 1996, and before October 1, 1997.	Nonrefundable credit. Part of the general business credit and therefore subject to the same carryback, carryover, and FIFO rules. Purpose is to encourage employment of individuals in specified groups.

- Ascertaining which employees and wages are covered by employment taxes and are subject to withholding for income taxes.
- Arriving at the amount to be paid and/or withheld.
- Reporting and paying employment taxes and income taxes withheld to the IRS on a timely basis through the use of proper forms.

▼ EXHIBIT 13-2
Withholding Classifications

Special Classes of Employment and Special Types of Payments	Treatment under Different Employment Taxes		
	Income Tax Withholding	**Social Security and Medicare**	**Federal Unemployment**
Family employees:			
a. Child employed by parent (or by partnership consisting only of parents) in a trade or business.	Withhold	Exempt until age 18	Exempt until age 21
b. Spouse employed by spouse.	Withhold	Taxable if in course of spouse's business	Exempt
c. Parent employed by a child.	Withhold	Taxable if in course of the child's business.	Exempt
Household employees (domestic service in private homes; farmers, see Circular A).	Exempt (withhold if both employer and employee voluntarily agree).	Taxable if paid $1,000 or more in cash in 1997. Exempt if performed by an individual under age 18 during any portion of the calendar year and is not the principal occupation of the employee.	Taxable if employer paid cash wages of $1,000 or more (for all household employees) in any quarter in the current or preceding calendar year.
Interns working in hospitals.	Withhold	Taxable	Exempt
Meals and lodging.	a. Meals—Subject to withholding and taxable unless furnished for employer's convenience and on the employer's premises. b. Lodging—Subject to withholding and taxable unless furnished on employer's premises, for the employer's convenience, and as a condition of employment.		
Ministers of churches performing duties as such.*	Exempt (withhold if both the minister and the church voluntarily agree).	Exempt (withhold if both the church and the minister voluntarily agree)	Exempt
Moving expense reimbursement:			
a. Qualified expenses.	Exempt, unless you have knowledge that the employee deducted the expenses in a prior year.		
b. Nonqualified expenses.	Withhold	Taxable	Taxable
Newspaper carriers under age 18.	Exempt (withhold if both employer and employee voluntarily agree).	Exempt	Exempt
Severance or dismissal pay.	Withhold	Taxable	Taxable
Tips, if less than $20 in a month.	Exempt	Exempt	Exempt
Worker's compensation.	Exempt	Exempt	Exempt

* In the typical case, ministers are considered to be self-employed rather than employees of the church.

Coverage Requirements. Circular E, Employer's Tax Guide (Publication 15) and Employer's Supplemental Tax Guide (Publication 15-A), issued by the IRS contain a discussion or listing of which employees and which wages require withholdings for income taxes and employment taxes. Excerpts from these publications appear in Exhibit 13-2. In working with Exhibit 13-2, consider the following observations:

TAX IN THE NEWS

CREATIVITY GONE AWRY LEADS TO TIME IN CONFINEMENT

Some people have found the lure of quick money too good to pass up. In various well-publicized schemes, individuals have obtained refunds from the government by filing false individual income tax returns. Essentially, the perpetrators gather and complete various phony employment documents, such as W–2s, which then serve as the basis for fictitious returns.

Other creative "taxpayers" have tried other approaches. For example, totally fake tax returns for bogus taxpayers, complete with Social Security numbers, have been filed reporting income not earned and income taxes not withheld for which a refund would be claimed. In other cases, taxpayers have claimed nonexistent dependents and then used the more beneficial head of household rate schedule to calculate their income tax refund. As reported by the popular television news magazine, *Dateline NBC*, such schemes have even been pursued by convicts already safely behind bars in various state and Federal prisons. These culprits would order the appropriate employment forms and tax returns from the IRS, complete them using fictitious data, and sit back in their cells and wait for refund checks to roll in. While these prisoners may have figured they had little to lose since they were already serving lengthy sentences, others caught by government officials may regret their activities for the rest of their lives.

One such scheme occurred in Norfolk, Virginia, in 1991. The perpetrators even had the audacity to file the returns through a commercial income tax preparer in order to receive a rapid refund loan. Recently, the fifty-third person was convicted in Federal court of participating in the scheme.

SOURCE: Adapted from Beverly N. Williams, "Norfolk Man is the 53rd Convicted in Tax Scheme," *Newport News Daily Press*, June 22, 1996, p. C3.

- The designation "Exempt" in the income tax withholding column does not mean that the amount paid is nontaxable to the employee. It merely relieves the employer from having to withhold.

EXAMPLE 28 Lee works for Yellow Corporation and has the type of job where tips are not common but do occur. If Lee's total tips amount to less than $20 per month, Yellow Corporation need not withhold Federal income taxes on the tips. Nevertheless, Lee must include the tips in his gross income. ▼

- In some cases, income tax withholding is not required but is voluntary. This is designated "Exempt (withhold if both employer and employee voluntarily agree)."

EXAMPLE 29 Pat is employed as a gardener by a wealthy family. In the past, he has encountered difficulty in managing his finances so as to be in a position to pay the income tax due every April 15. To ease the cash-flow problem that develops in April, Pat asks his employer to withhold income taxes from his wages. ▼

- The Social Security and Medicare (FICA) column refers to the employer's share. The same is true of the Federal Unemployment (FUTA) column since the employee does not contribute to this tax.

▼ TABLE 13-4
FICA Rates and Base

	Social Security Tax			Medicare Tax			
	Percent	×	Base Amount	+ Percent	×	Base Amount	= Maximum Tax
1990	6.20%	×	$51,300	+ 1.45%	×	$ 51,300	= $3,924.45
1991	6.20%	×	53,400	+ 1.45%	×	125,000	= 5,123.30
1992	6.20%	×	55,500	+ 1.45%	×	130,200	= 5,328.90
1993	6.20%	×	57,600	+ 1.45%	×	135,000	= 5,528.70
1994	6.20%	×	60,600	+ 1.45%	×	Unlimited	= Unlimited
1995	6.20%	×	61,200	+ 1.45%	×	Unlimited	= Unlimited
1996	6.20%	×	62,700	+ 1.45%	×	Unlimited	= Unlimited
1997	6.20%	×	65,400	+ 1.45%	×	Unlimited	= Unlimited
1998 on	6.20%	×	*	+ 1.45%	×	Unlimited	= Unlimited

*Not yet determined.

Amount of FICA Taxes. The FICA tax is comprised of two components: Social Security tax (old age, survivors, and disability insurance) *and* Medicare tax (hospital insurance). The tax rates and wage base under FICA have increased both frequently and substantially over the years. There appears to be every reason to predict that the rates and/or base amount will continue to rise in the future. As Table 13–4 shows, the top base amount differs for the Medicare portion and for the Social Security portion. Also note that Table 13–4 represents the employee's share of the tax. The employer must match the employee's portion.

Withholdings from employees must continue until the maximum base amount is reached. In 1997, for example, FICA withholding ceases for the Social Security portion (6.2 percent) once the employee has earned wages subject to FICA in the amount of $65,400. For the Medicare portion (1.45 percent), however, the employer is required to withhold on all wages without limit. This contrasts with years prior to 1994 when a maximum base existed for the Medicare portion also.

EXAMPLE 30 In 1997, Keshia earned a salary of $140,000 from her employer. Therefore, FICA taxes withheld from her salary are $4,055 ($65,400 × 6.2%) plus $2,030 ($140,000 × 1.45%) for a total of $6,085. In addition to paying the amount withheld from Keshia's salary to the government, her employer will also have to pay $6,085. ▼

In at least two situations, it is possible for an employee to have paid excess FICA taxes.

EXAMPLE 31 During 1997, Kevin changed employers in the middle of the year and earned $40,000 (all of which was subject to FICA) from each job. As a result, each employer withheld $3,060 [(6.2% × $40,000) + (1.45% × $40,000)] for a total of $6,120. Although each employer acted properly, Kevin's total FICA tax liability for the year is only $5,215 [(6.2% × $65,400) + (1.45% × $80,000)]. Thus, Kevin has overpaid his share of FICA taxes by $905 [$6,120 (amount paid) − $5,215 (amount of correct liability)]. He should claim this amount as a tax credit when filing his income tax return for 1997. The tax credit will reduce any income tax Kevin might owe or, possibly, generate a tax refund. ▼

EXAMPLE 32 During 1997, Lori earned $60,000 from her regular job and $20,000 from a part-time job (all of which was subject to FICA). As a result, one employer withheld $4,590 [(6.2% × $60,000)

+ (1.45% × $60,000)] while the other employer withheld $1,530 [(6.2% × $20,000) + (1.45% × $20,000)] for a total of $6,120. Lori's total FICA tax liability for the year is only $5,215 [(6.2% × $65,400) + (1.45% × $80,000)]. Thus, Lori has overpaid her share of FICA taxes by $905 [$6,120 (amount paid) − $5,215 (amount of correct liability)]. She should claim this amount as a tax credit when filing her income tax return for 1997. ▼

In Examples 31 and 32, the employee was subject to overwithholding. In both cases, however, the employee was able to obtain a credit for the excess withheld. The same result does not materialize for the portion paid by the employer. Since this amount is not refundable, in some situations employers may pay more FICA taxes than the covered employees.

The mere fact that a husband and wife are both employed does not, by itself, result in overwithholding of FICA taxes.

EXAMPLE 33 During 1997, Jim and Betty (husband and wife) are both employed, and each earns wages subject to FICA of $40,000. Accordingly, each has $3,060 FICA withheld [(6.2% × $40,000) + (1.45% × $40,000)] for a total of $6,120. Since neither spouse paid FICA tax on wages in excess of $65,400 (Social Security tax) [see Table 13–4], there is no overwithholding. ▼

A spouse employed by another spouse is subject to FICA. However, children under the age of 18 who are employed in a parent's trade or business are exempted.

ETHICAL CONSIDERATIONS

Being Paid Once Every Two Years

Sally is a CPA and the sole shareholder of her small public accounting practice, which has grown over the years. Sally has reached the point where she is financially comfortable with significant short-term and long-term savings balances. Because her practice involves a substantial amount of tax work, it is to her advantage to keep alert for possible tax savings strategies that she may be able to employ, either for her clients or for herself. One recent idea she has discovered involves manipulating the time at which her salary is paid in order to minimize the FICA taxes incurred by her corporation and herself.

In recent years, she has paid herself an annual salary of approximately $100,000 and the corresponding employer and employee portions of the FICA tax have been $11,009.60 (using the 1997 rates, the employer and employee portions of the FICA tax on $100,000 are calculated as [($65,400 × 6.2%) × 2 + ($100,000 × 1.45%) × 2]. Thus, over a two-year period, the FICA tax would aggregate to $22,019.20 ($11,009.60 × 2), based on an annual salary of $100,000 and without any changes in the FICA calculation. Alternatively, if Sally's corporation were to pay her a $200,000 salary *every other year*, the total FICA cost during the same two-year period would be $13,909.60 (using the 1997 rates, the employer and employee portions of the FICA tax on $200,000 are calculated as [($65,400 × 6.2%) × 2 + ($200,000 × 1.45%) × 2]. Therefore, if Sally were to implement this plan, her FICA tax savings would be $8,109.60 ($22,019.20 − $13,909.60). What are the ethical implications of Sally's plan?

Amount of Income Tax Withholding. Arriving at the amount to be withheld for income tax purposes is not so simple. It involves three basic steps:[28]

---

[28] The withholding provisions are contained in §§ 3401 and 3402. These Sections will not be referenced specifically in the discussion that follows.

- Have the employee complete Form W–4, Employee's Withholding Allowance Certificate.
- Determine the employee's payroll period.
- Compute the amount to be withheld, usually using either the wage-bracket tables or the percentage method.

Form W–4 reflects the employee's marital status and **withholding allowances.** Generally, it need not be filed with the IRS and is retained by the employer as part of the payroll records.

The employer need not verify the number of exemptions claimed. Any misinformation in the form will be attributed to the employee. However, if the employer has reason to believe that the employee made a false statement, the IRS District Director should be notified. In the meantime, the Form W–4 should be honored. Employees are subject to both civil and criminal penalties for filing false withholding statements.

On the current Form W–4 an employee may claim *withholding allowances* for the following: personal exemptions for self and spouse (unless either is claimed as a dependent of another person) and dependency exemptions. One *special withholding allowance* may be claimed if the employee is single and has only one job, if the employee is married and has only one job and the spouse is not employed, or if wages from a second job or a spouse's wages (or both) are $1,000 or less. An additional allowance is available if the employee expects to file using the head-of-household status or if the employee expects to claim a credit for child and dependent care expenses on qualifying expenditures of at least $1,500. An employee who plans to itemize deductions or claim adjustments to income (e.g., alimony, deductible IRA contributions) should use the worksheet provided on Form W–4 to determine the correct number of additional allowances.

To avoid having too little tax withheld, some employees may find it necessary to reduce their withholding allowances. This might be the case for an employee who has more than one job or who has other sources of income that are not subject to adequate withholding. Likewise, a married employee who has a working spouse or more than one job might wish to claim fewer allowances.

If both spouses of a married couple are employed, they may allocate their total allowances between themselves as they see fit. The same allocation procedure is required if a taxpayer has more than one job. In no event should the same allowance be claimed more than once at the same time. It is permissible to declare *fewer* allowances than the taxpayer is entitled to in order to increase the amount of withholding. Doing so, however, does not affect the number of exemptions allowable on the employee's income tax return. An employee is also permitted to have the employer withhold a certain dollar amount in addition to the required amount. This additional dollar amount can be arbitrary or calculated in accordance with a worksheet and tables on Form W–4.

EXAMPLE 34

Carl, who earns $15,000, is married to Carol, who earns $25,000. They have three dependent children and will claim the standard deduction. Together they should be entitled to five allowances [2 (for personal exemptions) + 3 (for dependency exemptions)]. The special withholding allowance is not available since both spouses earn more than $1,000. If Carl is the spouse first employed and his Form W–4 reflects five allowances, Carol's Form W–4 should report none. They could, however, reallocate their allowances between them as long as the total claimed does not exceed five. ▼

The period of service for which an employee is paid is known as the *payroll period*. Daily, weekly, biweekly, semimonthly, and monthly periods are the most common arrangements. If an employee has no regular payroll period, he or she is considered to be paid on a daily basis.

Once the allowances are known (as reflected on Form W–4) and the payroll period determined, the amount to be withheld for Federal income taxes can be computed. The computation usually is made by using the wage-bracket tables or the percentage method.

Wage-bracket tables are available for daily, weekly, biweekly, semimonthly, and monthly payroll periods for single (including heads of household) and married taxpayers. An extract of the tables dealing with married persons on a monthly payroll period is reproduced in Table 13–5. The data in Table 13–5 are for the period after December 31, 1996. Example 35 illustrates the use of withholding tables.

EXAMPLE 35

Tom is married and has three dependent children and no additional allowances for itemized deductions, adjustments to income, or credit for child and dependent care expenses. In his job with Pink Corporation, he earns $2,770 in May 1997. Assuming Tom's wife is not employed and all available allowances are claimed on Form W–4, Pink should withhold $138 a month from his wages. This amount is taken from the six allowances column in the $2,760–$2,800 wage bracket. The six allowances result from personal exemptions (two) plus the special withholding allowance (one) plus dependency exemptions (three). ▼

Although the wage-bracket table requires few, if any, calculations, the percentage method is equally acceptable. Its use may be necessary for payroll periods where no wage-bracket tables are available (quarterly, semiannual, and annual payroll periods) and where wages paid exceed the amount allowed for use of the wage-bracket tables. The percentage method is particularly useful when payroll computations are computerized. This method, however, requires the use of a conversion chart based on one withholding allowance. That is, the amount of one allowance is equal to the exemption amount divided by the number of payroll periods in a year. For example, the amount of one allowance for a taxpayer who is paid weekly is $50.96 ($2,650/52 payroll periods)—see Table 13–6.

To use the percentage method, proceed as follows:

Step 1. Multiply the amount of one allowance (as specified in the conversion chart in Table 13–6) by the employee's total allowances (taken from Form W–4).

Step 2. Subtract the product reached in step 1 from the employee's wages. The remainder is called "amount of wages."

Step 3. Using the result derived in step 2, compute the income tax withholding under the proper percentage-method table.

The table used in applying the percentage method for those with monthly payroll periods is reproduced in Table 13–7. An illustration of the percentage method follows.

EXAMPLE 36

Assume the same facts as in Example 35, except that Tom's income tax withholding is determined using the percentage method.

Step 1. $220.83 (amount of one allowance for a monthly payroll period) × 6 (total allowances) = $1,324.98.

Step 2. $2,770 (monthly salary) – $1,324.98 (step 1) = $1,445.02 (amount of wages).

Step 3. Referring to Table 13–7: 15% × $907.02 (excess of step 2 amount over $538) = $136.05. ▼

Note that the wage-bracket tables yield an amount for income tax withholding of $138 (refer to Example 35) while the percentage method results in $136.05

▼ TABLE 13-5
Withholding Table

MARRIED Persons—MONTHLY Payroll Period
(For Wages Paid in 1997)

If the wages are—		And the number of withholding allowances claimed is—										
At least	But less than	0	1	2	3	4	5	6	7	8	9	10
		The amount of income tax to be withheld is—										
$0	$540	0	0	0	0	0	0	0	0	0	0	0
540	560	2	0	0	0	0	0	0	0	0	0	0
560	580	5	0	0	0	0	0	0	0	0	0	0
580	600	8	0	0	0	0	0	0	0	0	0	0
600	640	12	0	0	0	0	0	0	0	0	0	0
640	680	18	0	0	0	0	0	0	0	0	0	0
680	720	24	0	0	0	0	0	0	0	0	0	0
720	760	30	0	0	0	0	0	0	0	0	0	0
760	800	36	3	0	0	0	0	0	0	0	0	0
800	840	42	9	0	0	0	0	0	0	0	0	0
840	880	48	15	0	0	0	0	0	0	0	0	0
880	920	54	21	0	0	0	0	0	0	0	0	0
920	960	60	27	0	0	0	0	0	0	0	0	0
960	1,000	66	33	0	0	0	0	0	0	0	0	0
1,000	1,040	72	39	6	0	0	0	0	0	0	0	0
1,040	1,080	78	45	12	0	0	0	0	0	0	0	0
1,080	1,120	84	51	18	0	0	0	0	0	0	0	0
1,120	1,160	90	57	24	0	0	0	0	0	0	0	0
1,160	1,200	96	63	30	0	0	0	0	0	0	0	0
1,200	1,240	102	69	36	3	0	0	0	0	0	0	0
1,240	1,280	108	75	42	9	0	0	0	0	0	0	0
1,280	1,320	114	81	48	15	0	0	0	0	0	0	0
1,320	1,360	120	87	54	21	0	0	0	0	0	0	0
1,360	1,400	126	93	60	27	0	0	0	0	0	0	0
1,400	1,440	132	99	66	33	0	0	0	0	0	0	0
1,440	1,480	138	105	72	39	6	0	0	0	0	0	0
1,480	1,520	144	111	78	45	12	0	0	0	0	0	0
1,520	1,560	150	117	84	51	18	0	0	0	0	0	0
1,560	1,600	156	123	90	57	24	0	0	0	0	0	0
1,600	1,640	162	129	96	63	30	0	0	0	0	0	0
1,640	1,680	168	135	102	69	36	3	0	0	0	0	0
1,680	1,720	174	141	108	75	42	9	0	0	0	0	0
1,720	1,760	180	147	114	81	48	15	0	0	0	0	0
1,760	1,800	186	153	120	87	54	21	0	0	0	0	0
1,800	1,840	192	159	126	93	60	27	0	0	0	0	0
1,840	1,880	198	165	132	99	66	33	0	0	0	0	0
1,880	1,920	204	171	138	105	72	39	6	0	0	0	0
1,920	1,960	210	177	144	111	78	45	12	0	0	0	0
1,960	2,000	216	183	150	117	84	51	18	0	0	0	0
2,000	2,040	222	189	156	123	90	57	24	0	0	0	0
2,040	2,080	228	195	162	129	96	63	30	0	0	0	0
2,080	2,120	234	201	168	135	102	69	36	3	0	0	0
2,120	2,160	240	207	174	141	108	75	42	9	0	0	0
2,160	2,200	246	213	180	147	114	81	48	15	0	0	0
2,200	2,240	252	219	186	153	120	87	54	21	0	0	0
2,240	2,280	258	225	192	159	126	93	60	27	0	0	0
2,280	2,320	264	231	198	165	132	99	66	33	0	0	0
2,320	2,360	270	237	204	171	138	105	72	39	5	0	0
2,360	2,400	276	243	210	177	144	111	78	45	11	0	0
2,400	2,440	282	249	216	183	150	117	84	51	17	0	0
2,440	2,480	288	255	222	189	156	123	90	57	23	0	0
2,480	2,520	294	261	228	195	162	129	96	63	29	0	0
2,520	2,560	300	267	234	201	168	135	102	69	35	2	0
2,560	2,600	306	273	240	207	174	141	108	75	41	8	0
2,600	2,640	312	279	246	213	180	147	114	81	47	14	0
2,640	2,680	318	285	252	219	186	153	120	87	53	20	0
2,680	2,720	324	291	258	225	192	159	126	93	59	26	0
2,720	2,760	330	297	264	231	198	165	132	99	65	32	0
2,760	2,800	336	303	270	237	204	171	138	105	71	38	5
2,800	2,840	342	309	276	243	210	177	144	111	77	44	11
2,840	2,880	348	315	282	249	216	183	150	117	83	50	17
2,880	2,920	354	321	288	255	222	189	156	123	89	56	23
2,920	2,960	360	327	294	261	228	195	162	129	95	62	29
2,960	3,000	366	333	300	267	234	201	168	135	101	68	35
3,000	3,040	372	339	306	273	240	207	174	141	107	74	41
3,040	3,080	378	345	312	279	246	213	180	147	113	80	47
3,080	3,120	384	351	318	285	252	219	186	153	119	86	53
3,120	3,160	390	357	324	291	258	225	192	159	125	92	59
3,160	3,200	396	363	330	297	264	231	198	165	131	98	65
3,200	3,240	402	369	336	303	270	237	204	171	137	104	71

▼ TABLE 13–6
Conversion Chart for 1997

Payroll Period	Amount of One Allowance
Daily	$ 10.19
Weekly	50.96
Biweekly	101.92
Semimonthly	110.42
Monthly	220.83
Quarterly	662.50
Semiannual	1,325.00
Annual	2,650.00

▼ TABLE 13–7
Table for Percentage Method of Withholding*

TABLE 4—MONTHLY Payroll Period

(a) SINGLE person (including head of household)—

If the amount of wages (after subtracting withholding allowances) is: The amount of income tax to withhold is:

Not over $221 . . . . $0

Over—	But not over—		of excess over—
$221	—$2,179	15%	—$221
$2,179	—$4,625	$293.70 plus 28%	—$2,179
$4,625	—$10,513	$978.58 plus 31%	—$4,625
$10,513	—$22,713	$2,803.86 plus 36%	—$10,513
$22,713	. . . . .	$7,195.86 plus 39.6%	—$22,713

(b) MARRIED person—

If the amount of wages (after subtracting withholding allowances) is: The amount of income tax to withhold is:

Not over $538 . . . . $0

Over—	But not over—		of excess over—
$538	—$3,788	15%	—$538
$3,788	—$7,738	$487.50 plus 28%	—$3,788
$7,738	—$13,000	$1,593.50 plus 31%	—$7,738
$13,000	—$22,942	$3,224.72 plus 36%	—$13,000
$22,942	. . . . .	$6,803.84 plus 39.6%	—$22,942

*This table is for wages paid in 1997.

(refer to Example 36). The difference occurs because the wage-bracket table amounts are derived by computing the withholding on the median wage within each bracket.

Reporting and Payment Procedures. Proper handling of employment taxes and income tax withholdings requires considerable compliance effort on the part of the employer. Among the Federal forms that have to be filed are the following:

Form Designation	Title
SS–4	Application for Employer Identification Number
W–2	Wage and Tax Statement
W–3	Transmittal of Wage and Tax Statements
940 or 940 EZ	Employer's Annual Federal Unemployment (FUTA) Tax Return
941	Employer's Quarterly Federal Tax Return

Form SS–4 is the starting point since it provides the employer with an identification number that must be used on all of the other forms filed with the IRS and the Social Security Administration. The number issued consists of nine digits and is hyphenated between the second and third digits (e.g., 72–1987316).

Form W–2 furnishes essential information to employees concerning wages paid, FICA, and income tax withholdings. Copies of Form W–2 are distributed to several parties for various purposes: to enable the employee to complete his or her income tax return, to inform the Social Security Administration of the amount of FICA wages earned by the employee, and to serve as a permanent record for the employer and employee of the payroll information contained on the form. Form W–2 must be furnished to an employee not later than January 31 of the following year. If an employee leaves a place of employment before the end of the year, Form W–2 can be given to him or her at any time after employment ends prior to the following January 31. However, if the terminated employee asks for Form W–2, it must be given to him or her within 30 days after the request or the final wage payment, whichever is later.

Form W–3 must accompany the copies of Forms W–2 filed by the employer with the Social Security Administration. Its basic purpose is to summarize and reconcile the amounts withheld for FICA and income taxes from *all* employees.

Form 940 (or Form 940 EZ) constitutes the employer's annual accounting for FUTA purposes. Generally, it must be filed on or before January 31 of the following year and must be accompanied by the payment of any undeposited FUTA due the Federal government.

Regardless of whether or not deposits[29] are required, most employers must settle their employment taxes every quarter. To do this, Form 941 must be filed on or before the last day of the month following the end of each calendar quarter.

Backup Withholding. Some types of payments made to individuals by banks or businesses are subject to backup withholding under certain conditions. Backup withholding is designed to ensure that income tax is collected on interest and other payments reported on a Form 1099. If backup withholding applies, the payer must withhold 31 percent of the gross amount. Backup withholding applies when the taxpayer does not give the business or bank his or her identification number in the required manner and in certain other situations.[30]

PROCEDURES APPLICABLE TO SELF-EMPLOYED PERSONS

6 LEARNING OBJECTIVE
Understand the payment procedures applicable to self-employed persons.

Although the following discussion largely centers on self-employed taxpayers, some of the procedures may be applicable to employed persons. In many cases, for example, employed persons may be required to pay estimated tax if they have income other than wages that is not subject to withholding. An employee may conduct a second trade or business in a self-employment capacity. Depending on the circumstances, the second job may require the payment of a self-employment tax. In addition, taxpayers whose income consists primarily of rentals, dividends, or interest (this list is not all-inclusive) may be required to pay estimated tax.

Estimated Tax for Individuals. **Estimated tax** is the amount of tax (including alternative minimum tax and self-employment tax) an individual expects to owe for the year after subtracting tax credits and income tax withheld. Any individual who has estimated tax for the year of $500 or more *and* whose withholding does not equal or exceed the required annual payment (discussed below) must make quarterly payments.[31] Otherwise, a penalty may be assessed. No quarterly payments are required (and no penalty will apply on an underpayment) if the taxpayer's estimated tax is under $500. No penalty will apply if the taxpayer had

---

[29] Deposit requirements are specified in each current issue of Circular E, *Employer's Tax Guide*, IRS Publication 15. Under current rules, most employers must make deposits on a monthly or semiweekly basis.

[30] § 3406(a).
[31] § 6654(c)(1).

no tax liability for the preceding tax year *and* the preceding tax year was a taxable year of 12 months *and* the taxpayer was a citizen or resident for the entire preceding tax year. In this regard, having no tax liability is not the same as having no additional tax to pay.

The required annual payment must first be computed. This is the *smaller* of the following amounts:

- Ninety percent of the tax shown on the current year's return.
- One hundred percent of the tax shown on the preceding year's return (the return must cover the full 12 months of the preceding year). The 100 percent requirement is increased to 110 percent if the AGI on the preceding year's return exceeds $150,000 ($75,000 if married filing separately).

In general, one-fourth of this required annual payment is due on April 15, June 15, and September 15 of the tax year and January 15 of the following year.

An equal part of withholding is deemed paid on each due date. Thus, the quarterly installment of the required annual payment reduced by the applicable withholding is the estimated tax to be paid. Payments are to be accompanied by the payment voucher for the appropriate date from Form 1040–ES.

Married taxpayers may make joint estimated tax payments even though a joint income tax return is not subsequently filed. In such event, the estimated tax payments may be applied against the separate return liability of the spouses as they see fit. If a husband and wife cannot agree on a division of the estimated tax payments, the Regulations provide that the payments are to be allocated in proportion to the tax liability on the separate returns.

Penalty on Underpayments. A nondeductible penalty is imposed on the amount of underpayment of estimated tax. The rate for this penalty is the same as the rate for underpayments of tax and is adjusted quarterly to reflect changes in the average prime rate.

An *underpayment* occurs when any installment (the sum of estimated tax paid and income tax withheld) is less than 25 percent of the required annual payment. The penalty is applied to the amount of the underpayment for the period of the underpayment.[32]

EXAMPLE 37

Marta made the following payments of estimated tax for 1997 and had no income tax withheld:

April 15, 1997	$1,400
June 16, 1997	2,300
September 15, 1997	1,500
January 15, 1998	1,800

Marta's actual tax for 1997 is $8,000, and her tax in 1996 was $10,000. Therefore, each installment should have been at least $1,800 [($8,000 × 90%) × 25%]. Of the payment on June 16, $400 will be credited to the unpaid balance of the first quarterly installment due on April 15,[33] thereby effectively stopping the underpayment penalty for the first quarterly period. Of the remaining $1,900 payment on June 16, $100 is credited to the September 15 payment, resulting in this third quarterly payment being $200 short. Then $200 of the January 15 payment is credited to the September 15 shortfall, ending the period of underpayment for

---

[32] § 6654(b)(2).
[33] Payments are credited to unpaid installments in the order in which the installments are required to be paid. § 6654(b)(3).

that portion due. The January 15, 1998, installment is now underpaid by $200, and a penalty will apply from January 15, 1998, to April 15, 1998 (unless paid sooner). Marta's underpayments for the periods of underpayment are as follows:

1st installment due:	$400 from April 15–June 16
2nd installment due:	Paid in full
3rd installment due:	$200 from September 15, 1997–January 15, 1998
4th installment due:	$200 from January 15–April 15, 1998

If a possible underpayment of estimated tax is indicated, Form 2210 (see Appendix B) should be filed to compute the penalty due or to justify that no penalty applies.

Self-Employment Tax. The tax on self-employment income is levied to provide Social Security and Medicare benefits (old age, survivors, and disability insurance and hospital insurance) for self-employed individuals. Individuals with net earnings of $400 or more from self-employment are subject to the **self-employment tax.**[34] For 1997, the self-employment tax is 15.3 percent on self-employment income up to $65,400 and 2.9 percent on self-employment income in excess of $65,400. In other words, for 1997 the self-employment tax is 12.4 percent of self-employment earnings up to $65,400 (for the Social Security portion) *plus* 2.9 percent of the total amount of self-employment earnings (for the Medicare portion)—see Table 13–8.

Currently, self-employed taxpayers are allowed a deduction from net earnings from self-employment, at one-half of the self-employment rate, for purposes of determining self-employment tax[35] *and* an income tax deduction for one-half the amount of self-employment tax paid.[36]

Determining the amount of self-employment tax to be paid for 1997 involves completing the steps in Figure 13–1. The result of step 3 or 4 is the amount of self-employment tax to be paid. For *income tax purposes,* the amount to be reported is net earnings from self-employment before the deduction for one-half of the self-employment tax. Then the taxpayer is allowed a deduction *for* AGI of one-half of the self-employment tax.

EXAMPLE 38

Using the format in Figure 13–1, the self-employment tax is determined for two taxpayers with net earnings from self-employment for 1997 as follows: Ned, $55,000 and Terry, $80,000.

TABLE 13–8
Self-Employment Tax: Social Security and Medicare Portions

Year		Tax Rate	Ceiling Amount
1997	Social Security portion	12.4%	$65,400
	Medicare portion	2.9%	Unlimited
	Aggregate rate	15.3%	
1996	Social Security portion	12.4%	$62,700
	Medicare portion	2.9%	Unlimited
	Aggregate rate	15.3%	

[34] § 6017.
[35] § 1402(a)(12).
[36] § 164(f).

▼ FIGURE 13–1
1997 Self-Employment Tax Worksheet

1. Net earnings from self-employment. _____
2. Multiply line 1 by 92.35%. _____
3. If the amount on line 2 is $65,400 or less, multiply the line 2 amount by 15.3%. This is the self-employment tax. _____
4. If the amount on line 2 is more than $65,400, multiply the excess of line 2 over $65,400 by 2.9% and add $10,006.20. This is the self-employment tax. _____

Ned's Self-Employment Tax Worksheet

1. Net earnings from self-employment.	$ 55,000.00
2. Multiply line 1 by 92.35%.	$ 50,792.50
3. If the amount on line 2 is $65,400 or less, multiply the line 2 amount by 15.3%. This is the self-employment tax.	$ 7,771.25
4. If the amount on line 2 is more than $65,400, multiply the excess over $65,400 by 2.9% and add $10,006.20. This is the self-employment tax.	

Terry's Self-Employment Tax Worksheet

1. Net earnings from self-employment.	$ 80,000.00
2. Multiply line 1 by 92.35%.	$ 73,880.00
3. If the amount on line 2 is $65,400 or less, multiply the line 2 amount by 15.3%. This is the self-employment tax.	
4. If the amount on line 2 is more than $65,400, multiply the excess over $65,400 by 2.9% and add $10,006.20. This is the self-employment tax.	$ 10,252.12

For income tax purposes, Ned has net earnings from self-employment of $55,000 and a deduction *for* AGI of $3,885.63 (one-half of $7,771.25). Terry has net earnings from self-employment of $80,000 and a deduction *for* AGI of $5,126.06 (one-half of $10,252.12). Both taxpayers benefit from the deduction for one-half of the self-employment tax paid. ▼

For 1996, the self-employment tax computations are similar to those for 1997. The only difference is that the tax base was lower for 1996 than it is for 1997 (see Table 13–8 and Figure 13–2).

If an individual also receives wages subject to FICA tax, the ceiling amount of the Social Security portion on which the self-employment tax is computed is reduced. Thus, self-employment tax may be reduced if a self-employed individual also receives FICA wages in excess of the ceiling amount.

EXAMPLE 39

In 1997, Kelly had $45,000 of net earnings from the conduct of a bookkeeping service (trade or business activity). She also received wages as an employee amounting to $25,000 during the year. The amount of Kelly's self-employment income subject to the Social Security portion (12.4%) is $40,400 ($65,400 − $25,000), producing a tax of $5,009.60 ($40,400 × 12.4%). All of Kelly's net self-employment earnings are subject to the Medicare portion of the self-employment tax of 2.9%. Therefore, the self-employment tax on this portion is $1,205.18 ($41,558 × 2.9%).

▼ FIGURE 13-2
1996 Self-Employment Tax Worksheet

1. Net earnings from self-employment. _____
2. Multiply line 1 by 92.35%. _____
3. If the amount on line 2 is $62,700 or less, multiply the line 2 amount by 15.3%. This is the self-employment tax. _____
4. If the amount on line 2 is more than $62,700, multiply the excess of line 2 over $62,700 by 2.9% and add $9,593.10. This is the self-employment tax. _____

	Social Security Portion
Ceiling amount	$ 65,400
Less: FICA wages	(25,000)
Net ceiling	$ 40,400
Net self-employment income ($45,000 × 92.35%)	$ 41,558
Lesser of net ceiling or net self-employment income	$ 40,400

Net earnings from self-employment include gross income from a trade or business less allowable trade or business deductions, the distributive share of any partnership income or loss derived from a trade or business activity, and net income from the rendering of personal services as an independent contractor. Gain or loss from the disposition of property (including involuntary conversions) is excluded from the computation of self-employment income unless the property involved is inventory.

FOREIGN TAX CREDIT

TAX PLANNING CONSIDERATIONS

7 LEARNING OBJECTIVE
Identify tax planning opportunities related to tax credits and payment procedures.

A U.S. citizen or resident working abroad (commonly referred to as an *expatriate*) may elect to take either a foreign tax credit or the foreign earned income exclusion. In cases where the income tax of a foreign country is higher than the U.S. income tax, the credit choice usually is preferable. If the reverse is true, electing the foreign earned income exclusion probably reduces the overall tax burden.

Unfortunately, the choice between the credit and the earned income exclusion is not without some limitations. The election of the foreign earned income exclusion, once made, can be revoked for a later year. However, once revoked, the earned income exclusion will not be available for a period of five years unless the IRS consents to an earlier date. This will create a dilemma for expatriates whose job assignments over several years shift between low- and high-bracket countries.

EXAMPLE 40
In 1996, Ira, a calendar year taxpayer, is sent by his employer to Saudi Arabia (a low-tax country). For 1996, therefore, Ira elects the foreign earned income exclusion. In 1997, Ira's employer transfers him to France (a high-tax country). Accordingly, he revokes the foreign earned income exclusion election for 1997 and chooses instead to use the foreign tax credit. If Ira is transferred back to Saudi Arabia (or any other low-tax country) within five years, he may not utilize the foreign earned income exclusion. ▼

CREDIT FOR CHILD AND DEPENDENT CARE EXPENSES

A taxpayer may incur employment-related expenses that also qualify as medical expenses (e.g., a nurse is hired to provide in-the-home care for an ill and incapacitated dependent parent). Such expenses may be either deducted as medical expenses (subject to the 7.5 percent limitation) or utilized in determining the credit for child and dependent care expenses. If the credit for child and dependent care expenses is chosen and the employment-related expenses exceed the limitation ($2,400, $4,800, or earned income, as the case may be), the excess may be considered a medical expense. If, however, the taxpayer chooses to deduct qualified employment-related expenses as medical expenses, any portion that is not deductible because of the 7.5 percent limitation may not be used in computing the credit for child and dependent care expenses.

EXAMPLE 41

Alicia, a single taxpayer, has the following tax position for the current tax year.

Adjusted gross income		$30,000
Potential itemized deductions *from* AGI—		
Other than medical expenses	$3,500	
Medical expenses	6,000	$ 9,500

All of Alicia's medical expenses were incurred to provide nursing care for her disabled father while she was working. The father lives with Alicia and qualifies as her dependent. ▼

What should Alicia do in this situation? One approach would be to use $2,400 of the nursing care expenses to obtain the maximum credit for child and dependent care expenses allowed of $480 (20% × $2,400). The balance of these expenses should be claimed as medical expenses. After a reduction of 7.5 percent of AGI, this would produce a medical expense deduction of $1,350 [$3,600 (remaining medical expenses) − (7.5% × $30,000)].

Another approach would be to claim the full $6,000 as a medical expense and forgo the credit for child and dependent care expenses. After the 7.5 percent adjustment of $2,250 (7.5% × $30,000), a deduction of $3,750 remains.

The choice, then, is between a credit of $480 plus a deduction of $1,350 or a credit of $0 plus a deduction of $3,750. Which is better, of course, depends on the relative tax savings involved.

One of the traditional goals of *family tax planning* is to minimize the total tax burden within the family unit. With proper planning and implementation, the credit for child and dependent care expenses can be used to help achieve this goal. For example, payments to certain relatives for the care of qualifying dependents and children qualify for the credit if the care provider is *not* a dependent of the taxpayer or the taxpayer's spouse or is *not* a child (under age 19) of the taxpayer. Thus, if the care provider is in a lower tax bracket than the taxpayer, the following benefits result:

- Income is shifted to a lower-bracket family member.
- The taxpayer qualifies for the credit for child and dependent care expenses.

In addition, the goal of minimizing the family income tax liability can be enhanced in some other situations, but only if the credit's limitations are recognized and avoided. For example, tax savings may still be enjoyed even if the qualifying expenditures incurred by a cash basis taxpayer have already reached the annual ceiling ($2,400 or $4,800). To the extent that any additional payments can be shifted into future tax years, the benefit from the credit may be preserved on these excess expenditures.

EXAMPLE 42

Andre, a calendar year and cash basis taxpayer, has spent $2,400 by December 1 on qualifying child care expenditures for his dependent 11-year-old son. The $200 that is due the care provider for child care services rendered in December does not generate a tax credit benefit if the amount is paid in the current year because the $2,400 ceiling has been reached. However, if the payment can be delayed until the next year, the total credit over the two-year period for which Andre is eligible may be increased. ▼

A similar shifting of expenditures to a subsequent year may be wise if the potential credit otherwise generated would exceed the tax liability available to absorb the credit.

ADJUSTMENTS TO INCREASE WITHHOLDING

The penalty for underpayment of estimated tax by individuals is computed for each quarter of the tax year. A taxpayer can play *catch-up* to a certain extent. Each quarterly payment is credited to the unpaid portion of any previous required installment. Thus, the penalty stops on that portion of the underpayment for the previous quarter. Since income tax withheld is assumed to have been paid evenly throughout the year and is allocated equally among the four installments in computing any penalty, a taxpayer who would otherwise be subject to a penalty for underpayment should increase withholdings late in the year. This can be done by changing the number of allowances claimed on Form W–4 or by special arrangement with the employer to increase the amount withheld.

A similar way to avoid (or reduce) a penalty for underpayment is to have the employer continue Social Security withholding beyond the base amount.

EXAMPLE 43

Rose, a calendar year taxpayer, earns $72,000 from her job. In late August 1997, she realizes that she will be subject to a penalty for underpayment of estimated tax due to income from outside sources. Consequently, she instructs her employer to continue FICA withholdings for the rest of 1997. If this is done, an extra $6,600 [$72,000 (annual salary) − $65,400 (base amount of the Social Security portion for 1997)] will be subject to the 6.2% Social Security portion of the FICA tax [7.65% (total FICA rate) − 1.45% (Medicare portion of the FICA rate)]. Thus, Rose generates an additional $409 (6.2% × $6,600) that will be deemed withheld ratably during 1997. ▼

ADJUSTMENTS TO AVOID OVERWITHHOLDING

Publication 505, Tax Withholding and Estimated Tax, contains worksheets that taxpayers may use to take advantage of special provisions for avoiding overwithholding. Extra exemptions for withholding purposes are allowed if the taxpayer has unusually large itemized deductions, deductions *for* AGI, or tax credits. Net losses from Schedules C, D, E, and F may be considered in computing the number of extra withholding exemptions. Net operating loss carryovers may also be considered in the computation. A taxpayer who is entitled to extra withholding exemptions for any of these reasons should file a new Form W–4, Employee's Withholding Allowance Certificate, with his or her employer.

KEY TERMS

Adoption expenses credit, 13–19

Business energy credits, 13–9

Credit for child and dependent care expenses, 13–20

Disabled access credit, 13–13

Earned income credit, 13–14

Employment taxes, 13–22

Estimated tax, 13–33

Foreign tax credit (FTC), 13–18

General business credit, 13–6

Low-income housing credit, 13–12

Nonrefundable credits, 13–5

Refundable credits, 13–5

Rehabilitation expenditures credit, 13–7

Rehabilitation expenditures credit recapture, 13–8

Research activities credit, 13–10

Self-employment tax, 13–35

Tax credits, 13–2

Tax credit for the elderly or disabled, 13–16

Withholding allowances, 13–29

Work opportunity tax credit, 13–9

PROBLEM MATERIALS

DISCUSSION QUESTIONS

1. Would an individual taxpayer receive greater benefit from deducting an expenditure or from taking a credit equal to 25% of the expenditure?

2. What is a refundable credit? Give examples. What is a nonrefundable credit? Give examples.

3. Discuss the order in which credits are offset against the tax liability. Why is the order in which credits are utilized important?

4. Discuss the treatment of unused general business credits.

5. John graduated from college several years ago with high hopes and expectations of enjoying a very successful business career. Almost as soon as he completed his final exams, he borrowed over $250,000 from a local bank (the loan was guaranteed by his parents) in order to make several "hot" investments. The investments, as expected, spun off huge tax losses and tax credits in their early years. More recently, however, John has begun to have doubts as to the wisdom of these investments as they have not begun to generate profits as promised. As a result, he is contemplating selling the investments, at yet another loss. Because his investments have not as yet produced any profits to support his lifestyle, he has been forced to live at home with his parents. Identify the relevant tax issues.

6. Vic is considering the purchase and renovation of an old building. He has heard about the tax credit for rehabilitation expenditures but does not know the specific rules applicable to the credit. He has asked you to explain the most important details to him. What will you tell Vic?

7. If property on which the tax credit for rehabilitation expenditures was claimed is prematurely disposed of or ceases to be qualified property, how is the tax liability affected in the year of the disposition or disqualification?

8. Discuss the purpose of the work opportunity tax credit. Who receives the tax benefits from the credit? Give examples of the types of individuals who, if hired, give rise to the credit.

9. What credit provisions in the tax law were enacted to encourage technological development in the United States?

10. Explain the alternatives a taxpayer has in claiming the deduction and credit for research and experimentation expenditures incurred.

11. Explain the purpose of the disabled access credit and describe the general characteristics of its computation.

12. Identify several examples of the type of structural changes to a building that qualify for the disabled access credit.

13. What three tests must be met for a child to be considered a qualifying child for purposes of the earned income credit? Describe.

14. Briefly discuss the requirements that must be satisfied for a taxpayer to qualify for the earned income tax credit.

15. Individuals who receive substantial Social Security benefits are usually not eligible for the tax credit for the elderly or disabled because these benefits effectively eliminate the base upon which the credit is computed. Explain.

16. What purpose is served by the overall limitation to the foreign tax credit?

17. Do all foreign taxes qualify for the U.S. foreign tax credit? Explain.

18. In general, when would an individual taxpayer find it more beneficial to take advantage of the foreign earned income exclusion rather than the foreign tax credit in computing his or her income tax liability?

19. Sally was recently called into the partner's office and offered a one-year assignment in her public accounting firm's Prague office. Realizing Sally will face incremental expenses while in Prague, such as for foreign income taxes and rent, the firm will try to make her "whole" from a financial perspective by increasing her salary to help offset the expenses she will incur while living overseas. If Sally takes the assignment, she will likely rent her personal residence and sell several major tangible assets such as her personal automobile. Identify the relevant tax issues.

20. Discuss, in general, the calculation of the adoption expenses credit.

21. Pete is not concerned about the credit for child and dependent care expenses because his AGI is considerably in excess of $20,000. Is Pete under a misconception regarding the tax law? Explain.

22. Polly and her spouse, Leo, file a joint return and expect to report AGI of $45,000 in the current year. Polly's employer offers a child and dependent care reimbursement plan that allows up to $2,500 of qualifying expenses to be reimbursed in exchange for a $2,500 reduction in the employee's salary. Because Polly and Leo have one minor child requiring child care that costs $2,500 each year, she is wondering if she should sign up for the program instead of taking advantage of the credit for child and dependent care expenses. Assuming Polly and Leo are in the 28% tax bracket, analyze the effect of the two alternatives. How would your answer differ if Polly and Leo's AGI was $20,000 instead of $45,000?

23. Discuss the rationale underlying the enactment of the following tax credits:
    a. Tax credit for rehabilitation expenditures.
    b. Low-income housing credit.
    c. Disabled access credit.
    d. Earned income credit.
    e. Foreign tax credit.
    f. Credit for child and dependent care expenses.

24. Sam and Martha have two preschool-age children. On several occasions during the current year, Sam and Martha took out-of-town trips due to Sam's business. While Sam and Martha were out of town, a 14-year-old neighbor cared for the children during the

day; at night, they stayed with their grandparents. Sam and Martha had a neighborhood teenager mow their lawn, but only once, because of the damage he did to Martha's flower garden. On a later out-of-town trip, they hired a professional lawn service to mow the lawn. Identify the relevant tax issues.

25. Elaborate rules exist that require employers to prepay various types of Federal taxes. Summarize the major issues that an employer must resolve if it is to comply with the requirements.

26. At a social function you attended in early July of 1997, you overhear a guest, the CEO of a corporation, remark, "Thank goodness this is the end of FICA for a while!" Interpret this remark.

27. Keith, a sole proprietor, owns and operates a grocery store. Keith's wife and his 17-year-old son work in the business and are paid wages. Will the wife and son be subject to FICA? Explain.

28. Although Vicki is entitled to four allowances, she claimed just one on her Form W–4.
    a. Why would Vicki claim fewer allowances than she is entitled to?
    b. Is this procedure permissible?
    c. Will this affect the number of personal and dependency exemptions Vicki can claim on her Federal income tax return?

29. Under what circumstances will the special withholding allowance be allowed for purposes of determining income tax withholding?

30. Describe the exposure (i.e., wage base and tax rate) that a self-employed individual has to the self-employment tax for 1997.

31. You read that self-employed taxpayers get a double deduction for one-half of the self-employment tax, not only as a deduction in computing the self-employment tax but also as a deduction *for* AGI. Is this true? Explain.

PROBLEMS

32. Carol has a tentative general business credit of $110,000 for 1997. Her net regular tax liability before the general business credit is $125,000, and her tentative minimum tax is $100,000. Compute Carol's allowable general business credit for the year.

33. Tan Corporation has the following general business credit carryovers:

1993	$10,000
1994	30,000
1995	10,000
1996	40,000
Total carryovers	$90,000

    If the general business credit generated by activities during 1997 equals $90,000 and the total credit allowed during the current year is $160,000 (based on tax liability), what amounts of the current general business credit and carryovers are utilized against the 1997 income tax liability? What is the amount of unused credit carried forward to 1998?

34. In January 1995, William purchased and placed into service a pre-1936 building that houses retail businesses. The cost was $200,000, of which $25,000 applied to the land. In modernizing the facility, William incurred $250,000 of renovations costs of the type that qualify for the rehabilitation credit. These improvements were placed into service in October 1997.
    a. Compute William's rehabilitation tax credit for 1997.
    b. Calculate the cost recovery deductions for the building and the renovation costs for 1997.

35. In the current year, Diane Lawson (123 Sunview Avenue, Jacksonville, FL 32231) acquires a qualifying historic structure for $250,000 (excluding the cost of land) with full

intentions of substantially rehabilitating the building. Write a letter to Diane and a memo to the tax files explaining the computation that determines the rehabilitation tax credit available to her and the impact on the depreciable basis, assuming either $245,000 or $255,000 is incurred for the rehabilitation project. Because Diane must decide whether to pursue the renovation plan costing $245,000 or the one costing $255,000, you should indicate in the letter and the memo the differences in cash flow to Diane arising from the tax consequences associated with the two renovation projects.

36. Red Company hires six individuals on January 15, 1997, qualifying Red for the work opportunity tax credit. Three of these individuals receive wages of $7,000 each during 1997 while the other three receive wages of $5,000 each.
    a. Calculate the amount of Red's work opportunity tax credit for 1997.
    b. Assume Red pays total wages of $120,000 to its employees during the year. How much of this amount is deductible in 1997 if the work opportunity tax credit is taken?

37. Matt, a calendar year taxpayer, informs you that during the year he incurs expenditures of $30,000 that qualify for the incremental research activities credit. In addition, it is determined that his base amount for the year is $22,800.
    a. Determine Matt's incremental research activities credit for the year.
    b. Matt is in the 28% tax bracket. Determine which approach to the research expenditures and the research activities credit (other than capitalization and subsequent amortization) would provide the greatest tax benefit to Matt.

38. In her eligible small business, Pat incurred the following expenditures during the current year to comply with the Americans with Disabilities Act:

Widening doorways and hallways	$8,000
Installing ramps	3,000

    These renovations were made to Pat's office building, which has been used in the business since 1975. Calculate the amount of the disabled access credit available to Pat's business.

39. Ahmed Zinna (16 Southside Drive, Charlotte, NC 28204), one of your clients, owns two retail establishments in downtown Charlotte, North Carolina, and has come to you seeking advice concerning the tax consequences of complying with the Americans with Disabilities Act. He understands that he needs to install various features at his stores (e.g., ramps, doorways, and restrooms that are handicapped accessible) to make them more accessible to disabled individuals. He inquires whether any tax credits will be available to help offset the cost of the necessary changes. He estimates the cost of the planned changes to his facilities as follows:

Location	Projected Cost
Oak Street	$18,000
Maple Avenue	8,000

    He reminds you that the Oak Street store was constructed in 1995 while the Maple Avenue store is in a building that was constructed in 1902. Ahmed operates his business as a sole proprietorship and has approximately eight employees at each location. Write a letter to Ahmed in which you summarize your conclusions concerning the tax consequences of his proposed capital improvements.

40. Which of the following individuals qualify for the earned income credit for 1997?
    a. Eduardo is single, 19 years of age, and has no dependents. His income consists of $8,000 of wages.
    b. Kate maintains a household for a dependent 12-year-old son and is eligible for head-of-household tax rates. Her income consists of $10,500 of salary and $300 of taxable interest.

c. Keith and Susan are married and file a joint return. Keith and Susan have no dependents. Their combined income consists of $18,500 of salary and $100 of taxable interest. Adjusted gross income is $18,600.
d. George is a 26-year-old single taxpayer. He has no dependents and generates earnings of $9,000.

41. Irene and Jerome, who qualify for the earned income credit, have one qualifying child who lives with them. Irene and Jerome earn salaries aggregating $20,000 during 1997. Calculate their earned income credit for the year.

42. Vern, a widower, lives in an apartment with his three minor children (ages 3, 4, and 5) whom he supports. Vern earned $19,500 during 1997. He contributed $500 to an IRA and uses the standard deduction. Calculate the amount, if any, of Vern's earned income credit.

43. Joyce, a widow, lives in an apartment with her two minor children (ages 8 and 10) whom she supports. Joyce earns $25,800 during 1997. She uses the standard deduction.
    a. Calculate the amount, if any, of Joyce's earned income credit.
    b. During the year, Joyce is offered a new job that has greater future potential than her current job. If she accepts the job offer, her earnings for the year would be $29,300; however, she will not qualify for the earned income credit. Using after-tax cash-flow calculations, determine whether Joyce should accept the new job offer.

44. Joe, age 68, and Emily, age 69, are married retirees who receive the following income and retirement benefits during the current year:

Fully taxable pension from Joe's former employer	$ 5,000
Dividends and interest	8,000
Social Security benefits	1,750
Total	$14,750

Assume Joe and Emily file a joint return, have no deductions *for* AGI, and do not itemize. Are they eligible for the tax credit for the elderly? If so, calculate the amount of the credit assuming their tax liability (before credits) is $150.

45. Kim, a U.S. citizen and resident, owns and operates a novelty goods business. During 1997, Kim has taxable income of $100,000, made up as follows: $50,000 from foreign sources and $50,000 from U.S. sources. In calculating taxable income, the standard deduction is used. The income from foreign sources is subject to foreign income taxes of $26,000. For 1997, Kim files a joint return claiming his three children as dependents.
    a. Assuming Kim chooses to claim the foreign taxes as an income tax credit, what is his income tax liability for 1997?
    b. Recently, Kim has become disenchanted with the location of his business and is considering moving his foreign operation to a different country. Based on his research, if he moves his business to his country of choice, all relevant revenues and costs would remain approximately the same except that the income taxes payable to that country would be only $10,000. Given that all of the foreign income taxes paid are available to offset the U.S. tax liability (whether he operates in a high-tax or a low-tax foreign jurisdiction), what impact will this have on his decision regarding the potential move?

46. Purple Corporation is an international wholesaler headquartered in the United States. Of its worldwide taxable income of $3 billion, $1.25 billion is foreign-sourced. Before any credits, Purple's U.S. income tax liability is $1.05 billion. If income taxes paid to foreign countries totaled $600 million, what is Purple's U.S. income tax liability after benefiting from the foreign tax credit?

47. Ann and Bill had been on the list of a local adoption agency for several years seeking to adopt a child. Finally, in 1997, good news came their way and an adoption seemed

imminent. They paid qualified adoption expenses of $2,000 in 1997 and $4,000 in 1998. Assume the adoption becomes final in 1998. Ann and Bill always file a joint income tax return.
   a. Determine the amount of the adoption expenses credit available to Ann and Bill assuming their combined annual income is $50,000. What year(s) will they benefit from the credit?
   b. Assuming Ann and Bill's modified AGI in 1997 and 1998 is $100,000, calculate the amount of the adoption expense credit.

48. Pat and Jeri are husband and wife, and both are gainfully employed. They have three children under the age of 13. During the current year, Pat earned $15,000, while Jeri earned $4,900. In order for them to work, they paid $5,800 to various unrelated parties to care for their children. Assuming Pat and Jeri file a joint return and their AGI is $20,000, what, if any, is their credit for child and dependent care expenses for the current year?

49. Jim and Jill are husband and wife and have two dependent children under the age of 13. They both are gainfully employed and during the current year earned salaries as follows: $12,000 (Jim) and $4,500 (Jill). To care for their children while they work, they pay Megan (Jim's mother) $5,600. Megan does not qualify as a dependent of Jim and Jill. Assuming Jim and Jill file a joint return, what, if any, is their credit for child and dependent care expenses?

50. Kevin and Jane are husband and wife and have one dependent child, age 9. Kevin is a full-time student for all of the current year, while Jane earns $18,000 as a nurse's aid. In order to provide care for their child while Kevin attends classes and Jane works, they pay Sara (Jane's 17-year-old sister) $2,300. Sara is not a dependent of Kevin and Jane. Assuming Kevin and Jane file a joint return, what, if any, is their credit for child and dependent care expenses?

51. In each of the following independent situations, determine the amount of FICA that should be withheld from the employee's 1997 salary by the employer:
   a. Harry earns a $40,000 salary, files a joint return, and claims four withholding allowances.
   b. Hazel earns a $80,000 salary, files a joint return, and claims four withholding allowances.
   c. Tracy earns a $160,000 salary, files a joint return, and claims four withholding allowances.
   d. Alicia's 17-year-old son, Carlos, earns $5,000 at the family business.

52. During 1997, Greg Cruz (1401 Orangedale Road, Troy, MI 48084) worked for Maple Corporation and Gray Company. He earned $60,000 at Maple Corporation where he was a full-time employee. Greg also worked part-time for Gray Company for wages of $30,000.
   a. Did Greg experience an overwithholding of FICA taxes? Write a letter to Greg and a memo for the tax files in which you explain your conclusion.
   b. Did Maple Corporation and Gray Company overpay the employer's portion of FICA? Explain.

53. In each of the following independent situations, determine the maximum withholding allowances permitted Eli (an employee) on Form W–4:
   a. Eli is single with no dependents.
   b. Eli is married to a nonemployed spouse, and they have no dependents.
   c. Eli is married to Vera, an employed spouse, and they have three dependent children. On the Form W–4 that she filed with the employer, Vera claimed zero allowances.
   d. Assume the same facts as in (c), except that Eli and Vera fully support Eli's mother, who lives with them. The mother (age 70 and blind) qualifies as their dependent. (Refer to Chapter 3.)
   e. Eli is single with no dependents but works for two employers, one on a full-time basis and the other on a part-time basis. The Form W–4 filed with the first employer

(the full-time job) reflects two withholding exemptions. The wages from each job exceed $1,000.

f. Assume the same facts as in (e), except that Eli is married to a nonemployed spouse.

54. Norm is married to a nonemployed spouse and has four dependents. He is employed by Beige Corporation and is paid a monthly salary of $2,620 ($31,440 per year). Using these facts, determine the amount to be withheld by Beige Corporation for Federal income tax purposes under the wage-bracket tables and under the percentage method for 1997.

55. Samantha, being self-employed, is required to make estimated payments of her tax liability for the year. Her tax liability for 1996 was $15,000. For 1997, Samantha ultimately determines that her income tax liability is $18,000. During the year, however, she made the following payments, totaling $13,000:

April 15, 1997	$ 4,500
June 16, 1997	2,800
September 15, 1997	4,100
January 15, 1998	1,600
	$13,000

Because she prepaid so little of her ultimate income tax liability, she now realizes that she may be subject to the penalty for underpayment of estimated tax. Determine Samantha's exposure to the penalty for underpayment of estimated tax.

56. During 1997, Helen, the owner of a store, had the following income and expenses:

Gross profit on sales	$63,000
Income from part-time job (subject to FICA)	24,000
Business expenses (related to store)	15,000
Fire loss on store building	1,200
Dividend income	200
Long-term capital gain on the sale of a stock investment	2,000

Compute Helen's self-employment tax using the format illustrated in the text.

57. In 1997, Fran has self-employed earnings of $150,000. Compute Fran's self-employment tax liability and the allowable income tax deduction for the self-employment tax paid using the format illustrated in the text.

CUMULATIVE PROBLEMS

58. Wade and Jane London are married and file a joint return. His Social Security number is 222-33-1111 and her Social Security number is 111-22-5555. They reside at 100 Olive Lane, Covington, LA 70400. They have two dependent children, Sean and Debra, ages 12 and 16, respectively. Wade is a self-employed businessman (sole proprietor of an unincorporated business), and Jane is a corporate executive. Wade has the following income and expenses from his business:

| Gross income | $280,000 |
| Business expenses | 166,000 |

Records related to Jane's employment provide the following information:

Salary	$130,000
Unreimbursed travel expenses (including $200 of meals)	1,000
Unreimbursed entertainment expenses	600

Other pertinent information relating to 1997 follows:

Proceeds from sale of stock acquired on July 15, 1997 (cost of $10,000) and sold on August 1	$ 8,000
Proceeds from sale of stock acquired on September 18, 1994 (cost of $6,000) and sold on October 5	4,800
Wages paid to full-time domestic worker for housekeeping and child supervision	10,000
Dividends ($6,000) and interest ($2,000) received	8,000
Total itemized deductions (not including any potential deductions above)	26,900
Federal income tax withheld	29,000
Estimated payments on Federal income tax	43,000

Compute the net tax payable or refund due for Wade and Jane London for 1997. Suggested software (if available): *TurboTax* or *MacInTax*.

59. Beth R. Jordan lives at 2322 Skyview Road, Mesa, AZ 85202. She is a tax accountant with Mesa Manufacturing Company. She also writes computer software programs for tax practitioners and has a part-time tax practice. Beth, age 35, is single and has no dependents. Her Social Security number is 111–35–2222. She wants to contribute $3 to the Presidential Election Campaign Fund.

During 1996, Beth earned a salary of $50,000 from her employer. She received interest of $290 from Home Federal Savings and Loan and $335 from Home State Bank. She received dividends of $500 from Gray Corporation, $400 from Blue Corporation, and $300 from Orange Corporation.

Beth received a $1,200 income tax refund from the state of Arizona on May 12, 1996. On her 1995 Federal income tax return, she reported total itemized deductions of $6,700, which included $2,000 of state income tax withheld by her employer.

Fees earned from her part-time tax practice in 1996 totaled $3,800. She paid $400 to have the tax returns processed by a computerized tax return service.

On February 1, 1996, Beth bought 500 shares of Gray Corporation common stock for $17.60 a share. On July 16, Beth sold the stock for $15 a share.

Beth bought a used utility vehicle for $3,000 on June 5, 1996. She purchased the vehicle from her brother-in-law, who was unemployed and was in need of cash. On November 2, 1996, she sold the vehicle to a friend for $3,400.

On January 2, 1985, Beth acquired 100 shares of Blue Corporation common stock for $30 a share. She sold the stock on December 19, 1996, for $75 a share.

During 1996, Beth received royalties of $14,000 on a software program she had written. Beth incurred the following expenditures in connection with her software-writing activities:

Cost of microcomputer (100% business use)	$7,000
Cost of printer (100% business use)	2,000
Furniture	3,000
Supplies	650
Fee paid to computer consultant	3,500

Beth elected to expense the maximum portion of the cost of the microcomputer, printer, and furniture allowed under the provisions of § 179. This equipment and furniture were placed in service on January 15, 1996.

Although her employer suggested that Beth attend a convention on current developments in corporate taxation, Beth was not reimbursed for the travel expenses of $1,420 she incurred in attending the convention. The $1,420 included $200 for the cost of meals.

During 1996, Beth paid $300 for prescription medicines and $2,875 in doctor bills, hospital bills, and medical insurance premiums. Her employer withheld state income tax of $1,954. Beth paid real property taxes of $1,766 on her home. Interest on her home mortgage was $3,845, and interest to credit card companies was $320. Beth contributed $20 each week to her church and $10 each week to the United Way. Professional dues and subscriptions totaled $350.

Beth's employer withheld Federal income taxes of $9,500 during 1996. Beth paid estimated taxes of $1,600. What is the amount of Beth's net tax payable or refund due for 1996? If Beth has a tax refund due, she wants to have it credited toward her 1997 income tax. If you use tax forms for your solution, you will need Forms 1040, 2106, and 4562 and Schedules A, B, C, D, and SE. Suggested software (if available): *TurboTax* or *MacInTax*.

RESEARCH PROBLEMS

*Note: **West's Federal Taxation on CD-ROM** can be used in preparing solutions to the Research Problems. Alternatively, tax research materials contained in a standard tax library can be used.*

Research Problem 1. A friend of yours, George Daley, who works full-time as an electrical engineer at the Johnson Space Center in Houston, Texas, approaches you about the tax implications of a decision that is on his mind. He explains that earlier in the year he inherited a working farm in Alabama from his father and now must decide whether to keep the farm going. George feels that giving up his secure, rewarding job in Houston to become an Alabama farmer is not in his best interests. Attempting to be a weekend farmer is also out of the question. The farm has been in his family for generations, and for sentimental reasons, George is hesitant to sell it. George has contacted a local farmer whom the family has known for years and has asked if he would be interested in sharecropping the land (i.e., George and the farmer would share the profits from the farming operation conducted by the local farmer). They have tentatively negotiated a satisfactory arrangement, particularly given George's inability to visit the farm regularly and his strong desire to keep the farm going and in his family. However, George is concerned that any income generated under such an arrangement would be subject to the self-employment tax in addition to the Federal income tax. George has decided that if he has to pay the self-employment tax, he will look at other options and will not pursue the sharecropping arrangement. What will George decide?

Research Problem 2. Sandy and John Via (12 Maple Avenue, Albany, NY 12205) are married, file a joint Federal income tax return, and have a 12-year-old son and a 10-year-old daughter. Sandy is currently in the U.S. Air Force and has been stationed in Germany for the entire year. John and their children have remained in the United States where John picks up work only on an irregular basis. In working on their Federal income tax return for 1996, John wonders if they qualify for the earned income credit. Sandy's income consists of salary of $18,000 (taxable) and food and lodging provided by the Air Force, valued at $7,000 (not taxable), while John's earnings for the current year total $5,000. John approaches you and asks your advice. Write a letter to Sandy and John that contains your conclusion and prepare a memo for the tax files.

Research Problem 3. Isabella, a lover of early twentieth-century American history and architecture, discovers a 1920s house in a downtown district of Atlanta during a recent visit. She decides not only to purchase and renovate this particular home, but also to move the structure to her hometown of Little Rock, Arkansas, so her community can enjoy its architectural features. Also, being aware of the availability of the tax credit for rehabilitation expenditures incurred on old structures, she wants to maximize her use of the provision once the renovation work begins in Arkansas. Comment on whether the renovation expenditures incurred will qualify for the tax credit for rehabilitation expenditures.

Research Problem 4. On graduating from the University of the Southeast with a Ph.D. in neurology, Sally learns that she has been awarded a postdoctoral fellowship from the university. This grant will enable her to pursue further study in her area of expertise dealing with the potential regeneration of atrophied nerve tissue. Besides the honor that the fellowship represents, Sally is excited about the opportunity to continue her studies, completely independent of the grantor. There is no requirement that Sally provide any services to the university in exchange for the grant. As she has been informed by the university's business office that she will receive a Form 1099–MISC at year-end reporting the grant proceeds as "nonemployee compensation," Sally is fully aware that the grant will be subject to Federal income taxation. However, the business office does not mention any exposure to the self-employment tax. Since the research grant proceeds will be reported to the IRS as "nonemployee compensation," Sally wonders whether she will be subject to the self-employment tax. What do you tell her?

Use the tax resources of the internet to address the following questions. Do not restrict your search to the World Wide Web, but include a review of newsgroups and general reference materials, practitioner sites and resources, primary sources of the tax law, chat rooms and discussion groups, and other opportunities.

Research Problem 5. Find several news reports concerning the government's effort to extend the use of the earned income credit to more of the taxpayers who qualify for it. Which agencies in your area are involved in this effort?

Research Problem 6. The foreign tax credit is especially valuable when a U.S. individual works in a country whose marginal income tax rates exceed those of the United States. List five countries whose tax rates on individuals exceed those of the U.S., and five where the corresponding U.S. rates are higher.

Research Problem 7. Download a copy of Form W-4 and complete the accompanying worksheet. File the worksheet with your employer if you discover that you currently are being under- or overwithheld.

TEAM PROJECT: ARTHUR ANDERSEN TAX CHALLENGE CASES

For more information on the Arthur Andersen Tax Challenge Cases, refer to Chapter 1, page 1–38.

Information related to tax issues and problems that are discussed in this chapter may be found in the

Day and Ball case on pages 2, 4, 5, 7, 11–13, 15, 29, 31, 32, and 36
Miller case on pages 1, 12–15

Read and analyze the case you have been assigned and *identify* any issues and problems that are related to material covered in this chapter. If the information provided in the case is complete, prepare answers for this part of the case at this time. If you need information that is contained in the later parts of the case, write a memo summarizing the questions or problems so you can prepare a complete answer at a later date.

PART V

PROPERTY TRANSACTIONS

Part V presents the tax treatment of sales, exchanges, and other dispositions of property. Included are the determination of the realized gain or loss, recognized gain or loss, and the classification of the recognized gain or loss as capital or ordinary. The topic of basis is evaluated both in terms of its effect on the calculation of the gain or loss and in terms of the determination of the basis of any contemporaneous or related subsequent acquisitions of property.

Chapter 14
Property Transactions: Determination of Gain or Loss and Basis Considerations

Chapter 15
Property Transactions: Nontaxable Exchanges

Chapter 16
Property Transactions: Capital Gains and Losses

Chapter 17
Property Transactions: Section 1231 and Recapture Provisions

CHAPTER 14

Property Transactions: Determination of Gain or Loss and Basis Considerations

LEARNING OBJECTIVES

After completing Chapter 14, you should be able to:

1. Understand the computation of realized gain or loss on property dispositions.

2. Distinguish between realized and recognized gain or loss.

3. Apply the recovery of capital doctrine.

4. Explain how basis is determined for various methods of asset acquisition.

5. Describe various loss disallowance provisions.

6. Identify tax planning opportunities related to selected property transactions.

OUTLINE

Determination of Gain or Loss, 14-3
Realized Gain or Loss, 14-3
Recognized Gain or Loss, 14-7
Nonrecognition of Gain or Loss, 14-7
Recovery of Capital Doctrine, 14-8
Basis Considerations, 14-9
Determination of Cost Basis, 14-9
Gift Basis, 14-12
Property Acquired from a Decedent, 14-15

Disallowed Losses, 14-17
Conversion of Property from Personal Use to Business or Income-Producing Use, 14-20
Additional Complexities in Determining Realized Gain or Loss, 14-21
Summary of Basis Adjustments, 14-23
Tax Planning Considerations, 14-23

Tax Consequences of Alice's Proposed Transaction, 14-23
Cost Identification and Documentation Considerations, 14-25
Selection of Property for Making Gifts, 14-25
Selection of Property for Making Bequests, 14-26
Disallowed Losses, 14-26

This chapter and the following three chapters are concerned with the income tax consequences of property transactions (the sale or other disposition of property). The following questions are considered with respect to the sale or other disposition of property:

- Is there a realized gain or loss?
- If so, is the gain or loss recognized?
- If the gain or loss is recognized, is it ordinary or capital?
- What is the basis of any replacement property that is acquired?

EXAMPLE 1

Alice owns a house that she received from her mother seven months ago. Her mother's cost for the house was $75,000. Alice is considering selling the house to her favorite nephew, Dan, for $75,000. Alice anticipates she will have no gain or loss on the transaction. She comes to you for advice.

As Alice's tax adviser, you need answers to the following questions:

- You are aware that Alice's mother died around the time Alice indicates she received the house from her mother. Did Alice receive the house by gift prior to her mother's death? If so, what was the mother's adjusted basis? If instead Alice inherited the house from her mother, what was the fair market value of the house on the date of her mother's death?
- Was the house Alice's principal residence during the period she owned it and was it her principal residence prior to receiving it from her mother?
- How long did Alice's mother own the house?
- What is the fair market value of the house?
- Does Alice intend for the transaction with Dan to be a sale or part sale and part gift?
- What does Alice intend to do with the sale proceeds?

Once you have the answers to these questions, you can advise Alice on the tax consequences of the proposed transaction. ▼

Chapters 14 and 15 discuss the determination of realized and recognized gain or loss and the basis of property. Chapters 16 and 17 cover the classification of the recognized gain or loss as ordinary or capital.

Determination of Gain or Loss

REALIZED GAIN OR LOSS

LEARNING OBJECTIVE 1
Understand the computation of realized gain or loss on property dispositions.

Realized gain or loss is measured by the difference between the amount realized from the sale or other disposition of property and the property's adjusted basis on the date of disposition. If the amount realized exceeds the property's adjusted basis, the result is a **realized gain.** Conversely, if the property's adjusted basis exceeds the amount realized, the result is a **realized loss.**[1]

EXAMPLE 2
Tab sells Swan Corporation stock with an adjusted basis of $3,000 for $5,000. Tab's realized gain is $2,000. If Tab had sold the stock for $2,000, he would have had a $1,000 realized loss. ▼

Sale or Other Disposition. The term *sale or other disposition* is defined broadly in the tax law and includes virtually any disposition of property. Thus, transactions such as trade-ins, casualties, condemnations, thefts, and bond retirements are treated as dispositions of property. The most common disposition of property is through a sale or exchange. The key factor in determining whether a disposition has taken place usually is whether an identifiable event has occurred[2] as opposed to a mere fluctuation in the value of the property.[3]

EXAMPLE 3
Lori owns Tan Corporation stock that cost $3,000. The stock has appreciated in value by $2,000 since Lori purchased it. Lori has no realized gain since mere fluctuation in value is not a disposition or identifiable event for tax purposes. Nor would Lori have a realized loss had the stock declined in value by $2,000. ▼

Amount Realized. The **amount realized** from a sale or other disposition of property is the sum of any money received plus the fair market value of other property received. The amount realized also includes any real property taxes treated as imposed on the seller that are actually paid by the buyer.[4] The reason for including these taxes in the amount realized is that by paying the taxes, the purchaser is, in effect, paying an additional amount to the seller of the property.

The amount realized also includes any liability on the property disposed of, such as a mortgage debt, if the buyer assumes the mortgage or the property is sold subject to the mortgage.[5] The amount of the liability is included in the amount realized even if the debt is nonrecourse and the amount of the debt is greater than the fair market value of the mortgaged property.[6]

EXAMPLE 4
Barry sells property on which there is a mortgage of $20,000 to Cole for $50,000 cash. Barry's amount realized from the sale is $70,000 if Cole assumes the mortgage or takes the property subject to the mortgage. ▼

---

[1] § 1001(a) and Reg. § 1.1001–1(a).
[2] Reg. § 1.1001–1(c)(1).
[3] *Lynch v. Turrish,* 1 USTC ¶18, 3 AFTR 2986, 38 S.Ct. 537 (USSC, 1918).
[4] § 1001(b) and Reg. § 1.1001–1(b). Refer to Chapter 10 for a discussion of this subject.
[5] *Crane v. Comm.,* 47–1 USTC ¶9217, 35 AFTR 776, 67 S.Ct. 1047 (USSC, 1947). Although a legal distinction exists between the direct assumption of a mortgage and taking property subject to a mortgage, the tax consequences in calculating the amount realized are the same.
[6] *Comm. v. Tufts,* 83–1 USTC ¶9328, 51 AFTR2d 83–1132, 103 S.Ct. 1826 (USSC, 1983).

TAX IN THE NEWS

WHAT IS THE AMOUNT REALIZED?

Determining the "amount realized" may be difficult, but usually can be done. The statutory definition is as follows: the sum of any money received plus the fair market value of property received. In a foreclosure sale, the amount realized includes the indebtedness discharged as the result of the foreclosure. In a real-world situation, however, the facts may not be nearly as clear as they are in a textbook situation.

In a recent case [*Wicker v. Comm.* 95–1 USTC ¶50,182, 75 AFTR2d 95–1701 (CA–8, 1995)], the Court of Appeals affirmed a Tax Court decision regarding the inability to calculate the "amount realized." In the case, both the IRS and the taxpayer could be viewed as losers or as winners, depending on one's perspective. The taxpayer had claimed a loss on his return associated with the foreclosure of mortgaged properties (i.e., the creditor accepted the mortgaged properties in exchange for the mortgage, with the properties being sold at a foreclosure sale). The IRS's position was that the foreclosure transaction produced a gain.

Because there was no evidence as to whether the loan was recourse or nonrecourse or the amount of the proceeds from the foreclosure sale, the Court concluded that the amount realized from the foreclosure could not be determined. Without a determination of the amount realized, it was not possible to ascertain if the foreclosure resulted in a gain or loss.

The **fair market value** of property received in a sale or other disposition has been defined by the courts as the price at which property will change hands between a willing seller and a willing buyer when neither is compelled to sell or buy.[7] Fair market value is determined by considering the relevant factors in each case.[8] An expert appraiser is often required to evaluate these factors in arriving at fair market value. When the fair market value of the property received cannot be determined, the value of the property surrendered may be used.[9]

In calculating the amount realized, selling expenses such as advertising, commissions, and legal fees relating to the disposition are deducted. The amount realized is the net amount received directly or indirectly by the taxpayer from the disposition of property in the form of cash or anything else of value.

Adjusted Basis. The **adjusted basis** of property disposed of is the property's original basis adjusted to the date of disposition.[10] Original basis is the cost or other basis of the property on the date the property is acquired by the taxpayer. *Capital additions* increase and *recoveries of capital* decrease the original basis so that on the date of disposition the adjusted basis reflects the unrecovered cost or other basis of the property.[11] Adjusted basis is determined as follows:

---

[7] *Comm. v. Marshman,* 60–2 USTC ¶9484, 5 AFTR2d 1528, 279 F.2d 27 (CA–6, 1960).
[8] *O'Malley v. Ames,* 52–1 USTC ¶9361, 42 AFTR 19, 197 F.2d 256 (CA–8, 1952).
[9] *U.S. v. Davis,* 62–2 USTC ¶9509, 9 AFTR2d 1625, 82 S.Ct. 1190 (USSC, 1962).
[10] § 1011(a) and Reg. § 1.1011–1.
[11] § 1016(a) and Reg. § 1.1016–1.

Cost (or other adjusted basis) on date of acquisition
+ Capital additions
− Capital recoveries
= Adjusted basis on date of disposition

Capital Additions. Capital additions include the cost of capital improvements and betterments made to the property by the taxpayer. These expenditures are distinguishable from expenditures for the ordinary repair and maintenance of the property that are neither capitalized nor added to the original basis (refer to Chapter 6). The latter expenditures are deductible in the current taxable year if they are related to business or income-producing property. Amounts representing real property taxes treated as imposed on the seller but paid or assumed by the buyer are part of the cost of the property.[12] Any liability on property that is assumed by the buyer is also included in the buyer's original basis of the property. The same rule applies if property is acquired subject to a liability. Amortization of the discount on bonds increases the adjusted basis of the bonds.[13]

Capital Recoveries. The following are examples of capital recoveries:

1. *Depreciation and cost recovery allowances.* The original basis of depreciable property is reduced by the annual depreciation charges (or cost recovery allowances) while the property is held by the taxpayer. The amount of depreciation that is subtracted from the original basis is the greater of the *allowed* or *allowable* depreciation on an annual basis.[14] In most circumstances, the allowed and allowable depreciation amounts are the same (refer to Chapter 8).
2. *Casualties and thefts.* A casualty or theft may result in the reduction of the adjusted basis of property.[15] The adjusted basis is reduced by the amount of the deductible loss. In addition, the adjusted basis is reduced by the amount of insurance proceeds received. However, the receipt of insurance proceeds may result in a recognized gain rather than a deductible loss. The gain increases the adjusted basis of the property.[16]

EXAMPLE 5 An insured truck used in a trade or business is destroyed in an accident. The adjusted basis is $8,000, and the fair market value is $6,500. Insurance proceeds of $6,500 are received. The amount of the casualty loss is $1,500 ($6,500 insurance proceeds − $8,000 adjusted basis). The adjusted basis is reduced by the $1,500 casualty loss and the $6,500 of insurance proceeds received. ▼

EXAMPLE 6 An insured truck used in a trade or business is destroyed in an accident. The adjusted basis is $6,500, and the fair market value is $8,000. Insurance proceeds of $8,000 are received. The amount of the casualty gain is $1,500 ($8,000 insurance proceeds − $6,500 adjusted basis). The adjusted basis is increased by the $1,500 casualty gain and is reduced by the $8,000 of insurance proceeds received ($6,500 basis before casualty + $1,500 casualty gain − $8,000 insurance proceeds = $0 basis). ▼

---

[12] Reg. §§ 1.1001−1(b)(2) and 1.1012−1(b). Refer to Chapter 10 for a discussion of this subject.
[13] See Chapter 16 for a discussion of bond discount and the related amortization.
[14] § 1016(a)(2) and Reg. § 1.1016−3(a)(1)(i).
[15] Refer to Chapter 7 for the discussion of casualties and thefts.
[16] Reg. § 1.1016−6(a).

3. *Certain corporate distributions.* A corporate distribution to a shareholder that is not taxable is treated as a return of capital, and it reduces the basis of the shareholder's stock in the corporation.[17] For example, if a corporation makes a cash distribution to its shareholders and has no earnings and profits, the distributions are treated as a return of capital. Once the basis of the stock is reduced to zero, the amount of any subsequent distributions is a capital gain if the stock is a capital asset. These rules are illustrated in Example 21 of Chapter 20.

ETHICAL CONSIDERATIONS
Reporting of a Distribution: Dividend versus Return of Capital

Rebecca purchased 100 shares of stock in Bluebird, Inc., on December 24, 1997, for $50,000. In January 1998, Rebecca receives a Form 1099 for 1997 from the corporation that indicates she should report dividend income of $2,000 on her tax return. While she did receive a check from Bluebird on January 4, 1998 (postmarked December 31), she believes that it is a return of capital. Therefore, she reduces her adjusted basis for the stock to $48,000 and reports no dividend income for 1997. Her justification is that the corporation reported a loss in its fourth quarter financial statements. Evaluate Rebecca's reporting of the $2,000 distribution.

4. *Amortizable bond premium.* The basis in a bond purchased at a premium is reduced by the amortizable portion of the bond premium.[18] Investors in taxable bonds may *elect* to amortize the bond premium, but the premium on tax-exempt bonds *must be* amortized.[19] The amount of the amortized premium on taxable bonds is permitted as an interest deduction. Therefore, the election produces the opportunity for an annual interest deduction to offset ordinary income in exchange for a larger capital gain or smaller capital loss on the disposition of the bond. No such interest deduction is permitted for tax-exempt bonds.

The amortization deduction is allowed for taxable bonds because the premium is viewed as a cost of earning the taxable interest from the bonds. The reason the basis of taxable bonds is reduced is that the amortization deduction is a recovery of the cost or basis of the bonds. The basis of tax-exempt bonds is reduced even though the amortization is not allowed as a deduction. No amortization deduction is permitted on tax-exempt bonds since the interest income is exempt from tax and the amortization of the bond premium merely represents an adjustment of the effective amount of such income.

EXAMPLE 7

Antonio purchases Eagle Corporation taxable bonds with a face value of $100,000 for $110,000, thus paying a premium of $10,000. The annual interest rate is 7%, and the bonds mature 10 years from the date of purchase. The annual interest income is $7,000

---

[17] § 1016(a)(4) and Reg. § 1.1016–5(a).

[18] § 1016(a)(5) and Reg. § 1.1016–5(b). The accounting treatment of bond premium amortization is the same as for tax purposes.

The amortization results in a decrease in the bond investment account.

[19] § 171(c).

Concept Summary 14–1

Recognized Gain or Loss

```
                              ┌─→ Realized ─→ Deferred (postponed) ─→ Recognized Gain
                 If amount is +    Gain         Gain or                  (taxable amount)
                                                Tax-Free Gain
Amount  ─→ Adjusted
Realized    Basis
                 If amount is -
                              └─→ Realized ─→ Deferred (postponed) ─→ Recognized Loss
                                  Loss         Loss or                  (deductible
                                                Disallowed Loss          amount)
```

(7% × $100,000). If Antonio elects to amortize the bond premium, the $10,000 premium is deducted over the 10-year period. Antonio's basis for the bonds is reduced each year by the amount of the amortization deduction. Note that if the bonds were tax-exempt, amortization of the bond premium and the basis adjustment would be mandatory. However, no deduction would be allowed for the amortization. ▼

RECOGNIZED GAIN OR LOSS

2 LEARNING OBJECTIVE
Distinguish between realized and recognized gain or loss.

Recognized gain is the amount of the realized gain included in the taxpayer's gross income.[20] A **recognized loss,** on the other hand, is the amount of a realized loss that is deductible for tax purposes.[21] As a general rule, the entire amount of a realized gain or loss is recognized.[22]

Concept Summary 14–1 summarizes the realized gain or loss and recognized gain or loss concepts.

NONRECOGNITION OF GAIN OR LOSS

In certain cases, a realized gain or loss is not recognized upon the sale or other disposition of property. One of the exceptions to the recognition of gain or loss involves nontaxable exchanges, which are covered in Chapter 15. Additional exceptions include losses realized upon the sale, exchange, or condemnation of personal use assets (as opposed to business or income-producing property) and gains realized upon the sale of a residence by taxpayers 55 years of age or older (see Chapter 15). In addition, realized losses from the sale or exchange of business or income-producing property between certain related parties are not recognized.[23]

---

[20] § 61(a)(3) and Reg. § 1.61–6(a).
[21] § 165(a) and Reg. § 1.165–1(a).
[22] § 1001(c) and Reg. § 1.1002–1(a).
[23] § 267(a)(1).

Sale, Exchange, or Condemnation of Personal Use Assets. A realized loss from the sale, exchange, or condemnation of personal use assets (e.g., a personal residence or an automobile not used at all for business or income-producing purposes) is not recognized for tax purposes. An exception exists for casualty or theft losses from personal use assets (see Chapter 7). In contrast, any gain realized from the sale or other disposition of personal use assets is, generally, fully taxable.

EXAMPLE 8 Freda sells an automobile, which is held exclusively for personal use, for $6,000. The adjusted basis of the automobile is $5,000. Freda has a realized and recognized gain of $1,000. ▼

EXAMPLE 9 Freda sells the automobile in Example 8 for $4,000. She has a realized loss of $1,000, but the loss is not recognized. ▼

RECOVERY OF CAPITAL DOCTRINE

LEARNING OBJECTIVE 3
Apply the recovery of capital doctrine.

Doctrine Defined. The **recovery of capital doctrine** is very significant and pervades all the tax rules relating to property transactions. The doctrine derives its roots from the very essence of the income tax—a tax on income. Therefore, as a general rule, a taxpayer is entitled to recover the cost or other original basis of property acquired and is not taxed on that amount.

The cost or other original basis of depreciable property is recovered through annual depreciation deductions. The basis is reduced as the cost is recovered over the period the property is held. Therefore, when property is sold or otherwise disposed of, it is the adjusted basis (unrecovered cost or other basis) that is compared to the amount realized from the disposition to determine realized gain or loss.

Relationship of the Recovery of Capital Doctrine to the Concepts of Realization and Recognition. If a sale or other disposition results in a realized gain, the taxpayer has recovered more than the adjusted basis of the property. Conversely, if a sale or other disposition results in a realized loss, the taxpayer has recovered less than the adjusted basis.

The general rules for the relationship between the recovery of capital doctrine and the realized and recognized gain and loss concepts are summarized as follows:

Rule 1. A realized gain that is *never recognized* results in the *permanent recovery* of more than the taxpayer's cost or other basis for tax purposes. For example, all or a portion of the realized gain on the sale of a personal residence by taxpayers 55 years of age or older can be excluded from gross income under § 121.

Rule 2. A realized gain on which *recognition is postponed* results in the *temporary recovery* of more than the taxpayer's cost or other basis for tax purposes. For example, an exchange of like-kind property under § 1031, an involuntary conversion under § 1033, and a replacement of a personal residence under § 1034 are all eligible for postponement treatment.

Rule 3. A realized loss that is *never recognized* results in the *permanent recovery* of less than the taxpayer's cost or other basis for tax purposes. For example, a loss on the sale of an automobile held for personal use is not deductible.

Rule 4. A realized loss on which *recognition is postponed* results in the *temporary recovery* of less than the taxpayer's cost or other basis for tax purposes. For example, the realized loss on the exchange of like-kind property under § 1031 is postponed.

These rules are illustrated in discussions to follow in this and the next chapter.

BASIS CONSIDERATIONS

DETERMINATION OF COST BASIS

LEARNING OBJECTIVE 4
Explain how basis is determined for various methods of asset acquisition.

The basis of property is generally the property's cost. Cost is the amount paid for the property in cash or other property.[24] This general rule follows logically from the recovery of capital doctrine; that is, the cost or other basis of property is to be recovered tax-free by the taxpayer.

A *bargain purchase* of property is an exception to the general rule for determining basis. A bargain purchase may result when an employer transfers property to an employee at less than the property's fair market value (as compensation for services) or when a corporation transfers property to a shareholder at less than the property's fair market value (a dividend). The basis of property acquired in a bargain purchase is the property's fair market value.[25] If the basis of the property were not increased by the bargain amount, the taxpayer would be taxed on this amount again at disposition.

EXAMPLE 10
Wade buys a machine from his employer for $10,000 on December 30. The fair market value of the machine is $15,000. Wade must include the $5,000 difference between cost and the fair market value of the machine in gross income for the taxable year. The bargain element represents additional compensation to Wade. His basis for the machine is $15,000, the machine's fair market value. ▼

Identification Problems. Cost identification problems are frequently encountered in securities transactions. For example, the Regulations require that the taxpayer adequately identify the particular stock that has been sold.[26] A problem arises when the taxpayer has purchased separate lots of stock on different dates or at different prices and cannot adequately identify the lot from which a particular sale takes place. In this case, the stock is presumed to come from the first lot or lots purchased (a FIFO presumption).[27] When securities are left in the custody of a broker, it may be necessary to provide specific instructions and receive written confirmation as to which securities are being sold.

EXAMPLE 11
Polly purchases 100 shares of Olive Corporation stock on July 1, 1995, for $5,000 ($50 a share) and another 100 shares of Olive stock on July 1, 1996, for $6,000 ($60 a share). She sells 50 shares of the stock on January 2, 1997. The cost of the stock sold, assuming Polly cannot adequately identify the shares, is $50 a share, or $2,500. This is the cost Polly will compare to the amount realized in determining the gain or loss from the sale. ▼

---

[24] § 1012 and Reg. § 1.1012–1(a).
[25] Reg. §§ 1.61–2(d)(2)(i) and 1.301–1(j).
[26] Reg. § 1.1012–1(c)(1).
[27] *Kluger Associates, Inc.*, 69 T.C. 925 (1978).

Allocation Problems. When a taxpayer acquires *multiple assets in a lump-sum purchase*, the total cost must be allocated among the individual assets.[28] Allocation is necessary because some of the assets acquired may be depreciable (e.g., buildings) and others not (e.g., land). In addition, only a portion of the assets acquired may be sold, or some of the assets may be capital or § 1231 assets that receive special tax treatment upon subsequent sale or other disposition. The lump-sum cost is allocated on the basis of the fair market values of the individual assets acquired.

EXAMPLE 12

Harry purchases a building and land for $800,000. Because of the depressed nature of the industry in which the seller was operating, Harry was able to negotiate a very favorable purchase price. Appraisals of the individual assets indicate that the fair market value of the building is $600,000 and that of the land is $400,000. Harry's basis for the building is $480,000 [($600,000/$1,000,000) × $800,000], and his basis for the land is $320,000 [($400,000/$1,000,000) × $800,000]. ▼

If a business is purchased and **goodwill** is involved, a special allocation rule applies. Initially, the purchase price is assigned to the assets, excluding goodwill, to the extent of their total fair market value. This assigned amount is allocated among the assets on the basis of the fair market value of the individual assets acquired. Goodwill is then assigned the residual amount of the purchase price. The resultant allocation is applicable to both the buyer and the seller.[29]

EXAMPLE 13

Rocky sells his business to Paul. They agree that the values of the individual assets are as follows:

Inventory	$ 50,000
Building	500,000
Land	200,000
Goodwill	150,000

After negotiations, Rocky and Paul agree on a sales price of $1 million. Applying the residual method with respect to goodwill results in the following allocation of the $1 million purchase price:

Inventory	$ 50,000
Building	500,000
Land	200,000
Goodwill	250,000

The residual method requires that all of the excess of the purchase price over the fair market value of the assets ($1,000,000 − $900,000 = $100,000) be allocated to goodwill. Without this requirement, the purchaser could allocate the excess pro rata to all of the assets, including goodwill, based on their respective fair market values. This would have resulted in only $166,667 [$150,000 + ($150,000 ÷ $900,000 × $100,000)] being assigned to goodwill. ▼

In the case of *nontaxable stock dividends*, the allocation depends upon whether the dividend is a common stock dividend on common stock or a preferred stock dividend on common stock. If the dividend is common on common, the cost

---

[28] Reg. § 1.61–6(a).

[29] § 1060.

of the original common shares is allocated to the total shares owned after the dividend.[30]

EXAMPLE 14 Susan owns 100 shares of Sparrow Corporation common stock for which she paid $1,100. She receives a 10% common stock dividend, giving her a new total of 110 shares. Before the stock dividend, Susan's basis was $11 per share ($1,100 ÷ 100 shares). The basis of each share after the stock dividend is $10 ($1,100 ÷ 110 shares). ▼

If the dividend is preferred stock on common, the cost of the original common shares is allocated between the common and preferred shares on the basis of their relative fair market values on the date of distribution.[31]

EXAMPLE 15 Fran owns 100 shares of Cardinal Corporation common stock for which she paid $1,000. She receives a stock dividend of 50 shares of preferred stock on her common stock. The fair market values on the date of distribution of the preferred stock dividend are $30 a share for common stock and $40 a share for preferred stock. Thus, the total fair market value is $3,000 ($30 × 100) for common stock and $2,000 ($40 × 50) for preferred stock. The basis of Fran's common stock after the dividend is $600, or $6 a share [($3,000/$5,000) × $1,000], and the basis of the preferred stock is $400, or $8 a share [($2,000/$5,000) × $1,000]. ▼

In the case of *nontaxable stock rights*, the basis of the rights is zero unless the taxpayer elects or is required to allocate a portion of the cost of the stock to the rights. If the fair market value of the rights is 15 percent or more of the fair market value of the stock, the taxpayer is required to allocate. If the value of the rights is less than 15 percent of the fair market value of the stock, the taxpayer may elect to allocate.[32] The result is that either the rights will have no basis or the cost of the stock on which the rights are received will be allocated between the stock and rights on the basis of their relative fair market values.

EXAMPLE 16 Donald receives nontaxable stock rights with a fair market value of $1,000. The fair market value of the stock on which the rights were received is $8,000 (cost $10,000). Donald does not elect to allocate. The basis of the rights is zero. If he exercises the rights, the basis of the new stock is the exercise (subscription) price. ▼

EXAMPLE 17 Assume the same facts as in Example 16, except the fair market value of the rights is $3,000. Donald must allocate because the value of the rights is 15% or more of the value of the stock ($3,000/$8,000 = 37.5%). The basis of the rights is $2,727 [($3,000/$11,000) × $10,000], and the basis of the stock is $7,273 [($8,000/$11,000) × $10,000]. If Donald exercises the rights, the basis of the new stock is the exercise (subscription) price plus the basis of the rights. If he sells the rights, he recognizes gain or loss to the extent of the difference between the amount realized and the basis of the rights. This allocation rule applies only when the rights are exercised or sold. Therefore, if the rights are allowed to lapse (expire), they have no basis, and the basis of the original stock is the stock's cost, $10,000. ▼

The holding period of nontaxable stock rights includes the holding period of the stock on which the rights were distributed. However, if the rights are exercised, the holding period of the newly acquired stock begins with the date the rights are exercised.[33] The significance of the holding period for capital assets is discussed in Chapter 16.

---

[30] §§ 305(a) and 307(a). The holding period of the new shares includes the holding period of the old shares. § 1223(5) and Reg. § 1.1223–1(e). See Chapter 16 for a discussion of the importance of the holding period.

[31] Reg. § 1.307–1(a).
[32] § 307(b).
[33] § 1223(5) and Reg. §§ 1.1223–1(e) and (f).

GIFT BASIS

When a taxpayer receives property as a gift, there is no cost to the recipient. Thus, under the cost basis provision, the donee's basis would be zero. However, this would violate the statutory intent that gifts are not subject to the income tax. With a zero basis, a sale by the donee would result in all of the amount realized being treated as realized gain. Therefore, a basis is assigned to the property received depending on the following:[34]

- The date of the gift.
- The basis of the property to the donor.
- The amount of the gift tax paid.
- The fair market value of the property.

Gift Basis Rules if No Gift Tax Is Paid. Property received by gift can be referred to as *dual basis* property; that is, the basis for gain and the basis for loss might not be the same amount. The present basis rules for gifts of property are as follows:

- If the donee subsequently disposes of gift property in a transaction that results in a gain, the basis to the donee is the same as the donor's adjusted basis.[35] The donee's basis in this case is referred to as the *gain basis*. Therefore, a *realized gain* results if the amount realized from the disposition exceeds the donee's gain basis.

EXAMPLE 18

Melissa purchased stock in 1996 for $10,000. She gave the stock to her son, Joe, in 1997, when the fair market value was $15,000. Assume no gift tax is paid on the transfer and Joe subsequently sells the property for $15,000. Joe's basis is $10,000, and he has a realized gain of $5,000. ▼

- If the donee subsequently disposes of gift property in a transaction that results in a loss, the basis to the donee is the *lower* of the donor's adjusted basis or fair market value on the date of the gift. The donee's basis in this case is referred to as the *loss basis*. Therefore, a *realized loss results* if the amount realized from the disposition is less than the donee's loss basis.

EXAMPLE 19

Burt purchased stock in 1996 for $10,000. He gave the stock to his son, Cliff, in 1997, when the fair market value was $7,000. Assume no gift tax is paid on the transfer. Cliff later sells the stock for $6,000. Cliff's basis is $7,000 (fair market value is less than donor's adjusted basis of $10,000), and the realized loss from the sale is $1,000 ($6,000 amount realized − $7,000 basis). ▼

The amount of the loss basis will *differ* from the amount of the gain basis only if at the date of the gift the adjusted basis of the property exceeds the property's fair market value. Note that the loss basis rule prevents the donee from receiving a tax benefit from the decline in value while the donor held the property. Therefore, in Example 19, Cliff has a loss of only $1,000 rather than a loss of $4,000. The $3,000 difference represents the decline in value while Burt held the property. Ironically, however, the gain basis rule may eventually result in the donee's being subject to income tax on the appreciation that occurred while the donor held the property, as illustrated in Example 18.

---

[34] § 102(a).
[35] § 1015(a) and Reg. § 1.1015−1(a)(1). See Reg. § 1.1015−1(a)(3) for cases in which the facts necessary to determine the donor's adjusted basis are unknown. Refer to Example 24 for the effect of depreciation deductions by the donee.

If the amount realized from sale or other disposition is *between* the basis for loss and the basis for gain, no gain or loss is realized.

EXAMPLE 20 Assume the same facts as in Example 19, except that Cliff sold the stock for $8,000. The application of the gain basis rule produces a loss of $2,000 ($8,000 − $10,000). The application of the loss basis rule produces a gain of $1,000 ($8,000 − $7,000). Therefore, Cliff recognizes neither a gain nor a loss because the amount realized is between the gain basis and the loss basis. ▼

Adjustment for Gift Tax. If gift taxes are paid by the donor, the donee's gain basis may exceed the adjusted basis of the property to the donor. This occurs only if the fair market value of the property at the date of the gift is greater than the donor's adjusted basis (the property has appreciated in value). The portion of the gift tax paid that is related to the appreciation is added to the donor's basis in calculating the donee's gain basis for the property. In this circumstance, the following formula is used for calculating the donee's gain basis:[36]

$$\text{Donee's gain basis} = \text{Donor's adjusted basis} + \left(\frac{\text{Unrealized appreciation}}{\text{Fair market value at date of gift}} \times \text{Gift tax paid} \right)$$

EXAMPLE 21 Bonnie made a gift of stock to Peggy in 1997, when the fair market value of the stock was $40,000. Bonnie had purchased the stock in 1982 for $10,000. Because the unrealized appreciation is $30,000 ($40,000 fair market value − $10,000 adjusted basis) and the fair market value is $40,000, three-fourths ($30,000/$40,000) of the gift tax paid is added to the basis of the property. If Bonnie paid gift tax of $4,000, Peggy's basis in the property is $13,000 [$10,000 + $3,000 (¾ of the $4,000 gift tax)]. ▼

EXAMPLE 22 Don made a gift of stock to Matt in 1997, when the fair market value of the stock was $40,000. Gift tax of $4,000 was paid by Don, who had purchased the stock in 1982 for $45,000. Because there is no unrealized appreciation at the date of the gift, none of the gift tax paid is added to Don's basis in calculating Matt's gain basis. Therefore, Matt's gain basis is $45,000. ▼

For *gifts made before 1977*, the full amount of the gift tax paid is added to the donor's basis. However, the ceiling on this total is the fair market value of the property at the date of the gift. Thus, in Example 21, if the gift had been made before 1977, the basis of the property would be $14,000 ($10,000 + $4,000). In Example 22, the gain basis would still be $45,000 ($45,000 + $0).

Holding Period. The **holding period** for property acquired by gift begins on the date the donor acquired the property if the gain basis rule applies.[37] The holding period starts on the date of the gift if the loss basis rule applies.[38] The significance of the holding period for capital assets is discussed in Chapter 16.

The following example summarizes the basis and holding period rules for gift property:

---

[36] § 1015(d)(6).
[37] § 1223(2) and Reg. § 1.1223−1(b).
[38] Rev.Rul. 59−86, 1959−1 C.B. 209.

EXAMPLE 23

Jill acquires 100 shares of Wren Corporation stock on December 30, 1982, for $40,000. On January 3, 1997, when the stock has a fair market value of $38,000, Jill gives it to Dennis and pays gift tax of $4,000. The basis is not increased by a portion of the gift tax paid because the property has not appreciated in value at the time of the gift. Therefore, Dennis's gain basis is $40,000. Dennis's basis for determining loss is $38,000 (fair market value) because the fair market value on the date of the gift is less than the donor's adjusted basis.

- If Dennis sells the stock for $45,000, he has a recognized gain of $5,000. The holding period for determining whether the capital gain is short term or long term begins on December 30, 1982, the date Jill acquired the property.
- If Dennis sells the stock for $36,000, he has a recognized loss of $2,000. The holding period for determining whether the capital loss is short term or long term begins on January 3, 1997, the date of the gift.
- If Dennis sells the property for $39,000, there is no gain or loss since the amount realized is less than the gain basis of $40,000 and more than the loss basis of $38,000. ▼

ETHICAL CONSIDERATIONS

Looking a Gift Horse in the Eye

Walter rarely sees his Uncle George because George is a devoted world traveler. On February 10, 1996, Walter received an envelope that George had mailed to him from Angola on December 23, 1995. The envelope contained 1,000 shares of stock of Lavender, Inc., and a Christmas card from George.

Walter is engaged to be married in December 1996. To finance the wedding (he and his fiancée have agreed that this is his responsibility) and the honeymoon, and to pay for the engagement ring, Walter sells the stock in October 1996 for $45,000.

In early April 1997, the accountant who is preparing Walter's tax return tells him that she needs to know his uncle's adjusted basis for the stock and the amount of any gift tax paid. Since Walter is unable to contact his uncle by April 15, 1997, he requests a filing extension on Form 4868. He does mail a letter to Uncle George requesting this information and thanking him for the gift. Walter is able to ascertain from a stock service that during the past 10 years, the stock price has ranged from $10 per share to $50 per share.

On August 10, 1997, Uncle George unexpectedly calls from Bosnia. He says he has not filed any type of Federal tax return in years. He thinks he won the stock in a poker game in Monaco about 15 years ago when another player used it to cover a $15,000 bet.

Walter wants to file his tax return by the August 15, 1997, due date. He does not think it is a good idea to tell the tax return preparer how his uncle acquired the stock or about his uncle's not filing tax returns. So he calls the accountant and tells her that his uncle's basis for the stock is $15,000 and that no gift taxes were paid.

Evaluate Walter's behavior.

Basis for Depreciation. The basis for depreciation on depreciable gift property is the donee's gain basis.[39] This rule is applicable even if the donee later sells the property at a loss and uses the loss basis rule in calculating the amount of the realized loss.

---

[39] § 1011 and Reg. §§ 1.1011–1 and 1.167(g)–1.

EXAMPLE 24

Vito gave a machine to Tina in 1997, when the adjusted basis was $32,000 (cost of $40,000 − accumulated depreciation of $8,000) and the fair market value was $26,000. No gift tax was paid. Tina's gain basis at the date of the gift is $32,000, and her loss basis is $26,000. During 1997, Tina deducts depreciation (cost recovery) of $10,240 ($32,000 × 32%). Therefore, at the end of 1997, Tina's gain basis and loss basis are calculated as follows:

	Gain Basis	Loss Basis
Donor's basis or fair market value	$ 32,000	$ 26,000
Depreciation	(10,240)	(10,240)
	$ 21,760	$ 15,760

PROPERTY ACQUIRED FROM A DECEDENT

General Rules. The basis of property acquired from a decedent is generally the property's fair market value at the date of death (referred to as the *primary valuation amount*).[40] The property's basis is the fair market value six months after the date of death if the executor or administrator of the estate *elects* the alternate valuation date for estate tax purposes. This amount is referred to as the *alternate valuation amount*.

EXAMPLE 25

Linda and various other family members inherited property from Linda's father, who died in 1997. At the date of death, her father's adjusted basis for the property Linda inherited was $35,000. The property's fair market value at date of death was $50,000. The alternate valuation date was not elected. Linda's basis for income tax purposes is $50,000. This is commonly referred to as a *stepped-up basis*. ▼

EXAMPLE 26

Assume the same facts as in Example 25, except the property's fair market value at date of death was $20,000. Linda's basis for income tax purposes is $20,000. This is commonly referred to as a *stepped-down basis*. ▼

If an estate tax return does not have to be filed because the estate is below the threshold amount for being subject to the estate tax, the alternate valuation date and amount are not available. Even if an estate tax return is filed and the executor elects the alternate valuation date, the six months after death date is available only for property that the executor has not distributed before this date. Any property distributed or otherwise disposed of by the executor during this six-month period will have an adjusted basis to the beneficiary equal to the fair market value on the date of distribution or other disposition.[41]

The alternate valuation date can be *elected only* if the election results in both the value of the gross estate and the estate tax liability being reduced below the amounts they would have been if the primary valuation date had been used. This provision prevents the alternate valuation election from being used to increase the basis of the property to the beneficiary for income tax purposes without simultaneously increasing the estate tax liability (because of estate tax deductions or credits).[42]

---

[40] § 1014(a).
[41] § 2032(a)(1) and Rev.Rul. 56–60, 1956–1 C.B. 443.
[42] § 2032(c).

EXAMPLE 27 Nancy inherited all the property of her father, who died in 1997. Her father's adjusted basis for the property at date of death was $35,000. The property's fair market value was $750,000 at date of death and $760,000 six months after death. The alternate valuation date cannot be elected because the value of the gross estate has increased during the six-month period. Nancy's basis for income tax purposes is $750,000. ▼

EXAMPLE 28 Assume the same facts as in Example 27, except the property's fair market value six months after death was $745,000. If the executor elects the alternate valuation date, Nancy's basis for income tax purposes is $745,000. ▼

EXAMPLE 29 Assume the same facts as in the previous example, except the property is distributed four months after the date of the decedent's death. At the distribution date, the property's fair market value is $747,500. Since the executor elected the alternate valuation date, Nancy's basis for income tax purposes is $747,500. ▼

For inherited property, both unrealized appreciation and decline in value are taken into consideration in determining the basis of the property for income tax purposes. Contrast this with the carryover basis rules for property received by gift.

Deathbed Gifts. The Code contains a provision designed to eliminate a tax avoidance technique referred to as *deathbed gifts*. If the time period between the date of the gift of appreciated property and the date of the donee's death is not longer than one year, the usual basis rule (stepped-up basis) for inherited property may not apply. The adjusted basis of such property inherited by the donor or his or her spouse from the donee shall be the same as the decedent's adjusted basis for the property rather than the fair market value at the date of death or the alternate valuation date.[43]

EXAMPLE 30 Ned gives stock to his uncle, Vern, in 1997. Ned's basis for the stock is $1,000, and the fair market value is $9,000. No gift tax is paid. Eight months later, Ned inherits the stock from Vern. At the date of Vern's death, the fair market value of the stock is $12,000. Ned's adjusted basis for the stock is $1,000. ▼

ETHICAL CONSIDERATIONS

Helping a Friend Increase Basis

Holly owns stock with an adjusted basis of $2,500 and a fair market value of $9,500. Holly expects the stock to continue to appreciate. Alice, Holly's best friend, has recently been operated on for cancer. Alice's physicians have told her that her life expectancy is between six months and one and a half years.

One day at lunch, the two friends were discussing their tax situations (both feel they pay too much), when Alice mentioned that she had read a newspaper article about a tax planning opportunity that might be suitable for Holly. Holly would make a gift of the appreciated stock to Alice. In her will, Alice would bequeath the stock to Holly. Since Alice is confident that she will live longer than a year, the basis of the stock to Holly would be the fair market value on the date of Alice's death. Alice would "feel good" because she had helped Holly "beat the tax system."

You are Holly's tax adviser. How will you respond to Alice's proposal to Holly?

---

[43] § 1014(e).

Survivor's Share of Property. Both the decedent's share and the survivor's share of *community property* have a basis equal to fair market value on the date of the decedent's death.[44] This result applies to the decedent's share of the community property because the property flows to the surviving spouse from the estate (fair market value basis for inherited property). Likewise, the surviving spouse's share of the community property is deemed to be acquired by bequest, devise, or inheritance from the decedent. Therefore, it also has a basis equal to fair market value.

EXAMPLE 31

Floyd and Vera reside in a community property state. They own community property (200 shares of Crow stock) that was acquired in 1974 for $100,000. Assume that Floyd dies in 1997, when the securities are valued at $300,000. One-half of the Crow stock is included in Floyd's estate. If Vera inherits Floyd's share of the community property, the basis for determining gain or loss is $300,000, determined as follows:

Vera's one-half of the community property (stepped up from $50,000 to $150,000 due to Floyd's death)	$150,000
Floyd's one-half of the community property (stepped up from $50,000 to $150,000 due to inclusion in his gross estate)	150,000
Vera's new basis	$300,000

In a *common law* state, only one-half of jointly held property of spouses (tenants by the entirety or joint tenants with rights of survivorship) is includible in the estate.[45] In such a case, no adjustment of the basis is permitted for the excluded property interest (the surviving spouse's share).

EXAMPLE 32

Assume the same facts as in the previous example, except that the property is jointly held by Floyd and Vera who reside in a common law state. Also assume that Floyd purchased the property and made a gift of one-half of the property when the stock was acquired, with no gift tax being paid. Only one-half of the Crow stock is included in Floyd's estate. Vera's basis for determining gain or loss in the excluded half is not adjusted upward for the increase in value to date of death. Therefore, Vera's basis is $200,000, determined as follows:

Vera's one-half of the jointly held property (carryover basis of $50,000)	$ 50,000
Floyd's one-half of the jointly held property (stepped up from $50,000 to $150,000 due to inclusion in his gross estate)	150,000
Vera's new basis	$200,000

Holding Period of Property Acquired from a Decedent. The holding period of property acquired from a decedent is *deemed to be long term* (held for the required long-term holding period). This provision applies regardless of whether the property is disposed of at a gain or a loss.[46]

DISALLOWED LOSSES

5 LEARNING OBJECTIVE
Describe various loss disallowance provisions.

Related Taxpayers. Section 267 provides that realized losses from sales or exchanges of property, directly or indirectly, between certain related parties are not recognized. This loss disallowance provision applies to several types of related-party transactions. The most common involve (1) members of a family and

---

[44] § 1014(b)(6). See the listing of community property states in Chapter 4.
[45] § 2040(b).
[46] § 1223(11).

(2) transactions between an individual and a corporation in which the individual owns, directly or indirectly, more than 50 percent in value of the corporation's outstanding stock. Section 707 provides a similar loss disallowance provision if the related parties are a partner and a partnership in which the partner owns, directly or indirectly, more than 50 percent of the capital interests or profits interests in the partnership. The rules governing the relationships covered by § 267 were discussed in Chapter 6. See Chapter 15 for the discussion of the special rules under § 1041 for property transfers between spouses or incident to divorce.

If income-producing or business property is transferred to a related taxpayer and a loss is disallowed, the basis of the property to the recipient is the property's cost to the transferee. However, if a subsequent sale or other disposition of the property by the original transferee results in a realized gain, the amount of gain is reduced by the loss that was previously disallowed.[47] This *right of offset* is not applicable if the original sale involved the sale of a personal use asset (e.g., the sale of a personal residence between related taxpayers). Likewise, this right of offset is available only to the original transferee (the related-party buyer).

EXAMPLE 33

Pedro sells business property with an adjusted basis of $50,000 to his daughter, Josefina, for its fair market value of $40,000.

- Pedro's realized loss of $10,000 is not recognized.
- How much gain will Josefina recognize if she sells the property for $52,000? Josefina recognizes a $2,000 gain. Her realized gain is $12,000 ($52,000 less her basis of $40,000), but she can offset Pedro's $10,000 loss against the gain.
- How much gain will Josefina recognize if she sells the property for $48,000? Josefina recognizes no gain or loss. Her realized gain is $8,000 ($48,000 less her basis of $40,000), but she can offset $8,000 of Pedro's $10,000 loss against the gain. Note that Pedro's loss can only offset Josefina's gain. It cannot create a loss for Josefina.
- How much loss will Josefina recognize if she sells the property for $38,000? Josefina recognizes a $2,000 loss, the same as her realized loss ($38,000 less $40,000 basis). Pedro's loss does not increase Josefina's loss. His loss can be offset only against a gain. Since Josefina has no realized gain, Pedro's loss cannot be used and is never recognized. This example assumes that the property is business or income producing to Josefina. If not, her $2,000 loss is personal and is not recognized. ▼

The loss disallowance rules are designed to achieve two objectives. First, the rules prevent a taxpayer from directly transferring an unrealized loss to a related taxpayer in a higher tax bracket who could receive a greater tax benefit from the recognition of the loss. Second, the rules eliminate a substantial administrative burden on the Internal Revenue Service as to the appropriateness of the selling price (fair market value or not). The loss disallowance rules are applicable even where the selling price is equal to fair market value and can be validated (e.g., listed stocks).

The holding period of the buyer for the property is not affected by the holding period of the seller. That is, the buyer's *holding period* includes only the period of time he or she has held the property.[48]

Wash Sales. Section 1091 stipulates that in certain cases, a realized loss on the sale or exchange of stock or securities is not recognized. Specifically, if a taxpayer sells or exchanges stock or securities and within 30 days before *or* after the date of the sale or exchange acquires substantially identical stock or securities, any loss

---

[47] § 267(d) and Reg. § 1.267(d)–1(a).

[48] §§ 267(d) and 1223(2) and Reg. § 1.267(d)–1(c)(3).

TAX IN THE NEWS

REPORTING OF WASH SALES

The IRS has increased the reporting responsibility for wash sales. Section 1091 denies a deduction for losses on wash sales. As part of this disallowance, the IRS now wants the wash sale reported on Schedule D (Capital Gains and Losses). According to the Schedule D instructions, the taxpayer should write "wash sale" and the amount of the disallowed loss on the line below the line where the sales transaction is reported.

realized from the sale or exchange is not recognized because the transaction is a **wash sale**.[49] The term *acquire* means acquire by purchase or in a taxable exchange and includes an option to purchase substantially identical securities. *Substantially identical* means the same in all important particulars. Corporate bonds and preferred stock are normally not considered substantially identical to the corporation's common stock. However, if the bonds and preferred stock are convertible into common stock, they may be considered substantially identical under certain circumstances.[50] Attempts to avoid the application of the wash sales rules by having a related taxpayer repurchase the securities have been unsuccessful.[51] The wash sales provisions do *not* apply to gains.

Recognition of the loss is disallowed because the taxpayer is considered to be in substantially the same economic position after the sale and repurchase as before the sale and repurchase. This disallowance rule does not apply to taxpayers engaged in the business of buying and selling securities.[52] Investors, however, are not allowed to create losses through wash sales to offset income for tax purposes.

Realized loss that is not recognized is added to the *basis* of the substantially identical stock or securities whose acquisition resulted in the nonrecognition of loss.[53] In other words, the basis of the replacement stock or securities is increased by the amount of the unrecognized loss. If the loss were not added to the basis of the newly acquired stock or securities, the taxpayer would never recover the entire basis of the old stock or securities.

The basis of the new stock or securities includes the unrecovered portion of the basis of the formerly held stock or securities. Therefore, the *holding period* of the new stock or securities begins on the date of acquisition of the old stock or securities.[54]

EXAMPLE 34

Bhaskar owns 100 shares of Green Corporation stock (adjusted basis of $20,000), 50 shares of which he sells for $8,000. Ten days later, he purchases 50 shares of the same stock for $7,000. Bhaskar's realized loss of $2,000 ($8,000 amount realized − $10,000 adjusted basis of

---

[49] § 1091(a) and Reg. §§ 1.1091–1(a) and (f).
[50] Rev.Rul. 56–406, 1956–2 C.B. 523.
[51] *McWilliams v. Comm.*, 47–1 USTC ¶9289, 35 AFTR 1184, 67 S.Ct. 1477 (USSC, 1947).
[52] Reg. § 1.1091–1(a).
[53] § 1091(d) and Reg. § 1.1091–2(a).
[54] § 1223(4) and Reg. § 1.1223–1(d).

50 shares) is not recognized because it resulted from a wash sale. Bhaskar's basis in the newly acquired stock is $9,000 ($7,000 purchase price + $2,000 unrecognized loss from the wash sale). ▼

The taxpayer may acquire less than the number of shares sold in a wash sale. In this case, the loss from the sale is prorated between recognized and unrecognized loss on the basis of the ratio of the number of shares acquired to the number of shares sold.[55]

CONVERSION OF PROPERTY FROM PERSONAL USE TO BUSINESS OR INCOME-PRODUCING USE

As discussed previously, losses from the sale of personal use assets are not recognized for tax purposes, but losses from the sale of business and income-producing assets are deductible. Can a taxpayer convert a personal use asset that has declined in value to business (or income-producing) use and then sell the asset to recognize a business (or income-producing) loss? The tax law prevents this by specifying that the *original basis for loss* on personal use assets converted to business or income-producing use is the *lower* of the property's adjusted basis or fair market value on the date of conversion.[56] The *gain basis* for converted property is the property's adjusted basis on the date of conversion. The tax law is not concerned with gains on converted property because gains are recognized regardless of whether property is business, income producing, or personal use.

EXAMPLE 35

Diane's personal residence has an adjusted basis of $75,000 and a fair market value of $60,000. Diane converts the personal residence to rental property. Her basis for loss is $60,000 (lower of $75,000 adjusted basis and fair market value of $60,000). The $15,000 decline in value is a personal loss and can never be recognized for tax purposes. Diane's basis for gain is $75,000. ▼

The basis for loss is also the *basis for depreciating* the converted property.[57] This is an exception to the general rule that provides that the basis for depreciation is the gain basis (e.g., property received by gift). This exception prevents the taxpayer from recovering a personal loss indirectly through depreciation of the higher original basis. After the property is converted, both its basis for loss and its basis for gain are adjusted for depreciation deductions from the date of conversion to the date of disposition. These rules apply only if a conversion from personal to business or income-producing use has actually occurred.

EXAMPLE 36

At a time when his personal residence (adjusted basis of $40,000) is worth $50,000, Keith converts one-half of it to rental use. Assume the property is not MACRS recovery property. At this point, the estimated useful life of the residence is 20 years, and there is no estimated salvage value. After renting the converted portion for five years, Keith sells the property for $44,000. All amounts relate only to the building; the land has been accounted for separately. Keith has a $2,000 realized gain from the sale of the personal use portion of the residence and a $7,000 realized gain from the sale of the rental portion. These gains are computed as follows:

---

[55] § 1091(b) and Reg. § 1.1091–1(c).
[56] Reg. § 1.165–9(b)(2).
[57] Reg. § 1.167(g)–1.

	Personal Use	Rental
Original basis for gain and loss—adjusted basis on date of conversion (fair market value is greater than the adjusted basis)	$20,000	$20,000
Depreciation—five years	None	5,000
Adjusted basis—date of sale	$20,000	$15,000
Amount realized	22,000	22,000
Realized gain	$ 2,000	$ 7,000

As discussed in Chapter 15, Keith may be able to defer recognition of part or all of the $2,000 gain from the sale of the personal use portion of the residence under § 1034. The $7,000 gain from the rental portion is recognized.

EXAMPLE 37

Assume the same facts as in the previous example, except that the fair market value on the date of conversion is $30,000 and the sales proceeds are $16,000. Keith has a $12,000 realized loss from the sale of the personal use portion of the residence and a $3,250 realized loss from the sale of the rental portion. These losses are computed as follows:

	Personal Use	Rental
Original basis for loss—fair market value on date of conversion (fair market value is less than the adjusted basis)	*	$15,000
Depreciation—five years	None	3,750
Adjusted basis—date of sale	$20,000	$11,250
Amount realized	8,000	8,000
Realized loss	$12,000	$ 3,250

*Not applicable.

The $12,000 loss from the sale of the personal use portion of the residence is not recognized. The $3,250 loss from the rental portion is recognized. ▼

ADDITIONAL COMPLEXITIES IN DETERMINING REALIZED GAIN OR LOSS

Amount Realized. The calculation of the amount realized may appear to be one of the least complex areas associated with property transactions. However, because numerous positive and negative adjustments may be required, the calculation of this amount can be complex and confusing. In addition, the determination of the fair market value of the items received by the taxpayer can be difficult. The following example provides insight into various items that can have an impact on the amount realized.

EXAMPLE 38

Ridge sells an office building and the associated land on October 1, 1997. Under the terms of the sales contract, Ridge is to receive $600,000 in cash. The purchaser is to assume Ridge's mortgage of $300,000 on the property. To enable the purchaser to obtain adequate financing to pay the $600,000, Ridge is to pay the $15,000 in points charged by the lender. The broker's commission on the sale is $45,000. The purchaser agrees to pay the $12,000 in property taxes for the entire year. The amount realized by Ridge is calculated as follows:

Selling price		
Cash	$600,000	
Mortgage assumed by purchaser	300,000	
Seller's property taxes paid by purchaser ($12,000 × 9/12)	9,000	$909,000
Less		
Broker's commission	$ 45,000	
Points paid by seller	15,000	(60,000)
Amount realized		$849,000

Adjusted Basis. Three types of items tend to complicate the determination of adjusted basis. First, the applicable tax provisions for calculating the adjusted basis are dependent on how the property was acquired (e.g., purchase, taxable exchange, nontaxable exchange, gift, inheritance). Second, if the asset is subject to depreciation, cost recovery, amortization, or depletion, adjustments must be made to the basis during the time period the asset is held by the taxpayer. Upon disposition of the asset, the taxpayer's records for both of these items may be deficient. For example, the donee does not know the amount of the donor's basis or the amount of gift tax paid by the donor, or the taxpayer does not know how much depreciation he or she has deducted. Third, the complex positive and negative adjustments encountered in calculating the amount realized are also involved in calculating the adjusted basis.

EXAMPLE 39

Jane purchased a personal residence in 1991. The purchase price and the related closing costs were as follows:

Purchase price	$125,000
Recording costs	140
Title fees and title insurance	815
Survey costs	115
Attorney's fees	750
Appraisal fee	60

Other relevant tax information for the house during the time Jane owned it follows:

- Constructed a swimming pool for medical reasons. The cost was $10,000, of which $3,000 was deducted as a medical expense.
- Added a solar heating system. The cost was $15,000.
- Deducted home office expenses of $6,000. Of this amount, $3,200 was for depreciation.

The adjusted basis for the house is calculated as follows:

Purchase price	$125,000
Recording costs	140
Title fees and title insurance	815
Survey costs	115
Attorney's fees	750
Appraisal fee	60
Swimming pool ($10,000 − $3,000)	7,000
Solar heating system	15,000
	$148,880
Less: Depreciation deducted on home office	(3,200)
Adjusted basis	$145,680

SUMMARY OF BASIS ADJUSTMENTS

Some of the more common items that either increase or decrease the basis of an asset appear in Concept Summary 14–2.

In discussing the topic of basis, a number of specific techniques for determining basis have been presented. Although the various techniques are responsive to and mandated by transactions occurring in the marketplace, they do possess enough common characteristics to be categorized as follows:

- The basis of the asset may be determined by reference to the asset's cost.
- The basis of the asset may be determined by reference to the basis of another asset.
- The basis of the asset may be determined by reference to the asset's fair market value.
- The basis of the asset may be determined by reference to the basis of the asset to another taxpayer.

TAX CONSEQUENCES OF ALICE'S PROPOSED TRANSACTION

TAX PLANNING CONSIDERATIONS

6 LEARNING OBJECTIVE
Identify tax planning opportunities related to selected property transactions.

In Example 1 earlier in the chapter, Alice's tax adviser asked a number of questions in order to advise her on a proposed transaction. Alice provided the following answers:

- Alice inherited the house from her mother. The fair market value of the house at the date of her mother's death, based on the estate tax return, was $200,000. Based on an appraisal, the house is worth $230,000. Alice's mother lived in the house for 48 years. According to the mother's attorney, her adjusted basis for the house was $75,000.
- As a child, Alice lived in the house for 10 years. She has not lived there during the 35 years she has been married.
- The house has been vacant during the seven months that Alice has owned it. She has been trying to decide whether she should sell it for its fair market value or sell it to her nephew for $75,000. Alice has suggested a $75,000 price for the sale to Dan because she believes this is the amount at which she will have no gain or loss.
- Alice intends to invest the $75,000 in stock.

You advise Alice that her adjusted basis for the house is the $200,000 fair market value on the date of her mother's death. If Alice sells the house for $230,000 (assuming no selling expenses), she would have a recognized gain of $30,000 ($230,000 amount realized − $200,000 adjusted basis). The house is a capital asset, and her holding period is long term since she inherited the house. Thus, the gain would be classified as a long-term capital gain. If, instead, Alice sells the house to her nephew for $75,000, she will have a part sale and part gift. The realized gain on the sale of $9,783 is recognized.

Amount realized	$ 75,000
Less: Adjusted basis	(65,217)*
Realized gain	$ 9,783
Recognized gain	$ 9,783

*[($75,000/$230,000) × $200,000] = $65,217.

The gain is classified as a long-term capital gain. Alice is then deemed to have made a gift to Dan of $155,000 ($230,000 − $75,000).

With this information, Alice can make an informed selection between the two options.

Concept Summary 14–2

Adjustments to Basis

Item	Effect	Refer to Chapter	Explanation
Amortization of bond discount.	Increase	16	Amortization is mandatory for certain taxable bonds and elective for tax-exempt bonds.
Amortization of bond premium.	Decrease	14	Amortization is mandatory for tax-exempt bonds and elective for taxable bonds.
Amortization of covenant not to compete.	Decrease	16	Covenant must be for a definite and limited time period. The amortization period is a statutory period of 15 years.
Amortization of intangibles.	Decrease	8	Even goodwill is now subject to amortization.
Assessment for local benefits.	Increase	10	To the extent not deductible as taxes (e.g., assessment for streets and sidewalks that increase the value of the property versus one for maintenance or repair or for meeting interest charges).
Bad debts.	Decrease	7	Only the specific charge-off method is permitted.
Capital additions.	Increase	14	Certain items, at the taxpayer's election, can be capitalized or deducted (e.g., selected medical expenses).
Casualty.	Decrease	7	For a casualty loss, the amount of the adjustment is the summation of the deductible loss and the insurance proceeds received. For a casualty gain, the amount of the adjustment is the insurance proceeds received reduced by the recognized gain.
Condemnation.	Decrease	15	See casualty explanation.
Cost recovery.	Decrease	8	§ 168 is applicable to tangible assets placed in service after 1980 whose useful life is expressed in terms of years.
Depletion.	Decrease	8	Use the greater of cost or percentage depletion. Percentage depletion can still be deducted when the basis is zero.
Depreciation.	Decrease	8	§ 167 is applicable to tangible assets placed in service before 1981 and to tangible assets not depreciated in terms of years.
Easement.	Decrease		If the taxpayer does not retain any use of the land, all of the basis is allocable to the easement transaction. However, if only part of the land is affected by the easement, only part of the basis is allocable to the easement transaction.
Improvements by lessee to lessor's property.	Increase	5	Adjustment occurs only if the lessor is required to include the fair market value of the improvements in gross income under § 109.
Imputed interest.	Decrease	18	Amount deducted is not part of the cost of the asset.
Inventory: lower of cost or market.	Decrease	18	Not available if the LIFO method is used.
Limited expensing under § 179.	Decrease	8	Occurs only if the taxpayer elects § 179 treatment.

Item	Effect	Refer to Chapter	Explanation
Medical capital expenditure permitted as a medical expense.	Decrease	10	Adjustment is the amount of the deduction (the effect on basis is to increase it by the amount of the capital expenditure net of the deduction).
Real estate taxes: apportionment between the buyer and seller.	Increase or decrease	10	To the extent the buyer pays the seller's pro rata share, the buyer's basis is increased. To the extent the seller pays the buyer's pro rata share, the buyer's basis is decreased.
Rebate from manufacturer.	Decrease		Since the rebate is treated as an adjustment to the purchase price, it is not included in the buyer's gross income.
Stock dividend.	Decrease	5	Adjustment occurs only if the stock dividend is nontaxable. While the basis per share decreases, the total stock basis does not change.
Stock rights.	Decrease	14	Adjustment to stock basis occurs only for nontaxable stock rights and only if the fair market value of the rights is at least 15% of the fair market value of the stock or, if less than 15%, the taxpayer elects to allocate the basis between the stock and the rights.
Theft.	Decrease	7	See casualty explanation.

COST IDENTIFICATION AND DOCUMENTATION CONSIDERATIONS

When multiple assets are acquired in a single transaction, the contract price must be allocated for several reasons. First, some of the assets may be depreciable while others are not. From the different viewpoints of the buyer and the seller, this may produce a tax conflict that needs to be resolved. That is, the seller prefers a high allocation for nondepreciable assets, whereas the purchaser prefers a high allocation for depreciable assets (see Chapters 16 and 17). Second, the seller needs to know the amount realized on the sale of the capital assets and the ordinary income assets so that the recognized gains and losses can be classified as capital or ordinary. For example, an allocation to goodwill or to a covenant not to compete (see Chapters 8, 16, and 17) produces different tax consequences to the seller. Third, the buyer needs the adjusted basis of each asset to calculate the realized gain or loss on a subsequent sale or other disposition of each asset.

SELECTION OF PROPERTY FOR MAKING GIFTS

A donor can achieve several tax advantages by making gifts of appreciated property. Income tax on the unrealized gain that would have occurred had the donor sold the property is avoided by the donor. A portion of this amount can be permanently avoided because the donee's adjusted basis is increased by part or all of any gift tax paid by the donor. Even without this increase in basis, the income tax liability on the sale of the property by the donee can be less than the income tax liability that would have resulted from the donor's sale of the property, if the donee is in a lower tax bracket than the donor. In addition, any subsequent appreciation during the time the property is held by the lower tax bracket donee results in a tax savings on the sale or other disposition of the property. Such gifts of appreciated property can be an effective tool in family tax planning.

Taxpayers should generally not make gifts of depreciated property (property that, if sold, would produce a realized loss) because the donor does not receive an income tax deduction for the unrealized loss element. In addition, the donee receives no benefit from this unrealized loss upon the subsequent sale of the property because of the loss basis rule. The loss basis rule provides that the donee's basis is the lower of the donor's basis or fair market value at the date of the gift. If the donor anticipates that the donee will sell the property upon receiving it, the donor should sell the property and take the loss deduction, assuming the loss is deductible. The donor can then give the proceeds from the sale to the donee.

SELECTION OF PROPERTY FOR MAKING BEQUESTS

A decedent's will should generally make bequests of appreciated property. Doing so enables both the decedent and the heir to avoid income tax on the unrealized gain because the recipient takes the fair market value as his or her basis.

Taxpayers generally should not make bequests of depreciated property (property that, if sold, would produce a realized loss) because the decedent does not receive an income tax deduction for the unrealized loss element. In addition, the heir will receive no benefit from this unrealized loss upon the subsequent sale of the property.

EXAMPLE 40

On the date of her death, Marta owned land held for investment purposes. The land had an adjusted basis of $600,000 and a fair market value of $100,000. If Marta had sold the property before her death, the recognized loss would have been $500,000. If Roger inherits the property and sells it for $60,000, the recognized loss will be $40,000 (the decline in value since Marta's death). In addition, regardless of the period of time Roger holds the property, the holding period is long term (see Chapter 16). ▼

From an income tax perspective, it is preferable to transfer appreciated property as a bequest rather than as a gift. This results because inherited property receives a step-up in basis, whereas property received by gift has a carryover basis to the donee. However, in making this decision, the estate tax consequences of the bequest should also be weighed against the gift tax consequences of the gift.

DISALLOWED LOSSES

Section 267 Disallowed Losses. Taxpayers should be aware of the desirability of avoiding transactions that activate the loss disallowance provisions for related parties. This is so even in light of the provision that permits the related-party buyer to offset his or her realized gain by the related-party seller's disallowed loss. Even with this offset, several inequities exist. First, the tax benefit associated with the disallowed loss ultimately is realized by the wrong party (the related-party buyer rather than the related-party seller). Second, the tax benefit of this offset to the related-party buyer does not occur until the buyer disposes of the property. Therefore, the longer the time period between the purchase and disposition of the property by the related-party buyer, the less the economic benefit. Third, if the property does not appreciate to at least its adjusted basis to the related-party seller during the time period the related-party buyer holds it, part or all of the disallowed loss is permanently lost. Fourth, since the right of offset is available only to the original transferee (the related-party buyer), all of the disallowed loss is permanently lost if the original transferee subsequently transfers the property by gift or bequest.

EXAMPLE 41

Tim sells property with an adjusted basis of $35,000 to Wes, his brother, for $25,000, the fair market value of the property. The $10,000 realized loss to Tim is disallowed by § 267. If Wes subsequently sells the property to an unrelated party for $37,000, he has a recognized gain of $2,000 (realized gain of $12,000 reduced by disallowed loss of $10,000). Therefore, from the perspective of the family unit, the original $10,000 realized loss ultimately is recognized. However, if Wes sells the property for $29,000, he has a recognized gain of $0 (realized gain of $4,000 reduced by disallowed loss of $4,000 necessary to offset the realized gain). From the perspective of the family unit, $6,000 of the realized loss of $10,000 is permanently wasted ($10,000 realized loss − $4,000 offset permitted). ▼

Wash Sales. The wash sales provisions can be avoided if the security is replaced within the statutory time period with a similar rather than a substantially identical security. For example, the sale of Bethlehem Steel common stock and a purchase of Inland Steel common stock is not treated as a wash sale. Such a procedure can enable the taxpayer to use an unrealized capital loss to offset a recognized capital gain. The taxpayer can sell the security before the end of the taxable year, offset the recognized capital loss against the capital gain, and invest the sales proceeds in a similar security.

Because the wash sales provisions do not apply to gains, it may be desirable to engage in a wash sale before the end of the taxable year. This recognized capital gain may be used to offset capital losses or capital loss carryovers from prior years. Since the basis of the replacement stock or securities will be the purchase price, the taxpayer in effect has exchanged a capital gain for an increased basis for the stock or securities.

KEY TERMS

Adjusted basis, 14–4
Amount realized, 14–3
Fair market value, 14–4
Goodwill, 14–10

Holding period, 14–13
Realized gain, 14–3
Realized loss, 14–3
Recognized gain, 14–7

Recognized loss, 14–7
Recovery of capital doctrine, 14–8
Wash sale, 14–19

PROBLEM MATERIALS

DISCUSSION QUESTIONS

1. Upon the sale or other disposition of property, what four questions should be considered for income tax purposes?

2. Define each of the following terms:
   a. Amount realized.
   b. Realized gain.
   c. Realized loss.

3. Which of the following would be treated as a "sale or other disposition"?
   a. Sale for cash.
   b. Sale on credit.
   c. Exchange.
   d. Involuntary conversion.
   e. Bond retirement.

4. Ivan invests in land and Grace invests in taxable bonds. The land appreciates by $5,000 each year, and the bonds earn interest of $5,000 each year. After holding the land and bonds for five years, Ivan and Grace sell them. There is a $25,000 realized gain on the sale of the land and no realized gain or loss on the sale of the bonds. Are the tax consequences to Ivan and Grace the same for each of the five years? Explain.

5. Carol and Dave each purchase 100 shares of stock of Burgundy, Inc., a publicly owned corporation, in July for $10,000 each. Carol sells her stock on December 31 for $14,000. Since Burgundy's stock is listed on a national exchange, Dave is able to ascertain that his shares are worth $14,000 on December 31. Does the tax law treat the appreciation in value of the stock differently for Carol and Dave? Explain.

6. If a taxpayer sells property for cash, the amount realized consists of the net proceeds from the sale. For each of the following, indicate the effect on the amount realized:
   a. The property is sold on credit.
   b. A mortgage on the property is assumed by the buyer.
   c. The buyer acquires the property subject to a mortgage of the seller.
   d. The seller pays real property taxes that are treated as imposed on the purchaser.
   e. Stock that has a basis to the purchaser of $6,000 and a fair market value of $10,000 is received by the seller as part of the consideration.

7. If the buyer pays real property taxes that are treated as imposed on the seller, what are the effects on the seller's amount realized and the buyer's adjusted basis for the property? If the seller pays real property taxes that are treated as imposed on the buyer, what are the effects on the seller's amount realized and the buyer's adjusted basis for the property?

8. Tom is negotiating to buy some land. Under the first option, Tom will give Sandra $70,000 and assume her mortgage on the land for $30,000. Under the second option, Tom will give Sandra $100,000, and she will immediately pay off the mortgage. Tom would like for his basis for the land to be as high as possible. Given this objective, which option should Tom select?

9. Edith purchases land from Gail. Edith gives Gail $40,000 in cash and agrees to pay Gail an additional $80,000 one year later plus interest at 8%.
   a. What is Edith's adjusted basis for the land at the date purchased?
   b. What is Edith's adjusted basis for the land one year later?

10. The taxpayer owns land and a building with an adjusted basis of $50,000 and a fair market value of $250,000. The property is subject to a mortgage of $400,000. Since the taxpayer is in arrears on the mortgage payments, the creditor is willing to accept the property in return for canceling the amount of the mortgage.
    a. How can the adjusted basis of the property be less than the amount of the mortgage?
    b. If the creditor's offer is accepted, what are the effects on the amount realized, the adjusted basis, and the realized gain or loss?
    c. Does it matter in (b) if the mortgage is recourse or nonrecourse?

11. Discuss the relationship between the adjusted basis and capital additions and between the adjusted basis and capital recoveries.

12. On August 16, 1997, Todd acquires land and a building for $300,000 to use in his sole proprietorship. Of the purchase price, $200,000 is allocated to the building, and $100,000 is allocated to the land. Cost recovery of $1,926 is deducted in 1997 for the building.
    a. What is the adjusted basis for the land and the building at the acquisition date?
    b. What is the adjusted basis for the land and the building at the end of 1997?

13. Abby owns stock in Orange Corporation and Blue Corporation. She receives a $1,000 distribution from both corporations. The instructions from Orange state that the $1,000 is a dividend. The instructions from Blue state that the $1,000 is not a dividend. What could cause the instructions to differ as to the tax consequences?

14. A taxpayer who acquires a taxable bond at a premium may elect to amortize the premium, whereas a taxpayer who acquires a tax-exempt bond at a premium must

amortize the premium. Why would a taxpayer make the amortization election for taxable bonds? What effect does the mandatory amortization of tax-exempt bonds have on taxable income?

15. Kara owns two assets that she is considering selling. One has appreciated in value by $3,000, and the other has declined in value by $3,000. Both assets are held for personal use. Kara believes that she should sell both assets in the same taxable year so that the loss of $3,000 can offset the gain of $3,000. Advise Kara regarding the tax consequences.

16. Ron sold a sailboat for a $5,000 loss in the current year because he was diagnosed as having skin cancer. His spouse wants him to sell his Harley Davidson motorcycle because her brother broke his leg while riding his motorcycle. Since Ron no longer has anyone to ride with, he is seriously considering accepting his wife's advice. Because the motorcycle is a classic, Ron has received two offers. Each offer would result in a $5,000 gain. Joe would like to purchase the motorcycle before Christmas, and Jeff would like to purchase it after New Year's. Identify the relevant tax issues Ron faces in making his decision.

17. Lee owns a life insurance policy that will pay $100,000 to Rita, his spouse, on his death. At the date of Lee's death, he had paid total premiums on the policy of $65,000. In accordance with § 101(a)(1), Rita excludes the $100,000 of insurance proceeds. Discuss the relationship, if any, between the § 101 exclusion and the recovery of capital doctrine.

18. For a bargain purchase, why is the adjusted basis of the property to the buyer equal to the fair market value of the property rather than the purchase price?

19. When a business is purchased and goodwill is involved, why is the adjusted basis of the goodwill determined using the residual method rather than the amount assigned to the goodwill in the purchase contract?

20. Discuss the differences in tax treatment when stock rights are allocated a cost basis and when stock rights have no cost basis. When does each of these situations occur?

21. Why does the Code contain both a gain basis rule and a loss basis rule for gift property? Under what circumstances will these rules produce different basis amounts?

22. Simon, who is retired, owns Teal, Inc., stock that has declined in value since he purchased it. He has decided to give the stock to his nephew, Fred, who is a high school teacher, or to sell the stock and give the proceeds to Fred. Because nearly all of his wealth is invested in tax-exempt bonds, Simon is in the 15% tax bracket. Fred will use the cash or the proceeds from his sale of the stock to make the down payment on the purchase of a house. Based on a recent conversation, Simon is aware that Fred is in the 28% bracket. Identify the tax issues relevant to Simon in deciding whether to give the stock or the sale proceeds to Fred.

23. In calculating the adjusted basis to the donee of property received by gift, why is it necessary to know if the gift was made before 1977 rather than after 1976?

24. Agnes has been diagnosed with a terminal disease. Her nephew, Stan, will graduate from college in May. She has stock worth $50,000 that she intends to give him as a graduation present. Since she may not be alive then, Agnes is considering giving the stock to him now (i.e., four months prior to graduation). If Agnes should die before making the gift, her will stipulates that Stan will receive the stock. Identify the relevant tax issues that Agnes should consider in making her decision.

25. Gary makes a gift of an appreciated building to Carmen. She dies three months later, and Gary inherits the building from her. During the period that Carmen held the building, she deducted depreciation and made a capital expenditure. What effect might these items have on Gary's basis for the inherited building?

26. Immediately before his death in 1997, Kirby sells securities (adjusted basis of $100,000) for their fair market value of $20,000. The sale was not to a related party. The securities were community property, and Kirby is survived by his wife, Zina, who inherits all of his property.
    a. Did Kirby act wisely? Why or why not?

b. Suppose the figures are reversed (sale for $100,000 of property with an adjusted basis of $20,000). Would the sale be wise? Why or why not?

27. Thelma inherited land from her Aunt Sadie on June 7, 1997. The land appreciated in value by 100% during the six months that Aunt Sadie owned it. The value has remained stable during the three months that Thelma has owned it, and she expects it to continue to do so in the near future. Although she would like to sell the land, Thelma has decided to delay the sale for another three months so that the gain will qualify for long-term capital gain treatment. Evaluate Thelma's understanding of the relevant tax issues.

28. What are related-party transactions, and why are they important?

29. What is a wash sale? Why isn't a realized loss recognized on a wash sale? How is the recovery of capital doctrine maintained?

30. Losses on the disposition of property used in a trade or business or held for investment are recognized whereas losses on the disposition of personal use property are disallowed. Is it possible to avoid this disallowance by reclassifying the personal use loss as a business or an investment loss through converting the personal use property to either trade or business property or investment property prior to the disposition?

PROBLEMS

31. Anne sold her home for $260,000 in 1997. Selling expenses were $15,000. She had purchased it in 1990 for $190,000. During the period of ownership, Anne had:

    - Deducted $50,500 office-in-home expenses, which included $14,500 in depreciation. (Refer to Chapter 9.)

    - Deducted a casualty loss of residential trees destroyed by a hurricane. The total loss was $19,000 (after the $100 floor and the 10%-of-AGI floor), and Anne's insurance company reimbursed her for $13,500. (Refer to Chapter 7.)

    - Paid street paving assessment of $7,000 and added sidewalks for $11,000.

    - Installed an elevator for medical reasons. The total cost was $20,000, and Anne deducted $12,000 as medical expenses. (Refer to Chapter 10.)

    - Received $7,500 from a utility company for an easement to install underground utility lines across the property.

    What is Anne's realized gain?

32. Kareem bought a rental house at the beginning of 1992 for $80,000, of which $10,000 is allocated to the land and $70,000 to the building. Early in 1994, he had a tennis court built in the backyard at a cost of $5,000. Kareem has deducted $32,200 for depreciation on the house and $1,300 for depreciation on the court. At the beginning of 1997, he sells the house and tennis court for $125,000 cash.
    a. What is Kareem's realized gain or loss?
    b. If an original mortgage of $20,000 is still outstanding and the buyer assumes the mortgage in addition to the cash payment, what is Kareem's realized gain or loss?
    c. If the buyer takes the property subject to the mortgage, what is Kareem's realized gain or loss?

33. Norm is negotiating the sale of a tract of his land to Pat. Use the following classification scheme to classify each of the items contained in the proposed sales contract:

    Legend

    DARN = Decreases amount realized by Norm
    IARN = Increases amount realized by Norm
    DABN = Decreases adjusted basis to Norm
    IABN = Increases adjusted basis to Norm
    DABP = Decreases adjusted basis to Pat
    IABP = Increases adjusted basis to Pat

a. Norm is to receive cash of $50,000.
b. Norm is to receive Pat's note payable for $25,000, payable in three years.
c. Pat assumes Norm's mortgage of $5,000 on the land.
d. Pat agrees to pay the realtor's sales commission of $8,000.
e. Pat agrees to pay the property taxes on the land for the entire year. If each party paid his or her respective share, Norm's share would be $1,000, and Pat's share would be $3,000.
f. Pat pays legal fees of $500.
g. Norm pays legal fees of $750.

34. Gayla owns a building (adjusted basis of $366,500 on January 1, 1997) that she rents to Len who operates a restaurant in the building. The municipal health department closed the restaurant for two months during 1997 because of health code violations. Under MACRS, the cost recovery deduction for 1997 would be $12,000. However, Gayla deducted cost recovery only for the 10 months the restaurant was open since she waived the rent income during the two-month period the restaurant was closed.
    a. What is the amount of the cost recovery deduction that Gayla should report on her 1997 income tax return?
    b. Calculate the adjusted basis of the building at the end of 1997.

35. Nell owns a personal use automobile that has an adjusted basis of $18,000. The fair market value of the automobile is $14,500. Nell's AGI is $40,000.
    a. Calculate the realized and recognized loss if Nell sells the automobile for $14,500.
    b. Calculate the realized and recognized loss if Nell exchanges the automobile for another automobile worth $14,500.
    c. Calculate the realized and recognized loss if the automobile is stolen and Nell receives insurance proceeds of $14,500.

36. Mitch's automobile, which is used exclusively in his business, is stolen. The adjusted basis is $30,000, and the fair market value is $33,000. Mitch's AGI is $50,000.
    a. If Mitch receives insurance proceeds of $33,000, what effect do the theft and the receipt of the insurance proceeds have on the adjusted basis of the automobile?
    b. If the automobile is not insured, what effect do the theft and the absence of insurance have on the adjusted basis of the automobile?

37. Aaron owns stock in Dove Corporation. His adjusted basis for the stock is $45,000. During the year, he receives a distribution from the corporation of $38,000 that is labeled a return of capital (i.e., Dove has no earnings and profits).
    a. Determine the tax consequences to Aaron.
    b. Assume instead that the amount of the distribution is $50,000. Determine the tax consequences to Aaron.
    c. Assume instead in (a) that the $38,000 distribution is labeled a taxable dividend (i.e., Dove has earnings and profits of at least $38,000).

38. Chee purchases Tan, Inc., bonds for $110,000 on January 2, 1997. The face value of the bonds is $100,000, the maturity date is December 31, 2001, and the annual interest rate is 8%. Chee will amortize the premium only if he is required to do so. Chee sells the bonds on July 1, 1999, for $109,000.
    a. Determine the interest income Chee should report for 1997.
    b. Calculate Chee's recognized gain or loss on the sale of the bonds in 1999.

39. Which of the following would definitely result in a recognized gain or loss?
    a. Kay sells her lakeside cabin, which has an adjusted basis of $100,000, for $150,000.
    b. Adam sells his personal residence, which has an adjusted basis of $150,000, for $100,000.
    c. Carl's personal residence is on the site of a proposed airport and is condemned by the city. Carl receives $55,000 for the house, which has an adjusted basis of $65,000.
    d. Olga's land is worth $40,000 at the end of the year. Olga had purchased the land six months earlier for $25,000.
    e. Vera's personal use vehicle is stolen. Her adjusted basis is $22,000. She receives a check from the insurance company for $23,000. Vera has decided that in the future she will use mass transit rather than owning an automobile.
    f. Jerry sells used clothing, adjusted basis of $500, to a thrift store for $50.

40. Tiffany sells the following assets during the year. All are held for personal use.
    - Car with an adjusted basis of $19,000 for $7,000.
    - Used clothing with an adjusted basis of $600 for $100.
    - Sailboat with an adjusted basis of $3,500 for $3,600.
    - Antique Chippendale chest with an adjusted basis of $10,000 for $14,000.

    Calculate Tiffany's realized and recognized gain or loss.

41. Hubert's personal residence is condemned as part of an urban renewal project. His adjusted basis for the residence is $200,000. He receives condemnation proceeds of $180,000 and invests the proceeds in stock.
    a. Calculate Hubert's realized and recognized gain or loss.
    b. If the condemnation proceeds are $225,000, what are Hubert's realized and recognized gain or loss?
    c. What are Hubert's realized and recognized gain or loss in (a) if the house was rental property?

42. Walt Barnes is a real estate agent for Governor's Farms, a residential real estate development. Because of his outstanding sales performance, Walt is permitted to buy a lot that normally would sell for $125,000 for $100,000. Walt is the only real estate agent for Governor's Farms who is permitted to do so.
    a. Does Walt have gross income from the transaction?
    b. What is Walt's adjusted basis for the land?
    c. Write a letter to Walt informing him of the tax consequences of his acquisition of the lot. His address is 100 Tower Road, San Diego, CA 92182.

43. Karen makes the following purchases and sales of stock:

Transaction	Date	Number of Shares	Company	Price per Share
Purchase	1–1–95	300	MDG	$ 75
Purchase	6–1–95	150	GRU	300
Purchase	11–1–95	60	MDG	70
Sale	12–3–95	180	MDG	70
Purchase	3–1–96	120	GRU	375
Sale	8–1–96	90	GRU	330
Sale	1–1–97	150	MDG	90
Sale	2–1–97	75	GRU	500

    Assuming that Karen is unable to identify the particular lots that are sold with the original purchase, what is the realized gain or loss on each type of stock as of:
    a. 7–1–95.
    b. 12–31–95.
    c. 12–31–96.
    d. 7–1–97.

44. Frank purchases 100 shares of Bluebird Corporation stock on June 3, 1997, for $150,000. On August 25, 1997, Frank purchases an additional 50 shares of Bluebird stock for $60,000. According to market quotations, Bluebird stock is selling for $1,100 per share on December 31, 1997. Frank sells 60 shares of Bluebird stock on March 1, 1998, for $51,000.
    a. What is the adjusted basis of Frank's Bluebird stock on December 31, 1997?
    b. What is Frank's recognized gain or loss from the sale of Bluebird stock on March 1, 1998, assuming the shares sold are from the shares purchased on June 3, 1997?
    c. What is Frank's recognized gain or loss from the sale of Bluebird stock on March 1, 1998, assuming Frank cannot adequately identify the shares sold?

45. Paula Andrews purchases the assets of a sole proprietorship from Seth. The adjusted basis of each of the assets on Seth's books and the fair market value of each asset as agreed to by Paula and Seth are as follows:

Asset	Seth's Adjusted Basis	FMV
Accounts receivable	$ –0–	$ 10,000
Notes receivable	15,000	20,000
Machinery and equipment	85,000	100,000
Building	100,000	300,000
Land	200,000	350,000

The purchase price is $900,000.
a. Calculate Seth's realized and recognized gain.
b. Determine Paula's basis for each of the assets.
c. Write a letter to Paula informing her of the tax consequences of the purchase. Her address is 300 Riverside Drive, Cincinnati, OH 45207.

46. Diane owns 1,000 shares of Robin, Inc., common stock with an adjusted basis of $100,000. During the year she receives the following distributions associated with the stock:

- $3,000 taxable cash dividend.
- 2% stock dividend in the form of 20 shares of preferred stock. The fair market value of the common stock was $110,000, and the fair market value of the preferred stock was $2,000.
- 5% stock dividend in the form of 50 shares of common stock. The fair market value of the 1,000 shares of common stock was $115,000.

Determine the tax consequences to Diane.

47. Shontelle owns 1,000 shares of Gray Corporation stock with a basis of $15,000 and a fair market value of $20,000. She receives nontaxable stock rights to purchase additional shares. The rights have a fair market value of $2,000.
    a. What is the basis of the stock and the basis of the stock rights?
    b. What is the holding period for the stock rights?
    c. What is the recognized gain or loss if the stock rights are sold for $2,000?
    d. What is the recognized gain or loss if the stock rights are allowed to lapse?

48. Rick received various gifts over the years. He has decided to dispose of the following assets that he received as gifts:
    a. In 1949, he received land worth $25,000. The donor's adjusted basis was $30,000. Rick sells the land for $87,000 in 1997.
    b. In 1955, he received stock in Gold Company. The donor's adjusted basis was $10,000. The fair market value on the date of the gift was $28,000. Rick sells the stock for $40,000 in 1997.
    c. In 1961, he received land worth $12,000. The donor's adjusted basis was $25,000. Rick sells the land for $8,000 in 1997.
    d. In 1994, he received stock worth $30,000. The donor's adjusted basis was $45,000. Rick sells the stock in 1997 for $39,000.

What is the realized gain or loss from each of the preceding transactions? Assume in each of the gift transactions that no gift tax was paid.

49. Beth received a car from Sam as a gift. Sam paid $18,000 for the car. He had used it for business purposes and had deducted $8,000 for depreciation up to the time he gave the car to Beth. The fair market value of the car is $6,000.
    a. Assuming Beth uses the car for business purposes, what is her basis for depreciation?
    b. If the estimated useful life is two years (from the date of the gift), what is her depreciation deduction for each year? Assume Beth elects the straight-line method.
    c. If Beth sells the car for $900 one year after receiving it, what is her gain or loss?
    d. If Beth sells the car for $6,000 one year after receiving it, what is her gain or loss?

50. In 1991, Ron receives a gift of property that has a fair market value of $100,000 on the date of the gift. The donor's adjusted basis for the property was $40,000. Assume the donor paid gift tax of $15,000 on the gift.
    a. What is Ron's basis for gain and loss and for depreciation?
    b. If Ron had received the gift of property in 1975, what would his basis be for gain and loss and for depreciation?

51. On September 18, 1997, Jerry received land and a building from his Uncle Ted as a gift. Uncle Ted's adjusted basis and the fair market value at the date of the gift were as follows:

	Adjusted Basis	FMV
Land	$100,000	$200,000
Building	80,000	100,000

    Uncle Ted paid gift tax of $45,000.
    a. Determine Jerry's adjusted basis for the land and building.
    b. Assume instead that the FMV of the land was $90,000 and the FMV of the building was $60,000. Determine Jerry's adjusted basis for the land and building.

52. Ira Cook is planning to make a charitable contribution of Crystal, Inc., stock worth $20,000 to the Boy Scouts. The stock Ira is considering contributing has an adjusted basis of $15,000. A friend has suggested that Ira sell the stock and contribute the $20,000 in proceeds rather than contribute the stock.
    a. Should Ira follow the friend's advice? Why?
    b. Assume the fair market value is only $13,000. In this case, should Ira follow the friend's advice? Why?
    c. Rather than make a charitable contribution to the Boy Scouts, Ira is going to make a gift to Nancy, his niece. Advise Ira regarding (a) and (b).
    d. Write a letter to Ira regarding whether in (a) he should sell the stock and contribute the cash or contribute the stock. He has informed you that he purchased the stock six years ago. Ira's address is 500 Ireland Avenue, De Kalb, IL 60115.

53. Dena inherits property from Mary, her mother. Mary's adjusted basis for the property is $100,000, and the fair market value is $725,000. Six months after Mary's death, the fair market value is $740,000. Dena is the sole beneficiary of Mary's estate.
    a. Can the executor of Mary's estate elect the alternate valuation date?
    b. What is Dena's basis for the property?

54. Earl's estate includes the following assets available for distribution to Robert, one of Earl's beneficiaries:

Asset	Earl's Adjusted Basis	FMV at Date of Death	FMV at Alternate Valuation Date
Cash	$10,000	$ 10,000	$ 10,000
Stock	40,000	125,000	60,000
Apartment building	60,000	300,000	325,000
Land	75,000	100,000	110,000

    The fair market value of the stock six months after Earl's death was $60,000. However, believing that the stock would continue to decline in value, the executor of the estate distributed the stock to Robert one month after Earl's death. Robert immediately sold the stock for $85,000.
    a. Determine Robert's basis for the assets if the primary valuation date and amount apply.
    b. Determine Robert's basis for the assets if the executor elects the alternate valuation date and amount.

55. Dan bought a hotel for $720,000 in January 1994. In January 1997, he died and left the hotel to Ed. Dan had deducted $42,000 of cost recovery on the hotel before his death. The fair market value in January 1997 was $780,000.
    a. What is the basis of the property to Ed?
    b. If the land is worth $240,000, what is Ed's basis for cost recovery?

56. Emily makes a gift of 100 shares of appreciated stock to her uncle, George, on January 5, 1997. The basis of the stock is $3,150, and the fair market value is $5,250. George dies on October 8, 1997. During the period that George held the stock, he received a 5% nontaxable stock dividend. Under the provisions of George's will, Emily inherits 100 shares of the stock. The value of the stock for Federal estate tax purposes is $55 per share.
    a. What is the basis of the inherited stock to Emily?
    b. What is the basis of the inherited stock to Emily if she had given the stock to George on January 5, 1996?

57. Larry and Grace live in Louisiana, a community property state. They own land (community property) that has an adjusted basis to them of $100,000. When Grace dies, Larry inherits her share of the land. At the date of Grace's death, the fair market value of the land is $140,000. Six months after Grace's death, the land is worth $150,000.
    a. What is Larry's basis for the land?
    b. What would Larry's basis for the land be if he and Grace lived in Virginia, a common law state, and Larry inherited Grace's share?

58. Joyce owns undeveloped real estate with an adjusted basis of $120,000. She sells the real estate to her sister, Iris, for its fair market value of $115,000.
    a. Calculate Joyce's realized and recognized gain or loss.
    b. If Iris later sells the real estate for $119,000, calculate her realized and recognized gain or loss.
    c. Assume instead that Joyce sold the real estate to Iris for its fair market value of $130,000. Calculate Joyce's realized and recognized gain or loss.
    d. Assume instead that Joyce sold the real estate to Hector, a friend, for its fair market value of $115,000.
    e. Advise Joyce whether she should sell the real estate to Iris or Hector for its fair market value of $115,000.

59. Ted owns a 60% capital and profits interest in TS Partnership, which sells property to Ted for $65,000. The partnership's adjusted basis for the property is $90,000.
    a. Calculate the realized and recognized loss to the partnership.
    b. Calculate the basis of the property to Ted.
    c. If Ted subsequently sells the property for $87,000, calculate his realized and recognized gain or loss.
    d. If Ted gives the property to his daughter, Donna, who subsequently sells it for $87,000, calculate Donna's realized and recognized gain or loss. Assume no gift tax is paid on the gift and the fair market value on the date of the gift is $80,000.
    e. Determine the tax consequences in (a) through (d) if Ted is a shareholder and TS is a corporation.

60. Susan owns 100 shares of Drake, Inc., stock with an adjusted basis of $50,000. On December 12, 1997, she sells the 100 shares for their fair market value of $45,000. On January 4, 1998, she purchases 125 shares of Drake stock for $57,500.
    a. What is Susan's realized and recognized gain or loss on the sale of the 100 shares sold on December 12, 1997?
    b. What is Susan's adjusted basis for the 125 shares purchased on January 4, 1998?
    c. How would your answers in (a) and (b) change if Susan purchased only 75 shares for $34,500 on January 4, 1998?
    d. How would your answers in (a) and (b) change if Susan purchased 125 shares on January 15, 1998, instead of January 4, 1998?

61. Kristy owns 100 shares of stock in Magenta Corporation. Her adjusted basis for the stock is $5,000. On December 21, Kristy sells the stock in the marketplace for $12,000. She purchases 100 shares of Magenta stock in the marketplace on January 5 of the following year for $12,000.

a. What is Kristy trying to achieve from a tax perspective?
b. Will she succeed?
c. Using the same data, except that Kristy's adjusted basis for the stock is $15,000, respond to (a) and (b).
d. Advise Kristy on how she can avoid any negative tax consequence encountered in (c).

62. James retires from a public accounting firm to enter private practice. He had bought a home two years earlier for $40,000. Upon opening his business, he converts one-fourth of his home into an office. The fair market value of the home on the date of conversion (January 1, 1992) is $75,000. The adjusted basis is $56,000 (ignore land). James lives and works in the home for six years (after converting it to business use) and sells it at the end of the sixth year. He deducted $2,630 of cost recovery using the statutory percentage method.
a. How much gain or loss is recognized if James sells the property for $44,000?
b. If he sells the property for $70,000?

63. Surendra's personal residence originally cost $180,000 (ignore land). After living in the house for five years, he converts it to rental property. At the date of conversion, the fair market value of the house is $150,000.
a. Calculate Surendra's basis for loss for the rental property.
b. Calculate Surendra's basis for depreciation for the rental property.
c. Calculate Surendra's basis for gain for the rental property.

64. Hun, age 93, has accumulated substantial assets during his life. Among his many assets are the following, which he is considering giving to Koji, his grandson.

Assets	Adjusted Basis	Fair Market Value
Red Corporation stock	$ 50,000	$700,000
Silver Corporation stock	70,000	71,000
Emerald Corporation stock	200,000	50,000

Hun has been in ill health for the past five years. His physician has informed him that he probably will not live for more than six months. Advise Hun which of the stocks should be transferred as gifts and which as bequests.

CUMULATIVE PROBLEMS

65. John Custer, age 35, is single. His Social Security number is 443–11–2222, and he resides at 150 Highway 51, Tangipahoa, LA 70443.

John has a five-year-old child, Kendra, who lives with her mother, Katy. John pays alimony of $15,000 per year to Katy and child support of $12,000. The $12,000 of child support covers 70 percent of Katy's costs of rearing Kendra. Kendra's Social Security number is 432–60–1000, and Katy's is 444–00–1234.

John's mother, Sally, lived with him until her death in early September 1997. He incurred and paid medical expenses for her of $9,000 and other support payments of $4,000. Sally's only sources of income were $3,000 of interest income on certificates of deposit and $2,400 of Social Security benefits, which she spent on her medical expenses and helping to maintain John's household. Sally's Social Security number was 400–10–2000.

John is employed by the Highway Department of the State of Louisiana in an executive position. His salary is $80,000. The appropriate amounts of Social Security and Medicare taxes were withheld. In addition, $16,000 was withheld for Federal income taxes, and $2,500 was withheld for state income taxes.

Upon the death of his Aunt Josie in December 1996, John, her only recognized heir, inherited the following assets:

Asset	Josie's Adjusted Basis	FMV at Date of Death
Car	$ 22,000	$ 14,000
Land—300 acres	150,000	600,000
IBM stock	50,000	125,000
Cash	33,000	33,000

Six months prior to her death, Josie gave John a beachhouse. Her adjusted basis for the beachhouse was $200,000, and the fair market value was $250,000. She paid a gift tax of $18,000.

During the year, John had the following transactions:

- On February 1, 1997, he sold for $40,000 Exxon stock that he inherited from his father four years ago. His father's adjusted basis was $20,000, and the fair market value at the date of the father's death was $35,000.

- The car John inherited from Josie was destroyed in a wreck on October 1, 1997. He had loaned the car to Katy to use for a two-week period while the engine in her car was being replaced. Fortunately, neither Katy nor Kendra was injured. John received insurance proceeds of $12,000, the fair market value of the car on October 1.

- On October 30, 1997, John gambled away the $33,000 he inherited on a riverboat casino in Biloxi. He had hoped this activity would help with the bouts of depression he had been suffering since Sally's death.

- On December 28, John sold the 300 acres of land to his brother, James, for its fair market value of $575,000. James planned on using the land for his dairy farm.

Other sources of income for John were as follows:

Dividend income	$20,000
Interest income:	
Guaranty Bank	11,000
City of Kentwood water bonds	12,000
Award from State of Louisiana for outstanding suggestion for highway beautification	6,000

Potential itemized deductions for John, in addition to items already mentioned, were:

Property taxes paid on his residence	$7,000
Property taxes paid on personalty	2,000
Estimated Federal income taxes paid	2,300
Estimated state income taxes paid	2,500
Charitable contributions	6,000
Mortgage interest on his residence	5,500
Orthodontic expenses for Kendra	3,000
Psychiatric expenses for John	2,000

Part 1—Tax Computation
Compute John's net tax payable or refund due for 1997. Suggested software (if available): *TurboTax* or *MacInTax*.

Part 2—Tax Planning
Assume that rather than selling the land to James, John is considering leasing it to him for $30,000 annually with the lease beginning on October 1, 1997. James would prepay

the lease payments through December 31, 1997. Thereafter, he would make monthly lease payments at the beginning of each month. What effect would this have on John's 1997 tax liability? What potential problem might John encounter? Write a letter to John in which you advise him of the tax consequences of leasing versus selling. Also, prepare a memo for the tax files.

66. Lori Ann (age 27) and Albert Welch (age 28) are married and file a joint return. They have one child, Margaret (age 3). Lori Ann's Social Security number is 366–55–2222, Albert's is 555–66–4300, and Margaret's is 555–77–7333. They reside at 400 Aspen Drive, Williamsburg, VA 23185.

Lori Ann is employed as an accountant at the College of William and Mary at an annual salary of $45,000. Albert is an executive with Historic Williamsburg and receives a salary of $40,000 annually. The appropriate amounts for FICA taxes were withheld. For Federal income taxes, $10,250 was withheld by Lori Ann's employer, and $7,000 was withheld by Albert's employer. For state income tax purposes, $1,800 was withheld by Lori Ann's employer, and $1,600 was withheld by Albert's employer.

Items of potential tax significance include the following:

- Albert received $1,500 of interest income on certificates of deposit and $400 of interest income on bonds issued by the City of Norfolk.

- Lori Ann received dividend income of $2,250 on Green, Inc., stock. She received the stock as a gift from her Aunt Jane three years ago when it was worth $9,500. Aunt Jane's adjusted basis was $1,000.

- On May 10, 1996, Albert sold land for $22,000 that he had inherited from his father in December 1993. His father's adjusted basis for the land was $12,000, and the fair market value on the date of the father's death was $26,000. Albert sold the land to his sister, Marge.

- On August 5, 1996, Lori Ann sold the Green, Inc., stock for $25,000.

- Lori Ann and Albert received rent income of $1,000 for their mountain getaway, which they rented for one week in December. During the year, they spent 80 days at their mountain home. Expenses associated with the mountain home for the year were as follows:

Property taxes	$1,500
Mortgage interest	1,200
Repairs, maintenance, and insurance	800
Utilities	600

They purchased the house in January 1993 for $100,000 with $20,000 being allocable to land.

- Potential itemized deductions, in addition to items already mentioned, were:

Charitable contributions	$ 900
Mortgage interest on residence	3,600
Real property taxes	1,300
Personal property taxes	300
State and local sales taxes	2,000
Medical expenses (less reimbursements)	350

- Albert receives a bonus of $4,000 in January 1997 associated with the outstanding performance of his unit in 1996.

- Lori Ann and Albert made estimated tax payments of $4,000.

Compute their net tax payable or refund due for 1996. If you use tax forms for your computations, you will need Form 1040 and Schedules A, B, and D. Suggested software (if available): *TurboTax* or *MacInTax*.

RESEARCH PROBLEMS

Note: ***West's Federal Taxation on CD-ROM*** *can be used in preparing solutions to the Research Problems. Alternatively, tax research materials contained in a standard tax library can be used.*

Research Problem 1. Amy sold land to Chuck two years ago for $200,000. Her adjusted basis for the land was $150,000. The consideration received for the land was $125,000 in cash and a debt instrument for $75,000. At the time of the sale, Amy reported a recognized gain of $50,000 ($200,000 amount realized − $150,000 adjusted basis).

In accordance with the sales agreement, Chuck pledged stock (Stock A) worth $75,000 as collateral for the note. The land was not pledged because Chuck was going to contribute it to a real estate partnership in which he would receive a 10% interest. Under the terms of the sales agreement, if the value of the stock declined below the principal amount of the note by at least $5,000, substitute collateral would be required. Because the value of the stock has declined, Chuck is required to substitute Stock B for Stock A. The value of Stock B exceeds the value of Stock A by $5,000.

Does Amy have a recognized gain or loss from the substitution?

Research Problem 2. Terry owns real estate with an adjusted basis of $600,000 and a fair market value of $1,100,000. The amount of the nonrecourse mortgage on the property is $2,500,000. Because of substantial past and projected future losses associated with the real estate development (occupancy rate of only 37% after three years), Terry deeds the property to the creditor.
a. What are the tax consequences to Terry?
b. Assume the data are the same, except the fair market value of the property is $2,525,000. Therefore, when Terry deeds the property to the creditor, she also receives $25,000 from the creditor. What are the tax consequences to Terry?

Partial list of research aids:
Rev.Rul. 76–111, 1976–1 C.B. 214.
Crane v. Comm., 47 USTC ¶9217, 35 AFTR 776, 67 S.Ct. 1047 (USSC, 1947).

Research Problem 3. Olaf gives stock worth $400,000 to Hazel. Olaf's adjusted basis in the stock is $50,000. The gift taxes due are $118,400. As a condition for receiving the gift of stock, Hazel agrees to pay the gift tax. The stock is transferred to Hazel on February 5, 1997.
a. What are the income tax consequences to Olaf?
b. What are the income tax consequences to Olaf if the gift was made on February 5, 1981?

Research Problem 4. As the result of a large inheritance from her grandmother, Beverly has a substantial investment portfolio. The securities are held in street name by her brokerage firm. Beverly's broker, Max, has standing oral instructions from her on sales transactions to sell the shares with the highest cost basis.

In October 1995, Beverly phoned Max and instructed him to sell 6,000 shares of Color, Inc. Her portfolio has 15,000 shares of Color, Inc., which were purchased in several transactions over a three-year period. At the end of each month, the brokerage firm provides Beverly with a monthly statement that includes sales transactions. It does not identify the specific certificates transferred.

In filing her 1995 income tax return, Beverly used the specific identification method to calculate the $90,000 gain on the sale of the Color shares. Now her 1995 return is being audited. The Revenue Agent has taken the position that under Reg. § 1.1012–1(c) Beverly should have used the FIFO method to report the sale of the Color shares. This would result in a recognized gain of $160,000. According to his interpretation of the Regulations, Beverly may not use the specific identification method and must use the FIFO method because the broker did not provide written confirmation of Beverly's sales instructions as required by the Regulations.

Beverly has come to you for tax advice.

Research Problem 5. Ruth Ames died on January 10, 1997. In filing the estate tax return, her executor, Melvin Sims, elects the primary valuation date and amount (fair market value on date of death). On March 12, 1997, Melvin invests $30,000 of cash that Ruth had in her money market account in acquiring 1,000 shares of Orange, Inc. ($30 per share). On January 10, 1997, Orange was selling for $29 per share. The stock is distributed to a beneficiary, Annette Rust, on June 1, 1997, when it is selling for $33 per share. Melvin would like for you to inform him at what amount the Orange shares should appear on the estate tax return and of Annette's adjusted basis for the stock. Write a letter to Melvin in which you respond to his inquiry and prepare a memo for the tax files. His address is 100 Center Lane, Salem, VA 24153.

Use the tax resources of the internet to address the following questions. Do not restrict your search to the World Wide Web, but include a review of newsgroups and general reference materials, practitioner sites and resources, primary sources of the tax law, chat rooms and discussion groups, and other opportunities.

Research Problem 6. The "step up in basis at death" rule of § 1014 is seen by many as an expensive tax loophole enjoyed by the wealthy.
  a. Find the latest estimates of the revenue loss to the Treasury that is attributable to this rule.
  b. How does Canada tax law determine the basis of property acquired from a decedent?
  c. Send an e-mail message to a member of the House Ways and Means Committee expressing a preference for the preservation of the current § 1014 rule or a modification to it.

TEAM PROJECT: ARTHUR ANDERSEN TAX CHALLENGE CASES

For more information on the Arthur Andersen Tax Challenge Cases, refer to Chapter 1, page 1–38.

Information related to tax issues and problems that are discussed in this chapter may be found in the

Day and Ball case on page 5

Read and analyze the case you have been assigned and *identify* any issues and problems that are related to material covered in this chapter. If the information provided in the case is complete, prepare answers for this part of the case at this time. If you need information that is contained in the later parts of the case, write a memo summarizing the questions or problems so you can prepare a complete answer at a later date.

CHAPTER 15

Property Transactions: Nontaxable Exchanges

LEARNING OBJECTIVES

After completing Chapter 15, you should be able to:

1. Understand the rationale for nonrecognition (postponement) of gain or loss in certain property transactions.

2. Apply the nonrecognition provisions and basis determination rules for like-kind exchanges.

3. Explain the nonrecognition provisions available on the involuntary conversion of property.

4. Describe the provisions for postponing recognition of gain on the sale and replacement of a personal residence.

5. Discuss the provisions for permanent exclusion of gain on the sale of a personal residence by taxpayers age 55 and older.

6. Identify other nonrecognition provisions contained in the Code.

7. Identify tax planning opportunities related to the nonrecognition provisions discussed in the chapter.

OUTLINE

General Concept of a Nontaxable Exchange, 15–2

Like-Kind Exchanges—§ 1031, 15–3

Like-Kind Property, 15–4
Exchange Requirement, 15–5
Boot, 15–5
Basis and Holding Period of Property Received, 15–7

Involuntary Conversions—§ 1033, 15–9

Involuntary Conversion Defined, 15–10
Computing the Amount Realized, 15–11
Replacement Property, 15–11
Time Limitation on Replacement, 15–13
Nonrecognition of Gain, 15–14
Involuntary Conversion of a Personal Residence, 15–15

Reporting Considerations, 15–15

Sale of a Residence—§ 1034, 15–16

Replacement Period, 15–16
Principal Residence, 15–18
Nonrecognition of Gain Requirements, 15–19
Capital Improvements, 15–20
Basis and Holding Period of the New Residence, 15–21
Reporting Procedures, 15–22

Sale of a Residence—§ 121, 15–23

Exclusion Requirements, 15–23
Relationship to Other Provisions, 15–24
Making and Revoking the Election, 15–24
Computation Procedure, 15–25

Other Nonrecognition Provisions, 15–26

Exchange of Stock for Property—§ 1032, 15–26
Certain Exchanges of Insurance Policies—§ 1035, 15–26
Exchange of Stock for Stock of the Same Corporation—§ 1036, 15–26
Certain Reacquisitions of Real Property—§ 1038, 15–26
Transfers of Property between Spouses or Incident to Divorce—§ 1041, 15–27
Rollovers into Specialized Small Business Investment Companies—§ 1044, 15–27

Tax Planning Considerations, 15–28

Like-Kind Exchanges, 15–28

Involuntary Conversions, 15–29
Sale of a Personal Residence, 15–29

---

1 **LEARNING OBJECTIVE**
Understand the rationale for nonrecognition (postponement) of gain or loss in certain property transactions.

GENERAL CONCEPT OF A NONTAXABLE EXCHANGE

A taxpayer who is going to replace a productive asset (e.g., machinery) used in a trade or business may structure the transactions as a sale of the old asset and the purchase of a new asset. Using this approach, any realized gain or loss on the asset sale is recognized. The basis of the new asset is its cost. Conversely, the taxpayer may be able to trade the old asset for the new asset. This exchange of assets may produce beneficial tax consequences by qualifying for nontaxable exchange treatment.

The tax law recognizes that nontaxable exchanges result in a change in the *form* but not in the *substance* of the taxpayer's relative economic position. The replacement property received in the exchange is viewed as substantially a continuation of the old investment.[1] Additional justification for nontaxable exchange treatment is that this type of transaction does not provide the taxpayer with the wherewithal to pay the tax on any realized gain.

The nonrecognition provisions for nontaxable exchanges do not apply to realized losses from the sale or exchange of personal use assets. Such losses are not recognized (are disallowed) because they are personal in nature and not because of any nonrecognition provision.

In a **nontaxable exchange,** realized gains or losses are not recognized. However, the nonrecognition is usually temporary. The recognition of gain or loss

---

[1] Reg. § 1.1002–1(c).

is *postponed* (deferred) until the property received in the nontaxable exchange is subsequently disposed of in a taxable transaction. This is accomplished by assigning a carryover basis to the replacement property.

EXAMPLE 1

Debra exchanges property with an adjusted basis of $10,000 and a fair market value of $12,000 for property with a fair market value of $12,000. The transaction qualifies for nontaxable exchange treatment. Debra has a realized gain of $2,000 ($12,000 amount realized − $10,000 adjusted basis). Her recognized gain is $0. Her basis in the replacement property is a carryover basis of $10,000. Assume the replacement property is nondepreciable. If Debra subsequently sells the replacement property for $12,000, her realized and recognized gain will be the $2,000 gain that was postponed (deferred) in the nontaxable transaction. If the replacement property is depreciable, the carryover basis of $10,000 is used in calculating depreciation. ▼

In some nontaxable exchanges, only part of the property involved in the transaction qualifies for nonrecognition treatment. If the taxpayer receives cash or other nonqualifying property, part or all of the realized gain from the exchange is recognized. In these instances, gain is recognized because the taxpayer has changed or improved his or her relative economic position and has the wherewithal to pay income tax to the extent of cash or other property received.

It is important to distinguish between a nontaxable disposition, as the term is used in the statute, and a tax-free transaction. First, a direct exchange is not required in all circumstances (e.g., replacement of involuntarily converted property or sale and replacement of a personal residence). Second, as previously mentioned, the term *nontaxable* refers to postponement of recognition via a carryover basis. In a *tax-free* transaction, the nonrecognition is permanent (e.g., see the discussion later in the chapter of the § 121 election by a taxpayer age 55 or over to exclude gain on the sale of a residence). Therefore, the basis of any property acquired in a tax-free transaction does not depend on the basis of the property disposed of by the taxpayer.

LIKE-KIND EXCHANGES—§ 1031

2 LEARNING OBJECTIVE
Apply the nonrecognition provisions and basis determination rules for like-kind exchanges.

Section 1031 provides for nontaxable exchange treatment if the following requirements are satisfied:[2]

- The form of the transaction is an exchange.
- Both the property transferred and the property received are held either for productive use in a trade or business or for investment.
- The property is like-kind property.

Like-kind exchanges include business for business, business for investment, investment for business, or investment for investment property. Property held for personal use, inventory, and partnership interests (both limited and general) do not qualify under the like-kind exchange provisions. Securities, even though held for investment, do not qualify for like-kind exchange treatment.

The nonrecognition provision for like-kind exchanges is *mandatory* rather than elective. A taxpayer who wants to recognize a realized gain or loss will have to structure the transaction in a form that does not satisfy the statutory requirements for a like-kind exchange. This topic is discussed further under Tax Planning Considerations.

---

[2] § 1031(a) and Reg. § 1.1031(a)–1(a).

LIKE-KIND PROPERTY

"The words 'like-kind' refer to the nature or character of the property and not to its grade or quality. One kind or class of property may not . . . be exchanged for property of a different kind or class."[3]

Although the term *like-kind* is intended to be interpreted very broadly, three categories of exchanges are not included. First, livestock of different sexes do not qualify as like-kind property. Second, real estate can be exchanged only for other real estate, and personalty can be exchanged only for other personalty. For example, the exchange of a machine (personalty) for an office building (realty) is not a like-kind exchange. *Real estate* (or realty) includes principally rental buildings, office and store buildings, manufacturing plants, warehouses, and land. It is immaterial whether real estate is improved or unimproved. Thus, unimproved land can be exchanged for an apartment house. Personalty includes principally machines, equipment, trucks, automobiles, furniture, and fixtures. Third, real property located in the United States exchanged for foreign real property (and vice versa) does not qualify as like-kind property.

EXAMPLE 2

Wade made the following exchanges during the taxable year:

a. Inventory for a machine used in business.
b. Land held for investment for a building used in business.
c. Stock held for investment for equipment used in business.
d. A business truck for a business truck.
e. An automobile used for personal transportation for an automobile used in business.
f. Livestock for livestock of a different sex.
g. Land held for investment in New York for land held for investment in London.

Exchanges (b), investment real property for business real property, and (d), business personalty for business personalty, qualify as exchanges of like-kind property. Exchanges (a), inventory; (c), stock; (e), personal use automobile (not held for business or investment purposes); (f), livestock of different sexes; and (g), U.S. and foreign real estate do not qualify. ▼

A special provision applies if the taxpayers involved in the exchange are *related parties* under § 267(b). To qualify for like-kind exchange treatment, the taxpayer and the related party must not dispose of the like-kind property received in the exchange within the two-year period following the date of the exchange. If such an early disposition does occur, the postponed gain is recognized as of the date of the early disposition. Dispositions due to death, involuntary conversions, and certain non-tax avoidance transactions are not treated as early dispositions.

Regulations dealing with § 1031 like-kind exchange treatment provide that if the exchange transaction involves multiple assets of a business (e.g., a television station for another television station), the determination of whether the assets qualify as like-kind property will not be made at the business level.[4] Instead, the underlying assets must be evaluated.

The Regulations also provide for greater specificity in determining whether depreciable tangible personal property is of a like kind or class. Such property held for productive use in a business is of a like class only if the exchanged property is within the same *general business asset class* (as specified by the IRS in Rev.Proc. 87–57 or as subsequently modified) or the same *product class* (as specified by the Department of Commerce). Property included in a general

---

[3] Reg. § 1.1031(a)–1(b).

[4] Reg. § 1.1031(j)–1.

business asset class is evaluated under this system rather than under the product class system.

The following are examples of general business asset classes:

- Office furniture, fixtures, and equipment.
- Information systems (computers and peripheral equipment).
- Airplanes.
- Automobiles and taxis.
- Buses.
- Light general-purpose trucks.
- Heavy general-purpose trucks.

These Regulations have made it more difficult for depreciable tangible personal property to qualify for § 1031 like-kind exchange treatment. For example, the exchange of office equipment for a computer does not qualify as an exchange of like-kind property. Even though both assets are depreciable tangible personal property, they are not like-kind property because they are in different general business asset classes.

EXCHANGE REQUIREMENT

The transaction must actually involve a direct exchange of property to qualify as a like-kind exchange. The sale of old property and the purchase of new property, even though like-kind, is generally not an exchange. However, if the two transactions are mutually dependent, the IRS may treat them as a like-kind exchange. For example, if the taxpayer sells an old business machine to a dealer and purchases a new one from the same dealer, like-kind exchange treatment could result.[5]

The taxpayer may want to avoid nontaxable exchange treatment. Recognition of gain gives the taxpayer a higher basis for depreciation (see Example 31). To the extent that such gains would, if recognized, either receive favorable capital gain treatment or be passive activity income that could offset passive activity losses, it may be preferable to avoid the nonrecognition provisions through an indirect exchange transaction. For example, a taxpayer may sell property to one individual and subsequently purchase similar property from another individual. The taxpayer may also want to avoid nontaxable exchange treatment so that a realized loss can be recognized.

BOOT

If the taxpayer in a like-kind exchange gives or receives some property that is not like-kind property, recognition may occur. Property that is not like-kind property, including cash, is referred to as **boot**. Although the term *boot* does not appear in the Code, tax practitioners commonly use it rather than saying "property that is not like-kind property."

The *receipt* of boot will trigger recognition of gain if there is realized gain. The amount of the recognized gain is the *lesser* of the boot received or the realized gain (realized gain serves as the ceiling on recognition).

EXAMPLE 3

Emily and Fran exchange machinery, and the exchange qualifies as like-kind under § 1031. Since Emily's machinery (adjusted basis of $20,000) is worth $24,000 and Fran's machine has a fair market value of $19,000, Fran also gives Emily cash of $5,000. Emily's recognized

---

[5] Rev.Rul. 61–119, 1961–1 C.B. 395.

TAX IN THE NEWS

RESIDENTIAL OR RENTAL? DEPENDS ON WHO WANTS TO KNOW!

A well-known, long-term member of Congress purchased a beach house on the North Carolina coast. After several years of renting the property, he decided to upgrade his investment. He wanted to acquire a particularly choice lot nearby and build a luxurious beach house on it. Rather than sell the old property and recognize a gain on the appreciation, he proceeded as follows:

- A like-kind exchange of the old beach house for the unimproved lot.
- The giving of boot to the owner of the lot to make up for the difference in values.

To finance the giving of boot and the later construction of a new beach house, the Congressman obtained financing from a local bank. In order to obtain funds on more favorable terms, the loan application stated that the new property would be used for residential purposes. Once the new beach house was built, in season it generated rent of as much as $5,000 per week.

For income tax purposes, the Congressman treated the swap as a like-kind exchange with the giving of boot. For this to be the case, both properties have to be held for investment purposes. For congressional disclosure purposes and on the loan application form, the properties were classified as residential (i.e., as a second home). Are different classifications (i.e., investment versus residential) appropriate for different purposes (i.e., income tax versus congressional disclosure and loan application)?

SOURCE: Adapted from Kenneth Harney, "Gephardt Plays the Tax Game," *Newport News Daily Press*, March 9, 1996, pp. E1 and E2. © 1996 *The Washington Post*. Reprinted with permission.

---

gain is $4,000, the lesser of the realized gain ($24,000 amount realized − $20,000 adjusted basis = $4,000) or the fair market value of the boot received ($5,000). ▼

EXAMPLE 4 Assume the same facts as in the previous example, except that Fran's machine is worth $21,000 (not $19,000). Under these circumstances, Fran gives Emily cash of $3,000 to make up the difference. Emily's recognized gain is $3,000, the lesser of the realized gain ($24,000 amount realized − $20,000 adjusted basis = $4,000) or the fair market value of the boot received ($3,000). ▼

The receipt of boot does not result in recognition if there is realized loss.

EXAMPLE 5 Assume the same facts as in Example 3, except the adjusted basis of Emily's machine is $30,000. Emily's realized loss is $6,000 ($24,000 amount realized − $30,000 adjusted basis = $6,000 realized loss). The receipt of the boot of $5,000 does not trigger recognition. Therefore, the recognized loss is $0. ▼

The *giving* of boot usually does not trigger recognition. If the boot given is cash, any realized gain or loss is not recognized.

EXAMPLE 6 Fred and Gary exchange equipment in a like-kind exchange. Fred receives equipment with a fair market value of $25,000 and Fred transfers equipment worth $21,000 (adjusted basis of $15,000) and cash of $4,000. Fred's realized gain is $6,000 ($25,000 amount realized − $15,000 adjusted basis − $4,000 cash). However, none of the realized gain is recognized. ▼

If, however, the boot given is appreciated or depreciated property, gain or loss is recognized to the extent of the differential between the adjusted basis and the fair market value of the boot. For this purpose, *appreciated or depreciated property* is defined as property whose adjusted basis is not equal to the fair market value.

EXAMPLE 7

Assume the same facts as in the previous example, except that Fred transfers equipment worth $10,000 (adjusted basis of $12,000) and boot worth $15,000 (adjusted basis of $9,000). Fred's realized gain appears to be $4,000 ($25,000 amount realized − $21,000 adjusted basis). Since realization previously has served as a ceiling on recognition, it appears that the recognized gain is $4,000 (lower of realized gain of $4,000 or amount of appreciation on boot of $6,000). However, the recognized gain actually is $6,000 (full amount of the appreciation on the boot). In effect, Fred must calculate the like-kind and boot parts of the transaction separately. That is, the realized loss of $2,000 on the like-kind property is not recognized ($10,000 fair market value − $12,000 adjusted basis), and the $6,000 realized gain on the boot is recognized ($15,000 fair market value − $9,000 adjusted basis). ▼

BASIS AND HOLDING PERIOD OF PROPERTY RECEIVED

If an exchange does not qualify as nontaxable under § 1031, gain or loss is recognized, and the basis of property received in the exchange is the property's fair market value. If the exchange qualifies for nonrecognition, the basis of property received must be adjusted to reflect any postponed (deferred) gain or loss. The *basis of like-kind property* received in the exchange is the property's fair market value less postponed gain or plus postponed loss. If the exchange partially qualifies for nonrecognition (if recognition is associated with boot), the basis of like-kind property received in the exchange is the property's fair market value less postponed gain or plus postponed loss. The *basis* of any *boot* received is the boot's fair market value.

If there is a postponed loss, nonrecognition creates a situation in which the taxpayer has recovered *less* than the cost or other basis of the property exchanged in an amount equal to the unrecognized loss. If there is a postponed gain, the taxpayer has recovered *more* than the cost or other basis of the property exchanged in an amount equal to the unrecognized gain.

EXAMPLE 8

Jaime exchanges a building (used in his business) with an adjusted basis of $30,000 and fair market value of $38,000 for land with a fair market value of $38,000. The land is to be held as an investment. The exchange qualifies as like-kind (an exchange of business real property for investment real property). Thus, the basis of the land is $30,000 (the land's fair market value of $38,000 less the $8,000 postponed gain on the building). If the land is later sold for its fair market value of $38,000, the $8,000 postponed gain is recognized. ▼

EXAMPLE 9

Assume the same facts as in the previous example, except that the building has an adjusted basis of $48,000 and fair market value of only $38,000. The basis in the newly acquired land is $48,000 (fair market value of $38,000 plus the $10,000 postponed loss on the building). If the land is later sold for its fair market value of $38,000, the $10,000 postponed loss is recognized. ▼

The Code provides an alternative approach for determining the basis of like-kind property received:

> Adjusted basis of like-kind property surrendered
> +Adjusted basis of boot given
> + Gain recognized
> − Fair market value of boot received
> − Loss recognized
> = *Basis of like-kind property received*

This approach is logical in terms of the recovery of capital doctrine. That is, the unrecovered cost or other basis is increased by additional cost (boot given) or decreased by cost recovered (boot received). Any gain recognized is included in the basis of the new property. The taxpayer has been taxed on this amount and is now entitled to recover it tax-free. Any loss recognized is deducted from the basis of the new property. The taxpayer has received a tax benefit on that amount.

The holding period of the property surrendered in the exchange carries over and *tacks on* to the holding period of the like-kind property received.[6] The logic of this rule is derived from the basic concept of the new property as a continuation of the old investment. The boot received has a new holding period (from the date of exchange) rather than a carryover holding period.

Depreciation recapture potential carries over to the property received in a like-kind exchange.[7] See Chapter 17 for a discussion of this topic.

The following comprehensive example illustrates the like-kind exchange rules.

EXAMPLE 10 Vicki exchanged the following old machines for new machines in five independent like-kind exchanges:

Exchange	Adjusted Basis of Old Machine	Fair Market Value of New Machine	Adjusted Basis of Boot Given	Fair Market Value of Boot Received
1	$4,000	$9,000	$ –0–	$ –0–
2	4,000	9,000	3,000	–0–
3	4,000	9,000	6,000	–0–
4	4,000	9,000	–0–	3,000
5	4,000	3,500	–0–	300

Vicki's realized and recognized gains and losses and the basis of each of the like-kind properties received are as follows:

Exchange	Realized Gain (Loss)	Recognized Gain (Loss)	Old Adj. Basis	+	Boot Given	+	Gain Recognized	–	Boot Received	=	New Basis
1	$5,000	$ –(0)–	$4,000	+	$ –0–	+	$ –0–	–	$ –0–	=	$ 4,000*
2	2,000	–(0)–	4,000	+	3,000	+	–0–	–	–0–	=	7,000*
3	(1,000)	–(0)–	4,000	+	6,000	+	–0–	–	–0–	=	10,000**
4	8,000	3,000	4,000	+	–0–	+	3,000	–	3,000	=	4,000*
5	(200)	–(0)–	4,000	+	–0–	+	–0–	–	300	=	3,700**

*Basis may be determined in gain situations under the alternative method by subtracting the gain not recognized from the fair market value of the new property:
$9,000 – $5,000 = $4,000 for exchange 1.
$9,000 – $2,000 = $7,000 for exchange 2.
$9,000 – $5,000 = $4,000 for exchange 4.

**In loss situations, basis may be determined by adding the loss not recognized to the fair market value of the new property:
$9,000 + $1,000 = $10,000 for exchange 3.
$3,500 + $200 = $3,700 for exchange 5.

The basis of the boot received is the boot's fair market value. ▼

---

[6] § 1223(1) and Reg. § 1.1223–1(a). For this carryover holding period rule to apply to like-kind exchanges after March 1, 1954, the like-kind property surrendered must have been either a capital asset or § 1231 property. See Chapters 16 and 17 for the discussion of capital assets and § 1231 property.

[7] Reg. §§ 1.1245–2(a)(4) and 1.1250–2(d)(1).

CHAPTER 15 Property Transactions: Nontaxable Exchanges

If the taxpayer either assumes a liability or takes property subject to a liability, the amount of the liability is treated as boot given. For the taxpayer whose liability is assumed or whose property is taken subject to the liability, the amount of the liability is treated as boot received. Example 11 illustrates the effect of such a liability. In addition, the example illustrates the tax consequences for both parties involved in the like-kind exchange.

EXAMPLE 11

Jane and Leo exchange real estate investments. Jane gives up property with an adjusted basis of $250,000 (fair market value $400,000) that is subject to a mortgage of $75,000 (assumed by Leo). In return for this property, Jane receives property with a fair market value of $300,000 (adjusted basis $200,000) and cash of $25,000.

- Jane's realized gain is $150,000. She gave up property with an adjusted basis of $250,000. Jane received $400,000 from the exchange ($300,000 fair market value of like-kind property plus $100,000 boot received). The boot received consists of the $25,000 cash received from Leo and Jane's mortgage of $75,000 that Leo assumes.
- Jane's recognized gain is $100,000. The realized gain of $150,000 is recognized to the extent of boot received.
- Jane's basis in the real estate received from Leo is $250,000. This basis can be computed by subtracting the postponed gain ($50,000) from the fair market value of the real estate received ($300,000). It can also be computed by adding the recognized gain ($100,000) to the adjusted basis of the real estate given up ($250,000) and subtracting the boot received ($100,000).
- Leo's realized gain is $100,000. Leo gave up property with an adjusted basis of $200,000 plus boot of $100,000 ($75,000 mortgage assumed + $25,000 cash) or a total of $300,000. Leo received $400,000 from the exchange (fair market value of like-kind property received).
- Leo has no recognized gain because he did not receive any boot. The entire realized gain of $100,000 is postponed.
- Leo's basis in the real estate received from Jane is $300,000. This basis can be computed by subtracting the postponed gain ($100,000) from the fair market value of the real estate received ($400,000). It can also be computed by adding the boot given ($75,000 mortgage assumed by Leo + $25,000 cash) to the adjusted basis of the real estate given up ($200,000).[8] ▼

INVOLUNTARY CONVERSIONS—§ 1033

3 LEARNING OBJECTIVE
Explain the nonrecognition provisions available on the involuntary conversion of property.

Section 1033 provides that a taxpayer who suffers an involuntary conversion of property may postpone recognition of *gain* realized from the conversion. The objective of this provision is to provide relief to the taxpayer who has suffered hardship and does not have the wherewithal to pay the tax on any gain realized from the conversion. Postponement of realized gain is permitted to the extent that the taxpayer *reinvests* the amount realized from the conversion in replacement property. The rules for nonrecognition of gain are as follows:

- If the amount reinvested in replacement property *equals or exceeds* the amount realized, realized gain is *not recognized.*
- If the amount reinvested in replacement property is *less than* the amount realized, realized gain *is recognized* to the extent of the deficiency.

---
[8] Example (2) of Reg. § 1.1031(d)–2 illustrates a special situation where both the buyer and the seller transfer liabilities that are assumed or property is acquired subject to a liability by the other party.

TAX IN THE NEWS

A Sound Investment—Not

A group of investors constructed a building and leased it to a city. This transaction is a normal event. The city later condemned the building so it would not have to make the lease payments. This is not a normal event.

In 1988, the investors paid $3.5 million to construct the building, which was then leased to the city of Sheridan, Colorado (population of 5,300), for $200,000 per year for use as the city hall. When the city experienced financial difficulties and tried to get out of the lease, the investors rejected an offer by the city. Consequently, the city exercised its right of eminent domain and condemned its own city hall.

Both the city and the trustee for the investors had the building appraised. As is frequently the case, the appraisers did not agree on the value. The city's appraiser valued the building at $600,000, while the investors' appraiser arrived at $2.8 million. Because the building was designed for governmental use, the city contended that it had much lower value than a private structure.

In final settlement, the city offered the investors $642,000. This amount results in a loss of $2.6 million for the investors. As the condemnation constitutes an involuntary conversion, the loss is deductible for Federal income tax purposes.

SOURCE: Adapted from Marcy Lamm, "Colorado Town Condemns City Hall in Effort to Avoid Lease Payments," *Wall Street Journal*, July 1, 1996, p. B7A.

If a *loss* occurs on an involuntary conversion, § 1033 does not modify the normal rules for loss recognition. That is, if a realized loss would otherwise be recognized, § 1033 does not change the result.

INVOLUNTARY CONVERSION DEFINED

An **involuntary conversion** results from the destruction (complete or partial), theft, seizure, requisition or condemnation, or the sale or exchange under threat or imminence of requisition or condemnation of the taxpayer's property.[9] To prove the existence of a threat or imminence of condemnation, the taxpayer must obtain confirmation that there has been a decision to acquire the property for public use. In addition, the taxpayer must have reasonable grounds to believe the property will be taken.[10] The property does not have to be sold to the authority threatening to condemn it to qualify for § 1033 postponement. If the taxpayer satisfies the confirmation and reasonable grounds requirements, he or she can sell the property to another party.[11] Likewise, the sale of property to a condemning authority by a taxpayer who acquired the property from its former owner with the knowledge that the property was under threat of condemnation also qualifies as an involuntary conversion under § 1033.[12] A voluntary act, such as a taxpayer destroying his or her own property by arson, is not an involuntary conversion.[13]

---

[9] § 1033(a) and Reg. §§ 1.1033(a)–1(a) and –2(a).
[10] Rev.Rul. 63–221, 1963–2 C.B. 332, and *Joseph P. Balistrieri*, 38 TCM 526, T.C.Memo. 1979–115.
[11] Rev.Rul. 81–180, 1981–2 C.B. 161.
[12] Rev.Rul. 81–181, 1981–2 C.B. 162.
[13] Rev.Rul. 82–74, 1982–1 C.B. 110.

COMPUTING THE AMOUNT REALIZED

The amount realized from the condemnation of property usually includes only the amount received as compensation for the property.[14] Any amount received that is designated as severance damages by both the government and the taxpayer is not included in the amount realized. *Severance awards* usually occur when only a portion of the entire property is condemned (e.g., a strip of land is taken to build a highway). Severance damages are awarded because the value of the taxpayer's remaining property has declined as a result of the condemnation. Such damages reduce the basis of the property. However, if either of the following requirements is satisfied, the nonrecognition provision of § 1033 applies to the severance damages.

- Severance damages are used to restore the usability of the remaining property.
- The usefulness of the remaining property is destroyed by the condemnation, and the property is sold and replaced at a cost equal to or exceeding the sum of the condemnation award, severance damages, and sales proceeds.

EXAMPLE 12

The government condemns a portion of Ron's farmland to build part of an interstate highway. Because the highway denies his cattle access to a pond and some grazing land, Ron receives severance damages in addition to the condemnation proceeds for the land taken. Ron must reduce the basis of the property by the amount of the severance damages. If the amount of the severance damages received exceeds the adjusted basis, Ron recognizes gain. ▼

EXAMPLE 13

Assume the same facts as in the previous example, except that Ron used the proceeds from the condemnation and the severance damages to build another pond and to clear woodland for grazing. Therefore, all the proceeds are eligible for § 1033 treatment. Thus, there is no possibility of gain recognition as the result of the amount of the severance damages received exceeding the adjusted basis. ▼

REPLACEMENT PROPERTY

The requirements for replacement property generally are more restrictive than those for like-kind property under § 1031. The basic requirement is that the replacement property be similar or related in service or use to the involuntarily converted property.[15]

Different interpretations of the phrase *similar or related in service or use* apply depending on whether the involuntarily converted property is held by an *owner-user* or by an *owner-investor* (e.g., lessor). A taxpayer who uses the property in his or her trade or business is subject to a more restrictive test in terms of acquiring replacement property. For an owner-user, the *functional use test* applies, and for an owner-investor, the *taxpayer use test* applies.

Taxpayer Use Test. The taxpayer use test for owner-investors provides the taxpayer with more flexibility in terms of what qualifies as replacement property than does the functional use test for owner-users. Essentially, the properties must be used by the taxpayer (the owner-investor) in similar endeavors. For example, rental property held by an owner-investor qualifies if replaced by other rental

---

[14] *Pioneer Real Estate Co.*, 47 B.T.A. 886 (1942), *acq.* 1943 C.B. 18.

[15] § 1033(a) and Reg. § 1.1033(a)–1.

Concept Summary 15–1

Replacement Property Tests

Type of Property and User	Like-Kind Test	Taxpayer Use Test	Functional Use Test
Land used by a manufacturing company is condemned by a local government authority.	X		
Apartment and land held by an investor are sold due to the threat or imminence of condemnation.	X		
An investor's rented shopping mall is destroyed by fire; the mall may be replaced by other rental properties (e.g., an apartment building).		X	
A manufacturing plant is destroyed by fire; replacement property must consist of another manufacturing plant that is functionally the same as the property converted.			X
Personal residence of taxpayer is condemned by a local government authority; replacement property must consist of another personal residence.			X

property, regardless of the type of rental property involved. The test is met when an investor replaces a manufacturing plant with a wholesale grocery warehouse if both properties are held for the production of rental income.[16] The replacement of a rental residence with a personal residence does not meet the test.[17]

Functional Use Test. Under this test, the taxpayer's use of the replacement property and of the involuntarily converted property must be the same. Replacing a manufacturing plant with a wholesale grocery warehouse, whether rented or not, does not meet this test. As indicated above, the IRS applies the taxpayer use test to owner-investors. However, the functional use test still applies to owner-users (e.g., a manufacturer whose manufacturing plant is destroyed by fire is required to replace the plant with another facility of similar functional use). Replacing a rental residence with a personal residence does not meet this test.

Special Rules. Under one set of circumstances, the broader replacement rules for like-kind exchanges are substituted for the narrow replacement rules normally used for involuntary conversions. This beneficial provision applies if business real property or investment real property is condemned. Therefore, the taxpayer has substantially more flexibility in selecting replacement property. For example, improved real property can be replaced with unimproved real property.

The rules concerning the nature of replacement property are illustrated in Concept Summary 15–1.

---

[16] *Loco Realty Co. v. Comm.*, 62–2 USTC ¶9657, 10 AFTR2d 5359, 306 F.2d 207 (CA–8, 1962).

[17] Rev.Rul. 70–466, 1970–2 C.B. 165.

TIME LIMITATION ON REPLACEMENT

The taxpayer normally has a two-year period after the close of the taxable year in which any gain is realized from the involuntary conversion to replace the property (*the latest date*).[18] This rule affords as much as three years from the date of realization of gain to replace the property if the realization of gain took place on the first day of the taxable year.[19] If the involuntary conversion involved the condemnation of real property used in a trade or business or held for investment, a three-year period is substituted for the normal two-year period. In this case, the taxpayer can actually have as much as four years from the date of realization of gain to replace the property.

EXAMPLE 14
Megan's warehouse is destroyed by fire on December 16, 1996. The adjusted basis is $325,000. Megan receives $400,000 from the insurance company on January 10, 1997. She is a calendar year taxpayer. The latest date for replacement is December 31, 1999 (the end of the taxable year in which realized gain occurred plus two years). The critical date is not the date the involuntary conversion occurred, but rather the date of gain realization. ▼

EXAMPLE 15
Assume the same facts as in the previous example, except Megan's warehouse is condemned. The latest date for replacement is December 31, 2000 (the end of the taxable year in which realized gain occurred plus three years). ▼

The *earliest date* for replacement typically is the date the involuntary conversion occurs. However, if the property is condemned, it is possible to replace the condemned property before this date. In this case, the earliest date is the date of the threat or imminence of requisition or condemnation of the property. The purpose of this provision is to enable the taxpayer to make an orderly replacement of the condemned property.

EXAMPLE 16
Assume the same facts as in Example 15. Megan can replace the warehouse before December 16, 1996 (the condemnation date). The earliest date for replacement is the date of the threat or imminence of requisition or condemnation of the warehouse. ▼

ETHICAL CONSIDERATIONS

Postponing Realized Gain from an Involuntary Conversion

Peggy, age 63 and in frail health, owns a furniture store in Petersburg. Due to competition from two large furniture retailers who opened stores in the Petersburg area during the past three years, Peggy's furniture store has been unprofitable.

Due to this lack of profitability as well as her advancing age, Peggy would like to retire. Unfortunately, she has been unable to locate a purchaser for her store. Her prayers seem to be answered when a tornado destroys her building and its contents. Fortunately, no one is injured or killed by the tornado.

Peggy anticipates that she can live on the insurance proceeds of $800,000 for the rest of her life. However, her realized gain on the involuntary conversion would produce a

---

[18] §§ 1033(a)(2)(B) and (g)(4) and Reg. § 1.1033(a)–2(c)(3).
[19] The taxpayer can apply for an extension of this time period anytime before its expiration [Reg. § 1.1033(a)–2(c)(3)]. Also, the period for filing the application for extension can be extended if the taxpayer shows reasonable cause.

combined state and Federal tax liability of approximately $175,000. In order to forgo paying this amount associated with her 1997 income tax returns, Peggy elects postponement treatment under § 1033, indicating that she intends to replace the involuntarily converted property with similar property even though she does not intend to do so. Her justification, based on her participation in a 12-step program, is that she lives "one day at a time."

Evaluate Peggy's election of § 1033 postponement under these circumstances.

NONRECOGNITION OF GAIN

Nonrecognition of gain can be either mandatory or elective, depending upon whether the conversion is direct (into replacement property) or into money (indirect).

Direct Conversion. If the conversion is directly into replacement property rather than into money, nonrecognition of realized gain is *mandatory*. In this case, the basis of the replacement property is the same as the adjusted basis of the converted property. Direct conversion is rare in practice and usually involves condemnations. The following example illustrates the application of the rules for direct conversions.

EXAMPLE 17

Lupe's property with an adjusted basis of $20,000 is condemned by the state. Lupe receives property with a fair market value of $50,000 as compensation for the property taken. Since the nonrecognition of realized gain is mandatory for direct conversions, Lupe's realized gain of $30,000 is not recognized, and the basis of the replacement property is $20,000 (adjusted basis of the condemned property). ▼

Conversion into Money. If the conversion is into money, at the election of the taxpayer, the realized gain is recognized only to the extent the amount realized from the involuntary conversion exceeds the cost of the qualifying replacement property.[20] This is the usual case, and nonrecognition (postponement) is *elective*. If the election is not made, the realized gain is recognized.

The basis of the replacement property is the property's cost less postponed (deferred) gain.[21] If the election to postpone gain is made, the holding period of the replacement property includes the holding period of the converted property.

Section 1033 applies *only to gains* and *not to losses*. Losses from involuntary conversions are recognized if the property is held for business or income-producing purposes. Personal casualty losses are recognized, but condemnation losses related to personal use assets (e.g., a personal residence) are neither recognized nor postponed.

Examples 18 and 19 illustrate the application of the involuntary conversion provisions.

EXAMPLE 18

Walt's building (used in his trade or business), with an adjusted basis of $50,000, is destroyed by fire in 1997. Walt is a calendar year taxpayer. In 1997, he receives an insurance reimbursement of $100,000 for the loss. Walt invests $80,000 in a new building.

- Walt has until December 31, 1999, to make the new investment and qualify for the nonrecognition election.

---

[20] § 1033(a)(2)(A) and Reg. § 1.1033(a)–2(c)(1).

[21] § 1033(b).

- Walt's realized gain is $50,000 ($100,000 insurance proceeds received − $50,000 adjusted basis of old building).
- Assuming the replacement property qualifies as similar or related in service or use, Walt's recognized gain is $20,000. He reinvested $20,000 less than the insurance proceeds received ($100,000 proceeds − $80,000 reinvested). Therefore, his realized gain is recognized to that extent.
- Walt's basis in the new building is $50,000. This is the building's cost of $80,000 less the postponed gain of $30,000 (realized gain of $50,000 − recognized gain of $20,000).
- The computation of realization, recognition, and basis would apply even if Walt was a real estate dealer and the building destroyed by fire was part of his inventory. Unlike § 1031, § 1033 generally does not exclude inventory. ▼

EXAMPLE 19

Assume the same facts as in the previous example, except that Walt receives only $45,000 (instead of $100,000) of insurance proceeds. He has a realized and recognized loss of $5,000. The basis of the new building is the building's cost of $80,000. If the destroyed building was held for personal use, the recognized loss is subject to the following additional limitations.[22] The loss of $5,000 is limited to the decline in fair market value of the property, and the amount of the loss is reduced first by $100 and then by 10% of adjusted gross income (refer to Chapter 7). ▼

INVOLUNTARY CONVERSION OF A PERSONAL RESIDENCE

The tax consequences of the involuntary conversion of a personal residence depend upon whether the conversion is a casualty or condemnation and whether a realized loss or gain results.

Loss Situations. If the conversion is a condemnation, the realized loss is not recognized. Loss from the condemnation of a personal use asset is never recognized. If the conversion is a casualty (a loss from fire, storm, etc.), the loss is recognized subject to the personal casualty loss limitations (refer to Chapter 7).

Gain Situations. If the conversion is a condemnation, the gain may be postponed under either § 1033 or § 1034. That is, the taxpayer may elect to treat the condemnation as a sale under the deferral of gain rules relating to the sale of a personal residence under § 1034 (presented subsequently). If the conversion is a casualty, the gain is postponed only under the involuntary conversion provisions.

REPORTING CONSIDERATIONS

Involuntary conversions from casualty and theft are reported first on Form 4684, Casualties and Thefts. Casualty and theft losses on personal use property for the individual taxpayer are carried from Form 4684 to Schedule A of Form 1040. For other casualty and theft items, the Form 4684 amounts are generally reported on Form 4797, Sales of Business Property, unless Form 4797 is not required. In the latter case, the amounts are reported directly on the tax return involved.

Except for personal use property, recognized gains and losses from involuntary conversions other than by casualty and theft are reported on Form 4797. As stated previously, if the property involved in the involuntary conversion (other than by casualty and theft) is personal use property, any realized loss is not recognized. Any realized gain is treated as gain on a voluntary sale.

---

[22] § 165(c)(3) and Reg. § 1.165−7.

SALE OF A RESIDENCE—§ 1034

4 LEARNING OBJECTIVE
Describe the provisions for postponing recognition of gain on the sale and replacement of a personal residence.

A realized loss from the sale of a **personal residence** is not recognized because the residence is personal use property. A realized gain is subject to taxation, however. The tax law includes two provisions under which all or part of the realized gain is either postponed or excluded from taxation. The first of these, § 1034, is discussed below. The second, § 121, is discussed later in the chapter.

Section 1034 provides for the *mandatory* nonrecognition of gain from the sale or exchange of a personal residence if the sales proceeds are reinvested in a replacement residence within a prescribed time period. Both the old and new residences must qualify as the taxpayer's principal residence. A houseboat or house trailer qualifies if it is used by the taxpayer as a principal residence.[23]

The reason for not recognizing gain when a residence is replaced by a new residence within the prescribed time period (discussed below) is that the new residence is viewed as a continuation of the investment. Also, if the proceeds from the sale are reinvested, the taxpayer does not have the wherewithal to pay tax on the realized gain. Beyond these fundamental concepts, Congress, in enacting § 1034, was concerned with the hardship of involuntary moves and the socially desirable objective of encouraging the mobility of labor.

REPLACEMENT PERIOD

For the nonrecognition treatment to apply, the old residence must be replaced by a new residence within a period *beginning two years before* the sale of the old residence and *ending two years after* the sale. This four-year period applies regardless of whether the new residence is purchased or constructed. The taxpayer must not only *acquire* the new residence during this period, but must *occupy* and use it as well. The occupancy requirement has been strictly construed by both the IRS and the courts, and even circumstances beyond a taxpayer's control do not excuse noncompliance.[24]

EXAMPLE 20

Gail sells her personal residence from which she realizes a gain of $50,000. She begins constructing a new residence immediately after the sale. However, unstable soil conditions and a trade union strike cause unforeseen delays. The new residence ultimately is completed and occupied by Gail 25 months after the sale of the old residence. Since the occupancy requirement has not been satisfied, § 1034 is inapplicable, and Gail must recognize a gain of $50,000 on the sale of the old residence. ▼

Taxpayers might be inclined to make liberal use of § 1034 as a means of speculating when the price of residential housing is rising. Without any time restriction on its use, § 1034 would permit deferral of gain on multiple sales of principal residences, each of which would result in an economic profit. The Code curbs this approach by precluding the application of § 1034 to any sales occurring within two years of its last use.

---

[23] Reg. § 1.1034–1(c)(3)(i).
[24] *James A. Henry,* 44 TCM 844, T.C.Memo. 1982–469, and *William F. Peck,* 44 TCM 1030, T.C.Memo. 1982–506.

TAX IN THE NEWS

IRS CONTINUES TO MAINTAIN STRICT INTERPRETATION OF § 1034

Section 1034 permits a taxpayer to postpone the recognition of the realized gain on the sale of his or her residence. To qualify for nonrecognition, the taxpayer must purchase and occupy a replacement residence that costs at least as much as the adjusted sales price of the old residence. In addition, this purchase and occupancy must occur within a four-year window that begins two years prior to the sales date and ends two years after the sales date.

A taxpayer who sold his residence purchased a new residence for an amount in excess of the adjusted sales price of the old residence. He signed the contract to buy the new residence six weeks before the expiration of the two-year period. Prior to the final settlement on the house and before the expiration of the two-year period, he occupied the house. However, the final settlement (signing of deeds, etc.) did not occur until shortly after the expiration of the two-year period.

The IRS has taken the position that it has no authority to ignore the statutory time period requirements. Therefore, the sale of the original residence does not qualify for § 1034 postponement treatment.

EXAMPLE 21

After Seth sells his principal residence (the first residence) in March 1996 for $150,000 (realized gain of $60,000), he buys and sells the following (all of which qualify as principal residences):

	Date of Purchase	Date of Sale	Amount Involved
Second residence	April 1996		$160,000
Second residence		May 1997	180,000
Third residence	June 1997		200,000

Because multiple sales have occurred within a period of two years, § 1034 does not apply to the sale of the second residence. Thus, the realized gain of $20,000 [$180,000 (selling price) − $160,000 (purchase price)] must be recognized. ▼

The two-year rule precluding multiple use of § 1034 could create a hardship where a taxpayer is transferred by his or her employer and has little choice in the matter. For this reason, § 1034 was amended to provide an exception to the two-year rule when the sale results from a change in the location of employment. To qualify for the exception, a taxpayer must meet the distance and length-of-employment requirements specified for the deduction of moving expenses under § 217.[25]

---

[25] Refer to Chapter 9 for the discussion of the rules governing the deduction for moving expenses.

EXAMPLE 22

Assume the same facts as in the previous example, except that in February 1997, Seth's employer transfers him to a job in another state. Consequently, the sale of the second residence and the purchase of the third residence were due to the relocation of employment. If Seth satisfies the distance and length-of-employment requirements of § 217, no gain is recognized on the sale of the first and second residences. ▼

The running of the time periods specified above (other than the two-year limit on multiple sales) is suspended during any time the taxpayer or spouse is on extended active duty (over 90 days or for an indefinite period) with the U.S. Armed Forces after the date the old residence is sold.[26] This suspension is limited to four years after the date the old residence is sold. A similar suspension is available to U.S. citizens who are employed outside the United States by nongovernmental employers (expatriates).[27]

EXAMPLE 23

Iris, an employee of Blue Corporation, sold her principal residence in Baltimore on July 5, 1997, because she had been transferred to the Berlin office on a one-year assignment. Iris returns to the United States on July 1, 1998, after completing the assignment. The latest date for a qualifying replacement is July 1, 2000 (i.e., two years after the end of the suspension period). ▼

EXAMPLE 24

Assume the same facts as in the previous example, except that the assignment is for a three-year period. Therefore, Iris returns to the United States on July 1, 2000, after completing the assignment. Two years after the end of the suspension period is July 1, 2002. However, since the suspension period exception cannot result in the replacement time period being extended beyond four years after the date the principal residence was sold, the latest date for a qualifying replacement is July 5, 2001. ▼

In one circumstance, the four-year limitation is extended for members of the U.S. Armed Forces. If they are stationed outside the United States or are required thereafter to reside in government quarters at a remote site, the four-year period is replaced with an eight-year period.[28]

PRINCIPAL RESIDENCE

Both the old and new residences must qualify as the taxpayer's principal residence. Whether property is the taxpayer's principal residence depends "... upon all the facts and circumstances in each case."[29]

EXAMPLE 25

Mitch sells his principal residence and moves to Norfolk, Virginia, where he is employed. He decides to rent an apartment in Norfolk because of its proximity to his place of employment. He purchases a beach house in Virginia Beach that he occupies most weekends. Mitch does not intend to live in the beach house other than on weekends. The apartment in Norfolk is his principal place of residence. Therefore, the purchase of the beach house does not qualify as an appropriate replacement. ▼

If the old residence ceases to be the taxpayer's principal residence before its sale, the nonrecognition provision does not apply. For example, if the taxpayer abandons the old residence before its sale, the residence no longer qualifies as a

---

[26] § 1034(h)(1).
[27] § 1034(k).
[28] § 1034(h)(2).
[29] Reg. § 1.1034–1(c)(3).

principal residence.[30] If the old residence is converted to other than personal use (e.g., rental) before its sale, the nonrecognition provision does not apply. If the residence is only partially converted to business use, gain from the sale of the personal use portion still qualifies for nonrecognition. It is possible to convert part of a principal residence to business use and later to convert that part back to being part of the principal residence (e.g., a home office).[31]

Temporarily renting out the old residence before sale does not necessarily terminate its status as the taxpayer's principal residence,[32] nor does temporarily renting out the new residence before it is occupied by the taxpayer. A related issue is whether a taxpayer who temporarily rents out the old residence while attempting to sell it is entitled to deduct expenses in excess of income relating to the rental. That is, is the old residence subject to the loss deduction rules for hobby loss activities? If it is, the deductions associated with the rental activity are limited to the rent income generated. In a divided opinion, the Tax Court concluded that since the property was considered to be the taxpayer's principal residence and as a result qualified for § 1034 postponement of gain, the property was subject to the hobby loss limitations. The Court of Appeals reversed the Tax Court and held that the hobby loss provisions did not apply.[33]

NONRECOGNITION OF GAIN REQUIREMENTS

Realized gain from the sale of the old residence is not recognized if the taxpayer reinvests an amount *at least equal* to the adjusted sales price of the old residence. Realized gain is recognized to the extent the taxpayer does not reinvest an amount at least equal to the adjusted sales price in a new residence. Therefore, the amount not reinvested is treated similarly to boot received in a like-kind exchange.

The **adjusted sales price** is the amount realized from the sale of the old residence less fixing-up expenses. The *amount realized* is the selling price less the selling expenses. *Selling expenses* include items such as the cost of advertising the property for sale, real estate broker commissions, legal fees in connection with the sale, and loan placement fees paid by the taxpayer as a condition of arranging financing for the buyer.

Fixing-up expenses are personal in nature and are incurred by the taxpayer to assist in the sale of the old residence. Fixing-up expenses include such items as ordinary repairs, painting, and wallpapering. To qualify as a fixing-up expense, the expense must (1) be incurred for work performed during the 90-day period ending on the date of the contract of sale, (2) be paid within 30 days after the date of the sale, and (3) not be a capital expenditure.

Although selling expenses are deductible in calculating the amount realized, fixing-up expenses are not. Therefore, fixing-up expenses do not have an impact on the calculation of realized gain or loss. However, since fixing-up expenses are deductible in calculating the adjusted sales price, they do have the potential for producing tax benefit in that they reduce the amount of the reinvestment required to qualify for nonrecognition treatment. Conversely, if a replacement residence is not acquired, the fixing-up expenses produce no tax benefit.

---

[30] *Richard T. Houlette*, 48 T.C. 350 (1967), and *Stolk v. Comm.*, 64–1 USTC ¶9228, 13 AFTR2d 535, 326 F.2d 760 (CA–2, 1964).
[31] Rev.Rul. 82–26, 1982–1 C.B. 114.
[32] *Robert W. Aagaard*, 56 T.C. 191 (1971), acq. 1971–2 C.B. 1; *Robert G. Clapham*, 63 T.C. 505 (1975); Rev.Rul. 59–72, 1959–1 C.B. 203; and Rev.Rul. 78–146, 1978–1 C.B. 260.
[33] *Bolaris v. Comm.*, 85–2 USTC ¶9822, 56 AFTR2d 85–6472, 776 F.2d 1428 (CA–9, 1985), rev'g. 81 T.C. 840 (1983).

TAX IN THE NEWS

JOINT OWNERSHIP AND A NEW SPOUSE: CAUTION IS NECESSARY

To obtain the full benefits of § 1034 deferral treatment on the sale of a residence, the taxpayer must reinvest in a replacement residence an amount at least equal to the adjusted sales price of the old residence. In a recent Tax Court case, the taxpayer thought she had done so, but the Tax Court disagreed.

The taxpayer and her former spouse, who jointly owned the house with her, sold their residence and calculated their realized gain as follows:

Amount realized	$356,000
Less: Adjusted basis	(216,000)
Realized gain	$140,000

The taxpayer thought that if she reinvested her $178,000 share of the net sales price, she would be able to defer the recognition of her $70,000 share of the realized gain.

She remarried prior to purchasing another residence. She and her new spouse jointly purchased a residence for $180,000. Since the purchase price exceeded her $178,000 share of the net sales price, she concluded that she had made a reinvestment adequate to defer her $70,000 share of the realized gain.

Not so according to the IRS. According to their position, since she purchased the house jointly with her new spouse, she had reinvested only $90,000. Therefore, her realized gain of $70,000 is recognized because this amount was less than her reinvestment deficiency of $88,000. Unfortunately, the Tax Court in *Jeanne G. Snowa*, 70 TCM 163, T.C. Memo. 1995–336, accepted the position of the IRS.

Reducing the amount of the required reinvestment by the amount of fixing-up expenses is another application of the wherewithal to pay concept. To the extent that the taxpayer has expended part of the funds received from the sale in preparing the old residence for sale, he or she does not have the funds available to reinvest in the new residence.

As previously mentioned, fixing-up expenses are not considered in determining realized gain. They are considered only in determining how much realized gain is to be postponed. In addition, fixing-up expenses have no direct effect on the basis of the new residence. Indirectly, though, through their effect on postponed gain, they can bring about a lesser basis for the new residence. The effects of fixing-up expenses on the computation of gain realized and recognized and on basis are illustrated in Figure 15–1 and in Example 26.

CAPITAL IMPROVEMENTS

Capital improvements are added to the adjusted basis of a personal residence. The adjusted basis is used in computing gain or loss on a subsequent sale or other disposition of the property. In calculating the cost of a replacement residence (for determining the nonrecognition of gain under § 1034), only capital improvements

▼ FIGURE 15–1
Sale-of-Residence Model

Step		
Step 1	Sales price − Selling expenses	= Amount realized
Step 2	Amount realized − Adjusted basis of old residence	= Realized gain
Step 3	Amount realized − Fixing-up expenses	= Adjusted sales price (amount that must be reinvested to avoid any recognized gain)
Step 4	Adjusted sales price − Cost of new residence	= Excess of adjusted sales price, if any, over cost
Step 5	Recognized gain	= Lesser of realized gain or excess determined in Step 4
Step 6	Gain not recognized (postponed)	= Realized gain − Recognized gain
Step 7	Basis of new residence	= Cost of new residence − Gain not recognized

made during a certain time period are counted. The time period begins two years before the date of sale of the old residence and ends two years after that date (the time period during which the old residence can be replaced).[34]

If the taxpayer receives a residence by gift or inheritance, the residence will not qualify as a replacement residence. However, if the taxpayer makes substantial capital expenditures (e.g., reconstruction or additions) to the property within the replacement time period, these expenditures do qualify.[35]

BASIS AND HOLDING PERIOD OF THE NEW RESIDENCE

The *basis* of the new residence is the cost of the new residence less the realized gain not recognized (postponed gain). If there is any postponed gain, the *holding period* of the new residence includes the holding period of the old residence.

Figure 15–1 summarizes the sale-of-residence concepts. Example 26 illustrates these concepts and the application of the nonrecognition provision.

---

[34] *Charles M. Shaw*, 69 T.C. 1034 (1978); Reg. § 1.1034–1(c)(4)(ii); and Rev.Rul. 78–147, 1978–1 C.B. 261.

[35] Reg. §§ 1.1034–1(b)(7) and (9) and 1.1034–1(c)(4)(i).

EXAMPLE 26

Kate, age 47, sells her personal residence (adjusted basis of $136,000) for $244,000. She receives only $229,400 after paying a brokerage fee of $14,600. Ten days before the sale, Kate incurred and paid for qualified fixing-up expenses of $3,400. Two months later, Kate acquires a new residence. Determine the gain, if any, she must recognize and the basis of the new residence under each of the following circumstances:

1. The new residence costs $230,000.
2. The new residence costs $210,000.
3. The new residence costs $110,000.

	1	2	3
Step 1: Sales price	$ 244,000	$ 244,000	$ 244,000
−Selling expenses	(14,600)	(14,600)	(14,600)
=Amount realized	$ 229,400	$ 229,400	$ 229,400
Step 2: Amount realized	$ 229,400	$ 229,400	$ 229,400
−Adjusted basis	(136,000)	(136,000)	(136,000)
=Realized gain	$ 93,400	$ 93,400	$ 93,400
Step 3: Amount realized	$ 229,400	$ 229,400	$ 229,400
−Fixing-up expenses	(3,400)	(3,400)	(3,400)
=Adjusted sales price	$ 226,000	$ 226,000	$ 226,000
Step 4: Adjusted sales price	$ 226,000	$ 226,000	$ 226,000
−Cost of new residence	(230,000)	(210,000)	(110,000)
=Excess of ASP over cost	$ −0−	$ 16,000	$ 116,000
Step 5: Recognized gain (lesser of Step 2 or Step 4)	$ −0−	$ 16,000	$ 93,400
Step 6: Realized gain	$ 93,400	$ 93,400	$ 93,400
−Recognized gain	(−0−)	(16,000)	(93,400)
=Postponed gain	$ 93,400	$ 77,400	$ −0−
Step 7: Cost of new residence	$ 230,000	$ 210,000	$ 110,000
−Postponed gain	(93,400)	(77,400)	(−0−)
=Basis of new residence	$ 136,600	$ 132,600	$ 110,000

None of the realized gain of $93,400 is recognized in the first case because the actual reinvestment of $230,000 exceeds the required reinvestment of $226,000. In the second case, the recognized gain is $16,000 because the required reinvestment of $226,000 exceeds the actual reinvestment of $210,000 by this amount. In the third case, the required reinvestment of $226,000 exceeds the actual reinvestment of $110,000 by $116,000. Since this amount is greater than the realized gain of $93,400, the realized gain of $93,400 is recognized, and § 1034 deferral does not apply. ▼

REPORTING PROCEDURES

The taxpayer is required to report the details of the sale of the residence on the tax return for the taxable year in which gain is realized, even if all of the gain is postponed. If a new residence is acquired and occupied before filing, a statement should be attached to the return showing the purchase date, the cost, and date of occupancy. Form 2119, Sale or Exchange of Your Home, is used to show the details of the sale and replacement, and the taxpayer should retain a copy permanently as support for the basis of the new residence. If a replacement residence has not been purchased by the time the return is filed, the taxpayer should submit the details of the purchase on the return of the taxable year during which it occurs. If the old residence is not replaced within the prescribed time period, or if some recognized gain results, the taxpayer must file an amended return for the year in which the sale took place.

Sale of a Residence—§ 121

5 Learning Objective
Discuss the provisions for permanent exclusion of gain on the sale of a personal residence by taxpayers age 55 and older.

Under the **Section 121 exclusion,** taxpayers age 55 or older who sell or exchange their principal residence may *elect to exclude* up to $125,000 ($62,500 for married individuals filing separate returns) of realized gain from the sale or exchange.[36] The election can be made *only once*.[37] This provision differs from § 1034 where nonrecognition is mandatory and may occur many times during a taxpayer's lifetime. Section 121 also differs from § 1034 in that it does not require the taxpayer to purchase a new residence. The excluded gain is never recognized, whereas the realized gain not recognized under § 1034 is postponed by subtracting it from the cost of the new residence in calculating the adjusted basis.

This provision is the only case in the tax law where a realized gain from the disposition of property that is not recognized is excluded rather than merely postponed. The provision allows the taxpayer a permanent recovery of more than the cost or other basis of the residence tax-free.

Congress enacted § 121 simply to relieve older citizens of the large tax they might incur from the sale of a personal residence. The dollar and age limitations restrict the benefit of § 121 to taxpayers who presumably have a greater need for increased tax-free dollars.

EXCLUSION REQUIREMENTS

The taxpayer must be at least age 55 before the date of the sale and have *owned* and *used* the residence as a principal residence for at least *three years* during the *five-year* period ending on the date of sale. The ownership and use periods do not have to be the same period of time. Short temporary absences (e.g., vacations) count as periods of use. If the residence is owned jointly by husband and wife, only one of the spouses is required to meet these requirements if a joint return is filed for the taxable year in which the sale took place.

In determining whether the ownership and use period requirements are satisfied, transactions affecting prior residences may be relevant. If a former residence is involuntarily converted and any gain is postponed under § 1033, the holding period of the former residence is added to the holding period of the replacement residence for § 121 purposes. However, if the realized gain is postponed under § 1034 (sale-of-residence provision), the holding period of the former residence is not added to the holding period of the replacement residence for § 121 purposes. In this instance, the holding period of the replacement residence begins with the acquisition date of the replacement residence.

---

[36] §§ 121(a), (b), and (c). For married taxpayers, each spouse must consent.

[37] § 121(b)(2) and Reg. § 1.121–2(b). Only one election may be made by married individuals.

EXAMPLE 27

Cole has lived in his residence since 1987. The residence is involuntarily converted in July 1997. He purchases a replacement residence in August 1997. When the replacement residence is subsequently sold, Cole includes the holding period of the involuntarily converted residence in determining whether he can satisfy the ownership and use requirements. ▼

EXAMPLE 28

Assume the same facts as in the previous example, except that Cole's residence was not involuntarily converted. Instead, he sold it so that he could move into a larger house. When the replacement residence is subsequently sold, Cole is not permitted to include the holding period of the old residence in determining whether he can satisfy the ownership and use requirements. ▼

ETHICAL CONSIDERATIONS

A Couple's Approach to the § 121 Exclusion

Bob and Sandra, both age 67, live in Houston, Texas, where each owns a personal residence on which the realized gain from a sale would be $125,000. They plan to marry and move to Williamsburg, Virginia. Not wanting the burdens of home ownership, they intend to rent a house.

Bob and Sandra both satisfy the requirements for the § 121 exclusion. Because of the soft real estate market in Houston, they have been unsuccessful in selling their personal residences. Being aware that a married couple can qualify only once for the § 121 exclusion, the realtor suggests the following plan. Bob will sell his house to Sandra, and Sandra will sell her house to Bob for the fair market value. Each will elect § 121 exclusion treatment. They will then marry and move to Williamsburg. Upon the subsequent sale of the houses to external buyers, the recognized gain, if any, will be minimal, since the adjusted basis of each house will have stepped up to the fair market value on the prior sale to each other.

Evaluate the realtor's proposal for Bob and Sandra.

RELATIONSHIP TO OTHER PROVISIONS

The taxpayer can treat an involuntary conversion of a principal residence as a sale for purposes of § 121. Any gain not excluded under § 121 is then subject to postponement under § 1033 or § 1034 (condemnation only), assuming the requirements of those provisions are met.

Any gain from the sale of a residence not excluded under § 121 is subject to postponement under § 1034, assuming the requirements of that provision are met. Examples 29 and 30 illustrate this relationship.

MAKING AND REVOKING THE ELECTION

The election not to recognize gain under § 121 may be made or revoked at any time before the statute of limitations expires. Therefore, the taxpayer generally has until the *later* of (1) three years from the due date of the return for the year the gain is realized or (2) two years from the date the tax is paid to make or revoke the election. The election is made by attaching a signed statement (showing all the details of the sale) to the return for the taxable year in which the sale took place. Form 2119 is used for this purpose. The election is revoked by filing a signed statement (showing the taxpayer's name, Social Security number, and taxable year for which the election was made) indicating the revocation.[38]

---

[38] Reg. §§ 1.121–4(b) and (c).

COMPUTATION PROCEDURE

The following examples illustrate the application of both the § 121 and § 1034 provisions.

EXAMPLE 29 Keith sells his personal residence (adjusted basis of $32,000) for $205,000, of which he receives only $195,400 after paying the selling expenses of $9,600. Ten days before the sale, he incurred and paid for qualified fixing-up expenses of $6,400. Keith is age 55 and elects the exclusion of gain under § 121. He does not acquire a replacement residence. ▼

EXAMPLE 30 Assume the same facts as in the previous example, except that Keith acquires a new residence for $40,000 within the prescribed time period.

The solutions to Examples 29 and 30 are as follows:

	Example 29	Example 30
Amount realized ($205,000 − $9,600)	$ 195,400	$ 195,400
Adjusted basis	(32,000)	(32,000)
Realized gain	$ 163,400	$ 163,400
§ 121 exclusion	(125,000)	(125,000)
Realized gain after exclusion	$ 38,400	$ 38,400
Amount realized	$ 195,400	$ 195,400
Fixing-up expenses	(6,400)	(6,400)
Adjusted sales price	$ 189,000	$ 189,000
§ 121 exclusion	(125,000)	(125,000)
Adjusted sales price after exclusion	$ 64,000	$ 64,000
Cost of new residence	(–0–)	(40,000)
Excess of adjusted sales price after the exclusion over reinvestment	$ 64,000	$ 24,000
Recognized gain (lower of realized gain after exclusion or above excess)	$ 38,400	$ 24,000
Realized gain after exclusion	$ 38,400	$ 38,400
Recognized gain	(38,400)	(24,000)
Postponed gain	$ –0–	$ 14,400
Cost of new residence	$ –0–	$ 40,000
Postponed gain	(–0–)	(14,400)
Basis of new residence	$ –0–	$ 25,600

▼

Comparing the results of Examples 29 and 30 provides insight into the relationship between § 1034 and § 121. If Keith had not made the election to postpone gain under § 121 in Example 29, his recognized gain would have been $163,400 (the realized gain). Thus, the election resulted in the permanent exclusion of the $125,000 of realized gain by reducing the recognized gain to $38,400. Further documentation of the permanent nature of the § 121 exclusion is provided in the calculation of the basis of the new residence in Example 30. The $40,000 cost of the residence is reduced only by the postponed gain of $14,400. That is, it is not reduced by the § 121 exclusion amount of $125,000. To postpone all of the $38,400 realized gain after the exclusion, Keith would have needed to reinvest $64,000 (the adjusted sales price after the exclusion). Also, note that the Example 29 results demonstrate that the realized gain after the exclusion is the ceiling on recognition.

OTHER NONRECOGNITION PROVISIONS

LEARNING OBJECTIVE 6
Identify other nonrecognition provisions contained in the Code.

The typical taxpayer experiences the sale of a residence or an involuntary conversion more frequently than the other types of nontaxable exchanges. Several additional nonrecognition provisions that are not as common are treated briefly in the remainder of this chapter.

EXCHANGE OF STOCK FOR PROPERTY—§ 1032

Under § 1032, a corporation does not recognize gain or loss on the receipt of money or other property in exchange for its stock (including treasury stock). In other words, a corporation does not recognize gain or loss when it deals in its own stock. This provision is consistent with the accounting treatment of such transactions.

CERTAIN EXCHANGES OF INSURANCE POLICIES—§ 1035

Under this provision, no gain or loss is recognized from the exchange of certain insurance contracts or policies. The rules relating to exchanges not solely in kind and the basis of the property acquired are the same as under § 1031. Exchanges qualifying for nonrecognition include the following:

- The exchange of life insurance contracts.
- The exchange of a life insurance contract for an endowment or annuity contract.
- The exchange of an endowment contract for another endowment contract that provides for regular payments beginning at a date not later than the date payments would have begun under the contract exchanged.
- The exchange of an endowment contract for an annuity contract.
- The exchange of annuity contracts.

EXCHANGE OF STOCK FOR STOCK OF THE SAME CORPORATION—§ 1036

A shareholder does not recognize gain or loss on the exchange of common stock solely for common stock in the same corporation or from the exchange of preferred stock for preferred stock in the same corporation. Exchanges between individual shareholders as well as between a shareholder and the corporation are included. The rules relating to exchanges not solely in kind and the basis of the property acquired are the same as under § 1031. For example, a nonrecognition exchange occurs when common stock with different rights, such as voting for nonvoting, is exchanged. A shareholder usually recognizes gain or loss from the exchange of common for preferred or preferred for common even though the stock exchanged is in the same corporation.

CERTAIN REACQUISITIONS OF REAL PROPERTY—§ 1038

Under this provision, no loss is recognized from the repossession of real property sold on an installment basis. Gain is recognized to a limited extent.

TRANSFERS OF PROPERTY BETWEEN SPOUSES OR INCIDENT TO DIVORCE—§ 1041

Section 1041 provides that transfers of property *between spouses or former spouses incident to divorce* are nontaxable transactions. Therefore, the basis to the recipient is a carryover basis. To be treated as incident to the divorce, the transfer must be related to the cessation of marriage or occur within one year after the date on which the marriage ceases.

Section 1041 also provides for nontaxable exchange treatment on property transfers *between spouses during marriage*. The basis to the recipient spouse is a carryover basis.

ETHICAL CONSIDERATIONS

Incident to Divorce or Not?

Randy and Judy are divorced in late 1996 after being married for 10 years. Several years ago they purchased a beach lot for $80,000. They planned to construct a beach house where they "could get away from it all" on weekends and holidays.

Eleven months after the divorce, Randy transfers his interest in the beach lot to Judy for $60,000 (i.e., 50 percent of the fair market value of $120,000). Since Randy is in a lower tax bracket than Judy (15 percent for Randy and 36 percent for Judy), they treat the sales transaction as not incident to the divorce. Randy recognizes a gain of $20,000 ($60,000 − $40,000), and Judy's adjusted basis is $100,000 ($40,000 + $60,000).

Evaluate Randy and Judy's treatment of the sales transaction.

ROLLOVERS INTO SPECIALIZED SMALL BUSINESS INVESTMENT COMPANIES—§ 1044

The Revenue Reconciliation Act of 1993 provides a postponement opportunity associated with the sale of publicly traded securities. If the amount realized is reinvested in the common stock or partnership interest of a specialized small business investment company (SSBIC), the realized gain is not recognized. Any amount not reinvested will trigger the recognition of the realized gain on the sale to the extent of the deficiency. The taxpayer must reinvest the proceeds within 60 days of the date of sale in order to qualify. In calculating the basis of the SSBIC stock, the amount of the purchase price is reduced by the amount of the postponed gain.

Statutory ceilings are imposed on the amount of realized gain that can be postponed for any taxable year as follows:

- Individual taxpayer: Lesser of:
  - $50,000 ($25,000 for married filing separately).
  - $500,000 ($250,000 for married filing separately) reduced by the amount of such nonrecognized gain in prior taxable years.
- Corporate taxpayer: Lesser of:
  - $250,000.
  - $1,000,000 reduced by the amount of such nonrecognized gain in prior taxable years.

Investors *ineligible* for this postponement treatment include partnerships, S corporations, estates, and trusts.

TAX PLANNING CONSIDERATIONS

7 LEARNING OBJECTIVE
Identify tax planning opportunities related to the nonrecognition provisions discussed in the chapter.

LIKE-KIND EXCHANGES

Since application of the like-kind exchange provisions is mandatory rather than elective, in certain instances it may be preferable to avoid qualifying for § 1031 nonrecognition. If the like-kind exchange provisions do not apply, the end result may be the recognition of capital gain in exchange for a higher basis in the newly acquired asset. Also, the immediate recognition of gain may be preferable in certain situations. Examples where immediate recognition is beneficial include the following:

- Taxpayer has unused net operating loss carryovers.
- Taxpayer has unused general business credit carryovers.
- Taxpayer has suspended or current passive activity losses.
- Taxpayer expects his or her effective tax rate to increase in the future.

EXAMPLE 31
Alicia disposes of a machine (used in her business) with an adjusted basis of $3,000 for $4,000. She also acquires a new business machine for $9,000. If § 1031 applies, the $1,000 realized gain is not recognized, and the basis of the new machine is reduced by $1,000 (from $9,000 to $8,000). If § 1031 does not apply, a $1,000 gain is recognized and may receive favorable capital gain treatment to the extent that the gain is not recognized as ordinary income due to the depreciation recapture provisions (see Chapter 17). In addition, the basis for depreciation on the new machine is $9,000 rather than $8,000 since there is no unrecognized gain. ▼

The application of § 1031 nonrecognition treatment should also be avoided when the adjusted basis of the property being disposed of exceeds the fair market value.

EXAMPLE 32
Assume the same facts as in the previous example, except the fair market value of the machine is $2,500. If § 1031 applies, the $500 realized loss is not recognized. To recognize the loss, Alicia should sell the old machine and purchase the new one. The purchase and sale transactions should be with different taxpayers. ▼

On the other hand, the like-kind exchange procedure can be utilized to control the amount of recognized gain.

EXAMPLE 33
Rex has property with an adjusted basis of $40,000 and a fair market value of $100,000. Sandra wants to buy Rex's property, but Rex wants to limit the amount of recognized gain on the proposed transaction. Sandra acquires other like-kind property (from an outside party) for $80,000. She then exchanges this property and $20,000 cash for Rex's property. Rex has a realized gain of $60,000 ($100,000 amount realized − $40,000 adjusted basis). His recognized gain is only $20,000, the lower of the $20,000 boot received or the $60,000 realized gain. Rex's basis for the like-kind property is $40,000 ($40,000 adjusted basis + $20,000 gain recognized − $20,000 boot received). If Rex had sold the property to Sandra for its fair market value of $100,000, the result would have been a $60,000 recognized gain ($100,000 amount realized − $40,000 adjusted basis) to him. It is permissible for Rex to identify the like-kind property that he wants Sandra to purchase.[39] ▼

---

[39] *Franklin B. Biggs,* 69 T.C. 905 (1978); Rev.Rul. 57–244, 1957–1 C.B. 247; Rev.Rul. 73–476, 1973–2 C.B. 300; *Starker v. U.S.,* 79–2 USTC ¶9541, 44 AFTR2d 79–5525, 602 F.2d 1341 (CA–9, 1979); and *Baird Publishing Co.,* 39 T.C. 608 (1962).

INVOLUNTARY CONVERSIONS

In certain cases, a taxpayer may prefer to recognize gain from an involuntary conversion. Keep in mind that § 1033, unlike § 1031 (dealing with like-kind exchanges), generally is an elective provision.

EXAMPLE 34

Ahmad has a $40,000 realized gain from the involuntary conversion of an office building. He reinvests the entire proceeds of $450,000 in a new office building. He does not elect to postpone gain under § 1033, however, because of an expiring net operating loss carryover that is offset against the gain. Therefore, none of the realized gain of $40,000 is postponed. By not electing § 1033 postponement, Ahmad's basis in the replacement property is the property's cost of $450,000 rather than $410,000 ($450,000 reduced by the $40,000 realized gain). ▼

SALE OF A PERSONAL RESIDENCE

Replacement Period Requirements.
Several problems arise in avoiding the recognition of gain on the sale of a principal residence. Most of these problems can be resolved favorably through appropriate planning procedures. However, a few represent situations where the taxpayer has to accept the adverse tax consequences and possesses little, if any, planning flexibility. One pitfall concerns the failure to reinvest *all* of the proceeds from the sale of the residence in a new principal residence.

EXAMPLE 35

Rita sells her principal residence in January 1995 for $150,000 (adjusted basis of $40,000). Shortly thereafter, she purchases for $100,000 a 50-year-old house in a historical part of the community and uses it as her principal residence. Rita intends to significantly renovate the property over a period of time and make it more suitable to her living needs. In December 1997, she enters into a contract with a home improvement company to carry out the renovation at a cost of $60,000. It is clear that only $100,000 of the proceeds from the sale of the old residence has been reinvested in a new principal residence on a *timely* basis. Of the realized gain of $110,000, therefore, $50,000 ($150,000 adjusted sales price – $100,000 reinvested) must be recognized.[40] ▼

One problem that a taxpayer may not be in a position to do anything about is the acquisition of property *before* the beginning of the replacement period. Recall that the replacement period begins two years before the sale and ends two years after the sale.

EXAMPLE 36

Tab's employer transfers him to a different city in July 1995, at which time Tab lists his house for sale with a realtor. Tab purchases a principal residence in the city to which he is transferred in September 1995. Because of market conditions, he is unable to sell his original residence until December 1997. Since the sale does not occur within two years of the purchase, the residence Tab bought in September 1995 is not a qualifying replacement residence. ▼

Principal Residence Requirement.
Section 1034 will not apply unless the property involved is the taxpayer's principal residence. A potential hurdle arises in cases where the residence has been rented and therefore has not been occupied

---

[40] It has been assumed that § 121 did not apply.

by the taxpayer for an extended period of time. Depending on the circumstances, the IRS may contend that the taxpayer has abandoned the property as his or her principal residence. The *key* to the abandonment issue is whether or not the taxpayer intended to reoccupy the property and use it as a principal residence upon returning to the locale. If the residence is, in fact, not reoccupied, the taxpayer should have a good reason to explain why it is not.

EXAMPLE 37

Lori's employer transfers her to another office out of the state on a three-year assignment. It is the understanding of the parties that the assignment is temporary, and upon its completion, Lori will return to the original job site. During her absence, she rents her principal residence and lives in an apartment at the new location. Lori has every intention of reoccupying her residence. However, when she returns from the temporary assignment, she finds that the residence no longer suits her needs. Specifically, the public school located nearby where she had planned to send her children has been closed. As a consequence, Lori sells the residence and replaces it with one more conveniently located to a public school. Under these circumstances, it would appear that Lori is in an excellent position to show that she has not abandoned the property as her principal residence. She can satisfactorily explain why she did not reoccupy the residence before its sale.[41]

The principal residence requirement can cause difficulty when a taxpayer works in two places and maintains more than one household. In such cases, the principal residence will be the location where the taxpayer lives most of the time.[42]

EXAMPLE 38

Hubert is a vice president of Green Corporation and in this capacity spends about an equal amount of time in the company's New York City and Miami offices. He owns a house in each location and expects to retire in about five years. At that time, he plans to sell his New York home and use some of the proceeds to make improvements on the Miami property. Both homes have appreciated in value since their acquisition, and Hubert expects the appreciation to continue. From a tax planning standpoint, Hubert should be looking toward the use of §§ 121 and 1034 to shelter some or all of the gain he will realize on the future sale of the New York City home.[43] To do this, he should arrange his affairs so as to spend more than six months each year at that location. Upon its sale, therefore, the New York home will be his principal residence. ▼

Section 121 Considerations.
Older individuals who may be contemplating a move from their home to an apartment should consider the following possibilities for minimizing or deferring taxes:

- Wait until age 55 to sell the residence and elect under § 121 to exclude up to $125,000 of the realized gain.
- Sell the personal residence under an installment contract to spread the gain over several years.[44]
- Sell the personal residence and purchase a condominium instead of renting an apartment, thereby permitting further deferral of the unrecognized gain.

---

[41] Rev.Rul. 78–146, 1978–1 C.B. 260. Compare *Rudolph M. Stucchi,* 35 TCM 1052, T.C.Memo. 1976–242.

[42] Rev.Rul. 77–298, 1977–2 C.B. 308.

[43] If Hubert qualifies, § 121 would allow the first $125,000 of gain to be excluded. Further gain might be avoided under § 1034 to the extent the sales proceeds are applied toward improvements on the Miami home.

[44] § 453(a). See the discussion of the installment method in Chapter 18.

The use of § 121 should be carefully considered. Although the use avoids the immediate recognition of gain, the election expends the full $125,000 allowed.

EXAMPLE 39
In 1997 Kate, age 55, sells her personal residence for an amount that yields a realized gain of $5,000. Presuming Kate does not plan to reinvest the sales proceeds in a new principal residence (take advantage of the deferral possibility of § 1034), should she avoid the recognition of this gain by utilizing § 121? Electing § 121 means that Kate will waste $120,000 of her lifetime exclusion. ▼

In this connection, the use of § 121 by one spouse precludes the other spouse from later taking advantage of the exclusion.

EXAMPLE 40
Assume the same facts as in the previous example, except that Kate was married to Wes at the time of the sale. Later, Kate and Wes are divorced and Wes marries Alice. If Kate has used the § 121 exclusion, it is unavailable to Wes and Alice even though either one of them may otherwise qualify. This result occurs because when Kate made the election for the 1997 sale, it was necessary for Wes to join with her in making the election even though the residence was owned separately by Kate. For Wes and Alice to be able to make the § 121 election, Wes and Kate must revoke their prior election. Another planning approach is for Alice to sell her residence before marrying Wes and to elect the exclusion on that sale. ▼

A taxpayer who is eligible to elect § 121 exclusion treatment may choose not to do so in order to remain eligible to elect it in the future. In arriving at this decision, consideration must be given to the probability that the taxpayer will satisfy the three-out-of-five-year ownership and use period requirements associated with a residence sale in the future. As previously mentioned, the holding period for the occupancy and use requirements carries over for a § 1033 involuntary conversion but not for a § 1034 sale.

Taxpayers should maintain records of both the purchase and sale of personal residences since the sale of one residence results in an adjustment of the basis of the new residence if the deferral provisions of § 1034 apply. Form 2119 should be filed with the tax return and a copy retained as support for the basis of the new residence. Detailed cost records should be retained for an indefinite period.

Chapter 15 has covered certain situations in which realized gains or losses are not recognized (nontaxable exchanges). Chapters 16 and 17 are concerned with the *classification* of recognized gains and losses. That is, if a gain or loss is recognized, is it an ordinary or capital gain or loss? Chapter 16 discusses the tax consequences of capital gains and losses.

KEY TERMS

Adjusted sales price, 15–19	Involuntary conversion, 15–10	Personal residence, 15–16
Boot, 15–5	Like-kind exchange, 15–3	Section 121 exclusion, 15–23
Fixing-up expenses, 15–19	Nontaxable exchange, 15–2	

PROBLEM MATERIALS

DISCUSSION QUESTIONS

1. What is the justification for nontaxable exchange treatment?

2. Distinguish between a loss that is not recognized on a nontaxable exchange and a loss that is not recognized on the sale or exchange of a personal use asset.

3. Distinguish between a nontaxable exchange and a tax-free transaction.

4. What are the three requirements that must be satisfied for a transaction to qualify for nontaxable exchange treatment under § 1031?

5. Can the exchange of personal use property for property held for productive use in a trade or business qualify for like-kind exchange treatment?

6. Amos owns a lathe that he uses in his trade or business. The adjusted basis is $40,000. Although the lathe is only two years old, Amos needs to replace it due to advances in technology. He exchanges the lathe and $20,000 in cash for a new lathe worth $50,000. May Amos elect not to treat the transaction as a like-kind exchange so that the realized loss of $10,000 can be recognized?

7. Which of the following qualify as like-kind exchanges under § 1031?
   a. Improved for unimproved real estate.
   b. Vending machine (used in business) for inventory.
   c. Rental house for personal residence.
   d. Business equipment for securities.
   e. Warehouse for office building (both used for business).
   f. Truck for computer (both used in business).
   g. Rental house for land (both held for investment).
   h. Ten shares of stock in Blue Corporation for 10 shares of stock in Red Corporation.
   i. Office furniture for office equipment (both used in business).
   j. General partnership interest in Green Partnership for general partnership interest in Brown Partnership.

8. Melissa owns a residential lot held for investment in Spring Creek that has appreciated substantially in value. She is considering exchanging the lot with her father for a residential lot in McComb that she also will hold for investment. Identify the relevant tax issues for Melissa.

9. Ross would like to dispose of some land that he acquired five years ago because he believes that it will not continue to appreciate. Its value has increased by $50,000 during the five-year period. He also intends to sell stock that has declined in value by $50,000 during the eight-month period he has owned it. Ross has four offers to acquire the stock and land:

Buyer number 1:	Exchange land.
Buyer number 2:	Purchase land for cash.
Buyer number 3:	Exchange stock.
Buyer number 4:	Purchase stock for cash.

   Identify the tax issues relevant to Ross in disposing of this land and stock.

10. What is boot, and how does it affect the recognition of gain or loss on a like-kind exchange when received by the taxpayer? How is the recognition of gain or loss affected when boot is given?

11. The receipt of boot in a § 1031 exchange triggers the recognition of realized gain. The gain recognition will affect the basis of the property received by the taxpayer.
    a. Discuss the relationship between the realized gain and the boot received if the boot received is greater than the realized gain.
    b. Discuss the relationship between the realized gain and the boot received if the boot received is less than the realized gain.

c. What effect does the recognition of gain have on the basis of the like-kind property received? Of the boot received?

12. In a like-kind exchange, the basis of the property received is the same as the adjusted basis of the property transferred. If boot is received, what effect does the boot have on the basis of the like-kind property received? If boot is given, what effect does the boot have on the basis of the like-kind property received?

13. In connection with like-kind exchanges, discuss each of the following:
    a. Realized gain.
    b. Realized loss.
    c. Recognized gain.
    d. Recognized loss.
    e. Postponed gain.
    f. Postponed loss.
    g. Basis of like-kind property received.
    h. Basis of boot received.

14. Aaron exchanges a machine used in his business for another machine and stock of Teal, Inc. Explain why the machine has a carryover holding period and the stock has a new (date of exchange) holding period.

15. Mortgaged real estate may be received in a like-kind exchange. If the taxpayer assumes the mortgage, what effect does the mortgage have on the recognition of realized gain? On the basis of the real estate received?

16. A taxpayer's appreciated property is involuntarily converted. She receives insurance proceeds equal to the fair market value of the property. What is the minimum amount the taxpayer must reinvest in qualifying property to defer recognition of realized gain?

17. Beth's retail store building is destroyed by a tornado. She receives insurance proceeds of $200,000, which is the appraised value of the building prior to its destruction. Her adjusted basis in the building is $225,000. What is the maximum amount that Beth can reinvest in another retail store building and still recognize the $25,000 loss?

18. Ed receives severance damages from the state government for a public road built across his property. Under what circumstances can the § 1033 involuntary conversion provision apply to prevent the recognition of gain?

19. Julia owns a shopping mall that she leases to tenants. The shopping mall is destroyed by a tornado. Is the functional use test or the taxpayer use test applied in terms of appropriate replacement property? Explain the differences between the two tests.

20. Rebecca, a calendar year taxpayer, owns an office building that she uses in her business. The building is involuntarily converted on June 15, 1997. On October 5, 1997, Rebecca receives proceeds large enough to produce a realized gain. What is the latest date she can replace the building if the form of the conversion is:
    a. A flood?
    b. A condemnation?
    c. A tornado?

21. What is the earliest date that a taxpayer can replace involuntarily converted property if the form of the conversion is:
    a. A casualty?
    b. A theft?
    c. A condemnation?

22. Bob is notified by the city public housing authority on October 5, 1997, that his apartment building is going to be condemned as part of an urban renewal project. On October 12, 1997, Carol offers to buy the building from Bob. Bob sells the building to Carol on October 30, 1997. Condemnation occurs on February 1, 1998, and Carol receives the condemnation proceeds from the city. Assume both Bob and Carol are calendar year taxpayers.
    a. What is the earliest date that Bob can dispose of the building and qualify for § 1033 postponement treatment?

b. Does the sale to Carol qualify as a § 1033 involuntary conversion?
c. What is the latest date that Carol can acquire qualifying replacement property and qualify for postponement of the realized gain?
d. What type of property will be qualifying replacement property?

23. A warehouse owned by Martha and used in her business (i.e., to store inventory) is being condemned by the city to provide a right of way for a highway. The warehouse has appreciated by $100,000 based on Martha's estimate of fair market value. In the negotiations, the city is offering $40,000 less than what Martha believes the property is worth. Alan, a real estate broker, has offered to purchase Martha's property for $25,000 more than the city's offer. Martha plans to invest the proceeds she will receive in an office building that she will lease to various tenants. Identify the relevant tax issues for Martha.

24. Gary sells his principal residence (the only one he has ever owned) at a gain. He replaces the old residence with a more expensive new principal residence one month after the sale. Gary would like to recognize the realized gain on the sale because he has a large investment loss on the sale of stock. Can he recognize the realized gain on the sale of his principal residence?

25. Samantha, who is age 39, would like to quit her job, sell her house, buy a sailboat, and sail the seven seas. The projected realized loss on the sale of her personal residence is $50,000. Is it possible for Samantha to recognize the loss or to elect to defer the loss?

26. What is the earliest date a principal residence that has been sold can be replaced and qualify for postponement treatment? The latest date?

27. Jim sells his principal residence on September 18, 1997. Although he does not replace it until August 19, 2001, the replacement qualifies for postponement treatment under § 1034. Discuss how this replacement could satisfy the residence replacement period requirement.

28. Sandy owns a residence that she acquired 19 months ago. It has appreciated by $40,000 during this period. Now, however, the school board has redrawn the boundaries for the school districts, and her son will have to transfer to a different high school for his senior year. Sandy is considering selling her residence and buying another one that will enable her son to remain in the same high school. Without this reason, she would not sell the house. Identify the relevant tax issues for Sandy.

29. Mort owns a beach house and a cabin in the mountains. He stays in each during different parts of the year. Mort also rents a townhouse in the city where he is employed. If Mort sells both the beach house and the cabin at a gain, how does he decide which of these properties is his principal residence?

30. Peggy has owned and occupied a house as her principal residence for 10 years. She purchases a new residence in March 1997. She initially listed her old residence with a realtor in January 1997. Needing the cash flow, she rents the old residence to Joe for a six-month period beginning in March. She sells the old residence to Paul upon the expiration of the rental period in September. Does the sale of the old residence in September qualify as the sale of a principal residence?

31. Define each of the following associated with the sale of a residence:
    a. Amount realized.
    b. Adjusted sales price.
    c. Fixing-up expenses.
    d. Realized gain.
    e. Recognized gain.
    f. Postponed gain.
    g. Basis of new residence.

32. Ned inherits a house from his aunt (value of $200,000 at the date of her death). He sells his principal residence for $125,000 and moves into the inherited house. Ned's realized gain on the sale is $30,000. Since the fair market value of the inherited property is

greater than the adjusted sales price of the house Ned sold, can he use § 1034 to postpone the recognition of the realized gain of $30,000?

33. What does the § 121 exclusion cover? Is it elective? Does the old residence have to be replaced?

34. How many times can § 121 exclusion treatment be elected by a taxpayer? If the taxpayer is filing a joint return with his or her spouse, do both taxpayers have to meet the ownership and use requirements?

35. Can any other provision be applied to any remaining gain that is not excluded under § 121?

PROBLEMS

36. Kay owns undeveloped land with an adjusted basis of $200,000. She exchanges it for other undeveloped land worth $230,000.
    a. What are Kay's realized and recognized gain or loss?
    b. What is Kay's basis in the undeveloped land she receives?

37. Kareem owns an automobile that he uses exclusively in his business. The adjusted basis is $19,000, and the fair market value is $16,000. Kareem exchanges the car for a car that he will use exclusively in his business.
    a. What are Kareem's realized and recognized gain or loss?
    b. What is his basis in the new car?
    c. What are the tax consequences to Kareem in (a) and (b) if he used the old car and will use the new car exclusively for personal purposes?

38. Tex Wall owns undeveloped land that he is holding for investment. His adjusted basis is $175,000. On October 7, 1997, he exchanges the land with his 23-year-old daughter, Paige, for other undeveloped land that he will hold for investment. The appraised value of Paige's land is $250,000.
    a. Calculate Tex's realized and recognized gain or loss from the exchange with Paige and on a subsequent sale of the land by Tex to Baxter, a real estate broker, for $300,000 on February 15, 1998.
    b. Calculate Tex's realized and recognized gain or loss on the exchange with Paige if Tex does not sell the land received from Paige, but Paige sells the land received from Tex on February 15, 1998. Calculate Tex's basis for the land on October 7, 1997, and on February 15, 1998.
    c. Write a letter to Tex advising him on how he could avoid any recognition of gain associated with the October 7, 1997, exchange prior to his actual sale of the land. His address is The Corral, El Paso, TX 79968.

39. Bonnie owns a personal computer that she uses exclusively in her business. The adjusted basis is $5,000. Bonnie transfers the personal computer and cash of $4,000 to Don for a laser printer worth $10,000 that she will use in her business.
    a. Calculate Bonnie's recognized gain or loss on the exchange.
    b. Calculate Bonnie's basis for the printer.

40. Chee exchanges a light-duty truck used exclusively in his business for a light-duty truck that will be used in his business. The adjusted basis for the old truck is $12,000, and the fair market value of the old truck is $10,000.
    a. Calculate Chee's recognized gain or loss on the exchange.
    b. Calculate Chee's basis for the truck he receives.
    c. How could Chee structure the transaction to produce better tax consequences?

41. Cary owns undeveloped land with an adjusted basis of $110,000. He exchanges it for an office building (fair market value of $120,000) and $40,000 in cash. He will use the building in his business.
    a. What is Cary's realized gain or loss?
    b. His recognized gain or loss?
    c. His basis in the office building?

42. Olga owns a machine that she uses in her business. The adjusted basis is $60,000, and the fair market value is $95,000. She exchanges it for another machine worth $70,000. Olga also receives stock worth $25,000.
    a. Calculate Olga's realized and recognized gain or loss on the exchange.
    b. Calculate Olga's basis for the new machine.
    c. Calculate Olga's basis for the stock she received.

43. Ed owns investment land with an adjusted basis of $35,000. Polly has offered to purchase the land from Ed for $175,000 for use in a real estate development. The amount offered by Polly is $10,000 in excess of what Ed perceives as the fair market value of the land. Ed would like to dispose of the land to Polly but does not want to incur the tax liability that would result. He identifies an office building with a fair market value of $175,000 that he would like to acquire. Polly purchases the office building and then exchanges the office building for Ed's land.
    a. Calculate Ed's realized and recognized gain on the exchange and his basis for the office building.
    b. Calculate Polly's realized and recognized gain on the exchange and her basis in the land.

44. What is the basis of the new property in each of the following exchanges?
    a. Apartment building held for investment (adjusted basis $150,000) for office building to be held for investment (fair market value $200,000).
    b. Land and building used as a barber shop (adjusted basis $30,000) for land and building used as a grocery store (fair market value $350,000).
    c. Office building (adjusted basis $30,000) for bulldozer (fair market value $42,000), both held for business use.
    d. IBM common stock (adjusted basis $14,000) for Exxon common stock (fair market value $18,000).
    e. Rental house (adjusted basis $90,000) for mountain cabin to be held for personal use (fair market value $115,000).

45. Norm owns Machine A, which he uses in his business. The adjusted basis of Machine A is $12,000, and the fair market value is $18,000. Norm is considering two options for the disposal of Machine A. Under the first option, Norm will transfer Machine A and $3,000 cash to Joan, a dealer, in exchange for Machine B, which has a fair market value of $21,000. Under the second option, Norm will sell Machine A for $18,000 to Tim, who is a dealer. Norm will then purchase Machine B from Joan for $21,000. Machine A and Machine B qualify as like-kind property.
    a. Calculate Norm's recognized gain or loss and the basis for Machine B under the first option.
    b. Calculate Norm's recognized gain or loss and the basis for Machine B under the second option.
    c. Advise Norm on which option he should select.

46. Gus exchanges real estate held for investment plus stock for real estate to be held for investment. The stock transferred has an adjusted basis of $15,000 and a fair market value of $10,000. The real estate transferred has an adjusted basis of $15,000 and a fair market value of $45,000. The real estate acquired has a fair market value of $55,000.
    a. What is Gus's realized gain or loss?
    b. His recognized gain or loss?
    c. The basis of the newly acquired real estate?

47. Agnes exchanges a warehouse and the related land with Damon for an office building and the related land. Agnes's adjusted basis for her warehouse and land is $420,000. The fair market value of Damon's office building and land is $410,000. Agnes's property has a $90,000 mortgage that Damon assumes.
    a. Calculate Agnes's realized and recognized gain or loss.
    b. Calculate Agnes's adjusted basis for the office building and land received.
    c. As an alternative, Damon has proposed that rather than assuming the mortgage, he will transfer cash of $90,000 to Agnes. Agnes would use the cash to pay off the mortgage. Advise Agnes on whether this alternative would be beneficial to her from a tax perspective.

48. Determine the realized, recognized, and postponed gain or loss and the new basis for each of the following like-kind exchanges:

	Adjusted Basis of Old Asset	Boot Given	Fair Market Value of New Asset	Boot Received
a.	$ 7,000	$ –0–	$12,000	$4,000
b.	14,000	2,000	15,000	–0–
c.	3,000	7,000	8,000	500
d.	22,000	–0–	32,000	–0–
e.	10,000	–0–	11,000	1,000
f.	10,000	–0–	8,000	–0–

49. Shontelle owns an apartment house that has an adjusted basis of $1,100,000 but is subject to a mortgage of $250,000. She transfers the apartment house to Dave and receives from him $125,000 in cash and an office building with a fair market value of $1,125,000 at the time of the exchange. Dave assumes the $250,000 mortgage on the apartment house.
   a. What is Shontelle's realized gain or loss?
   b. Her recognized gain or loss?
   c. The basis of the newly acquired office building?

50. Carmen's office building, which has an adjusted basis of $200,000, is destroyed by a tornado. Since Carmen's business has excess office space, she decides not to replace the office building, but instead to contribute the proceeds to the working capital of her business.
   a. If the insurance proceeds are $225,000, what is Carmen's recognized gain or loss?
   b. If the insurance proceeds are $180,000, what is Carmen's recognized gain or loss?

51. Albert owns 100 acres of land on which he grows spruce Christmas trees. His adjusted basis for the land is $100,000. He receives condemnation proceeds of $10,000 when the city's new beltway takes 5 acres along the eastern boundary of his property. He also receives a severance award of $6,000 associated with the possible harmful effects of exhaust fumes on his Christmas trees. Albert invests the $16,000 in a growth mutual fund.
   a. Determine the tax consequences to Albert of the condemnation proceeds.
   b. Determine the tax consequences to Albert of the severance award.

52. For each of the following involuntary conversions, indicate whether the property acquired qualifies as replacement property:
   a. Frank owns a shopping mall that is destroyed by a tornado. The space in the mall was rented to various tenants. Frank uses the insurance proceeds to build a shopping mall in a neighboring community where no property has been damaged by tornadoes.
   b. Ivan owns a warehouse that he uses in his business. The warehouse is destroyed by fire. Due to economic conditions in the area, Ivan decides not to rebuild the warehouse. Instead, he uses the insurance proceeds to build a warehouse to be used in his business in another state.
   c. Ridge's personal residence is condemned as part of a local government project to widen the highway from two lanes to four lanes. He uses the condemnation proceeds to purchase another personal residence.
   d. Juanita owns a building that she uses in her retail business. The building is destroyed by a hurricane. Due to an economic downturn in the area caused by the closing of a military base, she decides to rent space for her retail outlet rather than to replace the building. She uses the insurance proceeds to buy a four-unit apartment building in another city. A realtor in that city will handle the rental of the apartments for her.
   e. Susan and Rick's personal residence is destroyed by a tornado. Since they would like to travel, they decide not to acquire a replacement residence. Instead, they invest the insurance proceeds in a duplex that they rent to tenants.

53. The building that houses LaToya's designer clothing store is destroyed in a mud slide associated with a flood on June 27, 1997. LaToya had anticipated the flood and moved her inventory, furniture, and fixtures to a warehouse outside the floodplain on June 20, 1997. Her adjusted basis for the building is $150,000, and she receives insurance proceeds of $160,000 on July 15, 1997. LaToya intends to purchase another building for her store, but would like to have time to locate one in a safer location. Her taxable year ends on June 30.
   a. What are the earliest and latest dates that LaToya can make a qualified replacement?
   b. Assuming LaToya makes a qualified replacement costing $160,000, what are her realized gain, recognized gain, and basis for the replacement property?
   c. What are the earliest and latest dates that LaToya can make a qualified replacement if the form of the involuntary conversion is a condemnation by a governmental authority? She was officially notified of the pending condemnation on June 1, 1997.

54. Lynn's office building, which is used in her business, is destroyed by a hurricane in September 1997. The adjusted basis is $210,000. Lynn receives insurance proceeds of $390,000 in October 1997.
   a. Calculate Lynn's realized gain or loss, recognized gain or loss, and basis for the replacement property if she acquires an office building for $390,000 in October 1997.
   b. Calculate Lynn's realized gain or loss, recognized gain or loss, and basis for the replacement property if she acquires an office building for $350,000 in October 1997.
   c. Calculate Lynn's realized gain or loss and recognized gain or loss if she does not acquire replacement property.

55. Carlos's warehouse, which has an adjusted basis of $325,000 and a fair market value of $490,000, is condemned by an agency of the Federal government to make way for a highway interchange. The initial condemnation offer is $450,000. After substantial negotiations, the agency agrees to transfer to Carlos a surplus warehouse that he believes is worth $490,000.
   a. What are the recognized gain or loss and the basis of the replacement warehouse if Carlos's objective is to recognize as much gain as possible?
   b. Advise Carlos regarding what he needs to do by what date in order to achieve his objective.

56. What are the *maximum* postponed gain or loss and the basis for the replacement property for the following involuntary conversions?

	Property	Type of Conversion	Amount Realized	Adjusted Basis	Amount Reinvested
a.	Drugstore (business)	Casualty	$160,000	$130,000	$110,000
b.	Apartments (investment)	Condemned	100,000	125,000	175,000
c.	Grocery store (business)	Casualty	400,000	300,000	450,000
d.	Residence (personal)	Casualty	16,000	18,000	17,000
e.	Vacant lot (investment)	Condemned	240,000	160,000	220,000
f.	Residence (personal)	Casualty	20,000	18,000	19,000
g.	Residence (personal)	Condemned	18,000	20,000	26,000
h.	Apartments (investment)	Condemned	150,000	100,000	200,000

57. Rental property owned by Freda, a calendar year taxpayer, is destroyed by a tornado on January 1, 1997. Freda had originally paid $150,000 for the property, of which $125,000 was allocated to the building and $25,000 was allocated to the land. During the time Freda owned the property, MACRS deductions of $46,250 were taken. MACRS deductions of $57,500 would have been taken, except that Freda chose to forgo deductions of $11,250 one year when her tax return showed a net operating loss. Freda

receives insurance proceeds of $60,000 in November 1997. As a result of continuing negotiations with the insurance company, Freda receives additional proceeds of $35,000 in August 1998.
  a. What is Freda's adjusted basis for the property?
  b. What is Freda's realized gain or loss on the involuntary conversion in 1997? In 1998?
  c. What is the latest date that Freda can replace the involuntarily converted property to qualify for § 1033 postponement?
  d. What is the latest date that Freda can replace the involuntarily converted property to qualify for § 1033 postponement if the form of the involuntary conversion is a condemnation?

58. Cassandra's personal residence is condemned on October 31, 1997, as part of a plan to build a freeway around the city. Her adjusted basis is $125,000. She receives condemnation proceeds of $110,000 on November 19, 1997. Cassandra is a calendar year taxpayer. She purchases another personal residence on November 20, 1997, for $150,000.
  a. What are Cassandra's realized and recognized gain or loss?
  b. What is her adjusted basis for the new residence?

59. Milton listed his personal residence with a realtor on March 3, 1997, at a listed price of $250,000. He rejected several offers in the $200,000 range during the summer. Finally, on August 16, 1997, he and the purchaser signed a contract to sell for $235,000. The sale (i.e., closing) took place on September 7, 1997. The closing statement showed the following disbursements being made:

Realtor's commission	$ 14,000
Appraisal fee	500
Exterminator's certificate	300
Recording fees	400
Mortgage to First Bank	180,000
Cash to seller	39,800

Milton's adjusted basis for the house is $150,000.
  a. Calculate Milton's realized gain on the sale.
  b. What is the latest date that Milton can acquire a replacement residence in order to postpone any realized gain?

60. Tina, age 42, has lived in her residence for three years. Her adjusted basis is $130,000. In February 1995, she decides to move to another neighborhood to reduce her commuting time and lists her residence for sale for $225,000. In May 1995, she moves to another residence that she has purchased for $240,000 at the beginning of the month. By April 1997, she has still not sold her old residence due to market conditions. She is becoming concerned that she will not satisfy the two-year replacement provision. Therefore, she is considering moving back into her old residence and selling her new residence. She anticipates no difficulty in selling the new residence for $250,000.
  a. Advise Tina regarding whether she should (1) sell her new residence and move back into her old residence or (2) stay in her new residence and continue to try to sell her old residence.
  b. If Tina moves back into her old residence, what is her adjusted basis for the old residence?

61. Ted is a colonel in the U.S. Air Force who is stationed in Newport News, Virginia. He is being transferred to Turkey for a three-year tour of duty beginning on September 15, 1997. He sells his principal residence in Newport News on August 25, 1997, for $220,000. His adjusted basis is $120,000. The selling expenses are $12,000, and the fixing-up expenses are $3,000. He returns to the United States on September 15, 2000, and purchases a new residence for $210,000 in San Antonio, Texas, where he is now stationed.
  a. What is Ted's realized gain or loss?
  b. His recognized gain or loss?
  c. The basis of the residence?

62. On January 15, 1997, Kelly, a 48-year-old widow, buys a new residence for $200,000. On March 1, 1997, she sells for $249,000 her old residence, which had an adjusted basis of $140,000. Fixing-up expenses of $4,000 and selling expenses of $14,000 were incurred. Between April 1 and June 30, 1997, she constructs an addition to her new house at a cost of $15,000.
    a. What is Kelly's realized gain or loss?
    b. Kelly's recognized gain or loss?
    c. Kelly's basis for the new residence?

63. What are the realized, recognized, and postponed gain or loss, the new basis, and the adjusted sales price for each of the following? Assume that none of the taxpayers is 55 years of age or older.
    a. Susan sells her residence for $90,000. The adjusted basis was $55,000. The selling expenses were $5,000. The fixing-up expenses were $3,000. She did not reinvest in a new residence.
    b. Rocky sells his residence for $170,000. The adjusted basis was $120,000. The selling expenses were $4,000. The fixing-up expenses were $6,000. Rocky reinvested $160,000 in a new residence.
    c. Veneia sells her residence for $65,000. The adjusted basis was $35,000. The selling expenses were $1,000. The fixing-up expenses were $2,000. She reinvested $40,000.
    d. Barry sells his residence for $70,000. The adjusted basis was $65,000. The selling expenses were $6,000. He reinvested $80,000 in a new residence.
    e. Carl sells his residence for $100,000, and his mortgage is assumed by the buyer. The adjusted basis was $80,000; the mortgage, $50,000. The selling expenses were $4,000. The fixing-up expenses were $2,000. He reinvested $120,000 in a new residence.

64. Ned, age 47, sells his residence in Richmond on May 5, 1997, for $115,000. He incurs realtor's commissions of $6,900 and qualified fixing-up expenses of $2,000. His adjusted basis is $70,000. Ned sells the house because his employer assigns him to a temporary job in another state. Ned moves back to Richmond in December 1998. However, he has decided that he enjoys being relieved of the responsibilities of home ownership. Therefore, he rents an apartment and does not purchase another residence by May 5, 1999.
    a. What should Ned have reported on his 1997 return with respect to the sale of his residence?
    b. What should Ned do in 1999 when he has not replaced the residence within the required two-year period?

65. Pedro, age 57, is the sole owner of his principal residence. He has owned and occupied it for 10 years. He sells the house for a realized gain of $175,000. Pedro does not intend to acquire a replacement residence. Maria, his spouse, refuses to join him in making the § 121 election.
    a. Can Pedro elect the § 121 exclusion if he and Maria file a joint return? If so, what are the available amount of the exclusion and the recognized gain?
    b. Can Pedro elect the § 121 exclusion if he files a separate return? If so, what are the available amount of the exclusion and the recognized gain?
    c. If Maria joins Pedro in making the election, what are the available amount of the exclusion and the recognized gain on a joint return? On a separate return?

66. Pat sold his residence, which he had owned and occupied for 18 years. The adjusted basis was $130,000, and the selling price was $325,000. The selling expenses were $22,000, and the fixing-up expenses were $5,000. He reinvested $132,000 in a new residence. Pat is 57 years old.
    a. What are the realized, recognized, and postponed gain or loss, the new basis, and the adjusted sales price if his objective is to minimize the recognized gain?
    b. Based on the data provided, should Pat elect the § 121 exclusion?

67. Nell, Nina, and Nora Sanders, who are sisters, sell their principal residence in which they have lived for the past 20 years. The youngest of the sisters is age 58. The selling price is $555,000, selling expenses and legal fees are $15,000, and the adjusted basis is $60,000 (the fair market value of the residence when inherited from their parents 20

years ago). Since the sisters are going to live in rental housing, they do not plan to acquire another residence. Nell has contacted you on behalf of the three sisters regarding the tax consequences of the sale.

a. Write a letter to Nell advising her of the tax consequences and how taxes can be minimized. Nell's address is 100 Oak Avenue, Billings, MT 59101.

b. Prepare a memo for the tax files.

68. Jeff and Jill are divorced on August 1, 1997. According to the terms of the divorce decree, Jeff's ownership interest in the house is to be transferred to Jill in exchange for the release from marital rights. Before the divorce, the house was separately owned by Jeff. The adjusted basis and the fair market value at the date of the transfer are $175,000 and $200,000, respectively.

a. Does the transfer of the house produce recognized gain to either Jeff or Jill?

b. What is the basis of the house to Jill?

c. If the same transfer was made by Jeff to Jill for $200,000 and was not associated with a divorce, would either Jeff or Jill have recognized gain?

69. Sam, age 63, owns a residence in which he has lived for 20 years. The residence is destroyed by fire on August 8, 1997. The adjusted basis is $140,000, and the fair market value is $325,000. Sam receives insurance proceeds of $325,000 for the residence. He is trying to decide whether to purchase a comparable house. He anticipates that he will retire in two years and will move to a warmer climate where he will rent in case he decides to live in different places.

a. Advise Sam of the tax consequences of replacing versus not replacing the residence.

b. Which do you recommend to him?

CUMULATIVE PROBLEMS

70. Tammy Walker, age 37, is a self-employed accountant. Tammy's Social Security number is 333–40–1111. Her address is 101 Glass Road, Richmond, VA 23236. Her income and expenses associated with her accounting practice for 1997 are as follows:

Revenues (cash receipts during 1997)		$212,000
Expenses		
Salaries	$ 89,000	
Office supplies	2,100	
Postage	1,500	
Depreciation of equipment	25,000	
Telephone	800	
	$118,400	

Since Tammy is a cash method taxpayer, she does not record her receivables as revenue until she receives cash payment. At the beginning of 1997, her accounts receivable were $20,000, and the balance had decreased to $8,000 by the end of the year. The balance on December 31, 1997, would have been $14,000, except that an account for $6,000 had become uncollectible in November.

Tammy used one room in her 10-room house as the office for her accounting practice (400 square feet out of a total square footage of 4,000). She paid the following expenses related to the house during 1997:

Utilities	$4,000
Insurance	800
Property taxes	4,000
Repairs	1,400

Tammy had purchased the house on September 1, 1996, for $200,000. She sold her previous house on November 15, 1996, for $105,000. Her selling expenses had been $9,000, and qualified fixing-up expenses were $1,100. Tammy and her former husband, Lou, had purchased the house in 1993 for $80,000. Tammy had received Lou's 50% ownership interest as part of their divorce settlement in August 1995. Tammy had not used any part of the former residence as a home office.

Tammy has one child, Thomas, age 17. Thomas lives with his father during the summer and with Tammy for the rest of the year. Tammy can document that she spent $8,000 during 1997 for the child's support. The father normally provides about $2,000 per year, but this year he gave the child a new car for Christmas. The cost of the car was $18,000. The divorce decree is silent regarding the dependency exemption for the child.

Under the terms of the divorce decree, Tammy is to receive alimony of $900 per month. The payments will terminate at Tammy's death or if she should remarry.

Tammy provides part of the support of her mother, age 67. The total support for 1997 for her mother was as follows:

Social Security benefits	$5,300
From Tammy	1,700
From Bob, Tammy's brother	1,200
From Susan, Tammy's sister	1,800

Bob and Susan have both indicated their willingness to sign a multiple support waiver form if it will benefit Tammy.

Tammy's deductible itemized deductions during 1997, excluding any itemized deductions related to the house, were $13,000. She made estimated tax payments of $28,000.

Part 1—Tax Computation
Compute Tammy's lowest net tax payable or refund due for 1997. Suggested software (if available): *TurboTax* or *MacInTax*.

Part 2—Tax Planning
Tammy and her former husband have been discussing the $900 alimony he pays her each month. Due to a health problem of his new wife, he does not feel that he can afford to continue to pay the $900 each month. He is in the 15% tax bracket. If Tammy will agree to decrease the amount by 25%, he will agree that the amount paid is not alimony for tax purposes. Assume that the other data used in calculating Tammy's taxable income for 1997 will apply for her 1998 tax return. Write a letter to Tammy that contains your advice on whether she should agree to her former husband's proposal. Also prepare a memo for the tax files. Suggested software (if available): *TurboTax* or *MacInTax*.

71. Arnold Young, age 39, is single. He lives at 1507 Iris Lane, Tucson, AZ 85721. His Social Security number is 999–55–2000. Arnold does not wish to have $3 go to the Presidential Election Campaign Fund.

Arnold was divorced in 1993 after 15 years of marriage. He pays alimony of $36,000 a year to his former spouse, Carol. Carol's Social Security number is 999–33–3000. Arnold's son, Tom, who is age 13, resides with Carol. Arnold pays child support of $6,000 per year.

Arnold owns a sole proprietorship that is on the accrual method of accounting. His revenues and expenses for 1996 are as follows:

Sales revenue	$688,000
Cost of goods sold	430,000
Salary expense	90,000
Rent expense	24,000
Utilities	12,000

Telephone	3,000
Advertising	4,000
Bad debts	6,000
Depreciation	15,000
Insurance	7,000
Accounting and legal fees	4,000
Supplies	1,000

Other income received by Arnold includes the following:

Dividend income:	
Swan, Inc.	$8,000
Wren, Inc.	3,000
Interest income:	
First Bank	5,000
Second Bank	1,000
Lottery winnings (tickets purchased cost $700)	6,000

During the year, Arnold and his sole proprietorship had the following property transactions:

a. Sold Blue, Inc., stock for $27,000 on March 12, 1996. He had purchased the stock on September 5, 1993, for $30,000.
b. Received an inheritance of $50,000 from his Uncle Steve. Arnold used the $50,000 to purchase Green, Inc., stock on May 15, 1996.
c. Received Orange, Inc., stock worth $7,500 as a gift from his Aunt Jane on June 17, 1996. Her adjusted basis for the stock was $5,000. No gift taxes were paid on the transfer. Aunt Jane had purchased the stock on April 1, 1990. Arnold sold the stock on July 1, 1996, for $8,000.
d. On July 15, 1996, Arnold sold one-half of the Green, Inc., stock for $29,000.
e. Arnold is notified on August 1, 1996, that Yellow, Inc., stock he purchased from a colleague on September 1, 1995, for $20,000 is worthless. While he perceived the investment was risky, he did not anticipate that the corporation would declare bankruptcy.
f. On August 15, 1996, Arnold received a parcel of land in Phoenix worth $160,000 in exchange for a parcel of land he owned in Tucson. Since the Tucson parcel was worth $200,000, he also received $40,000 cash. Arnold's adjusted basis for the Tucson parcel was $190,000. He originally purchased it on September 18, 1993.
g. Sold the condominium in which he had been living for the past 10 years on December 1, 1996. He and Carol had purchased the condominium as joint owners for $120,000. Arnold had received Carol's ownership interest as part of the divorce proceedings. The fair market value at that time was $150,000. The sales price is $250,000, selling expenses are $15,000, and fixing-up expenses are $5,000. Although he has not yet purchased a replacement residence, negotiations are under way and are likely to be concluded during the first half of 1997. Arnold estimates that the purchase price will be about $235,000.

Arnold's itemized deductions are as follows:

Medical expenses (before the 7.5% floor)	$7,000
Property taxes on residence	5,000
State income taxes	6,000
Charitable contributions	10,000
Mortgage interest on residence	8,500

During the year, Arnold makes estimated Federal income tax payments of $20,000.

Compute Arnold's lowest net tax payable or refund due for 1996, assuming he makes any available elections that will reduce the tax. If you use tax forms for your computations, you will need Forms 1040, 2119, and 8824, and Schedules A, B, C, D, and SE. Suggested software (if available): *TurboTax* or *MacInTax*.

RESEARCH PROBLEMS

Note: ***West's Federal Taxation on CD-ROM*** *can be used in preparing solutions to the Research Problems. Alternatively, tax research materials contained in a standard tax library can be used.*

Research Problem 1. Sarah, age 37, and Ed, age 38, have been dating for three years. Their wedding date is two months away. They have found a house they would like to purchase as their principal residence for $400,000. The projected amount realized and realized gain on the sale of their current principal residences would be as follows:

	Sarah	Ed
Amount realized	$175,000	$200,000
Realized gain	40,000	90,000

Neither Sarah nor Ed would incur any fixing-up expenses.

Sarah and Ed will jointly purchase the new principal residence with Ed contributing his $200,000 net sales proceeds plus $50,000 in cash and Sarah contributing $150,000 of her $175,000 net sales proceeds. Can § 1034 be used to defer all of their realized gains?

Research Problem 2. Jeff and Andrea were married in 1981. In 1983, they purchased a residence on Glenn Avenue. In June 1993, in anticipation of a divorce, Jeff moved from the residence to a friend's house. He took personal belongings such as clothes, but left behind tools, heirlooms, and other items that he had acquired before the marriage. In September 1993, he moved into the home of his future wife, Melissa.

Jeff and Andrea were divorced on December 17, 1994, and on December 18, 1994, Jeff married Melissa. Jeff had continued to make the mortgage payments on the Glenn Avenue residence through June 1994. At the time he stopped making the mortgage payments, he started paying alimony and child support. Starting in the summer of 1994, Jeff and Andrea began splitting the cost of incidental expenses relating to the residence including property taxes, insurance, and utilities.

The divorce agreement provided that Andrea would have exclusive use of the residence for a two-year period ending December 17, 1996. The residence would be sold as soon as reasonably possible thereafter with the sales proceeds divided between Jeff and Andrea. Andrea would have exclusive temporary use of the residence until sold.

The Glenn Avenue residence was listed for sale in December 1996 and was sold in March 1997. Jeff's share of the realized gain was $120,000, and his share of the adjusted sales price was $170,000. In May 1997, Jeff and Melissa purchased a residence on Turtle Lane for $400,000. Jeff would like to defer the realized gain on the sale of the Glenn Avenue residence under § 1034. Can he do so?

Research Problem 3. Shelia, age 64, sold her Wren Lane residence in June 1992 for an adjusted sales price of $200,000. Her realized gain was $25,000. On her 1992 tax return, the tax return preparer, a CPA, reflected the exclusion of the $25,000 realized gain under § 121.

Shelia had purchased a smaller residence on First Street in a planned community in December 1991. The cost of this residence was $275,000.

In January 1997, Shelia sells the First Street residence for $360,000. She does not intend to purchase another residence. She would like to use the § 121 election to exclude the realized gain. Since the § 1034 sale-of-residence deferral is mandatory, she believes that the § 121 election on the sale of the Wren Lane residence is invalid. Therefore, Shelia believes that she is eligible to make the § 121 election on the sale of the First Street residence. In defense of her position, she also points out that she was unaware, until recently, that the § 121 election was made on her 1992 tax return.

Is Shelia eligible for the § 121 exclusion on her 1997 tax return?

Partial list of research aids:
§§ 121 and 1034.
Mary K. Robarts, 103 T.C. 72 (1994).

Research Problem 4. You are the new general manager of the Cleveland Indians, Inc. In order for the Indians to become a more serious contender to win the World Series, you believe that player changes are necessary. In particular, you believe that you need to improve your pitching staff. Discussions are in progress with the general manager of the Seattle Mariners. He has offered to trade Randy Johnson (an all-star pitcher) and $5 million to the Indians in exchange for Kenny Lofton (an all-star outfielder) and Albert Belle (an all-star outfielder). You have countered by expressing interest in receiving Johnson and Edgar Martinez (an all-star third baseman) rather than cash. You believe that if you are going to give up the speed provided by Lofton and the power of Belle, you need more than a starting pitcher in return. In addition, you vaguely remember from your MBA days that a player trade with no cash involved will provide better tax results. Before you finalize a trade, you need to know the tax consequences. Obtain a written opinion from your CPA on the way you should structure the trade. The mailing address is Jacobs Field, Cleveland, OH 44118.

Research Problem 5. Greenside Construction, Inc., is in the road construction business. Greenside exchanges a grader used in its road construction business and $20,000 in cash for a scraper to be used in its road construction business. The adjusted basis of the grader is $50,000, and the fair market value of the scraper is $85,000. What are the tax consequences to Greenside of the exchange transaction?

Use the tax resources of the internet to address the following questions. Do not restrict your search to the World Wide Web, but include a review of newsgroups and general reference materials, practitioner sites and resources, primary sources of the tax law, chat rooms and discussion groups, and other opportunities.

Research Problem 6. Find a financial calculator on the internet that can be used to help determine when to elect to use the exclusion of § 121. Use the calculator to address the issues raised in Problem 66.

Research Problem 7. A number of public policy think tanks, taxpayer unions, and other private interest groups have proposed changes to the tax rules that apply to the sale of principal residences. Summarize several of these proposals, including your assessment of the motivations underlying the suggested changes.

TEAM PROJECT: ARTHUR ANDERSEN TAX CHALLENGE CASES

For more information on the Arthur Andersen Tax Challenge Cases, refer to Chapter 1, page 1–38.

Information related to tax issues and problems that are discussed in this chapter may be found in the

Day and Ball case on pages 2, 3, and 5
Miller case on pages 3, 5, and 28

Read and analyze the case you have been assigned and *identify* any issues and problems that are related to material covered in this chapter. If the information provided in the case is complete, prepare answers for this part of the case at this time. If you need information that is contained in the later parts of the case, write a memo summarizing the questions or problems so you can prepare a complete answer at a later date.

CHAPTER

16

PROPERTY TRANSACTIONS: CAPITAL GAINS AND LOSSES

LEARNING OBJECTIVES

After completing Chapter 16, you should be able to:

1. Understand the rationale for separate reporting of capital gains and losses.

2. Distinguish capital assets from ordinary assets.

3. Understand the relevance of a sale or exchange to classification as a capital gain or loss and apply the special rules for the capital gain or loss treatment of the retirement of corporate obligations, options, patents, franchises, and lease cancellation payments.

4. Determine whether the holding period for a capital asset is long term or short term.

5. Describe the beneficial tax treatment for capital gains and the detrimental tax treatment for capital losses for noncorporate taxpayers.

6. Describe the tax treatment for capital gains and the detrimental tax treatment for capital losses for corporate taxpayers.

7. Identify tax planning opportunities arising from the sale or exchange of capital assets.

OUTLINE

General Considerations, 16-2
Rationale for Separate Reporting of Capital Gains and Losses, 16-2
General Scheme of Taxation, 16-3

Capital Assets, 16-3
Definition of a Capital Asset, 16-3
Effect of Judicial Action, 16-6
Statutory Expansions, 16-7

Sale or Exchange, 16-9
Worthless Securities and § 1244 Stock, 16-9
Special Rule—Retirement of Corporate Obligations, 16-9
Options, 16-10
Patents, 16-12

Franchises, Trademarks, and Trade Names, 16-13
Lease Cancellation Payments, 16-15

Holding Period, 16-16
Review of Special Holding Period Rules, 16-16
Special Rules for Short Sales, 16-17

Tax Treatment of Capital Gains and Losses of Noncorporate Taxpayers, 16-20
Treatment of Capital Gains, 16-21
Treatment of Capital Losses, 16-23
Reporting Procedures, 16-24

Tax Treatment of Capital Gains and Losses of Corporate Taxpayers, 16-27

Tax Planning Considerations, 16-27
Importance of Capital Asset Status, 16-27
Planning for Capital Asset Status, 16-27
Effect of Capital Asset Status in Transactions Other Than Sales, 16-28
Stock Sales, 16-29
Maximizing Benefits, 16-29
Year-End Planning, 16-30

GENERAL CONSIDERATIONS

RATIONALE FOR SEPARATE REPORTING OF CAPITAL GAINS AND LOSSES

1 LEARNING OBJECTIVE
Understand the rationale for separate reporting of capital gains and losses.

Fourteen years ago, a taxpayer purchased 100 shares of IBM stock for $17 a share. This year the taxpayer sells the shares for $97 a share. Should the $80 per share gain receive any special tax treatment? The $80 gain has built up over 14 years, so it may not be fair to tax it the same as income that was all earned this year.

What if the stock had been purchased for $97 per share and sold for $17 a share? Should the loss be fully deductible? The tax law has an intricate approach to answering these investment activity–related questions.

As you study this chapter, keep in mind that how investment-related gains and losses are taxed can dramatically affect whether taxpayers make investments and which investments are made. Except for a brief discussion in Chapter 3, earlier chapters dwelt on how to determine the amount of gain or loss from a property disposition, but did not discuss the classification of gains and losses. This chapter will focus on that topic.

The tax law requires **capital gains** and **capital losses** to be separated from other types of gains and losses. There are two reasons for this treatment. First, long-term capital gains may be taxed at a lower rate than ordinary gains. An *alternative tax computation* is used to determine the tax when taxable income includes net long-term capital gain. Capital gains and losses must therefore be matched with one another to see if a net long-term capital gain exists. The alternative tax computation is discussed later in the chapter under Tax Treatment of Capital Gains and Losses of Noncorporate Taxpayers.

The second reason the Code requires separate reporting of gains and losses and a determination of their tax character is that a net capital loss is only deductible up to $3,000 per year. Excess loss over the annual limit carries over and

TAX IN THE NEWS

CAMPAIGNING ON CAPITAL GAINS TAX CUTS

In the 1996 presidential election campaign, both candidates proposed changes in the taxation of capital gains. Candidate Bob Dole proposed reducing the tax rate on capital gains from a maximum of 28 percent to a maximum of 15 percent. President Bill Clinton did not propose any change in the capital gains rate, but would exclude all capital gains from the sale of a principal residence.

---

may be deductible in a future tax year. Capital gains and losses must be matched with one another to see if a net capital loss exists.

For these reasons, capital gains and losses must be distinguished from other types of gains and losses. Most of this chapter and the next chapter describe the intricate rules for determining what type of gains and losses the taxpayer has.

As a result of the need to distinguish and separately match capital gains and losses, the individual tax forms include very extensive reporting requirements for capital gains and losses. This chapter explains the principles underlying the forms. The forms are illustrated with examples at the end of the chapter.

GENERAL SCHEME OF TAXATION

Recognized gains and losses must be properly classified. Proper classification depends upon three characteristics:

- The tax status of the property.
- The manner of the property's disposition.
- The holding period of the property.

The three possible tax statuses are capital asset, § 1231 asset, or ordinary asset. Property disposition may be by sale, exchange, casualty, theft, or condemnation. The two holding periods are one year or less (short term) and more than one year (long term).

The major focus of this chapter is capital gains and losses. Capital gains and losses usually result from the disposition of a capital asset. The most common disposition is a sale of the asset. Capital gains and losses can also result from the disposition of § 1231 assets, which is discussed in Chapter 17.

CAPITAL ASSETS

DEFINITION OF A CAPITAL ASSET

2 LEARNING OBJECTIVE
Distinguish capital assets from ordinary assets.

Personal use assets and investment assets are the most common capital assets owned by individual taxpayers. Personal use assets usually include items such as clothing, recreation equipment, a residence, and automobiles. Investment assets usually include corporate stocks and bonds, government bonds, and vacant land. Remember, however, that losses from the sale or exchange of personal use assets are not recognized. Therefore, the classification of such losses as capital losses can be ignored.

Due to the historical preferential treatment of capital gains, taxpayers have preferred that gains be capital gains rather than ordinary gains. As a result, a great many statutes, cases, and rulings have accumulated in the attempt to define what is and what is not a capital asset.

Capital assets are not directly defined in the Code. Instead, § 1221 defines what is *not* a capital asset. A **capital asset** is property held by the taxpayer (whether or not it is connected with the taxpayer's business) that is *not* any of the following:

- Inventory or property held primarily for sale to customers in the ordinary course of a business. The Supreme Court, in *Malat v. Riddell*, defined *primarily* as meaning *of first importance* or *principally*.[1]
- Accounts and notes receivable acquired from the sale of inventory or acquired for services rendered in the ordinary course of business.
- Depreciable property or real estate used in a business.
- Certain copyrights; literary, musical, or artistic compositions; or letters, memoranda, or similar property held by (1) a taxpayer whose efforts created the property; (2) in the case of a letter, memorandum, or similar property, a taxpayer for whom it was produced; or (3) a taxpayer in whose hands the basis of the property is determined, for purposes of determining gain from a sale or exchange, in whole or in part by reference to the basis of such property in the hands of a taxpayer described in (1) or (2).
- U.S. government publications that are (1) received by a taxpayer from the U.S. government other than by purchase at the price at which they are offered for sale to the public or (2) held by a taxpayer whose basis, for purposes of determining gain from a sale or exchange, is determined by reference to a taxpayer described in (1).

The Code defines what is not a capital asset. From the preceding list, it is apparent that inventory, accounts and notes receivable, and most fixed assets of a business are not capital assets. The following discussion provides further detail on each part of the capital asset definition.

Inventory. What constitutes inventory is determined by the taxpayer's business.

EXAMPLE 1
Green Company buys and sells used cars. Its cars are inventory. Its gains from the sale of the cars are ordinary income. ▼

EXAMPLE 2
Soong sells her personal use automobile at a $500 gain. The automobile is a personal use asset and, therefore, a capital asset. The gain is a capital gain. ▼

Accounts and Notes Receivable. Collection of an accrual basis account receivable usually does not result in a gain or loss because the amount collected equals the receivable's basis. The sale of an account or note receivable may generate a gain or loss, and the gain or loss is ordinary because the receivable is not a capital asset. The sale of an accrual basis receivable may result in a gain or loss because it will probably be sold for more or less than its basis. A cash basis account receivable has no basis. Sale of such a receivable generates a gain. Collection of a cash basis receivable generates ordinary income rather than a gain. A gain usually requires a sale of the receivable. See the discussion of Sale or Exchange later in this chapter.

---

[1] 66–1 USTC ¶9317, 17 AFTR2d 604, 86 S.Ct. 1030 (USSC, 1966).

EXAMPLE 3

Oriole Company has accounts receivable of $100,000. Because it needs working capital, it sells the receivables for $83,000 to a financial institution. If Oriole is an accrual basis taxpayer, it has a $17,000 ordinary loss. Revenue of $100,000 would have been recorded and a $100,000 basis would have been established when the receivable was created. If Oriole is a cash basis taxpayer, it has $83,000 of ordinary income because it would not have recorded any revenue earlier; thus, the receivable has no tax basis. ▼

Business Fixed Assets.
Depreciable personal property and real estate (both depreciable and nondepreciable) used by a business are not capital assets. Thus, *business fixed assets* are generally not capital assets.

The Code has a very complex set of rules pertaining to such property. One of these rules is discussed under Real Property Subdivided for Sale in this chapter; the remainder of the rules are discussed in Chapter 17. Although business fixed assets are not capital assets, a long-term capital gain can sometimes result from their sale. Chapter 17 discusses the potential capital gain treatment for business fixed assets under § 1231.

Copyrights and Creative Works.
Generally, the person whose efforts led to the copyright or creative work has an ordinary asset, not a capital asset. *Creative works* include the works of authors, composers, and artists. Also, the person for whom a letter, memorandum, or other similar property was created has an ordinary asset. Finally, a person receiving a copyright, creative work, letter, memorandum, or similar property by gift from the creator or the person for whom the work was created has an ordinary asset.

EXAMPLE 4

Wanda is a part-time music composer. A music publisher purchases one of her songs for $5,000. Wanda has a $5,000 ordinary gain from the sale of an ordinary asset. ▼

EXAMPLE 5

Ed received a letter from the President of the United States in 1962. In the current year, Ed sells the letter to a collector for $300. Ed has a $300 ordinary gain from the sale of an ordinary asset (because the letter was created for Ed). ▼

EXAMPLE 6

Isabella gives a song she composed to her son. The son sells the song to a music publisher for $5,000. The son has a $5,000 ordinary gain from the sale of an ordinary asset. If the son inherits the song from Isabella, his basis for the song is its fair market value at Isabella's death. The song is a capital asset because the son's basis is not related to Isabella's basis for the song. ▼

(Patents are subject to special statutory rules discussed later in the chapter.)

U.S. Government Publications.
U.S. government publications received from the U.S. government (or its agencies) for a reduced price are not capital assets. This prevents a taxpayer from later donating the publications to charity and claiming a charitable contribution equal to the fair market value of the publications. A charitable contribution of a capital asset generally yields a deduction equal to the fair market value. A charitable contribution of an ordinary asset generally yields a deduction equal to less than the fair market value. If such property is received by gift from the original purchaser, the property is not a capital asset to the donee. (For a more comprehensive explanation of charitable contributions of property, refer to Chapter 10.)

TAX IN THE NEWS

IS THE ART IN CORPORATE OFFICES DEPRECIABLE?

On several occasions, the IRS has challenged the idea that valuable paintings used as decorations in corporate offices are depreciable. The IRS contends that if the paintings are not subject to wear and tear and are not obsolete, they should not be depreciable. The IRS is using various public forums (tax conferences and newspaper interviews) to put taxpayers on notice that such assets may be subject to increased scrutiny to determine whether they are actually used in the business or are held as an investment. Many corporations spend millions of dollars each year on expensive artworks to decorate their offices. The Forbes Magazine Collection of Fabergé eggs and other objects is an example.

EFFECT OF JUDICIAL ACTION

Court decisions play an important role in the definition of capital assets. Because the Code only lists categories of what are *not* capital assets, judicial interpretation is sometimes required to determine whether a specific item fits into one of those categories. The Supreme Court follows a literal interpretation of the categories. For instance, corporate stock is not mentioned in § 1221. Thus, corporate stock is *usually* a capital asset. However, what if corporate stock is purchased for resale to customers? Then it is *inventory* and not a capital asset because inventory is one of the categories in § 1221. (See the discussion of Dealers in Securities below.)

A Supreme Court decision was required to distinguish between capital asset and non-capital asset status when a taxpayer who did not normally acquire stock for resale to customers acquired stock with the intention of resale.[2] The Court decided that since the stock was not acquired primarily for sale to customers (the taxpayer did not sell the stock to its regular customers), the stock was a capital asset.

Often the crux of the capital asset determination hinges on whether the asset is held for investment purposes (capital asset) or business purposes (ordinary asset). The taxpayer's *use* of the property often provides objective evidence.

EXAMPLE 7

David's business buys an expensive painting. If the painting is used to decorate David's office and is not of investment quality, the painting is depreciable and, therefore, not a capital asset. If David's business is buying and selling paintings, the painting is inventory and, therefore, an ordinary asset. If the painting is of investment quality and the business purchased it for investment, the painting is a capital asset, even though it serves a decorative purpose in David's office. *Investment quality* generally means that the painting is expected to appreciate in value. ▼

Because of the uncertainty associated with capital asset status, Congress has enacted several Code Sections to clarify the definition. These statutory expansions of the capital asset definition are discussed in the following section.

---
[2] *Arkansas Best v. Comm.*, 88–1 USTC ¶9210, 61 AFTR2d 88–655, 108 S.Ct. 971 (USSC, 1988).

STATUTORY EXPANSIONS

Congress has often expanded the § 1221 general definition of what is *not* a capital asset.

Dealers in Securities. As a general rule, securities (stocks, bonds, and other financial instruments) held by a dealer are considered to be inventory and are not, therefore, subject to capital gain or loss treatment. A *dealer in securities* is a merchant (e.g., a brokerage firm) that regularly engages in the purchase and resale of securities to customers. The dealer must identify any securities being held for investment. Generally, if a dealer clearly identifies certain securities as held for investment purposes by the close of business on the acquisition date, gain from the securities' sale will be capital gain. However, the gain will not be capital gain if the dealer ceases to hold the securities for investment prior to the sale. Losses are capital losses if at any time the securities have been clearly identified by the dealer as held for investment.[3]

EXAMPLE 8

Tracy is a securities dealer. She purchases 100 shares of Swan stock. If Tracy takes no further action, the stock is inventory and an ordinary asset. If she designates in her records that the stock is held for investment, the stock is a capital asset. Tracy must designate the investment purpose by the close of business on the acquisition date. If Tracy maintains her investment purpose and later sells the stock, the gain or loss is capital gain or loss. If Tracy redesignates the stock as held for resale (inventory) and then sells it, any gain is ordinary, but any loss is capital loss. Stock designated as held for investment and then sold at a loss always yields a capital loss. ▼

ETHICAL CONSIDERATIONS

Capital Asset Status for Stock Held by Securities Dealers

A securities dealer purchases stock for her own account at 10:00 A.M. At the close of business that day, the stock has dropped slightly in price, so the dealer does not designate it as held for investment. By 10:30 A.M. the next morning, however, the value of the stock has risen substantially above the dealer's purchase price. Using her knowledge of computer programming, the dealer could manipulate the firm's computer records so that the stock will appear to have been designated as held for investment at the end of the previous day. She is absolutely certain that neither the firm nor the IRS will ever discover what she has done. Comment on the securities dealer's potential behavior and the motivation for it.

Real Property Subdivided for Sale. Substantial real property development activities may result in the owner being considered a dealer for tax purposes. Income from the sale of real estate property lots is treated as the sale of inventory (ordinary income) if the owner is considered to be a dealer. However, § 1237 allows real estate investors capital gain treatment if they engage *only* in *limited* development activities. To be eligible for § 1237 treatment, the following requirements must be met:

---

[3] §§ 1236(a) and (b) and Reg. § 1.1236–1(a).

- The taxpayer may not be a corporation.
- The taxpayer may not be a real estate dealer.
- No substantial improvements may be made to the lots sold. *Substantial* generally means more than a 10 percent increase in the value of a lot. Shopping centers and other commercial or residential buildings are considered substantial, while filling, draining, leveling, and clearing operations are not.
- The taxpayer must have held the lots sold for at least 5 years, except for inherited property. The substantial improvements test is less stringent if the property is held at least 10 years.

If the preceding requirements are met, all gain is capital gain until the tax year in which the *sixth* lot is sold. Sales of contiguous lots to a single buyer in the same transaction count as the sale of one lot. Beginning with the tax year the *sixth* lot is sold, some of the gain may be ordinary income. Five percent of the revenue from lot sales is potential ordinary income. That potential ordinary income is offset by any selling expenses from the lot sales. Practically, sales commissions often are at least 5 percent of the sales price, so none of the gain is treated as ordinary income.

Section 1237 does not apply to losses. A loss from the sale of subdivided real property is an ordinary loss unless the property qualifies as a capital asset under § 1221. The following example illustrates the application of § 1237.

EXAMPLE 9

Jack owns a large tract of land and subdivides it for sale. Assume Jack meets all the requirements of § 1237 and during the tax year sells the first 10 lots to 10 different buyers for $10,000 each. Jack's basis in each lot sold is $3,000, and he incurs total selling expenses of $4,000 on the sales. Jack's gain is computed as follows:

Selling price (10 × $10,000)		$100,000
Basis (10 × $3,000)		(30,000)
Excess over basis		$ 70,000
Five percent of selling price	$ 5,000	
Selling expenses	(4,000)	
Amount of ordinary income		$ 1,000
Five percent of selling price	$ 5,000	
Excess of expenses over 5% of selling price	–0–	(5,000)
Capital gain		65,000
Total gain ($70,000 − $4,000 selling expenses)		$66,000

Lump-Sum Distributions. A *lump-sum distribution* is generally a distribution of an employee's entire qualified pension or profit sharing plan balance within one tax year. The distribution must result from the employee's (1) death, (2) reaching age 59½, or (3) separation from service with an employer. TRA of 1986 repealed a provision that allowed a portion of a lump-sum distribution to be treated as capital gain. However, partial capital gain treatment may still be available because transition rules allow certain taxpayers to continue using prior law. See Chapter 19 for a further discussion of lump-sum distributions.

Nonbusiness Bad Debts. A loan not made in the ordinary course of business is classified as a nonbusiness receivable. In the year the receivable becomes completely worthless, it is a *nonbusiness bad debt,* and the bad debt is treated as a short-term capital loss. Even if the receivable was outstanding for more than one year, the loss is still a short-term capital loss. Chapter 7 discusses nonbusiness bad debts more thoroughly.

SALE OR EXCHANGE

3 LEARNING OBJECTIVE
Understand the relevance of a sale or exchange to classification as a capital gain or loss and apply the special rules for the capital gain or loss treatment of the retirement of corporate obligations, options, patents, franchises, and lease cancellation payments.

Recognition of capital gain or loss usually requires a sale or exchange of a capital asset. The Code uses the term **sale or exchange,** but does not define it. Generally, a property sale involves the receipt of money by the seller and/or the assumption by the purchaser of the seller's liabilities. An exchange involves the transfer of property for other property. Thus, an involuntary conversion (casualty, theft, or condemnation) is not a sale or exchange. In several situations, the determination of whether a sale or exchange has taken place has been clarified by the enactment of Code Sections that specifically provide for sale or exchange treatment.

Recognized gains or losses from the cancellation, lapse, expiration, or any other termination of a right or obligation with respect to personal property (other than stock) that is or would be a capital asset in the hands of the taxpayer are capital gains or losses.[4] See the discussion under Options later in the chapter for more details.

WORTHLESS SECURITIES AND § 1244 STOCK

Occasionally, securities such as stock and, especially, bonds may become worthless due to the insolvency of their issuer. If such a security is a capital asset, the loss is deemed to have occurred as the result of a sale or exchange on the *last day* of the tax year.[5] This last-day rule may have the effect of converting what otherwise would have been a short-term capital loss into a long-term capital loss. See Treatment of Capital Losses later in this chapter.

Section 1244 allows an ordinary deduction on disposition of stock at a loss. The stock must be that of a small business company, and the ordinary deduction is limited to $50,000 ($100,000 for married individuals filing jointly) per year. For a more detailed discussion, refer to Chapter 7.

SPECIAL RULE—RETIREMENT OF CORPORATE OBLIGATIONS

A debt obligation (e.g., a bond or note payable) may have a tax basis in excess of or less than its redemption value because it may have been acquired at a premium or discount. Consequently, the collection of the redemption value may result in a loss or gain. Generally, the collection of a debt obligation is *not* a sale or exchange. Therefore, any loss or gain cannot be a capital loss or gain because no sale or exchange has taken place. However, if the debt obligation was issued by a corporation or certain government agencies, the collection of the redemption value is treated as a sale or exchange.[6]

EXAMPLE 10

Fran acquires $1,000 of Osprey Corporation bonds for $980 in the open market. If the bonds are held to maturity, the $20 difference between Fran's collection of the $1,000 redemption value and her cost of $980 is treated as capital gain. If the obligation had been issued to Fran

---

[4] § 1234A.
[5] § 165(g)(1).
[6] § 1271.

by an individual instead of by a corporation, her $20 gain would be ordinary, since she did not sell or exchange the debt. ▼

Original Issue Discount. The benefit of the sale or exchange exception that allows a capital gain from the collection of certain obligations is reduced when the obligation has original issue discount. **Original issue discount (OID)** arises when the issue price of a debt obligation is less than the maturity value of the obligation. OID must generally be amortized over the life of the debt obligation using the effective interest method. The OID amortization increases the basis of the bond. Most new publicly traded bond issues do not carry OID since the stated interest rate is set to make the market price on issue the same as the bond's face amount. In addition, even if the issue price is less than the face amount, the difference is not considered to be OID if the difference is less than one-fourth of 1 percent of the redemption price at maturity multiplied by the number of years to maturity.[7]

In the case where OID does exist, it may or may not have to be amortized, depending upon the date the obligation was issued. When OID is amortized, the amount of gain upon collection, sale, or exchange of the obligation is correspondingly reduced. The obligations covered by the OID amortization rules and the method of amortization are presented in §§ 1272–1275. Similar rules for other obligations can be found in §§ 1276–1288.

EXAMPLE 11 Jerry purchases $10,000 of newly issued White Corporation bonds for $6,000. The bonds have OID of $4,000. Jerry must amortize the discount over the life of the bonds. The OID amortization *increases* his interest income. (The bonds were selling at a discount because the market rate of interest was greater than the bonds' interest rate.) After Jerry has amortized $1,800 of OID, he sells the bonds for $8,000. Jerry has a capital gain of $200 [$8,000 − ($6,000 cost + $1,800 OID amortization)]. The OID amortization rules prevent him from converting ordinary interest income into capital gain. Without the OID amortization, Jerry would have capital gain of $2,000 ($8,000 − $6,000 cost). ▼

OPTIONS

Frequently, a potential buyer of property wants some time to make the purchase decision, but wants to control the sale and/or the sale price in the meantime. **Options** are used to achieve these objectives. The potential purchaser (grantee) pays the property owner (grantor) for an option on the property. The grantee then becomes the option holder. The option usually sets a price at which the grantee can buy the property and expires after a specified period of time.

Sale of an Option. A grantee may sell or exchange the option rather than exercising it or letting it expire. Generally, the grantee's sale or exchange of the option results in capital gain or loss if the option property is (or would be) a capital asset to the grantee.[8]

EXAMPLE 12 Rosa wants to buy some vacant land for investment purposes. She cannot afford the full purchase price. Instead, she convinces the landowner (grantor) to sell her the right to purchase the land for $100,000 anytime in the next two years. Rosa (grantee) pays $3,000 to

---
[7] § 1273(a)(3).
[8] § 1234(a) and Reg. § 1.1234−1(a)(1). Stock options are discussed in Chapter 19.

obtain this option to buy the land. The option is a capital asset for Rosa because if she actually purchased the land, the land would be a capital asset. Three months after purchasing the option, Rosa sells it for $7,000. She has a $4,000 ($7,000 − $3,000) short-term capital gain on this sale since she held the option for one year or less. ▼

Failure to Exercise Options. If an option holder (grantee) fails to exercise the option, the lapse of the option is considered a sale or exchange on the option expiration date. Thus, the loss is a capital loss if the property subject to the option is (or would be) a capital asset in the hands of the grantee.

The grantor of an option on *stocks, securities, commodities, or commodity futures* receives short-term capital gain treatment upon the expiration of the option. Options on property other than stocks, securities, commodities, or commodity futures result in ordinary income to the grantor when the option expires. For example, an individual investor who owns certain stock (a capital asset) may sell a call option, entitling the buyer of the option to acquire the stock at a specified price higher than the value at the date the option is granted. The writer of the call receives a premium (e.g., 10 percent) for writing the option. If the price of the stock does not increase during the option period, the option will expire unexercised. Upon the expiration of the option, the grantor must recognize short-term capital gain. These provisions do not apply to options held for sale to customers (the inventory of a securities dealer).

Exercise of Options by Grantee. If the option is exercised, the amount paid for the option is added to the optioned property's selling price. This increases the gain (or reduces the loss) to the grantor resulting from the sale of the property. The grantor's gain or loss is capital or ordinary depending on the tax status of the property. The grantee adds the cost of the option to the basis of the property purchased.

EXAMPLE 13

On September 1, 1989, Wes purchases 100 shares of Eagle Company stock for $5,000. On April 1, 1997, he writes a call option on the stock, giving the grantee the right to buy the stock for $6,000 during the following six-month period. Wes (the grantor) receives a call premium of $500 for writing the call.

- If the call is exercised by the grantee on August 1, 1997, Wes has $1,500 ($6,000 + $500 − $5,000) of long-term capital gain from the sale of the stock. The grantee has a $6,500 ($500 option premium + $6,000 purchase price) basis for the stock.
- Assume that Wes decides to sell his stock prior to exercise for $6,000 and enters into a closing transaction by purchasing a call on 100 shares of Eagle Company stock for $5,000. Since the Eagle stock is selling for $6,000, Wes must pay a call premium of $1,000. He recognizes a $500 short-term capital loss [$1,000 (call premium paid) − $500 (call premium received)] on the closing transaction. On the actual sale of the Eagle stock, Wes has a long-term capital gain of $1,000 [$6,000 (selling price) − $5,000 (cost)]. The grantee is not affected by Wes's closing transaction. The original option is still in existence, and the grantee's tax consequences will depend on what action the grantee takes—exercising the option, letting the option expire, or selling the option.
- Assume that the original option expired unexercised. Wes has a $500 short-term capital gain equal to the call premium received for writing the option. This gain is not recognized until the option expires. The grantee has a loss from expiration of the option. The nature of the loss will depend upon whether the option was a capital asset or an ordinary asset. ▼

Concept Summary 16–1 summarizes the rules for options.

Concept Summary 16–1

Options

	Effect on	
Event	**Grantor**	**Grantee**
Option is granted.	Receives value and has a contract obligation (a liability).	Pays value and has a contract right (an asset).
Option expires.	Has a short-term capital gain if the option property is stocks, securities, commodities, or commodity futures. Otherwise, gain is ordinary income.	Has a loss (capital loss if option property would have been a capital asset for the grantee).
Option is exercised.	Amount received for option increases proceeds from sale of the option property.	Amount paid for option becomes part of the basis of the option property purchased.
Option is sold or exchanged by grantee.	Result depends upon whether option later expires or is exercised (see above).	Could have gain or loss (capital gain or loss if option property would have been a capital asset for the grantee).

PATENTS

Transfer of a **patent** is treated as the sale or exchange of a long-term capital asset when all substantial rights to the patent (or an undivided interest that includes all such rights) are transferred by a holder.[9] The transferor/holder may receive payment in virtually any form. Lump-sum or periodic payments are most common. The amount of the payments may also be contingent on the transferee/purchaser's productivity, use, or disposition of the patent. If the transfer meets these requirements, any gain or loss is *automatically a long-term* capital gain or loss. Whether the asset was a capital asset for the transferor, whether a sale or exchange occurred, and how long the transferor held the patent are not relevant.

This special long-term capital gain or loss treatment for patents is intended to encourage technological progress. Ironically, authors, composers, and artists are not eligible for capital gain treatment when their creations are transferred. Books, songs, and artists' works may be copyrighted, but copyrights and the assets they represent are not capital assets. Thus, the disposition of those assets by their creators usually results in ordinary gain or loss. The following example illustrates the special treatment for patents.

EXAMPLE 14

Diana, a druggist, invents a pill-counting machine, which she patents. In consideration of a lump-sum payment of $200,000 plus $10 per machine sold, Diana assigns the patent to Drug Products, Inc. Assuming Diana has transferred all substantial rights, the question of whether the transfer is a sale or exchange of a capital asset is not relevant. Diana automatically has a long-term capital gain from both the lump-sum payment and the $10 per machine royalty to the extent these proceeds exceed her basis for the patent. ▼

---
[9] § 1235.

Substantial Rights. To receive favorable capital gain treatment, all *substantial rights* to the patent (or an undivided interest in it) must be transferred. All substantial rights to a patent means all rights (whether or not then held by the grantor) that are valuable at the time the patent rights (or an undivided interest in the patent) are transferred. All substantial rights have not been transferred when the transfer is limited geographically within the issuing country or when the transfer is for a period less than the remaining life of the patent. The circumstances of the entire transaction, rather than merely the language used in the transfer instrument, are to be considered in deciding whether all substantial rights have been transferred.[10]

EXAMPLE 15

Assume Diana, the druggist in Example 14, only licensed Drug Products, Inc., to manufacture and sell the invention in Michigan. She retained the right to license the machine elsewhere in the United States. Diana has retained a substantial right and is not eligible for automatic long-term capital gain treatment. ▼

Holder Defined. The *holder* of a patent must be an *individual* and is usually the invention's creator. A holder may also be an individual who purchases the patent rights from the creator before the patented invention is reduced to practice. However, the creator's employer and certain parties related to the creator do not qualify as holders. Thus, in the common situation where an employer has all rights to an employee's inventions, the employer is not eligible for long-term capital gain treatment. More than likely, the employer will have an ordinary asset because the patent was developed as part of its business.

FRANCHISES, TRADEMARKS, AND TRADE NAMES

A mode of operation, a widely recognized brand name (trade name), and a widely known business symbol (trademark) are all valuable assets. These assets may be licensed (commonly known as franchising) by their owner for use by other businesses. Many fast-food restaurants (such as McDonald's and Taco Bell) are franchises. The franchisee usually pays the owner (franchisor) an initial fee plus a contingent fee. The contingent fee is often based upon the franchisee's sales volume.

For Federal income tax purposes, a **franchise** is an agreement that gives the franchisee the right to distribute, sell, or provide goods, services, or facilities within a specified area.[11] A franchise transfer includes the grant of a franchise, a transfer by one franchisee to another person, or the renewal of a franchise.

A franchise transfer is generally not a sale or exchange of a capital asset. Section 1253 provides that a transfer of a franchise, trademark, or trade name is not a transfer of a capital asset when the transferor retains any significant power, right, or continuing interest in the property transferred.

Significant Power, Right, or Continuing Interest. *Significant powers, rights, or continuing interests* include control over assignment, quality of products and services, sale or advertising of other products or services, and the right to require that substantially all supplies and equipment be purchased from the transferor. Also included are the right to terminate the franchise at will and the right to substantial contingent payments. Most modern franchising operations involve some or all of these powers, rights, or continuing interests.

---

[10] Reg. § 1.1235–2(b)(1).

[11] § 1253(b)(1).

In the unusual case where no significant power, right, or continuing interest is retained by the transferor, a sale or exchange may occur, and capital gain or loss treatment may be available. For capital gain or loss treatment to be available, the asset transferred must qualify as a capital asset.

EXAMPLE 16

Orange, Inc., a franchisee, sells the franchise to a third party. Payments to Orange are not contingent, and all significant powers, rights, and continuing interests are transferred. The gain (payments − adjusted basis) on the sale is a capital gain to Orange. ▼

Noncontingent Payments. When the transferor retains a significant power, right, or continuing interest, the transferee's noncontingent payments to the transferor are ordinary income to the transferor. The franchisee capitalizes the payments and amortizes them over 15 years. The amortization is subject to recapture under § 1245.[12]

EXAMPLE 17

Grey Company signs a 10-year franchise agreement with DOH Donuts. Grey (the franchisee) makes payments of $3,000 per year for the first 8 years of the franchise agreement—a total of $24,000. Grey cannot deduct $3,000 per year as the payments are made. Instead, Grey may amortize the $24,000 total over 15 years. Thus, Grey may deduct $1,600 per year for each of the 15 years of the amortization period. The same result would occur if Grey made a $24,000 lump-sum payment at the beginning of the franchise period. Assuming DOH Donuts (the franchisor) retains significant powers, rights, or a continuing interest, it will have ordinary income when it receives the payments from Grey. ▼

Contingent Payments. Whether or not the tranferor retains a significant power, right, or continuing interest, contingent franchise payments are ordinary income for the franchisor and an ordinary deduction for the franchisee. For this purpose, a payment qualifies as a contingent payment only if the following requirements are met:

- The contingent amounts are part of a series of payments that are paid at least annually throughout the term of the transfer agreement.
- The payments are substantially equal in amount or are payable under a fixed formula.

EXAMPLE 18

TAK, a spicy chicken franchisor, transfers an eight-year franchise to Otis. TAK retains a significant power, right, or continuing interest. Otis, the franchisee, agrees to pay TAK 15% of sales. This contingent payment is ordinary income to TAK and a business deduction for Otis as the payments are made. ▼

Sports Franchises. Professional sports franchises (e.g., the Detroit Tigers) are not covered by § 1253.[13] However, § 1056 restricts the allocation of sports franchise acquisition costs to player contracts. Player contracts are usually one of the major assets acquired with a sports franchise. These contracts last only for the time stated in the contract. Therefore, owners of sports franchises would like to allocate franchise acquisition costs disproportionately to the contracts so that the acquisition costs will be amortizable over the contracts' lives. Section 1056 prevents this by generally limiting the amount that can be allocated to player contracts to no more than 50 percent of the franchise acquisition cost. In addition, the seller of the sports franchise has ordinary income under § 1245 for the portion of the gain allocable to the disposition of player contracts.[14]

---

[12] See Chapter 17 for a discussion of the recapture provisions.
[13] § 1253(e).
[14] See Chapter 17 for a discussion of the recapture provisions.

Concept Summary 16-2

Franchises

	Effect on	
Event	**Franchisor**	**Franchisee**
Franchisor Retains Significant Powers and Rights		
Noncontingent payment	Ordinary income.	Capitalized and amortized over 15 years as an ordinary deduction; if franchise is sold, amortization is subject to recapture under § 1245.
Contingent payment	Ordinary income.	Ordinary deduction.
Franchisor Does *Not* Retain Significant Powers and Rights		
Noncontingent payment	Ordinary income if franchise rights are an ordinary asset; capital gain if franchise rights are a capital asset (unlikely).	Capitalized and amortized over 15 years as an ordinary deduction; if the franchise is sold, amortization is subject to recapture under § 1245.
Contingent payment	Ordinary income.	Ordinary deduction.

Concept Summary 16–2 summarizes the rules for franchises.

LEASE CANCELLATION PAYMENTS

The tax treatment of payments received for canceling a lease depends on whether the recipient is the **lessor** or the **lessee** and whether the lease is a capital asset or not.

Lessee Treatment. Lease cancellation payments received by a lessee are treated as an exchange.[15] Thus, these payments are capital gains if the lease is a capital asset. Generally, a lessee's lease is a capital asset if the property (either personalty or realty) is used for the lessee's personal use (e.g., his or her residence). A lessee's lease is an ordinary asset if the property is used in the lessee's trade or business.[16]

EXAMPLE 19
Mark owns an apartment building that he is going to convert into an office building. Vicki is one of the apartment tenants and receives $1,000 from Mark to cancel the lease. Vicki has a capital gain of $1,000 (which is long term or short term depending upon how long she has held the lease). Mark has an ordinary deduction of $1,000. ▼

Lessor Treatment. Payments received by a lessor for a lease cancellation are always ordinary income because they are considered to be in lieu of rental payments.[17]

EXAMPLE 20
Floyd owns an apartment building near a university campus. Hui-Fen is one of the tenants. Hui-Fen is graduating early and offers Floyd $800 to cancel the apartment lease. Floyd

---

[15] § 1241 and Reg. § 1.1241–1(a).
[16] Reg. § 1.1221–1(b).
[17] *Hort v. Comm.*, 41–1 USTC ¶9354, 25 AFTR 1207, 61 S.Ct. 757 (USSC, 1941).

accepts the offer. Floyd has ordinary income of $800. Hui-Fen has a nondeductible payment since the apartment was personal use property. ▼

HOLDING PERIOD

4 LEARNING OBJECTIVE
Determine whether the holding period for a capital asset is long term or short term.

Property must be held more than one year to qualify for long-term capital gain or loss treatment.[18] Property not held for the required long-term period results in short-term capital gain or loss. To compute the **holding period**, start counting on the day after the property was acquired and include the day of disposition.

EXAMPLE 21 Marge purchases a capital asset on January 15, 1996, and sells it on January 16, 1997. Marge's holding period is more than one year. If Marge had sold the asset on January 15, 1997, the holding period would have been exactly one year, and the gain or loss would have been short term. ▼

To be held for more than one year, a capital asset acquired on the last day of any month must not be disposed of until on or after the first day of the thirteenth succeeding month.[19]

EXAMPLE 22 Leo purchases a capital asset on February 29, 1996. If Leo sells the asset on February 28, 1997, the holding period is one year, and Leo will have a short-term capital gain or loss. If Leo sells the asset on March 1, 1997, the holding period is more than one year, and he will have a long-term capital gain or loss. ▼

REVIEW OF SPECIAL HOLDING PERIOD RULES

There are several special holding period rules.[20] The application of these rules depends on the type of asset and how it was acquired.

Nontaxable Exchanges. The holding period of property received in a like-kind exchange includes the holding period of the former asset if the property that has been exchanged is a capital asset or a § 1231 asset. In certain nontaxable transactions involving a substituted basis, the holding period of the former property is *tacked on* to the holding period of the newly acquired property.

EXAMPLE 23 Vern exchanges a business truck for another truck in a like-kind exchange. The holding period of the exchanged truck tacks on to the holding period of the new truck. ▼

EXAMPLE 24 Alicia sells her personal residence and acquires a new residence. If the transaction qualifies for nonrecognition of gain on the sale of a residence, the holding period of the new residence includes the holding period of the former residence. ▼

Certain Nontaxable Transactions Involving a Carryover of Another Taxpayer's Basis. A former owner's holding period is tacked on to the present owner's holding period if the transaction is nontaxable and the former owner's basis carries over to the present owner.

---

[18] § 1222.
[19] Rev.Rul. 66–7, 1966–1 C.B. 188.
[20] § 1223.

EXAMPLE 25 Kareem acquires 100 shares of Robin Corporation stock for $1,000 on December 31, 1989. He transfers the shares by gift to Megan on December 31, 1996, when the stock is worth $2,000. Kareem's basis of $1,000 becomes the basis for determining gain or loss on a subsequent sale by Megan. Megan's holding period begins with the date the stock was acquired by Kareem. ▼

EXAMPLE 26 Assume the same facts as in Example 25, except that the fair market value of the shares is only $800 on the date of the gift. The holding period begins on the date of the gift if Megan sells the stock for a loss. The value of the shares at the date of the gift is used in the determination of her basis for loss. If she sells the shares for $500 on April 1, 1997, Megan has a $300 recognized capital loss, and the holding period is from December 31, 1996, to April 1, 1997 (thus, the loss is short term). ▼

Certain Disallowed Loss Transactions. Under several Code provisions, realized losses are disallowed. When a loss is disallowed, there is no carryover of holding period. Losses can be disallowed under § 267 (sale or exchange between related taxpayers) and § 262 (sale or exchange of personal use assets) as well as other Code Sections. Taxpayers who acquire property in a disallowed loss transaction will have a new holding period begin and will have a basis equal to the purchase price.

EXAMPLE 27 Janet sells her personal automobile at a loss. She may not deduct the loss because it arises from the sale of personal use property. Janet purchases a replacement automobile for more than the selling price of her former automobile. Janet has a basis equal to the cost of the replacement automobile, and her holding period begins when she acquires the replacement automobile. ▼

Inherited Property. The holding period for inherited property is treated as long term no matter how long the property is actually held by the heir. The holding period of the decedent or the decedent's estate is not relevant for the heir's holding period.

EXAMPLE 28 Shonda inherits Blue Company stock from her father. She receives the stock on April 1, 1997, and sells it on November 1, 1997. Even though the stock was not held more than one year by Shonda, she receives long-term capital gain or loss treatment on the sale. ▼

SPECIAL RULES FOR SHORT SALES

The holding period of property sold short is determined under special rules provided in § 1233. A **short sale** occurs when a taxpayer sells borrowed property and repays the lender with substantially identical property either held on the date of the sale or purchased after the sale. Short sales usually involve corporate stock. The seller's objective is to make a profit in anticipation of a decline in the stock's price. If the price declines, the seller in a short sale recognizes a profit equal to the difference between the sales price of the borrowed stock and the price paid for the replacement stock.

A *short sale against the box* occurs when the stock is borrowed from a broker by a seller who already owns the same stock. The box is the safe deposit box where stock owners routinely used to keep stock certificates. Although today stockbrokers generally keep stock certificates for their customers, the terminology short sale against the box is still used.

TAX IN THE NEWS

A BIG SHORT SALE AGAINST THE BOX

"Short sales against the box" continue to be controversial. This technique allows gain to be deferred until the short sale is closed. Many wealthy taxpayers sell short against the box at the end of a tax year to defer gains until the next tax year. Several times in recent years, the IRS has encouraged Congress to outlaw this technique. The IRS contends that only very rich taxpayers use this technique and that it is merely a tax shelter for the wealthy. One recent example involved Estée Lauder and her son Ronald.

Estée and Ronald recently sold stock in Estée Lauder Companies in an initial public offering (IPO) for approximately $340 million. Because they sold short against the box, their current Federal tax liability associated with the sale is zero. This result occurs because the sales transaction will not close until they repay the borrowed stock that they delivered to the purchasers. Other family members were willing to loan the stock to Estée and Ronald, who pledged an equivalent number of Estée Lauder Companies shares as security.

If the short sale is not closed until after Estée and Ronald die, then neither they nor their heirs will ever pay Federal income tax on the transaction because of the step-up in basis rules associated with inherited property. Estée is said to be at least age 87 and Ronald is over 50.

SOURCE: Information from Allan Sloan, "Passing the Smell Test?" *Newsweek,* December 4, 1995, p. 57.

EXAMPLE 29

Chris does not own any shares of Brown Corporation. However, Chris sells 30 shares of Brown. The shares are borrowed from Chris's broker and must be replaced within 45 days. Chris has a short sale because he was short the shares he sold. He will *close* the short sale by purchasing Brown shares and delivering them to his broker. If the original 30 shares were sold for $10,000 and Chris later purchases 30 shares for $8,000, he has a gain of $2,000. Chris's hunch that the price of Brown stock would decline was correct. Chris was able to profit from selling high and buying low. If Chris had to purchase Brown shares for $13,000 to close the short sale, he would have a loss of $3,000. In this case, Chris has sold low and bought high—not the result he wanted! Chris would be making a short sale against the box if he borrowed shares from his broker to sell and then closed the short sale by delivering other Brown shares he owned at the time he made the short sale. ▼

A short sale gain or loss is a capital gain or loss to the extent that the short sale property constitutes a capital asset of the taxpayer. The gain or loss is not recognized until the short sale is closed. Generally, the holding period of the short sale property is determined by how long the property used to close the short sale was held. However, if *substantially identical property* (e.g., other shares of the same stock) is held by the taxpayer, the short-term or long-term character of the short sale gain or loss may be affected:

- If substantially identical property has *not* been held for the long-term holding period on the short sale date, the short sale *gain or loss* is short term.
- If substantially identical property has *been* held for the long-term holding period on the short sale date, the short sale *gain* is long term if the substantially identical property is used to close the short sale and short term if it is not used to close the short sale.

CHAPTER 16 Property Transactions: Capital Gains and Losses 16–19

Concept Summary 16–3

Short Sales of Securities

```
                    Has the taxpayer held substantially
                    identical securities for the required long-
                    term holding period at the date of the
                    short sale?
                         /                    \
                       Yes                    No
                        ↓                      ↓
    To the extent of the number of shares      Any gain or loss from the close of the
    sold short, any loss arising from the      short sale is short term.
    closing of the short sale is long-term
    loss regardless of the holding period
    of the securities used to close the
    short sale.
    If the securities held for the required
    long-term holding period are used to
    close the short sale, any gain is long
    term.
                        \                      /
                        And                  And
                          ↓                  ↓
    For the number of shares sold short, the
    holding period of substantially identical
    securities not held long term at the short
    sale date or acquired after the short sale
    date and before the closing date begins
    with the earlier of the date of sale of
    those securities or the closing date of the
    short sale. This holding period rule applies
    in the order of the acquisition dates of the
    substantially identical property.
```

- If substantially identical property has *been* held for the long-term holding period on the short sale date, the short sale *loss* is long term whether or not the substantially identical property is used to close the short sale.
- If substantially identical property is acquired *after* the short sale date and on or before the closing date, the short sale *gain or loss* is short term.

Concept Summary 16–3 summarizes the short sale rules.

These rules are intended to prevent the conversion of short-term capital gains into long-term capital gains and long-term capital losses into short-term capital losses. The following examples illustrate the application of the short sale rules.

Example 30

On January 4, 1997, Donald purchases five shares of Osprey Corporation common stock for $100. On April 14, 1997, he engages in a short sale of five shares of the same stock for $150. On August 15, Donald closes the short sale by repaying the borrowed stock with the five shares purchased on January 4. Donald has a $50 short-term capital gain from the short sale because he had not held substantially identical shares for the long-term holding period on the short sale date. ▼

EXAMPLE 31

Assume the same facts as in the previous example, except that Donald closes the short sale on January 28, 1998, by repaying the borrowed stock with five shares purchased on January 27, 1998, for $200. The stock used to close the short sale was not the property purchased on January 4, 1997, but since Donald held short-term property at the April 14, 1997, short sale date, the gain or loss from closing the short sale is short term. Donald has a $50 short-term capital loss ($200 cost of stock purchased January 27, 1998, and a short sale selling price of $150). ▼

EXAMPLE 32

Assume the same facts as in Example 31. On January 31, 1998, Donald sells for $200 the stock purchased January 4, 1997. Donald's holding period for that stock begins January 28, 1998, because the holding period portion of the short sale rules applies to the substantially identical property in order of acquisition. Donald has a short-term capital gain of $100 ($100 cost of stock purchased January 4, 1997, and a selling price of $200). ▼

EXAMPLE 33

On January 4, 1997, Rita purchases five shares of Owl Corporation common stock for $100. She purchases five more shares of the same stock on April 14, 1997, for $200. On January 17, 1998, she sells short five shares of the same stock for $150. On September 30, 1998, she repays the borrowed stock with the five shares purchased on April 14, 1997, and sells the five shares purchased on January 4, 1997, for $200. Rita has a $50 long-term capital loss from the short sale because she held substantially identical shares for more than one year on the date of the short sale. Rita has a $100 long-term capital gain from the sale of the shares purchased on January 4, 1997. ▼

TAX TREATMENT OF CAPITAL GAINS AND LOSSES OF NONCORPORATE TAXPAYERS

5 LEARNING OBJECTIVE
Describe the beneficial tax treatment for capital gains and the detrimental tax treatment for capital losses for noncorporate taxpayers.

All taxpayers net their capital gains and losses. Short-term gains and losses (if any) are netted against one another, and long-term gains and losses (if any) are netted against one another. The results will be net short-term gain or loss and net long-term gain or loss. If these two net positions are of opposite sign (one is a gain and one is a loss), they are netted against one another.

Six possibilities exist for the result after all possible netting has been completed. Three of these final results are gains, and three are losses. One possible result is a net long-term capital gain (NLTCG). Net long-term capital gains of noncorporate taxpayers are subject to beneficial treatment. A second possibility is a net short-term capital gain (NSTCG). Third, the netting may result in both NLTCG and NSTCG.

The NLTCG portion of these net results is subject to a 28 percent maximum tax rate. Since the maximum individual tax rate on non-NLTCG (ordinary income and NSTCG) income is 39.6 percent, the 28 percent maximum tax rate on NLTCG may reduce the tax rate by as much as 11.6 percentage points. The alternative tax computation (discussed in the next section of this chapter) is used to get this tax saving.

The last three results of the capital gain and loss netting process are losses. Thus, a fourth possibility is a net long-term capital loss (NLTCL). A fifth result is a net short-term capital loss (NSTCL). Finally, a sixth possibility includes both an NLTCL and an NSTCL. Neither NLTCLs nor NSTCLs are treated as ordinary losses. Treatment as an ordinary loss generally is preferable to capital loss treatment since ordinary losses are deductible in full while the deductibility of capital losses is subject to certain limitations. An individual taxpayer may deduct a maximum of $3,000 of net capital losses for a taxable year.[21]

TREATMENT OF CAPITAL GAINS

Computation of Net Capital Gain.
As just discussed, the *first step* in the computation is to net all long-term capital gains and losses and all short-term capital gains and losses. The result is the taxpayer's net long-term capital gain (NLTCG) or loss (NLTCL) and net short-term capital gain (NSTCG) or loss (NSTCL).

EXAMPLE 34

Some possible results of the first step in netting capital gains and losses are shown below. Assume that each case is independent (assume the taxpayer's only capital gains and losses are those shown in the given case).

Case	STCG	STCL	LTCG	LTCL	Result of Netting	Description of Result
A	$8,000	($5,000)			$ 3,000	NSTCG
B	2,000	(7,000)			(5,000)	NSTCL
C			$9,000	($1,000)	8,000	NLTCG
D			8,800	(9,800)	(1,000)	NLTCL

The *second step* in netting capital gains and losses requires offsetting any positive and negative amounts that remain after the first netting step. This procedure is illustrated in the following examples.

EXAMPLE 35

Assume that Sanjay had all the capital gains and losses specified in Cases B and C in Example 34:

Case C ($9,000 LTCG − $1,000 LTCL)	$ 8,000	NLTCG
Case B ($2,000 STCG − $7,000 STCL)	(5,000)	NSTCL
Excess of NLTCG over NSTCL	$ 3,000	

The excess of NLTCG over NSTCL is defined as **net capital gain (NCG)**. The result in Example 35 is a $3,000 NCG. There is an alternative tax computation when taxable income includes a NCG.

The **alternative tax** computation for the individual taxpayer taxes the NCG component of taxable income at a maximum tax rate of 28 percent. When taxable income including the NCG does not put the taxpayer into at least the 31 percent rate bracket, the alternative tax computation does not yield a tax benefit.

The NCG alternative tax is the summation of the following computations. It is illustrated in Example 36.

1. The tax computed using the regular rates on the greater of:
   a. Taxable income less the NCG, or
   b. The amount of taxable income taxed at a rate below 28 percent, plus
2. Twenty-eight percent of taxable income in excess of taxable income used in (1).

---

[21] § 1211(b).

EXAMPLE 36

Tim, an unmarried taxpayer, has taxable income (TI) of $175,000. The TI includes NCG of $50,000. Tim's regular tax liability for 1997 is $51,771 [($24,650 × 15%) + 28%($59,750 − $24,650) + 31%($124,650 − $59,750) + 36%($175,000 − $124,650)]. His alternative tax on the NCG is calculated as follows:

1. Tax on greater of:
   a. TI less NCG ($175,000 − $50,000)
   b. TI taxed below 28% ($24,650), plus $33,771
2. 28% of TI exceeding TI used in (1)
   [28% × ($175,000 − $125,000)]   14,000
   Alternative tax on TI including NCG $47,771

The NCG alternative tax saves Tim $4,000 ($51,771 − $47,771) in 1997. ▼

ETHICAL CONSIDERATIONS

Delaying a Marriage to Get a Tax Advantage

Jennifer and Fred have planned their wedding for December 10. Jennifer has a very large stock portfolio that includes stocks that have appreciated substantially in value and that have been held long term. Jennifer plans to sell the appreciated stocks and use the proceeds to purchase a home for Fred and herself. Jennifer's tax adviser has suggested that she sell these stocks before her wedding and that the wedding be postponed until next year. This tax strategy will result in significantly lower taxes for Jennifer because she will still be single at the end of the tax year in which she sells the stock. Fred feels that postponing the wedding for such "commercial" reasons is unromantic and unethical. What would you advise?

There is no special name for the excess of NSTCG over NLTCL, nor is there any special tax treatment. The nature of the gain is short term, and the gain is treated the same as ordinary gain and is included in the taxpayer's gross income.

EXAMPLE 37

Assume that Nora had all the capital gains and losses specified in Cases A and D in Example 34:

Case A ($8,000 STCG − $5,000 STCL)	$ 3,000	NSTCG
Case D ($8,800 LTCG − $9,800 LTCL)	(1,000)	NLTCL
Excess of NSTCG over NLTCL	$ 2,000	

▼

ETHICAL CONSIDERATIONS

Indexing Long-Term Capital Gains for Inflation

Tim, an economist, purchased a lot in a planned community for $100,000 in 1988. His intent at that time was to hold the land for investment. During the period from 1977 to 1987, golf course lots in the planned community had appreciated by 200 percent. Each year Tim pays real property taxes of $1,000 to the county. In addition, he pays $1,200 annually to the homeowners' association for maintenance of the community, security, and garbage collection. He deducts the property taxes on his Federal income tax return and capitalizes the homeowners' association fee.

Tim sells the lot at the end of 1997 for $160,000. Inflation for the 10-year period has been 30 percent. Tim is aware that the Internal Revenue Code of 1986 includes a number of statutory indexing provisions. Although one is not specifically provided for capital asset transactions, Tim feels that the appropriate way for the sale of the land to be taxed is as follows:

Adjusted basis of land:	
Cost	$100,000
Homeowners' association fees ($1,200 × 10 years)	12,000
Inflation adjustment ($100,000 × 30%)	30,000
	$142,000
Amount realized	$160,000
Adjusted basis	(142,000)
Recognized gain	$ 18,000

Since Tim's marginal tax rate is 28 percent, his tax liability associated with the sales transaction is $5,040 ($18,000 × 28%). What is your reaction to Tim's approach?

TREATMENT OF CAPITAL LOSSES

Computation of Net Capital Loss.
A **net capital loss (NCL)** results if capital losses exceed capital gains for the year. An NCL may be all long term, all short term, or part long and part short term.[22] The characterization of an NCL as long or short term is important in determining the capital loss deduction (discussed later in this chapter).

EXAMPLE 38

Three different individual taxpayers have the following capital gains and losses during the year:

Taxpayer	LTCG	LTCL	STCG	STCL	Result of Netting	Description of Result
Robert	$1,000	($2,800)	$1,000	($ 500)	($1,300)	NLTCL
Carlos	1,000	(500)	1,000	(2,800)	(1,300)	NSTCL
Troy	400	(1,200)	500	(1,200)	(1,500)	NLTCL ($800)
						NSTCL ($700)

Robert's NCL of $1,300 is all long term. Carlos's NCL of $1,300 is all short term. Troy's NCL is $1,500, $800 of which is long term and $700 of which is short term. ▼

Treatment of Net Capital Loss.
An NCL is deductible from gross income to the extent of $3,000 per tax year.[23] Capital losses exceeding the loss deduction limits carry forward indefinitely. Thus, although there may or may not be beneficial treatment for capital gains, there is *unfavorable* treatment for capital losses in terms of the $3,000 annual limitation on deducting NCL against ordinary

---

[22] Section 1222(10) defines a net capital loss as the net loss after the capital loss deduction. However, that definition confuses the discussion of net capital loss. Therefore, net capital loss is used here to mean the result after netting capital gains and losses and before considering the capital loss deduction. The capital loss deduction is discussed under Treatment of Net Capital Loss in this chapter.

[23] § 1211(b)(1). Married persons filing separate returns are limited to a $1,500 deduction per tax year.

income. If the NCL includes both long-term and short-term capital loss, the short-term capital loss is counted first toward the $3,000 annual limitation.

EXAMPLE 39 Burt has an NCL of $5,500, of which $2,000 is STCL and $3,500 is LTCL. Burt has a capital loss deduction of $3,000 [$2,000 of STCL and $1,000 of LTCL]. He has an LTCL carryforward of $2,500 ($3,500 − $1,000). ▼

Carryovers. Taxpayers are allowed to carry over unused capital losses indefinitely. The STCL and LTCL carried over retain their character as STCL or LTCL.

EXAMPLE 40 In 1997, Mark incurred $1,000 of STCL and $11,000 of LTCL. In 1998, Mark has a $400 LTCG.

- Mark's NCL for 1997 is $12,000. Mark deducts $3,000 ($1,000 STCL and $2,000 LTCL). He has $9,000 of LTCL carried forward to 1998.
- Mark combines the $9,000 LTCL carryforward with the $400 LTCG for 1998. He has an $8,600 NLTCL for 1998. Mark deducts $3,000 of LTCL in 1998 and carries forward $5,600 of LTCL to 1999. ▼

When a taxpayer has both a capital loss deduction and negative taxable income, a special computation of the capital loss carryover is required.[24] Specifically, the capital loss carryover is the NCL minus the lesser of:

- The capital loss deduction claimed on the return.
- The negative taxable income increased by the capital loss deduction claimed on the return and the personal and dependency exemption deduction.

Without this provision, some of the tax benefit of the capital loss deduction would be wasted when the deduction drives taxable income below zero.

EXAMPLE 41 In 1997, Joanne has a $13,000 NCL (all long term), a $2,650 personal exemption deduction, and $4,000 negative taxable income. The negative taxable income includes a $3,000 capital loss deduction. The capital loss carryover to 1998 is $11,350 computed as follows:

- The $4,000 negative taxable income is treated as a negative number, but the capital loss deduction and personal exemption deduction are treated as positive numbers.
- The normal ceiling on the capital loss deduction is $3,000.
- However, if the $3,000 capital loss deduction and the $2,650 exemption deduction are added back to the $4,000 negative taxable income, only $1,650 of the $3,000 capital loss deduction is needed to make taxable income equal to zero.
- Therefore, this special computation results in only $1,650 of the $13,000 NCL being consumed. The LTCL carryforward is $11,350 ($13,000 − $1,650). ▼

Concept Summary 16–4 summarizes the rules for noncorporate taxpayers' treatment of capital gains and losses.

REPORTING PROCEDURES

The following discusses only 1996 tax forms because the 1997 tax forms were not available at the time of this writing.

Capital gains and losses are reported on Schedule D of the 1996 Form 1040 (reproduced on page 16–26). Part I of Schedule D is used to report short-term capital gains and losses. Part II of Schedule D is used to report long-term capital

---

[24] § 1212(b).

Concept Summary 16–4

Noncorporate Taxpayer's Treatment of Net Capital Gain or Loss

Net Capital Gain Treatment Summarized

1. All long-term capital gain — 28% alternative tax, but it is not always beneficial.
2. All short-term capital gain — Taxable as ordinary income.
3. Part long-term and part short-term capital gain — Short-term capital gain portion taxable as ordinary income. 28% alternative tax is available for long-term capital gain portion, but it is not always beneficial.

Net Capital Loss Treatment Summarized

4. All long-term capital loss — $1 of loss used to make $1 of deduction. Deduction is *for* AGI and limited to $3,000 per year. Portion of loss not used to make deduction carries forward indefinitely.
5. All short-term capital loss — $1 of loss used to make $1 of deduction. Deduction is *for* AGI and limited to $3,000 per year. Portion of loss not used to make deduction carries forward indefinitely.
6. Part long-term and part short-term capital loss — Short-term losses used first to make $3,000 deduction.

---

gains and losses. Part III summarizes the results of Parts I and II. Part IV lists additional short-term capital gains and losses. It is a continuation of Part I. Part V lists additional long-term capital gains and losses. It is a continuation of Part II. The Form 1040 instructions have a Schedule D tax worksheet that is used for the alternative tax computation for net long-term capital gains. Parts IV and V of Schedule D and the Schedule D tax worksheet are not reproduced here.

Example 42

During 1996, Erlyne Smith (Social Security number, 466–36–4596) had the following sales of capital assets (a 1996 example has been used, since a 1997 form was unavailable):

Description	Date Acquired	Date Sold	Selling Price	Cost Basis*
100 shares of Apple Corp. common stock	10/21/96	12/3/96	$11,000	$10,000
300 shares of Orange Corp. preferred stock	7/29/96	11/25/96	5,000	5,500
2,000 shares of Peach Corp. common stock	1/31/89	12/12/96	8,000	7,000
40 shares of Pear Corp. common stock	6/11/89	12/5/96	16,000	18,800

*Includes selling expenses (e.g., brokerage commissions).

Note that Erlyne's tax position is the same as that of Robert in Example 38. Thus, Erlyne has a NLTCL of $1,800 (Part II of Schedule D) and an NSTCG of $500 (Part I of Schedule D). These amounts are combined (see Part III of Schedule D) for a NLTCL of $1,300. All of the $1,300 is deductible *for* AGI as a capital loss deduction. There is no remaining capital loss to carry over to 1997. In completing a Schedule D for Erlyne Smith, it was assumed that she had no capital loss carryovers from prior years. Her total stock sales of $40,000 ($11,000 + $5,000 + $8,000 + $16,000) were reported to her by her broker on a Form 1099–B. ▼

16–26 — **PART V** Property Transactions

SCHEDULE D (Form 1040) Department of the Treasury Internal Revenue Service (99)	**Capital Gains and Losses** ▶ Attach to Form 1040. ▶ See Instructions for Schedule D (Form 1040). ▶ Use lines 20 and 22 for more space to list transactions for lines 1 and 9.	OMB No. 1545-0074 **1996** Attachment Sequence No. **12**
Name(s) shown on Form 1040 *Erlyne Smith*		Your social security number 466 : 36 : 4596

Part I — Short-Term Capital Gains and Losses—Assets Held One Year or Less

(a) Description of property (Example: 100 sh. XYZ Co.)	(b) Date acquired (Mo., day, yr.)	(c) Date sold (Mo., day, yr.)	(d) Sales price (see page D-3)	(e) Cost or other basis (see page D-3)	(f) LOSS If (e) is more than (d), subtract (d) from (e)	(g) GAIN If (d) is more than (e), subtract (e) from (d)
1 100 shares Apple Corp. common	10/21/96	12/3/96	11,000	10,000		1,000
300 shares Orange Corp. preferred	7/29/96	11/25/96	5,000	5,500	500	

2 Enter your short-term totals, if any, from line 21 . . . . **2**		
3 **Total short-term sales price amounts.** Add column (d) of lines 1 and 2 . . . **3**	16,000	
4 Short-term gain from Forms 2119 and 6252, and short-term gain or loss from Forms 4684, 6781, and 8824 . . . . **4**		
5 Net short-term gain or loss from partnerships, S corporations, estates, and trusts from Schedule(s) K-1 . . . . **5**		
6 Short-term capital loss carryover. Enter the amount, if any, from line 9 of your 1995 Capital Loss Carryover Worksheet **6**		
7 Add lines 1 through 6 in columns (f) and (g) **7** (500)		1,000
8 **Net short-term capital gain or (loss).** Combine columns (f) and (g) of line 7 . . . . . ▶ **8**	500	

Part II — Long-Term Capital Gains and Losses—Assets Held More Than One Year

9 2,000 shares Peach Corp. common	1/31/89	12/12/96	8,000	7,000		1,000
40 shares Pear Corp. preferred	6/11/89	12/5/96	16,000	18,800	2,800	

10 Enter your long-term totals, if any, from line 23 . . . . **10**		
11 **Total long-term sales price amounts.** Add column (d) of lines 9 and 10 . . . **11**	24,000	
12 Gain from Form 4797; long-term gain from Forms 2119, 2439, and 6252; and long-term gain or loss from Forms 4684, 6781, and 8824 . . . . . **12**		
13 Net long-term gain or loss from partnerships, S corporations, estates, and trusts from Schedule(s) K-1 . . . . **13**		
14 Capital gain distributions **14**		
15 Long-term capital loss carryover. Enter the amount, if any, from line 14 of your 1995 Capital Loss Carryover Worksheet **15**		
16 Add lines 9 through 15 in columns (f) and (g) **16** (2,800)		1,000
17 **Net long-term capital gain or (loss).** Combine columns (f) and (g) of line 16 . . . . . ▶ **17** (1,800)		

Part III — Summary of Parts I and II

18 Combine lines 8 and 17. If a loss, go to line 19. If a gain, enter the gain on Form 1040, line 13. **Note:** *If both lines 17 and 18 are gains, see the* **Capital Gain Tax Worksheet** *on page 23* . .   **18** (1,300)

19 If line 18 is a loss, enter here and as a (loss) on Form 1040, line 13, the **smaller** of these losses:
   a The loss on line 18; **or**
   b ($3,000) or, if married filing separately, ($1,500) **19** (1,300)

Note: *See the* **Capital Loss Carryover Worksheet** *on page D-3 if the loss on line 18 exceeds the loss on line 19* **or** *if Form 1040, line 35, is a loss.*

For Paperwork Reduction Act Notice, see Form 1040 instructions.   Cat. No. 11338H   Schedule D (Form 1040) 1996

TAX TREATMENT OF CAPITAL GAINS AND LOSSES OF CORPORATE TAXPAYERS

6 LEARNING OBJECTIVE
Describe the tax treatment for capital gains and the detrimental tax treatment for capital losses for corporate taxpayers.

The treatment of a corporation's net capital gain or loss differs from the rules for individuals. Briefly, the differences are as follows:

- There is an NCG alternative tax rate of 35 percent.[25] However, since the maximum corporate tax rate is 35 percent, the alternative tax is not beneficial.
- Capital losses offset only capital gains. No deduction of capital losses is permitted against ordinary taxable income (whereas a $3,000 deduction is allowed to individuals).[26]
- There is a three-year carryback and a five-year carryover period for net capital losses.[27] Corporate carryovers and carrybacks are always treated as short term, regardless of their original nature.

EXAMPLE 43

Sparrow Corporation has a $15,000 NLTCL for the current year and $57,000 of ordinary taxable income. Sparrow may not offset the $15,000 NLTCL against its ordinary income by taking a capital loss deduction. The $15,000 NLTCL becomes a $15,000 STCL for carryback and carryover purposes. This amount may be offset by capital gains in the three-year carryback period or, if not absorbed there, offset by capital gains in the five-year carryforward period. ▼

The rules applicable to corporations are discussed in greater detail in Chapter 20.

TAX PLANNING CONSIDERATIONS

IMPORTANCE OF CAPITAL ASSET STATUS

Why is capital asset status important when net long-term capital gain is subject to a maximum 28 percent tax rate? The 11.6 percent difference between the maximum 39.6 percent regular tax rate and the maximum 28 percent net long-term capital gain tax rate may generate significant tax savings for taxpayers in the highest regular tax bracket (and to a lesser extent for taxpayers in the 31 percent and 36 percent tax brackets) who can receive income in the form of long-term capital gains. Thus, individuals who can receive income in the form of long-term capital gains have an advantage over taxpayers who cannot receive income in this form.

7 LEARNING OBJECTIVE
Identify tax planning opportunities arising from the sale or exchange of capital assets.

Capital asset status is also important because capital gains must be offset by capital losses. If a net capital loss results, the maximum deduction is $3,000 per year.

Consequently, capital gains and losses must be segregated from other types of gains and losses and must be reported separately on Schedule D of Form 1040.

PLANNING FOR CAPITAL ASSET STATUS

It is important to keep in mind that capital asset status often is a question of objective evidence. Thus, property that is not a capital asset to one party may qualify as a capital asset to another party.

---

[25] § 1201.
[26] § 1211(a).
[27] § 1212(a)(1).

EXAMPLE 44

Diane, a real estate dealer, transfers by gift a tract of land to Jeff, her son. The land was recorded as part of Diane's inventory (it was held for resale) and was therefore not a capital asset to her. Jeff, however, treats the land as an investment. The land is a capital asset in Jeff's hands, and any later taxable disposition of the property by him will yield a capital gain or loss. ▼

If proper planning is carried out, even a dealer may obtain long-term capital gain treatment on the sale of the type of property normally held for resale.

EXAMPLE 45

Jim, a real estate dealer, segregates tract A from the real estate he regularly holds for resale and designates the property as being held for investment purposes. The property is not advertised for sale and is disposed of several years later. The negotiations for the subsequent sale were initiated by the purchaser and not by Jim. Under these circumstances, it would appear that any gain or loss from the sale of tract A should be a capital gain or loss.[28] ▼

When a business is being sold, one of the major decisions usually concerns whether a portion of the sales price is for goodwill. For the seller, goodwill generally represents the disposition of a capital asset. Goodwill has no basis and represents a residual portion of the selling price that cannot be allocated reasonably to the known assets. The amount of goodwill thus represents capital gain. The buyer purchasing goodwill has a capitalizable, 15-year amortizable asset—a disadvantageous situation.

Prior to the Revenue Reconciliation Act (RRA) of 1993, the buyer would prefer that the residual portion of the purchase price be allocated to a covenant not to compete (a promise that the seller will not compete against the buyer by conducting a business similar to the one that the buyer has purchased). Payments for a covenant not to compete are ordinary income to the seller, but were ordinary deductions for the buyer over the life of the covenant. However, § 197 now provides that a covenant is amortized over the same 15-year period as goodwill.

EXAMPLE 46

Marcia is buying Jack's dry cleaning proprietorship. An appraisal of the assets indicates that a reasonable purchase price would exceed the value of the known assets by $30,000. If the purchase contract does not specify the nature of the $30,000, the amount will be for goodwill, and Jack will have a long-term capital gain of $30,000. Marcia will have a 15-year amortizable $30,000 asset. If Marcia is paying the extra $30,000 to prevent Jack from conducting another dry cleaning business in the area (a covenant not to compete), Jack will have $30,000 of ordinary income. Marcia will have a $30,000 deduction over the statutory 15-year amortization period rather than over the actual life of the covenant (e.g., 5 years). ▼

EFFECT OF CAPITAL ASSET STATUS IN TRANSACTIONS OTHER THAN SALES

The nature of an asset (capital or ordinary) is important in determining the tax consequences that result when a sale or exchange occurs. It may, however, be just as significant in circumstances other than a taxable sale or exchange. When a capital asset is disposed of, the result is not always a capital gain or loss. Rather, in general, the disposition must be a sale or exchange. Collection of a debt instru-

---

[28] *Toledo, Peoria & Western Railroad Co.,* 35 TCM 1663, T.C.Memo. 1976–366.

ment having a basis less than the face value results in an ordinary gain rather than a capital gain even though the debt instrument is a capital asset. The collection is not a sale or exchange. Sale of the debt shortly before the due date for collection will not produce a capital gain.[29] If selling the debt in such circumstances could produce a capital gain but collecting could not, the narrow interpretation of what constitutes a capital gain or loss would be frustrated. Another illustration of the sale or exchange principle involves a donation of certain appreciated property to a qualified charity. Recall that in certain circumstances, the measure of the charitable contribution is fair market value when the property, if sold, would have yielded a long-term capital gain (refer to Chapter 10 and the discussion of § 170(e)).

EXAMPLE 47

Sharon wants to donate a tract of unimproved land (basis of $40,000 and fair market value of $200,000) held for the required long-term holding period to State University (a qualified charitable organization). However, Sharon currently is under audit by the IRS for capital gains she reported on certain real estate transactions during an earlier tax year. Although Sharon is not a licensed real estate broker, the IRS agent conducting the audit is contending that she has achieved dealer status by virtue of the number and frequency of the real estate transactions she has conducted. Under these circumstances, Sharon would be well-advised to postpone the donation to State University until her status is clarified. If she has achieved dealer status, the unimproved land may be inventory (refer to Example 45 for another possible result), and Sharon's charitable contribution deduction would be limited to $40,000. If not, and if the land is held as an investment, Sharon's deduction is $200,000 (the fair market value of the property). ▼

STOCK SALES

The following rules apply in determining the date of a stock sale:

- The date the sale is executed is the date of the sale. The execution date is the date the broker completes the transaction on the stock exchange.
- The settlement date is the date the cash or other property is paid to the seller of the stock. This date is *not* relevant in determining the date of sale.

EXAMPLE 48

Lupe, a cash basis taxpayer, sells stock that results in a gain. The sale was executed on December 30, 1996. The settlement date is January 2, 1997. The date of sale is December 30, 1996 (the execution date). The holding period for the stock sold ends with the execution date. ▼

MAXIMIZING BENEFITS

Ordinary losses generally are preferable to capital losses because of the limitations imposed on the deductibility of net capital losses and the requirement that capital losses be used to offset capital gains. The taxpayer may be able to convert what would otherwise have been capital loss to ordinary loss. For example, business (but not nonbusiness) bad debts, losses from the sale or exchange of small business investment company stock, and losses from the sale or exchange of small business company stock all result in ordinary losses.[30]

Although capital losses can be carried over indefinitely, *indefinite* becomes definite when a taxpayer dies. Any loss carryovers not used by the taxpayer are

---

[29] *Comm. v. Percy W. Phillips*, 60–1 USTC ¶9294, 5 AFTR2d 855, 275 F.2d 33 (CA–4, 1960).

[30] §§ 166(d), 1242, and 1244. Refer to the discussion in Chapter 7.

permanently lost. That is, no tax benefit can be derived from the carryovers subsequent to death.[31] Therefore, the potential benefit of carrying over capital losses diminishes when dealing with older taxpayers.

It is usually beneficial to spread gains over more than one taxable year. In some cases, this can be accomplished through the installment sales method of accounting.

YEAR-END PLANNING

The following general rules can be applied for timing the recognition of capital gains and losses near the end of a taxable year:

- If the taxpayer already has recognized over $3,000 of capital loss, sell assets to generate capital gain equal to the excess of the capital loss over $3,000.

EXAMPLE 49 Kevin has already incurred a $7,000 STCL. Kevin should generate $4,000 of capital gain. The gain will offset $4,000 of the loss. The remaining loss of $3,000 can be deducted against ordinary income. ▼

- If the taxpayer already has recognized capital gain, sell assets to generate capital loss equal to the capital gain. The gain will not be taxed, and the loss will be fully *deductible* against the gain.
- If the taxpayer's ordinary taxable income is already in the 28 percent bracket, it would make sense to recognize long-term capital gain rather than ordinary income where the taxpayer has a choice between the two. Such gain is taxed at the alternative rate of 28 percent whereas ordinary income may be taxed under the regular tax rates at 31 percent or more.

KEY TERMS

Alternative tax, 16–21
Capital asset, 16–4
Capital gains, 16–2
Capital losses, 16–2
Franchise, 16–13
Holding period, 16–16
Lessee, 16–15
Lessor, 16–15
Net capital gain (NCG), 16–21
Net capital loss (NCL), 16–23
Options, 16–10
Original issue discount (OID), 16–10
Patent, 16–12
Sale or exchange, 16–9
Short sale, 16–17

PROBLEM MATERIALS

DISCUSSION QUESTIONS

1. What type of gain may be subject to beneficial tax treatment for noncorporate taxpayers?
2. Upon what three characteristics does proper classification of recognized gains and losses depend?

---
[31] Rev.Rul. 74–175, 1974–1 C.B. 52.

CHAPTER 16 Property Transactions: Capital Gains and Losses

3. Can the sale of personal use assets generally result in capital losses?

4. What broad class of assets is excluded from the capital asset category for tax purposes, but is labeled a capital asset in accounting textbooks for the capital asset budgeting decision?

5. Todd owns the following assets. Which of them are capital assets?
   a. Ten shares of Standard Motors common stock.
   b. A copyright on a song Todd wrote.
   c. A U.S. government savings bond.
   d. A note Todd received when he loaned $100 to a friend.
   e. A very rare copy of "Your Federal Income Tax" (a U.S. government publication that Todd purchased many years ago from the U.S. Government Printing Office).
   f. Todd's personal use automobile.
   g. A letter Todd received from a former U.S. President. Todd received the letter because he had complained to the President about the President's foreign policy.

6. Why doesn't the collection of an accrual basis account receivable usually result in a gain or loss?

7. Joanne purchases song copyrights from composers. What tax issues does Joanne face in determining whether the copyrights are capital assets for her?

8. Why do court decisions play an important role in the definition of capital assets?

9. In what circumstances may real estate held for resale receive capital gain treatment?

10. Jonathan lent $2,000 to a friend who became unemployed unexpectedly. Shortly thereafter, the friend took a new job in another state. After very diligent efforts to locate the friend, Jonathan was unable to find him, and payment of the loan is now 14 months overdue. Assuming the loan is fully noncollectible, what tax issues does Jonathan face?

11. Recognition of capital gain or loss usually requires a sale or exchange of a capital asset. Define "sale" and "exchange."

12. A corporate bond is worthless due to a bankruptcy on May 10. At what date does the tax loss occur? (Assume the bond was held by an individual for investment purposes.)

13. Why does the Code require amortization of original issue discount? What is the effect of this amortization on the interest income of the taxpayer owning the bond? On the adjusted basis?

14. David purchased a one-year option on 40 acres of farmland for $25,000. David's plans for the property did not work out, so he let the option expire unexercised. What tax issues does David face in determining how to treat the $25,000?

15. If a grantee of an option exercises the option, do the grantor's proceeds from the sale of the option property increase? Why?

16. When does the transfer of a patent result in long-term capital gain? Short-term capital gain? Ordinary income?

17. If an inventor's employer automatically has sole patent rights to the inventor's inventions, is the employer a holder of the patent?

18. What is a franchise? In practice, does the transfer of a franchise usually result in capital gain or loss treatment? Why or why not?

19. How does § 1056 restrict the allocation of sports franchise acquisition costs to player contracts?

20. For a lease cancellation to be treated as an exchange, does the lease have to be a capital asset? Why or why not?

21. What type of income does a landlord have on receiving a payment for cancellation of a lease?

22. A capital asset is purchased on the last day of the month. What is the first day that the holder may dispose of the asset and receive long-term treatment?

23. When is the former owner's holding period tacked on to the current owner's holding period?

24. Helen exchanges a computer used in her business for another computer that she will use in her business. The transaction qualifies as a like-kind exchange. Helen had held the computer given up in the exchange for four years. The computers are § 1231 assets. What is the holding period of the computer received in the exchange on the day of its acquisition?

25. Juan purchased corporate stock for $10,000 on April 10, 1996. On July 14, 1997, when the stock was worth $7,000, he gave it to his son, Miguel. What has to happen to the value of the property while Miguel holds it if Miguel is to tack Juan's holding period on to his own holding period?

26. John inherits stock on July 17, 1997. John's father had purchased the stock on April 10, 1996, for $12,000. The stock was worth $15,000 when the father died on December 20, 1996. The stock was worth $18,000 when John received it on July 17, 1997. When does John's holding period for the stock begin?

27. Define a short sale. Why does a seller enter into a short sale?

28. After all possible capital gain and loss netting is complete, what are the possibilities for outcomes that include a net long-term capital gain?

29. After all possible capital gain and loss netting is complete, what are the possibilities for outcomes that include a net long-term capital loss?

30. Sue and Ramon each have gross income of $150,000. Yet Sue contends that her gross income will be taxed at a lesser rate than Ramon's gross income. Assuming she is correct, what could explain this odd result?

31. A noncorporate taxpayer's taxable income, not including a $50,000 long-term capital gain, puts the taxpayer in the 36% bracket. Would all of the long-term capital gain be taxed at 28%?

32. When a noncorporate taxpayer has both a capital loss deduction and negative taxable income, why is a special computation of the capital loss carryover required?

33. Differentiate between the capital loss carryover rules for unused capital losses of individuals and corporations.

PROBLEMS

34. Nancy had three property transactions during the year. She sold a vacation home used for personal purposes at a $21,000 loss. The home had been held for five years and had never been rented. Nancy also sold an antique clock for $3,500 that she had inherited from her grandmother. The clock was valued in Nancy's grandmother's estate at $2,000. Nancy owned the clock for only four months. Nancy sold these assets to finance her full-time occupation as a songwriter. Near the end of the year, Nancy sold one of the songs she had written two years earlier. She received cash of $38,000 and a royalty interest in revenues derived from the merchandising of the song. Nancy had no tax basis for the song. Nancy had no other income and $18,000 in deductible songwriting expenses. Assuming the year is 1997, what is Nancy's adjusted gross income?

35. Revez owns an antique shop. He buys property from estates, often at much less than the retail value of the property. Recently, Revez sold for $4,000 an antique desk for which he had paid $125. Revez had held the desk in his shop for 15 months before selling it. Revez would like the gain on the sale of the desk to be a long-term capital gain. How can he achieve that objective?

36. Gary makes a gift to Barbara of the copyright on his song, "I Love the Spartans." The song has a basis of $20,000 to Gary. Gary had owned the copyright for two years. The copyright has a fair market value of $25,000 at the date of the gift. Three years after receiving the copyright, Barbara sells it to Jim for $30,000.

a. What is Barbara's recognized gain on the sale?
b. What is the nature of Barbara's gain?

37. Brenda Reynolds is a dealer in securities. She has spotted a fast-rising company and would like to buy and hold its stock for investment. The stock is currently selling for $45 per share, and Brenda thinks it will climb to $93 a share within two years. Brenda's co-workers have told her that there is "no way" she can get long-term capital gain treatment when she purchases stock because she is a securities dealer. Brenda has asked you to calculate her potential gain and tell her whether her co-workers are right. Draft a letter to Brenda responding to her request. Her address is 200 Morningside Drive, Hattisburg, MS 39406.

38. Gordon has owned a large tract of land for 15 years and subdivides it for sale. Assume Gordon meets all the requirements of § 1237. During the first year of sales, Gordon sells 20 lots for $20,000 each. His selling expenses are 7% of the sales price of each lot. Gordon has a basis of $11,000 in each lot. Compute Gordon's total gain from the sale of these lots and indicate the nature of the gain.

39. Sue has had a bad year with her investments. She lent a friend $3,700; the friend did not repay the loan when it was due, and then declared bankruptcy. The loan is totally uncollectible. Sue also was notified by her broker that the Willow corporate bonds she owned became worthless on October 13, 1997. She had purchased the bonds for $10,000 on October 10, 1996. Sue also had a $20,000 loss on the disposition of § 1244 corporate stock that she purchased several years ago. Sue is single.
a. What are the nature and amount of Sue's losses?
b. What is Sue's AGI for 1997 assuming she has $65,000 of ordinary gross income from sources other than those discussed above?
c. What are the nature and amount of Sue's loss carryforwards?

40. Fred purchases $100,000 of newly issued Gold Corporation bonds for $54,000. The bonds have original issue discount of $46,000. After Fred has held the bonds for two years and has amortized $14,000 of the original issue discount, he sells the bonds for $98,000. What is Fred's adjusted basis for the bonds when he sells them, and what are the amount and nature of the gain from the disposition of the bonds?

41. Samantha is in the business of buying song copyrights from struggling songwriters, holding those copyrights, and then reselling the songs to major record companies and singers. Samantha has a four-month option to purchase a song copyright. She paid $2,000 for this option. A famous singer has heard the song and is willing to buy the option from Samantha for $10,000. Samantha thinks the song may be worth $35,000 in six months. If Samantha exercises the option, she will have to pay $20,000 for the song. Assuming Samantha is in the 36% tax bracket, which of these alternatives will give her a better after-tax cash flow?

42. Marta is looking for vacant land to buy. She would hold the land as an investment. For $10,000, she is granted an 11-month option on January 1, 1997, to buy 10 acres of vacant land for $300,000. The owner (who is holding the land for investment) paid $12,000 for the land several years ago.
a. Does the landowner have gross income when $10,000 is received for granting the option?
b. Does Marta have an asset when the option is granted?
c. If the option lapses, does the landowner have a recognized gain? If so, what type of gain? Does Marta have a recognized loss? If so, what type of loss?
d. If the option is exercised and an additional $300,000 is paid for the land, how much recognized gain does the seller have? What type of gain? What is Marta's tax basis for the property?

43. Frank owns a patent on a part that Teal Corporation wishes to use as a component in a product it manufactures. Frank had purchased the patent from the inventor before the inventor reduced the patent to practice. Frank had intended to use the patented part in his business, but found that it was not suitable. Teal is willing to pay Frank $5,000 per month plus 1% of the manufactured cost of the part. How should Frank construct the

contract with Teal so that the $5,000 per month and 1% of manufactured cost are long-term capital gain?

44. Susan is the holder of a patent on a corn detassling machine. She sells all substantial rights to the patent for $88,000. Susan had developed the patented machine, but had not yet reduced it to practice. She had spent $93,000 developing the machine and obtaining the patent. What are the nature and amount of Susan's loss?

45. Freys, Inc., sells a 12-year franchise to Reynaldo. The franchise contains many restrictions on how Reynaldo may operate his store. For instance, Reynaldo cannot use less than Grade 10 Idaho potatoes, must fry the potatoes at a constant 410 degrees, dress store personnel in Freys-approved uniforms, and have a Freys sign that meets detailed specifications on size, color, and construction. When the franchise contract is signed, Reynaldo makes a noncontingent $40,000 payment to Freys. During the same year, Reynaldo pays Freys $25,000—14% of Reynaldo's sales. How does Freys treat each of these payments? How does Reynaldo treat each of the payments?

46. Irene lives in an apartment near her college campus. Her lease runs out in July 1998, but her landlord could sell the building if he can convince all the tenants to cancel their leases and move out by the end of 1997. The landlord has offered Irene $1,000 to cancel her lease. Irene's lease began on August 1, 1997. What tax factors should Irene consider in deciding whether to take the landlord's offer?

47. On August 10, 1997, Peter received 100 shares of Brown Corporation stock as a gift from his father, John. On that date, the stock was worth $18 per share. John had paid $23 per share for the stock on July 11, 1987. On December 20, 1997, Peter sold all of the shares for $16 per share. What are the amount and the nature of Peter's gain or loss from disposition of the Brown shares?

48. Dennis sells short 100 shares of ARC stock at $20 per share on January 15, 1997. He buys 200 shares of ARC stock on April 1, 1997, at $25 per share. On May 2, 1997, he closes the short sale by delivering 100 of the shares purchased on April 1.
    a. What are the amount and nature of Dennis's loss upon closing the short sale?
    b. When does the holding period for the remaining 100 shares begin?
    c. If Dennis sells (at $27 per share) the remaining 100 shares on January 20, 1998, what will be the nature of his gain or loss?

49. Elaine Case (single with no dependents) has the following transactions in 1997:

Adjusted gross income (exclusive of capital gains and losses)	$240,000
Long-term capital gain	12,000
Long-term capital loss	(5,000)
Short-term capital gain	19,000
Short-term capital loss	(23,000)

What is Elaine's net capital gain or loss? Draft a letter to Elaine describing how the net capital gain or loss will be treated on her tax return. Assume Elaine's income from other sources puts her in the 36% bracket. Elaine's address is 300 Ireland Avenue, Shepherdstown, WV 25443.

50. In 1997, Betty (head of household with three dependents) had an $18,000 loss from the sale of a personal residence. She also purchased from an individual inventor for $8,000 (and resold in two months for $7,000) a patent on a rubber bonding process. The patent had not yet been reduced to practice. Betty purchased the patent as an investment. Additionally, she had the following capital gains and losses from stock transactions:

Long-term capital loss	($ 3,000)
Long-term capital loss carryover from 1996	(12,000)
Short-term capital gain	21,000
Short-term capital loss	(6,000)

What is Betty's net capital gain or loss? Draft a letter to Betty explaining the tax treatment of the sale of her personal residence. Assume Betty's income from other sources puts her in the 36% bracket. Betty's address is 1120 West Street, Ashland, OR 97520.

51. For 1997, Nikko has *negative* taxable income of $6,000. In computing his taxable income, Nikko claimed a $3,000 short-term capital loss deduction, the standard deduction, one personal exemption, and two dependency exemptions. Nikko is 67 years old and had a net short-term capital loss for the year of $15,200. How much of Nikko's $15,200 of capital loss carries over to 1998?

52. For 1997, Ahmad completes the following stock transactions:

	Date Acquired	Cost	Date Sold	Selling Price
1,000 shares ABC	1/6/97	$4,000	8/2/97	$12,000
200 shares DEF	7/1/82	8,800	9/18/97	9,400
3,500 shares GHI	5/2/97	7,000	11/2/97	8,900
5,000 shares JKL	8/5/97	9,700	12/15/97	5,000

What is Ahmad's includible gain or deductible loss resulting from these stock sales?

53. Consuela, a head of household with two dependents, has the following 1997 transactions:

Adjusted gross income (exclusive of capital gains and losses)	$125,250
Long-term capital loss	(5,000)
Long-term capital gain	20,000
Short-term capital loss carryover	(2,000)

a. What is Consuela's net capital gain or loss?
b. What is Consuela's taxable income assuming she does not itemize?
c. What is Consuela's tax on taxable income?

54. Gold, Inc., has determined its 1997 taxable income as $45,000 before considering the results of its capital gain or loss transactions. Gold has a short-term capital loss of $4,000, a long-term capital loss of $18,000, and a short-term capital gain of $19,000. What is Gold's 1997 taxable income, and what (if any) are the amount and nature of its capital loss carryover?

55. June owns a sole proprietorship that Doria is going to purchase. They have agreed on a price for all the assets except goodwill and June's covenant not to compete against Doria. June is willing to give Doria a two-year covenant not to compete for only $1 of compensation, but would like $25,000 for the business goodwill. Doria would like to pay June $25,000 for the covenant not to compete and only $1 for the business goodwill. June is in the 36% tax bracket, and Doria is in the 31% tax bracket. Which of these approaches is better for June? For Doria?

CUMULATIVE PROBLEMS

56. Nikki Hassad is a graduate student at State University. She is single and has no dependents. During 1997, she had $5,500 wages from a full-time job she held until returning to school in August. Nikki received a $3,000 scholarship from State University and used all of the scholarship money to pay for tuition and fees. In June 1997, she won $135,000 with an instant lottery ticket and immediately invested in various stocks. The following table summarizes her stock transactions for 1997:

	Date Acquired	Cost	Date Sold	Selling Price
150 shares Clay	7/2/97	$5,000	12/11/97	$6,200
100 shares Gold	7/2/97	5,000	11/6/97	3,300
120 shares Iron	7/2/97	3,100	10/8/97	8,000
25 shares Sand	7/2/97	1,900		
100 shares Uranium	6/16/91	2,000	12/11/97	9,600

Nikki does not have many itemized deductions, so she will take the standard deduction. Her Social Security number is 393–86–4502, and she lives at 518 Marigold Lane, Okemos, MI 48864. She had $600 of Federal income tax withheld on her wages and $37,000 of Federal income tax withheld on her lottery winnings. She also made Federal estimated income tax payments of $3,500.

Compute Nikki's lowest legal tax liability for 1997. Suggested software (if available): *TurboTax* or *MacInTax*.

Draft a brief letter to Nikki describing (1) how long she must hold the Sand stock for it to become "long term," (2) what the 1998 tax consequences would be if she sold that stock for a $4,000 long-term capital gain, and (3) what would happen if she was eligible for the alternative tax on long-term capital gains. Also, prepare a memo for Nikki's tax file.

57. Sue Lowe lives at 1310 Meadow Lane, Lima, OH 23412 and her Social Security number is 312–55–8000. Sue is single and has a 10-year-old son, Kania. His Social Security number is 480–01–9030. Kania lives with Sue and she fully supports him. During 1996, Sue spent $2,700 on qualifying support for Kania at the Happy Daze Child Care Center, 18 Oak Lane, Lima, OH 23410. The center's identifying number is 38–6933367.

Sue owns the Lowe Enterprises sole proprietorship (38–1234567) which is located at 456 Hill Street, Lima, OH 23401. Her 1996 Form 1040 Schedule C for Lowe Enterprises shows net income of $30,000. Sue personally purchases health insurance on herself and Kania. The premiums are $3,000 per year.

Sue has an extensive stock portfolio and has prepared the following analysis:

Stock	Number of Shares	Date Purchased	Date Sold	Per Share Cost	Per Share Selling Price	Per Share Dividends
Blue	10	10/18/95	10/11/96	$80	$72	$3
Green	30	10/11/92	10/11/96	33	47	1
Purple	15	3/10/95	3/02/96	62	33	2
Yellow	100	4/11/89	4/02/96	18	46	1
Gold	35	7/12/95	10/11/96	7	12	0
White	100	10/11/95		82		1
Tan	20	4/02/95		15		0
Beige	17	4/11/89		11		0
Amber	75	3/10/94		43		2

Note: The per share cost includes commissions, and the per share selling price is net of commissions. Also, the per share dividends are the actual dividends received in 1996.

Sue had $800 of interest income from State of Ohio bonds and $600 of interest income on her Lima Savings Bank account. She also received $5,000 of alimony payments.

Sue itemizes her deductions and had the following items, which may be relevant to her return:

Item	Amount	Comment
Unreimbursed medical expenses for Sue and Kania (all for visits to doctors)	$1,786	Does not include health insurance premiums.
State income taxes paid	1,830	
Real property taxes on personal residence	3,230	
Interest paid on loans used to purchase stock held for investment	830	
Interest paid on home mortgage (Form 1098)	8,137	The loan is secured by the residence and was incurred when the home was purchased.
Charitable contributions	940	Cash paid to Sue's church.

Sue made a $6,000 Federal estimated income tax payment, does not wish any of her taxes to finance Presidential elections, has no foreign bank accounts or trusts, and wishes any refund to be applied against her 1997 taxes.

Compute Sue's net tax payable or refund due for 1996. If you use tax forms for your computations, you will need Form 1040 and Schedules A, B, C, D, and SE and Forms 2441 and 4952. Suggested software (if available): *TurboTax* or *MacInTax*.

RESEARCH PROBLEMS

*Note: **West's Federal Taxation on CD-ROM** can be used in preparing solutions to the Research Problems. Alternatively, tax research materials contained in a standard tax library can be used.*

Research Problem 1. Ali owns 100 shares of Brown Corporation stock. He purchased the stock at five different times and at five different prices per share as indicated:

Share Block	Number of Shares	Per Share Price	Purchase Date
A	10	$60	10/10/93
B	20	20	8/11/94
C	15	15	10/24/94
D	35	30	4/23/96
E	20	25	7/28/96

On April 28, 1997, Ali will sell 40 shares of Brown stock for $40 per share. All of Ali's shares are held by his stockbroker. The broker's records track when the shares were purchased. May Ali designate the shares he sells and, if so, which shares should he sell? Assume Ali wants to maximize his gain because he has a capital loss carryforward.

Research Problem 2. Clean Corporation runs a chain of dry cleaners. Borax is used heavily in Clean's dry cleaning process and has been in short supply several times in the past. Clean Corporation buys a controlling interest in Dig Corporation—a borax mining concern. Clean's sole reason for purchasing the Dig stock is to assure Clean of a continuous supply of borax if another shortage develops. Although borax must be refined before it is usable for dry cleaning purposes, a well-established commodities market exists for trading unrefined borax for refined borax. After owning the Dig stock for several years, Clean sells the stock at a loss because Dig is in difficult financial straits. Clean no longer needs to own Dig because Clean has obtained an alternative source of borax. What is the nature of Clean's loss on the disposition of the Dig Corporation stock? Write a letter to the controller, Salvio Guitterez, that contains your advice and prepare a memo for the tax files. The mailing address of Clean Corporation is 4455 Whitman Way, San Mateo, CA 44589.

Research Problem 3. Oak Corporation, a manufacturing company, hired several executives during 1997. The executives had homes in other cities when Oak hired them. If the executives were unable to sell those homes, they would be unable to buy replacement homes in Oak's area. Consequently, if the executives were unable to sell their homes within 30 days of listing them for sale, Oak bought the homes from the executives for 10% less than the list price. Oak immediately put the homes it purchased up for sale. Each home Oak purchased was sold at a loss. By the end of 1997, Oak did not own any homes, but had suffered a loss totaling $125,000. Oak is uncertain how to report the sale of the homes. Oak has a $32,000 short-term capital gain from stock investment transactions during 1997. What is the nature of the $125,000 loss on the sale of the homes? What is Oak's net capital gain or loss for 1997?

Partial list of research aids:
Rev.Rul. 82–204, 1982–2 CB 192.
Azar Nut Co., 91–1 USTC ¶50,257, 67 AFTR2d 91–987, 931 F.2d 314 (CA-5, 1991).

Use the tax resources of the internet to address the following questions. Do not restrict your search to the World Wide Web, but include a review of newsgroups and general reference materials, practitioner sites and resources, primary sources of the tax law, chat rooms and discussion groups, and other opportunities.

Research Problem 4. Go to a newsgroup frequented by inventors and patent consultants. Answer one of the queries there relative to the tax effects of buying and selling patents, receiving royalties thereon, or otherwise investing in new technology.

Research Problem 5. Download the text of one of the landmark Supreme Court cases defining capital asset status.

TEAM PROJECT: ARTHUR ANDERSEN TAX CHALLENGE CASES

For more information on the Arthur Andersen Tax Challenge Cases, refer to Chapter 1, page 1–38.

Information related to tax issues and problems that are discussed in this chapter may be found in the

Day and Ball case on pages 19 and 22
Miller case on pages 11, 20, 36, and 37

Read and analyze the case you have been assigned and *identify* any issues and problems that are related to material covered in this chapter. If the information provided in the case is complete, prepare answers for this part of the case at this time. If you need information that is contained in the later parts of the case, write a memo summarizing the questions or problems so you can prepare a complete answer at a later date.

CHAPTER

17

PROPERTY TRANSACTIONS: SECTION 1231 AND RECAPTURE PROVISIONS

LEARNING OBJECTIVES

After completing Chapter 17, you should be able to:

1. Understand the rationale for and the nature and treatment of gains and losses from the disposition of business assets.

2. Distinguish § 1231 assets from ordinary assets and capital assets and calculate the § 1231 gain or loss.

3. Determine when § 1245 recapture applies and how it is computed.

4. Determine when § 1250 recapture applies and how it is computed.

5. Understand considerations common to §§ 1245 and 1250.

6. Apply the special recapture provisions for related parties and IDC and be aware of the special recapture provision for corporations.

7. Describe and apply the reporting procedures for §§ 1231, 1245, and 1250.

8. Identify tax planning opportunities associated with §§ 1231, 1245, and 1250.

OUTLINE

Section 1231 Assets, 17–3
Relationship to Capital Assets, 17–3
Justification for Favorable Tax Treatment, 17–4
Property Included, 17–5
Property Excluded, 17–5
Special Rules for Certain § 1231 Assets, 17–5
General Procedure for § 1231 Computation, 17–8
Section 1245 Recapture, 17–12
Section 1245 Property, 17–14
Observations on § 1245, 17–15
Section 1250 Recapture, 17–16

Computing Recapture on Nonresidential Real Property, 17–16
Computing Recapture on Residential Rental Housing, 17–18
Section 1250 Recapture Situations, 17–19
Considerations Common to §§ 1245 and 1250, 17–20
Exceptions, 17–20
Other Applications, 17–21
Special Recapture Provisions, 17–23
Special Recapture for Corporations, 17–23

Gain from Sale of Depreciable Property between Certain Related Parties, 17–23
Intangible Drilling Costs, 17–23
Reporting Procedures, 17–24
Tax Planning Considerations, 17–29
Timing of § 1231 Gain, 17–29
Timing of Recapture, 17–29
Postponing and Shifting Recapture, 17–29
Avoiding Recapture, 17–30

Generic Motors Corporation sold machinery, office furniture, and unneeded production plants for $100 million last year. The corporation's disposition of these assets resulted in $60 million of gains and $13 million of losses. How are these gains and losses treated for tax purposes? Do any special tax rules apply? Could any of the gains and losses receive capital gain or loss treatment? This chapter answers these questions by explaining how to *classify* gains and losses from the disposition of assets that are used in the business rather than held for resale. Chapter 8 discussed how to *depreciate* such assets. Chapters 14 and 15 discussed how to determine the *adjusted basis* and the *amount* of gain or loss from their disposition.

A long-term capital gain was defined in Chapter 16 as the recognized gain from the sale or exchange of a capital asset held for the required long-term holding period.[1] This chapter is concerned with classification under § 1231, which applies to the sale or exchange of business properties and to certain involuntary conversions. The business properties are not capital assets because they are depreciable and/or are real property used in business or for the production of income. Section 1221(2) provides that such assets are not capital assets. Nonetheless, these business properties may be held for long periods of time and may be sold at a gain. Congress decided many years ago that such assets deserved *limited* capital gain–type treatment. Unfortunately, this limited capital gain–type treatment is very complex and difficult to understand.

Because the limited capital gain–type treatment sometimes gives too much tax advantage if assets are eligible for depreciation (or cost recovery), certain recapture rules may remove the capital gain treatment when depreciation is taken. Thus, this chapter also covers the recapture provisions that tax as ordinary income certain gains that might otherwise qualify for long-term capital gain treatment.

---

[1] The long-term holding period is more than one year.

TAX IN THE NEWS

READ THE FINE PRINT TO FIND THE TRUE TAX TREATMENT

During the 1996 presidential campaign, both the Republican and the Democratic candidate proposed a reduction in the tax rate on long-term capital gains. Only a very careful reading of the proposed tax legislation revealed that this tax break would not be available for most gains from the disposition of business fixed assets because these gains are generally taxed as ordinary gains.

SECTION 1231 ASSETS

RELATIONSHIP TO CAPITAL ASSETS

1 LEARNING OBJECTIVE
Understand the rationale for and the nature and treatment of gains and losses from the disposition of business assets.

Depreciable property and real property used in business are not capital assets.[2] Thus, the recognized gains from the disposition of such property (principally machinery, equipment, buildings, and land) would appear to be ordinary income rather than capital gain. Due to § 1231, however, *net gain* from the disposition of such property is sometimes *treated* as *long-term capital gain*. A long-term holding period requirement must be met; the disposition must generally be from a sale, exchange, or involuntary conversion; and certain recapture provisions must be satisfied for this result to occur. Section 1231 may also apply to involuntary conversions of capital assets. Since an involuntary conversion is not a sale or exchange, such a disposition would not normally result in a capital gain.

If the disposition of depreciable property and real property used in business results in a *net loss*, § 1231 *treats* the *loss* as an *ordinary loss* rather than as a capital loss. Ordinary losses are fully deductible *for* adjusted gross income (AGI). Capital losses are offset by capital gains, and, if any loss remains, the loss is deductible to the extent of $3,000 per year for individuals and currently is not deductible at all by regular corporations. It seems, therefore, that § 1231 provides the *best* of both potential results: net gain may be treated as long-term capital gain, and net loss is treated as ordinary loss.

EXAMPLE 1
Roberto sells business land and building at a $5,000 gain and business equipment at a $3,000 loss. Both properties were held for the long-term holding period. Roberto's net gain is $2,000, and that net gain may (depending on various recapture rules discussed later in this chapter) be treated as a long-term capital gain under § 1231. ▼

EXAMPLE 2
Samantha sells business equipment at a $10,000 loss and business land at a $2,000 gain. Both properties were held for the long-term holding period. Samantha's net loss is $8,000, and that net loss is an ordinary loss. ▼

---
[2] § 1221(2).

The rules regarding § 1231 treatment do *not* apply to *all* business property. Important in this regard are the holding period requirements and the fact that the property must be either depreciable property or real estate used in business. Nor is § 1231 necessarily limited to business property. Transactions involving certain capital assets may fall into the § 1231 category. Thus, § 1231 singles out only some types of business property.

As discussed in Chapter 16, there is beneficial tax treatment for long-term capital gains. Section 1231 requires netting of **§ 1231 gains and losses.** If the result is a gain, it may be treated as a long-term capital gain. The net gain is added to the "real" long-term capital gains (if any) and netted with capital losses (if any). Thus, the net § 1231 gain may eventually be eligible for beneficial capital gain treatment or help avoid the unfavorable net capital loss result. The § 1231 gain and loss netting may result in a loss. In this case, the loss is an ordinary loss and is deductible *for* AGI. Finally, § 1231 assets are treated the same as capital assets for purposes of the appreciated property charitable contribution provisions (refer to Chapter 10).

JUSTIFICATION FOR FAVORABLE TAX TREATMENT

The favorable capital gain/ordinary loss treatment sanctioned by § 1231 can be explained by examining several historical developments. Before 1938, business property had been included in the definition of capital assets. Thus, if such property was sold for a loss (not an unlikely possibility during the depression years), a capital loss resulted. If, however, the property was depreciable and could be retained for its estimated useful life, much (if not all) of its costs could be recovered in the form of depreciation. Because the allowance for depreciation was fully deductible whereas capital losses were not, the tax law favored those who did not dispose of an asset. Congress recognized this inequity when it removed business property from the capital asset classification. During the period 1938–1942, therefore, all such gains and losses were ordinary gains and losses.

With the advent of World War II, two developments in particular forced Congress to reexamine the situation regarding business assets. First, the sale of business assets at a gain was discouraged because the gain would be ordinary income. Gains were common because the war effort had inflated prices. Second, taxpayers who did not want to sell their assets often were required to because the government acquired them through condemnation. Often, as a result of the condemnation awards, taxpayers who were forced to part with their property experienced large gains and were deprived of the benefits of future depreciation deductions. Of course, the condemnations constituted involuntary conversions, so taxpayers could defer the gain by timely reinvestment in property that was "similar or related in service or use." But where was such property to be found in view of wartime restrictions and other governmental condemnations? The end result did not seem equitable: a large ordinary gain due to government action and no possibility of deferral due to government restrictions.

In recognition of these conditions, in 1942, Congress eased the tax bite on the disposition of some business property by allowing preferential capital gain treatment. Thus, the present scheme of § 1231 and the dichotomy of capital gain/ordinary loss treatment evolved from a combination of economic considerations existing in 1938 and 1942.

LEARNING OBJECTIVE 2
Distinguish § 1231 assets from ordinary assets and capital assets and calculate the § 1231 gain or loss.

PROPERTY INCLUDED

Section 1231 property includes the following:

- Depreciable or real property used in business or for the production of income (principally machinery and equipment, buildings, and land).
- Timber, coal, or domestic iron ore to which § 631 applies.
- Livestock held for draft, breeding, dairy, or sporting purposes.
- Unharvested crops on land used in business.
- Certain *purchased* intangible assets (such as patents and goodwill) that are eligible for amortization.

PROPERTY EXCLUDED

Section 1231 property does *not* include the following:

- Property not held for the long-term holding period. Since the benefit of § 1231 is long-term capital gain treatment, the holding period must correspond to the more-than-one-year holding period that applies to capital assets. Livestock must be held at least 12 months (24 months in some cases). Unharvested crops do not have to be held for the required long-term holding period, but the land must be held for the long-term holding period.
- Property where casualty losses exceed casualty gains for the taxable year. If a taxpayer has a net casualty loss, the individual casualty gains and losses are treated as ordinary gains and losses.
- Inventory and property held primarily for sale to customers.
- Copyrights; literary, musical, or artistic compositions, etc.; and certain U.S. government publications.
- Accounts receivable and notes receivable arising in the ordinary course of the trade or business.

SPECIAL RULES FOR CERTAIN § 1231 ASSETS

A rather diverse group of assets is included under § 1231. The following discussion summarizes the special rules for some of those assets.

Timber. A taxpayer can *elect* to treat the cutting of timber held for sale or for use in business as a sale or exchange.[3] If the taxpayer makes this election, the transaction qualifies under § 1231. The taxpayer must have owned the timber or a contract to cut it on the first day of the year and for the long-term holding period before the date the cutting takes place. The recognized § 1231 gain or loss is determined at the time the timber is cut and is equal to the difference between the timber's fair market value as of the first day of the taxable year and the adjusted basis for depletion. If a taxpayer sells the timber for more or less than the fair market value as of the first day of the taxable year in which it is cut, the difference is ordinary income or loss.

This provision was enacted to provide preferential treatment relative to the natural growth value of timber, which takes a relatively long time to mature. Congress believed this favorable treatment would encourage reforestation of

---
[3] § 631(a) and Reg. § 1.631–1.

Concept Summary 17-1

Section 1231 Netting Procedure

```
§1231 asset and long-term nonpersonal
use capital asset casualty* gains
         minus
§1231 asset and long-term nonpersonal
use capital asset casualty* losses
```

- **NET GAIN** → Net gain (add to § 1231 gains)
- **NET LOSS** → Items are treated separately:
  - Gains are ordinary income
  - §1231 asset losses are deductible *for* AGI
  - Other losses are deductible *from* AGI

§ 1231 gains minus § 1231 losses
- **NET LOSS** → (items treated separately as above)
- **NET GAIN** → **Lookback Provision:** Net gain is offset against nonrecaptured net §1231 losses from 5 prior tax years
  - Gain offset by lookback losses is ordinary gain
  - Remaining gain is LTCG

*Includes casualties and thefts.

---

timber lands. If a taxpayer disposes of timber held for the long-term holding period, either by sale or under a royalty contract (where the taxpayer retains an economic interest in the property), the disposal is treated as a sale of the timber. Therefore, any gain or loss qualifies under § 1231.

EXAMPLE 3

Several years ago, Tom purchased a tract of land with a substantial stand of trees on it. The land cost $40,000, and the timber cost $100,000. On the first day of 1997, the timber was appraised at $250,000. In August 1997, Tom cut the timber and sold it for $265,000. Tom elects to treat the cutting as a sale or exchange under § 1231. He has a $150,000 § 1231 gain ($250,000 − $100,000) and a $15,000 ordinary gain ($265,000 − $250,000).

What if the timber had been sold for $235,000? Tom would still have a $150,000 § 1231 gain, but would also have a $15,000 ordinary loss. The price for computation of § 1231 gain is the price at the beginning of the year. Any difference between that price and the sales price is ordinary gain or loss. Here, since the price declined by $15,000, Tom has an ordinary loss in that amount. ▼

Livestock. Cattle and horses must be held 24 months or more and other livestock must be held 12 months or more to qualify under § 1231.[4] The primary reason for enacting this provision was the considerable amount of litigation over the character of livestock (whether livestock was held primarily for sale to customers [ordinary income] or for use in a trade or business [§ 1231 property]). Poultry is not livestock for purposes of § 1231.

ETHICAL CONSIDERATIONS

Determining How Long an Asset Has Been Held

George, a dairy farmer sells a milk cow for $12,000. Normally, George does not sell his cows, but he received an offer he could not refuse for this "super milker." George is not sure exactly when the cow was born, but he does know that it is the calf of another cow he owns. Consequently, he has a zero tax basis for the cow that was sold. George owns 500 cows.

When George's tax adviser points out that the cow must have been held 24 months to be eligible for § 1231 treatment, George gets very upset. The tax adviser knows that George's records are a mess. George thinks the cow was born "within the last 27 months." After the tax adviser explains the tax benefits of the sale qualifying for § 1231 treatment, George decides the cow was more than 24 months old.

Section 1231 Assets Disposed of by Casualty or Theft. When § 1231 assets are disposed of by casualty or theft, a special netting rule is applied. For simplicity, the term *casualty* is used to mean both casualty and theft dispositions. First, the casualty gains and losses from § 1231 assets *and* the casualty gains and losses from **long-term nonpersonal use capital assets** are determined. A nonpersonal use capital asset might be an investment painting or a baseball card collection held by a nondealer in baseball cards.

Next, the § 1231 asset casualty gains and losses and the nonpersonal use capital asset casualty gains and losses are netted together (see Concept Summary 17–1). If the result is a *net loss,* the § 1231 casualty gains and the nonpersonal use capital asset casualty gains are treated as ordinary gains, the § 1231 casualty losses are deductible *for* AGI, and the nonpersonal use capital asset casualty losses are deductible *from* AGI subject to the 2 percent-of-AGI limitation.

If the result of the netting is a *net gain,* the net gain is treated as a § 1231 gain. Thus, a § 1231 asset disposed of by casualty may or may not get § 1231 treatment, depending on whether the netting process results in a gain or a loss. Also, a nonpersonal use capital asset disposed of by casualty may get § 1231 treatment or ordinary treatment, but will not get capital gain or loss treatment!

Personal use property casualty gains and losses are not subject to the § 1231 rules. If the result of netting these gains and losses is a gain, the net gain is a capital gain. If the netting results in a loss, the net loss is a deduction *from* AGI to the extent it exceeds 10 percent of AGI.

---

[4] Note that the holding period is "12 months or more" and not "more than 12 months."

TAX IN THE NEWS

HURRICANE BLOWS IN A GAIN

During the fall of 1996, a severe hurricane struck Wilmington, North Carolina, destroying the equipment in a business owner's store. Since the store equipment was insured for its replacement value and was fully depreciated, the store owner had a gain from this casualty event. After checking with her tax adviser, she realized that the gain was all going to be taxable as ordinary gain because of the depreciation recapture rules. Instead of recognizing the gain, however, she reinvested the insurance proceeds in store equipment and was able to postpone recognition of the gain (a § 1033 involuntary conversion).

Casualties, thefts, and condemnations are *involuntary conversions*. Involuntary conversion gains may be deferred if conversion proceeds are reinvested; involuntary conversion losses are recognized currently (refer to Chapter 15) regardless of whether the conversion proceeds are reinvested. Thus, the special netting process discussed above for casualties and thefts would not include gains that are not currently recognizable because the insurance proceeds are reinvested.

The special netting process for casualties and thefts also does not include condemnation gains and losses. Consequently, a § 1231 asset disposed of by condemnation will receive § 1231 treatment. This variation between recognized casualty and condemnation gains and losses sheds considerable light on what § 1231 is all about. Section 1231 has no effect on whether or not *realized* gain or loss is recognized. Instead, § 1231 merely dictates how such *recognized* gain or loss is *classified* (ordinary, capital, or § 1231) under certain conditions.

Personal use property condemnation gains and losses are not subject to the § 1231 rules. The gains are capital gains (because personal use property is a capital asset), and the losses are nondeductible because they arise from the disposition of personal use property.

GENERAL PROCEDURE FOR § 1231 COMPUTATION

The tax treatment of § 1231 gains and losses depends on the results of a rather complex *netting* procedure. The steps in this netting procedure are as follows.

Step 1: Casualty Netting. Net all recognized long-term gains and losses from casualties of § 1231 assets and nonpersonal use capital assets. Casualty gains result when insurance proceeds exceed the adjusted basis of the property. This casualty netting is beneficial because if there is a net gain, the gain may receive long-term capital gain treatment. If there is a net loss, it receives ordinary loss treatment.

   a. If the casualty gains exceed the casualty losses, add the excess to the other § 1231 gains for the taxable year.
   b. If the casualty losses exceed the casualty gains, exclude all casualty losses and gains from further § 1231 computation. If this is the case, all casualty gains are ordinary income. Section 1231 asset casualty losses are deductible *for* AGI. Other casualty losses are deductible *from* AGI.

Step 2: § 1231 Netting. After adding any net casualty gain from Step 1a to the other § 1231 gains and losses (including recognized § 1231 asset condemnation gains and losses), net all § 1231 gains and losses.

   a. If the gains exceed the losses, the net gain is offset by the "lookback" nonrecaptured § 1231 losses (see below) from the five prior tax years. To the extent of this offset, the net § 1231 gain is classified as ordinary gain. Any remaining gain is long-term capital gain.
   b. If the losses exceed the gains, all gains are ordinary income. Section 1231 asset losses are deductible *for* AGI. Other casualty losses are deductible *from* AGI.

Step 3: § 1231 Lookback Provision. The net § 1231 gain from Step 2a is offset by the nonrecaptured net § 1231 losses for the five preceding taxable years. For 1997, the lookback years are 1992, 1993, 1994, 1995, and 1996. To the extent of the nonrecaptured net § 1231 loss, the current year net § 1231 gain is ordinary income. The *nonrecaptured* net § 1231 losses are those that have not already been used to offset net § 1231 gains. Only the net § 1231 gain exceeding this net § 1231 loss carryforward is given long-term capital gain treatment. Concept Summary 17–1 summarizes the § 1231 computational procedure. Examples 6 and 7 illustrate the **§ 1231 lookback** provision.

Examples 4 through 7 illustrate the application of the § 1231 computation procedure.

EXAMPLE 4

During 1997, Ross had $125,000 of AGI before considering the following recognized gains and losses:

Capital Gains and Losses	
Long-term capital gain	$3,000
Long-term capital loss	(400)
Short-term capital gain	1,000
Short-term capital loss	(200)
Casualties	
Theft of diamond ring (owned four months)	($800)*
Fire damage to personal residence (owned 10 years)	(400)*
Gain from insurance recovery on fire loss to business building (owned two years)	200
§ 1231 Gains and Losses from Depreciable Business Assets Held Long Term	
Asset A	$ 300
Asset B	1,100
Asset C	(500)
Gains and Losses from Sale of Depreciable Business Assets Held Short Term	
Asset D	$ 200
Asset E	(300)

*As adjusted for the $100 floor on personal casualty losses.

Ross had no net § 1231 losses in tax years before 1997.

Disregarding the recapture of depreciation (discussed later in the chapter), Ross's gains and losses receive the following tax treatment:

- The diamond ring and the residence are personal use assets. Therefore, these casualties are not § 1231 transactions. The $800 (ring) plus $400 (residence) losses are potentially deductible *from* AGI. However, the total loss of $1,200 does not exceed 10% of AGI. Thus, only the business building (a § 1231 asset) casualty gain remains. The netting of the § 1231 asset and nonpersonal use capital asset casualty gains and losses contains only one item—the $200 gain from the business building. Consequently, there is a net gain and that gain is treated as a § 1231 gain (added to the § 1231 gains).
- The gains from § 1231 transactions (Assets A, B, and C and the § 1231 asset casualty gain) exceed the losses by $1,100 ($1,600 − $500). This excess is a long-term capital gain and is added to Ross's other long-term capital gains.
- Ross's net long-term capital gain is $3,700 ($3,000 + $1,100 from § 1231 transactions − $400 long-term capital loss). Ross's net short-term capital gain is $800 ($1,000 − $200). The result is capital gain net income of $4,500. The $3,700 net long-term capital gain portion is eligible for beneficial capital gain treatment, and the $800 net short-term capital gain is subject to tax as ordinary income.[5]
- Ross treats the gain and loss from Assets D and E (depreciable business assets held for less than the long-term holding period) as ordinary gain and loss.

Results of the Gains and Losses on Ross's Tax Computation

NLTCG	$ 3,700
NSTCG	800
Ordinary gain from sale of Asset D	200
Ordinary loss from sale of Asset E	(300)
AGI from other sources	125,000
AGI	$129,400

- Ross will have personal use property casualty losses of $1,200 [$800 (diamond ring) + $400 (personal residence)]. A personal use property casualty loss is deductible only to the extent it exceeds 10% of AGI. Thus, none of the $1,200 is deductible ($129,400 × 10% = $12,940). ▼

EXAMPLE 5

Assume the same facts as in Example 4, except the loss from Asset C was $1,700 instead of $500.

- The treatment of the casualty losses is the same as in Example 4.
- The losses from § 1231 transactions now exceed the gains by $100 ($1,700 − $1,600). As a result, the gains from Assets A and B and the § 1231 asset casualty gain are ordinary income, and the loss from Asset C is a deduction *for* AGI (a business loss). The same result can be achieved by simply treating the $100 net loss as a deduction *for* AGI.
- Capital gain net income is $3,400 ($2,600 long-term + $800 short-term). The $2,600 net long-term capital gain portion is eligible for beneficial capital gain treatment, and the $800 net short-term capital gain is subject to tax as ordinary income.

---

[5]Ross's taxable income (unless the itemized deductions and the personal exemption and dependency deductions are extremely large) will put him in at least the 31% bracket. Thus, the 28% alternative tax computation will yield a lower tax. See Example 36 in Chapter 16.

Results of the Gains and Losses on Ross's Tax Computation

NLTCG	$ 2,600
NSTCG	800
Net ordinary loss on Assets A, B, and C and § 1231 casualty gain	(100)
Ordinary gain from sale of Asset D	200
Ordinary loss from sale of Asset E	(300)
AGI from other sources	125,000
AGI	$128,200

- None of the personal use property casualty losses will be deductible since $1,200 does not exceed 10% of $128,200. ▼

EXAMPLE 6 Assume the same facts as in Example 4, except that Ross has a $700 nonrecaptured net § 1231 loss from 1996.

- The treatment of the casualty losses is the same as in Example 4.
- The 1997 net § 1231 gain of $1,100 is treated as ordinary income to the extent of the 1996 nonrecaptured § 1231 loss of $700. The remaining $400 net § 1231 gain is a long-term capital gain and is added to Ross's other long-term capital gains.
- Ross's net long-term capital gain is $3,000 ($3,000 + $400 from § 1231 transactions − $400 long-term capital loss). Ross's net short-term capital gain is still $800 ($1,000 − $200). The result is capital gain net income of $3,800. The $3,000 net long-term capital gain portion is eligible for beneficial capital gain treatment, and the $800 net short-term capital gain is subject to tax as ordinary income.

Results of the Gains and Losses on Ross's Tax Computation

NLTCG	$ 3,000
NSTCG	800
Ordinary gain from recapture of § 1231 losses	700
Ordinary gain from sale of Asset D	200
Ordinary loss from sale of Asset E	(300)
AGI from other sources	125,000
AGI	$129,400

- None of the personal use property casualty losses will be deductible since $1,200 does not exceed 10% of $129,400. ▼

EXAMPLE 7 Assume the same facts as in Example 4, except that Ross had a net § 1231 loss of $2,700 in 1995 and a net § 1231 gain of $300 in 1996.

- The treatment of the casualty losses is the same as in Example 4.
- The 1995 net § 1231 loss of $2,700 will have carried over to 1996 and been offset against the 1996 net § 1231 gain of $300. Thus, the $300 gain will have been classified as ordinary income, and $2,400 of nonrecaptured 1995 net § 1231 loss will carry over to 1997. The 1997 net § 1231 gain of $1,100 will be offset against this loss, resulting in $1,100 of ordinary income. The nonrecaptured net § 1231 loss of $1,300 ($2,400 − $1,100) carries over to 1998.

- Capital gain net income is $3,400 ($2,600 net long-term capital gain + $800 net short-term capital gain). The $2,600 net long-term capital gain portion is eligible for beneficial capital gain treatment, and the $800 net short-term capital gain is subject to tax as ordinary income.

Results of the Gains and Losses on Ross's Tax Computation	
NLTCG	$ 2,600
NSTCG	800
Ordinary gain from recapture of § 1231 losses	1,100
Ordinary gain from sale of Asset D	200
Ordinary loss from sale of Asset E	(300)
AGI from other sources	125,000
AGI	$129,400

- None of the personal use property casualty losses will be deductible since $1,200 does not exceed 10% of $129,400. ▼

SECTION 1245 RECAPTURE

3 LEARNING OBJECTIVE
Determine when § 1245 recapture applies and how it is computed.

Now that the basic rules of § 1231 have been introduced, it is time to add some complications. The Code contains two major *recapture* provisions—§§ 1245 and 1250. These provisions cause *gain* to be treated *initially* as ordinary gain. Thus, what may appear to be a § 1231 gain is ordinary gain instead. These recapture provisions may also cause a gain in a nonpersonal use casualty to be *initially* ordinary gain rather than casualty gain. Classifying gains (and losses) properly initially is important because improper initial classification may lead to incorrect mixing and matching of gains and losses. This section discusses the § 1245 recapture rules, and the next section discusses the § 1250 recapture rules.

ETHICAL CONSIDERATIONS

Does Applying the Recapture Rules Make a Difference?

Due to their complexity, the § 1245 and § 1250 recapture rules require careful study to obtain a complete understanding. It is much easier just to assume that the sale of business fixed assets results in capital gain or loss. Certainly, most taxpayers expect that result. Arnold, an overworked tax practitioner, concluded that quite often taxable income and tax liability are not affected by whether the recapture rules are properly applied or not. Therefore, he hypothesized that if ultimately there is *no difference* between tax liability with proper handling of recapture and tax liability without proper handling of recapture, is it not logical and practical for him simply to ignore the recapture rules?

Section 1245 requires taxpayers to treat all gain as ordinary gain unless the property is disposed of for more than was paid for it. This result is accomplished by requiring that all gain be treated as ordinary gain to the extent of the depreciation taken on the property disposed of. Section 1231 gain results only when the property is disposed of for more than its original cost. The excess of the

CHAPTER 17 Property Transactions: Section 1231 and Recapture Provisions 17–13

TAX IN THE NEWS

HARRIED CPA EXPLAINS THE UNEXPLAINABLE

During the spring of 1997, Judy Warren spent a very long day answering taxpayer questions on a radio call-in show. One caller had recently sold business equipment that had been held for more than one year. The caller thought there was a gain on the property disposition and simply wanted to know whether the gain would be taxed at ordinary income rates or capital gain rates. After the first four minutes of Judy's (necessarily) complex explanation, the show's moderator interjected, "I'm sure the rest of Judy's answer will be fascinating to our caller, but enough is enough for the rest of us. It's time for a commercial break."

sales price over the original cost is § 1231 gain. Section 1245 applies primarily to non-real estate property such as machinery, trucks, and office furniture. Section 1245 does not apply if property is disposed of at a loss. Generally, the loss will be a § 1231 loss unless the form of the disposition is a casualty.

EXAMPLE 8

Alice purchased a $100,000 business machine and deducted $70,000 depreciation before selling it for $80,000. If it were not for § 1245, the $50,000 gain would be § 1231 gain ($80,000 amount realized − $30,000 adjusted basis). Section 1245 prevents this potentially favorable result by treating as ordinary income (not as § 1231 gain) any gain to the extent of depreciation taken. In this example, the entire $50,000 gain would be ordinary income. If Alice had sold the machine for $120,000, she would have a gain of $90,000 ($120,000 amount realized − $30,000 adjusted basis). The § 1245 gain would be $70,000 (equal to the depreciation taken), and the § 1231 gain would be $20,000 (equal to the excess of the sales price over the original cost). ▼

Section 1245 recapture provides, in general, that the portion of recognized gain from the sale or other disposition of § 1245 property that represents depreciation (including § 167 depreciation, § 168 cost recovery, § 179 immediate expensing, and § 197 amortization) is *recaptured* as ordinary income. Thus, in Example 8, $50,000 of the $70,000 depreciation taken is recaptured as ordinary income when the business machine is sold for $80,000. Only $50,000 is recaptured rather than $70,000 because Alice is only required to recognize § 1245 recapture ordinary gain equal to the lower of the depreciation taken or the gain recognized.

The method of depreciation (e.g., accelerated or straight-line) does not matter. All depreciation taken is potentially subject to recapture. Thus, § 1245 recapture is often referred to as *full recapture*. Any remaining gain after subtracting the amount recaptured as ordinary income will usually be § 1231 gain. The remaining gain would be casualty gain if it were disposed of in a casualty event. If the business machine in Example 8 had been disposed of by casualty and the $80,000 received had been an insurance recovery, Alice would still have a gain of $50,000, and the gain would still be recaptured by § 1245 as ordinary gain. The § 1245 recapture rules apply before there is any casualty gain. Since all the $50,000 gain is recaptured, no casualty gain arises from the casualty.

Although § 1245 applies primarily to non-real estate property, it does apply to certain real estate. Nonresidential real estate acquired after 1980 and before 1987 and for which accelerated depreciation (the statutory percentage method of the

EXAMPLE 3 The ESOP of Gray Company borrows $100,000 from City Bank in January 1997. The loan is secured by the stock interest and is guaranteed by the company. The ESOP buys stock for the trust from a shareholder of Gray Company for $100,000. The shareholder has owned the stock for four years. The shares are then allocated among the employees' retirement accounts. The shareholder obtains capital gain treatment on the sale or can elect nonrecognition treatment if qualified replacement securities are purchased during a 15-month period. Gray Company makes deductible contributions to the ESOP, which, in turn, pays off the loan. ▼

QUALIFICATION REQUIREMENTS

2 LEARNING OBJECTIVE
Identify the qualification requirements for qualified plans.

To be *qualified*, and thereby to receive favorable tax treatment, a plan must satisfy the following requirements:

- Exclusive benefit requirement.
- Nondiscrimination requirements.
- Participation and coverage requirements.
- Vesting requirements.
- Distribution requirements.

These qualification rules are highly technical and numerous. Thus, an employer should submit a retirement plan to the IRS for a determination letter regarding the qualified status of the plan and trust. A favorable determination letter may be expected within 6 to 12 months, indicating that the plan meets the qualification requirements and that the trust is tax-exempt. However, the continued qualification of the plan depends upon its actual operations. Therefore, the operations of the plan should be reviewed periodically.

Exclusive Benefit Requirement. A pension, profit sharing, or stock bonus trust must be created by an employer for the exclusive benefit of employees or their beneficiaries. Under a prudent person concept, the IRS specifies four investment conditions for meeting the *exclusive benefit* requirement:[10]

- The cost of the investment must not exceed the fair market value at the time of purchase.
- A fair return commensurate with prevailing rates must be provided.
- Sufficient liquidity must be maintained to permit distributions in accordance with the terms of the qualified plan.
- The safeguards and diversity that a prudent investor would adhere to must be present.

Nondiscrimination Requirements. The contributions and benefits under a plan must *not discriminate* in favor of highly compensated employees. A plan is not considered discriminatory merely because the contributions and benefits on behalf of the employees are uniformly related to their compensation.[11] For example, a pension plan that provides for the allocation of employer contributions based upon a flat 3 percent of each employee's compensation would not be discriminatory even though highly paid employees receive greater benefits.

Qualified plans may be *integrated* with Social Security (employer FICA contributions for covered employees may be taken into account) to avoid giving lower-level employees proportionately greater benefits or contributions. Integrated plans may not reduce a participant's benefits or contributions to less than one-half of what they would have been without integration.

---

[10] § 401(a); Rev.Rul. 65–178, 1965–2 C.B. 94, and Rev.Rul. 73–380, 1973–2 C.B. 124.

[11] §§ 401(a)(4) and (5).

Participation and Coverage Requirements. A qualified plan must provide, at a minimum, that all employees in the covered group who are 21 years of age are eligible to participate after completing one year of service. A year of service is generally defined as the completion of 1,000 hours of service within a measuring period of 12 consecutive months. As an alternative, where the plan provides that 100 percent of an employee's accrued benefits will be vested upon entering the plan, the employee's participation may be postponed until the later of age 21 or two years from the date of employment.[12] Once the age and service requirements are met, an employee must begin participating no later than the *earlier* of the following:

- The first day of the first plan year beginning after the date upon which the requirements were satisfied.
- Six months after the date on which the requirements were satisfied.[13]

EXAMPLE 4 Coffee Corporation has a calendar year retirement plan covering its employees. The corporation adopts the most restrictive eligibility rules permitted. Wilma, age 21, is hired on January 31, 1996, and meets the service requirement over the next 12 months (completes at least 1,000 hours by January 31, 1997). Wilma must be included in this plan no later than July 31, 1997, because the 6-month limitation would be applicable. If the company had adopted the two-year participation rule, Wilma must be included in the plan no later than July 31, 1998. ▼

Since a qualified plan must be primarily for the benefit of employees and be nondiscriminatory, the plan has to cover a reasonable percentage of the company employees. A plan will be qualified only if it satisfies one of the following tests:[14]

- The plan benefits at least 70 percent of all non-highly compensated employees (the *percentage test*).
- The plan benefits a percentage of non-highly compensated employees equal to at least 70 percent of the percentage of highly compensated employees benefiting under the plan (the *ratio test*).
- The plan meets the *average benefits test*.

If a company has no highly compensated employees, the retirement plan will automatically satisfy the coverage rules.

To satisfy the *average benefits test*, the plan must benefit any employees who qualify under a classification set up by the employer and found by the Secretary of the Treasury not to be discriminatory in favor of highly compensated employees (the classification test). In addition, the average benefit percentage for non-highly compensated employees must be at least 70 percent of the average benefit percentage for highly compensated employees. The *average benefit percentage* means, with respect to any group of employees, the average of the benefit percentages calculated separately for each employee in the group. The term *benefit percentage* means the employer-provided contributions (including forfeitures) or benefits of an employee under all qualified plans of the employer, expressed as a percentage of that employee's compensation.

An employee is a **highly compensated employee** if, at any time during the year or the preceding year, the employee satisfies *either* of the following:[15]

- Was a 5 percent owner of the company.
- Received more than $80,000 (in 1996) in annual compensation from the employer *and* was a member of the top-paid group of the employer.[16]

---

[12] §§ 410(a)(1)(A) and (B).
[13] § 410(a)(4).
[14] § 410(b).
[15] §§ 401(a)(4) and 414(q).
[16] The $80,000 amount is to be indexed annually.

TABLE 19–1
Three-to-Seven-Year Vesting

Years of Service	Nonforfeitable Percentage
3	20%
4	40%
5	60%
6	80%
7 or more	100%

The top-paid group clause is applicable only if the employer elects to have it apply. An employee whose compensation is in the top 20 percent of the employees is a member of the top-paid group.

An additional *minimum participation* test must also be met. A plan must cover at least 40 percent of all employees or, if fewer, at least 50 employees on one representative day of the plan year. In determining all employees, nonresident aliens, certain union members, and employees not fulfilling the minimum age or years-of-service requirement of the plan may be excluded.[17]

EXAMPLE 5 Rust Corporation's retirement plan meets the 70% test (the percentage test) because 70% of all non-highly compensated employees are benefited. The company has 100 employees, but only 38 of these employees are covered by the plan. Therefore, this retirement plan does not meet the minimum participation requirement. ▼

Vesting Requirements. An employee's right to accrued benefits derived from his or her own contributions must be nonforfeitable from the date of contribution. The accrued benefits derived from employer contributions must be nonforfeitable in accordance with one of two alternative minimum vesting schedules. The purpose of the **vesting requirements** is to protect an employee who has worked a reasonable period of time for an employer from losing employer contributions because of being fired or changing jobs.

A plan will not be a qualified plan unless a participant's employer-provided benefits vest at least as rapidly as under one of *two alternative minimum vesting schedules*. To satisfy the *first alternative*, a participant must have a nonforfeitable right to 100 percent of his or her accrued benefits derived from employer contributions upon completion of five years of service (five-year or cliff vesting). The *second alternative* is satisfied if a participant has a nonforfeitable right at least equal to a percentage of the accrued benefits derived from employer contributions as depicted in Table 19–1 (graded vesting). Of the two alternatives, cliff vesting minimizes administration expenses for a company and provides more vesting for a long-term employee. Neither vesting schedule applies to top-heavy plans.

EXAMPLE 6 Mitch has six years of service completed as of February 2, 1997, his employment anniversary date. If his defined benefit plan has a five-year (cliff) vesting schedule, 100% of Mitch's accrued benefits are vested. If, however, the plan uses the graded vesting rule, Mitch's nonforfeitable percentage is 80%. ▼

Distribution Requirements. Uniform *minimum distribution rules* exist for all qualified defined benefit and defined contribution plans, Individual Retirement

---
[17] §§ 401(a)(26) and 410(b)(3) and (4).

Accounts (IRAs) and annuities, unfunded deferred compensation plans of state and local governments and tax-exempt employers, and tax-sheltered custodial accounts and annuities. After 1996, distributions to a participant must begin by April 1 of the calendar year *following the later* of (1) the calendar year in which the employee attains age 70½ or (2) the calendar year in which the employee retires. Thus, an employee can delay receiving distributions until retirement. However, distributions to a 5 percent owner or an IRA holder must begin no later than April 1 of the calendar year *following* the year in which the 5 percent owner or the IRA holder reaches age 70½.[18]

Minimum annual distributions must be made over the life of the participant or the lives of the participant and a designated individual beneficiary. The amount of the required minimum distribution for a particular year is determined by dividing the account balance as of December 31 of the prior year by the applicable life expectancy. The life expectancy of the owner and his or her beneficiary is based upon the expected return multiples in the Regulations, using ages attained within the calendar year the participant reaches age 70½.[19]

EXAMPLE 7

Beth reaches age 70½ in 1997, and she will also be age 71 in 1997. Her retirement account has a balance of $120,000 on December 31, 1996. If Beth is retired, a 5 percent owner, or an IRA holder, she must withdraw $7,843 for the 1997 calendar year, assuming her multiple is 15.3 ($120,000 ÷ 15.3). This distribution need not be made until April 1, 1998, but a second distribution must be made by December 31, 1998. ▼

Failure to make a minimum required distribution to a particular participant results in a 50 percent nondeductible excise tax on the excess in any taxable year of the amount that should have been distributed over the amount that actually was distributed. The tax is imposed on the individual required to take the distribution (the payee).[20] The Secretary of the Treasury is authorized to waive the tax for a given taxpayer year if the taxpayer is able to establish that the shortfall is due to reasonable error and that reasonable steps are being taken to remedy the shortfall.

If a taxpayer receives an *early distribution* from a qualified retirement plan, a 10 percent additional tax is levied on the full amount of any distribution includible in gross income.[21] For this purpose, the term qualified retirement plan includes a qualified defined benefit plan or defined contribution plan, a tax-sheltered annuity or custodial account, or an IRA. Certain distributions, however, are *not* treated as early distributions:

- Made on or after the date the employee attains age 59½.
- Made to a beneficiary (or the estate of an employee) on or after the death of the employee.
- Attributable to the employee's being disabled.
- Made as part of a scheduled series of substantially equal periodic payments (made not less frequently than annually) for the life of the participant (or the joint lives of the participant and the participant's beneficiary).
- Made to an employee after separation from service because of early retirement under the plan after attaining age 55. This exception to early distribution treatment does not apply to an IRA.
- Used to pay medical expenses to the extent that the expenses are deductible under § 213 (determined regardless of whether or not the taxpayer itemizes deductions).

---

[18] § 401(a)(9).
[19] Reg. § 1.72–9. Refer to Chapter 4.
[20] § 4974(a).
[21] § 72(t). See Ltr.Rul. 8837071.

The 15 percent excise tax imposed on excess distributions from qualified plans has been suspended for excess distributions received in 1997, 1998, and 1999.[22] Otherwise, the excess distribution tax is levied on the individual with respect to whom the excess distribution is made and is reduced by the amount of the tax imposed on early distributions (to the extent attributable to the excess distribution). An *excess distribution* is the aggregate amount of the retirement distributions during the taxable year for an individual to the extent that amount exceeds the greater of $150,000 or $112,500 (1997 indexed amount is $160,000). Thus, for 1997 the annual limitation is $160,000. Since the indexed $112,500 amount now exceeds the $150,000, the indexed amount is now the annual limit. The following distributions are *not* subject to this limitation:

- Any retirement distribution made after the death of the individual.
- Any retirement distribution payable to an alternate payee in conformance with a qualified domestic relations order.
- Any retirement distribution attributable to the employee's investment in the contract (after-tax contributions).
- Any retirement distribution not included in gross income by reason of a rollover contribution.

If the taxpayer elects lump-sum distribution treatment, the $160,000 limit is applied separately to the lump-sum distribution and is increased to five times the generally applicable limit with respect to that distribution (to $800,000).

EXAMPLE 8

Emily, age 65, has accumulated $960,000 in a defined contribution plan, $105,000 of which represents her own after-tax contributions. Receiving a lump-sum distribution after 1999 (assuming $160,000 indexed amount does not change) would result in an excise tax of $8,250.

Account balance	$ 960,000
Less after-tax contributions	(105,000)
Less lump-sum limitation	(800,000)
Amount subject to tax	$ 55,000
15% excise tax	× .15
Excise tax due	$ 8,250

If Emily receives the distribution in the form of an annuity over her expected lifetime of 20 years, her yearly distributions of $48,000 *plus* related interest would probably be less than the $160,000 annual distribution limit. Note that if the tax year is 1997, the excess distribution excise tax does not apply. ▼

TAX CONSEQUENCES TO THE EMPLOYEE AND EMPLOYER

3 LEARNING OBJECTIVE
Discuss the tax consequences of qualified plans.

In General. Although employer contributions to qualified plans are generally deductible immediately (subject to contribution and deductibility rules), these amounts are not subject to taxation until distributed to employees.[23] If benefits are paid with respect to an employee (to a creditor of the employee, a child of the employee, etc.), the benefits paid are treated as if paid to the employee. When benefits are distributed to employees, or paid with respect to an employee, the employer does not receive another deduction.

The tax benefit to the employee amounts to a substantial tax deferral and may be viewed as an interest-free loan from the government to the trust fund. Another advantage of a qualified plan is that any income earned by the trust is not taxable

---
[22] § 4981A.
[23] § 402(a)(1).

to the trust.[24] Employees, in effect, are taxed on such earnings when they receive the retirement benefits.

The taxation of amounts received by employees in periodic or installment payments is generally subject to the annuity rules in § 72 (refer to Chapter 4). Employee contributions have previously been subject to tax and are therefore included in the employee's *investment in the contract.* Two other alternative options are available for benefit distributions. A taxpayer may roll over the benefits into an IRA or another qualified employer retirement plan.[25] A taxpayer also may receive the distribution in a lump-sum payment.

Lump-Sum Distributions from Qualified Plans. The annuity rules do not apply to a **lump-sum distribution.** All such payments are taxed in one year. Since lump-sum payments have been accumulated over a number of years, bunching retirement benefits into one taxable year may impose a high tax burden because of progressive rates. To overcome this bunching effect, for many years the tax law has provided favorable treatment for certain lump-sum distributions. Major changes were made in the lump-sum distribution rules by TRA of 1986. Transitional provisions allow a participant who reached age 50 before January 1, 1986 (born before 1936) to elect the pre-1987 rules on a limited basis.

Under the pre-1987 rules, the taxable amount is allocated between a capital gain portion and an ordinary income portion (which may be subject to a special 10-year averaging treatment).[26] That portion attributable to the employee's service before 1974 qualifies for capital gain treatment. That portion attributable to the employee's service after 1973 is included as ordinary income when received and may be taxed under the 10-year averaging provision. An employee must be a plan participant for at least five years to take advantage of the 10-year averaging option. It is possible to defer tax on some or all of the distribution, provided that the employee elects to roll over the distribution by transferring the proceeds to an IRA or another qualified employer retirement plan.[27]

An employee may *elect* to treat all of the distribution as ordinary income subject to the 10-year forward averaging provision.[28] In some instances, ordinary income treatment is preferable to long-term capital gain treatment because of the favorable averaging technique.

Special preferential averaging treatment of qualified lump-sum distributions can be used only once during a recipient's lifetime. In the case of a small lump-sum distribution, a recipient may prefer to pay ordinary income tax on the amount and save the averaging election for a larger lump-sum distribution in the future.

To determine the tax on a lump-sum distribution, it is necessary to compute the taxable portion of the distribution by subtracting employee contributions and the net unrealized appreciation in the value of any distributed securities of the employer corporation.[29] The taxable amount is then reduced by a minimum distribution allowance to arrive at the amount that is eligible for the 10-year income averaging provisions.[30] The following portion of the lump-sum distribution is treated as a long-term capital gain:

---

[24] § 501(a).
[25] Refer to the subsequent discussion in this chapter under Individual Retirement Accounts (IRAs).
[26] § 402(e)(1)(C) of the IRC of 1954.
[27] § 402(a)(5).
[28] § 402(e)(4)(L).
[29] Section 402(e)(4)(J) provides that before any distribution a taxpayer may elect not to have this subtraction associated with employer securities apply.
[30] Section 402(e)(1)(D) defines the *minimum distribution allowance* as the smaller of $10,000 or one-half of the total taxable amount of the lump-sum distribution, reduced by 20% of the amount, if any, by which such total taxable amount exceeds $20,000. Thus, for lump-sum distributions of $70,000 or more, there will be no minimum distribution allowance.

$$\text{Taxable amount} \times \frac{\text{Years of service before 1974}}{\text{Total years of service}}$$
(computed without being reduced by the minimum distribution allowance)

The applicable capital gain rate is 20 percent.

After 1986, subject to the transition rule for recipients born before 1936 mentioned earlier, the 10-year forward averaging rule for lump-sum distributions is replaced by a 5-year forward averaging rule.[31] Only one lump-sum distribution received after age 59½ is eligible for the averaging treatment. Furthermore, capital gain treatment for lump-sum distributions (associated with participation before 1974) is repealed.

EXAMPLE 9

Esteban, age 65 and married, retires at the end of 1997 and receives a lump-sum distribution of $100,000 from his company's profit sharing plan. This plan includes $5,000 of his own contributions and $10,000 of unrealized appreciation on his employer's common stock. Esteban was a participant in the plan for 25 years. Since Esteban attained age 50 before January 1, 1986, he is eligible to elect the pre-1987 10-year forward averaging technique (using 1986 rates and the **zero bracket amount**). Refer to the computation model in Concept Summary 19–2.

Taxable portion of the lump-sum distribution		$85,000
Less: Minimum distribution allowance (½ of the taxable amount up to $20,000)	$ 10,000	
Less: 20% of the taxable amount in excess of $20,000: 20% × ($85,000 − $20,000)	(13,000)	
Minimum distribution allowance		–0–
Taxable amount		$85,000
Computation of tax under 10-year averaging: Long-term capital gain portion: $85,000 \times \dfrac{1 \text{ (service before 1974)}}{25 \text{ (total service years)}} = \$3,400 \times .20 =$		$ 680
Ordinary income portion: 10 times the tax on $10,640 [32] [1/10 ($85,000 − $3,400) + $2,480]		11,361
Tax on lump-sum distribution		$12,041

Thus, Esteban's capital gain on the distribution is $3,400 and is subject to a 20% capital gain rate. Here Esteban may wish to elect to treat the entire distribution as ordinary income using the 10-year forward averaging approach rather than taxing the capital gain portion at the 20% capital gain rate. The tax liability of $11,905 would be less than the previously calculated tax liability of $12,041. The capital gain on the unrealized appreciation in the employer's common stock is not taxable until Esteban sells the stock. In essence, the cost basis of the securities to the trust becomes the tax basis to the employee.[33] If Esteban keeps the securities until he dies, there may be some income tax savings on this gain to the extent his estate or heirs obtain a step-up in basis. ▼

---

[31] § 402(e)(1). The 5-year averaging for lump-sum distributions is repealed for tax years beginning after December 31, 1999. The grandfathered 10-year averaging and capital gains provisions for participants who attained age 50 by January 1, 1986, are retained.

[32] In making this tax computation, it is necessary to use the 1986 Tax Rate Schedule for single taxpayers and to add $2,480 (the zero bracket amount) to the taxable income. Thus, the tax was computed on $10,640, which is $8,160 (1/10 of $81,600) plus $2,480. Note that the tax rates provided in the instructions for Form 4972 (Tax on Lump-Sum Distributions) have already been adjusted for the zero bracket amount (i.e., it is not necessary to add the zero bracket amount in making the calculation).

[33] § 402(e)(4)(J).

> **CONCEPT SUMMARY 19-2**
>
> ## Model for Lump-Sum Distribution Computation
>
> 1. Start with the total lump-sum distribution and deduct any employee contributions and unrealized appreciation in employer securities.
> 2. Divide the result into the capital gain portion and the ordinary income portion.*
> 3. Multiply the capital gain portion by the capital gain rate of 20%.
> 4. Reduce the ordinary income portion by the minimum distribution allowance.
> 5. Divide the ordinary income portion into 5 or 10 equal portions, whichever is appropriate.
> 6. Compute the tax on the result in step 5 using the 1986 or current rate schedules (whichever is appropriate) for single taxpayers.
> 7. Multiply the resulting tax by 5 or 10, whichever is appropriate.
> 8. Add the results in steps 3 and 7.
>
> *In certain circumstances, none of the taxable amount of the distribution will be eligible for capital gain treatment. In other circumstances, the taxpayer may choose to treat none of the taxable amount as capital gain even though part could qualify.

If Esteban (in Example 9) uses the 5-year forward averaging provision instead, the following results are produced:

Taxable amount	$85,000
Computation of tax under 5-year averaging:	
Long-term capital gain portion:	
$85,000 \times \dfrac{1 \text{ (service before 1974)}}{25 \text{ (total service years)}} = \$3,400 \times .20 =$	$ 680
Ordinary income portion:	
5 times the tax on $16,320[35] [⅕ ($85,000 − $3,400)]	12,240
Tax on lump-sum distribution	$12,920

Thus, Esteban's capital gain on the distribution is $3,400 (the same as in the 10-year averaging calculation). The capital gain is subject to a 20 percent capital gain rate.[35] Once again the taxpayer may wish to elect to treat the entire distribution as ordinary income using the 5-year forward averaging approach rather than taxing the capital gain portion at the 20 percent capital gain rate. The tax liability of $12,750 would be less than the previously calculated tax liability of $12,920. Since the ordinary income tax under 10-year forward averaging is less than the ordinary income tax under 5-year forward averaging, it appears that Esteban's best alternative is to use the 10-year forward averaging provision and treat the capital gain as ordinary income.

---

[34] In making the tax computation, it is necessary to use the 1997 Tax Rate Schedule for single taxpayers.

[35] Note that since Esteban qualifies under the transition rules (attained age 50 before January 1, 1986), he is eligible to elect capital gain treatment in conjunction with 5-year forward averaging.

LIMITATIONS ON CONTRIBUTIONS TO AND BENEFITS FROM QUALIFIED PLANS

LEARNING OBJECTIVE 4
Calculate the limitations on contributions to and benefits from qualified plans.

In General. The limitations on contributions to and benefits from qualified plans appearing in § 415 must be written into a qualified plan. The plan terminates if these limits are exceeded. Section 404 sets the limits on deductibility applicable to the employer. The limit on the amount deductible under § 404 may have an impact on the amount the employer is willing to contribute. In fact, a defined benefit plan or defined contribution plan is not allowed a deduction for the amount that exceeds the § 415 limitations.[36]

Defined Contribution Plans. Under a *defined contribution plan* (money purchase pension, profit sharing, or stock bonus plan), the annual addition to an employee's account cannot exceed the smaller of $30,000 or 25 percent of the employee's compensation.[37] The $30,000 amount is to be indexed (in $5,000 increments).

Defined Benefit Plans. Under a *defined benefit plan,* the annual benefit payable to an employee is limited to the smaller of $125,000 (in 1997)[38] or 100 percent of the employee's average compensation for the highest three years of employment. This benefit limit is subject to a $10,000 *de minimis* floor. The $125,000 limitation is reduced actuarially if the benefits begin before the Social Security normal retirement age (currently age 65). The $125,000 amount is increased actuarially if the benefits begin after the Social Security normal retirement age. The dollar limit on annual benefits ($125,000) is reduced by one-tenth for each year of *participation* under 10 years by the employee. Furthermore, the 100 percent of compensation limitation and the $10,000 *de minimis* floor are reduced proportionately for a participant who has less than 10 years of *service* with the employer.[39]

EXAMPLE 10
Adam's average compensation for the highest three years of employment is $87,000. Although the § 415(b)(1) limitation does not limit the deduction, the defined benefit plan would not qualify if the plan provides for benefits in excess of the smaller of (1) $87,000 or (2) $125,000 for Adam in 1997 (assuming retirement age of 65). ▼

EXAMPLE 11
Peggy has participated for four years in a defined benefit plan and has six years of service with her employer. Her average compensation for the three highest years is $60,000. Her four years of participation reduce her dollar limitation to $50,000 ($125,000 × 4/10). Her six years of service reduce her 100% of compensation limitation to 60%. Therefore, her limit on annual benefits is $36,000 ($60,000 × 60%). ▼

For collectively bargained plans with at least 100 participants, the annual dollar limitation is the greater of $68,212 or one-half of the $125,000 monetary limit.

The amount of compensation that may be taken into account under any plan is limited to $160,000 (in 1997).[40] Thus, the benefits highly compensated individuals receive may be smaller as a percentage of their pay than those received by non-highly compensated employees.

EXAMPLE 12
Swan Corporation has a defined contribution plan with a 10% contribution formula. An employee earning less than $160,000 in 1997 would not be affected by this includible

---
[36] § 404(j).
[37] §§ 415(c) and (d).
[38] This amount is indexed annually.
[39] § 415(b).
[40] §§ 401(a)(17) and 404(l). This amount is to be indexed annually.

compensation limitation. However, an employee earning $320,000 in 1997 would have only 5% of compensation allocated to his or her account because of the $160,000 limit on includible compensation. ▼

Two methods can be used to determine the maximum deduction a corporation is permitted for contributions to pension plans. First, an aggregate cost method allows an actuarially determined deduction based on a level amount, or a level percentage, of compensation over the remaining future service of covered participants. Second, the employer is permitted to deduct the so-called normal cost plus no more than 10 percent of the past service costs.

The employer's contribution is deductible in the tax year such amounts are paid to the pension trust. However, both cash and accrual basis employers may defer the payment of contributions with respect to any tax year until the date fixed for filing the taxpayer's Federal income tax return for that year (including extensions).[41] In effect, the corporation is allowed a deduction to the extent it is compelled to make such contributions to satisfy the funding requirement. If an amount in excess of the allowable amount is contributed in any tax year, the excess may be carried forward and deducted in succeeding tax years (to the extent the carryover plus the succeeding year's contribution does not exceed the deductible limitation for that year).[42]

EXAMPLE 13

During 1997, Green Corporation contributes $17,500 to its qualified pension plan. Normal cost for this year is $7,200, and the amount necessary to pay retirement benefits on behalf of employee services before 1997 is $82,000 (past service costs). The corporation's maximum deduction would be $15,400. This amount consists of the $7,200 normal cost plus 10% ($8,200) of the past service costs. The corporation would have a $2,100 [$17,500 (contribution) − $15,400 (deduction)] contribution carryover. ▼

EXAMPLE 14

Assume in the previous example that Green Corporation has normal cost of $7,200 in 1998 and contributes $10,000 to the pension trust. The corporation's maximum deduction would be $15,400. Green Corporation may deduct $12,100, composed of this year's contribution ($10,000) plus the $2,100 contribution carryover. ▼

A 10 percent excise tax is imposed on nondeductible contributions. The tax is levied on the employer making the contribution. The tax applies to nondeductible contributions for the current year and any nondeductible contributions for the preceding year that have not been eliminated by the end of the current year (as a carryover or by being returned to the employer in the current year).[43]

Profit Sharing and Stock Bonus Plan Limitations. The maximum deduction permitted to an employer each year for contributions to profit sharing and stock bonus plans is 15 percent of the compensation paid or accrued with respect to plan participants. The amount of compensation that may be taken into account under a plan for an employee is $160,000 (in 1997). Any nondeductible excess, a so-called contribution carryover, may be carried forward indefinitely and deducted in subsequent years. The maximum deduction in any succeeding year is 15 percent of all compensation paid or accrued during that taxable year. An employer can circumvent the 15 percent limitation by establishing a money purchase pension plan as a supplement to the profit sharing or stock bonus plan. When

---

[41] §§ 404(a)(1) and (6).
[42] § 404(a)(1)(D).
[43] § 4972.

there are two or more plans, a maximum deduction of 25 percent of the compensation paid is allowable.[44]

ETHICAL CONSIDERATIONS

Personal Benefit versus Employees' Benefit

As an owner of a small business, Brotherhood, Inc., you are interested when your insurance adviser tells you about a new age-weighted and cross-tested profit sharing plan that satisfies the nondiscrimination requirements of Code § 401(a)(4). He points out that currently only $160,000 of your $250,000 salary is used to calculate your 15 percent annual contribution (e.g., limited to $24,000). Under the new plan, your limit will be 25 percent, up to $30,000.

By changing to this age-weighted and cross-tested plan, you can keep much of the annual contributions you currently make to the business retirement plan for your employees. You will be able to exclude many lower-paid employees and reduce the annual contributions made to the plan on behalf of rank-and-file employees.

Should you agree to this tax shelter, which blends rules for retirement savings plans with rules applicable to pension plans? Most of the affected employees are your friends, and you play softball with them on your company's team.

TOP-HEAVY PLANS

A special set of rules is imposed upon so-called top-heavy plans to discourage retirement plans from conferring disproportionate benefits upon key employees. Top-heaviness is determined on an annual basis.

In general, a **top-heavy plan** allocates more than 60 percent of the cumulative benefits to key employees; a plan may also be part of a top-heavy plan. *Key employees* are defined as follows:

- Officers. However, for purposes of this definition, only the smaller of (1) 50 officers or (2) three employees or 10 percent of all employees (whichever is greater) may be considered officers.
- The 10 employees owning the largest interest in the employer (using the constructive ownership rules of § 318).
- A greater-than-5 percent owner of the employer.
- A greater-than-1 percent owner of the employer with annual compensation in excess of $150,000.[45]

An employee need fall within only one of these categories to be classified as a key employee. However, a key employee does not include officers paid $45,000 or less a year. In addition, for purposes of the 10-employees provision, a key employee does not include an employee whose annual compensation from the employer is $30,000 or less. Employees receiving no compensation for five years are disregarded in testing for top-heavy status.

A top-heavy plan must provide for greater portability for participants who are non-key employees. An employee's right to the accrued benefits derived from employer contributions must become nonforfeitable under either of two vesting

---

[44] §§ 404(a)(3)(A) and (a)(7).

[45] § 416(i)(1).

TABLE 19–2
Top-Heavy Graded Vesting

Years of Service	Vested Percentage
2	20%
3	40%
4	60%
5	80%
6 or more	100%

schedules. Under the first schedule, an employee who has at least three years of service with the employer must have a nonforfeitable right to 100 percent of his or her accrued benefits derived from employer contributions. Under the second schedule, a six-year graded vesting schedule must be met (see Table 19–2).[46]

To prevent an employer from avoiding the top-heavy rules by establishing a one-person corporate shell, § 269A allows the IRS to allocate any income or deductions between a personal service corporation and its employee-owner. An employee-owner is any employee who owns more than 10 percent of the outstanding stock of the personal service corporation on any day during the tax year.

CASH OR DEFERRED ARRANGEMENT PLANS

General. A *cash or deferred arrangement plan,* hereafter referred to as a **§ 401(k) plan,** allows participants to elect either to receive up to $9,500 (in 1997)[47] in cash (taxed currently) or to have a contribution made on their behalf to a profit sharing or stock bonus plan. The plan may also be in the form of a salary-reduction agreement between an eligible participant and an employer under which a contribution will be made only if the participant elects to reduce his or her compensation or to forgo an increase in compensation.

Any pretax amount elected by the employee as a plan contribution is not includible in gross income and is 100 percent vested. Any employer contributions are tax deferred, as are earnings on contributions in the plan.

EXAMPLE 15

Sam participates in a § 401(k) plan of his employer. The plan permits the participants to choose between a full salary or a reduced salary where the reduction becomes a before-tax contribution to a retirement plan. Sam elects to contribute 10% of his annual compensation of $30,000 to the plan. Income taxes are paid on only $27,000. No income taxes are paid on the $3,000—or on any earnings—until it is distributed from the plan to Sam. The main benefit of a § 401(k) plan is that Sam can shift a portion of his income to a later taxable year. ▼

The maximum employee annual elective contribution to a § 401(k) plan is $9,500 (in 1997), but that amount is reduced dollar for dollar by other salary-reduction contributions to tax-sheltered annuities and simplified employee pension plans. Elective contributions in excess of the maximum limitation are taxable in the year of deferral. These amounts may be distributed from the plan tax-free before April 15 of the following year. Excess amounts not timely distributed will be taxable in the year of distribution, even though they were included in income in the year of deferral. Annual elective contributions are also limited by complicated nondiscrimination requirements and the defined contribution plan limitations.

A 10 percent excise tax is imposed on the employer for excess contributions not withdrawn from the plan within 2½ months after the close of the plan year.

---

[46] § 416(b).

[47] This amount is indexed annually. For 1996, the amount was $9,500.

The plan will lose its qualified status if these excess contributions (and any related income) are not withdrawn by the end of the plan year following the plan year in which the excess contributions were made.[48]

EXAMPLE 16

Carmen, an employee of a manufacturing corporation, defers $11,500 in a § 401(k) plan in 1997. The $2,000 excess deferral, along with the appropriate earnings, must be returned to Carmen by April 15, 1998. This $2,000 excess amount plus related income is taxable to her in 1997 and will be taxed again upon distribution (if made after April 15, 1998). There will be a 10% tax on Carmen's employer on any excess contributions not returned within 2½ months after the close of the plan year. ▼

ETHICAL CONSIDERATIONS

Everything Including the Kitchen Sink

Many § 401(k) and profit sharing plans have some strange assets stuffed away in them: bags of old coins, antique violins, parking lots, antique automobiles, and real estate. The reason is that § 401(k) plans and profit sharing plans are exempt from some pension plan rules, including diversification requirements. So these plans can invest most or all of the money in employer-related real estate or securities whereas pension plans are limited to only 10 percent in such assets. In addition, these plans are not insured by the Labor Department's Pension Benefit Guaranty Corporation.

For example, Color Tile, Inc., a Texas floor-covering chain, had a § 401(k) plan that invested heavily in Color Tile's own stores, and then leased the stores back to the company. Color Tile moved into Chapter 11 bankruptcy in 1996, and some stores stopped paying rent. Many workers were laid off, but they were not allowed to take their money out of their § 401(k) accounts. Then again, British Rail earned a 13.1 percent return per year over the 22-year life of the massive artwork collection inside its pension fund. The fund acquired more than 2,400 pieces over seven years.

Many companies have large holdings of their own stock in their retirement plans. Among these companies are WalMart Stores, Cooper Tire and Rubber, Hanson Industries, Nalco Chemicals, Banc One, and McDonald's.

Should companies invest a large percentage of § 401(k) plan money in company stores and their own stock?

SIMPLE Plans. Employers with 100 or fewer employees who do not maintain another qualified retirement plan may establish a *savings incentive match plan for employees* (SIMPLE plan).[49] The plan can be in the form of a § 401(k) plan or an IRA. Under the plan, employees are permitted to make elective contributions (i.e., a salary reduction approach) of up to $6,000 (to be indexed) per year, and employers generally are required to match the employee contributions up to 3 percent of the employee's compensation. The SIMPLE plan is not subject to the nondiscrimination and top-heavy rules that are normally applicable to § 401(k) plans.

All employees who received at least $5,000 in compensation from the employer during any two preceding years and who reasonably expect to receive at least $5,000 in compensation during the current year must be eligible to participate in the plan. The decision to participate is up to the employee. A self-employed individual may also participate in the plan.

---

[48] § 4979(a).

[49] § 408(p).

The contributions made by the employee must be expressed as a percentage of compensation rather than as a fixed dollar amount. The plan must not permit the elective employee contribution for the year to exceed $6,000 (to be indexed). Thus, the maximum amount that may be contributed to the plan for 1997 is $12,000. Generally, the employer must either match elective employee contributions up to 3 percent of the employee's compensation or provide nonmatching contributions of 2 percent of compensation for each eligible employee.

No other contributions may be made to the plan other than the employee elective contribution and the required employer matching contribution (or nonmatching contribution under the 2 percent rule). All contributions are fully vested.

Contributions to a SIMPLE plan by the employer generally are deductible by the employer. An employer is allowed a deduction for matching contributions only if the contributions are made by the due date (including extensions) for the employer's tax return. Contributions to a SIMPLE plan are excludible from the employee's gross income, and the SIMPLE plan is not subject to tax.

Distributions from a SIMPLE plan are taxed under the IRA rules. Tax-free rollovers can be made from one SIMPLE account to another. A SIMPLE account can be rolled over to an IRA tax-free after a two-year period has expired since the individual first participated in the plan. Withdrawals of contributions during the two-year period beginning on the date an employee first participates in the SIMPLE plan are subject to a 25 percent early withdrawal tax rather than the 10 percent early withdrawal tax that otherwise would apply.

RETIREMENT PLANS FOR SELF-EMPLOYED INDIVIDUALS

5 LEARNING OBJECTIVE
Understand the qualified plan (Keogh plan) available to a self-employed person.

Self-employed individuals (e.g., partners and sole proprietors) and their employees are eligible to receive qualified retirement benefits under what are known as **H.R. 10 (Keogh) plans.** Because of contribution limitations and other restrictions, self-employed plans previously were less attractive than corporate plans. Contributions and benefits of a self-employed person now are subject to the general corporate provisions. Basically, self-employed persons are on a parity with corporate employees. Consequently, Keogh plans can provide a self-employed person with an adequate retirement base.

A variety of funding vehicles can be used for Keogh investments, such as mutual funds, annuities, real estate shares, certificates of deposit, debt instruments, commodities, securities, and personal properties. Investment in most collectibles is not allowed in a self-directed plan. When an individual decides to make all investment decisions, a self-directed retirement plan is established. Otherwise the individual may prefer to invest the funds with a financial institution such as a broker, a bank, or a savings and loan institution.

COVERAGE REQUIREMENTS

Generally, the corporate coverage rules apply to Keogh plans. Thus, the percentage, ratio, and average benefits tests previously discussed also apply to self-employed plans. In addition, the more restrictive top-heavy plan rules apply to Keogh plans.[50] An individual covered under a qualified corporate plan as an employee may also establish a Keogh plan for earnings from self-employment.

---
[50] § 401(d).

> ### TAX IN THE NEWS
>
> **SELECTING BENEFIT OPTIONS**
>
> Many employers provide a benefits package from which an employee can select a certain dollar amount of fringe benefits (e.g., medical, dental, and life insurance, child care). Just because you selected certain options last year does not mean you should select the same ones this year. Your family situation may have changed, the options offered by your employer may have changed, or the tax law may have changed. As a result, you may find that some options have improved while others are less attractive. Typically, the options selected can be changed only once each year.
>
> The § 401(k) plan frequently is not among the benefits that are subject only to annual review. Many companies permit adjustments in contributions throughout the year. Not only can the contribution amounts be adjusted, but it is also possible to change the investment vehicles. So as not to overlook the opportunity to make changes in § 401(k) plans, it is a good idea to evaluate the § 401(k) plan at the same time other fringe benefits are evaluated.
>
> SOURCE: Adapted from Lynn Asinof, "Benefit-Option Plans: 'Tis the Season to be Selective," *Wall Street Journal*, November 15, 1996, pp. C1 and C2.

CONTRIBUTION LIMITATIONS

A self-employed individual may annually contribute the smaller of $30,000 or 25 percent of earned income to a *defined contribution* Keogh plan.[51] However, if the defined contribution plan is a profit sharing plan, a 15 percent deduction limit applies. Under a *defined benefit* Keogh plan, the annual benefit payable to an employee is limited to the smaller of $125,000 (in 1997) or 100 percent of the employee's average compensation for the three highest years of employment.[52] An employee includes a self-employed person. More restrictive rules apply to a top-heavy plan.

Earned income refers to net earnings from self-employment as defined in § 1402(a).[53] Net earnings from self-employment means the gross income derived by an individual from any trade or business carried on by that individual, less appropriate deductions, plus the distributive share of income or loss from a partnership.[54] Earned income is reduced by contributions to a Keogh plan on the individual's behalf and by 50 percent of any self-employment tax.[55]

EXAMPLE 17

Pat, a partner, has earned income of $130,000 in 1997 (after the deduction for one-half of self-employment tax, but before any Keogh contribution). The maximum contribution to a defined contribution plan is $26,000, calculated from the following formula: $130,000 − .25X = X$, where X is earned income reduced by Pat's Keogh contribution. Solving this equation, $X = \$104,000$; thus, the contribution limit is $.25 \times \$104,000 = \$26,000$. To achieve the maximum contribution of $30,000, Pat would have to earn at least $150,000. In essence, a self-employed individual can contribute 20% of *gross* earned income. (Pat could contribute only 13.043% of self-employment gross earned income if this were a profit sharing plan.) ▼

---

[51] § 415(c)(1).
[52] § 415(b)(1). This amount is indexed annually.
[53] § 401(c)(2).
[54] § 1402(a).
[55] §§ 401(c)(2)(A)(v) and 164(f).

TABLE 19-3
Phase-Out of IRA Deduction

AGI Filing Status	Phase-Out Begins	Phase-Out Ends
Single and head of household	$25,000	$35,000
Married, filing joint return	40,000	50,000
Married, filing separate return	–0–	10,000

Many Keogh plans will be considered top-heavy plans (refer to the previous discussion). For nondiscrimination purposes, the 25 percent limitation on the employee contribution is computed on the first $160,000 (in 1997) of earned income.

EXAMPLE 18

Terry, a self-employed accountant, has a money purchase plan with a contribution rate of 15% of compensation. Terry's earned income after the deduction for one-half of self-employment tax, but before the retirement contribution is $250,000. Terry's contribution would be limited to $20,870 ($160,000 − .15X = X), since X = $139,130 and .15 × $139,130 = $20,870. ▼

Although a Keogh plan must be established before the end of the year in question, contributions may be made up to the normal filing date for that year.

INDIVIDUAL RETIREMENT ACCOUNTS (IRAs)

GENERAL RULES

6 LEARNING OBJECTIVE
Describe the benefits of an Individual Retirement Account (IRA).

Employees not covered by another qualified plan can establish their own tax-deductible **Individual Retirement Accounts (IRAs).** The contribution ceiling is the smaller of $2,000 (or $4,000 for spousal IRAs) or 100 percent of compensation.[56] If the taxpayer or spouse is an active participant in another qualified plan, the IRA deduction limitation is phased out *proportionately* between certain adjusted gross income (AGI) ranges, as shown in Table 19–3.[57]

AGI is calculated taking into account any § 469 passive losses and § 86 taxable Social Security benefits and ignoring any § 911 foreign income exclusion, § 135 savings bonds interest exclusion, and the IRA deduction. There is a $200 floor on the IRA deduction limitation for individuals whose AGI is not above the phase-out range.

EXAMPLE 19

In 1997, Mr. and Mrs. Smith had compensation income of $27,000 and $20,000, respectively. Their AGI for 1997 was $47,000. Mr. Smith was an active participant in his employer's qualified retirement plan. Mr. and Mrs. Smith may *each* contribute $600 to an IRA. The deductible amount for each is reduced from $2,000 by $1,400 because of the phase-out mechanism:

$$\frac{\$7,000}{\$10,000} \times \$2,000 = \$1,400 \text{ reduction}$$

▼

---

[56] §§ 219(b)(1) and (c)(2).

[57] § 219(g). However, a special rule in § 219(g)(4) allows a married person filing a separate return to avoid the phase-out rules even though the spouse is an active participant. The individual must live apart from the spouse at all times during the taxable year and must not be an active participant in another qualified plan.

TAX IN THE NEWS

THE SOONER THE BETTER

The sooner you start a savings program, the greater the potential benefits. This is particularly so for an IRA where the earnings are tax deferred. So what is the single best day to make your IRA contribution? Most experts agree that it is on January 1 (or January 2 if your financial institution is closed on January 1).

Suppose you invest $2,000 in an IRA at the end of each year from age 21 through age 64 and the earnings rate is 10 percent annually. You will have accumulated $1.3 million at age 65. If you make the same contributions at the beginning of each year, however, you will have an extra $130,000 by age 65.

SOURCE: Adapted from "Funding Retirement: New Year IRA Tips," *Mutual Funds*, January 1997, p. 29.

EXAMPLE 20

An unmarried individual is an active participant in his employer's qualified retirement plan. With AGI of $34,500, he would normally have an IRA deduction limit of $100 {$2,000 − [($34,500 − $25,000)/$10,000 × $2,000]}. However, because of the special floor provision, a $200 IRA deduction is allowable. ▼

To the extent that an individual is ineligible to make a deductible contribution to an IRA, *nondeductible contributions* can be made to separate accounts.[58] The nondeductible contribution will be subject to the same dollar limits for deductible contributions of $2,000 of earned income ($4,000 for a spousal IRA). Income in the account accumulates tax-free until distributed. Only the account earnings will be taxed (account basis equals the contributions made by the taxpayer) upon distribution. A taxpayer may elect to treat deductible IRA contributions as nondeductible. If an individual has no taxable income for the year after taking into account other deductions, the election would be beneficial. The election is made on the individual's tax return for the taxable year to which the designation relates.

Simplified Employee Pension Plans. An employer may contribute to an IRA covering an employee an amount equal to the lesser of $30,000 or 15 percent of the employee's earned income. In such a plan, the corporation must make contributions for *each* employee who has reached age 21, has performed service for the employer during the calendar year and at least three of the five preceding calendar years, and has received at least $400 (in 1997) in compensation from the employer for the year.[59] Known as **simplified employee pension (SEP) plans,** these plans are subject to many of the same restrictions applicable to qualified plans (e.g., age and period-of-service requirements, top-heavy rules, and nondiscrimination limitations). Concept Summary 19–3 compares a SEP with a Keogh plan.

The amounts contributed to a SEP by an employer on behalf of an employee and the elective deferrals under a SEP are excludible from gross income. Elective

---

[58] § 408(o).
[59] §§ 408(j) and (k)(2). This amount is indexed annually. For 1996, the amount also was $400.

Concept Summary 19-3

Keogh Plan and SEP Compared

	Keogh	SEP
Form	Trust.	IRA.
Establishment	By end of year.	By extension due date of employer.
Type of plan	Qualified.	Qualified.
Contributions to plan	By extension due date.	By extension due date of employer.
Vesting rules	Qualified plan rules.	100% immediately.
Participants' rules	Flexible.	Stricter.
Lump-sum distributions and averaging	Yes, favorable 5-year or 10-year forward averaging.	No, ordinary income.
Deduction limitation	Varies.*	Smaller of $30,000** or 15% of earned income.
Self as trustee	Yes.	No.

*For a defined contribution pension plan, the limit is the smaller of $30,000 or 20% of self-employment income (after one-half of self-employment tax is deducted). A defined contribution profit sharing plan has a 13.043% deduction limit. A defined benefit Keogh plan's limit is the smaller of $125,000 (in 1997) or 100% of the employee's average compensation for the highest three years of employment.

**Since only $160,000 of income can be taken into consideration, the dollar limitation is effectively $24,000 ($160,000 × 15%).

---

deferrals under a SEP are subject to a statutory ceiling of $9,500 (in 1997).[60] Only $160,000 (in 1997) in compensation may be taken into account in making the SEP computation. An employer is permitted to elect to use its taxable year rather than the calendar year for purposes of determining contributions to a SEP.[61]

SIMPLE IRA. A SIMPLE plan can be in the form of an IRA. See the earlier discussion under SIMPLE Plans.

Spousal IRA. If both spouses work, each can individually establish an IRA. Deductible IRA contributions of up to $2,000 may be made by each spouse if the combined compensation of both spouses is at least equal to the contributed amount. Thus, if each spouse has compensation of at least $2,000, they each may contribute a maximum of $2,000. Likewise, if only one spouse is employed, they each may contribute a maximum of $2,000 if the employed spouse has compensation of at least $4,000. Finally, if both spouses are employed, but one has compensation of less than $2,000, they each may contribute a maximum of $2,000 if their combined compensation is at least $4,000.

---

[60] Elective deferrals by an employee were repealed by the Small Business Job Protection Act of 1996 effective after December 31, 1996. However, if the employer plan was established before January 1, 1997, contributions can continue to be made under the pre-repeal provisions.

[61] § 404(h)(1)(A). The $9,500 and $160,000 amounts are indexed annually.

For the spousal IRA provision to apply, a joint return must be filed.[62] The spousal IRA deduction is also proportionately reduced for active participants whose AGI exceeds the above target ranges.

EXAMPLE 21

Tony, who is married, is eligible to establish an IRA. He received $30,000 in compensation in 1997, and his spouse does not work outside the home. Tony can contribute up to $4,000 to two IRAs, to be divided in any manner between the two spouses, except that no more than $2,000 can be allocated to either spouse. ▼

EXAMPLE 22

Assume the same facts as in the previous example, except that Tony's wife has compensation income of $1,200. Without the spousal IRA provision, Tony could contribute $2,000 to his IRA, and his spouse could contribute only $1,200 to her IRA. With the spousal IRA provision, they both can contribute $2,000 to their IRAs. ▼

Alimony is considered to be earned income for purposes of IRA contributions. Thus, a person whose only income is alimony can contribute to an IRA.[63]

Timing of Contributions. Contributions (both deductible and nondeductible) can be made to an IRA anytime before the due date of the individual's tax return.[64] For example, an individual can establish and contribute to an IRA through April 15, 1998 (the return due date), and deduct this amount on his or her tax return for 1997. IRA contributions that are made during a tax return extension period do not satisfy the requirement of being made by the return due date. An employer can make contributions up until the time of the due date for filing the return (including extensions) and treat those amounts as a deduction for the prior year.[65] As noted earlier, a similar rule applies to Keogh plans. However, the Keogh plan must be established before the end of the tax year. Contributions to the Keogh plan may then be made anytime before the due date of the individual's tax return.

PENALTY TAXES FOR EXCESS CONTRIBUTIONS

A cumulative, nondeductible 6 percent excise penalty tax is imposed on the smaller of (1) any excess contributions or (2) the market value of the plan assets determined as of the close of the tax year. *Excess contributions* are any contributions that exceed the maximum limitation and contributions that are made during or after the tax year in which the individual reaches age 70½.[66] A taxpayer is not allowed a deduction for excess contributions. If the excess is corrected by contributing less than the deductible amount for a later year, a deduction then is allowable in the later year as a *makeup* deduction.

An excess contribution is taxable annually until returned to the taxpayer or reduced by the underutilization of the maximum contribution limitation in a subsequent year. The 6 percent penalty tax can be avoided if the excess amounts are returned.[67]

EXAMPLE 23

Nancy, age 55, establishes an IRA in 1997 and contributes $2,300 in cash to the plan. She has earned income of $22,000. Nancy is allowed a $2,000 deduction *for* AGI for 1997. Assuming the market value of the plan assets is at least $300, there is a nondeductible 6% excise penalty tax of $18 ($300 × 6%). The $300 may be subject to an additional penalty tax in future years if it is not returned to Nancy or reduced by underutilization of the $2,000 maximum contribution limitation. ▼

---

[62] § 219(c).
[63] § 219(f)(1).
[64] § 219(f)(3).
[65] § 404(h)(1)(B).
[66] §§ 4973(a)(1) and (b).
[67] §§ 408(d)(4) and 4973(b)(2).

TAXATION OF BENEFITS

A participant has a zero basis in the *deductible* contributions to an IRA because such contributions are not taxed currently.[68] Once retirement payments are received, they are ordinary income and are not subject to the 5-year or 10-year averaging allowed for lump-sum distributions. Payments made to a participant from *deductible* IRAs before age 59½ are subject to a nondeductible 10 percent penalty tax on such actual, or constructive, payments.[69] However, an individual may make penalty-free withdrawals to pay for medical expenses in excess of 7.5 percent of AGI. Further, an individual who has received unemployment compensation for at least 12 consecutive weeks may use IRA withdrawals to pay for health insurance for himself or herself, the spouse, and dependents without incurring the 10 percent penalty tax.[70]

All IRAs of an individual are treated as one contract, and all distributions during a taxable year are treated as one distribution. If an individual who previously has made both deductible and nondeductible IRA contributions makes a withdrawal from an IRA during a taxable year, the excludible amount must be calculated. The amount excludible from gross income for the taxable year is calculated by multiplying the amount withdrawn by a percentage. The percentage is calculated by dividing the individual's aggregate nondeductible IRA contributions by the aggregate balance of all of his or her IRAs (including rollover IRAs and SEPs).[71]

EXAMPLE 24

Carl, age 59, has a $12,000 deductible IRA and a $2,000 nondeductible IRA (without any earnings). Carl withdraws $1,000 from the nondeductible IRA. The excludible portion is $143 [($2,000/$14,000) × $1,000)], and the includible portion is $857 [($12,000/$14,000) × $1,000)]. Carl must pay a 10% penalty tax on a prorated portion considered withdrawn from the deductible IRA and earnings in either type of IRA. Thus, the 10% penalty tax is $85.70 (10% × $857). ▼

Rollovers. An IRA may be the recipient of a rollover from another qualified plan, including another IRA. Such a distribution from a qualified plan is not included in gross income if it is transferred within 60 days of receipt to an IRA or another qualified plan. For a series of distributions that constitute a lump-sum distribution, the 60-day period does not begin until the last distribution. Amounts received from IRAs may be rolled over tax-free only once in a 12-month period. If a person has more than one IRA, the one-year waiting period applies separately to each IRA.[72]

EXAMPLE 25

Nonemployer stock worth $60,000 is distributed to an employee from a qualified retirement plan. Hubert, the employee, sells the stock within 60 days for $60,000 and transfers one-half of the proceeds to an IRA. Hubert will have $30,000 of ordinary income, which is not eligible for 5-year or 10-year forward averaging or for the capital gain treatment for pre-1974 contributions. One-half of the distribution, or $30,000, does escape taxation because of the rollover. ▼

A tax-free rollover for distributions from qualified plans is an alternative to the taxable 5-year or 10-year forward averaging techniques. Any rollover amount

---

[68] § 408(d)(1).
[69] § 72(t). There are limited exceptions to the penalty on early distributions.
[70] §§ 72(t)(2)(B) and (D). For purposes of the unemployment provision, a self-employed individual who otherwise would have been eligible for unemployment compensation will qualify.
[71] § 408(d)(2).
[72] § 408(d)(3)(B) and Prop.Reg. 1.408–4(b)(4).

in an IRA may later be rolled over into another qualified plan if the IRA consists of only the amounts from the original plan. The amount of nondeductible employee contributions included in a distribution may not be rolled over, but that amount is tax-free because the contributions were made with after-tax dollars. Partial rollovers are allowed, but the maximum amount that may be rolled over may not exceed the portion of the distribution that is otherwise includible in gross income. Rollovers are not available for required distributions under the minimum distribution rules once age 70½ is reached.

EXAMPLE 26 Jane withdraws $1,500 from her IRA on May 2, 1997, but she redeposits it in the same IRA on June 28, 1997. Although the withdrawal and redeposit was a partial rollover and Jane may have used the funds for a limited time, this is a tax-free rollover.[73] ▼

A rollover is different from a direct transfer of funds from a qualified plan to an IRA or another qualified plan by a trustee or issuer. A direct transfer is not subject to the one-year waiting period and the withholding rules.[74] Further, in many states, IRA amounts are subject to claims of creditors, which is not the case for employer plans.

An employer must withhold 20 percent of any lump-sum distributions unless the transfer is a direct transfer to an IRA or another qualified plan.[75]

EXAMPLE 27 Kay receives a distribution from a qualified retirement plan. The amount of the distribution would have been $20,000, but Kay receives only $16,000 ($20,000 − $4,000) as a result of the 20% withholding provision. After several weeks, Kay decides to contribute $20,000 (the gross amount of the distribution) to her IRA. Since she received only $16,000, she will need to contribute $4,000 from another source in order to make a $20,000 contribution. Kay will be able to claim a refund for the $4,000 that was withheld when she files her tax return for the year. ▼

Distributions to an IRA are generally not eligible for 5- or 10-year averaging or capital gain treatment. An exception applies in the case of a *conduit IRA*, where the sole assets of a plan are rolled over into an IRA, and the assets are then rolled into a qualified plan. With a conduit IRA, the lump-sum distribution from the original plan is still eligible for the special tax treatments.

NONQUALIFIED DEFERRED COMPENSATION PLANS

UNDERLYING RATIONALE FOR TAX TREATMENT

7 LEARNING OBJECTIVE
Understand the rationale for nonqualified deferred compensation plans and the related tax treatment.

Nonqualified deferred compensation (NQDC) plans provide a flexible way for taxpayers, particularly those in the 36 or 39.6 percent tax brackets, to defer income taxes on income payments until a possible lower tax bracket year. Where the deferred compensation is credited with annual earnings until payment, the entire deferred compensation, not the after-tax amount, is generating investment income. Also, most NQDC plans do not have to meet the discrimination, funding, coverage, and other requirements of qualified plans. In addition to these advantages for the employee, the employer may not have a current cash outflow.

---

[73] Ltr.Rul. 9010007.
[74] Temp.Reg. 35.3405–1.
[75] § 3405(c).

The doctrine of constructive receipt is an important concept relating to the taxability of nonqualified deferred compensation.[76] In essence, if a taxpayer irrevocably earns income but may elect to receive it now or at a later date, the income is constructively received and is immediately taxed. Income is not constructively received, however, if the taxpayer's control over the amounts earned is subject to substantial limitations or restrictions.

Another important concept is the economic benefit theory. Although a taxpayer does not have a present right to income, the income will be taxable if a right in the form of a negotiable promissory note exists. Notes and other evidences of indebtedness received in payment for services constitute income to the extent of their fair market value at the time of the transfer.[77]

EXAMPLE 28

Eagle Corporation and Bill, a cash basis employee, enter into an employment agreement that provides an annual salary of $120,000 to Bill. Of this amount, $100,000 is to be paid in current monthly installments, and $20,000 is to be paid in 10 annual installments beginning at Bill's retirement or death. Although Eagle Corporation maintains a separate account for Bill, that account is not funded (Bill is merely an unsecured creditor of the corporation). The $20,000 is not considered constructively received and is deferred. Compensation of $100,000 is currently taxable to Bill and deductible to Eagle. The other $20,000 will be taxable and deductible when paid in future years. ▼

TAX TREATMENT TO THE EMPLOYER AND EMPLOYEE

The tax treatment of an NQDC plan depends on whether it is *funded* or *unfunded* and whether it is *forfeitable* or *nonforfeitable*. In an unfunded NQDC plan, the employee relies upon the company's mere promise to make the compensation payment in the future. An unfunded, unsecured promise to pay, not represented by a negotiable note, effectively defers the recognition of income. Thus, the employee is taxed later when the compensation is actually paid or made available.[78] Similarly, the employer is allowed a deduction when the employee recognizes income.[79]

The employer can set up an escrow account to accumulate deferred payments on behalf of the employee. These funds may be invested by the escrow agent for the benefit of the employee.[80] By avoiding income recognition until the benefits from the escrow custodial account are received, the employee postpones the tax. An escrow arrangement can be appropriate for a professional athlete or entertainer whose income is earned in a few peak years.

EXAMPLE 29

Ted, a professional athlete, is to receive a bonus for signing an employment contract. An NQDC plan is established to defer the income beyond Ted's peak income years. His employer transfers the bonus to an escrow agent who invests the funds in securities, etc., which may act as a hedge against inflation. The bonus is deferred for 10 years and becomes payable gradually in years 11 through 15. The bonus is taxable to Ted and deductible by his employer when Ted receives the payments in years 11 through 15. ▼

Generally, funded NQDC plans must be forfeitable to keep the compensation payments from being taxable immediately. In most instances, employees prefer to have some assurance that they will ultimately receive benefits from the NQDC

---

[76] § 451(a) and Reg. § 1.451–2.
[77] Reg. § 1.61–2(d)(4).
[78] Rev.Rul. 60–31, 1960–1 C.B. 174; Reg. § 1.451–2(a); *U.S. v. Basye*, 73–1 USTC ¶9250, 31 AFTR2d 73–802, 93 S.Ct. 1080 (USSC, 1973).
[79] §§ 404(a) and (d).
[80] Rev.Rul. 55–525, 1955–2 C.B. 543.

(that the plan provides for nonforfeitable benefits). In such instances, the plan will have to be unfunded to prevent immediate taxation to the employee. Note that most funded NQDC plans are subject to many of the provisions that apply to qualified plans.

When to Use an NQDC Arrangement. As a general rule, NQDC plans are more appropriate for executives in a financially secure company. Because of the need for currently disposable income, such plans are usually not appropriate for young employees.

An NQDC plan can reduce an employee's overall tax payments by deferring the taxation of income to later years (possibly when the employee is in a lower tax bracket). In effect, these plans may produce a form of income averaging. Further, NQDC plans may discriminate in favor of shareholders, officers, specific highly compensated key employees, or a single individual.

Certain disadvantages should be noted. Nonqualified plans are usually required to be unfunded, which means that an employee is not assured that funds ultimately will be available to pay the benefits. Also, the employer's tax deduction is postponed until the employee is taxed on those payments.

Golden Parachute Arrangements. Certain excessive severance payments to employees may be penalized. The Code denies a deduction to an employer who makes a payment of cash or property to an employee or independent contractor that satisfies both of the following conditions:

- The payment is contingent on a change of ownership of a corporation through a stock or asset acquisition.
- The aggregate present value of the payment equals or exceeds three times the employee's (or independent contractor's) average annual compensation.[81]

The law recognizes that a corporation may provide monetary benefits to key employees if those employees lose their jobs as a result of a change in ownership of the corporation. These payments may be unreasonable or not really for services rendered. The Code refers to such payments as **golden parachute payments,** a term that, in essence, means *excess severance pay*. The disallowed amount is the excess of the payment over a statutory base amount (a five-year average of taxable compensation if the taxpayer was an employee for the entire five-year period). Further, a 20 percent excise tax is imposed on the recipient on the receipt of these parachute payments, to be withheld at the time of payment.[82]

EXAMPLE 30

Irene, an executive, receives a golden parachute payment of $380,000 from her employer. Her average annual compensation for the most recent five tax years is $120,000. The corporation will be denied a deduction for $260,000 ($380,000 payment − $120,000 base amount). Irene's excise tax is $52,000 ($260,000 × 20%). ▼

Golden parachute payments do not include payments to or from qualified pension, profit sharing, stock bonus, annuity, or simplified employee pension plans. Also excluded is the amount of the payment that, in fact, represents reasonable compensation for personal services actually rendered or to be rendered. S corporations are not subject to the golden parachute rules. Generally, corporations that do not have stock that is readily tradable on an established securities market or elsewhere are also exempt. Such excluded payments are not

---

[81] § 280G. [82] § 4999.

taken into account when determining whether the threshold (the aggregate present value calculation) is exceeded.

Publicly Held Companies' Compensation Limitation. For purposes of both the regular income tax and the alternative minimum tax, the deductible compensation for the top five executives of publicly traded companies is limited to $1 million for each executive. A company is publicly held if the corporation has common stock listed on a national securities exchange.[83] This $1 million deduction limitation is decreased by any nondeductible golden parachute payments made to the employee during the same year.

This deduction limitation applies when the compensation deduction would otherwise be taken. For example, in the case of a nonqualified stock option (NQSO), which is discussed later in this chapter, the deduction is normally taken in the year the NQSO is exercised, even though the option was granted with respect to services performed in a prior year.

Certain types of compensation are *not* subject to this new deduction limit and are not taken into account in determining whether other compensation exceeds $1 million:

- Compensation payable on a commission basis.
- Compensation payable solely on account of the attainment of one or more performance goals when certain requirements involving the approval of outside directors and shareholders are met.
- Payments to a tax-qualified retirement plan (including salary reduction contributions).
- Amounts that are excludible from an executive's gross income (such as employer-provided health benefits and miscellaneous fringe benefits).

The most important exception is performance-based compensation. Compensation qualifies for this exception only if the following conditions are satisfied:

- The compensation is paid solely on account of the attainment of one or more performance goals.
- The performance goals are established by a compensation committee consisting solely of two or more outside directors.
- The material terms under which the compensation is to be paid (including the performance goals) are disclosed to and approved by the shareholders in a separate vote prior to payment.
- Prior to payment, the compensation committee certifies that the performance goals and any other material terms were in fact satisfied.

Compensation (other than stock options or other stock appreciation rights) is not treated as paid solely on account of the attainment of one or more performance goals unless the compensation is paid to the particular executive under a preestablished objective performance formula or standard that precludes discretion. In essence, a third party with knowledge of the relevant performance results could calculate the amount to be paid to the particular executive. A performance goal is broadly defined and includes, for example, any objective performance standard that is applied to the individual executive, a business unit (e.g., a division or a line of business), or the corporation as a whole. Performance standards could include increases in stock price, market share, sales, or earnings per share.

---

[83] § 162(m).

ETHICAL CONSIDERATIONS

Limiting Compensation for Executives But Not for Other Highly Paid Individuals

The top five executives of publicly traded corporations have a $1 million limit on deductible compensation. During 1995, chief executive officers in the financial services industry received the highest total compensation: median compensation of $1.5 million. Even with the limit, some CEOs received huge direct compensation. For example, the top wage earner in 1995 was Lawrence M. Coss of Green Tree Financial at $65.1 million, followed by John F. Welch, Jr., of General Electric at $22 million, Goodyear's Stanley C. Gault ($16.5 million), Compaq Computer's Eckhard Pfeiffer ($16.1 million), and Colgate-Palmolive's Reuben Mark ($15.1 million).

Yet other highly paid individuals are not subject to the $1 million compensation cap. Radio personality Paul Harvey lives comfortably on $13 million a year. A former streetcar conductor and Creole cook, Maya Angelou makes $4.3 million as a poet. Speaker Daniel Burrus pulls in $4 million, and Chef Roy Yamaguchi ($2 million) and Indian chief Skip Hayward ($1 million) also do well. Todd McFarlane, a comic book artist, makes $5 million, and Anthony Pellicano, a private investigator, makes $2 million. Sudan, a 14-year-old African lion, makes $800,000.

Similarly, many television and movie performers are receiving huge salaries (e.g., David Letterman at $14 million). Yet these entertainers and others not in the designated "top five" are not subject to the $1 million compensation cap. Some question the fairness of a policy that subjects business executives to a compensation limitation while allowing entertainers, sports stars, and others to be exempt from the limitation.

RESTRICTED PROPERTY PLANS

GENERAL PROVISIONS

LEARNING OBJECTIVE 8
Explain the value of restricted property plans.

A **restricted property plan** is an arrangement whereby an employer transfers property (e.g., stock of the employer-corporation) to a provider of services at no cost or at a bargain price. The purpose of a restricted stock plan is to retain the services of key employees who might otherwise leave. The employer hopes that such compensation arrangements will encourage company growth and attainment of performance objectives. Section 83 was enacted in 1969 to provide rules for the taxation of incentive compensation arrangements, which previously were governed by judicial and administrative interpretations. Although the following discussion refers to an employee as the provider of the services, the services need not be performed by an employee (§ 83 also applies to independent contractors).

As a general rule, if an employee performs services and receives property (e.g., stock), the fair market value of that property in excess of any amount paid by the employee is includible in his or her gross income. The time for inclusion is the earlier of (1) the time the property is no longer subject to a substantial risk of forfeiture or (2) the time the property is transferable by the employee. The fair market value of the property is determined without regard to any restriction, except a restriction that by its terms will never lapse.[84] Since the amount of the

---

[84] § 83(a)(1); *Miriam Sakol*, 67 T.C. 986 (1977); *T. M. Horwith*, 71 T.C. 932 (1979).

compensation is determined at the date that the restrictions lapse or when the property is transferable, the opportunity to generate capital gain treatment on the property is denied during a period when the ordinary income element is being deferred.

EXAMPLE 31

On October 1, 1993, Blue Corporation sold 100 shares of its stock to Ahmad, an employee, for $10 per share. At the time of the sale, the fair market value of the stock was $100 per share. Under the terms of the sale, each share of stock was nontransferable and subject to a substantial risk of forfeiture (which was not to lapse until October 1, 1997). Evidence of these restrictions was stamped on the face of the stock certificates. On October 1, 1997, the fair market value of the stock was $250 per share. Since the stock was nontransferable and was subject to a substantial risk of forfeiture, Ahmad did not include any compensation in gross income during 1993 (assuming no special election was made). Instead, Ahmad was required to include $24,000 of compensation in gross income [100 shares × ($250 − $10 per share)] during 1997. If for some reason the substantial risk of forfeiture had occurred (e.g., the plan required Ahmad to surrender the stock to the corporation if he voluntarily terminated his employment with the company before October 1, 1997) and Ahmad never received the stock certificates, he would have been allowed a capital loss of $1,000 (the extent of his investment). ▼

SUBSTANTIAL RISK OF FORFEITURE

A **substantial risk of forfeiture** exists if a person's rights to full enjoyment of property are conditioned upon the future performance, or the refraining from the performance, of substantial services by that individual.[85] For example, if an employee must return the property (receiving only his or her original cost, if any) should there be a failure to complete a substantial period of service (for any reason), the property is subject to a substantial risk of forfeiture. Another such situation exists when an employer can compel an employee to return the property due to a breach of a substantial covenant not to compete. Any substantial risk of forfeiture should be stated on the face of the stock certificates. Assuming that a substantial risk of forfeiture does not exist, the property received is valued at its fair market value, ignoring any restrictions, except for one instance dealing with closely held stock.

SPECIAL ELECTION AVAILABLE

An employee may elect within 30 days after the receipt of restricted property to recognize immediately as ordinary income the fair market value in excess of the amount paid for the property. Any appreciation in the value of the property after receipt is classified as capital gain instead of ordinary income. No deduction is allowed to the employee for taxes paid on the original amount included in income if the property is subsequently forfeited.[86] The employee is permitted to take a capital loss for any amounts that were actually paid for the property. Furthermore, in such a case, the employer must repay taxes saved by any compensation deduction taken in the earlier year.[87]

Any increase in value between the time the property is received and the time it becomes either nonforfeitable or transferable is taxed as ordinary income if the employee does not make a special election. However, if the employee elects to be

---

[85] § 83(c); Regulation § 1.83–3(c)(2) includes several examples of restricted property arrangements.

[86] § 83(b).
[87] Reg. §§ 1.83–6(c) and 2(a).

taxed immediately on the difference between the cost and fair market value on the date of issue, any future appreciation is treated as capital gain. In determining whether the gain is long term or short term, the holding period starts when the employee is taxed on the ordinary income.[88]

EXAMPLE 32

On July 1, 1987, Sparrow Company sold 100 shares of its preferred stock, worth $15 per share, to Diane (an employee) for $5 per share. The sale was subject to Diane's agreement to resell the preferred shares to the company for $5 per share if she terminated her employment during the following 10 years. Assume that the stock had a value of $25 per share on July 1, 1997, and Diane sold the stock for $30 per share on October 10, 1997. Diane made the special election to include the original spread (between the value of $15 in 1987 and the amount paid of $5) in income for 1987. Diane was required to recognize $1,000 of compensation income in 1987 ($15 − $5 = $10 × 100 shares), at which time her holding period in her stock began. Diane's tax basis in the stock was $1,500 ($1,000 + $500). When the preferred stock was sold in 1997, Diane recognized a $1,500 long-term capital gain ($30 × 100 shares − $1,500). ▼

EXAMPLE 33

Assume the same facts as in Example 32, except that Diane sells the stock in 1998 (rather than 1997). She would not recognize any gain in 1997 when the substantial risk of forfeiture lapses. Instead, Diane would recognize the $1,500 long-term capital gain in 1998. ▼

This special provision is usually not elected since it results in an immediate recognition of income and adverse tax consequences result from a subsequent forfeiture. However, the special election may be attractive in the following situations:

- The bargain element is relatively small.
- Substantial appreciation is expected in the future.
- A high probability exists that the restrictions will be met.

EMPLOYER DEDUCTIONS

At the time the employee is required to include the compensation in income, the employer is allowed a tax deduction for the same amount. The employer must withhold on this amount in accordance with § 3402. In the no-election situation, the deduction is limited to the fair market value of the restricted property (without regard to the restrictions) at the time the restrictions lapse, reduced by the amount originally paid for the property by the employee.[89] When the employee elects to be taxed immediately, the corporate deduction also is accelerated and deductible in like amount. In cases of deferred income recognition, the employer can receive a very sizable deduction if the property has appreciated.

EXAMPLE 34

On March 14, 1995, Gold Corporation sold to Harry, an employee, 10 shares of Gold common stock for $100 per share. Both the corporation and Harry were calendar year taxpayers. The common stock was subject to a substantial risk of forfeiture and was nontransferable; both conditions were to lapse on March 14, 1997. At the time of the sale, the fair market value of the common stock (without considering the restrictions) was $1,000 per share. On March 14, 1997, when the fair market value of the stock was $2,000 per share, the restrictions lapsed. Harry did not make a special election. In 1997, Harry realized ordinary income of $19,000 (10 shares at $2,000 per share less the $100 per share he had paid). Likewise, Gold Corporation was allowed a $19,000 compensation deduction in 1997. ▼

---

[88] § 1223(6).   [89] Reg. § 1.83–6(a).

EXAMPLE 35 In the previous example, assume that Harry had made the special election. Since he was taxed on $9,000 in 1995, the corporation was allowed to deduct a like amount in 1995. No deduction would be available in 1997.

STOCK OPTIONS

IN GENERAL

LEARNING OBJECTIVE 9
Differentiate the tax treatment of qualified and nonqualified stock options.

Various equity types of stock option programs are available for an employee's compensation package. Some authorities believe that some form of *equity kicker* is needed to attract new management, convert key officers into *partners* by giving them a share of the business, and retain the services of executives who might otherwise leave. Encouraging the managers of a business to have a proprietary interest in its successful operation should provide executives with a key motive to expand the company and improve its profits. In addition, under certain conditions, stock options may fall outside the $1 million limitation on the salaries of the top five executives of publicly traded companies.

A **stock option** gives an individual the right to purchase a stated number of shares of stock from a corporation at a certain price within a specified period of time. The optionee must be under no obligation to purchase the stock, and the option may be revocable by the corporation. The option must be in writing, and its terms must be clearly expressed.[90]

INCENTIVE STOCK OPTIONS

An equity type of stock option called an *incentive stock options (ISO)* is available for options granted after 1975 and exercised after 1980.[91] An ISO arrangement receives much the same tax treatment previously accorded to restricted and qualified stock option plans. There are no tax consequences when the option is granted, but the *spread* (the excess of the fair market value of the share at the date of exercise over the option price)[92] is a tax preference item for purposes of the alternative minimum tax. The determination of fair market value is made without regard to any lapse restrictions (a restriction that will expire after a period of time). After the option is exercised and when the stock is sold, any gain from the sale is taxed as a long-term capital gain if certain holding period requirements are met. To qualify as a long-term capital gain, the employee must not dispose of the stock within two years after the option is granted or within one year after acquiring the stock.[93] If the employee meets the holding period requirements, none of these transactions generates any business deduction for the employer.[94]

Since some beneficial treatment for long-term capital gains for the individual was restored beginning in 1991 and tax rates were increased in 1993, ISOs have regained some of their tax appeal on the gain side. In addition, an employee who has capital losses would prefer capital gain treatment.

---

[90] Reg. §§ 1.421–1(a)(1) and –7(a)(1).
[91] Qualified stock options were available under § 422 (prior to repeal by the Revenue Reconciliation Act of 1990) for certain qualified options granted before May 21, 1976. These qualified stock options had many of the statutory requirements of ISOs, but ISOs have a more favorable tax treatment.
[92] §§ 422(a), 421(a)(1), and 57(a)(3).
[93] § 422(a)(1).
[94] § 421(a)(2).

TAX IN THE NEWS

STOCK OPTIONS FOR SENIOR OFFICERS

Stock options are becoming an increasingly popular means of rewarding top executives. In 1995, for instance, U.S. corporations reserved 10 percent of their stock for options and outright grants to senior officers—three times as much as in the 1970s.

From a CEO's perspective, stock options have much to recommend them. If the company prospers, the options can be a bonanza, and even if the company's earnings and stock price plummet, none of the CEO's own money is at risk. Such opportunities are available only to CEO's and a handful of other top managers. According to Institutional Shareholder Services, an investment research firm, the top 15 executives in a company generally receive 97 percent of the options.

As some commentators are pointing out, however, the benefits of stock options do not extend to the common shareholders. While they risk their own money to buy the company's stock, stock options are diluting their equity. As for the argument that large stock option awards are necessary to lure and keep quality executives, one might consider the case of Westinghouse, which reportedly offered Michael Jordan a million share option to become CEO. So far, under Jordan's leadership, the price of Westinghouse stock has languished. While Jordan has not made any money on his options, he has not lost any either, and unlike many Westinghouse employees, he still has his job. Accordingly, the commentators suggest that if stock options are to be an inducement to performance, executives should buy them with their own money.

SOURCE: Adapted from Robert A. G. Monks, "Stock Options Don't Work. If CEOs Want Shares, Let'Em Buy Some," *Fortune*, September 18, 1995, pp. 230-31.

EXAMPLE 36

Wren Corporation granted an ISO for 100 shares of its stock to Rocky, an employee, on March 18, 1994. The option price was $100, and the fair market value was $100 on the date of the grant. Rocky exercised the option on April 1, 1996, when the market value of the stock was $200 per share. He sells the stock on April 6, 1997, for $300 per share. Rocky did not recognize any ordinary income on the date of the grant or the exercise date since the option qualified as an ISO. Wren received no compensation deduction. Rocky has a $10,000 tax preference item on the exercise date. He has a long-term capital gain of $20,000 [($300 − $100) × 100] upon the sale of the stock in 1997, because the one-year and two-year holding periods and other requirements have been met. ▼

As a further requirement for ISO treatment, the option holder must be an employee of the issuing corporation from the date the option is granted until 3 months (12 months if disabled) before the date of exercise. The holding period and the employee-status rules just described (the one-year, two-year, and three-month requirements) are waived in the case of the death of an employee.[95]

EXAMPLE 37

Assume the same facts as in the previous example, except that Rocky was not employed by Wren Corporation for six months before the date he exercised the options. Rocky must

---

[95] §§ 422(a)(2) and (c)(3). Exceptions are made for parent and subsidiary situations, corporate reorganizations, and liquidations. Also, in certain situations involving an insolvent employee, the holding period rules are modified.

recognize ordinary income to the extent of the spread, assuming there was no substantial risk of forfeiture. Thus, Rocky recognizes $10,000 [($200 − $100) × 100] of ordinary income on the exercise date, because he was not an employee of Wren Corporation at all times during the period beginning on the grant date and ending three months before the exercise date. Wren is allowed a deduction at the same time that Rocky reports the ordinary income. ▼

If the holding period requirements are not satisfied but all other conditions are met, the tax is still deferred to the point of the sale. However, the difference between the option price and the value of the stock at the date the option was exercised is treated as ordinary income. The difference between the amount realized for the stock and the value of the stock at the date of exercise is short-term or long-term capital gain, depending on the holding period of the stock itself. The employer is allowed a deduction equal to the amount recognized by the employee as ordinary income. The employee does not have a tax preference for alternative minimum tax purposes.

EXAMPLE 38

Assume the same facts as in Example 36, except that Rocky sells the stock on March 22, 1997, for $290 per share. Since Rocky did not hold the stock itself for at least one year, $10,000 of the gain is treated as ordinary income in 1997, and Wren Corporation is allowed a $10,000 compensation deduction in 1997. The remaining $9,000 is a short-term capital gain ($29,000 − $20,000). ▼

Qualification Requirements for Incentive Stock Option Plans.
An **incentive stock option (ISO)** is an option to purchase stock of a corporation granted to an individual for any reason connected with his or her employment.[96] The option is granted by the employer-corporation or by a parent or subsidiary corporation of the employer-corporation. An employee can use company stock to pay for the stock when exercising an option without disqualifying the ISO plan.

For an option to qualify as an ISO, the terms of the option itself must meet the following conditions:

- The option must be granted under a plan specifying the number of shares of stock to be issued and the employees or class of employees eligible to receive the options. The plan must be approved by the shareholders of the corporation within 12 months before or after the plan is adopted.
- The option must be granted within 10 years of the date the plan is adopted or of the date the plan is approved by the shareholders, whichever date is earlier.
- The option must by its terms be exercisable only within 10 years of the date it is granted.
- The option price must equal or exceed the fair market value of the stock at the time the option is granted. This requirement is deemed satisfied if there has been a good faith attempt to value the stock accurately, even if the option price is less than the stock value.
- The option by its terms must be nontransferable other than at death and must be exercisable during the employee's lifetime only by the employee.
- The employee must not, immediately before the option is granted, own stock representing more than 10 percent of the voting power or value of all classes of stock in the employer-corporation or its parent or subsidiary. (Here, the attribution rules of § 267 are applied in modified form.) However, the stock ownership limitation will be waived if the option price is at least

---
[96] § 422(b).

110 percent of the fair market value (at the time the option is granted) of the stock subject to the option and the option by its terms is not exercisable more than five years from the date it is granted.[97]

An overall limitation is imposed on the amount of ISOs that can be exercised in one year. This limit is set at $100,000 per year (based on the value of the stock determined at the time the option is granted) per employee.

NONQUALIFIED STOCK OPTIONS

A **nonqualified stock option (NQSO)** does not satisfy the statutory requirements for ISOs. In addition, a stock option that otherwise would qualify as an ISO will be treated as an NQSO if the terms of the stock option provide that it is not an ISO. If the NQSO has a readily ascertainable fair market value (e.g., the option is traded on an established exchange), the value of the option must be included in the employee's income at the date of grant. Thereafter, capital gain or loss is recognized only upon the disposal of the optioned stock. The employee's basis is the amount paid for the stock plus any amount reported as ordinary income. The employer obtains a corresponding tax deduction at the same time and to the extent that ordinary income is recognized by the employee.[98]

EXAMPLE 39

On February 1, 1996, Janet was granted an NQSO to purchase 100 shares of stock from her employer at $10 per share. On this date, the option was selling for $2 on an established exchange. Janet exercised the option on March 30, 1997, when the stock was worth $20 per share. On June 5, 1997, Janet sold the optioned stock for $22 per share.

- Janet must report ordinary income of $200 ($2 × 100 shares) on the date of grant (February 1, 1996), because the option has a readily ascertainable fair market value.
- Upon the sale of the stock (June 5, 1997), Janet must report a long-term capital gain of $1,000 [($22 − $12) × 100 shares].
- At the date of grant (February 1, 1996), the employer receives a tax deduction of $200, the amount of income reported by Janet. ▼

If an NQSO does not have a readily ascertainable fair market value, an employee does not recognize income at the grant date. However, as a general rule, ordinary income must be reported in the year of exercise (the difference between the fair market value of the stock at the exercise date and the option price).[99] The amount paid by the employee for the stock plus the amount reported as ordinary income becomes the basis. Any appreciation above that basis is taxed as a long-term capital gain upon disposition (assuming the stock is held for the required long-term holding period after exercise). The corporation receives a corresponding tax deduction at the same time and to the extent that ordinary income is recognized by the employee.

EXAMPLE 40

On February 3, 1995, Maria was granted an NQSO for 100 shares of common stock at $10 per share. On the date of the grant, there was no readily ascertainable fair market value for the option. Maria exercised the options on January 3, 1996, when the stock was selling for $15 per share. She sold one-half of the shares on April 15, 1996, and the other half on September 17, 1997. The sale price on both dates was $21 per share. Maria would not recognize any income on the grant date (February 3, 1995) but would recognize $500 ($1,500 − $1,000) of ordinary income on the exercise date (January 3, 1996). She would recognize a short-term capital gain

---

[97] § 422(c)(5).
[98] Reg. §§ 1.421–6(c), (d), (e), and (f); Reg. § 1.83–7.
[99] Reg. § 1.83–7(a); Reg. § 1.421–6(d).

of $300 on the sale of the first half in 1996 and a $300 long-term capital gain on the sale of the second batch of stock in 1997 [½($2,100 − $1,500)]. ▼

The major *advantages* of NQSOs can be summarized as follows:

- A tax deduction is available to the corporation without a cash outlay.
- The employee receives capital gain treatment on any appreciation in the stock starting either at the exercise date if the option does not have a readily ascertainable fair market value or at the date of grant if the option has a readily ascertainable fair market value.
- Options can be issued at more flexible terms than under ISO plans (e.g., longer exercise period and discount on exercise price).

A major *disadvantage* is that the employee must recognize ordinary income on the exercise of the option or at the date of grant without receiving cash to pay the tax.

TAX PLANNING CONSIDERATIONS

10 LEARNING OBJECTIVE
Identify tax planning opportunities available with deferred compensation.

DEFERRED COMPENSATION

With the higher 39.6 percent individual tax rate, taxpayers may try to lower their tax burden by participating in more deferred compensation arrangements. The $1 million annual limit on the compensation deduction for the top five executives of publicly traded companies may cause a shift into § 401(k) plans, qualified retirement plans, and especially nonqualified deferred compensation arrangements. However, the amount of compensation that can be taken into consideration for purposes of calculating contributions or benefits under a qualified pension or profit sharing plan has been reduced to $160,000. The increase to $2,000 for spousal IRAs and the new SIMPLE IRA and SIMPLE § 401(k) plan should encourage more participation in retirement vehicles.

The repeal of the five-year averaging after 1999 for qualified retirement plan distributions may encourage many employees to consider retiring over the next several years. The temporary suspension of the 15 percent excise tax on excess distributions during 1997, 1998, and 1999 may encourage individuals to take distributions from qualified plans. The expectation that individual tax rates may increase in future years likewise encourages distributions and the receipt of cash compensation in 1997.

QUALIFIED PLANS

Qualified plans provide maximum tax benefits for employers, because the employer receives an immediate tax deduction for contributions to such plans and the income that is earned on the contributions is not taxable to the employer. The employer contributions and the trust earnings are not taxed to the employees until those funds are made available to them.

Qualified plans are most appropriate where it is desirable to provide benefits for a cross section of employees. In some closely held corporations, the primary objective is to provide benefits for the officer-shareholder group and other highly paid personnel. The nondiscrimination requirements that must be met in a qualified plan may prevent such companies from attaining these objectives. Thus, a nonqualified arrangement may be needed as a supplement to, or used in lieu of, the qualified plan.

SELF-EMPLOYED RETIREMENT PLANS

A Keogh or IRA participant may make a deductible contribution for a tax year up to the time prescribed for filing the individual's tax return. A Keogh plan must have been established by the end of the tax year (e.g., December 31) to obtain a current deduction for the contribution made in the subsequent year. An individual can establish an IRA after the end of the tax year and still receive a current deduction for the contribution made in the subsequent year. However, since the deductibility of contributions to IRAs has been restricted for many middle-income and upper-income taxpayers, Keogh plans are likely to become more important.

INDIVIDUAL RETIREMENT ACCOUNTS

Fewer taxpayers are now allowed to make deductible contributions to IRAs. A working taxpayer not covered by another qualified plan may still deduct IRA contributions up to the smaller of $2,000 or 100 percent of earned income. If both spouses work, each may individually establish an IRA. Where only one spouse has earned income, an IRA may be established for the nonworking spouse. A total of $4,000 may then be contributed to the two IRAs as long as the combined compensation of both spouses is at least equal to the contributed amount.

A single working taxpayer covered by another retirement plan may deduct a $2,000 IRA contribution only if AGI is less than $25,000 a year. For married couples filing jointly, the ceiling is $40,000. The IRA deduction is reduced proportionately as AGI increases within a $10,000 phase-out range above the $25,000 and $40,000 ceilings.

IRA and Keogh participants can self-direct their investments into a wide variety of assets. The participant self-directs the investments into various assets even though the assets are under the control of a trustee or custodian. The acquisition of collectibles (e.g., art, gems, metals) by an IRA or self-directed Keogh or corporate plan is treated as a distribution (taxed). For an IRA or Keogh participant under age 59½, there is also a 10 percent premature distribution penalty.

COMPARISON OF § 401(k) PLAN WITH IRA

Most employees will find a § 401(k) plan more attractive than an IRA. Probably the biggest limitation of an IRA is the $2,000 maximum shelter. Under § 401(k), employees are permitted to shelter compensation up to $9,500 (in 1997).[100] The restrictions on deducting contributions to IRAs for many middle-income and upper-income taxpayers may cause many employees to utilize § 401(k) plans more frequently.

Another difference between § 401(k) plans and IRAs is the manner in which the money is treated. Money placed in an IRA may be tax deductible, whereas dollars placed in a § 401(k) plan are considered to be deferred compensation. Thus, a § 401(k) reduction may reduce profit sharing payments, group life insurance, and Social Security benefits. Concept Summary 19–4 compares a § 401(k) plan with an IRA.

NONQUALIFIED DEFERRED COMPENSATION (NQDC) PLANS

Nonqualified deferred compensation arrangements such as restricted property plans can be useful to attract executive talent or to provide substantial retirement benefits for executives. A restricted property plan may be used to retain a key employee of a closely held company when management continuity problems are anticipated. Without such employees, the untimely death or disability of one of

---

[100] This amount is indexed annually.

Concept Summary 19-4

Section 401(k) Plan and IRA Compared

	§ 401(k) Plan	IRA
Deduction limitation	Smaller of $9,500 (in 1997) or approximately 25% of total earnings. Limited by antidiscrimination requirements of § 401(k)(3).	$2,000 or 100% of compensation.
Distributions	Early withdrawal possible if for early retirement (55 or over) or to pay medical expenses.	10% penalty for early withdrawals, except for withdrawals to pay for certain medical expenses and health insurance.
Effect on gross earnings	Gross salary reduction, which may reduce profit sharing contributions, Social Security benefits, and group life insurance.	No effect.
Employer involvement	Must keep records; monitor for compliance with antidiscrimination test.	Minimal.
Lump-sum distributions	Favorable 5-year or 10-year forward averaging.	Ordinary income.
Timing of contribution	Within 30 days of plan year-end or due date of employer's return.*	Grace period up to due date of tax return (not including extensions).
Loans from plan	Yes.	No.

*Elective contributions must be made to the plan no later than 30 days after the end of the plan year, and nonelective contributions no later than the due date of the tax return (including extensions).

---

the owners might cause a disruption of the business with an attendant loss in value for his or her heirs. Such plans may discriminate in favor of officers and other highly paid employees. The employer, however, does not receive a tax deduction until the employee is required to include the deferred compensation in income (upon the lapse of the restrictions).

The principal advantage of NQDC plans is that the employee can defer the recognition of income to future periods when his or her income tax bracket may be lower (e.g., during retirement years). The time value benefits from the deferral of income should also be considered. However, with the trend toward increasing rates, an executive with a deferred compensation arrangement entered into in a prior year may wish to accelerate the income into 1997 since individual tax rates in future years may be even higher.

The principal disadvantage of NQDC plans could be the bunching effect that takes place on the expiration of the period of deferral. In some cases, planning can alleviate this result.

EXAMPLE 41

During 1997, Kelly, an executive, enters into an agreement to postpone a portion of her payment for current services until retirement. The deferred amount is not segregated from the company's general assets and is subject to normal business risk. The entire payment, not the after-tax amount, is invested in securities and variable annuity contracts. Kelly is not

Concept Summary 19-5

Incentive Stock Options and Nonqualified Stock Options Compared

	ISO	NQSO
Granted at any price	No	Yes
May have any duration	No	Yes
Governing Code Section	§ 422	§ 83
Spread subject to alternative minimum tax	Yes	No
Deduction to employer for spread	No	Yes
Type of gain/loss on disposal	Capital	Capital
Statutory amount ($100,000) limitation	Yes	No

taxed on the payment in 1997, and the company receives no deduction in 1997. If Kelly receives the deferred payment in a lump sum when she retires, the tax rates may be higher and more progressive than in 1997. Thus, Kelly may wish to arrange for a number of payments to be made to her or a designated beneficiary over a number of years. ▼

STOCK OPTIONS

Rather than paying compensation in the form of corporate stock, an alternative approach is to issue options to purchase stock at a specific price to an employee. Stock option plans are used more frequently by publicly traded companies than by closely held companies. This difference is due to the problems of determining the value of the stock of a company that is not publicly held.

Nonqualified stock options (NQSOs) are more flexible and less restrictive than incentive stock options (ISOs). For example, the holding period for an NQSO is not as long as that for an ISO. Further, the option price of an NQSO may be less than the fair market value of the stock at the time the option is granted. An NQSO creates an employer deduction that lowers the cost of the NQSO to the employer. The employer may pass along this tax savings to the employee in the form of a cash payment. Both the employer and the employee may be better off by combining NQSOs with additional cash payments rather than using ISOs. See Concept Summary 19-5.

FLEXIBLE BENEFIT PLANS

Employees may be permitted to choose from a package of employer-provided fringe benefits.[101] In these so-called **cafeteria benefit plans,** some of the benefits chosen by an employee may be taxable, and some may be statutory nontaxable benefits (e.g., health and accident insurance and group term life insurance).

Employer contributions made to a flexible plan are included in an employee's gross income only to the extent that the employee actually elects the taxable benefits. Certain nondiscrimination standards with respect to coverage, eligibility

---
[101] § 125.

for participation, contributions, and benefits must be met. Thus, such a plan must cover a fair cross section of employees. Also, a flexible plan cannot include an election to defer compensation, and a key employee is not exempt from taxation on the taxable benefits made available where more than 25 percent of the statutory nontaxable benefits are provided to key employees.

KEY TERMS

Cafeteria benefit plan, 19–41

Deferred compensation, 19–3

Defined benefit plan, 19–4

Defined contribution pension plan, 19–4

Employee stock ownership plan (ESOP), 19–6

Golden parachute payments, 19–29

Highly compensated employee, 19–8

H.R. 10 (Keogh) plan, 19–20

Incentive stock option (ISO), 19–36

Individual Retirement Account (IRA), 19–22

Lump-sum distribution, 19–12

Nonqualified deferred compensation (NQDC) plan, 19–27

Nonqualified stock option (NQSO), 19–37

Pension plan, 19–4

Profit sharing plan, 19–5

Restricted property plan, 19–31

Section 401(k) plan, 19–18

Simplified employee pension (SEP) plan, 19–23

Stock bonus plan, 19–6

Stock option, 19–34

Substantial risk of forfeiture, 19–32

Top-heavy plan, 19–17

Vesting requirements, 19–9

Zero bracket amount, 19–13

PROBLEM MATERIALS

DISCUSSION QUESTIONS

1. Describe the three basic types of qualified plans.
2. Compare and contrast qualified pension and profit sharing plans.
3. Determine whether each of the following independent statements best applies to a defined contribution plan (DCP), defined benefit plan (DBP), both (B), or neither (N):
   a. Includes an employee stock ownership plan (ESOP).
   b. Forfeitures can be allocated to the remaining participants' accounts.
   c. Requires greater reporting requirements and more actuarial and administrative costs.
   d. Forfeitures can revert to the employer.
   e. More favorable to employees who are older at the time the plan is adopted.
   f. Employee forfeitures can be used to reduce future contributions by the employer.
   g. May exclude employees who begin employment within five years of normal retirement age.
   h. Annual addition to each employee's account may not exceed the smaller of $30,000 or 25% of the employee's salary.
   i. The final benefit to a participant depends upon investment performance.
   j. To avoid penalties, the amount of annual contributions must meet minimum funding requirements.

4. Indicate whether the following statements apply to a pension plan (P), a profit sharing plan (PS), both (B), or neither (N):
   a. Forfeited amounts can be used to reduce future contributions by the employer.
   b. Allocation of forfeitures may discriminate in favor of the prohibited group (highly compensated employees).
   c. Forfeitures can revert to the employer.
   d. Forfeitures can increase plan benefits by allocating the forfeitures to participants.
   e. An annual benefit of $60,000 could be payable on behalf of a participant.
   f. More favorable to employees who are older at the time the qualified plan is adopted.

5. When will the $30,000 maximum annual contribution to a defined contribution plan be indexed?

6. What are the tax and financial advantages accruing to a company that adopts an employee stock ownership plan (ESOP) for employees?

7. List the qualification requirements that must be satisfied in order for a qualified plan to receive favorable tax treatment.

8. Is it possible to provide greater vested benefits for highly paid employees and still meet the nondiscrimination requirements under a qualified pension plan? Explain.

9. What causes an employee to be classified as a "highly compensated employee"?

10. When must a participant begin receiving distributions from a qualified plan?

11. Discuss the penalty for excess distributions from qualified plans.

12. Manuel plans to retire in 1997 at age 68. Identify any issues facing Manuel with respect to distributions from his qualified retirement plans.

13. Discuss the tax consequences to employee, employer, and the trust of a qualified pension or profit sharing plan.

14. Harvey Maxwell, who is age 67, is going to receive a lump-sum distribution from a qualified plan. He has asked you to provide him with a description of the alternatives available to him for taxing the lump-sum distribution. Draft a letter to Harvey in which you respond. He resides at 3000 East Glenn, Tulsa, OK 74104.

15. Which of the following would be considered a tax benefit or advantage of a qualified retirement plan?
    a. Certain lump-sum distributions may be subject to capital gain treatment.
    b. Employer contributions are currently deductible.
    c. Employee contributions are currently deductible.
    d. The qualified trust is tax-exempt as to all income (other than unrelated business income).
    e. In a lump-sum distribution, any capital gain tax on the portion attributable to any unrealized appreciation in the stock of the employer at the time of distribution is deferred until the time the employee disposes of the stock in a taxable transaction.
    f. Election may be made to allow a lump-sum distribution to be subject to a 5-year or 10-year forward averaging technique.

16. What ceiling limitations have been placed on employer contributions (relative to individual employees) to defined contribution and defined benefit plans?

17. What is the maximum deduction permitted to an employer each year for contributions to a profit sharing plan and a stock bonus plan?

18. Define the term *key employee* for purposes of a top-heavy plan.

19. Determine the 1997 indexed amounts for the following items:
    a. Maximum annual contribution to a defined contribution plan.
    b. Maximum annual benefits payable by a defined benefit plan.
    c. The $150,000 or $112,500 amounts for calculating the 15% excise tax imposed on excess distributions.
    d. The maximum amount of the annual contribution to a cash or deferred arrangement plan.

20. Frank Paterson calls you and asks about the differences between Keogh plans and Individual Retirement Accounts. Prepare a memo for the files about your discussion. Do not include the SIMPLE IRA in your presentation.

21. Can a § 401(k) plan avoid the nondiscrimination tests and the top-heavy rules?

22. Can an individual make withdrawals from an IRA without incurring the 10% penalty tax?

23. During his senior year in college, Mark is drafted by the Los Angeles Dodgers. When he graduates, he expects to sign a five-year contract in the range of $1.8 million per year. Mark plans to marry his girlfriend before he reports to the Dodger farm team in California. Identify the relevant tax issues facing this left-handed pitcher.

24. List some payments to employees that would not be considered golden parachute payments.

25. Currently, there is an absolute maximum limit of $1 million on the deductible compensation for each of the top five executives of publicly traded companies. Discuss the accuracy of this statement.

26. What is a substantial risk of forfeiture? Why is it necessary to impose this restriction on the transfer of restricted property?

27. Determine which of the following conditions would cause options to fall *outside* the qualification requirements for incentive stock options:
    a. The employee disposes of his stock within 15 months from the date of the granting of the options.
    b. The employee is allowed to exercise the options up to 12 years from the date the options are granted.
    c. The employee is transferred to the parent of the corporation six months before he exercises the options.
    d. The option price is 112% of the fair market value of the stock on the grant date, and the shareholder owns 15% of the stock.
    e. The option may be exercised by the employee's spouse in the event of the employee's death.

28. Would a 30-year-old corporate executive in the 39.6% tax bracket prefer an extra $20,000 bonus or the option to purchase $20,000 worth of securities for $8,000 from the employer under a nonqualified stock option plan in the current year?

29. Compare and contrast an IRA and a § 401(k) plan. Do not include SIMPLE plans in your analysis.

30. Amanda is the major owner and employee of a closely held corporation. She is in the 39.6% tax bracket, living in a state with a 6% income tax rate, and has a 7.65% FICA tax rate. She needs to determine how to receive compensation from her corporation. Identify relevant tax issues facing Amanda.

31. Indicate whether each of the following items is considered a nonqualified compensation plan (N), a qualified compensation plan (Q), or both (B):
    a. Individual Retirement Account.
    b. Incentive stock option.
    c. Group term life insurance.
    d. Cafeteria plan.
    e. Pension plan.
    f. Employee stock ownership plan.
    g. Nonqualified stock option.
    h. Keogh plan.
    i. Simplified employee pension plan.

PROBLEMS

32. Red Corporation has a total of 1,000 employees, of whom 700 are non-highly compensated. The retirement plan covers 300 non-highly compensated employees and 200 highly compensated employees. Does this plan satisfy the minimum coverage test?

33. Cardinal Corporation's pension plan benefits 620 of its 1,000 highly compensated employees. How many of its 620 non-highly compensated employees must benefit to meet the ratio test for the minimum coverage requirement?

34. A retirement plan covers 72% of the non-highly compensated individuals. The plan benefits 49 of the 131 employees. Determine if the participation requirement is met.

35. Robin, Inc., uses the three-to-seven-year graded vesting approach in its retirement plan. Calculate the nonforfeitable percentage for each of the following employees based on the years of service completed:

Participant	Years of Service
Sandy	2
Rod	4
Tony	6
Heather	8

36. Tyronne, age 46, is the sole remaining participant of a money purchase pension plan. The plan is terminated, and a $200,000 taxable distribution is made to Tyronne. Calculate the amount of any early distribution penalty tax for 1997.

37. Cheryl receives a $195,000 distribution from her qualified retirement plan in 1997. If this amount is not a lump-sum distribution, calculate the amount of any excess distribution penalty tax. Cheryl made no after-tax contributions to the plan. Assuming the 1997 indexed amount does not change, calculate any excess distribution penalty tax for 2000.

38. George received a distribution from a qualified plan that was entitled to capital gain treatment under § 402(a)(2). The 100 shares of the employer company stock received have a tax basis of $20 per share and a fair market value of $85 per share. George sold this stock five months after the distribution for $120 per share. Calculate the amount and character of any gain to George.

39. When Leif retires in 1997, he receives a lump-sum distribution of $50,000 from a noncontributory qualified pension plan. His active period of participation was from January 1, 1971, through December 31, 1978. Assume that Leif attained age 50 before January 1, 1986. If Leif files a joint return with his wife in 1997 and elects to use the 10-year forward averaging provision, calculate (a) his separate tax on this distribution and (b) the capital gain portion.

40. Yvonne Blair receives a $165,000 lump-sum distribution from a contributory pension plan in 1997; the distribution includes employer common stock with net unrealized appreciation of $30,000. Yvonne contributed $25,000 to the qualified plan while she was an active participant from February 10, 1973, to February 10, 1978. Yvonne attained age 50 before January 1, 1986. Yvonne wishes to know her tax consequences with respect to the lump-sum distribution. Write a letter to Yvonne that includes your calculations. Her address is 209 Barrett Street, Laramie, WY 82071.

41. Wade has been an active participant in a defined benefit plan for 21 years. During his last 5 years of employment, Wade earned $20,000, $32,000, $45,000, $50,000, and $70,000, respectively (representing his highest income years).
    a. Calculate Wade's maximum allowable benefits from this qualified plan (assume there are fewer than 100 participants).
    b. Assume that Wade's average compensation for his three high years is $135,000. Calculate Wade's maximum allowable benefits.

42. Determine the maximum annual benefits payable to an employee from a defined benefit plan in the following independent situations:
    a. Quincy, age 66, has been a participant for 13 years, and his highest average compensation for 3 years is $90,000.
    b. Wendy, age 67, has been a participant for 9 years (11 years of service), and her highest average compensation for 3 years is $90,000.
    c. Paul, age 68, has been a participant for 11 years in a collectively bargained plan with 238 participants. His highest average compensation for 3 years is $70,300.

43. The compensation paid by Orange Corporation to the plan participants of a profit sharing plan in 1997 was $33,300. During 1997, Orange Corporation contributed $10,000 to the plan.
    a. Calculate Orange Corporation's deductible amount for 1997.
    b. Calculate the amount of the contribution carryover from 1997.

44. A money purchase plan covers three employees: Samuel (who has annual compensation of $310,000), Mary (who has annual compensation of $140,000), and Larry (who has annual compensation of $50,000). If the contribution rate is 15%, what amount can be contributed to these employees' accounts?

45. During 1997, Keith is a key employee of a top-heavy pension plan. His salary is $275,000. Calculate Keith's maximum contribution to such a defined benefit plan.

46. Autumn Company's defined benefit plan allocates $300,000 of the $410,000 of cumulative benefits to key employees. The company has contacted you asking if the plan is in danger of being labeled a top-heavy plan. Prepare a memo for the tax files that includes your analysis and conclusions.

47. Blue, Inc., uses the six-year graded vesting schedule for its top-heavy retirement plan. Calculate the nonforfeitable percentage for each of the following non-key employees based on the years of service completed:

Participant	Years of Service
Dana	2
Gene	4
Samuel	5
Janet	7

48. Miguel, a single individual, participates in a SIMPLE § 401(k) plan of his employer. The plan permits participants to contribute a percentage of their salary. Miguel elects to contribute 6% of his annual compensation of $86,000 to the plan. On what amount of his salary are income taxes paid in 1997?

49. Susan earns $220,000 of self-employment net income (after the deduction for one-half of self-employment tax) in 1997 in a sole proprietorship.
    a. Calculate the maximum amount that Susan can deduct for contributions to a defined contribution Keogh plan.
    b. Suppose Susan contributes more than the allowable amount to the Keogh plan. What are the consequences to her?
    c. Can Susan retire and begin receiving Keogh payments at age 55?

50. Charlene is unmarried and is an active participant in a qualified IRA plan. Her modified AGI is $32,000.
    a. Calculate the amount that Charlene can contribute to the IRA and the amount she can deduct.
    b. Assume instead that Charlene is a participant in a SIMPLE IRA and that she elects to contribute 4% of her compensation to the account, while her employer contributes 3%. What amount will be contributed for 1997? What amount will be vested?

51. Answer the following independent questions with respect to IRA and § 401(k) contributions:
    a. Govind earns a salary of $24,000 and is not an active participant in any other qualified plan. His wife has $600 of compensation income. What is the maximum total deductible contribution to their IRAs?
    b. Danos is a participant in a SIMPLE § 401(k) plan. He contributes 6% of his salary of $31,000, and his employer contributes 4%. What amount will be contributed for the year? What amount will be vested?

52. Spring, Inc., pays bonuses to its key employees each year. The specific employees to receive bonuses and the amount of bonus for each recipient are determined on December 1 of each year. An employee eligible for a bonus may decide on or before November 15 of each year to postpone the receipt of the bonus until retirement or death. An employee electing to postpone receipt of a bonus is allowed to designate, at any time before retirement, the time and manner of the postretirement payments and to designate the persons to receive any amount payable after death. Separate accounts are not maintained for each employee. Under this compensation plan, Heather may elect to receive her $90,000 bonus in cash, or she may elect to defer the receipt of the bonus until 2001. Recommend to Heather which alternative to accept.

53. Nancy is an officer of a local bank that merges with another national bank (i.e., a change of ownership occurs). She loses her job as a result of the merger, but she receives a cash settlement of $590,000 from her employer. Her average annual compensation for the past five tax years is $200,000.
    a. What are the tax consequences to Nancy of the $590,000 payment?
    b. Assume instead that Nancy's five-year average annual compensation was $110,000, and she receives $390,000 in the settlement. What are the tax consequences to Nancy?

54. James, an executive, receives a $600,000 payment under a golden parachute agreement. James's base amount from Silver Corporation is $140,000.
    a. What amount is not deductible to Silver Corporation under § 280G?
    b. What total tax must James pay, assuming a 39.6% tax rate?
    c. Answer (a) and (b) assuming the payment is $400,000.

55. On February 20, 1997, Tim (an executive of Hawk Corporation) purchased 100 shares of Hawk stock (selling at $20 a share) for $10. A condition of the transaction was that Tim must resell the stock to Hawk at cost if he voluntarily leaves the company within five years of receiving the stock (assume this represents a substantial risk of forfeiture).
    a. Assuming that no special election is made under § 83(b), what amount, if any, is taxable to Tim in 1997?
    b. Five years later when the stock is selling for $40 a share, Tim is still employed by Hawk. What amount of ordinary income, if any, is taxable to Tim?
    c. What amount, if any, is deductible by Hawk as compensation expense five years later?
    d. Should Tim make the § 83(b) special election in 1997? What amount would be taxable in 1997 if he makes the special election?
    e. In (d), what amount would be deductible by Hawk five years later?
    f. Under (d), assume Tim sold all the stock six years later for $65 per share. How much capital gain is included in his gross income?
    g. In (d), what loss is available to Tim if he voluntarily resigns in 2000 before the five-year period and does not sell the stock back to the corporation?
    h. In (g), in the year Tim resigns, what amount, if any, would be taxable to Hawk Corporation?

56. On July 2, 1993, Black Corporation sold 1,000 of its common shares (worth $14 per share) to Earl, an employee, for $5 per share. The sale was subject to Earl's agreement to resell the shares to the corporation for $5 per share if his employment is terminated within the following four years. The shares had a value of $24 per share on July 2, 1997. Earl sells the shares for $31 per share on September 16, 1997. No special election under § 83(b) is made.

a. What amount, if any, will be taxed to Earl on July 2, 1993?
b. On July 2, 1997?
c. On September 16, 1997?
d. What deduction, if any, will Black Corporation obtain?
e. Assume the same facts but that Earl makes the election under § 83(b). What amount, if any, will be taxed to Earl on July 2, 1993?
f. Will the assumption made in (e) have any effect on any deduction Black Corporation will receive? Explain.

57. Rosa exercises incentive stock options for 100 shares of Copper Corporation stock at the option price of $100 per share on May 21, 1997, when the fair market value is $120 per share. She sells the 100 shares of common stock three and one-half years later for $140.
    a. Calculate the total long-term capital gain on this sale.
    b. Assume Rosa holds the stock seven months and sells the shares for $140 per share. Calculate any ordinary income on the sale.
    c. In (b), what amount can Copper Corporation deduct?
    d. Suppose Rosa holds the stock for two years and sells the shares for $115 per share. Calculate any capital gain on this transaction.
    e. In (a), assume the options are nonqualified options with a nonascertainable fair market value on the date of the grant. Calculate total long-term capital gain, if any, in the year of sale.
    f. In (e), assume that each option has an ascertainable fair market value of $10 on the date of the grant and no substantial risk of forfeiture exists. Calculate total long-term capital gain, if any, on the date of the sale.

58. On November 19, 1995, Rex is granted a nonqualified stock option to purchase 100 shares of Tan Company (on that date the stock is selling for $8 per share and the option price is $9 per share). Rex exercises the option on August 21, 1996, when the stock is selling for $10 per share. Five months later, Rex sells the shares for $11.50 per share.
    a. What amount is taxable to Rex in 1995?
    b. What amount is taxable to Rex in 1996?
    c. What amount and type of gain are taxable to Rex in 1997?
    d. What amount, if any, is deductible by Tan Company in 1996?
    e. What amount, if any, is recognized in 1997 if the stock is sold for $9.50 per share?

59. Sara Reid, the owner of a small business, is trying to decide whether to have a § 401(k) plan or a simplified employee pension plan. She is not interested in a SIMPLE § 401(k) plan. Her salary will be approximately $45,000, and she will have no employees. She asks you to provide her with information on the advantages and disadvantages of both types of plans and your recommendation. Draft a letter to Sara that contains your response. Her address is 1000 Canal Avenue, New Orleans, LA 70148.

60. Lou's employer provides a qualified cafeteria plan under which he can choose cash of $6,000 or health and accident insurance premiums worth approximately $5,000. If Lou is in the 39.6% tax bracket, advise him of his tax alternatives.

RESEARCH PROBLEMS

Note: ***West's Federal Taxation on CD-ROM*** *can be used in preparing solutions to the Research Problems. Alternatively, tax research materials contained in a standard tax library can be used.*

Research Problem 1. Mr. Sanjay Baker and his sister owned and operated a mail-order business in corporate form. The corporation used the homes of Mr. Baker and his sister for corporate mail-order activities (assembling, storing inventory, etc.). The corporation paid Mr. Baker and the sister rent for the use of the homes. The payments were deducted as rent and reported by the two parties on their tax returns. The IRS disallowed most of the deduction, contending that the rent was excessive. Is the excessive rent deductible as compensation? Write a letter to Mr. Baker that contains your advice and prepare a memo for the tax files. His address is 63 Rose Avenue, San Francisco, CA 94117.

Partial list of research aids:
Multnomah Operating Co., 57–2 USTC ¶9979, 52 AFTR 672, 248 F.2d 661 (CA–9, 1957).

Research Problem 2. Frank and Polly were married, but Frank died on February 25, 1997. During 1997, Frank earned $5,226 in wages, but Polly had no earned income. Neither had contributed any money to an IRA during 1997. What amount, if any, can be contributed to Frank's IRA and/or Polly's spousal IRA?

Research Problem 3. Six executives entered into elective deferred compensation agreements whereby, after rendering the necessary services, they are entitled to be paid deferred compensation plus incremental amounts designated as "interest." This "interest" is calculated by reference to a predetermined formula. On their retirement, the executives are entitled to receive the deferred compensation plus the incremental "interest" amounts. During 1997, the accrual method employer put $929,000 of deferred compensation into the deferred compensation accounts (DCAs) along with $177,500 of "interest." The DCAs were unfunded and unsecured. The employer intends to deduct the $177,500 as interest within the meaning of § 163. Is this the appropriate tax treatment?

Research Problem 4. What is the definition of "deferred compensation"? Are stock options and stock appreciation rights classified as deferred compensation? When is nonqualified deferred compensation taken into account as wages for FICA purposes?

Research Problem 5. What are stock appreciation rights? Outline the tax treatment.

Use the tax resources of the internet to address the following questions. Do not restrict your search to the World Wide Web, but include a review of newsgroups and general reference materials, practitioner sites and resources, primary sources of the tax law, chat rooms and discussion groups, and other opportunities.

Research Problem 6. Locate and download an internet retirement calculator. Use this program to help you answer the questions in Problems 50 and 51.

Research Problem 7. Contrast several advertisements offered by brokerage firms and other financial institutions promoting the SIMPLE retirement program. Do these solicitations correctly convey the details of the tax law?

Research Problem 8. Using newspaper and magazine articles, summarize the latest trends in the use of non-qualified deferred compensation and incentive stock options. Include in your analysis a key executive from at least one publicly traded corporation.

TEAM PROJECT: ARTHUR ANDERSEN TAX CHALLENGE CASES

For more information on the Arthur Andersen Tax Challenge Cases, refer to Chapter 1, page 1-38.

Information related to tax issues and problems that are discussed in this chapter may be found in the

Day and Ball case on pages 2, 3, 4, 5, and 30
Miller case on pages 2, 4, 5, 12-15, and 18-20

Read and analyze the case you have been assigned and *identify* any issues and problems that are related to material covered in this chapter. If the information provided in the case is complete, prepare answers for this part of the case at this time. If you need information that is contained in the later parts of the case, write a memo summarizing the questions or problems so you can prepare a complete answer at a later date.

PART VII
CORPORATIONS AND PARTNERSHIPS

The primary orientation of this text is toward basic tax concepts and the individual taxpayer. Although many of these tax concepts also apply to corporations and partnerships, numerous tax concepts apply specifically to corporations or partnerships. An overview of these provisions is presented in Part VII. Comprehensive coverage of these topics appears in *West's Federal Taxation: Corporations, Partnerships, Estates, and Trusts.*

Chapter 20
Corporations and Partnerships

CHAPTER 20

CORPORATIONS AND PARTNERSHIPS

LEARNING OBJECTIVES

After completing Chapter 20, you should be able to:

1. Identify those entities that are treated as corporations for Federal income tax purposes.

2. Contrast the income tax treatment of individuals with that applicable to corporations.

3. Recognize and calculate the tax deductions available only to corporations.

4. Determine the corporate tax liability and comply with various procedural and reporting requirements.

5. Understand the tax rules governing the formation of corporations.

6. Work with the tax rules governing the operation of corporations.

7. Recognize the tax rules governing the liquidation of corporations.

8. Appreciate the utility and effect of the Subchapter S election.

9. Understand the tax consequences of forming and operating a partnership.

10. Evaluate the advantages and disadvantages of the various forms for conducting a business.

OUTLINE

What Is a Corporation?, 20-3
Compliance with State Law, 20-3
The Association Approach, 20-3
Limited Liability Companies, 20-5
A Simple Way to Select Entity Status, 20-5
Income Tax Considerations, 20-5
General Tax Consequences of Different Forms of Business Entities, 20-5
Individuals and Corporations Compared—An Overview, 20-6
Specific Provisions Compared, 20-7
Deductions Available Only to Corporations, 20-10
Determination of Corporate Tax Liability, 20-12
Corporate Filing Requirements, 20-14

Reconciliation of Corporate Taxable Income and Accounting Income, 20-14
Forming the Corporation, 20-17
Capital Contributions, 20-17
Transfers to Controlled Corporations, 20-18
Operating the Corporation, 20-20
Dividend Distributions, 20-20
Stock Redemptions, 20-22
Liquidating the Corporation, 20-22
General Rule of § 331, 20-23
Exception to the General Rule, 20-23
Basis Determination—§§ 334 and 338, 20-23
Effect of the Liquidation on the Corporation, 20-24

The S Election, 20-24
Justification for the Election, 20-24
Operational Rules, 20-26
Partnerships, 20-29
Nature of Partnership Taxation, 20-29
Partnership Formation, 20-30
Partnership Operation, 20-32
Tax Planning Considerations, 20-34
Corporate versus Noncorporate Forms of Business Organization, 20-34
Regular Corporation versus S Status, 20-35
Use of an Entity to Reduce the Family Income Tax Burden, 20-35

Until now this text has concentrated on the Federal income taxation of individual taxpayers. However, even the most basic business decisions require some awareness of the tax implications of other business forms.

EXAMPLE 1

Gina and Tom are contemplating entering into a new business venture that will require additional capital investment by other parties. As the venture will involve financial risk, both Gina and Tom are concerned about personal liability. Further, they would prefer to avoid any income taxes at the entity level. Both Gina and Tom would like to take advantage of any losses the venture may generate during its formative period. ▼

In choosing the form for the venture, Gina and Tom will have to consider using a corporation. The corporate form limits a shareholder's liability to the amount invested in the stock. Regular corporations, however, are subject to the corporate income tax. Furthermore, losses incurred by corporations do not pass through to the shareholders. Perhaps the ideal solution would be to use the corporate form and elect to be taxed as an S corporation. The election would avoid the corporate income tax and permit the pass-through of losses while providing limited liability for the shareholders.

Although the resolution of the problem posed by Example 1 seems simple enough, it did not consider the possible use of a partnership. More important, the decision required *some* knowledge of corporations and the S corporation election. This chapter is intended to provide such knowledge by briefly reviewing the tax consequences of the various forms of business organization.

What Is a Corporation?

COMPLIANCE WITH STATE LAW

1 LEARNING OBJECTIVE
Identify those entities that are treated as corporations for Federal income tax purposes.

A company must comply with the specific requirements for corporate status under state law. For example, it is necessary to draft and file articles of incorporation with the state regulatory agency, be granted a charter, and issue stock to shareholders.

Compliance with state law, although important, is not the only requirement that must be met to qualify for corporate *tax* status. For example, a corporation qualifying under state law may be disregarded as a taxable entity if it is a mere sham lacking in economic substance. The key consideration is the degree of business activity conducted at the corporate level.

EXAMPLE 2
Gene and Mike are joint owners of a tract of unimproved real estate that they wish to protect from future creditors. Gene and Mike form Falcon Corporation, to which they transfer the land in return for all of the corporation's stock. The corporation merely holds title to the land and conducts no other activities. In all respects, Falcon Corporation meets the legal requirements of a corporation under applicable state law. Nevertheless, Falcon might not be recognized as a separate entity for corporate tax purposes under these facts.[1] ▼

EXAMPLE 3
Assume the same facts as in Example 2. In addition to holding title to the land, Falcon Corporation leases the property, collects rents, and pays the property taxes. Falcon probably would be treated as a corporation for Federal income tax purposes because of the scope of its activities. ▼

In some instances, the IRS has attempted to disregard (or collapse) a corporation in order to make the income taxable directly to the shareholders.[2] In other cases, the IRS has asserted that the corporation is a separate taxable entity so as to assess tax at the corporate level and to tax corporate distributions to shareholders as dividend income (double taxation).[3]

THE ASSOCIATION APPROACH

An organization not qualifying as a regular corporation under state law may nevertheless be taxed as a corporation under the association approach. The designation given to an entity under the state law is not controlling. For example, a partnership of physicians has been treated as an association even though state law prohibited the practice of medicine in the corporate form. The partnership thus was subject to the Federal income tax rules applicable to corporations.[4] Another sensitive area involves limited partnerships where the only general partner is a corporation. Unless certain prescribed guidelines are carefully followed, the IRS will treat the partnership as an association.[5]

---

[1] See *Paymer v. Comm.*, 45–2 USTC ¶9353, 33 AFTR 1536, 150 F.2d 334 (CA–2, 1945).
[2] *Floyd Patterson*, 25 TCM 1230, T.C.Memo. 1966–239, aff'd. in 68–2 USTC ¶9471, 22 AFTR2d 5810 (CA–2, 1968).
[3] *Raffety Farms Inc. v. U.S.*, 75–1 USTC ¶9271, 35 AFTR2d 75–811, 511 F.2d 1234 (CA–8, 1975).
[4] *U.S. v. Kintner*, 54–2 USTC ¶9626, 46 AFTR 995, 216 F.2d 418 (CA–5, 1954).
[5] Rev.Proc. 89–12, 1989–1 C.B. 798.

TAX IN THE NEWS

WHO IS TAXED ON A BASKETBALL STAR'S SALARY?

When he signed with the Houston Rockets, Allen Leavell agreed to be under their direction and control in carrying out all athletic activities required of him. Immediately after signing and upon the advice of his tax adviser, Allen formed the Leavell Corporation. Allen and Leavell Corporation contracted for the exclusive right to his services. Under the arrangement, all income Allen earned would belong to the corporation, and he would receive an annual salary. The amount of the salary was far less than the Rockets were paying Allen for playing point guard on the team.

During the years Allen played for the Rockets, his paychecks were turned over to the corporation, which reported those amounts on the Forms 1120 it filed. Upon audit by the IRS, Allen's pay from the Rockets was deemed taxed to him and not to Leavell Corporation.

In *Allen Leavell* [104 T.C. 140 (1995)], the Tax Court sided with the IRS. Income is taxed to whoever earns it. In this case, Allen (and not the corporation) earned the amounts paid by the Rockets. The Rockets were paying for services performed by Allen and not by his corporation.

Whether or not an entity will be considered an **association** for Federal income tax purposes depends upon the number of corporate characteristics it possesses. According to court decisions and the Regulations, corporate characteristics include the following:[6]

1. Associates.
2. An objective to carry on a business and divide the gains therefrom.
3. Continuity of life.
4. Centralized management.
5. Limited liability.
6. Free transferability of interests.

The Regulations state that an unincorporated organization shall not be classified as an association unless it possesses *more* corporate than noncorporate characteristics. In making this determination, the characteristics common to both corporate and noncorporate business organizations are to be disregarded. Both corporations and partnerships generally have associates (shareholders and partners) and an objective to carry on a business and divide the gains. Therefore, only if a partnership has at least three of attributes 3 through 6 will it be treated as an association (taxable as a corporation).

EXAMPLE 4 The Green Partnership agreement provides for the following: the partnership terminates with the withdrawal of a partner; all of the partners have authority to participate in the management of the partnership; all of the partners are individually liable for the debts of the partnership; and a partner may not freely transfer his or her interest in the partnership to another. None of corporate attributes 3 through 6 are present. Since the majority requirement of the Regulations is not satisfied, Green is not taxable as an association. ▼

---

[6] Reg. § 301.7701–2(a) prior to modification.

LIMITED LIABILITY COMPANIES

All U. S. states have adopted statutes allowing **limited liability companies.** These organizations have the corporate feature of limited liability, so the owners have no personal liability for the debts of the business. This type of organization is becoming increasingly popular for professional groups. In most cases, the owners want the organization to be treated as a partnership for Federal income tax purposes, so as to avoid the double tax resulting from operating as a corporation. Often, centralized management is present, but the other key corporate characteristics (i.e., continuity of life and free transferability of interests) are absent.

A SIMPLE WAY TO SELECT ENTITY STATUS

The advent of new types of entities due to the enactment of state laws (see the previous discussion of limited liability companies) has created administrative problems for the IRS and compliance costs for taxpayers. Upon the request of concerned taxpayers, each state statute has to be tested under the association criteria. The testing is necessary to ascertain whether the entity is to be treated as a corporation or as a partnership.

Hoping to curtail this time-consuming and costly evaluation process, in 1995 the IRS announced that it was considering amending existing Regulations.[7] Accordingly, Proposed Regulations were issued in May of 1996 and finalized in December 1996.[8] Under the so-called check-the-box rules, an entity can elect to be taxed either as a partnership or as a corporation regardless of its corporate or noncorporate characteristics. The status of existing entities will not be changed by the new rules. Further, the elective option is only available to *domestic* entities. The finalized Regulations became effective January 1, 1997.

The new rules will provide a simple and desirable solution for what has been a troublesome entity classification problem. They should prove particularly attractive to small businesses that want limited liability and pass-through treatment for tax purposes.

INCOME TAX CONSIDERATIONS

GENERAL TAX CONSEQUENCES OF DIFFERENT FORMS OF BUSINESS ENTITIES

2 LEARNING OBJECTIVE
Contrast the income tax treatment of individuals with that applicable to corporations.

A business operation may be conducted as a sole proprietorship, as a partnership, or in corporate form.

- Sole proprietorships are not separate taxable entities. The owner of the business reports all business transactions on his or her individual income tax return.
- Partnerships are not subject to the income tax. Under the *conduit* concept, the various tax attributes of the partnership's operations flow through to the individual partners to be reported on their personal income tax returns.
- The regular corporate form of doing business carries with it the imposition of the corporate income tax. The corporation is recognized as a separate taxpaying entity. Income is taxed to the corporation as earned and taxed again to the shareholders as dividends when distributed.

---
[7] Notice 95–14, 1995–1 C.B. 297.
[8] PS–43–95, I.R.B. 1996, No. 24, 20 and TD 8697, I.R.B. 1997, No. 2, 11 replacing Reg. §§ 301.7701–1, –2, and –3.

- A regular corporation may elect to be taxed as an S corporation. This special treatment is similar (although not identical) to the partnership rules. Income tax is generally avoided at the corporate level, and shareholders are taxed currently on the taxable income of the S corporation.

INDIVIDUALS AND CORPORATIONS COMPARED—AN OVERVIEW

Similarities between Corporate and Individual Tax Rules.
The gross income of a corporation is determined in much the same manner as for individuals. Both individuals and corporations are entitled to exclusions from gross income, such as interest on municipal bonds. Gains and losses from property transactions are also treated similarly. For example, whether a gain or loss is capital or ordinary depends on the nature and use of the asset rather than the type of taxpayer. Upon the sale or other taxable disposition of depreciable personalty, the recapture rules of § 1245 make no distinction between corporate and noncorporate taxpayers. In the case of the recapture of depreciation on real property (§ 1250), however, corporate taxpayers experience more severe tax consequences. As illustrated later, corporations must recognize as additional ordinary income 20 percent of the excess of the amount that would be recaptured under § 1245 over the amount recaptured under § 1250.

The business deductions of corporations parallel those available to individuals. Corporate deductions are allowed for all ordinary and necessary expenses paid or incurred in carrying on a trade or business. Corporations may also deduct interest, certain taxes, losses, bad debts, depreciation, cost recovery, charitable contributions subject to corporate limitation rules, net operating losses, research and experimental expenditures, and other less common deductions.

Many of the tax credits available to individuals, such as the foreign tax credit, can be claimed by corporations. Not available to corporations are certain credits that are personal in nature. Examples of credits not available to corporations include the credit for child and dependent care expenses, the credit for the elderly or disabled, and the earned income credit.

Corporations usually have the same choices of accounting periods as do individuals. Like an individual, a corporation may choose a calendar year or a fiscal year for reporting purposes. Corporations do enjoy greater flexibility in the election of a tax year. For example, corporations usually can have different tax years from those of their shareholders. Also, a newly formed corporation generally has a free choice of any approved accounting period without having to obtain the consent of the IRS. As noted in Chapter 18, however, personal service corporations are subject to severe restrictions on the use of a fiscal year.

The use of the cash method of accounting is denied to large corporations (those with average annual gross receipts in excess of $5 million). Smaller corporations as well as qualified personal service corporations and other corporations engaged in the trade or business of farming have a choice between the cash or accrual method of accounting for tax purposes. Both individuals and corporations that maintain inventory for sale to customers are required to use the accrual method of accounting for determining sales and cost of goods sold.

Dissimilarities.
Both noncorporate and corporate taxpayers are subject to progressive income tax rates. For individuals, the rates are 15, 28, 31, 36, and 39.6 percent. For corporations, the rates are 15, 25, 34, and 35 percent. Corporate taxpayers lose the benefits of the lower brackets (using a phase-out approach) once taxable income reaches a certain level. Noncorporate taxpayers, however, continue

to enjoy the benefits of the lower brackets even though they have reached the higher taxable income levels.

Both corporate and noncorporate taxpayers are subject to the alternative minimum tax (AMT). For AMT purposes, many adjustments and tax preference items are the same for both, but other adjustments and tax preferences apply only to corporations or only to individuals. Corporate tax rates are discussed later in the chapter. The AMT is discussed at length in Chapter 12. See also the coverage in *West's Federal Taxation: Corporations, Partnerships, Estates, and Trusts.*

All allowable corporate deductions are treated as business expenses. The determination of adjusted gross income, so essential for individuals, has no relevance to corporations. Corporations need not be concerned with classifying deductions into *deduction for* and *deduction from* categories.

SPECIFIC PROVISIONS COMPARED

Corporate and individual tax rules also differ in the following areas:

- Capital gains and losses.
- Recapture of depreciation.
- Charitable contributions.
- Net operating losses.
- Special deductions for corporations.

Capital Gains and Losses. Both corporate and noncorporate taxpayers are required to aggregate gains and losses from the taxable sale or exchange of capital assets. (Refer to Chapter 16 for a description of the netting process that takes place after the aggregation has been completed.) For net long-term capital gains, individual taxpayers enjoy an advantage (the alternative tax). In no event will the gains be taxed at a rate in excess of 28 percent. In the case of corporations, all capital gains are taxed using the rates for ordinary income. Therefore, the net long-term capital gains of a corporation could be taxed at a rate of 35 percent (the highest rate applicable to corporations).

Significant differences exist in the treatment of capital losses for income tax purposes. Individuals, for example, can annually deduct up to $3,000 of net capital losses against ordinary income. Corporations are not permitted to use net capital losses to offset ordinary income. Net capital losses can be used only to offset past or future capital gains.[9] Unlike individuals, corporations are not allowed an unlimited carryover period for capital losses. Instead, they may carry back excess capital losses to the three preceding years, applying them initially to the earliest year. If not exhausted by the carryback, remaining unused capital losses may be carried forward for a period of five years from the year of the loss.[10]

When carried back or forward, *both* short-term capital losses and long-term capital losses are treated as short-term capital losses by corporate taxpayers. For noncorporate taxpayers, a capital loss does not lose its identity. Thus, long-term capital losses of noncorporate taxpayers are carried forward as long-term capital losses, and short-term capital losses are carried forward as short-term capital losses.

▼ **EXAMPLE 5** Hawk Corporation, a calendar year taxpayer, incurs a long-term net capital loss of $5,000 for 1997. None of the capital loss may be deducted in 1997. Hawk may, however, carry the loss back to years 1994, 1995, and 1996 (in this order) and offset any capital gains recognized in

---

[9] §§ 1211(a) and (b).   [10] § 1212(a).

these years. If the carryback does not exhaust the loss, the loss may be carried forward to 1998, 1999, 2000, 2001, and 2002 (in this order). Such capital loss carrybacks or carryovers are treated as short-term capital losses. ▼

Recapture of Depreciation. Corporations selling depreciable real estate may have ordinary income in addition to that required by § 1250. Under § 291, the additional ordinary income element is 20 percent of the excess of the § 1245 recapture potential over the § 1250 recapture. As a result, the § 1231 gain is correspondingly decreased by the additional recapture.

EXAMPLE 6

Condor Corporation purchases residential real property on January 3, 1984, for $300,000. Accelerated cost recovery is taken in the amount of $270,000 before the property is sold on January 5, 1997, for $350,000. Straight-line cost recovery would have been $260,000 (using a 15-year recovery period under ACRS).

First, determine the realized gain:

Sales price		$350,000
Less adjusted basis:		
Cost of property	$ 300,000	
Less cost recovery	(270,000)	(30,000)
Realized gain		$320,000

Second, determine the § 1245 recapture potential. This is the lesser of $320,000 (realized gain) or $270,000 (cost recovery claimed). Third, determine the § 1250 recapture amount:

Cost recovery taken	$ 270,000
Less straight-line cost recovery	(260,000)
§ 1250 ordinary income	$ 10,000

Fourth, because the taxpayer is a corporation, determine the additional § 291 amount:

§ 1245 recapture potential	$270,000
Less § 1250 recapture amount	(10,000)
Excess § 1245 recapture potential	$260,000
Apply § 291 percentage	× 20%
Additional ordinary income under § 291	$ 52,000

Condor Corporation's realized and recognized gain of $320,000 is accounted for as follows:

Ordinary income under § 1250	$ 10,000
Ordinary income under § 291	52,000
§ 1231 gain	258,000
Total recognized gain	$320,000

▼

Charitable Contributions. Generally, a charitable contribution deduction is allowed only for the tax year in which the payment is made. However, an important exception is made for accrual basis corporations. The deduction may be claimed in the tax year *preceding* payment if the following conditions are satisfied:

- The contribution is authorized by the board of directors by the end of that tax year *and*
- The contribution is paid on or before the fifteenth day of the third month of the next tax year.[11]

---

[11] § 170(a)(2).

EXAMPLE 7 On December 28, 1997, the board of directors of Dove Corporation, a calendar year, accrual basis taxpayer, authorizes a $5,000 donation to a qualified charity. The donation is paid on March 14, 1998. Dove Corporation may claim the $5,000 donation as a deduction for 1997. As an alternative, Dove may claim the deduction in 1998 (the year of payment). ▼

Like individuals, corporations are not permitted an unlimited charitable contribution deduction. In any one year, a corporate taxpayer is limited to 10 percent of taxable income. For this purpose, taxable income is computed without regard to the charitable contribution deduction, any net operating loss carryback or capital loss carryback, or the dividends received deduction.[12] Any contributions in excess of the 10 percent limitation are carried forward to the five succeeding tax years. Any carryover must be added to subsequent contributions and is subject to the 10 percent limitation. In applying the limitation, the most recent contributions must be deducted first.[13]

EXAMPLE 8 During 1997, Eagle Corporation (a calendar year taxpayer) had the following income and expenses:

Income from operations	$140,000
Expenses from operations	110,000
Dividends received	10,000
Charitable contributions made in 1997	5,000

For purposes of the 10% limitation only, Eagle's taxable income is $40,000 ($140,000 − $110,000 + $10,000). Consequently, the allowable charitable contribution deduction for 1997 is $4,000 (10% × $40,000). The $1,000 unused portion of the contribution is carried forward to 1998, 1999, 2000, 2001, and 2002 (in that order) until exhausted. ▼

EXAMPLE 9 Assume the same facts as in Example 8. In 1998, Eagle Corporation has taxable income (after adjustments) of $50,000 and makes a charitable contribution of $4,800. The maximum deduction allowed for 1998 is $5,000 (10% × $50,000). The first $4,800 of the allowed deduction must be allocated to the 1998 contributions, and the $200 excess is carried over from 1997. The remaining $800 of the 1997 contribution is carried over to 1999, etc. ▼

As noted in Chapter 10, the deduction for charitable contributions of ordinary income property is limited to the lesser of the fair market value or the adjusted basis of the property. A special rule permits a corporation to contribute inventory (ordinary income property) to certain charitable organizations and receive a deduction equal to the adjusted basis plus one-half of the difference between the fair market value and the adjusted basis of the property.[14] In no event, however, may the deduction exceed twice the adjusted basis of the property. To qualify for this exception, the inventory must be used by the charity in its exempt purpose for the care of *children*, the *ill*, or the *needy*.

EXAMPLE 10 In the current year, Robin Company (a retail clothier) donates sweaters and overcoats to Sheltering Arms (a qualified charity caring for the homeless). The clothing is inventory and has a basis of $10,000 and a fair market value of $14,000. If Robin is a corporation, the charitable contribution that results is $12,000 [$10,000 (basis) + $2,000 (50% of the appreciation of $4,000)]. In contrast, if Robin is not a corporation, the charitable contribution is limited to $10,000 (basis). ▼

---

[12] § 170(b)(2).
[13] § 170(d)(2).
[14] § 170(e)(3).

Net Operating Losses. The computation of a net operating loss (NOL) for individuals was discussed in Chapter 7. Corporations are not subject to the complex adjustments required for individuals (e.g., a corporation has no adjustments for nonbusiness deductions or capital gains and losses). Corporations are subject to fewer adjustments than individuals are because a corporation's loss more clearly approximates a true economic loss. Artificial deductions (e.g., personal and dependency exemptions) that merely generate paper losses are not permitted for corporations.

In computing the NOL of a corporation, the dividends received deduction (discussed below) can be claimed in determining the amount of the loss.[15] Corporate NOLs may be carried back 3 years and forward 15 years (or taxpayers may elect to forgo the carryback period) to offset taxable income for those years.

EXAMPLE 11

In 1997, Wren Corporation has gross income of $200,000 and deductions of $300,000, excluding the dividends received deduction. Wren received taxable dividends of $100,000 from Exxon stock. Wren has an NOL of $170,000, computed as follows:

Gross income (including Exxon dividends)		$ 200,000
Less: Business deductions	$300,000	
Dividends received deduction (70% × $100,000)	70,000	(370,000)
Taxable income (loss)		($ 170,000)

EXAMPLE 12

Assume the same facts as in Example 11 and that Wren Corporation had taxable income of $40,000 in 1994. The NOL of $170,000 is carried back to 1994 (unless Wren elects not to carry back the loss to that year). The carryover to 1995 is $130,000, computed as follows:

Taxable income for 1994	$ 40,000
Less: NOL carryback from 1997	(170,000)
Carryover of unabsorbed 1997 loss	($ 130,000)

In Example 12, the carryback to 1994 might have been ill-advised if Wren Corporation had little, if any, taxable income in 1995 and 1996 and if it anticipated large amounts of taxable income in the immediate future. In that case, the *election to forgo* the carryback might generate greater tax savings. In this regard, three points should be considered. First, the time value of the tax refund that is lost by not using the carryback procedure must be considered. Second, the election to forgo an NOL carryback is irrevocable. Thus, it cannot be changed later if the future high profits do not materialize. Third, future increases or decreases in corporate income tax rates that can reasonably be anticipated should be considered.

DEDUCTIONS AVAILABLE ONLY TO CORPORATIONS

3 LEARNING OBJECTIVE
Recognize and calculate the tax deductions available only to corporations.

Dividends Received Deduction. The purpose of the **dividends received deduction** is to prevent triple taxation. Without the deduction, income paid to a corporation in the form of a dividend would be subject to taxation for a second time (once to the distributing corporation) with no corresponding deduction to the distributing corporation. A third level of tax would be assessed on the shareholders when the recipient corporation distributed the income to its shareholders.

---
[15] § 172(d).

Since the dividends received deduction may be less than 100 percent, the law provides only partial relief.

The amount of the dividends received deduction depends upon the percentage of ownership the recipient corporate shareholder holds in the corporation making the dividend distribution.[16] For dividends received or accrued, the *deduction percentage* is summarized as follows:

Percentage of Ownership by Corporate Shareholder	Deduction Percentage
Less than 20%	70%
20% or more (but less than 80%)	80%
80% or more	100%

The dividends received deduction may be limited to a percentage of the taxable income of a corporation computed without regard to the NOL deduction, the dividends received deduction, or any capital loss carryback to the current tax year. The percentage of taxable income limitation corresponds to the deduction percentage. Thus, if a corporate shareholder owns less than 20 percent of the stock in the distributing corporation, the dividends received deduction is limited to 70 percent of taxable income (as previously defined). However, this limitation does not apply if the corporation has an NOL for the current taxable year.[17]

In working with these myriad rules, the following steps need to be taken:

1. Multiply the dividends received by the deduction percentage.
2. Multiply the taxable income (as previously defined) by the deduction percentage.
3. The deduction is limited to the lesser of Step 1 or Step 2, unless subtracting the amount derived from Step 1 from taxable income (as previously defined) generates a negative number. If so, the amount derived in Step 1 should be used.

EXAMPLE 13

Crane, Osprey, and Gull Corporations, three unrelated calendar year corporations, have the following transactions for 1997:

	Crane Corporation	Osprey Corporation	Gull Corporation
Gross income from operations	$ 400,000	$ 320,000	$ 260,000
Expenses from operations	(340,000)	(340,000)	(340,000)
Dividends received from domestic corporations (less than 20% ownership)	200,000	200,000	200,000
Taxable income before the dividends received deduction	$ 260,000	$ 180,000	$ 120,000

In determining the dividends received deduction, use the step procedure just described:

---

[16] § 243(a).   [17] § 246(b).

	Crane Corporation	Osprey Corporation	Gull Corporation
Step 1: (70% × $200,000)	$140,000	$140,000	$140,000
Step 2:			
70% × $260,000 (taxable income)	$182,000		
70% × $180,000 (taxable income)		$126,000	
70% × $120,000 (taxable income)			$ 84,000
Step 3:			
Lesser of Step 1 or Step 2	$140,000	$126,000	
Generates an NOL			$140,000

Osprey Corporation is subject to the 70 percent of taxable income limitation. It does not qualify for the loss rule treatment, since subtracting $140,000 (Step 1) from $180,000 does not yield a loss. Gull Corporation qualifies for the loss rule treatment because subtracting $140,000 (Step 1) from $120,000 does yield a loss. In summary, each corporation has the following dividends received deduction for 1997: $140,000 for Crane, $126,000 for Osprey, and $140,000 for Gull. If a corporation already has an NOL before any dividends received deduction is claimed, the full dividends received deduction (as calculated in Step 1) is allowed.

Deduction of Organizational Expenditures. Under § 248, a corporation may elect to amortize organizational expenses over a period of 60 months or more. If the election is not made on a timely basis, the expenditures cannot be deducted until the corporation ceases to conduct business and liquidates. The election is made in a statement attached to the corporation's return for its first taxable year. The election covers all qualifying expenses *incurred* in the corporation's first year.[18]

Organizational expenditures include the following:

- Legal services incident to organization (e.g., drafting the corporate charter, bylaws, minutes of organizational meetings, terms of original stock certificates).
- Necessary accounting services.
- Expenses of temporary directors and of organizational meetings of directors and shareholders.
- Fees paid to the state of incorporation.

Expenditures connected with issuing or selling shares of stock or other securities (e.g., commissions, professional fees, and printing costs) or with the transfer of assets to a corporation do not qualify. These expenditures are generally added to the capital account and are not subject to amortization.

DETERMINATION OF CORPORATE TAX LIABILITY

4 LEARNING OBJECTIVE
Determine the corporate tax liability and comply with various procedural and reporting requirements.

Income Tax Rates. The Revenue Reconciliation Act of 1993 revised the corporate rate schedule for tax years beginning after 1992. The rates *were not changed for taxable income of $10 million or less.* For corporations with taxable income in excess

---

[18] A cash basis taxpayer need not have paid the expenses as long as they were incurred.

of $10 million, a rate of 35 percent applies to the excess. An additional tax at the rate of 3 percent (not to exceed $100,000) is imposed on taxable income in excess of $15 million.[19] In effect, the rate brackets on corporations are as follows:

Taxable Income	Tax Rate
Not over $50,000	15%
Over $50,000 but not over $75,000	25%
Over $75,000 but not over $100,000	34%
Over $100,000 but not over $335,000	39%*
Over $335,000 but not over $10,000,000	34%
Over $10,000,000 but not over $15,000,000	35%
Over $15,000,000 but not over $18,333,333	38%**
Over $18,333,333	35%

*Five percent of this rate represents a phase-out of the benefits of the lower tax rates on the first $75,000 of taxable income.
**Three percent of this rate represents a phase-out of the benefits of the lower tax rate (34% rather than 35%) on the first $10 million of taxable income.

EXAMPLE 14 A calendar year corporation has taxable income of $90,000 for 1997. The income tax liability is $18,850, determined as follows: $7,500 (15% × $50,000) + $6,250 (25% × $25,000) + $5,100 (34% × $15,000). ▼

ETHICAL CONSIDERATIONS

Where Do Deductions Belong?

Kirk and Darlene are the equal shareholders of Ruby Company, a C corporation. They are also the key employees of Ruby. The company is a wholesaler of costume jewelry. Because the business is very competitive, Kirk and Darlene must frequently entertain department store buyers.

When Kirk and Darlene realize that they are in a higher income tax bracket than Ruby, they enact, on behalf of Ruby, the following corporate resolution: "All entertainment expenses shall be the responsibility of the employee doing the entertaining and are not reimbursable."

Consequently, Kirk and Darlene deduct all entertainment expenses for the year on their individual income tax returns. Ruby Company claims none of these expenses and does not reimburse Kirk and Darlene for them.

Have the parties acted properly?

Qualified personal service corporations are taxed at a flat 35 percent rate on all taxable income. They do not enjoy the tax savings of the lower brackets. For this purpose, a *qualified* **personal service corporation** is one that is substantially employee owned and engages in one of the following activities: health, law, engineering, architecture, accounting, actuarial science, performing arts, or consulting.

---

[19] § 11(b).

Alternative Minimum Tax. Corporations are subject to an alternative minimum tax (AMT) that is structured in the same manner as that applicable to individuals. The AMT for corporations, as for individuals, defines a more expansive tax base than for the regular tax. Like individuals, corporations are required to apply a minimum tax rate to the expanded base and pay the difference between the tentative AMT liability and the regular tax. Many of the adjustments and tax preference items necessary to arrive at alternative minimum taxable income (AMTI) are the same for individuals and corporations. Although the objective of the AMT is the same for individuals and for corporations, the rate and exemptions are different. Computation of the AMT is discussed in Chapter 12.

CORPORATE FILING REQUIREMENTS

A corporation must file a return whether it has taxable income or not.[20] A corporation that was not in existence throughout an entire annual accounting period is required to file a return for the fraction of the year during which it was in existence. In addition, the corporation must file a return even though it has ceased to do business if it has valuable claims for which it will bring suit. It is relieved of filing returns once it ceases business and dissolves.

The corporate return is filed on Form 1120 unless the corporation is a small corporation entitled to file the shorter Form 1120–A. Among the *several* requirements for filing Form 1120–A are gross receipts (or sales) of less than $500,000 and total assets of less than $500,000. Corporations making the S corporation election (discussed later in the chapter) file on Form 1120S.

The return must be filed on or before the fifteenth day of the third month following the close of the corporation's tax year. Corporations can receive an automatic extension of six months for filing the corporate return by filing Form 7004 by the due date of the return. However, the IRS may terminate an extension by mailing a 10-day notice to the taxpayer corporation.[21]

A corporation must make payments of estimated tax unless its tax liability can reasonably be expected to be less than $500.[22] For 1997, the payments must equal 100 percent of the corporation's final tax. These payments may be made in four installments due on or before the fifteenth day of the fourth, sixth, ninth, and twelfth months of the corporate taxable year. The full amount of the unpaid tax is due on the date of the return. Failure to make the required estimated tax prepayments will result in a nondeductible penalty being imposed on the corporation. The penalty can be avoided, however, if any of various exceptions apply.[23]

RECONCILIATION OF CORPORATE TAXABLE INCOME AND ACCOUNTING INCOME

Taxable income and accounting net income are seldom the same amount. For example, a difference may arise if the corporation uses accelerated depreciation for tax purposes and straight-line depreciation for accounting purposes.

Many items of income for accounting purposes, such as proceeds from a life insurance policy on the death of a corporate officer and interest on municipal bonds, may not be includible in calculating taxable income. Some expense items for accounting purposes, such as expenses to produce tax-exempt income, estimated warranty reserves, a net capital loss, and Federal income taxes, are not deductible for tax purposes.

---

[20] § 6012(a)(2).
[21] § 6081.
[22] § 6655(f).
[23] See § 6655 for the penalty involved and the various exceptions.

Schedule M–1 on the last page of Form 1120 is used to reconcile accounting net income (net income after Federal income taxes) with taxable income (as computed on the corporate tax return before the deduction for a net operating loss and the dividends received deduction). In the left-hand column of Schedule M–1, net income per books is added to the following: the Federal income tax liability for the year, the excess of capital losses over capital gains (which cannot be deducted in the current year), income for tax purposes that is not income in the current year for accounting purposes, and expenses recorded on the books that are not deductible on the tax return. In the right-hand column, income recorded on the books that is not currently taxable or is tax-exempt and deductions for tax purposes that are not expenses for accounting purposes are totaled and subtracted from the left-hand column total to arrive at taxable income (before the net operating loss or dividends received deductions).

EXAMPLE 15

During 1997, Crow Corporation had the following transactions:

Net income per books (after tax)	$92,400
Taxable income	50,000
Federal income tax liability (15% × $50,000)	7,500
Interest income from tax-exempt bonds	5,000
Interest paid on loan, the proceeds of which were used to purchase the tax-exempt bonds	500
Life insurance proceeds received as a result of the death of a key employee	50,000
Premiums paid on key employee life insurance policy	2,600
Excess of capital losses over capital gains	2,000

For book and tax purposes, Crow determines depreciation under the straight-line method. Crow's Schedule M–1 for the current year follows.

Schedule M-1 Reconciliation of Income (Loss) per Books With Income per Return (See page 16 of instructions.)

1	Net income (loss) per books	92,400	7	Income recorded on books this year not included on this return (itemize): Tax-exempt interest $ 5,000 Life insurance proceeds on key employee $50,000	55,000
2	Federal income tax	7,500			
3	Excess of capital losses over capital gains	2,000			
4	Income subject to tax not recorded on books this year (itemize):				
5	Expenses recorded on books this year not deducted on this return (itemize):		8	Deductions on this return not charged against book income this year (itemize): a Depreciation . . . $ b Contributions carryover $	
a	Depreciation $				
b	Contributions carryover $				
c	Travel and entertainment $ Int. on tax-exempt bonds $500, Prem. on key employee ins. $2,600	3,100	9	Add lines 7 and 8	55,000
6	Add lines 1 through 5	105,000	10	Income (line 28, page 1)—line 6 less line 9	50,000

Schedule M–2 reconciles unappropriated retained earnings at the beginning of the year with unappropriated retained earnings at year-end. Beginning balance plus net income per books, as entered on line 1 of Schedule M–1, less dividend distributions during the year equals ending retained earnings. Other sources of increases or decreases in retained earnings are also listed on Schedule M–2.

EXAMPLE 16

Assume the same facts as in Example 15. Crow Corporation's beginning balance in unappropriated retained earnings is $125,000, and Crow distributed a cash dividend of $30,000 to its shareholders during the year. Based on these further assumptions, Crow has the following Schedule M-2 for the current year.

Schedule M-2 — Analysis of Unappropriated Retained Earnings per Books (Line 25, Schedule L)

1	Balance at beginning of year	125,000	5	Distributions:	a Cash	30,000
2	Net income (loss) per books	92,400			b Stock	
3	Other increases (itemize):				c Property	
			6	Other decreases (itemize):		
			7	Add lines 5 and 6		30,000
4	Add lines 1, 2, and 3	217,400	8	Balance at end of year (line 4 less line 7)		187,400

CONCEPT SUMMARY 20-1

Summary of Income Tax Consequences

	Individuals	Corporations
Computation of gross income	§ 61.	§ 61.
Computation of taxable income	§§ 62, 63(b) through (h).	§ 63(a). Concept of AGI has no relevance.
Deductions	Trade or business (§ 162); nonbusiness (§ 212); some personal and employee expenses (generally deductible as itemized deductions).	Trade or business (§ 162).
Charitable contributions	Limited in any tax year to 50% of AGI; 30% for long-term capital gain property unless election is made to reduce fair market value of gift; 20% for long-term capital gain property contributed to private nonoperating foundations.	Limited in any tax year to 10% of taxable income computed without regard to the charitable contribution deduction, net operating loss or capital loss carryback, and dividends received deduction.
	Time of deduction—year in which payment is made.	Time of deduction—year in which payment is made unless accrual basis taxpayer. Accrual basis corporation may take deduction in year preceding payment if contribution was authorized by board of directors by end of that year and contribution is paid by fifteenth day of third month of following year.
Casualty losses	$100 floor on nonbusiness casualty and theft losses; nonbusiness casualty and theft losses deductible only to extent losses exceed 10% of AGI.	Deductible in full.
Depreciation recapture for § 1250 property	Recaptured to extent accelerated depreciation exceeds straight-line.	20% of excess of amount that would be recaptured under § 1245 over amount recaptured under § 1250 is additional ordinary income under § 291.

	Individuals	**Corporations**
Net operating loss	Adjusted for nonbusiness deductions over nonbusiness income and for personal and dependency exemptions.	Generally no adjustments.
Dividend exclusion or deduction	None.	Generally 70% of dividends received.
Long-term capital gains	Taxed at a rate no higher than 28%.	Taxed using regular corporate rates.
Capital losses	Only $3,000 of capital loss can offset ordinary income; loss is carried forward indefinitely to offset capital gains or ordinary income up to $3,000; carryovers remain long term or short term (as the case may be).	Can offset only capital gains; carried back three years and forward five years; carrybacks and carryovers are treated as short-term losses.
Passive activity losses	Generally deductible only against income from passive activities.	For regular corporations, no limitation on deductibility. Personal service corporations and certain closely held corporations, however, are subject to same limitations as imposed on individuals. A closely held corporation is one where 5 or fewer individuals own more than 50% of the stock either directly or indirectly.
Alternative minimum tax	Applied at a graduated rate schedule of 26% and 28% to AMT base (taxable income as modified by certain adjustments plus preference items minus exemption amount); exemption allowed depending on filing status (e.g., $45,000 for married filing jointly); exemption phase-out begins when AMTI reaches a certain amount (e.g., $150,000 for married filing jointly).	Applied at a 20% rate to AMT base (taxable income as modified by certain adjustments plus preference items minus exemption amount); $40,000 exemption allowed but phase-out begins once AMTI reaches $150,000; adjustments and tax preference items similar to those applicable to individuals but also include 75% of adjusted current earnings (ACE) over AMTI.
Tax rates	Progressive with five rates (15%, 28%, 31%, 36%, and 39.6%).	Progressive with four rates (15%, 25%, 34%, and 35%); lower brackets phased out at higher levels.

Forming the Corporation

CAPITAL CONTRIBUTIONS

5 Learning Objective
Understand the tax rules governing the formation of corporations.

The receipt of money or property in exchange for capital stock produces neither recognized gain nor loss to the recipient corporation.[24] Gross income of a corporation does not include shareholders' contributions of money or property to the capital of the corporation.[25] Contributions by nonshareholders are also excluded from the gross income of a corporation.[26] The basis of the property (capital transfers by nonshareholders) to the corporation is zero.

---

[24] § 1032.
[25] § 118.
[26] *Edwards v. Cuba Railroad Co.*, 1 USTC ¶139, 5 AFTR 5398, 45 S.Ct. 614 (USSC, 1925).

EXAMPLE 17 A city donates land worth $200,000 to Cardinal Corporation as an inducement for it to locate in the city. The receipt of the land does not represent gross income. The land's basis to the corporation is zero. ▼

Thin Capitalization.
The advantages of capitalizing a corporation with debt may be substantial. Interest on debt is deductible by the corporation, while dividend payments are not. Further, the shareholders are not taxed on loan repayments unless the payments exceed basis. If a company is capitalized solely with common stock, subsequent repayments of such capital contributions are likely to be treated as dividends to the shareholders.

In certain instances, the IRS will contend that debt is really an equity interest (**thin capitalization**) and will deny the shareholders the tax advantages of debt financing. If the debt instrument has too many features of stock, it may be treated as a form of stock, and principal and interest payments are treated as dividends.[27]

The form of the instrument will not assure debt treatment, but failure to observe certain formalities in creating the debt may lead to an assumption that the purported debt is a form of stock. The debt should be in proper legal form, bear a legitimate rate of interest, have a definite maturity date, and be repaid on a timely basis. Payments should not be contingent upon earnings. Further, the debt should not be subordinated to other liabilities, and proportionate holdings of stock and debt should be avoided or minimized.

TRANSFERS TO CONTROLLED CORPORATIONS

Without special provisions in the Code, a transfer of property to a corporation in exchange for its stock would be a sale or exchange of property and would constitute a taxable transaction to the transferor shareholder. Section 351 provides for the nonrecognition of gain or loss upon such transfers of property if the transferors are in control of the corporation immediately after the transfer. Gain or loss is merely postponed in a manner similar to a like-kind exchange.[28] The following requirements must be met to qualify under § 351:

- The transferors must be in control of the corporation immediately after the exchange. *Control* is defined as ownership of at least 80 percent of the total combined voting power of all classes of stock entitled to vote and at least 80 percent of the total number of shares of all other classes of stock.[29]
- Realized gain (but not loss) is recognized to the extent that the transferors receive property other than stock. Such nonqualifying property is commonly referred to as *boot*.

If the requirements of § 351 are satisfied and no boot is involved, nonrecognition of gain or loss is *mandatory*.

Basis Considerations and Computation of Gain.
The nonrecognition of gain or loss is accompanied by a carryover of basis. The basis of stock received in a § 351 transfer is determined as follows:

- Start with the adjusted basis of the property transferred by the shareholder.
- Add any gain recognized by the shareholder as a result of the transfer.

---

[27] Section 385 lists several factors that might be used to determine whether a debtor-creditor relationship or a shareholder-corporation relationship exists.

[28] Refer to the discussion in Chapter 15.

[29] § 368(c).

- Subtract the fair market value of any boot received by the shareholder from the corporation.[30]

Shareholders who receive noncash boot have a basis in the property equal to the fair market value.

The basis of properties received by the corporation is the basis in the hands of the transferor increased by the amount of any gain recognized to the transferor shareholder.[31]

EXAMPLE 18

Ann and Lori form Bluejay Corporation. Ann transfers property with an adjusted basis of $30,000 and a fair market value of $60,000 for 50% of the stock. Lori transfers property with an adjusted basis of $40,000 and a fair market value of $60,000 for the remaining 50% of the stock. The realized gain ($30,000 for Ann and $20,000 for Lori) is not recognized on the transfer because the transfer qualifies under § 351. The basis of the stock to Ann is $30,000, and the basis of the stock to Lori is $40,000. Bluejay Corporation has a basis of $30,000 in the property transferred by Ann and a basis of $40,000 in the property transferred by Lori. ▼

EXAMPLE 19

Mike and John form Condor Corporation with the following investments: Mike transfers property (adjusted basis of $30,000 and fair market value of $70,000), and John transfers cash of $60,000. Each receives 50 shares of the Condor stock, but Mike also receives $10,000 in cash. Assume each share of the Condor stock is worth $1,200. Mike's realized gain is $40,000, determined as follows:

Value of the Condor stock received [50 (shares) × $1,200 (value per share)]	$ 60,000
Cash received	10,000
Amount realized	$ 70,000
Less basis of property transferred	(30,000)
Realized gain	$ 40,000

Mike's recognized gain is $10,000, the lesser of the realized gain ($40,000) or the fair market value of the boot received ($10,000). Mike's basis in the Condor stock is $30,000, computed as follows:

Basis in the property transferred	$ 30,000
Plus recognized gain	10,000
	$ 40,000
Less boot received	(10,000)
Basis to Mike of the Condor stock	$ 30,000

Condor Corporation's basis in the property transferred by Mike is $40,000 [$30,000 (basis of the property to Mike) + $10,000 (gain recognized by Mike)]. John neither realizes nor recognizes gain or loss and will have a basis of $60,000 in the Condor stock. ▼

The receipt of stock for the performance of *services* always results in ordinary income to the transferor shareholder. An example might be an attorney who does not charge a fee for incorporating a business but instead receives the value equivalent in stock of the newly formed corporation. The basis of stock received for the performance of services is equal to the fair market value of the services.

---

[30] § 358(a).   [31] § 362(a).

OPERATING THE CORPORATION

DIVIDEND DISTRIBUTIONS

6 LEARNING OBJECTIVE
Work with the tax rules governing the operation of corporations.

Corporate distributions of cash or property to shareholders are treated as ordinary dividend income to the extent the corporation has accumulated *or* current earnings and profits (E & P).[32] In determining the source of the distribution, a dividend is deemed to have been made initially from current E & P.

EXAMPLE 20

As of January 1, 1997, Teal Corporation has a deficit in accumulated E & P of $30,000. For tax year 1997, it has current E & P of $10,000. In 1997, the corporation distributes $5,000 to its shareholders. The $5,000 distribution is treated as a taxable dividend, since it is deemed to have been made from current E & P. This is the case even though Teal still has a deficit in its accumulated E & P at the end of 1997. ▼

If a corporate distribution is not covered by E & P (either current or past), it is treated as a return of capital (refer to the discussion of the recovery of capital doctrine in Chapter 4). This treatment allows the shareholder to apply the amount of the distribution against the basis of the stock investment and therefore represents a nontaxable return of capital. Any amount received in excess of the stock basis is classified as a capital gain (if the stock is a capital asset in the hands of the shareholder).

EXAMPLE 21

When Mallard Corporation has no E & P (either current or accumulated), it distributes cash of $30,000 to its sole shareholder, Helen. The basis of Helen's stock investment is $20,000. Based on these facts, the $30,000 distribution Helen receives is accounted for as follows:

Return of capital (nontaxable)	$20,000
Capital gain	10,000
Total amount of distribution	$30,000

After the distribution, Helen has a basis of zero in her stock investment. ▼

Concept of Earnings and Profits. The term **earnings and profits** is not defined in the Code, although § 312 does include certain transactions that affect E & P. Although E & P and the accounting concept of retained earnings have certain similarities, they differ in numerous respects. For example, although a nontaxable stock dividend is treated as a capitalization of retained earnings for accounting purposes, it does not decrease E & P for tax purposes. Taxable dividends do reduce E & P but cannot yield a deficit. Referring to Example 21, after the distribution, Mallard Corporation's E & P remains zero rather than being a negative amount.

Generally, *current E & P* for a taxable year is taxable income plus or minus certain adjustments (e.g., an addition is made for tax-exempt income). Federal income taxes are subtracted from taxable income in arriving at current E & P. *Accumulated E & P* is the sum of the corporation's past current E & P that has not been distributed as dividends. A detailed discussion of the concept of E & P is beyond the scope of this chapter.

---

[32] § 316.

Property Dividends. A distribution of property to a shareholder is measured by the fair market value of the property on the date of distribution. The shareholder's basis in the property received is also the fair market value.[33]

EXAMPLE 22 Drake Corporation has E & P of $60,000. It distributes land with a fair market value of $50,000 (adjusted basis of $30,000) to its sole shareholder, Art. Art has a taxable dividend of $50,000 and a basis in the land of $50,000. ▼

A corporation that distributes appreciated property to its shareholders as a dividend must recognize the amount of the appreciation as gain.[34]

EXAMPLE 23 Assume the same facts as in Example 22. Drake Corporation must recognize a gain of $20,000 on the distribution it made to Art. ▼

However, if the property distributed has a basis in excess of its fair market value, the distributing corporation cannot recognize any loss.

Constructive Dividends. Many taxpayers mistakenly assume that dividend consequences do not take place unless the distribution carries the formalities of a dividend (declaration date, record date, payment date). They further assume that dividends must be paid out to all shareholders on a pro rata basis. This may not be the case when closely held corporations are involved. Here, the key to dividend treatment depends upon whether the shareholders derive a benefit from the corporation that cannot be otherwise classified (e.g., reasonable salary). The following are examples of **constructive dividends**:

- Salaries paid to shareholder-employees that are not reasonable (refer to Example 6 in Chapter 6).
- Interest on debt owed by the corporation to shareholders that is reclassified as equity because the corporation is thinly capitalized (refer to the earlier discussion in this chapter).
- Excessive rent paid by a corporation for the use of shareholder property. The arm's length standard is used to test whether the rent is excessive (refer to Example 23 in Chapter 1).
- Advances to shareholders that are not bona fide loans.
- Interest-free (or below-market) loans to shareholders. In this situation, the dividend component is the difference between the interest provided for, if any, and that calculated using the market rate.
- Shareholder use of corporate property for less than an arm's length rate.
- Absorption by the corporation of a shareholder's personal expenses.
- Bargain purchase of corporate property by shareholders.

Like regular dividends, constructive dividends must be covered by E & P to carry dividend income consequences to the shareholders. As noted above, however, constructive dividends need not be available to all shareholders on a pro rata basis.

Although dividends reduce the E & P of a corporation, they are not deductible for income tax purposes. In this regard, certain constructive dividends could have subtle tax consequences for all parties concerned.

---

[33] § 301.
[34] The tax consequences to a corporation of nonliquidating distributions to shareholders are covered in § 311.

EXAMPLE 24

Grouse Corporation makes a loan to one of its shareholders, Hal. No interest is provided for, but application of the market rate would produce $20,000 of interest for the term of the loan. Presuming the loan is bona fide, the following results occur:

- Hal has dividend income of $20,000.
- Grouse Corporation has interest income of $20,000.
- Hal might obtain an interest deduction of $20,000.

Not only does Grouse Corporation have to recognize income of $20,000, but it also obtains no income tax deduction for the $20,000 constructive dividend. ▼

EXAMPLE 25

Assume the same facts as in Example 24, except that the loan to Hal was not bona fide. In this event, the full amount of the loan is regarded as a dividend to Hal. Therefore, the interest element is not a factor, since no bona fide loan ever existed. ▼

STOCK REDEMPTIONS

If a corporation redeems a shareholder's stock (a **stock redemption**), one of two possible outcomes occurs:

- The redemption may qualify as a sale or exchange under § 302 or § 303. In that case, capital gain or loss treatment usually applies to the qualifying shareholders.
- The redemption will be treated as a dividend under § 301, provided the distributing corporation has E & P.

EXAMPLE 26

Reba owns 300 shares of Snipe Corporation stock as an investment. The shares have a basis to Reba of $100 each, for a total of $30,000. When the fair market value of a share is $200, Snipe redeems 200 of Reba's shares. If the redemption qualifies for sale or exchange treatment, the result is a capital gain to Reba of $20,000 [$40,000 (redemption price) – $20,000 (basis in 200 shares)]. Reba's basis in the remaining 100 shares is $10,000 [$30,000 (basis in the original shares) – $20,000 (basis in the shares redeemed)]. ▼

EXAMPLE 27

Assume the same facts as in Example 26, except that the redemption does not qualify for sale or exchange treatment. Presuming adequate E & P, the redemption results in $40,000 dividend income. Reba's basis in the remaining 100 shares now becomes $30,000, or $300 per share. ▼

A stock redemption qualifies as a sale or exchange if it meets any of the safe harbors of § 302 or § 303.

LIQUIDATING THE CORPORATION

7 LEARNING OBJECTIVE
Recognize the tax rules governing the liquidation of corporations.

Unlike dividend distributions or stock redemptions, where the distributing corporation continues its operations, **liquidating distributions** occur during the termination of the business. All debts are paid, and any remaining corporate assets are distributed pro rata to the shareholders in exchange for their stock. Once these distributions are completed, the corporation undergoing liquidation will cease to be a separate tax entity.

GENERAL RULE OF § 331

Under the general rule, the shareholders recognize gain or loss in a corporate liquidation. The amount of recognized gain or loss is measured by the difference between the fair market value of the assets received from the corporation and the adjusted basis of the stock surrendered. The shareholders recognize capital gain or loss if the stock is a capital asset.[35]

EXAMPLE 28

Pursuant to a complete liquidation, Starling Corporation distributes $100,000 in cash to Edna, one of its shareholders. If Edna's basis in the stock surrendered is $40,000, she must recognize a gain of $60,000. If Edna held the stock as an investment, the $60,000 gain is capital gain—either short term or long term (depending on the holding period). ▼

EXCEPTION TO THE GENERAL RULE

Section 332 is an exception to the general rule that the shareholder recognizes gain or loss on a corporate liquidation. If a parent corporation liquidates a subsidiary corporation in which it owns at least 80 percent of the voting power and value of the stock, no gain or loss is recognized by the parent company. The subsidiary must distribute all of its property in complete liquidation of all of its stock within the taxable year or within three years from the close of the tax year in which the first distribution occurred.

BASIS DETERMINATION—§§ 334 AND 338

General Rule. Where gain or loss is recognized upon the complete liquidation of a corporation, the basis of the property received by the shareholders is the property's fair market value.[36]

Subsidiary Liquidation Basis Rules. The general rule is that the property received by the parent corporation in a complete liquidation of its subsidiary under § 332 has the same basis it had in the hands of the subsidiary (a carryover basis).[37] The parent's basis in the stock of the liquidated subsidiary disappears.

EXAMPLE 29

Swallow, the parent corporation, has a basis of $20,000 in the stock of Shrike Corporation, a subsidiary in which it owns 85% of all classes of stock. Swallow purchased the stock of Shrike Corporation 10 years ago. In the current year, Swallow liquidates Shrike Corporation and receives assets worth $50,000 with a tax basis to Shrike of $40,000. Swallow Corporation would have a basis of $40,000 in the assets, with a potential gain upon sale of $10,000. Swallow's original $20,000 basis in the Shrike stock disappears. ▼

An exception to the carryover of basis rule is provided in § 338. Under this exception, the parent company may elect to receive a basis for the assets equal to the adjusted basis of the stock of the subsidiary. In effect, the initial acquisition of the subsidiary is treated as if the parent company had acquired the assets (rather than the stock) of the subsidiary.

---

[35] If the stock is held as an investment, which is usually the case, gain or loss will be capital. Stock owned by a broker probably will be inventory and therefore will not constitute a capital asset. Thus, the gain or loss on this type of stock is ordinary and not capital.

[36] § 334(a).
[37] § 334(b)(1).

EFFECT OF THE LIQUIDATION ON THE CORPORATION

Having examined what happens to the shareholder upon the liquidation of a corporation, what happens at the corporate level? Here, § 336 applies to dictate the tax consequences to the corporation being liquidated.

Under § 336, the distributing corporation recognizes gain or loss upon complete liquidation. In this regard, it does not matter whether the corporation distributes the property in-kind (*as is*) to the shareholders or first sells the property and then distributes the proceeds.

EXAMPLE 30

Pursuant to a complete liquidation, Grackle Corporation distributes the following assets to its shareholders: undeveloped land held as an investment (basis of $150,000 and fair market value of $140,000) and marketable securities (basis of $160,000 and fair market value of $200,000). Since Grackle is treated as if it had sold the property, a gain of $40,000 results from the securities, and a loss of $10,000 results from the land. ▼

ETHICAL CONSIDERATIONS

Necessity for Filing a Corporate Tax Return

For many years, Hanna has owned and operated several apartment buildings. In 1990 and upon the advice of her attorney, Hanna transferred the apartment buildings to a newly formed corporation. Her main reason for incorporating the business was to achieve limited liability.

Every year since 1990, Hanna has prepared and filed a Form 1120 for the corporation. No corporate income tax has been paid because, after the deduction of various expenses (including Hanna's salary), the corporation has zero taxable income.

In 1997, Hanna decides that filing Form 1120 is a waste of time. Instead, she will report all of the financial activities of the apartment business on her own individual Form 1040.

Has Hanna acted properly or should she first liquidate the corporation?

The deductibility of losses may be restricted by the related-party rules (refer to Chapter 6) if certain conditions exist (e.g., the distributions are not pro rata).[38]

A wholly owned subsidiary corporation does not recognize gain or loss when the parent corporation uses the carryover basis option of § 334(b)(1). The reason for the special treatment is that the subsidiary's basis (and all other tax attributes) in the assets carries over to the parent corporation.

THE S ELECTION

JUSTIFICATION FOR THE ELECTION

LEARNING OBJECTIVE 8
Appreciate the utility and effect of the Subchapter S election.

Numerous nontax reasons exist for operating a business in the corporate form (e.g., limited liability). Consequently, the existence of income tax disadvantages (e.g., double taxation of corporate income and shareholder dividends) should not deter business people from using the corporate form. To prevent tax considerations from interfering with the exercise of sound business judgment, Congress enacted Subchapter S of the Code.

---

[38] § 336(d).

To qualify for **S corporation** status, the corporation must be a **small business corporation**.[39] This includes any corporation that has the following characteristics:

- Is a domestic corporation.
- Has no more than 75 shareholders.
- Has as its shareholders only individuals, estates, and certain trusts.
- Does not have a nonresident alien as a shareholder.
- Has only one class of stock outstanding.

These characteristics must continue to exist if an electing S corporation is to maintain S status.

Making the Election.
The election is made by filing Form 2553, and *all* shareholders must consent. For this purpose, husbands and wives are counted as a single shareholder.

To be effective for the current year, the election must be filed anytime during the preceding taxable year or on or before the fifteenth day of the third month of the current year.[40]

EXAMPLE 31 — Heron, a calendar year taxpayer, is a regular corporation that wishes to elect S status for 1997. If the election is filed anytime from January 1, 1996, through March 15, 1997, it will be effective for 1997. ▼

Legislation enacted in 1996 gives the IRS the authority to waive invalid S elections (e.g., inadvertent failure to obtain all the necessary shareholder consents to the original election) and to treat late elections as timely.

Loss of the Election.
The S election may be terminated *voluntarily* (a majority of the shareholders file to revoke the election) or *involuntarily*. An involuntary termination may occur in *any* of the following ways:

- The corporation ceases to qualify as a small business corporation (e.g., the number of shareholders exceeds 75, or a partnership becomes a shareholder).
- The corporation has passive investment income (e.g., interest, dividends) in excess of 25 percent of gross receipts for a period of three consecutive years. This possibility applies only if the corporation was previously a regular corporation and has earnings and profits from that period.

If the holders of a *majority* of the shares consent to a voluntary revocation of S status, the election to revoke must be made on or before the fifteenth day of the third month of the tax year to be effective for that year.

EXAMPLE 32 — The shareholders of Stork Corporation, a calendar year S corporation, elect to revoke the election on January 4, 1997. Assuming the election is duly executed and timely filed, Stork will become a regular corporation for calendar year 1997. If the election to revoke is not made until June 1997, Stork will not become a regular corporation until calendar year 1998. ▼

Suppose the shareholders in Example 32 file the election to revoke on January 4, 1997, but do not want the revocation to take place until 1998. If the election so specifies, Stork Corporation will cease to have S status as of January 1, 1998.

---

[39] § 1361(b). [40] § 1362.

TAX IN THE NEWS

ONE QUESTIONABLE USE OF S CORPORATION STATUS

The IRS has stepped up its audits of S corporations to catch owners who cheat on FICA self-employment taxes. In partnerships, limited liability companies, and sole proprietorships, all income flowing to the partners or owners is subject to FICA taxes. In S corporations, only amounts designated as salaries are so subject. Distributions of profits are not subject to FICA taxes. Thus, owner-employees of S corporations may attempt to reduce (or avoid) self-employment taxes by curtailing salaries and maximizing profits. In such cases, the IRS can reclassify as salaries some of the profit pass-through to properly reflect the value of the services rendered to the corporation.

SOURCE: Peter Weaver, "Heightened Scrutiny for S Corporations," *Nation's Business*, February 1995, p. 37.

In the case where S status is lost because of a disqualifying act (involuntarily), the loss of the election takes effect as of the date on which the event occurs.

EXAMPLE 33 Crow Corporation has been a calendar year S corporation for several years. On August 13, 1997, one of its shareholders sells her stock to Kite Corporation. Since Crow Corporation no longer satisfies the definition of a small business corporation (it has another corporation as a shareholder), the election has been involuntarily terminated. For calendar year 1997, therefore, Crow will be an S corporation through August 12 and a regular corporation from August 13 through December 31, 1997. ▼

In the event the election is lost through a violation of the passive investment income limitation, the loss of S status starts at the beginning of the next tax year.

Barring certain exceptions, the loss of the election after 1996 places the corporation in a five-year holding period before S status can be reelected.

OPERATIONAL RULES

The S corporation is primarily a tax-reporting rather than a taxpaying entity. In this respect, the entity is taxed much like a partnership.[41] Under the conduit concept, the taxable income and losses of an S corporation flow through to the shareholders who report them on their personal income tax returns.

To ascertain the annual tax consequences to each shareholder, it is necessary to carry out two steps at the S corporation level. First, all corporate transactions that will flow through to the shareholders on an *as is* basis under the conduit approach must be set aside. Second, what remains is aggregated as the taxable income of the S corporation and is allocated to each shareholder on a per-share and per-day of stock ownership basis.[42]

---

[41] This is not to imply that an S corporation is always free from the income tax. For example, a tax may be imposed on certain built-in gains or certain excessive passive investment income.

[42] § 1366.

Separately Stated Items.
The following are some of the items that do not lose their identity as they pass through the S corporation and are therefore picked up by each shareholder on an *as is* basis:

- Tax-exempt income.
- Long-term and short-term capital gains and losses.
- Section 1231 gains and losses.
- Charitable contributions.
- Foreign tax credits.
- Depletion.
- Nonbusiness income or loss under § 212.
- Intangible drilling costs.
- Investment interest, income, and expenses covered under § 163(d).
- Certain portfolio income.
- Passive activity gains, losses, and credits under § 469.
- AMT adjustments and tax preference items.

These items are separately stated because each may lead to a different tax result when combined with a particular shareholder's other transactions.

EXAMPLE 34 Arnold and Jean are equal shareholders in Lark Corporation (an S corporation). For calendar year 1997, each must account for one-half of a corporate short-term capital gain of $6,000. Arnold has no other capital asset transactions, and Jean has a short-term capital loss of $3,000 from the sale of stock in IBM Corporation. In terms of overall effect, the difference between the two taxpayers is significant. Although both must report the short-term capital gain pass-through, Jean will neutralize its inclusion in gross income by offsetting it with the $3,000 short-term capital loss from the sale of the IBM stock. For Arnold, the short-term capital gain pass-through results in a $3,000 increase in his taxable income. ▼

Taxable Income.
After the separately stated items have been removed, the balance represents the taxable income of the S corporation. In arriving at taxable income, the dividends received deduction and the net operating loss deduction are not allowed. An S corporation does come under the regular corporate rules, however, for purposes of amortization of organizational expenditures.

Once taxable income has been determined, it passes through to each shareholder as of the last day of the S corporation's tax year.

EXAMPLE 35 Harrier Corporation, a calendar year S corporation, had the following transactions during the current year:

Sales		$ 40,000
Cost of goods sold		(23,000)
Other income		
*Tax-exempt interest	$ 300	
*Long-term capital gain	500	800
Other expenses		
*Charitable contributions	$ 400	
Advertising expense	1,500	
Other operating expenses	2,000	
*Short-term capital loss	150	(4,050)
Net income per books		$ 13,750

When the items that are to be separately stated (those preceded by an asterisk [*]) and shown *as is* by each shareholder are withdrawn, Harrier has the following taxable income:

Sales		$ 40,000
Cost of goods sold		(23,000)
Other expenses		
Advertising expense	$1,500	
Other operating expenses	2,000	(3,500)
Taxable income		$ 13,500

▼

EXAMPLE 36

If Oscar owned 10% of the stock in Harrier Corporation (refer to Example 35) during all of the current year, he must account for the following:

Separately stated items	
Tax-exempt interest	$ 30
Long-term capital gain	50
Charitable contributions	40
Short-term capital loss	15
Taxable income (10% of $13,500)	1,350

Some of the separately stated items need not be reported on Oscar's individual income tax return (e.g., the tax-exempt interest). Others must be reported but may not lead to tax consequences. Oscar picks up his share of Harrier's taxable income ($1,350) as ordinary income. ▼

Treatment of Losses. As previously noted, separately stated loss items (e.g., capital losses, § 1231 losses) flow through to the shareholders on an *as is* basis. Their treatment by a shareholder depends on the shareholder's individual income tax position. If the S corporation's taxable income determination results in an operating loss, it also passes through to the shareholders. As is the case with separately stated items, the amount of the loss each shareholder receives depends on the stock ownership during the year.

EXAMPLE 37

In 1997, Oriole Corporation (a calendar year S corporation) incurred an operating loss of $36,500. During 1997, Jason's ownership in Oriole was as follows: 20% for 200 days and 30% for 165 days. Jason's share of the loss is determined as follows:

[$36,500 × (200/365)] × 20% =	$4,000
[$36,500 × (165/365)] × 30% =	4,950
Total loss for Jason	$8,950

Presuming the basis limitation does not come into play (see the following discussion), Jason deducts $8,950 in arriving at adjusted gross income. ▼

Basis Determination. A shareholder's *basis* in the stock of an S corporation, like that of a regular corporation, is the original investment plus additional capital contributions less return of capital distributions. At this point, however, the symmetry disappears. Generally, basis is increased by the pass-through of income items (including those separately stated) and decreased by the loss items (including those separately stated).[43]

---

[43] § 1367.

EXAMPLE 38
In 1997, Warbler Corporation is formed with an investment of $100,000, of which Janice contributed $20,000 for a 20% stock interest. A timely S election is made, and for 1997, Warbler earns taxable income of $15,000. Janice's basis in her stock investment now becomes $23,000 [$20,000 (original capital contribution) + $3,000 (the 20% share of the corporation's taxable income assigned to Janice)]. ▼

Distributions by an S corporation reduce the basis of a shareholder's stock investment. However, if the amount of the distribution exceeds basis, the excess normally receives capital gain treatment.

As previously noted, operating losses of an S corporation pass through to the shareholders and reduce the basis in their stock investment. Because the basis of the stock cannot fall below zero, an excess loss is then applied against the basis of any loans the shareholder may have made to the corporation.

EXAMPLE 39
Flamingo Corporation, a calendar year S corporation, has an operating loss of $60,000 for 1997. Norman, a 50% shareholder, has an adjusted basis of $25,000 in his stock investment and has made loans to the corporation of $5,000. Based on these facts, Norman may take full advantage of the $30,000 loss (50% of $60,000) on his 1997 individual income tax return. Norman's basis in the stock and the loans must be reduced accordingly, and both will be zero after the pass-through. ▼

In the event the basis limitation precludes an operating loss from being absorbed, the loss can be carried forward and deducted when and if it is covered by basis.

EXAMPLE 40
Assume the same facts as in Example 39, except that Norman had not made any loans to Flamingo Corporation. Further assume that Flamingo has taxable income of $15,000 in the following year (1998). Norman's tax situation for 1997 and 1998 is summarized as follows:

Ordinary loss for 1997	$25,000
Income to be reported in 1998 (50% of $15,000)	7,500
Restoration of stock basis in 1998 (50% of $15,000)	7,500
Loss allowed for 1998 ($30,000 − $25,000)	5,000
Basis in stock account after 1998 ($7,500 − $5,000)	2,500

Thus, Norman's unabsorbed loss of $5,000 from 1997 carries over to 1998 and is applied against the $7,500 of ordinary income for that year. ▼

PARTNERSHIPS

NATURE OF PARTNERSHIP TAXATION

9 LEARNING OBJECTIVE
Understand the tax consequences of forming and operating a partnership.

Unlike corporations, partnerships are not considered separate taxable entities. Each member of a partnership is subject to income tax on his or her distributive share of the partnership's income, even if an actual distribution is not made. The tax return (Form 1065) required of a partnership serves only to provide information necessary in determining the character and amount of each partner's distributive share of the partnership's income and expense. Because a partnership acts as a conduit, items that pass through to the partners do not lose their identity. For example, tax-exempt income earned by a partnership is picked up by the partners as tax-exempt income. In this regard, partnerships function in much the same fashion as S corporations, which also serve as conduits.

A partnership is considered a separate taxable entity for purposes of making various elections and selecting its taxable year, method of depreciation, and accounting method. A partnership is also treated as a separate legal entity under civil law with the right to own property in its own name and to transact business free from the personal debts of its partners.

PARTNERSHIP FORMATION

Recognition of Gain or Loss. The general rule is that no gain or loss is recognized by a partnership or any of its partners on the contribution of property in exchange for a capital interest in the partnership.[44] The general rule also applies to all subsequent contributions of property.

There are certain exceptions to the nonrecognition of gain or loss rule including the following:

- If a partner transfers property to the partnership and receives money or other consideration (boot) as a result, the transaction will be treated as a sale or exchange rather than as a contribution of capital. Realized gain is recognized to the extent of the fair market value of the boot received.
- If a partnership interest is received in exchange for services rendered or to be rendered by the partner to the partnership, the fair market value of the transferred capital interest is regarded as compensation for services rendered. In such cases, the recipient of the capital interest must recognize the amount as ordinary income in the year actually or constructively received.
- If property that is subject to a liability in excess of its basis is contributed to a partnership, the contributing partner may recognize gain.

Basis of a Partnership Interest. The contributing *partner's basis* in the partnership interest received is the sum of money contributed plus the adjusted basis of any other property transferred to the partnership.[45]

EXAMPLE 41 In return for the contribution of property (with a basis of $50,000 and a fair market value of $80,000) and cash of $10,000 to the Brown Partnership, Marcia receives a 10% capital interest worth $90,000. Although Marcia has a realized gain of $30,000 ($90,000 − $60,000) on the transfer, none of the gain is recognized. The basis of her interest in the Brown Partnership is $60,000 [$50,000 (basis of property contributed) + $10,000 (cash contribution)]. ▼

A partner's basis in the partnership interest is determined without regard to any amount reflected on the partnership's books as capital, equity, or a similar account.

EXAMPLE 42 Marge and Clyde form the equal Blue Partnership with a cash contribution of $30,000 from Marge and a property contribution (adjusted basis of $18,000 and fair market value of $30,000) from Clyde. Although the books of the Blue Partnership may reflect a credit of $30,000 to each partner's capital account, only Marge has a tax basis of $30,000 in her partnership interest. Clyde's tax basis in his partnership interest is $18,000, the amount of his tax basis in the property contributed to the partnership. ▼

After its initial determination, the basis of a partnership interest is subject to continuous fluctuations. A partner's basis is increased by additional contributions

---

[44] § 721. [45] § 722.

and the sum of his or her current and prior years' distributive share of the following:

- Taxable income of the partnership, including capital gains.
- Tax-exempt income of the partnership.
- The excess of the deductions for depletion over the basis of the partnership's property subject to depletion.[46]

Similarly, the basis of a partner's interest is decreased, but not below zero, by distributions of partnership property and by the sum of the current and prior years' distributive share of the following:

- Partnership losses, including capital losses.
- Partnership expenditures that are not deductible in computing taxable income or loss and that are not capital expenditures.

Changes in the liabilities (including trade accounts payable, bank loans, etc.) of a partnership also affect the basis of a partnership interest. A partner's basis is increased by his or her assumption of partnership liabilities and by his or her pro rata share of liabilities incurred by the partnership. Likewise, the partner's basis is decreased by the amount of any personal liabilities assumed by the partnership and by the pro rata share of any decreases in the liabilities of the partnership.

EXAMPLE 43

Tony, Martha, and Carolyn form the Orange Partnership with the following contributions: cash of $50,000 from Tony for a 50% interest in capital and profits, cash of $25,000 from Martha for a 25% interest, and property valued at $33,000 from Carolyn for a 25% interest. The property contributed by Carolyn has an adjusted basis of $15,000 and is subject to a mortgage of $8,000, which is assumed by the partnership. Carolyn's basis in her interest in the Orange Partnership is $9,000, determined as follows:

Adjusted basis of Carolyn's contributed property	$15,000
Less portion of mortgage assumed by Tony and Martha and treated as a distribution of money to Carolyn (75% of $8,000)	(6,000)
Basis of Carolyn's interest in Orange Partnership	$ 9,000

EXAMPLE 44

Assuming the same facts as in Example 43, Tony and Martha have a basis in their partnership interests of $54,000 and $27,000, respectively.

	Tony	Martha
Cash contribution	$50,000	$25,000
Plus portion of mortgage assumed and treated as an additional cash contribution:		
(50% of $8,000)	4,000	
(25% of $8,000)		2,000
Basis of interest in Orange Partnership	$54,000	$27,000

Partnership's Basis in Contributed Property. The *basis of property* contributed to a partnership by a partner is the adjusted basis of the property to the contributing partner at the time of the contribution.[47] Additionally, the holding

---

[46] § 705(a).

[47] § 723.

period of the property for the partnership includes the period during which the property was held by the contributing partner. This is logical, since the partnership's basis in the property is the same basis the property had in the hands of the partner.[48]

EXAMPLE 45

In 1997, Roger contributed equipment with an adjusted basis of $10,000 and fair market value of $30,000 to the Red Partnership in exchange for a one-third interest in the partnership. No gain or loss is recognized by Roger. The basis in the equipment is $10,000 to the Red Partnership. If Roger had acquired the equipment in 1986, the holding period for the Red Partnership would include the period from 1986 through 1997. ▼

PARTNERSHIP OPERATION

Measuring and Reporting Partnership Income.
Although a partnership is not subject to Federal income taxation, it is required to determine its taxable income and file an income tax return for information purposes.[49] The tax return, Form 1065, is due on the fifteenth day of the fourth month following the close of the taxable year of the partnership.

In measuring and reporting partnership income, certain transactions must be segregated and reported separately on the partnership return. Items such as charitable contributions, capital gains and losses, and foreign taxes are excluded from partnership taxable income and are allocated separately to the partners.[50] These items must be segregated and allocated separately because they affect the computation of various exclusions, deductions, and credits at the individual partner level. For example, one of the partners may have made personal charitable contributions in excess of the ceiling limitations on his or her individual tax return. Therefore, partnership charitable contributions are excluded from partnership taxable income and are reported separately on the partnership return.

A second step in the measurement and reporting process is the computation of the partnership's ordinary income or loss. The taxable income of a partnership is computed in the same manner as the taxable income of an individual taxpayer. However, a partnership is not allowed the following deductions:[51]

- The deduction for personal and dependency exemptions.
- The deduction for taxes paid to foreign countries or possessions of the United States.
- The deduction for charitable contributions.
- The deduction for net operating losses.
- The additional itemized deductions allowed individuals in §§ 211 through 219.

The partnership's ordinary income or loss and each of the items requiring separate treatment are reported in the partnership's information return and allocated to the partners in accordance with their distributive shares.

Limitation on Partner's Share of Losses.
A partner's deduction of the distributive share of partnership losses (including capital losses) could be limited. The limitation is the adjusted basis of the partnership interest at the end of the partnership year in which the losses were incurred.

---

[48] § 1223(2).
[49] § 6031.
[50] § 702(a).
[51] § 703(a).

The limitation for partnership loss deductions is similar to that applicable to losses of S corporations. Like S corporation losses, partnership losses may be carried forward by the partner and utilized against future increases in the basis of the partnership interest. Such increases might result from additional capital contributions to the partnership, from additional partnership liabilities, or from future partnership income.

EXAMPLE 46
Florence and Donald do business as the Green Partnership, sharing profits and losses equally. All parties use the calendar year for tax purposes. As of January 1, 1997, Florence's basis in her partnership interest is $25,000. The partnership sustained an operating loss of $80,000 in 1997 and earned a profit of $70,000 in 1998. For the calendar year 1997, Florence may claim only $25,000 of her $40,000 distributive share of the partnership loss (one-half of the $80,000 loss). As a result, the basis in her partnership interest is reduced to zero as of January 1, 1998, and she must carry forward the remaining $15,000 of partnership losses. ▼

EXAMPLE 47
Assuming the same facts as in Example 46, what are the income tax consequences for Florence in 1998? Since the partnership earned a profit of $70,000 for the calendar year 1998, Florence reports income from the partnership of $20,000 ($35,000 distributive share of income for 1998 less the $15,000 loss not allowed for 1997). The adjusted basis of her partnership interest now becomes $20,000. ▼

Transactions between Partner and Partnership. A partner engaging in a transaction with the partnership is generally regarded as a nonpartner or outsider. However, the Code includes certain exceptions to prevent unwarranted tax avoidance. For instance, losses from the sale or exchange of property are disallowed if they arise in either of the following cases:

- Between a partnership and a person whose direct or indirect interest in the capital or profits of the partnership is more than 50 percent.
- Between two partnerships in which the same persons own more than a 50 percent interest in the capital or profits.[52]

If one of the purchasers later sells the property, any gain realized will be recognized only to the extent that it exceeds the loss previously disallowed.

EXAMPLE 48
Pat owns a 60% interest in the capital and profits of the Rose Partnership. In the current year, Pat sells property with an adjusted basis of $50,000 to the partnership for its fair market value of $35,000. The $15,000 loss is not deductible since Pat's ownership interest is more than 50%. If the Rose Partnership later sells the property for $40,000, none of the $5,000 (sale price of $40,000 less adjusted basis to partnership of $35,000) gain will be recognized since it is offset by $5,000 of the previously disallowed loss of $15,000. The unused loss of $10,000, however, is of no tax benefit either to the partnership or to Pat. ▼

Payments made by a partnership to one of its partners for services rendered or for the use of capital, to the extent they are determined without regard to the income of the partnership, are treated by the partnership in the same manner as payments made to a person who is not a partner. Referred to as **guaranteed payments,** these are generally deductible by the partnership as a business expense.[53] The payments must be reported as ordinary income by the receiving partner. Their deductibility distinguishes guaranteed payments from a partner's distributive share of income that is not deductible by the partnership.

---

[52] § 707(b)(1).   [53] § 707(c).

EXAMPLE 49

Under the terms of the Silver Partnership agreement, Kim is entitled to a fixed annual salary of $18,000 without regard to the income of the partnership. He is also to share in the profits and losses of the partnership as a one-third partner. After deducting the guaranteed payment, the partnership has $36,000 of ordinary income. Kim must include $30,000 as ordinary income on his income tax return for his tax year with or within which the partnership tax year ends ($18,000 guaranteed payment + $12,000 one-third distributive share of partnership income). ▼

Other Partnership Considerations. Complex tax provisions involving liquidating and nonliquidating distributions and the sale of a partnership interest are beyond the scope of this text and are discussed in depth in *West's Federal Taxation: Corporations, Partnerships, Estates, and Trusts.*

TAX PLANNING CONSIDERATIONS

CORPORATE VERSUS NONCORPORATE FORMS OF BUSINESS ORGANIZATION

10 LEARNING OBJECTIVE
Evaluate the advantages and disadvantages of the various forms for conducting a business.

The decision to use the corporate form in conducting a trade or business must be weighed carefully. Besides the nontax aspects of the corporate form (limited liability, continuity of life, free transferability of interests, centralized management), tax ramifications play an important role in any such decision. Close attention should be paid to the following:

1. The corporate form means the imposition of the corporate income tax. Corporate-source income will be taxed twice—once as earned by the corporation and again when distributed to the shareholders. Since dividends are not deductible, a strong incentive exists in a closely held corporation to structure corporate distributions in a deductible form. The shareholders may bail out profits in the form of salaries, interest, or rents. These procedures lead to a multitude of problems, one of which, the reclassification of debt as equity, has been discussed. The problems of unreasonable salaries and rents were discussed in Chapter 6.
2. The applicable income tax rates also affect the choice of the form for doing business. Unfortunately, because of the wide range of possibilities involved (15 to 39.6 percent for individuals and 15 to 35 percent for corporations), this factor must be considered on a case-by-case basis. For example, the corporate form is very appealing if the anticipated taxable income falls within the 25 percent bracket while the shareholder's individual bracket is 39.6 percent. Here, the time value of the taxes saved (by not distributing dividends and postponing the effect of the double tax) could make operating a business in the corporate form advantageous.
3. Corporate-source income loses its identity as it passes through the corporation to the shareholders. Thus, items possessing preferential tax treatment (e.g., interest on municipal bonds) are not taxed as such to the shareholders.
4. As noted earlier, it may be difficult for shareholders to recover some or all of their investment in the corporation without an ordinary income result. Recall that most corporate distributions are treated as dividends to the extent of the corporation's earnings and profits. Structuring the capital of the corporation to include debt is a partial solution to this problem. Thus, the shareholder-creditor could recoup part of his or her investment through the tax-free payment of principal. Too much debt, however, may lead to the debt being reclassified as equity.
5. Corporate losses cannot be passed through to the shareholders.
6. The liquidation of a corporation may generate tax consequences to both the corporation and its shareholders.

7. The corporate form provides the shareholders with the opportunity to be treated as employees for tax purposes if they render services to the corporation. This status makes a number of attractive tax-sheltered fringe benefits available (e.g., group term life insurance). These benefits are not available to partners and sole proprietors.

REGULAR CORPORATION VERSUS S STATUS

Due to the pass-through concept, the use of S status generally avoids the income tax at the corporate level, bringing the individual income tax into play. As noted in item 2 in the previous section, the differential between the rates applicable to noncorporate and corporate taxpayers makes this a factor to be considered. The S election enables a business to operate in the corporate form, avoid the corporate income tax, and, depending on taxable income, possibly take advantage of the lower rates usually applicable to individuals. Also, losses incurred at the corporate level pass through to the shareholders, who will utilize them on their individual returns (compare with item 5).

Electing S status can present several problems. First, the election is available only to small business corporations. Consequently, many corporations will not qualify for the election. Second, S corporations are subject to the rules governing regular corporations unless otherwise specified in the Code. For example, if an S corporation carries out a stock redemption or is liquidated, the rules covering regular corporations apply. Third, some states do not recognize S status for purposes of state and local taxation. Therefore, an S corporation might be subject to a state franchise tax (refer to Chapter 1) or a state or local income tax.

USE OF AN ENTITY TO REDUCE THE FAMILY INCOME TAX BURDEN

One objective of tax planning is to keep the income from a business within the family unit but to disperse the income in such a manner as to minimize the overall tax burden. To the extent feasible, therefore, income should be shifted from higher-bracket to lower-bracket family members.

Unfortunately, the income from property (a business) cannot be shifted to another without also transferring an interest in the property. If, for example, a father wants to assign income from his sole proprietorship to his children, he must form a partnership or incorporate the business.[54] In either case, the transfer of the interest may be subject to the Federal gift tax. But any potential gift tax can be eliminated or controlled through judicious use of the annual exclusion, the election to split gifts (for married donors), and the unified tax credit (refer to the discussion of the Federal gift tax in Chapter 1).

Consequently, the first problem to be resolved becomes which form of business organization will best fit the objective of income shifting. For the partnership form, one major obstacle arises. Family partnership rules preclude the assignment of income to a family member unless capital is a material income-producing factor.[55] If not, the family member must contribute substantial or vital services. Ordinarily, capital is not a material income-producing factor if the income

---

[54] Income shifting will not work, however, if the minor is under 14 years of age. In such cases, net unearned income (refer to the discussion in Chapter 3) of the child is taxed at the parents' tax rate. § 1(g).

[55] § 704(e).

of the business consists principally of compensation for personal services performed by members or employees of the partnership. Conversely, capital is a material income-producing factor if the operation of the business entails a substantial investment in physical assets (e.g., inventory, plant, machinery, or equipment).

Income shifting through the use of a partnership, therefore, may be ineffectual if a personal service business is involved. In fact, it could be hopeless if the assignees are minors. The use of the corporate form usually involves no such impediment. Regardless of the nature of the business, a gift of stock carries with it the attributes of ownership. Thus, dividends paid on stock are taxed to the owner of the stock.

But what if the corporate form is utilized and the S election is made? A new hurdle arises. The Code authorizes the IRS to make adjustments in situations where shareholders are not being adequately compensated for the value of their services or capital provided to an S corporation in a family setting.[56] Thus, an S corporation suffers from the same vulnerability that exists with family partnerships.

ETHICAL CONSIDERATIONS

Does a Shifting of Income Occur?

Several years ago, Roy incorporated his sole proprietorship and made an election under Subchapter S. Since then, Roy has been paying himself an annual salary of $90,000. In 1997, Roy makes a gift of 10 percent of the stock to each of his four children. All of the children are over 13 but less than 21 years of age, and none work in the business. For 1997 and subsequent years, Roy reduces his salary to $50,000.

What is Roy trying to accomplish? Will it work?

A further factor that favors the corporate form (either a regular or an S corporation) as a device for income splitting is the ease with which it can be carried out. Presuming the entity already exists, the transfer of stock merely requires an entry in the corporation's stock ledger account. In contrast, a gift of a partnership interest probably requires an amendment to the articles of copartnership. If minors are to be the assignees (donees), a state's Uniform Gifts to Minors Act provides a useful and flexible means of holding a stock interest until the assignees become adults.[57] In the case of a partnership interest, however, a guardianship may have to be set up to achieve the same flexibility. In summary, the transfer of stock is more convenient and, since it usually avoids legal problems, can be less expensive.

Regardless of the form of organization used for the business, income shifting will not take place unless the transfer is complete.[58] If the donor continues to exercise control over the interest transferred and does not recognize and protect the ownership rights of the donee, the IRS may argue that the transfer is ineffective for tax purposes. In that case, the income from the transferred interest continues to be taxed to the donor.

---

[56] § 1366(e).
[57] The Uniform Gifts to Minors Act is explained in Chapter 4.
[58] *Ginsberg v. Comm.*, 74–2 USTC ¶9660, 34 AFTR2d 74–5760, 502 F.2d 965 (CA–6, 1974), and *Michael F. Beirne*, 61 T.C. 268 (1973).

KEY TERMS

Association, 20-4
Constructive dividends, 20-21
Dividends received deduction, 20-10
Earnings and profits, 20-20
Guaranteed payments, 20-33
Limited liability companies, 20-5
Liquidating distribution, 20-22
Organizational expenditures, 20-12
Personal service corporation, 20-13
S corporation, 20-25
Small business corporation, 20-25
Stock redemption, 20-22
Thin capitalization, 20-18

PROBLEM MATERIALS

DISCUSSION QUESTIONS

1. What is the role of state law in determining whether or not an entity will be classified as a corporation for Federal income tax purposes?
2. Under what circumstances might the disregard of the corporate entity produce a favorable result for the IRS?
3. When will an entity be classified as a corporation under the association approach?
4. Why are limited liability companies advantageous?
5. How would the Regulations dealing with the "check-the-box" rules be beneficial to the IRS? To taxpayers?
6. Would a corporation such as General Motors be affected by the "check-the-box" rules promulgated by the Regulations? Why or why not?
7. Can corporations use the cash method of accounting? Explain.
8. Are the tax brackets applied differently in any way to individuals and corporations in higher taxable income levels?
9. Are the net long-term capital gains of individual taxpayers taxed in the same manner as those of corporate taxpayers? Explain.
10. Contrast the corporate tax rules for deducting net capital losses with the rules for individuals. Are the corporate capital loss rules *more or less* favorable than the capital loss provisions for individuals? Why?
11. Do corporations have to recapture more depreciation than noncorporate taxpayers? Explain.
12. Is it ever possible for a corporation to deduct some (or all) of the appreciation on inventory donated to charity? Explain.
13. In computing an NOL, corporations are subject to fewer adjustments than are individuals. Explain.
14. Why would a corporation elect not to carry back an NOL to a particular year?
15. What is the rationale for the dividends received deduction for corporate shareholders?
16. Mallard Corporation was formed in December 1996 and plans to use the cash basis of accounting. Mallard incurred one-half of its organizational expenses in December 1996 and one-half in January 1997. The payment of these expenses also occurred in these two months. Do you recognize any income tax problem?

17. Snipe Corporation is wholly owned by Regis, who is its CEO. For the past several years, Snipe has reported taxable income as follows: $75,100 (1995), $74,900 (1996), and $74,800 (1997). Snipe has a policy of paying its CEO a year-end bonus that varies in amount. Do you discern any potential income tax problems?

18. All corporations are taxed at a rate of 35%. Comment on the validity of this statement.

19. What purpose does the Schedule M–1 reconciliation of Form 1120 serve for the taxpayer? For the IRS?

20. To encourage a corporation to open a manufacturing facility in the community, a city donates land to the corporation. Does the donation generate income to the corporation? What basis will the corporation have in the land?

21. Why is it usually advantageous to capitalize a corporation by using debt? Is it possible that the debt will be reclassified as equity? Why?

22. Several persons plan to start a business that will be conducted by a newly formed corporation. One of the organizers, however, desires to recognize gain on the appreciated property he transfers to the corporation. What do you suggest?

23. When a corporation receives property in a nontaxable exchange under § 351, what is its income tax basis in the property?

24. In return for the performance of legal services, Imelda receives stock in newly formed Swallow Corporation. What is Imelda's income tax situation for this stock?

25. How do the following transactions affect the earnings and profits of a corporation?
    a. A nontaxable stock dividend issued to the shareholders.
    b. Receipt of interest on municipal bonds.
    c. Federal corporate income tax liability.

26. When is a distribution by a corporation to its shareholders treated by the shareholders as a return of capital? When can a shareholder have a capital gain on a distribution received from a corporation?

27. A corporation distributes a property dividend to its shareholders.
    a. Is any gain or loss recognized by the distributing corporation?
    b. What basis will the shareholders have in the property?

28. The stock of Loon Corporation is owned equally by a brother and two sisters: Cole, Alma, and Kara. During the year, the following transactions occur.
    a. Cole buys property from Loon Corporation.
    b. Alma rents property to Loon Corporation.
    c. Kara borrows money from Loon Corporation.
    d. Loon Corporation pays interest on bonds it sold to Cole, Alma, and Kara.

    Discuss any potential tax problems that these transactions might involve.

29. What difference does it make whether a corporation's redemption of its stock qualifies as a sale or exchange?

30. What is the usual tax effect to a shareholder when the corporation liquidates?

31. Since Mario incorporated his sole proprietorship and had the corporation make an S election, he has reduced his overall tax liability. How can this be?

32. Both Kimberly and Edward are shareholders in Emerald Company, an S corporation. During the current year, Emerald had losses. These losses benefited Kimberly but not Edward. How can you explain this result?

33. Compare the nonrecognition of gain or loss on contributions to a partnership with the similar provision found in corporate formation (§ 351). What are the major differences and similarities?

34. Under what circumstances does the receipt of a partnership interest result in the recognition of ordinary income? What is the effect of this on the partnership and the other partners?

35. How is a contributing partner's basis in a partnership interest determined?

36. What transactions or events will cause a partner's basis in his or her partnership interest to fluctuate continuously?

37. Describe the two-step approach used in determining partnership income. Why is the computation necessary?

38. To what extent can a partner deduct his or her distributive share of partnership losses? What happens to any unused losses?

39. What are guaranteed payments? When might such payments be used?

40. Cecil is the sole shareholder of Stilt Corporation (an S corporation). In order to shift income to lower-bracket family members, Cecil gives 40% of the stock in Stilt to his four children. Cecil's children are all minors, and none of them works for the corporation. Do you see any potential tax problems?

PROBLEMS

41. Cardinal Corporation has net short-term capital gains of $5,000 and net long-term capital losses of $45,000 during 1997. Taxable income from other sources is $200,000. Prior years' transactions included the following:

1993	Net short-term capital gains	$20,000
1994	Net long-term capital gains	10,000
1995	Net short-term capital gains	15,000
1996	Net long-term capital gains	10,000

    a. How are the capital gains and losses treated on the 1997 tax return?
    b. Compute the capital loss carryback to the carryback years.
    c. Compute the amount of capital loss carryover, if any, and designate the years to which the loss may be carried.

42. Starling Corporation acquired residential rental property on January 3, 1986, for $100,000. The property was depreciated using the accelerated method and a 19-year recovery period under ACRS. Depreciation in the amount of $66,375 was claimed. Straight-line depreciation for the period would have been $58,221. Starling sold the property on January 1, 1997, for $110,000. What is the gain on the sale, and how is it taxed?

43. Assume the property in Problem 42 was a commercial building and Starling Corporation used the straight-line method of depreciation with a 19-year recovery period under ACRS. What would be the gain on the sale, and how would it be taxed?

44. During 1997, Canary Corporation, a calendar year taxpayer, had the following income and expenses:

Income from operations	$225,000
Expenses from operations	165,000
Dividends from domestic corporations	15,000
NOL carryover from 1996	4,500

    On May 1, 1997, Canary made a contribution to a qualified charitable organization of $10,500 in cash (not included in any of the items listed above).
    a. Determine Canary's deduction for charitable contributions for 1997.
    b. What happens to any portion of the contribution not deductible in 1997?

45. Warbler Company is a wholesale grocery business. During 1997, it donated canned and dried food (held as inventory) to the local Goodwill branch. The basis of the food is $15,000, and it has a fair market value of $16,500. Based on the following assumptions, what amount qualifies as a charitable contribution?

a. Warbler Company is a sole proprietorship.
b. Warbler Company is a regular corporation.

46. During 1997, Raven Corporation had net income from operations of $200,000. In addition, Raven received dividends in the following amounts: $10,000 from Flicker Corporation and $20,000 from Blackbird Corporation. Raven owns 14% of the stock of Flicker and 40% of the stock of Blackbird. Determine Raven Corporation's dividends received deduction for 1997.

47. In each of the following independent situations, determine the dividends received deduction. Assume that none of the corporate shareholders owns 20% or more of the stock in the corporation paying the dividends.

	Gold Corporation	Silver Corporation	Rust Corporation
Income from operations	$ 700,000	$ 800,000	$ 700,000
Expenses of operations	(600,000)	(900,000)	(740,000)
Qualifying dividends	100,000	200,000	200,000

48. In each of the following independent situations, determine the corporation's income tax liability. Assume that all corporations use a calendar year for tax purposes, and that the tax year involved is 1997.

	Taxable Income
Peacock Corporation	$ 30,000
Sparrow Corporation	105,000
Robin Corporation	300,000
Nighthawk Corporation	10,000,000
Jay Corporation (a qualified personal service corporation)	50,000

49. Using the following legend, classify each statement accordingly:

Legend

I = Applies to the income taxation of individuals.

C = Applies to the income taxation of regular corporations.

B = Applies to the income taxation of both individuals and regular corporations.

N = Applies to the income taxation of neither individuals nor regular corporations.

a. Net capital losses can be carried back.
b. Net capital losses can be carried over indefinitely.
c. Net capital losses can offset other income.
d. Net long-term capital gains can be taxed at a rate in excess of 28%.
e. A cash basis taxpayer cannot deduct charitable contributions until the year of payment.
f. A dividends received deduction may be available.
g. The application of § 1250 (the recapture of depreciation claimed on certain real property) may yield less ordinary income.
h. The concept of adjusted gross income (AGI) is relevant.
i. Percentage limitations do not restrict the amount of charitable deductions that can be claimed in any one tax year.
j. Casualty losses are deductible in full.
k. Tax rates are progressive.

CHAPTER 20 Corporations and Partnerships

50. Pam, Gail, and Wyatt form the Godwit Corporation with the following investments:

	Basis	Fair Market Value	Number of Shares Issued
From Pam—			
Cash	$50,000	$50,000	50
From Gail—			
Land	50,000	60,000	45
From Wyatt—			
Services		5,000	5

In addition to stock, Gail received $15,000 in cash from the corporation. Wyatt received his 5 shares for performing legal and accounting services in forming the corporation. Assume each share of Godwit Stock is worth $1,000.
   a. How much gain (or loss) must Gail recognize?
   b. What basis will Gail have in the stock?
   c. What basis will Godwit Corporation have in the land?
   d. How much gain, if any, must Wyatt recognize?
   e. What basis will he have in the stock?

51. Zina and Walter form the Amber Corporation with the following investments:

	Basis	Fair Market Value	Number of Shares Issued
From Zina—			
Cash	$200,000	$200,000	200
From Walter—			
Land	250,000	230,000	200

In addition to stock, Walter received $30,000 in cash. Assume each share of Amber stock is worth $1,000.
   a. How much gain (or loss) must Walter recognize?
   b. What basis will Walter have in the stock?
   c. What basis will Amber Corporation have in the land?

52. Jane, the sole shareholder of Plover Corporation, has a basis of $20,000 in her stock investment. At a time when Plover Corporation has E & P of $14,000, it distributes cash of $30,000 to Jane. What are the tax consequences to Jane of the $30,000 distribution?

53. The stock of Sandpiper Corporation is held equally by Russ and Erlyne. The shareholders would like to receive, as a dividend, value of $100,000 each. The corporation has the following assets it can spare:

Asset	Adjusted Basis to Sandpiper Corporation	Fair Market Value
Land (parcel A)	$ 60,000	$100,000
Land (parcel B)	130,000	100,000

Both assets are held as investments. Sandpiper Corporation has a capital loss carryover from the previous year of $10,000 and has accumulated E & P in excess of $1 million.
Russ and Erlyne have come to you for advice. Suggest an attractive tax plan to carry out what the parties want. Write a letter (addressed to Sandpiper Corporation at P.O. Box 1150, St. Louis, MO 63130) describing your plan and its tax consequences.

54. At a time when Longspur Corporation has ample E & P, it redeems 500 of Cynthia's 1,500 shares for their fair market value of $500,000 ($1,000 for each share). All of Cynthia's shares were acquired 10 years ago as an investment and have an adjusted basis of $150,000 ($100 for each share).
    a. Describe the tax effect of the redemption if it qualifies for sale or exchange treatment.
    b. Describe the tax effect of the redemption if it does not qualify for sale or exchange treatment.

55. In the current year, Shearwater Corporation is liquidated under the general rules of § 331. The company distributes its only asset (land with a fair market value of $100,000 and adjusted basis of $20,000) to Oscar, who holds all of the Shearwater stock as an investment. Oscar's basis in the Shearwater stock is $60,000. Shearwater Corporation has E & P of $10,000.
    a. What are the amount and character of the gain or loss recognized by Oscar upon receiving the land in exchange for the stock?
    b. What is Oscar's basis in the land?
    c. Is there any tax effect to Shearwater Corporation? Explain.

56. Ten years ago, Albatross Corporation purchased all of the stock of Kingbird Corporation for $100,000. In the current year, Kingbird has a basis in its assets of $300,000 and a fair market value of $400,000. Albatross liquidates Kingbird Corporation and receives all of its assets. The exception to the carryover basis rule does not apply.
    a. Does Albatross Corporation recognize any gain as a result of the liquidation?
    b. What is Albatross Corporation's basis for the assets it receives from Kingbird Corporation?

57. During 1997, Crimson Corporation (a calendar year, accrual basis S corporation) had the following transactions:

Sales	$500,000
Cost of goods sold	300,000
Salaries	80,000
Charitable contributions	6,000
Capital gain (short term)	3,000
Advertising	5,000
Interest on City of Tulsa bonds	2,000

    a. Determine Crimson Corporation's separately stated items for 1997.
    b. Determine Crimson Corporation's taxable income for 1997.

58. Julius Walker owns all of the stock of Mockingbird Corporation, a calendar year S corporation. For calendar year 1997, Mockingbird anticipates an operating loss of $20,000 and could, if deemed worthwhile, sell a stock investment that would generate a $3,000 long-term capital loss. Julius has an adjusted basis of $5,000 in the Mockingbird stock. He anticipates no capital asset transactions and expects to be in the 36% tax bracket in 1997.
    a. Can you recommend a course of action that can save Julius taxes for 1997?
    b. Write a letter to Julius explaining your recommendations. Julius's address is Box 429, Normal, AL 35762.

59. In 1997, Heron Corporation (a calendar year S corporation) had an NOL of $73,000. Otto, a calendar year individual, held stock in Heron Corporation as follows: 40% for 200 days and 60% for 165 days. Based on these facts, what is Otto's loss pass-through for 1997?

60. Sam, Bob, and Clara form the Beige Partnership on January 1, 1997. In exchange for a 30% capital interest, Sam transfers property (basis of $14,000, fair market value of $25,000) subject to a liability of $10,000. The liability is assumed by the partnership. Bob transfers property (basis of $24,000, fair market value of $15,000) for a 30% capital interest, and Clara transfers cash of $20,000 for the remaining 40% capital interest.

a. How much gain must Sam recognize on the transfer?
b. What is Sam's basis in his partnership interest?
c. How much loss may Bob recognize on the transfer?
d. What is Bob's basis in his partnership interest?
e. What is Clara's basis in her partnership interest?
f. What basis will the Beige Partnership have in the property transferred by Sam? The property transferred by Bob?
g. What would be the tax consequences to Sam if the basis of the property he contributed is only $9,000?

61. As of January 1, 1996, Victor had a basis of $26,000 in his 25% capital interest in the Gray Partnership. He and the partnership use the calendar year for tax purposes. The partnership incurred an operating loss of $120,000 for 1996 and a profit of $80,000 for 1997.
    a. How much, if any, loss may Victor recognize for 1996?
    b. How much income must Victor recognize for 1997?
    c. What basis will Victor have in his partnership interest as of January 1, 1997?
    d. What basis will Victor have in his partnership interest as of January 1, 1998?
    e. What year-end tax planning would you suggest to ensure that a partner could deduct all of his or her share of any partnership losses?

62. Sarah owns a 51% interest in the capital and profits of the Rose Partnership. In 1996, Sarah sells property (adjusted basis of $120,000) to the partnership for the property's fair market value of $109,000. In 1997, Rose Partnership sells the same property to an outsider for $112,000.
    a. What are Sarah's tax consequences on the 1996 sale?
    b. What are Rose Partnership's tax consequences on the 1997 sale?

RESEARCH PROBLEMS

Note: **West's Federal Taxation on CD-ROM** *can be used in preparing solutions to the Research Problems. Alternatively, tax research materials contained in a standard tax library can be used.*

Research Problem 1. Rick and Alex (unrelated) are the equal shareholders of Aqua Corporation. A few years before his death, Alex divorced his wife, Wanda. The divorce proceeding was quite unpleasant, and many felt that Wanda's property settlement was inadequate under the circumstances. In his will, Alex leaves his half of the Aqua stock to Rick. Feeling bad about Wanda's economic plight, Rick has Aqua declare a $200,000 severance bonus on behalf of Alex. The bonus is paid to Wanda.
What are the tax issues involved, and how should they be resolved?

Partial list of research aids:
Montgomery Engineering Co. v. U.S., 64–2 USTC ¶9618, 13 AFTR2d 1747, 230 F.Supp. 838 (D.Ct.N.J., 1964).

Research Problem 2. Leonora incorporates her retail clothing business. She transfers all her business assets (total basis of $100,000 and fair market value of $95,000) along with business liabilities of $10,000 and a personal note in the amount of $15,000 to the corporation for 100% of its stock. The note is for money borrowed from the bank six months before incorporation to finance improvements on her home. What are the tax consequences of the transfer?

Research Problem 3. Several years ago, Mike Dalton incorporated his sole proprietorship and immediately made an election under Subchapter S. Mike lives in El Paso, Texas, and is married to Consuela, a citizen of Mexico. Since Consuela's father is ill and requires constant care, she lives with him across the border in Ciudad Juarez.
This year, the IRS audits the Forms 1120S filed by Mike's corporation and disallows its Subchapter S status. What could be the cause of the disallowance?

Research Problem 4. Ms. Marge Bland and a number of her friends want to diversify their investment portfolios. With this in mind, they form a partnership to which they transfer appreciated securities. Each transferor receives an interest in the new partnership proportionate to the value of the securities transferred. Will the creation of the partnership be tax-free? Why or why not?

a. Prepare a letter to Ms. Bland giving your advice. Ms. Bland's address is 349 Azalea Drive, Athens, GA 30602.

b. Prepare a memo for your firm's client files.

APPENDIX A
Tax Rate Schedules and Tables

1996	Income Tax Rate Schedules	A-2
1997	Income Tax Rate Schedules	A-2
1996	Tax Tables	A-3

1996 Tax Rate Schedules

Single—Schedule X

If taxable income is: Over—	But not over—	The tax is:	of the amount over—
$0	$ 24,000	...............15%	$0
24,000	58,150	$3,600.00 + 28%	24,000
58,150	121,300	13,162.00 + 31%	58,150
121,300	263,750	32,738.50 + 36%	121,300
263,750	....	84,020.50 + 39.6%	263,750

Married filing jointly or Qualifying widow(er)—Schedule Y-1

If taxable income is: Over—	But not over—	The tax is:	of the amount over—
$0	$ 40,100	...............15%	$0
40,100	96,900	$6,015.00 + 28%	40,100
96,900	147,700	21,919.00 + 31%	96,900
147,700	263,750	37,667.00 + 36%	147,700
263,750	....	79,445.00 + 39.6%	263,750

Head of household—Schedule Z

If taxable income is: Over—	But not over—	The tax is:	of the amount over—
$0	$ 32,150	...............15%	$0
32,150	83,050	$4,822.50 + 28%	32,150
83,050	134,500	19,074.50 + 31%	83,050
134,500	263,750	35,024.00 + 36%	134,500
263,750	....	81,554.00 + 39.6%	263,750

Married filing separately—Schedule Y-2

If taxable income is: Over—	But not over—	The tax is:	of the amount over—
$0	$ 20,050	...............15%	$0
20,050	48,450	$3,007.50 + 28%	20,050
48,450	73,850	10,959.50 + 31%	48,450
73,850	131,875	18,833.50 + 36%	73,850
131,875	....	39,722.50 + 39.6%	131,875

1997 Tax Rate Schedules

Single—Schedule X

If taxable income is: Over—	But not over—	The tax is:	of the amount over—
$0	$ 24,650	...............15%	$0
24,650	59,750	$3,697.50 + 28%	24,650
59,750	124,650	13,525.50 + 31%	59,750
124,650	271,050	33,644.50 + 36%	124,650
271,050	....	86,348.50 + 39.6%	271,050

Married filing jointly or Qualifying widow(er)—Schedule Y-1

If taxable income is: Over—	But not over—	The tax is:	of the amount over—
$0	$ 41,200	...............15%	$0
41,200	99,600	$6,180.00 + 28%	41,200
99,600	151,750	22,532.00 + 31%	99,600
151,750	271,050	38,698.50 + 36%	151,750
271,050	....	81,646.50 + 39.6%	271,050

Head of household—Schedule Z

If taxable income is: Over—	But not over—	The tax is:	of the amount over—
$0	$ 33,050	...............15%	$0
33,050	85,350	$4,957.50 + 28%	33,050
85,350	138,200	19,601.50 + 31%	85,350
138,200	271,050	35,985.00 + 36%	138,200
271,050	....	83,811.00 + 39.6%	271,050

Married filing separately—Schedule Y-2

If taxable income is: Over—	But not over—	The tax is:	of the amount over—
$0	$ 20,600	...............15%	$0
20,600	49,800	$3,090.00 + 28%	20,600
49,800	75,875	11,266.00 + 31%	49,800
75,875	135,525	19,349.25 + 36%	75,875
135,525	....	40,823.25 + 39.6%	135,525

1996 Tax Table

Use if your taxable income is less than $100,000.
If $100,000 or more, use the Tax Rate Schedules.

Example. Mr. and Mrs. Brown are filing a joint return. Their taxable income on line 37 of Form 1040 is $25,300. First, they find the $25,300–25,350 income line. Next, they find the column for married filing jointly and read down the column. The amount shown where the income line and filing status column meet is $3,799. This is the tax amount they should enter on line 38 of their Form 1040.

Sample Table

At least	But less than	Single	Married filing jointly*	Married filing separately	Head of a household
			Your tax is—		
25,200	25,250	3,943	3,784	4,457	3,784
25,250	25,300	3,957	3,791	4,471	3,791
25,300	25,350	3,971	(3,799)	4,485	3,799
25,350	25,400	3,985	3,806	4,499	3,806

If line 37 (taxable income) is—		And you are—			
At least	But less than	Single	Married filing jointly*	Married filing separately	Head of a household
			Your tax is—		
0	5	0	0	0	0
5	15	2	2	2	2
15	25	3	3	3	3
25	50	6	6	6	6
50	75	9	9	9	9
75	100	13	13	13	13
100	125	17	17	17	17
125	150	21	21	21	21
150	175	24	24	24	24
175	200	28	28	28	28
200	225	32	32	32	32
225	250	36	36	36	36
250	275	39	39	39	39
275	300	43	43	43	43
300	325	47	47	47	47
325	350	51	51	51	51
350	375	54	54	54	54
375	400	58	58	58	58
400	425	62	62	62	62
425	450	66	66	66	66
450	475	69	69	69	69
475	500	73	73	73	73
500	525	77	77	77	77
525	550	81	81	81	81
550	575	84	84	84	84
575	600	88	88	88	88
600	625	92	92	92	92
625	650	96	96	96	96
650	675	99	99	99	99
675	700	103	103	103	103
700	725	107	107	107	107
725	750	111	111	111	111
750	775	114	114	114	114
775	800	118	118	118	118
800	825	122	122	122	122
825	850	126	126	126	126
850	875	129	129	129	129
875	900	133	133	133	133
900	925	137	137	137	137
925	950	141	141	141	141
950	975	144	144	144	144
975	1,000	148	148	148	148

1,000

At least	But less than	Single	Married filing jointly*	Married filing separately	Head of a household
1,000	1,025	152	152	152	152
1,025	1,050	156	156	156	156
1,050	1,075	159	159	159	159
1,075	1,100	163	163	163	163
1,100	1,125	167	167	167	167
1,125	1,150	171	171	171	171
1,150	1,175	174	174	174	174
1,175	1,200	178	178	178	178
1,200	1,225	182	182	182	182
1,225	1,250	186	186	186	186
1,250	1,275	189	189	189	189
1,275	1,300	193	193	193	193
1,300	1,325	197	197	197	197
1,325	1,350	201	201	201	201
1,350	1,375	204	204	204	204
1,375	1,400	208	208	208	208
1,400	1,425	212	212	212	212
1,425	1,450	216	216	216	216
1,450	1,475	219	219	219	219
1,475	1,500	223	223	223	223
1,500	1,525	227	227	227	227
1,525	1,550	231	231	231	231
1,550	1,575	234	234	234	234
1,575	1,600	238	238	238	238
1,600	1,625	242	242	242	242
1,625	1,650	246	246	246	246
1,650	1,675	249	249	249	249
1,675	1,700	253	253	253	253
1,700	1,725	257	257	257	257
1,725	1,750	261	261	261	261
1,750	1,775	264	264	264	264
1,775	1,800	268	268	268	268
1,800	1,825	272	272	272	272
1,825	1,850	276	276	276	276
1,850	1,875	279	279	279	279
1,875	1,900	283	283	283	283
1,900	1,925	287	287	287	287
1,925	1,950	291	291	291	291
1,950	1,975	294	294	294	294
1,975	2,000	298	298	298	298

2,000

At least	But less than	Single	Married filing jointly*	Married filing separately	Head of a household
2,000	2,025	302	302	302	302
2,025	2,050	306	306	306	306
2,050	2,075	309	309	309	309
2,075	2,100	313	313	313	313
2,100	2,125	317	317	317	317
2,125	2,150	321	321	321	321
2,150	2,175	324	324	324	324
2,175	2,200	328	328	328	328
2,200	2,225	332	332	332	332
2,225	2,250	336	336	336	336
2,250	2,275	339	339	339	339
2,275	2,300	343	343	343	343
2,300	2,325	347	347	347	347
2,325	2,350	351	351	351	351
2,350	2,375	354	354	354	354
2,375	2,400	358	358	358	358
2,400	2,425	362	362	362	362
2,425	2,450	366	366	366	366
2,450	2,475	369	369	369	369
2,475	2,500	373	373	373	373
2,500	2,525	377	377	377	377
2,525	2,550	381	381	381	381
2,550	2,575	384	384	384	384
2,575	2,600	388	388	388	388
2,600	2,625	392	392	392	392
2,625	2,650	396	396	396	396
2,650	2,675	399	399	399	399
2,675	2,700	403	403	403	403
2,700	2,725	407	407	407	407
2,725	2,750	411	411	411	411
2,750	2,775	414	414	414	414
2,775	2,800	418	418	418	418
2,800	2,825	422	422	422	422
2,825	2,850	426	426	426	426
2,850	2,875	429	429	429	429
2,875	2,900	433	433	433	433
2,900	2,925	437	437	437	437
2,925	2,950	441	441	441	441
2,950	2,975	444	444	444	444
2,975	3,000	448	448	448	448

3,000

At least	But less than	Single	Married filing jointly*	Married filing separately	Head of a household
3,000	3,050	454	454	454	454
3,050	3,100	461	461	461	461
3,100	3,150	469	469	469	469
3,150	3,200	476	476	476	476
3,200	3,250	484	484	484	484
3,250	3,300	491	491	491	491
3,300	3,350	499	499	499	499
3,350	3,400	506	506	506	506
3,400	3,450	514	514	514	514
3,450	3,500	521	521	521	521
3,500	3,550	529	529	529	529
3,550	3,600	536	536	536	536
3,600	3,650	544	544	544	544
3,650	3,700	551	551	551	551
3,700	3,750	559	559	559	559
3,750	3,800	566	566	566	566
3,800	3,850	574	574	574	574
3,850	3,900	581	581	581	581
3,900	3,950	589	589	589	589
3,950	4,000	596	596	596	596

4,000

At least	But less than	Single	Married filing jointly*	Married filing separately	Head of a household
4,000	4,050	604	604	604	604
4,050	4,100	611	611	611	611
4,100	4,150	619	619	619	619
4,150	4,200	626	626	626	626
4,200	4,250	634	634	634	634
4,250	4,300	641	641	641	641
4,300	4,350	649	649	649	649
4,350	4,400	656	656	656	656
4,400	4,450	664	664	664	664
4,450	4,500	671	671	671	671
4,500	4,550	679	679	679	679
4,550	4,600	686	686	686	686
4,600	4,650	694	694	694	694
4,650	4,700	701	701	701	701
4,700	4,750	709	709	709	709
4,750	4,800	716	716	716	716
4,800	4,850	724	724	724	724
4,850	4,900	731	731	731	731
4,900	4,950	739	739	739	739
4,950	5,000	746	746	746	746

Continued on next page

* This column must also be used by a qualifying widow(er).

1996 Tax Table—Continued

At least	But less than	Single	Married filing jointly*	Married filing separately	Head of a household
5,000					
5,000	5,050	754	754	754	754
5,050	5,100	761	761	761	761
5,100	5,150	769	769	769	769
5,150	5,200	776	776	776	776
5,200	5,250	784	784	784	784
5,250	5,300	791	791	791	791
5,300	5,350	799	799	799	799
5,350	5,400	806	806	806	806
5,400	5,450	814	814	814	814
5,450	5,500	821	821	821	821
5,500	5,550	829	829	829	829
5,550	5,600	836	836	836	836
5,600	5,650	844	844	844	844
5,650	5,700	851	851	851	851
5,700	5,750	859	859	859	859
5,750	5,800	866	866	866	866
5,800	5,850	874	874	874	874
5,850	5,900	881	881	881	881
5,900	5,950	889	889	889	889
5,950	6,000	896	896	896	896
6,000					
6,000	6,050	904	904	904	904
6,050	6,100	911	911	911	911
6,100	6,150	919	919	919	919
6,150	6,200	926	926	926	926
6,200	6,250	934	934	934	934
6,250	6,300	941	941	941	941
6,300	6,350	949	949	949	949
6,350	6,400	956	956	956	956
6,400	6,450	964	964	964	964
6,450	6,500	971	971	971	971
6,500	6,550	979	979	979	979
6,550	6,600	986	986	986	986
6,600	6,650	994	994	994	994
6,650	6,700	1,001	1,001	1,001	1,001
6,700	6,750	1,009	1,009	1,009	1,009
6,750	6,800	1,016	1,016	1,016	1,016
6,800	6,850	1,024	1,024	1,024	1,024
6,850	6,900	1,031	1,031	1,031	1,031
6,900	6,950	1,039	1,039	1,039	1,039
6,950	7,000	1,046	1,046	1,046	1,046
7,000					
7,000	7,050	1,054	1,054	1,054	1,054
7,050	7,100	1,061	1,061	1,061	1,061
7,100	7,150	1,069	1,069	1,069	1,069
7,150	7,200	1,076	1,076	1,076	1,076
7,200	7,250	1,084	1,084	1,084	1,084
7,250	7,300	1,091	1,091	1,091	1,091
7,300	7,350	1,099	1,099	1,099	1,099
7,350	7,400	1,106	1,106	1,106	1,106
7,400	7,450	1,114	1,114	1,114	1,114
7,450	7,500	1,121	1,121	1,121	1,121
7,500	7,550	1,129	1,129	1,129	1,129
7,550	7,600	1,136	1,136	1,136	1,136
7,600	7,650	1,144	1,144	1,144	1,144
7,650	7,700	1,151	1,151	1,151	1,151
7,700	7,750	1,159	1,159	1,159	1,159
7,750	7,800	1,166	1,166	1,166	1,166
7,800	7,850	1,174	1,174	1,174	1,174
7,850	7,900	1,181	1,181	1,181	1,181
7,900	7,950	1,189	1,189	1,189	1,189
7,950	8,000	1,196	1,196	1,196	1,196
8,000					
8,000	8,050	1,204	1,204	1,204	1,204
8,050	8,100	1,211	1,211	1,211	1,211
8,100	8,150	1,219	1,219	1,219	1,219
8,150	8,200	1,226	1,226	1,226	1,226
8,200	8,250	1,234	1,234	1,234	1,234
8,250	8,300	1,241	1,241	1,241	1,241
8,300	8,350	1,249	1,249	1,249	1,249
8,350	8,400	1,256	1,256	1,256	1,256
8,400	8,450	1,264	1,264	1,264	1,264
8,450	8,500	1,271	1,271	1,271	1,271
8,500	8,550	1,279	1,279	1,279	1,279
8,550	8,600	1,286	1,286	1,286	1,286
8,600	8,650	1,294	1,294	1,294	1,294
8,650	8,700	1,301	1,301	1,301	1,301
8,700	8,750	1,309	1,309	1,309	1,309
8,750	8,800	1,316	1,316	1,316	1,316
8,800	8,850	1,324	1,324	1,324	1,324
8,850	8,900	1,331	1,331	1,331	1,331
8,900	8,950	1,339	1,339	1,339	1,339
8,950	9,000	1,346	1,346	1,346	1,346
9,000					
9,000	9,050	1,354	1,354	1,354	1,354
9,050	9,100	1,361	1,361	1,361	1,361
9,100	9,150	1,369	1,369	1,369	1,369
9,150	9,200	1,376	1,376	1,376	1,376
9,200	9,250	1,384	1,384	1,384	1,384
9,250	9,300	1,391	1,391	1,391	1,391
9,300	9,350	1,399	1,399	1,399	1,399
9,350	9,400	1,406	1,406	1,406	1,406
9,400	9,450	1,414	1,414	1,414	1,414
9,450	9,500	1,421	1,421	1,421	1,421
9,500	9,550	1,429	1,429	1,429	1,429
9,550	9,600	1,436	1,436	1,436	1,436
9,600	9,650	1,444	1,444	1,444	1,444
9,650	9,700	1,451	1,451	1,451	1,451
9,700	9,750	1,459	1,459	1,459	1,459
9,750	9,800	1,466	1,466	1,466	1,466
9,800	9,850	1,474	1,474	1,474	1,474
9,850	9,900	1,481	1,481	1,481	1,481
9,900	9,950	1,489	1,489	1,489	1,489
9,950	10,000	1,496	1,496	1,496	1,496
10,000					
10,000	10,050	1,504	1,504	1,504	1,504
10,050	10,100	1,511	1,511	1,511	1,511
10,100	10,150	1,519	1,519	1,519	1,519
10,150	10,200	1,526	1,526	1,526	1,526
10,200	10,250	1,534	1,534	1,534	1,534
10,250	10,300	1,541	1,541	1,541	1,541
10,300	10,350	1,549	1,549	1,549	1,549
10,350	10,400	1,556	1,556	1,556	1,556
10,400	10,450	1,564	1,564	1,564	1,564
10,450	10,500	1,571	1,571	1,571	1,571
10,500	10,550	1,579	1,579	1,579	1,579
10,550	10,600	1,586	1,586	1,586	1,586
10,600	10,650	1,594	1,594	1,594	1,594
10,650	10,700	1,601	1,601	1,601	1,601
10,700	10,750	1,609	1,609	1,609	1,609
10,750	10,800	1,616	1,616	1,616	1,616
10,800	10,850	1,624	1,624	1,624	1,624
10,850	10,900	1,631	1,631	1,631	1,631
10,900	10,950	1,639	1,639	1,639	1,639
10,950	11,000	1,646	1,646	1,646	1,646
11,000					
11,000	11,050	1,654	1,654	1,654	1,654
11,050	11,100	1,661	1,661	1,661	1,661
11,100	11,150	1,669	1,669	1,669	1,669
11,150	11,200	1,676	1,676	1,676	1,676
11,200	11,250	1,684	1,684	1,684	1,684
11,250	11,300	1,691	1,691	1,691	1,691
11,300	11,350	1,699	1,699	1,699	1,699
11,350	11,400	1,706	1,706	1,706	1,706
11,400	11,450	1,714	1,714	1,714	1,714
11,450	11,500	1,721	1,721	1,721	1,721
11,500	11,550	1,729	1,729	1,729	1,729
11,550	11,600	1,736	1,736	1,736	1,736
11,600	11,650	1,744	1,744	1,744	1,744
11,650	11,700	1,751	1,751	1,751	1,751
11,700	11,750	1,759	1,759	1,759	1,759
11,750	11,800	1,766	1,766	1,766	1,766
11,800	11,850	1,774	1,774	1,774	1,774
11,850	11,900	1,781	1,781	1,781	1,781
11,900	11,950	1,789	1,789	1,789	1,789
11,950	12,000	1,796	1,796	1,796	1,796
12,000					
12,000	12,050	1,804	1,804	1,804	1,804
12,050	12,100	1,811	1,811	1,811	1,811
12,100	12,150	1,819	1,819	1,819	1,819
12,150	12,200	1,826	1,826	1,826	1,826
12,200	12,250	1,834	1,834	1,834	1,834
12,250	12,300	1,841	1,841	1,841	1,841
12,300	12,350	1,849	1,849	1,849	1,849
12,350	12,400	1,856	1,856	1,856	1,856
12,400	12,450	1,864	1,864	1,864	1,864
12,450	12,500	1,871	1,871	1,871	1,871
12,500	12,550	1,879	1,879	1,879	1,879
12,550	12,600	1,886	1,886	1,886	1,886
12,600	12,650	1,894	1,894	1,894	1,894
12,650	12,700	1,901	1,901	1,901	1,901
12,700	12,750	1,909	1,909	1,909	1,909
12,750	12,800	1,916	1,916	1,916	1,916
12,800	12,850	1,924	1,924	1,924	1,924
12,850	12,900	1,931	1,931	1,931	1,931
12,900	12,950	1,939	1,939	1,939	1,939
12,950	13,000	1,946	1,946	1,946	1,946
13,000					
13,000	13,050	1,954	1,954	1,954	1,954
13,050	13,100	1,961	1,961	1,961	1,961
13,100	13,150	1,969	1,969	1,969	1,969
13,150	13,200	1,976	1,976	1,976	1,976
13,200	13,250	1,984	1,984	1,984	1,984
13,250	13,300	1,991	1,991	1,991	1,991
13,300	13,350	1,999	1,999	1,999	1,999
13,350	13,400	2,006	2,006	2,006	2,006
13,400	13,450	2,014	2,014	2,014	2,014
13,450	13,500	2,021	2,021	2,021	2,021
13,500	13,550	2,029	2,029	2,029	2,029
13,550	13,600	2,036	2,036	2,036	2,036
13,600	13,650	2,044	2,044	2,044	2,044
13,650	13,700	2,051	2,051	2,051	2,051
13,700	13,750	2,059	2,059	2,059	2,059
13,750	13,800	2,066	2,066	2,066	2,066
13,800	13,850	2,074	2,074	2,074	2,074
13,850	13,900	2,081	2,081	2,081	2,081
13,900	13,950	2,089	2,089	2,089	2,089
13,950	14,000	2,096	2,096	2,096	2,096

* This column must also be used by a qualifying widow(er).

Continued on next page

Tax Rate Schedules and Tables

A–5

1996 Tax Table—Continued

If line 37 (taxable income) is—		And you are—				If line 37 (taxable income) is—		And you are—				If line 37 (taxable income) is—		And you are—			
At least	But less than	Single	Married filing jointly *	Married filing separately	Head of a household	At least	But less than	Single	Married filing jointly *	Married filing separately	Head of a household	At least	But less than	Single	Married filing jointly *	Married filing separately	Head of a household
		Your tax is—						Your tax is—						Your tax is—			
14,000						**17,000**						**20,000**					
14,000	14,050	2,104	2,104	2,104	2,104	17,000	17,050	2,554	2,554	2,554	2,554	20,000	20,050	3,004	3,004	3,004	3,004
14,050	14,100	2,111	2,111	2,111	2,111	17,050	17,100	2,561	2,561	2,561	2,561	20,050	20,100	3,011	3,011	3,015	3,011
14,100	14,150	2,119	2,119	2,119	2,119	17,100	17,150	2,569	2,569	2,569	2,569	20,100	20,150	3,019	3,019	3,029	3,019
14,150	14,200	2,126	2,126	2,126	2,126	17,150	17,200	2,576	2,576	2,576	2,576	20,150	20,200	3,026	3,026	3,043	3,026
14,200	14,250	2,134	2,134	2,134	2,134	17,200	17,250	2,584	2,584	2,584	2,584	20,200	20,250	3,034	3,034	3,057	3,034
14,250	14,300	2,141	2,141	2,141	2,141	17,250	17,300	2,591	2,591	2,591	2,591	20,250	20,300	3,041	3,041	3,071	3,041
14,300	14,350	2,149	2,149	2,149	2,149	17,300	17,350	2,599	2,599	2,599	2,599	20,300	20,350	3,049	3,049	3,085	3,049
14,350	14,400	2,156	2,156	2,156	2,156	17,350	17,400	2,606	2,606	2,606	2,606	20,350	20,400	3,056	3,056	3,099	3,056
14,400	14,450	2,164	2,164	2,164	2,164	17,400	17,450	2,614	2,614	2,614	2,614	20,400	20,450	3,064	3,064	3,113	3,064
14,450	14,500	2,171	2,171	2,171	2,171	17,450	17,500	2,621	2,621	2,621	2,621	20,450	20,500	3,071	3,071	3,127	3,071
14,500	14,550	2,179	2,179	2,179	2,179	17,500	17,550	2,629	2,629	2,629	2,629	20,500	20,550	3,079	3,079	3,141	3,079
14,550	14,600	2,186	2,186	2,186	2,186	17,550	17,600	2,636	2,636	2,636	2,636	20,550	20,600	3,086	3,086	3,155	3,086
14,600	14,650	2,194	2,194	2,194	2,194	17,600	17,650	2,644	2,644	2,644	2,644	20,600	20,650	3,094	3,094	3,169	3,094
14,650	14,700	2,201	2,201	2,201	2,201	17,650	17,700	2,651	2,651	2,651	2,651	20,650	20,700	3,101	3,101	3,183	3,101
14,700	14,750	2,209	2,209	2,209	2,209	17,700	17,750	2,659	2,659	2,659	2,659	20,700	20,750	3,109	3,109	3,197	3,109
14,750	14,800	2,216	2,216	2,216	2,216	17,750	17,800	2,666	2,666	2,666	2,666	20,750	20,800	3,116	3,116	3,211	3,116
14,800	14,850	2,224	2,224	2,224	2,224	17,800	17,850	2,674	2,674	2,674	2,674	20,800	20,850	3,124	3,124	3,225	3,124
14,850	14,900	2,231	2,231	2,231	2,231	17,850	17,900	2,681	2,681	2,681	2,681	20,850	20,900	3,131	3,131	3,239	3,131
14,900	14,950	2,239	2,239	2,239	2,239	17,900	17,950	2,689	2,689	2,689	2,689	20,900	20,950	3,139	3,139	3,253	3,139
14,950	15,000	2,246	2,246	2,246	2,246	17,950	18,000	2,696	2,696	2,696	2,696	20,950	21,000	3,146	3,146	3,267	3,146
15,000						**18,000**						**21,000**					
15,000	15,050	2,254	2,254	2,254	2,254	18,000	18,050	2,704	2,704	2,704	2,704	21,000	21,050	3,154	3,154	3,281	3,154
15,050	15,100	2,261	2,261	2,261	2,261	18,050	18,100	2,711	2,711	2,711	2,711	21,050	21,100	3,161	3,161	3,295	3,161
15,100	15,150	2,269	2,269	2,269	2,269	18,100	18,150	2,719	2,719	2,719	2,719	21,100	21,150	3,169	3,169	3,309	3,169
15,150	15,200	2,276	2,276	2,276	2,276	18,150	18,200	2,726	2,726	2,726	2,726	21,150	21,200	3,176	3,176	3,323	3,176
15,200	15,250	2,284	2,284	2,284	2,284	18,200	18,250	2,734	2,734	2,734	2,734	21,200	21,250	3,184	3,184	3,337	3,184
15,250	15,300	2,291	2,291	2,291	2,291	18,250	18,300	2,741	2,741	2,741	2,741	21,250	21,300	3,191	3,191	3,351	3,191
15,300	15,350	2,299	2,299	2,299	2,299	18,300	18,350	2,749	2,749	2,749	2,749	21,300	21,350	3,199	3,199	3,365	3,199
15,350	15,400	2,306	2,306	2,306	2,306	18,350	18,400	2,756	2,756	2,756	2,756	21,350	21,400	3,206	3,206	3,379	3,206
15,400	15,450	2,314	2,314	2,314	2,314	18,400	18,450	2,764	2,764	2,764	2,764	21,400	21,450	3,214	3,214	3,393	3,214
15,450	15,500	2,321	2,321	2,321	2,321	18,450	18,500	2,771	2,771	2,771	2,771	21,450	21,500	3,221	3,221	3,407	3,221
15,500	15,550	2,329	2,329	2,329	2,329	18,500	18,550	2,779	2,779	2,779	2,779	21,500	21,550	3,229	3,229	3,421	3,229
15,550	15,600	2,336	2,336	2,336	2,336	18,550	18,600	2,786	2,786	2,786	2,786	21,550	21,600	3,236	3,236	3,435	3,236
15,600	15,650	2,344	2,344	2,344	2,344	18,600	18,650	2,794	2,794	2,794	2,794	21,600	21,650	3,244	3,244	3,449	3,244
15,650	15,700	2,351	2,351	2,351	2,351	18,650	18,700	2,801	2,801	2,801	2,801	21,650	21,700	3,251	3,251	3,463	3,251
15,700	15,750	2,359	2,359	2,359	2,359	18,700	18,750	2,809	2,809	2,809	2,809	21,700	21,750	3,259	3,259	3,477	3,259
15,750	15,800	2,366	2,366	2,366	2,366	18,750	18,800	2,816	2,816	2,816	2,816	21,750	21,800	3,266	3,266	3,491	3,266
15,800	15,850	2,374	2,374	2,374	2,374	18,800	18,850	2,824	2,824	2,824	2,824	21,800	21,850	3,274	3,274	3,505	3,274
15,850	15,900	2,381	2,381	2,381	2,381	18,850	18,900	2,831	2,831	2,831	2,831	21,850	21,900	3,281	3,281	3,519	3,281
15,900	15,950	2,389	2,389	2,389	2,389	18,900	18,950	2,839	2,839	2,839	2,839	21,900	21,950	3,289	3,289	3,533	3,289
15,950	16,000	2,396	2,396	2,396	2,396	18,950	19,000	2,846	2,846	2,846	2,846	21,950	22,000	3,296	3,296	3,547	3,296
16,000						**19,000**						**22,000**					
16,000	16,050	2,404	2,404	2,404	2,404	19,000	19,050	2,854	2,854	2,854	2,854	22,000	22,050	3,304	3,304	3,561	3,304
16,050	16,100	2,411	2,411	2,411	2,411	19,050	19,100	2,861	2,861	2,861	2,861	22,050	22,100	3,311	3,311	3,575	3,311
16,100	16,150	2,419	2,419	2,419	2,419	19,100	19,150	2,869	2,869	2,869	2,869	22,100	22,150	3,319	3,319	3,589	3,319
16,150	16,200	2,426	2,426	2,426	2,426	19,150	19,200	2,876	2,876	2,876	2,876	22,150	22,200	3,326	3,326	3,603	3,326
16,200	16,250	2,434	2,434	2,434	2,434	19,200	19,250	2,884	2,884	2,884	2,884	22,200	22,250	3,334	3,334	3,617	3,334
16,250	16,300	2,441	2,441	2,441	2,441	19,250	19,300	2,891	2,891	2,891	2,891	22,250	22,300	3,341	3,341	3,631	3,341
16,300	16,350	2,449	2,449	2,449	2,449	19,300	19,350	2,899	2,899	2,899	2,899	22,300	22,350	3,349	3,349	3,645	3,349
16,350	16,400	2,456	2,456	2,456	2,456	19,350	19,400	2,906	2,906	2,906	2,906	22,350	22,400	3,356	3,356	3,659	3,356
16,400	16,450	2,464	2,464	2,464	2,464	19,400	19,450	2,914	2,914	2,914	2,914	22,400	22,450	3,364	3,364	3,673	3,364
16,450	16,500	2,471	2,471	2,471	2,471	19,450	19,500	2,921	2,921	2,921	2,921	22,450	22,500	3,371	3,371	3,687	3,371
16,500	16,550	2,479	2,479	2,479	2,479	19,500	19,550	2,929	2,929	2,929	2,929	22,500	22,550	3,379	3,379	3,701	3,379
16,550	16,600	2,486	2,486	2,486	2,486	19,550	19,600	2,936	2,936	2,936	2,936	22,550	22,600	3,386	3,386	3,715	3,386
16,600	16,650	2,494	2,494	2,494	2,494	19,600	19,650	2,944	2,944	2,944	2,944	22,600	22,650	3,394	3,394	3,729	3,394
16,650	16,700	2,501	2,501	2,501	2,501	19,650	19,700	2,951	2,951	2,951	2,951	22,650	22,700	3,401	3,401	3,743	3,401
16,700	16,750	2,509	2,509	2,509	2,509	19,700	19,750	2,959	2,959	2,959	2,959	22,700	22,750	3,409	3,409	3,757	3,409
16,750	16,800	2,516	2,516	2,516	2,516	19,750	19,800	2,966	2,966	2,966	2,966	22,750	22,800	3,416	3,416	3,771	3,416
16,800	16,850	2,524	2,524	2,524	2,524	19,800	19,850	2,974	2,974	2,974	2,974	22,800	22,850	3,424	3,424	3,785	3,424
16,850	16,900	2,531	2,531	2,531	2,531	19,850	19,900	2,981	2,981	2,981	2,981	22,850	22,900	3,431	3,431	3,799	3,431
16,900	16,950	2,539	2,539	2,539	2,539	19,900	19,950	2,989	2,989	2,989	2,989	22,900	22,950	3,439	3,439	3,813	3,439
16,950	17,000	2,546	2,546	2,546	2,546	19,950	20,000	2,996	2,996	2,996	2,996	22,950	23,000	3,446	3,446	3,827	3,446

* This column must also be used by a qualifying widow(er).

Continued on next page

1996 Tax Table—Continued

At least	But less than	Single	Married filing jointly *	Married filing separately	Head of a household	At least	But less than	Single	Married filing jointly *	Married filing separately	Head of a household	At least	But less than	Single	Married filing jointly *	Married filing separately	Head of a household
23,000						**26,000**						**29,000**					
23,000	23,050	3,454	3,454	3,841	3,454	26,000	26,050	4,167	3,904	4,681	3,904	29,000	29,050	5,007	4,354	5,521	4,354
23,050	23,100	3,461	3,461	3,855	3,461	26,050	26,100	4,181	3,911	4,695	3,911	29,050	29,100	5,021	4,361	5,535	4,361
23,100	23,150	3,469	3,469	3,869	3,469	26,100	26,150	4,195	3,919	4,709	3,919	29,100	29,150	5,035	4,369	5,549	4,369
23,150	23,200	3,476	3,476	3,883	3,476	26,150	26,200	4,209	3,926	4,723	3,926	29,150	29,200	5,049	4,376	5,563	4,376
23,200	23,250	3,484	3,484	3,897	3,484	26,200	26,250	4,223	3,934	4,737	3,934	29,200	29,250	5,063	4,384	5,577	4,384
23,250	23,300	3,491	3,491	3,911	3,491	26,250	26,300	4,237	3,941	4,751	3,941	29,250	29,300	5,077	4,391	5,591	4,391
23,300	23,350	3,499	3,499	3,925	3,499	26,300	26,350	4,251	3,949	4,765	3,949	29,300	29,350	5,091	4,399	5,605	4,399
23,350	23,400	3,506	3,506	3,939	3,506	26,350	26,400	4,265	3,956	4,779	3,956	29,350	29,400	5,105	4,406	5,619	4,406
23,400	23,450	3,514	3,514	3,953	3,514	26,400	26,450	4,279	3,964	4,793	3,964	29,400	29,450	5,119	4,414	5,633	4,414
23,450	23,500	3,521	3,521	3,967	3,521	26,450	26,500	4,293	3,971	4,807	3,971	29,450	29,500	5,133	4,421	5,647	4,421
23,500	23,550	3,529	3,529	3,981	3,529	26,500	26,550	4,307	3,979	4,821	3,979	29,500	29,550	5,147	4,429	5,661	4,429
23,550	23,600	3,536	3,536	3,995	3,536	26,550	26,600	4,321	3,986	4,835	3,986	29,550	29,600	5,161	4,436	5,675	4,436
23,600	23,650	3,544	3,544	4,009	3,544	26,600	26,650	4,335	3,994	4,849	3,994	29,600	29,650	5,175	4,444	5,689	4,444
23,650	23,700	3,551	3,551	4,023	3,551	26,650	26,700	4,349	4,001	4,863	4,001	29,650	29,700	5,189	4,451	5,703	4,451
23,700	23,750	3,559	3,559	4,037	3,559	26,700	26,750	4,363	4,009	4,877	4,009	29,700	29,750	5,203	4,459	5,717	4,459
23,750	23,800	3,566	3,566	4,051	3,566	26,750	26,800	4,377	4,016	4,891	4,016	29,750	29,800	5,217	4,466	5,731	4,466
23,800	23,850	3,574	3,574	4,065	3,574	26,800	26,850	4,391	4,024	4,905	4,024	29,800	29,850	5,231	4,474	5,745	4,474
23,850	23,900	3,581	3,581	4,079	3,581	26,850	26,900	4,405	4,031	4,919	4,031	29,850	29,900	5,245	4,481	5,759	4,481
23,900	23,950	3,589	3,589	4,093	3,589	26,900	26,950	4,419	4,039	4,933	4,039	29,900	29,950	5,259	4,489	5,773	4,489
23,950	24,000	3,596	3,596	4,107	3,596	26,950	27,000	4,433	4,046	4,947	4,046	29,950	30,000	5,273	4,496	5,787	4,496
24,000						**27,000**						**30,000**					
24,000	24,050	3,607	3,604	4,121	3,604	27,000	27,050	4,447	4,054	4,961	4,054	30,000	30,050	5,287	4,504	5,801	4,504
24,050	24,100	3,621	3,611	4,135	3,611	27,050	27,100	4,461	4,061	4,975	4,061	30,050	30,100	5,301	4,511	5,815	4,511
24,100	24,150	3,635	3,619	4,149	3,619	27,100	27,150	4,475	4,069	4,989	4,069	30,100	30,150	5,315	4,519	5,829	4,519
24,150	24,200	3,649	3,626	4,163	3,626	27,150	27,200	4,489	4,076	5,003	4,076	30,150	30,200	5,329	4,526	5,843	4,526
24,200	24,250	3,663	3,634	4,177	3,634	27,200	27,250	4,503	4,084	5,017	4,084	30,200	30,250	5,343	4,534	5,857	4,534
24,250	24,300	3,677	3,641	4,191	3,641	27,250	27,300	4,517	4,091	5,031	4,091	30,250	30,300	5,357	4,541	5,871	4,541
24,300	24,350	3,691	3,649	4,205	3,649	27,300	27,350	4,531	4,099	5,045	4,099	30,300	30,350	5,371	4,549	5,885	4,549
24,350	24,400	3,705	3,656	4,219	3,656	27,350	27,400	4,545	4,106	5,059	4,106	30,350	30,400	5,385	4,556	5,899	4,556
24,400	24,450	3,719	3,664	4,233	3,664	27,400	27,450	4,559	4,114	5,073	4,114	30,400	30,450	5,399	4,564	5,913	4,564
24,450	24,500	3,733	3,671	4,247	3,671	27,450	27,500	4,573	4,121	5,087	4,121	30,450	30,500	5,413	4,571	5,927	4,571
24,500	24,550	3,747	3,679	4,261	3,679	27,500	27,550	4,587	4,129	5,101	4,129	30,500	30,550	5,427	4,579	5,941	4,579
24,550	24,600	3,761	3,686	4,275	3,686	27,550	27,600	4,601	4,136	5,115	4,136	30,550	30,600	5,441	4,586	5,955	4,586
24,600	24,650	3,775	3,694	4,289	3,694	27,600	27,650	4,615	4,144	5,129	4,144	30,600	30,650	5,455	4,594	5,969	4,594
24,650	24,700	3,789	3,701	4,303	3,701	27,650	27,700	4,629	4,151	5,143	4,151	30,650	30,700	5,469	4,601	5,983	4,601
24,700	24,750	3,803	3,709	4,317	3,709	27,700	27,750	4,643	4,159	5,157	4,159	30,700	30,750	5,483	4,609	5,997	4,609
24,750	24,800	3,817	3,716	4,331	3,716	27,750	27,800	4,657	4,166	5,171	4,166	30,750	30,800	5,497	4,616	6,011	4,616
24,800	24,850	3,831	3,724	4,345	3,724	27,800	27,850	4,671	4,174	5,185	4,174	30,800	30,850	5,511	4,624	6,025	4,624
24,850	24,900	3,845	3,731	4,359	3,731	27,850	27,900	4,685	4,181	5,199	4,181	30,850	30,900	5,525	4,631	6,039	4,631
24,900	24,950	3,859	3,739	4,373	3,739	27,900	27,950	4,699	4,189	5,213	4,189	30,900	30,950	5,539	4,639	6,053	4,639
24,950	25,000	3,873	3,746	4,387	3,746	27,950	28,000	4,713	4,196	5,227	4,196	30,950	31,000	5,553	4,646	6,067	4,646
25,000						**28,000**						**31,000**					
25,000	25,050	3,887	3,754	4,401	3,754	28,000	28,050	4,727	4,204	5,241	4,204	31,000	31,050	5,567	4,654	6,081	4,654
25,050	25,100	3,901	3,761	4,415	3,761	28,050	28,100	4,741	4,211	5,255	4,211	31,050	31,100	5,581	4,661	6,095	4,661
25,100	25,150	3,915	3,769	4,429	3,769	28,100	28,150	4,755	4,219	5,269	4,219	31,100	31,150	5,595	4,669	6,109	4,669
25,150	25,200	3,929	3,776	4,443	3,776	28,150	28,200	4,769	4,226	5,283	4,226	31,150	31,200	5,609	4,676	6,123	4,676
25,200	25,250	3,943	3,784	4,457	3,784	28,200	28,250	4,783	4,234	5,297	4,234	31,200	31,250	5,623	4,684	6,137	4,684
25,250	25,300	3,957	3,791	4,471	3,791	28,250	28,300	4,797	4,241	5,311	4,241	31,250	31,300	5,637	4,691	6,151	4,691
25,300	25,350	3,971	3,799	4,485	3,799	28,300	28,350	4,811	4,249	5,325	4,249	31,300	31,350	5,651	4,699	6,165	4,699
25,350	25,400	3,985	3,806	4,499	3,806	28,350	28,400	4,825	4,256	5,339	4,256	31,350	31,400	5,665	4,706	6,179	4,706
25,400	25,450	3,999	3,814	4,513	3,814	28,400	28,450	4,839	4,264	5,353	4,264	31,400	31,450	5,679	4,714	6,193	4,714
25,450	25,500	4,013	3,821	4,527	3,821	28,450	28,500	4,853	4,271	5,367	4,271	31,450	31,500	5,693	4,721	6,207	4,721
25,500	25,550	4,027	3,829	4,541	3,829	28,500	28,550	4,867	4,279	5,381	4,279	31,500	31,550	5,707	4,729	6,221	4,729
25,550	25,600	4,041	3,836	4,555	3,836	28,550	28,600	4,881	4,286	5,395	4,286	31,550	31,600	5,721	4,736	6,235	4,736
25,600	25,650	4,055	3,844	4,569	3,844	28,600	28,650	4,895	4,294	5,409	4,294	31,600	31,650	5,735	4,744	6,249	4,744
25,650	25,700	4,069	3,851	4,583	3,851	28,650	28,700	4,909	4,301	5,423	4,301	31,650	31,700	5,749	4,751	6,263	4,751
25,700	25,750	4,083	3,859	4,597	3,859	28,700	28,750	4,923	4,309	5,437	4,309	31,700	31,750	5,763	4,759	6,277	4,759
25,750	25,800	4,097	3,866	4,611	3,866	28,750	28,800	4,937	4,316	5,451	4,316	31,750	31,800	5,777	4,766	6,291	4,766
25,800	25,850	4,111	3,874	4,625	3,874	28,800	28,850	4,951	4,324	5,465	4,324	31,800	31,850	5,791	4,774	6,305	4,774
25,850	25,900	4,125	3,881	4,639	3,881	28,850	28,900	4,965	4,331	5,479	4,331	31,850	31,900	5,805	4,781	6,319	4,781
25,900	25,950	4,139	3,889	4,653	3,889	28,900	28,950	4,979	4,339	5,493	4,339	31,900	31,950	5,819	4,789	6,333	4,789
25,950	26,000	4,153	3,896	4,667	3,896	28,950	29,000	4,993	4,346	5,507	4,346	31,950	32,000	5,833	4,796	6,347	4,796

* This column must also be used by a qualifying widow(er).

Continued on next page

Tax Rate Schedules and Tables

1996 Tax Table—Continued

If line 37 (taxable income) is—		And you are—				If line 37 (taxable income) is—		And you are—				If line 37 (taxable income) is—		And you are—			
At least	But less than	Single	Married filing jointly *	Married filing separately	Head of a household	At least	But less than	Single	Married filing jointly *	Married filing separately	Head of a household	At least	But less than	Single	Married filing jointly *	Married filing separately	Head of a household
		Your tax is—						Your tax is—						Your tax is—			

32,000 / 35,000 / 38,000

32,000	32,050	5,847	4,804	6,361	4,804	35,000	35,050	6,687	5,254	7,201	5,628	38,000	38,050	7,527	5,704	8,041	6,468
32,050	32,100	5,861	4,811	6,375	4,811	35,050	35,100	6,701	5,261	7,215	5,642	38,050	38,100	7,541	5,711	8,055	6,482
32,100	32,150	5,875	4,819	6,389	4,819	35,100	35,150	6,715	5,269	7,229	5,656	38,100	38,150	7,555	5,719	8,069	6,496
32,150	32,200	5,889	4,826	6,403	4,830	35,150	35,200	6,729	5,276	7,243	5,670	38,150	38,200	7,569	5,726	8,083	6,510
32,200	32,250	5,903	4,834	6,417	4,844	35,200	35,250	6,743	5,284	7,257	5,684	38,200	38,250	7,583	5,734	8,097	6,524
32,250	32,300	5,917	4,841	6,431	4,858	35,250	35,300	6,757	5,291	7,271	5,698	38,250	38,300	7,597	5,741	8,111	6,538
32,300	32,350	5,931	4,849	6,445	4,872	35,300	35,350	6,771	5,299	7,285	5,712	38,300	38,350	7,611	5,749	8,125	6,552
32,350	32,400	5,945	4,856	6,459	4,886	35,350	35,400	6,785	5,306	7,299	5,726	38,350	38,400	7,625	5,756	8,139	6,566
32,400	32,450	5,959	4,864	6,473	4,900	35,400	35,450	6,799	5,314	7,313	5,740	38,400	38,450	7,639	5,764	8,153	6,580
32,450	32,500	5,973	4,871	6,487	4,914	35,450	35,500	6,813	5,321	7,327	5,754	38,450	38,500	7,653	5,771	8,167	6,594
32,500	32,550	5,987	4,879	6,501	4,928	35,500	35,550	6,827	5,329	7,341	5,768	38,500	38,550	7,667	5,779	8,181	6,608
32,550	32,600	6,001	4,886	6,515	4,942	35,550	35,600	6,841	5,336	7,355	5,782	38,550	38,600	7,681	5,786	8,195	6,622
32,600	32,650	6,015	4,894	6,529	4,956	35,600	35,650	6,855	5,344	7,369	5,796	38,600	38,650	7,695	5,794	8,209	6,636
32,650	32,700	6,029	4,901	6,543	4,970	35,650	35,700	6,869	5,351	7,383	5,810	38,650	38,700	7,709	5,801	8,223	6,650
32,700	32,750	6,043	4,909	6,557	4,984	35,700	35,750	6,883	5,359	7,397	5,824	38,700	38,750	7,723	5,809	8,237	6,664
32,750	32,800	6,057	4,916	6,571	4,998	35,750	35,800	6,897	5,366	7,411	5,838	38,750	38,800	7,737	5,816	8,251	6,678
32,800	32,850	6,071	4,924	6,585	5,012	35,800	35,850	6,911	5,374	7,425	5,852	38,800	38,850	7,751	5,824	8,265	6,692
32,850	32,900	6,085	4,931	6,599	5,026	35,850	35,900	6,925	5,381	7,439	5,866	38,850	38,900	7,765	5,831	8,279	6,706
32,900	32,950	6,099	4,939	6,613	5,040	35,900	35,950	6,939	5,389	7,453	5,880	38,900	38,950	7,779	5,839	8,293	6,720
32,950	33,000	6,113	4,946	6,627	5,054	35,950	36,000	6,953	5,396	7,467	5,894	38,950	39,000	7,793	5,846	8,307	6,734

33,000 / 36,000 / 39,000

33,000	33,050	6,127	4,954	6,641	5,068	36,000	36,050	6,967	5,404	7,481	5,908	39,000	39,050	7,807	5,854	8,321	6,748
33,050	33,100	6,141	4,961	6,655	5,082	36,050	36,100	6,981	5,411	7,495	5,922	39,050	39,100	7,821	5,861	8,335	6,762
33,100	33,150	6,155	4,969	6,669	5,096	36,100	36,150	6,995	5,419	7,509	5,936	39,100	39,150	7,835	5,869	8,349	6,776
33,150	33,200	6,169	4,976	6,683	5,110	36,150	36,200	7,009	5,426	7,523	5,950	39,150	39,200	7,849	5,876	8,363	6,790
33,200	33,250	6,183	4,984	6,697	5,124	36,200	36,250	7,023	5,434	7,537	5,964	39,200	39,250	7,863	5,884	8,377	6,804
33,250	33,300	6,197	4,991	6,711	5,138	36,250	36,300	7,037	5,441	7,551	5,978	39,250	39,300	7,877	5,891	8,391	6,818
33,300	33,350	6,211	4,999	6,725	5,152	36,300	36,350	7,051	5,449	7,565	5,992	39,300	39,350	7,891	5,899	8,405	6,832
33,350	33,400	6,225	5,006	6,739	5,166	36,350	36,400	7,065	5,456	7,579	6,006	39,350	39,400	7,905	5,906	8,419	6,846
33,400	33,450	6,239	5,014	6,753	5,180	36,400	36,450	7,079	5,464	7,593	6,020	39,400	39,450	7,919	5,914	8,433	6,860
33,450	33,500	6,253	5,021	6,767	5,194	36,450	36,500	7,093	5,471	7,607	6,034	39,450	39,500	7,933	5,921	8,447	6,874
33,500	33,550	6,267	5,029	6,781	5,208	36,500	36,550	7,107	5,479	7,621	6,048	39,500	39,550	7,947	5,929	8,461	6,888
33,550	33,600	6,281	5,036	6,795	5,222	36,550	36,600	7,121	5,486	7,635	6,062	39,550	39,600	7,961	5,936	8,475	6,902
33,600	33,650	6,295	5,044	6,809	5,236	36,600	36,650	7,135	5,494	7,649	6,076	39,600	39,650	7,975	5,944	8,489	6,916
33,650	33,700	6,309	5,051	6,823	5,250	36,650	36,700	7,149	5,501	7,663	6,090	39,650	39,700	7,989	5,951	8,503	6,930
33,700	33,750	6,323	5,059	6,837	5,264	36,700	36,750	7,163	5,509	7,677	6,104	39,700	39,750	8,003	5,959	8,517	6,944
33,750	33,800	6,337	5,066	6,851	5,278	36,750	36,800	7,177	5,516	7,691	6,118	39,750	39,800	8,017	5,966	8,531	6,958
33,800	33,850	6,351	5,074	6,865	5,292	36,800	36,850	7,191	5,524	7,705	6,132	39,800	39,850	8,031	5,974	8,545	6,972
33,850	33,900	6,365	5,081	6,879	5,306	36,850	36,900	7,205	5,531	7,719	6,146	39,850	39,900	8,045	5,981	8,559	6,986
33,900	33,950	6,379	5,089	6,893	5,320	36,900	36,950	7,219	5,539	7,733	6,160	39,900	39,950	8,059	5,989	8,573	7,000
33,950	34,000	6,393	5,096	6,907	5,334	36,950	37,000	7,233	5,546	7,747	6,174	39,950	40,000	8,073	5,996	8,587	7,014

34,000 / 37,000 / 40,000

34,000	34,050	6,407	5,104	6,921	5,348	37,000	37,050	7,247	5,554	7,761	6,188	40,000	40,050	8,087	6,004	8,601	7,028
34,050	34,100	6,421	5,111	6,935	5,362	37,050	37,100	7,261	5,561	7,775	6,202	40,050	40,100	8,101	6,011	8,615	7,042
34,100	34,150	6,435	5,119	6,949	5,376	37,100	37,150	7,275	5,569	7,789	6,216	40,100	40,150	8,115	6,022	8,629	7,056
34,150	34,200	6,449	5,126	6,963	5,390	37,150	37,200	7,289	5,576	7,803	6,230	40,150	40,200	8,129	6,036	8,643	7,070
34,200	34,250	6,463	5,134	6,977	5,404	37,200	37,250	7,303	5,584	7,817	6,244	40,200	40,250	8,143	6,050	8,657	7,084
34,250	34,300	6,477	5,141	6,991	5,418	37,250	37,300	7,317	5,591	7,831	6,258	40,250	40,300	8,157	6,064	8,671	7,098
34,300	34,350	6,491	5,149	7,005	5,432	37,300	37,350	7,331	5,599	7,845	6,272	40,300	40,350	8,171	6,078	8,685	7,112
34,350	34,400	6,505	5,156	7,019	5,446	37,350	37,400	7,345	5,606	7,859	6,286	40,350	40,400	8,185	6,092	8,699	7,126
34,400	34,450	6,519	5,164	7,033	5,460	37,400	37,450	7,359	5,614	7,873	6,300	40,400	40,450	8,199	6,106	8,713	7,140
34,450	34,500	6,533	5,171	7,047	5,474	37,450	37,500	7,373	5,621	7,887	6,314	40,450	40,500	8,213	6,120	8,727	7,154
34,500	34,550	6,547	5,179	7,061	5,488	37,500	37,550	7,387	5,629	7,901	6,328	40,500	40,550	8,227	6,134	8,741	7,168
34,550	34,600	6,561	5,186	7,075	5,502	37,550	37,600	7,401	5,636	7,915	6,342	40,550	40,600	8,241	6,148	8,755	7,182
34,600	34,650	6,575	5,194	7,089	5,516	37,600	37,650	7,415	5,644	7,929	6,356	40,600	40,650	8,255	6,162	8,769	7,196
34,650	34,700	6,589	5,201	7,103	5,530	37,650	37,700	7,429	5,651	7,943	6,370	40,650	40,700	8,269	6,176	8,783	7,210
34,700	34,750	6,603	5,209	7,117	5,544	37,700	37,750	7,443	5,659	7,957	6,384	40,700	40,750	8,283	6,190	8,797	7,224
34,750	34,800	6,617	5,216	7,131	5,558	37,750	37,800	7,457	5,666	7,971	6,398	40,750	40,800	8,297	6,204	8,811	7,238
34,800	34,850	6,631	5,224	7,145	5,572	37,800	37,850	7,471	5,674	7,985	6,412	40,800	40,850	8,311	6,218	8,825	7,252
34,850	34,900	6,645	5,231	7,159	5,586	37,850	37,900	7,485	5,681	7,999	6,426	40,850	40,900	8,325	6,232	8,839	7,266
34,900	34,950	6,659	5,239	7,173	5,600	37,900	37,950	7,499	5,689	8,013	6,440	40,900	40,950	8,339	6,246	8,853	7,280
34,950	35,000	6,673	5,246	7,187	5,614	37,950	38,000	7,513	5,696	8,027	6,454	40,950	41,000	8,353	6,260	8,867	7,294

* This column must also be used by a qualifying widow(er).

Continued on next page

1996 Tax Table—Continued

If line 37 (taxable income) is—		And you are—				If line 37 (taxable income) is—		And you are—				If line 37 (taxable income) is—		And you are—			
At least	But less than	Single	Married filing jointly *	Married filing separately	Head of a house-hold	At least	But less than	Single	Married filing jointly *	Married filing separately	Head of a house-hold	At least	But less than	Single	Married filing jointly *	Married filing separately	Head of a house-hold
		Your tax is—						Your tax is—						Your tax is—			

41,000

41,000	41,050	8,367	6,274	8,881	7,308
41,050	41,100	8,381	6,288	8,895	7,322
41,100	41,150	8,395	6,302	8,909	7,336
41,150	41,200	8,409	6,316	8,923	7,350
41,200	41,250	8,423	6,330	8,937	7,364
41,250	41,300	8,437	6,344	8,951	7,378
41,300	41,350	8,451	6,358	8,965	7,392
41,350	41,400	8,465	6,372	8,979	7,406
41,400	41,450	8,479	6,386	8,993	7,420
41,450	41,500	8,493	6,400	9,007	7,434
41,500	41,550	8,507	6,414	9,021	7,448
41,550	41,600	8,521	6,428	9,035	7,462
41,600	41,650	8,535	6,442	9,049	7,476
41,650	41,700	8,549	6,456	9,063	7,490
41,700	41,750	8,563	6,470	9,077	7,504
41,750	41,800	8,577	6,484	9,091	7,518
41,800	41,850	8,591	6,498	9,105	7,532
41,850	41,900	8,605	6,512	9,119	7,546
41,900	41,950	8,619	6,526	9,133	7,560
41,950	42,000	8,633	6,540	9,147	7,574

42,000

42,000	42,050	8,647	6,554	9,161	7,588
42,050	42,100	8,661	6,568	9,175	7,602
42,100	42,150	8,675	6,582	9,189	7,616
42,150	42,200	8,689	6,596	9,203	7,630
42,200	42,250	8,703	6,610	9,217	7,644
42,250	42,300	8,717	6,624	9,231	7,658
42,300	42,350	8,731	6,638	9,245	7,672
42,350	42,400	8,745	6,652	9,259	7,686
42,400	42,450	8,759	6,666	9,273	7,700
42,450	42,500	8,773	6,680	9,287	7,714
42,500	42,550	8,787	6,694	9,301	7,728
42,550	42,600	8,801	6,708	9,315	7,742
42,600	42,650	8,815	6,722	9,329	7,756
42,650	42,700	8,829	6,736	9,343	7,770
42,700	42,750	8,843	6,750	9,357	7,784
42,750	42,800	8,857	6,764	9,371	7,798
42,800	42,850	8,871	6,778	9,385	7,812
42,850	42,900	8,885	6,792	9,399	7,826
42,900	42,950	8,899	6,806	9,413	7,840
42,950	43,000	8,913	6,820	9,427	7,854

43,000

43,000	43,050	8,927	6,834	9,441	7,868
43,050	43,100	8,941	6,848	9,455	7,882
43,100	43,150	8,955	6,862	9,469	7,896
43,150	43,200	8,969	6,876	9,483	7,910
43,200	43,250	8,983	6,890	9,497	7,924
43,250	43,300	8,997	6,904	9,511	7,938
43,300	43,350	9,011	6,918	9,525	7,952
43,350	43,400	9,025	6,932	9,539	7,966
43,400	43,450	9,039	6,946	9,553	7,980
43,450	43,500	9,053	6,960	9,567	7,994
43,500	43,550	9,067	6,974	9,581	8,008
43,550	43,600	9,081	6,988	9,595	8,022
43,600	43,650	9,095	7,002	9,609	8,036
43,650	43,700	9,109	7,016	9,623	8,050
43,700	43,750	9,123	7,030	9,637	8,064
43,750	43,800	9,137	7,044	9,651	8,078
43,800	43,850	9,151	7,058	9,665	8,092
43,850	43,900	9,165	7,072	9,679	8,106
43,900	43,950	9,179	7,086	9,693	8,120
43,950	44,000	9,193	7,100	9,707	8,134

44,000

44,000	44,050	9,207	7,114	9,721	8,148
44,050	44,100	9,221	7,128	9,735	8,162
44,100	44,150	9,235	7,142	9,749	8,176
44,150	44,200	9,249	7,156	9,763	8,190
44,200	44,250	9,263	7,170	9,777	8,204
44,250	44,300	9,277	7,184	9,791	8,218
44,300	44,350	9,291	7,198	9,805	8,232
44,350	44,400	9,305	7,212	9,819	8,246
44,400	44,450	9,319	7,226	9,833	8,260
44,450	44,500	9,333	7,240	9,847	8,274
44,500	44,550	9,347	7,254	9,861	8,288
44,550	44,600	9,361	7,268	9,875	8,302
44,600	44,650	9,375	7,282	9,889	8,316
44,650	44,700	9,389	7,296	9,903	8,330
44,700	44,750	9,403	7,310	9,917	8,344
44,750	44,800	9,417	7,324	9,931	8,358
44,800	44,850	9,431	7,338	9,945	8,372
44,850	44,900	9,445	7,352	9,959	8,386
44,900	44,950	9,459	7,366	9,973	8,400
44,950	45,000	9,473	7,380	9,987	8,414

45,000

45,000	45,050	9,487	7,394	10,001	8,428
45,050	45,100	9,501	7,408	10,015	8,442
45,100	45,150	9,515	7,422	10,029	8,456
45,150	45,200	9,529	7,436	10,043	8,470
45,200	45,250	9,543	7,450	10,057	8,484
45,250	45,300	9,557	7,464	10,071	8,498
45,300	45,350	9,571	7,478	10,085	8,512
45,350	45,400	9,585	7,492	10,099	8,526
45,400	45,450	9,599	7,506	10,113	8,540
45,450	45,500	9,613	7,520	10,127	8,554
45,500	45,550	9,627	7,534	10,141	8,568
45,550	45,600	9,641	7,548	10,155	8,582
45,600	45,650	9,655	7,562	10,169	8,596
45,650	45,700	9,669	7,576	10,183	8,610
45,700	45,750	9,683	7,590	10,197	8,624
45,750	45,800	9,697	7,604	10,211	8,638
45,800	45,850	9,711	7,618	10,225	8,652
45,850	45,900	9,725	7,632	10,239	8,666
45,900	45,950	9,739	7,646	10,253	8,680
45,950	46,000	9,753	7,660	10,267	8,694

46,000

46,000	46,050	9,767	7,674	10,281	8,708
46,050	46,100	9,781	7,688	10,295	8,722
46,100	46,150	9,795	7,702	10,309	8,736
46,150	46,200	9,809	7,716	10,323	8,750
46,200	46,250	9,823	7,730	10,337	8,764
46,250	46,300	9,837	7,744	10,351	8,778
46,300	46,350	9,851	7,758	10,365	8,792
46,350	46,400	9,865	7,772	10,379	8,806
46,400	46,450	9,879	7,786	10,393	8,820
46,450	46,500	9,893	7,800	10,407	8,834
46,500	46,550	9,907	7,814	10,421	8,848
46,550	46,600	9,921	7,828	10,435	8,862
46,600	46,650	9,935	7,842	10,449	8,876
46,650	46,700	9,949	7,856	10,463	8,890
46,700	46,750	9,963	7,870	10,477	8,904
46,750	46,800	9,977	7,884	10,491	8,918
46,800	46,850	9,991	7,898	10,505	8,932
46,850	46,900	10,005	7,912	10,519	8,946
46,900	46,950	10,019	7,926	10,533	8,960
46,950	47,000	10,033	7,940	10,547	8,974

47,000

47,000	47,050	10,047	7,954	10,561	8,988
47,050	47,100	10,061	7,968	10,575	9,002
47,100	47,150	10,075	7,982	10,589	9,016
47,150	47,200	10,089	7,996	10,603	9,030
47,200	47,250	10,103	8,010	10,617	9,044
47,250	47,300	10,117	8,024	10,631	9,058
47,300	47,350	10,131	8,038	10,645	9,072
47,350	47,400	10,145	8,052	10,659	9,086
47,400	47,450	10,159	8,066	10,673	9,100
47,450	47,500	10,173	8,080	10,687	9,114
47,500	47,550	10,187	8,094	10,701	9,128
47,550	47,600	10,201	8,108	10,715	9,142
47,600	47,650	10,215	8,122	10,729	9,156
47,650	47,700	10,229	8,136	10,743	9,170
47,700	47,750	10,243	8,150	10,757	9,184
47,750	47,800	10,257	8,164	10,771	9,198
47,800	47,850	10,271	8,178	10,785	9,212
47,850	47,900	10,285	8,192	10,799	9,226
47,900	47,950	10,299	8,206	10,813	9,240
47,950	48,000	10,313	8,220	10,827	9,254

48,000

48,000	48,050	10,327	8,234	10,841	9,268
48,050	48,100	10,341	8,248	10,855	9,282
48,100	48,150	10,355	8,262	10,869	9,296
48,150	48,200	10,369	8,276	10,883	9,310
48,200	48,250	10,383	8,290	10,897	9,324
48,250	48,300	10,397	8,304	10,911	9,338
48,300	48,350	10,411	8,318	10,925	9,352
48,350	48,400	10,425	8,332	10,939	9,366
48,400	48,450	10,439	8,346	10,953	9,380
48,450	48,500	10,453	8,360	10,967	9,394
48,500	48,550	10,467	8,374	10,983	9,408
48,550	48,600	10,481	8,388	10,998	9,422
48,600	48,650	10,495	8,402	11,014	9,436
48,650	48,700	10,509	8,416	11,029	9,450
48,700	48,750	10,523	8,430	11,045	9,464
48,750	48,800	10,537	8,444	11,060	9,478
48,800	48,850	10,551	8,458	11,076	9,492
48,850	48,900	10,565	8,472	11,091	9,506
48,900	48,950	10,579	8,486	11,107	9,520
48,950	49,000	10,593	8,500	11,122	9,534

49,000

49,000	49,050	10,607	8,514	11,138	9,548
49,050	49,100	10,621	8,528	11,153	9,562
49,100	49,150	10,635	8,542	11,169	9,576
49,150	49,200	10,649	8,556	11,184	9,590
49,200	49,250	10,663	8,570	11,200	9,604
49,250	49,300	10,677	8,584	11,215	9,618
49,300	49,350	10,691	8,598	11,231	9,632
49,350	49,400	10,705	8,612	11,246	9,646
49,400	49,450	10,719	8,626	11,262	9,660
49,450	49,500	10,733	8,640	11,277	9,674
49,500	49,550	10,747	8,654	11,293	9,688
49,550	49,600	10,761	8,668	11,308	9,702
49,600	49,650	10,775	8,682	11,324	9,716
49,650	49,700	10,789	8,696	11,339	9,730
49,700	49,750	10,803	8,710	11,355	9,744
49,750	49,800	10,817	8,724	11,370	9,758
49,800	49,850	10,831	8,738	11,386	9,772
49,850	49,900	10,845	8,752	11,401	9,786
49,900	49,950	10,859	8,766	11,417	9,800
49,950	50,000	10,873	8,780	11,432	9,814

* This column must also be used by a qualifying widow(er).

Continued on next page

Tax Rate Schedules and Tables

1996 Tax Table—Continued

If line 37 (taxable income) is— At least	But less than	Single	Married filing jointly *	Married filing separately	Head of a household	If line 37 (taxable income) is— At least	But less than	Single	Married filing jointly *	Married filing separately	Head of a household	If line 37 (taxable income) is— At least	But less than	Single	Married filing jointly *	Married filing separately	Head of a household
50,000						**53,000**						**56,000**					
50,000	50,050	10,887	8,794	11,448	9,828	53,000	53,050	11,727	9,634	12,378	10,668	56,000	56,050	12,567	10,474	13,308	11,508
50,050	50,100	10,901	8,808	11,463	9,842	53,050	53,100	11,741	9,648	12,393	10,682	56,050	56,100	12,581	10,488	13,323	11,522
50,100	50,150	10,915	8,822	11,479	9,856	53,100	53,150	11,755	9,662	12,409	10,696	56,100	56,150	12,595	10,502	13,339	11,536
50,150	50,200	10,929	8,836	11,494	9,870	53,150	53,200	11,769	9,676	12,424	10,710	56,150	56,200	12,609	10,516	13,354	11,550
50,200	50,250	10,943	8,850	11,510	9,884	53,200	53,250	11,783	9,690	12,440	10,724	56,200	56,250	12,623	10,530	13,370	11,564
50,250	50,300	10,957	8,864	11,525	9,898	53,250	53,300	11,797	9,704	12,455	10,738	56,250	56,300	12,637	10,544	13,385	11,578
50,300	50,350	10,971	8,878	11,541	9,912	53,300	53,350	11,811	9,718	12,471	10,752	56,300	56,350	12,651	10,558	13,401	11,592
50,350	50,400	10,985	8,892	11,556	9,926	53,350	53,400	11,825	9,732	12,486	10,766	56,350	56,400	12,665	10,572	13,416	11,606
50,400	50,450	10,999	8,906	11,572	9,940	53,400	53,450	11,839	9,746	12,502	10,780	56,400	56,450	12,679	10,586	13,432	11,620
50,450	50,500	11,013	8,920	11,587	9,954	53,450	53,500	11,853	9,760	12,517	10,794	56,450	56,500	12,693	10,600	13,447	11,634
50,500	50,550	11,027	8,934	11,603	9,968	53,500	53,550	11,867	9,774	12,533	10,808	56,500	56,550	12,707	10,614	13,463	11,648
50,550	50,600	11,041	8,948	11,618	9,982	53,550	53,600	11,881	9,788	12,548	10,822	56,550	56,600	12,721	10,628	13,478	11,662
50,600	50,650	11,055	8,962	11,634	9,996	53,600	53,650	11,895	9,802	12,564	10,836	56,600	56,650	12,735	10,642	13,494	11,676
50,650	50,700	11,069	8,976	11,649	10,010	53,650	53,700	11,909	9,816	12,579	10,850	56,650	56,700	12,749	10,656	13,509	11,690
50,700	50,750	11,083	8,990	11,665	10,024	53,700	53,750	11,923	9,830	12,595	10,864	56,700	56,750	12,763	10,670	13,525	11,704
50,750	50,800	11,097	9,004	11,680	10,038	53,750	53,800	11,937	9,844	12,610	10,878	56,750	56,800	12,777	10,684	13,540	11,718
50,800	50,850	11,111	9,018	11,696	10,052	53,800	53,850	11,951	9,858	12,626	10,892	56,800	56,850	12,791	10,698	13,556	11,732
50,850	50,900	11,125	9,032	11,711	10,066	53,850	53,900	11,965	9,872	12,641	10,906	56,850	56,900	12,805	10,712	13,571	11,746
50,900	50,950	11,139	9,046	11,727	10,080	53,900	53,950	11,979	9,886	12,657	10,920	56,900	56,950	12,819	10,726	13,587	11,760
50,950	51,000	11,153	9,060	11,742	10,094	53,950	54,000	11,993	9,900	12,672	10,934	56,950	57,000	12,833	10,740	13,602	11,774
51,000						**54,000**						**57,000**					
51,000	51,050	11,167	9,074	11,758	10,108	54,000	54,050	12,007	9,914	12,688	10,948	57,000	57,050	12,847	10,754	13,618	11,788
51,050	51,100	11,181	9,088	11,773	10,122	54,050	54,100	12,021	9,928	12,703	10,962	57,050	57,100	12,861	10,768	13,633	11,802
51,100	51,150	11,195	9,102	11,789	10,136	54,100	54,150	12,035	9,942	12,719	10,976	57,100	57,150	12,875	10,782	13,649	11,816
51,150	51,200	11,209	9,116	11,804	10,150	54,150	54,200	12,049	9,956	12,734	10,990	57,150	57,200	12,889	10,796	13,664	11,830
51,200	51,250	11,223	9,130	11,820	10,164	54,200	54,250	12,063	9,970	12,750	11,004	57,200	57,250	12,903	10,810	13,680	11,844
51,250	51,300	11,237	9,144	11,835	10,178	54,250	54,300	12,077	9,984	12,765	11,018	57,250	57,300	12,917	10,824	13,695	11,858
51,300	51,350	11,251	9,158	11,851	10,192	54,300	54,350	12,091	9,998	12,781	11,032	57,300	57,350	12,931	10,838	13,711	11,872
51,350	51,400	11,265	9,172	11,866	10,206	54,350	54,400	12,105	10,012	12,796	11,046	57,350	57,400	12,945	10,852	13,726	11,886
51,400	51,450	11,279	9,186	11,882	10,220	54,400	54,450	12,119	10,026	12,812	11,060	57,400	57,450	12,959	10,866	13,742	11,900
51,450	51,500	11,293	9,200	11,897	10,234	54,450	54,500	12,133	10,040	12,827	11,074	57,450	57,500	12,973	10,880	13,757	11,914
51,500	51,550	11,307	9,214	11,913	10,248	54,500	54,550	12,147	10,054	12,843	11,088	57,500	57,550	12,987	10,894	13,773	11,928
51,550	51,600	11,321	9,228	11,928	10,262	54,550	54,600	12,161	10,068	12,858	11,102	57,550	57,600	13,001	10,908	13,788	11,942
51,600	51,650	11,335	9,242	11,944	10,276	54,600	54,650	12,175	10,082	12,874	11,116	57,600	57,650	13,015	10,922	13,804	11,956
51,650	51,700	11,349	9,256	11,959	10,290	54,650	54,700	12,189	10,096	12,889	11,130	57,650	57,700	13,029	10,936	13,819	11,970
51,700	51,750	11,363	9,270	11,975	10,304	54,700	54,750	12,203	10,110	12,905	11,144	57,700	57,750	13,043	10,950	13,835	11,984
51,750	51,800	11,377	9,284	11,990	10,318	54,750	54,800	12,217	10,124	12,920	11,158	57,750	57,800	13,057	10,964	13,850	11,998
51,800	51,850	11,391	9,298	12,006	10,332	54,800	54,850	12,231	10,138	12,936	11,172	57,800	57,850	13,071	10,978	13,866	12,012
51,850	51,900	11,405	9,312	12,021	10,346	54,850	54,900	12,245	10,152	12,951	11,186	57,850	57,900	13,085	10,992	13,881	12,026
51,900	51,950	11,419	9,326	12,037	10,360	54,900	54,950	12,259	10,166	12,967	11,200	57,900	57,950	13,099	11,006	13,897	12,040
51,950	52,000	11,433	9,340	12,052	10,374	54,950	55,000	12,273	10,180	12,982	11,214	57,950	58,000	13,113	11,020	13,912	12,054
52,000						**55,000**						**58,000**					
52,000	52,050	11,447	9,354	12,068	10,388	55,000	55,050	12,287	10,194	12,998	11,228	58,000	58,050	13,127	11,034	13,928	12,068
52,050	52,100	11,461	9,368	12,083	10,402	55,050	55,100	12,301	10,208	13,013	11,242	58,050	58,100	13,141	11,048	13,943	12,082
52,100	52,150	11,475	9,382	12,099	10,416	55,100	55,150	12,315	10,222	13,029	11,256	58,100	58,150	13,155	11,062	13,959	12,096
52,150	52,200	11,489	9,396	12,114	10,430	55,150	55,200	12,329	10,236	13,044	11,270	58,150	58,200	13,170	11,076	13,974	12,110
52,200	52,250	11,503	9,410	12,130	10,444	55,200	55,250	12,343	10,250	13,060	11,284	58,200	58,250	13,185	11,090	13,990	12,124
52,250	52,300	11,517	9,424	12,145	10,458	55,250	55,300	12,357	10,264	13,075	11,298	58,250	58,300	13,201	11,104	14,005	12,138
52,300	52,350	11,531	9,438	12,161	10,472	55,300	55,350	12,371	10,278	13,091	11,312	58,300	58,350	13,216	11,118	14,021	12,152
52,350	52,400	11,545	9,452	12,176	10,486	55,350	55,400	12,385	10,292	13,106	11,326	58,350	58,400	13,232	11,132	14,036	12,166
52,400	52,450	11,559	9,466	12,192	10,500	55,400	55,450	12,399	10,306	13,122	11,340	58,400	58,450	13,247	11,146	14,052	12,180
52,450	52,500	11,573	9,480	12,207	10,514	55,450	55,500	12,413	10,320	13,137	11,354	58,450	58,500	13,263	11,160	14,067	12,194
52,500	52,550	11,587	9,494	12,223	10,528	55,500	55,550	12,427	10,334	13,153	11,368	58,500	58,550	13,278	11,174	14,083	12,208
52,550	52,600	11,601	9,508	12,238	10,542	55,550	55,600	12,441	10,348	13,168	11,382	58,550	58,600	13,294	11,188	14,098	12,222
52,600	52,650	11,615	9,522	12,254	10,556	55,600	55,650	12,455	10,362	13,184	11,396	58,600	58,650	13,309	11,202	14,114	12,236
52,650	52,700	11,629	9,536	12,269	10,570	55,650	55,700	12,469	10,376	13,199	11,410	58,650	58,700	13,325	11,216	14,129	12,250
52,700	52,750	11,643	9,550	12,285	10,584	55,700	55,750	12,483	10,390	13,215	11,424	58,700	58,750	13,340	11,230	14,145	12,264
52,750	52,800	11,657	9,564	12,300	10,598	55,750	55,800	12,497	10,404	13,230	11,438	58,750	58,800	13,356	11,244	14,160	12,278
52,800	52,850	11,671	9,578	12,316	10,612	55,800	55,850	12,511	10,418	13,246	11,452	58,800	58,850	13,371	11,258	14,176	12,292
52,850	52,900	11,685	9,592	12,331	10,626	55,850	55,900	12,525	10,432	13,261	11,466	58,850	58,900	13,387	11,272	14,191	12,306
52,900	52,950	11,699	9,606	12,347	10,640	55,900	55,950	12,539	10,446	13,277	11,480	58,900	58,950	13,402	11,286	14,207	12,320
52,950	53,000	11,713	9,620	12,362	10,654	55,950	56,000	12,553	10,460	13,292	11,494	58,950	59,000	13,418	11,300	14,222	12,334

* This column must also be used by a qualifying widow(er).

Continued on next page

1996 Tax Table—Continued

If line 37 (taxable income) is—		And you are—				If line 37 (taxable income) is—		And you are—				If line 37 (taxable income) is—		And you are—			
At least	But less than	Single	Married filing jointly *	Married filing separately	Head of a household	At least	But less than	Single	Married filing jointly *	Married filing separately	Head of a household	At least	But less than	Single	Married filing jointly *	Married filing separately	Head of a household
		Your tax is—						Your tax is—						Your tax is—			

59,000

59,000	59,050	13,433	11,314	14,238	12,348
59,050	59,100	13,449	11,328	14,253	12,362
59,100	59,150	13,464	11,342	14,269	12,376
59,150	59,200	13,480	11,356	14,284	12,390
59,200	59,250	13,495	11,370	14,300	12,404
59,250	59,300	13,511	11,384	14,315	12,418
59,300	59,350	13,526	11,398	14,331	12,432
59,350	59,400	13,542	11,412	14,346	12,446
59,400	59,450	13,557	11,426	14,362	12,460
59,450	59,500	13,573	11,440	14,377	12,474
59,500	59,550	13,588	11,454	14,393	12,488
59,550	59,600	13,604	11,468	14,408	12,502
59,600	59,650	13,619	11,482	14,424	12,516
59,650	59,700	13,635	11,496	14,439	12,530
59,700	59,750	13,650	11,510	14,455	12,544
59,750	59,800	13,666	11,524	14,470	12,558
59,800	59,850	13,681	11,538	14,486	12,572
59,850	59,900	13,697	11,552	14,501	12,586
59,900	59,950	13,712	11,566	14,517	12,600
59,950	60,000	13,728	11,580	14,532	12,614

60,000

60,000	60,050	13,743	11,594	14,548	12,628
60,050	60,100	13,759	11,608	14,563	12,642
60,100	60,150	13,774	11,622	14,579	12,656
60,150	60,200	13,790	11,636	14,594	12,670
60,200	60,250	13,805	11,650	14,610	12,684
60,250	60,300	13,821	11,664	14,625	12,698
60,300	60,350	13,836	11,678	14,641	12,712
60,350	60,400	13,852	11,692	14,656	12,726
60,400	60,450	13,867	11,706	14,672	12,740
60,450	60,500	13,883	11,720	14,687	12,754
60,500	60,550	13,898	11,734	14,703	12,768
60,550	60,600	13,914	11,748	14,718	12,782
60,600	60,650	13,929	11,762	14,734	12,796
60,650	60,700	13,945	11,776	14,749	12,810
60,700	60,750	13,960	11,790	14,765	12,824
60,750	60,800	13,976	11,804	14,780	12,838
60,800	60,850	13,991	11,818	14,796	12,852
60,850	60,900	14,007	11,832	14,811	12,866
60,900	60,950	14,022	11,846	14,827	12,880
60,950	61,000	14,038	11,860	14,842	12,894

61,000

61,000	61,050	14,053	11,874	14,858	12,908
61,050	61,100	14,069	11,888	14,873	12,922
61,100	61,150	14,084	11,902	14,889	12,936
61,150	61,200	14,100	11,916	14,904	12,950
61,200	61,250	14,115	11,930	14,920	12,964
61,250	61,300	14,131	11,944	14,935	12,978
61,300	61,350	14,146	11,958	14,951	12,992
61,350	61,400	14,162	11,972	14,966	13,006
61,400	61,450	14,177	11,986	14,982	13,020
61,450	61,500	14,193	12,000	14,997	13,034
61,500	61,550	14,208	12,014	15,013	13,048
61,550	61,600	14,224	12,028	15,028	13,062
61,600	61,650	14,239	12,042	15,044	13,076
61,650	61,700	14,255	12,056	15,059	13,090
61,700	61,750	14,270	12,070	15,075	13,104
61,750	61,800	14,286	12,084	15,090	13,118
61,800	61,850	14,301	12,098	15,106	13,132
61,850	61,900	14,317	12,112	15,121	13,146
61,900	61,950	14,332	12,126	15,137	13,160
61,950	62,000	14,348	12,140	15,152	13,174

62,000

62,000	62,050	14,363	12,154	15,168	13,188
62,050	62,100	14,379	12,168	15,183	13,202
62,100	62,150	14,394	12,182	15,199	13,216
62,150	62,200	14,410	12,196	15,214	13,230
62,200	62,250	14,425	12,210	15,230	13,244
62,250	62,300	14,441	12,224	15,245	13,258
62,300	62,350	14,456	12,238	15,261	13,272
62,350	62,400	14,472	12,252	15,276	13,286
62,400	62,450	14,487	12,266	15,292	13,300
62,450	62,500	14,503	12,280	15,307	13,314
62,500	62,550	14,518	12,294	15,323	13,328
62,550	62,600	14,534	12,308	15,338	13,342
62,600	62,650	14,549	12,322	15,354	13,356
62,650	62,700	14,565	12,336	15,369	13,370
62,700	62,750	14,580	12,350	15,385	13,384
62,750	62,800	14,596	12,364	15,400	13,398
62,800	62,850	14,611	12,378	15,416	13,412
62,850	62,900	14,627	12,392	15,431	13,426
62,900	62,950	14,642	12,406	15,447	13,440
62,950	63,000	14,658	12,420	15,462	13,454

63,000

63,000	63,050	14,673	12,434	15,478	13,468
63,050	63,100	14,689	12,448	15,493	13,482
63,100	63,150	14,704	12,462	15,509	13,496
63,150	63,200	14,720	12,476	15,524	13,510
63,200	63,250	14,735	12,490	15,540	13,524
63,250	63,300	14,751	12,504	15,555	13,538
63,300	63,350	14,766	12,518	15,571	13,552
63,350	63,400	14,782	12,532	15,586	13,566
63,400	63,450	14,797	12,546	15,602	13,580
63,450	63,500	14,813	12,560	15,617	13,594
63,500	63,550	14,828	12,574	15,633	13,608
63,550	63,600	14,844	12,588	15,648	13,622
63,600	63,650	14,859	12,602	15,664	13,636
63,650	63,700	14,875	12,616	15,679	13,650
63,700	63,750	14,890	12,630	15,695	13,664
63,750	63,800	14,906	12,644	15,710	13,678
63,800	63,850	14,921	12,658	15,726	13,692
63,850	63,900	14,937	12,672	15,741	13,706
63,900	63,950	14,952	12,686	15,757	13,720
63,950	64,000	14,968	12,700	15,772	13,734

64,000

64,000	64,050	14,983	12,714	15,788	13,748
64,050	64,100	14,999	12,728	15,803	13,762
64,100	64,150	15,014	12,742	15,819	13,776
64,150	64,200	15,030	12,756	15,834	13,790
64,200	64,250	15,045	12,770	15,850	13,804
64,250	64,300	15,061	12,784	15,865	13,818
64,300	64,350	15,076	12,798	15,881	13,832
64,350	64,400	15,092	12,812	15,896	13,846
64,400	64,450	15,107	12,826	15,912	13,860
64,450	64,500	15,123	12,840	15,927	13,874
64,500	64,550	15,138	12,854	15,943	13,888
64,550	64,600	15,154	12,868	15,958	13,902
64,600	64,650	15,169	12,882	15,974	13,916
64,650	64,700	15,185	12,896	15,989	13,930
64,700	64,750	15,200	12,910	16,005	13,944
64,750	64,800	15,216	12,924	16,020	13,958
64,800	64,850	15,231	12,938	16,036	13,972
64,850	64,900	15,247	12,952	16,051	13,986
64,900	64,950	15,262	12,966	16,067	14,000
64,950	65,000	15,278	12,980	16,082	14,014

65,000

65,000	65,050	15,293	12,994	16,098	14,028
65,050	65,100	15,309	13,008	16,113	14,042
65,100	65,150	15,324	13,022	16,129	14,056
65,150	65,200	15,340	13,036	16,144	14,070
65,200	65,250	15,355	13,050	16,160	14,084
65,250	65,300	15,371	13,064	16,175	14,098
65,300	65,350	15,386	13,078	16,191	14,112
65,350	65,400	15,402	13,092	16,206	14,126
65,400	65,450	15,417	13,106	16,222	14,140
65,450	65,500	15,433	13,120	16,237	14,154
65,500	65,550	15,448	13,134	16,253	14,168
65,550	65,600	15,464	13,148	16,268	14,182
65,600	65,650	15,479	13,162	16,284	14,196
65,650	65,700	15,495	13,176	16,299	14,210
65,700	65,750	15,510	13,190	16,315	14,224
65,750	65,800	15,526	13,204	16,330	14,238
65,800	65,850	15,541	13,218	16,346	14,252
65,850	65,900	15,557	13,232	16,361	14,266
65,900	65,950	15,572	13,246	16,377	14,280
65,950	66,000	15,588	13,260	16,392	14,294

66,000

66,000	66,050	15,603	13,274	16,408	14,308
66,050	66,100	15,619	13,288	16,423	14,322
66,100	66,150	15,634	13,302	16,439	14,336
66,150	66,200	15,650	13,316	16,454	14,350
66,200	66,250	15,665	13,330	16,470	14,364
66,250	66,300	15,681	13,344	16,485	14,378
66,300	66,350	15,696	13,358	16,501	14,392
66,350	66,400	15,712	13,372	16,516	14,406
66,400	66,450	15,727	13,386	16,532	14,420
66,450	66,500	15,743	13,400	16,547	14,434
66,500	66,550	15,758	13,414	16,563	14,448
66,550	66,600	15,774	13,428	16,578	14,462
66,600	66,650	15,789	13,442	16,594	14,476
66,650	66,700	15,805	13,456	16,609	14,490
66,700	66,750	15,820	13,470	16,625	14,504
66,750	66,800	15,836	13,484	16,640	14,518
66,800	66,850	15,851	13,498	16,656	14,532
66,850	66,900	15,867	13,512	16,671	14,546
66,900	66,950	15,882	13,526	16,687	14,560
66,950	67,000	15,898	13,540	16,702	14,574

67,000

67,000	67,050	15,913	13,554	16,718	14,588
67,050	67,100	15,929	13,568	16,733	14,602
67,100	67,150	15,944	13,582	16,749	14,616
67,150	67,200	15,960	13,596	16,764	14,630
67,200	67,250	15,975	13,610	16,780	14,644
67,250	67,300	15,991	13,624	16,795	14,658
67,300	67,350	16,006	13,638	16,811	14,672
67,350	67,400	16,022	13,652	16,826	14,686
67,400	67,450	16,037	13,666	16,842	14,700
67,450	67,500	16,053	13,680	16,857	14,714
67,500	67,550	16,068	13,694	16,873	14,728
67,550	67,600	16,084	13,708	16,888	14,742
67,600	67,650	16,099	13,722	16,904	14,756
67,650	67,700	16,115	13,736	16,919	14,770
67,700	67,750	16,130	13,750	16,935	14,784
67,750	67,800	16,146	13,764	16,950	14,798
67,800	67,850	16,161	13,778	16,966	14,812
67,850	67,900	16,177	13,792	16,981	14,826
67,900	67,950	16,192	13,806	16,997	14,840
67,950	68,000	16,208	13,820	17,012	14,854

* This column must also be used by a qualifying widow(er).

Continued on next page

1996 Tax Table—Continued

At least	But less than	Single	Married filing jointly*	Married filing separately	Head of a household	At least	But less than	Single	Married filing jointly*	Married filing separately	Head of a household	At least	But less than	Single	Married filing jointly*	Married filing separately	Head of a household
68,000						**71,000**						**74,000**					
68,000	68,050	16,223	13,834	17,028	14,868	71,000	71,050	17,153	14,674	17,958	15,708	74,000	74,050	18,083	15,514	18,897	16,548
68,050	68,100	16,239	13,848	17,043	14,882	71,050	71,100	17,169	14,688	17,973	15,722	74,050	74,100	18,099	15,528	18,915	16,562
68,100	68,150	16,254	13,862	17,059	14,896	71,100	71,150	17,184	14,702	17,989	15,736	74,100	74,150	18,114	15,542	18,933	16,576
68,150	68,200	16,270	13,876	17,074	14,910	71,150	71,200	17,200	14,716	18,004	15,750	74,150	74,200	18,130	15,556	18,951	16,590
68,200	68,250	16,285	13,890	17,090	14,924	71,200	71,250	17,215	14,730	18,020	15,764	74,200	74,250	18,145	15,570	18,969	16,604
68,250	68,300	16,301	13,904	17,105	14,938	71,250	71,300	17,231	14,744	18,035	15,778	74,250	74,300	18,161	15,584	18,987	16,618
68,300	68,350	16,316	13,918	17,121	14,952	71,300	71,350	17,246	14,758	18,051	15,792	74,300	74,350	18,176	15,598	19,005	16,632
68,350	68,400	16,332	13,932	17,136	14,966	71,350	71,400	17,262	14,772	18,066	15,806	74,350	74,400	18,192	15,612	19,023	16,646
68,400	68,450	16,347	13,946	17,152	14,980	71,400	71,450	17,277	14,786	18,082	15,820	74,400	74,450	18,207	15,626	19,041	16,660
68,450	68,500	16,363	13,960	17,167	14,994	71,450	71,500	17,293	14,800	18,097	15,834	74,450	74,500	18,223	15,640	19,059	16,674
68,500	68,550	16,378	13,974	17,183	15,008	71,500	71,550	17,308	14,814	18,113	15,848	74,500	74,550	18,238	15,654	19,077	16,688
68,550	68,600	16,394	13,988	17,198	15,022	71,550	71,600	17,324	14,828	18,128	15,862	74,550	74,600	18,254	15,668	19,095	16,702
68,600	68,650	16,409	14,002	17,214	15,036	71,600	71,650	17,339	14,842	18,144	15,876	74,600	74,650	18,269	15,682	19,113	16,716
68,650	68,700	16,425	14,016	17,229	15,050	71,650	71,700	17,355	14,856	18,159	15,890	74,650	74,700	18,285	15,696	19,131	16,730
68,700	68,750	16,440	14,030	17,245	15,064	71,700	71,750	17,370	14,870	18,175	15,904	74,700	74,750	18,300	15,710	19,149	16,744
68,750	68,800	16,456	14,044	17,260	15,078	71,750	71,800	17,386	14,884	18,190	15,918	74,750	74,800	18,316	15,724	19,167	16,758
68,800	68,850	16,471	14,058	17,276	15,092	71,800	71,850	17,401	14,898	18,206	15,932	74,800	74,850	18,331	15,738	19,185	16,772
68,850	68,900	16,487	14,072	17,291	15,106	71,850	71,900	17,417	14,912	18,221	15,946	74,850	74,900	18,347	15,752	19,203	16,786
68,900	68,950	16,502	14,086	17,307	15,120	71,900	71,950	17,432	14,926	18,237	15,960	74,900	74,950	18,362	15,766	19,221	16,800
68,950	69,000	16,518	14,100	17,322	15,134	71,950	72,000	17,448	14,940	18,252	15,974	74,950	75,000	18,378	15,780	19,239	16,814
69,000						**72,000**						**75,000**					
69,000	69,050	16,533	14,114	17,338	15,148	72,000	72,050	17,463	14,954	18,268	15,988	75,000	75,050	18,393	15,794	19,257	16,828
69,050	69,100	16,549	14,128	17,353	15,162	72,050	72,100	17,479	14,968	18,283	16,002	75,050	75,100	18,409	15,808	19,275	16,842
69,100	69,150	16,564	14,142	17,369	15,176	72,100	72,150	17,494	14,982	18,299	16,016	75,100	75,150	18,424	15,822	19,293	16,856
69,150	69,200	16,580	14,156	17,384	15,190	72,150	72,200	17,510	14,996	18,314	16,030	75,150	75,200	18,440	15,836	19,311	16,870
69,200	69,250	16,595	14,170	17,400	15,204	72,200	72,250	17,525	15,010	18,330	16,044	75,200	75,250	18,455	15,850	19,329	16,884
69,250	69,300	16,611	14,184	17,415	15,218	72,250	72,300	17,541	15,024	18,345	16,058	75,250	75,300	18,471	15,864	19,347	16,898
69,300	69,350	16,626	14,198	17,431	15,232	72,300	72,350	17,556	15,038	18,361	16,072	75,300	75,350	18,486	15,878	19,365	16,912
69,350	69,400	16,642	14,212	17,446	15,246	72,350	72,400	17,572	15,052	18,376	16,086	75,350	75,400	18,502	15,892	19,383	16,926
69,400	69,450	16,657	14,226	17,462	15,260	72,400	72,450	17,587	15,066	18,392	16,100	75,400	75,450	18,517	15,906	19,401	16,940
69,450	69,500	16,673	14,240	17,477	15,274	72,450	72,500	17,603	15,080	18,407	16,114	75,450	75,500	18,533	15,920	19,419	16,954
69,500	69,550	16,688	14,254	17,493	15,288	72,500	72,550	17,618	15,094	18,423	16,128	75,500	75,550	18,548	15,934	19,437	16,968
69,550	69,600	16,704	14,268	17,508	15,302	72,550	72,600	17,634	15,108	18,438	16,142	75,550	75,600	18,564	15,948	19,455	16,982
69,600	69,650	16,719	14,282	17,524	15,316	72,600	72,650	17,649	15,122	18,454	16,156	75,600	75,650	18,579	15,962	19,473	16,996
69,650	69,700	16,735	14,296	17,539	15,330	72,650	72,700	17,665	15,136	18,469	16,170	75,650	75,700	18,595	15,976	19,491	17,010
69,700	69,750	16,750	14,310	17,555	15,344	72,700	72,750	17,680	15,150	18,485	16,184	75,700	75,750	18,610	15,990	19,509	17,024
69,750	69,800	16,766	14,324	17,570	15,358	72,750	72,800	17,696	15,164	18,500	16,198	75,750	75,800	18,626	16,004	19,527	17,038
69,800	69,850	16,781	14,338	17,586	15,372	72,800	72,850	17,711	15,178	18,516	16,212	75,800	75,850	18,641	16,018	19,545	17,052
69,850	69,900	16,797	14,352	17,601	15,386	72,850	72,900	17,727	15,192	18,531	16,226	75,850	75,900	18,657	16,032	19,563	17,066
69,900	69,950	16,812	14,366	17,617	15,400	72,900	72,950	17,742	15,206	18,547	16,240	75,900	75,950	18,672	16,046	19,581	17,080
69,950	70,000	16,828	14,380	17,632	15,414	72,950	73,000	17,758	15,220	18,562	16,254	75,950	76,000	18,688	16,060	19,599	17,094
70,000						**73,000**						**76,000**					
70,000	70,050	16,843	14,394	17,648	15,428	73,000	73,050	17,773	15,234	18,578	16,268	76,000	76,050	18,703	16,074	19,617	17,108
70,050	70,100	16,859	14,408	17,663	15,442	73,050	73,100	17,789	15,248	18,593	16,282	76,050	76,100	18,719	16,088	19,635	17,122
70,100	70,150	16,874	14,422	17,679	15,456	73,100	73,150	17,804	15,262	18,609	16,296	76,100	76,150	18,734	16,102	19,653	17,136
70,150	70,200	16,890	14,436	17,694	15,470	73,150	73,200	17,820	15,276	18,624	16,310	76,150	76,200	18,750	16,116	19,671	17,150
70,200	70,250	16,905	14,450	17,710	15,484	73,200	73,250	17,835	15,290	18,640	16,324	76,200	76,250	18,765	16,130	19,689	17,164
70,250	70,300	16,921	14,464	17,725	15,498	73,250	73,300	17,851	15,304	18,655	16,338	76,250	76,300	18,781	16,144	19,707	17,178
70,300	70,350	16,936	14,478	17,741	15,512	73,300	73,350	17,866	15,318	18,671	16,352	76,300	76,350	18,796	16,158	19,725	17,192
70,350	70,400	16,952	14,492	17,756	15,526	73,350	73,400	17,882	15,332	18,686	16,366	76,350	76,400	18,812	16,172	19,743	17,206
70,400	70,450	16,967	14,506	17,772	15,540	73,400	73,450	17,897	15,346	18,702	16,380	76,400	76,450	18,827	16,186	19,761	17,220
70,450	70,500	16,983	14,520	17,787	15,554	73,450	73,500	17,913	15,360	18,717	16,394	76,450	76,500	18,843	16,200	19,779	17,234
70,500	70,550	16,998	14,534	17,803	15,568	73,500	73,550	17,928	15,374	18,733	16,408	76,500	76,550	18,858	16,214	19,797	17,248
70,550	70,600	17,014	14,548	17,818	15,582	73,550	73,600	17,944	15,388	18,748	16,422	76,550	76,600	18,874	16,228	19,815	17,262
70,600	70,650	17,029	14,562	17,834	15,596	73,600	73,650	17,959	15,402	18,764	16,436	76,600	76,650	18,889	16,242	19,833	17,276
70,650	70,700	17,045	14,576	17,849	15,610	73,650	73,700	17,975	15,416	18,779	16,450	76,650	76,700	18,905	16,256	19,851	17,290
70,700	70,750	17,060	14,590	17,865	15,624	73,700	73,750	17,990	15,430	18,795	16,464	76,700	76,750	18,920	16,270	19,869	17,304
70,750	70,800	17,076	14,604	17,880	15,638	73,750	73,800	18,006	15,444	18,810	16,478	76,750	76,800	18,936	16,284	19,887	17,318
70,800	70,850	17,091	14,618	17,896	15,652	73,800	73,850	18,021	15,458	18,826	16,492	76,800	76,850	18,951	16,298	19,905	17,332
70,850	70,900	17,107	14,632	17,911	15,666	73,850	73,900	18,037	15,472	18,843	16,506	76,850	76,900	18,967	16,312	19,923	17,346
70,900	70,950	17,122	14,646	17,927	15,680	73,900	73,950	18,052	15,486	18,861	16,520	76,900	76,950	18,982	16,326	19,941	17,360
70,950	71,000	17,138	14,660	17,942	15,694	73,950	74,000	18,068	15,500	18,879	16,534	76,950	77,000	18,998	16,340	19,959	17,374

* This column must also be used by a qualifying widow(er).

Continued on next page

1996 Tax Table—Continued

At least	But less than	Single	Married filing jointly*	Married filing separately	Head of a household	At least	But less than	Single	Married filing jointly*	Married filing separately	Head of a household	At least	But less than	Single	Married filing jointly*	Married filing separately	Head of a household
77,000						**80,000**						**83,000**					
77,000	77,050	19,013	16,354	19,977	17,388	80,000	80,050	19,943	17,194	21,057	18,228	83,000	83,050	20,873	18,034	22,137	19,068
77,050	77,100	19,029	16,368	19,995	17,402	80,050	80,100	19,959	17,208	21,075	18,242	83,050	83,100	20,889	18,048	22,155	19,082
77,100	77,150	19,044	16,382	20,013	17,416	80,100	80,150	19,974	17,222	21,093	18,256	83,100	83,150	20,904	18,062	22,173	19,098
77,150	77,200	19,060	16,396	20,031	17,430	80,150	80,200	19,990	17,236	21,111	18,270	83,150	83,200	20,920	18,076	22,191	19,113
77,200	77,250	19,075	16,410	20,049	17,444	80,200	80,250	20,005	17,250	21,129	18,284	83,200	83,250	20,935	18,090	22,209	19,129
77,250	77,300	19,091	16,424	20,067	17,458	80,250	80,300	20,021	17,264	21,147	18,298	83,250	83,300	20,951	18,104	22,227	19,144
77,300	77,350	19,106	16,438	20,085	17,472	80,300	80,350	20,036	17,278	21,165	18,312	83,300	83,350	20,966	18,118	22,245	19,160
77,350	77,400	19,122	16,452	20,103	17,486	80,350	80,400	20,052	17,292	21,183	18,326	83,350	83,400	20,982	18,132	22,263	19,175
77,400	77,450	19,137	16,466	20,121	17,500	80,400	80,450	20,067	17,306	21,201	18,340	83,400	83,450	20,997	18,146	22,281	19,191
77,450	77,500	19,153	16,480	20,139	17,514	80,450	80,500	20,083	17,320	21,219	18,354	83,450	83,500	21,013	18,160	22,299	19,206
77,500	77,550	19,168	16,494	20,157	17,528	80,500	80,550	20,098	17,334	21,237	18,368	83,500	83,550	21,028	18,174	22,317	19,222
77,550	77,600	19,184	16,508	20,175	17,542	80,550	80,600	20,114	17,348	21,255	18,382	83,550	83,600	21,044	18,188	22,335	19,237
77,600	77,650	19,199	16,522	20,193	17,556	80,600	80,650	20,129	17,362	21,273	18,396	83,600	83,650	21,059	18,202	22,353	19,253
77,650	77,700	19,215	16,536	20,211	17,570	80,650	80,700	20,145	17,376	21,291	18,410	83,650	83,700	21,075	18,216	22,371	19,268
77,700	77,750	19,230	16,550	20,229	17,584	80,700	80,750	20,160	17,390	21,309	18,424	83,700	83,750	21,090	18,230	22,389	19,284
77,750	77,800	19,246	16,564	20,247	17,598	80,750	80,800	20,176	17,404	21,327	18,438	83,750	83,800	21,106	18,244	22,407	19,299
77,800	77,850	19,261	16,578	20,265	17,612	80,800	80,850	20,191	17,418	21,345	18,452	83,800	83,850	21,121	18,258	22,425	19,315
77,850	77,900	19,277	16,592	20,283	17,626	80,850	80,900	20,207	17,432	21,363	18,466	83,850	83,900	21,137	18,272	22,443	19,330
77,900	77,950	19,292	16,606	20,301	17,640	80,900	80,950	20,222	17,446	21,381	18,480	83,900	83,950	21,152	18,286	22,461	19,346
77,950	78,000	19,308	16,620	20,319	17,654	80,950	81,000	20,238	17,460	21,399	18,494	83,950	84,000	21,168	18,300	22,479	19,361
78,000						**81,000**						**84,000**					
78,000	78,050	19,323	16,634	20,337	17,668	81,000	81,050	20,253	17,474	21,417	18,508	84,000	84,050	21,183	18,314	22,497	19,377
78,050	78,100	19,339	16,648	20,355	17,682	81,050	81,100	20,269	17,488	21,435	18,522	84,050	84,100	21,199	18,328	22,515	19,392
78,100	78,150	19,354	16,662	20,373	17,696	81,100	81,150	20,284	17,502	21,453	18,536	84,100	84,150	21,214	18,342	22,533	19,408
78,150	78,200	19,370	16,676	20,391	17,710	81,150	81,200	20,300	17,516	21,471	18,550	84,150	84,200	21,230	18,356	22,551	19,423
78,200	78,250	19,385	16,690	20,409	17,724	81,200	81,250	20,315	17,530	21,489	18,564	84,200	84,250	21,245	18,370	22,569	19,439
78,250	78,300	19,401	16,704	20,427	17,738	81,250	81,300	20,331	17,544	21,507	18,578	84,250	84,300	21,261	18,384	22,587	19,454
78,300	78,350	19,416	16,718	20,445	17,752	81,300	81,350	20,346	17,558	21,525	18,592	84,300	84,350	21,276	18,398	22,605	19,470
78,350	78,400	19,432	16,732	20,463	17,766	81,350	81,400	20,362	17,572	21,543	18,606	84,350	84,400	21,292	18,412	22,623	19,485
78,400	78,450	19,447	16,746	20,481	17,780	81,400	81,450	20,377	17,586	21,561	18,620	84,400	84,450	21,307	18,426	22,641	19,501
78,450	78,500	19,463	16,760	20,499	17,794	81,450	81,500	20,393	17,600	21,579	18,634	84,450	84,500	21,323	18,440	22,659	19,516
78,500	78,550	19,478	16,774	20,517	17,808	81,500	81,550	20,408	17,614	21,597	18,648	84,500	84,550	21,338	18,454	22,677	19,532
78,550	78,600	19,494	16,788	20,535	17,822	81,550	81,600	20,424	17,628	21,615	18,662	84,550	84,600	21,354	18,468	22,695	19,547
78,600	78,650	19,509	16,802	20,553	17,836	81,600	81,650	20,439	17,642	21,633	18,676	84,600	84,650	21,369	18,482	22,713	19,563
78,650	78,700	19,525	16,816	20,571	17,850	81,650	81,700	20,455	17,656	21,651	18,690	84,650	84,700	21,385	18,496	22,731	19,578
78,700	78,750	19,540	16,830	20,589	17,864	81,700	81,750	20,470	17,670	21,669	18,704	84,700	84,750	21,400	18,510	22,749	19,594
78,750	78,800	19,556	16,844	20,607	17,878	81,750	81,800	20,486	17,684	21,687	18,718	84,750	84,800	21,416	18,524	22,767	19,609
78,800	78,850	19,571	16,858	20,625	17,892	81,800	81,850	20,501	17,698	21,705	18,732	84,800	84,850	21,431	18,538	22,785	19,625
78,850	78,900	19,587	16,872	20,643	17,906	81,850	81,900	20,517	17,712	21,723	18,746	84,850	84,900	21,447	18,552	22,803	19,640
78,900	78,950	19,602	16,886	20,661	17,920	81,900	81,950	20,532	17,726	21,741	18,760	84,900	84,950	21,462	18,566	22,821	19,656
78,950	79,000	19,618	16,900	20,679	17,934	81,950	82,000	20,548	17,740	21,759	18,774	84,950	85,000	21,478	18,580	22,839	19,671
79,000						**82,000**						**85,000**					
79,000	79,050	19,633	16,914	20,697	17,948	82,000	82,050	20,563	17,754	21,777	18,788	85,000	85,050	21,493	18,594	22,857	19,687
79,050	79,100	19,649	16,928	20,715	17,962	82,050	82,100	20,579	17,768	21,795	18,802	85,050	85,100	21,509	18,608	22,875	19,702
79,100	79,150	19,664	16,942	20,733	17,976	82,100	82,150	20,594	17,782	21,813	18,816	85,100	85,150	21,524	18,622	22,893	19,718
79,150	79,200	19,680	16,956	20,751	17,990	82,150	82,200	20,610	17,796	21,831	18,830	85,150	85,200	21,540	18,636	22,911	19,733
79,200	79,250	19,695	16,970	20,769	18,004	82,200	82,250	20,625	17,810	21,849	18,844	85,200	85,250	21,555	18,650	22,929	19,749
79,250	79,300	19,711	16,984	20,787	18,018	82,250	82,300	20,641	17,824	21,867	18,858	85,250	85,300	21,571	18,664	22,947	19,764
79,300	79,350	19,726	16,998	20,805	18,032	82,300	82,350	20,656	17,838	21,885	18,872	85,300	85,350	21,586	18,678	22,965	19,780
79,350	79,400	19,742	17,012	20,823	18,046	82,350	82,400	20,672	17,852	21,903	18,886	85,350	85,400	21,602	18,692	22,983	19,795
79,400	79,450	19,757	17,026	20,841	18,060	82,400	82,450	20,687	17,866	21,921	18,900	85,400	85,450	21,617	18,706	23,001	19,811
79,450	79,500	19,773	17,040	20,859	18,074	82,450	82,500	20,703	17,880	21,939	18,914	85,450	85,500	21,633	18,720	23,019	19,826
79,500	79,550	19,788	17,054	20,877	18,088	82,500	82,550	20,718	17,894	21,957	18,928	85,500	85,550	21,648	18,734	23,037	19,842
79,550	79,600	19,804	17,068	20,895	18,102	82,550	82,600	20,734	17,908	21,975	18,942	85,550	85,600	21,664	18,748	23,055	19,857
79,600	79,650	19,819	17,082	20,913	18,116	82,600	82,650	20,749	17,922	21,993	18,956	85,600	85,650	21,679	18,762	23,073	19,873
79,650	79,700	19,835	17,096	20,931	18,130	82,650	82,700	20,765	17,936	22,011	18,970	85,650	85,700	21,695	18,776	23,091	19,888
79,700	79,750	19,850	17,110	20,949	18,144	82,700	82,750	20,780	17,950	22,029	18,984	85,700	85,750	21,710	18,790	23,109	19,904
79,750	79,800	19,866	17,124	20,967	18,158	82,750	82,800	20,796	17,964	22,047	18,998	85,750	85,800	21,726	18,804	23,127	19,919
79,800	79,850	19,881	17,138	20,985	18,172	82,800	82,850	20,811	17,978	22,065	19,012	85,800	85,850	21,741	18,818	23,145	19,935
79,850	79,900	19,897	17,152	21,003	18,186	82,850	82,900	20,827	17,992	22,083	19,026	85,850	85,900	21,757	18,832	23,163	19,950
79,900	79,950	19,912	17,166	21,021	18,200	82,900	82,950	20,842	18,006	22,101	19,040	85,900	85,950	21,772	18,846	23,181	19,966
79,950	80,000	19,928	17,180	21,039	18,214	82,950	83,000	20,858	18,020	22,119	19,054	85,950	86,000	21,788	18,860	23,199	19,981

* This column must also be used by a qualifying widow(er).

Continued on next page

Tax Rate Schedules and Tables

A–13

1996 Tax Table—*Continued*

If line 37 (taxable income) is—		And you are—				If line 37 (taxable income) is—		And you are—				If line 37 (taxable income) is—		And you are—			
At least	But less than	Single	Married filing jointly *	Married filing separately	Head of a household	At least	But less than	Single	Married filing jointly *	Married filing separately	Head of a household	At least	But less than	Single	Married filing jointly *	Married filing separately	Head of a household
		Your tax is—						Your tax is—						Your tax is—			

86,000

86,000	86,050	21,803	18,874	23,217	19,997
86,050	86,100	21,819	18,888	23,235	20,012
86,100	86,150	21,834	18,902	23,253	20,028
86,150	86,200	21,850	18,916	23,271	20,043
86,200	86,250	21,865	18,930	23,289	20,059
86,250	86,300	21,881	18,944	23,307	20,074
86,300	86,350	21,896	18,958	23,325	20,090
86,350	86,400	21,912	18,972	23,343	20,105
86,400	86,450	21,927	18,986	23,361	20,121
86,450	86,500	21,943	19,000	23,379	20,136
86,500	86,550	21,958	19,014	23,397	20,152
86,550	86,600	21,974	19,028	23,415	20,167
86,600	86,650	21,989	19,042	23,433	20,183
86,650	86,700	22,005	19,056	23,451	20,198
86,700	86,750	22,020	19,070	23,469	20,214
86,750	86,800	22,036	19,084	23,487	20,229
86,800	86,850	22,051	19,098	23,505	20,245
86,850	86,900	22,067	19,112	23,523	20,260
86,900	86,950	22,082	19,126	23,541	20,276
86,950	87,000	22,098	19,140	23,559	20,291

87,000

87,000	87,050	22,113	19,154	23,577	20,307
87,050	87,100	22,129	19,168	23,595	20,322
87,100	87,150	22,144	19,182	23,613	20,338
87,150	87,200	22,160	19,196	23,631	20,353
87,200	87,250	22,175	19,210	23,649	20,369
87,250	87,300	22,191	19,224	23,667	20,384
87,300	87,350	22,206	19,238	23,685	20,400
87,350	87,400	22,222	19,252	23,703	20,415
87,400	87,450	22,237	19,266	23,721	20,431
87,450	87,500	22,253	19,280	23,739	20,446
87,500	87,550	22,268	19,294	23,757	20,462
87,550	87,600	22,284	19,308	23,775	20,477
87,600	87,650	22,299	19,322	23,793	20,493
87,650	87,700	22,315	19,336	23,811	20,508
87,700	87,750	22,330	19,350	23,829	20,524
87,750	87,800	22,346	19,364	23,847	20,539
87,800	87,850	22,361	19,378	23,865	20,555
87,850	87,900	22,377	19,392	23,883	20,570
87,900	87,950	22,392	19,406	23,901	20,586
87,950	88,000	22,408	19,420	23,919	20,601

88,000

88,000	88,050	22,423	19,434	23,937	20,617
88,050	88,100	22,439	19,448	23,955	20,632
88,100	88,150	22,454	19,462	23,973	20,648
88,150	88,200	22,470	19,476	23,991	20,663
88,200	88,250	22,485	19,490	24,009	20,679
88,250	88,300	22,501	19,504	24,027	20,694
88,300	88,350	22,516	19,518	24,045	20,710
88,350	88,400	22,532	19,532	24,063	20,725
88,400	88,450	22,547	19,546	24,081	20,741
88,450	88,500	22,563	19,560	24,099	20,756
88,500	88,550	22,578	19,574	24,117	20,772
88,550	88,600	22,594	19,588	24,135	20,787
88,600	88,650	22,609	19,602	24,153	20,803
88,650	88,700	22,625	19,616	24,171	20,818
88,700	88,750	22,640	19,630	24,189	20,834
88,750	88,800	22,656	19,644	24,207	20,849
88,800	88,850	22,671	19,658	24,225	20,865
88,850	88,900	22,687	19,672	24,243	20,880
88,900	88,950	22,702	19,686	24,261	20,896
88,950	89,000	22,718	19,700	24,279	20,911

89,000

89,000	89,050	22,733	19,714	24,297	20,927
89,050	89,100	22,749	19,728	24,315	20,942
89,100	89,150	22,764	19,742	24,333	20,958
89,150	89,200	22,780	19,756	24,351	20,973
89,200	89,250	22,795	19,770	24,369	20,989
89,250	89,300	22,811	19,784	24,387	21,004
89,300	89,350	22,826	19,798	24,405	21,020
89,350	89,400	22,842	19,812	24,423	21,035
89,400	89,450	22,857	19,826	24,441	21,051
89,450	89,500	22,873	19,840	24,459	21,066
89,500	89,550	22,888	19,854	24,477	21,082
89,550	89,600	22,904	19,868	24,495	21,097
89,600	89,650	22,919	19,882	24,513	21,113
89,650	89,700	22,935	19,896	24,531	21,128
89,700	89,750	22,950	19,910	24,549	21,144
89,750	89,800	22,966	19,924	24,567	21,159
89,800	89,850	22,981	19,938	24,585	21,175
89,850	89,900	22,997	19,952	24,603	21,190
89,900	89,950	23,012	19,966	24,621	21,206
89,950	90,000	23,028	19,980	24,639	21,221

90,000

90,000	90,050	23,043	19,994	24,657	21,237
90,050	90,100	23,059	20,008	24,675	21,252
90,100	90,150	23,074	20,022	24,693	21,268
90,150	90,200	23,090	20,036	24,711	21,283
90,200	90,250	23,105	20,050	24,729	21,299
90,250	90,300	23,121	20,064	24,747	21,314
90,300	90,350	23,136	20,078	24,765	21,330
90,350	90,400	23,152	20,092	24,783	21,345
90,400	90,450	23,167	20,106	24,801	21,361
90,450	90,500	23,183	20,120	24,819	21,376
90,500	90,550	23,198	20,134	24,837	21,392
90,550	90,600	23,214	20,148	24,855	21,407
90,600	90,650	23,229	20,162	24,873	21,423
90,650	90,700	23,245	20,176	24,891	21,438
90,700	90,750	23,260	20,190	24,909	21,454
90,750	90,800	23,276	20,204	24,927	21,469
90,800	90,850	23,291	20,218	24,945	21,485
90,850	90,900	23,307	20,232	24,963	21,500
90,900	90,950	23,322	20,246	24,981	21,516
90,950	91,000	23,338	20,260	24,999	21,531

91,000

91,000	91,050	23,353	20,274	25,017	21,547
91,050	91,100	23,369	20,288	25,035	21,562
91,100	91,150	23,384	20,302	25,053	21,578
91,150	91,200	23,400	20,316	25,071	21,593
91,200	91,250	23,415	20,330	25,089	21,609
91,250	91,300	23,431	20,344	25,107	21,624
91,300	91,350	23,446	20,358	25,125	21,640
91,350	91,400	23,462	20,372	25,143	21,655
91,400	91,450	23,477	20,386	25,161	21,671
91,450	91,500	23,493	20,400	25,179	21,686
91,500	91,550	23,508	20,414	25,197	21,702
91,550	91,600	23,524	20,428	25,215	21,717
91,600	91,650	23,539	20,442	25,233	21,733
91,650	91,700	23,555	20,456	25,251	21,748
91,700	91,750	23,570	20,470	25,269	21,764
91,750	91,800	23,586	20,484	25,287	21,779
91,800	91,850	23,601	20,498	25,305	21,795
91,850	91,900	23,617	20,512	25,323	21,810
91,900	91,950	23,632	20,526	25,341	21,826
91,950	92,000	23,648	20,540	25,359	21,841

92,000

92,000	92,050	23,663	20,554	25,377	21,857
92,050	92,100	23,679	20,568	25,395	21,872
92,100	92,150	23,694	20,582	25,413	21,888
92,150	92,200	23,710	20,596	25,431	21,903
92,200	92,250	23,725	20,610	25,449	21,919
92,250	92,300	23,741	20,624	25,467	21,934
92,300	92,350	23,756	20,638	25,485	21,950
92,350	92,400	23,772	20,652	25,503	21,965
92,400	92,450	23,787	20,666	25,521	21,981
92,450	92,500	23,803	20,680	25,539	21,996
92,500	92,550	23,818	20,694	25,557	22,012
92,550	92,600	23,834	20,708	25,575	22,027
92,600	92,650	23,849	20,722	25,593	22,043
92,650	92,700	23,865	20,736	25,611	22,058
92,700	92,750	23,880	20,750	25,629	22,074
92,750	92,800	23,896	20,764	25,647	22,089
92,800	92,850	23,911	20,778	25,665	22,105
92,850	92,900	23,927	20,792	25,683	22,120
92,900	92,950	23,942	20,806	25,701	22,136
92,950	93,000	23,958	20,820	25,719	22,151

93,000

93,000	93,050	23,973	20,834	25,737	22,167
93,050	93,100	23,989	20,848	25,755	22,182
93,100	93,150	24,004	20,862	25,773	22,198
93,150	93,200	24,020	20,876	25,791	22,213
93,200	93,250	24,035	20,890	25,809	22,229
93,250	93,300	24,051	20,904	25,827	22,244
93,300	93,350	24,066	20,918	25,845	22,260
93,350	93,400	24,082	20,932	25,863	22,275
93,400	93,450	24,097	20,946	25,881	22,291
93,450	93,500	24,113	20,960	25,899	22,306
93,500	93,550	24,128	20,974	25,917	22,322
93,550	93,600	24,144	20,988	25,935	22,337
93,600	93,650	24,159	21,002	25,953	22,353
93,650	93,700	24,175	21,016	25,971	22,368
93,700	93,750	24,190	21,030	25,989	22,384
93,750	93,800	24,206	21,044	26,007	22,399
93,800	93,850	24,221	21,058	26,025	22,415
93,850	93,900	24,237	21,072	26,043	22,430
93,900	93,950	24,252	21,086	26,061	22,446
93,950	94,000	24,268	21,100	26,079	22,461

94,000

94,000	94,050	24,283	21,114	26,097	22,477
94,050	94,100	24,299	21,128	26,115	22,492
94,100	94,150	24,314	21,142	26,133	22,508
94,150	94,200	24,330	21,156	26,151	22,523
94,200	94,250	24,345	21,170	26,169	22,539
94,250	94,300	24,361	21,184	26,187	22,554
94,300	94,350	24,376	21,198	26,205	22,570
94,350	94,400	24,392	21,212	26,223	22,585
94,400	94,450	24,407	21,226	26,241	22,601
94,450	94,500	24,423	21,240	26,259	22,616
94,500	94,550	24,438	21,254	26,277	22,632
94,550	94,600	24,454	21,268	26,295	22,647
94,600	94,650	24,469	21,282	26,313	22,663
94,650	94,700	24,485	21,296	26,331	22,678
94,700	94,750	24,500	21,310	26,349	22,694
94,750	94,800	24,516	21,324	26,367	22,709
94,800	94,850	24,531	21,338	26,385	22,725
94,850	94,900	24,547	21,352	26,403	22,740
94,900	94,950	24,562	21,366	26,421	22,756
94,950	95,000	24,578	21,380	26,439	22,771

* This column must also be used by a qualifying widow(er).

Continued on next page

1996 Tax Table—*Continued*

If line 37 (taxable income) is—		And you are—				If line 37 (taxable income) is—		And you are—			
At least	But less than	Single	Married filing jointly *	Married filing separately	Head of a house-hold	At least	But less than	Single	Married filing jointly *	Married filing separately	Head of a house-hold
		Your tax is—						Your tax is—			
95,000						**98,000**					
95,000	95,050	24,593	21,394	26,457	22,787	98,000	98,050	25,523	22,268	27,537	23,717
95,050	95,100	24,609	21,408	26,475	22,802	98,050	98,100	25,539	22,283	27,555	23,732
95,100	95,150	24,624	21,422	26,493	22,818	98,100	98,150	25,554	22,299	27,573	23,748
95,150	95,200	24,640	21,436	26,511	22,833	98,150	98,200	25,570	22,314	27,591	23,763
95,200	95,250	24,655	21,450	26,529	22,849	98,200	98,250	25,585	22,330	27,609	23,779
95,250	95,300	24,671	21,464	26,547	22,864	98,250	98,300	25,601	22,345	27,627	23,794
95,300	95,350	24,686	21,478	26,565	22,880	98,300	98,350	25,616	22,361	27,645	23,810
95,350	95,400	24,702	21,492	26,583	22,895	98,350	98,400	25,632	22,376	27,663	23,825
95,400	95,450	24,717	21,506	26,601	22,911	98,400	98,450	25,647	22,392	27,681	23,841
95,450	95,500	24,733	21,520	26,619	22,926	98,450	98,500	25,663	22,407	27,699	23,856
95,500	95,550	24,748	21,534	26,637	22,942	98,500	98,550	25,678	22,423	27,717	23,872
95,550	95,600	24,764	21,548	26,655	22,957	98,550	98,600	25,694	22,438	27,735	23,887
95,600	95,650	24,779	21,562	26,673	22,973	98,600	98,650	25,709	22,454	27,753	23,903
95,650	95,700	24,795	21,576	26,691	22,988	98,650	98,700	25,725	22,469	27,771	23,918
95,700	95,750	24,810	21,590	26,709	23,004	98,700	98,750	25,740	22,485	27,789	23,934
95,750	95,800	24,826	21,604	26,727	23,019	98,750	98,800	25,756	22,500	27,807	23,949
95,800	95,850	24,841	21,618	26,745	23,035	98,800	98,850	25,771	22,516	27,825	23,965
95,850	95,900	24,857	21,632	26,763	23,050	98,850	98,900	25,787	22,531	27,843	23,980
95,900	95,950	24,872	21,646	26,781	23,066	98,900	98,950	25,802	22,547	27,861	23,996
95,950	96,000	24,888	21,660	26,799	23,081	98,950	99,000	25,818	22,562	27,879	24,011
96,000						**99,000**					
96,000	96,050	24,903	21,674	26,817	23,097	99,000	99,050	25,833	22,578	27,897	24,027
96,050	96,100	24,919	21,688	26,835	23,112	99,050	99,100	25,849	22,593	27,915	24,042
96,100	96,150	24,934	21,702	26,853	23,128	99,100	99,150	25,864	22,609	27,933	24,058
96,150	96,200	24,950	21,716	26,871	23,143	99,150	99,200	25,880	22,624	27,951	24,073
96,200	96,250	24,965	21,730	26,889	23,159	99,200	99,250	25,895	22,640	27,969	24,089
96,250	96,300	24,981	21,744	26,907	23,174	99,250	99,300	25,911	22,655	27,987	24,104
96,300	96,350	24,996	21,758	26,925	23,190	99,300	99,350	25,926	22,671	28,005	24,120
96,350	96,400	25,012	21,772	26,943	23,205	99,350	99,400	25,942	22,686	28,023	24,135
96,400	96,450	25,027	21,786	26,961	23,221	99,400	99,450	25,957	22,702	28,041	24,151
96,450	96,500	25,043	21,800	26,979	23,236	99,450	99,500	25,973	22,717	28,059	24,166
96,500	96,550	25,058	21,814	26,997	23,252	99,500	99,550	25,988	22,733	28,077	24,182
96,550	96,600	25,074	21,828	27,015	23,267	99,550	99,600	26,004	22,748	28,095	24,197
96,600	96,650	25,089	21,842	27,033	23,283	99,600	99,650	26,019	22,764	28,113	24,213
96,650	96,700	25,105	21,856	27,051	23,298	99,650	99,700	26,035	22,779	28,131	24,228
96,700	96,750	25,120	21,870	27,069	23,314	99,700	99,750	26,050	22,795	28,149	24,244
96,750	96,800	25,136	21,884	27,087	23,329	99,750	99,800	26,066	22,810	28,167	24,259
96,800	96,850	25,151	21,898	27,105	23,345	99,800	99,850	26,081	22,826	28,185	24,275
96,850	96,900	25,167	21,912	27,123	23,360	99,850	99,900	26,097	22,841	28,203	24,290
96,900	96,950	25,182	21,927	27,141	23,376	99,900	99,950	26,112	22,857	28,221	24,306
96,950	97,000	25,198	21,942	27,159	23,391	99,950	100,000	26,128	22,872	28,239	24,321
97,000											
97,000	97,050	25,213	21,958	27,177	23,407						
97,050	97,100	25,229	21,973	27,195	23,422						
97,100	97,150	25,244	21,989	27,213	23,438						
97,150	97,200	25,260	22,004	27,231	23,453						
97,200	97,250	25,275	22,020	27,249	23,469						
97,250	97,300	25,291	22,035	27,267	23,484						
97,300	97,350	25,306	22,051	27,285	23,500			$100,000 or over — use the Tax Rate Schedules on page A-2			
97,350	97,400	25,322	22,066	27,303	23,515						
97,400	97,450	25,337	22,082	27,321	23,531						
97,450	97,500	25,353	22,097	27,339	23,546						
97,500	97,550	25,368	22,113	27,357	23,562						
97,550	97,600	25,384	22,128	27,375	23,577						
97,600	97,650	25,399	22,144	27,393	23,593						
97,650	97,700	25,415	22,159	27,411	23,608						
97,700	97,750	25,430	22,175	27,429	23,624						
97,750	97,800	25,446	22,190	27,447	23,639						
97,800	97,850	25,461	22,206	27,465	23,655						
97,850	97,900	25,477	22,221	27,483	23,670						
97,900	97,950	25,492	22,237	27,501	23,686						
97,950	98,000	25,508	22,252	27,519	23,701						

* This column must also be used by a qualifying widow(er).

APPENDIX B
Tax Forms

Form 1040EZ	Income Tax Return for Single and Joint Filers With No Dependents	**B–3**
Form 1040A	U.S. Individual Income Tax Return (Short Form)	**B–5**
Schedule 1	Interest and Dividend Income	**B–7**
Form 1040	U.S. Individual Income Tax Return	**B–8**
Schedules A & B	Itemized Deductions; Interest and Dividend Income	**B–10**
Schedule C	Profit or Loss from Business	**B–12**
Schedule D	Capital Gains and Losses	**B–14**
Schedule E	Supplemental Income and Loss	**B–16**
Schedule EIC	Earned Income Credit	**B–18**
Schedule R	Credit for the Elderly or the Disabled	**B–20**
Schedule SE	Self-Employment Tax	**B–22**
Form 1040-ES	Estimated Tax for Individuals	**B–24**
Form 2106	Employee Business Expenses	**B–30**
Form 2106-EZ	Unreimbursed Employee Business Expenses	**B–32**
Form 2119	Sale of Your Home	**B–33**
Form 2120	Multiple Support Declaration	**B–34**
Form 2210	Underpayment of Estimated Tax by Individuals, Estates, and Trusts	**B–35**
Form 2441	Child and Dependent Care Expenses	**B–38**

Form 3800	General Business Credit	B–40
Form 3903	Moving Expenses	B–42
Form 4255	Recapture of Investment Credit	B–44
Form 4562	Depreciation and Amortization	B–46
Form 4684	Casualties and Thefts	B–48
Form 4797	Sales of Business Property	B–50
Form 4868	Application for Automatic Extension of Time to File U.S. Individual Income Tax Return	B–52
Form 4952	Investment Interest Expense Deduction	B–56
Form 4972	Tax on Lump-Sum Distributions	B–58
Form 6251	Alternative Minimum Tax—Individuals	B–60
Form 6252	Installment Sale Income	B–61
Form 8283	Noncash Charitable Contributions	B–62
Form 8332	Release of Claim to Exemption for Child of Divorced or Separated Parents	B–64
Form 8582	Passive Activity Loss Limitations	B–65
Form 8606	Nondeductible IRAs (Contributions, Distributions, and Basis)	B–68
Form 8615	Tax for Children Under Age 14 Who Have Investment Income of More Than $1,300	B–70
Form 8824	Like-Kind Exchanges	B–72
Form 8829	Expenses for Business Use of Your Home	B–74

Tax Forms   B–3

Department of the Treasury—Internal Revenue Service

Form 1040EZ **Income Tax Return for Single and Joint Filers With No Dependents** (99) **1996**   OMB No. 1545-0675

Use the IRS label here

Your first name and initial — Last name

If a joint return, spouse's first name and initial — Last name

Home address (number and street). If you have a P.O. box, see page 7. — Apt. no.

City, town or post office, state, and ZIP code. If you have a foreign address, see page 7.

Your social security number

Spouse's social security number

Presidential Election Campaign (See page 7.)

Note: *Checking "Yes" will not change your tax or reduce your refund.*

Do you want $3 to go to this fund? ▶ Yes ☐ No ☐

If a joint return, does your spouse want $3 to go to this fund? ▶ Yes ☐ No ☐

Dollars | Cents

Income

Attach Copy B of Form(s) W-2 here. Enclose, but do not attach, any payment with your return.

1 Total wages, salaries, and tips. This should be shown in box 1 of your W-2 form(s). Attach your W-2 form(s).   1

2 Taxable interest income of $400 or less. If the total is over $400, you cannot use Form 1040EZ.   2

3 Unemployment compensation (see page 9).   3

4 Add lines 1, 2, and 3. This is your **adjusted gross income.** If under $9,500, see page 9 to find out if you can claim the earned income credit on line 8.   4

Note: *You must check Yes or No.*

5 Can your parents (or someone else) claim you on their return?
   Yes. Enter amount from worksheet on back.   **No.** If **single,** enter 6,550.00. If **married,** enter 11,800.00. See back for explanation.   5

6 Subtract line 5 from line 4. If line 5 is larger than line 4, enter 0. This is your **taxable income.** ▶ 6

Payments and tax

7 Enter your Federal income tax withheld from box 2 of your W-2 form(s).   7

8 **Earned income credit** (see page 9). Enter type and amount of nontaxable earned income below.
   Type _____ $ _____   8

9 Add lines 7 and 8 (do not include nontaxable earned income). These are your **total payments.**   9

10 **Tax.** Use the amount on **line 6** to find your tax in the tax table on pages 20–24 of the booklet. Then, enter the tax from the table on this line.   10

Refund

Have it sent directly to your bank account! See page 13 and fill in 11b, c, and d.

11a If line 9 is larger than line 10, subtract line 10 from line 9. This is your **refund.**   11a

▶ b Routing number

▶ c Type
   Checking ☐   Savings ☐

d Account number

Amount you owe

12 If line 10 is larger than line 9, subtract line 9 from line 10. This is the **amount you owe.** See page 13 for details on how to pay and what to write on your payment.   12

I have read this return. Under penalties of perjury, I declare that to the best of my knowledge and belief, the return is true, correct, and accurately lists all amounts and sources of income I received during the tax year.

Sign here

Keep copy for your records.

Your signature — Spouse's signature if joint return

Date — Your occupation — Date — Spouse's occupation

For Official Use Only

For Privacy Act and Paperwork Reduction Act Notice, see page 5.   Cat. No. 11329W   Form 1040EZ (1996)

1996 Form 1040EZ page 2

Use this form if
- Your filing status is single or married filing jointly.
- You do not claim any dependents.
- You had **only** wages, salaries, tips, taxable scholarship or fellowship grants, unemployment compensation, or Alaska Permanent Fund dividends, and your taxable interest income was $400 or less. **But** if you earned tips, including allocated tips, that are not included in box 5 and box 7 of your W-2, you may not be able to use Form 1040EZ. See page 8.
- You did not receive any advance earned income credit payments.
- You (and your spouse if married) were under 65 on January 1, 1997, and not blind at the end of 1996.
- Your taxable income (line 6) is less than $50,000.

If you are not sure about your filing status, see page 7. If you have questions about dependents, use Tele-Tax topic 354 (see page 18). If you **can't use this form,** use Tele-Tax topic 352 (see page 18).

Filling in your return
For tips on how to avoid common mistakes, see page 3.

Because this form is read by a machine, please print your numbers inside the boxes like this:

`9 8 7 6 5 4 3 2 1 0` Do not type your numbers. Do not use dollar signs.

If you received a scholarship or fellowship grant or tax-exempt interest income, such as on municipal bonds, see the booklet before filling in the form. Also, see the booklet if you received a Form 1099-INT showing income tax withheld or if tax was withheld from your Alaska Permanent Fund dividends.

Remember, you must report all wages, salaries, and tips even if you do not get a W-2 form from your employer. You must also report all your taxable interest income, including interest from banks, savings and loans, credit unions, etc., even if you do not get a Form 1099-INT.

Worksheet for dependents who checked "Yes" on line 5

Use this worksheet to figure the amount to enter on line 5 if someone can claim you (or your spouse if married) as a dependent, even if that person chooses not to do so. To find out if someone can claim you as a dependent, use Tele-Tax topic 354 (see page 18).

- **A.** Enter the amount from line 1 on the front. **A.** _____
- **B.** Minimum standard deduction. **B.** 650.00
- **C.** Enter the LARGER of line A or line B here. **C.** _____
- **D.** Maximum standard deduction. If single, enter 4,000.00; if married, enter 6,700.00. **D.** _____
- **E.** Enter the SMALLER of line C or line D here. This is your standard deduction. **E.** _____
- **F.** Exemption amount.
  - If single, enter 0.
  - If married and both you and your spouse can be claimed as dependents, enter 0.
  - If married and only one of you can be claimed as a dependent, enter 2,550.00. **F.** _____
- **G.** Add lines E and F. Enter the total here and on line 5 on the front. **G.** _____

If you checked "No" on line 5 because no one can claim you (or your spouse if married) as a dependent, enter on line 5 the amount shown below that applies to you.

- Single, enter 6,550.00. This is the total of your standard deduction (4,000.00) and personal exemption (2,550.00).
- Married, enter 11,800.00. This is the total of your standard deduction (6,700.00), exemption for yourself (2,550.00), and exemption for your spouse (2,550.00).

Mailing your return

Mail your return by **April 15, 1997.** Use the envelope that came with your booklet. If you do not have that envelope, see page 28 for the address to use.

Paid preparer's use only

See page 14.

Under penalties of perjury, I declare that I have examined this return, and to the best of my knowledge and belief, it is true, correct, and accurately lists all amounts and sources of income received during the tax year. This declaration is based on all information of which I have any knowledge.

| Preparer's signature ▶ | Date | Check if self-employed ☐ | Preparer's SSN |

| Firm's name (or yours if self-employed) and address ▶ | | EIN | |
| | | ZIP code | |

Tax Forms B–5

Form 1040A (99)   Department of the Treasury—Internal Revenue Service
U.S. Individual Income Tax Return 1996   IRS Use Only—Do not write or staple in this space.

OMB No. 1545-0085

Label (See page 15.) Use the IRS label. Otherwise, please print in **ALL CAPITAL LETTERS**.

LABEL HERE

- Your first name / Init. / Last name
- If a joint return, spouse's first name / Init. / Last name
- Home address (number and street). If you have a P.O. box, see page 15. / Apt. no.
- City, town or post office. If you have a foreign address, see page 15. / State / ZIP code

Your social security number

Spouse's social security number

For Privacy Act and Paperwork Reduction Act Notice, see page 9.

Presidential Election Campaign Fund (See page 15.)   Yes   No
Do you want $3 to go to this fund?
If a joint return, does your spouse want $3 to go to this fund?

Note: Checking "Yes" will not change your tax or reduce your refund.

1 ☐ Single
2 ☐ Married filing joint return (even if only one had income)
3 ☐ Married filing separate return. Enter spouse's social security number above and full name here. ▶
4 ☐ Head of household (with qualifying person). (See page 16.) If the qualifying person is a child but not your dependent, enter this child's name here. ▶
5 ☐ Qualifying widow(er) with dependent child (year spouse died ▶ 19). (See page 16.)

6a ☐ **Yourself.** If your parent (or someone else) can claim you as a dependent on his or her tax return, **do not** check box 6a.
 b ☐ **Spouse**

 c **Dependents.** If more than six dependents, see page 17.

(1) First name Last name	(2) Dependent's social security number. If born in Dec. 1996, see page 18.	(3) Dependent's relationship to you	(4) No. of months lived in your home in 1996

No. of boxes checked on lines 6a and 6b

No. of your children on line 6c who:
• lived with you
• did not live with you due to divorce or separation (see page 18)

Dependents on 6c not entered above

Add numbers entered in boxes above

 d Total number of exemptions claimed ▶

7 Wages, salaries, tips, etc. This should be shown in box 1 of your W-2 form(s). Attach Form(s) W-2.   **7 $**

8a Taxable interest income. If over $400, attach Schedule 1.   **8a $**
 b Tax-exempt interest. DO NOT include on line 8a.   **8b $**

9 Dividends. If over $400, attach Schedule 1.   **9 $**

10a Total IRA distributions.   **10a $**   10b Taxable amount (see page 20).   **10b $**

11a Total pensions and annuities.   **11a $**   11b Taxable amount (see page 20).   **11b $**

12 Unemployment compensation.   **12 $**

13a Social security benefits.   **13a $**   13b Taxable amount (see page 22).   **13b $**

14 Add lines 7 through 13b (far right column). This is your **total income.** ▶   **14 $**

15a Your IRA deduction (see page 22).   **15a $**
 b Spouse's IRA deduction (see page 22).   **15b $**
 c Add lines 15a and 15b. These are your **total adjustments.**   **15c $**

16 Subtract line 15c from line 14. This is your **adjusted gross income.** If under $28,495 (under $9,500 if a child did not live with you), see the instructions for line 29c on page 29. ▶   **16 $**

Attach Copy B of W-2 and 1099-R here.   Cat. No. 11327A   1996 Form 1040A page 1

1996 Form 1040A page 2

17	Enter the amount from line 16.	17 $
18a	Check if: ☐ You were 65 or older ☐ Blind / ☐ Spouse was 65 or older ☐ Blind Enter number of boxes checked ▶ 18a	
b	If you are married filing separately and your spouse itemizes deductions, see page 26 and check here . . . . ▶ 18b ☐	
19	Enter the **standard deduction** for your filing status. **But** see page 26 if you checked any box on line 18a or b **OR** someone can claim you as a dependent. • Single—4,000 • Married filing jointly or Qualifying widow(er)—6,700 • Head of household—5,900 • Married filing separately—3,350	19 $
20	Subtract line 19 from line 17. If line 19 is more than line 17, enter 0.	20 $
21	Multiply $2,550 by the total number of exemptions claimed on line 6d.	21 $
22	Subtract line 21 from line 20. If line 21 is more than line 20, enter 0. This is your **taxable income. If you want the IRS to figure your tax, see page 26.** ▶	22 $
23	Find the tax on the amount on line 22 (see page 26).	23 $
24a	Credit for child and dependent care expenses. Attach Schedule 2. 24a $	
b	Credit for the elderly or the disabled. Attach Schedule 3. 24b $	
c	Add lines 24a and 24b. These are your **total credits.**	24c $
25	Subtract line 24c from line 23. If line 24c is more than line 23, enter 0.	25 $
26	Advance earned income credit payments from Form(s) W-2.	26 $
27	Household employment taxes. Attach Schedule H.	27 $
28	Add lines 25, 26, and 27. This is your **total tax.** ▶	28 $
29a	Total Federal income tax withheld from Forms W-2 and 1099. 29a $	
b	1996 estimated tax payments and amount applied from 1995 return. 29b $	
c	**Earned income credit.** Attach Schedule EIC if you have a qualifying child. 29c $ Nontaxable earned income: amount ▶ $ and type ▶	
d	Add lines 29a, 29b, and 29c (do not include nontaxable earned income). These are your **total payments.** ▶	29d $
30	If line 29d is more than line 28, subtract line 28 from line 29d. This is the amount you **overpaid.**	30 $
31a	Amount of line 30 you want **refunded to you.** If you want it sent directly to your bank account, see page 35 and fill in 31b, c, and d.	31a $
b	Routing number	
	c Type: ☐ Checking ☐ Savings	
d	Account number	
32	Amount of line 30 you want **applied to your 1997 estimated tax.** 32 $	
33	If line 28 is more than line 29d, subtract line 29d from line 28. This is the **amount you owe.** For details on how to pay, including what to write on your payment, see page 36.	33 $
34	Estimated tax penalty (see page 36). 34 $	

Sign here

Under penalties of perjury, I declare that I have examined this return and accompanying schedules and statements, and to the best of my knowledge and belief, they are true, correct, and accurately list all amounts and sources of income I received during the tax year. Declaration of preparer (other than the taxpayer) is based on all information of which the preparer has any knowledge.

▶ Your signature   Date   Your occupation

Keep a copy of this return for your records.

▶ Spouse's signature. If joint return, BOTH must sign.   Date   Spouse's occupation

Paid preparer's use only

Preparer's signature ▶   Date   Check if self-employed ☐   Preparer's SSN

Firm's name (or yours if self-employed) and address ▶   EIN   ZIP code

1996 Form 1040A page 2

**Schedule 1
(Form 1040A)**
Department of the Treasury—Internal Revenue Service
(99) **Interest and Dividend Income for Form 1040A Filers**

1996

OMB No. 1545-0085

Name(s) shown on Form 1040A: First and initial(s) | Last | Your social security number

Part I Interest Income (See pages 19 and 50.)

Note: *If you received a Form 1099–INT, Form 1099–OID, or substitute statement from a brokerage firm, enter the firm's name and the total interest shown on that form.*

1 List name of payer. If any interest is from a seller-financed mortgage and the buyer used the property as a personal residence, see page 50 and list this interest first. Also, show that buyer's social security number and address.

Amount

1 $
$
$
$
$
$
$
$
$
$
$

2 Add the amounts on line 1. 2 $

3 Excludable interest on series EE U.S. savings bonds issued after 1989 from Form 8815, line 14. You **must** attach Form 8815 to Form 1040A. 3 $

4 Subtract line 3 from line 2. Enter the result here and on Form 1040A, line 8a. 4 $

Part II Dividend Income (See pages 20 and 50.)

Note: *If you received a Form 1099–DIV or substitute statement from a brokerage firm, enter the firm's name and the total dividends shown on that form.*

5 List name of payer

Amount

5 $
$
$
$
$
$
$
$
$
$
$

6 Add the amounts on line 5. Enter the total here and on Form 1040A, line 9. 6 $

For Paperwork Reduction Act Notice, see Form 1040A instructions. Cat. No. 12075R 1996 Schedule 1 (Form 1040A)

Appendix B

Form 1040 — Department of the Treasury—Internal Revenue Service
U.S. Individual Income Tax Return **1996** (99) IRS Use Only—Do not write or staple in this space.

For the year Jan. 1–Dec. 31, 1996, or other tax year beginning , 1996, ending , 19   OMB No. 1545-0074

Label (See page 11.)

Your first name and initial | Last name | Your social security number

If a joint return, spouse's first name and initial | Last name | Spouse's social security number

Use the IRS label. Otherwise, please print or type.

Home address (number and street). If you have a P.O. box, see page 11. | Apt. no.

For help finding line instructions, see pages 2 and 3 in the booklet.

City, town or post office, state, and ZIP code. If you have a foreign address, see page 11.

Presidential Election Campaign (See page 11.) ▶

Do you want $3 to go to this fund? . . . .   Yes | No
If a joint return, does your spouse want $3 to go to this fund? . . . . .

Note: Checking "Yes" will not change your tax or reduce your refund.

Filing Status
Check only one box.

1 Single
2 Married filing joint return (even if only one had income)
3 Married filing separate return. Enter spouse's social security no. above and full name here. ▶
4 Head of household (with qualifying person). (See instructions.) If the qualifying person is a child but not your dependent, enter this child's name here. ▶
5 Qualifying widow(er) with dependent child (year spouse died ▶ 19   ). (See instructions.)

Exemptions

6a ☐ **Yourself.** If your parent (or someone else) can claim you as a dependent on his or her tax return, **do not** check box 6a . . . .

b ☐ **Spouse** . . . .

c **Dependents:**
(1) First name   Last name | (2) Dependent's social security number. If born in Dec. 1996, see inst. | (3) Dependent's relationship to you | (4) No. of months lived in your home in 1996

If more than six dependents, see the instructions for line 6c.

No. of boxes checked on lines 6a and 6b ___
No. of your children on line 6c who:
• lived with you ___
• did not live with you due to divorce or separation (see instructions) ___
Dependents on 6c not entered above ___
Add numbers entered on lines above ▶ ☐

d Total number of exemptions claimed . . . .

Income

Attach Copy B of your Forms W-2, W-2G, and 1099-R here.

If you did not get a W-2, see the instructions for line 7.

Enclose, but do not attach, any payment. Also, please enclose Form 1040-V (see the instructions for line 62).

7   Wages, salaries, tips, etc. Attach Form(s) W-2 . . . . | 7
8a Taxable interest. Attach Schedule B if over $400 . . . . . . | 8a
b   Tax-exempt interest. DO NOT include on line 8a   . . | 8b |
9   Dividend income. Attach Schedule B if over $400 . . . . . . | 9
10 Taxable refunds, credits, or offsets of state and local income taxes (see instructions) | 10
11 Alimony received . . . . | 11
⑫ Business income or (loss). Attach Schedule C or C-EZ . . . . | ⑫
⑬ Capital gain or (loss). If required, attach Schedule D | 13
⑭ Other gains or (losses). Attach Form 4797 . . . . | 14
15a Total IRA distributions . . | 15a | b Taxable amount (see inst.) | 15b
16a Total pensions and annuities | 16a | b Taxable amount (see inst.) | 16b
⑰ Rental real estate, royalties, partnerships, S corporations, trusts, etc. Attach Schedule E | 17
18 Farm income or (loss). Attach Schedule F . . . . | 18
19 Unemployment compensation . . . . | 19
20a Social security benefits . | 20a | b Taxable amount (see inst.) | 20b
21 Other income. List type and amount—see instructions _____ | 21
22 Add the amounts in the far right column for lines 7 through 21. This is your **total income** ▶ | 22

Adjusted Gross Income

If line 31 is under $28,495 (under $9,500 if a child did not live with you), see the instructions for line 54.

㉓a Your IRA deduction (see instructions) . . . . . . | 23a
b   Spouse's IRA deduction (see instructions) . . . . . | 23b
㉔ Moving expenses. Attach Form 3903 or 3903-F . . . | 24
㉕ One-half of self-employment tax. Attach Schedule SE . | 25
26 Self-employed health insurance deduction (see inst.) . . | 26
㉗ Keogh & self-employed SEP plans. If SEP, check ▶ ☐ | 27
㉘ Penalty on early withdrawal of savings . . . . . . | 28
㉙ Alimony paid. Recipient's SSN ▶ _____ | 29
30 Add lines 23a through 29 . . . . | 30
31 Subtract line 30 from line 22. This is your **adjusted gross income** . . . . . . ▶ | 31

For Privacy Act and Paperwork Reduction Act Notice, see page 7.   Cat. No. 11320B   Form **1040** (1996)

Form 1040 (1996) Page **2**

Tax Computation

32	Amount from line 31 (adjusted gross income)	32	
33a	Check if: ☐ **You** were 65 or older, ☐ Blind; ☐ **Spouse** was 65 or older, ☐ Blind. Add the number of boxes checked above and enter the total here ▶ 33a		
b	If you are married filing separately and your spouse itemizes deductions or you were a dual-status alien, see instructions and check here ▶ 33b ☐		
34	Enter the larger of your: **Itemized deductions** from Schedule A, line 28, **OR** **Standard deduction** shown below for your filing status. **But** see the instructions if you checked any box on line 33a or b **or** someone can claim you as a dependent. • Single—$4,000 • Married filing jointly or Qualifying widow(er)—$6,700 • Head of household—$5,900 • Married filing separately—$3,350	34	
35	Subtract line 34 from line 32	35	
36	If line 32 is $88,475 or less, multiply $2,550 by the total number of exemptions claimed on line 6d. If line 32 is over $88,475, see the worksheet in the inst. for the amount to enter	36	
37	**Taxable income.** Subtract line 36 from line 35. If line 36 is more than line 35, enter -0-	37	
38	**Tax.** See instructions. Check if total includes any tax from a ☐ Form(s) 8814 b ☐ Form 4972 ▶	38	

If you want the IRS to figure your tax, see the instructions for line 37.

Credits

39	Credit for child and dependent care expenses. Attach Form 2441	39	
40	Credit for the elderly or the disabled. Attach Schedule R	40	
41	Foreign tax credit. Attach Form 1116	41	
42	Other. Check if from a ☐ Form 3800 b ☐ Form 8396 c ☐ Form 8801 d ☐ Form (specify) _____	42	
43	Add lines 39 through 42	43	
44	Subtract line 43 from line 38. If line 43 is more than line 38, enter -0- ▶	44	

Other Taxes

45	Self-employment tax. Attach Schedule SE	45	
46	Alternative minimum tax. Attach Form 6251	46	
47	Social security and Medicare tax on tip income not reported to employer. Attach Form 4137	47	
48	Tax on qualified retirement plans, including IRAs. If required, attach Form 5329	48	
49	Advance earned income credit payments from Form(s) W-2	49	
50	Household employment taxes. Attach Schedule H	50	
51	Add lines 44 through 50. This is your **total tax** ▶	51	

Payments

Attach Forms W-2, W-2G, and 1099-R on the front.

52	Federal income tax withheld from Forms W-2 and 1099	52	
53	1996 estimated tax payments and amount applied from 1995 return	53	
54	**Earned income credit.** Attach Schedule EIC if you have a qualifying child. Nontaxable earned income: amount ▶ _____ and type ▶ _____	54	
55	Amount paid with Form 4868 (request for extension)	55	
56	Excess social security and RRTA tax withheld (see inst.)	56	
57	Other payments. Check if from a ☐ Form 2439 b ☐ Form 4136	57	
58	Add lines 52 through 57. These are your **total payments** ▶	58	

Refund

Have it sent directly to your bank account! See inst. and fill in 60b, c, and d.

59	If line 58 is more than line 51, subtract line 51 from line 58. This is the amount you **OVERPAID**	59	
60a	Amount of line 59 you want **REFUNDED TO YOU** ▶	60a	
▶ b	Routing number _____ c Type: ☐ Checking ☐ Savings		
▶ d	Account number _____		
61	Amount of line 59 you want **APPLIED TO YOUR 1997 ESTIMATED TAX** ▶	61	

Amount You Owe

62	If line 51 is more than line 58, subtract line 58 from line 51. This is the **AMOUNT YOU OWE**. For details on how to pay and use **Form 1040-V**, see instructions ▶	62	
63	Estimated tax penalty. Also include on line 62	63	

Sign Here

Keep a copy of this return for your records.

Under penalties of perjury, I declare that I have examined this return and accompanying schedules and statements, and to the best of my knowledge and belief, they are true, correct, and complete. Declaration of preparer (other than taxpayer) is based on all information of which preparer has any knowledge.

▶ Your signature | Date | Your occupation

▶ Spouse's signature. If a joint return, BOTH must sign. | Date | Spouse's occupation

Paid Preparer's Use Only

Preparer's signature ▶	Date	Check if self-employed ☐	Preparer's social security no.
Firm's name (or yours if self-employed) and address ▶		EIN	
		ZIP code	

Schedule A—Itemized Deductions

SCHEDULES A&B (Form 1040)
Department of the Treasury
Internal Revenue Service (99)

(Schedule B is on back)
▶ Attach to Form 1040. ▶ See Instructions for Schedules A and B (Form 1040).

OMB No. 1545-0074
1996
Attachment Sequence No. **07**

Name(s) shown on Form 1040 — Your social security number

Medical and Dental Expenses
Caution: *Do not include expenses reimbursed or paid by others.*
1. Medical and dental expenses (see page A-1)
2. Enter amount from Form 1040, line 32.
3. Multiply line 2 above by 7.5% (.075)
4. Subtract line 3 from line 1. If line 3 is more than line 1, enter -0-

Taxes You Paid
(See page A-1.)
5. State and local income taxes
6. Real estate taxes (see page A-2)
7. Personal property taxes
8. Other taxes. List type and amount ▶
9. Add lines 5 through 8

Interest You Paid
(See page A-2.)

Note: Personal interest is not deductible.

10. Home mortgage interest and points reported to you on Form 1098
11. Home mortgage interest not reported to you on Form 1098. If paid to the person from whom you bought the home, see page A-2 and show that person's name, identifying no., and address ▶
12. Points not reported to you on Form 1098. See page A-3 for special rules
13. Investment interest. If required, attach Form 4952. (See page A-3.)
14. Add lines 10 through 13

Gifts to Charity
If you made a gift and got a benefit for it, see page A-3.
15. Gifts by cash or check. If you made any gift of $250 or more, see page A-3
16. Other than by cash or check. If any gift of $250 or more, see page A-3. If over $500, you **MUST** attach Form 8283
17. Carryover from prior year
18. Add lines 15 through 17

Casualty and Theft Losses
19. Casualty or theft loss(es). Attach Form 4684. (See page A-4.)

Job Expenses and Most Other Miscellaneous Deductions
(See page A-4 for expenses to deduct here.)
20. Unreimbursed employee expenses—job travel, union dues, job education, etc. If required, you **MUST** attach Form 2106 or 2106-EZ. (See page A-4.) ▶
21. Tax preparation fees
22. Other expenses—investment, safe deposit box, etc. List type and amount ▶
23. Add lines 20 through 22
24. Enter amount from Form 1040, line 32.
25. Multiply line 24 above by 2% (.02)
26. Subtract line 25 from line 23. If line 25 is more than line 23, enter -0-

Other Miscellaneous Deductions
27. Other—from list on page A-4. List type and amount ▶

Total Itemized Deductions
28. Is Form 1040, line 32, over $117,950 (over $58,975 if married filing separately)?
    NO. Your deduction is not limited. Add the amounts in the far right column for lines 4 through 27. Also, enter on Form 1040, line 34, the **larger** of this amount or your standard deduction.
    YES. Your deduction may be limited. See page A-5 for the amount to enter.

For Paperwork Reduction Act Notice, see Form 1040 instructions. Cat. No. 11330X Schedule A (Form 1040) 1996

Schedules A&B (Form 1040) 1996   OMB No. 1545-0074   Page **2**

Name(s) shown on Form 1040. Do not enter name and social security number if shown on other side.   **Your social security number**

Schedule B—Interest and Dividend Income

Attachment Sequence No. 08

Part I
Interest Income

(See page B-1.)

Note: *If you had over $400 in taxable interest income, you must also complete Part III.*

1. List name of payer. If any interest is from a seller-financed mortgage and the buyer used the property as a personal residence, see page B-1 and list this interest first. Also, show that buyer's social security number and address ▶

   Amount

Note: If you received a Form 1099-INT, Form 1099-OID, or substitute statement from a brokerage firm, list the firm's name as the payer and enter the total interest shown on that form.

2. Add the amounts on line 1
3. Excludable interest on series EE U.S. savings bonds issued after 1989 from Form 8815, line 14. You MUST attach Form 8815 to Form 1040
4. Subtract line 3 from line 2. Enter the result here and on Form 1040, line 8a ▶

Part II
Dividend Income

(See page B-1.)

Note: *If you had over $400 in gross dividends and/or other distributions on stock, you must also complete Part III.*

5. List name of payer. Include gross dividends and/or other distributions on stock here. Any capital gain distributions and nontaxable distributions will be deducted on lines 7 and 8 ▶

   Amount

Note: If you received a Form 1099-DIV or substitute statement from a brokerage firm, list the firm's name as the payer and enter the total dividends shown on that form.

6. Add the amounts on line 5
7. Capital gain distributions. Enter here and on Schedule D*.
8. Nontaxable distributions. (See the inst. for Form 1040, line 9.)
9. Add lines 7 and 8
10. Subtract line 9 from line 6. Enter the result here and on Form 1040, line 9 ▶

    *If you do not need Schedule D to report any other gains or losses, see the instructions for Form 1040, line 13.

Part III
Foreign Accounts and Trusts

(See page B-1.)

You must complete this part if you **(a)** had over $400 of interest or dividends; **(b)** had a foreign account; or **(c)** received a distribution from, or were a grantor of, or a transferor to, a foreign trust.

    Yes   No

11a. At any time during 1996, did you have an interest in or a signature or other authority over a financial account in a foreign country, such as a bank account, securities account, or other financial account? See page B-1 for exceptions and filing requirements for Form TD F 90-22.1
 b. If "Yes," enter the name of the foreign country ▶
12. During 1996, did you receive a distribution from, or were you the grantor of, or transferor to, a foreign trust? If "Yes," see page B-2 for other forms you may have to file

For Paperwork Reduction Act Notice, see Form 1040 instructions.   Schedule B (Form 1040) 1996

SCHEDULE C (Form 1040)

Department of the Treasury
Internal Revenue Service (99)

Profit or Loss From Business
(Sole Proprietorship)

▶ Partnerships, joint ventures, etc., must file Form 1065.
▶ Attach to Form 1040 or Form 1041. ▶ See Instructions for Schedule C (Form 1040).

OMB No. 1545-0074

1996

Attachment Sequence No. 09

Name of proprietor | Social security number (SSN)

A	Principal business or profession, including product or service (see page C-1)	B Enter principal business code (see page C-6) ▶
C	Business name. If no separate business name, leave blank.	D Employer ID number (EIN), if any
E	Business address (including suite or room no.) ▶ .... City, town or post office, state, and ZIP code	
F	Accounting method: (1) ☐ Cash (2) ☐ Accrual (3) ☐ Other (specify) ▶	
G	Did you "materially participate" in the operation of this business during 1996? If "No," see page C-2 for limit on losses.	☐ Yes ☐ No
H	If you started or acquired this business during 1996, check here . . . . ▶ ☐	

Part I Income

1	Gross receipts or sales. **Caution:** If this income was reported to you on Form W-2 and the "Statutory employee" box on that form was checked, see page C-2 and check here . . . . . ▶ ☐	1	
2	Returns and allowances	2	
3	Subtract line 2 from line 1	3	
4	Cost of goods sold (from line 42 on page 2)	4	
5	**Gross profit.** Subtract line 4 from line 3	5	
6	Other income, including Federal and state gasoline or fuel tax credit or refund (see page C-2)	6	
7	**Gross income.** Add lines 5 and 6 ▶	7	

Part II Expenses. Enter expenses for business use of your home **only** on line 30.

8	Advertising	8		19 Pension and profit-sharing plans	19	
9	Bad debts from sales or services (see page C-3)	9		20 Rent or lease (see page C-4):		
				a Vehicles, machinery, and equipment	20a	
10	Car and truck expenses (see page C-3)	10		b Other business property	20b	
				21 Repairs and maintenance	21	
11	Commissions and fees	11		22 Supplies (not included in Part III)	22	
12	Depletion	12		23 Taxes and licenses	23	
13	Depreciation and section 179 expense deduction (not included in Part III) (see page C-3)	13		24 Travel, meals, and entertainment:		
				a Travel	24a	
				b Meals and entertainment		
14	Employee benefit programs (other than on line 19)	14		c Enter 50% of line 24b subject to limitations (see page C-4)		
15	Insurance (other than health)	15				
16	Interest:					
a	Mortgage (paid to banks, etc.)	16a		d Subtract line 24c from line 24b	24d	
b	Other	16b		25 Utilities	25	
17	Legal and professional services	17		26 Wages (less employment credits)	26	
				27 Other expenses (from line 48 on page 2)	27	
18	Office expense	18				
28	**Total expenses** before expenses for business use of home. Add lines 8 through 27 in columns ▶				28	
29	Tentative profit (loss). Subtract line 28 from line 7				29	
30	Expenses for business use of your home. Attach **Form 8829**				30	
31	**Net profit or (loss).** Subtract line 30 from line 29.					
	• If a profit, enter on **Form 1040, line 12,** and ALSO on **Schedule SE, line 2** (statutory employees, see page C-5). Estates and trusts, enter on Form 1041, line 3.				31	
	• If a loss, you MUST go on to line 32.					
32	If you have a loss, check the box that describes your investment in this activity (see page C-5).					
	• If you checked 32a, enter the loss on **Form 1040, line 12,** and ALSO on **Schedule SE, line 2** (statutory employees, see page C-5). Estates and trusts, enter on Form 1041, line 3.				32a ☐ All investment is at risk. 32b ☐ Some investment is not at risk.	
	• If you checked 32b, you MUST attach **Form 6198.**					

For Paperwork Reduction Act Notice, see Form 1040 instructions. Cat. No. 11334P Schedule C (Form 1040) 1996

Schedule C (Form 1040) 1996 Page **2**

Part III — Cost of Goods Sold (see page C-5)

33 Method(s) used to value closing inventory: **a** ☐ Cost   **b** ☐ Lower of cost or market   **c** ☐ Other (attach explanation)

34 Was there any change in determining quantities, costs, or valuations between opening and closing inventory? If "Yes," attach explanation . . . . ☐ Yes   ☐ No

35 Inventory at beginning of year. If different from last year's closing inventory, attach explanation . . | 35 |

36 Purchases less cost of items withdrawn for personal use . . . . | 36 |

37 Cost of labor. Do not include salary paid to yourself . . . . | 37 |

38 Materials and supplies . . . . | 38 |

39 Other costs . . . . | 39 |

40 Add lines 35 through 39 . . . . | 40 |

41 Inventory at end of year . . . . | 41 |

42 **Cost of goods sold.** Subtract line 41 from line 40. Enter the result here and on page 1, line 4 . . | 42 |

Part IV — Information on Your Vehicle. Complete this part **ONLY** if you are claiming car or truck expenses on line 10 and are not required to file Form 4562 for this business. See the instructions for line 13 on page C-3 to find out if you must file.

43 When did you place your vehicle in service for business purposes? (month, day, year) ▶ ..../......./....... .

44 Of the total number of miles you drove your vehicle during 1996, enter the number of miles you used your vehicle for:

   a Business ....   **b** Commuting ....   **c** Other ....

45 Do you (or your spouse) have another vehicle available for personal use? . . . . ☐ Yes   ☐ No

46 Was your vehicle available for use during off-duty hours? . . . . ☐ Yes   ☐ No

47a Do you have evidence to support your deduction? . . . . ☐ Yes   ☐ No

   b If "Yes," is the evidence written? . . . . ☐ Yes   ☐ No

Part V — Other Expenses. List below business expenses not included on lines 8–26 or line 30.

48 **Total other expenses.** Enter here and on page 1, line 27 . . . . | 48 |

SCHEDULE D
(Form 1040)

Department of the Treasury
Internal Revenue Service (99)

Capital Gains and Losses

▶ Attach to Form 1040. ▶ See Instructions for Schedule D (Form 1040).
▶ Use lines 20 and 22 for more space to list transactions for lines 1 and 9.

OMB No. 1545-0074

1996

Attachment Sequence No. **12**

Name(s) shown on Form 1040

Your social security number

Part I — Short-Term Capital Gains and Losses—Assets Held One Year or Less

	(a) Description of property (Example: 100 sh. XYZ Co.)	(b) Date acquired (Mo., day, yr.)	(c) Date sold (Mo., day, yr.)	(d) Sales price (see page D-3)	(e) Cost or other basis (see page D-3)	(f) LOSS If (e) is more than (d), subtract (d) from (e)	(g) GAIN If (d) is more than (e), subtract (e) from (d)
1							
2	Enter your short-term totals, if any, from line 21		2				
3	**Total short-term sales price amounts.** Add column (d) of lines 1 and 2 . . .		3				
4	Short-term gain from Forms 2119 and 6252, and short-term gain or loss from Forms 4684, 6781, and 8824				4		
5	Net short-term gain or loss from partnerships, S corporations, estates, and trusts from Schedule(s) K-1				5		
6	Short-term capital loss carryover. Enter the amount, if any, from line 9 of your 1995 Capital Loss Carryover Worksheet				6		
7	Add lines 1 through 6 in columns (f) and (g)				7	( )	
8	**Net short-term capital gain or (loss).** Combine columns (f) and (g) of line 7 . . . . . ▶				8		

Part II — Long-Term Capital Gains and Losses—Assets Held More Than One Year

9							
10	Enter your long-term totals, if any, from line 23		10				
11	**Total long-term sales price amounts.** Add column (d) of lines 9 and 10 . . .		11				
12	Gain from Form 4797; long-term gain from Forms 2119, 2439, and 6252; and long-term gain or loss from Forms 4684, 6781, and 8824				12		
13	Net long-term gain or loss from partnerships, S corporations, estates, and trusts from Schedule(s) K-1				13		
14	Capital gain distributions				14		
15	Long-term capital loss carryover. Enter the amount, if any, from line 14 of your 1995 Capital Loss Carryover Worksheet				15		
16	Add lines 9 through 15 in columns (f) and (g)				16	( )	
17	**Net long-term capital gain or (loss).** Combine columns (f) and (g) of line 16 . . . . . ▶				17		

Part III — Summary of Parts I and II

18	Combine lines 8 and 17. If a loss, go to line 19. If a gain, enter the gain on Form 1040, line 13. **Note:** *If both lines 17 and 18 are gains, see the **Capital Gain Tax Worksheet** on page 23* . .	18
19	If line 18 is a loss, enter here and as a (loss) on Form 1040, line 13, the **smaller** of these losses:	
a	The loss on line 18; **or**	
b	($3,000) or, if married filing separately, ($1,500)	19 ( )
	Note: *See the **Capital Loss Carryover Worksheet** on page D-3 if the loss on line 18 exceeds the loss on line 19 **or** if Form 1040, line 35, is a loss.*	

For Paperwork Reduction Act Notice, see Form 1040 instructions.   Cat. No. 11338H   Schedule D (Form 1040) 1996

Schedule D (Form 1040) 1996 — Attachment Sequence No. **12** — Page **2**

Name(s) shown on Form 1040. Do not enter name and social security number if shown on other side. | Your social security number

Part IV — Short-Term Capital Gains and Losses—Assets Held One Year or Less *(Continuation of Part I)*

(a) Description of property (Example: 100 sh. XYZ Co.)	(b) Date acquired (Mo., day, yr.)	(c) Date sold (Mo., day, yr.)	(d) Sales price (see page D-3)	(e) Cost or other basis (see page D-3)	(f) LOSS If (e) is more than (d), subtract (d) from (e)	(g) GAIN If (d) is more than (e), subtract (e) from (d)
20						

21 Short-term totals. Add columns (d), (f), and (g) of line 20. Enter here and on line 2. | 21

Part V — Long-Term Capital Gains and Losses—Assets Held More Than One Year *(Continuation of Part II)*

(a) Description of property	(b) Date acquired	(c) Date sold	(d) Sales price	(e) Cost or other basis	(f) LOSS	(g) GAIN
22						

23 Long-term totals. Add columns (d), (f), and (g) of line 22. Enter here and on line 10. | 23

SCHEDULE E
(Form 1040)

Department of the Treasury
Internal Revenue Service (99)

Supplemental Income and Loss
(From rental real estate, royalties, partnerships, S corporations, estates, trusts, REMICs, etc.)
▶ Attach to Form 1040 or Form 1041. ▶ See Instructions for Schedule E (Form 1040).

OMB No. 1545-0074

1996

Attachment Sequence No. **13**

Name(s) shown on return | Your social security number

Part I — Income or Loss From Rental Real Estate and Royalties
Note: *Report income and expenses from your business of renting personal property on* **Schedule C** *or* **C-EZ** *(see page E-1). Report farm rental income or loss from* **Form 4835** *on page 2, line 39.*

1 Show the kind and location of each **rental real estate property:**

A ....
B ....
C ....

2 For each rental real estate property listed on line 1, did you or your family use it for personal purposes for more than the greater of 14 days or 10% of the total days rented at fair rental value during the tax year? (See page E-1.)

	Yes	No
A		
B		
C		

Income:

			Properties			Totals
		A	B	C		(Add columns A, B, and C.)
3	Rents received	3				3
4	Royalties received	4				4

Expenses:

5	Advertising	5				
6	Auto and travel (see page E-2)	6				
7	Cleaning and maintenance	7				
8	Commissions	8				
9	Insurance	9				
10	Legal and other professional fees	10				
11	Management fees	11				
12	Mortgage interest paid to banks, etc. (see page E-2)	12				12
13	Other interest	13				
14	Repairs	14				
15	Supplies	15				
16	Taxes	16				
17	Utilities	17				
18	Other (list) ▶	18				
19	Add lines 5 through 18	19				19
20	Depreciation expense or depletion (see page E-2)	20				20
21	Total expenses. Add lines 19 and 20	21				
22	Income or (loss) from rental real estate or royalty properties. Subtract line 21 from line 3 (rents) or line 4 (royalties). If the result is a (loss), see page E-2 to find out if you must file **Form 6198**	22				
23	Deductible rental real estate loss. **Caution:** *Your rental real estate loss on line 22 may be limited. See page E-3 to find out if you must file* **Form 8582**. *Real estate professionals must complete line 42 on page 2*	23 ( )	( )	( )		
24	**Income.** Add positive amounts shown on line 22. **Do not** include any losses					24
25	**Losses.** Add royalty losses from line 22 and rental real estate losses from line 23. Enter the total losses here					25 ( )
26	**Total rental real estate and royalty income or (loss).** Combine lines 24 and 25. Enter the result here. If Parts II, III, IV, and line 39 on page 2 do not apply to you, also enter this amount on Form 1040, line 17. Otherwise, include this amount in the total on line 40 on page 2					26

For Paperwork Reduction Act Notice, see Form 1040 instructions.   Cat. No. 11344L   Schedule E (Form 1040) 1996

Tax Forms B–17

Schedule E (Form 1040) 1996   Attachment Sequence No. **13**   Page **2**

Name(s) shown on return. Do not enter name and social security number if shown on other side.   **Your social security number**

Note: *If you report amounts from farming or fishing on Schedule E, you must enter your gross income from those activities on line 41 below. Real estate professionals must complete line 42 below.*

Part II — Income or Loss From Partnerships and S Corporations
Note: If you report a loss from an at-risk activity, you MUST check either column (e) or (f) of line 27 to describe your investment in the activity. See page E-4. If you check column (f), you must attach **Form 6198.**

27	(a) Name	(b) Enter **P** for partnership; **S** for S corporation	(c) Check if foreign partnership	(d) Employer identification number	Investment At Risk? (e) All is at risk	(f) Some is not at risk
A						
B						
C						
D						
E						

	Passive Income and Loss		Nonpassive Income and Loss		
	(g) Passive loss allowed (attach **Form 8582** if required)	(h) Passive income from **Schedule K–1**	(i) Nonpassive loss from **Schedule K–1**	(j) Section 179 expense deduction from **Form 4562**	(k) Nonpassive income from **Schedule K–1**
A					
B					
C					
D					
E					
28a Totals					
b Totals					

29	Add columns (h) and (k) of line 28a	29	
30	Add columns (g), (i), and (j) of line 28b	30	( )
31	Total partnership and S corporation income or (loss). Combine lines 29 and 30. Enter the result here and include in the total on line 40 below	31	

Part III — Income or Loss From Estates and Trusts

32	(a) Name	(b) Employer identification number
A		
B		

	Passive Income and Loss		Nonpassive Income and Loss	
	(c) Passive deduction or loss allowed (attach **Form 8582** if required)	(d) Passive income from **Schedule K–1**	(e) Deduction or loss from **Schedule K–1**	(f) Other income from **Schedule K–1**
A				
B				
33a Totals				
b Totals				

34	Add columns (d) and (f) of line 33a	34	
35	Add columns (c) and (e) of line 33b	35	( )
36	Total estate and trust income or (loss). Combine lines 34 and 35. Enter the result here and include in the total on line 40 below	36	

Part IV — Income or Loss From Real Estate Mortgage Investment Conduits (REMICs)—Residual Holder

37	(a) Name	(b) Employer identification number	(c) Excess inclusion from **Schedules Q,** line 2c (see page E-4)	(d) Taxable income (net loss) from **Schedules Q,** line 1b	(e) Income from **Schedules Q,** line 3b

| 38 | Combine columns (d) and (e) only. Enter the result here and include in the total on line 40 below | 38 | |

Part V — Summary

39	Net farm rental income or (loss) from **Form 4835.** Also, complete line 41 below	39	
40	**TOTAL** income or (loss). Combine lines 26, 31, 36, 38, and 39. Enter the result here and on Form 1040, line 17 ▶	40	
41	**Reconciliation of Farming and Fishing Income.** Enter your **gross** farming and fishing income reported on Form 4835, line 7; Schedule K–1 (Form 1065), line 15b; Schedule K–1 (Form 1120S), line 23; and Schedule K–1 (Form 1041), line 13 (see page E-4)	41	
42	**Reconciliation for Real Estate Professionals.** If you were a real estate professional (see page E-3), enter the net income or (loss) you reported anywhere on Form 1040 from all rental real estate activities in which you materially participated under the passive activity loss rules . . .	42	

SCHEDULE EIC
(Form 1040A or 1040)

Department of the Treasury
Internal Revenue Service (99)

Earned Income Credit
(Qualifying Child Information)
▶ Attach to Form 1040A or 1040.
▶ See instructions on back.

OMB No. 1545-0074

1996

Attachment
Sequence No. **43**

Name(s) shown on return: First and initial(s) | Last | Your social security number

Before You Begin . . .

- See the instructions for Form 1040A, line 29c, or Form 1040, line 54, to find out if you can take this credit.
- If you can take the credit, fill in the Earned Income Credit Worksheet in the Form 1040A or Form 1040 instructions to figure your credit. **But if you want the IRS to figure it for you, see instructions on back.**

Then, you **must** complete and attach Schedule EIC only if you have a qualifying child (see boxes on back).

Information About Your Qualifying Child or Children

If you have more than two qualifying children, you only have to list two to get the maximum credit.

Caution: *If you do not attach Schedule EIC and fill in all the lines that apply, it will take us longer to process your return and issue your refund.*

		(a) Child 1	(b) Child 2
		First name / Last name	First name / Last name
1	Child's name		
2	Child's year of birth	19 ___	19 ___
3	If the child was born **before 1978** AND—		
a	was **under age 24** at the end of 1996 **and** a student, check the "Yes" box, **OR** . . .	☐ Yes	☐ Yes
b	was permanently and totally disabled (see back), check the "Yes" box	☐ Yes	☐ Yes
4	Enter the child's social security number. If born in December 1996, see instructions on back		
5	Child's relationship to you (for example, son, grandchild, etc.) . .		
6	Number of months child lived with you in the United States in 1996 . .	___ months	___ months

TIP: Do you want the earned income credit added to your take-home pay in 1997? To see if you qualify, get **Form W-5** from your employer or by calling the IRS at 1-800-TAX-FORM (1-800-829-3676).

For Paperwork Reduction Act Notice, see Form 1040A or 1040 instructions.

Cat. No. 13339M

Schedule EIC (Form 1040A or 1040) 1996

Instructions

Purpose of Schedule

If you can take the earned income credit and have a qualifying child, use Schedule EIC to give information about that child. To figure the amount of your credit, use the worksheet in the instructions for Form 1040A, line 29c, or Form 1040, line 54.

If you want the IRS to figure the credit for you, print "EIC" next to line 29c of Form 1040A or line 54 of Form 1040. Also, enter the amount and type of any nontaxable earned income in the spaces provided on Form 1040A, line 29c, or Form 1040, line 54, and attach Schedule EIC to your return.

Line 1

Enter each qualifying child's name.

Line 3a

If your child was born **before 1978** but was under age 24 at the end of 1996 and a student, put a checkmark in the "Yes" box.

Your child was a **student** if he or she—

- Was enrolled as a full-time student at a school during any 5 months of 1996, or
- Took a full-time, on-farm training course during any 5 months of 1996. The course had to be given by a school or a state, county, or local government agency.

A **school** includes technical, trade, and mechanical schools. It does not include on-the-job training courses or correspondence schools.

Line 3b

If your child was born **before 1978** and was permanently and totally disabled during any part of 1996, put a checkmark in the "Yes" box.

A person is **permanently and totally disabled** if **both** of the following apply.

1. He or she cannot engage in any substantial gainful activity because of a physical or mental condition.

2. A doctor determines the condition has lasted or can be expected to last continuously for at least a year or can lead to death.

Line 4

You must enter your child's social security number (SSN) on line 4 unless he or she was born in December 1996 or was born and died in 1996. If you do not enter the correct SSN, at the time we process your return, we may reduce or disallow your credit. If your child was born in December 1996 and does not have an SSN, enter "12/96" on line 4. If your child was born and died in 1996 and did not have an SSN, print "Died" on line 4.

If your child does not have an SSN, apply for one by filing **Form SS-5** with your local Social Security Administration (SSA) office. It usually takes about 2 weeks to get a number. If your child will not have an SSN by April 15, 1997, you can get an automatic 4-month extension by filing Form 4868 with the IRS by that date.

Line 6

Enter the number of months your child lived with you in your home in the United States during 1996. (If you were in the military on extended active duty outside the United States, your home is considered to be in the United States during that duty period.) Do not enter more than 12. Count temporary absences, such as for school, vacation, or medical care, as time lived in your home. If the child lived with you for more than half of 1996 but less than 7 months, enter "07" on this line.

Exception. If your child, including a foster child, was born or died in 1996 and your home was the child's home for the entire time he or she was alive during 1996, enter "12" on line 6.

Qualifying Child

A **qualifying child** is a child who:

is your:	AND	was (at the end of 1996):	AND	who:
son daughter adopted child grandchild stepchild or foster child		under age 19 or under age 24 and a full-time student or any age and permanently and totally disabled		lived with you in the U.S. for more than half of 1996* (or all of 1996 if a foster child*)

*If the child did not live with you for the required time (for example, was born in 1996), see the **Line 6** instructions above.

If the child was married or is also a qualifying child of another person (other than your spouse if filing a joint return), special rules apply. For details, see the instructions for Form 1040A, line 29c, or Form 1040, line 54. Also, the child must have an SSN (as defined in those instructions) unless he or she was born in December 1996 or was born and died in 1996.

Schedule R (Form 1040)

Credit for the Elderly or the Disabled

Department of the Treasury
Internal Revenue Service (99)

▶ Attach to Form 1040. ▶ See separate instructions for Schedule R.

OMB No. 1545-0074

1996

Attachment Sequence No. **16**

Name(s) shown on Form 1040

Your social security number

You may be able to take this credit and reduce your tax if by the end of 1996:
- You were age 65 or older, **OR**
- You were under age 65, you retired on **permanent and total** disability, and you received taxable disability income.

But you must also meet other tests. See the separate instructions for Schedule R.

Note: *In most cases, the IRS can figure the credit for you. See the instructions.*

Part I — Check the Box for Your Filing Status and Age

If your filing status is:	And by the end of 1996:	Check only one box:
Single, Head of household, or Qualifying widow(er) with dependent child	**1** You were 65 or older	1 ☐
	2 You were under 65 and you retired on permanent and total disability	2 ☐
Married filing a joint return	**3** Both spouses were 65 or older	3 ☐
	4 Both spouses were under 65, but only one spouse retired on permanent and total disability	4 ☐
	5 Both spouses were under 65, and both retired on permanent and total disability	5 ☐
	6 One spouse was 65 or older, and the other spouse was under 65 and retired on permanent and total disability	6 ☐
	7 One spouse was 65 or older, and the other spouse was under 65 and **NOT** retired on permanent and total disability	7 ☐
Married filing a separate return	**8** You were 65 or older and you lived apart from your spouse for all of 1996	8 ☐
	9 You were under 65, you retired on permanent and total disability, and you lived apart from your spouse for all of 1996	9 ☐

Did you check box 1, 3, 7, or 8?
- Yes ⟶ Skip Part II and complete Part III on back.
- No ⟶ Complete Parts II and III.

Part II — Statement of Permanent and Total Disability (Complete **only** if you checked box 2, 4, 5, 6, or 9 above.)

IF: 1 You filed a physician's statement for this disability for 1983 or an earlier year, or you filed a statement for tax years after 1983 and your physician signed line B on the statement, **AND**

2 Due to your continued disabled condition, you were unable to engage in any substantial gainful activity in 1996, check this box ▶ ☐

- If you checked this box, you do not have to file another statement for 1996.
- If you **did not** check this box, have your physician complete the statement below.

Physician's Statement (See instructions at bottom of page 2.)

I certify that _____
Name of disabled person

was permanently and totally disabled on January 1, 1976, or January 1, 1977, **OR** was permanently and totally disabled on the date he or she retired. If retired after 1976, enter the date retired. ▶ _____

Physician: Sign your name on **either** line A or B below.

A The disability has lasted or can be expected to last continuously for at least a year . . . . _____

Physician's signature _____ Date _____

B There is no reasonable probability that the disabled condition will ever improve . . . . _____

Physician's signature _____ Date _____

Physician's name _____ Physician's address _____

For Paperwork Reduction Act Notice, see Form 1040 instructions. Cat. No. 11359K Schedule R (Form 1040) 1996

Schedule R (Form 1040) 1996

Part III — Figure Your Credit

10 If you checked (in Part I):   Enter:
  Box 1, 2, 4, or 7 . . . . $5,000
  Box 3, 5, or 6 . . . . $7,500   **10**
  Box 8 or 9 . . . . $3,750

  Did you check box 2, 4, 5, 6, or 9 in Part I?
  — Yes → You **must** complete line 11.
  — No → Enter the amount from line 10 on line 12 and go to line 13.

11 If you checked:
  • Box 6 in Part I, add $5,000 to the taxable disability income of the spouse who was under age 65. Enter the total.
  • Box 2, 4, or 9 in Part I, enter your taxable disability income.
  • Box 5 in Part I, add your taxable disability income to your spouse's taxable disability income. Enter the total.   **11**
  TIP: For more details on what to include on line 11, see the instructions.

12 If you completed line 11, enter the **smaller** of line 10 or line 11; **all others,** enter the amount from line 10 . . . .   **12**

13 Enter the following pensions, annuities, or disability income that you (and your spouse if filing a joint return) received in 1996:

  a Nontaxable part of social security benefits, and Nontaxable part of railroad retirement benefits treated as social security. See instructions.   **13a**

  b Nontaxable veterans' pensions, and Any other pension, annuity, or disability benefit that is excluded from income under any other provision of law. See instructions.   **13b**

  c Add lines 13a and 13b. (Even though these income items are not taxable, they **must** be included here to figure your credit.) If you did not receive any of the types of nontaxable income listed on line 13a or 13b, enter -0- on line 13c **13c**

14 Enter the amount from Form 1040, line 32   **14**

15 If you checked (in Part I):   Enter:
  Box 1 or 2 . . . . $7,500
  Box 3, 4, 5, 6, or 7 . . . . $10,000   **15**
  Box 8 or 9 . . . . $5,000

16 Subtract line 15 from line 14. If zero or less, enter -0- **16**

17 Enter one-half of line 16 . . . .   **17**

18 Add lines 13c and 17 . . . .   **18**

19 Subtract line 18 from line 12. If zero or less, **stop;** you **cannot** take the credit. Otherwise, go to line 20 . . . .   **19**

20 Multiply line 19 by 15% (.15). Enter the result here and on Form 1040, line 40. **Caution:** *If you file Schedule C, C-EZ, D, E, or F (Form 1040), your credit may be limited. See the instructions for line 20 for the amount of credit you can claim* **20**

Instructions for Physician's Statement

Taxpayer
If you retired after 1976, enter the date you retired in the space provided in Part II.

Physician
A person is permanently and totally disabled if **both** of the following apply:
  1. He or she cannot engage in any substantial gainful activity because of a physical or mental condition, and
  2. A physician determines that the disability has lasted or can be expected to last continuously for at least a year or can lead to death.

SCHEDULE SE (Form 1040) Department of the Treasury Internal Revenue Service (99)	**Self-Employment Tax** ▶ See Instructions for Schedule SE (Form 1040). ▶ Attach to Form 1040.	OMB No. 1545-0074 **1996** Attachment Sequence No. **17**
Name of person with **self-employment** income (as shown on Form 1040)	Social security number of person with **self-employment** income ▶	

Who Must File Schedule SE

You must file Schedule SE if:

- You had net earnings from self-employment from **other than** church employee income (line 4 of Short Schedule SE or line 4c of Long Schedule SE) of $400 or more, **OR**
- You had church employee income of $108.28 or more. Income from services you performed as a minister or a member of a religious order **is not** church employee income. See page SE-1.

Note: *Even if you had a loss or a small amount of income from self-employment, it may be to your benefit to file Schedule SE and use either "optional method" in Part II of Long Schedule SE. See page SE-3.*

Exception. If your only self-employment income was from earnings as a minister, member of a religious order, or Christian Science practitioner **and** you filed Form 4361 and received IRS approval not to be taxed on those earnings, **do not** file Schedule SE. Instead, write "Exempt–Form 4361" on Form 1040, line 45.

May I Use Short Schedule SE or MUST I Use Long Schedule SE?

```
                        ┌─────────────────────────────────────┐
                        │ DID YOU RECEIVE WAGES OR TIPS IN 1996? │
                        └─────────────────────────────────────┘
                          No │                              │ Yes
                             ▼                              ▼
   ┌────────────────────────────────────────┐    ┌────────────────────────────────────────┐
   │ Are you a minister, member of a        │    │ Was the total of your wages and tips   │
   │ religious order, or Christian Science  │Yes │ subject to social security or railroad │ Yes
   │ practitioner who received IRS approval │───▶│ retirement tax plus your net earnings  │───▶
   │ not to be taxed on earnings from these │    │ from self-employment more than $62,700?│
   │ sources, but you owe self-employment   │    └────────────────────────────────────────┘
   │ tax on other earnings?                 │                  │ No
   └────────────────────────────────────────┘                  ▼
                          No │                     ┌────────────────────────────────────────┐
                             ▼              ◀ No ─│ Did you receive tips subject to social │ Yes
   ┌────────────────────────────────────────┐     │ security or Medicare tax that you did  │───▶
   │ Are you using one of the optional      │ Yes │ not report to your employer?           │
   │ methods to figure your net earnings    │──▶  └────────────────────────────────────────┘
   │ (see page SE-3)?                       │
   └────────────────────────────────────────┘
                          No │
                             ▼
   ┌────────────────────────────────────────┐
   │ Did you receive church employee income │ Yes
   │ reported on Form W-2 of $108.28 or more?│──▶
   └────────────────────────────────────────┘
                          No │
                             ▼
   ┌────────────────────────────────────────┐    ┌────────────────────────────────────────┐
   │ YOU MAY USE SHORT SCHEDULE SE BELOW    │    │ YOU MUST USE LONG SCHEDULE SE ON THE BACK │
   └────────────────────────────────────────┘    └────────────────────────────────────────┘
```

Section A—Short Schedule SE. Caution: *Read above to see if you can use Short Schedule SE.*

1	Net farm profit or (loss) from Schedule F, line 36, and farm partnerships, Schedule K-1 (Form 1065), line 15a	1
2	Net profit or (loss) from Schedule C, line 31; Schedule C-EZ, line 3; and Schedule K-1 (Form 1065), line 15a (other than farming). Ministers and members of religious orders see page SE-1 for amounts to report on this line. See page SE-2 for other income to report	2
3	Combine lines 1 and 2	3
4	**Net earnings from self-employment.** Multiply line 3 by 92.35% (.9235). If less than $400, **do not** file this schedule; you do not owe self-employment tax ▶	4
5	**Self-employment tax.** If the amount on line 4 is: • $62,700 or less, multiply line 4 by 15.3% (.153). Enter the result here and on **Form 1040, line 45.** • More than $62,700, multiply line 4 by 2.9% (.029). Then, add $7,774.80 to the result. Enter the total here and on **Form 1040, line 45.**	5
6	**Deduction for one-half of self-employment tax.** Multiply line 5 by 50% (.5). Enter the result here and on **Form 1040, line 25**	6	

For Paperwork Reduction Act Notice, see Form 1040 instructions.   Cat. No. 11358Z   Schedule SE (Form 1040) 1996

Tax Forms B–23

Schedule SE (Form 1040) 1996 — Attachment Sequence No. **17** — Page **2**

Name of person with **self-employment** income (as shown on Form 1040) | Social security number of person with **self-employment** income ▶

Section B—Long Schedule SE

Part I Self-Employment Tax

Note: *If your only income subject to self-employment tax is* **church employee income,** *skip lines 1 through 4b. Enter -0- on line 4c and go to line 5a. Income from services you performed as a minister or a member of a religious order* **is not** *church employee income. See page SE-1.*

A If you are a minister, member of a religious order, or Christian Science practitioner **and** you filed Form 4361, but you had $400 or more of **other** net earnings from self-employment, check here and continue with Part I . . . . . . ▶ ☐

1. Net farm profit or (loss) from Schedule F, line 36, and farm partnerships, Schedule K-1 (Form 1065), line 15a. **Note:** *Skip this line if you use the farm optional method. See page SE-3* . . | **1** |

2. Net profit or (loss) from Schedule C, line 31; Schedule C-EZ, line 3; and Schedule K-1 (Form 1065), line 15a (other than farming). Ministers and members of religious orders see page SE-1 for amounts to report on this line. See page SE-2 for other income to report. **Note:** *Skip this line if you use the nonfarm optional method. See page SE-3.* . . . . | **2** |

3. Combine lines 1 and 2 . . . . | **3** |

4a. If line 3 is more than zero, multiply line 3 by 92.35% (.9235). Otherwise, enter amount from line 3 | **4a** |
  b. If you elected one or both of the optional methods, enter the total of lines 15 and 17 here . . | **4b** |
  c. Combine lines 4a and 4b. If less than $400, **do not** file this schedule; you do not owe self-employment tax. **Exception.** If less than $400 and you had **church employee income,** enter -0- and continue ▶ | **4c** |

5a. Enter your **church employee income** from Form W-2. **Caution:** *See page SE-1 for definition of church employee income* . . | **5a** | |
  b. Multiply line 5a by 92.35% (.9235). If less than $100, enter -0- . . . . | **5b** |

6. **Net earnings from self-employment.** Add lines 4c and 5b . . . . | **6** |

7. Maximum amount of combined wages and self-employment earnings subject to social security tax or the 6.2% portion of the 7.65% railroad retirement (tier 1) tax for 1996 . . . . . . | **7** | 62,700 | 00 |

8a. Total social security wages and tips (total of boxes 3 and 7 on Form(s) W-2) and railroad retirement (tier 1) compensation . . . . . . | **8a** | |
  b. Unreported tips subject to social security tax (from Form 4137, line 9) | **8b** | |
  c. Add lines 8a and 8b . . . . | **8c** |

9. Subtract line 8c from line 7. If zero or less, enter -0- here and on line 10 and go to line 11 . ▶ | **9** |

10. Multiply the **smaller** of line 6 or line 9 by 12.4% (.124) . . . . | **10** |

11. Multiply line 6 by 2.9% (.029) . . . . | **11** |

12. **Self-employment tax.** Add lines 10 and 11. Enter here and on **Form 1040, line 45** . . . | **12** |

13. **Deduction for one-half of self-employment tax.** Multiply line 12 by 50% (.5). Enter the result here and on **Form 1040, line 25** . . . . | **13** | |

Part II Optional Methods To Figure Net Earnings (See page SE-3.)

Farm Optional Method. You may use this method **only** if:
- Your gross farm income[1] was not more than $2,400, **or**
- Your gross farm income[1] was more than $2,400 and your net farm profits[2] were less than $1,733.

14. Maximum income for optional methods . . . . | **14** | 1,600 | 00 |

15. Enter the **smaller** of: two-thirds (⅔) of gross farm income[1] (not less than zero) or $1,600. Also, include this amount on line 4b above . . . . | **15** |

Nonfarm Optional Method. You may use this method **only** if:
- Your net nonfarm profits[3] were less than $1,733 and also less than 72.189% of your gross nonfarm income,[4] **and**
- You had net earnings from self-employment of at least $400 in 2 of the prior 3 years.

Caution: You may use this method no more than five times.

16. Subtract line 15 from line 14 . . . . | **16** |

17. Enter the **smaller** of: two-thirds (⅔) of gross nonfarm income[4] (not less than zero) **or** the amount on line 16. Also, include this amount on line 4b above . . . . | **17** |

[1] From Schedule F, line 11, and Schedule K-1 (Form 1065), line 15b.
[2] From Schedule F, line 36, and Schedule K-1 (Form 1065), line 15a.
[3] From Schedule C, line 31; Schedule C-EZ, line 3; and Schedule K-1 (Form 1065), line 15a.
[4] From Schedule C, line 7; Schedule C-EZ, line 1; and Schedule K-1 (Form 1065), line 15c.

Form 1040-ES — Estimated Tax for Individuals

OMB No. 1545-0087

1997

Department of the Treasury
Internal Revenue Service

This package is primarily for first-time filers of estimated tax.

Paperwork Reduction Act Notice

We ask for the information on the payment vouchers to carry out the Internal Revenue laws of the United States. You are required to give us the information. We need it to ensure that you are complying with these laws and to allow us to figure and collect the right amount of tax.

You are not required to provide the information requested on a form that is subject to the Paperwork Reduction Act unless the form displays a valid OMB control number. Books or records relating to a form or its instructions must be retained as long as their contents may become material in the administration of any Internal Revenue law. Generally, tax returns and return information are confidential, as required by Internal Revenue Code section 6103.

The time needed to complete the worksheets and prepare and file the payment vouchers will vary depending on individual circumstances. The estimated average time is: **Recordkeeping,** 1 hr., 19 min.; **Learning about the law,** 18 min.; **Preparing the worksheets and payment vouchers,** 49 min.; **Copying, assembling, and sending the payment voucher to the IRS,** 10 min. If you have comments concerning the accuracy of these time estimates or suggestions for making this package simpler, we would be happy to hear from you. You can write to the Tax Forms Committee, Western Area Distribution Center, Rancho Cordova, CA 95743-0001. **DO NOT** send the payment vouchers to this address. Instead, see **Where To File Your Payment Voucher** on page 5.

Purpose of This Package

Use this package to figure and pay your estimated tax. Estimated tax is the method used to pay tax on income that is not subject to withholding; for example, earnings from self-employment, interest, dividends, rents, alimony, etc. In addition, if you do not elect voluntary withholding, you should make estimated tax payments on unemployment compensation and the taxable part of your social security benefits. See the 1996 instructions for your tax return for more details on income that is taxable.

This package is primarily for first-time filers who are or may be subject to paying estimated tax. This package can also be used if you did not receive or have lost your preprinted 1040-ES package. The estimated tax worksheet on page 4 will help you figure the correct amount to pay. The payment vouchers in this package are for crediting your estimated tax payments to your account correctly. Use the **Record of Estimated Tax Payments** on page 5 to keep track of the payments you have made and the number and amount of your remaining payments.

After we receive your first payment voucher from this package, we will mail you a 1040-ES package with your name, address, and social security number preprinted on each payment voucher. Use the preprinted vouchers to make your **remaining** estimated tax payments for the year. This will speed processing, reduce processing costs, and reduce the chance of errors.

Do not use the vouchers in this package to notify the IRS of a **change of address.** If you have a new address, order **Form 8822,** Change of Address, by calling 1-800-TAX-FORM (1-800-829-3676). Send the completed form to the Internal Revenue Service Center where you filed your last tax return. The Service Center will update your record and send you new preprinted payment vouchers.

Note: *Continue to use your old preprinted payment vouchers to make payments of estimated tax until you receive the new vouchers.*

Who Must Make Estimated Tax Payments

In most cases, you must make estimated tax payments if you expect to owe, after subtracting your withholding and credits, at least $500 in tax for 1997, and you expect your withholding and credits to be less than the **smaller** of:

1. 90% of the tax shown on your 1997 tax return, or

2. The tax shown on your 1996 tax return (110% of that amount if you are not a farmer or a fisherman and the adjusted gross income shown on that return is more than $150,000 or, if married filing separately for 1997, more than $75,000).

However, if you did not file a 1996 tax return or that return did not cover all 12 months, item 2 above does not apply.

For this purpose, household employment taxes are not included when figuring the tax shown on your tax return and are not required to be included when figuring your estimated tax payments. However, you may choose to include these taxes when paying estimated tax to avoid a large balance due at the time your tax return is due.

Exception. You do not have to pay estimated tax if you were a U.S. citizen or resident alien for all of 1996 and you had no tax liability for the full 12-month 1996 tax year.

The estimated tax rules apply to:

- U.S. citizens and residents,
- Residents of Puerto Rico, the Virgin Islands, Guam, the Commonwealth of the Northern Mariana Islands, and American Samoa, and
- Nonresident aliens (use Form 1040-ES (NR)).

If you also receive salaries and wages, you may be able to avoid having to make estimated tax payments by asking your employer to take more tax out of your earnings. To do this, file a new **Form W-4,** Employee's Withholding Allowance Certificate, with your employer.

Caution: *You may not make joint estimated tax payments if you or your spouse is a nonresident alien, you are separated under a decree of divorce or separate maintenance, or you and your spouse have different tax years.*

Additional Information You May Need

Most of the information you will need can be found in:

Pub. 505, Tax Withholding and Estimated Tax.

Other available information:

Pub. 553, Highlights of 1996 Tax Changes, and

Instructions for the 1996 Form 1040 or 1040A.

To order forms and publications, call 1-800-TAX-FORM (1-800-829-3676). If you have a personal computer and a modem, you can also get forms and publications electronically. For details, see page 5 of the Instructions for Form 1040 or page 5 of the Instructions for Form 1040A.

If you have tax questions, call 1-800-829-1040 for assistance.

Tax Law Changes Effective for 1997

Use your 1996 tax return as a guide in figuring your 1997 estimated tax, but be sure to consider the changes noted in this section. For more information on changes that may affect your 1997 estimated tax, see Pub. 553.

Voluntary Withholding on Social Security and Other Federal Payments. Beginning in 1997, you can choose to have Federal income tax withheld on social security benefits; tier 1 railroad retirement benefits; unemployment compensation; certain crop disaster payments; and Commodity Credit Corporation loans. To make this choice, see **Form W-4V,** Voluntary Withholding Request.

Increase in IRA Deduction for Certain Spouses. For tax years beginning after 1996, the limit on the maximum IRA deduction for a married couple filing a joint return has increased for the spouse with the smaller compensation. The deduction limit for the spouse with the smaller compensation is equal to the smaller of **(a)** $2,000, or **(b)** the compensation of both spouses reduced by the amount of the IRA deduction claimed by the other spouse. As a result of this change, the limit on nondeductible contributions to IRAs also has increased.

Section 179 Expense Deduction Increased. For 1997, the deduction to expense certain property under section 179 generally has been increased to $18,000.

Cat. No. 11340T

(Continued on page 2)

New Savings Incentive Match Plans for Employees of Small Employers (SIMPLE Retirement Plans). For tax years beginning after 1996, an employer (including a self-employed individual) who employs no more than 100 employees who received at least $5,000 compensation from the employer in the prior year and who does not maintain another employer-sponsored retirement plan can adopt a SIMPLE retirement plan. Contributions to the plan generally are deductible by the employer and excludable from the employee's income. A SIMPLE plan, like an IRA, is not subject to tax. Distributions from the plan generally are taxed under the rules that apply to IRAs.

Credit or Exclusion for Adoption Expenses. A tax credit of up to $5,000 ($6,000 for a child with special needs) is allowed for qualified adoption expenses paid or incurred after 1996. The credit generally is allowed for the year following the year the expenses were paid. However, the credit is allowed in the same year the expenses were paid or incurred if the expenses were paid or incurred in the year the adoption becomes final. No expenses for a foreign adoption qualify for the credit unless the adoption becomes final, and these expenses are taken into account only for the year the adoption becomes final. The credit begins to phase out for taxpayers whose modified adjusted gross income (AGI) is more than $75,000, and is fully phased out for taxpayers with modified AGI of $115,000 or more. Under rules similar to those for the credit, amounts paid by an employer under an adoption assistance program may be excludable from an employee's income.

Self-Employed Health Insurance Deduction Increased. For 1997, the self-employed health insurance deduction is increased to 40% of health insurance expenses.

Medical Savings Accounts. Beginning in 1997, self-employed individuals and eligible employees covered by a high-deductible health insurance plan may be eligible to open a medical savings account (MSA). Only a limited number of taxpayers will be eligible to participate in MSAs. Within limits, contributions to an MSA are deductible and are excludable if made by the employer of an eligible individual. Earnings from an MSA are tax deferred. Distributions from an MSA for medical expenses are not taxable.

Long-Term Care Insurance. Beginning in 1997, amounts received under a qualified long-term care insurance policy are excludable from income, subject to certain dollar limits. Also, premiums for long-term care insurance that do not exceed certain dollar limits and unreimbursed costs for long-term care of an individual, spouse, or dependent are treated as medical expenses when figuring the itemized deduction for medical expenses.

Receipt of Accelerated Death Benefits or Sale of a Life Insurance Contract. Beginning in 1997, amounts received by the insured **(a)** under a life insurance contract or **(b)** for the sale or assignment of a life insurance contract to a qualified viatical settlement provider generally are excluded from income, provided that the insured is either terminally or chronically ill. For a chronically ill individual, however, the exclusion for periodic payments is subject to certain dollar limits and other special rules apply.

Credit for Increasing Research Activities. You cannot take this credit into account when figuring your 1997 estimated tax payments.

Standard Deduction for 1997. If you do not itemize your deductions, you may take the 1997 standard deduction listed below:

Filing Status	Standard Deduction
Married filing jointly or Qualifying widow(er)	$6,900
Head of household	$6,050
Single	$4,150
Married filing separately	$3,450

Caution: If you can be claimed as a dependent on another person's 1997 return, your standard deduction is the greater of $650 or your earned income, up to the standard deduction amount.

An additional amount is added to the standard deduction if:

1. You are an unmarried individual (single or head of household) and are:

65 or older or blind	$1,000
65 or older and blind	$2,000

2. You are a married individual (filing jointly or separately) or a qualifying widow(er) and are:

65 or older or blind	$800
65 or older and blind	$1,600
Both spouses 65 or older	$1,600*
Both spouses 65 or older and blind	$3,200*

* If married filing separately, these amounts apply only if you can claim an exemption for your spouse.

1997 Tax Rate Schedules

Caution: *Do not use these Tax Rate Schedules to figure your 1996 taxes. Use only to figure your 1997 estimated taxes.*

Single—Schedule X

If line 5 is: Over—	But not over—	The tax is:	of the amount over—
$0	$24,650	15%	$0
24,650	59,750	$3,697.50 + 28%	24,650
59,750	124,650	13,525.50 + 31%	59,750
124,650	271,050	33,644.50 + 36%	124,650
271,050		86,348.50 + 39.6%	271,050

Head of household—Schedule Z

If line 5 is: Over—	But not over—	The tax is:	of the amount over—
$0	$33,050	15%	$0
33,050	85,350	$4,957.50 + 28%	33,050
85,350	138,200	19,601.50 + 31%	85,350
138,200	271,050	35,985.00 + 36%	138,200
271,050		83,811.00 + 39.6%	271,050

Married filing jointly or Qualifying widow(er)—Schedule Y-1

If line 5 is: Over—	But not over—	The tax is:	of the amount over—
$0	$41,200	15%	$0
41,200	99,600	$6,180.00 + 28%	41,200
99,600	151,750	22,532.00 + 31%	99,600
151,750	271,050	38,698.50 + 36%	151,750
271,050		81,646.50 + 39.6%	271,050

Married filing separately—Schedule Y-2

If line 5 is: Over—	But not over—	The tax is:	of the amount over—
$0	$20,600	15%	$0
20,600	49,800	$3,090.00 + 28%	20,600
49,800	75,875	11,266.00 + 31%	49,800
75,875	135,525	19,349.25 + 36%	75,875
135,525		40,823.25 + 39.6%	135,525

To Figure Your Estimated Tax Use

- The **1997 Estimated Tax Worksheet** on page 4.
- The instructions below for the worksheet on page 4.
- The **1997 Tax Rate Schedules** on page 2.
- Your 1996 tax return and instructions as a guide to figuring your income, deductions, and credits (but be sure to consider the tax law changes noted earlier).

If you receive your income unevenly throughout the year (e.g., you operate your business on a seasonal basis), you may be able to lower or eliminate the amount of your required estimated tax payment for one or more periods by using the annualized income installment method. See Pub. 505 for details.

To amend or correct your estimated tax, see **Amending Estimated Tax Payments** on this page.

Instructions for Worksheet on Page 4

Line 1—Use your 1996 tax return and instructions as a guide to figuring the adjusted gross income you expect in 1997 (but be sure to consider the tax law changes noted earlier). For more details on figuring your adjusted gross income, see **Expected Adjusted Gross Income** in Pub. 505. If you are self-employed, be sure to take into account the deduction for one-half of your self-employment tax.

Line 7—Additional Taxes. Enter the additional taxes from **Form 4972**, Tax on Lump-Sum Distributions, or **Form 8814**, Parents' Election To Report Child's Interest and Dividends.

Line 9—Credits. See the 1996 Form 1040, lines 39 through 43, or Form 1040A, lines 24a and 24b, and the related instructions.

Line 11—Self-Employment Tax. If you and your spouse make joint estimated tax payments and you both have self-employment income, figure the self-employment tax for each of you separately. Enter the total on line 11. When figuring your estimate of 1997 net earnings from self-employment, be sure to use only 92.35% of your total net profit from self-employment.

Line 12—Other Taxes. Except as noted below, enter any other taxes, such as alternative minimum tax, tax on accumulation distribution of trusts, and the tax on early distributions from **(a)** a qualified retirement plan (including your IRA), **(b)** an annuity, or **(c)** a modified endowment contract entered into after June 20, 1988.

Do not include tax on recapture of a Federal mortgage subsidy, social security and Medicare tax on unreported tip income, household employment taxes, or uncollected employee social security and Medicare or RRTA tax on tips or group-term life insurance. These taxes are not required to be paid until your income tax return is due (not including extensions).

Payment Due Dates

You may pay all of your estimated tax by April 15, 1997, or in four equal amounts by the dates shown below:

1st payment	April 15, 1997
2nd payment	June 16, 1997
3rd payment	Sept. 15, 1997
4th payment	Jan. 15, 1998*

*You do not have to make the payment due January 15, 1998, if you file your 1997 tax return by February 2, 1998, **AND** pay the entire balance due with your return.

Note: *Payments are due by the dates indicated whether or not you are outside the United States and Puerto Rico.*

If, after March 31, 1997, you have a large change in income, deductions, additional taxes, or credits that requires you to start making estimated tax payments, you should figure the amount of your estimated tax payments by using the annualized income installment method, as explained in Pub. 505. Although your payment due dates will be the same as shown above, the payment amounts will vary based on your income, deductions, additional taxes, and credits for the months ending before each payment due date. As a result, this method may allow you to skip or lower the amount due for one or more payments. If you use the annualized income installment method, be sure to file **Form 2210**, Underpayment of Estimated Tax by Individuals, Estates, and Trusts, with your 1997 tax return, even if no penalty is owed.

Farmers and Fishermen. If at least two-thirds of your gross income for 1996 or 1997 is from farming or fishing, you may do one of the following:

- Pay all of your estimated tax by January 15, 1998, or
- File your 1997 Form 1040 by March 2, 1998, and pay the total tax due. In this case, 1997 estimated payments are not required.

Fiscal Year Taxpayers. You are on a fiscal year if your 12-month tax period ends on any day except December 31. Due dates for fiscal year taxpayers are the 15th day of the 4th, 6th, and 9th months for your current fiscal year and the 1st month of the following fiscal year. If any payment date falls on a Saturday, Sunday, or legal holiday, use the next business day.

Amending Estimated Tax Payments

To change or amend your estimated payments, refigure your total estimated payments due (line 16 of the worksheet on page 4). Then use the worksheets under **Amended estimated tax** in Chapter 2 of Pub. 505 to figure the payment due for each remaining payment period. If an estimated tax payment for a previous period is less than one-fourth of your amended estimated tax, you may owe a penalty when you file your return.

When a Penalty Is Applied

In some cases, you may owe a penalty when you file your return. The penalty is imposed on each underpayment for the number of days it remains unpaid. A penalty may be applied if you did not pay enough estimated tax or you did not make the payments on time or in the required amount. A penalty may apply even if you have an overpayment on your tax return.

The penalty may be waived under certain conditions. See Pub. 505 for details.

How To Complete and Use the Payment Voucher

There is a separate payment voucher for each due date. Please be sure you use the voucher with the correct due date shown in the upper right corner. Complete and send in the voucher **only** if you are making a payment. To complete your voucher:

- Type or print your name, address, and social security number in the space provided on the voucher. If filing a joint voucher, also enter your spouse's name and social security number. List the names and social security numbers in the same order on the joint voucher as you will on your joint return. If you and your spouse plan to file separate returns, file separate vouchers instead of a joint voucher.
- Enter on the payment line of the voucher only the amount you are sending in. When making payments of estimated tax, be sure to take into account any 1996 overpayment that you choose to credit against your 1997 tax, but do not include the overpayment amount on this line.
- Enclose your payment, making the check or money order payable to: "Internal Revenue Service" (not "IRS").
- Write your social security number and "1997 Form 1040-ES" on your check or money order.
- Do not staple or attach your payment to the voucher.
- Mail your payment voucher to the address shown on page 5 for the place where you live.
- Fill in the **Record of Estimated Tax Payments** on page 5 for your files.

If you changed your name and made estimated tax payments using your old name, attach a statement to the front of your 1997 tax return. List all of the estimated tax payments you and your spouse made for 1997, the address where you made the payments, and the name(s) and social security number(s) under which you made the payments.

Paying Electronically

If you want, you can use the Electronic Federal Tax Payment System (EFTPS) to make your estimated tax payments. EFTPS is a safe, fast, and convenient way to make your payments. No checks to write! To use EFTPS, you must first apply. The application process may take several weeks. For EFTPS information, call **1-800-945-8400** or **1-800-555-4477**.

1997 Estimated Tax Worksheet (keep for your records)

1	Enter amount of adjusted gross income you expect in 1997 (see instructions)	1
2	• If you plan to itemize deductions, enter the estimated total of your itemized deductions. **Caution:** If line 1 above is over $121,200 ($60,600 if married filing separately), your deduction may be reduced. See Pub. 505 for details. • If you do not plan to itemize deductions, see **Standard Deduction for 1997** on page 2, and enter your standard deduction here.	2
3	Subtract line 2 from line 1	3
4	Exemptions. Multiply $2,650 by the number of personal exemptions. If you can be claimed as a dependent on another person's 1997 return, your personal exemption is not allowed. **Caution:** If line 1 above is over $181,800 ($151,500 if head of household; $121,200 if single; $90,900 if married filing separately), see Pub. 505 to figure the amount to enter	4
5	Subtract line 4 from line 3	5
6	**Tax.** Figure your tax on the amount on line 5 by using the 1997 Tax Rate Schedules on page 2. DO NOT use the Tax Table or the Tax Rate Schedules in the 1996 Form 1040 or Form 1040A instructions. **Caution:** If you have a net capital gain and line 5 is over $99,600 ($85,350 if head of household; $59,750 if single; $49,800 if married filing separately), see Pub. 505 to figure the tax	6
7	Additional taxes (see instructions)	7
8	Add lines 6 and 7	8
9	Credits (see instructions). Do not include any income tax withholding on this line	9
10	Subtract line 9 from line 8. Enter the result, but not less than zero	10
11	Self-employment tax (see instructions). Estimate of 1997 net earnings from self-employment $_____ ; if **$65,400 or less,** multiply the amount by 15.3%; if **more than $65,400,** multiply the amount by 2.9%, add $8,109.60 to the result, and enter the total. **Caution:** If you also have wages subject to social security tax, see Pub. 505 to figure the amount to enter	11
12	Other taxes (see instructions)	12
13a	Add lines 10 through 12	13a
b	Earned income credit and credit from **Form 4136**	13b
c	Subtract line 13b from line 13a. Enter the result, but not less than zero. **THIS IS YOUR TOTAL 1997 ESTIMATED TAX** ▶	13c
14a	Multiply line 13c by 90% (66⅔% for farmers and fishermen)	14a
b	Enter the tax shown on your 1996 tax return (110% of that amount if you are not a farmer or a fisherman and the adjusted gross income shown on that return is more than $150,000 or, if married filing separately for 1997, more than $75,000)	14b
c	Enter the **smaller** of line 14a or 14b. **THIS IS YOUR REQUIRED ANNUAL PAYMENT TO AVOID A PENALTY** ▶ **Caution:** Generally, if you do not prepay (through income tax withholding and estimated tax payments) at least the amount on line 14c, you may owe a penalty for not paying enough estimated tax. To avoid a penalty, make sure your estimate on line 13c is as accurate as possible. Even if you pay the required annual payment, you may still owe tax when you file your return. If you prefer, you may pay the amount shown on line 13c. For more details, see Pub. 505.	14c
15	Income tax withheld and estimated to be withheld during 1997 (including income tax withholding on pensions, annuities, certain deferred income, etc.)	15
16	Subtract line 15 from line 14c. (Note: *If zero or less, or line 13c minus line 15 is less than $500, stop here. You are not required to make estimated tax payments.*)	16
17	If the first payment you are required to make is due April 15, 1997, enter ¼ of line 16 (minus any 1996 overpayment that you are applying to this installment) here and on your payment voucher(s)	17

Page 4

Record of Estimated Tax Payments (see page 3 for payment due dates)

Payment number	(a) Date	(b) Check or money order number	(c) Amount paid	(d) 1996 overpayment credit applied	(e) Total amount paid and credited (add (c) and (d))
1					
2					
3					
4					
Total. ▶					

Where To File Your Payment Voucher

Mail your payment voucher to the Internal Revenue Service at the address shown below for the place where you live. **Do not** mail your tax return to this address. Also, do not mail your estimated tax payments to the address shown in the Form 1040 or 1040A instructions.

Note: For proper delivery of your estimated tax payment to a P.O. box, you must include the box number in the address. Also, note that only the U.S. Postal Service can deliver to P.O. boxes.

If you live in:	Use this address:
New Jersey, New York (New York City and counties of Nassau, Rockland, Suffolk, and Westchester)	P.O. Box 162 Newark, NJ 07101-0162
New York (all other counties), Connecticut, Maine, Massachusetts, New Hampshire, Rhode Island, Vermont	P.O. Box 371999 Pittsburgh, PA 15250-7999
Delaware, District of Columbia, Maryland, Pennsylvania, Virginia	P.O. Box 8318 Philadelphia, PA 19162-8318
Florida, Georgia, South Carolina	P.O. Box 105900 Atlanta, GA 30348-5900
Indiana, Kentucky, Michigan, Ohio, West Virginia	P.O. Box 7422 Chicago, IL 60680-7422
Alabama, Arkansas, Louisiana, Mississippi, North Carolina, Tennessee	P.O. Box 1219 Charlotte, NC 28201-1219
Illinois, Iowa, Minnesota, Missouri, Wisconsin	P.O. Box 970006 St. Louis, MO 63197-0006
Kansas, New Mexico, Oklahoma, Texas	P.O. Box 970001 St. Louis, MO 63197-0001
Alaska, Arizona, California (counties of Alpine, Amador, Butte, Calaveras, Colusa, Contra Costa, Del Norte, El Dorado, Glenn, Humboldt, Lake, Lassen, Marin, Mendocino, Modoc, Napa, Nevada, Placer, Plumas, Sacramento, San Joaquin, Shasta, Sierra, Siskiyou, Solano, Sonoma, Sutter, Tehama, Trinity, Yolo, and Yuba), Colorado, Idaho, Montana, Nebraska, Nevada, North Dakota, Oregon, South Dakota, Utah, Washington, Wyoming	P.O. Box 510000 San Francisco, CA 94151-5100
California (all other counties), Hawaii	P.O. Box 54030 Los Angeles, CA 90054-0030
American Samoa	P.O. Box 8318 Philadelphia, PA 19162-8318
The Commonwealth of the Northern Mariana Islands	P.O. Box 8318 Philadelphia, PA 19162-8318
Puerto Rico (or if excluding income under section 933)	P.O. Box 8318 Philadelphia, PA 19162-8318
Guam: Nonpermanent residents	P.O. Box 8318 Philadelphia, PA 19162-8318
Permanent residents*	Department of Revenue and Taxation Government of Guam P.O. Box 23607 GMF, GU 96921

* You must prepare separate vouchers for estimated income tax and self-employment tax payments. Send the income tax vouchers to the Guam address and the self-employment tax vouchers to the address for Guam nonpermanent residents shown above.

Virgin Islands: Nonpermanent residents	P.O. Box 8318 Philadelphia, PA 19162-8318
Permanent residents*	V.I. Bureau of Internal Revenue 9601 Estate Thomas Charlotte Amalie St. Thomas, VI 00802

* You must prepare separate vouchers for estimated income tax and self-employment tax payments. Send the income tax vouchers to the Virgin Islands address and the self-employment tax vouchers to the address for Virgin Islands nonpermanent residents shown above.

All APO and FPO addresses	P.O. Box 8318 Philadelphia, PA 19162-8318
Foreign country: U.S. citizens and those filing Form 2555, Form 2555-EZ, or Form 4563	P.O. Box 8318 Philadelphia, PA 19162-8318

---- Tear off here ----

Form 1040-ES
Department of the Treasury
Internal Revenue Service

1997 Payment Voucher 4

OMB No. 1545-0087

File only if you are making a payment of estimated tax. Return this voucher with check or money order payable to the **"Internal Revenue Service."** Please write your social security number and "1997 Form 1040-ES" on your check or money order. Do not send cash. Enclose, but do not staple or attach, your payment with this voucher.

Calendar year—Due Jan. 15, 1998

Amount of payment

$ _____

Please type or print

Your first name and initial	Your last name	Your social security number
If joint payment, complete for spouse		
Spouse's first name and initial	Spouse's last name	Spouse's social security number
Address (number, street, and apt. no.)		
City, state, and ZIP code. (If a foreign address, enter city, province or state, postal code, and country.)		

For Paperwork Reduction Act Notice, see instructions on page 1.

Tax Forms B–29

Form **1040-ES**
Department of the Treasury
Internal Revenue Service

1997 Payment Voucher **3**

OMB No. 1545-0087

File only if you are making a payment of estimated tax. Return this voucher with check or money order payable to the **"Internal Revenue Service."** Please write your social security number and "1997 Form 1040-ES" on your check or money order. Do not send cash. Enclose, but do not staple or attach, your payment with this voucher.

Calendar year—Due Sept. 15, 1997

Amount of payment

Please type or print

Your first name and initial	Your last name	Your social security number
If joint payment, complete for spouse			
Spouse's first name and initial	Spouse's last name	Spouse's social security number
Address (number, street, and apt. no.)		
City, state, and ZIP code. (If a foreign address, enter city, province or state, postal code, and country.)		

$ _____

For Paperwork Reduction Act Notice, see instructions on page 1.

- Tear off here -

Form **1040-ES**
Department of the Treasury
Internal Revenue Service

1997 Payment Voucher **2**

OMB No. 1545-0087

File only if you are making a payment of estimated tax. Return this voucher with check or money order payable to the **"Internal Revenue Service."** Please write your social security number and "1997 Form 1040-ES" on your check or money order. Do not send cash. Enclose, but do not staple or attach, your payment with this voucher.

Calendar year—Due June 16, 1997

Amount of payment

Please type or print

Your first name and initial	Your last name	Your social security number
If joint payment, complete for spouse			
Spouse's first name and initial	Spouse's last name	Spouse's social security number
Address (number, street, and apt. no.)		
City, state, and ZIP code. (If a foreign address, enter city, province or state, postal code, and country.)		

$ _____

For Paperwork Reduction Act Notice, see instructions on page 1.

- Tear off here -

Form **1040-ES**
Department of the Treasury
Internal Revenue Service

1997 Payment Voucher **1**

OMB No. 1545-0087

File only if you are making a payment of estimated tax. Return this voucher with check or money order payable to the **"Internal Revenue Service."** Please write your social security number and "1997 Form 1040-ES" on your check or money order. Do not send cash. Enclose, but do not staple or attach, your payment with this voucher.

Calendar year—Due April 15, 1997

Amount of payment

Please type or print

Your first name and initial	Your last name	Your social security number
If joint payment, complete for spouse			
Spouse's first name and initial	Spouse's last name	Spouse's social security number
Address (number, street, and apt. no.)		
City, state, and ZIP code. (If a foreign address, enter city, province or state, postal code, and country.)		

$ _____

For Paperwork Reduction Act Notice, see instructions on page 1. Page 7

Form **2106**	**Employee Business Expenses**	OMB No. 1545-0139
Department of the Treasury Internal Revenue Service (99)	▶ See separate instructions. ▶ Attach to Form 1040.	**1996** Attachment Sequence No. **54**

Your name	Social security number	Occupation in which expenses were incurred

Part I — Employee Business Expenses and Reimbursements

STEP 1   Enter Your Expenses

		Column A Other Than Meals and Entertainment	**Column B** Meals and Entertainment
1	Vehicle expense from line 22 or line 29		
2	Parking fees, tolls, and transportation, including train, bus, etc., that **did not** involve overnight travel or commuting to and from work . .		
3	Travel expense while away from home overnight, including lodging, airplane, car rental, etc. **Do not** include meals and entertainment		
4	Business expenses not included on lines 1 through 3. **Do not** include meals and entertainment		
5	Meals and entertainment expenses (see instructions)		
6	**Total expenses.** In Column A, add lines 1 through 4 and enter the result. In Column B, enter the amount from line 5		

Note: *If you were not reimbursed for any expenses in Step 1, skip line 7 and enter the amount from line 6 on line 8.*

STEP 2   Enter Amounts Your Employer Gave You for Expenses Listed in STEP 1

7	Enter amounts your employer gave you that were **not** reported to you in box 1 of Form W-2. Include any amount reported under code "L" in box 13 of your Form W-2 (see instructions) . . .		

STEP 3   Figure Expenses To Deduct on Schedule A (Form 1040)

8	Subtract line 7 from line 6		
	Note: *If **both columns** of line 8 are zero, **stop here.** If Column A is less than zero, report the amount as income on Form 1040, line 7.*		
9	In Column A, enter the amount from line 8. In Column B, multiply the amount on line 8 by 50% (.50). If either column is zero or less, enter -0- in that column		
10	Add the amounts on line 9 of both columns and enter the total here. **Also, enter the total on Schedule A (Form 1040).** (Qualified performing artists and individuals with disabilities, see the instructions for special rules on where to enter the total.) . . . . ▶		

For Paperwork Reduction Act Notice, see instructions.   Cat. No. 11700N   Form **2106** (1996)

Form 2106 (1996) Page **2**

Part II Vehicle Expenses (See instructions to find out which sections to complete.)

Section A—General Information

			(a) Vehicle 1	(b) Vehicle 2
11	Enter the date vehicle was placed in service	11	/ /	/ /
12	Total miles vehicle was driven during 1996	12	miles	miles
13	Business miles included on line 12	13	miles	miles
14	Percent of business use. Divide line 13 by line 12	14	%	%
15	Average daily round trip commuting distance	15	miles	miles
16	Commuting miles included on line 12	16	miles	miles
17	Other personal miles. Add lines 13 and 16 and subtract the total from line 12	17	miles	miles
18	Do you (or your spouse) have another vehicle available for personal purposes?		☐ Yes	☐ No
19	If your employer provided you with a vehicle, is personal use during off-duty hours permitted? ☐ Yes ☐ No ☐ Not applicable
20	Do you have evidence to support your deduction?		☐ Yes	☐ No
21	If "Yes," is the evidence written?		☐ Yes	☐ No

Section B—Standard Mileage Rate (Use this section only if you own the vehicle.)

| 22 | Multiply line 13 by 31¢ (.31). Enter the result here and on line 1. (Rural mail carriers, see instructions.) | 22 | |

Section C—Actual Expenses

			(a) Vehicle 1	(b) Vehicle 2
23	Gasoline, oil, repairs, vehicle insurance, etc.	23		
24a	Vehicle rentals	24a		
b	Inclusion amount (see instructions)	24b		
c	Subtract line 24b from line 24a	24c		
25	Value of employer-provided vehicle (applies only if 100% of annual lease value was included on Form W-2—see instructions)	25		
26	Add lines 23, 24c, and 25	26		
27	Multiply line 26 by the percentage on line 14	27		
28	Depreciation. Enter amount from line 38 below	28		
29	Add lines 27 and 28. Enter total here and on line 1	29		

Section D—Depreciation of Vehicles (Use this section only if you own the vehicle.)

			(a) Vehicle 1	(b) Vehicle 2
30	Enter cost or other basis (see instructions)	30		
31	Enter amount of section 179 deduction (see instructions)	31		
32	Multiply line 30 by line 14 (see instructions if you elected the section 179 deduction)	32		
33	Enter depreciation method and percentage (see instructions)	33		
34	Multiply line 32 by the percentage on line 33 (see instructions)	34		
35	Add lines 31 and 34	35		
36	Enter the limitation amount from the table in the line 36 instructions	36		
37	Multiply line 36 by the percentage on line 14	37		
38	Enter the **smaller** of line 35 or line 37. Also, enter this amount on line 28 above	38		

Form 2106-EZ
Department of the Treasury
Internal Revenue Service (99)

Unreimbursed Employee Business Expenses
▶ See instructions on back.
▶ Attach to Form 1040.

OMB No. 1545-1441

1996

Attachment Sequence No. **54A**

Your name | Social security number | Occupation in which expenses were incurred

Part I — General Information

You May Use This Form ONLY if All of the Following Apply:

- You are an employee deducting expenses attributable to your job.
- You **do not** get reimbursed by your employer for any expenses (amounts your employer included in box 1 of your Form W-2 are not considered reimbursements).
- If you are claiming vehicle expense,
  - **a** You own your vehicle, and
  - **b** You are using the standard mileage rate for 1996 **and** also used it for the year you first placed the vehicle in service.

Part II — Figure Your Expenses

1. Vehicle expense using the standard mileage rate. Complete Part III and multiply line 8a by 31¢ (.31) **1**
2. Parking fees, tolls, and transportation, including train, bus, etc., that **did not** involve overnight travel or commuting to and from work **2**
3. Travel expense while away from home overnight, including lodging, airplane, car rental, etc. **Do not** include meals and entertainment **3**
4. Business expenses not included on lines 1 through 3. **Do not** include meals and entertainment . **4**
5. Meals and entertainment expenses: $ _____ x 50% (.50) **5**
6. **Total expenses.** Add lines 1 through 5. Enter here and **on line 20 of Schedule A (Form 1040).** (Qualified performing artists and individuals with disabilities, see the instructions for special rules on where to enter this amount.) **6**

Part III — Information on Your Vehicle. Complete this part ONLY if you are claiming vehicle expense on line 1.

7. When did you place your vehicle in service for business purposes? (month, day, year) ▶ _____ / _____ / _____

8. Of the total number of miles you drove your vehicle during 1996, enter the number of miles you used your vehicle for:

   a Business _____ **b** Commuting _____ **c** Other _____

9. Do you (or your spouse) have another vehicle available for personal use? . . . . ☐ Yes ☐ No

10. Was your vehicle available for use during off-duty hours? . . . . ☐ Yes ☐ No

11a. Do you have evidence to support your deduction? . . . . ☐ Yes ☐ No

   b If "Yes," is the evidence written? . . . . ☐ Yes ☐ No

For Paperwork Reduction Act Notice, see back of form.   Cat. No. 20604Q   Form **2106-EZ** (1996)

Form **2119**	**Sale of Your Home**	OMB No. 1545-0072
Department of the Treasury Internal Revenue Service	▶ Attach to Form 1040 for year of sale. ▶ See separate instructions. ▶ Please print or type.	**1996** Attachment Sequence No. **20**

Your first name and initial. If a joint return, also give spouse's name and initial.	Last name	Your social security number
Fill in Your Address Only If You Are Filing This Form by Itself and Not With Your Tax Return	Present address (no., street, and apt. no., rural route, or P.O. box no. if mail is not delivered to street address)	Spouse's social security number
	City, town or post office, state, and ZIP code	

Part I — Gain on Sale

1. Date your former main home was sold (month, day, year) ▶ **1** __ / __ / __
2. Have you bought or built a new main home? ☐ Yes ☐ No
3. If any part of either main home was ever rented out or used for business, check here ▶ ☐ and see page 3.
4. Selling price of home. Do not include personal property items you sold with your home — **4**
5. Expense of sale (see page 3) — **5**
6. Subtract line 5 from line 4 — **6**
7. Adjusted basis of home sold (see page 3) — **7**
8. **Gain on sale.** Subtract line 7 from line 6 — **8**

Is line 8 more than zero?
— Yes ▶ If line 2 is "Yes," you **must** go to Part II or Part III, whichever applies. If line 2 is "No," go to line 9.
— No ▶ **Stop** and attach this form to your return.

9. If you haven't replaced your home, do you plan to do so within the **replacement period** (see page 1)? ☐ Yes ☐ No
   - If line 9 is "Yes," stop here, attach this form to your return, and see **Additional Filing Requirements** on page 1.
   - If line 9 is "No," you **must** go to Part II or Part III, whichever applies.

Part II — One-Time Exclusion of Gain for People Age 55 or Older
By completing this part, you are electing to take the one-time exclusion (see page 2). If you are not electing to take the exclusion, go to Part III now.

10. Who was age 55 or older on the date of sale? ☐ You ☐ Your spouse ☐ Both of you
11. Did the person who was 55 or older own and use the property as his or her main home for a total of at least 3 years of the 5-year period before the sale? See page 2 for exceptions. If "No," go to Part III now ☐ Yes ☐ No
12. At the time of sale, who owned the home? ☐ You ☐ Your spouse ☐ Both of you
13. Social security number of spouse at the time of sale if you had a different spouse from the one above. If you were not married at the time of sale, enter "None" ▶ **13**
14. **Exclusion.** Enter the **smaller** of line 8 or $125,000 ($62,500 if married filing separate return). Then, go to line 15 — **14**

Part III — Adjusted Sales Price, Taxable Gain, and Adjusted Basis of New Home

15. If line 14 is blank, enter the amount from line 8. Otherwise, subtract line 14 from line 8 — **15**
    - If line 15 is zero, stop and attach this form to your return.
    - If line 15 is more than zero and line 2 is "Yes," go to line 16 now.
    - If you are reporting this sale on the installment method, stop and see page 4.
    - All others, stop and **enter the amount from line 15 on Schedule D, col. (g), line 4 or line 12.**
16. Fixing-up expenses (see page 4 for time limits) — **16**
17. If line 14 is blank, enter amount from line 16. Otherwise, add lines 14 and 16 — **17**
18. **Adjusted sales price.** Subtract line 17 from line 6 — **18**
19a. Date you moved into new home ▶ __ / __ / __ **b** Cost of new home (see page 4) — **19b**
20. Subtract line 19b from line 18. If zero or less, enter -0- — **20**
21. **Taxable gain.** Enter the **smaller** of line 15 or line 20 — **21**
    - If line 21 is zero, go to line 22 and attach this form to your return.
    - If you are reporting this sale on the installment method, see the line 15 instructions and go to line 22.
    - All others, **enter the amount from line 21 on Schedule D, col. (g), line 4 or line 12,** and go to line 22.
22. Postponed gain. Subtract line 21 from line 15 — **22**
23. **Adjusted basis of new home.** Subtract line 22 from line 19b — **23**

Sign Here Only If You Are Filing This Form by Itself and Not With Your Tax Return

Under penalties of perjury, I declare that I have examined this form, including attachments, and to the best of my knowledge and belief, it is true, correct, and complete.

Your signature _____ Date _____ Spouse's signature _____ Date _____

If a joint return, both must sign.

For Paperwork Reduction Act Notice, see separate instructions.   Cat. No. 11710J   Form **2119** (1996)

Form 2120 — Multiple Support Declaration

Form 2120
(Rev. November 1996)
Department of the Treasury
Internal Revenue Service

Multiple Support Declaration

▶ Attach to Form 1040 or Form 1040A of Person Claiming the Dependent.

OMB No. 1545-0071

Attachment Sequence No. **50**

Name of person claiming the dependent

Social security number

During the calendar year 19 ...., I paid over 10% of the support of

_____
Name of person

I could have claimed this person as a dependent except that I did not pay over 50% of his or her support. I understand that the person named above is being claimed as a dependent on the income tax return of

_____
Name

_____
Address

I agree not to claim this person as a dependent on my Federal income tax return for any tax year that began in this calendar year.

_____   _____
Your signature   Your social security number

_____   _____
Date   Address (number, street, apt. no.)

_____
City, state, and ZIP code

Instructions

Paperwork Reduction Act Notice

We ask for the information on this form to carry out the Internal Revenue laws of the United States. You are required to give us the information. We need it to ensure that you are complying with these laws and to allow us to figure and collect the right amount of tax.

You are not required to provide the information requested on a form that is subject to the Paperwork Reduction Act unless the form displays a valid OMB control number. Books or records relating to a form or its instructions must be retained as long as their contents may become material in the administration of any Internal Revenue law. Generally, tax returns and return information are confidential, as required by Internal Revenue Code section 6103.

The time needed to complete and file this form will vary depending on individual circumstances. The estimated average time is: **Recordkeeping,** 7 minutes; **Learning about the law or the form,** 2 minutes; **Preparing the form,** 7 minutes; and **Copying, assembling, and sending the form to the IRS,** 10 minutes.

If you have comments concerning the accuracy of these time estimates or suggestions for making this form simpler, we would be happy to hear from you. You can write or call the IRS. See the instructions of the tax return with which this form is filed.

Purpose of Form

Form 2120 is used for two purposes:

1. When two or more individuals together pay over 50% of another person's support, one of them can claim the person as a dependent for tax purposes. Any person who pays over 10% but less than 50% and **does not** claim the dependent must complete and sign a Form 2120 or similar statement and give it to the person claiming the dependent.

2. The person **claiming** the dependent attaches all of the Form(s) 2120 to his or her tax return. See **How To File** below.

Who Can Claim the Dependent

Generally, to claim someone as a dependent, you must pay over 50% of that person's living expenses (support).

Even if you don't pay over half of another person's support, you may still be able to claim him or her as a dependent if **all five** of the following apply and all others who paid over 10% agree not to claim the person as a dependent.

1. You and one or more other eligible person(s) together paid over half of another person's support.

2. You paid over 10% of the support.

3. No one alone paid over half of the person's support.

4. The other four dependency tests are met. See **Dependents** in the Form 1040 or Form 1040A instructions.

5. Each other eligible person who paid over 10% of support completes **Form 2120** or similar statement.

An **eligible person** is someone who could have claimed another person as a dependent except that he or she did not pay over half of that person's support.

How To File

The person claiming the dependent must attach all the completed and signed Form(s) 2120 or similar statement(s) to his or her tax return. The name and social security number of the person claiming the dependent must be at the top of each Form 2120 or similar statement.

Additional Information

See **Pub. 501,** Exemptions, Standard Deduction, and Filing Information, for more information.

Cat. No. 11712F

Form **2120** (Rev. 11-96)

Form **2210**	**Underpayment of Estimated Tax by Individuals, Estates, and Trusts**	OMB No. 1545-0140
Department of the Treasury Internal Revenue Service	▶ See separate instructions. ▶ Attach to Form 1040, 1040A, 1040NR, 1040NR-EZ, or 1041.	**19**96 Attachment Sequence No. 06

Name(s) shown on tax return	Identifying number

Note: *In most cases, you **do not** need to file Form 2210. The IRS will figure any penalty you owe and send you a bill. File Form 2210 **only** if one or more boxes in Part I apply to you. If you do not need to file Form 2210, you still may use it to figure your penalty. Enter the amount from line 20 or line 36 on the penalty line of your return, but **do not** attach Form 2210.*

Part I — Reasons for Filing—If 1a, b, or c below applies to you, you may be able to lower or eliminate your penalty. But you MUST check the boxes that apply and file Form 2210 with your tax return. If 1d below applies to you, check that box and file Form 2210 with your tax return.

1   Check whichever boxes apply (if none apply, see the **Note** above):

   a ☐ You request a **waiver.** In certain circumstances, the IRS will waive all or part of the penalty. See **Waiver of Penalty** on page 2 of the instructions.

   b ☐ You use the **annualized income installment method.** If your income varied during the year, this method may reduce the amount of one or more required installments. See page 4 of the instructions.

   c ☐ You had Federal income tax withheld from wages and, for estimated tax purposes, you treat the withheld tax as paid on the dates it was actually withheld, instead of in equal amounts on the payment due dates. See the instructions for line 22 on page 3.

   d ☐ Your required annual payment (line 13 below) is based on your 1995 tax and you filed or are filing a joint return for either 1995 or 1996 but not for both years.

Part II — Required Annual Payment

2	Enter your 1996 tax after credits (see page 2 of the instructions)	2
3	Other taxes (see page 2 of the instructions)	3
4	Add lines 2 and 3	4
5	Earned income credit **5**	
6	Credit for Federal tax paid on fuels **6**	
7	Add lines 5 and 6	7
8	Current year tax. Subtract line 7 from line 4	8
9	Multiply line 8 by 90% (.90) **9**	
10	Withholding taxes. **Do not** include any estimated tax payments on this line (see page 2 of the instructions)	10
11	Subtract line 10 from line 8. If less than $500, stop here; **do not** complete or file this form. You do not owe the penalty	11
12	Enter the tax shown on your 1995 tax return (110% of that amount if the adjusted gross income shown on that return is more than $150,000, or if married filing separately for 1996, more than $75,000). **Caution:** See page 2 of the instructions	12
13	**Required annual payment.** Enter the **smaller** of line 9 or line 12	13

Note: *If line 10 is equal to or more than line 13, stop here; you do not owe the penalty. Do not file Form 2210 unless you checked box 1d above.*

Part III — Short Method (**Caution:** *See page 2 of the instructions to find out if you can use the short method. If you checked box **1b** or **c** in Part I, skip this part and go to Part IV.*)

14	Enter the amount, if any, from line 10 above **14**	
15	Enter the total amount, if any, of estimated tax payments you made **15**	
16	Add lines 14 and 15	16
17	**Total underpayment for year.** Subtract line 16 from line 13. If zero or less, stop here; you do not owe the penalty. Do not file Form 2210 unless you checked box 1d above	17
18	Multiply line 17 by .05914	18
19	• If the amount on line 17 was paid **on or after** 4/15/97, enter -0-.	
	• If the amount on line 17 was paid **before** 4/15/97, make the following computation to find the amount to enter on line 19. Amount on line 17 × Number of days paid before 4/15/97 × .00025	19
20	**PENALTY.** Subtract line 19 from line 18. Enter the result here and on Form 1040, line 63; Form 1040A, line 34; Form 1040NR, line 63; Form 1040NR-EZ, line 26; or Form 1041, line 26 ▶	20

For Paperwork Reduction Act Notice, see page 1 of separate instructions.   Cat. No. 11744P   Form **2210** (1996)

Form 2210 (1996) — Page 2

Part IV — Regular Method (See page 2 of the instructions if you are filing Form 1040NR or 1040NR-EZ.)

Section A—Figure Your Underpayment

Payment Due Dates: (a) 4/15/96, (b) 6/15/96, (c) 9/15/96, (d) 1/15/97

21. **Required installments.** If box 1b applies, enter the amounts from Schedule AI, line 26. Otherwise, enter ¼ of line 13, Form 2210, in each column

22. **Estimated tax paid and tax withheld** (see page 3 of the instructions). For column (a) only, also enter the amount from line 22 on line 26. If line 22 is equal to or more than line 21 for all payment periods, stop here; you do not owe the penalty. Do not file Form 2210 unless you checked a box in Part I
    Complete lines 23 through 29 of one column before going to the next column.

23. Enter amount, if any, from line 29 of previous column

24. Add lines 22 and 23

25. Add amounts on lines 27 and 28 of the previous column

26. Subtract line 25 from line 24. If zero or less, enter -0-. For column (a) only, enter the amount from line 22

27. If the amount on line 26 is zero, subtract line 24 from line 25. Otherwise, enter -0-

28. **Underpayment.** If line 21 is equal to or more than line 26, subtract line 26 from line 21. Then go to line 23 of next column. Otherwise, go to line 29 ▶

29. **Overpayment.** If line 26 is more than line 21, subtract line 21 from line 26. Then go to line 23 of next column

Section B—Figure the Penalty (Complete lines 30 through 35 of one column before going to the next column.)

Rate Period 1 — April 16, 1996—June 30, 1996

30. Number of days FROM the date shown above line 30 TO the date the amount on line 28 was paid **or** 6/30/96, whichever is earlier
    Column (a): 4/15/96 Days: ___ ; Column (b): 6/15/96 Days: ___

31. $\dfrac{\text{Underpayment on line 28 (see page 4 of the instructions)} \times \text{Number of days on line 30}}{366} \times .08$ ▶ $ ___ $ ___

Rate Period 2 — July 1, 1996—December 31, 1996

32. Number of days FROM the date shown above line 32 TO the date the amount on line 28 was paid **or** 12/31/96, whichever is earlier
    Column (a): 6/30/96 Days: ___ ; Column (b): 6/30/96 Days: ___ ; Column (c): 9/15/96 Days: ___

33. $\dfrac{\text{Underpayment on line 28 (see page 4 of the instructions)} \times \text{Number of days on line 32}}{366} \times .09$ ▶ $ ___ $ ___ $ ___

Rate Period 3 — January 1, 1997—April 15, 1997

34. Number of days FROM the date shown above line 34 TO the date the amount on line 28 was paid **or** 4/15/97, whichever is earlier
    Column (a): 12/31/96 Days: ___ ; Column (b): 12/31/96 Days: ___ ; Column (c): 12/31/96 Days: ___ ; Column (d): 1/15/97 Days: ___

35. $\dfrac{\text{Underpayment on line 28 (see page 4 of the instructions)} \times \text{Number of days on line 34}}{365} \times .09$ ▶ $ ___ $ ___ $ ___ $ ___

36. **PENALTY.** Add all amounts on lines 31, 33, and 35 in all columns. Enter the total here and on Form 1040, line 63; Form 1040A, line 34; Form 1040NR, line 63; Form 1040NR-EZ, line 26; or Form 1041, line 26 ▶ 36 $ ___

Form 2210 (1996) — Page 3

Schedule AI—Annualized Income Installment Method (see pages 4 and 5 of the instructions)

Estates and trusts, **do not** use the period ending dates shown to the right. Instead, use the following: 2/29/96, 4/30/96, 7/31/96, and 11/30/96.

	(a) 1/1/96–3/31/96	(b) 1/1/96–5/31/96	(c) 1/1/96–8/31/96	(d) 1/1/96–12/31/96

Part I — Annualized Income Installments
Caution: *Complete lines 20–26 of one column before going to the next column.*

#	Description	(a)	(b)	(c)	(d)
1	Enter your adjusted gross income for each period (see instructions). (Estates and trusts, enter your taxable income without your exemption for each period.)				
2	Annualization amounts. (Estates and trusts, see instructions.)	4	2.4	1.5	1
3	Annualized income. Multiply line 1 by line 2				
4	Enter your itemized deductions for the period shown in each column. If you do not itemize, enter -0- and skip to line 7. (Estates and trusts, enter -0-, skip to line 9, and enter the amount from line 3 on line 9.)				
5	Annualization amounts	4	2.4	1.5	1
6	Multiply line 4 by line 5 (see instructions if line 3 is more than $58,975)				
7	In each column, enter the full amount of your standard deduction from Form 1040, line 34, or Form 1040A, line 19 (Form 1040NR or 1040NR-EZ filers, enter -0-. **Exception:** Indian students and business apprentices, enter standard deduction from Form 1040NR, line 33 or Form 1040NR-EZ, line 10.)				
8	Enter the **larger** of line 6 or line 7				
9	Subtract line 8 from line 3				
10	In each column, multiply $2,550 by the total number of exemptions claimed (see instructions if line 3 is more than $88,475). (Estates and trusts and Form 1040NR or 1040NR-EZ filers, enter the exemption amount shown on your tax return.)				
11	Subtract line 10 from line 9				
12	Figure your tax on the amount on line 11 (see instructions)				
13	Form 1040 filers only, enter your self-employment tax from line 35 below				
14	Enter other taxes for each payment period (see instructions)				
15	Total tax. Add lines 12, 13, and 14				
16	For each period, enter the same type of credits as allowed on Form 2210, lines 2, 5, and 6 (see instructions)				
17	Subtract line 16 from line 15. If zero or less, enter -0-				
18	Applicable percentage	22.5%	45%	67.5%	90%
19	Multiply line 17 by line 18				
20	Add the amounts in all preceding columns of line 26	▓			
21	Subtract line 20 from line 19. If zero or less, enter -0-				
22	Enter ¼ of line 13 on page 1 of Form 2210 in each column				
23	Enter amount from line 25 of the preceding column of this schedule	▓			
24	Add lines 22 and 23 and enter the total				
25	Subtract line 21 from line 24. If zero or less, enter -0-				▓
26	Enter the **smaller** of line 21 or line 24 here and on Form 2210, line 21 ▶				

Part II — Annualized Self-Employment Tax

#	Description	(a)	(b)	(c)	(d)
27a	Net earnings from self-employment for the period (see instructions)				
b	Annualization amounts	4	2.4	1.5	1
c	Multiply line 27a by line 27b				
28	Social security tax limit	$62,700	$62,700	$62,700	$62,700
29	Enter actual wages subject to social security tax or the 6.2% portion of the 7.65% railroad retirement (tier 1) tax				
30	Annualization amounts	4	2.4	1.5	1
31	Multiply line 29 by line 30				
32	Subtract line 31 from line 28. If zero or less, enter -0-				
33	Multiply the smaller of line 27c or line 32 by .124				
34	Multiply line 27c by .029				
35	Add lines 33 and 34. Enter the result here and on line 13 above ▶				

Form **2441**	**Child and Dependent Care Expenses**	OMB No. 1545-0068
Department of the Treasury Internal Revenue Service (99)	▶ Attach to Form 1040. ▶ See separate instructions.	**1996** Attachment Sequence No. **21**

Name(s) shown on Form 1040 | Your social security number

You need to understand the following terms to complete this form: **Qualifying Person(s), Dependent Care Benefits, Qualified Expenses,** and **Earned Income.** See **Important Terms** on page 1 of the Form 2441 instructions.

Part I Persons or Organizations Who Provided the Care—You **must** complete this part.
(If you need more space, use the bottom of page 2.)

1	(a) Care provider's name	(b) Address (number, street, apt. no., city, state, and ZIP code)	(c) Identifying number (SSN or EIN)	(d) Amount paid (see instructions)

2 Add the amounts in column (d) of line 1 . . . . **2**

3 Enter the number of **qualifying persons** cared for in 1996 . . . . ▶ ☐

Did you receive **dependent care benefits?**
— NO ⟶ Complete only Part II below.
— YES ⟶ Complete Part III on the back now.

Caution: *If the care was provided in your home, you may owe employment taxes. See the instructions for Form 1040, line 50.*

Part II Credit for Child and Dependent Care Expenses

4 Enter the amount of **qualified expenses** you incurred and paid in 1996. DO NOT enter more than $2,400 for one qualifying person or $4,800 for two or more persons. If you completed Part III, enter the amount from line 25 . . . . **4**

5 Enter YOUR **earned income** **5**

6 If married filing a joint return, enter YOUR SPOUSE'S earned income (if student or disabled, see the instructions); **all others,** enter the amount from line 5 . . . . **6**

7 Enter the **smallest** of line 4, 5, or 6 . . . . **7**

8 Enter the amount from Form 1040, line 32 . . . . **8**

9 Enter on line 9 the decimal amount shown below that applies to the amount on line 8

If line 8 is—		Decimal amount is	If line 8 is—		Decimal amount is
Over	But not over		Over	But not over	
$0	10,000	.30	$20,000	22,000	.24
10,000	12,000	.29	22,000	24,000	.23
12,000	14,000	.28	24,000	26,000	.22
14,000	16,000	.27	26,000	28,000	.21
16,000	18,000	.26	28,000	No limit	.20
18,000	20,000	.25			

9 X .

10 Multiply **line 7** by the decimal amount on line 9. Enter the result. Then, see the instructions for the amount of credit to enter on Form 1040, line 39 . . . . **10**

For Paperwork Reduction Act Notice, see separate instructions. Cat. No. 11862M   Form **2441** (1996)

Form 2441 (1996) Page **2**

Part III Dependent Care Benefits—Complete this part **only** if you received these benefits.

11 Enter the total amount of **dependent care benefits** you received for 1996. This amount should be shown in box 10 of your W-2 form(s). DO NOT include amounts that were reported to you as wages in box 1 of Form(s) W-2 . . . . **11**

12 Enter the amount forfeited, if any. See the instructions **12**

13 Subtract line 12 from line 11 . . . . **13**

14 Enter the total amount of **qualified expenses** incurred in 1996 for the care of the qualifying person(s) **14**

15 Enter the **smaller** of line 13 or 14 . . . . **15**

16 Enter YOUR **earned income** **16**

17 If married filing a joint return, enter YOUR SPOUSE'S earned income (if student or disabled, see the line 6 instructions); if married filing a separate return, see the instructions for the amount to enter; **all others,** enter the amount from line 16 . . **17**

18 Enter the **smallest** of line 15, 16, or 17 . . . . **18**

19 **Excluded benefits.** Enter here the **smaller** of the following:
  • The amount from line 18, or
  • $5,000 ($2,500 if married filing a separate return **and** you were required to enter your spouse's earned income on line 17). **19**

20 **Taxable benefits.** Subtract line 19 from line 13. Also, include this amount on Form 1040, line 7. On the dotted line next to line 7, write "DCB" **20**

To claim the child and dependent care credit, complete lines 21–25 below, and lines 4–10 on the front of this form.

21 Enter the amount of qualified expenses you incurred and paid in 1996. DO NOT include on this line any excluded benefits shown on line 19 . . . . **21**

22 Enter $2,400 ($4,800 if two or more qualifying persons) . . . **22**

23 Enter the amount from line 19 . . . . **23**

24 Subtract line 23 from line 22. If zero or less, **STOP.** You cannot take the credit. **Exception.** If you paid 1995 expenses in 1996, see the line 10 instructions **24**

25 Enter the **smaller** of line 21 or 24 here **and** on line 4 on the front of this form **25**

Form **3800**	**General Business Credit**	OMB No. 1545-0895
Department of the Treasury Internal Revenue Service	▶ Attach to your tax return. ▶ See separate instructions.	**1996** Attachment Sequence No. 22

Name(s) shown on return | Identifying number

Part I — Tentative Credit

1a	Current year investment credit (Form 3468, Part I)	1a
b	Current year work opportunity credit (Form 5884, Part I)	1b
c	Current year credit for alcohol used as fuel (Form 6478)	1c
d	Current year credit for increasing research activities (Form 6765, Part I)	1d
e	Current year low-income housing credit (Form 8586, Part I)	1e
f	Current year enhanced oil recovery credit (Form 8830, Part I)	1f
g	Current year disabled access credit (Form 8826, Part I)	1g
h	Current year renewable electricity production credit (Form 8835, Part I)	1h
i	Current year Indian employment credit (Form 8845, Part I)	1i
j	Current year credit for employer social security and Medicare taxes paid on certain employee tips (Form 8846, Part I)	1j
k	Current year orphan drug credit (Form 8820, Part I)	1k
l	Current year credit for contributions to selected community development corporations (Form 8847, Part I)	1l
m	Current year trans-Alaska pipeline liability fund credit (see instructions)	1m
n	**Current year general business credit.** Add lines 1a through 1m	1n
2	Passive activity credits included on line 1n (see instructions)	2
3	Subtract line 2 from line 1n	3
4	Passive activity credits allowed for 1996 (see instructions)	4
5	Carryforward of general business, WIN, or ESOP credit to 1996 (see instructions for the schedule to attach)	5
6	Carryback of general business credit to 1996 (see instructions)	6
7	**Tentative general business credit.** Add lines 3 through 6	7

Part II — General Business Credit Limitation Based on Amount of Tax

8	Regular tax before credits: • Individuals. Enter amount from Form 1040, line 38 • Corporations. Enter amount from Form 1120, Schedule J, line 3 (or Form 1120-A, Part I, line 1) • Other filers. Enter regular tax before credits from your return	8
9a	Credit for child and dependent care expenses (Form 2441, line 10)	9a
b	Credit for the elderly or the disabled (Schedule R (Form 1040), line 20)	9b
c	Mortgage interest credit (Form 8396, line 11)	9c
d	Foreign tax credit (Form 1116, line 32, or Form 1118, Sch. B, line 12)	9d
e	Possessions tax credit (Form 5735)	9e
f	Credit for fuel from a nonconventional source	9f
g	Qualified electric vehicle credit (Form 8834, line 19)	9g
h	Add lines 9a through 9g	9h
10	Net regular tax. Subtract line 9h from line 8	10
11	Alternative minimum tax: • Individuals. Enter amount from Form 6251, line 28 • Corporations. Enter amount from Form 4626, line 15 • Estates and trusts. Enter amount from Form 1041, Schedule I, line 41	11
12	Net income tax. Add lines 10 and 11	12
13	Tentative minimum tax (see instructions): • Individuals. Enter amount from Form 6251, line 26 • Corporations. Enter amount from Form 4626, line 13 • Estates and trusts. Enter amount from Form 1041, Schedule I, line 37	13
14	If line 10 is more than $25,000, enter 25% (.25) of the excess (see instructions)	14
15	Enter the greater of line 13 or line 14	15
16	Subtract line 15 from line 12. If zero or less, enter -0-	16
17	**General business credit allowed for current year.** Enter the **smaller** of line 7 or line 16 here and on Form 1040, line 42; Form 1120, Schedule J, line 4d; Form 1120-A, Part I, line 2a; Form 1041, Schedule G, line 2c; or the applicable line of your return. **Individuals, estates, and trusts:** See instructions if the credit for increasing research activities is claimed. **C corporations:** See instructions for Schedule A if any regular investment credit carryforward is claimed. See the instructions if the corporation has had a post-1986 "ownership change."	17

For Paperwork Reduction Act Notice, see page 2 of this form.   Cat. No. 12392F   Form **3800** (1996)

Form 3800 (1996) Page **2**

Schedule A— Additional General Business Credit Allowed By Section 38(c)(2) (Before Repeal by the Revenue Reconciliation Act of 1990)—Only Applicable to C Corporations

18	Enter the portion of the credit shown on line 5 that is attributable to the regular investment credit under section 46 (before amendment by the Revenue Reconciliation Act of 1990)	18
19	Tentative minimum tax (from line 13)	19
20	Multiply line 19 by 25% (.25)	20
21	Enter the amount from line 16	21
22	Enter the portion of the credit shown on line 7 that is NOT attributable to the regular investment credit under section 46 (before amendment by the Revenue Reconciliation Act of 1990)	22
23	Subtract line 22 from line 21 (if zero or less, enter -0-)	23
24	Subtract line 23 from line 18 (if zero or less, enter -0-)	24
25	For purposes of this line only, refigure the amount on line 11, Form 4626, by using zero on line 6, Form 4626, and enter the result here .	25
26	Multiply line 25 by 10% (.10)	26
27	Net income tax (from line 12)	27
28	General business credit (from line 17)	28
29	Subtract line 28 from line 27	29
30	Subtract line 26 from line 29	30
31	Enter the smallest of line 20, line 24, or line 30	31
32	Subtract line 31 from line 19	32
33	Enter the greater of line 14 or line 32	33
34	Subtract line 33 from line 27	34
35	Enter the smaller of line 10 or line 34. Enter this amount also on line 17 instead of the amount previously figured on that line. Write "Sec. 38(c)(2)" in the margin next to your entry on line 17 .	35
36	If line 34 is greater than line 35, enter the excess here and see the instructions on how to claim the additional credit	36

Paperwork Reduction Act Notice

We ask for the information on this form to carry out the Internal Revenue laws of the United States. You are required to give us the information. We need it to ensure that you are complying with these laws and to allow us to figure and collect the right amount of tax.

You are not required to provide the information requested on a form that is subject to the Paperwork Reduction Act unless the form displays a valid OMB control number. Books or records relating to a form or its instructions must be retained as long as their contents may become material in the administration of any Internal Revenue law. Generally, tax returns and return information are confidential, as required by Code section 6103.

The time needed to complete and file this form will vary depending on individual circumstances. The estimated average time is:

Recordkeeping . . . 12 hr., 12 min.
Learning about the
law or the form . . . . 1 hr.
Preparing and sending
the form to the IRS . . 1 hr., 14 min.

If you have comments concerning the accuracy of these time estimates or suggestions for making this form simpler, we would be happy to hear from you. You can write to the IRS at the address listed in the instructions for the tax return with which this form is filed.

Form **3903**	**Moving Expenses**	OMB No. 1545-0062
Department of the Treasury Internal Revenue Service	▶ Attach to Form 1040. ▶ See instructions on back.	**1996** Attachment Sequence No. **62**

Name(s) shown on Form 1040	Your social security number

Caution: *If you are a member of the armed forces, see the instructions before completing this form.*

1. Enter the number of miles from your **old home** to your **new workplace** . . **1** _____ miles
2. Enter the number of miles from your **old home** to your **old workplace** . . **2** _____ miles
3. Subtract line 2 from line 1. Enter the result but not less than zero . . . . **3** _____ miles

   Is line 3 at least 50 miles?

   Yes ▶ Go to line 4. Also, see **Time Test** in the instructions.

   No ▶ You **cannot** deduct your moving expenses. Do not complete the rest of this form.

4. Transportation and storage of household goods and personal effects (see instructions) . . . **4** _____
5. Travel and lodging expenses of moving from your old home to your new home. **Do not** include meals (see instructions). . . . . **5** _____
6. Add lines 4 and 5 . . . . **6** _____
7. Enter the total amount your employer paid for your move (including the value of services furnished in kind) that is **not** included in the wages box (box 1) of your W-2 form. This amount should be identified with code **P** in box 13 of your W-2 form. . . . . **7** _____

   Is line 6 more than line 7?

   Yes ▶ Go to line 8.

   No ▶ You **cannot** deduct your moving expenses. If line 6 is less than line 7, subtract line 6 from line 7 and include the result in income on Form 1040, line 7.

8. Subtract line 7 from line 6. Enter the result here and on Form 1040, line 24. This is your **moving expense deduction**. . . . . **8** _____

For Paperwork Reduction Act Notice, see back of form.   Cat. No. 12490K   Form **3903** (1996)

Form 3903 (1996) page **2**

Paperwork Reduction Act Notice

We ask for the information on this form to carry out the Internal Revenue laws of the United States. You are required to give us the information. We need it to ensure that you are complying with these laws and to allow us to figure and collect the right amount of tax.

You are not required to provide the information requested on a form that is subject to the Paperwork Reduction Act unless the form displays a valid OMB control number. Books or records relating to a form or its instructions must be retained as long as their contents may become material in the administration of any Internal Revenue law. Generally, tax returns and return information are confidential, as required by Internal Revenue Code section 6103.

The time needed to complete and file this form will vary depending on individual circumstances. The estimated average time is:

Recordkeeping . . . . 33 min.
Learning about the law or the form . . . . . . 7 min.
Preparing the form . . . . 13 min.
Copying, assembling, and sending the form to the IRS . . 20 min.

If you have comments concerning the accuracy of these time estimates or suggestions for making this form simpler, we would be happy to hear from you. You can write or call the IRS. See the Instructions for Form 1040.

General Instructions

Purpose of Form

Use Form 3903 to figure your moving expense deduction if you moved to a new principal place of work (workplace) within the United States or its possessions. If you qualify to deduct expenses for more than one move, use a separate Form 3903 for each move.

For more details, get **Pub. 521,** Moving Expenses.

Note: *Use* **Form 3903-F,** *Foreign Moving Expenses, instead of this form if you are a U.S. citizen or resident alien who moved to a new principal workplace outside the United States or its possessions.*

Other Forms You May Have To File

If you sold your main home in 1996, you must file **Form 2119,** Sale of Your Home, to report the sale.

Who May Deduct Moving Expenses

If you moved to a different home because of a change in job location, you may be able to deduct your moving expenses. You may be able to take the deduction whether you are self-employed or an employee. But you must meet certain tests explained next.

Distance Test.—Your new principal workplace must be at least 50 miles farther from your old home than your old workplace was. For example, if your old workplace was 3 miles from your old home, your new workplace must be at least 53 miles from that home. If you did not have an old workplace, your new workplace must be at least 50 miles from your old home. The distance between the two points is the shortest of the more commonly traveled routes between them.

Time Test.—If you are an employee, you must work full time in the general area of your new workplace for at least 39 weeks during the 12 months right after you move. If you are self-employed, you must work full time in the general area of your new workplace for at least 39 weeks during the first 12 months and a total of at least 78 weeks during the 24 months right after your move.

You may deduct your moving expenses even if you have not met the time test before your return is due. You may do this if you expect to meet the 39-week test by the end of 1997 or the 78-week test by the end of 1998. If you deduct your moving expenses on your 1996 return but do not meet the time test, you will have to either:

● Amend your 1996 tax return by filing **Form 1040X,** Amended U.S. Individual Income Tax Return, or

● Report the amount of your 1996 moving expense deduction that reduced your 1996 income tax as income in the year you cannot meet the test. For more details, see **Time Test** in Pub. 521.

If you do not deduct your moving expenses on your 1996 return and you later meet the time test, you may take the deduction by filing an amended return for 1996. To do this, use Form 1040X.

Exceptions to the Time Test.—The time test does not have to be met if any of the following apply:

● Your job ends because of disability.

● You are transferred for your employer's benefit.

● You are laid off or discharged for a reason other than willful misconduct.

● You meet the requirements (explained later) for retirees or survivors living outside the United States.

● You are filing this form for a decedent.

Members of the Armed Forces

If you are in the armed forces, you do not have to meet the **distance and time tests** if the move is due to a permanent change of station. A permanent change of station includes a move in connection with and within 1 year of retirement or other termination of active duty.

How To Complete the Form.—First, complete lines 4 through 6 using your actual expenses. **Do not** reduce your expenses by any reimbursements or allowances you received from the government in connection with the move. Also, do not include any expenses for moving services that were provided by the government. If you and your spouse and dependents are moved to or from different locations, treat the moves as a single move.

Next, enter on line 7 the total reimbursements and allowances you received from the government in connection with the expenses you claimed on lines 4 and 5. **Do not** include the value of moving services provided by the government. Then, complete line 8 if applicable.

Retirees or Survivors Living Outside the United States

If you are a retiree or survivor who moved to a home in the United States or its possessions and you meet the following requirements, you are treated as if you moved to a new workplace located in the United States. You are subject to the distance test. Use this form instead of Form 3903-F to figure your moving expense deduction.

Retirees.—You may deduct moving expenses for a move to a new home in the United States when you actually retire if both your old principal workplace and your old home were outside the United States.

Survivors.—You may deduct moving expenses for a move to a home in the United States if you are the spouse or dependent of a person whose principal workplace at the time of death was outside the United States. In addition, the expenses must be for a move **(a)** that begins within 6 months after the decedent's death, and **(b)** from a former home outside the United States that you lived in with the decedent at the time of death.

Reimbursements

If your employer paid for any part of your move, your employer must give you a statement showing a detailed breakdown of reimbursements or payments for moving expenses. Your employer may use **Form 4782,** Employee Moving Expense Information, or his or her own form.

You may choose to deduct moving expenses in the year you are reimbursed by your employer, even though you paid the expenses in a different year. However, special rules apply. Also, if you were reimbursed for expenses incurred before 1994, you must use the **1994** Form 3903. See **How To Report** in Pub. 521.

Specific Instructions

You may deduct the following expenses you incurred in moving your family and dependent household members. Do not deduct expenses for employees such as a maid, nanny, or nurse.

Line 4.—Enter the actual cost to pack, crate, and move your household goods and personal effects. You may also include the cost to store and insure household goods and personal effects within any period of 30 days in a row after the items were moved from your old home and before they were delivered to your new home.

Line 5.—Enter the costs of travel from your old home to your new home. These include transportation and lodging on the way. Include costs for the day you arrive. Although not all the members of your household have to travel together or at the same time, you may only include expenses for one trip per person.

If you use your own car(s), you may figure the expenses by using either:

● Actual out-of-pocket expenses for gas and oil, or

● Mileage at the rate of 10 cents a mile.

You may add parking fees and tolls to the amount claimed under either method. Keep records to verify your expenses.

B–44 Appendix B

Form **4255**
(Rev. April 1994)
Department of the Treasury
Internal Revenue Service

Recapture of Investment Credit

▶ Attach to your income tax return.

OMB No. 1545-0166
Expires 4-30-97
Attachment
Sequence No. **65**

Name(s) as shown on return

Identifying number

Properties	Type of property—State whether rehabilitation, energy, reforestation, or transition property. (See the Instructions for Form 3468 for the year the investment credit property was placed in service for definitions.) If rehabilitation property, also show type of building. If energy property, show type.
A	
B	
C	
D	

Original Investment Credit

Computation Steps: (See Specific Instructions)	Properties			
	A	B	C	D
1 Original rate of credit				
2 Date property was placed in service				
3 Cost or other basis				
4 Original estimated useful life or class of property .				
5 Applicable percentage				
6 Original qualified investment (Multiply line 3 by the percentage on line 5.)				
7 Original credit (Multiply line 6 by the percentage on line 1.)				
8 Date property ceased to be qualified investment credit property				
9 Number of full years between the date on line 2 and the date on line 8				

Computation of Recapture Tax

10 Recapture percentage (from instructions)				
11 Tentative recapture tax (Multiply line 7 by the percentage on line 10.)				

12 Add line 11, columns A through D . . . .
13 Enter the recapture tax from property ceasing to be at risk, or for which there was an increase in nonqualified-nonrecourse financing (Attach separate computation.) . . . .
14 Add lines 12 and 13 . . . .
15 Portion of original credit (line 7) not used to offset tax in any year, plus any carryback and carryforward of credits you can now apply to the original credit year because you have freed up tax liability in the amount of the tax recaptured (Do not enter more than line 14—see instructions.) . . . .
16 Total increase in tax. Subtract line 15 from line 14. Enter here and on the appropriate line of your tax return

Paperwork Reduction Act Notice

We ask for the information on this form to carry out the Internal Revenue laws of the United States. You are required to give us the information. We need it to ensure that you are complying with these laws and to allow us to figure and collect the right amount of tax.

The time needed to complete and file this form will vary depending on individual circumstances. The estimated average time is:

Recordkeeping . . . . 7 hr., 53 min.
Learning about the law or the form . . . . 2 hr., 23 min.
Preparing, copying, assembling, and sending the form to the IRS . . . 2 hr., 37 min.

If you have comments concerning the accuracy of these time estimates or suggestions for making this form more simple, we would be happy to hear from you. You can write to both the IRS and the Office of Management and Budget at the addresses listed in the instructions for the tax return with which this form is filed.

General Instructions

Section references are to the Internal Revenue Code before amendment by the Revenue Reconciliation Act of 1990 (RRA of 1990), unless otherwise noted.

Purpose of Form

Use Form 4255 to figure the increase in tax for the recapture of investment credit claimed.

You must refigure the credit if you claimed it in an earlier year, but disposed of the property before the end of the recapture period or the useful life you used to figure the original credit, whichever applies. Refigure the credit for all property (except nonrecovery placed in service before 1991) when the property ceases to be investment credit property before the end of 5 full years after the property is placed in service (recapture period). For nonrecovery property placed in service before 1991, refigure the credit when the property ceases to be investment credit property before the end of the useful life used to figure the credit. See the line 10 instructions for details.

You must also refigure the credit if you returned leased property (on which you had taken a credit) to the lessor before the end of the recapture period or useful life.

Cat. No. 41488C

Form **4255** (Rev. 4-94)

Form 4255 (Rev. 4-94) Page **2**

If you claim investment credit for property and the percentage of business use in a later year falls below the percentage for the year the property was placed in service, you are treated as having disposed of part of the property and may have to recapture part of the investment credit.

You must refigure the credit if you changed the use of property so that it no longer qualifies as investment credit property. For example, you must refigure the credit if you change the use of property from business use to personal use, or if there is any decrease in the percentage of business use of investment credit property. See sections 50(a)(2) (as amended by the RRA of 1990), 47(a)(3), 47(a)(5)(C), and 49(e)(2) for information on recapture for progress expenditure property. Also, see the instructions for line 13 regarding recapture if property ceases to be at risk, or if there is an increase in nonqualified-nonrecourse financing related to certain at-risk property.

An election to be treated as an S corporation does not automatically trigger recapture of investment credit taken before the election was effective. However, the S corporation is liable for any recapture of investment credit taken before the election.

If property on which you took both regular and energy investment credit ceases to be energy credit property but still qualifies as regular investment credit property, only refigure the energy investment credit. However, if you took both credits, and you dispose of the property, or the property ceases to be both energy and regular investment credit property, you must refigure both credits.

If you are an S corporation, a partnership, or an estate or trust that allocated any or all of the investment credit to your shareholders, partners, or beneficiaries, you must provide the information they need to refigure the credit. See Regulations sections 1.47-4, 1.47-5, and 1.47-6.

Partners, shareholders, and beneficiaries.—If your Schedule K-1 shows recapture of investment credit claimed in an earlier year, you will need your copy of the original Form 3468 to complete lines 1 through 9 of this Form 4255.

Special rules.—If you claimed a credit on the following kinds of property, see the sections listed below before you complete Form 4255:

Property	Section
Motion picture films and video tapes	47(a)(8)
Ships	46(g)(4)

If you took any nonconventional source fuel credit, see section 29(b)(4).

Note: *The RRA of 1990 changed the rules for property eligible for the rehabilitation credit under section 47, as amended by the RRA of 1990. Increase the basis of this property by 100% of the recapture amount. For details, see sections 50(c)(2) and 50(c)(3), as amended by the RRA of 1990.*

Specific Instructions

Note: *Do not figure the recapture tax on lines 1 through 12 for property ceasing to be at risk, or if there is an increase in nonqualified-nonrecourse financing related to certain at-risk property. Figure the recapture tax for these properties on separate schedules and enter the recapture tax on line 13. Include any unused credit for these properties on line 15.*

Lines A through D.—Describe the property for which you must refigure the credit.

Complete lines 1 through 11 for each property on which you are refiguring the credit. Use a separate column for each item. If you must recapture both the energy investment credit and the regular investment credit for the same item, use a separate column for each credit. If you need more columns, use additional Forms 4255, or other schedules that include all the information shown on Form 4255. Enter the total from the separate sheets on line 12.

Line 1.—Enter the rate you used to figure the original credit from the Form 3468 that you filed.

See section 46(b)(4) for the rates for qualified rehabilitation expenditures made after 1981.

Line 2.—Enter the day, month, and year that the property was available for service.

Line 3.—Enter the cost or other basis that you used to figure the original credit.

Line 4.—Enter the estimated useful life that you used to figure the original credit for the property.

Line 5.—Enter the applicable percentage that you used to figure the original qualified investment from the Form 3468 that you filed.

Generally, the applicable percentage will be 100% for property eligible for the investment credit under section 46, as amended by the RRA of 1990.

Line 8.—Generally, this will be the date you disposed of the property. See Regulations section 1.47-1(c) for more information.

Line 9.—Do not enter partial years. If the property was held less than 12 months, enter zero.

Line 10.—Enter the recapture percentage from the following tables:

Property placed in service after 12/31/90 and recovery property

If number of full years on line 9 of Form 4255 is:	The recapture percentage is:
0	100
1	80
2	60
3	40
4	20
5 or more	0

Nonrecovery property placed in service before 1991

If number of full years on line 9 of Form 4255 is:	The recapture percentage for property with an original useful life of: 5 or more but less than 7 years is:	7 or more years is:
4	50	66.6
5	0	33.3
6	0	33.3
7 or more	0	0

Line 12.—If you have used more than one Form 4255, or separate sheets to list additional items on which you figured an increase in tax, write to the left of the entry space "Tax from attached, $ ...." Include the amount in the total for line 12.

Line 13.—For certain taxpayers, the basis or cost of property is limited to the amount the taxpayer is at risk for the property at yearend. The basis or cost must be reduced by the amount of any "nonqualified-nonrecourse financing" related to the property at yearend. If property ceases to be at risk in a later year, or if there is an increase in nonqualified-nonrecourse financing, recapture may be required. See section 49(b), as amended by the RRA of 1990, for details. Attach a separate computation schedule to figure the recapture tax and enter the total tax on line 13.

Line 15.—If you did not use all the credit you originally figured, either in the year you figured it or in a carryback or carryforward year, you do not have to recapture the amount of the credit you did not use. In refiguring the credit for the original credit year, be sure to include any carryforwards from previous years, plus any carrybacks arising within the 3 taxable years after the original credit year that are now allowed because the recapture and recomputation of the original credit made available some additional tax liability in that year. See Regulations section 1.47-1(d) and Rev. Rul. 72-221 1972-1 C.B. 15, for details.

Note: *You must also take into account any applicable 35% reduction in credit under section 49(c)(2) when computing the amount to enter on line 15.*

Figure the unused portion on a separate sheet and enter it on this line. Do not enter more than the recapture tax on line 14.

Note: *Be sure to adjust your current unused credit to reflect any unused portion of the original credit that was entered on line 15 of this form.*

Printed on recycled paper

Form **4562**	**Depreciation and Amortization**	OMB No. 1545-0172
Department of the Treasury Internal Revenue Service (99)	(Including Information on Listed Property) ▶ See separate instructions. ▶ Attach this form to your return.	**1996** Attachment Sequence No. **67**

Name(s) shown on return	Business or activity to which this form relates	Identifying number

Part I — Election To Expense Certain Tangible Property (Section 179) (Note: If you have any "listed property," complete Part V before you complete Part I.)

1	Maximum dollar limitation. If an enterprise zone business, see page 2 of the instructions	1	$17,500
2	Total cost of section 179 property placed in service. See page 2 of the instructions	2	
3	Threshold cost of section 179 property before reduction in limitation	3	$200,000
4	Reduction in limitation. Subtract line 3 from line 2. If zero or less, enter -0-	4	
5	Dollar limitation for tax year. Subtract line 4 from line 1. If zero or less, enter -0-. If married filing separately, see page 2 of the instructions	5	

(a) Description of property	(b) Cost (business use only)	(c) Elected cost
6		

7	Listed property. Enter amount from line 27	7	
8	Total elected cost of section 179 property. Add amounts in column (c), lines 6 and 7	8	
9	Tentative deduction. Enter the smaller of line 5 or line 8	9	
10	Carryover of disallowed deduction from 1995. See page 2 of the instructions	10	
11	Business income limitation. Enter the smaller of business income (not less than zero) or line 5 (see instructions)	11	
12	Section 179 expense deduction. Add lines 9 and 10, but do not enter more than line 11	12	
13	Carryover of disallowed deduction to 1997. Add lines 9 and 10, less line 12 ▶	13	

Note: *Do not use Part II or Part III below for listed property (automobiles, certain other vehicles, cellular telephones, certain computers, or property used for entertainment, recreation, or amusement). Instead, use Part V for listed property.*

Part II — MACRS Depreciation For Assets Placed in Service ONLY During Your 1996 Tax Year (Do Not Include Listed Property.)

Section A—General Asset Account Election

14 If you are making the election under section 168(i)(4) to group any assets placed in service during the tax year into one or more general asset accounts, check this box. See page 2 of the instructions . . . . ▶ ☐

Section B—General Depreciation System (GDS) (See page 3 of the instructions.)

(a) Classification of property	(b) Month and year placed in service	(c) Basis for depreciation (business/investment use only—see instructions)	(d) Recovery period	(e) Convention	(f) Method	(g) Depreciation deduction
15a 3-year property						
b 5-year property						
c 7-year property						
d 10-year property						
e 15-year property						
f 20-year property						
g 25-year property			25 yrs.		S/L	
h Residential rental property			27.5 yrs. 27.5 yrs.	MM MM	S/L S/L	
i Nonresidential real property			39 yrs.	MM MM	S/L S/L	

Section C—Alternative Depreciation System (ADS) (See page 4 of the instructions.)

16a Class life					S/L	
b 12-year			12 yrs.		S/L	
c 40-year			40 yrs.	MM	S/L	

Part III — Other Depreciation (Do Not Include Listed Property.) (See page 4 of the instructions.)

17	GDS and ADS deductions for assets placed in service in tax years beginning before 1996	17	
18	Property subject to section 168(f)(1) election	18	
19	ACRS and other depreciation	19	

Part IV — Summary (See page 4 of the instructions.)

20	Listed property. Enter amount from line 26	20	
21	**Total.** Add deductions on line 12, lines 15 and 16 in column (g), and lines 17 through 20. Enter here and on the appropriate lines of your return. Partnerships and S corporations—see instructions	21	
22	For assets shown above and placed in service during the current year, enter the portion of the basis attributable to section 263A costs	22	

For Paperwork Reduction Act Notice, see page 1 of the separate instructions. Cat. No. 12906N Form **4562** (1996)

Form 4562 (1996) Page **2**

Part V — Listed Property—Automobiles, Certain Other Vehicles, Cellular Telephones, Certain Computers, and Property Used for Entertainment, Recreation, or Amusement

Note: *For any vehicle for which you are using the standard mileage rate or deducting lease expense, complete **only** 23a, 23b, columns (a) through (c) of Section A, all of Section B, and Section C if applicable.*

Section A—Depreciation and Other Information (Caution: *See page 5 of the instructions for limitations for automobiles.*)

23a Do you have evidence to support the business/investment use claimed? ☐ Yes ☐ No   23b If "Yes," is the evidence written? ☐ Yes ☐ No

(a) Type of property (list vehicles first)	(b) Date placed in service	(c) Business/ investment use percentage	(d) Cost or other basis	(e) Basis for depreciation (business/investment use only)	(f) Recovery period	(g) Method/ Convention	(h) Depreciation deduction	(i) Elected section 179 cost
24 Property used more than 50% in a qualified business use (See page 5 of the instructions.):								
		%						
		%						
		%						
25 Property used 50% or less in a qualified business use (See page 5 of the instructions.):								
		%			S/L –			
		%			S/L –			
		%			S/L –			

26 Add amounts in column (h). Enter the total here and on line 20, page 1 . . . . . . | 26 |
27 Add amounts in column (i). Enter the total here and on line 7, page 1 . . . . | 27 |

Section B—Information on Use of Vehicles

Complete this section for vehicles used by a sole proprietor, partner, or other "more than 5% owner," or related person.
If you provided vehicles to your employees, first answer the questions in Section C to see if you meet an exception to completing this section for those vehicles.

	(a) Vehicle 1	(b) Vehicle 2	(c) Vehicle 3	(d) Vehicle 4	(e) Vehicle 5	(f) Vehicle 6
28 Total business/investment miles driven during the year (DO NOT include commuting miles)						
29 Total commuting miles driven during the year						
30 Total other personal (noncommuting) miles driven						
31 Total miles driven during the year. Add lines 28 through 30						
	Yes No	Yes No	Yes No	Yes No	Yes No	Yes No
32 Was the vehicle available for personal use during off-duty hours?						
33 Was the vehicle used primarily by a more than 5% owner or related person?						
34 Is another vehicle available for personal use?						

Section C—Questions for Employers Who Provide Vehicles for Use by Their Employees

*Answer these questions to determine if you meet an exception to completing Section B for vehicles used by employees who **are not** more than 5% owners or related persons.*

	Yes	No
35 Do you maintain a written policy statement that prohibits all personal use of vehicles, including commuting, by your employees?		
36 Do you maintain a written policy statement that prohibits personal use of vehicles, except commuting, by your employees? See page 6 of the instructions for vehicles used by corporate officers, directors, or 1% or more owners		
37 Do you treat all use of vehicles by employees as personal use?		
38 Do you provide more than five vehicles to your employees, obtain information from your employees about the use of the vehicles, and retain the information received?		
39 Do you meet the requirements concerning qualified automobile demonstration use? See page 6 of the instructions . .		

Note: *If your answer to 35, 36, 37, 38, or 39 is "Yes," you need not complete Section B for the covered vehicles.*

Part VI — Amortization

(a) Description of costs	(b) Date amortization begins	(c) Amortizable amount	(d) Code section	(e) Amortization period or percentage	(f) Amortization for this year
40 Amortization of costs that begins during your 1996 tax year:					
41 Amortization of costs that began before 1996				41	
42 **Total.** Enter here and on "Other Deductions" or "Other Expenses" line of your return . . .				42	

Form **4684**	**Casualties and Thefts**	OMB No. 1545-0177
Department of the Treasury Internal Revenue Service	▶ See separate instructions. ▶ Attach to your tax return. ▶ Use a separate Form 4684 for each different casualty or theft.	**1996** Attachment Sequence No. **26**

Name(s) shown on tax return | Identifying number

SECTION A—Personal Use Property (Use this section to report casualties and thefts of property **not** used in a trade or business or for income-producing purposes.)

1 Description of properties (show type, location, and date acquired for each):
   Property **A** ....
   Property **B** ....
   Property **C** ....
   Property **D** ....

Properties (Use a separate column for each property lost or damaged from one casualty or theft.)

		A	B	C	D
2	Cost or other basis of each property				
3	Insurance or other reimbursement (whether or not you filed a claim). See instructions				
	Note: If line 2 is **more than** line 3, skip line 4.				
4	Gain from casualty or theft. If line 3 is **more than** line 2, enter the difference here and skip lines 5 through 9 for that column. See instructions if line 3 includes insurance or other reimbursement you did not claim, or you received payment for your loss in a later tax year				
5	Fair market value **before** casualty or theft				
6	Fair market value **after** casualty or theft				
7	Subtract line 6 from line 5				
8	Enter the **smaller** of line 2 or line 7				
9	Subtract line 3 from line 8. If zero or less, enter -0-				

10	Casualty or theft loss. Add the amounts on line 9. Enter the total	10	
11	Enter the amount from line 10 or $100, whichever is **smaller**	11	
12	Subtract line 11 from line 10	12	
	Caution: Use only one Form 4684 for lines 13 through 18.		
13	Add the amounts on line 12 of all Forms 4684	13	
14	Combine the amounts from line 4 of all Forms 4684	14	
15	• If line 14 is **more than** line 13, enter the difference here and on Schedule D. Do not complete the rest of this section (see instructions). • If line 14 is **less than** line 13, enter -0- here and continue with the form. • If line 14 is **equal to** line 13, enter -0- here. Do not complete the rest of this section.	15	
16	If line 14 is **less than** line 13, enter the difference	16	
17	Enter 10% of your adjusted gross income (Form 1040, line 32). Estates and trusts, see instructions	17	
18	Subtract line 17 from line 16. If zero or less, enter -0-. Also enter result on Schedule A (Form 1040), line 19. Estates and trusts, enter on the "Other deductions" line of your tax return	18	

For Paperwork Reduction Act Notice, see page 1 of separate instructions.   Cat. No. 12997O   Form **4684** (1996)

Tax Forms B–49

Form 4684 (1996) Attachment Sequence No. **26** Page **2**

Name(s) shown on tax return. Do not enter name and identifying number if shown on other side. Identifying number

SECTION B—Business and Income-Producing Property (Use this section to report casualties and thefts of property used in a trade or business or for income-producing purposes.)

Part I Casualty or Theft Gain or Loss (Use a separate Part I for each casualty or theft.)

19 Description of properties (show type, location, and date acquired for each):
   Property **A** ....
   Property **B** ....
   Property **C** ....
   Property **D** ....

Properties (Use a separate column for each property lost or damaged from one casualty or theft.)

		A	B	C	D
20	Cost or adjusted basis of each property . . .				
21	Insurance or other reimbursement (whether or not you filed a claim). See the instructions for line 3 . **Note:** *If line 20 is **more than** line 21, skip line 22.*				
22	Gain from casualty or theft. If line 21 is **more than** line 20, enter the difference here and on line 29 or line 34, column (c), except as provided in the instructions for line 33. Also, skip lines 23 through 27 for that column. See the instructions for line 4 if line 21 includes insurance or other reimbursement you did not claim, or you received payment for your loss in a later tax year				
23	Fair market value **before** casualty or theft . . .				
24	Fair market value **after** casualty or theft . . .				
25	Subtract line 24 from line 23				
26	Enter the **smaller** of line 20 or line 25 . . . . **Note:** *If the property was totally destroyed by casualty or lost from theft, enter on line 26 the amount from line 20.*				
27	Subtract line 21 from line 26. If zero or less, enter -0-				

28 Casualty or theft loss. Add the amounts on line 27. Enter the total here and on line 29 **or** line 34 (see instructions).   **28**

Part II Summary of Gains and Losses (from separate Parts I)

(a) Identify casualty or theft	(b) Losses from casualties or thefts		(c) Gains from casualties or thefts includible in income
	(i) Trade, business, rental or royalty property	(ii) Income-producing property	

Casualty or Theft of Property Held One Year or Less

29 _____ ( ) ( ) ( )
    _____ ( ) ( ) ( )
30 Totals. Add the amounts on line 29 . . . . **30** ( ) ( ) ( )
31 Combine line 30, columns (b)(i) and (c). Enter the net gain or (loss) here and on Form 4797, line 15. If Form 4797 is not otherwise required, see instructions **31**
32 Enter the amount from line 30, column (b)(ii) here and on Schedule A (Form 1040), line 22. Partnerships, S corporations, estates and trusts, see instructions **32**

Casualty or Theft of Property Held More Than One Year

33 Casualty or theft gains from Form 4797, line 34 . . . .   **33**
34 _____ ( ) ( ) ( )
    _____ ( ) ( ) ( )
35 Total losses. Add amounts on line 34, columns (b)(i) and (b)(ii) . . . **35** ( ) ( )
36 Total gains. Add lines 33 and 34, column (c) **36**
37 Add amounts on line 35, columns (b)(i) and (b)(ii) **37**
38 If the loss on line 37 is **more than** the gain on line 36:
   a Combine line 35, column (b)(i) and line 36, and enter the net gain or (loss) here. Partnerships and S corporations see the note below. All others enter this amount on Form 4797, line 15. If Form 4797 is not otherwise required, see instructions **38a**
   b Enter the amount from line 35, column (b)(ii) here. Partnerships and S corporations see the note below. Individuals enter this amount on Schedule A (Form 1040), line 22. Estates and trusts, enter on the "Other deductions" line of your tax return   **38b**
39 If the loss on line 37 **is equal to** or **less than** the gain on line 36, combine these lines and enter here. Partnerships, see the note below. All others, enter this amount on Form 4797, line 3 . . . .   **39**

Note: *Partnerships, enter the amount from line 38a, 38b, or line 39 on Form 1065, Schedule K, line 7. S corporations, enter the amount from line 38a or 38b on Form 1120S, Schedule K, line 6.*

Form 4797

Sales of Business Property
(Also Involuntary Conversions and Recapture Amounts Under Sections 179 and 280F(b)(2))

▶ Attach to your tax return. ▶ See separate instructions.

Department of the Treasury
Internal Revenue Service (99)

OMB No. 1545-0184

1996

Attachment Sequence No. **27**

Name(s) shown on return | Identifying number

1 Enter here the gross proceeds from the sale or exchange of real estate reported to you for 1996 on Form(s) 1099-S (or a substitute statement) that you will be including on line 2, 11, or 22 .... **1**

Part I — Sales or Exchanges of Property Used in a Trade or Business and Involuntary Conversions From Other Than Casualty or Theft—Property Held More Than 1 Year

(a) Description of property	(b) Date acquired (mo., day, yr.)	(c) Date sold (mo., day, yr.)	(d) Gross sales price	(e) Depreciation allowed or allowable since acquisition	(f) Cost or other basis, plus improvements and expense of sale	(g) LOSS If (f) is more than (d) plus (e), subtract the sum of (d) and (e) from (f)	(h) GAIN If (d) plus (e) is more than (f), subtract (f) from the sum of (d) and (e)
2							

3 Gain, if any, from Form 4684, line 39 .... **3**
4 Section 1231 gain from installment sales from Form 6252, line 26 or 37 ..... **4**
5 Section 1231 gain or (loss) from like-kind exchanges from Form 8824 ...... **5**
6 Gain, if any, from line 34, from other than casualty or theft **6**
7 Add lines 2 through 6 in columns (g) and (h) .... **7** ( )
8 Combine columns (g) and (h) of line 7. Enter gain or (loss) here, and on the appropriate line as follows: **8**

Partnerships—Enter the gain or (loss) on Form 1065, Schedule K, line 6. Skip lines 9, 10, 12, and 13 below.

S corporations—Report the gain or (loss) following the instructions for Form 1120S, Schedule K, lines 5 and 6. Skip lines 9, 10, 12, and 13 below, unless line 8 is a gain and the S corporation is subject to the capital gains tax.

All others—If line 8 is zero or a loss, enter the amount on line 12 below and skip lines 9 and 10. If line 8 is a gain and you did not have any prior year section 1231 losses, or they were recaptured in an earlier year, enter the gain as a long-term capital gain on Schedule D and skip lines 9, 10, and 13 below.

9 Nonrecaptured net section 1231 losses from prior years (see instructions) **9**
10 Subtract line 9 from line 8. If zero or less, enter -0-. Also enter on the appropriate line as follows (see instructions): **10**

S corporations—Enter this amount on Schedule D (Form 1120S), line 13, and skip lines 12 and 13 below.

All others—If line 10 is zero, enter the amount from line 8 on line 13 below. If line 10 is more than zero, enter the amount from line 9 on line 13 below, and enter the amount from line 10 as a long-term capital gain on Schedule D.

Part II — Ordinary Gains and Losses

11 Ordinary gains and losses not included on lines 12 through 18 (include property held 1 year or less):

12 Loss, if any, from line 8 .... **12**
13 Gain, if any, from line 8, or amount from line 9 if applicable **13**
14 Gain, if any, from line 33 .... **14**
15 Net gain or (loss) from Form 4684, lines 31 and 38a **15**
16 Ordinary gain from installment sales from Form 6252, line 25 or 36 .... **16**
17 Ordinary gain or (loss) from like-kind exchanges from Form 8824 .... **17**
18 Recapture of section 179 expense deduction for partners and S corporation shareholders from property dispositions by partnerships and S corporations (see instructions) **18**
19 Add lines 11 through 18 in columns (g) and (h) .... **19** ( )
20 Combine columns (g) and (h) of line 19. Enter gain or (loss) here, and on the appropriate line as follows: ... **20**
 a For all except individual returns: Enter the gain or (loss) from line 20 on the return being filed.
 b For individual returns:
  (1) If the loss on line 12 includes a loss from Form 4684, line 35, column (b)(ii), enter that part of the loss here and on line 22 of Schedule A (Form 1040). Identify as from "Form 4797, line 20b(1)." See instructions ... **20b(1)**
  (2) Redetermine the gain or (loss) on line 20, excluding the loss, if any, on line 20b(1). Enter here and on Form 1040, line 14 . **20b(2)**

For Paperwork Reduction Act Notice, see page 1 of separate instructions. Cat. No. 13086I Form **4797** (1996)

Form 4797 (1996) Page **2**

Part III — Gain From Disposition of Property Under Sections 1245, 1250, 1252, 1254, and 1255

21 **(a)** Description of section 1245, 1250, 1252, 1254, or 1255 property: | **(b)** Date acquired (mo., day, yr.) | **(c)** Date sold (mo., day, yr.)

A
B
C
D

Relate lines 21A through 21D to these columns	▶	Property A	Property B	Property C	Property D
22 Gross sales price (**Note:** See line 1 before completing.)	22				
23 Cost or other basis plus expense of sale	23				
24 Depreciation (or depletion) allowed or allowable	24				
25 Adjusted basis. Subtract line 24 from line 23	25				
26 Total gain. Subtract line 25 from line 22	26				
27 If section 1245 property:					
a Depreciation allowed or allowable from line 24	27a				
b Enter the **smaller** of line 26 or 27a	27b				
28 If section 1250 property: If straight line depreciation was used, enter -0- on line 28g, except for a corporation subject to section 291.					
a Additional depreciation after 1975 (see instructions)	28a				
b Applicable percentage multiplied by the **smaller** of line 26 or line 28a (see instructions)	28b				
c Subtract line 28a from line 26. If residential rental property or line 26 is not more than line 28a, skip lines 28d and 28e	28c				
d Additional depreciation after 1969 and before 1976	28d				
e Enter the **smaller** of line 28c or 28d	28e				
f Section 291 amount (corporations only)	28f				
g Add lines 28b, 28e, and 28f	28g				
29 If section 1252 property: Skip this section if you did not dispose of farmland or if this form is being completed for a partnership.					
a Soil, water, and land clearing expenses	29a				
b Line 29a multiplied by applicable percentage (see instructions)	29b				
c Enter the **smaller** of line 26 or 29b	29c				
30 If section 1254 property:					
a Intangible drilling and development costs, expenditures for development of mines and other natural deposits, and mining exploration costs (see instructions)	30a				
b Enter the **smaller** of line 26 or 30a	30b				
31 If section 1255 property:					
a Applicable percentage of payments excluded from income under section 126 (see instructions)	31a				
b Enter the **smaller** of line 26 or 31a (see instructions)	31b				

Summary of Part III Gains. Complete property columns A through D through line 31b before going to line 32.

32 Total gains for all properties. Add property columns A through D, line 26	32
33 Add property columns A through D, lines 27b, 28g, 29c, 30b, and 31b. Enter here and on line 14	33
34 Subtract line 33 from line 32. Enter the portion from casualty or theft on Form 4684, line 33. Enter the portion from other than casualty or theft on Form 4797, line 6	34

Part IV — Recapture Amounts Under Sections 179 and 280F(b)(2) When Business Use Drops to 50% or Less
See instructions.

		(a) Section 179	(b) Section 280F(b)(2)
35 Section 179 expense deduction or depreciation allowable in prior years	35		
36 Recomputed depreciation. See instructions	36		
37 Recapture amount. Subtract line 36 from line 35. See the instructions for where to report	37		

1996 Form 4868

Department of the Treasury — Internal Revenue Service

General Instructions

Purpose of Form

Use Form 4868 to apply for 4 more months to file **Form 1040EZ, Form 1040A,** or **Form 1040.**

To get the extra time you **MUST:**

- Properly estimate your 1996 tax liability using the information available to you,
- Enter your tax liability on line 6a of Form 4868, **AND**
- File Form 4868 by the regular due date of your return.

You are not required to send a payment of the tax you estimate as due. However, it will benefit you to pay as much as you can. Any remittance you send with your application for extension will be treated as a payment of tax.

You do not have to explain why you are asking for the extension. We will contact you only if your request is denied.

Do not file Form 4868 if you want the IRS to figure your tax or you are under a court order to file your return by the regular due date.

If you need an additional extension, see **If You Need Additional Time** on this page.

Note: *An extension of time to file your 1996 calendar year income tax return also extends the time to file a gift or generation-skipping transfer (GST) tax return (Form 709 or 709-A) for 1996.*

Out of the Country

If you already had 2 extra months to file because you were a U.S. citizen or resident and were out of the country, use this form to obtain an additional 2 months to file. Write "Taxpayer Abroad" across the top of Form 4868. "Out of the country" means either **(a)** you live outside the United States and Puerto Rico **and** your main place of work is outside the United States and Puerto Rico, **or (b)** you are in military or naval service outside the United States and Puerto Rico.

When To File Form 4868

File Form 4868 by April 15, 1997. Fiscal year taxpayers, file Form 4868 by the regular due date of the return.

If you had 2 extra months to file your return because you were out of the country, file Form 4868 by June 16, 1997, for a 1996 calendar year return.

How To Send In Your Payment

- When sending a payment with Form 4868, use the addresses in the middle column under **Where To File** on page 2.
- Make your check or money order payable to "Internal Revenue Service" (not "IRS"). Do not send cash.
- Write your social security number, daytime phone number, and "1996 Form 4868" on the front of your check or money order.
- Do not staple or attach your payment to the form.

If You Need Additional Time

If the automatic extension does not give you enough time, you can ask for additional time later. But you will have to give a good reason, and it must be approved by the IRS. To ask for the additional time, you must **either:**

1. File **Form 2688,** Application for Additional Extension of Time To File U.S. Individual Income Tax Return, or

2. Explain your reason in a letter. Mail it to the address in the right column under **Where To File** on page 2.

File Form 4868 **before** you file Form 2688 or write a letter asking for more time. Only in cases of undue hardship will the IRS approve your request for an additional extension without receiving Form 4868 first. Ask early for this extra time. Then, you can still file your return on time if your request is not approved.

For Paperwork Reduction Act Notice, see page 3.   Cat. No. 13141W   Form **4868** (1996)

▼ DETACH HERE ▼

Form 4868
Department of the Treasury
Internal Revenue Service

Application for Automatic Extension of Time To File U.S. Individual Income Tax Return

OMB No. 1545-0188

1996

1 Your name(s) (see instructions)

Address (see instructions)

City, town or post office, state, and ZIP code

3 Your social security number

4 Spouse's social security no.

2a Amount due— Add lines 6c, d, and e ▶ $ _____

b Amount you are paying ▶ $ _____

5 I request an automatic 4-month extension of time to August 15, 1997, to file my individual tax return for the calendar year 1996 or to _____ , 19 ___ , for the fiscal tax year ending _____ , 19 ___ .

6 **Individual Income Tax Return**—See instructions.

a Total income tax liability for 1996 . . . $ _____

b Total payments for 1996 . . . . . . $ _____

c **Balance.** Subtract 6b from 6a . . . $ _____

Gift/GST Tax Return(s)—See instructions.

Check here **ONLY** if filing a gift or GST tax return . . . .   Yourself ▶ ☐   Spouse ▶ ☐

d Your gift/GST tax payment . . . $ _____

e Your spouse's gift/GST tax payment $ _____

Form 4868 (1996)

Where To File

If you live in:	And you are making a payment, send Form 4868 with your payment to IRS:	And you are NOT making a payment, send Form 4868 to Internal Revenue Service Center:
Florida, Georgia, South Carolina	P.O. Box 105073 Atlanta, GA 30348-5073	Atlanta, GA 39901
New Jersey, New York (*New York City and counties of Nassau, Rockland, Suffolk, and Westchester*)	P.O. Box 22423 Newark, NJ 07101-2423	Holtsville, NY 00501
New York (*all other counties*), Connecticut, Maine, Massachusetts, New Hampshire, Rhode Island, Vermont	P.O. Box 371410 Pittsburgh, PA 15250-7410	Andover, MA 05501
Illinois, Iowa, Minnesota, Missouri, Wisconsin	P.O. Box 970028 St. Louis, MO 63197-0028	Kansas City, MO 64999
Delaware, District of Columbia, Maryland, Pennsylvania, Virginia	P.O. Box 7990 Philadelphia, PA 19162-7990	Philadelphia, PA 19255
Indiana, Kentucky, Michigan, Ohio, West Virginia	P.O. Box 6252 Chicago, IL 60680-6252	Cincinnati, OH 45999
Kansas, New Mexico, Oklahoma, Texas	P.O. Box 970027 St. Louis, MO 63197-0027	Austin, TX 73301
Alaska, Arizona, California (*counties of Alpine, Amador, Butte, Calaveras, Colusa, Contra Costa, Del Norte, El Dorado, Glenn, Humboldt, Lake, Lassen, Marin, Mendocino, Modoc, Napa, Nevada, Placer, Plumas, Sacramento, San Joaquin, Shasta, Sierra, Siskiyou, Solano, Sonoma, Sutter, Tehama, Trinity, Yolo, and Yuba*), Colorado, Idaho, Montana, Nebraska, Nevada, North Dakota, Oregon, South Dakota, Utah, Washington, Wyoming	P.O. Box 7122 San Francisco, CA 94120-7122	Ogden, UT 84201
California (*all other counties*), Hawaii	P.O. Box 54916 Los Angeles, CA 90054-0916	Fresno, CA 93888
Alabama, Arkansas, Louisiana, Mississippi, North Carolina, Tennessee	P.O. Box 1236 Charlotte, NC 28201-1236	Memphis, TN 37501
American Samoa or Puerto Rico (*or exclude income under section 933*); are a nonpermanent resident of Guam or the Virgin Islands; have an APO, FPO, or foreign address; are a dual status alien; or file Form 2555, 2555-EZ, or 4563	P.O. Box 7990 Philadelphia, PA 19162-7990	Philadelphia, PA 19255
Guam: Permanent residents	Send Form 4868 and payments to:	Department of Revenue and Taxation Government of Guam P.O. Box 23607 GMF, GU 96921
Virgin Islands: Permanent residents	Send Form 4868 and payments to:	V.I. Bureau of Internal Revenue 9601 Estate Thomas Charlotte Amalie St. Thomas, VI 00802

Form 4868 (1996) Page **3**

Filing Your Tax Return

You may file your tax return any time before the extension expires. But remember, Form 4868 does not extend the time to pay taxes. If you do not pay the amount due by the regular due date, you will owe interest. You may also be charged penalties.

Do not attach a copy of Form 4868 to your return.

For your convenience, we have included an extra copy of Form 4868. However, only one needs to be filed.

Interest

You will owe interest on any tax not paid by the regular due date of your return. The interest runs until you pay the tax. Even if you had a good reason for not paying on time, you will still owe interest.

Late Payment Penalty

The penalty is usually ½ of 1% of any tax (other than estimated tax) not paid by the regular due date. It is charged for each month or part of a month the tax is unpaid. The maximum penalty is 25%.

The late payment penalty will not be charged if you can show reasonable cause for not paying on time. Attach a statement to your return fully explaining the reason. **Do not** attach the statement to Form 4868.

You are considered to have "reasonable cause" for the period covered by this automatic extension if at least 90% of your actual 1996 tax liability is paid before the regular due date of your return through withholding, estimated tax payments, or with Form 4868.

Late Filing Penalty

A penalty is usually charged if your return is filed after the due date (including extensions). It is usually 5% of the tax not paid by the regular due date for each month or part of a month your return is late. Generally, the maximum penalty is 25%. If your return is more than 60 days late, the minimum penalty is $100 or the balance of the tax due on your return, whichever is smaller. You might not owe the penalty if you have a good reason for filing late. Attach a statement to your return fully explaining the reason. **Do not** attach the statement to Form 4868.

How To Claim Credit for Payment Made With This Form

When you file your return, include the amount of any payment you sent with Form 4868 on the appropriate line of your tax return. If you file Form 1040EZ, the instructions for line 9 of that form will tell you how to report the payment. If you file Form 1040A, see the instructions for line 29d. If you file Form 1040, enter the payment on line 55.

If you and your spouse each filed a separate Form 4868 but later file a joint return for 1996, enter the total paid with both Forms 4868 on the appropriate line of your joint return.

If you and your spouse jointly filed Form 4868 but later file separate returns for 1996, you may enter the total amount paid with Form 4868 on either of your separate returns. Or you and your spouse may divide the payment in any agreed amounts. Be sure each separate return has the social security numbers of both spouses.

Paperwork Reduction Act Notice

We ask for the information on this form to carry out the Internal Revenue laws of the United States. You are required to give us the information. We need it to ensure that you are complying with these laws and to allow us to figure and collect the right amount of tax.

You are not required to provide the information requested on a form that is subject to the Paperwork Reduction Act unless the form displays a valid OMB control number. Books or records relating to a form or its instructions must be retained as long as their contents may become material in the administration of any Internal Revenue law. Generally, tax returns and return information are confidential, as required by Internal Revenue Code section 6103.

The time needed to complete and file this form will vary depending on individual circumstances. The estimated average time is: **Recordkeeping,** 26 min.; **Learning about the law or the form,** 12 min.; **Preparing the form,** 17 min.; and **Copying, assembling, and sending the form to the IRS,** 10 min.

If you have comments concerning the accuracy of these time estimates or suggestions for making this form simpler, we would be happy to hear from you. You can write to the Tax Forms Committee, Western Area Distribution Center, Rancho Cordova, CA 95743-0001. **DO NOT** send the form to this address. Instead, see **Where To File** on page 2.

▼ DETACH HERE ▼   (This is an extra copy. File only one Form 4868.)

| Form **4868** Department of the Treasury Internal Revenue Service | **Application for Automatic Extension of Time To File U.S. Individual Income Tax Return** | OMB No. 1545-0188 **1996** |

1 Your name(s) (see instructions)

Address (see instructions)

City, town or post office, state, and ZIP code

3 Your social security number

4 Spouse's social security no.

2a Amount due— Add lines 6c, d, and e . ▶ $ _____

b Amount you are paying ▶ $

5 I request an automatic 4-month extension of time to August 15, 1997, to file my individual tax return for the calendar year 1996 or to _____ , 19 ___ , for the fiscal tax year ending _____ , 19 ___ .

6 Individual Income Tax Return—See instructions.

a Total income tax liability for 1996 . . . $ _____

b Total payments for 1996 . . . . . $ _____

c **Balance.** Subtract 6b from 6a . . . $ _____

Gift/GST Tax Return(s)—See instructions.
Check here **ONLY** if filing a gift or GST tax return . . . . } Yourself ▶ ☐ Spouse ▶ ☐

d Your gift/GST tax payment . . . $ _____

e Your spouse's gift/GST tax payment $

Specific Instructions

How To Complete Form 4868

Box 1

Enter your name(s) and address. If you plan to file a joint return, include both spouses' names in the order in which they will appear on the return.

If you want correspondence regarding this extension to be sent to you at an address other than your own or to an agent acting for you, include the agent's name, if any, and enter that address instead.

If you changed your name after you filed your last return because of marriage, divorce, etc., be sure to report this to your local Social Security Administration office before filing Form 4868. This prevents delays in processing your extension request.

If you changed your mailing address after you filed your last return, you should use **Form 8822,** Change of Address, to notify the IRS of the change. Showing a new address on Form 4868 will not update your record. You can get Form 8822 by calling 1-800-TAX-FORM (1-800-829-3676).

Line 2

Enter the total of lines 6c, d, and e on line 2a. On line 2b, enter the amount of your check or money order. If you are paying your entire estimate of tax liability, both lines should be the same.

Lines 3 and 4

If you plan to file jointly, enter on line 3 the SSN that you will show first on your return. Enter your spouse's SSN on line 4.

Line 6a—Total Income Tax Liability for 1996

This is the amount you expect to enter on Form 1040EZ, line 10; Form 1040A, line 28; or Form 1040, line 51. If you expect this amount to be zero, enter zero.

Caution: *You can estimate this amount, but be as exact as you can with the information you have. If we later find that your estimate was not reasonable, the extension will be null and void.*

Line 6b—Total Payments for 1996

This is the amount you expect to enter on Form 1040EZ, line 9; Form 1040A, line 29d; or Form 1040, line 58 (excluding line 55).

Line 6c—Balance

Subtract line 6b from line 6a. If line 6b is more than line 6a, enter zero.

If you find you cannot pay the amount shown on line 6c, you can still get the extension. But you should pay as much as you can to limit the amount of interest you will owe. Also, you may be charged the late payment penalty on the unpaid tax from the regular due date of your return. See **Late Payment Penalty** on page 3.

Lines 6d and 6e—Gift or GST Tax Return(s)

Fill in this part only if you or your spouse plan to file Form 709 or 709-A **and** you are also using Form 4868 to apply for an extension of time to file your 1996 **calendar year** income tax return. **Do not** include income tax on lines 6d and 6e.

Enter the amount of gift and GST tax you (or your spouse) are paying on these lines. If your spouse files a **separate** Form 4868, **do not** check the box for your spouse; enter on your form only the total gift and GST tax **you** are paying. Pay in full with this form to avoid interest and penalties.

Form **4952**
Department of the Treasury
Internal Revenue Service (99)

Investment Interest Expense Deduction

▶ Attach to your tax return.

OMB No. 1545-0191

1996

Attachment Sequence No. **12A**

Name(s) shown on return

Identifying number

Part I — Total Investment Interest Expense

1. Investment interest expense paid or accrued in 1996. See instructions . . . . | 1 |
2. Disallowed investment interest expense from 1995 Form 4952, line 7 . . . . | 2 |
3. **Total investment interest expense.** Add lines 1 and 2 . . . . | 3 |

Part II — Net Investment Income

4a. Gross income from property held for investment (excluding any net gain from the disposition of property held for investment) . . . . | 4a |

b. Net gain from the disposition of property held for investment . . . | 4b |

c. Net capital gain from the disposition of property held for investment | 4c |

d. Subtract line 4c from line 4b. If zero or less, enter -0- . . . . | 4d |

e. Enter all or part of the amount on line 4c that you elect to include in investment income. Do not enter more than the amount on line 4b. See instructions . . . . ▶ | 4e |

f. Investment income. Add lines 4a, 4d, and 4e. See instructions . . . . | 4f |

5. Investment expenses. See instructions . . . . | 5 |

6. **Net investment income.** Subtract line 5 from line 4f. If zero or less, enter -0- . . . . . | 6 |

Part III — Investment Interest Expense Deduction

7. Disallowed investment interest expense to be carried forward to 1997. Subtract line 6 from line 3. If zero or less, enter -0- . . . . | 7 |

8. **Investment interest expense deduction.** Enter the smaller of line 3 or 6. See instructions . | 8 |

Section references are to the Internal Revenue Code unless otherwise noted.

Paperwork Reduction Act Notice

We ask for the information on this form to carry out the Internal Revenue laws of the United States. You are required to give us the information. We need it to ensure that you are complying with these laws and to allow us to figure and collect the right amount of tax.

You are not required to provide the information requested on a form that is subject to the Paperwork Reduction Act unless the form displays a valid OMB control number. Books or records relating to a form or its instructions must be retained as long as their contents may become material in the administration of any Internal Revenue law. Generally, tax returns and return information are confidential, as required by section 6103.

The time needed to complete and file this form will vary depending on individual circumstances. The estimated average time is:

Recordkeeping . . . . . . 13 min.
Learning about the law or the form . . . . . 15 min.
Preparing the form . . . . . 21 min.
Copying, assembling, and sending the form to the IRS . . 10 min.

If you have comments concerning the accuracy of these time estimates or suggestions for making this form simpler, we would be happy to hear from you. See the instructions for the tax return with which this form is filed.

General Instructions

Purpose of Form

Interest expense paid by an individual, estate, or trust on a loan allocable to property held for investment may not be fully deductible in the current year. Use Form 4952 to figure the amount of investment interest expense deductible for the current year and the amount, if any, to carry forward to future years.

For more details, get **Pub. 550,** Investment Income and Expenses.

Who Must File

If you are an individual, estate, or a trust, and you claim a deduction for investment interest expense, you must complete and attach Form 4952 to your tax return, unless **all** the following apply.

- Your only investment income was from interest or dividends.
- You have no other deductible expenses connected with the production of interest or dividends.
- Your investment interest expense is not more than your investment income.
- You have no disallowed investment interest expense from 1995.

Allocation of Interest Expense Under Temporary Regulations Section 1.163-8T

If you paid or accrued interest on a loan and used the loan proceeds for more than one purpose, you may have to allocate the interest paid. This is necessary because different rules apply to investment interest, personal interest, trade or business interest, home mortgage interest, and passive activity interest. Get **Pub. 535,** Business Expenses.

Cat. No. 13177Y

Form **4952** (1996)

Specific Instructions
Part I—Total Investment Interest Expense
Line 1
Enter the investment interest paid or accrued during the tax year, regardless of when you incurred the indebtedness. Investment interest is interest paid or accrued on a loan (or part of a loan) that is allocable to property held for investment (as defined below).

Include investment interest expense reported to you on Schedule K-1 from a partnership or an S corporation. Include amortization of bond premium on taxable bonds purchased after October 22, 1986, but before January 1, 1988, unless you elected to offset amortizable bond premium against the interest payments on the bond. A taxable bond is a bond on which the interest is includible in gross income.

Investment interest expense **does not** include the following:

- Home mortgage interest.
- Interest expense that is properly allocable to a passive activity. Generally, a passive activity is any business activity in which you **do not** materially participate and any rental activity. See the separate instructions for **Form 8582**, Passive Activity Loss Limitations, for more details.
- Any interest expense that is capitalized, such as construction interest subject to section 263A.
- Interest expense related to tax-exempt interest income under section 265.

Property held for investment.—Property held for investment includes property that produces income (unless derived in the ordinary course of a trade or business) from interest, dividends, annuities, or royalties; and gains from the disposition of property that produces those types of income or is held for investment. However, it does not include an interest in a passive activity.

Property held for investment also includes an interest in an activity of conducting a trade or business in which you did not materially participate and that is not a passive activity. For example, a working interest in an oil or gas property that you held directly or through an entity that did not limit your liability is property held for investment if you did not materially participate in the activity.

Part II—Net Investment Income
Line 4a
Gross income from property held for investment to enter on line 4a includes income (unless derived in the ordinary course of a trade or business) from:

- Interest,
- Dividends (except Alaska Permanent Fund dividends),
- Annuities, and
- Royalties.

If you are filing **Form 8814**, Parents' Election To Report Child's Interest and Dividends, part or all of your child's income may be included on line 4a. See Form 8814 for details.

Also, include on line 4a net income from the following passive activities:

- Rental of substantially nondepreciable property,
- Equity-financed lending activities, and
- Acquisition of certain interests in a pass-through entity licensing intangible property.

See Regulations section 1.469-2(f)(10) for details.

Also include on line 4a (or 4b, if applicable) net passive income from a passive activity of a publicly traded partnership (as defined in section 469(k)(2)). See Notice 88-75, 1988-2 C.B. 386, for details.

Include investment income reported to you on Schedule K-1 from a partnership or an S corporation. Also include net investment income from an estate or a trust.

Do not include on line 4a any net gain from the disposition of property held for investment. Instead, enter this amount on line 4b.

Line 4b
Net gain from the disposition of property held for investment is the excess, if any, of total gains over total losses from the disposition of property held for investment. When figuring this amount, include capital gain distributions from mutual funds.

Line 4c
Net capital gain from the disposition of property held for investment is the excess, if any, of net long-term capital gain over net short-term capital loss from the disposition of property held for investment. When figuring this amount, include capital gain distributions from mutual funds.

Line 4e
Net capital gain from the disposition of property held for investment is excluded from investment income. However, you may elect to include in investment income all or part of the net capital gain from the disposition of property held for investment. If you make the election, you also must reduce the amount of net capital gain eligible for the 28% maximum capital gains rate by the amount of net capital gain you included in investment income. Therefore, you should consider the effect on your tax using the maximum capital gains rate before making this election. You must make the election no later than the due date (including extensions) of your income tax return. Once made, the election may not be revoked without IRS consent.

To make the election, enter all or part of the amount on line 4c, but not more than the amount on line 4b, that you elect to include in investment income. Also enter this amount on line 3 of the **Capital Gain Tax Worksheet** in the Form 1040 instructions, or on line 37b of Schedule D (Form 1041), if applicable.

Line 5
Investment expenses are your allowed deductions, other than interest expense, directly connected with the production of investment income. For example, depreciation or depletion allowed on assets that produce investment income is an investment expense.

Include investment expenses reported to you on Schedule K-1 from a partnership or an S corporation.

Investment expenses **do not** include any deductions taken into account in determining your income or loss from a passive activity.

If you have investment expenses that are included as a miscellaneous itemized deduction on Schedule A (Form 1040), line 22, you may not have to use the entire amount for purposes of Form 4952, line 5. The 2% adjusted gross income limitation on Schedule A (Form 1040), line 25, may reduce the amount you must enter on Form 4952, line 5.

To figure the amount to use, compare the amount of the investment expenses included on Schedule A (Form 1040), line 22, with the total miscellaneous expenses on Schedule A (Form 1040), line 26. The smaller of **(a)** the investment expenses included on Schedule A (Form 1040), line 22, or **(b)** the total on Schedule A (Form 1040), line 26, is the amount of investment expenses included as a miscellaneous itemized deduction to use when figuring Form 4952, line 5.

Example. Assume Schedule A, line 22, includes investment expenses of $3,000, and line 26 is $1,300 after the 2% adjusted gross income limitation. Investment expenses from Schedule A of $1,300 are used to figure the amount of investment expenses for line 5. If investment expenses of $800 were included on line 22 and line 26 was $1,300, investment expenses from Schedule A of $800 would be used.

Part III—Investment Interest Expense Deduction
Line 8
This is the amount you may deduct as investment interest expense.

Individuals.—Generally, enter the amount from line 8 on Schedule A (Form 1040), line 13, even if all or part of it is attributable to a partnership or an S corporation. If any portion of this amount is attributable to royalties, enter that part of the interest expense on Schedule E (Form 1040). If any portion is attributable to a trade or business in which you did not materially participate and that is not a passive activity, enter that part of the interest expense on the schedule where you report other expenses for that trade or business.

Estates and trusts.—Enter the amount from line 8 on Form 1041, line 10.

Form 6198.—If any portion of the deductible investment interest expense is attributable to an activity for which you are not at risk, you must also use **Form 6198**, At-Risk Limitations, to figure your deductible investment interest expense. Enter the portion attributable to the at-risk activity on Form 6198, line 4. Reduce Form 4952, line 8, by the amount entered on Form 6198. See Form 6198 and its instructions for more details, especially the instructions for line 4 of that form.

Alternative minimum tax (AMT).—Deductible interest expense is an adjustment for the AMT. Get **Form 6251**, Alternative Minimum Tax—Individuals, or Form 1041, Schedule I, for estates and trusts.

Form **4972**	**Tax on Lump-Sum Distributions**	OMB No. 1545-0193
Department of the Treasury Internal Revenue Service	From Qualified Retirement Plans ▶ Attach to Form 1040 or Form 1041. ▶ See separate instructions.	**1996** Attachment Sequence No. **28**

Name of recipient of distribution	Identifying number

Part I — Complete this part to see if you qualify to use Form 4972

			Yes	No
1	Was this a distribution of a plan participant's entire balance from all of an employer's qualified plans of one kind (pension, profit-sharing, or stock bonus)? If "No," do not use this form.	1		
2	Did you roll over any part of the distribution? If "Yes," do not use this form.	2		
3	Was this distribution paid to you as a beneficiary of a plan participant who died after reaching age 59½ (or who had been born before 1936)?.	3		
4	Were you a plan participant who received this distribution after reaching age 59½ **and** having been in the plan for at least 5 years before the year of the distribution?.	4		
	If you answered "No" to both questions 3 **and** 4, do not use this form.			
5a	Did you use Form 4972 after 1986 for a previous distribution from your own plan? If "Yes," do not use this form for a 1996 distribution from your own plan.	5a		
b	If you are receiving this distribution as a beneficiary of a plan participant who died, did you use Form 4972 for a previous distribution received for that plan participant after 1986? If "Yes," you may not use the form for this distribution.	5b		

Part II — Complete this part to choose the 20% capital gain election (See instructions.) Do not complete this part unless the participant was born **before** 1936.

6	Capital gain part from box 3 of Form 1099-R.	6	
7	Multiply line 6 by 20% (.20).	7	
	If you also choose to use Part III, go to line 8. Otherwise, include the amount from line 7 in the total on Form 1040, line 38, or Form 1041, Schedule G, line 1b, whichever applies.		

Part III — Complete this part to choose the 5- or 10-year tax option (See instructions.)

8	Ordinary income from Form 1099-R, box 2a minus box 3. If you did not complete Part II, enter the taxable amount from box 2a of Form 1099-R	8	
9	Death benefit exclusion for a beneficiary of a plan participant who died before August 21, 1996	9	
10	Total taxable amount. Subtract line 9 from line 8.	10	
11	Current actuarial value of annuity (from Form 1099-R, box 8).	11	
12	Adjusted total taxable amount. Add lines 10 and 11. If this amount is $70,000 or more, **skip** lines 13 through 16, and enter this amount on line 17.	12	
13	Multiply line 12 by 50% (.50), but **do not** enter more than $10,000	13	
14	Subtract $20,000 from line 12. If the result is less than zero, enter -0-	14	
15	Multiply line 14 by 20% (.20)	15	
16	Minimum distribution allowance. Subtract line 15 from line 13.	16	
17	Subtract line 16 from line 12.	17	
18	Federal estate tax attributable to lump-sum distribution.	18	
19	Subtract line 18 from line 17.	19	
	If line 11 is blank, skip lines 20 through 22 and go to line 23.		
20	Divide line 11 by line 12 and enter the result as a decimal.	20	
21	Multiply line 16 by the decimal on line 20.	21	
22	Subtract line 21 from line 11.	22	

For Paperwork Reduction Act Notice, see separate instructions.   Cat. No. 13187U   Form **4972** (1996)

Form 4972 (1996) — Page 2

Part III 5- or 10-year tax option—CONTINUED

5-year tax option

23	Multiply line 19 by 20% (.20)	23
24	Tax on amount on line 23. Use the Tax Rate Schedule for the 5-Year Tax Option in the instructions	24
25	Multiply line 24 by five (5). If line 11 is blank, skip lines 26 through 28, and enter this amount on line 29	25
26	Multiply line 22 by 20% (.20)	26
27	Tax on amount on line 26. Use the Tax Rate Schedule for the 5-Year Tax Option in the instructions	27
28	Multiply line 27 by five (5)	28
29	Subtract line 28 from line 25. (Multiple recipients, see page 3 of the instructions.) . . .	29

Note: *Complete lines 30 through 36 ONLY if the participant was born before 1936. Otherwise, enter the amount from line 29 on line 37.*

10-year tax option

30	Multiply line 19 by 10% (.10)	30
31	Tax on amount on line 30. Use the Tax Rate Schedule for the 10-Year Tax Option in the instructions	31
32	Multiply line 31 by ten (10). If line 11 is blank, skip lines 33 through 35, and enter this amount on line 36	32
33	Multiply line 22 by 10% (.10)	33
34	Tax on amount on line 33. Use the Tax Rate Schedule for the 10-Year Tax Option in the instructions	34
35	Multiply line 34 by ten (10)	35
36	Subtract line 35 from line 32. (Multiple recipients, see page 3 of the instructions.) . . .	36
37	Compare lines 29 and 36. Generally, you should enter the **smaller** amount here (see instructions) . . . . ▶	37
38	Tax on lump-sum distribution. Add lines 7 and 37. Also, include in the total on Form 1040, line 38, or Form 1041, Schedule G, line 1b, whichever applies . . . . ▶	38

Form **6251**	**Alternative Minimum Tax—Individuals**	OMB No. 1545-0227
Department of the Treasury Internal Revenue Service	► See separate instructions. ► Attach to Form 1040 or Form 1040NR.	**1996** Attachment Sequence No. **32**

Name(s) shown on Form 1040 | Your social security number

Part I — Adjustments and Preferences

1	If you itemized deductions on Schedule A (Form 1040), go to line 2. Otherwise, enter your standard deduction from Form 1040, line 34, here and go to line 6	1
2	Medical and dental. Enter the smaller of Schedule A (Form 1040), line 4 **or** 2½% of Form 1040, line 32	2
3	Taxes. Enter the amount from Schedule A (Form 1040), line 9	3
4	Certain interest on a home mortgage not used to buy, build, or improve your home	4
5	Miscellaneous itemized deductions. Enter the amount from Schedule A (Form 1040), line 26	5
6	Refund of taxes. Enter any tax refund from Form 1040, line 10 or line 21	6 ( )
7	Investment interest. Enter difference between regular tax and AMT deduction	7
8	Post-1986 depreciation. Enter difference between regular tax and AMT depreciation	8
9	Adjusted gain or loss. Enter difference between AMT and regular tax gain or loss	9
10	Incentive stock options. Enter excess of AMT income over regular tax income	10
11	Passive activities. Enter difference between AMT and regular tax income or loss	11
12	Beneficiaries of estates and trusts. Enter the amount from Schedule K-1 (Form 1041), line 8	12
13	Tax-exempt interest from private activity bonds issued after 8/7/86	13
14	Other. Enter the amount, if any, for each item below and enter the total on line 14.	
	a Charitable contributions **h** Loss limitations	
	b Circulation expenditures **i** Mining costs	
	c Depletion **j** Patron's adjustment	
	d Depreciation (pre-1987) **k** Pollution control facilities	
	e Installment sales **l** Research and experimental	
	f Intangible drilling costs **m** Tax shelter farm activities	
	g Long-term contracts **n** Related adjustments	14
15	**Total Adjustments and Preferences.** Combine lines 1 through 14	15

Part II — Alternative Minimum Taxable Income

16	Enter the amount from **Form 1040, line 35.** If less than zero, enter as a (loss)	16
17	Net operating loss deduction, if any, from Form 1040, line 21. Enter as a positive amount	17
18	If Form 1040, line 32, is over $117,950 (over $58,975 if married filing separately), and you itemized deductions, enter the amount, if any, from line 9 of the worksheet for Schedule A (Form 1040), line 28	18 ( )
19	Combine lines 15 through 18	19
20	Alternative tax net operating loss deduction. See page 5 of the instructions	20
21	**Alternative Minimum Taxable Income.** Subtract line 20 from line 19. (If married filing separately and line 21 is more than $165,000, see page 5 of the instructions.)	21

Part III — Exemption Amount and Alternative Minimum Tax

22 **Exemption Amount.** (If this form is for a child under age 14, see page 6 of the instructions.)

If your filing status is:	And line 21 is not over:	Enter on line 22:	
Single or head of household	$112,500	$33,750	
Married filing jointly or qualifying widow(er)	150,000	45,000	22
Married filing separately	75,000	22,500	

If line 21 is **over** the amount shown above for your filing status, see page 6 of the instructions.

23	Subtract line 22 from line 21. If zero or less, enter -0- here and on lines 26 and 28	23
24	If line 23 is $175,000 or less ($87,500 or less if married filing separately), multiply line 23 by 26% (.26). Otherwise, multiply line 23 by 28% (.28) and subtract $3,500 ($1,750 if married filing separately) from the result	24
25	Alternative minimum tax foreign tax credit. See page 6 of the instructions	25
26	Tentative minimum tax. Subtract line 25 from line 24	26
27	Enter your tax from Form 1040, line 38 (excluding any amount from Form 4972), minus any foreign tax credit from Form 1040, line 41	27
28	**Alternative Minimum Tax.** (If this form is for a child under age 14, see page 7 of the instructions.) Subtract line 27 from line 26. If zero or less, enter -0-. Enter here and on Form 1040, line 46	28

For Paperwork Reduction Act Notice, see separate instructions.   Cat. No. 13600G   Form **6251** (1996)

Tax Forms B–61

Form **6252**	**Installment Sale Income**	OMB No. 1545-0228
Department of the Treasury Internal Revenue Service	▶ See separate instructions. ▶ Attach to your tax return. ▶ Use a separate form for each sale or other disposition of property on the installment method.	**19**96 Attachment Sequence No. **79**

Name(s) shown on return | Identifying number

1 Description of property ▶ ....
2a Date acquired (month, day, year) ▶ __/__/__   b Date sold (month, day, year) ▶ __/__/__
3 Was the property sold to a related party after May 14, 1980? See instructions. If "No," skip line 4 . . . ☐ Yes ☐ No
4 Was the property you sold to a related party a marketable security? If "Yes," complete Part III. If "No,"
   complete Part III for the year of sale and the 2 years after the year of sale . . . . ☐ Yes ☐ No

Part I **Gross Profit and Contract Price.** Complete this part for the year of sale only.

5 Selling price including mortgages and other debts. Do not include interest whether stated or unstated | 5
6 Mortgages and other debts the buyer assumed or took the property subject
   to, but not new mortgages the buyer got from a bank or other source . | 6
7 Subtract line 6 from line 5 . . . . | 7
8 Cost or other basis of property sold . . . . | 8
9 Depreciation allowed or allowable . . . . | 9
10 Adjusted basis. Subtract line 9 from line 8 . . . . | 10
11 Commissions and other expenses of sale . . . . | 11
12 Income recapture from Form 4797, Part III. See instructions . . | 12
13 Add lines 10, 11, and 12 . . . . | 13
14 Subtract line 13 from line 5. If zero or less, **stop here.** Do not complete the rest of this form . | 14
15 If the property described on line 1 above was your main home, enter the total of lines 14 and
   22 from Form 2119. Otherwise, enter -0- . . . . | 15
16 **Gross profit.** Subtract line 15 from line 14 . . . . | 16
17 Subtract line 13 from line 6. If zero or less, enter -0- . . . . | 17
18 **Contract price.** Add line 7 and line 17 . . . . | 18

Part II **Installment Sale Income.** Complete this part for the year of sale and any year you receive a payment or
have certain debts you must treat as a payment on installment obligations.

19 Gross profit percentage. Divide line 16 by line 18. For years after the year of sale, see instructions | 19
20 **For year of sale only:** Enter amount from line 17 above; otherwise, enter -0- . . . . | 20
21 Payments received during year. See instructions. Do not include interest whether stated or unstated | 21
22 Add lines 20 and 21 . . . . | 22
23 Payments received in prior years. See instructions. Do not include
   interest whether stated or unstated . . . . | 23
24 **Installment sale income.** Multiply line 22 by line 19 . . . . | 24
25 Part of line 24 that is ordinary income under recapture rules. See instructions . . . . | 25
26 Subtract line 25 from line 24. Enter here and on Schedule D or Form 4797. See instructions . | 26

Part III **Related Party Installment Sale Income.** Do not complete if you received the final payment this tax year.

27 Name, address, and taxpayer identifying number of related party ....
   ....
28 Did the related party, during this tax year, resell or dispose of the property ("second disposition")? . . . ☐ Yes ☐ No
29 If the answer to question 28 is "Yes," complete lines 30 through 37 below unless one of the following conditions is
   met. Check only the box that applies.
 a ☐ The second disposition was more than 2 years after the first disposition (other than dispositions
     of marketable securities). If this box is checked, enter the date of disposition (month, day, year) ▶ __/__/__
 b ☐ The first disposition was a sale or exchange of stock to the issuing corporation.
 c ☐ The second disposition was an involuntary conversion where the threat of conversion occurred after the first disposition.
 d ☐ The second disposition occurred after the death of the original seller or buyer.
 e ☐ It can be established to the satisfaction of the Internal Revenue Service that tax avoidance was not a principal purpose
     for either of the dispositions. If this box is checked, attach an explanation. See instructions.
30 Selling price of property sold by related party . . . . | 30
31 Enter contract price from line 18 for year of first sale . . . . | 31
32 Enter the **smaller** of line 30 or line 31 . . . . | 32
33 Total payments received by the end of your 1996 tax year. See instructions . . . . | 33
34 Subtract line 33 from line 32. If zero or less, enter -0- . . . . | 34
35 Multiply line 34 by the gross profit percentage on line 19 for year of first sale . . . . . . | 35
36 Part of line 35 that is ordinary income under recapture rules. See instructions . . . . . . | 36
37 Subtract line 36 from line 35. Enter here and on Schedule D or Form 4797. See instructions . | 37

For Paperwork Reduction Act Notice, see separate instructions.   Cat. No. 13601R   Form **6252** (1996)

Form **8283** (Rev. October 1995) Department of the Treasury Internal Revenue Service	**Noncash Charitable Contributions** ▶ Attach to your tax return if you claimed a total deduction of over $500 for all contributed property. ▶ See separate instructions.	OMB No. 1545-0908 Attachment Sequence No. **55**
Name(s) shown on your income tax return		Identifying number

Note: *Figure the amount of your contribution deduction before completing this form. See your tax return instructions.*

Section A—List in this section **only** items (or groups of similar items) for which you claimed a deduction of $5,000 or less. Also, list certain publicly traded securities even if the deduction is over $5,000 (see instructions).

Part I Information on Donated Property—If you need more space, attach a statement.

1	(a) Name and address of the donee organization	(b) Description of donated property
A		
B		
C		
D		
E		

Note: *If the amount you claimed as a deduction for an item is $500 or less, you do not have to complete columns (d), (e), and (f).*

	(c) Date of the contribution	(d) Date acquired by donor (mo., yr.)	(e) How acquired by donor	(f) Donor's cost or adjusted basis	(g) Fair market value	(h) Method used to determine the fair market value
A						
B						
C						
D						
E						

Part II Other Information—Complete line 2 if you gave less than an entire interest in property listed in Part I. Complete line 3 if restrictions were attached to a contribution listed in Part I.

2   If, during the year, you contributed less than the entire interest in the property, complete lines a – e.
  a Enter the letter from Part I that identifies the property ▶ _____ . If Part II applies to more than one property, attach a separate statement.
  b Total amount claimed as a deduction for the property listed in Part I: **(1)** For this tax year ▶ _____
     (2) For any prior tax years ▶ _____ .
  c Name and address of each organization to which any such contribution was made in a prior year (complete only if different than the donee organization above):
     Name of charitable organization (donee)

     Address (number, street, and room or suite no.)

     City or town, state, and ZIP code

  d For tangible property, enter the place where the property is located or kept ▶ _____
  e Name of any person, other than the donee organization, having actual possession of the property ▶ _____

3 If conditions were attached to any contribution listed in Part I, answer questions a – c and attach the required statement (see instructions).   Yes No
  a Is there a restriction, either temporary or permanent, on the donee's right to use or dispose of the donated property? . . . .
  b Did you give to anyone (other than the donee organization or another organization participating with the donee organization in cooperative fundraising) the right to the income from the donated property or to the possession of the property, including the right to vote donated securities, to acquire the property by purchase or otherwise, or to designate the person having such income, possession, or right to acquire? . . . .
  c Is there a restriction limiting the donated property for a particular use? . . . .

For Paperwork Reduction Act Notice, see separate instructions.   Cat. No. 62299J   Form **8283** (Rev. 10-95)

Tax Forms B–63

Form 8283 (Rev. 10-95) Page **2**

Name(s) shown on your income tax return | Identifying number

Section B—Appraisal Summary—List in this section only items (or groups of similar items) for which you claimed a deduction of more than $5,000 per item or group. **Exception.** Report contributions of certain publicly traded securities only in Section A.

If you donated art, you may have to attach the complete appraisal. See the **Note** in Part I below.

Part I Information on Donated Property—To be completed by the taxpayer and/or appraiser.

4 Check type of property:
- ☐ Art* (contribution of $20,000 or more)
- ☐ Art* (contribution of less than $20,000)
- ☐ Real Estate
- ☐ Coin Collections
- ☐ Gems/Jewelry
- ☐ Books
- ☐ Stamp Collections
- ☐ Other

*Art includes paintings, sculptures, watercolors, prints, drawings, ceramics, antique furniture, decorative arts, textiles, carpets, silver, rare manuscripts, historical memorabilia, and other similar objects.

Note: *If your total art contribution deduction was $20,000 or more, you must attach a complete copy of the signed appraisal. See instructions.*

5	**(a)** Description of donated property (if you need more space, attach a separate statement)	**(b)** If tangible property was donated, give a brief summary of the overall physical condition at the time of the gift	**(c)** Appraised fair market value
A		
B		
C		
D		

	(d) Date acquired by donor (mo., yr.)	**(e)** How acquired by donor	**(f)** Donor's cost or adjusted basis	**(g)** For bargain sales, enter amount received	See instructions
					(h) Amount claimed as a deduction	**(i)** Average trading price of securities
A						
B						
C						
D						

Part II Taxpayer (Donor) Statement—List each item included in Part I above that is separately identified in the appraisal as having a value of $500 or less. See instructions.

I declare that the following item(s) included in Part I above has to the best of my knowledge and belief an appraised value of not more than $500 (per item). Enter identifying letter from Part I and describe the specific item. See instructions. ▶ _____

Signature of taxpayer (donor) ▶   Date ▶

Part III Declaration of Appraiser

I declare that I am not the donor, the donee, a party to the transaction in which the donor acquired the property, employed by, or related to any of the foregoing persons, or married to any person who is related to any of the foregoing persons. And, if regularly used by the donor, donee, or party to the transaction, I performed the majority of my appraisals during my tax year for other persons.

Also, I declare that I hold myself out to the public as an appraiser or perform appraisals on a regular basis; and that because of my qualifications as described in the appraisal, I am qualified to make appraisals of the type of property being valued. I certify that the appraisal fees were not based on a percentage of the appraised property value. Furthermore, I understand that a false or fraudulent overstatement of the property value as described in the qualified appraisal or this appraisal summary may subject me to the penalty under section 6701(a) (aiding and abetting the understatement of tax liability). I affirm that I have not been barred from presenting evidence or testimony by the Director of Practice.

Sign Here
Signature ▶   Title ▶   Date of appraisal ▶
Business address (including room or suite no.)   Identifying number
City or town, state, and ZIP code

Part IV Donee Acknowledgment—To be completed by the charitable organization.

This charitable organization acknowledges that it is a qualified organization under section 170(c) and that it received the donated property as described in Section B, Part I, above on ▶ _____
(Date)

Furthermore, this organization affirms that in the event it sells, exchanges, or otherwise disposes of the property described in Section B, Part I (or any portion thereof) within 2 years after the date of receipt, it will file **Form 8282**, Donee Information Return, with the IRS and give the donor a copy of that form. This acknowledgment does not represent agreement with the claimed fair market value.

Name of charitable organization (donee) | Employer identification number
Address (number, street, and room or suite no.) | City or town, state, and ZIP code
Authorized signature | Title | Date

Printed on recycled paper

Form **8332**	**Release of Claim to Exemption**	OMB No. 1545-0915
(Rev. June 1996) Department of the Treasury Internal Revenue Service	**for Child of Divorced or Separated Parents** ▶ **ATTACH** to noncustodial parent's return **EACH YEAR** exemption claimed.	Attachment Sequence No. **51**

Name(s) of parent claiming exemption   Social security number

Part I — Release of Claim to Exemption for Current Year

I agree not to claim an exemption for _____
                                                    Name(s) of child (or children)

for the tax year 19____.

_____   _____   _____
Signature of parent releasing claim to exemption   Social security number   Date

If you choose not to claim an exemption for this child (or children) for future tax years, complete Part II.

Part II — Release of Claim to Exemption for Future Years (If completed, see **Noncustodial Parent** below.)

I agree not to claim an exemption for _____
                                                    Name(s) of child (or children)

for the tax year(s) _____.
                          (Specify. See instructions.)

_____   _____   _____
Signature of parent releasing claim to exemption   Social security number   Date

General Instructions

Paperwork Reduction Act Notice.—We ask for the information on this form to carry out the Internal Revenue laws of the United States. You are required to give us the information. We need it to ensure that you are complying with these laws and to allow us to figure and collect the right amount of tax.

You are not required to provide the information requested on a form that is subject to the Paperwork Reduction Act unless the form displays a valid OMB control number. Books or records relating to a form or its instructions must be retained as long as their contents may become material in the administration of any Internal Revenue law. Generally, tax returns and return information are confidential, as required by Internal Revenue Code section 6103.

The time needed to complete and file this form will vary depending on individual circumstances. The estimated average time is: **Recordkeeping**, 7 min.; **Learning about the law or the form**, 5 min.; **Preparing the form**, 7 min.; and **Copying, assembling, and sending the form to the IRS**, 14 min.

If you have comments concerning the accuracy of these time estimates or suggestions for making this form simpler, we would be happy to hear from you. See the instructions for the tax return with which this form is filed.

Purpose of Form.—If you are a **custodial parent**, you may use this form to release your claim to your child's exemption. To do so, complete this form and give it to the **noncustodial parent** who will claim the child's exemption. Then, the noncustodial parent must attach this form or a similar statement to his or her tax return EACH YEAR the exemption is claimed.

You are the **custodial parent** if you had custody of the child for most of the year. You are the **noncustodial parent** if you had custody for a shorter period of time or did not have custody at all.

Instead of using this form, you (the custodial parent) may use a similar statement as long as it contains the same information required by this form.

Children of Divorced or Separated Parents.—Special rules apply to determine if the support test is met for children of parents who are divorced or legally separated under a decree of divorce or separate maintenance or separated under a written separation agreement. The rules also apply to children of parents who did not live together at any time during the last 6 months of the year, even if they do not have a separation agreement.

The general rule is that the custodial parent is treated as having provided over half of the child's support if:

1. The child received over half of his or her total support for the year from both of the parents, **AND**

2. The child was in the custody of one or both of his or her parents for more than half of the year.

Note: *Public assistance payments, such as Aid to Families with Dependent Children, are not support provided by the parents.*

If both **1** and **2** above apply, and the other four dependency tests in your tax return instruction booklet are also met, the custodial parent can claim the child's exemption.

Exception. The general rule does not apply if **any** of the following apply:

● The custodial parent agrees not to claim the child's exemption by signing this form or similar statement. The noncustodial parent **must** attach this form or similar statement to his or her tax return for the tax year. See **Custodial Parent** later.

● The child is treated as having received over half of his or her total support from a person under a multiple support agreement (**Form 2120**, Multiple Support Declaration).

● A pre-1985 divorce decree or written separation agreement states that the noncustodial parent can claim the child as a dependent. But the noncustodial parent must provide at least $600 for the child's support during the year. This rule does not apply if the decree or agreement was changed after 1984 to say that the noncustodial parent cannot claim the child as a dependent.

Additional Information.—For more details, get **Pub. 504**, Divorced or Separated Individuals.

Specific Instructions

Custodial Parent.—You may agree to release your claim to the child's exemption for the current tax year or for future years, or both.

● Complete **Part I** if you agree to release your claim to the child's exemption for the current tax year.

● Complete **Part II** if you agree to release your claim to the child's exemption for any or all future years. If you do, write the specific future year(s) or "all future years" in the space provided in Part II.

Noncustodial Parent.—Attach Form 8332 or similar statement to your tax return for the tax year in which you claim the child's exemption. You may claim the exemption **only** if the other four dependency tests in your tax return instruction booklet are met.

Note: *If the custodial parent completed Part II, you **must** attach a copy of this form to your tax return for each future year in which you claim the exemption.*

Cat. No. 13910F   Form **8332** (Rev. 6-96)

Form **8582**	**Passive Activity Loss Limitations**	OMB No. 1545-1008
Department of the Treasury Internal Revenue Service (99)	▶ See separate instructions. ▶ Attach to Form 1040 or Form 1041.	**1996** Attachment Sequence No. **88**

Name(s) shown on return | Identifying number

Part I — 1996 Passive Activity Loss
Caution: *See the instructions for Worksheets 1 and 2 on page 8 before completing Part I.*

Rental Real Estate Activities With Active Participation (For the definition of active participation see **Active Participation in a Rental Real Estate Activity** on page 4 of the instructions.)

- **1a** Activities with net income (from Worksheet 1, column (a)) . . . **1a** ____
- **b** Activities with net loss (from Worksheet 1, column (b)) . . . . **1b** (____)
- **c** Prior year unallowed losses (from Worksheet 1, column (c)) . . **1c** (____)
- **d** Combine lines 1a, 1b, and 1c . . . . **1d** ____

All Other Passive Activities

- **2a** Activities with net income (from Worksheet 2, column (a)) . . . **2a** ____
- **b** Activities with net loss (from Worksheet 2, column (b)) . . . . **2b** (____)
- **c** Prior year unallowed losses (from Worksheet 2, column (c)) . . **2c** (____)
- **d** Combine lines 2a, 2b, and 2c . . . . **2d** ____

3 Combine lines 1d and 2d. If the result is net income or zero, see the instructions for line 3 on page 9. If this line and line 1d are losses, go to line 4. Otherwise, enter -0- on line 9 and go to line 10 . **3** ____

Part II — Special Allowance for Rental Real Estate With Active Participation
Note: *Enter all numbers in Part II as positive amounts. See page 9 of the instructions for examples.*

4 Enter the **smaller** of the loss on line 1d or the loss on line 3 . . . . **4** ____

5 Enter $150,000. If married filing separately, see page 9 of the instructions . . . . **5** ____

6 Enter modified adjusted gross income, but not less than zero (see page 9 of the instructions) . . . . **6** ____

Note: *If line 6 is equal to or greater than line 5, skip lines 7 and 8, enter -0- on line 9, and then go to line 10. Otherwise, go to line 7.*

7 Subtract line 6 from line 5 . . . . **7** ____

8 Multiply line 7 by 50% (.5). **Do not** enter more than $25,000. If married filing separately, see page 9 of the instructions . . . . **8** ____

9 Enter the **smaller** of line 4 or line 8 . . . . **9** ____

Part III — Total Losses Allowed

10 Add the income, if any, on lines 1a and 2a and enter the total . . . . **10** ____

11 **Total losses allowed from all passive activities for 1996.** Add lines 9 and 10. See pages 10 and 11 of the instructions to find out how to report the losses on your tax return . . . . . **11** ____

For Paperwork Reduction Act Notice, see separate instructions.   Cat. No. 63704F   Form **8582** (1996)

Form 8582 (1996) Page **2**

Caution: *The worksheets are not required to be filed with your tax return and may be detached before filing Form 8582. Keep a copy of the worksheets for your records.*

Worksheet 1—For Form 8582, Lines 1a, 1b, and 1c (See page 8 of the instructions.)

Name of activity	Current year		Prior year	Overall gain or loss	
	(a) Net income (line 1a)	(b) Net loss (line 1b)	(c) Unallowed loss (line 1c)	(d) Gain	(e) Loss
Total. Enter on Form 8582, lines 1a, 1b, and 1c. ▶					

Worksheet 2—For Form 8582, Lines 2a, 2b, and 2c (See page 8 of the instructions.)

Name of activity	Current year		Prior year	Overall gain or loss	
	(a) Net income (line 2a)	(b) Net loss (line 2b)	(c) Unallowed loss (line 2c)	(d) Gain	(e) Loss
Total. Enter on Form 8582, lines 2a, 2b, and 2c. ▶					

Worksheet 3—Use this worksheet if an amount is shown on Form 8582, line 9 (See page 9 of the instructions.)

Name of activity	Form or schedule to be reported on	(a) Loss	(b) Ratio	(c) Special allowance	(d) Subtract column (c) from column (a)
Total ▶			1.00		

Worksheet 4—Allocation of Unallowed Losses (See page 10 of the instructions.)

Name of activity	Form or schedule to be reported on	(a) Loss	(b) Ratio	(c) Unallowed loss
Total ▶			1.00	

Worksheet 5—Allowed Losses (See page 10 of the instructions.)

Name of activity	Form or schedule to be reported on	(a) Loss	(b) Unallowed loss	(c) Allowed loss
Total ▶				

Form 8582 (1996) Page **3**

Worksheet 6—Activities With Losses Reported on Two or More Different Forms or Schedules (See page 10 of the instructions.)

Name of Activity:	(a)	(b)	(c) Ratio	(d) Unallowed loss	(e) Allowed loss
Form or Schedule To Be Reported on:					
1a Net loss plus prior year unallowed loss from form or schedule . ▶					
b Net income from form or schedule . . . . ▶					
c Subtract line 1b from line 1a. If zero or less, enter -0- ▶					
Form or Schedule To Be Reported on:					
1a Net loss plus prior year unallowed loss from form or schedule . ▶					
b Net income from form or schedule . . . . ▶					
c Subtract line 1b from line 1a. If zero or less, enter -0- ▶					
Form or Schedule To Be Reported on:					
1a Net loss plus prior year unallowed loss from form or schedule . ▶					
b Net income from form or schedule . . . . ▶					
c Subtract line 1b from line 1a. If zero or less, enter -0- ▶					
Total . . . . ▶			1.00		

B–68 Appendix B

Form **8606** Department of the Treasury Internal Revenue Service	**Nondeductible IRAs** **(Contributions, Distributions, and Basis)** ▶ Please see What Records Must I Keep? on page 2. ▶ Attach to Form 1040, Form 1040A, or Form 1040NR.	OMB No. 1545-1007 **19**96 Attachment Sequence No. **47**

Name. If married, file a separate Form 8606 for each spouse who is required to file Form 8606. See instructions. | Your social security number

Fill in Your Address Only If You Are Filing This Form by Itself and Not With Your Tax Return ▶

Home address (number and street, or P.O. box if mail is not delivered to your home) | Apt. no.

City, town or post office, state, and ZIP code

Contributions, Nontaxable Distributions, and Basis

1. Enter your IRA contributions for 1996 that you choose to be nondeductible. Include those made during 1/1/97–4/15/97 that were for 1996. See instructions **1**
2. Enter your total IRA basis for 1995 and earlier years. See instructions **2**
3. Add lines 1 and 2 . . . . **3**

Did you receive any IRA distributions (withdrawals) in 1996? — No ▶ Enter the amount from line 3 on line 12. Then, **stop** and read **When and Where To File** on page 2.
— Yes ▶ Go to line 4.

4. Enter only those contributions included on line 1 that were made during 1/1/97–4/15/97. This amount will be the same as line 1 if all of your nondeductible contributions for 1996 were made in 1997 by 4/15/97. See instructions **4**
5. Subtract line 4 from line 3 . . . . **5**
6. Enter the total value of **ALL** your IRAs as of 12/31/96 plus any outstanding rollovers. See instructions **6**
7. Enter the total IRA distributions received during 1996. Do not include amounts rolled over before 1/1/97. See instructions **7**
8. Add lines 6 and 7 . . . . **8**
9. Divide line 5 by line 8 and enter the result as a decimal (to at least two places). Do not enter more than "1.00" . . . . **9** × .
10. Multiply line 7 by line 9. This is the amount of your **nontaxable distributions for 1996** **10**
11. Subtract line 10 from line 5. This is the **basis in your IRA(s) as of 12/31/96** **11**
12. Add lines 4 and 11. This is your **total IRA basis for 1996 and earlier years** **12**

Taxable Distributions for 1996

13. Subtract line 10 from line 7. Enter the result here and on Form 1040, line 15b; Form 1040A, line 10b; or Form 1040NR, line 16b, whichever applies **13**

Sign Here Only If You Are Filing This Form by Itself and Not With Your Tax Return — Under penalties of perjury, I declare that I have examined this form, including accompanying attachments, and to the best of my knowledge and belief, it is true, correct, and complete.

▶ Your signature ▶ Date

Section references are to the Internal Revenue Code.

Paperwork Reduction Act Notice

We ask for the information on this form to carry out the Internal Revenue laws of the United States. You are required to give us the information. We need it to ensure that you are complying with these laws and to allow us to figure and collect the right amount of tax.

You are not required to provide the information requested on a form that is subject to the Paperwork Reduction Act unless the form displays a valid OMB control number. Books or records relating to a form or its instructions must be retained as long as their contents may become material in the administration of any Internal Revenue law. Generally, tax returns and return information are confidential, as required by section 6103.

The time needed to complete and file this form will vary depending on individual circumstances. The estimated average time is: **Recordkeeping,** 26 min.; **Learning about the law or the form,** 7 min.; **Preparing the form,** 21 min.; and **Copying, assembling, and sending the form to the IRS,** 20 min.

If you have comments concerning the accuracy of these time estimates or suggestions for making this form simpler, we would be happy to hear from you. See the instructions for the tax return with which this form is filed.

General Instructions

Purpose of Form

Use Form 8606 to report your IRA contributions that you choose to be nondeductible. For example, if you cannot deduct all of your contributions because of the income limits for IRAs, you may want to make nondeductible contributions.

Also use Form 8606 to figure the basis in your IRA(s) and the taxable part of any distributions you received in 1996 if you have ever made nondeductible contributions.

Your **basis** is the total of all your nondeductible IRA contributions minus the total of all nontaxable IRA distributions received. It is to your advantage to keep track of your basis because it is used to figure the nontaxable part of future distributions.

Note: *To figure your deductible IRA contributions, see the Instructions for Form 1040, or Form 1040A, whichever applies.*

Who Must File

You must file Form 8606 for 1996 if:

- You made nondeductible contributions to your IRA for 1996, **or**
- You received IRA distributions in 1996 **and** you have ever made nondeductible contributions to any of your IRAs.

Cat. No. 63966F Form **8606** (1996)

Form 8606 (1996) — Page 2

What Records Must I Keep?

To verify the nontaxable part of distributions from your IRA, keep a copy of this form together with copies of the following forms and records until all distributions are made from your IRA(s):

- Page 1 of Forms 1040 (or Forms 1040A, 1040NR, or 1040-T) filed for each year you make a nondeductible contribution.
- Forms 5498 or similar statements received each year showing contributions you made.
- Forms 5498 or similar statements received showing the value of your IRA(s) for each year you received a distribution.
- Forms 1099-R and W-2P received for each year you received a distribution.

When and Where To File

Attach Form 8606 to your 1996 Form 1040, 1040A, or 1040NR.

If you are required to file Form 8606 but you are not required to file an income tax return, you still **must** file Form 8606. Send it to the Internal Revenue Service at the same time and place you would otherwise file Form 1040, 1040A, or 1040NR.

Penalty for Not Filing

If you are required to file Form 8606 but do not do so, you will have to pay a $50 penalty for each failure to file this form unless you can show reasonable cause.

Penalty for Overstatement

If you overstate your nondeductible contributions for any tax year, you must pay a $100 penalty for each overstatement unless it was due to reasonable cause.

Additional Information

For more details on nondeductible contributions, IRA basis, and distributions, get **Pub. 590,** Individual Retirement Arrangements (IRAs).

Amending Form 8606

After you file your return, you may change a nondeductible contribution made on a prior year's return to a deductible contribution or vice versa. To do this, complete a new Form 8606 showing the revised information and attach it to **Form 1040X,** Amended U.S. Individual Income Tax Return. Send both of these forms to the Internal Revenue Service Center for your area as shown in the Form 1040X instructions.

Specific Instructions

Note: *If you received an IRA distribution in 1996 and you also made IRA contributions for 1996 that may not be fully deductible because of the income limits, you need to make a special computation before completing this form. For details, including how to complete Form 8606, see* **Tax Treatment of Distributions** *in Chapter 6 of Pub. 590.*

Name and Social Security Number

If you file a joint return on Form 1040, or Form 1040A, enter the name and social security number of the spouse whose IRA information is shown.

Line 1

If you used IRA Worksheet 2 in the Form 1040 or Form 1040A instructions, include the following on line 1 of Form 8606.

- The amount shown on line 10 of IRA Worksheet 2 (Form 1040) or line 8 of IRA Worksheet 2 (Form 1040A) that you choose to make nondeductible.
- The part, if any, of the amount shown on line 9 of IRA Worksheet 2 (Form 1040) or line 7 of IRA Worksheet 2 (Form 1040A) that you choose to make nondeductible. You cannot take a deduction for the part included on line 1.

Note: *Enter any nondeductible contributions for your* **nonworking spouse** *from the appropriate lines of IRA Worksheet 2 on line 1 of your spouse's* **separate** *Form 8606.*

If none of your contributions are deductible, you may choose to make nondeductible contributions up to $2,000 (but not more than your earned income). Enter on line 1 of Form 8606 your contributions that you choose to make nondeductible.

If contributions were also made to your nonworking spouse's IRA, you may choose to make nondeductible contributions up to $2,250 (but not more than your earned income). Enter on line 1 of your Form 8606 the total nondeductible contributions you are making to your IRA. Enter the balance on line 1 of your nonworking spouse's Form 8606. Do not enter more than $2,000 on either your or your spouse's Form 8606. Also, the total of the two amounts cannot be more than $2,250.

If you used IRA Worksheet 1 in the Form 1040 or Form 1040A instructions but choose not to deduct the full amount shown on line 3 of that worksheet, subtract the amount you are deducting from the amount on line 3. Enter the result on line 1 of your Form 8606.

If contributions were made to your nonworking spouse's IRA but you choose not to deduct the full amount shown on line 8 of IRA Worksheet 1, subtract the amount you are deducting for your nonworking spouse from the amount on line 8. Enter the result on line 1 of your nonworking spouse's Form 8606.

Line 2

If this is the first year you are required to file Form 8606, enter zero. If you filed a **1995, 1994,** or **1993** Form 8606, enter the amount from line 12 of the **last** Form 8606 you filed. If you did not file a 1995, 1994, or 1993 Form 8606 but you filed a Form 8606 for any other year after **1988,** enter the amount from line 14 of the **last** Form 8606 you filed. Otherwise, enter the total of the amounts from lines 7 and 16 of your **1988** Form 8606. Or, if you didn't file a 1988 Form 8606, enter the total of the amounts from lines 4 and 13 of your **1987** Form 8606.

Line 4

If you made contributions in 1996 and 1997 that are for 1996, you may choose to apply the contributions made in 1996 first to nondeductible contributions and then to deductible contributions, or vice versa. But the amount on line 1 minus the amount on line 4 cannot be more than the IRA contributions you actually made in 1996.

Example. You made contributions of $1,000 in 1996 and $1,000 in 1997 of which $1,500 are deductible and $500 are nondeductible. You choose $500 of your contribution in 1996 to be nondeductible. In this case, the $500 would be entered on line 1, but not on line 4, and would become part of your basis for 1996.

Line 5

Although the 1996 IRA contributions you made during 1/1/97–4/15/97 (line 4) can be treated as nondeductible for purposes of line 1, they are not included in your basis for purposes of figuring the nontaxable part of any distributions you received in 1996. This is why you subtract line 4 from line 3.

Line 6

Enter the total value of **ALL** your IRAs as of 12/31/96 **plus** any outstanding rollovers. You should receive a statement by 1/31/97 for each IRA account showing the value on 12/31/96. A **rollover** is a tax-free distribution from one IRA that is contributed to another IRA. The rollover must be completed within 60 days of receiving the distribution from the first IRA. An **outstanding rollover** is any amount distributed to you from one IRA within 60 days of the end of 1996 (between Nov. 2 and Dec. 31) that you did not roll over to another IRA by 12/31/96, but that you roll over to another IRA in 1997 within the normal 60-day rollover period.

Line 7

Do not include on line 7:

- Distributions received in 1996 and rolled over to another IRA by 12/31/96,
- Outstanding rollovers included on line 6,
- Contributions under section 408(d)(4) returned to you on or before the due date of the return, or
- Excess contributions under section 408(d)(5) returned to you after the due date of the return.

Line 11

This is the total of your nondeductible IRA contributions made in 1996 and earlier years minus the total of any nontaxable IRA distributions received in those years.

Line 12

This is the total of your IRA basis as of 12/31/96 and any nondeductible IRA contributions for 1996 that you made in 1997 by 4/15/97.

This amount will be used on Form 8606 in future years if you make nondeductible IRA contributions or receive distributions.

Form **8615**	**Tax for Children Under Age 14 Who Have Investment Income of More Than $1,300**	OMB No. 1545-0998
Department of the Treasury Internal Revenue Service	▶ Attach ONLY to the child's Form 1040, Form 1040A, or Form 1040NR.	1996 Attachment Sequence No. **33**

Child's name shown on return | Child's social security number

A Parent's name (first, initial, and last). **Caution:** See instructions on back before completing. | **B** Parent's social security number

C Parent's filing status (check one):
☐ Single ☐ Married filing jointly ☐ Married filing separately ☐ Head of household ☐ Qualifying widow(er)

Step 1 — Figure child's net investment income

1. Enter child's investment income, such as taxable interest and dividend income. See instructions. If this amount is $1,300 or less, **stop;** do not file this form **1**
2. If the child DID NOT itemize deductions on Schedule A (Form 1040 or Form 1040NR), enter $1,300. If the child ITEMIZED deductions, see instructions **2**
3. Subtract line 2 from line 1. If the result is zero or less, **stop;** do not complete the rest of this form but ATTACH it to the child's return **3**
4. Enter child's **taxable** income from Form 1040, line 37; Form 1040A, line 22; or Form 1040NR, line 36 . . . . ▶ **4**
5. Enter the **smaller** of line 3 or line 4 . . . . ▶ **5**

Step 2 — Figure tentative tax based on the tax rate of the parent listed on line A

6. Enter parent's **taxable** income from Form 1040, line 37; Form 1040A, line 22; Form 1040EZ, line 6; TeleFile Tax Record, line J; Form 1040NR, line 36; or Form 1040NR-EZ, line 13. If the parent transferred property to a trust, see instructions **6**
7. Enter the total net investment income, if any, from Forms 8615, line 5, of ALL OTHER children of the parent identified above. **Do not** include the amount from line 5 above . . **7**
8. Add lines 5, 6, and 7 . . . . **8**
9. Tax on line 8 based on the **parent's** filing status. See instructions. If from Capital Gain Tax Worksheet, enter amount from line 4 of that worksheet here ▶ _____ **9**
10. Enter parent's tax from Form 1040, line 38; Form 1040A, line 23; Form 1040EZ, line 10; TeleFile Tax Record, line J; Form 1040NR, line 37; or Form 1040NR-EZ, line 14. If from **Capital Gain Tax Worksheet,** enter amount from line 4 of that worksheet here ▶ _____ **10**
11. Subtract line 10 from line 9. If line 7 is blank, enter on line 13 the amount from line 11; skip lines 12a and 12b **11**
12a. Add lines 5 and 7 . . . . **12a**
   b. Divide line 5 by line 12a. Enter the result as a decimal (rounded to two places) . . . . . **12b** × .
13. Multiply line 11 by line 12b . . . . ▶ **13**

Step 3 — Figure child's tax—If lines 4 and 5 above are the same, enter -0- on line 15 and go to line 16.

14. Subtract line 5 from line 4 . . . . **14**
15. Tax on line 14 based on the **child's** filing status. See instructions. If from Capital Gain Tax Worksheet, enter amount from line 4 of that worksheet here ▶ _____ **15**
16. Add lines 13 and 15 . . . . **16**
17. Tax on line 4 based on the **child's** filing status. See instructions. If from Capital Gain Tax Worksheet, check here . . . . ▶ ☐ **17**
18. Enter the **larger** of line 16 or line 17 here and on Form 1040, line 38; Form 1040A, line 23; or Form 1040NR, line 37 . . . . ▶ **18**

General Instructions

Purpose of Form.—For children under age 14, investment income over $1,300 is taxed at the parent's rate if the parent's rate is higher than the child's rate. If the child's investment income is more than $1,300, use this form to figure the child's tax.

Investment Income.—As used on this form, "investment income" includes all taxable income other than earned income as defined on page 2. It includes taxable interest, dividends, capital gains, rents, royalties, etc. It also includes pension and annuity income and income (other than earned income) received as the beneficiary of a trust.

Who Must File.—Generally, Form 8615 must be filed for any child who was under age 14 on January 1, 1997, had more than $1,300 of investment income, and is required to file a tax return. If neither parent was alive on December 31, 1996, do not use Form 8615. Instead, figure the child's tax in the normal manner.

Note: The parent may be able to elect to report the child's interest and dividends on his or her return. If the parent makes this election, the child will not have to file a return or Form 8615. For more details, get **Form 8814,** *Parents' Election To Report Child's Interest and Dividends.*

Additional Information.—For more details, get **Pub. 929,** Tax Rules for Children and Dependents.

Incomplete Information for Parent.—If the parent's taxable income or filing status or the net investment income of the parent's other children is not known by the

For Paperwork Reduction Act Notice, see back of form. | Cat. No. 64113U | Form **8615** (1996)

Form 8615 (1996) Page 2

due date of the child's return, reasonable estimates may be used. Write "Estimated" on the appropriate line(s) of Form 8615. For more details, see Pub. 929.

Amended Return.—If after the child's return is filed the parent's taxable income is changed or the net investment income of any of the parent's other children is changed, the child's tax must be refigured using the adjusted amounts. If the child's tax is changed as a result of the adjustment(s), file **Form 1040X,** Amended U.S. Individual Income Tax Return, to correct the child's tax.

Alternative Minimum Tax.—A child whose tax is figured on Form 8615 may owe the alternative minimum tax. For details, get **Form 6251,** Alternative Minimum Tax—Individuals, and its instructions.

Line Instructions

Section references are to the Internal Revenue Code.

Lines A and B.—If the child's parents were married to each other and filed a joint return, enter the name and social security number (SSN) of the parent who is listed first on the joint return. For example, if the father's name is listed first on the return and his SSN is entered in the block labeled "Your social security number," enter his name on line A and his SSN on line B.

If the parents were married but filed separate returns, enter the name and SSN of the parent who had the **higher** taxable income. If you do not know which parent had the higher taxable income, see Pub. 929.

If the parents were unmarried, treated as unmarried for Federal income tax purposes, or separated either by a divorce or separate maintenance decree, enter the name and SSN of the parent who had custody of the child for most of the year (the custodial parent).

Exception. If the custodial parent remarried and filed a joint return with his or her new spouse, enter the name and SSN of the person listed first on the joint return, even if that person is not the child's parent. If the custodial parent and his or her new spouse filed separate returns, enter the name and SSN of the person with the **higher** taxable income, even if that person is not the child's parent.

Note: *If the parents were unmarried but lived together during the year with the child, enter the name and SSN of the parent who had the **higher** taxable income.*

Line 1.—If the child had no earned income (defined later), enter the child's adjusted gross income from Form 1040, line 32; Form 1040A, line 17; or Form 1040NR, line 32.

If the child had earned income, use the following worksheet to figure the amount to enter on line 1. But if the child files **Form 2555,** Foreign Earned Income, or **Form 2555-EZ,** Foreign Earned Income Exclusion, has a net loss from self-employment, or claims a net operating loss deduction, **do not** use the worksheet below. Instead, use the worksheet in Pub. 929 to figure the amount to enter on line 1.

Worksheet (keep a copy for your records)

1. Enter the amount from the child's Form 1040, line 22; Form 1040A, line 14; or Form 1040NR, line 23, whichever applies . . . _____
2. Enter the child's **earned income** (defined below) plus any deduction the child claims on Form 1040, line 28; or Form 1040NR, line 28, whichever applies _____
3. Subtract line 2 from line 1. Enter the result here and on Form 8615, line 1 . . _____

Earned income includes wages, tips, and other payments received for personal services performed. Generally, it is the total of the amounts reported on Form 1040, lines 7, 12, and 18; Form 1040A, line 7; or Form 1040NR, lines 8, 13, and 19.

Line 2.—If the child itemized deductions, enter the **greater** of:

- $650 plus the portion of the amount on Schedule A (Form 1040), line 28; or Schedule A (Form 1040NR), line 17, that is directly connected with the production of the investment income on Form 8615, line 1; **OR**
- $1,300.

Line 6.—If the parent's taxable income is less than zero, enter zero on line 6. If the parent filed a joint return, enter the taxable income shown on that return even if the parent's spouse is not the child's parent. If the parent transferred property to a trust that sold or exchanged the property during the year at a gain, include any gain that was taxed to the trust under section 644 in the amount entered on line 6. Enter "Section 644" and the amount to the right of the line 6 entry. Also, see the instructions for line 10.

Line 9.—Figure the tax using the Tax Table, Tax Rate Schedules, or the Capital Gain Tax Worksheet, whichever applies. If any net capital gain is included on lines 5, 6, and/or 7, the tax on the amount on line 8 may be less if the Capital Gain Tax Worksheet can be used to figure the tax. See Pub. 929 for details on how to figure the net capital gain included on line 8 and how to complete the worksheet. The Capital Gain Tax Worksheet should be used if:

the parent's filing status is:	AND	the amount on Form 8615, line 8, is over:
• Single		$58,150
• Married filing jointly or Qualifying widow(er)		$96,900
• Married filing separately		$48,450
• Head of household		$83,050

If the Capital Gain Tax Worksheet is used to figure the tax, enter on Form 8615, line 9, the amount from line 13 of that worksheet. Also, enter the amount from line 4 of that worksheet in the space next to line 9 of Form 8615.

Line 10.—If the parent filed a joint return, enter the tax shown on that return even if the parent's spouse is not the child's parent. If the parent filed Form 8814, enter "Form 8814" and the total tax from line 8 of Form(s) 8814 in the space next to line 10 of Form 8615.

If line 6 includes any gain taxed to a trust under section 644, add the tax imposed under section 644(a)(2)(A) to the tax shown on the parent's return and enter the total on line 10. Also, enter "Section 644" next to line 10.

Line 15.—Figure the tax using the Tax Table, Tax Rate Schedule X, or the Capital Gain Tax Worksheet, whichever applies. If line 14 is more than $58,150 and includes any net capital gain, the tax may be less if the Capital Gain Tax Worksheet is used to figure the tax. See Pub. 929 for details on how to figure the net capital gain included on line 14 and how to complete the worksheet.

Line 17.—Figure the tax as if these rules did not apply. For example, if the child can use the Capital Gain Tax Worksheet to figure his or her tax, complete that worksheet.

Paperwork Reduction Act Notice.—We ask for the information on this form to carry out the Internal Revenue laws of the United States. You are required to give us the information. We need it to ensure that you are complying with these laws and to allow us to figure and collect the right amount of tax.

You are not required to provide the information requested on a form that is subject to the Paperwork Reduction Act unless the form displays a valid OMB control number. Books or records relating to a form or its instructions must be retained as long as their contents may become material in the administration of any Internal Revenue law. Generally, tax returns and return information are confidential, as required by Code section 6103.

The time needed to complete and file this form will vary depending on individual circumstances. The estimated average time is: **Recordkeeping,** 13 min.; **Learning about the law or the form,** 12 min.; **Preparing the form,** 45 min.; and **Copying, assembling, and sending the form to the IRS,** 17 min.

If you have comments concerning the accuracy of these time estimates or suggestions for making this form simpler, we would be happy to hear from you. See the instructions for the tax return with which this form is filed.

Form **8824**	**Like-Kind Exchanges**	OMB No. 1545-1190
Department of the Treasury Internal Revenue Service	(and nonrecognition of gain from conflict-of-interest sales) ▶ See separate instructions. ▶ Attach to your tax return. ▶ Use a separate form for each like-kind exchange.	**1996** Attachment Sequence No. **49**

Name(s) shown on tax return | Identifying number

Part I — Information on the Like-Kind Exchange

Note: *If the property described on line 1 or line 2 is real property located outside the United States, indicate the country.*

1 Description of like-kind property given up ▶ ....

2 Description of like-kind property received ▶ ....

3 Date like-kind property given up was originally acquired (month, day, year) . . . . . . 3 / /
4 Date you actually transferred your property to other party (month, day, year) . . . . . 4 / /
5 Date the like-kind property you received was identified (month, day, year). See instructions . 5 / /
6 Date you actually received the like-kind property from other party (month, day, year) . . . 6 / /
7 Was the exchange made with a related party? If "Yes," complete Part II. If "No," go to Part III. See instructions.
  a ☐ Yes, in this tax year   b ☐ Yes, in a prior tax year   c ☐ No.

Part II — Related Party Exchange Information

8 Name of related party | Related party's identifying number

Address (no., street, and apt., room, or suite no.)

City or town, state, and ZIP code | Relationship to you

9 During this tax year (and before the date that is 2 years after the last transfer of property that was part of the exchange), did the related party sell or dispose of the like-kind property received from you in the exchange? ☐ Yes ☐ No

10 During this tax year (and before the date that is 2 years after the last transfer of property that was part of the exchange), did you sell or dispose of the like-kind property you received? . . . . ☐ Yes ☐ No

If both lines 9 and 10 are "No" and this is the year of the exchange, go to Part III. If either line 9 or line 10 is "Yes," the deferred gain or (loss) from line 24 **must** be reported on your return this tax year, **unless** one of the exceptions on line 11 applies. See **Related Party Exchanges** in the instructions.

11 If one of the exceptions below applies to the disposition, check the applicable box:
  a ☐ The disposition was after the death of either of the related parties.
  b ☐ The disposition was an involuntary conversion, and the threat of conversion occurred after the exchange.
  c ☐ You can establish to the satisfaction of the IRS that neither the exchange nor the disposition had tax avoidance as its principal purpose. If this box is checked, attach an explanation. See instructions.

Part III — Realized Gain or (Loss), Recognized Gain, and Basis of Like-Kind Property Received

Caution: *If you transferred and received (a) more than one group of like-kind properties, or (b) cash or other (not like-kind) property, see instructions under **Multi-Asset Exchanges**.*

Note: *Complete lines 12 through 14 ONLY if you gave up property that was not like-kind. Otherwise, go to line 15.*

12 Fair market value (FMV) of other property given up 12
13 Adjusted basis of other property given up 13
14 Gain or (loss) recognized on other property given up. Subtract line 13 from line 12. Report the gain or (loss) in the same manner as if the exchange had been a sale . . 14
15 Cash received, FMV of other property received, plus net liabilities assumed by other party, reduced (but not below zero) by any exchange expenses you incurred. See instructions 15
16 FMV of like-kind property you received 16
17 Add lines 15 and 16 17
18 Adjusted basis of like-kind property you gave up, net amounts paid to other party, plus any exchange expenses **not** used on line 15. See instructions 18
19 **Realized gain or (loss).** Subtract line 18 from line 17 19
20 Enter the smaller of line 15 or line 19, but not less than zero 20
21 Ordinary income under recapture rules. Enter here and on Form 4797, line 17. See instructions . 21
22 Subtract line 21 from line 20. If zero or less, enter -0-. If more than zero, enter here and on Schedule D or Form 4797, unless the installment method applies. See instructions 22
23 **Recognized gain.** Add lines 21 and 22 23
24 Deferred gain or (loss). Subtract line 23 from line 19. If a related party exchange, see instructions . 24
25 **Basis of like-kind property received.** Subtract line 15 from the sum of lines 18 and 23 . . 25

For Paperwork Reduction Act Notice, see separate instructions.   Cat. No. 12311A   Form **8824** (1996)

Form 8824 (1996) Page **2**

Name(s) shown on tax return. Do not enter name and social security number if shown on other side. | **Your social security number**

Part IV — Section 1043 Conflict-of-Interest Sales. See instructions. Attach a copy of your certificate of divestiture.

Note: *This part is only to be used by officers or employees of the executive branch of the Federal Government for reporting nonrecognition of gain under section 1043 on the sale of property to comply with the conflict-of-interest requirements. This part can be used only if the cost of the replacement property exceeds the basis of the divested property.*

26 Description of divested property ▶

27 Description of replacement property ▶

28 Date divested property was sold (month, day, year) . . . . | 28 | / /

29 Sales price of divested property. See instructions . . . . . . | 29 |

30 Basis of divested property . . . . | 30 |

31 **Realized gain.** Subtract line 30 from line 29 . . . . | 31 |

32 Cost of replacement property purchased within 60 days after date of sale . . . . | 32 |

33 Subtract line 32 from line 29. If zero or less, enter -0- . . . . | 33 |

34 Ordinary income under recapture rules. Enter here and on Form 4797, line 11. See instructions | 34 |

35 Subtract line 34 from line 33. If zero or less, enter -0-. If more than zero, enter here and on Schedule D or Form 4797. See instructions . . . . | 35 |

36 **Recognized gain.** Add lines 34 and 35 . . . . | 36 |

37 Deferred gain. Subtract line 36 from line 31 . . . . | 37 |

38 **Basis of replacement property.** Subtract line 37 from line 32 . . . . | 38 |

Form 8829 — Expenses for Business Use of Your Home

Form **8829**
Department of the Treasury
Internal Revenue Service (99)

▶ File only with Schedule C (Form 1040). Use a separate Form 8829 for each home you used for business during the year.
▶ See separate instructions.

OMB No. 1545-1266
1996
Attachment Sequence No. **66**

Name(s) of proprietor(s) | Your social security number

Part I — Part of Your Home Used for Business

1. Area used regularly and exclusively for business, regularly for day care, or for storage of inventory or product samples. See instructions ... **1**
2. Total area of home ... **2**
3. Divide line 1 by line 2. Enter the result as a percentage ... **3** %
   - For day-care facilities not used exclusively for business, also complete lines 4–6.
   - All others, skip lines 4–6 and enter the amount from line 3 on line 7.
4. Multiply days used for day care during year by hours used per day . **4** hr.
5. Total hours available for use during the year (366 days × 24 hours). See instructions **5** 8,784 hr.
6. Divide line 4 by line 5. Enter the result as a decimal amount ... **6** .
7. Business percentage. For day-care facilities not used exclusively for business, multiply line 6 by line 3 (enter the result as a percentage). All others, enter the amount from line 3 ▶ **7** %

Part II — Figure Your Allowable Deduction

8. Enter the amount from Schedule C, line 29, **plus** any net gain or (loss) derived from the business use of your home and shown on Schedule D or Form 4797. If more than one place of business, see instructions **8**

See instructions for columns (a) and (b) before completing lines 9–20. | (a) Direct expenses | (b) Indirect expenses

9. Casualty losses. See instructions ... **9**
10. Deductible mortgage interest. See instructions . **10**
11. Real estate taxes. See instructions ... **11**
12. Add lines 9, 10, and 11 ... **12**
13. Multiply line 12, column (b) by line 7 ... **13**
14. Add line 12, column (a) and line 13 ... **14**
15. Subtract line 14 from line 8. If zero or less, enter -0- . **15**
16. Excess mortgage interest. See instructions ... **16**
17. Insurance ... **17**
18. Repairs and maintenance ... **18**
19. Utilities ... **19**
20. Other expenses. See instructions ... **20**
21. Add lines 16 through 20 ... **21**
22. Multiply line 21, column (b) by line 7 ... **22**
23. Carryover of operating expenses from 1995 Form 8829, line 41 . . **23**
24. Add line 21 in column (a), line 22, and line 23 ... **24**
25. Allowable operating expenses. Enter the **smaller** of line 15 or line 24 ... **25**
26. Limit on excess casualty losses and depreciation. Subtract line 25 from line 15 ... **26**
27. Excess casualty losses. See instructions ... **27**
28. Depreciation of your home from Part III below ... **28**
29. Carryover of excess casualty losses and depreciation from 1995 Form 8829, line 42 **29**
30. Add lines 27 through 29 ... **30**
31. Allowable excess casualty losses and depreciation. Enter the **smaller** of line 26 or line 30 . . **31**
32. Add lines 14, 25, and 31 ... **32**
33. Casualty loss portion, if any, from lines 14 and 31. Carry amount to **Form 4684**, Section B . . **33**
34. Allowable expenses for business use of your home. Subtract line 33 from line 32. Enter here and on Schedule C, line 30. If your home was used for more than one business, see instructions ▶ **34**

Part III — Depreciation of Your Home

35. Enter the **smaller** of your home's adjusted basis or its fair market value. See instructions ... **35**
36. Value of land included on line 35 ... **36**
37. Basis of building. Subtract line 36 from line 35 ... **37**
38. Business basis of building. Multiply line 37 by line 7 ... **38**
39. Depreciation percentage. See instructions ... **39** %
40. Depreciation allowable. Multiply line 38 by line 39. Enter here and on line 28 above. See instructions **40**

Part IV — Carryover of Unallowed Expenses to 1997

41. Operating expenses. Subtract line 25 from line 24. If less than zero, enter -0- ... **41**
42. Excess casualty losses and depreciation. Subtract line 31 from line 30. If less than zero, enter -0- **42**

For Paperwork Reduction Act Notice, see page 1 of separate instructions.   Cat. No. 13232M   Form **8829** (1996)

APPENDIX C
Glossary of Tax Terms

The words and phrases in this glossary have been defined to reflect their conventional use in the field of taxation. The definitions may therefore be incomplete for other purposes.

A

Abandoned spouse. The abandoned spouse provision enables a married taxpayer with a dependent child whose spouse did not live in the taxpayer's home during the last six months of the tax year to file as a head of household rather than as married filing separately.

Accelerated cost recovery system (ACRS). A method in which the cost of tangible property is recovered over a prescribed period of time. Enacted by the Economic Recovery Tax Act (ERTA) of 1981 and substantially modified by the Tax Reform Act (TRA) of 1986 (the modified system is referred to as MACRS), the approach disregards salvage value, imposes a period of cost recovery that depends upon the classification of the asset into one of various recovery periods, and prescribes the applicable percentage of cost that can be deducted each year. § 168.

Accelerated death benefits. The amount received from a life insurance policy by the insured who is terminally ill or chronically ill. Any realized gain may be excluded from the gross income of the insured if the policy is surrendered to the insurer or is sold to a licensed viatical settlement provider. § 101(g).

Accelerated depreciation. Various methods of depreciation that yield larger deductions in the earlier years of the life of an asset than the straight-line method. Examples include the double declining-balance and the sum-of-the-years' digits methods of depreciation. § 167.

Accident and health benefits. Employee fringe benefits provided by employers through the payment of health and accident insurance premiums or the establishment of employer-funded medical reimbursement plans. Employers generally are entitled to a deduction for such payments, whereas employees generally exclude the fringe benefits from gross income. §§ 105 and 106.

Accountable plan. An accountable plan is a type of expense reimbursement plan that requires an employee to render an adequate accounting to the employer and return any excess reimbursement or allowance. If the expense qualifies, it will be treated a deduction *for* AGI.

Accounting income. The accountant's concept of income is generally based upon the realization principle. Financial accounting income may differ from taxable income (e.g., accelerated depreciation might be used for Federal income tax and straight-line depreciation for financial accounting purposes). Differences are included in a reconciliation of taxable and accounting income on Schedule M–1 of Form 1120 for corporations. Seventy-five percent of the excess of adjusted current earnings over alternative minimum taxable income is an adjustment for alternative minimum tax purposes for a corporation. See *alternative minimum tax* and *economic income*.

Accounting method. The method under which income and expenses are determined for tax purposes. Major accounting methods are the cash basis and the accrual basis. Special methods are available for the reporting of gain on installment sales, recognition of income on construction projects (the completed contract and percentage of completion methods), and the valuation of inventories (last-in, first-out and first-in, first-out). §§ 446–474. See also *accrual method, cash receipts method, completed contract method, percentage of completion method*, etc.

Accounting period. The period of time, usually a year, used by a taxpayer for the determination of tax liability. Unless a fiscal year is chosen, taxpayers must determine and pay their income tax liability by using the calendar year (January 1 through December 31) as the period of measurement. An example of a fiscal year is July 1 through June 30. A change in accounting period (e.g., from a calendar year to a fiscal year) generally requires the consent of the IRS. A new taxpayer, such as a newly formed corporation or an estate created upon the death of an individual taxpayer, is free to select either a calendar or a fiscal year without the consent of the IRS. Limitations exist on the accounting period that may be selected by a partnership, an S corporation, and a personal service corporation. §§ 441–444.

Accrual basis. See *accrual method*.

Accrual method. A method of accounting that reflects expenses incurred and income earned for any one tax year. In contrast to the cash basis of accounting, expenses do not have to be paid to be deductible nor does income have to be received to be taxable. Unearned income (e.g., prepaid interest and rent) generally is taxed in the year of receipt regardless of the method of accounting used by the taxpayer. § 446(c)(2). See also *accounting method, cash receipts method,* and *unearned income.*

Accumulated earnings tax. A special tax imposed on corporations that accumulate (rather than distribute) their earnings beyond the reasonable needs of the business. The tax is imposed on accumulated taxable income and is imposed in addition to the corporate income tax. §§ 531–537.

ACE adjustment. See *adjusted current earnings (ACE) adjustment* and *business untaxed reported profits.*

Acquiescence. In agreement with the result reached. The IRS follows a policy of either acquiescing (*A, Acq.*) or nonacquiescing (*NA, Nonacq.*) in the results reached in certain judicial decisions.

Acquisition indebtedness. Debt incurred in acquiring, constructing, or substantially improving a qualified residence of the taxpayer. The interest on such loans is deductible as *qualified residence interest.* However, interest on such debt is deductible only on the portion of the indebtedness that does not exceed $1,000,000 ($500,000 for married persons filing separate returns). § 163(h)(3). See also *home equity loans.*

ACRS. See *accelerated cost recovery system.*

Active income. Active income includes wages, salary, commissions, bonuses, profits from a trade or business in which the taxpayer is a material participant, gain on the sale or other disposition of assets used in an active trade or business, and income from intangible property if the taxpayer's personal efforts significantly contributed to the creation of the property. The passive activity loss rules require classification of income and losses into three categories with active income being one of them.

Active participation. A term that is relevant for both the at-risk rules and the passive activity loss rules associated with rental real estate activities. For the at-risk rules, the following factors indicate active participation: (1) making decisions involving the operation or management of the activity, (2) performing services for the activity, and (3) hiring and discharging employees. For the passive activity loss rules, the taxpayer must participate in the making of management decisions in a significant and bona fide sense.

Additional depreciation. The excess of the amount of depreciation actually deducted over the amount that would have been deducted had the straight-line method been used. § 1250(b). See also *Section 1250 recapture.*

Adjusted basis. The cost or other basis of property reduced by depreciation (cost recovery) allowed or allowable and increased by capital improvements. See also *basis* and *realized gain or loss.*

Adjusted current earnings (ACE) adjustment. An adjustment in computing corporate alternative minimum taxable income (AMTI), computed at 75 percent of the excess of adjusted current earnings and profits computations over unadjusted AMTI. ACE computations reflect longer and slower cost recovery deductions and other restrictions on the timing of certain recognition events. Exempt interest, life insurance proceeds, and other receipts that are included in earnings and profits but not in taxable income also increase the ACE adjustment. If unadjusted AMTI exceeds adjusted current earnings and profits, the ACE adjustment is negative. The negative adjustment is limited to the aggregate of the positive adjustments under ACE for prior years, reduced by any previously claimed negative adjustments. See also *alternative minimum tax, business untaxed reported profits,* and *earnings and profits.*

Adjusted gross income (AGI). A determination peculiar to individual taxpayers. Generally, it represents gross income less business expenses, expenses attributable to the production of rent or royalty income, the allowed capital loss deduction, and certain personal expenses (deductions for AGI). § 62. See also *gross income.*

Adjusted sales price. The amount realized from the sale of a residence reduced by the fixing-up expenses is the adjusted sales price. An amount equal to the adjusted sales price must be reinvested in a replacement residence to defer the recognition of the realized gain on the sale of a residence. See also *amount realized, fixing-up expense,* and *realized gain or loss.*

Adoption expenses credit. The provision is intended to assist taxpayers who incur nonrecurring costs directly associated with the adoption process such as legal costs, social service review costs, and transportation costs. Up to $5,000 ($6,000 for a child with special needs) of costs incurred to adopt an eligible child qualify for the credit. An individual claims a credit in the year that follows the year in which the taxpayer pays or incurs the expenses. The credit can also be claimed in the year in which the adoption becomes final for expenses paid or incurred in that year. § 23.

Ad valorem tax. A tax imposed on the value of property. The most familiar ad valorem tax is that imposed by states, counties, and cities on real estate. Ad valorem taxes can, however, be imposed upon personal property (e.g., a motor vehicle tax based on the value of an automobile). §§ 164(a)(1) and (2).

Advance payments. In general, prepayments for services or goods are includible in gross income upon receipt of the advance payments (for both accrual and cash basis taxpayers). However, Rev.Proc. 71–21 (1971–2 C.B. 549) provides guidelines for the deferral of tax on certain advance payments providing specific conditions are met.

AFTR. Published by Research Institute of America (formerly by Prentice-Hall), *American Federal Tax Reports* contains all of the Federal tax decisions issued by the U.S. District Courts, U.S. Court of Federal Claims, U.S. Courts of Appeals, and U.S. Supreme Court.

AFTR2d. The second series of the *American Federal Tax Reports*.

AFTR3d. The third series of the *American Federal Tax Reports*.

Alimony and separate maintenance payments. Alimony and separate maintenance payments are includible in the gross income of the recipient and are deductible by the payor. The payments must be made in discharge of a legal obligation arising from a marital or family relationship. Child support and voluntary payments are not treated as alimony. Alimony is deductible *for* AGI. §§ 62(10), 71, and 215. See also *child support payments*.

Alimony recapture. The amount of alimony that previously has been included in the gross income of the recipient and deducted by the payor that now is deducted by the recipient and included in the gross income of the payor as the result of front-loading. § 71(f).

All events test. For accrual method taxpayers, income is earned when (1) all the events have occurred that fix the right to receive the income and (2) the amount can be determined with reasonable accuracy. Accrual of income cannot be postponed simply because a portion of the income may have to be returned in a subsequent period. The all events test also is utilized to determine when expenses can be deducted by an accrual basis taxpayer. The application of the test could cause a variation between the treatment of an item for accounting and for tax purposes. For example, a reserve for warranty expense may be properly accruable under generally accepted accounting principles but not be deductible under the Federal income tax law. Because of the application of the all events test, the deduction becomes available in the year the warranty obligation becomes fixed and the amount is determinable with reasonable certainty. See also *economic performance test*. Reg. §§ 1.446–1(c)(1)(ii) and 1.461–1(a)(2).

Alternate valuation date. Property passing from a person by reason of death may be valued for death tax purposes as of the date of death or the alternate valuation date. The alternate valuation date is six months from the date of death or the date the property is disposed of by the estate, whichever comes first. To use the alternate valuation date, the executor or administrator of the estate must make an affirmative election. The election of the alternate valuation date is not available unless it decreases both the amount of the gross estate *and* the estate tax liability. §§ 1014(a) and 2032.

Alternative depreciation system (ADS). A cost recovery system that produces a smaller deduction than would be calculated under ACRS or MACRS. The alternative system must be used in certain instances and can be elected in other instances. § 168(g). See also *cost recovery allowance*.

Alternative minimum tax (AMT). The alternative minimum tax is imposed only to the extent it exceeds the regular income tax (in effect, the tax liability is the greater of the tax liability calculated using the AMT rules and that calculated using the regular income tax rules). The AMT rates (26 and 28 percent for the individual taxpayer and 20 percent for the corporate taxpayer) are applied to the AMT base. The AMT base is calculated by modifying taxable income as follows: (1) add tax preferences, (2) add certain adjustments, (3) deduct certain adjustments, and (4) deduct the exemption amount. §§ 55–59. See also *adjusted current earnings (ACE) adjustment* and *business untaxed reported profits*.

Alternative minimum tax credit. The AMT can result from timing differences that give rise to positive adjustments in calculating the AMT base. To provide equity for the taxpayer when these timing differences reverse, the regular tax liability may be reduced by a tax credit for prior year's minimum tax liability attributable to timing differences. § 53.

Alternative tax. An option that is allowed in computing the tax on net capital gain. The rate is 35 percent of net capital gain for corporations and 28 percent for noncorporate taxpayers. For 1988 through 1990, the alternative tax did not produce a beneficial result. For 1991 and thereafter, the alternative tax can produce beneficial results for the noncorporate taxpayer because the regular tax rates can be as high as 39.6 percent. §§ 1(h) and 1201. See also *net capital gain*.

Alternative tax NOL deduction (ATNOLD). In calculating the AMT, the taxpayer is allowed to deduct NOL carryovers and carrybacks. A special calculation, referred to as the ATNOLD, is required for this purpose. The regular income tax is modified for AMT adjustments and preferences to produce the ATNOLD. § 56(d).

Amortization. The allocation (and charge to expense) of the cost or other basis of an intangible asset over a statutory period of 15 years. Examples of amortizable intangibles include patents, copyrights, covenants not to compete, acquired goodwill, and leasehold interests. See also *estimated useful life* and *goodwill*.

Amount realized. The amount received by a taxpayer on the sale or other disposition of property. The amount realized is the sum of the cash and the fair market value of any property or services received, plus any related debt assumed by the buyer. Determining the amount realized is the starting point for arriving at realized gain or loss. The amount realized is defined in § 1001(b) and the related Regulations. See also *realized gain or loss* and *recognized gain or loss*.

AMT adjustments. In calculating AMTI, certain adjustments are added to or deducted from taxable income. These adjustments generally reflect timing differences. § 56.

AMT exclusions. A credit that can be used to reduce the regular tax liability in future tax years is available in connection with the AMT (*AMT credit*). The credit is applicable only with respect to the AMT that results from timing differences. It is not available in connection with AMT exclusions, which include the standard deduction, personal exemptions, medical expenses deductible in calculating the regular income tax that are not deductible in computing the AMT, other itemized deductions that are not allowable for AMT purposes, excess percentage depletion, and tax-exempt interest on specified private activity bonds.

Annuity. A fixed sum payable to a person at specified intervals for a specific period of time or for life. Payments represent a partial return of capital and a return (interest) on the capital investment. Therefore, an exclusion ratio must be used to compute the amount of nontaxable income. The exclusion ratio is used until the annuitant has recovered his or her investment in the annuity contract. Thereafter, all of the annuity payments received are included in gross income. If the annuitant dies before his or her investment is recovered, a deduction is allowed. § 72. See also *qualified pension or profit sharing plan*.

Appellate court. For Federal tax purposes, appellate courts include the Courts of Appeals and the Supreme Court. If the party losing in the trial (or lower) court is dissatisfied with the result, the dispute may be carried to the appropriate appellate court. See also *Court of Appeals* and *trial court*.

Arm's length transaction. The standard under which unrelated parties would determine an exchange price for a transaction. Suppose, for example, Cardinal Corporation sells property to its sole shareholder for $10,000. In testing whether the $10,000 is an "arm's length" price, one would ascertain the price that would have been negotiated between the corporation and an unrelated party in a bargained exchange.

Asset Depreciation Range (ADR) system. A system of estimated useful lives for categories of tangible assets prescribed by the IRS. The system provides a range for each category that extends from 20 percent above to 20 percent below the guideline class lives prescribed by the IRS.

Assignment of income. A procedure whereby a taxpayer attempts to avoid the recognition of income by assigning the property that generates the income to another. Such a procedure will not avoid the recognition of income by the taxpayer making the assignment if it can be said that the income was earned at the point of the transfer. In this case, usually referred to as an anticipatory assignment of income, the income will be taxed to the person who earns it.

Association. An organization treated as a corporation for Federal tax purposes even though it may not qualify as such under applicable state law. An entity designated as a trust or a partnership, for example, may be classified as an association if it clearly possesses corporate attributes. Corporate attributes include centralized management, continuity of life, free transferability of interests, and limited liability. § 7701(a)(3).

At-risk limitation. Under the at-risk rules, a taxpayer's deductible losses from an activity for any taxable year are limited to the amount the taxpayer has at risk at the end of the taxable year. The initial amount considered at risk is generally the sum of the amount of cash and the adjusted basis of property contributed to the activity and amounts borrowed for use in the activity for which the taxpayer is personally liable or has pledged as security property not used in the activity.

Attribution. Under certain circumstances, the tax law applies attribution (construction ownership) rules to assign to one taxpayer the ownership interest of another taxpayer. If, for example, the stock of Gold Corporation is held 60 percent by Marsha and 40 percent by Sid, Marsha may be deemed to own 100 percent of Gold Corporation if she and Sid are mother and son. In that case, the stock owned by Sid is attributed to Marsha. See, for example, §§ 267 and 318.

Audit. Inspection and verification of a taxpayer's return or other transactions possessing tax consequences. See also *correspondence audit, field audit,* and *office audit*.

Automatic mileage method. See *automobile expenses*.

Automobile expenses. Automobile expenses are generally deductible only to the extent the automobile is used in business or for the production of income. Personal commuting expenses are not deductible. The taxpayer may deduct actual expenses (including depreciation and insurance), or the standard (automatic) mileage rate may be used (27.5 cents per mile for 1991, 28 cents per mile for 1992, 28 cents per mile for 1993, 29 cents per mile for 1994, 30 cents per mile for 1995, 31 cents per mile for 1996, and 31.5 cents per mile for 1997) during any one year. Automobile expenses incurred for medical purposes or in connection with job-related moving expenses are deductible to the extent of actual out-of-pocket expenses or at the rate of 10 cents per mile (12 cents for charitable activities). See also *transportation expenses*.

B

Bad debts. A deduction is permitted if a business account receivable subsequently becomes partially or completely worthless, providing the income arising from the debt previously was included in income. Available methods are the specific charge-off method and the reserve method. However, except for certain financial institutions, TRA of 1986 repealed the use of the reserve method for 1987 and thereafter. If the reserve method is used, partially or totally worthless accounts are charged to the reserve. A nonbusiness bad debt deduction is allowed as a short-term capital loss if the loan did not arise in connection with the creditor's trade or business activities. Loans between related parties (family members) generally are classified as nonbusiness. § 166. See also *nonbusiness bad debts*.

Basis. The acquisition cost assigned to an asset for income tax purposes. For assets acquired by purchase, the basis is the cost (§ 1012). Special rules govern the basis of property received by virtue of another's death (§ 1014) or by gift (§ 1015), the basis of stock received on a transfer of property to a controlled corporation (§ 358), the basis of the property transferred to the corporation (§ 362), and the basis of property received upon the liquidation of a corporation (§§ 334 and 338). See also *adjusted basis*.

Book value. The net amount of an asset after reduction by a related reserve. The book value of accounts receivable, for example, is the face amount of the receivables less the reserve for bad debts. The book value of a building is the cost less the accumulated depreciation.

Boot. Cash or property of a type not included in the definition of a nontaxable exchange. The receipt of boot will cause an otherwise nontaxable transfer to become taxable to the extent of the lesser of the fair market value of such boot or the realized gain on the transfer. Examples of nontaxable exchanges that could be partially or completely taxable due to the receipt of boot include transfers to controlled corporations [§ 351(b)] and like-kind exchanges [§ 1031(b)]. See also *realized gain or loss* and *recognized gain or loss*.

Bribes and illegal payments. Section 162 denies a deduction for bribes or kickbacks, fines and penalties paid to a government official or employee for violation of law, and two-thirds of the treble damage payments made to claimants for violation of the antitrust law. Denial of a deduction for bribes and illegal payments is based upon the judicially established principle that allowing such payments would be contrary to public policy.

B.T.A. The Board of Tax Appeals was a trial court that considered Federal tax matters. This court is now the U.S. Tax Court.

Burden of proof. The requirement in a lawsuit to show the weight of evidence and thereby gain a favorable decision. Except in cases of tax fraud, the burden of proof in a tax case generally is on the taxpayer.

Business bad debt. A debt created or acquired in connection with a trade or business of the taxpayer, or a debt the loss from the worthlessness of which is incurred in the taxpayer's trade or business. A business bad debt is deducted as an ordinary deduction.

Business energy credit. See *energy tax credit—business property*.

Business expenses. See *trade or business expenses*.

Business gifts. Business gifts are deductible only to the extent that each gift does not exceed $25 per person per year. Exceptions are made for gifts costing $4 or less and for certain employee awards. § 274(b).

Business untaxed reported profits. Such profits are a positive adjustment for purposes of the corporate alternative minimum tax. For taxable years beginning after 1989, the amount is 75 percent of the excess of adjusted current earnings over the alternative minimum taxable income (AMTI). This adjustment was replaced in 1990 with the ACE adjustment. §§ 56(c)(1) and (g). See also *adjusted current earnings (ACE) adjustment* and *alternative minimum tax*.

C

Cafeteria benefit plan. An employee benefit plan under which an employee is allowed to select from among a variety of employer-provided fringe benefits. Some of the benefits may be taxable and some may be statutory nontaxable benefits (e.g., health and accident insurance and group term life insurance). The employee is taxed only on the taxable benefits selected. A cafeteria benefit plan is also referred to as a flexible benefit plan. § 125.

Cafeteria plan. See *cafeteria benefit plan*.

Canons of taxation. Criteria used in the selection of a tax base that were originally discussed by Adam Smith in *The Wealth of Nations*. Canons of taxation include equality, convenience, certainty, and economy.

Capital asset. Broadly speaking, all assets are capital except those specifically excluded by the Code. Major categories of noncapital assets include property held for resale in the normal course of business (inventory), trade accounts and notes receivable, and depreciable property and real estate used in a trade or business (§ 1231 assets). § 1221. See also *capital gain* and *capital loss*.

Capital contributions. Various means by which a shareholder makes additional funds available to the corporation (placed at the risk of the business) without the receipt of additional stock. Such contributions are added to the basis of the shareholder's existing stock investment and do not generate income to the corporation. § 118.

Capital expenditure. An expenditure that should be added to the basis of the property improved. For income tax purposes, this generally precludes a full deduction for the expenditure in the year paid or incurred. Any capital recovery in the form of a tax deduction must come in the form of depreciation. § 263.

Capital gain. The gain from the sale or exchange of a capital asset. See also *capital asset* and *net capital gain*.

Capital gain net income. If the total capital gains for the tax year exceed the total capital losses, the result is capital gain net income. Note that the term does not distinguish between the long-term and short-term gains. § 1222(9). See also *net capital gain*.

Capital gain or loss holding period. The period of time that a capital asset is held by the taxpayer. To qualify for long-term treatment, the asset must be held for more than one year. See also *holding period*.

Capital gain property. Property contributed to a charitable organization that, if sold rather than contributed, would have resulted in long-term capital gain to the donor. See also *ordinary income property*.

Capital loss. The loss from the sale or exchange of a capital asset. See also *capital asset*.

Cash basis. See *accounting method* and *cash receipts method*.

Cash equivalent doctrine. Generally, a cash basis taxpayer does not report income until cash is constructively or actually received. Under the cash equivalent doctrine, cash basis taxpayers are required to report income if they receive the equivalent of cash (e.g., property is received) in a taxable transaction.

Cash method. See *cash receipts method.*

Cash receipts method. A method of accounting under which the taxpayer generally reports income when cash is collected and reports expenses when cash payments are made. However, for fixed assets, the cash basis taxpayer claims deductions through depreciation or amortization in the same manner as an accrual basis taxpayer. Prepaid expenses must be capitalized and amortized if the life of the asset extends "substantially beyond" the end of the tax year. See also *constructive receipt.*

Casualty loss. A casualty is defined as "the complete or partial destruction of property resulting from an identifiable event of a sudden, unexpected or unusual nature" (e.g., floods, storms, fires, auto accidents). Individuals may deduct a casualty loss only if the loss is incurred in a trade or business or in a transaction entered into for profit or arises from fire, storm, shipwreck, or other casualty or from theft. Individuals usually deduct personal casualty losses as itemized deductions subject to a $100 nondeductible amount and to an annual floor equal to 10 percent of adjusted gross income that applies after the $100 per casualty floor has been applied. Special rules are provided for the netting of certain casualty gains and losses. See also *disaster area loss* and *Section 1231 gains and losses.*

C corporation. A corporation that has not elected conduit treatment under § 1361. See also *S corporation status.*

Cert. den. By denying the Writ of Certiorari, the U.S. Supreme Court refuses to accept an appeal from a U.S. Court of Appeals. The denial of certiorari does not, however, mean that the U.S. Supreme Court agrees with the result reached by the lower court.

Certiorari. Appeal from a U.S. Court of Appeals to the U.S. Supreme Court is by Writ of Certiorari. The Supreme Court does not have to accept the appeal and usually does not (*cert. den.*) unless there is a conflict among the lower courts that needs to be resolved or a constitutional issue is involved.

Change in accounting method. A change in the taxpayer's method of accounting (e.g., from FIFO to LIFO) generally requires prior approval from the IRS. Generally, a request must be filed within 180 days after the beginning of the taxable year of the desired change. In some instances, the permission for change will not be granted unless the taxpayer agrees to certain adjustments prescribed by the IRS.

Change in accounting period. A taxpayer must obtain the consent of the IRS before changing his or her tax year. Income for the short period created by the change must be annualized.

Charitable contributions. Contributions are deductible (subject to various restrictions and ceiling limitations) if made to qualified nonprofit charitable organizations. A cash basis taxpayer is entitled to a deduction solely in the year of payment. Accrual basis corporations may accrue contributions at year-end if payment is properly authorized before the end of the year and payment is made within two and one-half months after the end of the year. § 170.

Child and dependent care expenses credit. A tax credit ranging from 20 percent to 30 percent of employment-related expenses (child and dependent care expenses) for amounts of up to $4,800 is available to individuals who are employed (or deemed to be employed) and maintain a household for a dependent child under age 13, disabled spouse, or disabled dependent. § 21.

Child support payments. Payments for child support do not constitute alimony and are therefore not includible in gross income by the recipient or deductible as alimony by the payor. Generally, none of the amounts paid are regarded as child support unless the divorce decree or separation agreement specifically calls for child support payments. However, if the amount of the payment to the former spouse would be reduced upon the happening of a contingency related to a child (e.g., the child attains age 21 or dies), the amount of the future reduction in the payment will be deemed child support for post-1984 agreements and decrees. § 71(c). See also *alimony and separate maintenance payments.*

Circuit Court of Appeals. See *Court of Appeals.*

Circulation expenditures. Expenditures of establishing or increasing the circulation of a periodical that may be either expensed or capitalized. If such expenses are expensed, an adjustment will occur for AMT purposes, since the expenses are deducted over a three-year period for AMT purposes. Over the three-year period, both positive and negative AMT adjustments will be produced. § 173. See also *AMT adjustments.*

Claim of right doctrine. A judicially imposed doctrine applicable to both cash and accrual basis taxpayers that holds that an amount is includible in income upon actual or constructive receipt if the taxpayer has an unrestricted claim to the payment. For the tax treatment of amounts repaid when previously included in income under the claim of right doctrine, see § 1341.

Claims Court. One of three Federal trial courts that consider Federal tax controversy. Now known as the U.S. Court of Federal Claims, appeal from this court (formerly to the U.S. Supreme Court) now goes to the Court of Appeals for the Federal Circuit. See also *trial court.*

Clear reflection of income. The IRS has the authority to redetermine a taxpayer's income using a method that clearly reflects income if the taxpayer's method does not do so. § 446(b). In addition, the IRS may apportion or allocate income among various related businesses if income is not "clearly reflected." § 482.

Closely held corporation. A corporation where the stock ownership is not widely dispersed. Instead, a few shareholders are in control of corporate policy and are in a position to benefit personally from that policy.

Community property. Louisiana, Texas, New Mexico, Arizona, California, Washington, Idaho, Nevada, and Wisconsin have community property systems. The rest of the states are classified as common law jurisdictions. The difference between common law and community property systems centers around the property rights possessed by married persons. In a common law system, each spouse owns whatever he or she earns. Under a community property system, one-half of the earnings of each spouse is considered owned by the other spouse. Assume, for example, Alice and Jeff are husband and wife and their only income is the $50,000 annual salary Jeff receives. If they live in New York (a common law state), the $50,000 salary belongs to Jeff. If, however, they live in Texas (a community property state), the $50,000 salary is divided equally, in terms of ownership, between Jeff and Alice. See also *separate property.*

Compensatory damages. Damages received or paid by the taxpayer can be classified as compensatory damages or as punitive damages. Compensatory damages are those paid to compensate one for harm caused by another. Compensatory damages are excludible from the recipient's gross income. See also *punitive damages.*

Completed contract method. A method of reporting gain or loss on certain long-term contracts. Under this method of accounting, gross income and expenses are recognized in the tax year in which the contract is completed. Reg. § 1.451–3. Limitations exist on a taxpayer's ability to use the completed contract method. § 460. See also *long-term contract* and *percentage of completion method.*

Component depreciation. The process of dividing an asset (e.g., a building) into separate components or parts for the purpose of calculating depreciation. The advantage of dividing an asset into components is to use shorter depreciation lives for selected components under § 167. Generally, the same cost recovery period must be used for all the components of an asset under § 168.

Condemnation. The taking of property by a public authority. The property is condemned as the result of legal action, and the owner is compensated by the public authority. The power to condemn property is known as the right of eminent domain.

Conduit concept. An approach assumed by the tax law in the treatment of certain entities and their owners. Specific tax characteristics pass through the entity without losing their identity. For example, items of income and expense, capital gains and losses, tax credits, etc., realized by a partnership pass through the partnership (a conduit) and are subject to taxation at the partner level. Also, in an S corporation, certain items pass through and are reported on the returns of the shareholders.

Constructive dividends. In addition to dividends formally declared by the board of directors of a corporation (i.e., declaration date, record date, and payment date), a shareholder may receive a distribution that does not have the formalities of a dividend but is treated as a dividend. Examples include salaries paid to shareholder-employees that are not reasonable and the shareholder use of corporate property for less than an arm's length rate.

Constructive ownership. See *attribution.*

Constructive receipt. If income is unqualifiedly available, it will be subject to the income tax even though it is not physically in the taxpayer's possession. An example is accrued interest on a savings account. Under the constructive receipt of income concept, the interest will be taxed to a depositor in the year it is available rather than the year actually withdrawn. The fact that the depositor uses the cash basis of accounting for tax purposes is irrelevant. See Reg. § 1.451–2.

Consumer interest. Interest expense of the taxpayer of a personal nature (not trade or business interest, investment interest, qualified residence interest, or passive activity interest). TRA of 1986 provided that no deduction is permitted for consumer interest. However, the provision was not fully effective until 1991. § 163(h). See also *qualified residence interest.*

Contributions to the capital of a corporation. See *capital contributions.*

Convention expenses. Travel expenses incurred in attending a convention are deductible if the meetings are related to a taxpayer's trade or business or job-related activities. If, however, the convention trip is primarily for pleasure, no deduction is permitted for transportation expenses. Likewise, if the expenses are for attending a convention related to the production of income (§ 212), no deduction is permitted. Specific limitations are provided for foreign convention expenses. See § 274(n) for the limitations on the deductions for meals. § 274(h).

Correspondence audit. An audit conducted by the IRS by mail. Typically, the IRS writes to the taxpayer requesting the verification of a particular deduction, exemption, or credit. The completion of a special form or the remittance of copies of records or other support is all that is requested of the taxpayer. To be distinguished from a *field audit* or an *office audit.*

Cost depletion. Depletion that is calculated based on the adjusted basis of the asset. The adjusted basis is divided by the expected recoverable units to determine the depletion per unit. The depletion per unit is multiplied by the units sold during the tax year to calculate cost depletion. See also *percentage depletion.*

Cost recovery allowance. The portion of the cost of an asset written off under ACRS (or MACRS), which replaced the depreciation system as a method for writing off the cost of an asset for most assets placed in service after 1980 (after 1986 for MACRS). § 168. See also *alternative depreciation system.*

Cost recovery period. A period specified in the Code for writing off the cost of an asset under ACRS or MACRS.

Court of Appeals. Any of 13 Federal courts that consider tax matters appealed from the U.S. Tax Court, U.S. Court of Federal Claims, or a U.S. District Court. Appeal from a U.S. Court of Appeals is to the U.S. Supreme Court by Writ of Certiorari. See also *appellate court.*

Court of Federal Claims. See *Claims Court.*

Court of original jurisdiction. The Federal courts are divided into courts of original jurisdiction and appellate courts. The dispute between the taxpayer and the IRS is first considered by a court of original jurisdiction (i.e., a trial court). The four Federal courts of original jurisdiction are the U.S. Tax Court, U.S. District Court, the Court of Federal Claims, and the Small Cases Division of the U.S. Tax Court. See *Court of Appeals.*

Credit for child and dependent care expenses. See *child and dependent care expenses credit.*

D

Death benefit. A payment made by an employer to the beneficiary or beneficiaries of a deceased employee on account of the death of the employee.

Death tax. See *estate tax.*

Declaration of estimated tax. A procedure whereby individuals and corporations are required to make quarterly installment payments of estimated tax. Individuals are required to make the declaration and file quarterly payments of the estimated tax if certain requirements are met. In 1997, a declaration is not required for an individual whose estimated tax is reasonably expected to be less than $500.

Deductions for adjusted gross income. See *adjusted gross income.*

Deductions from adjusted gross income. See *itemized deductions.*

Deferred compensation. Compensation that will be taxed when received or upon the removal of certain restrictions on receipt and not when earned. Contributions by an employer to a qualified pension or profit sharing plan on behalf of an employee are an example. The contributions will not be taxed to the employee until the funds are made available or distributed to the employee (e.g., upon retirement). See also *qualified pension or profit sharing plan.*

Deficiency. Additional tax liability owed by a taxpayer and assessed by the IRS. See also *statutory notice of deficiency.*

Defined benefit plan. Qualified plans can be dichotomized into defined benefit plans and defined contribution plans. Under a defined benefit plan, a formula defines the benefits employees are to receive. The formula usually includes years of service, employee compensation, and some stated percentage. The employer must make annual contributions based on actuarial computations that will be sufficient to pay the vested retirement benefits. See also *defined contribution plan* and *pension plan.*

Defined contribution plan. Qualified plans can be dichotomized into defined benefit plans and defined contribution plans. Under a defined contribution plan, a separate account is maintained for each covered employee. The employee's benefits under the plan are based solely on (1) the amount contributed and (2) income from the fund that accrues to the employee's account. The plan defines the amount the employer is required to contribute (e.g., a flat dollar amount, an amount based on a special formula, or an amount equal to a certain percentage of compensation). See also *defined benefit plan* and *pension plan.*

Defined contribution pension plan. See *defined contribution plan.*

De minimis fringe. Benefits provided to employees that are too insignificant to warrant the time and effort required to account for the benefits received by each employee and the value of those benefits. Such amounts are excludible from the employee's gross income. § 132.

Dependency exemption. See *personal and dependency exemptions.*

Depletion. The process by which the cost or other basis of a natural resource (e.g., an oil or gas interest) is recovered upon extraction and sale of the resource. The two ways to determine the depletion allowance are the cost and percentage (or statutory) methods. Under the cost method, each unit of production sold is assigned a portion of the cost or other basis of the interest. This is determined by dividing the cost or other basis by the total units expected to be recovered. Under the percentage (or statutory) method, the tax law provides a special percentage factor for different types of minerals and other natural resources. This percentage is multiplied by the gross income from the interest to arrive at the depletion allowance. §§ 613 and 613A.

Depreciation. The deduction of the cost or other basis of a tangible asset over the asset's estimated useful life. § 167. For intangible assets, see *amortization.* For natural resources, see *depletion.* Also see *estimated useful life.* The depreciation system was replaced by ACRS for most assets placed in service after 1980 (by MACRS for most assets placed in service after 1986) but still applies for assets placed in service before 1981. See also *recapture of depreciation.*

Determination letter. Upon the request of a taxpayer, a District Director will comment on the tax status of a completed transaction. Determination letters are most frequently used to clarify employee versus self-employed status, to determine whether a pension or profit sharing plan qualifies under the Code, and to determine the tax-exempt status of certain nonprofit organizations.

Direct charge-off method. See *specific charge-off method.*

Disabled access credit. A tax credit whose purpose is to encourage small businesses to make their businesses more accessible to disabled individuals. The credit is equal to 50 percent of the eligible expenditures that exceed $250 but do not exceed $10,250. Thus, the maximum amount for the credit is $5,000. The adjusted basis for depreciation is reduced by the amount of the credit. To qualify, the facility must have been placed in service before November 6, 1990. § 44. See also *general business credit*.

Disaster area loss. A casualty sustained in an area designated as a disaster area by the President of the United States. In such an event, the disaster loss may be treated as having occurred in the taxable year immediately preceding the year in which the disaster actually occurred. Thus, immediate tax benefits are provided to victims of a disaster. § 165(i). See also *casualty loss*.

Dissent. To disagree with the majority. If, for example, Judge Brown disagrees with the result reached by Judges Charles and Davis (all of whom are members of the same court), Judge Brown could issue a dissenting opinion.

District Court. A Federal District Court is a trial court for purposes of litigating (among others) Federal tax matters. It is the only trial court where a jury trial can be obtained. See also *trial court*.

Dividends received deduction. A deduction allowed a shareholder that is a corporation for dividends received from a domestic corporation. The percentage applied in calculating the dividends received deduction varies according to the percentage of stock ownership. If the stock ownership percentage is less than 20 percent, the percentage is 70 percent of the dividends received. If the stock ownership percentage is at least 20 percent but less than 80 percent, the percentage is 80 percent. If the stock ownership percentage is at least 80 percent, the percentage is 100 percent. §§ 243–246A.

Dollar value LIFO. An inventory technique that focuses on the dollars invested in the inventory rather than the particular items on hand each period. Each inventory item is assigned to a pool. A pool is a collection of similar items and is treated as a separate inventory. At the end of the period, each pool is valued in terms of prices at the time LIFO was adopted (base period prices), whether or not the particular items were actually on hand in the year LIFO was adopted, to compare with current prices to determine if there has been an increase or decrease in inventories.

E

Earned income. Income from personal services as distinguished from income generated by property. See §§ 32 and 911 and the related Regulations.

Earned income credit. A refundable tax credit whose purpose is to provide assistance to certain low-income individuals. To receive the most beneficial treatment, the taxpayer must have qualifying children. However, it is possible to qualify for the credit without having a child. To calculate the credit for a taxpayer with one or more children for 1997, a statutory rate of 34.0 percent for one child (40.0 percent for two or more children) is multiplied by the earned income (subject to a statutory maximum of $6,500 with one qualifying child or $9,140 with two or more qualifying children). Once the earned income exceeds $11,930, the credit is phased out using a 15.98 percent rate for one qualifying child and a 21.06 percent rate for two or more qualifying children. For the qualifying taxpayer without children, the credit is calculated on a maximum earned income of $4,340 applying a 7.65 percent rate with the phaseout beginning at $5,430 applying the same rate. § 32.

Earnings and profits. A tax concept peculiar to corporate taxpayers that measures economic capacity to make a distribution to shareholders that is not a return of capital. Such a distribution will result in dividend income to the shareholders to the extent of the corporation's current and accumulated earnings and profits.

Economic income. The change in the taxpayer's net worth, as measured in terms of market values, plus the value of the assets the taxpayer consumed during the year. Because of the impracticality of this income model, it is not used for tax purposes. See also *accounting income*.

Economic performance test. One of the requirements that must be satisfied in order for an accrual basis taxpayer to deduct an expense. The accrual basis taxpayer first must satisfy the all events test. That test is not deemed satisfied until economic performance occurs. This occurs, when property or services are provided to the taxpayer or, in the case in which the taxpayer is required to provide property or services, whenever the property or services are actually provided by the taxpayer. See also *all events test*.

Education expenses. Employees may deduct education expenses if such items are incurred either (1) to maintain or improve existing job-related skills or (2) to meet the express requirements of the employer or the requirements imposed by law to retain employment status. The expenses are not deductible if the education is required to meet the minimum educational standards for the taxpayer's job or if the education qualifies the individual for a new trade or business. Reg. § 1.162–5.

Educational savings bonds. United States Series EE bonds whose proceeds are used for qualified higher educational expenses for the taxpayer, the taxpayer's spouse, or a dependent. The interest may be excluded from gross income, provided the taxpayer's adjusted gross income does not exceed certain amounts. § 135.

Employee expenses. The deductions *for* adjusted gross income include reimbursed expenses and certain expenses of performing artists. All other employee expenses are deductible *from* adjusted gross income. § 62. See also *trade or business expenses*.

Employee stock ownership plan (ESOP). A type of defined contribution plan that qualifies as a tax-exempt employee trust. The ESOP must invest primarily in qualifying

employer securities. A major benefit of an ESOP to the employer corporation is that it can contribute stock rather than cash and receive a tax deduction equal to the fair market value of the stock.

Employment taxes. Employment taxes are those taxes that an employer must pay on account of its employees. Employment taxes include FICA (Federal Insurance Contributions Act) and FUTA (Federal Unemployment Tax Act) taxes. Employment taxes are paid to the IRS in addition to income tax withholdings at specified intervals. Such taxes can be levied on the employees, the employer, or both. See also *FICA tax* and *FUTA tax*.

Energy tax credit—business property. A 10 percent tax credit is available to businesses that invest in certain energy property. The purpose of the credit is to create incentives for conservation and to penalize the increased use of oil and gas. The business energy tax credit applies to equipment with an estimated useful life of at least three years that uses fuel or feedstock other than oil or natural gas (e.g., solar, geothermal). §§ 46(2) and 48(a). See also *estimated useful life* and *investment tax credit*.

Entertainment expenses. These expenses are deductible only if they are directly related to or associated with a trade or business. Various restrictions and documentation requirements have been imposed upon the deductibility of entertainment expenses to prevent abuses by taxpayers. See, for example, the provision contained in § 274(n) that disallows 50 percent of entertainment expenses. § 274.

Estate tax. A tax imposed on the right to transfer property by reason of death. Thus, an estate tax is levied on the decedent's estate and not on the heir receiving the property. §§ 2001 and 2002. See also *inheritance tax*.

Estimated tax. The amount of tax (including alternative minimum tax and self-employment tax) an individual expects to owe for the year after subtracting tax credits and income tax withheld. The estimated tax must be paid in installments at designated intervals (e.g. for the individual taxpayer, by April 15, June 15, September 15, and January 15 of the following year).

Estimated useful life. The period over which an asset will be used by a particular taxpayer. Although the period cannot be longer than the estimated physical life of an asset, it could be shorter if the taxpayer does not intend to keep the asset until it wears out. Assets such as goodwill do not have an estimated useful life. The estimated useful life of an asset is essential to measuring the annual tax deduction for depreciation and amortization. An asset subject to ACRS or MACRS is written off over a specified cost recovery period rather than over its estimated useful life. In addition, most intangibles are now amortized over a 15-year statutory period.

Excise tax. A tax on the manufacture, sale, or use of goods or on the carrying on of an occupation or activity. Also a tax on the transfer of property. Thus, the Federal estate and gift taxes are, theoretically, excise taxes.

Extraordinary personal services. These are services provided by individuals where the customers' use of the property is incidental to their receipt of the services. For example, a patient's use of a hospital bed is incidental to his or her receipt of medical services. This is one of the six exceptions to determine whether an activity is a passive rental activity.

F

Fair market value. The amount at which property would change hands between a willing buyer and a willing seller, neither being under any compulsion to buy or sell and both having reasonable knowledge of the relevant facts. Reg. § 20.2031–1(b).

F.3d. An abbreviation for the Third Series of the *Federal Reporter*, the official series where decisions of the U.S. Claims Court (before October 1982) and the U.S. Courts of Appeals are published.

F.Supp. The abbreviation for the *Federal Supplement*, the official series where the reported decisions of the U.S. District Courts are published.

Federal district court. See *district court*.

FICA tax. An abbreviation for Federal Insurance Contributions Act, commonly referred to as the Social Security tax. The FICA tax is comprised of the Social Security tax (old age, survivors, and disability insurance) and the Medicare tax (hospital insurance) and is imposed on both employers and employees. The employer is responsible for withholding from the employee's wages the Social Security tax at a rate of 6.2 percent on a maximum wage base of $65,400 (for 1997) and the Medicare tax at a rate of 1.45 percent (no maximum wage base). The employer is required to match the employee's contribution. See also *employment taxes*.

Field audit. An audit by the IRS conducted on the business premises of the taxpayer or in the office of the tax practitioner representing the taxpayer. To be distinguished from a *correspondence audit* or an *office audit*.

Finalized regulation. See *regulations*.

First-in, first-out (FIFO). An accounting method for determining the cost of inventories. Under this method, the inventory on hand is deemed to be the sum of the cost of the most recently acquired units. See also *last-in, first-out (LIFO)*.

Fiscal year. A fiscal year is a 12-month period ending on the last day of a month other than December. In certain circumstances, a taxpayer is permitted to elect a fiscal year instead of being required to use a calendar year. See also *accounting period* and *taxable year*.

Fixing-up expense. An expense that is incurred to assist in the sale of a residence and is deductible in calculating the adjusted sales price. Fixing-up expenses include such items as ordinary repairs, painting, and wallpapering. To qualify, the expense must (1) be incurred on work performed during the 90-day period ending on the date of the contract of sale, (2) be paid within 30 days after the date of the sale, and (3) not be a capital expenditure. § 1034. See also *adjusted sales price.*

Flat tax. In its pure form, it would replace the graduated income tax rates with a single rate (e.g., 17 percent). All deductions are eliminated, and a large personal exemption is allowed to remove low-income and many middle-income taxpayers from the application of the tax.

Flexible spending plan. An employee benefit plan that allows the employee to take a reduction in salary in exchange for the employer paying benefits that can be provided by the employer without the employee being required to recognize income (e.g., medical and child-care benefits).

Foreign earned income exclusion. The foreign earned income exclusion is a relief provision that applies to U.S. citizens working in a foreign country. To qualify for the exclusion, the taxpayer must be either a bona fide resident of the foreign country or present in the country for 330 days during any 12 consecutive months. The exclusion is limited to $70,000 per year. § 911.

Foreign tax credit or deduction. Both individual taxpayers and corporations may claim a foreign tax credit on income earned and subject to tax in a foreign country or U.S. possession. As an alternative to the credit, a deduction may be taken for the foreign taxes paid. §§ 27, 164, and 901–905.

Franchise. An agreement that gives the transferee the right to distribute, sell, or provide goods, services, or facilities within a specified area. The cost of obtaining a franchise may be amortized over a statutory period of 15 years. In general, the franchisor's gain on the sale of franchise rights is an ordinary gain because the franchisor retains a significant power, right, or continuing interest in the subject of the franchise. §§ 197 and 1253.

Franchise tax. A tax levied on the right to do business in a state as a corporation. Although income considerations may come into play, the tax usually is based on the capitalization of the corporation.

Fringe benefits. Compensation or other benefits received by an employee that are not in the form of cash. Some fringe benefits (e.g., accident and health plans, group term life insurance) may be excluded from the employee's gross income and therefore are not subject to the Federal income tax.

Fruit and tree metaphor. The courts have held that an individual who earns income from property or services cannot assign that income to another. For example, a father cannot assign his earnings from commissions to his child and escape income tax on those amounts.

FUTA tax. An employment tax levied on employers. Jointly administered by the Federal and state governments, the tax provides funding for unemployment benefits. FUTA applies at a rate of 6.2 percent in 1997 on the first $7,000 of covered wages paid during the year for each employee. The Federal government allows a credit for FUTA paid (or allowed under a merit rating system) to the state. The credit cannot exceed 5.4 percent of the covered wages. See also *employment taxes.*

G

General business credit. The summation of various non-refundable business credits, including the investment tax credit, jobs credit, research activities credit, low-income housing credit, and disabled access credit. The amount of general business credit that can be used to reduce the tax liability is limited to the taxpayer's net income tax reduced by the greater of (1) the tentative minimum tax or (2) 25 percent of the net regular tax liability that exceeds $25,000. Unused general business credits can be carried back 3 years and forward 15 years. § 38.

Gift. A transfer of property for less than adequate consideration. Gifts usually occur in a personal setting (such as between members of the same family). Gifts are excluded from the income tax but may be subject to the *gift tax.*

Gift tax. A tax imposed on the transfer of property by gift. The tax is imposed upon the donor of a gift and is based upon the fair market value of the property on the date of the gift. §§ 2501–2524.

Golden parachute payments. A severance payment to employees that meets the following requirements: (1) the payment is contingent on a change of ownership of a corporation through a stock or asset acquisition and (2) the aggregate present value of the payment equals or exceeds three times the employee's average annual compensation. To the extent the severance payment meets these conditions, a deduction is disallowed to the employer for the excess of the payment over a statutory base amount (a five-year average of compensation if the taxpayer was an employee for the entire five-year period). In addition, a 20 percent excise tax is imposed on the employee who receives the excess severance pay. §§ 280G and 4999.

Goodwill. The ability of a business to generate income in excess of a normal rate on assets due to superior managerial skills, market position, new product technology, etc. In the purchase of a business, goodwill represents the difference between the purchase price and the fair market value of the net assets acquired. Goodwill is an intangible asset that possesses an indefinite life. However, since acquired goodwill is a § 197 intangible asset, it is amortized over a 15-year statutory period. Self-created goodwill cannot be amortized. Reg. § 1.167(a)–3. See also *amortization.*

Government bonds issued at a discount. Certain U.S. government bonds (Series E and EE) are issued at a discount and do not pay interest during the life of the bonds. Instead, the bonds are redeemable at increasing fixed amounts. Thus, the difference between the purchase price and the amount received upon redemption represents interest income to the holder. A cash basis taxpayer may defer recognition of gross income until the bonds are redeemed. For Series EE savings bonds issued after 1989, the interest otherwise taxable at redemption can be excluded if the bonds are qualified educational savings bonds. As an alternative to deferring recognition of gross income until the bonds are redeemed, the taxpayer may elect to include in gross income on an annual basis the annual increase in the value of the bonds. § 454.

Gross income. Income subject to the Federal income tax. Gross income does not include income for which the Code permits exclusion treatment (e.g., interest on municipal bonds). For a manufacturing or merchandising business, gross income means gross profit (gross sales or gross receipts less cost of goods sold). § 61 and Reg. § 1.61–3(a).

Group term life insurance. Life insurance coverage permitted by an employer for a group of employees. Such insurance is renewable on a year-to-year basis and does not accumulate in value (i.e., no cash surrender value is built up). The premiums paid by the employer on the insurance are not taxed to an employee on coverage of up to $50,000 per person. § 79 and Reg. § 1.79–1(a).

Guaranteed payments. Payments made by a partnership to one of its partners for services rendered or for the use of capital, to the extent the payments are determined without regard to the income of the partnership. Such payments generally are deductible by the partnership as a business expense and are reported as ordinary income by the recipient partner. § 707(c).

H

Half-year convention. The half-year convention is a cost recovery convention that assumes all property is placed in service at mid-year and thus provides for a half-year's cost recovery for that year.

Head of household. An unmarried individual who maintains a household for another and satisfies certain conditions set forth in § 2(b). Such status enables the taxpayer to use a set of income tax rates [see § 1(b)] that are lower than those applicable to other unmarried individuals [§ 1(c)] but higher than those applicable to surviving spouses and married persons filing a joint return [§ 1(a)]. See also *tax rate schedules*.

Highly compensated employee. The employee group is generally divided into two categories for fringe benefit (including pension and profit sharing plans) purposes. These are (1) highly compensated employees and (2) non-highly compensated employees. For most fringe benefits, if the fringe benefit plan discriminates in favor of highly compensated employees, it will not be a qualified plan with respect, at a minimum, to the highly compensated employees.

Hobby loss. A nondeductible loss arising from a personal hobby as contrasted with an activity engaged in for profit. Generally, the law provides a rebuttable presumption that an activity is engaged in for profit if profits are earned during any three or more years during a five-year period. § 183. See also *vacation home*.

Holding period. The period of time property has been held for income tax purposes. The holding period is crucial in determining whether gain or loss from the sale or exchange of a capital asset is long term or short term. § 1223. See also *capital gain or loss holding period*.

Home equity loans. Loans that utilize the personal residence of the taxpayer as security. The interest on such loans is deductible as *qualified residence interest*. However, interest is deductible only on the portion of the loan that does not exceed the lesser of (1) the fair market value of the residence, reduced by the *acquisition indebtedness*, or (2) $100,000 ($50,000 for married persons filing separate returns). A major benefit of a home equity loan is that there are no tracing rules regarding the use of the loan proceeds. § 163(h)(3).

Home office expenses. See *office-in-the-home expenses*.

H.R. 10 (Keogh) plan. See *self-employment retirement plan*.

Hybrid method. A combination of the accrual and cash methods of accounting. That is, the taxpayer may account for some items of income on the accrual method (e.g., sales and cost of goods sold) and other items (e.g., interest income) on the cash method.

I

Imputed interest. For certain long-term sales of property, the IRS can convert some of the gain from the sale into interest income if the contract does not provide for a minimum rate of interest to be paid by the purchaser. The application of this procedure has the effect of forcing the seller to recognize less long-term capital gain and more ordinary income (interest income). §§ 483 and 1274 and the Regulations thereunder. In addition, interest income and interest expense are imputed (deemed to exist) on interest-free or below-market rate loans between certain related parties. § 7872. See also *interest-free loans*.

Incentive stock option (ISO). A type of stock option that receives favorable tax treatment. If various qualification requirements can be satisfied, there are no recognition tax consequences when the stock option is granted. However, the spread (the excess of the fair market value at the date of exercise over the option price) is a tax preference item for purposes of the alternative minimum tax. The gain on disposition of the stock resulting from the exercise of the stock option will be classified as long-term capital gain if certain holding period requirements are met (the employee must not dispose of the stock within two years after the option is granted or within one year after acquiring the stock). § 422. See *nonqualified stock option (NQSO)*.

Income. For tax purposes, an increase in wealth that has been realized.

Independent contractor. A self-employed person as distinguished from one who is employed as an employee.

Individual retirement account (IRA). Individuals with earned income who are not active participants in qualified retirement plans are permitted to set aside up to 100 percent of their salary per year (generally not to exceed $2,000 or $4,000 for a spousal IRA) for a retirement account. The amount set aside can be deducted by the taxpayer and will be subject to income tax only upon withdrawal. Specific requirements are established for the withdrawal of such funds, and penalties are provided for failure to comply. If the employee is an active participant in a qualified retirement plan, the IRA deduction is phased out once adjusted gross income exceeds certain amounts. Even if the IRA deduction has been completely phased out, the taxpayer can still make a nondeductible contribution. § 219. See also *simplified employee pension plan.*

Inheritance tax. An excise tax levied on the heir based on the value of property received from a decedent. See also *estate tax.*

Installment method. A method of accounting enabling a taxpayer to spread the recognition of gain on the sale of property over the payout period. Under this procedure, the seller computes the gross profit percentage from the sale (the gain divided by the contract price) and applies it to each payment received to arrive at the gain to be recognized. §§ 453 and 453A.

Intangible drilling and development costs (IDC). Taxpayers may elect to expense or capitalize (subject to amortization) intangible drilling and development costs. However, ordinary income recapture provisions apply to oil and gas properties on a sale or other disposition if the expense method is elected. §§ 263(c) and 1254(a).

Interest-free loans. Bona fide loans that carry no interest (or a below-market rate). If made in a nonbusiness setting, the imputed interest element is treated as a gift from the lender to the borrower. If made by a corporation to a shareholder, a constructive dividend could result. In either event, the lender may recognize interest income, and the borrower may be able to deduct interest expense. § 7872.

Interpretive regulation. A Regulation issued by the Treasury Department that purports to explain the meaning of a particular Code Section. An interpretive Regulation is given less deference than a legislative Regulation. See also *legislative regulation* and *procedural regulation.* § 7805.

Investigation of a new business. Expenditures by taxpayers who are not engaged in a trade or business incurred in the evaluation of prospective business activities (acquiring an existing business or entering into a new trade or business). If the expenditures are general, it is the position of the IRS that no deduction is permitted even if the investigation is abandoned because the taxpayer is not engaged in a trade or business. The courts, however, have permitted a loss deduction providing the expenditures were specific.

Investment income. Gross income from interest, dividends, annuities, and royalties not derived in the ordinary course of a trade or business. Net capital gain attributable to the disposition of property producing these types of income normally is not included in investment income. However, a taxpayer may elect to include the capital gains as investment income if the net capital gain qualifying for the *alternative tax* is reduced by an equivalent amount. See also *investment interest.*

Investment indebtedness. If funds are borrowed by noncorporate taxpayers for the purpose of purchasing or continuing to hold investment property, some portion of the interest expense deduction may be disallowed. The interest deduction is generally limited to net investment income. Amounts that are disallowed may be carried forward and treated as investment interest of the succeeding year. § 163(d).

Investment interest. Payment for the use of funds used to acquire assets that produce investment income. The deduction for investment interest is limited to *net investment income* for the tax year. See also *investment income.*

Investment tax credit (ITC). A tax credit that usually was equal to 10 percent (unless a reduced credit was elected) of the qualified investment in tangible personalty used in a trade or business. If the tangible personalty had a recovery period of five years or more, the full cost of the property qualified for the credit. Only 60 percent of cost qualified for property with a recovery period of three years. However, the regular investment tax credit was repealed by TRA of 1986 for property placed in service after December 31, 1985. §§ 46–48. See also *general business credit, recapture of investment tax credit,* and *Section 38 property.*

Involuntary conversion. The loss or destruction of property through theft, casualty, or condemnation. Any gain realized on an involuntary conversion can, at the taxpayer's election, be postponed (deferred) for Federal income tax purposes if the owner reinvests the proceeds within a prescribed period of time in property that is similar or related in service or use. § 1033. See also *nontaxable exchange.*

IRA. See *individual retirement account.*

Itemized deductions. Certain personal expenditures allowed by the Code as deductions *from* adjusted gross income. Examples include certain medical expenses, interest on home mortgages, state income taxes, and charitable contributions. Itemized deductions are reported on Schedule A of Form 1040. Certain miscellaneous itemized deductions are reduced by 2 percent of the taxpayer's adjusted gross income. In addition, a taxpayer whose adjusted gross income exceeds $100,000 ($50,000 for married filing separately) must reduce the itemized deductions by 3 percent of the excess of adjusted gross income over $100,000. For 1997, the indexed amount for the $100,000 is $121,200, and the indexed amount for the $50,000 is $60,600. Medical, casualty and theft, and investment interest deductions are not subject to the 3 percent reduction. The 3 percent reduction may not reduce itemized deductions that are subject to the reduction to below 20 percent of their initial amount. §§ 63(d), 67, and 68.

K

Keogh plan. See *self-employment retirement plan*.

Kiddie tax. To reduce the tax savings that result from shifting income from parents to children, the net unearned income of a child under age 14 is taxed at the marginal tax rate of the parent(s). For the provision to apply, the child must have at least one living parent and unearned income of more than $1,300 for the tax year. § 1(g). See also *unearned income*.

L

Last-in, first-out (LIFO). An accounting method for valuing inventories for tax purposes. Under this method, it is assumed that the inventory on hand is valued at the cost of the earliest acquired units. § 472 and the related Regulations. See also *first-in, first-out (FIFO)*.

Least aggregate deferral method. An algorithm set forth in the Regulations to determine the tax year for a partnership with partners whose tax years differ. The tax year that produces the least aggregate deferral of income for the partners is selected.

Legislative regulation. Some Code Sections give the Secretary of the Treasury or his delegate the authority to prescribe Regulations to carry out the details of administration or to otherwise complete the operating rules. Regulations issued pursuant to this type of authority truly possess the force and effect of law. In effect, Congress is almost delegating its legislative powers to the Treasury Department. See also *interpretive regulation* and *procedural regulation*.

Lessee. One who rents property from another. In the case of real estate, the lessee is also known as the tenant.

Lessor. One who rents property to another. In the case of real estate, the lessor is also known as the landlord.

Letter rulings. Issued upon a taxpayer's request, by the National Office of the IRS, they describe how the IRS will treat a proposed transaction for tax purposes. They apply only to the taxpayer who asks for and obtains the ruling, but post-1984 rulings may be substantial authority for purposes of avoiding the accuracy-related penalties. The IRS limits the issuance of letter rulings to restricted, preannounced areas of taxation.

Life insurance proceeds. Generally, life insurance proceeds paid to a beneficiary upon the death of the insured are exempt from Federal income tax. An exception is provided when a life insurance contract has been transferred for valuable consideration to another individual who assumes ownership rights. In that case, the proceeds are income to the assignee to the extent that the proceeds exceed the amount paid for the policy plus any subsequent premiums paid. Insurance proceeds may be subject to the Federal estate tax if the decedent retained any incidents of ownership in the policy before death or if the proceeds are payable to the decedent's estate. §§ 101 and 2042.

Like-kind exchange. An exchange of property held for productive use in a trade or business or for investment (except inventory, stocks and bonds, and partnership interests) for other investment or trade or business property. Unless non-like-kind property is received (boot), the exchange will be nontaxable. § 1031. See also *boot* and *nontaxable exchange*.

Limited expensing. See *Section 179 expensing*.

Limited liability company. An organization that combines the corporate characteristic of limited liability with treatment as a partnership for Federal income tax purposes.

Liquidating distribution. A distribution of assets by a corporation associated with the termination of the business. See also *liquidation of a corporation*.

Liquidation of a corporation. In a complete or partial liquidation of a corporation, amounts received by the shareholders in exchange for their stock are usually treated as a sale or exchange of the stock resulting in capital gain or loss treatment. § 331. Special rules apply to the liquidation of a subsidiary under § 332. Generally, a liquidation is a taxable event to the corporation. § 336. Special rules apply to a parent corporation that is liquidating a subsidiary. § 337.

Listed property. The term listed property includes (1) any passenger automobile, (2) any other property used as a means of transportation, (3) any property of a type generally used for purposes of entertainment, recreation, or amusement, (4) any computer or peripheral equipment (with an exception for exclusive business use), (5) any cellular telephone (or other similar telecommunications equipment), and (6) any other property of a type specified in the Regulations. If listed property is predominantly used for business, the taxpayer is allowed to use the statutory percentage method of cost recovery. Otherwise, the straight-line cost recovery method must be used. § 280F.

Long-term care insurance. Insurance that helps pay the cost of care when the insured is unable to care for himself or herself. Such insurance is generally thought of as insurance against the cost of an aged person entering a nursing home. The employer can provide the insurance and the premiums may be excluded from the employee's gross income. § 7702B.

Long-term contract. A building, installation, construction, or manufacturing contract that is entered into but not completed within the same tax year. A manufacturing contract is a long-term contract only if the contract is to manufacture (1) a unique item not normally carried in finished goods inventory or (2) items that normally require more than 12 calendar months to complete. The two available methods to account for long-term contracts are the percentage of completion method and the completed contract method. The completed contract method can be used only in limited circumstances. § 460. See also *completed contract method* and *percentage of completion method*.

Long-term nonpersonal use capital assets. Includes investment property with a long-term holding period. Such property disposed of by casualty or theft may receive § 1231 treatment. See also *Section 1231 gains and losses*.

Lower of cost or market. An elective inventory method, whereby the taxpayer may value inventories at the lower of the taxpayer's actual cost or the current replacement cost of the goods. This method cannot be used in conjunction with the LIFO inventory method.

Low-income housing. Low-income housing is rental housing that is a dwelling unit for low- or moderate-income individuals or families. Beneficial tax treatment is in the form of the *low-income housing credit*. § 42. See also *accelerated cost recovery system (ACRS)*.

Low-income housing credit. Beneficial treatment to owners of low-income housing is provided in the form of a tax credit. The calculated credit is claimed in the year the building is placed in service and in the following nine years. § 42. See also *general business credit*.

Lump-sum distribution. Payment of the entire amount due at one time rather than in installments. Such distributions often occur from qualified pension or profit sharing plans upon the retirement or death of a covered employee. The recipient of a lump-sum distribution may recognize both long-term capital gain and ordinary income upon the receipt of the distribution. The ordinary income portion may be subject to a special 5-year or 10-year income averaging provision. § 402(e).

M

MACRS. See *accelerated cost recovery system (ACRS)*.

Majority interest partners. Partners who have more than a 50 percent interest in partnership profits and capital, counting only those partners who have the same taxable year, are referred to as majority interest partners. The term is of significance in determining the appropriate taxable year of a partnership. § 706(b). See also *accounting period* and *principal partner*.

Marital deduction. A deduction allowed upon the transfer of property from one spouse to another. The deduction is allowed under the Federal gift tax for lifetime (inter vivos) transfers or under the Federal estate tax for death (testamentary) transfers. §§ 2056 and 2523.

Marriage penalty. The additional tax liability that results for a married couple compared with what their tax liability would be if they were not married and filed separate returns.

Material participation. If an individual taxpayer materially participates in a nonrental trade or business activity, any loss from that activity is treated as an active loss that can be offset against active income. Material participation is achieved by meeting any one of seven tests provided in the Regulations.

Medical expenses. Medical expenses of an individual, spouse, and dependents are allowed as an itemized deduction to the extent that such amounts (less insurance reimbursements) exceed 7.5 percent of adjusted gross income. § 213.

Medical savings account. A plan available to employees of small firms (50 or fewer employees) with high deductible health insurance. The employee can place money in the fund and then deduct the contributions (within limits) from gross income. If the employer contributes to the fund, the employee can exclude the contribution from gross income. Income earned from the fund and withdrawals for medical care are not subject to tax. §§ 106(b) and 220.

Mid-month convention. The mid-month convention is a cost recovery convention that assumes property is placed in service in the middle of the month that it is actually placed in service.

Mid-quarter convention. The mid-quarter convention is a cost recovery convention that assumes property placed in service during the year is placed in service at the middle of the quarter in which it is actually placed in service. The mid-quarter convention applies if more than 40 percent of the value of property (other than eligible real estate) is placed in service during the last quarter of the year.

Miscellaneous itemized deductions. A special category of itemized deductions that includes such expenses as professional dues, tax return preparation fees, job-hunting costs, unreimbursed employee business expenses, and certain investment expenses. Such expenses are deductible only to the extent they exceed 2 percent of adjusted gross income. § 67. See also *itemized deductions*.

Mitigation of the annual accounting period concept. Various tax provisions that provide relief from the effect of the finality of the annual accounting period concept. For example, the *net operating loss* provisions provide relief to a taxpayer whose business profits and losses for different taxable years fluctuate. See also *accounting period*.

Modified accelerated cost recovery system (MACRS). See *accelerated cost recovery system (ACRS)*.

Moving expenses. A deduction *for AGI* is permitted to employees and self-employed individuals provided certain tests are met. The taxpayer's new job must be at least 50 miles farther from the old residence than the old residence was from the former place of work. In addition, an employee must be employed on a full-time basis at the new location for 39 weeks in the 12-month period following the move. Deductible moving expenses include the cost of moving the household and personal effects, transportation, and lodging expenses during the move. The cost of meals during the move are not deductible. Qualified moving expenses that are paid (or reimbursed) by the employer can be excluded from the employee's gross income. In this case, the related deduction by the employee is not permitted. §§ 62(a)(15), 132(a)(6), and 217.

Multiple support agreement. To qualify for a dependency exemption, the support test must be satisfied. This requires that over 50 percent of the support of the potential dependent be provided by the taxpayer. Where no one person provides more than 50 percent of the support, a multiple support agreement enables a taxpayer to still qualify for the dependency exemption. Any person who contributed more than 10 percent of the support is entitled to claim the exemption if each person in the group who contributed more than 10 percent files a written consent (Form 2120). Each person who is a party to the multiple support agreement must meet all the other requirements for claiming the dependency exemption. § 152(c). See also *personal and dependency exemptions*.

N

National sales tax. Intended as a replacement for the current Federal income tax. Unlike a value added tax (VAT), which is levied on the manufacturer, it would be imposed on the consumer upon the final sale of goods and services. To keep the tax from being regressive, low-income taxpayers would be granted some kind of credit or exemption.

Necessary. Appropriate and helpful in furthering the taxpayer's business or income-producing activity. §§ 162(a) and 212. See also *ordinary*.

Net capital gain. The excess of the net long-term capital gain for the tax year over the net short-term capital loss. The net capital gain of an individual taxpayer is eligible for the alternative tax. § 1222(11). See also *alternative tax*.

Net capital loss. The excess of the losses from sales or exchanges of capital assets over the gains from sales or exchanges of such assets. Up to $3,000 per year of the net capital loss may be deductible by noncorporate taxpayers against ordinary income. The excess net capital loss carries over to future tax years. For corporate taxpayers, the net capital loss cannot be offset against ordinary income, but it can be carried back 3 years and forward 5 years to offset net capital gains. §§ 1211, 1212, and 1221(10).

Net investment income. The excess of *investment income* over investment expenses. Investment expenses are those deductible expenses directly connected with the production of investment income. Investment expenses do not include investment interest. The deduction for *investment interest* for the tax year is limited to net investment income. § 163(d).

Net operating loss. To mitigate the effect of the annual accounting period concept, § 172 allows taxpayers to use an excess loss of one year as a deduction for certain past or future years. In this regard, a carryback period of 3 years and a carryforward period of 15 years are allowed. See also *mitigation of the annual accounting period concept*.

Net worth method. An approach used by the IRS to reconstruct the income of a taxpayer who fails to maintain adequate records. Under this approach, the gross income for the year is the increase in net worth of the taxpayer (assets in excess of liabilities) with appropriate adjustment for nontaxable receipts and nondeductible expenditures. The net worth method often is used when tax fraud is suspected.

Ninety-day letter. See *statutory notice of deficiency*.

No-additional-cost services. Services that the employer may provide the employee at no additional cost to the employer. Generally, the benefit is the ability to utilize the employer's excess capacity (vacant seats on an airliner). Such amounts are excludible from the recipient's gross income. § 132.

Nonaccountable plan. An expense reimbursement plan that does not have an accountability feature. The result is that employee expenses must be claimed as deductions *from* AGI. An exception is moving expenses, which are deductions *for* AGI. See also *accountable plan*.

Nonacquiescence. Announcement of disagreement by the IRS on the result reached in certain judicial decisions. Sometimes abbreviated *Nonacq.* or *NA*. See also *acquiescence*.

Nonbusiness bad debts. A bad debt loss not incurred in connection with a creditor's trade or business. The loss is deductible as a short-term capital loss and is allowed only in the year the debt becomes entirely worthless. In addition to family loans, many investor losses fall into the classification of nonbusiness bad debts. § 166(d). See also *bad debts*.

Nonqualified deferred compensation (NQDC) plans. Compensation arrangements that are frequently offered to executives. Such plans may include stock options, restricted stock, etc. Often, an executive may defer the recognition of taxable income. The employer, however, does not receive a tax deduction until the employee is required to include the compensation in income. See also *restricted property plan*.

Nonqualified stock option (NQSO). A type of stock option that does not satisfy the statutory requirements of an incentive stock option. If the NQSO has a readily ascertainable fair market value (e.g., the option is traded on an established exchange), the value of the option must be included in the employee's gross income at the date of the grant. Otherwise, the employee does not recognize income at the grant date. Instead, ordinary income is recognized in the year of exercise of the option. See also *incentive stock option (ISO)*.

Nonrecourse debt. An obligation on which the endorser is not personally liable. An example of a nonrecourse debt is a mortgage on real estate acquired by a partnership without the assumption of any liability on the mortgage by the partnership or any of the partners. The acquired property generally is pledged as collateral for the loan.

Nonrefundable credit. A nonrefundable credit is a credit that is not paid if it exceeds the taxpayer's tax liability.

Some nonrefundable credits qualify for carryback and carryover treatment. See also *refundable credit*.

Nontaxable exchange. A transaction in which realized gains or losses are not recognized. The recognition of gain or loss is postponed (deferred) until the property received in the nontaxable exchange is subsequently disposed of in a taxable transaction. Examples are § 1031 like-kind exchanges, § 1033 involuntary conversions, and § 1034 sale of a residence. See also *involuntary conversion* and *like-kind exchange*.

O

Occupational tax. A tax imposed on various trades or businesses. A license fee that enables a taxpayer to engage in a particular occupation.

Office audit. An audit by the IRS of a taxpayer's return that is conducted in the agent's office. To be distinguished from a *correspondence audit* or a *field audit*.

Office-in-the-home expenses. Employment and business-related expenses attributable to the use of a residence (e.g., den or office) are allowed only if the portion of the residence is exclusively used on a regular basis as a principal place of business of the taxpayer or as a place of business that is used by patients, clients, or customers. If the expenses are incurred by an employee, the use must be for the convenience of the employer as opposed to being merely appropriate and helpful. § 280A.

One-year rule for prepaid expenses. Taxpayers who use the cash method are required to use the accrual method for deducting certain prepaid expenses (i.e., must capitalize the item and can deduct only when used). If a prepayment will not be consumed or expire by the end of the tax year following the year of payment, the prepayment must be capitalized and prorated over the benefit period. Conversely, if the prepayment will be consumed by the end of the tax year following the year of payment, it can be expensed when paid. To obtain the current deduction under the one-year rule, the payment must be a required payment rather than a voluntary payment.

Open transaction. A judicially imposed doctrine that allows the taxpayer to defer all gain until he or she has collected an amount equal to the adjusted basis of assets transferred pursuant to an exchange transaction. This doctrine has been applied where the property received in an exchange has no ascertainable fair market value due to the existence of contingencies. The method is permitted only in very limited circumstances. See also *recovery of capital doctrine*.

Options. The sale or exchange of an option to buy or sell property results in capital gain or loss if the property is a capital asset. Generally, the closing of an option transaction results in short-term capital gain or loss to the writer of the call and the purchaser of the call option. § 1234.

Ordinary. Common and accepted in the general industry or type of activity in which the taxpayer is engaged. It comprises one of the tests for the deductibility of expenses incurred or paid in connection with a trade or business; for the production or collection of income; for the management, conservation, or maintenance of property held for the production of income; or in connection with the determination, collection, or refund of any tax. §§ 162(a) and 212. See also *necessary*.

Ordinary and necessary. See *necessary* and *ordinary*.

Ordinary income property. Property contributed to a charitable organization that, if sold rather than contributed, would have resulted in other than long-term capital gain to the donor (i.e., ordinary income property and short-term capital gain property). Examples are inventory and capital assets held for less than the long-term holding period.

Organizational expenses. A corporation may elect to amortize organizational expenses over a period of 60 months or more. Certain expenses of organizing a company do not qualify for amortization (e.g., expenditures connected with issuing or selling stock or other securities). § 248.

Original issue discount (OID). The difference between the issue price of a debt obligation (e.g., a corporate bond) and the maturity value of the obligation when the issue price is *less than* the maturity value. OID represents interest and must be amortized over the life of the debt obligation using the effective interest method. The difference is not considered to be original issue discount for tax purposes when it is less than one-fourth of 1 percent of the redemption price at maturity multiplied by the number of years to maturity. §§ 1272 and 1273(a)(3).

Outside salesperson. An outside salesperson solicits business away from the employer's place of business on a full-time basis. The employment-related expenses of an outside salesperson are itemized deductions unless reimbursed by the employer. If reimbursed, such expenses are deductible *for* AGI.

P

Partnerships. A partnership is treated as a conduit and is not subject to taxation. Various items of partnership income, expenses, gains, and losses flow through to the individual partners and are reported on the partners' personal income tax returns.

Passive activity. A trade or business activity in which the taxpayer does not materially participate is subject to limitations on the deduction of losses and credits. Rental activities (subject to exceptions) and limited partnership interests are inherently passive. Relief from passive activity limitation treatment is provided in certain situations, such as for certain rental real estate if the taxpayer actively participates in the activity. The annual ceiling on the relief is $25,000. § 469. See also *portfolio income*.

Passive investment income. As defined in § 1362(d)(3)(D), passive investment income means gross receipts from royalties, certain rents, dividends, interest, annuities, and gains from the sale or exchange of stock and securities. Revocation of the S corporation election may occur in certain cases when the S corporation has passive investment income in excess of 25 percent of gross receipts for a period of three consecutive years.

Passive loss. Any loss from (1) activities in which the taxpayer does not materially participate or (2) rental activities (subject to certain exceptions). Net passive losses cannot be used to offset income from nonpassive sources. Rather, they are suspended until the taxpayer either generates net passive income (and a deduction of the losses is allowed) or disposes of the underlying property (at which time the loss deductions are allowed in full). One relief provision allows landlords who actively participate in the rental activities to deduct up to $25,000 of passive losses annually. However, a phaseout of the $25,000 amount commences when the landlord's AGI exceeds $100,000. See also *portfolio income.*

Patent. A patent is an intangible asset that may be amortized over a statutory 15-year period as a § 197 intangible. The sale of a patent usually results in favorable long-term capital gain treatment. §§ 197 and 1235.

Pension plan. A type of deferred compensation arrangement that provides for systematic payments of definitely determinable retirement benefits to employees who meet the requirements set forth in the plan. See also *defined benefit plan* and *defined contribution plan.*

Percentage depletion. Percentage depletion is depletion based on a statutory percentage applied to the gross income from the property. The taxpayer deducts the greater of cost depletion or percentage depletion. § 613. See also *cost depletion.*

Percentage of completion method. A method of reporting gain or loss on certain long-term contracts. Under this method of accounting, the gross contract price is included in income as the contract is being completed. § 460 and Reg. § 1.451–3. See also *completed contract method* and *long-term contract.*

Personal and dependency exemptions. The tax law provides an exemption for each individual taxpayer and an additional exemption for the taxpayer's spouse if a joint return is filed. An individual may also claim a dependency exemption for each dependent, provided certain tests are met. The amount of the personal and dependency exemptions is $2,550 in 1996 and $2,650 in 1997. The amount is indexed for inflation. The exemption is subject to phaseout once adjusted gross income exceeds certain statutory threshold amounts. §§ 151 and 152.

Personal casualty gain. The recognized gain from any involuntary conversion of personal use property arising from fire, storm, shipwreck, or other casualty, or from theft. See also *personal casualty loss.*

Personal casualty loss. The recognized loss from any involuntary conversion of personal use property arising from fire, storm, shipwreck, or other casualty, or from theft. See also *personal casualty gain.*

Personal exemption. See *personal and dependency exemptions.*

Personal expenses. Expenses of an individual for personal reasons that are not deductible unless specifically provided for under the tax law. § 262.

Personal property. Generally, all property other than real estate. It is sometimes referred to as personalty when real estate is termed realty. Personal property also can refer to property that is not used in a taxpayer's trade or business or held for the production or collection of income. When used in this sense, personal property can include both realty (e.g., a personal residence) and personalty (e.g., personal effects such as clothing and furniture).

Personal residence. The sale of a personal residence generally results in the recognition of capital gain (but not loss). However, the gain may be deferred if the adjusted sales price of the old residence is reinvested in the purchase of a new residence within certain prescribed time periods. Also, taxpayers age 55 or older may exclude $125,000 of the gain from tax, provided certain requirements are met. §§ 1034 and 121. See also *Section 121 exclusion.*

Personal service corporation (PSC). A corporation the principal activity of which is the performance of personal services (e.g., health, law, engineering, architecture, accounting, actuarial science, performing arts, or consulting), with such services being substantially performed by the employee-owners.

Personalty. All property other than realty (real estate). Personalty usually is categorized as tangible or intangible property. Tangible personalty includes such assets as machinery and equipment, automobiles and trucks, and office equipment. Intangible personalty includes stocks and bonds, goodwill, patents, trademarks, and copyrights. See also *personal property.*

Points. Loan origination fees that may be deductible as interest by a buyer of property. A seller of property who pays points reduces the selling price by the amount of the points paid for the buyer. While the seller is not permitted to deduct this amount as interest, the buyer may do so. See *prepaid interest* for the timing of the interest deduction.

Pollution control facilities. A certified pollution control facility, the cost of which may be amortized over a 60-month period if the taxpayer elects. § 169.

Portfolio income. The term is relevant in applying the limitation on passive activity losses and credits. Although normally considered passive in nature, for this purpose portfolio income is treated as nonpassive. Therefore, net passive losses and credits cannot be offset against portfolio income. Examples of portfolio income are interest, dividends, annuities, and certain royalties. § 469. See also *passive activity.*

Precedent. A previously decided court decision that is recognized as authority for the disposition of future decisions.

Prepaid expenses. Cash basis as well as accrual basis taxpayers usually are required to capitalize prepayments for rent, insurance, etc., that cover more than one year. Deductions are taken during the period the benefits are received.

Prepaid interest. In effect, the Code places cash basis taxpayers on an accrual basis for purposes of recognizing a deduction for prepaid interest. Thus, interest paid in advance is deductible as an interest expense only as it accrues. The one exception to this rule involves the interest element when a cash basis taxpayer pays points to obtain financing for the purchase of a principal residence (or to make improvements thereto) if the payment of points is an established business practice in the area in which the indebtedness is incurred and the amount involved is not excessive. § 461(g). See also *points*.

Principal partner. A partner with a 5 percent or greater interest in partnership capital or profits. § 706(b)(3). See also *majority interest partners*.

Private activity bond. Interest on state and local bonds is excludible from gross income. § 103. Certain such bonds are labeled private activity bonds. Although the interest on such bonds is excludible for regular income tax purposes, it is treated as a tax preference in calculating the AMT. See also *alternative minimum tax (AMT)*.

Prizes and awards. The fair market value of a prize or award generally is includible in gross income. However, exclusion is permitted if the prize or award is made in recognition of religious, charitable, scientific, educational, artistic, literary, or civic achievement, and the recipient transfers the award to a qualified governmental unit or a nonprofit organization. In that case, the recipient must be selected without any action on his or her part to enter a contest or proceeding, and the recipient must not be required to render substantial future services as a condition of receiving the prize or award. § 74.

Procedural regulation. A Regulation issued by the Treasury Department that is a housekeeping-type instruction indicating information that taxpayers should provide the IRS as well as information about the internal management and conduct of the IRS itself. See also *interpretive regulation* and *legislative regulation*.

Profit sharing plan. A deferred compensation plan established and maintained by an employer to provide for employee participation in the company's profits. Contributions are paid from the employer's current or accumulated profits to a trustee. Separate accounts are maintained for each participant employee. The plan must provide a definite, predetermined formula for allocating the contributions among the participants. It also must include a definite, predetermined formula for distributing the accumulated funds after a fixed number of years, on the attainment of a stated age, or on the occurrence of certain events such as illness, layoff, or retirement.

Proposed regulation. A Regulation issued by the Treasury Department in proposed, rather than final, form. The interval between the proposal of a Regulation and its finalization permits taxpayers and other interested parties to comment on the propriety of the proposal. See also *regulations* and *temporary regulation*.

Public policy limitation. See *bribes and illegal payments*.

Punitive damages. Damages received or paid by the taxpayer can be classified as compensatory damages or as punitive damages. Punitive damages are those awarded to punish the defendant for gross negligence or the intentional infliction of harm. Such damages are includible in gross income. § 104. See also *compensatory damages*.

Q

Qualified employee discounts. Discounts offered employees on merchandise or services that the employer ordinarily sells or provides to customers. The discounts must be generally available to all employees. In the case of property, the discount cannot exceed the employer's gross profit (the sales price cannot be less than the employer's cost). In the case of services, the discounts cannot exceed 20 percent of the normal sales price. § 132.

Qualified pension or profit sharing plan. An employer-sponsored plan that meets the requirements of § 401. If these requirements are met, none of the employer's contributions to the plan will be taxed to the employee until distributed to him or her (§ 402). The employer will be allowed a deduction in the year the contributions are made (§ 404). See also *annuity* and *deferred compensation*.

Qualified real property business indebtedness. Indebtedness that was incurred or assumed by the taxpayer in connection with real property used in a trade or business and is secured by such real property. The taxpayer must not be a C corporation. For qualified real property business indebtedness, the taxpayer may elect to exclude some or all of the income realized from cancellation of debt on qualified real property. If the election is made, the basis of the property must be reduced by the amount excluded. The amount excluded cannot be greater than the excess of the principal amount of the outstanding debt over the fair market value (net of any other debt outstanding on the property) of the property securing the debt.

Qualified residence interest. A term relevant in determining the amount of interest expense the individual taxpayer may deduct as an itemized deduction for what otherwise would be disallowed as a component of personal interest (consumer interest). Qualified residence interest consists of interest paid on qualified residences (principal residence and one other residence) of the taxpayer. Debt that qualifies as qualified residence interest is limited to $1 million of debt to acquire, construct, or substantially improve qualified residences (acquisition indebtedness) plus $100,000 of other debt secured by qualified residences (home equity indebtedness). The home equity indebtedness may not exceed the fair market value of a qualified residence reduced by the acquisition indebtedness for that residence. § 163(h)(3). See also *consumer interest* and *home equity loans.*

Qualified state tuition program. A program established by the individual states that allows a resident to prepay college tuition for a beneficiary. When the tuition is used, the beneficiary must recognize income equal to the difference between the amount placed in the fund and the charges for tuition at the time it is used using an annuity-type approach. § 529.

Qualified transportation fringes. Transportation benefits provided by the employer to the employee. Such benefits include (1) transportation in a commuter highway vehicle between the employee's residence and the place of employment, (2) a transit pass, and (3) qualified parking. Qualified transportation fringes are excludible from the employee's gross income to the extent categories (1) and (2) above do not exceed $65 per month and category (3) does not exceed $170 per month. These amounts are indexed annually for inflation. § 132.

Qualified tuition reduction plan. A type of fringe benefit plan that is available to employees of nonprofit educational institutions. Such employees (and the spouse and dependent children) are allowed to exclude a tuition waiver pursuant to a qualified tuition reduction plan from gross income. The exclusion applies to undergraduate tuition. In limited circumstances, the exclusion also applies to the graduate tuition of teaching and research assistants. § 117(d).

R

RAR. A Revenue Agent's Report, which reflects any adjustments made by the agent as a result of an audit of the taxpayer. The RAR is mailed to the taxpayer along with the 30-day letter, which outlines the appellate procedures available to the taxpayer.

Realized gain or loss. The difference between the amount realized upon the sale or other disposition of property and the adjusted basis of the property. § 1001. See also *adjusted basis* and *recognized gain or loss.*

Realty. All real estate, including land and buildings. Permanent improvements to a building (fixtures) become realty if their removal would cause significant damage to the property. An example of a fixture is the installation of a central air conditioning or heating system to a building. Thus, personalty can become realty through the fixture reclassification.

Reasonable needs of the business. See *accumulated earnings tax.*

Reasonableness. The Code includes a reasonableness requirement with respect to the deduction of salaries and other compensation for services. What constitutes reasonableness is a question of fact. If an expense is unreasonable, the amount that is classified as unreasonable is not allowed as a deduction. The question of reasonableness generally arises with respect to closely held corporations where there is no separation of ownership and management. § 162(a)(1).

Recapture. To recover the tax benefit of a deduction or a credit previously taken.

Recapture of depreciation. Upon the disposition of depreciable property used in a trade or business, gain or loss is determined measured by the difference between the consideration received (the amount realized) and the adjusted basis of the property. Before the enactment of the recapture of depreciation provisions of the Code, any such gain recognized could be § 1231 gain and usually qualified for long-term capital gain treatment. The recapture provisions of the Code (e.g., §§ 1245 and 1250) may operate to convert some or all of the previous § 1231 gain into ordinary income. The justification for recapture of depreciation is that it prevents a taxpayer from deducting depreciation at ordinary income rates and having the related gain on disposition taxed at capital gain rates. The recapture of depreciation rules do not apply when the property is disposed of at a loss. See also *residential rental property, Section 1231 gains and losses, Section 1245 recapture,* and *Section 1250 recapture.*

Recapture of investment tax credit. When investment tax credit property is disposed of or ceases to be used in the trade or business of the taxpayer, some or all of the investment tax credit claimed on the property may be recaptured as additional tax liability. The amount of the recapture is the difference between the amount of the credit originally claimed and what should have been claimed in light of the length of time the property was actually held or used for qualifying purposes. § 50. See also *investment tax credit.*

Recapture potential. Reference is to property that, if disposed of in a taxable transaction, would result in the recapture of depreciation (§§ 1245 or 1250) and/or of the investment tax credit (§ 50).

Recognized gain or loss. The portion of realized gain or loss that is considered in computing taxable income. See also *realized gain or loss.*

Recovery of capital doctrine. When a taxable sale or exchange occurs, the seller may be permitted to recover his or her investment (or other adjusted basis) in the property before gain or loss is recognized. See also *open transaction.*

Refundable credit. A refundable credit is a credit that is paid to the taxpayer even if the amount of the credit (or credits) exceeds the taxpayer's tax liability. See also *nonrefundable credit.*

Regulations. Treasury Department Regulations represent the position of the IRS as to how the Internal Revenue Code is to be interpreted. Their purpose is to provide taxpayers and IRS personnel with rules of general and specific application to the various provisions of the tax law. Regulations are published in the *Federal Register* and in all tax services. See also *interpretive regulation, legislative regulation, procedural regulation,* and *proposed regulation.*

Rehabilitation expenditures credit. A credit that is based on expenditures incurred to rehabilitate industrial and commercial buildings and certified historic structures. The credit, an extension of the regular investment tax credit, is intended to discourage businesses from moving from older, economically distressed areas to newer locations and to encourage the preservation of historic structures. § 47. See *rehabilitation expenditures credit recapture.*

Rehabilitation expenditures credit recapture. When property that qualifies for the rehabilitation expenditures credit is disposed of or ceases to be used in the trade or business of the taxpayer, some or all of the tax credit claimed on the property may be recaptured as additional tax liability. The amount of the recapture is the difference between the amount of the credit claimed originally and what should have been claimed in light of the length of time the property was actually held or used for qualifying purposes. § 50. See *rehabilitation expenditures credit.*

Related party. Includes certain family members and controlled entities (i.e., partnerships and corporations). §§ 267, 707(b), and 1239. See also *related-party transactions.*

Related-party transactions. The tax law places restrictions upon the recognition of gains and losses between related parties because of the potential for abuse. For example, restrictions are placed on the deduction of losses from the sale or exchange of property between related parties. In addition, under certain circumstances, related-party gains that would otherwise be classified as capital gain are classified as ordinary income. §§ 267, 707(b), and 1239. See also *related party.*

Rental activity. Any activity where payments are received principally for the use of tangible property is a rental activity. Temporary Regulations provide that in certain circumstances activities involving rentals of real and personal property are not to be *treated* as rental activities. The Temporary Regulations list six exceptions.

Research activities credit. A tax credit whose purpose is to encourage research and development. It consists of two components: the incremental research activities credit and the basic research credit. The incremental research activities credit is equal to 20 percent of the excess of qualified research expenditures over the base amount. The basic research credit is equal to 20 percent of the excess of basic research payments over the base amount. § 41. See also *general business credit.*

Research and experimental expenditures. The Code provides three alternatives for the tax treatment of research and experimentation expenditures. They may be expensed in the year paid or incurred, deferred subject to amortization, or capitalized. If the taxpayer does not elect to expense such costs or to defer them subject to amortization (over 60 months), the expenditures must be capitalized. § 174. Two types of research activities credits are available: the basic research credit and the incremental research activities credit. The rate for each type is 20 percent. § 41. See also *research activities credit.*

Reserve for bad debts. A method of accounting whereby an allowance is permitted for estimated uncollectible accounts. Actual write-offs are charged to the reserve, and recoveries of amounts previously written off are credited to the reserve. The Code permits only certain financial institutions to use the reserve method. § 166. See also *specific charge-off method.*

Reserve method. See *reserve for bad debts.*

Reserves for estimated expenses. Except in the limited case for bad debts, reserves for estimated expenses (e.g., warranty service costs) are not permitted for tax purposes even though such reserves are appropriate for financial accounting purposes. See also *all events test.*

Residential rental property. Buildings for which at least 80 percent of the gross rents are from dwelling units (e.g., an apartment building). This type of building is distinguished from nonresidential (commercial or industrial) buildings in applying the recapture of depreciation provisions. The term also is relevant in distinguishing between buildings that are eligible for a 27.5-year life versus a 39-year (or 31.5-year) life for MACRS purposes. Generally, residential buildings receive preferential treatment. §§ 168(e)(2) and 1250. See also *recapture of depreciation.*

Residential rental real estate. See *residential rental property.*

Restricted property plan. An arrangement whereby an employer transfers property (usually stock) to an employee at a bargain price (for less than the fair market value). If the transfer is accompanied by a substantial risk of forfeiture and the property is not transferable, no compensation results to the employee until the restrictions disappear. An example of a substantial risk of forfeiture would be a requirement that the employee return the property if his or her employment is terminated within a specified period of time. § 83. See also *nonqualified deferred compensation (NQDC) plans* and *substantial risk of forfeiture.*

Retirement of corporate obligations. The retirement of corporate and certain government obligations is considered to be a sale or exchange. Gain or loss, upon the retirement of a corporate obligation, therefore, is treated as capital gain or loss rather than as ordinary income or loss. §§ 1271–1275.

Return of capital doctrine. See *recovery of capital doctrine.*

Revenue neutrality. A description that characterizes tax legislation when it neither increases nor decreases the revenue result. Thus, any tax revenue losses are offset by tax revenue gains.

Revenue Procedure. A matter of procedural importance to both taxpayers and the IRS concerning the administration of the tax law is issued by the National Office of the IRS as a Revenue Procedure (abbreviated Rev.Proc.). A Revenue Procedure is first published in an *Internal Revenue Bulletin* (I.R.B.) and later transferred to the appropriate *Cumulative Bulletin* (C.B.). Both the *Internal Revenue Bulletin* and the *Cumulative Bulletin* are published by the U.S. Government Printing Office.

Revenue Ruling. A Revenue Ruling (abbreviated Rev.Rul.) is issued by the National Office of the IRS to express an official interpretation of the tax law as applied to specific transactions. It is more limited in application than a Regulation. A Revenue Ruling is first published in an *Internal Revenue Bulletin* (I.R.B.) and later transferred to the appropriate *Cumulative Bulletin* (C.B.). Both the *Internal Revenue Bulletin* and the *Cumulative Bulletin* are published by the U.S. Government Printing Office.

S

Sale or exchange. A requirement for the recognition of capital gain or loss. Generally, the seller of property must receive money or relief from debt in order to have sold the property. An exchange involves the transfer of property for other property. Thus, *collection* of a debt is neither a sale nor an exchange. The term *sale or exchange* is not defined by the Code.

Sales tax. A transaction tax imposed upon the sale of goods. It usually is based on a specified percentage of the value of the property sold. A sales tax is to be distinguished from an excise tax, since a sales tax applies to a broad variety of commodities.

Salvage value. The estimated amount a taxpayer will receive upon the disposition of an asset used in the taxpayer's trade or business. Salvage value is relevant in calculating depreciation under § 167, but is not relevant in calculating cost recovery under § 168.

Scholarships. Scholarships are generally excluded from the gross income of the recipient unless the payments are a disguised form of compensation for services rendered. However, the Code imposes restrictions on the exclusion. The recipient must be a degree candidate. The excluded amount is limited to amounts used for tuition, fees, books, supplies, and equipment required for courses of instruction. Amounts received for room and board are not eligible for the exclusion. § 117.

S corporation. See *S corporation status*.

S corporation status. An elective provision permitting certain small business corporations (§ 1361) and their shareholders to elect (§ 1362) to be treated for income tax purposes in accordance with the operating rules of §§ 1363–1379. Of major significance are the facts that S status avoids the corporate income tax and corporate losses can be claimed by the shareholders. See also *C corporation*.

Section 38 property. Property that qualified for the investment tax credit. Generally, this included all tangible property (other than real estate) used in a trade or business. § 48 prior to repeal by the Revenue Reconciliation Act of 1990. See also *investment tax credit*.

Section 121 exclusion. An exclusion of $125,000 of realized gain available to taxpayers who are age 55 or over associated with the sale of their principal residence. The taxpayer must have owned and occupied the residence for at least three years during the five-year period ending on the date of sale. The exclusion treatment is elective, and the election can be made only once. If married, both spouses must consent to the election. § 121. See also *personal residence*.

Section 179 expensing. The ability to deduct a capital expenditure in the year an asset is placed in service rather than over the asset's useful life or cost recovery period. The annual ceiling on the deduction is $17,500 for 1996 and $18,000 for 1997. The ceiling amount is increased each year until it reaches $25,000 for 2003 and thereafter. However, the deduction is reduced dollar for dollar when § 179 property placed in service during the taxable year exceeds $200,000. In addition, the amount expensed under § 179 cannot exceed the aggregate amount of taxable income derived from the conduct of any trade or business by the taxpayer.

Section 401(k) plan. A cash or deferred arrangement plan that allows participants to elect to receive up to $9,500 in 1997 in cash (taxed currently) or to have a contribution made on their behalf to a profit sharing or stock bonus plan (excludible from gross income). The plan may also be in the form of a salary reduction agreement between the participant and the employer.

Section 1231 assets. Depreciable assets and real estate used in a trade or business and held for the required long-term holding period. Under certain circumstances, the classification also includes timber, coal, domestic iron ore, livestock (held for draft, breeding, dairy, or sporting purposes), and unharvested crops. § 1231(b).

Section 1231 gains and losses. If the net result of the combined gains and losses from the taxable dispositions of § 1231 assets plus the net gain from the involuntary conversion of nonpersonal use assets is a gain, the gains and losses from § 1231 assets are treated as long-term capital gains and losses. In arriving at § 1231 gains, however, the depreciation recapture provisions (e.g., §§ 1245 and 1250) are first applied to produce ordinary income. If the net result of the combination is a loss, the gains and losses from § 1231 assets are treated as ordinary gains and losses. § 1231(a). See also *recapture of depreciation*.

Section 1231 lookback. In order for gain to be classified as § 1231 gain, the gain must survive the § 1231 lookback. To the extent of nonrecaptured § 1231 losses for the five prior tax years, the gain is classified as ordinary income. § 1231(c).

Section 1231 property. See *Section 1231 assets*.

Section 1244 stock. Stock issued under § 1244 by qualifying small business corporations. If § 1244 stock is disposed of at a loss or becomes worthless, the shareholders may claim an ordinary loss rather than the usual capital loss. The annual ceiling on the ordinary loss treatment is $50,000 ($100,000 for married individuals filing jointly). See also *worthless securities.*

Section 1245 property. Property that is subject to the recapture of depreciation under § 1245. For a definition of § 1245 property, see § 1245(a)(3). See also *Section 1245 recapture.*

Section 1245 recapture. Upon a taxable disposition of § 1245 property, all depreciation claimed on the property after 1961 is recaptured as ordinary income (but not to exceed the recognized gain from the disposition). See also *recapture of depreciation.*

Section 1250 property. Real estate that is subject to the recapture of depreciation under § 1250. For a definition of § 1250 property, see § 1250(c). See also *Section 1250 recapture.*

Section 1250 recapture. Upon a taxable disposition of § 1250 property, some or all of the additional depreciation claimed on the property may be recaptured as ordinary income. Various recapture rules apply depending upon the type of property (residential or nonresidential real estate) and the date acquired. Generally, the additional depreciation is recaptured in full to the extent of the gain recognized. See also *additional depreciation* and *recapture of depreciation.*

Self-employment retirement plan. A designation for retirement plans available to self-employed taxpayers. Also referred to as H.R. 10 and Keogh plans. Under such plans, a taxpayer may deduct each year up to either 20 percent of net earnings from self-employment or $30,000, whichever is less. If the plan is a profit sharing plan, the percentage is 13.043 percent.

Self-employment tax. In 1997, a tax of 12.4 percent is levied on individuals with net earnings from self-employment (up to $65,400) to provide Social Security benefits (i.e., the old age, survivors, and disability insurance portion) for such individuals. In addition, in 1997, a tax of 2.9 percent is levied on individuals with net earnings from self-employment (with no statutory ceiling) to provide Medicare benefits (i.e., the hospital insurance portion) for such individuals. If a self-employed individual also receives wages from an employer that are subject to FICA, the self-employment tax will be reduced if total income subject to Social Security is more than $65,400. A partial deduction is allowed in calculating the self-employment tax. Individuals with net earnings of $400 or more from self-employment are subject to this tax. §§ 1401 and 1402.

Separate property. In a community property jurisdiction, separate property is the property that belongs entirely to one of the spouses. Generally, it is property acquired before marriage or acquired after marriage by gift or inheritance. See also *community property.*

Severance tax. A tax imposed upon the extraction of natural resources.

Short sale. A short sale occurs when a taxpayer sells borrowed property (usually stock) and repays the lender with substantially identical property either held on the date of the short sale or purchased after the sale. No gain or loss is recognized until the short sale is closed, and such gain or loss is generally short term. § 1233.

Short taxable year (short period). A tax year that is less than 12 months. A short taxable year may occur in the initial reporting period, in the final tax year, or when the taxpayer changes tax years.

Significant participation activity. There are seven tests to determine whether an individual has achieved material participation in an activity, one of which is based on more than 500 hours of participation in significant participation activities. A significant participation activity is one in which the individual's participation exceeds 100 hours during the year.

Simplified employee pension (SEP) plan. An employer may make contributions to an employee's IRA in amounts not exceeding the lesser of 15 percent of compensation or $30,000 per individual. These employer-sponsored simplified employee pensions are permitted only if the contributions are nondiscriminatory and are made on behalf of all employees who have attained age 21 and have worked for the employer during at least three of the five preceding calendar years. § 219(b). See also *individual retirement account (IRA).*

Small business corporation. A corporation that satisfies the definition of § 1361(b), § 1244(c)(3), or both. Satisfaction of § 1361(b) permits an S corporation election, and satisfaction of § 1244 enables the shareholders of the corporation to claim an ordinary loss. See also *S corporation status* and *Section 1244 stock.*

Small business stock. See *small business corporation.*

Small cases division. A subsidiary division of the U.S. Tax Court. The jurisdiction of the Small Cases division is limited to small claims (i.e., claims of $10,000 or less). The proceedings of the Small Cases Division are informal, and the findings cannot be appealed.

Specific charge-off method. A method of accounting for bad debts in which a deduction is permitted only when an account becomes partially or completely worthless. See also *reserve for bad debts.*

Standard deduction. The individual taxpayer can either itemize deductions or take the standard deduction. The amount of the standard deduction depends on the taxpayer's filing status (single, head of household, married filing jointly, surviving spouse, or married filing separately). For 1997, the amount of the standard deduction ranges from $3,450 to $6,900. Additional standard deductions of either $800 (for married taxpayers) or $1,000 (for single taxpayers) are available if the taxpayer is either blind or age 65 or over. Limitations exist on the amount of the standard deduction of a taxpayer who is another taxpayer's dependent. Beginning in 1989, the standard deduction amounts are adjusted for inflation each year. § 63(c). See also *zero bracket amount*.

Statute of limitations. Provisions of the law that specify the maximum period of time in which action may be taken on a past event. Code §§ 6501–6504 contain the limitation periods applicable to the IRS for additional assessments, and §§ 6511–6515 relate to refund claims by taxpayers.

Statutory employee. Statutory employees are considered self-employed independent contractors for purposes of reporting income and expenses on their tax returns. Generally, a statutory employee must meet three tests:

- It is understood from a service contract that the services will be performed by the person.
- The person does not have a substantial investment in facilities (other than transportation) used to perform the services.
- The services involve a continuing relationship with the person for whom they are performed.

For further information on statutory employees, see Circular E *Employer's Tax Guide* (IRS Publication 15).

Statutory notice of deficiency. Commonly referred to as the 90-day letter, this notice is sent to a taxpayer upon request, upon the expiration of the 30-day letter, or upon exhaustion by the taxpayer of his or her administrative remedies before the IRS. The notice gives the taxpayer 90 days in which to file a petition with the U.S. Tax Court. If a petition is not filed, the IRS will issue a demand for payment of the assessed deficiency. §§ 6211–6216. See also *thirty-day letter*.

Stock bonus plan. A type of deferred compensation plan in which the employer establishes and maintains the plan and contributes employer stock to the plan for the benefit of employees. The contributions need not be dependent on the employer's profits. Any benefits of the plan are distributable in the form of employer stock, except that distributable fractional shares may be paid in cash.

Stock option. The right to purchase a stated number of shares of stock from a corporation at a certain price within a specified period of time. §§ 421 and 422. See also *incentive stock option (ISO)* and *nonqualified stock option (NQSO)*.

Stock redemption. The redemption of the stock of a shareholder by the issuing corporation is treated as a sale or exchange of the stock if the redemption is not a dividend. §§ 301 and 302.

Substantial risk of forfeiture. A term that is associated with a restricted property plan. Generally, an employee who receives property (e.g., stock of the employer-corporation) from the employer at a bargain price or at no cost must include the bargain element in gross income. However, the employee currently does not have to do so if there is a substantial risk of forfeiture. A substantial risk of forfeiture exists if a person's rights to full enjoyment of property are conditioned upon the future performance, or the refraining from the performance, of substantial services by the individual. § 83. See also *restricted property plan*.

Super-full absorption costing rules. See *uniform capitalization rules*.

Surviving spouse. The joint return tax rates apply for a surviving spouse. Such rates apply for the two tax years after the tax year of the death of the spouse. To qualify as a surviving spouse, the taxpayer must maintain a household for a dependent child. § 2.

T

Targeted jobs tax credit. See *work opportunity tax credit*.

Taxable year. The annual period over which income is measured for income tax purposes. Most individuals use a calendar year, but many businesses use a fiscal year based on the natural business year. See also *accounting period* and *fiscal year*.

Tax avoidance. The minimization of one's tax liability by taking advantage of legally available tax planning opportunities. Tax avoidance can be contrasted with tax evasion, which entails the reduction of tax liability by illegal means.

Tax benefit rule. A provision that limits the recognition of income from the recovery of an expense or loss properly deducted in a prior tax year to the amount of the deduction that generated a tax benefit. § 111.

Tax Court. The U.S. Tax Court is one of three trial courts of original jurisdiction that decide litigation involving Federal income, estate, or gift taxes. It is the only trial court where the taxpayer need not first pay the deficiency assessed by the IRS. The Tax Court will not have jurisdiction over a case unless the statutory notice of deficiency (90-day letter) has been issued by the IRS and the taxpayer files the petition for hearing within the time prescribed.

Tax credits. Tax credits are amounts that directly reduce a taxpayer's tax liability. The tax benefit received from a tax credit is not dependent on the taxpayer's marginal tax rate, whereas the benefit of a tax deduction or exclusion is dependent on the taxpayer's tax bracket.

Tax credit for the elderly or disabled. An elderly (age 65 and over) or disabled taxpayer may receive a tax credit amounting to 15 percent of $5,000 ($7,500 for qualified married individuals filing jointly). This amount is reduced by Social Security benefits, excluded pension benefits, and one-half of the taxpayer's adjusted gross income in excess of $7,500 ($10,000 for married taxpayers filing jointly). § 22.

Tax-free exchange. Transfers of property specifically exempted from Federal income tax consequences. Examples are a transfer of property to a controlled corporation under § 351(a) and a like-kind exchange under § 1031(a). The recognition of gain or loss is postponed, rather than being permanently excluded, through the assignment of a carryover basis to the replacement property. See also *nontaxable exchange*.

Tax home. Since travel expenses of an employee are deductible only if the taxpayer is away from home, the deductibility of such expenses rests upon the definition of tax home. The IRS position is that tax home is the business location, post, or station of the taxpayer. If an employee is temporarily reassigned to a new post for a period of one year or less, the taxpayer's home should be his or her personal residence, and the travel expenses should be deductible. If the assignment is for more than two years, the IRS position is that it is indefinite or permanent and the taxpayer is therefore not in travel status. If the assignment is for between one and two years, the IRS position is that the location of the tax home will be determined on the basis of the facts and circumstances. The courts are in conflict regarding what constitutes a person's home for tax purposes. For such costs paid or incurred after December 31, 1992, the Energy Policy Act of 1992 provides that the taxpayer shall not be treated as temporarily away from home if the employment period exceeds one year. Thus, in this situation, the tax home will be the place of employment. See also *travel expenses*.

Tax preferences. Those items set forth in § 57 that may result in the imposition of the alternative minimum tax. See also *alternative minimum tax (AMT)*.

Tax rate schedules. Rate schedules appearing in Appendix A that are used by upper-income taxpayers and those not permitted to use the tax table. Separate rate schedules are provided for married individuals filing jointly, head of household, single taxpayers, estates and trusts, and married individuals filing separate returns. § 1.

Tax research. The method used to determine the best available solution to a situation that possesses tax consequences. Both tax and nontax factors are considered.

Tax shelters. The typical tax shelter generated large losses in the early years of the activity. Investors would offset these losses against other types of income and, therefore, avoid paying income taxes on this income. These tax shelter investments could then be sold after a few years and produce capital gain income, which is taxed at a lower rate than ordinary income. The passive activity loss rules and the at-risk rules now limit tax shelter deductions.

Tax table. A tax table appearing in Appendix A that is provided for taxpayers with less than $100,000 of taxable income. Separate columns are provided for single taxpayers, married taxpayers filing jointly, head of household, and married taxpayers filing separately. § 3.

Technical advice memoranda (TAMs). TAMs are issued by the National Office of the IRS in response to questions raised by IRS field personnel during audits. They deal with completed rather than proposed transactions and are often requested for questions related to exempt organizations and employee plans.

Temporary regulation. A Regulation issued by the Treasury Department in temporary form. When speed is critical, the Treasury Department issues Temporary Regulations, which take effect immediately. These Regulations have the same authoritative value as final Regulations and may be cited as precedent for three years. Temporary Regulations are also issued as Proposed Regulations. See also *proposed regulation* and *regulations*.

Theft loss. A loss from larceny, embezzlement, and robbery. It does not include misplacement of items. See also *casualty loss*.

Thin capitalization. When debt owed by a corporation to its shareholders is large relative to its capital structure (stock and shareholder equity), the IRS may contend that the corporation is thinly capitalized. In effect, this means that some or all of the debt will be reclassified as equity. The immediate result is to disallow any interest deduction to the corporation on the reclassified debt. To the extent of the corporation's earnings and profits, interest payments and loan repayments on the reclassified debt are treated as dividends to the shareholders. § 385.

Thirty-day letter. A letter that accompanies a Revenue Agent's Report (RAR) issued as a result of an IRS audit of a taxpayer (or the rejection of a taxpayer's claim for refund). The letter outlines the taxpayer's appeal procedure before the IRS. If the taxpayer does not request any such procedures within the 30-day period, the IRS will issue a *statutory notice of deficiency* (the 90-day letter).

Timber. Special rules apply to the recognition of gain from the sale of timber. A taxpayer may elect to treat the cutting of timber that is held for sale or use in a trade or business as a sale or exchange. If the holding period requirements are met, the gain is recognized as § 1231 gain and may therefore receive long-term capital gain treatment. § 631.

Top-heavy plan. A type of retirement plan that primarily benefits key employees. Such plans allocate more than 60 percent of the cumulative benefits to key employees. Special rules are imposed to discourage retirement plans from conferring disproportionate benefits on key employees.

Trade or business expenses. Deductions *for* AGI that are attributable to a taxpayer's business or profession. Some employee expenses may also be treated as trade or business expenses. See also *employee expenses*.

Transportation expenses. Transportation expenses for an employee include only the cost of transportation (taxi fares, automobile expenses, etc.) in the course of employment when the employee is not away from home in travel status. Commuting expenses are not deductible. See also *automobile expenses*.

Travel expenses. Travel expenses include meals (subject to a 50 percent disallowance) and lodging and transportation expenses while away from home in the pursuit of a trade or business (including that of an employee). See also *tax home*.

Trial court. The court of original jurisdiction; the first court to consider litigation. In Federal tax controversies, trial courts include U.S. District Courts, the U.S. Tax Court, and the U.S. Court of Federal Claims. See also *appellate court*.

U

Unearned income. Also referred to as investment income, it includes such income as interest, dividends, capital gains, rents, royalties, and pension and annuity income. See also *kiddie tax*.

Unearned (prepaid) income. For tax purposes, prepaid income (e.g., rent) is taxable in the year of receipt. In certain cases involving advance payments for goods and services, income may be deferred. See Rev.Proc. 71–21 (1971–2 C.B. 549) and Reg. § 1.451–5. See also *accrual method*.

Uniform capitalization rules. Under § 263A, the Regulations provide a set of rules that all taxpayers (regardless of the particular industry) can use to determine the items of cost (and means of allocating those costs) that must be capitalized with respect to the production of tangible property.

Unreasonable compensation. Under § 162(a)(1), a deduction is allowed for "reasonable" salaries or other compensation for personal services actually rendered. To the extent compensation is excessive ("unreasonable"), no deduction will be allowed. The problem of unreasonable compensation usually is limited to closely held corporations where the motivation is to pay out profits in some form deductible to the corporation. Deductible compensation, therefore, becomes an attractive substitute for nondeductible dividends when the shareholders are also employees of the corporation.

U.S. Court of Federal Claims. See *Claims Court*.

Use tax. A use tax is an ad valorem tax, usually at the same rate as the sales tax, on the use or consumption of tangible personalty. The purpose of a use tax is to prevent the avoidance of a sales tax.

U.S. Supreme Court. The highest appellate court or the court of last resort in the Federal court system and in most states. Only a small number of tax decisions of the U.S. Courts of Appeal are reviewed by the U.S. Supreme Court under its certiorari procedure. The Supreme Court usually grants certiorari to resolve a conflict among the Courts of Appeal (e.g., two or more appellate courts have assumed opposing positions on a particular issue) or when the tax issue is extremely important (e.g., size of the revenue loss to the Federal government).

U.S. Tax Court. See *Tax Court*.

USTC. Published by Commerce Clearing House, *U.S. Tax Cases* contain all of the Federal tax decisions issued by the U.S. District Courts, U.S. Court of Federal Claims, U.S. Courts of Appeals, and the U.S. Supreme Court.

V

Vacation home. The Code places restrictions upon taxpayers who rent their residences or vacation homes for part of the tax year. The restrictions may result in a scaling down of expense deductions for the taxpayers. § 280A. See also *hobby loss*.

Value added tax (VAT). A national sales tax that taxes the increment in value as goods move through the production process. A VAT is much used in other countries, but has not yet been incorporated as part of the U.S. Federal tax structure.

Vesting requirements. A qualified deferred compensation arrangement must satisfy a vesting requirement. Under this provision, an employee's right to accrued plan benefits derived from employer contributions must be nonforfeitable in accordance with one of two vesting time period schedules.

W

Wash sale. A loss from the sale of stock or securities that is disallowed because the taxpayer within 30 days before or after the sale has acquired stock or securities that are substantially identical to those sold. § 1091.

Wherewithal to pay. This concept recognizes the inequity of taxing a transaction when the taxpayer lacks the means with which to pay the tax. Under it, there is a correlation between the imposition of the tax and the ability to pay the tax. It is particularly suited to situations in which the taxpayer's economic position has not changed significantly as a result of the transaction.

Withholding allowances. The number of withholding allowances serves as the basis for determining the amount of income taxes withheld from an employee's salary or wages. The more withholding allowances claimed, the less income tax withheld by an employer. An employee may claim withholding allowances for personal exemptions for self and spouse (unless claimed as a dependent of another person), dependency exemptions, and special withholding allowances.

Working condition fringe. A type of fringe benefit received by the employee that is excludible from the employee's gross income. It consists of property or services provided (paid or reimbursed) by the employer for which the employee could take a tax deduction if the employee had paid for them. § 132.

Work opportunity tax credit. Employers are allowed a tax credit equal to 35 percent of the first $6,000 of wages (per eligible employee) for the first year of employment. Eligible employees include certain hard-to-employ individuals (e.g., qualified ex-felons, high risk youth, food stamp recipients, and veterans). The employer's deduction for wages is reduced by the amount of the credit taken. For qualified summer youth employees, the 35 percent rate is applied to the first $3,000 of qualified wages. §§ 51 and 52.

Worthless securities. A loss (usually capital) is allowed for a security that becomes worthless during the year. The loss is deemed to have occurred on the last day of the year. Special rules apply to securities of affiliated companies and small business stock. § 165. See also *Section 1244 stock*.

Writ of certiorari. See *certiorari*.

Z

Zero bracket amount. A deduction that was generally available to all individual taxpayers in arriving at taxable income. It represented the equivalent of the standard deduction for taxable years before 1987. The taxpayer did not take a deduction for the zero bracket amount because it was built into the tax tables and tax rate schedules. Because the amount was built in, if the taxpayer itemized deductions, only the excess itemized deductions (amount of the itemized deductions in excess of the zero bracket amount) were deductible. TRA of 1986 repealed the zero bracket amount and replaced it with the standard deduction for 1987 and thereafter. The zero bracket amount for 1986 is presently used in the 10-year forward averaging calculation for lump-sum distributions. § 63(c). See also *standard deduction*.

APPENDIX D-1
Table of Code Sections Cited

[See Title 26 U.S.C.A.]

I.R.C. Sec.	This Work Page	I.R.C. Sec.	This Work Page
1	2–7, 18–6	47	13–17
1(a)	3–24	48(q)	8–7
1(g)	3–19, 20–35	50(c)	13–8
1–5	2–6	51	13–10, 13–24
2	2–7, 2–8	53	12–24
2(a)	2–6, 3–26	55	12–3
2(a)(1)(A)	2–6, 2–7	55(b)(1)	12–8
2(b)	3–26	55(b)(1)(B)	12–27
2(b)(1)(A)	3–26	55(d)	12–7
2(b)(1)(B)	3–26	55(d)(2)	12–27
5	2–6	56	12–4, 12–30
11	2–6	56(a)(1)	12–10
11(b)	20–13	56(a)(2)	12–11
11–12	2–6	56(a)(3)	12–12
12(d)	2–7	56(a)(4)	12–15
21	13–20, 13–23	56(a)(5)	12–11
21(c)	13–22	56(a)(7)	12–13
22	13–16, 13–23	56(b)(1)(A)	12–17
23	13–19, 13–23	56(b)(1)(B)	12–17
23(b)(1)	13–19	56(b)(1)(C)	12–18
23(d)(3)	13–19	56(b)(1)(D)	12–17
26(a)	12–8	56(b)(1)(E)	12–20
27	13–18, 13–23	56(b)(1)(F)	12–17
31	13–23	56(b)(2)(A)(i)	12–9
32	13–14, 13–23	56(b)(3)	12–13
32(a)(2)(B)	13–15	56(c)	12–28
32(c)(5)	13–15	56(g)	12–28
38	13–23	56(g)(2)	12–29
38(c)	13–6	56(g)(6)	12–28
39(a)(1)	13–7	57	12–5, 12–30
41	7–18, 13–10, 13–24	57(a)(1)	12–20
41(b)(3)(A)	13–11	57(a)(2)	12–21
41(d)	13–11	57(a)(3)	19–34
41(e)	13–12	57(a)(5)	12–21
42	13–12, 13–24	57(a)(6)	12–22
44	13–14, 13–24	57(a)(7)	12–23
46	13–24	58	12–30

I.R.C. Sec.	This Work Page
59(e)(2)(A)	12–9
59(e)(2)(D)	12–12
59(e)(2)(E)	12–12
61	4–2, 20–16
61(a)	3–3
61(a)(12)	5–33
61(a)(3)	14–7
62	3–5, 6–3
62 63(b)–(h)	20–16
62(a)(1)	6–31, 7–15, 9–3
62(a)(1) or (3)	6–31
62(a)(1) or (4)	6–31
62(a)(15)	6–31, 9–13
62(a)(2)	9–21
62(a)(2)(A)	6–31
62(a)(2)(B)	6–31
62(a)(4)	6–5, 6–31, 7–15
62(b)	9–21
63(a)	20–16
63(c)(1)	3–7
63(c)(5)	3–9
63(c)(6)	3–9
63(d)	6–4, 10–14
66	2–41, 4–19
67	5–23, 6–31, 9–25
67(b)(3)	7–15
71	4–20
71(b)(1)	4–20
71(c)(2)	4–23
71(f)	4–21
71(f)(5)(A)	4–22
71(f)(5)(C)	4–22
71–90	4–19
72	19–12
72(b)	4–31
72(d)	4–31
72(e)(3)	4–28
72(q)	4–29
72(t)	19–10, 19–26
72(t)(2)(B)	19–26
72(t)(2)(D)	19–26
73	4–14
74	4–32
74(b)	4–32
74(c)	4–33, 5–3
79	4–33, 5–3
79(d)	4–34, 5–25
83	19–31, 19–41
83(a)	4–10
83(a)(1)	19–31
83(b)	19–32, 19–47, 19–48
83(c)	19–32
85	4–34
86	4–34, 5–3, 19–22
101	5–3, 14–29
101 through 150	5–4

I.R.C. Sec.	This Work Page
101(a)	5–6
101(a)(1)	14–29
101(g)	5–3, 5–7
102	5–3, 5–4
102(a)	14–12
102(c)	5–5
103	5–3, 5–48, 6–29
103(a)	5–28
103(b)	5–29
104	5–3
104(a)(1)	5–12
104(a)(2)	5–11
104(a)(3)	5–13
105	5–3, 5–14
105(a)	5–13
105(b)	5–13
105(c)	5–13
105(h)	5–14, 5–25
106	5–3, 5–13
106(b)	5–3, 5–14
107	5–3, 5–17
108	5–3, 5–33
108(a)	5–33
108(b)	5–33
108(c)	5–33
108(e)	5–33
108(e)(5)	5–33
108(e)(6)	5–34
108(f)	5–34
108(g)	5–33
109	5–3, 5–4, 14–24
111	5–3, 5–32, 12–43
111(a)	5–32
112	5–3
117	4–32, 5–3, 9–15
117(a)	2–32, 5–9
117(b)	5–9
117(d)	5–10
118	20–17
119	5–3, 5–15, 5–21
119(a)	5–15
119(d)	5–17
121	5–3, 14–8, 15–2, 15–3, 15–16, 15–23, 15–24, 15–25, 15–29, 15–30, 15–31, 15–35, 15–40, 15–44, 15–45
121(a)	15–23
121(b)(2)	15–23
121(b)	15–23
121(c)	15–23
123	5–3
125	5–3, 5–19, 19–41
125(f)	5–19
127	5–3, 5–18, 9–15
127(b)(2)	5–25
129	5–3, 5–18
131	5–3

Table of Code Sections Cited

I.R.C. Sec.	This Work Page
132	5–3, 5–20
132(a)(6)	9–13
132(c)	5–22
132(d)	5–23
132(f)	5–23
132(g)	9–13
132(j)(1)	5–24, 5–25
132(j)(3)	5–23
132(j)(4)	5–18
134	5–3, 5–18
135	5–3, 5–30, 19–22
137	5–3, 5–18
141	12–21
151(c)(1)	3–14
151(c)(1)	2–32
151(c)(1)(B)	2–24, 2–32
151(c)(2)	2–30, 2–32, 3–15
151(d)	2–24
151(d)(2)	2–30, 2–32
152(a)	2–32, 3–14, 3–26
152(b)(2)	3–14
152(b)(5)	2–49, 3–14
152(c)	3–12
152(d)	2–24, 3–42
152(e)	3–13
162	6–3, 6–5, 6–6, 6–13, 6–31, 6–34, 20–16
162(a)	6–5, 6–31, 9–3, 9–8
162(a)(f)	6–46
162(a)(1)	6–7
162(a)(2)	6–31
162(c)	6–12
162(c)(1)	6–6
162(c)(2)	9–37
162(e)	6–14
162(f)	6–12
162(g)	6–12
162(l)	10–8
162(m)	6–14, 19–30
163	19–49
163(a)	6–31, 10–14
163(d)	6–31, 20–27
163(h)	6–31
163(h)(3)	10–15
164	10–10, 10–11, 13–18
164(a)(1)	6–31
164(a)(2)	6–31
164(a)(3)	6–31
164(f)	13–35, 19–21
165	6–7
165(a)	14–7
165(c)	7–9
165(c)(1)	6–31
165(c)(3)	6–31, 7–13, 15–15
165(g)	7–7
165(g)(1)	16–9
165(h)	7–12, 7–16

I.R.C. Sec.	This Work Page
165(h)(4)(E)	7–13
165(i)	7–14, 18–10
165(k)	7–12
165(l)	7–6
166	6–31
166(a)	7–3
166(d)	16–29
167	8–2, 8–3, 14–24, 17–13
168	8–2, 14–24, 17–13
168(b)	8–8, 8–13
168(c)	8–13
168(b)(5)	8–15
168(d)(3)	8–10
168(d)(4)(A)	8–9
168(e)	8–8, 8–13
168(e)(2)(A)	17–18
168(e)(3)	8–23
168(f)	8–4
168(g)	8–23
168(g)(3)(B)	8–23
170	6–31, 10–19, 17–20
170(a)(2)	20–8
170(b)(2)	20–9
170(c)	10–20, 10–21
170(d)(2)	20–9
170(e)	16–29
170(e)(1)(A)	10–47, 17–20
170(e)(1)(B)	17–20
170(e)(3)	20–9
170(f)(8)	10–22
170(i)	10–20
170(j)	10–20
170(l)	10–20
171(c)	14–6
172	7–20, 18–10
172(d)	7–22, 20–10
173(a)	12–9
174	7–17, 13–11
174(b)(2)	7–18
179	2–48, 8–1, 8–15, 8–16, 8–17, 8–19, 8–24, 8–29, 8–43, 8–44, 8–45, 8–46, 8–47, 8–48, 8–49, 8–50, 9–7, 9–26, 13–47, 14–24, 17–13, 17–14, 17–19, 17–21, 17–24, 17–30, 18–43
179(b)	8–15
179(a)	8–15
183	2–18, 6–17, 6–33
183(b)(2)	6–17
183(d)	6–17
1843(c)(2)	4–22
195	6–16
197	6–26, 8–24, 8–45, 16–28, 17–13, 17–19
197(a)	8–24
211	2–6
211–219	20–32
212	3–6, 6–3, 6–4, 6–5, 6–6, 6–29, 6–31, 9–20, 9–25, 10–28, 20–16, 20–27

I.R.C. Sec.	This Work Page
212(1)	2–6
212(3)	10–6
213	6–31, 19–10
213(a)	6–25
213(d)(1)(A)	10–4
213(d)(2)	10–7
215	4–20
217	5–24, 5–26, 15–17, 15–18
217(a)	9–11
217(b)	9–12
219	6–3
219(b)(1)	19–22
219(c)	19–25
219(c)(2)	19–22
219(f)(1)	19–25
219(f)(3)	19–25
219(g)	19–22
219(g)(4)	19–22
220	5–14
241	2–6
243(a)	20–11
246(b)	20–11
248	20–12
262	6–25, 6–31, 10–2, 10–27, 16–17
263A	18–32
263A(d)	18–13
263(a)(1)	6–26
263(c)	17–23
265	6–29, 6–45
265(a)(2)	10–18
267	6–27, 6–28, 14–17, 14–18, 14–26, 14–27, 16–17, 19–36
267(a)(1)	6–27, 14–7
267(b)	15–4, 18–23
267(d)	14–18
269A	19–18
269A(b)(2)	11–11
274	8–21
274(a)(1)(A)	9–16
274(a)(3)	9–18
274(b)(1)	9–18
274(c)	9–10
274(d)	8–21, 9–22
274(d)	9–37
274(e)(2)	9–16
274(e)(9)	9–16
274(e)(4)	9–16
274(h)(1)	9–9
274(i)	8–21
274(j)	4–33
274(k)	9–17
274(k)(1)(B)	9–17
274(l)	9–18
274(m)(2)	9–9
274(m)(3)	9–9
274(n)	9–16

I.R.C. Sec.	This Work Page
274(n)(2)	9–16
275	10–11
276	6–14
280A	6–19, 6–46
280A–280H	2–6
280A(c)(1)	9–19
280A(d)	6–20, 6–23
280A(g)	6–20
280C(c)	13–11
280E	6–13, 6–14
280F	8–17, 17–24
280F(a)(2)	8–19
280F(b)(2)	8–20
280F(b)(3)	8–20
280F(b)(4)	8–18
280F(d)(1)	8–19
280F(d)(4)	8–18
280F(d)(5)	8–18
280G	19–29, 19–47
280H	18–6
291	17–38, 20–8, 20–16
291(a)(1)	17–23
301	20–21, 20–22
301(c)	5–29
302	20–22
303	20–22
305(a)	5–30, 14–11
305(b)	5–30
307(a)	14–11
307(b)	14–11
311	20–21
311(b)	17–21
312	20–20
316	20–20
316(a)	5–29
318	19–17
318(a)	18–23
331	20–2, 20–23, 20–42
332	17–20, 20–23
334	20–2, 20–23
334(a)	20–23
334(b)(1)	20–23, 20–24
336	20–24
336(d)	20–24
338	20–2, 20–23
341(e)	2–26
351	17–20, 18–26, 20–18, 20–19, 20–38
358(a)	20–19
362(a)	20–19
368(c)	20–18
385	20–18
401(a)	19–6, 19–7
401(a)(17)	19–15
401(a)(26)	19–9
401(a)(4)	19–7, 19–8, 19–17
401(a)(5)	19–7

Table of Code Sections Cited

I.R.C. Sec.	This Work Page
401(a)(9)	19–10
401(c)(2)	19–21
401(c)(2)(A)(v)	19–21
401(d)	19–20
401(k)	19–2, 19–3, 19–18, 19–19, 19–21, 19–38, 19–39, 19–40, 19–42, 19–44, 19–46, 19–47, 19–48
401(k)(3)	19–40
402(a)(1)	19–11
402(a)(2)	19–45
402(a)(5)	19–12
402(e)(1)	19–13
402(e)(1)(C)	19–12
402(e)(1)(D)	19–12
402(e)(4)(J)	19–12, 19–13
402(e)(4)(L)	19–12
404	19–15
404(a)(1)	19–16
404(a)(6)	19–16
404(a)(1)(D)	19–16
404(a)(3)(A)	19–17
404(a)(7)	19–17
404(d)	19–28
404(h)(1)(A)	19–24
404(h)(1)(B)	19–25
404(j)	19–15
404(l)	19–15
408(d)(1)	19–26
408(d)(2)	19–26
408(d)(3)(B)	19–26
408(d)(4)	19–25
408(j)	19–23
408(k)(2)	19–23
408(o)	19–23
408(p)	19–19
409(h)(1)	19–6
410(a)(1)(A)	19–8
410(a)(1)(B)	19–8
410(a)(4)	19–8
410(b)	19–8
410(b)(3)	19–9
410(b)(4)	19–9
414(i)	19–4
414(j)	19–4
414(q)	19–8
415	19–15
415(b)	19–15
415(b)(1)	19–15, 19–21
415(c)	19–15
415(c)(1)	19–21
416(b)	19–18
416(i)(1)	19–17
421	4–22
421(a)	12–13
421(a)(1)	19–34
421(a)(2)	19–34

I.R.C. Sec.	This Work Page
422	19–34, 19–41
422(a)	19–34
422(a)(1)	19–34
422(a)(2)	19–35
422(c)(3)	19–35
422(b)	19–36
422(c)(5)	19–37
422(e)	4–23
441(a)(d)	4–7
441(c)	18–3
441(f)	18–3
441(i)	18–6
442	18–7
443(b)(1)	18–9
443(b)(2)	18–10
444	18–5, 18–6
444(c)	18–6
446	18–11
446(a)	6–9
446(b)	4–8, 4–12, 18–11
446(b)(e)	6–9
446(c)	18–16
446(d)	18–11
446(e)	4–8
446(f)	18–17
447	18–12
447(c)	18–12
448	6–10
448(a)	18–12
448(b)	18–12
448(d)(2)	11–11
448(d)(5)	18–15
451(a)	19–28
451(d)	18–10
453	2–35
453A	4–8
453(a)	15–30, 18–20, 18–26
453(a)(b)	4–8
453B(a)	18–26
453B(c) (d)(g)	18–26
453B(f)(2)	18–26
453(b)	18–19
453(d)	18–27
453(d)(3)	18–27
453(e)	18–23
453(e)(2)	18–24
453(e)(2)(B)	18–24
453(e)(6)(7)	18–24
453(f)(1)	18–23
453(g)	18–25
453(i)	8–19, 17–21
453(l)	18–19
453(l)(2)	18–20
454(a)	4–12
460	18–28
460(b)(1)(A)	18–30

I.R.C. Sec.	This Work Page
460(b)(2)	18–31
460(b)(5)	18–31
460(f)	18–27
461(g)(1)	10–18
461(g)(2)	10–16
461(h)	6–10, 18–13
461(h)(3)(A)	6–10
461(h)(4)	18–13
464	18–12
464(c)	18–12
465(b)(1)	11–4
465(b)(6)	11–5
465(e)	11–5
468	18–14
469	6–19, 11–6, 11–11, 11–15, 11–18, 11–19, 19–22, 20–27
469(a)	11–10
469(b)	11–9
469(c)(2)	11–19
469(c)(7)	11–22
469(c)(7)(A)	11–36
469(c)(7)(B)	11–23
469(d)(2)	11–9
469(f)	11–26
469(g)(2)	11–25
469(g)(3)	11–26
469(i)	11–24
469(i)(6)	11–24
469(j)(2)	11–11
469(j)(5)	11–24
469(j)(6)	11–26
469(j)(8)	11–19
471	18–32
471(a)	18–31
472(c)	12–29, 18–37
472(d)	18–37
481(b)	18–18
483	18–22, 18–24
483(e)	18–24
501	10–21
501(a)	19–12
529	5–3, 5–31
530	9–3
585	18–15
611(a)	8–27
612	8–26
613	8–29
613A	8–27
613A(c)	12–20
613(a)	8–27
616(a)	12–11
617(a)	12–11
631	17–5
631(a)	17–5
652(a)	4–17
662(a)	4–17

I.R.C. Sec.	This Work Page
702(a)	20–32
703(a)	20–32
704(e)	20–35
705(a)	20–31
706(a)	4–16
706(b)(1)(B)	18–4
706(b)(1)(C)	18–5
706(b)(3)	18–4
707	14–18
707(b)(1)	20–33
707(c)	20–33
708(a)	2–48
721	11–26, 17–21, 20–30
722	20–30
723	20–31
901–908	13–18
904	13–19
904(c)	13–19
911	5–3, 5–31, 19–22
911(a)	5–25
911(c)	5–27
911(d)	5–27
912(1)(C)	6–45
1001(a)	14–3
1001(b)	14–3
1001(c)	14–7
1011	14–14
1011(a)	14–4
1012	14–9
1014(a)	14–15
1014(b)(6)	14–17
1014(e)	14–16
1015(a)	14–12
1015(d)(6)	14–13
1016(a)	14–4
1016(a)(2)	14–5
1016(a)(4)	14–6
1016(a)(5)	14–6
1017	5–33
1031	11–26, 14–8, 14–9, 15–2, 15–3, 15–4, 15–5, 15–7, 15–11, 15–15, 15–26, 15–28, 15–29, 15–32, 17–21, 17–35
1031(a)	15–3
1032	15–2, 15–26, 19–6, 20–17
1033	14–8, 15–2, 15–9, 15–10, 15–11, 15–14, 15–15, 15–23, 15–24, 15–29, 15–31, 15–33, 15–34, 15–39, 17–8, 17–21
1033(a)	15–10, 15–11
1033(a)(2)(A)	15–14
1033(a)(2)(B)	15–13
1033(b)	15–14
1033(g)(4)	15–13
1034	10–15, 14–8, 14–21, 15–2, 15–15, 15–16, 15–17, 15–19, 15–20, 15–22, 15–23, 15–24, 15–25, 15–29, 15–30, 15–31, 15–34, 15–35, 15–44, 15–45

Table of Code Sections Cited

I.R.C. Sec.	This Work Page
1034(h)(1)	15–18
1034(h)(2)	15–18
1034(k)	15–18
1035	15–2, 15–26
1036	15–2, 15–26
1038	15–2, 15–26
1041	4–20, 14–18, 15–2, 15–27, 18–23
1042(c)(4)	19–6
1044	15–2, 15–27
1056	16–14, 16–31
1060	14–10
1091	14–18, 14–19
1091(a)	14–19
1091(b)	14–20
1091(d)	14–19
1202	5–3, 12–25
1211(a)	16–27
1211(a)(b)	20–7
1211(b)	16–21
1211(b)(1)	16–23
1212(a)	20–7
1212(a)(1)	16–27
1212(b)	16–24
1221	3–28, 16–4, 16–6, 16–7, 16–8
1221(1)	2–6
1221(2)	17–2, 17–3
1221(3)	10–47
1222	16–16
1222(10)	16–23
1223	16–16
1223(1)	15–8
1223(11)	14–17
1223(2)	14–13, 14–18, 20–32
1223(4)	14–19
1223(5)	14–11
1223(6)	19–33
1231	6–26, 10–24, 14–10, 15–8, 16–3, 16–5, 16–16, 16–32, 17–1, 17–2, 17–3, 17–4, 17–5, 17–6, 17–7, 17–8, 17–9, 17–10, 17–11, 17–12, 17–13, 17–14, 17–15, 17–16, 17–17, 17–18, 17–19, 17–20, 17–21, 17–22, 17–24, 17–25, 17–29, 17–30, 17–31, 17–32, 17–33, 17–34, 17–36, 17–37, 18–22, 20–8, 20–27, 20–28
1233	16–17
1233(a)	2–35
1233(b)(2)	2–35
1234A	16–9
1234(a)	16–10
1235	16–12
1236(a)(b)	16–7
1237	16–7, 16–8, 16–33
1239	17–23
1239(b)(c)	18–25
1241	16–15
1242	16–29

I.R.C. Sec.	This Work Page
1244	7–1, 7–7, 7–8, 7–9, 7–27, 7–28, 7–30, 7–34, 7–35, 7–36, 16–2, 16–9, 16–29, 16–33
1245	8–6, 16–14, 16–15, 17–1, 17–2, 17–12, 17–13, 17–14, 17–15, 17–16, 17–19, 17–20, 17–21, 17–22, 17–24, 17–29, 17–30, 17–31, 17–32, 17–35, 17–38, 18–19, 18–22, 18–46, 20–6, 20–8, 20–16
1245(b)(1)	17–20
1245(b)(2)	17–20
1245(b)(3)	17–20, 17–21
1245(d)	17–21
1250	17–1, 17–2, 17–12, 17–14, 17–16, 17–17, 17–18, 17–19, 17–20, 17–21, 17–23, 17–24, 17–29, 17–30, 17–31, 17–32, 17–35, 18–19, 18–22, 18–46, 20–6, 20–8, 20–16, 20–40
1250(a)(1)	17–18
1250(a)(1)(B)	17–19
1250(a)(2)	17–18
1250(d)(1)	17–20
1250(d)(2)	17–20
1250(d)(3)	17–20, 17–21
1250(i)	17–21
1253	16–13, 16–14
1253(b)(1)	16–13
1253(e)	16–14
1254	17–24
1271	16–9
1272(a)	18–22
1272(a)(2)	4–11
1272(a)(3)	4–11, 18–24
1272–1275	16–10
1273(a)	4–11, 18–22
1273(a)(3)	16–10
1274	18–22
1274(a)	18–22
1274A	18–24
1274A(c)	18–24
1274(a)	18–24
1274(c)(3)(A)	18–24
1274(c)(3)(B)	18–24
1274(c)(3)(C)	18–24
1274(c)(3)(F)	18–24
1274(d)(1)	18–22
1276–1288	16–10
1341	18–10
1361(a)	4–17
1361(b)	20–25
1361–1379	2–6
1362	20–25
1366	4–17, 20–26
1366(e)	20–36
1367	20–28
1371(a)(1)	2–48
1378(a)(b)	18–5
1378(b)(2)	18–5

I.R.C. Sec.	This Work Page	I.R.C. Sec.	This Work Page
1402(a)	19–21	6654	3–18, 13–22
1402(a)(12)	13–35	6654(b)(2)	13–34
2032(a)(1)	14–15	6654(b)(3)	13–34
2032(c)	14–15	6654(c)(1)	13–33
2040(b)	14–17	6655	20–14
2503(a)	2–48	6655(f)	20–14
3401	13–28	6656	13–22
3402	3–18, 13–28, 19–33	6659	10–48
3403	13–22	6661	2–30
3405(c)	19–27	6662	2–8, 2–30
3406(a)	13–33	6662(a)	2–28
4972	19–16	6662(b)(1)	2–28, 9–37
4973(a)(1)	19–25	6662(b)(3)	10–48
4973(b)(1)	19–25	6662(c)	2–28
4973(b)(2)	19–25	7482(a)(c)	2–18
4974(a)	19–10	7519	18–6
4975(e)(7)	19–6	7519(b)	18–6
4979(a)	19–19	7702B	5–3, 5–15
4981A	19–11	7703(a)(1)	3–43
4999	19–29	7805	2–8
6001	9–37	7805(a)	2–9
6012(a)(1)	3–21	7805(e)	2–9
6012(a)(2)	20–14	7852(d)	2–7
6017	13–35	7872(a)(1)	4–24
6031	20–32	7872(b)(2)(f)(2)	4–25
6072(a)	3–23	7872(c)	4–25
6081	20–14	7872(c)(2)	4–26
6110	2–11	7872(c)(3)	4–28
6110(j)(3)	2–12	7872(d)	4–26
6621	18–26		

APPENDIX D-2
Table of Regulations Cited

Temporary Treasury Regulations

Temp.Reg. Sec.	This Work Page
1.263A–1(a)	18–33
1.263A–1(h)(5)	18–33
1.263A–1T(b)(3)(iii)(A)(1)	18–28
1.417(e)–1T(d)	2–9
1.469–1T(e)(3)(ii)	11–19
1.469–1T(e)(3)(iv)	11–20
1.469–1T(e)(3)(vi)(B)–(E)	11–20
1.469–5T(a)	11–15
1.469–5T(b)(2)	11–18
1.469–5T(e)(3)(ii)	11–19
1.469–5T(f)(3)	11–18
1.706–1T(a)(2)	18–4
15a.453–1(b)(2)(iii)	18–21
15a.453–1(d)	18–27
15a.453–1(d)(4)	18–27
35.3405–1	19–27

Treasury Regulations

Reg. Sec.	This Work Page
1.2	2–8
1.61–12	4–6
1.61–1(a)	4–6
1.61–2 T(j)	5–25
1.61–2(d)(2)(i)	14–9
1.61–2(d)(4)	19–28
1.61–3(a)	6–14, 9–37
1.61–6(a)	14–7, 14–10
1.61–9(c)	4–15
1.67–1T(a)(1)(iv)	6–18
1.72–7(c)(1)	5–8
1.72–9	4–28, 19–10
1.79–3(d)(2)	4–33
1.83–2(a)	19–32
1.83–3(c)(2)	19–32

Treasury Regulations

Reg. Sec.	This Work Page
1.83–6(a)	19–33
1.83–6(c)	19–32
1.83–7	19–37
1.83–7(a);	19–37
1.101–7T	5–8
1.106–1	5–13
1.107–1	5–17
1.117–2(a)	5–8
1.117–6(b)(2)	5–9
1.117–6(c)(3)(i)	5–9
1.117–6(d)	5–10
1.117–6(h)	5–9
1.119–1(c)(1)	5–16
1.119–1(f)	5–16
1.121–2(b)	15–23
1.121–4(b)	15–24
1.121–4(c)	15–24
1.132–1(b)	5–21
1.132–2	5–21
1.151–3(a)	3–14
1.151–3(b)	2–30, 2–32
1.151–3(b)(c)	3–14
1.152–1(c)	2–24, 2–32, 3–11
1.162–12(a)	18–13
1.162–17(b)(4)	9–22
1.162–21(b)	6–46
1.162–2(b)(1)	9–10
1.162–5(b)(2)(3)	9–14
1.162–5(b)(2)(iii)	9–14
1.162–5(b)(3)(ii)	9–14
1.162–8	6–7
1.164–4(a)	10–12
1.165–1(a)	14–7
1.165–1(d)(2)	7–10
1.165–1(d)(2)(i)	7–11
1.165–7	15–15
1.165–7(a)(2)(ii)	7–13

Treasury Regulations

Reg. Sec.	This Work Page
1.165–8(a)(2)	7–10
1.165–8(d)	7–10
1.165–9(b)(2)	14–20
1.166	7–3
1.166–1(e)	7–3
1.166–5(d)	7–5
1.167(g)–1	14–14, 14–20
1.170A–1(e)	10–48
1.170A–4(b)(1)	17–20
1.170A–4(b)(3)(ii)(b)	10–25
1.170–4(A)(b)(2)(ii)(C)	2–48
1.172–3(a)	7–22
1.174–2(a)(1)	7–17
1.179–1(e)	8–17
1.183–1(b)(1)	6–18
1.183–2(b)(1)–(9)	6–17
1.212–1(d)	6–6
1.212–1(f)	9–14
1.212–1(g)	6–5
1.213–1(e)(1)(v)	10–5
1.263(a)–1(b)	6–26
1.263A–1(b)(12)	18–33
1.267(d)–1(a)	14–18
1.267(d)–1(c)(3)	14–18
1.274–4	9–10
1.274–5T(c)(3)	9–22
1.280A–3(c)	6–20
1.280A–3(d)(4)	6–22
1.280F–6T(e)	8–18
1.280F–7T(a)	8–21
1.301–1(j)	14–9
1.307–1(a)	14–11
1.401–1(b)	19–6
1.401–1(b)(1)(iii)	19–6
1.401–1(b)(2)	19–6
1.401–4(a)(1)(iii)	19–6
1.408–4(b)(4)	19–26
1.421–1(a)(1)	19–34
1.421–6(c)	19–37
1.421–6(d)	19–37
1.421–6(e)	19–37
1.421–6(f)	19–37
1.421–7(a)(1)	19–34
1.441–1(b)(1)(ii)	18–3
1.441–1(b)(3)	18–7
1.441–1(b)(4)	18–7
1.441–1(e)(2)	18–3
1.442–1(b)(1)	18–7
1.442–1(c)(1)	18–7
1.443–1(a)(2)	18–10
1.446–1(a)(1)	18–11, 18–16
1.446–1(a)(2)	6–9
1.446–1(a)(3)(c)(1)(i)	4–8

Treasury Regulations

Reg. Sec.	This Work Page
1.446–1(a)(4)(i)	18–11, 18–12
1.446–1(c)(1)(iv)(b)	18–11
1.446–1(c)(2)(i)	4–7
1.446–1(e)(2)(ii)	18–16
1.446–1(e)(2)(ii)(b)	18–16
1.446–1(e)(3)	18–16
1.451–1(a)	4–9, 18–11, 18–13
1.451–2	19–28
1.451–2(a)	4–9, 19–28
1.451–2(b)	4–10
1.451–3	4–8
1.451–3(b)	18–27
1.451–3(b)(2)	18–28
1.451–3(c)(3)	18–31
1.451–3(d)(2)(ii)–(vii)	18–30
1.451–3(d)(9)	18–28
1.451–5	4–38, 18–30
1.451–5(b)	4–13
1.451–5(c)	4–13
1.461–1(a)	6–9
1.461–1(a)(1)	18–12
1.461–4(g)(2)–(6)	18–15
1.461–5(c)	18–15
1.469–4	11–12
1.469–4(c)(3)	11–12
1.469–4(d)	11–14
1.469–4(f)	11–13
1.469–9	11–23
1.469–9(e)	11–36
1.471–1–2	18–31
1.471–2(c)	18–34
1.471–3(b)	18–32
1.471–4(b)	18–32
1.471–4(c)	18–34
1.471–6(a)	18–12
1.472–2(c)	18–36
1.472–2(e)	18–37
1.472–3(a)	18–36
1.472–4	18–34
1.472–5	18–36
1.472–8	18–35
1.611–1(b)	8–25
1.631–1	17–5
1.641(a)–0(c)	2–16
1.6661–3(b)(2)	2–30
1.672(b)–1	2–48
1.706–1(a)	18–4
1.706–1(a)(1)	4–16
1.871–2(b)	5–27
1.1001–1(a)	14–3
1.1001–1(b)	14–3
1.1001–1(b)(2)	14–5
1.1001–1(c)(1)	14–3

Treasury Regulations

Reg. Sec.	This Work Page
1.1001–2(a)	5–32
1.1002–1(a)	14–7
1.1002–1(c)	15–2
1.1011–1	14–4, 14–14
1.1012–1(a)	14–9
1.1012–1(b)	14–5
1.1012–1(c)	14–39
1.1012–1(c)(1)	14–9
1.1015–1(a)(1)	14–12
1.1015–1(a)(3)	14–12
1.1016–1	14–4
1.1016–3(a)(1)(i)	14–5
1.1016–5(a)	14–6
1.1016–5(b)	14–6
1.1016–6(a)	14–5
1.1031(a)–1(a)	15–3
1.1031(a)–1(b)	15–4
1.1031(d)–2	15–9
1.1031(j)–1	15–4
1.1033(a)–1	15–11
1.1033(a)–1(a)	15–10
1.1033(a)–2(a)	15–10
1.1033(a)–2(c)(1)	15–14
1.1033(a)–2(c)(3)	15–13
1.1034–1(b)(7)	15–21
1.1034–1(b)(9)	15–21
1.1034–1(c)(3)	15–18
1.1034–1(c)(3)(i)	15–16
1.1034–1(c)(4)(i)	15–21
1.1034–1(c)(4)(ii)	15–21
1.1091–1(a)	14–19
1.1091–1(a)(f)	14–19
1.1091–1(f)	14–19
1.1091–1(c)	14–20

Treasury Regulations

Reg. Sec.	This Work Page
1.1091–2(a)	14–19
1.1221–1(b)	16–15
1.1223–1(a)	15–8
1.1223–1(b)	14–13
1.1223–1(d)	14–19
1.1223–1(e)	14–11
1.1223–1(f)	14–11
1.1234–1(a)(1)	16–10
1.1235–2(b)(1)	16–13
1.1236–1(a)	16–7
1.1241–1(a)	16–15
1.1245–1(c)–6(b)	17–21
1.1245–2(a)(4)	15–8
1.1245–2(a)(4)–2(c)(2)	17–20
1.1245–4(a)(1)	17–20
1.1245–4(c)	17–20, 17–21
1.1250–1(a)(4) –1(b)(4)–1(c)(2)	17–21
1.1250–1(d)(1)(i)(c)	17–18
1.1250–2(d)(1)	15–8
1.1250–2(d)(1)(3)–3(c)(3)	17–20
1.1250–3(a)(1)	17–20
1.1250–3(c)	17–20, 17–21
1.6013–1(a)(1)	3–32
1.6013–4(a)(1)	3–43
1.6081–4	3–23
1.7872–2(b)(1)(i)	4–26
20.2031–7(F)	2–48
31.3401(c)–(1)(b)	9–3
301.6114–1	2–7
301.6712–1	2–7
301.7701–1	20–5
301.7701–2	20–5
301.7701–2(a)	20–4
301.7701–3	20–5

Appendix D-3
Table of Revenue Procedures and Revenue Rulings Cited

Revenue Procedure

Rev.Proc.	This Work Page
71–21	4–13, 4–14, 4–38, 4–53
77–37	2–47
83–35	8–6
84–74	18–36
85–16	18–8
87–1	2–29
87–32	18–8, 18–37
87–56	8–8, 8–23, 8–50, 12–11
87–57	8–37, 8–42, 15–4
87–59	2–42
89–12	20–3
92–20	18–18, 18–36
92–71	6–29
94–27	10–17, 10–34
96–54	9–6
97–3	2–11

Revenue Rulings

Rev.Rul.	This Work Page
54–567	2–30
55–261	10–6
55–525	19–28
56–406	14–19
56–60	14–15
57–244	15–28
57–344	3–11
57–345	10–11
57–418	6–16
58–419	3–11
59–72	15–19
59–86	14–13
60–31	19–28
61	4–4
61–119	15–5

Revenue Rulings

Rev.Rul.	This Work Page
61–186	3–42
62–102	5–5
63–221	15–10
63–232	7–10
64–221	3–42
65–178	19–7
65–34	2–30
66–7	16–16
67–297	10–16
68–212	10–6
68–662	6–13
68–99	4–53
69–292	9–14
70–466	15–12
70–622	10–11
71–190	10–13
71–425	5–3
72–25	4–53
72–312	4–15
72–545	6–25
72–592	7–9
73–380	19–7
73–476	15–28
74–164	2–46
74–175	16–30
74–503	2–42
74–78	9–14
75–14	6–18
75–168	9–7
75–380	9–5
75–448	5–10
76–111	14–39
76–282	18–36
77–298	15–30
78–146	15–19, 15–30
78–147	15–21
78–325	2–48

Revenue Rulings

Rev.Rul.	This Work Page
78–340	10–5
78–39	6–9
79–379	4–16
80	5–15
80–335	6–9
80–52	4–10
81–180	15–10
81–181	15–10
82–196	5–13
82–202	5–33
82–204	16–38
82–208	10–13
82–227	18–27

Rev.Rul.	This Work Page
82–26	15–19
82–74	15–10
87–106	10–6
87–22	10–17
87–57	18–5, 18–8
90–23	9–6
91–31	5–48
94–24	9–19
94–47	9–6
96–6	13–13
96–28	2–10
190	9–6

APPENDIX E
Citator Example

ILLUSTRATION OF THE USE OF THE CITATOR

BACKGROUND

The *Federal Tax Citator* is a separate multivolume service with monthly supplements.[1] Cases reported by the *Citator* are divided into the various issues involved. Since the researcher may be interested in only one or two issues, only those cases involving the particular issue need to be checked.

The *Federal Tax Citator* includes the following volumes, each of which covers a particular period of time:

- Volume 1 (1863–1941)
- Volume 2 (1942–1948)
- Volume 3 (1948–1954)
- Volume 1, Second Series (1954–1977)
- Volume 2, Second Series (1978–1989)
- Cumulative Supplement, Second Series (1990–1996)
- Monthly cumulative supplements (paperback)

Through the use of symbols, the *Citator* indicates whether a decision has been followed, explained, criticized, questioned, or overruled by a later court decision. These symbols are reproduced in Figure E–1.

EXAMPLE

Determine the background and validity of *Adda v. Comm.*, 37 AFTR 654, 171 F.2d 457 (CA–4, 1948).

SOLUTION

Turning directly to the case itself (reproduced as Figure E–2), note the two issues involved (issues 1 and 2). For purposes of emphasis, these issues have been bracketed and identified by a marginal notation in the figure. The reason for the division of the issues becomes apparent when the case is traced through the *Citator*.

Refer to Volume 3 of the First Series (covering the period from October 7, 1948, through July 29, 1954) of the *Federal Tax Citator*. The case reference is located on page 5505, which is reproduced in Figure E–3.

Correlating the symbols in Figure E–1 with the shaded portion of Figure E–3 reveals the following information about *Adda v. Comm.*:

---

[1] Features in the *Federal Tax Citator* that do not appear in the CCH *Citator* include the following: (1) distinguishes between the various issues in the case, (2) lists all court decisions that cite the court decision being researched, (3) indicates the relationship (e.g., explained, criticized, followed, or overruled) between the court decision being researched and subsequent decisions, and (4) pinpoints the exact page on which one court decision is cited by another court decision. Prior to the acquisition of Prentice-Hall Information Services, the *Federal Tax Citator* was published by Prentice-Hall. The *Federal Tax Citator* is now published by Research Institute of America.

▼ FIGURE E-1

Citator Symbols*
COURT DECISIONS
Judicial History of the Case

a	affirmed (by decision of a higher court)
d	dismissed (appeal to a higher court dismissed)
m	modified (decision modified by a higher court, or on rehearing)
r	reversed (by a decision of a higher court)
s	same case (e.g., on rehearing)
rc	related case (companion cases and other cases arising out of the same subject matter are so designated)
x	certiorari denied (by the Supreme Court of the United States)
(C or G)	The Commissioner or Solicitor General has made the appeal
(T)	Taxpayer has made the appeal
(A)	Tax Court's decision acquiesced in by Commissioner
(NA)	Tax Court's decision nonacquiesced in by Commissioner
sa	same case affirmed (by the cited case)
sd	same case dismissed (by the cited case)
sm	same case modified (by the cited case)
sr	same case reversed (by the cited case)
sx	same case—certiorari denied

Syllabus of the Cited Case

iv	four (on all fours with the cited case)
f	followed (the cited case followed)
e	explained (comment generally favorable, but not to a degree that indicates the cited case is followed)
k	reconciled (the cited case reconciled)
n	dissenting opinion (cited in a dissenting opinion)
g	distinguished (the cited case distinguished either in law or on the facts)
l	limited (the cited case limited to its facts. Used when an appellate court so limits a prior decision, or a lower court states that in its opinion the cited case should be so limited)
c	criticized (adverse comment on the cited case)
q	questioned (the cited case not only criticized, but its correctness questioned)
o	overruled

*Reproduced from the *Federal Tax 2nd Citator* with the permission of the publisher, Research Institute of America, Englewood Cliffs, NJ 07632.

- Application for certiorari (appeal to the U.S. Supreme Court) filed by the taxpayer (T) on March 1, 1949.
- Certiorari was denied (x) by the U.S. Supreme Court on April 18, 1949.
- The trial court decision is reported in 10 T.C. 273 and was affirmed on appeal (sa) to the Fourth Court of Appeals.
- During the time frame of Volume 3 of the *Citator* (October 7, 1948, through July 29, 1954), one decision (*Milner Hotels, Inc.*) has agreed "on all fours with the cited case" (iv). One decision (*Comm. v. Nubar*) has limited the cited case

Citator Example   E–3

▼ FIGURE E–2

> ADDA v. COMMISSIONER OF INTERNAL REVENUE   457
> Cite as 171 F.2d 457
>
> **ADDA v. COMMISSIONER OF INTERNAL REVENUE.**
> No. 5796.
> United States Court of Appeals
> Fourth Circuit.
> Dec. 3, 1948.
>
> **ISSUE 1**
>
> 1. Internal revenue ⇐792
>
> Where nonresident alien's brother residing in United States traded for alien's benefit on commodity exchanges in United States at authorization of alien, who vested full discretion in brother with regard thereto, and many transactions were effected through different brokers, several accounts were maintained, and substantial gains and losses realized, transactions constituted a "trade or business," profits of which were "capital gains" taxable as income to the alien. 26 U.S.C.A. § 211(b).
>
> See Words and Phrases, Permanent Edition, for other judicial constructions and definitions of "Capital Gains" and "Trade or Business".
>
> **ISSUE 2**
>
> 2. Internal revenue ⇐792
>
> The exemption of a nonresident alien's commodity transactions in the United States provided for by the Internal Revenue Code does not apply where alien has agent in United States using his own discretion in effecting transactions for alien's account. 26 U.S.C.A. § 211(b).
>
> On Petition to Review the Decision of The Tax Court of the United States.
>
> Petition by Fernand C. A. Adda to review a decision of the Tax Court redetermining a deficiency in income tax imposed by the Commissioner of Internal Revenue.
>
> Decision affirmed.
>
> Rollin Browne and Mitchell B. Carroll, both of New York City, for petitioner.
>
> Irving I. Axelrad, Sp. Asst. to Atty. Gen. (Theron Lamar Caudle, Asst. Atty. Gen., and Ellis N. Slack and A. F. Prescott, Sp. Assts. to Atty. Gen., on the brief), for respondent.
>
> Before PARKER, Chief Judge, and SOPER and DOBIE, Circuit Judges.
>
> PER CURIAM.
>
> [1, 2] This is a petition by a non-resident alien to review a decision of the Tax Court. Petitioner is a national of Egypt, who in the year 1941 was residing in France. He had a brother who at that time was residing in the United States and who traded for petitioner's benefit on commodity exchanges in the United States in cotton, wool, grains, silk, hides and copper. This trading was authorized by petitioner who vested full discretion in his brother with regard thereto, and it resulted in profits in the sum of $193,857.14. The Tax Court said: "While the number of transactions or the total amount of money involved in them has not been stated, it is apparent that many transactions were effected through different brokers, several accounts were maintained, and gains and losses in substantial amounts were realized. This evidence shows that the trading was extensive enough to amount to a trade or business, and the petitioner does not contend, nor has he shown, that the transactions were so infrequent or inconsequential as not to amount to a trade or business." We agree with the Tax Court that, for reasons adequately set forth in its opinion, this income was subject to taxation, and that the exemption of a non-resident alien's commodity transactions in the United States, provided by section 211(b) of the Internal Revenue Code, 26 U.S.C.A. § 211(b), does not apply to a case where the alien has an agent in the United States using his own discretion in effecting the transactions for the alien's account. As said by the Tax Court, "Through such transactions the alien is engaging in trade or business within the United States, and the profits on these transactions are capital gains taxable to him." Nothing need be added to the reasoning of the Tax Court in this connection, and the decision will be affirmed on its opinion.
>
> Affirmed.

to its facts (1) and two decisions (*The Scottish American Investment Co., Ltd.* and *Zareh Nubar*) have distinguished the cited case on issue number one (g-1).

Reference to Volume 1 of the *Citator* Second Series (covering the period from 1954 through 1977) shows the *Adda v. Comm.* case on page 25, which is reproduced in Figure E–4.

▼ FIGURE E-3

» Adamson — Adler « 5505

ADAMSON, JAMES H. & MARION C. v U. S., — F Supp —, 36 AFTR 1529, 1946 P.-H. ¶ 72,418 (DC Calif) (See Adamson v U. S.)
ADAMSON, R. R., MRS. — BTA —, 1934 (P.-H.) BTA Memo. Dec. ¶ 34,370
ADAMSON v U. S., 26 AFTR 1188 (DC Calif, Sept 8, 1939)
  iv—Coggan, Linus C., 1939 (P.-H.) BTA Memo. Dec. page 39—806
ADAMSON; U. S. v, 161 F(2d) 942, 35 AFTR 1404 (CCA 9)
  1—Lazier v U. S., 170 F(2d) 524, 37 AFTR 545, 1948 P.-H. page 73,174 (CCA 8)
  1—Grace Bros., Inc. v Comm., 173 F(2d) 178, 37 AFTR 1014, 1949 P.-H. page 72,433 (CCA 9)
  1—Briggs; Hofferbert v, 178 F(2d) 744, 38 AFTR 1219, 1950 P.-H. page 72,267 (CCA 4)
  1—Rogers v Comm., 180 F(2d) 720, 39 AFTR 115, 1950 P.-H. page 72,531 (CCA 3)
  1—Lamar v Granger, 99 F Supp 41, 40 AFTR 270, 1951 P.-H. page 72,945 (DC Pa)
  1—Herbert v Riddell, 103 F Supp 383, 41 AFTR 975, 1952 P.-H. page 72,383 (DC Calif)
  1—Hudson, Galvin, 20 TC 737, 20-1953 P.-H. TC 418
ADAMSON v U. S., — F Supp —, 36 AFTR 1529, 1946 P.-H. ¶ 72,418 (DC Calif, Jan 28, 1946)
ADAMS-ROTH BAKING CO., 8 BTA 458
  1—Gunderson Bros. Engineering Corp., 16 TC 129, 16-1951 P.-H. TC 72
ADAMSTON FLAT GLASS CO. v COMM., 162 F(2d) 875, 35 AFTR 1579 (CCA 6)
  4—Forrest Hotel Corp. v. Fly, 112 F Supp 789, 43 AFTR 1080, 1953 P.-H. page 72,856 (DC Miss)
ADDA v COMM., 171 F(2d) 457, 37 AFTR 654, 1948 P.-H. ¶ 72,655 (CCA 4, Dec 3, 1948)
Cert. filed, March 1, 1949 (T)
No cert. (G) 1949 P-H ¶ 71,050
  x—Adda v Comm., 336 US 952, 69 S Ct 883, 93 L Ed 1107, April 18, 1949 (T)
  sa—Adda, Fernand C. A., 10 TC 273 (No. 33), ¶ 10.33 P.-H. TC 1948
  iv—Milner Hotels, Inc., N. Y., 173 F (2d) 567, 37 AFTR 1170, 1949 P.-H. page 72,528 (CCA 6)
  1—Nubar; Comm. v, 185 F(2d) 588, 39 AFTR 1315, 1950 P.-H. page 73,423 (CCA 4)
  g-1—Scottish Amer. Invest. Co., Ltd., The, 12 TC 59, 12-1949 P.-H. TC 32
  g-1—Nubar, Zareh, 13 TC 579, 13-1949 P.-H. TC 318
ADDA, FERNAND C. A., 10 TC 273 (No. 33), ¶ 10.33 P.-H. TC 1948 (A) 1948-2 CB 1
  a—Adda v Comm., 171 F(2d) 457, 37 AFTR 654, 1948 P.-H. ¶ 72,655 (CCA 4)
  1—Nubar; Comm. v, 185 F(2d) 588, 39 AFTR 1315, 1950 P.-H. page 73,423 (CCA 4)
  g-1—Scottish Amer. Invest. Co., Ltd., The, 12 TC 59, 12-1949 P.-H. TC 32
  g-1—Nubar, Zareh, 13 TC 579, 13-1949 P.-H. TC 318
ADDA, FERNAND C. A., 10 TC 1291 (No. 168), ¶ 10.168 P.-H. TC 1948 (A) 1953-1 CB 3, 1953 P.-H. ¶ 76,453 (NA) 1948-2 CB 5, 1948 P.-H. ¶ 76,434 withdrawn
  1—Scottish Amer. Invest. Co., Ltd., The, 12 TC 59, 12-1949 P.-H. TC 32
ADDA INC., 9 TC 199 (A) 1949-1 CB 1, 1949 P.-H. ¶ 76,260 (NA) 1947-2 CB 6 withdrawn
  a—Adda, Inc.; Comm. v, 171 F(2d) 367, 37 AFTR 641, 1948 P.-H. ¶ 72,654 (CCA 2)
  a—Adda, Inc.; Comm. v, 171 F(2d) 367, 37 AFTR 641, 1949 P.-H. ¶ 72,303 (CCA 2)
  e-1—G.C.M. 26069, 1949-2 CB 38, 1949 P.-H. page 76,226
  3—Koshland, Execx.; U.S. v, 208 F(2d) 640, — AFTR —, 1953 P.-H. page 73,597 (CCA 9)
  4—Kent, Otis Beall, 1954 (P. H.) TC Memo. Dec. page 54—47

ADDA, INC.; COMM. v, 171 F(2d) 367, 37 AFTR 641, 1948 P.-H. ¶ 72,654 (CCA 2, Dec 6, 1948)
  sa—Adda, Inc., 9 TC 199
  s—Adda, Inc.; Comm. v, 171 F(2d) 367, 37 AFTR 641, 1949 P.-H. ¶ 72,303 (CCA 2) reh. den.
  e-1—G.C.M. 26069, 1949-2 CB 39, 1949 P.-H. page 76,227
  e-2—G.C.M. 26069, 1949-2 CB 39, 1949 P.-H. page 76,227
ADDA, INC.; COMM. v, 171 F(2d) 367, 37 AFTR 641, 1949 P.-H. ¶ 72,303 (CCA 2, Dec 6, 1948) reh. den.
  sa—Adda, Inc., 9 TC 199
  s—Adda, Inc.; Comm. v, 171 F(2d) 367, 37 AFTR 641, 1948 P.-H. ¶ 72,654 (CCA 2)
ADDISON-CHEVROLET SALES, INC. v CHAMBERLAIN, L. A. & NAT. BANK OF WASH., THE, — F Supp —, — AFTR —, 1954 P.-H. ¶ 72,550 (DC DC) (See Campbell v Chamberlain)
ADDISON v COMM., 177 F(2d) 521, 38 AFTR 821, 1949 P.-H. ¶ 72,637 (CCA 8, Nov 3, 1949)
  sa—Addison, Irene D., — TC —, 1948 (P.-H.) TC Memo. Dec. ¶ 48,177
  1—Roberts, Supt. v U. S., 115 Ct Cl 439, 87 F Supp 937, 38 AFTR 1314, 1950 P.-H. page 72,292
  1—Cold Metal Process Co., The, 17 TC 934, 17-1951 P.-H. TC 512
  1—Berger, Samuel & Lillian, 1954 (P.-H.) TC Memo. Dec. page 54—232
  2—Urquhart, George Gordon & Mary F., 20 TC 948, 20-1953 P.-H. TC 536
ADDISON, IRENE D., — TC —, 1948 (P.-H.) TC Memo. Dec. ¶ 48,177
App (T) Jan 14, 1949 (CCA 8)
  a—Addison v Comm., 177 F(2d) 521, 38 AFTR 821, 1949 P.-H. ¶ 72,637 (CCA 8)
  1—Urquhart, George Gordon & Mary F., 20 TC 948, 20-1953 P.-H. TC 536
ADDITON, HARRY L. & ANNIE S., 3 TC 427
  1—Lum, Ralph E., 12 TC 379, 12-1949 P.-H. TC 204
  1—Christie, John A. & Elizabeth H., — TC —, 1949 (P.-H.) TC Memo. Dec. page 49—795
ADDRESSOGRAPH - MULTIGRAPH CORP., 1945 (P.-H.) TC Memo. Dec. ¶ 45,058
  f-10—Rev. Rul. 54-71, 1954 P.-H. page 76.453
ADDRESSOGRAPH-MULTIGRAPH CORP. v U. S., 112 Ct Cl 201, 78 F Supp 111, 37 AFTR 53, 1948 P.-H. ¶ 72,504 (June 1, 1948)
No cert (G) 1949 P.-H. ¶ 71,041
  1—New Oakmont Corp., The v U. S., 114 Ct Cl 686, 86 F Supp 901, 38 AFTR 924, 1949 P.-H. page 73,181
ADELAIDE PARK LAND, 25 BTA 211
  g-1—Amer. Security & Fidelity Corp., — BTA —, 1940 (P.-H.) BTA Memo. Dec. page 40—571
ADELPHI PAINT & COLOR WORKS, INC., 18 BTA 436
  1—Neracher, William A., — BTA —, 1939 (P.-H.) BTA Memo. Dec. page 39—69
  1—Lyman-Hawkins Lumber Co., — BTA —, 1939 (P.-H.) BTA Memo. Dec. page 39—350
ADEMAN v U. S., 174 F(2d) 283, 37 AFTR 1406 (CCA 9, April 25, 1949)
ADICONIS, NOELLA L. (PATNAUDE), 1953 (P.-H.) TC Memo. Dec. ¶ 53,305
ADJUSTMENT BUREAU OF ST. LOUIS ASSN., OF CREDIT MEN, 21 BTA 232
  1—Cook County Loss Adjustment Bureau, — BTA —, 1940 (P.-H.) BTA Memo. Dec. page 40—331
ADKINS, CHARLES I., — BTA —, 1933 (P.-H.) BTA Memo. Dec. ¶ 33,457
ADLER v COMM., 77 F(2d) 733, 16 AFTR 162 (CCA 5)
  g-2—McEuen v Comm., 196 F(2d) 130, 41 AFTR 1172, 1952 P.-H. page 72,604 (CCA 5)

Copyright 1955 by Prentice-Hall, Inc.—Federal Tax Citator

Reproduced from the *Federal Taxes 2nd Citator* with permission of the publisher, Research Institute of America, Englewood Cliffs, N.J. 07632.

FIGURE E-4

ADASKAVICH—ADELSON   25

ADASKAVICH, STEPHEN A. v U.S., 39 AFTR2d 77-517, 422 F Supp 276 (DC Mont) (See Wiegand, Charles J, Jr v U S.)
AD. AURIEMA, INC., 1943 P-H TC Memo ¶ 43,422
  e-1—Miller v U S., 13 AFTR2d 1515, 166 Ct Cl 257, 331 F2d 859
ADAY v SUPERIOR CT. OF ALAMEDA COUNTY, 8 AFTR2d 5367, 13 Cal Reptr 415, 362 P2d 47 (Calif, 5-11-61)
ADCO SERVICE, INC., ASSIGNEE v CYBERMATICS, INC., 36 AFTR2d 75-6342 (NJ) (See Adco Service, Inc., Assignee v Graphic Color Plate)
ADCO SERVICE, INC., ASSIGNEE v GRAPHIC COLOR PLATE, 36 AFTR2d 75-6342 (NJ, Supr Ct, 11-10-75)
ADCO SERVICE, INC., ASSIGNEE v GRAPHIC COLOR PLATE, INC., 36 AFTR2d 75-6342 (NJ) (See Adco Service, Inc., Assignee v Graphic Color Plate)
ADDA v COMM., 171 F2d 457, 37 AFTR 654 (USCA 4)
  Rev. Rul. 56-145, 1956-1 CB 613
  1—Balanovski, U.S. v, 236 F2d 304, 49 AFTR 2013 (USCA 2)
  1—Liang, Chang Hsiao, 23 TC 1045, 23-1955 P-H TC 624
  f-1—Asthmanefrin Co., Inc., 25 TC 1141, 25-1956 P-H TC 639
  g-1—de Vegvar, Edward A. Neuman, 28 TC 1061, 28-1957 P-H TC 599
  g-1—Purvis, Ralph E. & Patricia Lee, 1974 P-H TC Memo 74-669
  k-1—deKrause, Piedad Alvarado, 1974 P-H TC Memo 74-1291
  1—Rev. Rul. 56-392, 1956-2 CB 971
ADDA, FERNAND C.A., 10 TC 273, ¶ 10,133 P-H TC 1948
  1—Balanovski, U.S. v, 236 F2d 303, 49 AFTR 2012 (USCA 2)
  1—Liang, Chang Hsiao, 23 TC 1045, 23-1955 P-H TC 624
  g-1—de Vegvar, Edward A. Neuman, 28 TC 1061, 28-1957 P-H TC 599
  g-1—Purvis, Ralph E. & Patricia Lee, 1974 P-H TC Memo 74-669
  k-1—deKrause, Piedad Alvarado, 1974 P-H TC Memo 74-1291
ADDA, INC., 9 TC 199
  Pardee, Marvin L., Est. of, 49 TC 152, 49 P-H TC 107 [See 9 TC 206-208]
  f-1—Asthmanefrin Co., Inc., 25 TC 1141, 25-1956 P-H TC 639
  1—Keil Properties, Inc. (Dela), 24 TC 1117, 24-1955 P-H TC 615
  1—Saffan, Samuel, 1957 P-H TC Memo 57—701
  1—Rev. Rul. 56-145, 1956-1 CB 613
  1—Rev. Rul. 56-392, 1956-2 CB 971
  4—Midler Court Realty, Inc., 61 TC 597, 61 P-H TC 368
ADDA, INC.; COMM. v, 171 F2d 367, 37 AFTR 641 (USCA 2)
  1—Pardee, Marvin L., Est. of, 49 TC 152, 49 P-H TC 107
  1—Saffan, Samuel, 1957 P-H TC Memo 57-701
  2—Midler Court Realty, Inc., 61 TC 597, 61 P-H TC 368
ADDELSTON, ALBERT A. & SARAH M., 1965 P-H TC Memo ¶ 65,215
ADDISON v COMM., 177 F2d 521, 38 AFTR 821 (USCA 8)
  g-1—Industrial Aggregate Co. v U.S., 6 AFTR2d 5963, 284 F2d 645 (USCA 8)
  1—Sturgeon v McMahon, 155 F Supp 630, 52 AFTR 789 (DC NY)
  1—Gilmore v U.S., 16 AFTR2d 5211, 5213, 245 F Supp 384, 386 (DC Calif)
  1—Waldheim & Co., Inc., 25 TC 599, 25-1955 P-H TC 332
  g-1—Galewitz, Samuel & Marian, 50 TC 113, 50 P-H TC 79
  1—Buder, G. A., Est. of, 1963 P-H TC Memo 63-345
  e-1—Rhodes, Lynn E. & Martha E., 1963 P-H TC Memo 63-1374
  2—Shipp v Comm., 217 F2d 402, 46 AFTR 1170 (USCA 9)

ADDISON—Contd.
  g-2—Industrial Aggregate Co. v U.S., 6 AFTR2d 5964, 284 F2d 645 (USCA 8)
  e-2—Buder, Est. of v Comm., 13 AFTR2d 1238, 330 F2d 443 (USCA 8)
  2—Iowa Southern Utilities Co. v Comm., 14 AFTR2d 5063, 333 F2d 385 (USCA 8)
  2—Kelly, Daniel, S.W., 23 TC 687, 23-1955 P-H TC 422
  f-2—Morgan, Joseph P., Est. of, 37 TC 36, 37, 37-1961 P-H TC 26, 27
  n-2—Woodward, Fred W. & Elsie M., 49 TC 385, 49 P-H TC 270
ADDISON, IRENE D., 1948 P-H TC Memo ¶ 48,177
  1—Waldheim & Co., Inc., 25 TC 599, 25-1955 P-H TC 332
  f-1—Morgan, Joseph P., Est. of, 37 TC 36, 37, 37-1961 P-H TC 26, 27
  1—Buder, G. A., Est. of, 1963 P-H TC Memo 63-345
  e-1—Rhodes, Lynn E. & Martha E., 1963 P-H TC Memo 63-1374
ADDISON, JOHN MILTON, BKPT; U.S. v, 20 AFTR2d 5630, 384 F2d 748 (USCA 5) (See Rochelle Jr., Trtee; U.S. v)
ADDRESSOGRAPH - MULTIGRAPH CORP., 1945 P-H TC Memo ¶ 45,058
  Conn. L. & P. Co., The v U.S., 9 AFTR2d 679, 156 Ct Cl 312, 314, 299 F2d 264
  Copperhead Coal Co., Inc., 1958 P-H TC Memo 58-33
  1—Seas Shipping Co., Inc. v Comm., 19 AFTR2d 596, 371 F2d 529 (USCA 2)
  e-1—Hitchcock, E. R., Co., The v U.S., 35 AFTR2d 75-1207, 514 F2d 487 (USCA 2)
  f-2—Vulcan Materials Co. v U.S., 25 AFTR2d 70-446, 308 F Supp 57 (DC Ala)
  f-3—Marlo Coil Co., 1969 P-H 58,133 (Ct Cl Comr Rep)
  4—United Gas Improvement Co. v Comm., 240 F2d 318, 50 AFTR 1354 (USCA 3)
  10—St. Louis Co. (Del) (in Dissolution) v U.S., 237 F2d 156, 50 AFTR 257 (USCA 3)
ADDRESSOGRAPH - MULTIGRAPH CORP. v U.S., 112 Ct Cl 201, 78 F Supp 111, 37 AFTR 53
  f-1—St. Joseph Lead Co. v U.S., 9 AFTR2d 712, 299 F2d 350 (USCA 2)
  e-1—Central & South West Corp. v U.S., 1968 P-H 58,175 (Ct Cl Comr Rep)
  1—Smale & Robinson, Inc. v U.S., 123 F Supp 469, 46 AFTR 375 (DC Calif)
  1—St. Joseph Lead Co. v U.S., 7 AFTR2d 401, 190 F Supp 640 (DC NY)
  1—Eisenstadt Mfg. Co., 28 TC 230, 28-1957 P-H TC 132
  f-2—St. Joseph Lead Co. v U.S., 9 AFTR2d 712, 299 F2d 350 (USCA 2)
  f-3—Consol. Coppermines Corp. v U.S., 8 AFTR2d 5873, 155 Ct Cl 736, 296 F2d 745
ADELAIDE PARK LAND, 25 BTA 211
  g—Custom Component Switches, Inc. v U.S., 19 AFTR2d 560 (DC Calif) [See 25 BTA 215]
  O'Connor, John C., 1957 P-H TC Memo 57-190
ADELBERG, MARVIN & HELEN, 1971 P-H TC Memo ¶ 71,015
ADELMAN v U.S., 27 AFTR2d 71-1464, 440 F2d 991 (USCA 9, 5-3-71)
  sa—Adelman v U.S., 24 AFTR2d 69-5769, 304 F Supp 599 (DC Calif)
ADELMAN v U.S., 24 AFTR2d 69-5769, 304 F Supp 599 (DC Calif, 9-30-69)
  a—Adelman v U.S., 27 AFTR2d 71-1464, 440 F2d 991 (USCA 9)
ADELSON, SAMUEL; U.S. v, 52 AFTR 1798 (DC RI) (See Sullivan Co., Inc.; U.S. v)
ADELSON v U.S., 15 AFTR2d 246, 342 F2d 332 (USCA 9, 1-13-65)
  sa—Adelson v U.S., 12 AFTR2d 5010, 221 F Supp 31 (DC Calif)
  g-1—Greenlee, L. C. & Gladys M., 1966 P-H TC Memo 66-985
  f-1—Cochran, Carol J., 1973 P-H TC Memo 73-459
  f-1—Marchionni, Siro L., 1976 P-H TC Memo 76-1321
  f-2—Krist, Edwin F. v Comm., 32 AFTR2d 73-5663, 483 F2d 1351 (USCA 2)
  f-2—Fugate v U.S., 18 AFTR2d 5607, 259 F Supp 401 (DC Tex) [See 15 AFTR2d 249, 342 F2d 335]

Reproduced from the *Federal Taxes 2nd Citator* with permission of the publisher, Research Institute of America, Englewood Cliffs, N.J. 07632.

Correlating the symbols in Figure E–1 with the shaded portion of Figure E–4 reveals the following additional information about *Adda v. Comm.*:

- The case was cited without comment in two rulings and two cases: Rev.Rul. 56–145 , Rev.Rul. 56–392 , *Balanovski,* and *Liang.*
- It was followed in *Asthmanefrin Co.* (f-1).
- It was distinguished in *de Vegvar* and *Purvis* (g-1).
- It was reconciled in *deKrause* (k-1).

Reference to the "Court Decisions" section of Volume 2, Second Series of the *Citator* (covering the period from 1978 through 1989) shows that *Adda v. Comm.* was cited in *Judith C. Connelly* and *Robert E. Cleveland,* with each case limited to its facts (1). This page (22) is reproduced in Figure E–5.

The *Citator* includes a cumulative supplement (i.e., 1990–1996), and a cumulative monthly supplement is published each month. Be sure to refer to these supplements, or very recent citations might be overlooked. No citations appear in the supplements for *Adda v. Comm.*

Except as otherwise noted, it appears that *Adda v. Comm.* has withstood the test of time.

▼ **FIGURE E-5**

22   ADAMSON—ADELSON

ADAMSON, LEE A., 1981 PH TC Memo ¶ 81,285 (See Petty, R. M. & Allene A.)
ADAMSON, RAY P., 1981 PH TC Memo ¶ 81,285 (See Petty, R. M. & Allene A.)
ADAMSON, ROY & CATHERINE, 1986 PH TC Memo ¶ 86,489
   f-1—Dew, James Edward, 91 PH TC 626, 91 PH TC 310
   e-1—Telfeyan, Louis & Lynn, 1988 PH TC Memo 88-2146
   e-1—Bullock, Kenneth & Gail, 1988 PH TC Memo 88-2706
ADAMSON, SANDRA L., 1981 PH TC Memo ¶ 81,285 (See Petty, R. M. & Allene A.)
ADAMSON; U.S. v, 161 F2d 942, 35 AFTR 1404 (USCA 9)
   e-1—Inco Electroenergy Corp., 1987 PH TC Memo 87-2295
ADAMUCCI, RICHARD, 1987 PH TC Memo ¶ 87,378 (See Batastini, Paul J. & Amelia)
ADCOCK, HOMER & DOROTHY, 1982 PH TC Memo ¶ 82,206
   e-1—Kauffman, Wilma G., 1982 PH TC Memo 82-2193
   e-1—Scallen, Stephen B. & Chacke Y., 1987 PH TC Memo 87-2134
ADDA v COMM., 171 F2d 457, 37 AFTR 654 (USCA 4)
   1—Connelly, Judith C., 1982 PH TC Memo 82-2866
   1—Cleveland, Robert E., 1983 PH TC Memo 83-1223
ADDA, FERNAND C.A., 10 TC 273, ¶ 10.133 PH TC 1948
   1—Connelly, Judith C., 1982 PH TC Memo 82-2866
   1—Cleveland, Robert E., 1983 PH TC Memo 83-1223
ADDA, INC., 9 TC 199
   e—Hodges, Irene McLaughlin & Thomas Lyman, 1985 PH TC Memo 85-2062 [See 9 TC 210-211)
   1—Security Bancorp, Inc. v U.S., 48 AFTR2d 81-5514 (DC Mich)
   4—Watson Land Co., 1983 PH TC Memo 83-744
ADDA, INC.; COMM. v, 171 F2d 367, 37 AFTR 641 (USCA 2)
   Security Bancorp, Inc. v U.S., 48 AFTR2d 81-5514 (DC Mich)
   Watson Land Co., 1983 PH TC Memo 83-744
   e—Hodges, Irene McLaughlin & Thomas Lyman, 1985 PH TC Memo 85-2062
ADDEO, ARTHUR J., Jr. & MARY, 1984 PH TC Memo ¶ 84,493
   e-1—Brown, Stewart L., 1986 PH TC Memo 86-1153
ADDINGTON, DOUGLAS F., 1986 PH TC Memo ¶ 86,358 (See Hoak, Roderick C. & Cornelia)
ADDINGTON, WILLIAM H. & DONNA L., 1980 PH TC Memo ¶ 80,046
   a—Court Order, 10-20-81, 663 F2d 104 (USCA 5)
   d—1981 PH 61,000 (USCA 10)
ADDISON, ALBERT I., 1979 PH TC Memo ¶ 79,317
   e-1—Ridenour, Harry P., Jr. v U.S., 52 AFTR2d 83-5589, 3 Cl Ct 134
   e-1—Reinhardt, Jules & Marilyn D., 85 TC 526, 85 PH TC 299
ADDISON INTERNAT., INC., 90 TC 1207, ¶ 90.78 PH TC
   a—Addison Internat., Inc. v Comm., 64 AFTR2d 89-5747, 887 F2d 660 (USCA 6)
   rc—Rocky Mountain Associates Internat., Inc., 90 TC 1241, 1242, 90 PH TC 637, 638
   g-1—Butka, David J. & Sabine I., 91 TC 130, 91 PH TC 66
ADDISON INTERNAT., INC. v COMM., 64 AFTR2d 89-5747, 887 F2d 660 (USCA 6, 10-10-89)
   sa—Addison Internat., Inc., 90 TC 1207, ¶ 90.78 PH TC
ADDRESSOGRAPH-MULTIGRAPH CORP., 1945 PH TC Memo ¶ 45,058
   1—Buffalo Wire Works Co., Inc., 74 TC 938, 74 PH TC 509
   g-1—Maier Brewing Co., 1987 PH TC Memo 87-1978
ADEE, ALLEN R., TRUST NO. 1 v U.S., 52 AFTR2d 83-6437 (DC Kan, 7-19-83)
ADEE, DONALD P., TRUSTEE v U.S., 52 AFTR2d 83-6437 (DC Kan) (See Adee, Allen R., Trust No. 1 v U.S.)
ADEE, JACK R., TRUSTEE v U.S., 52 AFTR2d 83-6437 (DC Kan) (See Adee, Allen R., Trust No. 1 v U.S.)

ADELBERG, MARVIN & HELEN M., 1985 PH TC Memo ¶ 85,597
   a—Court Order, 1-21-87, 811 F2d 1507 (USCA 9)
   e-1—Chao, Wen Y. & Ching J., 92 TC 1144, 92 PH TC 577
   e-1—Nicklo, Joseph J., 1988 PH TC Memo 88-1199
ADELEKE, JOEL & CATHERINE A., 1980 PH TC Memo ¶ 80,479
   e-1—Pike-Biegunski, Maciej Jan & Denise Nadine, 1984 PH TC Memo 84-1123
ADELMAN v U.S., 27 AFTR2d 71-1464, 440 F2d 991 (USCA 9)
   e-1—Barbados #7 Ltd., 92 TC 813, 92 PH TC 409
ADELMAN v U.S., 24 AFTR2d 69-5769, 304 F Supp 599 (DC Calif)
   e-2—Barbados #7 Ltd., 92 TC 813, 92 PH TC 409
ADELSON, SHELDON G. v U.S., 54 AFTR2d 84-5428, 737 F2d 1569 (USCA Fed, 6-28-84)
   remg—Adelson, Sheldon G. v U.S., 52 AFTR2d 83-5211 (Cl Ct)
   s—Adelson, Sheldon G. v U.S., 51 AFTR2d 83-574 (Cl Ct) 535 F Supp 1082
   s—Adelson, Sheldon G. v U.S., 54 AFTR2d 84-5959, 6 Cl Ct 102
   rc—Adelson, Sheldon G. v U.S., 57 AFTR2d 86-736, 782 F2d 1010 (USCA Fed)
   rc—Adelson, Sheldon G. v U.S., 59 AFTR2d 87-993, 12 Cl Ct 231
   e-1—Larson, Roger Roy, In re, 62 AFTR2d 88-5801, 862 F2d 117 (USCA 7)
   e-1—Raab, George S. v I.R.S., 57 AFTR2d 86-715, 86-716 (DC Pa)
ADELSON, SHELDON G. v U.S., 57 AFTR2d 86-736, 782 F2d 1010 (USCA Fed, 1-29-86)
   remd—Adelson, Sheldon G. v U.S., 54 AFTR2d 84-5959, 6 Cl Ct 102
   rc—Adelson, Sheldon G. v U.S., 54 AFTR2d 84-5428, 737 F2d 1569 (USCA Fed)
   rc—Adelson, Sheldon G. v U.S., 52 AFTR2d 83-5211, 2 Cl Ct 591
   rc—Adelson, Sheldon G. v U.S., 51 AFTR2d 83-574, 1 Cl Ct 61, 553 F Supp 1082
   rc—Adelson, Sheldon G. v U.S., 59 AFTR2d 87-993, 12 Cl Ct 231
ADELSON, SHELDON G. v U.S., 51 AFTR2d 83-574, 1 Cl Ct 61, 553 F Supp 1082 (12-27-82)
   s—Adelson, Sheldon G. v U.S., 54 AFTR2d 84-5428, 737 F2d 1569 (USCA Fed)
   s—Adelson, Sheldon G. v U.S., 52 AFTR2d 83-5211, 2 Cl Ct 591
   rc—Adelson, Sheldon G. v U.S., 57 AFTR2d 86-736, 782 F2d 1010 (USCA Fed)
   rc—Adelson, Sheldon G. v U.S., 54 AFTR2d 84-5959, 6 Cl Ct 102
   rc—Adelson, Sheldon G. v U.S., 59 AFTR2d 87-993, 12 Cl Ct 231
   e-1—Mann, Guy L. Est. of, 53 AFTR2d 84-1304, 731 F2d 273 (USCA 5)
ADELSON, SHELDON G. v U.S., 52 AFTR2d 83-5211, 2 Cl Ct 591 (6-14-83)
   remd—Adelson, Sheldon G. v U.S., 54 AFTR2d 84-5428, 737 F2d 1569 (USCA Fed)
   s—Adelson, Sheldon G. v U.S., 51 AFTR2d 83-574 (Cl Ct) 553 F Supp 1082
   rc—Adelson, Sheldon G. v U.S., 57 AFTR2d 86-736, 782 F2d 1010 (USCA Fed)
   rc—Adelson, Sheldon G. v U.S., 54 AFTR2d 84-5959, 6 Cl Ct 102
   rc—Adelson, Sheldon G. v U.S., 59 AFTR2d 87-993, 12 Cl Ct 231
ADELSON, SHELDON G. v U.S., 54 AFTR2d 84-5959, 6 Cl Ct 102 (9-12-84)
   remd—Adelson, Sheldon G. v U.S., 57 AFTR2d 86-736, 782 F2d 1010 (USCA Fed)
   s—Adelson, Sheldon G. v U.S., 54 AFTR2d 84-5428, 737 F2d 1569 (USCA Fed)
   rc—Adelson, Sheldon G. v U.S., 51 AFTR2d 83-574, 1 Cl Ct 61, 553 F Supp 1082
   rc—Adelson, Sheldon G. v U.S., 52 AFTR2d 83-5211, 2 Cl Ct 591
   rc—Adelson, Sheldon G. v U.S., 59 AFTR2d 87-993, 12 Cl Ct 231

Reproduced from the *Federal Tax 2nd Citator* with the permission of the publisher, Research Institute of America, Englewood Cliffs, NJ 07632.

APPENDIX F
Comprehensive Tax Return Problems

PROBLEM 1

1. Adam J. and Ginger C. Clay are married and file a joint return for 1996. Adam is age 51 and Ginger is 49. Adam is employed by Oracle Corporation as a chemist. Ginger is a registered nurse in charge of the oncology unit at St. Anne's Hospital. Both live at 4396 Scenic Road, San Diego, CA 92184.

2. The Clay's have three children: Paul (age 23), Julie (age 22), and Heather (age 18), who live with them. Paul is a full-time law student at San Diego State University and earned $3,100 from a summer job. Julie is a full-time nursing student at the same university and earned $3,300 from part-time nursing jobs. Heather finished high school in 1995 and has not decided on a career. In 1996, however, she did earn $3,700 as a tour guide at the San Diego zoo. The Clay's furnish more than 50% of the support of their three children.

3. For all of 1996, Adam's widowed mother, Cora Clay, was confined to the Medical Arms Manor, a full-service nursing home. Cora suffers from an advanced stage of Alzheimer's disease and requires constant supervision and daily medication. [Medical Arms Manor was recommended by Cora's physician.] Adam and his two unmarried sisters (Fran and Iris) all contribute toward their mother's support. The cost of supporting Cora for 1996 is as follows:

Medical Arms Manor (room and board and general nursing care)	$24,000
Prescription drugs	2,000
Doctor bills	4,000

Of the total support, Adam furnished 40% and each of his sisters furnished 20%. The remaining 20% came from Cora's assets. Included in the share provided by Adam is the payment for Cora's drugs ($2,000) and doctor bills ($4,000). Both Fran and Iris complete Forms 2120 (Multiple Support Agreement) on March 1, 1997, awarding the dependency exemption for Cora to Adam. Fran and Iris live at 318 Vista Drive, San Diego, CA 92184.

4. On July 1, 1995, and prior to entering the nursing home, Cora gave Adam her personal residence including its furnishings. No gift tax was due on the transfer. The property was converted to rental property on the same date. Information regarding the property is summarized below.

	Adjusted Basis to Cora	FMV on July 1, 1995
House	$45,000	$120,000
Land	5,000	10,000
Furnishings	12,000	8,000

On July 1, 1995, Adam listed the property (furnished) for rent, but a suitable tenant was not found until February 1, 1996. The house was then occupied under the following terms: renewable one-year lease at $700 per month (payable on the first of each month), damage deposit (refundable) of $600, and the last month's rent in advance. The tenant has complied with all of the terms of the lease agreement.

The rental house is located at 3690 Bay Area Boulevard, San Diego, CA 92184. It is a 15-year-old, single-story, stucco dwelling built on a concrete foundation.

Out of pocket expenses as to the property for 1996 are as follows:

Property taxes	$1,700
Special street paving assessment	500
Repairs	220
Casualty insurance premiums	1,000

Utilities and yard maintenance are the responsibility of the tenant. Depreciation is claimed under the MACRS method.

5. The Clays have the following non-salary income:

Winnings from state lottery (losses were $700)		$ 400
Interest on CD (Wells Fargo)		6,000
Interest on money market account (Bank of America)		3,500
Dividends—		
Exxon	$2,400	
Xerox	1,400	3,800
Gibraltar life insurance proceeds		100,000

The life insurance proceeds were paid to Ginger as the designated beneficiary of a policy Ginger's father had on his life. Ginger's father died in August 1996; the proceeds were paid the following month.

6. The Clays had the following stock transactions:

Description of Property	Date Acquired	Date Sold	Sales Price	Cost or Other Basis
Union Oil	9/18/94	4/8/96	$11,000	$18,000
ADM	11/20/96	12/9/96	32,000	(see below)
West Mining	7/10/95	(see below)		15,000

The Clays purchased Union Oil as a speculative investment. However, when it significantly dropped in price on April 8, they became concerned and sold the stock. The same stock was repurchased on May 2, 1996, for $9,000, when the Clays thought it had "bottomed out."

Ginger inherited the ADM stock from her father. The stock was purchased by the father in 1990 for $21,000 and had a fair market value of $31,800 when he died.

Adam bought the West Mining stock on a tip from a friend who worked at the company. Although the stock was already depressed and the company was rumored to be in financial difficulty, the friend thought that an eventual reorganization or liquidation would realize much more for the shareholders than the stock's listed price. In February 1996, West Mining filed for bankruptcy. In the same month, it was announced by management that the company's assets were not enough to pay all creditors. In short, the shareholders would receive nothing; the stock was worthless.

7. Although Adam is mainly involved in manufacturing, he does, on occasion, do consulting for his employer. When one of Oracle's customers has a problem with a product, Adam may be sent out to investigate the matter. The employer estimates the expenses Adam might have for each trip and provides him with an allowance. Oracle

does not require its consulting chemists to account for the allowances. However, Adam maintains records and receipts for each trip.

A summary of these allowances and expenses appears below.

Allowance provided by employer ($11,000 − $3,080 income tax withholding)		$7,920
Expenses paid by Adam—		
Air fare	$4,100	
Lodging	1,600	
Meals	1,500	
Ground transportation	105	$7,305

8. Other expenditures for 1996 are as follows:

Medical (not including Cora)—		
Prescribed drugs	$ 305	
Doctor bills	4,400	
Medical insurance premiums	2,100	
Reimbursements from medical insurance (for 1996 expenses)	(600)	$6,205
Taxes—		
State income tax withheld from wages (Adam $3,000; Ginger, $2,900)	$5,900	
Property taxes on personal residence	2,800	8,700
Mortgage interest on personal residence		4,100
Charitable contributions (appropriate documentation received)		
To church	$1,800	
United Way	1,500	3,300
Other—		
Professional dues (Ginger $300; Adam $250)	$ 550	
Professional journals (Ginger $220; Adam $180)	400	
Safety shoes and glasses (Adam)	120	
Nurse uniforms	320	
Laundry of uniforms	220	1,610

The doctor bills ($4,400) included $3,200 for dental restorative work to correct Ginger's overbite problem. Dental work is not covered by the Clay's medical insurance.

The state income taxes listed above do not include $150 the Clays had to pay to the state of California in 1996 for tax year 1995. The Clays estimate they will receive a $100 refund (in 1997) on the $5,900 withheld in 1996.

9. Salaries and Federal income tax withholdings for Adam and Ginger are summarized below:

	Compensation	Federal Income Tax Withholding
Adam:		
Salary	$52,000	$5,900
Expense allowance	11,000	3,080
Ginger	48,000	5,200

On a timely basis, the Clays made four quarterly estimated Federal income tax payments of $700 each. The proper social security tax and Medicare tax amounts have been withheld from wages and allowances.

10. Relevant social security numbers are:

Person	Number
Adam J. Clay	546-19-5021
Ginger C. Clay	547-20-1960
Julie Clay	550-41-6582
Heather Clay	551-19-1642
Paul Clay	557-83-4693
Cora Clay	572-11-3641
Fran Clay	546-42-7011
Iris Clay	546-19-6001

11. The Clays do not wish to designate a contribution to the Presidential Election fund. If they have overpaid, any refund is to be applied toward the 1997 Federal income tax liability.

Requirements

You are to prepare a joint Federal income tax return for the Clays for 1996.

PROBLEM 2

1. Bill H. Alford, age 42, is divorced and lives alone at 1260 Elm Street, Cincinnati, OH 45221. He provides more than half of the cost of maintaining a household for Alice Alford, who lives in an apartment nearby. Alice, age 68, is Bill's widowed mother and qualifies as his dependent.

2. Bill and Marcia were married eighteen years ago and were divorced in 1993. Marcia was awarded custody of their only child, Peter, now twelve years old. Under the divorce decree, Bill must pay Marcia $400 each month until Peter reaches age 21 or dies (whichever occurs first). Upon the occurrence of either event, the monthly payment becomes $100. Since Bill and Marcia have been alternating claiming Peter as a dependent, Marcia did complete and send to Bill a Form 8332 for 1996. Bill sent Marcia the required $4,800 ($400 × 12 months) for 1996. Furthermore, he sent Marcia an additional $1,100 for dental work she had done on her teeth. He also paid an optometrist/optician $300 for Peter's eye exams and prescription glasses.

3. Bill is a licensed hair stylist and beautician and operates his own salon under the business name of "Bill's Creations." Although it varies as to number, Bill's business consists of four to six stations operated by himself and other licensed beauticians. The beauticians who work in the salon are treated as independent contractors. In this regard, each has his or her own telephone line. They maintain their own appointment books, have their own customers, and collect and keep the fees charged. For the use of the work stations and various facilities (e.g., hair dryers, shampoo sinks, waiting area), each pays Bill a monthly rental. Bill does not control their work hours, although most choose to follow Bill's own work schedule.

4. Bill's Creations is well-known for its selection and quality of men's hairpieces (i.e., toupees) and women's wigs. The business also sells a considerable quantity of beauty products (e.g., conditioners, shampoos, curling irons). Some of these items are sold to other beauticians but most are sold to regular patrons and walk-in customers.

5. Bill's Creations is located at 4620 Grant Street, Cincinnati, OH 45221. The employer identification number is 31–0009521; the professional activity code for beauticians is 8110.

6. The building in which the business is located is rented under a long-term lease for $1,300 each month. Bill pays his own utilities. Before Bill moved in, the landlord customized the facilities so as to be suited for its intended use. The only employee Bill has is a shampoo person, who also performs light janitorial services. Bill hires an outside service to do the heavier janitorial duties. Likewise, a local accounting group is on retainer to keep the financial records and prepare the tax returns for the business.

7. Bill's Creations had the following receipts for 1996:

Sales of cosmetics	$16,200
Sales of hairpieces, wigs	27,500
Fees received from patrons by Bill (including tips received)	33,350
Rent charged other beauticians	23,100

The amounts shown for the retail sales of cosmetics, hairpieces, and wigs, include state sales tax.

8. Bill's Creations has the following expenses for 1996:

Purchases of cosmetics	$ 8,980
Purchases of hairpieces, wigs	12,200
Operating supplies (shampoo, permanent wave solution, color, etc.)	5,200
Rent for building	15,600
Utilities and telephone	6,000
Payroll expense	4,800
Payroll taxes (FICA, FUTA, state unemployment)	490
Sales taxes remitted to state	2,250
Health insurance coverage for employee	825
City of Cincinnati occupation permit for 1996	500
State beautician license fee	250
Liability insurance premiums (coverage is for calendar years 1996–1998)	6,000
Casualty insurance on business furnishings and equipment for 1996	1,300
Janitorial services	2,300
Accounting services	3,900
Waiting room furniture	2,800
Magazine subscriptions for waiting room	210
Advertising	830
Fine paid to city of Cincinnati	200

9. Bill decided to completely renovate the furnishings in his waiting room. Consequently, he spent $2,800 for chairs, sofa, lamps, coffee table, etc., all placed in service on April 20, 1996. The old furnishings were given to patrons or thrown away. The old furniture was completely depreciated and had a zero tax basis. Bill has always followed a policy of claiming as much depreciation as soon as possible. All of his other business assets (e.g., hair driers, work-station chairs) have been fully depreciated by 1996.

10. The fine paid to the city was assessed by the Sanitation Department. Bill had failed, in accordance with a city ordinance, to separate the trash of the business into recyclable and nonrecyclable bins.

11. In late 1995, a transient customer visiting the city had purchased a hairpiece from the business for $290. The customer's check was not deposited until early 1996 and ultimately proved fraudulent. The sale was reported on Bill's 1995 tax return. Bill has no doubt that he will never collect the $290 due him.

12. Bill maintains an inventory as to the merchandise he sells. The business inventories (based on the lower of cost or market) are as follows:

	12/31/95	12/31/96
Hairpieces and wigs	$3,000	$2,800
Cosmetics	2,100	2,000

13. In 1996, Bill was audited by both the city and the state as to his 1995 income tax returns. As a result of the audit, he had to pay the city an additional $110 but he received a refund from the state of $170.

14. Except for the inventory and purchases accounts, Bill operates the business on a cash method. Customers pay for services as rendered. Sales income is recorded when the merchandise is sold. Bill does not extend credit but does accept payment by charge card and check (see item 11 above).

15. Bill's medical expenses for 1996, and not mentioned elsewhere, included the following:

Gall bladder operation (includes hospital and surgeon's charges) for Alice	$2,000
Annual physical for Bill	500
Dentist charges for Bill (includes crown, bridges, fillings, etc.)	4,100
Hernia operation (includes hospital and surgeon's charges)	3,000
Prescription medicines	400
Medical insurance premiums	800

In November of 1996, Bill purchased a medical insurance policy. The policy does not cover anyone but Bill and his one employee (see item 6 above). The premium for the employee coverage is stated separately at item 8. Also, the policy does not apply to dental bills. Bill filed a claim with the insurance company in late December. He received a check in January of 1997 which, after the appropriate deductible, was for $300.

16. Bill's other expenses are listed below:

Property taxes on residence	$3,600
Interest on home mortgage	5,050
Annual dues for membership in the American Association of Beauticians	150
Professional journals	200

17. Bill has always itemized his deductions because even without substantial medical expenses, his deductions from adjusted gross income have exceeded the standard deductions.

18. Bill had no stock transactions in 1996 but he does have a $3,500 long-term capital loss carryover from 1995.

19. Bill's other income for 1996 is summarized below:

Interest income from a savings account at United Bank	$6,100
Cash dividend from General Electric	4,300

20. Bill made estimated tax payments for 1996 as follows:

City income tax	$ 650
Ohio income tax	2,600
Federal income and self-employment taxes (paid $1,400 quarterly)	5,600

21. Relevant social security numbers are—

Bill Alford	268–01–5869
Alice Alford	301–42–2657
Marcia Alford	300–52–7981
Peter Alford	302–64–1826

Requirements

You are to prepare Bill's Federal income tax return for 1996. Bill wants to designate that $3 be directed to the Presidential Election Campaign fund. If he has overpaid his 1996 taxes, he wants to have the amount applied to his 1997 estimated tax.

Appendix G
Table of Cases Cited

A

Aagaard, Robert W., 15–19
Alexander, Kenneth J., 12-16
Allen, Mary Francis, 7–10
American Automobile Association v. U.S., 4–13
Anderson, Comm. v., 5–16
Andrew Crispo Gallery, Inc. v. Comm., 18–20
Anton, M. G., 4–16
Appeal of (see name of party)
Apollo Computer, Inc. v. U.S., 2–21
Arcade Realty Co., 10–18
Arkansas Best Corp. v. Comm., 16–6
Armantrout, Richard T., 5–10
Armstrong v. Phinney, 5–15
Artnell Co. v. Comm., 4–13
Associated Industries of Missouri v. Lohman, 1–10
Augustus v. Comm., 2–28
Azar Nut Co., 16–38

B

Baird Publishing Co., 15–28
Baist, George A., 9–28
Balistrieri, Joseph P., 15–10
Bassett, Robert S., 10–9
Basye, U.S. v., 19–28
Baxter v. Comm., 4–10
Beatty, John D., 2–19, 9–37
Bedell v. Comm., 4–8
Beirne, Michael F., 20–36
Bhalla, C. P., 5–8
Biggs, Franklin B., 15–28
Bingler v. Johnson, 5–8
Boise Cascade Corp. v. U.S., 4–13
Bolaris v. Comm., 15–19
Bolton v. Comm., 6–22
Bonaire Development Co. v. Comm., 6–10
Bowman, Loy E., 7–7
Brown, Landis G., 7–37
Brown v. Helvering, 4–9
Bruun, Helvering v., 5–4
Burnet v. Sanford & Brooks Co., 4–9, 18–13

C

Carr, Jack D., 2–20
Carter, Estate of v. Comm., 5–5
Carahan, William A., 18–50
Caruth Corp. v. U.S., 4–16
Charley v. Comm., 4–5
Christine, William M., 12–43
Clapham, Robert G., 15–19
Cohan v. Comm., 9–37
Cohen, Theodore H., 4–10
Comm. v. (see opposing party)
Consolidated-Hammer Dry Plate & Film Co. v. Comm., 4–13
Continental Trust Co., 10–18
Correll, U.S. v., 9–7
Cowden v. Comm., 4–10
Crane v. Comm., 14–3, 14–39
Crowther, Charles, 2–48

D

Daly, Estate of, 5–5
Davidson, Collin J., 9–14
Davis, U.S. v., 4–20, 14–4
Delman, Estate of, 5–32
Delp, F. S., 10–6
Deputy v. du Pont, 6–6
Doak, Comm. v., 5–15
Donruss, U.S. v., 2–22
Doyle v. Mitchell Bros. Co., 4–6
Dreicer v. Comm. v., 2–18
Duberstein, Comm. v., 2–18, 5–5, 10–20
Dunn & McCarthy v. Comm., 6–6
Dyer, J. Raymond, 6–6

E

Edwards v. Cuba R. Co., 20–17
Eisner v. Macomber, 4–4, 5–30
Estate of (see name of party)

G–1

F

Farm Service Cooperative, 2–48
Faulconer v. Comm., 6–33
Fausner v. Comm., 9–5
Fay v. Helvering, 7–10
Finkbohner v. U.S., 2–21
Fischer, L. M., 4–10
Flint v. Stone Tracy Co., 1–3
Frank, Morton, 6–16
F.W. Woolworth Co., 2–8

G

Galt v. Comm., 4–15
Ginsberg v. Comm., 20–36
Goldberg, Harry H., 6–25
Golsen, Jack E., 2–17
Goode v. Comm., 7–37
Groetzinger v. Comm., 7–2, 7–26
Guenther, Kenneth W., 9–28

H

Hawkins, C. A., 5–11
Heininger, Comm. v., 6–6
Helvering v. (see opposing party)
Henry, James A., 15–16
Highland Farms, Inc. v. Comm., 18–14
Hillsboro Nat. Bank v. Comm., 6–9
Horst, Helvering v., 4–15
Hort v. Comm., 16–15
Horwith, T. M., 19–31
Houlette, Richard T., 15–19

I

Indianapolis Power & Light Co., Comm. v., 4–13
Industrial Valley Bank & Trust Co., 2–29

J

Jacobson, Comm. v., 5–33
James v. U.S., 4–3

K

Kahler, C. F., 4–8
Keller v. Comm., 6–10
Kennedy, Jr. v. Comm., 6–7
Kieselbach v. Comm., 5–29
Kintner, U.S. v., 20–3
Kirby Lumber Co., U.S. v., 4–6, 5–33
Kluger Associates, Inc., 14–9
Korn Industries, Inc. v. U.S., 18–17
Kowalski, Comm. v., 5–16

L

Lazisky, Albert A., 2–48
Leavell, Allen, 20–4

Lee, Harold K., 3–43
Lesslie, Thomas E., 10–34
Lester v. Comm., 4–23
Levien, Francis, 2–48
Lewis, U.S. v., 18–10
Lincoln Electric Co., Comm. v., 6–7
Lindeman, J. B., 5–16
Loco Realty Co. v. Comm., 15–12
Longue Vue Foundation, 2–48
Lucas v. Earl, 4–14
Lucas v. North Texas Lumber Co., 4–9
Lynch v. Turrish, 14–3

M

Maid of the Mist Corporation and Affiliated Corporations, 2–48
Malat v. Riddell, 16–4
Mantell, John, 4–12
Marshman, Comm. v., 14–4
Max Sobel Wholesale Liquors, 9–37
McCrary, Ronald W., 10–48
McWilliams v. Comm., 6–27, 14–19
Merchants' Loan & Trust Co. v. Smietanka, 4–3
Merians, Sidney, 2–48
Miller, Harris M., 2–8
Miller, J. O., 8–50
Mitnick, Moses (Also Known as Eddie Lewis), 9–8
Montgomery Engineering v. U.S., 20–43
Morris Trusts, Estelle, 2–16
Mulherin, Brian C., 9–28
Multnomah Operating Co., 19–49

N

National Muffler Dealers Ass'n, Inc. v. U.S., 2–28
Neuhoff, Ann R., 2–29
New Colonial Ice Co. v. Helvering, 6–2
Newman, Comm. v., 2–34
Nico, Severino R., 2–29
North American Oil Consolidated v. Burnet, 4–9, 18–10

O

Old Colony R. Co. v. Comm., 10–14
O'Malley v. Ames, 14–4

P

Page v. Rhode Island Hospital Trust Co., 6–9
Papineau, G. A., 5–15
Patterson, Floyd, 20–3
Pauli, Karl, 2–20
Paymer v. Comm., 20–3
Peacock, Cassius L., III, 3–14
Peck, William F., 15–16
Pfeifer, Donald R., 10–5
Phillips, Comm. v., 16–29
Pioneer Real Estate Co., 15–11

Pollock v. Farmers' Loan & Trust Co., 1-3, 5-28
Pulvers v. Comm., 7-10

R

Raffety Farms Inc. v. U.S., 20-3
Riach v. Frank, 10-6
Robarts, Mary K., 15-45
Robertson v. U.S., 5-5
Rogers, U.S. v., 7-10
Rose, Erie H., 10-12
Rosenberg v. Comm., 7-10
Rowan Companies, Inc. v. U.S., 5-15
Rubnitz, Alan A., 10-34
Rutkin v. U.S., 4-4

S

Sakol, Miriam, 19-31
Sanford, William F., 9-37
Sargent v. Comm., 4-14
Schlude v. Comm., 4-13
Schuster's Express Inc., 2-43
Shackelford, Betty J., 3-43
Sharer, Mary Lee, 3-27
Shaw, Charles M., 15-21
Sheehy, P. F. and A. G., 7-19
Sherman, Stephen G., 9-27
Shopmaker v. U.S., 7-10
Simons-Eastern Co. v. U.S., 2-21, 2-25
Simpson v. U.S., 5-6
Smith v. Comm., 4-24
Snow v. Comm., 7-18
Snowa, Jeanne G., 15-20
Soliman, Comm. v., 9-19
Solomon, Stephen L., 7-10
South Carolina v. Baker, 5-28
Stark, Nelda C., 2-29
Starker v. U.S., 15-28
Stolk v. Comm., 15-19
Strauss, Julia A., 4-8
Stucchi, Rudolph M., 15-30
Sullivan, Comm. v., 6-13

T

Tank Truck Rentals, Inc. v. Comm., 6-11
Tauferner v. U.S., 9-5
Tellier, Comm. v., 6-13
Thor Power Tool Co. v. Comm., 4-6, 18-32, 18-34
Toledo, Peoria & Western Railroad Company, 16-28
Tomerlin Trust, James O., 2-8
Tougher v. Comm., 5-16
Tufts v. Comm., 2-48, 14-3
Tyler, W. David, 9-23

U

United States Trust Co. of New York v. Anderson, 5-29
United States v. (see opposing party)
Untermann, John T., 2-49

V

Veenstra & DeHavaan Coal Co., 4-13
Vogel Fertilizer Co., U.S. v., 2-28

W

Ward, Dwight A., 6-16
Washington, Alexander, 4-20
Welch v. Helvering, 6-6
Whitaker, William T., 9-22
White, William C., 3-13
Wicker v. Comm., 14-4
Wilkerson, Donald L., 10-34
Wisconsin Cheeseman, Inc. v. U.S., 6-29
Withers, LaVar M., 10-35

Y

York v. Comm., 6-16

Z

Zabolotny v. Comm., 2-47, 2-48
Zaninovich v. Comm., 6-9, 18-12
Zarin v. Comm., 4-2

APPENDIX H
Depreciation

INTRODUCTION

Cost recovery, amortization, and depletion are presented in Chapter 8. For most fixed assets (e.g., machinery, equipment, furniture, fixtures, buildings) placed in service after December 31, 1980, the Economic Recovery Tax Act of 1981 (ERTA) has replaced the depreciation system with the cost recovery system.[1] The general relationship between the depreciation system and the cost recovery system is summarized in Exhibit H–1.

Despite ERTA, a discussion of § 167 depreciation is still relevant for two reasons. First, assets that were placed in service prior to 1981 are still in use. Second, certain assets placed in service after 1980 are not eligible to use the cost recovery system (ACRS and MACRS) and therefore must be depreciated. They include property placed in service after 1980 whose life is not based on years (e.g., units-of-production method).

DEPRECIATION

Section 167 permits a depreciation deduction in the form of a reasonable allowance for the exhaustion, wear and tear, and obsolescence of business property and property held for the production of income (e.g., rental property held by an investor).[2] Obsolescence refers to normal technological change due to reasonably foreseeable economic conditions. If rapid or abnormal obsolescence occurs, a taxpayer may change to a shorter estimated useful life if there is a "clear and

▼ EXHIBIT H–1
Depreciation and Cost Recovery: Relevant Time Periods

System	Date Property Is Placed in Service
§ 167 depreciation	Before January 1, 1981, and *certain* property placed in service after December 31, 1980.
Original accelerated cost recovery system (ACRS)	After December 31, 1980, and before January 1, 1987.
Modified accelerated cost recovery system (MACRS)	After December 31, 1986.

---

[1] Depreciation is covered in § 167, and cost recovery (ACRS and MACRS) is covered in § 168.

[2] § 167(a) and Reg. § 1.167(a)–1.

convincing basis for the redetermination." Depreciation deductions are *not* permitted for personal use property.

The taxpayer must adopt a reasonable and consistent plan for depreciating the cost or other basis of assets over the estimated useful life of the property (e.g., the taxpayer cannot arbitrarily defer or accelerate the amount of depreciation from one year to another). The basis of the depreciable property must be reduced by the depreciation allowed and by not less than the allowable amount.[3] The *allowed* depreciation is the depreciation actually taken, whereas the *allowable* depreciation is the amount that could have been taken under the applicable depreciation method. If the taxpayer does not claim any depreciation on property during a particular year, the basis of the property still must be reduced by the amount of depreciation that should have been deducted (the allowable depreciation).

EXAMPLE 1

On January 1, Ted paid $7,500 for a truck to be used in his business. He chose a five-year estimated useful life, no salvage value, and straight-line depreciation. Thus, the allowable depreciation deduction was $1,500 per year. However, depreciation actually taken (allowed) was as follows:

Year 1	$1,500
Year 2	–0–
Year 3	–0–
Year 4	1,500
Year 5	1,500

The adjusted basis of the truck must be reduced by the amount of allowable depreciation of $7,500 ($1,500 × 5 years) even though Ted claimed only $4,500 depreciation during the five-year period. Therefore, if Ted sold the truck at the end of Year 5 for $1,000, he would recognize a $1,000 gain, since the adjusted basis of the truck is zero. ▼

QUALIFYING PROPERTY AND BASIS FOR DEPRECIATION

The use rather than the character of property determines whether a depreciation deduction is permitted. Property must be used in a trade or business or held for the production of income to qualify as depreciable.

EXAMPLE 2

Carol is a self-employed CPA who maintains her office in a room in her home. The room, which is used exclusively for her business, comprises 20% of the square footage of her house. Carol is permitted a depreciation deduction only for the business use part of the house. No depreciation deduction is permitted for the 80% of the square footage of her house that is used as her residence. ▼

The basis for depreciation generally is the adjusted cost basis used to determine gain if the property is sold or otherwise disposed of.[4] However, if personal use assets are converted to business or income-producing use, the basis for depreciation *and* for loss is the *lower* of the adjusted basis or fair market value at the time of the conversion of the property.[5] As a result of this lower of basis

---

[3] § 1016(a)(2) and Reg. § 1.167(a)–10(a).
[4] § 167(c).
[5] Reg. § 1.167(g)–1.

rule, losses that occurred while the property was personal use property will not be recognized for tax purposes through the depreciation of the property.

EXAMPLE 3

Hans acquires a personal residence for $130,000. Four years later, when the fair market value is only $125,000, he converts the property to rental use. The basis for depreciation is $125,000, since the fair market value is less than the adjusted basis. The $5,000 decline in value is deemed to be personal (since it occurred while the property was held for personal use) and therefore nondeductible. ▼

The Regulations provide that tangible property is depreciable only to the extent that the property is subject to wear and tear, decay or decline from natural causes, exhaustion, and obsolescence.[6] Thus, land and inventory are not depreciable, but land improvements are depreciable (e.g., paved surfaces, fences, landscaping).

OTHER DEPRECIATION CONSIDERATIONS

In determining the amount of the depreciation deduction, the following additional considerations need to be addressed:

- The salvage value of the asset.
- The choice of depreciation methods.
- The useful life of the asset.

For property subject to depreciation under § 167, taxpayers generally must take into account the **salvage value** (assuming there is a salvage value) of an asset in calculating depreciation. An asset cannot be depreciated below its salvage value. However, the Code permits a taxpayer to disregard salvage value for amounts up to 10 percent of the basis in the property. This provision applies to tangible personal property (other than livestock) with an estimated useful life of three years or more.[7]

EXAMPLE 4

Green Company acquired a machine for $10,000 in 1980 with an estimated salvage value of $3,000 after 17 years. The company may disregard salvage value to the extent of $1,000 and compute the machine's depreciation based upon a cost of $10,000 less $2,000 salvage value. The adjusted basis may be reduced to $2,000 (depreciation of $8,000 may be taken) even though the actual salvage value is $3,000. ▼

This provision was incorporated into the law to reduce the number of IRS-taxpayer disputes over the amount of the salvage value that should be used.

Another consideration is the *choice of depreciation methods* from among the several allowed. The following alternative depreciation methods are permitted for property placed into service before January 1, 1981, and for the aforementioned property placed in service after December 31, 1980, for which cost recovery is not permitted:

- The straight-line (SL) method (cost basis less salvage value ÷ estimated useful life).
- The declining-balance method (DB) using a rate not to exceed twice the straight-line rate. Common methods include 200 percent DB (double-declining balance), 150 percent DB, and 125 percent DB. Salvage value is not taken into account under any of the declining-balance methods. However,

---
[6] Reg. § 1.167(a)–2.   [7] Reg. §§ 1.167(a)–1(c) and (f)–1.

no further depreciation can be claimed once net book value (cost minus depreciation) and salvage value are the same.
- The sum-of-the-years' digits method (SYD).
- Any other consistent method that does not result in greater total depreciation being claimed during the first two-thirds of the useful life than would have been allowable under the double-declining balance method. Permissible methods include machine hours and the units-of-production method.

EXAMPLE 5

On January 1, 1980, Diego acquired a new machine to be used in his business. The asset cost $10,000 with an estimated salvage value of $2,000 and a four-year estimated useful life.[8] The following amounts of depreciation could be deducted, depending on the method of depreciation used:

	1980	1981	1982	1983
1. Straight-line: $10,000 cost less ($2,000 salvage value reduced by 10% of cost) ÷ 4 years	$2,250	$2,250	$2,250	$2,250
2. Double-declining balance:				
a. $10,000 × 50% (twice the straight-line rate)	5,000			
b. ($10,000 − $5,000) × 50%		2,500		
c. ($10,000 − $5,000 − $2,500) × 50%			1,250	
d. ($10,000 − $5,000 − $2,500 − $1,250) × 50%				250[9]
3. Sum-of-the-years' digits:* $10,000 cost less ($2,000 salvage value reduced by 10% of cost) or $9,000				
a. $9,000 × 4/10	3,600			
b. $9,000 × 3/10		2,700		
c. $9,000 × 2/10			1,800	
d. $9,000 × 1/10				900

*The formula for the sum-of-the-years' digits (SYD) method is

$$\text{Cost} - \text{Salvage value} \times \frac{\text{Remaining life at the beginning of the year}}{\text{Sum-of-the-years' digits of the estimated life}}$$

In this example, the denominator for SYD is 1 + 2 + 3 + 4, or 10. The numerator is 4 for Year 1 (the number of years left at the beginning of Year 1), 3 for Year 2, etc. The denominator can be calculated by the following formula:

$$S = \frac{Y(Y + 1)}{2} \text{ where } Y = \text{estimated useful life}$$

$$S = \frac{4(4 + 1)}{2} = 10$$

EXAMPLE 6

Using the depreciation calculations in Example 5, the depreciation reserve (accumulated depreciation) and net book value at the end of 1983 are as follows:

	Cost −	Depreciation =	Net Book Value*
Straight-line	$10,000	$9,000	$1,000
Double-declining balance	10,000	9,000	1,000
Sum-of-the-years' digits	10,000	9,000	1,000

*Note that an asset may not be depreciated below its salvage value even when a declining-balance method is used.

---

[8] A four-year life is used to illustrate the different depreciation methods. Note that an asset placed in service in 1980 must have a useful life of at least 18 years in order for depreciation to be deducted in 1997.

[9] Total depreciation taken cannot exceed cost minus estimated salvage value ($1,000 in this example).

In 1969, Congress placed certain restrictions on the use of accelerated methods for new and used realty that are subject to the depreciation rules under § 167. These restrictions were imposed to reduce the opportunities for using real estate investments as tax shelters. The use of accelerated depreciation frequently resulted in the recognition of ordinary tax losses on economically profitable real estate ventures.

The following methods were permitted for residential and nonresidential real property:

	Nonresidential Real Property (Commercial and Industrial Buildings, Etc.)	**Residential Real Property (Apartment Buildings, Etc.)**
New property acquired after July 24, 1969, and generally before January 1, 1981	150% DB, SL	200% DB, SYD, 150% DB, or SL
Used property acquired after July 24, 1969, and generally before January 1, 1981	SL	125% DB (if estimated useful life is 20 years or greater) or SL

Congress chose to permit accelerated methods (200 percent declining-balance and sum-of-the-years' digits) for new residential rental property. Presumably, the desire to stimulate construction of new housing units justified the need for such accelerated methods.

Restrictions on the use of accelerated methods were not imposed on new tangible personalty (e.g., machinery, equipment, and automobiles). However, the 200 percent declining-balance and sum-of-the-years' digits methods were not permitted for used tangible personal property. The depreciation methods permitted for *used* tangible personal property were as follows:

	Useful Life of Three Years or More	**Useful Life of Less Than Three Years**
Used tangible personal property acquired after July 24, 1969, and generally before January 1, 1981	150% DB, SL	SL

Since the acquisition of used property does not result in any net addition to gross private investment in our economy, Congress chose not to provide as rapid accelerated depreciation for used property.

The determination of a *useful life* for a depreciable asset often led to disagreement between taxpayers and the IRS. One source of information was the company's previous experience and policy with respect to asset maintenance and utilization. Another source was the guideline lives issued by the IRS.[10] In 1971, the IRS guideline life system was modified and liberalized by the enactment of the **Asset Depreciation Range (ADR) system.**[11]

---

[10] Rev.Proc. 72–10, 1972–1 C.B. 721, superseded by Rev.Proc. 83–35, 1983–1 C.B. 745.

[11] Reg. § 1.167(a)–11.

KEY TERMS

Asset Depreciation Range (ADR) system, H–5

Salvage value, H–3

INDEX

A

Abandoned spouse rules, 3:26–27
Accelerated cost recovery system (ACRS and MACRS)
  alternative depreciation system (ADS), 8:23–24
  business and personal use of automobiles and other listed property, 8:17–18
    change from predominantly business use, 8:20–21
    leased automobiles, 8:21
    not used predominantly in business, 8:19–20
    substantiation requirements, 8:21–22
    used predominantly in business, 8:18–19
  eligible property under ACRS or MACRS, 8:5
  election to expense assets, 8:15
    annual limitations, 8:16–17
    conversion to personal use, 8:17
    effect on basis, 8:17
  personalty
    classification of property (ACRS), 8:5–7
    classification of property (MACRS), 8:8–10
    mid-quarter convention, 8:10–11
    reduction of basis for investment tax credit, 8:7–8
  realty
    ACRS, 8:11–12
    MACRS, 8:13–14
  straight-line election
    ACRS, 8:14–15
    MACRS, 8:15
  general considerations, 8:4
    cost recovery allowed or allowable, 8:4–5
    cost recovery basis for personal use assets converted to business or income-producing use, 8:5
    relevant time periods, 8:3
    reporting procedures, 8:29
    tables, 8:35–43
    tax planning, 8:33–34
Accelerated death benefits, 5:6–7
ACCESS, 2:38
Access expenditures, eligible for disabled access credit, 13:14

Accident and health insurance benefits from policy purchased by taxpayer, 5:13
  long-term care insurance benefits, 5:14–15
  provided by employer, 5:15
    medical reimbursement plans, 5:15–16
  See also Employee fringe benefits
Accountable employee business expense reimbursement plan, 9:21–22
  deemed substantiation, 9:23
  substantiation, 9:22–23
Accountant's Index, 2:26
Accounting income, 4:4, 20:14–16
Accounting methods, 4:7–9, 18:11
  change of method, 18:16, 18:19
    change from incorrect method, 18:17
    correction of error, 18:16
    disposition of net adjustment, 18:18
    net adjustments due to change, 18:17–18
  inventories, 18:31–37
  special methods, 18:18
    long-term contracts, 18:27–31
  tax planning for, 18:38–40
  timing of expense recognition in, 6:9
  See also Accrual method of accounting; Cash receipts method of accounting; Completed contract method of accounting; Hybrid method of accounting; Installment method of accounting
Accounting periods, 18:3
  business purpose, 18:5
  changes in, 18:7
    IRS requirements, 18:7–8
    making the election, 18:7
  mitigation of annual accounting period concept, 18:10
    restoration of amounts received under a claim of right, 18:10
  partnerships, 18:4–5
  personal service corporations, 18:6–7
  required tax payments, 18:5–6
  S corporations, 18:4–5
  taxable periods of less than one year, 18:8–10
Accounting and Tax Index, The, 2:26
Accounts and notes receivable, as capital asset, 16:5

Accrual method of accounting, 4:8–9
  all events test for income, 18:13–14
  economic performance test for deductions, 18:13, 18:14–15
  exceptions applicable to
    deferral of advance payments for goods, 4:13
    deferral of advance payments for services, 4:13–14
    prepaid income, 4:12–13
  recurring items in, 6:10
  reserves, 6:11, 18:15
  timing of expense recognition, 6:10–11
Acquiescence, 2:20
Acquisition indebtedness, 10:15–16
ACRS. *See* Accelerated cost recovery system (ACRS and MACRS)
Actions on Decisions, 2:29
Active income, 11:6
Active participation in rental real estate activities, 11:24
Activity not engaged in for profit. *See* Hobby losses
Ad valorem taxes, 1:6, 10:11–12
  on personalty, 1:7–8
  on realty, 1:6–7
Additional depreciation, 17:16
Adjusted basis, 14:4–5, 14:22, 14:23
Adjusted current earnings (ACE) adjustment, 12:28–30
Adjusted gross income (AGI), 3:5–6
  charitable contribution calculation, 10:23–26
  classification of interest expense, 10:18–19
  deductions for, 3:5–6, 6:2–5, 7:2
    expenses of self-employed persons, 9:3
  deductions from, 6:2–3, 7:2
    employee expenses, 9:3
  medical expense calculation, 10:2–4
  net operating losses and, 7:24–25
  Social Security calculation, 4:35–36
  two-percent floor calculation, 9:25–26, 10:27–28
  See also Gross Income; Income
Adjusted sales price (of personal residence), 15:19
Adoption expenses tax credit, 13:19–20
Age, extra standard deduction for persons over 65, 3:7, 3:22

I–1

Age test, for earned income credit, **13**:16
Agent, income received by, **4**:16
Alimony, **19**:25
Alimony recapture, **4**:21–23
Alimony and separate maintenance payments, **4**:19–20
  child support, **4**:23
  deduction of, **4**:19
  front-loading, **4**:21–23
  inclusion in gross income, **4**:19
  post-1984 agreements and decrees, **4**:20–21
  tax planning for, **4**:39–40
All events test, **6**:10
  for deductions, **18**:13–14
  for income, **18**:13–14
Allocable parental tax, **3**:19–20
Alternate valuation amount, **14**:15
Alternative capital gains tax, **16**:21–23
Alternative depreciation system (ADS), **8**:23–24
Alternative minimum tax adjustments, **12**:4
Alternative minimum tax (AMT), **12**:2
  AMT computation, **12**:23–24
  AMT credit, **12**:24, **12**:27
  corporate, **12**:27
    AMT adjustments
      applicable only to corporations, **12**:28–30
      applicable to individuals and corporations, **12**:27–28
    exemption, **12**:31
    other aspects, **12**:31
    tax preferences, **12**:30–31
  corporate versus noncorporate treatment, **20**:7, **20**:14
  individual, **12**:25–26
    AMT adjustments
      adjusted gain or loss, **12**:13–14
      alternative tax net operating loss deduction, **12**:15–16
      circulation expenditures, **12**:9
      depreciation of post-1986 personal property, **12**:10–11
      depreciation of post-1986 real property, **12**:9–10
      direction of, **12**:9
      expenditures requiring 10-year write-off for AMT purposes, **12**:11–12
      incentive stock options (ISOs), **12**:12–13
      itemized deductions, **12**:16–19
      other adjustments, **12**:20
      passive activity losses, **12**:14–15
      pollution control facilities, **12**:11
      use of completed contract method of accounting, **12**:12
  AMT formula for alternative minimum taxable income (AMTI), **12**:3–4
    adjustments, **12**:4–5
    tax preferences, **12**:5–6
  AMT formula (other components), **12**:6–7
    AMT rate schedule, **12**:8

    exemption amount, **12**:7
    regular tax liability, **12**:8–9
  AMT preferences, **12**:20
    depreciation, **12**:21–22
    fifty percent exclusion for certain small business stock, **12**:23
    intangible drilling costs, **12**:20–21
    interest on private activity bonds, **12**:21
    percentage depletion, **12**:20
  municipal bonds and, **12**:22
  tax planning for, **12**:31–33
Alternative minimum tax credit, **12**:24, **12**:27
Alternative minimum tax exclusions, **12**:27
Alternative minimum taxable income (AMTI), **12**:3
  See also Alternative minimum tax (AMT)
Alternative tax NOL deduction (ATNOLD), **12**:15–16
American Institute of CPAs, ethical guidelines, **1**:23–24
Americans with Disabilities Act, **13**:3
Amortizable bond premiums as capital recovery, **14**:6–7
Amortizable Section 197 intangible, **8**:24
Amortization, **8**:3, **8**:24–25
  Form 4562, **8**:30–31
  of research and experimental expenditures, **7**:19–20
Amount realized from sale or other disposition, **14**:3–4
Annual accounting period concept, **1**:28–29
  mitigation of, **18**:10
Annuities
  income from, **4**:28
    collection on and after annuity starting date, **4**:29–31
    collection before annuity starting date, **4**:28–29
    one life-expected return multiples, **4**:30
    simplified method for distributions from qualified retirement plans, **4**:31
    taxation of, **4**:32
    unrecovered investment in, **10**:28
Appellate courts, **2**:15–19, **2**:21
Appropriate economic unit, **11**:12
Archer, Bill, **1**:18
Armey, Dick, **1**:17
Arm's length concept, **1**:33
Assets
  amortizable Section 197 intangibles, **8**:24
  business, **17**:2
  capital, **16**:2–30
  classification of, **1**:7–8
  expensing of, **8**:15–17
  investment, **16**:4
  personal use, **14**:8, **16**:4
  Section 1231, **17**:3–12
  valuation of, **4**:4
Assignment of income, **4**:14

Associated with business test for entertainment expenses, **9**:16–17, **9**:28
Associations, taxed as corporations, **20**:3–4
At-risk limits, **11**:3, **11**:4–6
  See also Passive loss rules
Audit process
  selection of returns, **1**:18–19
  settlement procedures, **1**:20–21
  types of audits, **1**:19–20
Automatic mileage method of auto expense computation, **9**:6–7
Automobiles
  change from predominantly business use, **8**:20–21
  computation of auto expenses, **9**:6–7
  leased, **8**:21
  luxury, **8**:17–19
  not used predominantly in business, **8**:19
  used predominantly in business, **8**:18–19
Average benefits test, for qualified plans, **19**:8
Awards, **4**:32–33

B

Backup withholding, **13**:33
Bad debts, **7**:3
  business versus nonbusiness, **7**:4–5
  deduction of, **7**:8
  loans between related parties, **7**:5
  loss of deposits in insolvent financial institutions, **7**:6
  nonbusiness, **16**:8–9
  specific chargeoff method, **7**:3–4
Bankruptcy, **7**:4
  IRS actions after declaration of, **2**:15
Basic research, **13**:12
Basic research payments, **13**:12
Basis
  adjusted, **14**:4–5, **14**:22, **14**:23
  determination of cost basis, **14**:9
    allocation problems, **14**:10–11
    identification problems, **14**:9
  gain basis, **14**:12, **14**:20
  of gift, **14**:12–15
  of partnership interest, **20**:30–31
  of personal residence, **15**:21–22
  of property acquired from decedent, **14**:15–17
  of property contributed to partnership, **20**:31–32
  of property received in like-kind exchange, **15**:7–9
  reduction of for investment tax credit, **8**:7–8
  in S corporations, **20**:28–29
  stepped-down, **14**:15
  stepped-up, **14**:15
  in subsidiary liquidation situations, **20**:23
  summary of adjustments to, **14**:23–25
  of transfers to controlled corporations, **20**:18–19
Below-market interest, **4**:23–28
Benefit received rule, **10**:20

Bequests, **14**:27
Blindness, extra standard deduction for, **3**:7, **3**:22
Blue Cross/Blue Shield organizations, AMT adjustment for, **12**:28
Bluebook, **2**:30
Board of Tax Appeals, **2**:20
Bonds, amortizable bond premium as capital recovery, **14**:6–7
Boot, in like-kind exchange, **15**:5–7
Bracket creep, **1**:29
Business assets, **17**:2
  See also Section 1231 assets
Business bad debts, **7**:5
Business energy credits, **13**:9
Business entity
  choice of, **20**:4, **20**:5
  See also Forms of doing business
Business expense, **6**:5–7
Business fixed assets, not considered as capital assets, **16**:5
Business gifts, **9**:18–19
Business meals, **9**:17–18

C

Cafeteria benefit plans, **5**:18–19, **19**:41
Calendar year, **18**:5
Capital additions, **14**:4, **14**:5
Capital assets
  definition of, **3**:29, **16**:3–4
    accounts and notes receivable, **16**:4–5
    business fixed assets, **16**:5
    copyrights and creative works, **16**:5
    inventory, **16**:4
    U.S. government publications, **16**:5
  effect of judicial action, **16**:6
  holding period, **16**:16
    short sales, **16**:17–20
    special holding period rules, **16**:16
      certain disallowed loss transactions, **16**:17
      certain nontaxable transactions involving carryover of another taxpayer's basis, **16**:16–17
      inherited property, **16**:17
      nontaxable exchanges, **16**:16
  long-term nonpersonal use, **17**:7–8
  relationship of to Section 1231 assets, **17**:3–4
  sale or exchange of, **16**:9
    franchises, trademarks, and trade names, **16**:13, **16**:15
      contingent payments, **16**:14
      noncontingent payments, **16**:14
      significant power, right, or continuing interest, **16**:13–14
      sports franchises, **16**:14–15
    lease cancellation payments, **16**:15–16
    options, **16**:10–12
    patents, **16**:12–13
    retirement of corporate obligations (special rule), **16**:9–10
      original issue discount, **16**:10
    worthless securities and Section 1244 stock, **16**:9

statutory expansions, **16**:7
  dealers in securities, **16**:7
  lump-sum distributions, **16**:8
  nonbusiness bad debts, **16**:8–9
  real property subdivided for sale, **16**:7–8
tax planning
  capital asset status, **16**:27–28, **16**:27–29
  effect of capital asset status in transactions other than sales, **16**:28–29
  maximizing benefits, **16**:29–30
  stock sales, **16**:29
  year-end planning, **16**:30
See also Capital gains; Capital losses
Capital contributions, **20**:17–18
Capital expenditures
  disallowance of deductions for, **6**:26–27
  tax planning for, **6**:33
Capital gain property, **10**:24–25
  limitations on charitable contribution of, **10**:24–25
Capital gains, **16**:2–3
  computation of net capital gains, **3**:29, **16**:21–23
  nonbusiness, **7**:22
  reporting procedures, **16**:25–26
  tax treatment of, **20**:7
    corporate taxpayers, **16**:27
    noncorporate taxpayers, **16**:20–23, **16**:25
See also Capital assets
Capital improvements, to personal residence, **15**:20–21
Capital loss deduction, **16**:20
Capital losses, **16**:2–3
  computation of net capital losses, **3**:29
  limitation on
    corporate, **3**:30
    noncorporate, **3**:29–30
  tax treatment of, **20**:7–8
    corporate taxpayers, **16**:27
    noncorporate taxpayers, **16**:20, **16**:23–25
See also Capital assets
Capital recoveries, **14**:4, **14**:5–7
Carry backs and carry forwards
  net capital gains and losses, **16**:23–25
  net operating losses (NOL), **7**:20–21
Cash or deferred arrangement plan (Section 401[k] plan), **19**:18–19
Cash receipts method of accounting, **4**:8, **18**:11–12
  exceptions applicable to
    amounts received under an obligation to repay, **4**:12
    constructive receipt, **4**:9–11
    original issue discount, **4**:11
    Series E and EE bonds, **4**:11–12
  farming, **18**:12–13
  restrictions on use of, **18**:12
  tax planning for, **4**:38, **18**:38–39
  timing of expense recognition, **6**:9–10
Casualty, as capital recovery, **14**:5
Casualty gains, **7**:15–17

Casualty losses, **7**:9–10, **7**:17
  documentation of, **7**:26
  events that are not casualties, **7**:10
  measuring the amount of loss
    amount of loss, **7**:12–13
    multiple losses, **7**:14–15
    reduction for $100 and 10 percent-of-AGI floors, **7**:13–14
  personal casualty gains and losses, **7**:15–17
  Section 1231 assets, **17**:7–8
  statutory framework for deduction of, **7**:15
  theft losses, **7**:10–11
  when to deduct, **7**:11
    disaster area losses, **7**:12
Casualty netting, **17**:8
CCH's Federal Tax Service, **2**:25
CD-ROM tax services, **2**:36–37
Certainty, in tax structure, **1**:5
Charitable contributions, **10**:19
  of appreciated property, **10**:27
  corporate treatment of, **20**:8–9
  criteria for a gift, **10**:20
    benefit received rule, **10**:20
    contribution of services, **10**:20–21
    nondeductible items, **10**:21
  limitation on deduction, **10**:23
    capital gain property, **10**:24–25
    contribution carryovers, **10**:26
    fifty percent ceiling, **10**:25
    ordinary income property, **10**:23–24
    thirty percent ceiling, **10**:25–26
    twenty percent ceiling, **10**:26
  qualified organizations, **10**:21
  recapture and, **17**:20
  record-keeping and valuation requirements, **10**:22
  tax planning for, **10**:34–36
  time of deduction, **10**:20–21
Child
  personal services of, **4**:14
  under age 14, income of taxed at parents' rate, **3**:19–21
Child and dependent care expenses, tax credit for, **13**:20
  calculation of, **13**:21–22
  dependent care assistance program, **13**:22
  earned income ceiling, **13**:21
  eligibility, **13**:20
  eligible employment-related expenses, **13**:20–21
  noncustodial parent able to deduct medical expenses paid for child, **10**:7
  reporting requirements, **13**:22
  tax planning, **13**:38–39
Child support, **4**:23
Chronic illness, accelerated death benefits and, **5**:6–7
Circuit Court of Appeals, **2**:15–17
Circulation expenditures, **12**:4, **12**:9
Citizenship test (dependency exemption), **3**:15
Claim of right doctrine, **10**:28, **18**:10
Claims Court Reporter, **2**:21

Clear business purpose test for entertainment expenses, 9:17–18
Client letter, 2:33
Closely held C corporations, passive loss rules and, 11:11
Club dues, 9:18
Comm. v. Duberstein, 5:5
Commerce Clearing House (CCH), 2:20
Commissioner of Internal Revenue, 1:18
Commissioner v. Newman, 2:34
Common law states, survivor's share of property, 14:17
Community property states, 1:30–31, 4:17–19
　spouses living apart, 4:18–19
　survivor's share of property, 14:17
　tax planning in, 4:39
Commuter highway vehicle, 5:23
Commuting expenses, 9:5–6
　See also Travel expenses
Compensation, reasonable, 6:7
Compensation-related loans, 4:28
Compensatory damages, 5:11
　personal injury, 5:11
　punitive damages, 5:11–12
Completed contract method, 18:28, 18:30
　tax planning, 18:38
Completed contract method of accounting, AMT adjustment for, 12:12
Computer-assisted tax research, 2:35–36
Congress
　tax credits created by, 13:3–4
　tax legislative process in, 2:4–5
　treatment of business assets determined by, 17:4
Constructive dividends, 20:21–22
Constructive ownership, 6:28
Constructive receipt, 4:9–11, 18:11–12
Contingent payments, 16:14
Controlled corporations, transfers to, 20:18–19
Convenience, in tax structure, 1:4, 1:5
Conventions, travel to, 9:9
Copyrights, as capital assets, 16:5
Corporate distributions, as capital recovery, 14:6
Corporate obligations, retirement of, 16:9–10
Corporate stock, as capital asset, 16:6
Corporation-shareholder loans, 4:28
Corporations
　association approach, 20:3–4
　compliance with state law, 20:3
　formation
　　capital contributions, 20:17–18
　　thin capitalization, 20:18
　　transfers to controlled corporations, 20:18
　　　basis considerations and computation of gain, 20:18–19
　income tax considerations, 20:16–17
　corporate filing requirements, 20:14
　deductions available only to corporations
　　deduction of organizational expenditures, 20:12
　　dividends received deduction, 20:10–12
　determination of corporate tax liability
　　alternative minimum tax, 20:14
　　income tax rates, 20:12–13
　　individuals and corporations compared, 20:6–7, 20:16–17
　　reconciliation of corporate taxable income and accounting income, 20:14–15
　　specific provisions compared, 20:7
　　　capital gains and losses, 20:7–8
　　　charitable contributions, 20:8–9
　　　net operating losses, 20:10
　　　recapture and depreciation, 20:8
　limited liability companies, 20:5
　liquidation, 20:22
　　basis determination (Sections 334 and 338), 20:23
　　　subsidiary liquidation basis rules, 20:23
　　effect of on corporation, 20:24
　　exception to the general rule, 20:23
　　general rule of Section 331, 20:23
　operations
　　dividend distributions, 20:20
　　　constructive dividends, 20:21–22
　　　earnings and profits, 20:20–21
　　　property dividends, 20:21
　　　stock redemptions, 20:21–22
　retirement of obligations of, 16:9–10
　special recapture for, 17:23
　tax planning, 20:34–35
　See also S corporations
Correspondence audit, 1:19–20
Cosmetic surgery, 10:4
Cost basis, determination of, 14:9–11
Cost depletion, 8:26–27
Cost recovery allowances, as capital recovery, 14:5
Cost recovery system. *See* Accelerated cost recovery system (ACRS and MACRS)
Courts, influence of on tax law, 1:32–33
Covenant not to compete, as amortizable asset, 8:24
Creative works, as capital assets, 16:5
Credits. *See* Tax credits
Cumulative Bulletin (C.B.), 2:10, 2:19, 2:20
Current participation tests, 11:15–17
Current Tax Payment Act, 1:4
Customs duties, 1:17

D

Damages, 5:11–13
　taxation of, 5:12
De minimis fringes, 5:23, 5:24–25, 9:16
De minimis rule, percentage of completion method of accounting, 18:31
Dealers in securities, 16:7
Death
　disposition of passive interest at, 11:25–26
　recapture and, 17:20
Death benefits, 5:5–6
　accelerated, 5:6–7
Death taxes, 1:10–11
Deathbed gifts, 14:16
Debt discharge, 5:32–34
Decedent, income in respect of, 10:28
Deductions
　from adjusted gross income, 6:2–3
　for adjusted gross income, 6:2–5
　　itemized deductions, 6:4
　　　deductible personal expenses, 6:5
　　Section 212 expenses, 6:4–5
　all events and economic performance tests for, 18:13–15
　business and nonbusiness losses, 6:7
　classification of, 6:2–3, 6:31
　compared to tax credits, 3:18
　disallowance possibilities, 6:11
　　deductions for capital expenditures, 6:26–27
　　excessive executive compensation, 6:14–15
　　expenditures incurred for taxpayer's benefit or obligation, 6:23–25
　　expenses and interest relating to tax-exempt income, 6:29–30
　　hobby losses, 6:16–19
　　investigation of a business, 6:15–16
　　personal expenditures, 6:25–26
　　political contributions and lobbying activities, 6:14
　　public policy limitation, 6:11–12
　　　expenses related to illegal business, 6:13–14
　　　legal expenses incurred in defense of civil or criminal penalties, 6:12–13
　　related-party transactions, 6:27–28
　　rental of vacation homes, 6:19–23
　　substantiation requirements, 6:28–29
　itemized, 3:6
　　AMT and, 12:16–17
　　　cutback adjustment, 12:17
　　　housing interest, 12:18
　　　interest in general, 12:17
　　　investment interest, 12:18–19
　　　medical expenses, 12:17
　　average amounts of, 10:3
　　charitable contributions, 10:19–27
　　interest, 10:13–19
　　limitations on
　　　miscellaneous deductions not subject to 2 percent floor, 9:25–26
　　　miscellaneous deductions subject to 2 percent floor, 9:25
　　medical expenses, 3:32–33, 10:4–10
　　miscellaneous, 10:27–28
　　other miscellaneous deductions, 10:28–29
　　overall limitation on, 10:29, 10:31–32
　　tax planning for, 10:32–36
　　taxes, 10:10–13
　nonbusiness, 7:22
　reporting procedures, 6:7–8, 8:29–30
　standard, 3:7–8, 3:9, 3:22
　tax planning for
　　capital expenditures, 6:33

excessive executive compensation, 6:32
  hobby losses, 6:32–33
  shifting deductions, 6:32
  time value of deductions, 6:30–32
  unreasonable compensation, 6:32
  timing of expense recognition
    accrual method requirements, 6:10–11
    cash method requirements, 6:9–10
    method of accounting, 6:9
  trade or business and production of income expenses, 6:5–6
    ordinary and necessary requirement, 6:6
    reasonableness requirement, 6:7
Deemed substantiation, of employee business expenses, 9:22–23
Defendant, 2:19
Deferred compensation, 19:2–4
  individual retirement accounts, 19:20–26
  nonqualified deferred compensation plans, 19:27–31
  qualified pension, profit sharing, and stock bonus plans, 19:4–20
  restricted property plans, 19:31–34
  retirement plans for self-employed individuals, 19:20
  stock options, 19:34–38
  tax planning, 19:38
Deferred taxes, interest on, 18:26
Deficiency, payment of, 2:15
Deficit Reduction Act (1984), 8:12
Defined benefit plan, 19:4, 19:5, 19:15–16
Defined contribution pension plan, 19:4–5
Defined contribution plan, 19:5, 19:15
Department of the Treasury, 1:18
Dependency exemptions, 3:10–11
  citizenship or residency test, 3:15
  gross income test, 3:14
  joint return test, 3:15
  phase-out of, 3:15–16
  relationship or member-of-the-household test, 3:14–15
  support test, 3:11–13
  tax planning for, 3:31–33
Dependent care assistance program, 13:22
Dependents
  filing requirements for, 3:22–23
  medical expenses incurred for, 10:6–7
  special limitations for individuals who can be claimed as, 3:9–10
  tax credit for care expenses, 13:20–22
Depletion, 8:3, 8:25–26
  intangible drilling and development costs (IDC), 8:26–27
  methods of, 8:26
    cost depletion, 8:26–27
    effect of IDC on depletion, 8:28–29
    percentage depletion, 8:27–28
  tax planning, 8:34
Deposits, 7:6
  loss of due to insolvency of financial institution, 7:6

Depreciable tangible personal property, in like-kind exchanges, 15:4–5
Depreciation, 8:2–3
  additional, 17:16
  as AMT preference item, 12:22–23
  as capital recovery, 14:5
  Form 4562, 8:30–31
  gift basis for, 14:14–15
  recapture of in corporations, 20:8
  See also Accelerated cost recovery system; Recapture
Determination letters, 2:11–12
Disabled access credit, 13:13–14
Disabled taxpayers, tax credit for, 13:16–18
Disallowed losses, 14:17–20, 14:27–28, 16:17
Disaster area losses, 7:12
Disguised compensation, scholarships as, 5:9–10
Distance test, for moving expenses, 9:11–12
Dividends, 4:15–16, 5:29
  constructive, 20:21–22
  distribution of, 20:19–22
  property, 20:21
    recapture and, 17:21–23
  stock, 5:30
Dividends received deduction, 20:10–12
Divorce
  noncustodial parent able to deduct medical expenses paid, 10:7
  tax issues, 4:19–23
Dollar value LIFO, 18:35–36
Domestic entities, 20:5
Domestic travel, 9:10
Drug dealers, deduction of expenses of, 6:13–14
Dual basis property, 14:12

E

E-mail, 2:39–40
Early distribution, from qualified plan, 19:10
Earned income credit, 13:14–15
  advance payment, 13:16
  earned income credit table, 13:15
  eligibility requirements, 13:15–16
Earnings and profits, 20:20–21
Economic income, 4:3
Economic performance test, 6:10
  for deductions, 18:14–15
Economic Recovery Tax Act of 1981 (ERTA), 8:2
Economy, in tax structure, 1:5
Education, travel as form of, 9:9
Education expenses, 9:13–14
  classification of specific items, 9:15
  maintaining or improving existing skills, 9:14
  other provisions, 9:15
  requirements imposed by law or by employer for retention of employment, 9:14
  tax planning for, 9:27
Educational institutions, employees of, campus housing provided for, 5:17

Educational savings bonds, 4:11–12, 4:37, 4:38–39, 5:30–31
Eisner v. Macomber, 4:4
Elderly taxpayers, tax credit for, 13:16–18
Eligible access expenditures, 13:14
Employee
  cash or other property received by, 5:5
  compared to self-employed individual, 9:2–4
  death benefits, 5:6–8
    accelerated, 5:6–7
  of educational institution, 5:17
  expenses of, 9:3, 9:4
    classification, 9:21
      accountable plans, 9:21–23, 9:22–23
      nonaccountable plans, 9:23–24
      reporting procedures, 9:24
    contributions to Individual Retirement Accounts, 9:21
    education, 9:13–15, 9:27–28
    entertainment, 9:15–19, 9:28
    miscellaneous, 9:20–21
    moving expenses, 9:11–13
    office in the home, 9:19–21
    shifting deductions between employer and employee, 9:26
    transportation, 9:5–7, 9:26–27
    travel, 9:7–11, 9:27
    unreimbursed business expenses, 9:28
  highly compensated, 19:8–9
  personal services of, 4:14
  statutory, 9:4
Employee achievement awards, 4:33
Employee fringe benefits, 5:18
  cafeteria plans, 5:18–19
  flexible spending plans, 5:19
  general classes of excluded benefits, 5:19–20, 5:26
    de minimis fringes, 5:23, 5:24–25, 9:16
    no-additional-cost services, 5:21
    nondiscrimination provisions, 5:24–25
    qualified employee discounts, 5:21–22
    qualified moving expense reimbursements, 5:24
    qualified transportation fringes, 5:23–24
    working condition fringes, 5:23
  tax planning for, 5:34–35
  taxable, 5:25
  See also Accident and health insurance benefits
Employee stock ownership plans (ESOPs), 19:6–7
Employer-employee relationship, 9:4
Employer-sponsored accident and health plans, 5:13–15
Employment taxes, 13:22, 13:24
  amount of FICA taxes, 13:27–28
  amount of income tax withholding, 13:28–30, 13:32
  backup withholding, 13:33

coverage requirements, **13**:25–27
reporting procedures, **13**:32–33
Energy credits, **13**:9
Entertainment expenses, **9**:15
  classification of, **9**:16–17
  dollar limitations, **9**:16
  restrictions upon deductibility
    business gifts, **9**:18–19
    business meals, **9**:17–18
    club dues, **9**:18
    ticket purchased for entertainment, **9**:18
  tax planning for, **9**:28
Entity status
  change of, **20**:5
  See also Forms of doing business
Equality, in tax structure, **1**:4, **1**:5
ERTA. *See* Economic Recovery Tax Act of 1981 (ERTA)
Estate taxes, **1**:11–12
Estates, income from, **4**:17
Estimated tax, **13**:33–34
Excess cost recovery, **8**:20–21
Excessive executive compensation, **6**:14–15, **6**:31
Excise taxes
  federal, **1**:8–9
  state, **1**:9
Exclusion amount, for annuity, **4**:29
Exclusion ratio, for annuity, **4**:31
Exclusive benefit requirement, **19**:7
Exemptions
  dependency, **3**:10–16
  personal, **3**:10
  phase-out of, **3**:15–16
Expected return, on annuity, **4**:29–31
Expensing of assets, **8**:15–17
Extraordinary personal services, **11**:20

F

Facts and circumstances test, **11**:17–18
Fair market value, **14**:4
Family businesses, tax planning for, **20**:35–36
Farming, **18**:12–13
Federal Claims Reporter, **2**:21
Federal District Court, **2**:13, **2**:14–15, **2**:17
  citations of, **2**:21
Federal estate tax on income in respect of a decedent, **10**:28
Federal Income, Gift and Estate Taxation, **2**:25
Federal income tax. *See* Income tax
Federal Insurance Contributions Act (FICA). *See* FICA taxes
Federal Register, **2**:9
Federal Second Series (F.2d), **2**:21
Federal Tax Articles, **2**:25
Federal Tax Coordinator 2d, **2**:25
Federal Third Series (F.3d), **2**:21
Federal Unemployment Tax Act (FUTA). *See* FUTA taxes
Fees, distinguished from taxes, **10**:11
Fellowships, **5**:9–11
FICA taxes, **1**:16, **13**:22, **13**:26–28
Field audit, **1**:20
FIFO (first in, first out), **18**:35

FIFO method, applied to carryovers, carrybacks, and utilization of tax credits, **13**:7
Fifty percent organizations, **10**:25
Filing status, **13**:24–26
Finalized Regulations, **2**:8–9
Fiscal year, **18**:3
Fixing-up expenses, **15**:19–20
Fixtures, **1**:6
Flat tax, **1**:17–18
Flexible spending plans, **5**:19
Foreign earned income, **5**:25, **5**:27–28
Foreign earned income exclusion, **5**:25, **5**:27–28
Foreign Sales Corporations (FSCs), **1**:25
Foreign tax credit (FTC), **13**:18–19
  tax planning for, **13**:37
Foreign tax credits, AMT and, **12**:31
Foreign travel, **9**:10–11
Form 940 (940 EZ) (Employer's Annual Federal Unemployment Tax Return), **13**:32
Form 970 (Application to Use LIFO Inventory Method), **18**:36
Form 1040, **6**:8
Form 1120, **20**:14
Form 1120-A, **20**:14
Form 3115 (Application for Change in Accounting Method), **18**:16
Form 4562 (Depreciation and Amortization), **8**:30–31
Form 4797 (Sale of Business Property), **17**:26–27
Form 6251 (Alternative Minimum Tax—Individuals), **12**:26
Form SS-4 (Application for Employer Identification Number), **13**:32
Form W-2 (Wage and Tax Statement), **13**:32
Form W-3 (Transmittal of Wage and Tax Statements), **13**:32
Form W-4 (withholding allowances), **13**:29–32
Forms of doing business
  tax consequences of, **20**:5–6, **20**:34–35
  See also Corporations; Partnerships; S corporations
Franchise taxes, **1**:17
Franchises, **8**:24, **16**:13–14
  sports franchises, **16**:14–15
Fraud, **1**:23
Fringe benefits. *See* Employee fringe benefits
Fruit and tree metaphor, **4**:14
Functional use test (involuntary conversions), **15**:12
FUTA taxes, **1**:16, **13**:22, **13**:26–28

G

GAAP. *See* Generally accepted accounting principles (GAAP)
Gain basis, **14**:12, **14**:20
Gains
  adjusted, for AMT, **12**:13–14
  capital gains, **3**:29
    capital loss limitation, **3**:29–30
    computation of net capital gains, **3**:29

  definition of capital asset, **3**:29
  in involuntary conversion of personal residence, **15**:15
  nonrecognition of, **14**:7–8
    in involuntary conversions, **15**:14–15
    sale, exchange, or condemnation of personal use assets, **14**:8
    in sale of personal residence, **15**:15, **15**:19–20
  from property transactions (in general), **3**:27–28
  realized, **14**:3
    adjusted basis, **14**:4–5, **14**:22
    amount realized, **14**:3–4, **14**:21–22
    capital additions, **14**:5
    capital recoveries, **14**:5–7
    sale or other disposition, **14**:3–4
  recognized, **14**:7
  recovery of capital doctrine, **14**:8–9
  Section 1231, **17**:4
  in transfers to controlled corporations, **20**:18–19
Gambling losses and winnings, **10**:28
General business tax credit, **13**:6–7
  treatment of unused credits, **13**:7
General Counsel Memoranda (GCMs), **2**:12
General Explanation of the Act, **2**:30
General sales taxes, **1**:9
Generally accepted accounting principles (GAAP), **18**:32
Geothermal energy property, tax credit for, **13**:9
Gift loans, **4**:26–28
Gift taxes, **1**:12–13, **14**:12, **14**:13
  adjustment for, **14**:13
Gifts
  basis of, **14**:12
    adjustment for gift tax, **14**:13
    basis for depreciation, **14**:14–15
    holding period, **14**:13–14
    rules if no gift tax is paid, **14**:12–13
  criteria for, **10**:20
  deathbed, **14**:16
  definition of, **5**:5
  disposition of passive interest by, **11**:26
  recapture potential of, **17**:20
  received by employees, **5**:5
  tax planning for, **14**:26–27
  See also Charitable contributions
Golden parachute, **19**:29–30
Golsen decision, **2**:17
Goods, deferral of advance payments for, **4**:13
Goodwill, **8**:24, **14**:10
Goodwill entertainment expenses, **9**:16–17, **9**:28
Groetzinger case, **7**:2, **7**:26
Gross estate, **1**:11
Gross income, **3**:3–5, **4**:3
  accounting and tax concepts of, **4**:4–6
  economic and accounting concepts of, **4**:3–4
  form of receipt, **4**:6
  items specifically excluded from, **3**:4, **5**:2–4, **5**:26

compensation for injuries and
  sickness, **5:**11–13
dividends, **5:**29–30
educational savings bonds, **5:**30–31
employee death benefits, **5:**6–8
employer-sponsored accident and
  health plans, **5:**13–15
foreign earned income, **5:**25,
  5:27–28
gifts and inheritances, **5:**4–6
income from discharge of
  indebtedness, **5:**32–34
interest on certain state and local
  government obligations, **5:**28–29
life insurance proceeds, **5:**6–8
meals and lodging, **5:**15–18
other employee fringe benefits,
  5:18–25
qualified state tuition programs,
  5:31
scholarships, **5:**8–11
statutory authority, **5:**4
tax benefit rule, **5:**32
items specifically included in, **3:**4, **4:**19
  alimony and separate maintenance
    payments, **4:**19–23
  annuities, **4:**28–32
  child support, **4:**23
  group term life insurance, **4:**33–34
  imputed interest on below-market
    loans, **4:**25–28
  prizes and awards, **4:**32–33
  Social Security benefits, **4:**34–36
  unemployment compensation, **4:**34
recovery of capital doctrine, **4:**6–7
year of inclusion
  accounting methods, **4:**7–9
  exceptions applicable to accrual
    basis taxpayers, **4:**12–14
  exceptions applicable to cash basis
    taxpayers, **4:**9–12
  taxable year, **4:**7
See also Adjusted gross income;
  Income
Gross income test, dependency
  exemption, **3:**14–15, **3:**32
Group term life insurance, **4:**33–34

H

Half-year convention, **8:**7
Hand, Learned, **2:**34
Handicapped persons, impairment-
  related work expenses of, **10:**28
Hazard of litigation, **1:**20
Head of household, tax rates for, **3:**26
Health insurance, value of excluded
  from gross income, **5:**13–15
Health Insurance Portability and
  Accountability Act of 1996, **10:**10
Highly compensated employee,
  19:8–9
Hobby losses, **6:**16
  determining amount of deduction,
    6:17–19
  general rules, **6:**17
  presumptive rule of Section 183, **6:**17
  tax planning for, **6:**32–33
Holding period

certain disallowed loss transactions,
  16:17
certain nontaxable transactions
  involving carryover of another
  taxpayer's basis, **16:**16–17
disallowed losses between related
  taxpayers, **14:**18
inherited property, **16:**17
for long-term capital gain or loss
  treatment, **16:**16–20
nontaxable exchanges, **16:**16
of personal residence, **15:**21–22
of property acquired by gift, **14:**13–14
of property acquired from a decedent,
  14:17
of property received in like-kind
  exchange, **15:**7–9
Holmes, Oliver Wendell, **4:**14
Home equity loans, **10:**16
Home office expenses, **9:**19–21
Home pages, **2:**37–38
House Ways and Means Committee, **2:**4,
  2:5, **2:**30
H.R. 10 (Keogh) plans, **19:**20–22, **19:**24,
  19:38–39
Hybrid method of accounting, **4:**9, **18:**16

I

Illegal business, deduction of expense
  related to, **6:**13–14
Improvements made by lessee, **5:**4
Imputed interest, **4:**23–28, **18:**22–23
  exceptions and limitations, **4:**26–28
  tax avoidance and other
    below-market loans, **4:**25–28
Incentive stock options (ISOs), **12:**12–13,
  19:34–37
Inclusion amount (in gross income), **8:**21
Income, **3:**3, **4:**3
  accounting and tax concepts of,
    4:4–6
  accounting versus taxable, **20:**14–15
  active, **11:**6
  all events test for, **18:**13–14
  alternative minimum taxable (AMTI),
    12:3
  assignment of, **4:**14
  in community property states,
    4:17–19
  from discharge of indebtedness,
    5:32–34
  investment, **3:**19
  nonbusiness, **7:**22
  portfolio, **11:**6
  prepaid, **4:**12–13
  in respect of decedent, **10:**28
  sources of
    from partnerships, S corporations,
      trusts, and estates, **4:**16–17
    personal services, **4:**14
    property, **4:**14–16
    received by an agent, **4:**16
  tax-exempt, **6:**29–30, **12:**22
  unearned income of children under
    age 14 taxed at parents' rate,
    3:19–21
See also Adjusted gross income; Gross
  income; Taxable income

Income tax, **1:**13–14
  federal, **1:**14
  formula for individuals, **1:**14
  history of, **1:**2–3
  local, **1:**15
  as mass tax, **1:**4
  net, **13:**6
  state, **1:**14–15
Income Tax Act of 1913, **5:**4
Indebtedness, income from discharge of,
  5:32–34
Independent contractors, **9:**2–4
  See also Self-employed persons
Individual Retirement Accounts (IRAs),
  1:26, **19:**22–23
  compared to Keogh plan, **19:**24,
    19:38–39, **19:**40
  as deduction for AGI, **9:**21
  penalty tax for excess contributions,
    19:25
  SIMPLE IRA, **19:**24
  simplified employee pension (SEP)
    plans, **19:**23–24
  spousal IRA, **19:**23–24
  tax planning for, **19:**39, **19:**40
  taxation of benefits, **19:**26
    rollovers, **19:**26–27
  timing of contributions, **19:**25
Inflation, **1:**29
Inheritance tax, **1:**11
Inherited property, **16:**17
Injuries, benefits paid on account of,
  5:13–15
Innocent spouse relief, **4:**19
Insolvency, **7:**6
Installment method of accounting, **1:**29,
  18:19
  computing the gain for the period,
    18:20–22
  disposition of installment obligations,
    18:26
  electing out of installment method,
    18:27–28
  eligibility and calculations, **18:**19–20
  imputed interest, **18:**22–23
  interest on deferred taxes, **18:**26
  nonelective aspect, **18:**20
  related-party sales of depreciable
    property, **18:**25–26
  related-party sales of nondepreciable
    property, **18:**23–25
Installment sales
  interest on, **18:**24
  of passive activities, **11:**26
  recapture and, **17:**21
Insurance
  group term life insurance exclusion,
    4:33–34
  medical, deductibility of premiums,
    10:8
Insurance claim, timeliness of, **7:**13
Insurance policies, certain exchanges of
  (Section 1035), **15:**26
Intangible assets, amortization of,
  6:26–27, **8:**24
Intangible drilling and development
  costs (IDC), **8:**26–27
  as AMT preference item, **12:**20–21

effect of on depletion, **8**:28–29
recapture and, **17**:23–24
Interest, **4**:23–28, **18**:22–23
AMT and, **12**:18–19
on below-market loans, **4**:25–28
deductibility of, **10**:13
allowed and disallowed items, **10**:14
interest paid for services, **10**:16–17
interest paid to related parties, **10**:18
investment interest, **10**:14–15
prepayment penalty, **10**:17
qualified residence interest, **10**:13, **10**:15–16
tax-exempt securities, **10**:18
classification of interest expense, **10**:18–19
restrictions on deductibility and timing considerations, **10**:18
prepaid interest, **10**:18
taxpayer's obligation, **10**:18
time of deduction, **10**:18
tax planning for, **10**:33–34
on deferred taxes, **18**:26
imputed, **4**:23–28, **18**:22–23
on installment sales, **18**:24
on private activity bonds, **12**:21
termination of running of (in tax cases), **2**:15
Interest income, **4**:15
from certain state and local government obligations, **5**:28–29
Interest rates, on taxes and tax refunds, **1**:22
Internal Revenue Bulletin (I.R.B.), **2**:10, **2**:20
Internal Revenue Code (IRC)
of 1939, **1**:3, **2**:3
of 1954, **1**:3, **2**:3
of 1986, **1**:3, **2**:3
arrangement of, **2**:6
citing, **2**:6–7
interpreting, **2**:26–27
Internal Revenue Service (IRS), **1**:31
administrative feasibility, **1**:31–32
Appeals Division, **1**:20
field organization of, **1**:18
method of accounting prescribed by, **4**:8
as protector of the revenue, **1**:31
Internet, the, **2**:37–40
Interpretive Regulations, **2**:28
Inventories, **18**:31–32
definition of capital asset and, **16**:6
determining inventory cost, **18**:32
determining cost (specific identification, FIFO, LIFO), **18**:34–35
dollar-value LIFO, **18**:35–36
lower of cost or market, **18**:34
uniform capitalization, **18**:32–34
LIFO election, **18**:37–38
tax planning for, **18**:38
Inventory, as capital asset, **16**:4

Investigation of a business, expenses incurred in, **6**:15–16
Investment assets, **16**:4
Investment income, **10**:14
from reinvestment of life insurance proceeds, **5**:8
tax planning for, **5**:35
Investment interest, **10**:13, **10**:14
AMT and, **12**:18–19
Investment tax credit (ITC), reduction of basis for, **8**:7–8
Involuntary conversions, **15**:9–10, **17**:8
computing the amount realized, **15**:11
defined, **15**:10–11
nonrecognition of gain, **15**:14
conversion into money, **15**:14–15
direct conversion, **15**:14
of personal residence, **15**:15
gain situations, **15**:15
loss situations, **15**:15
recapture and, **17**:21
replacement property, **15**:11–12
functional use test, **15**:12
special rules, **15**:12
taxpayer use test, **15**:11–12
reporting considerations, **15**:15
tax planning for, **15**:29
time limitation on replacement, **15**:13–14
IRS Letter Rulings Reports, **2**:11
Itemized deductions. *See* Deductions, itemized

J

Joint Committee on Taxation, **2**:30
Joint Conference Committee, **2**:4, **2**:5
Joint return test (dependency exemption), **3**:15, **3**:31–32
Jury trial, in tax cases, **2**:14–15

K

Keogh (H.R. 10) plans, **19**:20–22, **19**:24, **19**:38
compared to IRAs, **19**:24, **19**:38–39, **19**:40
Kiddie tax, **3**:19

L

Lease cancellation payments, **16**:15–16
Leasehold improvements, **5**:4
Least aggregate deferral method, **18**:4–5
Legal expenses incurred in defense of civil or criminal penalties, **6**:12–13
Legislative Regulations, **2**:28
Lessee, improvements made by, **5**:4
Letter Ruling Review, **2**:11
Letter rulings, **2**:9, **2**:11
LEXIS, **2**:36
Life insurance, tax planning for, **5**:34
Life insurance proceeds, **5**:5–6
accelerated death benefits, **5**:6–7
transfer for valuable consideration, **5**:7–8
LIFO (last in, first out), **18**:35
dollar-value LIFO, **18**:35–36
tax planning, **18**:38–39

LIFO election, **18**:36–37
Like-kind exchanges, **15**:3
basis and holding period of property received, **15**:7–9
boot, **15**:5–7
exchange requirement, **15**:5
like-kind property, **15**:4–5
recapture and, **17**:21
tax planning for, **15**:28
Limited expensing. *See* Expensing of assets
Limited liability companies, **20**:5
Limited partners, **11**:18–19
Listed property, cost recovery for, **8**:17–22
Livestock, as Section 1231 asset, **17**:7
Living expenses, **6**:5, **10**:2
Loans
below-market, **4**:23–28
compensation-related, **4**:28
corporation-shareholder, **4**:28
gift, **4**:26–28
Lobbying expenditures, **6**:14
Local income taxes, **1**:15, **10**:13
Lodging exclusion, **5**:15–18
Long-term capital gains (LTCG), **3**:29, **17**:2, **17**:3–4
Long-term capital losses (LTCL), **3**:29
Long-term care insurance benefits, **5**:14–15
Long-term contracts, **18**:27–28, **18**:29
completed contract method, **18**:28, **18**:30
lookback provisions, **18**:31
percentage of completion method, **18**:30–31
Long-term nonpersonal use capital assets, **17**:7
Lookback provisions
long-term contracts, **18**:31
Section 1231, **17**:9–12
Losses
adjusted, for AMT, **12**:13–14
business and nonbusiness, **6**:7
capital losses, **3**:29
capital loss limitation, **3**:29–30
computation of net capital losses, **3**:29
definition of capital asset, **3**:29
disallowed
related taxpayers, **14**:17–18
tax planning for, **14**:27–28
wash sales, **14**:18–20, **14**:27
of individuals, **7**:8–9
casualty losses, **7**:11–17, **7**:17
events that are not casualties, **7**:10
personal casualty gains and losses, **7**:15–17
statutory framework for deduction, **7**:15
theft losses, **7**:10–11
nonrecognition of, **14**:7–8
in involuntary conversion of personal residence, **15**:15
sale, exchange, or condemnation of personal use assets, **14**:8

from property transactions (in general), **3:**27–28
realized, **14:**3
    adjusted basis, **14:**4–5, **14:**22
    amount realized, **14:**3–4, **14:**21–22
    capital additions, **14:**5
    capital recoveries, **14:**5–7
    sale or other disposition, **14:**3–4
recognized, **14:**7
recovery of capital doctrine, **14:**8–9
in related-party transactions, **6:**27–28
in S corporations, **20:**28
Section 1231, **17:**4
suspended, **11:**7–9
Lottery winnings, **10:**28
Low-income housing credit, **13:**12–13
Lower of cost or market (replacement cost), **18:**34
Lucas v. Earl, **4:**14
Lump-sum distributions, **19:**12–14
    as capital assets, **16:**8
Luxury automobiles, 8, 17–19

M

MACRS. *See* Accelerated cost recovery system (ACRS and MACRS)
Majority interest partner, **18:**4
Malat v. Riddell, **16:**4
Marriage penalty, **3:**24–26, **3:**25
Married
    filing jointly, **3:**24–26
    filing separately, **3:**24
Mass tax, **1:**4
Material participation, **11:**14–15
    current participation, **11:**15–17
    facts and circumstances test, **11:**17–18
    limited partners, **11:**18–19
    participation defined, **11:**18
    prior participation, **11:**17
    in real property trade or business, **11:**22–23, **11:**24
Meals and lodging
    furnished for the convenience of the employer, **5:**15
    for the convenience of the employer, **5:**16
    on the employer's business premises, **5:**16
    furnished by employer, **5:**15–16
    required as a condition of employment, **5:**16–17
    other housing exclusions
    employees of educational institutions, **5:**17
    military personnel, **5:**18
    ministers of the gospel, **5:**17–18
Medical expenses, **10:**2–4
    AMT adjustment for, **12:**17
    capital expenditures, **10:**5–6
    defined, **10:**4–5
    incurred for spouse and dependents, **10:**6–7
    medical insurance premiums, **10:**8
    reimbursements, **10:**9–10
    tax planning for, **3:**32–33, **10:**32–33
    transportation, meal, and lodging expenses, **10:**7–8
    tuition expenses included in, **10:**5
    year of deduction, **10:**8–9
Medical savings account (MSA), **5:**14, **10:**10
Medicare tax, **13:**26, **13:**26–27, **13:**27
Member-of-the-household test (dependency exemption), **3:**14–15
Memorandum decisions, **2:**19
Merchant Marine capital construction fund adjustment, **12:**28
Merten's Law of Federal Income Taxation, **2:**25
Mid-month convention, **8:**12
Mid-quarter convention, **8:**10–11
Military personnel, **5:**18
Millionaires provision, **6:**14–15
Minimum distribution rules, **19:**10–11
Minimum tax. *See* Alternative minimum tax (AMT)
Ministers of the gospel, **5:**17–18
Miscellaneous itemized deductions, **10:**27–29
Modified accelerated cost recovery system (MACRS). *See* Accelerated cost recovery system (ACRS and MACRS)
Modified adjusted gross income (MAGI), **4:**34
    phaseout of interest income exclusion and, **5:**30–31
    Social Security benefits and, **4:**35–36
Moving expenses, **9:**11
    distance test, **9:**11–12
    tax planning for, **9:**27
    time test, **9:**12
    treatment of, **9:**12–13
Multiple support agreement, **3:**12–13
Multiple taxation, **1:**27–28
Municipal bonds, AMT and, **12:**22

N

National sales tax, **1:**18
Natural business year, **18:**7–8
Net capital gain (NCG), **16:**21–22, **16:**25
Net capital loss (NCL), **16:**23–25
Net income tax, **13:**6
Net investment income, **10:**14–15
Net long-term capital gain (NLTCG), **3:**29, **16:**20
Net long-term capital loss (NLTCL), **3:**29, **16:**20
Net operating losses (NOL), **7:**19–20, **7:**26
    calculation of remaining NOL, **7:**25
    carryback and carryover periods, **7:**20–21
    computation of, **7:**21–24
    corporate treatment of, **20:**10
    deduction of, **1:**28–29
    election to forgo carryback, **7:**21
    recomputation of tax liability for year to which NOL is carried, **7:**24–25
    sequence of use of, **7:**21
    tax planning for, **7:**27
Net regular tax liability, **13:**6
Net short-term capital gain (NSTCG), **3:**29, **16:**20
Net short-term capital loss (NSTCL), **3:**29, **16:**20
Net unearned income, **3:**19
Netting
    casualty, **17:**8
    Section 1231, **17:**9, **17:**22
Newsgroups, **2:**38–39
No-additional-cost services, **5:**21
Nonaccountable plan for reimbursement of employee business expenses, **9:**23–24
    failure to comply with accountable plan requirements, **9:**24
    unreimbursed expenses, **9:**23
Nonacquiescence, **2:**20
Nonbusiness bad debts, **7:**4–5
    as capital assets, **16:**8–9
Nonbusiness capital gains, **7:**22
Nonbusiness deductions, **7:**22
Nonbusiness expenses, **3:**6
Nonbusiness income, **7:**22
Noncompete agreement, as amortizable asset, **8:**24
Noncontingent payments, **16:**14
Nondiscrimination provisions (employee fringe benefits), **5:**24–25
Nonoperating foundation, **10:**24
Nonqualified deferred compensation (NQDC) plans, **19:**27–28
    tax planning for, **19:**39–41
    tax treatment to employer and employee, **19:**28–29
    golden parachute, **19:**29–30
    publicly held companies' compensation limitation, **19:**30–31
    when to use NQDC arrangement, **19:**29
Nonqualified stock option (NQSO), **19:**30, **19:**35–36
Nonrecourse financing, **11:**5
Nonrefundable tax credits, **13:**5–6
Nonresidential real property, computing recapture on, **17:**16–18
Nontaxable economic benefits, **4:**36
Nontaxable exchanges, **15:**2–3
    certain exchanges of insurance policies (Section 1035), **15:**26
    certain reacquisitions of real property, **15:**26
    exchange of stock for property (Section 1032), **15:**26
    exchange of stock for stock of the same corporation (Section 1036), **15:**26
    holding period rules for, **16:**16
    involuntary conversions (Section 1033), **15:**9–15
    like-kind (Section 1031), **15:**3–9
    of passive activity, **11:**26
    rollovers into specialized small business investment companies (Section 1044), **15:**27
    sale of personal residence (Section 121), **15:**23–25
    sale of personal residence (Section 1034), **15:**16–23

tax planning for
  involuntary conversions, **15:**29
  like-kind exchanges, **15:**28
  sale of personal residence, **15:**28–31
  transfers of property between spouses or incident to divorce (Section 1041), **15:**27
Nontaxable stock dividends, **14:**10–11
Nontaxable stock rights, **14:**11
Nontaxable transactions
  involving carryover of another taxpayer's basis, **16:**16–17
  recapture and, **17:**20–21
Nursing home expenses, **10:**5

O

Obligation to repay, amounts received under, **4:**12
Occupational taxes, **1:**17
Office audit, **1:**20
Office in the home expenses, **9:**19–21
On-line tax services, **2:**37–38
One other residence, **10:**15
One-year rule for prepaid expenses, **18:**12
Operating foundation, **10:**24
Optional straight-line method of cost recovery, **8:**7
Options, **16:**10, **16:**12
  exercise of by grantee, **16:**11
  failure to exercise, **16:**11
  sale of, **16:**10–11
Ordinary income property, **10:**23–24
Ordinary and necessary requirement, **6:**6
Organizational expenditures, deduction of, **20:**12
Original issue discount, **4:**11, **16:**10

P

Partial recapture, **17:**16
Participation, in activity, **11:**18
Partnerships, **4:**16
  accounting period for, **18:**4–5
  formation
    basis of partnership interest, **20:**30–31
    partnership's basis in contributed property, **20:**31–32
    recognition of gain or loss, **20:**30
  operations
    measuring and reporting income, **20:**32
      limitation on partner's share of losses, **20:**32–33
        other partnership considerations, **20:**34
        transactions between partner and partnership, **20:**33–34
  taxation of, **20:**29–30
Passenger automobile, **8:**18–19
Passive activity losses and credits, **11:**3–6
Passive credits, **11:**9–10
Passive loss rules, **11:**3–4, **11:**27
  AMT and, **12:**14–15
  classification and impact of passive income and losses, **11:**6–7
    carryover of passive credits, **11:**9–10

carryover of suspended losses, **11:**8–9
general impact, **11:**7
impact of suspended losses, **11:**7–8
passive credits, **11:**9
dispositions of passive interests, **11:**25
  at death, **11:**25–26
  by gift, **11:**26
  installment sale, **11:**26
  nontaxable exchange, **11:**26
  passive activity changes to active, **11:**26
interaction of at-risk and passive activity limits, **11:**21–22
passive activities defined, **11:**11
  identification of activity, **11:**11–13
  regrouping of activities, **11:**13
  special grouping rules for rental activities, **11:**13–14
  material participation, **11:**14–15
    current participation, **11:**15–17
    facts and circumstances test, **11:**17–18
    limited partners, **11:**18–19
    participation defined, **11:**18
    prior participation, **11:**17
  rental activities, **11:**19–21
special passive activity rules for real estate activities, **11:**22
  material participation in real property trade or business, **11:**22–23
  rental real estate activities, **11:**23–25
tax planning, **11:**27–28
taxpayers subject to, **11:**10
  closely held C corporations, **11:**11
  personal service corporations, **11:**10–11
Patents, **16:**12–13
  holder defined, **16:**13
  substantial rights, **16:**13
Pay-as-you-go tax system, **1:**4, **1:**31–32
Payroll period, **13:**29
Penalties, for lack of compliance, **1:**22
Pension plans, **19:**4–5, **19:**5
Per diem allowance for employee business expense, **9:**23
Percentage of completion method, **18:**30–31
Percentage depletion, **8:**27–28
  as AMT preference item, **12:**20
Percentage test, for qualified plans, **19:**8
Personal casualty gains and losses, **7:**15–17
Personal exemption deduction, **3:**10–16
Personal expenditures
  deductible, **6:**5, **10:**2
  disallowance of deduction for, **6:**25–26
Personal injury, damages for, **5:**11
Personal property, AMT adjustment for depreciation of, **12:**10–11
Personal residence
  involuntary conversion of, **15:**15
  sale of
    Section 121, **15:**23
      computation procedure, **15:**25
      exclusion requirements, **15:**23–24

making and revoking the election, **15:**24
relationship to other provisions, **15:**24
Section 1034, **15:**16
  basis and holding period of new residence, **15:**21–22
  capital improvements, **15:**20–21
  nonrecognition of gain requirements, **15:**19–20
  principal residence, **15:**18–19
  replacement period, **15:**16–18
  reporting procedures, **15:**22–23
  tax planning for, **15:**29–31
Personal service corporation (PSC)
  accounting period for, **18:**6–7
  passive loss rules and, **11:**10–11
  taxation of qualified PSC, **20:**13
Personal services, **4:**14
  of child, **4:**14
  of employee, **4:**14
Personal use assets, sale, exchange, or condemnation of, **14:**8
Personal use property, **8:**3, **8:**5, **16:**4
  casualty gains and losses, **17:**7
  condemnation of, **17:**8
Personalty, **1:**7–8
  ad valorem taxes on, **1:**7–8
  recovery periods and methods, **8:**3–4, **8:**5–11
  tangible, **10:**24–25
Petitioner, **2:**19
Plaintiff, **2:**19
Points, **10:**17
Political contributions, **6:**14
Political expediency, **1:**30
Pollock v. Farmers' Loan and Trust Co., **1:**3
Pollution control facilities, AMT adjustment for, **12:**11
Portfolio income, **11:**6
Precedents, **2:**17
Prepaid income, **4:**12–13
  tax deferral and, **4:**38
Prepaid interest, **10:**18
Prepayment penalty, **10:**17
Primary residence, **6:**23
Primary valuation amount, **14:**15
Principal partner, **18:**4
Principal residence, **10:**15, **15:**18–19, **15:**29–30
  See also Personal residence
Prior participation tests, **11:**17
Private activity bonds, interest on as AMT preference item, **12:**21
Private Letter Rulings, **2:**11
Private nonoperating foundation, **10:**24
Private operating foundation, **10:**24
Prizes and awards, income from, **4:**32–33
Procedural Regulations, **2:**28
Profit sharing plans, **19:**5–6, **19:**16–17
Progressive taxes, **1:**5
Property
  acquired from a decedent, **14:**15–16, **14:**26
    deathbed gifts, **14:**16
    holding period, **14:**17
    survivor's share of property, **14:**17

amount realized from sale or other disposition of, **14**:3–4
bargain purchase of, **14**:8
capital gain property, **10**:24–25
contributed to partnership, **20**:31–32
contributions of appreciated property, **10**:27
conversion of from personal use to business or income-producing use, **14**:20–21
depreciable tangible personal, in like-kind exchange, **15**:4–5
dual basis, **14**:12
exchange of stock for, **15**:26
fair market value of, **14**:4
held primarily for investment, **11**:20
held for sale to customers, **11**:21
income from, **4**:14–15
   dividends, **4**:15–16
   interest, **4**:15
inherited, **16**:17
like-kind, **15**:4–5, **15**:7–9
listed, **8**:17–22
lodging rented for convenience of employer, **11**:21
ordinary income property, **10**:23–24
personal use, **8**:3, **8**:5, **16**:4, **17**:7, **17**:8
recovery periods and methods *See* Accelerated cost recovery system (ACRS and MACRS)
replacement (in involuntary conversion), **15**:11–12
sale of
   depreciable between related parties, **18**:25
   nondepreciable between related parties, **18**:23–25
Section 1231, **17**:5
Section 1245, **17**:14–15
Section 1250, **17**:16
tangible personal, **8**:15–17, **15**:4–5
tax planning for transactions involving, **14**:25–27
transfer of between spouses or incident to divorce, **15**:27
used in a trade or business, **11**:21
See also Basis; Gains; Involuntary conversions; Losses
Property dividends, **20**:21
   recapture and, **17**:21–23
Property taxes, **1**:6–8, **10**:11–13
Proportional taxes, **1**:5
Proposed Regulations, **2**:8
Public Law 99–121, **8**:12
Publicly held companies, compensation limitation for, **19**:30–31
Punitive damages, **5**:12–13

Q

Qualified employee discounts, **5**:21–22
Qualified financial institution (for purpose of deduction of lost deposits), **7**:6
Qualified higher education expenses, **5**:30–31
Qualified housing interest, **12**:18

Qualified individual (for deduction of loss of deposits in insolvent financial institution), **7**:6
Qualified moving expense reimbursements, **5**:24
Qualified nonrecourse financing, **11**:5
Qualified parking, **5**:23
Qualified pension, profit sharing, and stock bonus plans, **19**:4
   cash or deferred arrangement plans generally, **19**:18–19
   SIMPLE plans, **19**:19–20, **19**:24
   limitations on contributions to and benefits from, **19**:15
   defined benefit plans, **19**:15–16
   defined contribution plans, **19**:15
   profit sharing and stock bonus plans, **19**:16–17
   qualification requirements, **19**:7
   distribution, **19**:9–11
   exclusive benefit, **19**:7
   nondiscrimination, **19**:7
   participation and coverage, **19**:8–9
   vesting, **19**:9
   tax consequences to employer and employee, **19**:11–12
   lump-sum distributions from qualified plans, **19**:12–14
   tax planning for, **19**:38
   top-heavy plans, **19**:17–18
   types of plans, **19**:4
      employee stock ownership plans (ESOPs), **19**:6–7
      pension plans, **19**:4–5
      profit sharing plans, **19**:5–6
      stock bonus plans, **19**:6
Qualified personal service corporation, taxation of, **20**:13
Qualified real property business indebtedness, **5**:33
Qualified rental period, **6**:23
Qualified residence, **10**:15
Qualified residence interest, **10**:13, **10**:15–16, **12**:18
Qualified state tuition programs, **5**:31
Qualified summer youth employee, **13**:10
Qualified transportation fringes, **5**:23–24
Qualified tuition reduction plans, **5**:10–11

R

Ratio test, for qualified plans, **19**:8
Real estate, rental real estate activities, **11**:23–25
Real property
   certain reacquisitions of (Section 1038), **15**:26
   nonresidential, computing recapture on, **17**:16–18
   post-1986, AMT adjustment for depreciation of, **12**:9–10
   subdivided for sale, treated as capital asset, **16**:7–8
Real property taxes, apportionment between buyer and seller, **10**:12–13
Real property trade or business, material participation in, **11**:23–24

Realized gain, **14**:3, **14**:7, **14**:22
Realized loss, **14**:3, **14**:7, **14**:22
Realty
   ad valorem taxes on, **1**:6–7
   cost recovery periods and methods for, **8**:3–4, **8**:11–14
Reasonable prospect of recovery doctrine, **7**:11, **7**:13–14
Reasonableness requirement, **6**:7
Recapture, **17**:22
   of alimony, **4**:21–23
   exceptions, **17**:20–21
      certain nontaxable transactions, **17**:20–21
      charitable transfers, **17**:20
      death, **17**:20
      gifts, **17**:20
      like-kind exchanges and involuntary conversions, **17**:21
   gain from sale of depreciable property between certain related parties, **17**:23
   intangible drilling and development costs (IDC), **17**:23–24
   other applications, **17**:21
      installment sales, **17**:21
      property dividends, **17**:21–23
   partial, **17**:16
   of rehabilitation expenditures tax credit, **13**:8–9
   reporting procedures, **17**:24–28
   Section 1245, **17**:12–15
   Section 1250, **17**:16–19
   Sections 1245 and 1250 compared, **17**:19
   special recapture for corporations, **17**:23, **20**:8
   tax planning for, **17**:29–30
Recognized gain, **14**:7
Recognized loss, **14**:7
Recovery of capital doctrine, **4**:6–7, **4**:18, **14**:8–9
Recurring item exception, **18**:14–15
Recurring items, in accrual method of accounting, **6**:10
Refinancing, points paid for, **10**:17
Refund, computation of, **3**:18
Refundable tax credits, **13**:5–6
Refunds, limitations on, **1**:21
Regrouping of activities for passive loss rules, **11**:13
Regular decisions, **2**:19
Regular tax liability, **13**:6
Rehabilitation expenditures credit, **13**:7–9
Rehabilitation expenditures credit recapture, **13**:8–9
Related parties
   disallowed losses, **14**:17–18
   interest paid to, **10**:18
   like-kind exchanges between, **15**:4
   loans between, **7**:5, **7**:26
   recapture on gain from sale of depreciable property between, **17**:23
   sale of depreciable property, **18**:25
   sale of nondepreciable property, **18**:23–25
   shifting income to, **4**:38–39

tax planning for, installment sales, **18**:38
transactions between, **6**:27
  losses, **6**:27–28
    relationship and constructive ownership, **6**:28
  unpaid expenses and interest, **6**:27–28
Relationship test
  for dependency exemption, **3**:14–15
  for earned income credit, **13**:15
Rental, of vacation home, **6**:19–23
Rental activities
  defined, **11**:19–21
  special grouping rules for, **11**:15
Rental real estate activities, **11**:23–25, **11**:24–26
Repairs, cost of, **7**:13
Replacement cost (lower of cost or market), **18**:34
Replacement property tests, **15**:12
Research activities credit, **13**:10
  basic research credit, **13**:12
  incremental research activities credit, **13**:11–12
Research expenditures, defined, **13**:11
Research and experimental expenditures, **7**:17–18
  deferral and amortization method, **7**:19–20
  expense method, **7**:18
  research activities credit, **13**:10–12
Research Institute of America (RIA), **2**:20
Reserve method for computing deductions for bad debts, **7**:3–4
Reserves, in accrual method of accounting, **6**:11, **18**:15–16
Residence. *See* Personal residence; Vacation homes
Residency test
  for dependency exemption, **3**:15
  for earned income credit, **13**:15–16
Residential rental housing, computing recapture on, **17**:18
Residential rental real estate, cost recovery periods for, **8**:13–14
Respondent, **2**:19
Restricted property plan, **19**:31–32
  employer deductions, **19**:33–34
  special election available, **19**:32–33
  substantial risk of forfeiture, **19**:32
Revenue Act of 1913, **1**:3
Revenue Act of 1916, **1**:11
Revenue Act of 1948, **1**:31
Revenue Agent's Report (RAR), **1**:20
Revenue neutrality, **1**:24–25
Revenue Procedures, **2**:9–10
Revenue Reconciliation Act of 1993, **5**:24, **8**:24
  amortization of intangibles, **6**:26–27
  corporate tax rate structure, **20**:12–13
  excessive executive compensation, **6**:15
  lobbying expenditures, **6**:14
  specialized small business investment companies, **15**:27

Revenue Rulings, **2**:9–10
  assessing validity of, **2**:28–29
Rollovers, of IRAs, **19**:26–27

S

S corporations
  accounting period for, **18**:4–5
  income of, **4**:17
  justification for the election, **20**:24–25
    loss of the election, **20**:25–26
    making the election, **20**:25
  operational rules, **20**:26
    basis determination, **20**:28–29
    separately stated items, **20**:26–27
    taxable income, **20**:27–28
    treatment of losses, **20**:28
  tax planning, **20**:35
  See also Corporations
Sale or exchange, **16**:9
  See also Capital assets
Sale of personal residence. *See* Personal residence
Sales tax, national, **1**:18
Savings bonds. *See* Educational savings bonds
Savings incentive match plan for employees (SIMPLE plan), **19**:19–20, **19**:24
Schedule A, comprehensive example, **10**:29, **10**:30
Schedule C (Profit or Loss from Business), **8**:29, **8**:32
Schedule D (Capital Gains and Losses), **16**:26
Schedule M-1, **20**:15
Schedule M-2, **20**:15–16
Scholarships, **5**:8–9
  disguised compensation, **5**:9–10
  qualified tuition reduction plans, **5**:10–11
  timing issues, **5**:10
Second residence, **10**:15
Section 121 exclusion, **15**:23–24, **15**:30–31
Section 179 (expensing of assets), **8**:15–17
Section 183 presumptive rule, **6**:17
Section 212 expenses, **6**:4–5
Section 331 (corporate liquidations), **20**:22–24
Section 334 (basis determination), **20**:23
Section 338 (basis determination), **20**:23
Section 401(k) plans, **19**:18–19, **19**:39, **19**:40
Section 1031 (like-kind exchanges), **15**:3–9
Section 1033 (involuntary conversions), **15**:9–15
Section 1034 (sale of residence), **15**:16–23
Section 1231 assets
  computation procedure, **17**:6, **17**:8
    casualty netting, **17**:8
    Section 1231 lookback procedure, **17**:9–12
    Section 1231 netting, **17**:9, **17**:22
  justification for favorable tax treatment, **17**:4

  netting procedure, **17**:6
  property included and excluded, **17**:5
  relationship to capital assets, **17**:3–4
  reporting procedures, **17**:24–28
  special rules, **17**:5
    assets disposed of by casualty or theft, **17**:7–8
    livestock, **17**:7
    timber, **17**:5–7
  tax planning for, **17**:29
Section 1231 gains and losses, **17**:4
Section 1231 lookback, **17**:9–12
Section 1231 property, **17**:5
Section 1244 stock, **7**:8–9, **7**:27, **16**:9
Section 1245 property, **17**:14–15
Section 1245 recapture, **17**:12–14
  compared to Section 1250 recapture, **17**:19
  exceptions, **17**:20–21
  observations on, **17**:15
  other applications, **17**:21–23
  property covered by, **17**:14–15
Section 1250 property, **17**:16
Section 1250 recapture, **17**:16
  compared to Section 1245 recapture, **17**:19
  computing on nonresidential real property, **17**:16–18
  computing on residential real property, **17**:18
  exceptions, **17**:20–21
  other applications, **17**:21–23
  qualifying situations, **17**:19
Securities
  dealers in, **16**:7
  sale of, **16**:29
  short sale of, **16**:17–20
  tax-exempt, **10**:18
Self-employed persons, **9**:2–4
  expenses of, **9**:3
  medical insurance premiums as deductible expense, **10**:8
  retirement plans for, **19**:20
    contribution limitations, **19**:21
    coverage requirements, **19**:20
    Keogh compared to IRA, **19**:24
    tax planning, **19**:38, **19**:39
  tax payment by, **13**:33
    estimated tax, **13**:33–34
    penalty on underpayments, **13**:34–35
    self-employment tax, **13**:35–37
    tax planning, **13**:39
Self-employment tax, **13**:35–37
Senate, **2**:4, **2**:5
Senate Finance Committee, **2**:4, **2**:5, **2**:30
Separately stated items, **20**:26–27
Series E and EE bonds, **4**:11–12, **5**:30–31
  as tax management tool, **4**:37, **4**:38–39
Series H bonds, **4**:37
Services
  contribution of, **10**:20
  deferral of advance payments for, **4**:13–14
  interest paid for, **10**:16–17
Severance awards, **15**:11
Severance taxes, **1**:10

Short sale against the box, **16:**17
Short sales, **16:**17–20
Short taxable year (short period), **18:**8–10
Short-term capital gains (STCG), **3:**29
Short-term capital losses (STCL), **3:**29
Sickness, benefits paid on account of, **5:**13–15
Significant participation activity, **11:**16–17
Significant power, right, or continuing interest, **16:**13–14
SIMPLE plans, **19:**19–20, **19:**24
Simplified employee pension (SEP) plans, **19:**23–24
Sixteenth Amendment, **1:**3, **2:**3, **4:**3
Small business, encouragement of, **1:**26
Small business corporation, **20:**25
  See also S corporations
Small Business Job Protection Act, **1:**26
Small business stock, **7:**8–9, **7:**27
  as AMT preference item, **12:**23
Small Cases Division, U.S. Tax Court, **2:**13
Smith, Adam, **1:**4
Social Security benefits, **4:**34–36
Social Security calculations, **4:**34–36
Social Security tax, **13:**22, **13:**26, **13:**26–27, **13:**27
Solar energy property, tax credit for, **13:**9
Special interest legislation, **1:**30
Specialized small business investment company (SSBIC), **15:**27
Specific chargeoff method of accounting for bad debts, **7:**3–4
Sports franchises, **8:**24, **16:**14–15
Spousal IRA, **19:**24–25
Spouses
  medical expenses incurred for, **10:**6–7
  transfers of property between (or incident to divorce), **15:**27
Standard deduction, **3:**7–8, **3:**22
  individuals not eligible for, **3:**9
Standard Federal Tax Reporter, **2:**25
Stare decisis, doctrine of, **2:**13–14
State income taxes, **1:**14–15, **10:**13
Statute of limitations, **1:**21
Statutory employees, **9:**4
Statutory percentage method of cost recovery, **8:**7, **8:**13
Stepped-down basis, **14:**15
Stepped-up basis, **14:**15
Stock
  corporate, as capital asset, **16:**6
  exchange of for property (Section 1032), **15:**26
  exchange of for stock in same corporation (Section 1036), **15:**26
  nontaxable stock rights, **14:**11
  rollovers into specialized small business investment companies (Section 1044), **15:**27
  sale of, **16:**29
Stock bonus plans, **19:**6, **19:**16–17
Stock dividends, **5:**30
  nontaxable, **14:**10–11

Stock options, **19:**34
  incentive stock options, **19:**34–37
  nonqualified stock options, **19:**37–38
  tax planning for, **19:**41
Stock redemptions, **20:**22
Stock rights, **14:**11
Straight-line method of cost recovery, **8:**6, **8:**14–15, **8:**16
Subchapter S, **20:**24
Substantial rights (patents), **16:**13
Substantial risk of forfeiture, **19:**32
Sudden event, **7:**9
Super-full absorption costing system, **18:**32–33
Support test (dependency exemption), **3:**11–13, **3:**32
Supreme Court
  accounting and tax concepts of income, **4:**5–6
  gifts, **5:**5
  recovery of capital doctrine, **4:**6–7
Supreme Court Reporter, **2:**21
Surviving spouse status, **3:**26
Suspended losses, **11:**7–9

T

Tangible personal property, depreciable expensing of, **8:**15–17
  in like-kind exchange, **15:**4–5
Tangible personalty, **10:**24–25
Tax administration
  audit process, **1:**18–21
  interest and penalties, **1:**22
  Internal Revenue Service (IRS), **1:**18
  statute of limitations, **1:**21
  tax practice, **1:**23–24
Tax avoidance, **2:**34–35
  below-market loans and, **4:**25–28
Tax avoidance loans, **4:**25–28
Tax base, **1:**5
Tax benefit rule, **5:**32, **10:**9
Tax Court of the United States Reports, **2:**19–20
Tax credits, **3:**18, **13:**2–3, **13:**23–24
  adoption expenses tax credit, **13:**19–20
  business energy credits, **13:**9
  child and dependent care expenses, **13:**20–22
  disabled access credit, **13:**13–14
  earned income credit, **13:**14–16
  elderly or disabled taxpayers, **13:**16–18
  foreign tax credit, **13:**18–19
  general business credit, **13:**6–7
  low-income housing credit, **13:**12–13
  refundable versus nonrefundable credits, **13:**5–6
  rehabilitation expenditures, **13:**7–9
  research activities credit, **13:**10–12
  tax policy considerations, **13:**3–4
  work opportunity tax credit, **13:**9–10
Tax deferral, **4:**36–37
  cash basis, **4:**38
  prepaid income, **4:**38
  selection of investments, **4:**37–38

Tax determination
  computation of net taxes payable or refund due, **3:**18
  tax rate schedule method, **3:**16–17
  tax table method, **3:**16
  unearned income of children under age 14 taxed at parents' rate, **3:**19
    election to claim certain unearned income on parent's return, **3:**20–21
    net unearned income, **3:**19
    other provisions, **3:**21
    tax determination, **3:**19–20
Tax evasion, **2:**34–35
Tax file memorandum, **2:**30–32
Tax filing, **3:**21–22
  filing requirements for dependents, **3:**22–23
  filing status, **3:**24–25
    abandoned spouse rules, **3:**26–27
    rates for heads of household, **3:**26
    rates for married individuals, **3:**24–26
    rates for single taxpayers, **3:**24
  selecting the proper form, **3:**23
  when and where to file, **3:**23
Tax formula, **3:**2, **3:**3
  application of, **3:**8
  components
    adjusted gross income, **3:**5–6
    deductions for adjusted gross income, **3:**5–6
    exclusions, **3:**3, **3:**4
    gross income, **3:**3–5
    income (broadly conceived), **3:**3
    itemized deductions, **3:**6
    standard deduction, **3:**7–8
  dependency exemptions, **3:**10–16
  individuals not eligible for standard deduction, **3:**9
  personal exemptions, **3:**10
  special limitations for individuals who can be claimed as dependents, **3:**9–10
  tax planning and, **3:**30–33
Tax holiday, **1:**7
Tax home, determining, **9:**8
Tax law **1:**24
  administrative sources of, **2:**7–8, **2:**8
    letter rulings, **2:**11
    other administrative pronouncements, **2:**11–12
    Revenue Rulings and Revenue Procedures, **2:**9–11
    Treasury Department Regulations, **2:**8–9
  assessing validity of, **2:**26–30
  courts' influence on, **1:**32–33
  economic considerations, **1:**25–26
  equity considerations, **1:**27–29
  IRS influence on, **1:**31–32
  judicial sources of, **2:**13–14, **2:**22
    appellate courts, **2:**15–19
    judicial citations, **2:**19
      U.S. District Court, Court of Federal Claims, and courts of appeal, **2:**20–21

U.S. Supreme Court, **2:**21–22
U.S. Tax Court, **2:**19–20
trial courts, **2:**14–15, **2:**16
political considerations, **1:**29–31
revenue needs, **1:**24–25
social considerations, **1:**26–27
sources of, **2:**2
statutory sources of, **2:**3–4
 arrangement of IRC, **2:**6
 citing IRC, **2:**6–7
 effect of tax treaties, **2:**7
 legislative process, **2:**4–5
Tax Management Portfolios, **2:**25
Tax Notes, **2:**11
Tax payment, **13:**22
procedures applicable to employers, **13:**22, **13:**24
 amount of FICA taxes, **13:**27–28
 amount of income tax withholding, **13:**28–33
 backup withholding, **13:**33
 coverage requirements, **13:**25–27
 reporting and payment procedures, **13:**32–33
procedures applicable to self-employed persons, **13:**34
 estimated tax, **13:**33–34
 penalty on underpayments, **13:**34–35
 self-employment tax, **13:**35–37
Tax periodicals, **2:**25–26
Tax planning, **2:**31–32
alimony, **4:**39–40
alternative minimum tax, **12:**31–33
amortization, **8:**34
cafeteria benefit plans, **19:**41
capital assets, **16:**27–29
cash method of accounting, **4:**38, **18:**37
casualty losses, **7:**27
charitable contributions, **10:**34–36
child and dependent care expenses, **13:**38–39
community property, **4:**39
completed contract method, **18:**39
cost recovery, **8:**33–34
deductible taxes, **10:**33
deferred compensation, **19:**37–40
dependency exemption, **3:**31–32
 gross income test, **3:**32
 relationship to deduction for medical expenses, **3:**32–33
 support test, **3:**32
depletion, **8:**34
documentation, **7:**26
education expenses, **9:**27–28
electronic tax research, **2:**35–40
employee benefits, **5:**34–35
entertainment expenses, **9:**28
excessive executive compensation, **6:**32
family businesses, **20:**35–36
follow-up procedures, **2:**34
foreign tax credit (FTC), **13:**37
forms of doing business, **20:**34–35
hobby losses, **6:**32–33
Individual Retirement Accounts (IRAs), **19:**38–39, **19:**39, **19:**40
installment method of accounting, **18:**37–38
interest deduction, **10:**33–34
inventories, **18:**38
investment income, **5:**35
itemized deductions, **10:**32–36
life insurance, **5:**34
medical deductions, **10:**32–33
minor children's income, **3:**31
moving expenses, **9:**27
net operating losses, **7:**27
nonqualified deferred compensation plans, **19:**39–40
nontax considerations, **2:**33
nontaxable economic benefits, **4:**36
passive losses, **11:**27–28
practical application, **2:**34–35
property transactions, **14:**25–27
qualified plans, **19:**38
regular corporations, **20:**35
related parties, **18:**38
S corporations, **20:**35
Section 401(k) plans, **19:**39, **19:**40
self-employed individuals, **9:**26, **13:**39
self-employed retirement plans, **19:**38–39
shifting deductions, **6:**32
shifting deductions between employer and employee, **9:**26
shifting income to relatives, **4:**38–39
small business stock, **7:**27
stock options, **19:**41
stock sales, **16:**29
tax deferral, **4:**36–37
tax rate differentials, **3:**30–31
taxable year, **18:**37
time value of deductions, **6:**30
transportation expenses, **9:**26–27
travel expenses, **9:**27
unreasonable compensation, **6:**32
unreimbursed employee business expenses, **9:**28
Tax practice, **1:**23
ethical guidelines, **1:**23–24
statutory penalties imposed on preparers, **1:**24
Tax preferences, AMT, **12:**3–4, **12:**5–6
Tax preparers, statutory penalties imposed upon, **1:**24
Tax Rate Schedules, **3:**16–17
Tax rates, **1:**5, **3:**30–31
Tax Reform Act (TRA) of 1986, **1:**30, **2:**3, **8:**2
Tax research, **2:**23, **2:**24
arriving at the solution or at alternative solutions, **2:**30
assessing the validity of tax law sources, **2:**26
 interpreting the IRC, **2:**26–27
 judicial sources, **2:**29
 other administrative sources, **2:**28–29
 other sources, **2:**29–30
 Treasury Regulations, **2:**27–28
communicating, **2:**31–32
electronic, **2:**36
 CD-ROM services, **2:**36–37
 Internet, **2:**37–40
 on-line systems, **2:**37, **2:**38
identifying the problem, **2:**23
locating appropriate tax law sources, **2:**24–25
 tax periodicals, **2:**25–26
 working with tax services, **2:**25
refining the problem, **2:**23–24
Tax services, **2:**25
Tax shelters, **11:**2–4
Tax structure
criteria used in selection of, **1:**4–5
incidence of taxation, **1:**5–6
tax base, **1:**5
tax rates, **1:**5
Tax Table, **3:**16
Tax treaties, **2:**7
Tax-exempt income, expenses and interest relating to, **6:**29–30
Tax-exempt securities, **10:**18
Taxable estate, **1:**11
Taxable income, **1:**5, **3:**2–3, **20:**14–15
in S corporation, **20:**27–28
Taxable year, **4:**7, **18:**3, **18:**37
Taxation
canons of, **1:**4–5
history of
 early periods, **1:**2–3
 historical trends, **1:**3–4
 revenue acts, **1:**3
incidence of, **1:**5–6
Taxes
customs duties, **1:**17
death taxes, **1:**10–11
 federal estate tax, **1:**11
 state death taxes, **1:**11–12
deductibility of, **10:**11
 property taxes, **10:**11–13
 state and local income taxes, **10:**13
 tax planning for, **10:**33
distinguished from fees, **10:**11
employment taxes, **1:**15–16
 FICA taxes, **1:**16
franchise taxes, **1:**17
gift taxes, **1:**12
 federal gift tax, **1:**12–13
 state gift taxes, **1:**13
income taxes, **1:**13–14
occupational taxes, **1:**17
progressive, **1:**5
property (ad valorem) taxes, **1:**6–8
proportional, **1:**5
proposed, **1:**17
 flat tax, **1:**17–18
 national sales tax, **1:**18
 value added tax (VAT), **1:**18
transaction taxes, **1:**8
 federal excise taxes, **1:**8–9
 general sales taxes, **1:**9–10
 severance taxes, **1:**10
 state excise taxes, **1:**9–10
Taxpayer use test (involuntary conversions), **15:**11–12
Taxpayer's benefit or obligation, expenses incurred for, **6:**23–25
Technical Advice Memoranda (TAMs), **2:**11, **2:**12

Technical and Miscellaneous Revenue Act of 1988, **2**:7
Temporary assignments, travel to, **9**:8
Temporary Regulations, **2**:9
Tentative minimum tax, **13**:6
Term certain, **4**:30
Terminal illness, accelerated death benefits and, **5**:6–7
Theft losses, **7**:10–11, **7**:26
    capital recovery and, **14**:5
    Section 1231 assets, **17**:7–8
Thin capitalization, **20**:18
Thor Power Tool Co. v. Comm., **18**:32, **18**:34
Tickets purchased for entertainment, deductibility of, **9**:18
Timber, as Section 1231 asset, **17**:5–7
Time test, for moving expenses, **9**:12
Top-heavy plans, **19**:17–18
Trade or business expense, **6**:5–7
Trade names, **8**:24, **16**:13–14
Trademarks, **8**:24, **16**:13–14
Transportation expenses
    commuting expenses, **9**:5–6
    computation of automobile expenses, **9**:6–7
    qualified expenditures, **9**:5
    tax planning for, **9**:26–27
Travel expenses, **9**:7
    away-from-home requirement, **9**:7
        determining tax home, **9**:8
        temporary assignments, **9**:8
    combined business and pleasure travel, **9**:10
        domestic, **9**:10
        foreign, **9**:10–11
    restrictions on, **9**:8
        conventions, **9**:9
        education, **9**:9
    tax planning for, **9**:27
    See also Commuting expenses

Treasury Decisions (TDs), **2**:11
Treasury Department Regulations, **2**:8–9
    assessing validity of, **2**:27–28
Treaties, **2**:7
Trial courts, **2**:14–15, **2**:16
Trusts, income from, **4**:17
Tuition, deductible as medical expense, **10**:5
Two percent limitation, **9**:25, **10**:27–29

U

Unearned income, of children under 14, **3**:19–21
Unemployment compensation, **4**:34
Unexpected event, **7**:9
Unified transfer tax credit, **1**:12
Unified transfer tax schedule, **1**:12
Uniform capitalization, **18**:32–34
Uniform Gifts to Minors Act, **4**:38–39
United States Board of Tax Appeals Reports (B.T.A.), **2**:20
United States Reports, Lawyer's Edition, **2**:22
United States Supreme Court Reports, **2**:21
United States Tax Reporter, **2**:25
Unreasonable compensation, **6**:32
Unreimbursed employee business expenses, **9**:28
U.S. Court of Federal Claims, **2**:13, **2**:14, **2**:17
    citations of, **2**:21
U.S. government publications, as capital assets, **16**:5
U.S. Supreme Court, **2**:17, **2**:18
    appeals to, **2**:18–19
    citations of, **2**:21–22
    writ of certiorari, **2**:18
U.S. Tax Court, **2**:13
    appeals from, **2**:17–18
    citations of, **2**:19–20

Small Cases Division, **2**:13
Use or lose plans, **5**:19
Use tax, **1**:9–10

V

Vacation homes
    rental of, **6**:19–20, **6**:23
        conversion to rental property, **6**:23
        personal/rental use, **6**:21–23
        primarily personal use, **6**:20
        primarily rental use, **6**:20–21
Value added tax (VAT), **1**:18
Vesting requirements, in qualified plans, **19**:9

W

Wagering, **10**:28
Wash sales, **14**:18–20, **14**:27
WESTLAW, **2**:38
Wherewithal to pay concept, **1**:28
Withholding
    allowances for, **13**:28–30
    backup, **13**:33
    classifications of, **13**:25
    income tax, **13**:28–30, **13**:32
    table for, **13**:31
    tax planning for, **13**:39
Withholding allowances, **13**:29
Work opportunity tax credit, **13**:9–10
Workers' compensation, **5**:12
Working condition fringes, **5**:23
World Wide Web, **2**:37–38
Worthless securities, **7**:7
    sale or exchange of, **16**:9
    small business stock, **7**:8–9
Writ of certiorari, **2**:18

Z

Zero bracket amount, **19**:13

AMT Formula for Individuals

Regular Taxable Income	
Plus or minus:	Adjustments
Plus:	Tax preferences
Equals:	Alternative minimum taxable income
Minus:	Exemption
Equals:	Alternative minimum tax base
Times:	26% and 28% graduated rates
Equals:	Tentative minimum tax before foreign tax credit
Minus:	Alternative minimum tax foreign tax credit
Equals:	Tentative minimum tax
Minus:	Regular income tax liability
Equals:	Alternative minimum tax (if amount is positive)

AMT Exemption Phase-Out for Individuals

Filing Status	Exemption	Phase-out Begins at	Ends at
Married, filing jointly	$45,000	$150,000	$330,000
Single or head of household	33,750	112,500	247,500
Married, filing separately	22,500	75,000	165,000

AMT Formula for Corporations

Regular Taxable Income before NOL Deduction	
Plus or minus:	Adjustments (except ACE adjustment)
Plus:	Tax preferences
Equals:	AMTI before ATNOL deduction and ACE adjustment
Plus or minus:	ACE adjustment
Equals:	Alternative minimum taxable income (AMTI) before ATNOL deduction
Minus:	ATNOL deduction (limited to 90% of AMTI before ATNOL deduction)
Equals:	Alternative minimum taxable income (AMTI)
Minus:	Exemption
Equals:	Alternative minimum tax base
Times:	20% rate
Equals:	AMT before AMT foreign tax credit
Minus:	AMT foreign tax credit (possibly limited to 90% of AMT before AMT foreign tax credit)
Equals:	Tentative minimum tax
Minus:	Regular income tax liability before credits minus regular foreign tax credit
Equals:	Alternative minimum tax (AMT) if positive